W9-BTE-785

Dictionary of the Middle Ages

AMERICAN COUNCIL OF LEARNED SOCIETIES

The American Council of Learned Societies, organized in 1919 for the purpose of advancing the study of the humanities and of the humanistic aspects of the social sciences, is a nonprofit federation comprising forty-five national scholarly groups. The Council represents the humanities in the United States in the International Union of Academies, provides fellowships and grants-in-aid, supports research-and-planning conferences and symposia, and sponsors special projects and scholarly publications.

MEMBER ORGANIZATIONS

AMERICAN PHILOSOPHICAL SOCIETY, 1743
AMERICAN ACADEMY OF ARTS AND SCIENCES, 1780
AMERICAN ANTIQUARIAN SOCIETY, 1812
AMERICAN ORIENTAL SOCIETY, 1842
AMERICAN NUMISMATIC SOCIETY, 1858
AMERICAN PHILOLOGICAL ASSOCIATION, 1869
ARCHAEOLOGICAL INSTITUTE OF AMERICA, 1879
SOCIETY OF BIBLICAL LITERATURE, 1880
MODERN LANGUAGE ASSOCIATION OF AMERICA, 1883
AMERICAN HISTORICAL ASSOCIATION, 1884
AMERICAN ECONOMIC ASSOCIATION, 1885
AMERICAN FOLKLORE SOCIETY, 1888
AMERICAN DIALECT SOCIETY, 1889
AMERICAN PSYCHOLOGICAL ASSOCIATION, 1892
ASSOCIATION OF AMERICAN LAW SCHOOLS, 1900
AMERICAN PHILOSOPHICAL ASSOCIATION, 1901
AMERICAN ANTHROPOLOGICAL ASSOCIATION, 1902
AMERICAN POLITICAL SCIENCE ASSOCIATION, 1903
BIBLIOGRAPHICAL SOCIETY OF AMERICA, 1904
ASSOCIATION OF AMERICAN GEOGRAPHERS, 1904
HISPANIC SOCIETY OF AMERICA, 1904
AMERICAN SOCIOLOGICAL ASSOCIATION, 1905
AMERICAN SOCIETY OF INTERNATIONAL LAW, 1906
ORGANIZATION OF AMERICAN HISTORIANS, 1907
AMERICAN ACADEMY OF RELIGION, 1909
COLLEGE ART ASSOCIATION OF AMERICA, 1912
HISTORY OF SCIENCE SOCIETY, 1924
LINGUISTIC SOCIETY OF AMERICA, 1924
MEDIAEVAL ACADEMY OF AMERICA, 1925
AMERICAN MUSICOLOGICAL SOCIETY, 1934
SOCIETY OF ARCHITECTURAL HISTORIANS, 1940
ECONOMIC HISTORY ASSOCIATION, 1940
ASSOCIATION FOR ASIAN STUDIES, 1941
AMERICAN SOCIETY FOR AESTHETICS, 1942
AMERICAN ASSOCIATION FOR THE ADVANCEMENT OF SLAVIC STUDIES, 1948
METAPHYSICAL SOCIETY OF AMERICA, 1950
AMERICAN STUDIES ASSOCIATION, 1950
RENAISSANCE SOCIETY OF AMERICA, 1954
SOCIETY FOR ETHNOMUSICOLOGY, 1955
AMERICAN SOCIETY FOR LEGAL HISTORY, 1956
AMERICAN SOCIETY FOR THEATRE RESEARCH, 1956
SOCIETY FOR THE HISTORY OF TECHNOLOGY, 1958
AMERICAN COMPARATIVE LITERATURE ASSOCIATION, 1960
AMERICAN SOCIETY FOR EIGHTEENTH-CENTURY STUDIES, 1969
ASSOCIATION FOR JEWISH STUDIES, 1969

David and Goliath. Byzantine miniature from the Paris Psalter, 10th century. PARIS, BIBLIOTHÈQUE NATIONALE, MS GR.139, fol. 4v

Dictionary of the Middle Ages

JOSEPH R. STRAYER, *EDITOR IN CHIEF*

Volume 9

MYSTERY RELIGIONS—POLAND

CHARLES SCRIBNER'S SONS • NEW YORK

Library of Congress Cataloging in Publication Data
Main entry under title:

Dictionary of the Middle Ages.

Includes bibliographies and index.
1. Middle Ages—Dictionaries. I. Strayer,
Joseph Reese, 1904–
D114.D5 1982 909.07 82-5904
ISBN 0-684-16760-3 (v. 1)
ISBN 0-684-17022-1 (v. 2)
ISBN 0-684-17023-X (v. 3)
ISBN 0-684-17024-8 (v. 4)
ISBN 0-684-18161-4 (v. 5)
ISBN 0-684-18168-1 (v. 6)
ISBN 0-684-18169-X (v. 7)
ISBN 0-684-18274-2 (v. 8)
ISBN 0-684-18275-0 (v. 9)

Published simultaneously in Canada
by Collier Macmillan Canada, Inc.

3 5 7 9 11 13 15 17 19 M/C 20 18 16 14 12 10 8 6 4

PRINTED IN THE UNITED STATES OF AMERICA.

The *Dictionary of the Middle Ages* has been produced with
support from the National Endowment for the Humanities.

The paper in this book meets the guidelines for
permanence and durability of the Committee on
Production Guidelines for Book Longevity of the
Council on Library Resources.

Maps prepared by Sylvia Lehrman.

Editorial Board

Advisory Committee

Editorial Staff

JOHN F. FITZPATRICK, *MANAGING EDITOR*

JONATHAN G. ARETAKIS, *Associate Editor*

DANIEL J. CALTO, *Editorial Assistant*

NORMA FRANKEL, *Associate Editor*

SANDRA D. KNIGHT, *Administrative Assistant*

ANJU MAKHIJANI, *Production Manager*

BETH ANN McCABE, *Senior Editorial Assistant*

DAVID J. BABIN, *Assistant Photo Editor*

JEFFREY L. BENEKE, *Associate Editor*

LESLEY ANN BENEKE, *Associate Editor*

ILENE COHEN, *Associate Editor*

EDWARD FERRARO, *Associate Editor*

EMILY GARLIN, *Proofreader*

GEOFFREY B. GNEUHS, *Assistant Editor*

ROBERT HALASZ, *Associate Editor*

ROBERT K. HAYCRAFT, *Associate Editor*

PAMELA NICELY, *Assistant Editor*

W. KIRK REYNOLDS, *Proofreader*

JACK RUMMEL, *Proofreader*

IRINA RYBACEK, *Associate Editor*

SAM TANENHAUS, *Proofreader*

DEBBIE TAYLOR, *Photo Editor*

TERENCE WALZ, *Associate Editor*

WILLIAM K. WEST, *Associate Editor*

ELIZABETH I. WILSON, *Associate Editor*

G. MICHAEL McGINLEY, *DIRECTOR, REFERENCE BOOKS DIVISION*

Contributors to Volume 9

WILLIAM Y. ADAMS
University of Kentucky
Nubia

DOROTHY AFRICA
O'Sinaich, Cellach;
Patrick, St.

MANSOUR J. AJAMI
Princeton University
Nadīm, Ibn al-

GUSTAVE ALEF
University of Oregon
Novgorod

THEODORE M. ANDERSSON
Stanford University
Niebelungenlied; Norse, Kings' Sagas; Oddrun Ar Grátr

AVERY ANDREWS
George Washington University, Washington, D.C.
Pera-Galata

MICHAEL ANGOLD
University of Edinburgh
Nicaea, Empire of;
Nymphaion

YOM TOV ASSIS
Hebrew University of Jerusalem
Oath, More Judaico

LEVON AVDOYAN
Library of Congress
Patmut^{c}iwn (Erkrin) Tarōnoy

PETER J. AWN
Columbia University
Mysticism, Islamic

SUSAN M. BABBITT
American Philosophical Society
Nicopolis

TERENCE BAILEY
University of Western Ontario
Neuma; Noeannoe

JOHN W. BALDWIN
The Johns Hopkins University
Peter the Chanter; Philip II Augustus

JOHN W. BARKER
University of Wisconsin
Nikolaos Kavasilas

CARL F. BARNES, JR.
Notre Dame de Paris, Cathedral of; Oriel Window; Orphrey; Pierre de Montreuil; Pierre des Champs

ELIEZER BASHAN
Bar-Ilan University
Nasi

ÜLKÜ Ü. BATES
Hunter College, City University of New York
Otaq

ROBERT BEDROSIAN
Orbēlean, Step^{c}anos

JEANETTE M. A. BEER
Purdue University
Picard Language, Picard Literature

HAIM BEINART
Hebrew University of Jerusalem
New Christians

HANS BEKKER-NIELSEN
Odense Universitet
Páls Saga Biskups

ALDO S. BERNARDO
State University of New York at Binghamton
Petrarch

LIONEL BIER
Brooklyn College
Naqsh-i Rustam; Paikuli

JANE BISHOP
Nicholas I, Pope

THOMAS N. BISSON
University of California, Berkeley
Peace of God, Truce of God

ROBERT J. BLANCH
Northeastern University
Pearl

CALVIN M. BOWER
University of Notre Dame
Paraphonista; Perfectio

EDMUND A. BOWLES
Organ

WILLIAM M. BOWSKY
University of California
Podesta

MARY BOYCE
Pahlavi Literature

DENIS J. M. BRADLEY
Georgetown University
Philosophy and Theology, Western European: to Mid Twelfth Century

STEPHEN F. BROWN
Boston College
Neoplatonism; Philosophy and Theology, Western European: Late Medieval

KEVIN BROWNLEE
Dartmouth College
Philippe de Novare

LESLIE BRUBAKER
Wheaton College, Norton, Mass.
Octateuch; Opus

CONTRIBUTORS TO VOLUME 9

Anglicanum; Orant; Pala D'Oro; Palimpsest; Palmette; Parousia; Pendentive; Pentateuch

FRANÇOIS BUCHER
Florida State University
Parler Family

RICHARD W. BULLIET
Columbia University
Nishapur

ROBERT W. BURCHFIELD
Oxford English Dictionaries
Ormulum

CHARLES S. F. BURNETT
Warburg Institute, University of London
Plato of Tivoli

DAVID BURR
Virginia Polytechnic Institute and State University
Peter John Olivi

ROBERT G. CALKINS
Cornell University
Pleurant

DANIEL CALLAM
St. Thomas More College
Paradise, Western Concept of

AVERIL CAMERON
King's College, University of London
Paschale Chronicon

JAMES E. CATHEY
University of Massachusetts, Amherst
Norns

GRETEL CHAPMAN
Nicholas of Verdun

COLIN CHASE
University of Toronto, Centre for Medieval Studies
Paul the Deacon

CHARLES D. CHAVEL
Naḥmanides, Moses

MARJORIE CHIBNALL
Cambridge University
Ordericus Vitalis

V. CHRISTIDES
Navies, Islamic

CAROL J. CLOVER
University of California, Berkeley
Njáls Saga; Norse Flyting

MARK R. COHEN
Princeton University
Nadīm, Ibn al-; Nagid; People of the Book

SIDNEY L. COHEN
Louisiana State University
Oseberg Find

THOMAS H. CONNOLLY
University of Pennsylvania
Old Roman Chant

LAWRENCE I. CONRAD
The Wellcome Institute for the History of Medicine
Najd; Plagues in the Islamic World

DEMETRIOS J. CONSTANTELOS
Stockton State University
Orphanotrophos; Patriarch

JOHN J. CONTRENI
Purdue University
Peter of Pisa

MADELEINE PELNER COSMAN
City College of New York
Pharmacopeia

WILLIAM J. COURTENAY
University of Wisconsin
Nominalism; Ockham, William of

EDWARD J. COWAN
University of Guelph, Ontario
Parliament, Scottish

GLYNNIS M. CROPP
Massey University, New Zealand
Partimen

BERNARD CULLEN
The Queen's University of Belfast
Pelagius

JOSEPH DAN
Hebrew University of Jerusalem
Philosphy and Theology, Jewish: In Northern Europe

MICHAEL T. DAVIS
Mount Holyoke College
Pallium; Paludamentum; Passion Cycle; Paten; Peter Urseolus, St.; Peter von Prachtatitz; Pilgrim's Guide

NORMAN DAVIS
Merton College, Oxford
Paston Letters, the

PETER F. DEMBOWSKI
University of Chicago
Philippe Mousket

LUCY DER MANUELIAN
Noravank^{c} at Amału; Ōjun

WILLIAM J. DIEBOLD
Nomen Sacrum; Pericopes

WACHTANG DJOBADZE
California State University, Los Angeles
Nikorc^{c}minda; Oški

JERRILYNN DODDS
Columbia University
Plateresque Style

ANN DOOLEY
St. Michael's College, University of Toronto
Ó Brolcháin, Maol Íosa; Ó Dálaigh, Donnchadh Mór; Ó Dálaigh, Gofraidh Fionn; Ó Dálaigh, Muiredach Albanach

KATHERINE FISCHER DREW
Rice University
Odoacer; Ostrogoths

DIANE L. DROSTE
University of Toronto, Centre for Medieval Studies
Plica

WILLIAM HUSE DUNHAM, JR.
Parliament, English

WILLIAM DUNPHY
St. Michael's College, University of Toronto
Philosophy and Theology, Western European: Thirteenth-Century Crisis

RICHARD A. DWYER
Florida International University
Ovid in the Middle Ages

CONTRIBUTORS TO VOLUME 9

LAWRENCE M. EARP
University of Wisconsin-Madison
Petrus de Cruce

STEVEN G. ELLIS
University College of Galway
Parliament, Irish

MARCIA J. EPSTEIN
University of Calgary
Peire Vidal; Play of Daniel; Play of Herod

STEVEN EPSTEIN
University of Colorado
Pisa

JOHN H. ERICKSON
St. Vladimir's Seminary
Nomocanon; Paterikon

MICHAEL VAN ESBROECK
Société des Bollandistes
Nino, St.

THEODORE EVERGATES
Western Maryland College
Nobles and Nobility; Pierre de Fontaines

ROBERT FALCK
University of Toronto
Organum; O Roma Nobilis; Planctus

ANN E. FARKAS
Pecherskaya Lavra; Pokrov

JEFFREY FEATHERSTONE
Harvard University
Nikephoros, Patriarch

S. C. FERRUOLO
Stanford University
Nigel of Longchamp; Placentinus

R. S. FIELD
Yale University
Niello

JOHN V. A. FINE, JR.
University of Michigan
Peter and Asen; Peter of Bulgaria

EVELYN SCHERABON FIRCHOW
University of Minnesota
Nithard; Poeta Saxo

RUTH H. FIRESTONE
University of Missouri
Ortnit

PATRICK K. FORD
Center for the Study of Comparative Folklore and Mythology, University of California, Los Angeles
Mythology, Celtic

JEROLD C. FRAKES
University of Southern California
Philip the Chancellor

JOHN B. FREED
Illinois State University
Otto III, Emperor; Nuremberg

PAUL FREEDMAN
Vanderbilt University
Oliba

EDWARD FRUEH
Columbia University
Norbert of Iburg; Onulf of Speyer

ASTRIK L. GABRIEL
University of Notre Dame
Paris, University of

STEPHEN GARDNER
Sackler Museum, Harvard University
Nicholas of Ely; Old Sarum; Orchard, William

NINA G. GARSOÏAN
Columbia University
Naχarar; Naχčawan; Nersēs I the Great, St.; Nersēs II Aštarakacʿi; Nersēs III Išχanecʿi; Nisibis; Ostikan; Pahlawuni; Paulicians; Pʿawstos Buzand; Pʿilartos Varažnuni

ADELHEID M. GEALT
Indiana University
Nanni di Banco; Nardo di Cione; Niccolò di Buonaccorso; Niccolò di Pietro Gerini; Orcagna, Andrea; Panel Painting; Paolo di Giovanni Fei; Paolo Veneziano; Pietro da Rimini

DENO J. GEANAKOPLOS
Yale University
Pelagonia

CHRISTIAN GELLINEK
University of Florida
Orendel

MOSHE GIL
Tel-Aviv University
Palestine; Pilgrimage, Jewish

DOROTHY F. GLASS
State University of New York at Buffalo
Niccolò da Verona; Oderisi, Pietro

JOSCELYN GODWIN
Colgate University
Mystery Religions

PETER B. GOLDEN
Rutgers University
Niẓām al-Mulk

ROBERT S. GOTTFRIED
Rutgers University
Plagues, European

ANTHONY GRAFTON
Princeton University
Nicolaus de Tudeschis

EDWARD GRANT
Indiana University
Oresme, Nicole

KATHLEEN GREENFIELD
Albright College
Peckham, John

JAMES GRIER
University of Waterloo, Ontario
Neume

KAAREN GRIMSTAD
University of Minnesota
Njǫrðr

MARY GRIZZARD
University of New Mexico
Nisart, Pedro; Oliphant

FINNBOGI GUÐMUNDSSON
Orkneyinga Saga

JEAN-MARIE GY, O.P.
Couvent Saint-Jacques, Paris
Papal Curia, Liturgy of

CONTRIBUTORS TO VOLUME 9

JAMES HANKINS
Harvard University
PLATO IN THE MIDDLE AGES

NATHALIE HANLET
ODA OF CANTERBURY

JOSEPH HARRIS
Harvard University
NORNA-GESTS ÞÁTTR

RALPH S. HATTOX
Emory University
OSMAN I

ROBERT K. HAYCRAFT
PALIOTTO OF S. AMBROGIO

KNUT HELLE
University of Bergen, Norway
NORWAY

HEATHER HENDERSON
University of Toronto
Ó HUIGINN, TADHG DALL;
Ó HUIGINN, TADHG ÓG

JOHN BELL HENNEMAN
Princeton University Library
PHILIP VI OF VALOIS

JOHN H. HILL
PETER THE HERMIT

ROBERT HILLENBRAND
University of Edinburgh
PISHTAQ

J. N. HILLGARTH
Pontifical Institute of Mediaeval Studies, Toronto
PETER IV THE CEREMONIOUS

DAVID L. HOOVER
New York University
OLD ENGLISH LANGUAGE

JASPER HOPKINS
University of Minnesota
NICHOLAS OF CUSA

GEORGE F. HOURANI
State University of New York at Buffalo
PHILOSOPHY AND THEOLOGY, ISLAMIC

NORMAN HOUSLEY
University of Liverpool
PILGRIMAGE, WESTERN EUROPEAN

HALIL INALCIK
University of Chicago
OTTOMANS

JEAN IRIGOIN
PAPER, INTRODUCTION OF

ALFRED L. IVRY
Brandeis University
PHILOSOPHY AND THEOLOGY, JEWISH: ISLAMIC WORLD

WILLIAM E. JACKSON
University of Virginia
OTTO VON BOTENLAUBEN

W. T. H. JACKSON
Columbia University
ODO OF MEUN; OTTO OF BAMBERG, ST.

MICHAEL JACOFF
Brooklyn College, City University of New York
NICCOLÒ DA BOLOGNA; PACINO DI BONAGUIDA

JAMES L. JOHN
Cornell University
PALEOGRAPHY, WESTERN EUROPEAN

D. W. JOHNSON
Catholic University of America
NESTORIANISM; NESTORIUS

GEORGE FENWICK JONES
University of Maryland
OSWALD VON WOLKENSTEIN

JENNIFER E. JONES
NATIVITY; NIMBUS; NOLI ME TANGERE; PENTECOST; PIETÀ; PLATYTERA

CHRISTIANE L. JOOST-GAUGIER
University of New Mexico
PISANELLO, ANTONIO

WILLIAM CHESTER JORDAN
Princeton University
ORDINANCE (FRENCH AND ENGLISH); PAGUS; PASTOUREAUX; PASTURE, RIGHTS OF

WALTER EMIL KAEGI, JR.
University of Chicago
NOTITIA DIGNITATUM; OPSIKION, THEME OF

RICHARD W. KAEUPER
University of Rochester
NISI PRIUS; OYER AND TERMINER, TRAILBASTON; PEASANTS' REBELLION

IOLI KALAVREZOU-MAXEINER
University of California, Los Angeles
PARIS PSALTER

MARIANNE E. KALINKE
University of Illinois at Urbana-Champaign
PARCEVALS SAGA; PARTALOPA SAGA

FRANCIS KELLEY
St. Bonaventure University
PETER AUREOLI

THOMAS E. KELLY
Purdue University
PERLESVAUS

MARILYN KAY KENNEY
OWAIN GWYNEDD

FRANCES KIANKA
Dumbarton Oaks
NIKEPHOROS GREGORAS

JOSEPH A. KICKLIGHTER
Auburn University
PARLEMENT OF PARIS

RICHARD KIECKHEFER
Northwestern University
PAPACY, ORIGINS AND DEVELOPMENT OF

DALE KINNEY
Bryn Mawr College
ODO OF METZ; OLD ST. PETER'S, ROME; PISA CATHEDRAL

ALAN E. KNIGHT
Pennsylvania State University
PASSION PLAYS, FRENCH

PAUL W. KNOLL
University of Southern California, Los Angeles
PIAST DYNASTY; POLAND

BARIŠA KREKIĆ
University of California, Los Angeles
OCHRID

CONTRIBUTORS TO VOLUME 9

VALERIE M. LAGORIO
University of Iowa
Mysticism, Christian: Continental (Women); Mysticism, English

ANGELIKI LAIOU
Harvard University
Palaiologoi; Paroikoi; Penetes

IAN LANCASHIRE
Erindale College University of Toronto at Mississauga
N-Town Plays

DAMIAN RIEHL LEADER
University of Toronto, Centre for Medieval Studies
Oxford University

R. WILLIAM LECKIE, JR.
University of Toronto, Centre for Medieval Studies
Nennius

JOHN LE PATOUREL
University of Leeds
Normans and Normandy

ROBERT E. LERNER
Northwestern University
Otto of Freising; Otto I the Great; Paschal II, Pope

ARTHUR LEVINE
University of Toronto
Old Hall MS

DAVID C. LINDBERG
University of Wisconsin
Optics, Western European

JOHN LINDOW
University of California, Berkeley
Odin

LARS LÖNNROTH
Göteborgs Universitet
Oddr Snorrason; Óláfs Saga Helga; Óláfs Saga Tryggvasonar

JOHN E. LYNCH
Catholic University of America
Oath

BRYCE LYON
Brown University
Pipe Rolls

MICHAEL McCORMICK
Dumbarton Oaks/The Johns Hopkins University
Papyrus; Parchment; Pecia; Philip of Harvengt; Pocketbooks

DAVID R. McLINTOCK
University of London
Old High German Literature; Otfrid von Weissenburg; Petruslied

HARRY J. MAGOULIAS
Wayne State University
Niketas Choniates

HENRY MAGUIRE
University of Illinois at Urbana-Champaign
Nikolaos Mesarites

GEORGE P. MAJESKA
University of Maryland
Nevsky, Alexander; Oleg; Olga/Helen; Omophorion; Orarion; Papert; Pelena; Peter, Master; Pilgrimage, Russian; Plashchanitsa; Pogost

KRIKOR H. MAKSOUDIAN
Nersēs IV Šnorhali; Nersēs Lambronacʿi; Petros Getadarj

STEPHEN MANNING
University of Kentucky
Pastourelle

HARRY J. MARGOULIAS
Niketas Choniates

THOMAS F. MATHEWS
New York University
Parekklesion

RALPH WHITNEY MATHISEN
University of South Carolina
Orientius; Orosius; Patrician, Roman; Paulinus of Aquileia, St.; Paulinus of Béziers; Paulinus of Nola, St.; Paulinus of Pella; Paulinus of Périgueux

E. ANN MATTER
University of Pennsylvania
Origen, Paschasius Radbertus of Corbie, St.

BRIAN MERRILEES
University of Toronto
Orthographia Gallica; Oxford Psalter; Passiun Seint Edmund, La; Petite Philosophie, La

JOHN MEYENDORFF
Fordham University
Mysticism, Byzantine; Nil Sorsky, St., Pentarchy; Permanent Synod; Peter; Philotheos Kokkinos

STEPHEN MURRAY
Columbia University
Parler Family

JOHN W. NESBITT
Dumbarton Oaks Research Center
Nomisma

STEPHEN G. NICHOLS, JR.
University of Pennsylvania
Peire Cardenal

W. F. H. NICOLAISEN
State University of New York at Binghamton
Nechtan; Picts

THOMAS F. X. NOBLE
University of Virginia
Pepin I; Pepin II; Pepin III and the Donation of Pepin; Poitiers, Battle of

JOHN T. NOONAN, JR.
University of California, Berkeley
Paucapalea

RICHARD O'GORMAN
University of Iowa
Nouvelle

PÁDRAIG P. Ó NÉILL
University of North Carolina
Ogham

THOMAS H. OHLGREN
Purdue University
Oswald of Ramsey

NICOLAS OIKONOMIDES
Université de Montreal
Nikephoros II Phokas; Philotheos; Phokas

CONTRIBUTORS TO VOLUME 9

ERIC L. ORMSBY
McGill University
PARADISE, ISLAMIC

ROBERT OUSTERHOUT
University of Illinois at Urbana-Champaign
NAOS; NYMPHAEUM; ORATORY; PASTOPHORY

HERMANN PÁLSSON
University of Edinburgh
ÖRVAR-ODDS SAGA

PETER PARTNER
Winchester College, England
PAPAL STATES

JOSEPH F. PATROUCH
University of Dayton
PECOCK, REGINALD

PIERRE J. PAYER
PENANCE AND PENITENTIALS

FRANKLIN J. PEGUES
Ohio State University
NOGARET, GUILLAUME DE

DAVID PELTERET
New College, University of Toronto
NINIAN, ST.

KENNETH PENNINGTON
Syracuse University
PETRI EXCEPTIONES

ALEJANDRO ENRIQUE PLANCHART
University of California
ODINGTON, WALTER

JAMES F. POWERS
College of the Holy Cross
NAVARRE, KINGDOM OF

JAMES M. POWELL
Syracuse University
NAPLES; PALERMO; PETER'S PENCE; PIERO DELLA VIGNA; PIRMIN, ST.

WALTER H. PRINCIPE
Pontifical Institute of Mediaeval Studies, Toronto
PHILOSOPHY AND THEOLOGY, WESTERN EUROPEAN: TWELFTH CENTURY TO AQUINAS

CHARLES M. RADDING
Loyola University, Chicago
ORDEALS

THOMAS RENNA
Saginaw Valley State College
ODILO OF CLUNY, ST.; ODO OF CLUNY, ST.

ELIZABETH REVELL
Huron College
PETER OF BLOIS

ROGER E. REYNOLDS
Pontifical Institute of Mediaeval Studies, Toronto
NARBONNE RITE; ORDINALE; ORDINARIUS LIBER; ORDINATION, CLERICAL; ORDINES ROMANI

A. G. RIGG
University of Toronto, Centre for Medieval Studies
PARODY, LATIN; PETER RIGA

ELAINE GOLDEN ROBISON
NICOLAITISM; ODINGTON, WALTER; PETER OF SPAIN; PETER PEREGRINUS OF MARICOURT

HELEN ROLFSON, O.S.F.
St. John's University, Collegeville, Minnesota
MYSTICISM, CHRISTIAN: LOW COUNTRIES

LINDA C. ROSE
NAXOS, DUCHY OF; NIKEPHOROS BRYENNIOS; PALLADIOS; PHILIPPOPOLIS; PHILOSTORGIOS

RHIMAN A. ROTZ
Indiana University, Northwest
PATRICIAN, URBAN

DANIEL RUSSELL
University of Pittsburgh
OVIDE MORALISÉ

JAMES R. RUSSELL
Columbia University
PARTHIANS

A. I. SABRA
Harvard University
OPTICS, ISLAMIC

ERNEST H. SANDERS
Columbia University
NOTRE DAME SCHOOL; PEROTINUS

T. A. SANDQUIST
University of Toronto
OUTLAWRY

NICOLAS SCHIDLOVSKY
Smithsonian Institution
OKTOECHOS

JAMES A. SCHULTZ
Yale University
OSWALD, ST.: GERMAN EPICS

IRFAN SHAHÎD
Georgetown University
NAJRĀN

DANUTA SHANZER
University of California
NEMESIANUS, MARCUS AURELIUS OLYMPIUS

LON R. SHELBY
Southern Illinois University at Carbondale
PILGRAM, ANTON

CHARLES R. SHRADER
NATO Defense College
NOTGER OF LIÈGE

S. A. SHUISKII
Princeton University
NAVIGATION: INDIAN OCEAN, RED SEA; NIKITIN, AFANASY; PILGRIMAGE, ISLAMIC

LARRY SILVER
Northwestern University
OIL PAINTING; NOTKE, BERNT; PACHER, MICHAEL; PLEYDENWURFF, HANS

ECKEHARD SIMON
Harvard University
NEIDHART "VON REUENTAL"

BARRIE SINGLETON
Courtauld Institute, University of London
PARES, JOHN

JAMES SNYDER
Bryn Mawr College
OUWATER, ALBERT VAN

CONTRIBUTORS TO VOLUME 9

PRISCILLA P. SOUCEK
New York University
NAQSH; NAQSH ḤADĪDA; NASKHĪ; NASTAᶜLIQ; PALEOGRAPHY, ARABIC AND PERSIAN

JAY L. SPAULDING
Michigan State University
NILE

E. G. STANLEY
Pembroke College, Oxford
OWL AND THE NIGHTINGALE, THE

RUTH STEINER
Catholic University of America
OFFERTORY; PLAINSONG, SOURCES OF

JOSEPH R. STRAYER
Princeton University
NECKHAM, ALEXANDER; NICHOLAS OF AUTRECOURT; NICHOLAS OF CLAMANGES; ODOFREDUS; PHILIP IV THE FAIR; PIERRE DUBOIS; PLANTAGENETS

LARRY E. SULLIVAN
Lehman College, City University of New York
PARIS

RICHARD E. SULLIVAN
Michigan State University
PARISH

SANDRA CANDEE SUSMAN
PIERO DI GIOVANNI TEDESCO; PISANO, ANDREA

DONALD W. SUTHERLAND
University of Iowa
PETTY ASSIZES, ENGLISH

R. N. SWANSON
University of Birmingham
NUNCIO, PAPAL

EDITH DUDLEY SYLLA
North Carolina State University
PHYSICS

EDWARD A. SYNAN
Pontifical Institute of Mediaeval Studies, Toronto
PHILOSOPHY AND THEOLOGY, WESTERN EUROPEAN: TERMINOLOGY

JOSEPH SZÖVÉRFFY
Wissenchaftskolleg zu Berlin
NOTKER BALBULUS; POETRY, LITURGICAL

PETRUS W. TAX
University of North Carolina
NOTKER TEUTONICUS; OTLOH OF ST. EMMERAM; PLEIER, DER

JOHN TAYLOR
University of Leeds
PALATINATES

MICHAEL D. TAYLOR
University of Houston
PISANO, GIOVANNI; PISANO, NICOLA

ROBERT TAYLOR
Victoria College, University of Toronto
PEIRE D'ALVERNHA

FRANK TOBIN
University of Nevada
MYSTICISM, CHRISTIAN: GERMAN

WARREN T. TREADGOLD
Hillsdale College
NIKEPHOROS I; PHOTIOS

RICHARD W. UNGER
University of British Columbia
NAVIES, WESTERN

MILOŠ VELIMIROVIĆ
University of Virginia
OKTOECHOS; PLAINSONG, EASTERN EUROPE

CHARLES VERLINDEN
NAVIGATION, WESTERN EUROPEAN

CHRYSOGONUS WADDELL
Abbey of Gethsemani
PETER THE VENERABLE

STEPHEN WAGLEY
PLENITUDO POTESTATIS

ELLEN T. WEHNER
University of Toronto
NICOLE BOZON; ORNEMENT DES DAMES; PETER LANGTOFT; PETER PECKHAM; PHILIPPE DE THAON

MARTIN WERNER
Temple University
PICTISH ART

L. G. WESTERINK
State University of New York at Amherst
NIKOLAOS I MYSTIKOS, PATRIARCH; PHILOSOPHY AND THEOLOGY, BYZANTINE

ESTELLE WHELAN
NĀᶜŪRA; ORTUQIDS

GREGORY WHITTINGTON
New York University
NARTHEX; NAVE; NICHE; OPUS ALEXANDRINUM; OPUS FRANCIGENUM; OPUS MIXTUM; OPUS RETICULATUM; OPUS SECTILE; PILASTER; PILASTER STRIP

GERNOT WIELAND
University of British Columbia
PAPIAS

JOHN WILLIAMS
University of Pittsburgh
OBECO; PEDRO DE CÓRDOBA; PETRUS

BRUCIA WITTHOFT
Framingham State College
NERI DI FIORAVANTI; NIVARDUS OF FLEURY

MARTHA WOLFF
Art Institute of Chicago
PLAYING CARDS, MASTER OF THE

KENNERLY M. WOODY
PETER DAMIAN, ST.

MARK A. ZIER
University of Toronto
NICHOLAS OF LYRA; PETER COMESTOR; PETER LOMBARD; PETER THE DEACON OF MONTE CASSINO

RONALD EDWARD ZUPKO
Marquette University
OUNCE; PECK; PENNY; PERCH

Dictionary of the Middle Ages

Dictionary of the Middle Ages

MYSTERY RELIGIONS. Although the term "mystery religions" is usually reserved for certain cults of antiquity (notably those of Eleusis, Dionysus, Orpheus, Isis and Osiris, Serapis, Mithras, Attis, and Cybele), there were several movements and cults in the Middle Ages that fulfilled the conditions requisite to being designated mystery religions. These are: (1) being restricted in membership; (2) requiring the performance of initiatic and other ceremonies under conditions of secrecy; and (3) promising spiritual privileges to their members.

Since both medieval Christianity and Islam were universal religions, they had the function, from which the ancient mysteries were exempt, of providing a doctrine and a practice, or liturgy, that could accommodate everyone without distinction. Openly proselytizing, their goal was to increase their membership, whereas in the ancient mysteries the approach had been from the other direction. Under such conditions both religions divided at a very early stage—perhaps from the outset—into an exoteric form suitable for the commonality of believers, and an esoteric form for the elect. Esoteric Christianity and esoteric Islam were, in effect, continuations of the mysteries of antiquity, but with a difference. As soon as temporal power was joined to spiritual authority (in the case of Christianity, with the conversion of the emperor Constantine in 312) the exoteric church became the established church, whose authorities regarded esotericists not as an initiated elite but often as unbelievers or heretics. Initiatic groups then had to contend with climates very different from the easy tolerance of the pagan Roman Empire, and their secrecy was as much a matter of self-preservation as of principle.

The experiences of mystery cultists are a phenomenon that recurs everywhere and at all times, be it within the framework of an established religion or outside it. There are always some who seek a more intense spiritual experience and are more curious about theological, cosmological, and psychological matters than the majority of believers. While the first aspiration can sometimes be satisfied without human assistance and within the orthodox system, there are certain aids such as personal contact, meditation techniques, and ritual practices which may further or intensify such experiences. The understanding of how and why these are efficacious leads to doctrines not easily comprehended by those who lack the experiences. Both the techniques and the theories seem strange, occult, and often threatening to the outsider, who is therefore excluded both to protect the initiates from ridicule and persecution, and for his own protection from unguided dabbling or intellectual confusion. If this is recognized as the raison d'être of esoteric mysteries in general, the degree to which this type of religion was present in the Middle Ages can be rightly judged, and one can appreciate Henry Corbin's statement: "There is a common ground between the ancient mystery religions, whose adepts are initiated into a mystery, and the initiatory brotherhoods within the revealed religions, whose adepts are initiated into a gnosis."

CHRISTIANITY AS A MYSTERY RELIGION

The question may arise as to what extent Catholic or Orthodox Christianity itself is a mystery religion. It fulfills some of the conditions enumerated above: initiatic and other ceremonies are performed, although publicly, and spiritual benefits are promised. Jesus Christ resembles mystery-saviors such as Dionysus, Orpheus, Mithras, Osiris, Attis, and Adonis in being an incarnate son of God who knew human suffering and death, and with whom the religion offers a personal relationship, even an identification; while the central Christian

MYSTERY RELIGIONS

sacraments of baptism and the Eucharist are so similar to pagan ones that there must be either a mutual influence or a common drawing on some fund of universal symbolic meaning. But the special purpose of Christianity appears to have been to throw open at least some aspects of the mysteries to all people without distinction and without secrecy. Thus all people, including slaves, sinners, and idiots, are offered the chance of attaining the Kingdom of Heaven, where "the last shall be first"—a "catholicity" whose obverse is the compulsion of everyone alike to accept the official version of this mystery.

Within Christianity esoteric movements have periodically surfaced in which the resemblance to the pagan mysteries is still stronger. The first one of the medieval period was the quest for the Holy Grail, whose mythology bears consideration in this context from a purely phenomenological point of view. To summarize: The Grail is the object of a quest that may or may not succeed in this life. It is concealed, guarded, and eventually removed from the world, or else sequestered in the Orient. It is perhaps a cup of plenty, or immortality, or of Christ's blood; perhaps the emerald eye of Lucifer before his fall; perhaps a stone "in exile." A group of ascetic warriors assembles to guard it in a semisubstantial temple, another group to seek for it. These present a phenomenology closely akin to that of alchemy, with all the ambiguity and multiple layers of mythology that also mark the alchemical quest and its object. It is impossible to say, in the case of the Grail material, how much is inner and how much outer history, just as in alchemy one cannot tell whether the operations described are supposed to be physical, psychic, or spiritual. In both cases, all that is certain is that there is a quest which leads, even in this life, to something that cannot or may not be described in rational language: hence the "mystery," the "keeping silent."

The Grail mythology borrows elements from ancient Celtic paganism, from Christianity both Celtic and Roman, and from Islam. Again like alchemy, it concerns a secret without confessional boundaries: it is its own religion in the sense of being a means to reconnect man with his origin. The exoteric religions are merely a support to it. While one cannot isolate "Grailists" as one can Sufis or Templars, this highly developed mythology points to the existence of more or less organized conclaves of devotees to this particular form of quest—one that regards the healing of the world as the concomitant duty of one who is seeking to heal his own exiled state.

The initiations of the Grail then become the archetypal spiritual path of the sacred warrior, seldom realized in practice, but always present as an ideal in medieval chivalry. Perhaps its closest realization was in the Order of the Temple (Templars), whose knights, at least in the early period, were engaged in some form of activity, still not fully explained, connected with the site of Solomon's Temple in Jerusalem. They were certainly an initiatic organization and some of their tenets and rites may well have been heretical in the eyes of the Roman church. The relations they fostered with the Islamic world went far beyond the obvious one of crusading: the work of Dante alone proves that philosophical exchanges took place under their auspices. The Templars are among the most visible signs of the underground currents which connect Islamic esotericism, the Fedele d'Amore (servants of love), the secret society to which Dante is said by Guénon to have belonged, and what were much later called the Rosicrucians.

The dualistic heresies such as Bogomils and Cathars cannot be considered mystery religions because they embraced whole peoples and claimed to be the true and potentially universal church. The qualifications of their initiates were not gnostic but purely ascetic.

MYSTERIES WITHIN ISLAM

Although heresy was always regarded in the Muslim world with great severity, the absence of a central church and hierarchy of professional clergy permitted the flourishing of an Islamic gnosis or esotericism to which the medieval Christian world offers no parallel. The transmission of esoteric doctrines and powers, in any tradition, has always taken place individually, either in the context of a mystery initiation or in the relationship of master to pupil. The Christian in need of spiritual advice turned naturally to the clergy; the Muslim, on the other hand, turned to a more or less recognized imam (model or prototype), who was beholden to no ecclesiastical superiors. While it is necessary to distinguish the separate existence of an actual sect, such as the Druzes, from the circle or spiritual progeny of an orthodox Sufi master, the intention of the aspirant or pupil remains the same: the dedication of life to a spiritual goal that remains a "mystery" until realized.

Another important difference was the relation-

MYSTERY RELIGIONS

ship of Islam with the pagan past. Quite soon after the first period of extreme revulsion against paganism, concerted efforts were made to rescue Greek learning and science. The form in which these legacies were found was colored by the general tendencies of very late paganism toward what can broadly be called hermeticism: a blend of Neoplatonic philosophy with syncretistic religion and the occult sciences of theurgy, alchemy, and astrology. These pre-Islamic religions, with their strong mystical content and literature descriptive of interior states, could not be ignored by esoterically inclined Muslims, to whom the validity of the Jewish and Christian revelations was already an article of faith. Sometimes their influences were successfully absorbed into orthodoxy; at other times—especially when completely unorthodox beliefs such as polytheism or reincarnation were concerned—they formed separate sects.

A cosmic system which promises successive rebirths on earth to the mass of humanity, but holds out the possibility, for the few who can attain it, of permanent liberation from the world of time and matter, is common to the ancient mystery religions as well as to Buddhism and Hinduism. We treat here four sects within the Islamic domain which share these assumptions.

The Druzes. According to Druze doctrine, al-Ḥākim and Ḥamza proclaimed that the time had come to supersede both the Sunnis' literal interpretation of the Koran, and the Shiites' allegorical interpretation; to open mankind to what Ḥamza called "a spiritual doctrine without any ritualistic impositions" (Epistle 13), in which, according to Makarim, man seeks to realize himself "in God, the absolute Reality, the only Existent and the only Real, the One Whom no one can realize in himself unless he moves away from his own self that separates and alienates him from the Unity that comprises all existence." This Unity will eventually be reestablished in an Apocalypse which will be experienced by those prepared for it as Paradise, by the unprepared as Hell.

The Druze's search for the divine Unity is a mystical one, informed by a philosophical nondualism. The path extends through successive reincarnations, one life not being sufficient for full realization of the Truth; but the moment of accepting the Call by pledging one's allegiance in writing is considered as the initiation into the ultimate stage of evolution, marked by the highest refinement of philosophy and ending in the highest goal attainable by man, that of conscious absorption into the Divine Unity. Present-day Druzes believe themselves to be reincarnations of those who then accepted the Call in the eleventh century. But the majority of mankind was not ready to understand this doctrine, hence its failure to become universal, the persecution of its followers from the outset, and the secrecy and close clannishness practiced by Druzes ever since.

Whether this sketch of contemporary Druze beliefs (based on Makarim) reflects the situation of medieval Druzism cannot be ascertained; but unless there has been some influence in the intervening centuries from Sufism or from further east (one observes, for instance, striking correspondences with Advaita Vedanta, and, in the Druze incarnational theosophy which is too involved to summarize here, with Tibetan Buddhism) it is more plausible than the previous accounts of Westerners working mainly from limited and prejudicial Muslim sources. We are still without any evidence concerning the secret initiations and rites that have been suspected by outsiders.

The Nuṣayrīs. As in the case of the Druzes, knowledge of the medieval Nuṣayrīs is largely a matter of induction from modern sources, particularly the testimony of a nineteenth-century apostate, Sulaiman Effendi. The clear evidences of pre-Islamic religion prove that there must have been some doctrinal continuity from long before the eleventh century, when they were mentioned in a refutation by the Druze founder Ḥamza. They were, like the Druzes, a hereditary sect, accepting no converts except Shiites (who shared some of their devotion to ᶜAlī). They celebrated mysteries and initiations which carried vows of absolute secrecy and which, in contrast to the Islamic prohibition, used consecrated wine.

The Nuṣayrīs resemble most the syncretistic mystery religions of the Roman Empire. From Shiite Islam they accepted the imamate, though authorities differ on whether they were twelvers or seveners. But their devotion to ᶜAlī went much further than any Shiite would allow. They applied to him the Christian doctrine of incarnation, calling him God's *maᶜnā* (creative mind or logos) and asserting that "there is no god but ᶜAlī ibn Abi Ṭālib." They allowed many other incarnations, ranging from Adam to the camel of Saleh (Koran 7:73, 26:155). At the core of Nuṣayrī theology (most complex in its ramifications, though simple

MYSTERY RELIGIONS

in its essence) is the Trinity shown in the accompanying table.

While a parallel with the Christian Trinity is just recognizable here, the Nuṣayrīs' identification of these three Persons with heavenly bodies (usually Sky, Sun, and Moon respectively, but varying with the subsects) betrays a closer origin in the Palmyrene Trinity of Baal Shamin (Sky god), Malakbel (Sun god), and Aglibol (Moon god). Their religion therefore seems to be rooted in the ancient paganism of Palmyra, to whose empire their region originally belonged.

The Nuṣayrīs expected only seven reincarnations before attaining the realm of ᶜAlī among the stars—a clear echo of the hermetic ascent through the spheres of the seven planets, culminating in the attainment of the transcendent eighth sphere. They also awaited the apocalyptic return of ᶜAlī from the sun to the earth. Their mysteries seem to have consisted of the delivery of a doctrinal Book of the Summary and the teaching of prayers, including the invocation "AMS" (initials of the last incarnation). Their ceremonies employed wine (as did the sacred banquets of the ancient Palmyrenes), incense, herbs, and prayers, some of them beautiful, others consisting of virulent curses on all other sects.

The Sabaeans of Ḥarrān. The Nuṣayrīs had a tradition that the elect stand at the gate of Ḥarrān and there receive the just, who will inhabit heaven. Ḥarrān has an immensely long history as a center of trade routes, metallurgy, alchemy, astrolatry, and hermetic religion—one thing, presumably, having led to another. In 830, in response to the caliph al-Maᵓmūn's challenge, the inhabitants claimed to be Sabaeans, a sect whose approving mention in Koran 2:62, 5:69, and 22:17 allowed them the status of "people of the book." They were in fact more pagan than Muslim, being worshipers of star gods, of Hermes and Agathodaemon, practitioners of astrological rituals and of alchemy. This survival of hermeticism in the bosom of Islam was possible because these divinities had been accepted into the prophetic canon by identification with Idris and Seth.

In the early Abbasid period a school of translators flourished in Ḥarrān under the guidance of Thābit ibn Qurra, specializing in Greek mathematical and astronomical texts. Both these sciences were highly developed there, and Pythagoras himself was regarded as the ancestor of the community. The Sabaean doctrines of the cosmos and human fate are close to his. Seven spiritual beings rule over the seven planets, which in turn direct the material universe, where Divine Light meets the darkness of evil. The human soul is consubstantial with the divine, but forgets its powers because of the admixture of matter. The universe proceeds in great cycles of 36,425 years, in each of which the human soul reincarnates under conditions determined by its previous conduct, unless through great effort it has completely emancipated itself from matter and escaped to join the pure souls in the timeless heaven. This appears to have been the more philosophical and esoteric side of Ḥarranian belief. Al-Shahrastānī divides them into two sects, the "spirituals" and the "idolaters," presumably referring respectively to these philosophical and ritual elements.

The Ikhwān al-Ṣafāᵓ. The avowed heirs of the Ḥarranian Sabaeans were the community in Basra known as the Ikhwān al-Ṣafāᵓ (Brethren of Purity), whom F. E. Peters calls "part of that Gnostic elite which in many times and many cultures has bent its efforts toward recovering the secret truths necessary for salvation. . . . They knew that the joys of Paradise had nothing to do with houris; it was assimilation to the One, and man need not wait upon death to attain it." The fifty-second and last volume of the Ikhwān's Encyclopedia, devoted to theurgy and magic, acknowledges the Sabaeans and is connected with the magical treatise of Ḥarranian origin known to the Renaissance in Latin under the name of *Picatrix.* The Ikhwān also celebrated a hermetic liturgy, including the reading of a "cosmic text" facing the Pole Star, and psalms and prayers attributed to Plato and Aristotle. Their Encyclopedia was read by the Druzes, the secret sect of Assassins, and most Sufi schools. The identity and nonliterary activity of the Ikhwān remains enigmatic, but they were evidently a group in which the main

The Nuṣayrī Trinity

Names Given in Initiation	Incarnational Type	Last Incarnation
Eternal archetypal deity	*asas* (foundation)	ᶜAlī ibn Abi Ṭālib
Expressed deity	*nāṭiq* (utterer) or *ism* (name)	Muḥammad
Communicator	*bāb* (gate)	Salmān al-Fārisī

object of the classical mysteries—the transformation of the individual through ritual and gnosis—was pursued in the new context of the Islamic revelation.

JUDAISM AS A MYSTERY RELIGION

In one sense, Judaism was a mystery religion within the Roman, Christian, and Islamic worlds: it was a nonproselytizing community whose members considered themselves in a special relationship with God, which could be entered by sincere converts on acceptance of initiation and a way of life permeated with ritual. It was in this sense that late Roman syncretism could accept Judaism as just one among many such cults. But in a deeper sense Judaism possessed its own mysteries in the cabala, which interprets the scriptures in an esoteric and symbolic sense, reading its own doctrines into the Torah. In this it resembles the Neoplatonic reading of Homer, the Sufi reading of the Koran, and certain Christian mystical interpretations of both Testaments. The doctrines of the medieval cabala incorporated ideas common to all mysteries of the hermetic type, for example, emanation, cosmic cycles, reincarnation, numerology, correspondences of microcosm and macrocosm. It envisaged the human race as arising from the sinking of divine sparks into matter, and the potential for their liberation either through the universal messianic redemption, or sooner through individual gnosis.

BIBLIOGRAPHY

Henry Corbin, "Rituel Sabéen et exegèse ismaelienne du rituel," in *Eranos-Jahrbuch,* **19** (1950), *Creative Imagination in the Sufism of Ibn ᶜArabī,* Ralph Manheim, trans. (1969), and "L'Imago Templi face aux normes profanes," in *Eranos-Jahrbuch,* **43** (1974); Joscelyn Godwin, *Mystery Religions in the Ancient World* (1981); René Guénon, *L'ésotérisme de Dante* (1925); Stephen Howarth, *The Knights Templar* (1982); Sāmī Nasīb Makārim, *The Druze Faith* (1974); John Matthews, *The Grail* (1981); Seyyed Hossein Nasr, *An Introduction to Islamic Cosmological Doctrines,* rev. ed. (1978); F. E. Peters, *Allah's Commonwealth: A History of Islam in the Near East, 600–1100 A.D.* (1973); Bernard H. Springett, *Secret Sects of Syria and the Lebanon* (1922).

JOSCELYN GODWIN

[See also **Abbasids; ᶜAlī ibn Abī Ṭālib; Assassins; Basra; Bogomilism; Cabala; Cathars; Chivalry, Orders of; Druzes; Encyclopedias and Dictionaries, Arabic and Persian; Grail, Legend of; Hākim bi-Amr Allāh, al-; Imam; Koran; Maᵓmūn, al-; Neoplatonism; Sabaeans; Sects, Islamic; Shiᶜa; Sunna.**]

MYSTICISM, CHRISTIAN. The subject of Christian mysticism is treated below in five separate articles: **Byzantine, Continental (Women), English, German,** and **Low Countries.** Additional discussions are cited in cross-references at the end of each essay.

MYSTICISM, CHRISTIAN: BYZANTINE. The word "mysticism" is widely used to designate the spirituality represented, in Byzantine tradition, by such authors as Origen, Gregory of Nyssa, and Maximus the Confessor. Whereas it is methodologically possible in studying the Western Christian tradition to draw a clear distinction between mysticism and theology, such a distinction is hardly admissible at all in Eastern, and particularly Byzantine, Christianity. All historians recognize today that, in the words of Jaroslav Pelikan, "one distinctive feature of the doctrinal history of Greek Christianity . . . was the role of mysticism." It is also possible to say that, for a Byzantine, Christian faith was identical with personal experience, and the latter was understood as being shared with others, as tradition and common teaching of the church. Thus, Vladimir Lossky could write: "If the mystical experience is a personal working out of the content of the common faith, theology is an expression, for the profit of all, of that which can be experienced by everyone."

One can legitimately wonder, therefore, whether the term "mysticism"—in its usual distinctive contemporary meaning, implying subjectivism and individual emotionalism—is applicable at all to the Eastern Christian tradition. In Greek patristics, the adjective "mystical" (*mystikos*) points most frequently to the hidden and transcendent character of divine existence, and only secondarily to the human perception of it. The short treatise "On Mystical Theology" by the unknown author who wrote in the early sixth century under the pseudonym of Dionysius the Areopagite is actually about divine transcendence: It affirms that God is totally unattainable by human senses or reason, that he is not an object of created perception at all, and that, therefore, knowledge of God is, indeed, a mysteri-

MYSTICISM, BYZANTINE

ous "communion," implying not only intellectual purification (as in Platonism), but a detachment from anything that is not God.

This goal and method is proposed not only to individual ascetics but to any theologian and, actually, any believer. Since the term "detachment" in this context implies individual effort, however, those who devoted their lives to it (essentially the monks) were generally recognized as spiritual leaders par excellence, and the specifically monastic spirituality tended to become a general example for all Christians. Consequently, the various trends of that spirituality influenced theology and the church in a decisive way.

These remarks concerning religious knowledge, understood in terms of mystical communion, imply a general recognition in Byzantine Christianity that truth is accessible, in a particular way, through the personal experience of the saints. This recognition does not exclude the teaching authority of the institutional and sacramental hierarchy of the church, but it presupposes that doctrinal pronouncements of bishops, or councils, lack final validity without their "reception" by all the believers. The numerous cases of popular, particularly monastic, opposition to synodal and, indeed, imperial pronouncements in the history of Christian Byzantium show that the external authority of the church magisterium—certainly essential ecclesiologically—was not seen as a substitute for the direct experience of the faith itself; rather institutional authority and mystical experience are the necessary and mutually validating poles of religious knowledge.

THE ORIGENISTIC AND EVAGRIAN TREND

The thought of Origen, the greatest of Christian philosophers and apologists of the third century, is based on the principle of convergence between Neoplatonic mysticism and Christian experience. The biblical idea of creation applies, according to Origen, not to an event happening in time, but to the existence of an eternal world of "intellects" whose original destiny was to participate in the divine essence of the Creator, but who fell away from God through a misuse of their freedom. This basic presupposition served as a foundation for monastic spirituality and asceticism in the writings of Evagrius Ponticus (346–399), who spent most of his life as a monk in the desert of Scete in Egypt and and was the first intellectual to interpret the popular monastic experience of the time in terms of Greek philosophical concepts. Evagrius is well known particularly for his formulation of the doctrine of "mental" or "intellectual" prayer. Identifying human existence in general with that of the intellect, destined to union with God, he defined permanent prayer as "the proper activity of the mind." The Evagrian doctrine of permanent prayer, which presupposed a struggle against "thoughts" and "passions"—that is, against all forms of attraction to things which are not God, and which Evagrius describes with an extraordinary knowledge of human psychology—became the foundation of spirituality, in all its forms, in the Christian East. Although Evagrius himself was posthumously condemned (together with Origen) by the Second Council of Constantinople (553) for his heretical christological views, his writings on prayer never lost their influence and popularity. They were preserved in manuscripts attributed to Orthodox authors, particularly St. Nilus of Sinai.

Equally influential in Byzantine spirituality were the writings of the Cappadocian fathers, particularly St. Gregory of Nyssa (*d. ca.* 394). Also influenced by Origen, they were more careful than Evagrius in maintaining, against Platonism, the biblical doctrine of creation and the idea of absolute divine transcendence. For Gregory of Nyssa, man, even in mystical rapture, cannot attain the essence of God, but participates only in divine energy—a self-giving activity of the Trinity. And since divine being is inexhaustible, the ascent of man is infinite "from glory to glory," as the experience of love. Together with the other Cappadocians, Gregory always expressed his doctrine of union with God in terms of *apophatic* (or "negative") theology: God is distinct from all creatures, and his being can be expressed only by saying "what he is not," not what he is. In spiritual terms, the mystics experience this transcendence when they speak of the divine darkness, which precedes the vision of God as light. Following Origen, Gregory uses the biblical narrative which describes Moses, seeing God in a cloud, as a model for the path followed by every Christian mystic. A similar approach to mysticism is found in the writings of Pseudo-Dionysius.

THE CHARISMATIC TREND: PSEUDO-MACARIUS

After Evagrius, the greatest influence in the history of spirituality in the Byzantine world was exercised by the writings known under the pseudonym of Macarius of Egypt. The author lived in eastern Asia Minor at the end of the fourth century, and his spiritual teaching was close to that of the Cappadocian fathers. In contrast with Evagrius, however, he did not identify human existence with its intellectual sphere only, but considered man as a psychosomatic whole, placing the center of human life in the heart. From this anthropology follows an understanding of salvation, or "deification," based on the sacraments of baptism and the Eucharist, which involve both the spirit and the body in a process leading to the resurrection. The spirituality of Macarius, based on the doctrine of the Incarnation and, therefore, on Christology and pneumatology, led to a new understanding of mental prayer: it became, more specifically, the "prayer of Jesus," based on the constant invocation of the name of Jesus, interpreted as the name of God incarnate. In this form, it appears in the writings of numerous spiritual and mystical Byzantine authors of the Middle Ages, including Diadochus of Photice (mid fifth century), John Climacus (*d. ca.* 649), and many others, whose writings were eventually included in the collection known as the *Philokalia.*

One of the most important messages contained in the writings of Pseudo-Macarius is his affirmation that communion with God happens "as an experience and with assurance," that such a conscious experience is available to all Christians and that it constitutes a necessary element of an authentic faith. This charismatic element, and other features of Macarian thought, has led some modern scholars to identify the author as one of the leaders of the dualistic Messalian sect (Symeon of Mesopotamia). The sect, condemned by several councils, was a charismatic monastic movement opposed to the institutional church. Whether or not this identification is historically demonstrable, the importance and influence of "Macarius" helped to counteract the Platonizing trend, going back to Evagrius, while preserving in Eastern Christendom the importance of personal experience, as distinct from institutional authoritarianism.

SYMEON THE NEW THEOLOGIAN

Following the tradition of Pseudo-Macarius, the monk Symeon, abbot of the monastery of St. Mamas in Constantinople (949–1022), maintained in medieval Byzantium the idea that conscious experience is the true sign of authentic Christian faith. Whereas practically all other Byzantine spiritual writers, even those who defended the principle of a conscious vision of God, refrained from describing their own visions directly, Symeon wrote in the first person. He can therefore be seen as a mystic in the usual sense of the word. Author of catechetical sermons addressed to his monks and of hymns reflecting poetically his experiences and teachings, he entered into repeated conflicts with ecclesiastical authorities on such issues as allowing nonordained monks to hear confessions and the unilateral canonization of his spiritual father, Symeon the Pious, in the liturgical ordo of his community. Some of his hymns, if understood literally, challenge the validity of sacraments performed by unworthy ministers. Symeon himself was a priest, however, and his insistence on the centrality of the sacraments, and particularly of the Eucharist, still separates him from nonecclesial and sectarian charismatics such as the Messalians. His message is that of a prophet; and as with all prophets and mystics, he is more concerned with communicating his message on the sensible experience of God than with theological exactness. Nevertheless, not only did his writings become extremely popular among Byzantine Christians, but he himself entered history with the title of "New Theologian," which puts him in line with John the Evangelist and Gregory of Nazianzus (also known in Byzantium as "the theologian").

HESYCHASM IN THE LATE BYZANTINE PERIOD

The terms *hesychia* (quietude) and hesychast have served to designate monastic hermits since the fourth century. In the late Byzantine period, however, the principles involved in contemplative monasticism and its discipline were hotly disputed. A psychosomatic method of continuous prayer, associated with the names of Nikephoros the Hesychast (thirteenth century) and Gregory of Sinai (*d.* 1359), involved an association of the Jesus Prayer with the rhythm of breathing. It was attacked by Barlaam of Calabria and defended on theological grounds by the most eminent theologian of that period, Gregory Palamas. The major issue involved in the debate was the experiential nature of the faith and the problem of whether communion with God was, in Christ, fully real or only symbolic. The victory of hesychasm was sanctioned by several councils of the period (1341, 1347, and 1351). This victory was followed by a revival of sacramental spirituality and mysticism, of which Nikolaos Kavasilas, author of *The Life in Christ,* is the best exponent.

BIBLIOGRAPHY
I. Hausherr, "L'hesychasme, étude de spiritualité," in *Orientalia christiana periodica,* **22** (1956); Vladimir Lossky, *The Vision of God* (1963), and *The Mystical Theology of the Eastern Church,* 2nd ed. (1976); John Meyendorff, *St. Gregory Palamas and Orthodox Spirituality* (1976); Jaroslav Pelikan, *The Christian Tradition,* I, *The Emergence of the Catholic Tradition, 100–600* (1971); *The Philokalia,* G. E. H. Palmer, Philip Sherrard, Kallistos Ware, eds. and trans., 3 vols. (1981–1984).

JOHN MEYENDORFF

[See also **Barlaam of Calabria; Byzantine Church; Councils (Ecumenical); Gregory of Nyssa, St.; Gregory Palamas; Hesychasm; Maximus the Confessor, St.; Nikolaos Kavasilas; Origen; Pseudo-Dionysius the Areopagite; Symeon the New Theologian, St.**]

MYSTICISM, CHRISTIAN: CONTINENTAL (WOMEN)

GENERAL BACKGROUND

The continental women mystics must be viewed in their historical, cultural, and religious context: Hildegard of Bingen and Elizabeth of Schönau in the twelfth century, which was marked by secular and religious wars, rampant millenarianism, and the decline of Benedictine monasticism; the *mulieres sanctae* (holy women) of the Low Countries, the Helfta mystics, Marguerite d'Oingt, and Angela of Foligno in the thirteenth century, which saw the ascendancy of the Cistercian and mendicant orders, the *Frauenfrage* (women's question) and *Frauenbewegung* (women's movement) phenomena, the beguine and beghard movements, and widespread heresy; the Dominican nuns in Bavaria and Switzerland, Birgitta of Sweden, and Catherine of Siena in the fourteenth century, with its continuation of church abuses that cried out for reform, the Black Death, the *Gottesfreunde* and *Devotio Moderna,* and temporal and ecclesiastical struggles which resulted in the Great Western Schism; and, finally, at the waning of the Middle Ages, Catherine of Genoa.

The responses of these women mystics to their age and their resultant impact on the society and culture of the Middle Ages are remarkable, especially given the inferior status of women at the time. According to Lucia of the Incarnation:

> When we turn now to the direct contribution of woman, we are struck by the fact that, whenever she left her vast kingdom of silence and revealed her genius in a more outstanding way, it was almost always in the religious sphere; and here her contribution bears more characteristically that of a charismatic vocation than in the case of man. She does not speak on her own account, but as an instrument; in this way, again, profoundly true to her nature. But in so doing, each time she reveals her unmistakable individuality.

This theme of the universal mystical experience and the idiosyncratic nature of each individual's response to it is manifest in the lives of these women mystics, who represented all social classes and religious and secular ways of life, whose revelations ranged from autobiographical accounts of their experiences to monitory prophecies and calls for reform, to treatises on the *via mystica* (mystic way); and whose lives and writings reveal several striking similarities.

(1) All were reluctant to record their mystical experiences (which were unsought) owing to their sense of inadequacy, lack of education, or fear of insufficient discernment of spirits and stirrings on their part, which could result in delusion or, worse, heresy. Invariably they ascribed their visions and auditions to a special seeing with the soul and hearing with the ears of inner understanding. Hildegard of Bingen, for example, classified herself as a *homo simplex* (artless human) and merely a mouthpiece for the *Verbum Dei* (Word of God). All were encouraged to write or dictate their accounts by their spiritual directors or a divine dictum, or both.

(2) The majority led lives of extreme asceticism, and were afflicted with protracted illnesses, a fact which is given undue importance by many critics who tend to impute their ecstasies to poor health.

(3) All were under the guidance of learned spiritual directors, capable of imparting doctrinal and theological learning, and of assessing the validity of the mystic's experience.

(4) As their formal schooling was generally limited—an astonishing fact when one considers the cosmic visions of Hildegard of Bingen, the mystical insights of Angela of Foligno, and the theological complexity of Catherine of Siena—their biographers and hagiographers stressed the operation of divine inspiration and infused knowledge, thereby assigning a *dictante Spiritu Sancto* (dictated by the Holy Spirit) authority to their writings. Because most of them did not know Latin, they dictated

The Creation (left) and Vicissitudes of the Soul (heaven, the tribulations of life, hell). Miniature from the *Scivias* of Hildegard of Bingen, 1141–1150. WIESBADEN, HESSISCHE LANDESBIBLIOTHEK, MS 1

their experiences to a secretary, usually their spiritual advisor, who then translated the material into Latin. This transmission process raises the question of scribal interpolation and emendation.

(5) Their writings are far more imaginative, colorful, sensuous, and descriptive than those of their male counterparts, are frequently cast in the dialogue mode, and, in many instances, are closely linked with the *Opus Dei*.

(6) Their spirituality was predominantly Christocentric, with a special affinity for the infant Jesus, Christ crucified, and the Eucharist, and also incorporated *Brautmystik* (bride mysticism) elements, the "play of love" between the soul and God, Trinitarian exemplarism, and a strong core of Marian piety.

(7) In addition to enriching the *depositum fidei* (deposit of faith) with their contemplative and expiatory prayers, all were impeccably orthodox in their beliefs and support of the institutional church and its sacraments.

(8) As a group, they were imbued with a high degree of social responsibility, evinced by their strong moral condemnation of temporal and ecclesiastical abuses and injustice, active opposition to heresy, vigorous apostolates among clergy and laity, spiritual counseling, and dedication to the corporeal works of mercy, particularly for the sick, indigent, and dispossessed. Thus their mystical vocation conjoined the active and contemplative lives in the spirit of *libertas cordis* (freedom of the heart), whereby, according to Kenneth Wapnick:

> The mystic now no longer finds his involvement with the world to be abhorrent, but, in fact, seems to welcome the opportunity to move in the social world he had abandoned. This seeming paradox becomes understandable when one considers it was not the

> world the mystic was renouncing, but merely his attachments and needs relating to it, which precluded the development of his personal asocial experience. Once he was able to abandon these dependent, social needs, and felt freed of the social world, he experienced the freedom to live within society in conjunction with his inner strivings, rather than experiencing society's customs and institutions as obstacles to his self-fulfillment.

This *Wirkeinheit* or working union with God and the resultant social action represent the fulfillment of the *via mystica.*

Although the majority of the women mystics were not officially canonized, Gertrude of Helfta, Catherine of Siena, Catherine of Genoa, Birgitta of Sweden, and Dorothea of Montau being notable exceptions, they were all eventually included in the Roman Martyrology. It should also be noted that, with few exceptions, they have been undeservedly neglected by scholars.

WESTERN AND CENTRAL GERMANY

Hildegard of Bingen. The recipient of heavenly visions from the age of five onward, Hildegard of Bingen (1098–1179) first joined the Benedictine house at Disibodenberg, becoming abbess in 1136, and subsequently established a convent at Rupertsberg, near Bingen, where she remained until her death. Hildegard not only served as abbess and foundress, but also was a visionary, prophet, natural scientist, skilled infirmarian, poetess, musician, and social and ecclesial activist. Her canon includes the *Liber simplicis medicinae* (*Liber subtilitatum diversarum naturarum creaturarum* which comprehended both *Causae et curae* and *Physica*) the *Ordo Virtutum* (in part III, visio 13, of the *Scivias*), a liturgical drama set to music, which is the earliest known morality play; an *Explication of the Rule of St. Benedict; The Life of St. Rupert* and *The Life of St. Disibode;* an *Expositio* on the Gospels; *Explanatio symboli sancti Athanasii; Solutiones triginta octo quaestionum; Lingua ignota;* and a large collection of *Letters.*

In her own and succeeding ages, her fame resided in part with her mystical and prophetic writings: the *Scivias* or *Scito vias Domini,* written between 1141 and 1150 and consisting of twenty-six detailed symbolic and allegorical visions (some of which were translated into thirty-five miniatures executed under her supervision), coupled with chiliastic warnings directed against both secular and religious corruption; the *Liber vitae meritorum,* a treatise on the moral order, composed between 1158 and 1163; and the *Liber Divinorum operum simplics hominis* or *De operatione Dei* (1163–1173). Hildegard's mystical visions were not limited to the *unio mystica* (mystic union), but, seen in the shadow or cloud of the *lux vivens* (living light), encompassed the macrocosm (Creation), the microcosm (man), and the transcosm (God).

An even greater measure of fame was accorded to this "Sybil of the Rhine" for her prophetic powers and apostolic missions of instruction and reform throughout Germany and France, which commanded the respect and approbation of monarchs, prelates such as Pope Eugenius III and Bernard of Clairvaux, and countless numbers of lesser lay and religious figures.

Elizabeth of Schönau. Hildegard's influence can be seen in the life and writings of her contemporary Elizabeth of Schönau (1129–1164), a prophetic visionary and strong advocate for church reform, who served as the superior of the nuns at the double monastery at Schönau, under Abbot Hildelin. Her mystical experiences, which occurred between 1152 and 1160, were dictated to her brother Eckbert, a Benedictine monk, and include: *Visiones,* a liturgically oriented account of her visions and auditions of Christ, the Blessed Virgin, and saints; *Liber viarum Dei,* patterned on Hildegard's *Scivias;* the *Visiones de resurrectione Beatae Mariae Virginis,* attesting to the Assumption of the Blessed Virgin; and the legend of St. Ursula and her band of 11,000 virgin martyrs, one of the best-known hagiographic stories of the Middle Ages. Her works were disseminated throughout Europe, and also reached England, through a redaction by Roger of Ford in the 1170's.

Mechthild of Hackeborn, Mechthild of Magdeburg, Gertrude the Great. The three thirteenth-century German mystics, Mechthild of Hackeborn, Mechthild of Magdeburg, and Gertrude the Great, were associated with the Cistercian/Benedictine convent at Helfta, which, under the forty-year abbatial tenure of Gertrude of Hackeborn, was an intellectual, spiritual, and mystical center.

Mechthild of Hackeborn (1241–1299) was charged not only with assisting her sister Abbess Gertrude, but also with such conventual tasks as teaching, counseling, training novices, and directing the choir (for which she was called "God's Nightingale"). Her close friend Gertrude the Great compiled the accounts of Mechthild's ascetic life, visions, and ecstasies into the seven-part *Liber*

MYSTICISM, CONTINENTAL

specialis gratiae, which is infused with a joyful spirit of praise and love of God, and participates in the *Brautmystik* school of mystical writings, colored by the chivalric and minnesang traditions. Along with other Helfta religious, and especially Gertrude, Mechthild was instrumental in promoting the cult of the Sacred Heart. Her *Liber* was circulated on the Continent and in England, where a Middle English translation, *The Booke of Gostlye Grace,* often referred to as the "Maude Book," was a popular devotional work.

After leaving her aristocratic family to become a beguine about 1230, Mechthild of Magdeburg (1210–1282/1294) became a Dominican tertiary, under the spiritual direction of Henry of Halle, a disciple of Albert the Great. In 1250, after years of ascetic and prayerful living, she began to record the particulars of her mystical life, which were then edited and rearranged by Henry into *Das fliessende Licht der Gottheit* (The flowing light of the Godhead). Because of her outspoken denunciations of immoral conduct in both church and state, for which she was persecuted and even accused of heresy, she took refuge at Helfta around 1270–1271, and, having lost her sight, dictated the conclusion of her book to the nuns. Shortly after her death, Henry produced a Latin translation of her book, *Lux divinitatis fluens in corda veritatis,* and a subsequent High German version by Henry of Nördlingen was circulated among the *Gottesfreunde* in southern Germany and Switzerland, including the Waldschwestern recluses at Einsiedeln.

In addition to recounting Mechthild's spiritual journey from purgation through illumination to union with God, the *Flowing Light* is a devotional work of extraordinary beauty and, at the same time, a jeremiad against societal and ecclesial inequities. Like Hildegard of Bingen and Mechthild of Hackeborn, Mechthild of Magdeburg was an inclusivist, encompassing all of creation in her visions.

Gertrude the Great (1256–1301/1302), who came to Helfta at the age of five, avidly pursued higher learning until a spiritual crisis in 1281. This marked the beginning of her mystical vocation, which resulted in the invisible stigmata, like Catherine of Siena, and, later, the wound of divine love, a privilege later to be accorded to Teresa of Ávila. At Christ's behest, she wrote *The Messenger or Herald of God's Loving Kindness* (*Legatus divinae pietatis,* or *Insinuationes*), as well as the ascetical-mystical *Spiritual Exercises,* composed for the Helfta community. Only Book 2 of the *Insinuationes* was actually composed by Gertrude, Book 1 being a posthumous tribute to the saint, but it is believed that she dictated the last three books to members of the community. While following the contemplative life, Gertrude was actively engaged in conventual tasks and in her apostolate to the laity and clergy. Like the two Mechthilds, she promoted the cult of the Sacred Heart of Jesus, a devotion also promulgated by Lutgard of Aywières and other Low Country ecstatics.

THE LOW COUNTRIES

As a result of the *Frauenfrage, Frauenbewegung,* and *cura monialium* (the charge laid to the religious orders, especially the Cistercians and Dominicans, to assume the spiritual care of women monastics in convents), a large number of *mulieres sanctae* in the Low Countries and elsewhere in Europe attached themselves to Cistercian and Dominican houses, or became associated with the semireligious beguine movement, which, in its emphasis on apostolic poverty and Christian perfection, anticipated the *Gottesfreunde,* Brethren of the Common Life, and *devotio moderna* of the fourteenth and fifteenth centuries. The women mystics of the Low Countries, with vocations as lay women, tertiaries, religious, recluses, and beguines, were particularly noteworthy: Mary of Oignies (*d.* 1213), Christine of St. Tronde, called "Mirabilis" (*d.* 1224), Yvette of Huy (*d.* 1228), Ida of Nivelles (*d. ca.* 1231), Margaret of Ypres (*d.* 1237), Lutgard of Aywières (*d.* 1246), Hadewijch (*fl.* 1250), Alice of Schaarbeek (*d.* 1250), Juliana of Cornillion (*d.* 1258), Ida of Leeuw (*d.* 1260), Eve of St. Martin (*d.* 1265), Beatrice of Nazareth (*d.* 1268), Ida of Louvain (*d.* 1300), Christine of Stommeln (*d.* 1312), Elizabeth of Spalbeck (*d.* 1316), and Gertrude of Oosten (*d.* 1358). All led lives of heroic virtue, extreme asceticism, and deep spirituality, extolled in what might be termed the *Vitae matrum* (Lives of holy women) by hagiographers such as Jacques de Vitry (Mary of Oignies), Peter of Dacia (Christine of Stommeln), Thomas de Cantimpré (Lutgard of Aywières, Christine of St. Trond, Margaret Ypres), and Hugh de Floreffe (Yvette of Huy). In addition to following the *via mystica,* these holy women were, like their sister mystics, occupied with campaigns against social evils, church laxity, and heresy, as well as with spiritual counseling and social service.

 MYSTICISM, CONTINENTAL

Mary of Oignies and Christine of Stommeln both fulfilled the role of *pia mater* for a zealous circle of followers; Lutgard of Aywières and Alice of Schaarbeek championed the devotion to the Sacred Heart; Juliana of Cornillon and Eve of St. Martin were instrumental in establishing the feast of Corpus Christi; and, consonant with the spirit of *imitatio Christi,* Mary of Oignies, Ida of Louvain, Christine of Stommeln, Elizabeth of Spalbeek, and Gertrude of Oosten all received the stigmata.

Of the Low Countries group, perhaps the best known are Beatrice of Nazareth, a Cistercian nun (*ca.* 1200–1268), and the beguine Hadewijch (*fl.* 1250), both exponents of love mysticism, which drew upon the Bernardian *Brautmystik* and the chivalric concept of *Minne* to express the centrality of love of the exemplar Christ to the spiritual life. Beatrice authored a spiritual autobiography, subsequently translated into Latin by William of Afflighem, and an excerpt therefrom, entitled *The Seven Ways or Degrees of Love (Van Seven Manieren van Heiligher Minnen).* The tract outlines the theopathic states of the progressive spiritual life, leading to the soul's passivity in the realm of higher contemplation, annihilation, union, and a longing for death which alone would bring full union with God.

At one time erroneously identified with the heretical beguine Bloemardinne of Brussels (*d.* 1336), Hadewijch left fourteen visions, thirty-one letters addressed to an anonymous young beguine, forty-five strophic poems which are adjudged her greatest work, and sixteen poems in *rimes plates.* Employing the metaphor of a duel to describe the soul's ascent to God, who is Love, Hadewijch was influenced by Bernard of Clairvaux, William of St. Thierry, Richard of St. Victor, and Neoplatonic Trinitarian exemplarism, and, in turn, exerted a great influence on Jan van Ruusbroec.

FRANCE

Despite the opportunities for Christian women to seek fulfillment in religious life, there is little evidence of women contemplatives in France during the early Middle Ages. Only Liutberga of Wendhausen (*d.* 860?) is singled out in this regard. In the later Middle Ages, only Marguerite d'Oingt and the beguine Margaret Porete have received any significant mention. Born into a noble Beaujolais family, Marguerite d'Oingt (*d.* 1310) entered the Carthusian house of Poleteins near Lyon and subsequently was appointed prioress, a position she held until her death. Her canon of writings is composed of the *Pagina meditationum,* a series of Latin meditations on Christ's Passion, sin, hell, God's grace, and the Motherhood of Christ, a theme shared especially with Julian of Norwich; and of several works in Provençal: the *Speculum,* telling of her visions of Christ, the Trinity, and heaven; the *Life of St. Beatrix d'Ornacieux,* which shows many similarities with Marguerite's own affective spirituality; and five letters.

Margaret Porete (*d.* 1310) has been credited with the *Miroir des simples ames,* a manual on the progressive spiritual life structured as a dialogue, which concentrates on the higher stages of contemplation, union, and the mystical marriage. Because of its seeming espousal of tenets of the Free Spirit heresy, both the work and its author were condemned and burned in 1310. Despite its putative heterodoxy, the work was translated into Middle English by M.N. in the fifteenth century, possibly through the agency of the Carthusians, but those passages which might be interpreted as unorthodox were carefully glossed by the translator. In 1491, M. N.'s Middle English version was translated into Latin by Richard Methley of Mount Grace Charterhouse, who also glossed the suspect sections. Both M. N. and Methley, along with the three French theologians who approved the original French text, were obviously convinced of the *Mirror's* orthodoxy, a position which is questioned today by such critics as Edmund Colledge and Romana Guarnieri.

SOUTHERN GERMANY AND SWITZERLAND

The efflorescence of women mystics in Alemannic Switzerland and southwestern Germany during the late thirteenth and fourteenth centuries received its impetus generally from the *Frauenfrage* and *Frauenbewegung,* but more particularly from the *cura monialium* of the mendicant orders. In addition to assuming the spiritual responsibility for semireligious communities, the Dominicans were charged with the direction and guidance of cloistered women religious in this locale. To carry out this responsibility they assigned some of their most outstanding men, such as Henry Suso, who introduced the nuns to theological speculation and mystical contemplation. It is important to note that many of the nuns were from the upper classes or aristocracy, capable of bringing substantial dowries to the convents, and also were well educated. At the beginning of the fourteenth century, there were over seventy Dominican convents in this geographical area, several of which were noted centers of mysticism: Töss near Winterthur, Katharinental by Diessenhofen, Oetenbach near Zurich, Engeltal and Maria-Medingen near Nuremberg, Adelhausen in Freiburg, Kirchberger near Sulz, Weiler by Esslingen, and the Alsatian house at Schönensteinbach. Interestingly enough, many of these convents, such as Töss and St. Katharinental, originally were *Gotteshäuser* (houses of God) or beguinages.

A second major influence was the socio-religious phenomenon known as the *Gottesfreunde,* whose practical mysticism espoused individualism, self-renunciation, the feasibility of *unio mystica* between God and man, and the essential equality of lay and religious Christians. Among the leaders of this movement who were particularly important in the southern Dominican houses were Henry Suso and Henry of Nördlingen, laypersons such as members of the Golden Ring in Basel, and, among the nuns, Elsbeth Stagel, Suso's spiritual daughter, at Töss; Margaret Ebner at Maria-Medingen, associated with Henry of Nördlingen; and Christine Ebner and Adelhaid Langmann of Engeltal.

These religious led the mixed life of intense ascesis, penance, prayer, and contemplation, coupled with participation in convent life, counseling, charitable works, and literary activity, which consisted in recording sermons, setting down their own mystical experiences as well as those of *consorores* (sister mystics), and extensive letter writing. Because of their penitential austerities and, in some cases, excessive subjectivity and sentimentality, as well as the physical and psychic tensions generated by the whole community, these women have been rather unfairly castigated by later critics as hysterical, pathological, repressed, totally imitative, or, at best, uninspired.

Their literary productivity was varied and usually represented the collaboration of two nuns or a monk and a nun. Several wrote revelations of their mystical life. Examples are the *Diarium* of Margaret Ebner (*d.* 1351), recounting her contemplative experience from 1312 to 1348, actually written down by the prioress Elizabeth Scheppach and edited by Henry of Nördlingen; *Von der Gnaden Ueberlast* by Christine Ebner (*d.* 1356); and the *Offenbarungen* of Adelhaid Langmann (*d.* 1375). The correspondence between these cloistered nuns and a wide circle of other religious, clergy, and laity affords illuminating accounts of the mystical atmosphere and practices in the convents and the religious milieu of the age, as well as contemporary historical events like papal/imperial struggles, the interdict, and Black Death. Noteworthy in this regard are Henry of Nördlingen's correspondence with Margaret Ebner and her contemporaries, which is the first collection of letters in the German language, and the communications of Elsbeth Stagel and Henry Suso. The most illustrious of this group of women mystics was Elsbeth Stagel, who was as important in Henry Suso's life as Clare was to Francis of Assisi. Not only did she encourage him to write his *vita* and collect his letters, but she also translated some of his Latin works into the vernacular.

A third important literary legacy from these nuns are the *vitae sororum (Schwesternbücher),* which were collections of the spiritual and mystical biographies of the sisters, written by Anna von Munzingen, Elsbeth Stagel, and Katherine von Gebweiler, among others. The *vitae* were intended to provide edifying exemplars of the ascetic-mystical vocation for the later nuns at Adelhausen, Töss, Engeltal, Unterlinden, Weiler, Katharinental, and Oetenbach, and represent a distinct genre of religious writing. While the chronicles have been derogated as pedestrian and derivative in their language, possibly because they lack the lyric flights and intensity of a Mechthild of Magdeburg or a Henry Suso, Hester Ghering's careful study suggests that such criticism is unjust, and that they indeed made a definite contribution to the mystical language of the later Middle Ages by affording a complete terminology of practical, as opposed to speculative, mysticism. Furthermore, answering the charge that the accounts of supernatural manifestations—which were the central concern of the *vitae*—appear unauthentic, Ghering demonstrates that they encompass all phases of the ongoing mystical life. An even stronger apologia for the importance and validity of these works is offered in Walter Blank's *Die Nonnenviten des 14. Jahrhunderts.*

Another important fourteenth-century German mystic is St. Dorothea of Montau, patronness of Prussia (1347–1394). Like Birgitta of Sweden, whom she admired greatly, she was married and widowed, went on pilgrimages, and simultaneously led a contemplative life. Toward the end of her life she was enclosed in the cathedral wall at Marienwerder, where, like the English recluse Julian of Norwich, she was sought after as a spiritual counselor by her "even Christians." Her experiences, recorded by her spiritual director, John of Marienwerder (1343–1417), are contained in her *vita,* the *Septililium* or *Seven Graces,* and the liturgically oriented *Liber de Festis.* Her spirituality is similar to that of Birgitta and Catherine of Siena, and, according to some scholars, may have exerted an influence on Margery Kempe of Lynn.

ITALY

The flowering of feminine mysticism in Germany and Switzerland was paralleled in Italy, again under the impetus of the Dominican and Franciscan orders. Approximately 100 known *mulieres sanctae,* following a variety of lay and religious ways of life, appeared between 1200 and 1400, among them St. Verdiana, Bd. Gherardesca of Pisa, St. Humiliana, St. Umiltà of Florence, Bd. Beneventua of Friuli, Bd. Margaret of Faenza, Bd. Aldobrandesca of Siena, Bd. Santuccia of Gubbio, Bd. Margaret of Cortona, Bd. Agnesa of Montepulciano, Bd. Giuliana Falconiere, Bd. Margherita of Città di Castello, Bd. Giustina of Arezzo. The most famous of these Italian visionaries were Bd. Angela of Foligno, St. Catherine of Siena, and, in the fifteenth century, St. Catherine of Genoa.

Angela of Foligno. In her spiritual autobiography, entitled *Memoriale de fra Arnaldo,* Angela of Foligno (1248–1309) depicts her earlier life as a wife and mother as one of indulgence, vanity, and, at best, lukewarm Christianity. Converted about 1285 by a dream of St. Francis of Assisi, she made a general confession to her relative, Fra Arnaldo da Foligno, OFM, who subsequently became her spiritual advisor and the transcriber and Latin translator of her revelations. Her spiritual conversion turned her to a life of asceticism, penance, and contemplation, together with unflagging work at the leper hospital and related social service. Finally, in 1291, following the death of her husband, children, and mother, she became a Franciscan tertiary and, en route to Assisi, received a revelation from the Holy Spirit, stating that she would be God's instrument, a vocation which would bring great fame to her and even greater glory to God. At Fra Arnaldo's insistence, she dictated the account of her spiritual *itinerarium* from 1285 to 1296, which she arranged into thirty steps to perfection to accord with the hidden years of Christ's earthly life. After 1296, she directed her energies into her spiritual maternity to cenacles of souls in Italy and elsewhere, an activity which resulted in her *Istruzioni salutifere* and an extensive correspondence. For her theological and mystical acumen and her work with her priest "sons," she was given the titles "Mother of Souls" and "Mistress of Theologians," and was lauded by one of her spiritual sons, Ubertino da Casale, in his *Arbor vitae crucifixae Jesu.*

Catherine of Siena. Catherine of Siena (1347–1380) not only pursued the *via mystica* but also was immersed in the active life as a teacher, theologian, social worker, reformer, peacemaker, advisor to secular and ecclesiastical rulers, and leader of the cause to end the Babylonian Captivity and return the papacy to Rome. This extraordinarily gifted woman became a Dominican tertiary or *mantellata* at sixteen, and four years later was mystically espoused to Christ. Eight years later, in 1375, she received the stigmata, which, at her request, were invisible. Through her sanctity, charisma, and zealous efforts for church and social reform, she gathered a following of lay and religious disciples, called *la bella brigata* or *Caterinati,* one member of which was William Flete, the noted English Augustinian recluse. Although her rigorous apostolate to effect the *santo passaggio* (holy passage or holy return to Rome) ended in failure with the Great Western Schism, she continued to work for the reform of the Dominican order and other causes of her earthly mission until her death in Rome in 1380, at the age of thirty-three.

Catherine's works include 382 *Letters,* twenty-six *Prayers,* and the *Dialogue,* also known as the *Book of Divine Providence,* an extended colloquy between her soul and God. This record of her mystical life is centered around Christ crucified, his salvific Sacred Blood, and divine love, experienced to the fullest in union and translated into service in behalf of her fellow Christians and of the church, as Christ's mystical body. Her *Dialogue* and the *vita* written by her confessor Raymond of Capua, later to become master general of the Dominicans, were disseminated throughout the Continent and in England, where a Middle English translation of the *Dialogue,* called *The Orcherd of Syon,* was prepared for the Birgittine nuns at Syon Abbey.

Catherine was canonized in 1461, designated by the church as patronness of Italy, together with Francis of Assisi, in 1939, and proclaimed a doctor of the church in 1970, along with Teresa of Ávila.

Catherine of Genoa. The third great Italian woman mystic, Catherine of Genoa (1447–1510), was born into an aristocratic Genoese family, was pressured into marriage at the age of sixteen, and, in 1473, experienced a dramatic second conversion to a life of rigorous ascesis, penance, and contemplation. Her husband agreed to a continent marriage, and both focused their energies on nursing the sick poor, and particularly the plague victims, at the Pammatone Hospital. Like Catherine of Siena, she fulfilled the demands of the mystical life, with a special devotion to the Eucharistic Presence of Christ, and of the active life of social service and church reform. She also attracted a devoted band of disciples, one of whom, Ettore Vernazza, inspired by Catherine, founded the Oratory of Divine Love, dedicated to the reform of the church and care of the poor. Unlike many of her sister mystics, Catherine had no spiritual director until approximately eleven years before her death, when Dom Cattaneo Marabotto assumed this responsibility. She died in 1510, surrounded by her *circolo,* and was canonized in 1733.

Catherine's teachings are found in a *Vita,* the *Trattato* or *Purgation and Purgatory,* concerned with spiritual purgation in this life and the next, and the psychomachian *Dialogo* or *Spiritual Dialogue,* all of which were written by her followers, most probably Dom Marabotto and Ettore Vernazza, who drew upon her accounts of her mystical experiences and the inner life, as well as her spiritual advice.

Birgitta of Sweden. St. Birgitta of Sweden (1303–1373) is often associated with Catherine of Siena, owing to her commitment to moral reform and to the *santo passaggio.* Married to a Swedish nobleman at fourteen and mother of eight children, Birgitta led an ascetic life under the direction of Master Matthias (*d.* 1351), the foremost theologian in Sweden. After her husband's death in 1344, she began to lead an intense life of prayer and contemplation, and, like Hildegard of Bingen, to experience revelations calling for reform of church and secular governments. She was also commanded by Christ to found a new religious order, the Order of the Most Holy Savior, dedicated to the Blessed Virgin, which subsequently flourished throughout Europe, with major houses at Vadstena, Lübeck, and Syon Abbey, established by Henry V at Isleworth, England, in 1415.

At God's direction, she proceeded to Rome in 1349, where her forceful intervention in papal, ecclesiastical, and secular affairs resulted in great hostility toward her on the one hand, but, on the other, earned her the title "protectress of the Holy See." Birgitta had several spiritual directors in Rome, the most important being Alphonse of Pecha, bishop of Jaen, who served as her confessor, advisor, collaborator and editor of her *Revelations,* and as the leading force for her canonization. After a pilgrimage to the Holy Land, which occasioned a number of visions of Christ and the Blessed Virgin, Birgitta died in Rome in 1373, and her remains were translated to the mother house of her order at Vadstena.

Owing to the efforts of her daughter Katherine, who was the first superior at Vadstena, the *Defensorium* of the English cardinal Adam Easton, and, above all, Alphonse of Pecha, with his *Epistola Solitarii ad Reges,* Birgitta's canonization occurred in 1391, and was reaffirmed in 1419. Yet she remained a controversial figure and was attacked during the conciliar movement by John Gerson, with his *De probatione spiritum,* and by Matthias Döring in his *Probate spiritus.* With the apologias of Alphonse and Easton, however, and bolstered by Cardinal John Torquemada's *Defensione,* Birgitta's cause prevailed.

Her major writings are her 700 *Revelations* or *Liber celestis,* which were widely circulated and received with special favor in England; the *Rule of St. Savior;* and the *Sermo angelicus* or lessons for the Birgittine Night Office.

An inspired visionary, spiritual force, and prophetess, Birgitta exemplifies the mixed life of the true mystic, combining the activity of the human spirit with the Divine Will of God, and joins her mystical *consorores* in imparting their timeless message of human dignity, hope, and love.

BIBLIOGRAPHY

General Background. "Women in the Kingdom of God," in *Month,* 241 (1980); Caroline Bunum, *Jesus as Mother* (1982), and *The Religious Significance of Good to Medieval Women* (1987); John E. Crean, "Studies in Fourteenth Century Mystical Terminology: The Middle High German of Meister Eckhart and the Middle Netherlandic of Jan van Ruusbroec" (diss., Yale, 1966); Peter Dronke, *Women Writers of the Middle Ages* (1984); Lina Eckenstein, *Women Under Monasticism* (1896); Richard Kieckhefer, "Mysticism and Social Consciousness in the Fourteenth Century," in *University of Ottawa Quarterly,* 48 (1978); Lucia of the Incarnation, "The Western Spiritual Tradition," in *Way,* suppl. 16 (1972); Lucy Menzies, *Mirrors of the Holy: Ten Studies in Sanctity* (1928); Ray C. Petry, "Social Responsibility and the Late Medieval Mystics," in *Church History,* 21 (1952); Wolfgang Riehle, *The Middle English Mystics,*

Bernard Standring, trans. (1981); Richard W. Southern, *Western Society and the Church in the Middle Ages* (1970); Kenneth Wapnick, "Mysticism and Schizophrenia," in *Journal of Transpersonal Psychology,* **1** (1969); Wendy M. Wright, "The Feminine Dimension and Consciousness," in *Studia mystica,* **3** (1980).

Western and central Germany: Hildegard of Bingen (Sources). Pudentiana Barth, and Joseph Schmidt-Görg, eds., Hildegard von Bingen, *Lieder* (1969); Adelgundis Führkötter, ed., *Les miniatures du Scivias: La connaissance des voies de Sainte Hildegarde de Bingen, tirées du codex de Rupertsberg* (1977), and *Hildegardis Scivias,* 2 vols. (1978); Bruce Hozeski, ed. and trans., *Hildegard of Bingen's Scivias* (1985); Heinrich Schipperges, trans., *Hildegard von Bingen: Welt und Mensch. Das Buch De operatione Dei* (1965), and *Hildegard von Bingen: Der Mensch in der Verantwortung. Das Buch der Lebensverdienste* (1972).

Hildegard of Bingen (Studies). David Baumgardt, "The Concept of Mysticism: Analysis of a Letter Written by Hildegard of Bingen to Guibert of Gembloux," in *Review of Religion,* **12** (1948); Peter Dronke, "Hildegard of Bingen as Poetess and Dramatist," in *Poetic Individuality in the Middle Ages* (1970); Adelgundis Fuhrkotter, *Das Leben der heiligen Hildegard* (1968); Barbara L. Grant, "Five Liturgical Songs by Hildegard von Bingen (1098–1179)," in *Signs: Journal of Women in Culture and Society,* **5** (1980), and "Hildegard and Wisdom," in *14th-century English Mystics Newsletter,* **7** (1981); Bruce Hozeski, "*Ordo Virtutum:* Hildegard of Bingen's Liturgical Morality Play," in *Annuale medievale,* **13** (1972), and "Hildegard of Bingen's *Ordo Virtutum:* The Earliest Discovered Liturgical Morality Play," in *American Benedictine Review,* **26** (1975); C. C. Martindale, "'Shadow of Living Light': Two Medieval Mystics," in *Month,* **185** (1948); Barbara Newman, "O Feminea Forma: God and Woman in the Works of St. Hildegard" (diss., Yale, 1981); Bernhard W. Scholz, "Hildegard von Bingen on the Nature of Woman," in *American Benedictine Review,* **31** (1980); Charles J. Singer, "The Scientific Views and Visions of Saint Hildegard," in *Studies in the History and Methods of Science* (1917, repr. 1955); Francesca M. Steele, *The Life and Visions of St. Hildegard* (1914).

Elizabeth of Schönau. Ruth J. Dean, "Manuscripts of St. Elizabeth of Schönau in England," in *Modern Language Review,* **32** (1937), and "Elizabeth, Abbess of Schönau, and Roger of Ford," in *Modern Philology,* **41** (1944).

Mechthild of Hackeborn (Sources). Revelationes selectae (1854); Theresa A. Halligan, ed., *The Booke of Gostlye Grace of Mechtild of Hackeborn* (1979).

Mechthild of Hackeborn (Studies). N. F. Blake, "Revelations of St. Matilda," in *Notes & Queries,* **218** (1973); Theresa A. Halligan, "The Revelations of St. Matilda in English: *The Booke of Gostlye Grace,*" in *Notes & Queries,* **21** (1974); Arthur R. McGratty, *The Sacred Heart, Yesterday and Today* (1951).

Mechthild of Magdeburg (Sources). Lucy Menzies, trans., *The Revelations of Mechthild of Magdeburg (1210–1297); or The Flowing Light of the Godhead* (1953).

Mechthild of Magdeburg (Studies). Eric Colledge, "Mechthild of Magdeburg," in *Month,* **25** (1961); Odo Egres, "Mechthild von Magdeburg: *The Flowing Light of God,*" in *Cistercians in the Late Middle Ages,* E. Rozanne Elder, ed. (1981); Edmund G. Gardner, *Dante and the Mystics* (1913); Alice Kemp-Welch, "A Thirteenth-century Mystic and Beguine: Mechthild of Magdeburg," in *Of Six Medieval Women* (1913); William M. Kimbrel, Jr., "Mechthild of Magdeburg: The Transformational Character of Mystical Poetry," in *Massachusetts Studies in English,* **6** (1978).

Gertrude the Great (Sources). St. Gertrude, *The Life and Revelations of Saint Gertrude,* by a member of the Order of Poor Clares (1857, repr. 1952), and *The Exercises of Saint Gertrude,* edited by a Benedictine nun of Regina Laudis (1956).

Gertrude the Great (Studies). Gilbert Dolan, *St. Gertrude the Great* (1913); Pierre Doyère, "Gertrude d'Helfta," in *Dictionnaire de spiritualité,* VI, 331–339; Sr. Mary Jeremy, "'Similitudes' in the Writing of Saint Gertrude of Helfta," in *Mediaeval Studies,* **19** (1957), and *Scholars and Mystics* (1962); J. Leclercq, "Liturgy and Mental Prayer in the Life of St. Gertrude," in *Sponsa Regis,* **31** (1960); Michael Oliver, *St. Gertrude the Great* (1930).

Frauenfrage, Frauenbewegung, Gottesfreunde (Studies). Brenda M. Bolton, "Mulieres Sanctae," in *Women in Medieval Society,* Susan M. Stuard, ed. (1976); Norman Cohn, *The Pursuit of the Millennium* (1957); John B. Freed, "Urban Development and the *Cura monialium* in Thirteenth-century Germany," in *Viator,* **3** (1972), and *The Friars and German Society in the Thirteenth Century* (1977); Rufus M. Jones, *The Flowering of Mysticism: The Friends of God in the Fourteenth Century* (1939); Ernest W. McDonnell, *The Beguines and Beghards in Medieval Culture* (1954); Anna Groh Seeholtz, *Friends of God: Practical Mystics of the Fourteenth Century* (1934).

Low Countries. Stephanus Axters, *The Spirituality of the Old Low Countries,* Donald Attwater, trans. (1954); Brenda M. Bolton, "*Vitae matrum:* A Further Aspect of the Frauenfrage," in Derek Baker, ed., *Medieval Women* (1978), 253–273; Eric Colledge, ed. and trans., *Mediaeval Netherlands Religious Literature* (1965); Michael Goodich, "The Contours of Female Piety in Later Medieval Hagiography," in *Church History,* **50** (1981); Herbert Thurston, "The Transition Period of Catholic Mysticism," in *Month,* **150** (1922), and "The Case of Blessed Christine von Stommeln," in *Month,* **156** (1928).

Beatrice of Nazareth. F. Sherwood Taylor, trans.,

Beatrice of Nazareth: The Seven Steps of the Ladder of Spiritual Love (1943).

Hadewijch. Frances Gooday, "Mechthild of Magdeburg and Hadewijch of Antwerp: A Comparison," in *Ons Geestelijk Erf,* **48** (1974); Colomba Hart, "Hadewijch of Brabant," in *American Benedictine Review,* **13** (1962), and *idem,* ed. and trans., Hadewych, *The Complete Works* (1980).

France: Marguerite d'Oingt. Antonin Duraffour, Pierre Gardette, and Paulette Durdilly, eds., *Les oeuvres de Marguerite d'Oingt* (1965); Roland Maisonneuve, "L'Experience mystique et visionnaire de Marguerite d'Oingt (d. 1310), Moniale Chartreuse," in James Hogg, ed., *Kartäusermystik und -Mystiker,* I (1981), 81–102; Suzanne F. Wemple, *Women in Frankish Society: Marriage and the Cloister 500 to 900* (1981).

Margaret Porete (Sources). C. Crawford, ed., *A Mirror for Simple Souls* (1981); Marilyn Doiron, ed., "Margaret Porete: *The Mirror of Simple Souls,* a Middle English Translation," in *Archivio italiano per la storia della pietà,* **5** (1968).

Margaret Porete (Studies). E. Colledge, "Liberty of Spirit: *The Mirror of Simple Souls,*" in *Theology of Renewal,* Laurence K. Shook, ed. (1968), and, with R. Guarnieri, "The Glosses by M N and Richard Methley to *The Mirror of Simple Souls,*" in *Archivio italiano per la storia della pietà,* **5** (1968); Gordon Leff, *Heresy in the Later Middle Ages: The Relation of Heterodoxy to Dissent c. 1250–1450,* I (1967); Eleanor McLaughlin, "The Heresy of the Free Spirit and Late Medieval Mysticism," in *Medievalia et humanistica,* n.s. **4** (1973).

Southern Germany and Switzerland. Jeanne Ancelet-Hustache, *La vie mystique d'un monastère de Dominicaines au moyen âge d'après la chronique de Töss* (1928), and "Les 'Vitae Sororum' d'Unterlinden," in *Archives d'histoire doctrinale et littéraire du moyen âge,* **5** (1931); Walter Blank, *Die Nonnenviten des 14. Jahrhunderts* (diss., Freiburg, 1962); Hester McNeal Reed Gehring, "The Language of Mysticism in South German Dominican Convent Chronicles of the Fourteenth Century" (diss., Univ. of Michigan, 1957); Hugo Kuhn, *Rittertum und Mystik* (1963).

Italy: Angela of Foligno. G. M. Alcan, *The Spiritual Amour of S. Catherine of Bologna Together with the Way of the Cross by B. Angela of Foligno* (1926); Elizabeth Petroff, *Consolation of the Blessed* (1979), and *Medieval Women's Visionary Literature* (1986); Paul Lachance, trans., *The Book of Divine Consolation of Angela of Foligno* (1987); Mary G. Steegman, trans., *The Book of Divine Consolation of the Blessed Angela of Foligno* (1909, repr. 1966).

Algar Thorold, *An Essay in Aid of the Better Appreciation of Catholic Mysticism, Illustrated From the Writings of Blessed Angela of Foligno* (1900); Evelyn Underhill, *A Franciscan Mystic of the Thirteenth Century* (1912), and "Two Franciscan Mystics: Jacopone da Todi and Angela of Foligno," in *St. Francis of Assisi, 1226–1926: Essays in Commemoration,* Walter Seton, ed. (1926).

Catherine of Siena (Sources). Kenelm Foster and Mary John Ronayne, eds. and trans., *Catherine: Selected Writings of St. Catherine of Siena* (1980); Suzanne Noffke, trans., *The Dialogue* (1980); Vida D. Scudder, ed. and trans., *Selected Letters of Catherine Benincasa: Saint Catherine of Siena as Seen in Her Letters* (1927).

Catherine of Siena (Studies). Mary Denise, "*The Orchard of Syon:* An Introduction," in *Traditio,* **14** (1958); Jean David Finley, *Catherine of Siena, Woman of Faith* (1980); Kenelm Foster, "St. Catherine's Teaching on Christ," in *Life of the Spirit,* **16** (1962); Edmund G. Gardner, *Saint Catherine of Siena: A Study in the Religion, Literature, and History of the Fourteenth Century in Italy* (1907); Igino Giordani, *Saint Catherine of Siena,* Thomas J. Tobin, trans. (1975); Alvaro M. Grion, "The Mystical Personality of St. Catherine of Siena," Mark Barron, trans., in *Cross and Crown,* **2** (1950); Phyllis Hodgson, "*The Orcherd of Syon* and the English Mystical Tradition," in *Proceedings of the British Academy,* **50** (1964); Johannes Jorgensen, *Saint Catherine of Siena,* Ingeborg Lund, trans. (1938); Arrigo Levasti, *My Servant, Catherine,* Dorothy M. White, trans. (1954); Raymond of Capua, *St. Catherine of Siena,* George Lamb, trans. (1960; repr. 1980); Sigrid Undset, *St. Catherine of Siena,* Kate Austin Lund, trans. (1954).

Catherine of Genoa (Sources). C. Balfour, and H. D. Irvine, trans., *St. Catherine of Genoa: The Treatise on Purgatory and the Dialogue* (1946); Serge Hughes, trans., *Purgation and Purgatory: The Spiritual Dialogue* (1979).

Catherine of Genoa (Studies). Barnabas Ahern, "Christian Perfection, Contemplation, and Purgatory," in *American Ecclesiastical Review,* **118** (1948); Friedrich von Hügel, *The Mystical Element of Religion as Studied in Saint Catherine of Genoa and Her Friends,* 2 vols. (1908, repr. 1961).

Birgitta of Sweden (Sources). John H. Blunt, ed., *The Myroure of Oure Ladye* (1873); William P. Cummings, ed., *The Revelations of Saint Birgitta* (1929); Ernest Graf, trans., *Revelations and Prayers of St. Bridget of Sweden* (1928).

Birgitta of Sweden (Studies). E. Colledge, "*Epistola solitarii ad reges:* Alphonse of Pecha as Organizer of Birgittine and Urbanist Propaganda," in *Mediaeval Studies,* **17** (1956); Johannes Jørgensen, *Saint Bridget of Sweden,* Ingeborg Lund, trans., 2 vols. (1954); Edith Peacey, *Saint Birgitta of Sweden* (1934); Helen Redpath, *God's Ambassadress: St. Bridget of Sweden* (1947).

VALERIE M. LAGORIO

[See also **Albertus Magnus; Angela of Foligno; Babylonian Captivity; Beguines and Beghards; Benedictines; Bernard of Clairvaux, St.; Birgitta, St.; Black Death;**

Brethren of the Common Life; Carthusians; Chivalry; Cistercian Order; Devotio Moderna; Dominicans; Francis of Assisi, St.; Free Spirit; Gerson, John; Hadewijch; Hagiography; Hildegard of Bingen, St.; Jacques de Vitry; Julian of Norwich; Kempe, Margery; Mechthild of Magdeburg; Mendicant Orders; Millennialism; Minnesingers; Mysticism (various articles); Richard of St. Victor; Schism, Great; Suso (Seuse), Heinrich; Thomas of Cantimpré; William of St. Thierry.]

MYSTICISM, CHRISTIAN: ENGLISH

BACKGROUND AND PRECURSORS

The history of Christianity reveals an ongoing mystical continuum extending from the earliest era to the present day. Leading a life of contemplation and prayer, the mystics not only enrich the *depositum fidei* (deposit of faith) of the church as they follow the mystical way, but concomitantly are actively fulfilling roles as prophet, reformer of church and society, teacher, and spiritual guide for their fellow Christians. The mystical life can be defined as the interior spiritual journey of the individual soul through purgation, a penitential and ascetical process dedicated to cleansing the soul of sin and stripping away selfhood; illumination, consisting of the advancing life of prayer and contemplation; and experiential union with God, which is always one of love, and which can only be attained by God's grace. As the ultimate extension of the mystical love between God and the soul, the mystic becomes God's instrument for active service to humanity.

The late thirteenth and fourteenth centuries witnessed an extraordinary flowering of mysticism in England and on the Continent, which can be ascribed in part to the temper of the age. It was a time of political and ecclesiastical struggles and warfare, abuses and laxity in the church, the Babylonian Captivity and Great Western Schism, widespread heresy, and natural calamities like the Black Death.

This mystical renascence drew on such patristic and medieval spiritual traditions as the life of ascesis and prayer of the Desert Fathers and Western monasticism, and the teachings of Augustine, Pseudo-Dionysius, Hugh and Richard of St. Victor, Bonaventure, Thomas Aquinas, and Bernard of Clairvaux. The great fourteenth-century English mystics—Richard Rolle, the anonymous author of *The Cloud of Unknowing* and its companion tracts, Walter Hilton, Julian of Norwich, and Margery Kempe—participated not only in these traditions, but also in a large corpus of indigenous devotional and mystical works of Anglo-Saxon and post-Conquest times.

While little attention has been focused on the insular antecedents of Middle English mysticism, recent scholarship has explored Pseudo-Dionysian influence on Anglo-Saxon prose and poetry, and the basic tenets of mystical theology, such as the three stages of contemplative life and the importance of divinely infused grace, have been found in Bede's writings. Anselm of Canterbury's *Proslogion* and other works, along with the Anselmian meditations *An Orison of Our Lord, A Love Song of Our Lord,* and *The Wooing of Our Lord,* the so-called Wooing Group, reveal an affective devotion to Christ's passion which becomes a major characteristic of the later English mystics. Both Bede and Anselm also propagated the Augustinian concept of Trinitarian exemplarism—the soul as God's image and likeness, and the sinful soul's separation from and return to God, an image theology which is central to Hilton's *Scale of Perfection.* Influenced by Bernard, William of St. Thierry, and Augustine, Ethelred of Rievaulx's *Mirror of Love* (*Speculum caritatis*) stresses the dichotomy between caritas and cupiditas, the centrality of Christ's humanity to the spiritual life, and the compatibility of the active and contemplative lives. His *Letter to His Sister* (*De institutione inclusarum*) teaches the achievement of contemplation through the solitary life of prayer, and thus anticipates the *Rule of the Anchoresses* (*Ancrene riwle*) (*ca.* 1200) and later works of spiritual guidance addressed to women religious, such as Rolle's *Form of Living* and Book I of Hilton's *Scale.*

Strictly speaking, the *Ancrene riwle,* which was written in English, Anglo-Norman, and Latin, does not deal extensively with the higher reaches of contemplation, but is important to the history of English mysticism for its careful delineation of the Purgative Way, which, in its final stages, leads to the fuller life of divine love. Edmund Rich's *Mirror of Holy Church* (*Speculum ecclesiae*), which also appeared in trilingual versions, combined religious instructions for novices, the mystical theology of acquired and infused contemplation, and the efficacy of Christocentric meditation. Other early evidence of mystical instruction and a concomitant stress on affective piety is seen in the lives of Godric of Finchale and Christina of Markyate, Adam of Dryburgh's (or Adam Scotus') *Fourfold Exercise of the Cell,* Stephen of Sawley's (Étienne de Sawley's) *Threefold Exercise,* and Thomas of Hales's lyrical *Love Rune,* which, like the Wooing Group, sets forth a Bernardian *Brautmystik* (bride mysticism) with Christ as the wooer and lover of the soul.

In addition to this rich indigenous background, the fourteenth-century English mystics benefited from and drew upon a vast corpus of instructive manuals for priests, penitential and devotional treatises, moral and didactic literature, and sermons, which represented an important influence on all literary activities in medieval England, and, moreover, helped to provide a trained and receptive audience for the writings of the mystics.

CHARACTERISTICS OF THE ENGLISH MYSTICS

The individual English mystics differed in temperament and in their concept and treatment of the *via mystica* (mystic way). At the same time, however, sharing in the above traditional and native legacies, they were marked as a group by the following characteristics, which they all possessed in varying degrees.

(1) They shared an independence from organized religious life and a predilection for the solitary life. With the exception of Walter Hilton, who unsuccessfully attempted a solitary vocation, and Margery Kempe, the major writers were solitaries. Moreover, Rolle, Hilton, and the *Cloud* author wrote treatises for those entering or living the eremitic life, which was the most conducive to contemplation. And in the fifteenth century, the Carthusians, whose rule stressed the primacy of the contemplative way, were to serve as a major channel for the writing and dissemination of mystical texts.

(2) They manifested a decided anti-intellectualism and a concomitant emphasis on affective piety. The mystics shared a distrust of the argumentations of Scholasticism, learning for its own sake, and the intellectual pride resulting therefrom. This is not to say that the English group was uneducated. Rolle studied at Oxford, and his works, both Latin and English, reveal his knowledge of many of the traditional authorities and rhetorical theory. Both the *Cloud* author and Hilton were skilled theologians, adhering more to Thomas Aquinas than to the Scotist and Nominalist trends at the universities. Despite Julian's protest that she was "unlettered," she was versed in the Fathers, theology, and the teachings of the church, while Margery Kempe exemplified the religious knowledge and pious practices of the devout layperson of her age. In general, the English mystics were not given to abstract speculation, and, owing to the inefficacy of discursive thought in contemplation, emphasized the affective power of the soul over reason, and extolled divinely infused knowledge over acquired knowledge.

(3) They exhibited a devotion to Christ's sacred humanity and passion, and to the holy name of Jesus. With the possible exception of the *Cloud* author, the English mystical canon had a *Passio Domini* concentration, as envinced by Rolle's *Meditations on the Passion* and lyrics addressed to Jesus, Julian's *Revelations of Divine Love,* which grew out of her visions of the crucified Christ, and Walter Hilton's *Scale.* In his *Epistle of Privy Counsel,* even the *Cloud* author points to the importance of meditating on the passion. This devotion to the suffering Christ was not unique to the mystics, but was manifest in the visual arts, sculpture, drama, and devotional and homiletic literature of the period. Yet for the mystics, Christ's passion provided the ultimate exemplar of the self-abnegation, conformity to God's will, and selfless love requisite for contemplation and union.

(4) The English mystics revealed in their writings a strict orthodoxy. In his *Judica me Deus* and *Melos amoris,* Richard Rolle inveighed against the corruption of the clergy, an anticlericalism prevalent in much of the secular and religious literature of the fourteenth century. Nevertheless, he adhered strictly to the teaching and traditions of the church and the contemplative life. Julian's mystical doctrine on sin, the primacy of love, and the motherhood of God is both profound and orthodox. The writings of both the *Cloud* author and Walter Hilton, informed by a fullness of doctrinal truth and a contemplative knowledge of God, are totally free from any tinge of antinomianism, illuminism, or quietism. Margery Kempe, enthusiast though she may have been, was trained and guided by learned friars and priests, and successfully defended her beliefs and practices before several ecclesiastical tribunals.

(5) They appear to have been free from the influence of contemporary continental mystics. Since the five leading English mystics came from eastern and northern England, it has been conjectured that some or all were influenced by the

teachings of the Rhenish and Flemish *Gottesfreunde* group, which could have entered England through mercantile or monastic channels. Julian of Norwich and, to a greater extent, Margery Kempe have been linked with continental women ecstatics and visionaries. It is true that many continental mystical texts were introduced by religious orders, especially the Carthusians and Birgittines. Yet no direct influence on the English group has been established, and it is the consensus that similarities of doctrine and expression can be ascribed to a common background of tradition, mystical theology, and contemplative experience.

(6) Their writings were in the vernacular. Excepting the Latin writings of Rolle and Hilton, all of the English mystics wrote in the vernacular. Their use of English rather than Latin for spiritual works not only contributed to the continuity of English prose, but also indicated the presence of a literate religious and lay audience. Although there are several instances where an English work is translated into Latin, presumably for learned religious, the converse is more generally true. In addition to clarity of expression, common sense, and sincerity, the mystic's English works reveal a lively penchant for pithy statement and colloquialisms, but they also achieve lyric and artistic heights, as seen especially in Rolle and Julian. Above all, the mystics' writing in English indicate their concern to communicate their personal experiences and teach their "even Christians," whether a limited audience attempting the contemplative life, or a broader spectrum of the devout.

RICHARD ROLLE OF HAMPOLE

Richard Rolle (*ca.* 1300–1349) was the pioneer among the fourteenth-century English mystics, anticipating many of their teachings on the active and contemplative life, the centrality of the suffering Christ and the holy name to meditation and prayer, the primacy of love in contemplation, and the unitive experience as a direct gift from God. His productivity, versatility, and literary skill are manifest in his Latin and English works, the latter earning critical accolades for Rolle as a master of English prose. His solitary vocation, intense spirituality, and commitment to guiding the ascetic and spiritual lives of his followers, both by his example and his teachings, resulted in his widespread popularity and influence in England and abroad, and in posthumous claims for his sanctity. The foregoing encomium, however, needs to be qualified, for the young Rolle's idiosyncratic way of life, his contentious personality, and his emotional spirituality, with its concentration on the perceptibile love of God (*amor sensibilis*), were censured by his religious contemporaries and by such later critics as the *Cloud* author and Hilton, who considered his spiritual teaching immature and even harmful. Their criticisms did not go unanswered by Rolle's admirers, as evidenced in Thomas Basset's impassioned *Defense Against Detractors of Richard Rolle,* which appeared in 1400. Modern critics have tended to classify Rolle as a great writer, but a less than great mystic.

Rolle's genuine Latin canon includes: *Canticum amoris* (an alliterative poem praising the Virgin), *Judica me Deus, Melos amoris* (*Melum contemplativorum*), and *Job* (his juvenilia); *Canticles, Super threnos, Super apocalypsim, Super orationem dominicam, Super mulierem fortem, Super symbolorum apostolorum, De Dei misericordia, Latin Psalter, Super Psalmum, Contra amatores mundi, Super magnificat* (in Latin and English), *Incendium amoris,* and *De ēmendatione vitae.* The *Judica me deus* and *Melos* contain many autobiographical references, such as his distaste for liturgical pomp, his self-righteous anger toward his patrons and the clergy, and his apology for his eremitic life. Rolle's life is also recounted in the *Officium* and *Miracula,* composed at Hampole Priory toward the end of the fourteenth century to advance his canonization. The *Canticles,* particularly the *Encomium nominis Jesu,* initiates Rolle's devotion to the holy name of Jesus, which is a leitmotif in his writings. The following is from his *Ego dormio* (I sleep):

> And I pray all of you who desire to be God's lover that you love this name Jesus, and think it in your heart, so that you shall never forget it, wherever you may be. And truly I say to you that you shall find much joy and comfort therefrom; and for the love with which you love Jesus, so tenderly and so specially, you shall be filled with grace on earth, and be Christ's beloved servant in heaven. For nothing pleases God as much as the true love of this name Jesus. [Allen, ed., *English Writings of Richard Rolle*]

The *Encomium* also tells of his temptation by a woman devil (reminiscent of similar accounts in the *Vitae patrum*), an event which could reflect Rolle's misogynism. Yet in the *Incendium amoris,* he upholds the propriety of chaste friendships with women. The *Incendium* and the *De emendatione vitae,* both works of Rolle's maturity, retrospectively recall his experiences of mystical love and rapture. They were subsequently translated into English as the *Fire of Love* and *Amending of Life* by the Carmelite Richard Misyn about 1434.

Rolle's vernacular prose works, which are all assigned to his later years, are the English Psalter, most probably his first work in English; two versions of the *Meditations on the Passion;* five short prose tracts: *The Bee and the Stork, Desire and Delight, Ghostly Gladness, The Seven Gifts of the Holy Ghost,* and *Commentary on the Decalogue;* and the epistles *Ego dormio* (*ca.* 1343), *The Commandment,* and *The Form of Living* (1348). Some manuscripts of the English Psalter suffered Lollard interpolations, but this did not affect the popularity of Rolle's original, which remained the orthodox English Psalter until the Dissolution. The Psalter and the later three epistles were addressed to individual women religious, Rolle's favorite disciple being the anchoress Margaret Kirkeby. The epistles, like the *Amending of Life,* outline Rolle's three degrees of love—insuperable in meditation, inseparable in contemplation, and singular in joyful union—and, along with the *Fire of Love,* attest to his progress on the *via mystica:*

> Certainly the perfect solitary burns intensely in divine love, and while he is snatched away, beyond himself, in the going forth of his spirit through contemplation, he is lifted up, rejoicing, to the jubilant songs of the singers and their heavenly music. And certainly such a man is made like the seraphim, burning especially within himself with incomparable and most constant love. His heart is transfigured by divine fire; burning and shining with extreme fervor, he is carried into his Beloved. [*Fire of Love*]

Like his prose works, Rolle's mystical lyrics stress the intimate union between Jesus and the soul, and the *Passio Domini/Quia amore langueo* themes.

Because of Rolle's reputation as a mystic and author, his works were frequently included in compilations, such as the *Poor Caitiff;* and a large number of devotional and mystical writings were wrongly assigned to him. Prominent among such doubtful ascriptions are *The Pater Noster of Richard Hermit, The Holy Boke Gratia Dei, The Prick of Conscience,* and *Speculum vitae.*

As noted above, the major detractions directed against Rolle in his own and later times concern his headstrong youthful behavior, anticlericalism, anti-intellectualism, and sensuous or supra-sensuous mystical experiences. One cannot deny the impulsiveness and arrogance which characterized much of Rolle's early years. Yet, his conversion and flight from Oxford, pursuit of the solitary life, purported persecution by secular and monastic clergy, and apostolic preaching and teaching take on a different light when viewed as biblical *imitatio*—Rolle's conscious effort to pattern his life on exemplars like Christ, Paul, David, and Job. Rolle's antipathy for the clergy was directed against their worldliness and corruption, and did not, as some have claimed, constitute an open revolt against church authority. The theory that he was a recalcitrant priest, rather than a lay hermit, has also been discounted. Despite his outspoken distrust of higher learning, Rolle had a university education—at one time he was erroneously reputed to have studied theology at the Sorbonne—and was well versed in the Scriptures, theology, and traditional teaching on faith and the contemplative life. His erudition can be seen in his familiarity with Augustine, Gregory, Bernard, the Victorines, Peter Lombard, and other church authorities. His essentially affective approach to the mystical life and stress on psychophysical manifestations of heat (*calor*), sweetness (*dulcor*), and song (*canor*) may reflect not only his temperament, but also his desire to communicate in finite language the ineffable joy and fullness of love experienced in union with God. For varying reasons, such as the relative spontaneity of his mystical ascent, a number of critics hold that Rolle never achieved the unitive stage. Perhaps Rolle would answer them:

> The love of God takes up to itself with marvelous rejoicing the soul of the man whom it perfectly penetrates and sets it truly ablaze by the fire of the Holy Spirit, and does not permit it to stray for a moment from the memory of so great a love. It ties the spirit of the lover so that it does not fly away toward vain things and continually tends in to the Beloved. . . . But what do I say about these things to those others who, although they are chosen, nevertheless have not had that potion? I wonder now and then about myself, because I have spoken concerning the excellence of the lovers of God, as if anyone who wanted to would be strong enough to ascend that reality, when it is not done by flying nor by running but by Christ's loving and elevating and accepting. Actually the smallness of my natural capacity does not know how to open up that which, like a stutterer, I have tried in every way to show. Nevertheless, I was compelled to say something concerning the ineffable, so that those listening or reading might desire to imitate. [*Fire of Love*]

THE *CLOUD* AUTHOR

The anonymous author of *The Cloud of Unknowing* and its six cognate tracts was the first great English spiritual director among the mystics. There have been numerous conjectures about his identity and his religious vocation, whether a friar, monk, recluse, or secular priest. All that is known is that he was a learned priest, obviously an experienced contemplative, and, based on the lexicon and dialect of the manuscripts, located in the East Midlands. Moreover, he was gifted with a felicitous prose style, a capacity to express the complex simply, and a wry sense of humor, which is especially evident when he describes the pious posturings of the pseudocontemplatives.

Some scholars have identified Walter Hilton as the *Cloud* author, based in part on the mistaken assignment of the *Cloud* to Hilton by the noted Carthusian editor James Grenehalgh of Sheen Charterhouse, a hundred years after Hilton's death. This hypothesis has been questioned by Phyllis Hodgson, J. P. H. Clark, and others, who point to the differences in the two men's theology and psychology, approaches to and treatment of the contemplative life, style, and, above all, temperament and intellect. Like the identity of its author, the dating of the *Cloud* corpus is uncertain, but, as the *Cloud* criticizes Rolle's mystical excesses and is, in turn, criticized by Walter Hilton, it must have been composed during the latter half of the fourteenth century.

The *Cloud* author stands alone among the English group in his espousal of the apophatic or negative way of mysticism, based on the Pseudo-Dionysian tenet of God's unknowability. Because of this approach, the *Cloud* has enjoyed a recent popularity among lay and religious scholars, seeking to synthesize Eastern and Western mysticism. Although various sources are assigned to or cited in the *Cloud* series, among them Augustine, Bernard, Thomas Aquinas, the *De adhaerendo Deo* from the school of Albertus Magnus, and the *Ladder of Monks* (*Scala claustralium*) of Guigo II of Grand Chartreuse (*d.* 1188), the author is primarily indebted to Pseudo-Dionysius' *Mystical Theology*, and Richard of St. Victor's *Benjamin major* and *Benjamin minor*.

The Cloud of Unknowing is a manual on the achievement of contemplation, addressed to an unnamed young disciple who has already completed the foundation work of self-discipline, meditation, and prayer. It is also written for those leading the mixed life, that is, charitably active in the external world, but inclined toward contemplation. Although, like many of his precursors and contemporaries, the *Cloud* author upheld the supremacy of the contemplative over the active life, he joined Walter Hilton in advancing the possibility of a synthesis of the two. The *Cloud* basically outlines an ongoing process of ascesis and self-renunciation until the soul, pointed above the "cloud of forgetting," that is, divorced from the world of the senses, discursive reason, and self, and below the "cloud of unknowing" which surrounds God, plunges into the latter cloud with the naked intention of longing and love, aided by divine grace:

> When you first begin, you find only darkness and as it were a cloud of unknowing. You don't know what this means except that in your will you feel a simple steadfast intention reaching out towards God. Do what you will, this darkness and this cloud remain between you and God, and stop you both from seeing him in the clear light of rational understanding, and from experiencing his loving sweetness in your affection. Reconcile yourself to wait in darkness as long as is necessary, but still go on longing after him whom you love. For if you are to feel him or to see him in this life, it must always be in this cloud, in this darkness. And if you will work hard at what I tell you, I believe that through God's mercy you will achieve this very thing. [cap. 3]

In cap. 7, the author also recommends that this intention be summed up in one word, such as "Love" or "God," very much like a medieval mantra.

Of the six cognate treatises, three are derivative: *The Discerning of Spirits,* taken from two sermons of Bernard of Clairvaux; *The Study of Wisdom,* a summary of Richard of St. Victor's *Benjamin minor;* and *Denis Hid Divinity,* translated from Pseudo-Dionysius' *Mystical Theology* and Thomas Gallus' *Commentary*. The other three are original: *The Epistle of Privy Counsel,* a continuation of the *Cloud,* iterates many of the *Cloud*'s doctrines, such as God's transcendence, the difficult course of self-renunciation, and the soul's union with God in humility and love. *The Epistle on Prayer* delineates the prayer of pure contemplation, or perfect love, and *The Epistle of Discretion in the Stirrings of the Soul* expands on the discussion of discernment in matters of silence, fasting, and solitude contained in cap. 42 of the *Cloud.* Based on a careful examination of the subject matter, language, and style of

MYSTICISM, ENGLISH

these six works, Phyllis Hodgson has conclusively established a single authorship for the entire group (*Deonise Hid Diuinite*).

WALTER HILTON

The third great English mystic is Walter Hilton (*d. ca.* 1395/1396), an Augustinian canon regular at the priory of St. Peter at Thurgarton, Nottinghamshire. Little is known of his life, but it is believed that he studied canon law, and that, at one time, he attempted a solitary vocation prior to joining the Thurgarton community in the mid 1380's. Like the *Cloud* author, Hilton was a gifted theologian, experienced contemplative, and outstanding spiritual director and teacher, apprehensive about the sensuous and emotional aspects of Rolle's spirituality, and concerned more with the practical side of the progressive spiritual life than with the abstract speculation of his continental confreres Eckhart and Ruusbroec.

Hilton's Latin canon includes: *Epistola de utilitate et prerogativis religionis* or *Epistola aurea* (On the profit and prerogatives of religious life or The golden letter), encouraging one Adam Horsley to pursue a monastic vocation, and, at the same time, counteracting Wyclif's opposition to the religious life; *De adoracione imaginum* (On the adoration of images), another anti-Wycliffite work, upholding the veneration of images as an aid to devout worship and advancement in the spiritual life; *Epistola ad quemdam seculo renunciare volentem* (To one wishing to renounce the world), exhorting an anonymous lawyer friend not to undertake a religious vocation for which he was unfitted, but to remain in the world; *Epistola ad solitarium de lectione, intentione, oratione et aliis* (Of reading, intention, and prayer); and *De imagine peccati* (Of the image of sin).

His English works are *Of Angels's Song*, warning against sense-oriented manifestations of the mystical experience; *Eight Chapters on Perfection*, translated from a work by Louis de Fontibus; *On the Mixed Life*, instructing a noble layman on how to combine the outward works of charity of the active life with the interior life of contemplation; and *The Scale of Perfection*. Also ascribed to him with some degree of certainty are *The Goad of Love*, a translation and adaptation of James of Milan's *Stimulus Amoris;* and *Commentaries* on Psalm 90, *Qui habitat*, Psalm 91, *Bonum est*, and the *Benedictus*, all three of which have also been assigned to Richard Rolle.

The Scale of Perfection is perhaps the most influential treatise of the English mystical canon, and the only one to treat the comprehensive spiritual life. In this work, Hilton is indebted ultimately to Augustine's teaching on the stages of the soul's ascent to contemplation, and also his image theology. The central concept in the *Scale*, in fact, is concerned with how the *Imago peccati* has supplanted the *Imago Dei* in the soul, and how the *Imago Dei* can be restored, or, using Hilton's term, "reformed," in part in this life, but totally only in heaven. The *Scale* is composed of two books, which were originally written as separate works, and which vary greatly in scope and style. Book I exists in two main versions, with the second revision marked by Christocentric additions. Like Rolle's *Form of Living*, the first book is addressed to an anchoress, but, like the *Cloud*, is suited to others pursuing and leading the contemplative life. The emphasis in this book is on the reforming of the soul in faith, when it is in a state of grace, and following the way of purgation and illumination. Book II, addressed to a wider audience, speaks to the reforming of the soul in faith and feeling, effected by grace and much corporeal and spiritual effort. The central metaphor of Book II is the pilgrimage of the soul toward Jerusalem, the City of Peace, or contemplation. En route, the soul passes through a spiritual night, but gains its contemplative goal with the aid of infused knowledge and unformed love, which is identified with the Holy Ghost:

> Show me, then, a soul who through the inspiration of grace has had his spiritual eyes opened to beholding Jesus, who has been separated and drawn out from the love of the world to the extent that he has purity and poverty of spirit, inward spiritual rest, silence and peace in conscience, loftiness of thought, solitude and privacy of heart, the waking sleep of the spouse, who has lost the delight and joys of this world, being caught up with the delight of Heavenly savor, ever thirsting and spiritually seeking for the blessed presence of Jesus, and I dare boldly declare that this soul burns entirely with love and shines with spiritual light and is worthy to receive the name and honor of the spouse. For this soul has been reformed in experience, made able and ready for contemplation. [cap. 41]

The *Scale* was not only widely read in the fifteenth and sixteenth centuries, as evinced by the large number of manuscripts and early printed editions, but was also translated into Latin by the Carmelite Thomas Fishlake or Fyslawe around

MYSTICISM, ENGLISH

1400, undoubtedly for a religious audience. The fact that there is no critical edition of *The Scale of Perfection* reflects the complexity of its Middle English and Latin manuscript traditions.

DAME JULIAN OF NORWICH

Dame Julian (1342–1416/1423), an anchoress and mystic, left as her spiritual legacy the *Revelations of Divine Love* or *Showings,* which has been acclaimed as one of the major spiritual works of the Middle Ages.

As a girl, Julian wished for three gifts from God: an ever-deepening devotion to Christ's passion; a serious illness at age thirty, which would inflict great physical and spiritual pain and would bring her to the brink of death, as preparation for a holy death and union with God; and three wounds—true contrition, loving compassion, and an affective longing for God and conformance of her will with God's. The fulfillment of these wishes is recounted in the *Revelations.* On 8 May 1373, when she was thirty, she lay dying from a mortal illness, attended by her mother and friends. As the local priest held a crucifix before her eyes, she began to experience a series of sixteen visions or showings, and was miraculously cured. These visions, which focused on the crucified Christ, occurred over a five-hour period, with the sixteenth taking place on the following evening. Her account of this experience appeared in a short version of the *Revelations,* recorded shortly after the event, and a long version, set down after twenty years of insightful meditation.

Manuscript evidence indicates that the *Revelations* did not enjoy a large audience, there being only one fifteenth-century copy of the short version, three postmedieval manuscripts and two extracts of the long version, and the Serenus Cressy edition of the long text, published in 1670. This last edition attests to the continuing interest in Julian on the part of the exiled Benedictine communities on the Continent. The renascence of interest in the *Revelations* in the late nineteenth century has continued throughout the twentieth.

Although both texts were dictated to an amanuensis—a practice also followed by the other women mystics—Julian's claim that she was "unlettered" is belied by her profound grasp of church teachings and Scriptures, her familiarity with earlier and contemporary mystical authorities, and her extraordinary literary gifts. In accounting for her visions, she states:

> All this blessed teaching of our Lord God was shown in three parts, that is to say by bodily vision, and by words formed in my understanding and by spiritual vision. About the bodily vision I have said as I saw, as truly as I am able. And about the words, I have repeated them just as our Lord revealed them to me. And about the spiritual vision, I have told a part, but I can never tell it in full. [cap. 73]

Similar explanations are given by Margery Kempe and the continental women mystics.

A comparison of the two texts reveals that the long version is more concerned with the significance of the visions, shows a greater assurance on Julian's part, and has two important additions: the central allegory of the lord and the servant (caps. 51–57) and the excursus on the motherhood of God (caps. 58–61):

> And so Jesus is our true Mother in nature by our first creation, and he is our true Mother by grace by his taking our created nature. All the lovely works and all the sweet loving offices of beloved motherhood are appropriated to the second person, for in him we have this godly will, whole and safe forever, both in nature and in grace, from his own goodness proper to him. [cap. 59]

Like its precursor, the long version proclaims Julian's message of joy in Christ, sorrow for sin, and God's love, not to a restricted audience of contemplatives, but to her fellow Christians "who desire to be Christ's lovers."

Julian's language is simple and moving: Christ is homely and courteous; all creation resides in a hazelnut held in the palm of her hand; and God is seen in a point. Yet she explores and elucidates the deepest mysteries and theological concerns of Christianity—creation, redemption, Divine Providence, the nature of sin, the paradox of evil (sin) and God's all-embracing love, the indwelling of the Trinity at the apex of the soul, the Mystical Body of Christ, the motherhood of God invested in Christ as wisdom, and man's spiritual childhood. And, iterating Christ's great consolation and assurance to mankind that "All shall be well, and all shall be well, and all manner thing shall be well," Julian ends her *Revelations:*

> What, do you wish to know your Lord's meaning in this thing? Know it well, love was his meaning. Who reveals it to you? Love. What did he reveal to you? Love. Why does he reveal it to you? For love. Remain in this, and you will know more of the same. But you will never know different, without end. . . . And I saw

very certainly in this and in everything that before God made us he loved us, which love was never abated and never will be. And in this love he had done all his works, and in this love he has made all things profitable to us, and in this love our life is everlasting. . . . In this love we have our beginning, and all this shall we see in God without end. [cap. 86]

MARGERY KEMPE OF LYNN

Margery Kempe (*ca.* 1373–after 1438) is as controversial a figure today as she was in her own time, owing to her highly idiosyncratic religious experience. She was and has been adjudged a saint, a hypocrite, a fanatic, a neurotic, a heretic, and a genuine though lesser mystic, as well as a real-life counterpart of Chaucer's Wife of Bath. Certainly her *Book* presents evidence for all of these claims.

An extract of her *Book,* entitled *A shorte treatyse of contemplacyon taught by our lorde ihesu Cryste, or taken out of the boke of Margerie Kempe of Lynn,* was printed by Wynkyn de Worde around 1501. The unique manuscript of the entire text, however, was lost until 1934, when it was discovered among the manuscript holdings of the Butler-Bowdon family, who had received it from the Carthusians at Mount Grace Charterhouse. It was identified as the missing *Book* by Hope Emily Allen.

Margery had little or no formal education, and, like Julian of Norwich and the continental women visionaries, dictated her book. Actually her first amanuensis had lived for a long time in the Lowlands, and consequently wrote in a mixture of English and a Dutch vernacular which made it almost impossible to read. It was later revised by a priest at her request and possibly under her supervision, and the Butler-Bowdon manuscript is a mid-fifteenth-century copy made by a man named Salthows. This complex copying tradition raises the possibility of scribal contributions and interpolations, especially in the case of the second scribe.

The Book of Margery Kempe has been acclaimed as the first autobiography in the English language, and as a speculum of medieval life and religious practices in England, on the Continent, and in the Holy Land. These generic classifications have undoubtedly been assigned to the *Book* because it records Margery's secular life as wife of a Lynn burgess and unsuccessful businesswoman, her conversion and continuing visions of Christ and other mystical experiences, her emotional public weepings and wailings which often disrupted religious services, to the general discomfiture of the presiding clerics and her fellow Christians, her extraordinary journeys and pilgrimages, and her equally extraordinary, successful defenses of her orthodoxy before critical ecclesiasts. It should be remembered that Margery's model for her opus was probably the saint's *vita,* which was an established genre in her time.

Hope Emily Allen, among others, has placed Margery in the mainstream of native and continental piety, suggesting her affinity with Birgitta of Sweden (1302/1303–1373), whom Margery admired and emulated, Dorothea of Montau (1347–1394), and the Lowland women mystics such as Mary of Oignies (*d.* 1213). Although uneducated, Margery drew on church doctrine, the Scriptures, and the writings of her coeval mystics. She also received support, instruction, and spiritual guidance from a series of holy priests, clerks, and friars, along with the approbation of Julian of Norwich, whose solitary, contemplative life accorded with the pattern followed by other women mystics, but only served to accentuate Margery's boisterous personality, way of life, and emotional spirituality.

Although recent criticisms have veered away from Herbert Thurston's assessment of Margery as a "queer mystic," or Butler-Bowdon's "difficult and morbid religious enthusiast," they are far from sharing the sympathetic views of E. I. Watkin regarding her sincerity, holiness, and genuine mysticism. Yet this more benign judgment is upheld by a careful reading of her mystical life, which stresses penance and asceticism; a great attention to discerning of spirits and stirrings; constant recourse to spiritual directors; the gift of tears, admittedly in copious measure; the progressive life of meditation and prayer combined with charitable works; concern for the spiritual welfare of the Christian community expressed through expiatory and intecessory prayers; an ardent spirit of reform directed against temporal and spiritual abuses; a cheerful willingness to suffer for Christ's sake; a longing for death which alone would bring perfect union with God; and continuing visions, auditions, and "dalliances" with Christ, the Blessed Virgin, and the saints who would "illuminate her ghostly sight with understanding." Again and again, she refers to her experiences of high contemplation, which she is unable to relate:

MYSTICISM, ENGLISH

> They were so holy and so high that she was abashed to tell them to any creature, and also they were so high above her bodily wits that she might never express them with her bodily tongue, as she felt them. [cap. 83]

One must also consider that her *Book* was a retrospective account dictated to a scribe who knew little of the *via mystica.* As a final note in Margery's defense, her *Book* was written at Christ's command so that "many a man shall be turned to Me and believe there-in," and with His assurance that she would be "full merry" in heaven because of her mixed life of action and contemplation on earth:

> And therfore, daughter, thou beguilest both the devil and the world with thy holy thoughts, and it is right great folly for the people of the world to judge thy heart, which no man may know, but God alone. [cap. 84]

SECONDARY FIGURES AND WORKS

In addition to the five leading English mystics, there were secondary, in the sense of lesser-known, writers and anonymous mystical texts, written in English and Latin.

Prominent among these secondary figures were William of Nassington (or Nassyngton, *d.* 1354), a high diocesan official of York and Durham, who is credited with the *Speculum vitae* (Mirror of life), a long poem in the summa tradition, which has a derivative prose version, *The Mirror to Unlearned Men and Women,* and with the *Tractate on the Trinity and Unity,* excerpted from Edmund Rich's *Mirror of Holy Church;* and the Carthusian Richard Methley, author of *To Hugh Hermit: An Epistle on the Solitary Life Nowadays.* Anonymous works in English, several of which were composed for nuns, include The *Cleansing of Man's Soul* and *Contemplations of the Dread and Love of God,* both penitential treatises on the Purgative Way; *A Talking of the Love of God,* an affective meditation drawn from the Wooing Group; and two allegories of the progressive spiritual life, *The Desert of Religion,* which is heavily indebted to the *Speculum vitae,* and *A Devout Treatise Called the Tree and XII Fruits of the Holy Ghost.*

Despite the ascendancy of English over Latin as the linguistic medium for mystical and devotional writings, works also continued to be written in Latin for an audience of learned clerics and monastics. William Flete, an English Augustinian, left England in 1359 to lead a life of retirement at Lecceto, near Siena. Prior to his departure, he wrote *De remediis contra temptaciones* (On remedies against temptations), a popular spiritual manual on purgation. Although there is little evidence of Flete's mysticism, he was closely associated with Catherine of Siena and her circle, and thus linked the English and Italian mystical schools. John Whiterig (*d.* 1371), also called the Monk-Solitary of Farne, who left the Benedictine community at Durham for a hermitage on the island of Inner Farne, wrote a series of Latin meditations featuring devotion to the Sacred Heart and reflecting his contemplative experiences. His writings point to the possibility of a much larger Anglo-Latin mystical and devotional corpus which remains to be discovered. Richard Methley of Mount Grace Charterhouse, who translated *The Cloud of Unknowing* and the "M. N." version of *The Mirror of Simple Souls* into Latin, also wrote the *Experimentum veritatis* and three autobiographical treatises on the mystical life: *Scola amoris languidi, Dormitorium dilecti dilecti,* and *Refectorium salutis.*

TRANSLATIONS

Again reflecting the lay and clerical demand for spiritual texts in English, a large number of Latin works, both insular and continental, were translated and incorporated into the English mystical canon in the late fourteenth and fifteenth centuries.

Translations of Latin works composed in England include Ethelred of Rievaulx's *De institutione inclusarum,* which became the *Letter to His Sister* or *A Rule of Life for a Recluse,* also called *Informacio Aelredi abbatis monasterij de Rievalle ad sororem suam inclusarum;* Edmund Rich's influential *Speculum ecclesiae,* retitled *Mirror of Holy Church;* Stephen of Sawley's (Étienne de Sawley's) *Speculum novitii,* which formed the basis of *On Daily Work,* one of the four treatises in *The Holy Boke Gratia Dei;* William Flete's *De remediis contra temptaciones,* which, known as *Remedies Against Temptations,* appeared in three accretive Middle English versions; and, as noted above, Richard Rolle's *Incendium amoris* and *De emendatione vitae,* translated by Richard Misyn into *The Fire of Love* and *Amending of Life* respectively.

The many English translations of continental works can be ascribed in great measure to the efforts of the Carthusians, who also promoted and disseminated the teachings of the medieval mystics, and to the Birgittine Order at Syon Abbey, founded by Henry V in 1415.

Of the German and Flemish mystical texts, Henry Suso's *Büchlein der ewigen Weisheit* was translated into the Latin *Horologium sapientiae,* thence into the *Treatise of the Seven Points of True Love and Everlasting Wisdom.* Jan van Ruusbroec's *Van den blinkenden Steen* and *Die geestelijke Brülocht* became the *Treatise of Perfection of the Sons of God and the Chastising of God's Children,* a large portion of which was incorporated into the *Disce mori* and *Ignorancia sacerdotum.* This translation process of vernacular original to Latin to English was the usual pattern for the majority of continental works introduced into England.

The writings of leading continental women mystics were also well represented. In addition to the Middle English version of the *Revelations* of the Benedictine abbess and visionary Elizabeth of Schönau (*d.* 1165), the *Liber specialis gratie* of Mechthild of Hackeborn, a thirteenth-century Benedictine nun at Helfta, Germany, appeared as *The Book of Ghostly Grace,* also known as the *Mauldeboke.* Moreover, there were English versions of the *vitae* of three other thirteenth-century ecstatics: Elizabeth of Spalbeek (*d.* 1316), Christine of St. Tronde, called "Mirabilis" (*d.* 1224), and Mary of Oignies (*d.* 1213). Margaret Porete's (*d.* 1310) *Mirror of Simple Souls,* portions of which were deemed heretical by continental clerics, was translated by one M. N. in the middle or late fourteenth century, with special glosses for obscure or suspect passages. Birgitta of Sweden's *Revelations* were "Englished" for the Syon nuns, as was Catherine of Siena's *Dialogue,* retitled *The Orcherd of Syon,* and her *Life.*

Among other continental Latin texts which were translated in toto or incorporated into Middle English mystical works were: the *Scala paradisi* or *Scala claustralium* of Guigo II of Grande Chartreuse, into *A Ladder of Four Rungs,* also called *The Ladder of Monks;* David of Augsburg's *De exterioris et interioris hominis compositione,* into the *Rule for Novices* (*Formula noviciorum*); Gerard of Liège's *De doctrina cordis* into *Doctrine of the Heart;* and Peter of Blois's *Duodecim utilitates tribulationis,* into *The Twelve Profits of Tribulation* and several derivative works. In addition, the mystical canon can encompass *The Abbey of the Holy Ghost,* taken from *L'Abbaye du Saint Esprit* and *Abbacia de Sancto Spiritu,* a work upholding the mixed life, and a companion English work, *The Charter of the Abbey of the Holy Ghost; The Mirror of the Blessed Life of Jesus Christ,* translated by Nicholas Love of Mount Grace Charterhouse from the Pseudo-Bonaventuran *Meditationes vitae Christi;* and Thomas à Kempis' *Imitation of Christ,* representative of the practical mysticism of the Devotio Moderna movement.

COMPILATIONS

The following compilations, predominantly composed in the fifteenth century, represent still other components of the English mystical corpus, often combining the writings of English and continental mystics with catechetical and devotional material: *Of Active Life and Contemplative Declaration* and *Way to Contemplation* (*Via ad contemplacionem*), both of Carthusian provenance; *The Holy Boke Gratia Dei,* made up of four works: *On Grace, Our Daily Work, On Prayer,* and *Meditations on the Passion and of Three Arrows of Doomsday,* all of which were wrongly ascribed to Richard Rolle; *Of the Knowledge of Ourselves and God,* a florilegium on the contemplative life; the *Disce mori* and its derivative *Ignorancia sacerdotum; the Poor Caitiff;* the *Treatise of Love;* and the Latin *Speculum spiritualium.*

THE ONGOING TRADITION

The Reformation did not completely stifle the message of the medieval English mystics, whose writings continued to be emulated, published, and read by such sixteenth-century figures as Thomas More, John Fisher, Giles Brewse, Richard Whytford, and Benet Canfield, as well as the Recusants in England and abroad. Giles Brewse's *The Homely Presence of Christ,* Richard Whytford's *The Pipe or Tonne of the Life of Perfection,* and Benet Canfield's *Rule of Perfection* all link the fourteenth-century mystics with Reformation spirituality. Yet the Dissolution and subsequent diaspora of religious orders and their libraries resulted in the loss of manuscripts, or their consignment to the private sector for safekeeping, as with Margery Kempe's *Book,* or their transfer to the exiled Carthusian, Birgittine, and Benedictine houses on the Continent. The English Benedictines, and particularly the Cambrai community and scriptorium, were an important channel for the preservation of medieval spiritual texts during the seventeenth century. Not only were the English mystical writings brought over and copied, as attested to by Fr. Augustine Baker's well-known letter to Sir Robert Cotton, but derivative works were composed, such as Fr. Baker's *Sancta Sophia* and his rescensions of the *Cloud* and *Remedies Against Temptations;* Dame Gertrude More's *Spiritual Exercises;* and Fr. Serenus Cressy's editing and publishing of the *Sancta Sophia,* Hilton's *Scale,* and Julian's *Revelations.*

It might seem that post-Reformation antipathy toward "Popish" texts and the more intellectual orientation of Counter-Reformation spirituality might have done away with the medieval English mystical legacy. According to T. A. Birrell's seminal study, "English Catholic Mystics in Non-Catholic Circles," however, the authentic Western mystical tradition embodied in the writings of the English mystics has continued from the post-Reformation/Recusant era to the present day and forms an integral part of our total spiritual and cultural heritage.

BIBLIOGRAPHY

General reference works. A. E. Doyle, "A Survey of the Origins and Circulation of Theological Writings in English in the Fourteenth, Fifteenth, and Early Sixteenth Centuries" (diss., Cambridge Univ., 1953); *14th-century English Mystics Newsletter,* Valerie Lagorio and Ritamary Bradley, eds. (1975–1983); and *Mystics Quarterly* (1984–); Peter S. Jolliffe, *A Check-List of Middle English Prose Writings of Spiritual Guidance* (1974); Valerie Lagorio and Ritamary Bradley, *The 14th-century English Mystics: A Comprehensive Annotated Bibliography* (1981).

Background and precursors. Cuthbert Butler, *Western Mysticism,* 2nd ed. (1951); Ray C. Petry, "Social Responsibility and the Late Medieval Mystics," in *Church History,* **21** (1952), and *idem,* ed., *Late Medieval Mysticism* (1957); Gerard Sitwell, *Spiritual Writers of the Middle Ages* (1961); Evelyn Underhill, *Mysticism* (1911, repr. 1961); and *The Mystics of the Church* (1925, repr. 1964); James Walsh, ed., *Pre-Reformation English Spirituality* (1965); Robert C. Zaehner, *Mysticism, Sacred and Profane* (1957, repr. 1975).

General studies and anthologies. Gerald W. Bullett, *The English Mystics* (1950); Rotha M. Clay, *The Hermits and Anchorites of England* (1914); Thomas W. Coleman, *English Mystics of the Fourteenth Century* (1971); Eric Colledge, ed., *The Mediaeval Mystics of England* (1961), with an excellent introduction; Marion Glasscoe, ed., *The Medieval Mystical Tradition in England* (1980, repr. 1982, 1984); Geraldine E. Hodgson, *English Mystics* (1922); Clare Kirchberger, ed., *The Coasts of the Country* (1952); David Knowles, *The English Mystical Tradition* (1961); Valerie Lagorio, "New Avenues of Research on the English Mystics," in Marion Glasscoe, ed., *The Medieval Mystical Tradition in England* (1980), and "Problems in Middle English Mystical Prose," in Anthony S. G. Edwards, ed., *Middle English Prose: Essays on Bibliographical Problems* (1981); Conrad Pepler, *The English Religious Heritage* (1958); Wolfgang Riehle, *The Middle English Mystics* (1981); Martin Thornton, *English Spirituality* (1963); George W. Tuma, *The Fourteenth-century English Mystics: A Comparative Analysis,* 2 vols. (1977).

Richard Rolle of Hampole (Sources). Hope Emily Allen, ed., *English Writings of Richard Rolle, Hermit of Hampole* (1931, repr. 1979); Emile J. F. Arnould, ed., *The Melos Amoris of Richard Rolle of Hampole* (1967); Frances Comper, ed., *The Life of Richard Rolle Together with an Edition of His English Lyrics* (1928, repr. 1969); Margaret Deanesly, ed., *The Incendium amoris of Richard Rolle* (1915, repr. 1974); M. L. del Mastro, trans., *The Fire of Love and The Amending of Life* (1981); Carl Horstmann, ed., *Yorkshire Writers: Richard Rolle of Hampole,* 2 vols. (1895–1896, repr. 1978); Gabriel Liegey, "The *Canticum Amoris* of Richard Rolle," in *Traditio,* **12** (1956), and "Richard Rolle's 'Carmen Prosaicum,' An Edition and Commentary" in *Mediaeval Studies,* **19** (1957); Harald Lindkvist, ed., *Richard Rolle's "Meditatio de Passione Domini"* (1917); Nicole Marzac, ed., *Richard Rolle de Hampole (1300–1349): Vie et oeuvres suivies du Tractatus Super Apocalypsim* (1968); Paul F. Theiner, ed., *The Contra Amatores Mundi* (1968); J. Ullmann, ed., "Studien zu Richard Rolle de Hampole," in *Englische Studien,* **7** (1884), editions of *Meditations on the Passion* and *Speculum Vitae.*

Richard Rolle of Hampole (Studies). John A. Alford, "The Biblical Identity of Richard Rolle," in *14th-century English Mystics Newsletter,* **2** (1976), and "Biblical *Imitatio* in the Writings of Richard Rolle," in *ELH: A Journal of English Literary History,* **40** (1973); Hope Emily Allen, *The Authorship of the Prick of Conscience* (1910), "The *Speculum Vitae:* Addendum," in *Publications of the Modern Language Association,* **32,** n.s. **25** (1917), and *Writings Ascribed to Richard Rolle, Hermit of Hampole, and Materials for His Biography* (1927); A. I. Doyle, "Carthusian Participation in the Movement of Works of Richard Rolle Between England and Other Parts of Europe in the 14th and 15th Centuries," in *Kartäusermystik und -mystiker* (Analecta Cartusiana, 55) (1981); Dorothy Everett, "The Middle English Prose Psalter of Richard Rolle of Hampole" in *Modern Language Review,* **17** (1922) and **18** (1923); Geraldine Hodgson, *The Sanity of Mysticism: A Study of Richard Rolle* (1926, repr. 1976); Mary F. Madigan, *The Passio Domini Theme in the Works of Richard Rolle* (1978); Michael Sargent, "Contemporary Criticism of Richard Rolle," in *Kartäusermystik und -mystiker* (Analecta Cartusiana, 55) (1981); John P. Schneider, *The Prose*

Style of Richard Rolle of Hampole (1906); Lois K. Smedick, "Parallelism and Pointing in Rolle's Rhythmical Style," in *Mediaeval Studies,* **41** (1979); Rosemary Woolf, "Richard Rolle and the Mystical School," in *The Religious Lyric in the Middle Ages* (1968), 159–179.

The Cloud author (Editions and studies). J. P. H. Clark, "*The Cloud of Unknowing,* Walter Hilton, and St. John of the Cross: A Comparison," in *Downside Review,* **96** (1978), and "Sources and Theology in *The Cloud of Unknowing,*" in *Downside Review,* **98** (1980); H. D. Egan, "Christian Apophatic and Kataphatic Mysticisms," in *Theological Studies,* **39** (1978); Helen L. Gardner, "Walter Hilton and the Authorship of *The Cloud of Unknowing,*" in *Review of English Studies,* **9** (1933), and review of Phyllis Hodgson, in *Medium aevum,* **16** (1947); Phyllis Hodgson, ed., *The Cloud of Unknowing and The Book of Privy Counseling* (1944, repr. 1973), *Deonise Hid Diuinite and Other Treatises on Contemplative Prayer Related to The Cloud of Unknowing* (1955, repr. 1958), "Walter Hilton and 'The Cloud of Unknowing': A Problem of Authorship Reconsidered," in *Modern Language Review,* **50** (1955), and *The Cloud of Unknowing and Related Tracts* (1982); David Knowles, "The Excellence of the *Cloud,*" in *Downside Review,* **52** (1934); Robert Llewelyn, "The Treatment of Distractions and *The Cloud of Unknowing,*" in *14th-century English Mystics Newsletter,* **7** (1981); Patrick F. O'Connell, "The Person and Work of Christ in *The Cloud of Unknowing,*" in *Contemplative Review,* **14** (1981); N. O'Donoghue, "This Noble Noughting and This High Alling: Self-relinquishment in *The Cloud of Unknowing,*" *Journal of Studies in Mysticism,* **2** (1979); Constantino Sarmiento Nieva, *The Transcending God* (1971); James Walsh, "The Cloud of Unknowing," in *Month,* n.s. **30** (1963); Clifton Wolters, ed., *The Cloud of Unknowing, and Other Works* (1970), with an excellent introduction.

Walter Hilton. Walter H. Beale, "Walter Hilton and the Concept of the 'Medled Lyf,'" in *American Benedictine Review,* **26** (1975); J. P. H. Clark, "The 'Lightsome Darkness'—Aspects of Walter Hilton's Theological Background," in *Downside Review,* **95** (1977), "Walter Hilton and 'Liberty of Spirit,'" in *Downside Review,* **96** (1978), "Intention in Walter Hilton," in *Downside Review,* **97** (1979), and "Action and Contemplation in Walter Hilton," in *Downside Review,* **97** (1979); M. L. del Mastro, ed, *The Stairway to Perfection* (1979); Helen L. Gardner, "Walter Hilton and the Mystical Tradition of England," in *Essays and Studies by Members of the English Association,* **22** (1937); S. S. Hussey, "Latin and English in *The Scale of Perfection,*" in *Mediaeval Studies,* **35** (1973); Dorothy Jones, ed., *Minor Works of Walter Hilton* (1929); Harold J. Kane, *A Critical Edition of the Prickyng of Love,* 2 vols. (1983); Clare Kirchberger, ed., *The Goad of Love* (1952), and "Scruples at Confession: A Modern English Translation of Part of the *Epistola ad Quemdam Saeculo Renunciare Volentem,*" in *Life of the Spirit,* **10** (1956); Fumio Kuriyagawa, ed., *Walter Hilton's Eight Chapters on Perfection* (1967); Joseph E. Milosh, *The Scale of Perfection and the English Mystical Tradition* (1966); Joy Russell-Smith, "Walter Hilton and a Tract in Defense of the Veneration of Images," in *Dominican Studies,* **7** (1954); Leo Sherley-Price, ed., *The Scale of Perfection* (1975), Gerard Sitwell, "Contemplation in *The Scale of Perfection,*" in *Downside Review,* **67** (1949), **68** (1950), and **69** (1950); Toshiyuki Takamiya, ed., *Of Angels' Song* (1977); Björn Wallner, ed., *An Exposition of "Qui Habitat" and "Bonum Est" in English* (1954), and *A Commentary on the "Benedictus"* (1957).

Julian of Norwich. A. M. Allchin, "Julian of Norwich—Today," in *14th-century English Mystics Newsletter,* **6** (1980); Frances Beer, ed., *Julian of Norwich's Revelations of Divine Love* (1978), short version; Ritamary Bradley, "The Motherhood Theme in Julian of Norwich," in *14-century English Mystics Newsletter,* **2** (1976), and "Patristic Background of the Motherhood Similitude in Julian of Norwich," in *Christian Scholar's Review,* **8** (1978); Caroline Bynum, "Jesus as Mother and Abbot as Mother: Some Themes in Twelfth-century Cistercian Writing," in *Harvard Theological Review,* **70** (1977); Andre Cabussut, "Une dévotion médiévale peu connue: La dévotion à Jésus nôtre mère," in *Revue d'ascétique et de mystique,* **25** (1949); Edmund and James Walsh Colledge, eds., *A Book of Showings to the Anchoress Julian of Norwich,* 2 vols. (1978), critical edition of both versions, and *Showings* (1978); Enid Dinnis, "Juliana's Bread," in *Catholic World,* **116** (1922–1923); M. L. del Mastro, ed., *The Revelations of Divine Love by Julian of Norwich* (1977); Marion Glasscoe, ed., *A Revelation of Love* (1976), long version; Eleanor McLaughlin, "'Christ My Mother': Feminine Naming and Metaphor in Medieval Spirituality," in *Nashotah Review,* **15** (1975); Roland Maisonneuve, "L'univers visionnaire de Julian de Norwich" (diss., Sorbonne, 1978); Paul Molinari, *Julian of Norwich: The Teaching of a Fourteenth-century Mystic* (1958); C. Brant Pelphrey, *Love Was His Meaning: The Mystical Theology of Julian of Norwich* (1981); Conrad Pepler, "The Mystical Body in the English Mystics," in *Clergy Review,* **23** (1943); Anna Maria Reynolds, "Love Is His Meaning," in *Clergy Review,* **58** (1973), "'Courtesy' and 'Homeliness' in the *Revelations* of Julian of Norwich," in *14th-century English Mystics Newsletter,* **5** (1979), and *On Julian of Norwich and in Defence of Margery Kempe* (1979).

Margery Kempe. Clara W. Atkinson, *Mystic and Pilgrim: The Book and the World* (1983); Roberta Bux Bosse, "Margery Kempe's Tarnished Reputation: A Reassessment," in *14th-century English Mystics Newsletter,* **5** (1979); George Burns, "Margery Kempe Reviewed," in

Month, **171** (1938); William Butler-Bowdon, ed., *The Book of Margery Kempe* (1936, repr. 1954); Katherine Cholmeley, *Margery Kempe, Genius and Mystic* (1947); Louise Collis, *Memoirs of a Medieval Woman: The Life and Times of Margery Kempe* (1964); Sanford B. and Hope Emily Allen Meech, eds., *The Book of Margery Kempe* (1940, repr. 1961); Martin Thornton, *Margery Kempe: An Example in the English Pastoral Tradition* (1960); Barry Windeatt, *The Book of Margery Kempe* (1985).

Secondary figures. F. G. A. M. Aarts, *Þe Pater Noster of Richard Ermyte* (1967); Hope Emily Allen, "*The Desert of Religion:* Addendum," in *Archiv,* **127** (1911); Edmund Colledge and Noel Chadwick, "*Remedies Against Temptations:* The Third English Version of William Flete," in *Archivio italiano per la storia della pietà,* **5** (1958); Frances Comper, ed., *Contemplations of the Dread and Love of God* (1916); Hugh Farmer, ed. and trans., *The Monk of Farne* (1961); Benedict Hackett, E. Colledge, and Noel Chadwick, "William Flete's *De Remediis Contra Temptaciones* in Its Latin and English Rescensions: The Growth of a Text," in *Mediaeval Studies,* **26** (1964); James Hogg, ed., *Richard Methley: To Hew Heremyte. A Pystyl of Solytary Lyfe Nowadayes* (Analecta Cartusiana, **31**) (1977), and *Mount Grace Charterhouse and Late Medieval English Spirituality* (Analecta Cartusiana, **82**) (1980); W. Hübner, "*The Desert of Religion,*" in *Archiv,* **126** (1911); Margery Morgan, "*A Talking of the Love of God* and the Continuity of Stylistic Tradition in Middle English Prose Meditations," in *Review of English Studies,* n.s. **3** (1952); Venetia Nelson, "An Introduction to the *Speculum Vitae,*" in *Essays in Literature* (Denver), **2** (1974); W. A. Pantin, "The Monk-Solitary of Farne: A Fourteenth-century English Mystic," in *English Historical Review,* **59** (1944); Michael G. Sargent, "The Self-verification of Visionary Phenomena: Richard Methley's *Experimentum Veritatis,*" in *Kartäusermystik und -mystiker,* II (Analecta Cartusiana, 55) (1981); Lois Smedick, "Cursus in Middle English: *A Talkyng of þe Loue of God Reconsidered,*" in *Mediaeval Studies,* **37** (1975); John W. Smeltz, "*Speculum Vitae:* An Edition of British Museum Manuscript Royal 17C. viii" (diss., Duquesne Univ., 1977); E. V. Stover, "*A Myrrour to Lewde Men and Wymmen*" (diss., Univ. of Pennsylvania, 1951); Meredith Thompson, ed., *Þe Wohunge of Ure Lauerd and Other Pieces* (1958, repr. 1970); J. J. Vaissier, ed., *A Devout Treatyse Called the Tree and XII Frutes of the Holy Ghost* (1960); M. Salvina Westra, ed., *A Talking of the Love of God* (1950).

Translations. Joyce Bazire and Eric Colledge, eds., *The Chastising of God's Children and The Treatise of Perfection of the Sons of God* (1957); Mary Patrick Candon, "*The Doctrine of the Hert,* Edited from the Manuscripts with Introduction and Notes" (diss., Fordham, 1963); Edmund Colledge, "*Epistola Solitarii ad Reges:* Alphonse of Pecha as Organizer of Birgittine and Urbanist Propaganda," in *Mediaeval Studies,* **17** (1956), and with Romana Guarnieri, "The Glosses of 'M. N.' and Richard Methley to *The Mirror of Simple Souls,*" in *Archivio italiano per la storia della pietà,* **5** (1968); William P. Cumming, ed., *The Revelations of Saint Birgitta* (1929); David of Augsburg, *Spiritual Life and Progress,* Dominic Devas, ed. and trans., 2 vols. (1937); Marilyn Doiron, "Margaret Porete: *The Mirror of Simple Souls:* A Middle English Translation," in *Archivio italiano per la storia della pietà,* **5** (1968); Helen P. Forshaw, "St. Edmund's *Speculum:* A Classic of Western Spirituality," in *Archives d'histoire doctrinale et littéraire du moyen âge,* **39** (1972); Theresa A. Halligan, ed., *The Booke of Gostlye Grace of Mechtild of Hackeborn* (1979); Phyllis Hodgson, "A Ladder of Foure Ronges by the Whiche Men Mowe Wele Clyme to Heven: A Study of the Prose Style of a Middle English Translation," in *Modern Language Review,* **44** (1949), and with Gabriel Liegey, eds., *The Orcherd of Syon* (1966); Carl Horstmann, ed., "*Informacio. Alredi Abbatis Monasterij de Rieualle ad Sororem Suam Inclusarum:* Translata de Latino in Anglicum per Thomam N. (Aus MS. Vernon fol.a-k)," in *Englische Studien,* 7 (1884), "Prosalegenden: Die Legenden des MS. Douce 114," in *Anglia,* **8** (1885), lives of Elizabeth of Spalbeek, Christina Mirabilis, Mary of Oignies, and Catherine of Siena, and "*Orologium Sapientiae* or *The Seven Poyntes of Trewe Wisdom,* aus MS. Douce 114," in *Anglia,* **10** (1888); Peter S. Jolliffe, "Middle English Translations of *De Exterioris et Interioris Hominis Compositione,*" in *Mediaeval Studies,* **36** (1974), containing *Formula Noviciorum;* Clare Kirchberger, ed., *The Mirror of Simple Souls* (1927); Roger Lovatt, "The *Imitation of Christ* in Late Medieval England," in *Transactions of the Royal Historical Society,* 5th ser., **18** (1968); Elizabeth Salter, *Nicholas Love's "Myrrour of the Blessed Lyf of Jesu Christ"* (1974); Michael G. Sargent, "The Transmission by the English Carthusians of Some Late Medieval Spiritual Writings," in *Journal of Ecclesiastical History,* **27** (1976); Thomas à Kempis, *The Imitation of Christ,* E. M. Blaiklock, trans. (1979); Evelyn Underhill, ed., *The Adornment of the Spiritual Marriage, The Sparkling Stone, The Book of Supreme Truth,* C. A. Wynschenk, trans. (1916).

Compilations. Mary Luke Arntz, ed., *Richard Rolle and Þe Holy Boke Gratia Dei: An Edition with Commentary* (1981); Mary Teresa Brady, "*The Pore Caitiff,* Edited from MS. Harley 2336, with Introduction and Notes" (diss., Fordham, 1954); John H. Fisher, ed., *The Tretyse of Loue* (1951, repr. 1970); Peter S. Jolliffe, "Two Middle English Tracts on the Contemplative Life," in *Mediaeval Studies,* **37** (1975), *Of Actyf Lyfe and Contemplatyf Declaracion* and *Via ad Contemplacionem.*

The ongoing traditions. T. A. Birrell, "English Catholic Mystics in Non-Catholic Circles," in *Downside*

Review, **94** (1976); Kent Emery, "Benet of Canfield: Counter-Reformation Spirituality and Its Medieval Origins" (diss., Toronto, 1976); Anthony Low, *Augustine Baker* (1970); D. Lunn, "Augustine Baker (1575–1641) and the English Mystical Tradition," in *Journal of Ecclesiastical History,* **26** (1975); Marion Norman, "Dame Gertrude More and the English Mystical Tradition," in *Recusant History,* **13** (1976); Benedict Weld-Blundell, ed., *The Inner Life and Writings of Dame Gertrude More,* 2 vols. (1910–1911); Richard Whytford, *The Pype or Tonne of the Lyfe of Perfection,* James Hogg, ed. (1980).

VALERIE M. LAGORIO

[See also **Albertus Magnus; Anchorites; Ancrene Riwle; Anselm of Canterbury; Aquinas, St. Thomas; Augustine, St.; Babylonian Captivity; Bede; Benedictines; Bernard of Clairvaux, St.; Birgitta, St.; Black Death; Bonaventure, St.; Carthusians; Devotio Moderna; Duns Scotus, John; Eckhart, Meister; Ethelred of Rievaulx, St.; Hugh of St. Victor; Julian of Norwich; Kempe, Margery; Lollards; Middle English Literature; Nominalism; Peter Lombard; Peter of Blois; Pseudo-Dionysius; Richard of St. Victor; Ruusbroec, Jan Van; Schism, Great; Scholasticism; Suso, Heinrich; Thomas à Kempis; Thomas of Hales; William of St. Thierry; Wyclif, John; Wynkyn de Worde.**]

MYSTICISM, CHRISTIAN: GERMAN The flowering of mysticism in German-speaking countries in the late thirteenth and fourteenth centuries was in part a reaction to political and social calamities, such a famines, plagues, conflict between pope and emperor, and wars, which caused pessimism about the value and possibility of earthly happiness and a stable civil order as well as intense interest in the life of the soul and union with God as its final goal. Large numbers of women especially sought spiritual fulfillment either as nuns or as lay persons living a life directed to goals similar to those of religious orders. Many of these people possessed great aptitude for and sensitivity to profound religious truths. The intellectual climate was also favorable for a turn to mysticism. In the previous decades, in such figures as the Dominicans Albertus Magnus (*d.* 1280) and Thomas Aquinas (*d.* 1274) and the Franciscan Bonaventure (*d.* 1274), philosophy and theology had reached their peak, especially at the University of Paris, in exploring the nature of God and the world to the extent that these are knowable for the human mind working according to rational concepts and logic. Further progress would be sought by attempting to go beyond the limits of rational thought and by emphasizing the affective, ethical, and personal aspects of religious experience. In 1267 a papal bull entrusted Dominican friars with the instruction of nuns. In 1303 there were 65 convents of Dominican nuns alone (7 in Strasbourg) in the area of the Dominican province Teutonia (chiefly along the Rhine). These complementary factors—a large qualified audience and gifted spiritual guides—resulted in a body of sermons and religious writings of high quality and wide appeal.

The Rhineland, both along the upper Rhine (Strasbourg, Cologne, and Switzerland) and in the Low Countries, was the principal area where mysticism thrived. In the Low Countries the best known mystical writer was Jan van Ruusbroec (1293–1381). Women mystics, such as Hildegard of Bingen (1098–1179), Elizabeth of Schönau (1126–1164), Mechthild of Magdeburg (1207–1282), Mechthild of Hackeborn (1241–1299), Gertrude the Great (1256–1302), and Hadevijch of Antwerp (*fl.* 1350) represent the Rhineland but other areas within German speaking lands as well. Exclusive of the Low Countries, well known German speaking male mystics were members of the newer religious orders of Franciscans and Dominicans. The most renowned spiritual force among the Franciscans was David of Augsburg (*ca.* 1200–1272), but it was definitely the three Dominicans, Meister Eckhart, Johannes Tauler, and Heinrich Suso, whose fame and influence were most far reaching.

MEISTER ECKHART (CA. 1260–CA. 1328)

Born in a village called Hochheim, near either Erfurt or Gotha, in Thuringia in central Germany, Eckhart entered the Dominican order in Erfurt quite young and probably studied in Paris in the late 1270's and in Cologne about 1280. In 1293–1294 he was lecturer on Peter Lombard's *Sentences* in Paris. He achieved prominence as both a religious superior (prior in Erfurt *ca.* 1294–1300, vicar general 1316 and 1322, and provincial 1303–1311) and as professor of theology, twice occupying a chair at the University of Paris (1302–1303 and 1311–1313). The title *Meister* is the German equivalent of master (*magister*) and refers to his having completed this highest academic degree. Especially after his second tenure in Paris his activities included preaching in the vernacular to houses of religious women and probably to lay

MYSTICISM, GERMAN

audiences first in Strasbourg and then in Cologne. In 1326 an ecclesiastical court under Henry of Virneburg, the archbishop of Cologne, began investigating charges of heresy against him. As the proceedings dragged on, Eckhart appealed to the pope and early in 1327 traveled to the papal court in Avignon. He died, probably there, before 30 April 1328 and before the end of the papal investigation. On 27 March 1329, Pope John XXII issued the bull *In agro dominico,* which faulted him with clouding the minds of the uneducated and, though mentioning that he was reconciled to the church before his death, condemned twenty-eight articles representing a broad sampling of his works. Despite the condemnation, Eckhart retained the respect and admiration of such persons as his religious brothers Johannes Tauler and Heinrich Suso, as well as Cardinal Nicholas of Cusa (1401–1464). Due to his condemnation, however, he most often appears as an opponent of orthodoxy in the writings of late medieval theologians when mentioned at all. His thought reappears in baroque religious poetry, especially in that of Angelus Silesius (Johannes Scheffler) and Daniel Czepko. Since the rediscovery of his works in the early nineteenth century, interest in him has remained strong, although he has often been misunderstood and misrepresented.

Eckhart's German works include sermons, eighty-six of which have been published in the nearly completed critical edition by Joseph Quint. He also wrote three treatises, *Reden der Unterscheidung* (Counsels on discernment), *Von abegescheidenheit* (On detachment), and *Buch der göttlichen Trostung* (The book of divine consolation). The latter, published together with the sermon *Von dem edeln menschen* (Of the nobleman), was also known as *Liber "Benedictus."* The main Latin work of Eckhart is the incomplete *Opus tripartitum,* which was to consist of the *Opus propositionum* (Work of propositions), with about 1,000 philosophical and theological propositions and their demonstrations, the *Opus quaestionum* (Work of questions), with lectures and disputations, and the *Opus expositionum* (Work of commentaries), with sermons and Bible commentaries. Extant are two prologues (general prologue and introduction to the first section), over fifty sermons (the so-called *Opus sermonum* in the third part), and commentaries on Genesis (two), Exodus, Wisdom, Ecclesiasticus, and the Gospel of John. Nothing survives from the second part of the work. Several other texts by Eckhart have been preserved, including the *Pariser quaestiones* and documents relating to his trial in Cologne and Avignon.

Although one should not overemphasize the differences between the Latin and the German works, the former center more on his philosophical-theological explanations of the nature of God, man, and the world. The latter stress man's spiritual path to union with God. What they have in common is the attempt to uncover hidden truths beneath the surface or literal sense of Holy Scripture. These interpretations, which often have little connection to the literal sense, show the workings of a rich and original mind gifted in both thought and expression.

What distinguishes Eckhart most from other medieval mystics is his attempt to explain the nature of God, creature, and their union in terms of Scholasticism, the academic philosophy and theology of the age. This has earned him the title speculative mystic. Although his doctrines were long considered to coincide largely with those of Thomas Aquinas and although he quotes with approval a large number of Christian, Islamic, Jewish, and classical thinkers, scholars now generally agree that in its core his distinctive thought derives from the traditions of Christian Neoplatonism. Augustine appears most frequently in his works. Pseudo-Dionysius and Moses Maimonides provide essential impulses. It is misleading to speak of a clearly developed Eckhartian system, but his major tenets display consistency.

According to Eckhart, the human intellect can attain some knowledge of God by calling him existence, one, true, good and the like; but what is not grasped through these names is greater than what is grasped. Calling God good is like calling the sun black. He is better described as nameless, or by saying what he is *not:* that he is *not* corporeal, *not* in time, *not* visible, and so on. It is especially illegitimate to apply one term, like "being," to both God and creature. If being is applied to creatures, God is not being but rather the "purity of being." If God is described as being, then creatures are best termed a "pure nothing." In themselves creatures are totally dependent on God's being. Any being they have on their own is at best a sign pointing to real being, God. Or they are like mirrors, empty in themselves but capable of reflecting an image of God. If Eckhart stresses the infinite distance separating God and creature, he is equally insistent that they are one and inseparable. The nothingness that

MYSTICISM, GERMAN

creatures are in their separation from God is balanced by the higher existence beyond the transitoriness of the world that they enjoy in him. This higher or virtual existence in the mind of God in which the creature is indistinct from, and utterly one with, the divinity provides the foundation for his thoughts on mystical union. This dialectic of seeing the God-creature relationship as both oneness and separation overcomes in part the limitations of human concepts.

Eckhart's explanation of how one achieves union denies none of the doctrines of traditional Christian morality and asceticism. However, certain accents are clearly his own. The redemptive act of the suffering God-man Christ receives much less emphasis than the role of Christ in the Trinity and the process through which we become sons of God and even, as he dares to say, the same Son. Also, external actions and ascetical practices are deemphasized in favor of a correct inner disposition based on the aforementioned insight into the nothingness of creatures in themselves and the all-embracing being of God. This disposition is called detachment and requires that one free oneself from a possessive attitude to all things including one's own intellect, will, and very being. To the extent that one is able to divest oneself of one's creaturely nothingness one can be called the just man whose being derives totally from justice. And God is justice. Or he will describe this process as the birth of the Son in the soul by which the creature is subsumed into the very workings of the Trinity, both giving birth to and being born the Son. The goal of union is achieved when one has overcome one's separateness from God, which came about through creation, and achieves the breakthrough into the ground or desert solitude of the divinity, where one becomes what one always was, is, and will be.

The language of Eckhart's vernacular works is generally credited with being a major impulse in the development of abstract concepts and philosophical vocabulary in German. His works are the first in German to express so successfully difficult philosophical, religious, and mystical thoughts and they remain unequalled in the whole period of medieval German. His belief that God and all that is touched by what is divine can never find adequate expression in logical progression and conceptual thought had important consequences for his use of language. Since he considered all philosophical explanations to be at best partial explanations, he was not much concerned with inconsistencies or apparent contradictions that arise when one compares his different descriptions of God and union with him. Because of the limitations of philosophy he frequently employs literary and rhetorical means as alternate modes of expression. Images and rhetorical devices, especially those stressing the alogical, such as paradox, hyperbole, antithesis, parallelism, chiasmus, accumulation, intensification, and the like, are often preferred to scholastic terminology to express his favorite mystical themes.

Eckhart has little in common with mystics emphasizing dark nights of the soul, moments of rapture, or primarily emotional ecstatic experiences of oneness with God. His mysticism is concerned with the constant state of the creature and rests on his intensely experienced realization that oneness with God is both an expression of man's true metaphysical state and a goal toward which one must strive.

JOHN TAULER (CA. 1300–1361)

Tauler was born in Strasbourg, where he was active most of his life except for periods in Basel and Cologne. The son of a wealthy townsman, he entered the Dominican order about 1315 and studied seven or eight years in Strasbourg and three years in Cologne. The rest of his life was devoted to pastoral work. He attained a reputation for preaching in convents and before lay audiences. He had connections to other religious figures, notably to Margarethe Ebner, a Dominican nun, and Heinrich von Nördlingen, an itinerant preacher and Ebner's spritual counselor. Tauler also became the confessor of Rulman Merswin, a wealthy Strasbourg merchant with spiritual ambitions. His extant authenticated works consist of about eight sermons and one letter to Margarethe Ebner. Also, because of his fame, many additional works were falsely attributed to him. His reputation and influence remained strong in the centuries following his death. Among his admirers was Martin Luther.

Although he shows a dependence on and admiration for Meister Eckhart, the contrasts are equally striking. Probably in part because of Eckhart's condemnation he avoids highly speculative topics and displays at times an almost anti-intellectual attitude, warning against the delights of "tasty wisdom." While incorporating some of Eckhart's thought and terminology into his own sermons, he is careful to render them clearly orthodox. In speaking of the birth of God in the soul or man's becoming one with God, he emphasizes the central role of grace. Although he mentions the ground of the soul as the place where union with God takes place, it is a union of wills rather than of being that he stresses. Untypically for a Dominican he considers the will a more important faculty than the intellect and subordinates the value of the person engaged in academic pursuits (*lesemeister*) to one teaching the practice of the spiritual life (*lebemeister*). In interpreting Scripture he avoids the unusual, preferring to follow traditional lines. A sharp critic of what he considered the doctrinal and moral evils of the times, Tauler distanced himself from the heresies of certain beghards and beguines and from the pantheism of the Brethren of the Free Spirit. Equally severe was his criticism of abuses within the church, especially of the worldliness of the clergy. In ascetical matters he warned against exaggerated external practices that could become an end in themselves and thus impede spiritual progress.

The central concern of Tauler's mystical doctrine is not union with God but rather the path to this union and what steps along the purgative and illuminative ways one can take to prepare for the grace of union. For this reason he is usually considered the master of mystical ethics and the spiritual psychologist helping his hearers to distinguish true religious attitudes from false ones. One must free oneself from attachments to creatures and especially from attachment to self. This doctrine is not antiworldly but demands rather that the world be transformed supernaturally. Self-denial and the leaving of self are difficult because persons seeking spiritual perfection are vulnerable to self-deception and a false sense of security. Esteeming themselves because of their piety, they remain victims of self-will and are pursuing their own selfish purposes instead of being open to the guidance of the divine will. Thus *gelassenheit,* the free and complete letting-go of all aspects of self, which results from true self-knowledge, is the first important step in developing the inner man. To this negative approach of liberation from self corresponds the positive following of Christ in humility and suffering. God humiliated himself by assuming the nothingness of human nature. We must imitate this humility by giving up ourselves and sinking into the abyss of nothingness where union is possible. His sober and critical spirit advocating true spiritual reform and a mysticism of inward experience moderated by practical norms has won him many admirers, including Martin Luther.

Tauler's language is not without rhetorical features but is mostly temperate and down-to-earth. Although some of his mystical terminology is borrowed from the scholastic world of Eckhart, he uses such concepts in contexts that deemphasize their philosophical validity to the advantage of their application to individual religious experience. His images are generally taken from everyday life and the simple professions. His eloquence rests mainly on simplicity and directness.

HEINRICH SUSO (CA. 1295–1366)

Suso was born probably in Constance into a distinguished family. His father, Heinrich von Berg, was a knight, and his mother came from the patrician family Süs (or Süse), the name that he later adopted. Suso entered the Dominican order in Constance at the age of thirteen. His entry was aided, contrary to canon law, by a gift to the order, a fact that caused him grave doubts about his salvation until he was reassured regarding the validity of his vocation by Meister Eckhart. He experienced a conversion to higher spiritual goals after five years as a Dominican and then studied in Cologne, probably in the early 1320's, when Eckhart was teaching there. From Cologne he returned to Constance, where he stayed until 1339. That year he was exiled with most of his fellow Dominicans to Diessenhofen for siding with the pope against the emperor, and from 1347 or 1348 until his death he was in Ulm.

Neither a professor nor a noted preacher, Suso was best known for the holiness of his life (he was beatified in 1831) and for pastoral work in convents and among spiritually minded lay persons. In addition to his relationships to mystically inclined nuns, Suso had contact with Johannes Tauler, Heinrich von Nördlingen, and a group of mystics called the Friends of God (*Gottesfreunde*). Suso's *Life* (or *Vita*) has been called the first autobiography in German but the extent of its authenticity is disputed. Some of it is similar to stereotyped hagiography and legend, which casts doubt on many interesting incidents related, such as his meeting a man in the woods who insists that Suso hear his confession and relates that he had murdered a priest on that very spot; or his being accused by a relapsed spiritual daughter of fathering her illegitimate child. Much of the *Life* was written down by his spiritual daughter Elsbeth Stagel, a nun in Töss, Switzerland, based on conversations with him. The rest was probably added after their deaths by other

MYSTICISM, GERMAN

nuns. Most modern critics consider it generally reliable.

Stagel also collected twenty-eight of Suso's letters in the *Book of Letters.* A second collection, *The Little Book of Letters,* consists of extracts from the larger collection, with most personal elements removed; it is thus a set of discourses on spiritual topics. Of the four sermons in the Bihlmeyer edition two are considered genuine, two questionable.

The Little Book of Truth, written in dialogue form, treats questions of speculative mysticism. The influence of Eckhart and of the attacks on him are evident. Several incriminated doctrines are touched upon and presented in an orthodox light. Suso especially emphasizes that in mystical union God and creature remain metaphysically separate even if it seems otherwise to one experiencing it. He also refutes claims by the Brethren of the Free Spirit that Eckhartian doctrines justify their pantheism and unconventional moral doctrines.

Suso's masterpiece, *The Little Book of Eternal Wisdom,* is a devotional manual that attained great popularity. It is mostly a series of dialogues between the Servant of Wisdom (Suso) and Eternal Wisdom (Christ), envisioned as suffering on the cross. Suso is careful to point out that these should not be thought of as real visions. He has rather chosen to emphasize visual impressions for these tender conversations to make them more attractive. Because he considered works composed in the vernacular to lack permanence, Suso also wrote a modified Latin version of *The Little Book of Eternal Wisdom,* entitled *Horologium sapientiae* (The clock of wisdom). He probably also wanted to present it to the non-German father general of his order because his orthodoxy had apparently been impugned at some previous time.

The central theme of his works is that one must free oneself (*entbilden*) from creatures, form oneself (*bilden*) with Christ, and transform oneself (*überbilden*) in God. The highest stage occurs when one loses oneself in the divine being. He relates that he has experienced mystical ecstasy but denies that one can achieve this by one's own efforts. He avoids theological sophistication in reaction to scholastic rationalism and stresses personal warmth in the relationship between God and his creature. For sources he prefers to draw upon the kindred spirit of Bernard of Clairvaux or the Song of Songs rather than the learned doctors of his own order. Human love and emotion are essential terms for understanding this union. It is the human Christ who suffered and died with whom he converses. Suffering in union with Christ is a sure path to God.

Suso is the lyricist among the Dominican mystics and borrows terms from the poetry of courtly love and chivalry. He is the knight in the service of Christ and seeks to perform spiritual feats to win the love of his lady, Eternal Truth. Though his form remains prose, poetic elements abound. His visual imagination gives his imagery vivid authenticity and intensity. Love of his native surroundings and his appreciation of the beauties of nature that his works reveal rest on his seeing them as revelations of God's glory. His works contributed much to the development of religious thought and expression, especially in Germany and the Low Countries.

BIBLIOGRAPHY

Editions and translations

Eckhart. Die deutschen Werke, Joseph Quint, ed. (1958–); *Die lateinischen Werke,* Joseph Koch *et al.*, eds., 5 vols. (1936–1964); Edmund Colledge, O.S.A., and Bernard McGinn, trans., *Meister Eckhart: The Essential Sermons, Commentaries, Treatises, and Defense* (1981), containing McGinn's "Theological Summary," the best introduction to Eckhart's thought; Matthew Fox, O.P. ed., *Breakthrough: Meister Eckhart's Creation Spirituality, in New Translation* (1980), with much false information and questionable interpretation, but translations are satisfactory; Bernard McGinn, ed. and trans., *Meister Eckhart: Preacher and Teacher* (1987).

Tauler. Predigten, Ferdinand Vetter, ed. (1910, repr. 1968); Elizabeth Strakosch, trans., *Signposts to Perfection* (1958).

Suso. Deutsche Schriften, Karl Bihlmeyer, ed. (1907, repr. 1961); *The Life of the Servant,* James M. Clark, trans. (1952); *Little Book of Eternal Wisdom* and *Little Book of Truth,* James M. Clark, ed. and trans. (1953).

Studies

General. James M. Clark, *The Great German Mystics: Eckhart, Tauler, Suso* (1949, repr. 1969, 1970); Friedrich W. Wentzlaff-Eggebert, *Deutsche Mystik zwischen Mittelalter und Neuzeit,* 3rd ed. (1969), with a bibliography.

Eckhart. Jeanne Ancelet-Hustache, *Master Eckhart and the Rhineland Mystics,* Hilda Graef, trans. (1957); Richard Kieckhefer, "Meister Eckhart's Conception of Union with God," in *Harvard Theological Review,* **71** (1978); Bernard McGinn, "Eckhart's Condemnation Reconsidered," in *Thomist,* **44** (1980), and "The God Beyond God," in *Journal of Religion,* **61** (1981); Frank Tobin, *Meister Eckhart: Thought and Language* (1986); previously published works on Eckhart listed in Thomas F. O'Meara, O.P., *et al.*, "An Eckhart Bibliography," in *Thomist,* **42** (1978).

Tauler. Steven E. Ozment, *Homo Spiritualis: A Com-*

MYSTICISM: LOW COUNTRIES

parative Study of the Anthropology of Johannes Tauler, Jean Gerson, and Martin Luther (1509–1516) in the Context of Their Theological Thought (1969).

Suso. Ephrem Filthaut, ed., *Heinrich Seuse: Studien zum 600. Todestag, 1366–1966* (1966); Anne-Marie Holenstein-Hasler, "Studien zur Vita Heinrich Seuses," in *Zeitschrift für schweizerische Kirchengeschichte,* **62** (1968).

FRANK TOBIN

[See also **Aquinas, St. Thomas; Beguines and Beghards; Dominicans; Eckhart, Meister; Free Spirit, Heresy of; Neoplatonism; Suso, Heinrich; Tauler, Johannes.**]

MYSTICISM, CHRISTIAN: LOW COUNTRIES

JAN VAN RUUSBROEC (1293–1381)

Life. Little is known of Jan van Ruusbroec's early life. According to his first biographer, Henricus Pomerius (*d.* 1469), Ruusbroec left home at the age of eleven and began studies preparatory to priesthood with his uncle, Jan Hinckaert, canon of the St. Gudule church in Brussels. There is no evidence that he did university studies. Ruusbroec's work, however, gives proof of appreciable philosophical and theological formation. Ordained in 1317, he served as chaplain at St. Gudule's until 1343, where his duties included saying Mass, praying the daily Divine Office, and preaching the word of God. Pomerius relates that Ruusbroec took an active part in counteracting certain heretical groups of pantheists and quietists, members of the Brethren of the Free Spirit. His earliest writings date from this period. They were in the vernacular (Middle Netherlandic); as his Carthusian contemporary Gerard of Hérinnes (*d.* 1377) explained, "In those days, there was great need for spiritual writing in the language of the people." Some of Ruusbroec's writings were responses to specific requests for clarification and direction, for example, for the Carthusians of Hérinnes or for Margriet van Meerbeke of the Brussels Poor Clares.

The second major period of Ruusbroec's life began with a move in 1343 to the Forest of Soignes south of Brussels, where he retired with Jan Hinckaert and Francis van Coudenberg, both of whom belonged to the St. Gudule chapter of canons. There, Jan III, duke of Brabant (*r.* 1312–1355), accorded them a vacant hermitage, which eventually became the Groenendael monastery. The reasons for the move are not altogether clear. Speculations range from political motives (refuge from enemies among the "false mystics") to the threat to piety in having to bear with a confrere's unmusical voice in choir; more probably it was the desire to find an atmosphere congenial to deeper contemplation, retirement, and seclusion. There seems to have been no plan to found a religious community; the three secular priests simply wanted to praise God in relative solitude. This state was not to endure; the ambiguous status of the three hermits attracted unfavorable attention. Coudenberg went to consult the Victorines (at the Abbey of St. Victor) in Paris, who recommended that they become Canons Regular of St. Augustine. Their decision to do so was approved by the bishop of Cambrai. They took their vows in 1350. Coudenbergh was the first superior and Ruusbroec the first prior. Eight new members joined them immediately. The Groenendael priory was eventually affiliated with the Victorines of Paris, but the relationship was never particularly close. In 1412, however, the priory joined the Congregation of Windesheim, which was influential in the spread of the Modern Devotion.

Works. Ruusbroec's writings have been called "the most completely theological ever composed by a mystic," and he himself has been characterized as "the greatest phenomenologist of the encounter between God and man." The writings include:

(1) *Het rijcke der ghelieven* (The realm lovers), probably dating between 1330 and 1340, describes the spiritual life as a progression toward God by the operation of the gifts of the Holy Spirit.

(2) *Die gheestelike brulocht* (The spiritual espousals) also belongs to the Brussels period. Ruusbroec's masterpiece and his most translated work, it is a mystical exposition of the text: "Behold, the Bridegroom comes; go out to meet Him," and gives a complete description of mystical states which are authentic, as opposed to their counterfeits. It was translated into Latin before 1360 by Willem Jordaens of the Groenendael monastery.

(3) *Vanden blinckenden steen* (The sparkling stone) was also probably a Brussels work. Written at the request of a Carthusian brother, this short work is related to the doctrine of previous writings, especially the *Espousals.* This was also translated into Latin by Jordaens.

(4) *Vanden vier becoringhen* (The four temptations) describes pitfalls for beginners in the spiritual life (living according to the flesh, hypocrisy, exaggerated confidence in one's own knowledge,

MYSTICISM: LOW COUNTRIES

and flight into laziness and false emptiness in prayer). This was translated into Latin by a Norbertine (Premonstratensian).

(5) *Vanden kerstenen ghelove* (The Christian faith) is a brief exposition of the articles of the creed, linking both theology and spirituality in a sort of catechism.

(6) *Vanden gheesteliken tabernakel* (The spiritual tabernacle), Ruusbroec's longest treatise, was begun in Brussels and completed in Groenendael. An extensive spiritual allegory on the biblical accounts of the construction and significance of the Ark of the Covenant, it was extremely popular from the fourteenth through the seventeenth centuries.

(7) *Dat boecsken der verclaringhe* (The little book of enlightenment), written at the request of Gerard of Hérinnes, who had requested clarification of problematic passages of the *Die gheestelike brulocht* text, especially concerning expressions such as "union without differentiation," is also an important treatise on the characteristics of the false mystics of his time. It dates from about 1363.

(8) *Vanden seven sloten* (The seven enclosures) is one of the several works composed for Sister Margriet van Meerbeke between 1346 and 1361, including one letter and three important treatises. *Enclosures* (1346) explains how a Poor Clare nun passes a day of prayer and work in ever deeper union with the Lord. The work has a highly Eucharistic character. It covers not only religious asceticism but also the highest reaches of the mystical life, to which the young nun was called. It has been termed "the most beautiful jewel of Netherlandic prose, together with the *Sparkling Stone*" (A. Deblaere).

(9) *Een spieghel der eewigher salicheit* (Mirror of eternal blessedness), written in 1359, is a treatise regarded by some as Ruusbroec's most mature work. Written for one of his directees (possibly Margriet), *Mirror* is based on Eucharistic mysticism. Geert Groote (*d.* 1384), founder of the Brethren of the Common Life, translated it into Latin.

(10) *Vanden seven trappen* (The seven steps on the ladder of spiritual love) was also written for a religious; references to Christ the celestial cantor may well reflect the fact that Margriet was the cantress of her community. She is invited to deeper understanding of her vocation of mystical union with the Lord in her "common" life (that is, a life of contemplation and of action). Both Jordaens and Groote translated this into Latin.

(11) *Vanden XII beghinen* (The twelve beguines) is a long book in four parts which were probably written independently and then collected and published by the Groenendael community shortly before Ruusbroec's death. In an opening poem, each strophe on the spiritual life is recited by one of twelve beguines.

(12) A collection of seven letters or fragments of letters completes Ruusbroec's works. The first was addressed to Margriet van Meerbeke; the second, to Lady Machteld, widow of a knight; a third was written for three Cologne Carthusian hermits on the subject of the eremitical life. The remaining four were for women of varying states of life. All show Ruusbroec in his role as spiritual director.

Doctrine. Most of Ruusbroec's writings are on the interior life, giving direction especially to those in whom he had discerned mystical grace. The grace of direct, passive, conscious awareness of the presence of God in the soul, he taught, cannot be merited, for God gives it to whom He wills, as He wills, and when He wills. The difference between a mystic and an ordinary Christian is that what every Christian knows by faith of the indwelling God, a mystic knows by experience. Such an experience is passive, the result of grace and not of technique. Ruusbroec describes the way in which the grace of God transforms human reality; the human partner in the God-man encounter is transfigured by God's grace at every level of human existence. The beatific vision is reserved for the life of heaven; here on earth the mystic, even one having reached the transforming union, lives the life of faith and of virtue. Ruusbroec presents a spirituality that is at once Trinitarian, Christocentric, biblical, dynamic, and deeply human. In so doing, he proved himself to be the greatest spiritual writer in the history of Netherlandish literature.

OTHER NETHERLANDISH MYSTICS AND FOLLOWERS OF RUUSBROEC

The early Groenendael community flourished with fervent religious, some of whom continued to write in the same vein as their spiritual master. One of these was Jan van Leeuwen (*d.* 1378), also known as "the good cook." He wrote of the high regard in which Ruusbroec held the writings of the Antwerp beguine Hadewijch. He also wrote a little treatise on Meister Eckhart, but doing no more than echoing passages condemned by Pope John XXII. Willem Jordaens (*d.* 1396) entered Groenendael in 1352 as a master of theology. In addition to translating the works of Ruusbroec into Latin, he also wrote *De mystieke mondkus* (The mystic kiss). Godfried van Wevel entered Groenendael around 1360, where he was frequently called upon to do spiritual direction. He is author of *Vanden VII dogheden* (The seven virtues), long attributed to Ruusbroec himself. A friend of Ruusbroec, the Carthusian Gerard of Hérinnes, translated several of Ruusbroec's treatises; he also left us a charming literary portrait of the Groenendael mystic. Ruusbroec's regard for this monk of Hérinnes is manifested by the fact that Ruusbroec, at an advanced age, walked almost thirty miles to speak with him. Ruusbroec's works subsequently circulated widely in Carthusian monasteries. One of the many early visitors to Groenendael may have been the renowned Dominican preacher Johannes Tauler (*d.* 1361). There is no doubt, however, about the visit from Geert Groote, whose name is forever linked, along with that of Florens Radewijns (*d.* 1400), to the origins of the new spiritual movement in the Low Countries known as the Devotio Moderna. This movement is most famous for having produced the *Imitatio Christi* (Imitation of Christ) by Thomas à Kempis (*d.* 1471), but it is also rich with many other writings, few of which have yet been translated into English. The writings of Ruusbroec spread rapidly among the Brethren of the Common Life, the Carthusians, the Gottesfreunde (Friends of God), the Friars Minor, and, of course, among monasteries with which Groenendael was intimately associated in the Windesheim congregation. One of Ruusbroec's disciples, Jan van Schoonhoven (*d.* 1432), became his staunch defender when Jordaens' translation of the *Espousals* came to the attention of Jean Charlier (John Gerson, *d.* 1429), chancellor of the University of Paris. Gerson suspected the work of pantheist tendencies and apparently was not moved by van Schoonhoven's careful defense of his master. All the more interesting, then, that Laurentius Surius (*d.* 1578), a Carthusian of Cologne, began in 1549 a new Latin translation of the mystic's complete works precisely in order to counteract the growing Protestantism in his country.

BIBLIOGRAPHY

Sources. Henricus Pomerius, *De origine monasterii Viridisvallis. Una cum vitis B. Joannis Rusbrochii primi prioris hujus monasterii, et aliquot coaetaneorum ejus* (1885), repr. in *Analecta bollandiana,* IV (1885), 257–334; Jan van Ruusbroec, *Werken,* 4 vols. (1944–1948), and *Opera omnia,* I, *Boecsken der verclaringhe,* II, *Vanden seven sloten,* III, *Die geestelike brulocht* (1981–).

Studies. Stephaan G. Axters, *Geschiedenis van de vroomheid in de Nederlanden,* II, *De eeuw van Ruusbroec* (1953), III, *De moderne devotie* (1956), and *The Spirituality of the Old Low Countries,* Donald Attwater, trans. (1954); Paul Mommaers, *The Land Within: The Process of Possessing and Being Possessed by God According to the Mystic Jan van Ruysbroeck,* David N. Smith, trans. (1975); Jean Orcibal, *Saint Jean de la Croix et les mystiques Rhéno-flamands* (1966); Paul Verdeyen, *Ruusbroec en zign mystiek* (1981).

HELEN ROLFSON, OSF

[See also **Augustinian Canons; Brethren of the Common Life; Carthusians; Devotio Moderna; Eckhart, Meister; Gerson, John; Groote, Geert; Hadewijch of Antwerp; Premonstratensians; Ruusbroec, Jan van; Thomas à Kempis.**]

MYSTICISM, ISLAMIC, is also known as Sufism, a term most probably derived from the Arabic *ṣūf* (wool). The early ascetics of Islam, the Sufis, wore coarse woolen garments to signify their rejection of the material world.

The Islamic mystical tradition springs from the Koran. Although the predominant vision of God in the Koran is that of an omnipotent creator, lawgiver, and judge who wields terrifying power, yet is eternally compassionate, a careful study of the text reveals a far more complex God-man relationship.

One of the most crucial Koranic verses for Sufis (7:172) describes the establishment of the primordial covenant between God and the souls of men and women in a time before the creation of the world. The goal of every Islamic mystic is to reestablish this loving intimacy between the Lord of the Worlds and the human soul confirmed on the "day of *alast,*" the day when God proclaimed his lordship and the souls of mankind acquiesced in an act of perfect surrender (*islām*).

Not only does the Koran affirm the existence of this unique covenant established before created time, but it also confronts the believer with God's pervasive presence within the created universe. Nothing exists except by God's direct intervention; neither nature nor mankind acts by its own power, for all depends directly on God.

Two major methods of Koran interpretation have held prominence from the early days of the

MYSTICISM, ISLAMIC

umma, the Islamic community: *tafsīr* and *taʾwīl.* The method of *tafsīr* explicates the text on the bases of language, grammar, law, history, and dogma. Often several points of view are presented, with no one view necessarily predominant. On the other hand, *taʾwīl,* the method often associated with the Shiite community and Sufi commentators, emphasizes the search for the esoteric, hidden meaning of the Divine Word. The lines between these two approaches, however, are not always distinct, especially in the early stages of the development of commentary literature. The work of the early exegete Muqātil ibn Sulaymān (*d.* 767), for example, employed literal and historical analysis together with the imaginative use of allegory and myth, thus opening the way for less literalist interpretations of the Koran text.

The influence of the sixth imam, Jaʿfar al-Ṣādiq (*d.* 765), is equally formative. Whereas Muqātil turned to the imagination to elucidate an obscure verse, Jaʿfar sees the verse as a symbolic allusion that refers to the experiences of the spiritual life. Thus, an understanding of the text is not dependent solely on its self-revelatory quality; equally important is the interior state of the interpreter. One has insight, therefore, in direct proportion to one's spiritual sensitivity and development. This establishes a dynamic interrelationship between individual and text, in which each is perceived as a living reality, one capable of increasing spiritual awareness through progress along the Sufi path (*ṭarīqa*), the other revealing itself as a Word whose depths can never fully be plumbed.

The earliest stimuli for the burgeoning Sufi tradition should not, however, be localized in the text of the Koran alone; social and political forces were at work as well. The transfer of the capital of the nascent Islamic empire from Mecca to Damascus with the establishment of the Umayyad dynasty in the mid seventh century is symbolic of a dramatic new ambiance with which Islam had to cope. The comparatively spartan tribal life in the Arabian peninsula gave way to the sophisticated, cosmopolitan atmosphere of a wealthy urban metropolis. The relative opulence of the early Umayyad period may have given impetus to the ascetics who preached detachment from worldly goods and power—in fact, from all earthly attainments—as a prerequisite for creating a suitable environment in which to cultivate the experience of God's immanence.

One of the major centers for this eighth-to-ninth-century phenomenon was the province of Khorāsān, especially the former Buddhist city of Balkh. From Balkh came the renowned mystic Ibrāhīm ibn Adham (*d.* 776/790), whose life, as recounted in Muslim hagiographic sources, closely resembles that of the Buddha. He is perhaps best remembered for his insistence on *tawakkul,* total dependence on God for one's physical and spiritual needs.

Another center for early Sufism was Iraq, especially the cities of Baghdad, Basra, and Al-Kufa. Ḥasan al-Baṣrī (*d.* 728), Rābiʿa al-ʿAdawīya (*d.* 801), and Ḥārith ibn Asad al-Muḥāsibī (*d.* 857) left lasting impressions on the embryonic Sufi movement in this region of the empire.

Ḥasan influenced a broad range of religious sciences ranging from *ḥadīth* (traditions) to ascetical theology. To Rābiʿa is attributed the introduction of love mysticism into what was predominantly an ascetic movement. She is still revered as one of the preeminent women saints in Islam.

Egypt also produced significant figures of early Sufism, most notably Dhu 'l-Nūn al-Miṣrī, who was born of Nubian parents at Akhmīm in Upper Egypt and died at Giza, near modern Cairo, in 859. The details of his life are obscure and overlaid with hagiographic embellishments, as are the lives of most of the early Sufis. Tradition credits him with introducing the notion of gnosis (*maʿrifa*) into Sufism and providing the first classification of the stations (*maqāmāt*) and states (*aḥwāl*) of the Sufi Path. Dhu 'l-Nūn was a master of the Arabic language, a skill exemplified by the epigrams and prayers attributed to him.

Renunciation and detachment are often understood to be ideals concerning primarily the individual's dealings with the material realm: food, clothing, money, sex. More sophisticated understandings of the role of detachment, however, emphasize emotional and psychological life as the most significant areas of concern. It is this realization that provided the impetus for highly sophisticated treatments of various aspects of human psychology by masters such as al-Muḥāsibī, who introduced the examination of conscience into Sufi practice.

The effort to provide the novice with organized treatments of the theoretical foundations of the Sufi life was not restricted to the realm of psychology but touched on every dimension of the spiritual life. The late tenth and the eleventh centuries saw the production of important manuals of the mystical

MYSTICISM, ISLAMIC

Path. Each attempts to categorize and elucidate the spiritual and psychological experiences encountered at every stage of the Path. In addition, a great deal of helpful, practical advice is imparted by the well-tested master to the new initiate.

Several of the most important manuals sprang from the fertile environment of Khorāsān: the *Kitāb al-taᶜarruf* of Abū Bakr Muḥammad al-Kalābādhī (*d. ca.* 990), the *Kitāb al-lumaᶜ* of Abū Naṣr ᶜAbd Allāh ibn ᶜAlī al-Sarrāj from Ṭūs (*d.* 988), and *al-Risālat al-Qushayrīya* (or *al-Risāla fī ᶜilm al-taṣawwuf*) of Abu 'l-Qāsim ᶜAbd al-Karīm al-Qushayrī (*d.* 1074). From farther east came the first significant manual in the Persian language, the *Kashf al-maḥjūb* (Unveiling of the hidden), written in Lahore by ᶜAlī ibn ᶜUthmān al-Jullābī al-Hujwīrī (*d. ca.* 1071). To this formidable group must be added Abū Ṭālib Muḥammad ibn ᶜAlī al-Ḥārithī al-Makkī (*d.* 996), whose work, the *Qūt al-qulūb* (The food of the hearts), influenced both Abū Ḥāmid al-Ghazālī and Jalāl al-Dīn Rūmī.

A didactic literary genre of a different sort, hagiography, attained prominence during the same period. The early Koran commentators and street preachers often focused on the lives of the prophets for inspiration. This interest spawned works known as *qiṣaṣ al-anbiyāᵓ* (tales of the prophets), compilations of lively pedagogic prophetic fables. So too the Sufi community cherished the lives of its prominent members as role models. Collections of the lives of Sufis offer a wealth of practical guidance in the form of the preserved sayings and teachings of particular masters as well as details about their lives.

Abū ᶜAbd al-Raḥmān al-Sulamī (*d.* 1021) from Nishapur is credited with the first systematic history of the lives of the great Sufis who preceded him. This influential hagiographic work, the *Ṭabaqāt al-ṣūfīya* (The classes of the Sufis), underwent amplification and revision in the eleventh century at the hands of ᶜAbdallāh Anṣārī (*d.* 1089), who translated it into Persian as well, and later by ᶜAbd al-Raḥmān ibn Aḥmad Jāmī (*d.* 1492) in his *Nafaḥat al-uns*. The most complete source book for the lives of the early masters is the ten-volume *Ḥilyat al-awliyāᵓ* (The ornament of the saints) of Abū Nuᶜaym al-Iṣfahānī (*d.* 1037), without which a great deal of historical and mythical data about the lives of the early mystics would be lost.

The development of ascetic, theoretical, and hagiographic literature in Sufism must be viewed as companion to and parallel with the development of a far more provocative expression of mystical experience: the ecstatic utterance. It is here that one encounters the most problematic and most intriguing attempts by the mystics to convey in words the ultimately ineffable experience of union with the Beloved.

Ecstasy in Sufism originates from the very foundations of the movement. Abū Yazīd (Bāyezīd) al-Bisṭāmī (*d.* 874 or 877–878) is the most prominent early exponent of this startling, if not shocking, mode of mystical expression. While he himself wrote nothing, his sayings were preserved by his disciples and became the object of careful scrutiny by more sober Sufis, notably Abu 'l-Qāsim al-Junayd (*d.* 910). Al-Bisṭāmī's cries of "Glory to me!" "How great is my majesty!" and similar seemingly self-divinizing expressions of ecstasy raised dramatically from the Muslim community the question of the exact nature of mystical union.

It is not possible here to delve deeply into the issue of whether such expressions are to be taken as metaphysical statements of actual identity with God, or are to be seen as dramatic metaphors expressing the mystic's conviction that the intimacy experienced is of such a nature that it is *as if* one were identified with the deity. Suffice it to say that such ecstatic utterances, especially when voiced in a public forum where the uninitiated might be grievously misled, continually vexed the non-Sufi segment of the Islamic community, and contributed to the growing tensions between Sufis and learned doctors of law and theology.

Although al-Bisṭāmī is the first recorded ecstatic of significant influence, his utterances are overshadowed by those of the most famous of the Baghdad mystics, Ḥusayn ibn Manṣūr al-Ḥallāj, who was put to death by order of the Abbasid caliph al-Muqtadir in 922. Al-Ḥallāj's "ana 'l-ḥaqq" (I am the Divine Truth) rings through the history of Sufism as the paradigmatic ecstatic utterance.

Al-Ḥallāj's mystical paradoxes range far beyond the single subject of union with the Divine; it is to him that one must turn to discover the first elaborations of the complex tragedy surrounding the mythic personality of Iblīs, the Islamic devil figure. For al-Ḥallāj, Iblīs is satanic yet tragic victim, condemned yet perfect in loving devotion, tempter but also teacher.

The use of paradox to cut through to the core of the Sufi experience in dramatic fashion is a technique that many renowned Sufis used to express the

MYSTICISM, ISLAMIC

essentially supprarational quality of the mystical experience. Logic, philosophy, theology—all the religious sciences, especially those that rely heavily on rational discourse—are inadequate to encompass in verbal expressions the essence of Sufi ecstasy.

Even some very traditionally minded Sufis became experts at this science of the conjunction of opposites. ᶜAbdallāh Anṣārī of Herāt (*d.* 1089), an expert in *ḥadīth* and an archconservative in his literalist Ḥanbalite interpretations of the Koran and Islamic law, is the most renowned example of this type of fundamentalist mystic. He proclaimed both freedom and predestination. The pious Sufi must strive with all his or her power, Anṣārī insists, to attain the goal of union with the Beloved; yet, as he affirms in the *Munājāt* (Intimate conversations), it is clear from the outset that God has arranged all beforehand. Adam sinned in paradise, it is true, but who, Anṣārī asks, provided him with the tree of wheat? God, of course. So too Iblīs' refusal to bow to the newly created Adam as God commanded is blamed ultimately on God himself.

In his discussion of ethics, Anṣārī perceives no objective basis for distinguishing between good and evil other than the fundamental principle that whatever God wills for the individual is good, no matter whether that be condemnation or blessing, disease or health, destruction or salvation. Consequently, what appears good to the majority may actually be bad for the individual, and vice versa.

The intensity of loving union proclaimed by Anṣārī rivals that of any of the ecstatic mystics. He admits, however, that his more acceptable way of expressing his intimacy with the Beloved is what protected his position in the community. In the *Munājāt* he compares his own experience of union with that of al-Ḥallāj; the difference is that al-Hallāj announced it imprudently to the uninitiated, while Anṣārī speaks softly and remains devoted to the most conservative interpretations of the religious sciences.

The tension in the history of Sufism between the sober school and the ecstatic, "drunken" mystics is dramatically encapsulated in the lives of two brothers of the eleventh–twelfth centuries whose intellectual brilliance and religious perspicacity have left indelible marks on the shape of Islamic religious life. The elder and by far the more famous of the two is the mystic-theologian Abū Ḥāmid Muḥammad ibn Muḥammad al-Ghazālī (*d.* 1111). Born in 1058 at Ṭūs in Khorāsān, al-Ghazālī became a skilled practitioner of the traditional religious sciences of law and theology, and a spokesman for the Ashᶜarite school, which became identified with the mainstream of Islamic philosophical theology.

Al-Ghazālī's patron, the influential vizier Niẓām al-Mulk, appointed him professor at the Niẓāmīya at Baghdad in 1091. Beginning in 1095, however, he underwent a spiritual crisis; his life as prominent scholar appeared to him devoid of the personal religious experience that he felt essential to his survival. It was at this juncture that he abandoned his academic career to dedicate himself wholeheartedly to the Sufi path. His personal struggle is poignantly documented in his autobiography, *al-Munqidh min al-ḍalāl* (What saves from error), in which he also addresses the questions of philosophy's relation to revelation, the difference between intellectual and experiential religion, and man's innate capacity to attain suprarational knowledge and experience.

What makes al-Ghazālī especially significant for the history of Sufism, apart from his inherent brilliance, is his ability to reconcile his commitment to the traditional religious sciences with his newfound personal religious experience. He is perhaps the most eloquent spokesman for a sober mysticism based upon and in conformity with, the law, philosophy, and theology of the mainstream Sunni community. His magnum opus, the *Iḥyā ᶜulūm al-dīn* (The revivification of the religious sciences), remains one of the most influential treatises on Islamic religious life. Its topics range from the exoteric religious structures of the community and their implications for the individual Muslim to the ideals and practices of the exponents of a moderate Sufism.

Al-Ghazālī's commitment to a sober mysticism is best witnessed by his willingness to return to his teaching post in 1106 at the urgings of Fakhr al-Mulk, son of Niẓām al-Mulk and vizier to the Seljuk sultan. His mysticism did not necessitate his remaining on the fringe of the community either intellectually or physically, but challenged him to integrate his personal religious experience within the broader framework of the Islamic *umma*.

Al-Ghazālī's younger brother Aḥmad al-Ghazālī (*d.* 1126) was no less intelligent, nor less trained in the intellectual pursuits of law and theology. Yet Aḥmad was far more inclined toward the role of the charismatic street preacher than that of the staid academic. His writings cannot compete in

MYSTICISM, ISLAMIC

range or quantity with those of his brother. Yet the mystical writings that have survived, especially his Persian work on mystical love, *Sawāniḥ* (Aphorisms on love), and the stories of his life preserved by hagiographers testify to his skill in capturing and analyzing the dynamism of the mystical love relationship. Where Abū Ḥāmid strained to describe his mystical experience in a carefully constructed religious prose style acceptable to the mainstream Muslim community, Aḥmad wrote in the exuberant style of the ecstatic that was sure to rankle the more conservative lawyer-theologians.

Aḥmad's spiritual heritage lived on in a brilliant young disciple, ᶜAyn al-Quḍāt al-Hamadānī. Born in 1098 at Hamadān in western Iran, he was in his late twenties when Aḥmad died. Despite his youth, his writings reflect the skill of a seasoned spiritual guide as well as the passion of the youthful ecstatic. His works surpass those of his master in poetical refinement and general accessibility.

ᶜAyn al-Quḍāt is second only to al-Ḥallāj in both his creative use of the Iblīs motif and the dramatic quality of his death. The tragedy of self-destruction that is so much a part of the Iblīs tradition in Islamic mysticism was, ironically, mirrored in the life of ᶜAyn al-Quḍāt. As a practitioner of the science of opposites, he far surpasses both al-Ḥallāj and his spiritual master, Aḥmad al-Gahazālī. He juxtaposes the images of black light and white light to capture the ambivalence of the Sufi experiences within the divine. God is both destructive power and the luminous source of guidance. The Beloved possesses both an enticing curl (=Iblīs) that seduces the unwary Sufi and a mole (=Muḥammad) that leads the wayfarer to the right path. Yet both curl and mole spring from the Beloved's face.

ᶜAyn al-Quḍāt discovers the most appropriate expression of the conjunction of opposites in God in the Muslim confession of faith, *lā ilāha ill' allāh*. To experience *lā ilāha* ("there is no god") is to be engulfed by the realm of darkness over which Iblīs reigns. Many Sufis are lost forever in *lā ilāha*. Only the truly adept emerge into the realm of *ill' allāh* ("but God"), the station of divine intimacy. ᶜAyn al-Quḍāt insists, however, that both experiences must be seen as essential dimensions of one and the same God.

ᶜAyn al-Quḍāt's charismatic personality attracted many disciples and inflamed the hostility of the more traditionally minded, who branded his teaching heterodox in complaints to the ruling Seljuk authorities. He was imprisoned at Baghdad and later in Hamadān. While in Baghdad he wrote an apologia of his life and teachings, in an effort to discredit the charges of heresy laid against him. His attempt failed, and following his transfer to Hamadān, he was put to death in grisly fashion in May 1131. He was thirty-three years old.

A contemporary of ᶜAyn al-Quḍāt, the Ghaznavid poet Abu 'l-Majd Majdūd Sanāʾī, was the first to put the rhyming couplets of the *mathnawī* form at the service of didactic religious literature. It had originally been made famous by the epic poet Firdawsī in his *Shāhnāma* (The epic of the kings). The general outline of Sanāʾī's *mathnawī*—mystical teaching interspersed with illustrative fables, anecdotes, proverbs, and the like—became the literary model for much of the mystical literature that followed.

The recapitulation of mystical themes reached a unique level of comprehensiveness in the *mathnawī*s of the famed druggist and spiritual guide of Nishapur, Farīd al-Dīn ᶜAṭṭār (*d. ca.* 1230). His works should not be seen as simply résumés of the Sufi tradition of the past. On the contrary, ᶜAṭṭār was a master of spiritual perspicacity, a litterateur, and a skilled storyteller. His *mathnawī*s, in contrast with those of Sanāʾī and Jalāl al-Dīn Rūmī, give evidence of well-planned and carefully executed structure. Traditional themes, anecdotes, and fables undergo subtle transformation at the hands of this accomplished practitioner of both literary and mystical arts.

The third great master of the *mathnawi*, and possibly the greatest of the Persian mystical poets, is Jalāl al-Dīn Rūmī (*d.* 1273). He was born in 1207 at Balkh, the city in Khorāsān known from the earliest days of Sufism as a center of mysticism. By 1228 his family had settled in Ikonion (Konya) in Anatolia.

The most formative years in Rūmī's life were between 1244 and 1248, when he was under the personal influence of the enigmatic Shams al-Dīn Tabrīzī. The obsessive quality of their relationship alienated Rūmī from his family, friends, and disciples. Eventually Shams disappeared; the evidence implies murder, possibly with the cooperation of one of Rūmī's sons.

Even though the physical presence of Shams had faded, the love Rūmī experienced became more ardent and acted as catalyst for his astonishingly prolific literary output. The intimacy between lover

MYSTICISM, ISLAMIC

and beloved was such that Rūmī wrote his poetry under the name of Shamsi Tabrīzī, the "Sun of Tabrīz."

At the urging of his favorite disciple, Ḥusāmuddīn Çelebī, Rūmī began, in the later part of his life, to put down his teachings and mystical vision in writing. Once complete, Rūmī's *Mathnawī* exceeded 25,000 lines. It has been so revered by the Islamic community that it is often described as the Persian Koran.

The important literary and theoretical advances of twelfth- and thirteenth-century Sufism exemplified in the works of Sanāʾī, ʿAṭṭār, and Rūmī must share the stage with one of the most creative geniuses of Islamic philosophical theology and mysticism, Muḥyī 'l-Dīn ibn ʿArabī (*d.* 1240). Born at Murcia, Spain, in 1165, Ibn ʿArabī received his early training in mysticism under the guidance of two female spiritual masters. His travels led him from Spain to North Africa, Mecca, and eventually to Damascus, where he spent the rest of his life.

Ibn ʿArabī's literary output was prodigious; the physical volume and intellectual density of his work make any definitive analysis of his thought a goal yet to be achieved. Nevertheless, his basic metaphysical stance, summarized in his concept of *waḥdat al-wujūd* (the unity of being), has had tremendous formative influence on the shape Sufism has taken since the thirteenth century. *Waḥdat al-wujūd* has often been equated with metaphysical monism or pantheism by Ibn ʿArabī's commentators. While there is much evidence to substantiate such a view, Ibn ʿArabī's own perspective seems more nuanced; God is not identified substantially with his creation, for he himself transcends the very quality of substance, as, in fact, he transcends all categories.

In Ibn ʿArabī's scheme of things, creation results from God's longing to be known and loved. "I was a hidden treasure," explains God in a famous Sufi *ḥadīth*, "and I longed to be known so I created the world." Creation thus becomes the mirror of the Divine Essence. Yet, as existents, created realities are not identical with God, but only reflections of his attributes. The intimacy between God and his creation is analogous to that between God and his creative spirit, which he breathes forth. Or, as ʿAbd al-Karīm al-Jīlī (*d. ca.* 1428), one of Ibn ʿArabī's later adherents, describes it, the created universe is like ice and God is the water from which the ice is formed. Neither of these images should be seen as

Allegory of the travelers and the elephant from the *Mathnawī* of Rūmī. Some travelers (Greed), having slain the young elephant of Righteousness, are attacked by its mother, Judgment, who tramples only the guilty travelers. Miniature in Tabrīz style, *ca.* 1530. BY PERMISSION OF THE BRITISH LIBRARY, LONDON, MS ADD. 27263, fol. 134

static but, rather, as dynamic processes. As breath is exhaled and inhaled, and as ice melts and re-forms, so does God continually create and annihilate, emanate and call back his creation to its trancendent origin.

The only true existent is God; although creation functions as his mirror, it still yearns to return to the source from which it sprung. Al Jīlī is credited with the elaboration of the theory of the perfect man (*al-insān al-kāmil*), the reality in which God is most perfectly manifest. The essence that has manifested itself in creation now returns to itself through the perfect man. When this process is finally complete, all the paradoxes and the tension of opposites that so characterize Sufi experience will be resolved. Heaven and hell, reward and punishment will become empty concepts at the final return, for all will be one.

The broad influence of Ibn ʿArabī on post-thirteenth-century Sufism can scarcely be overrated. It would not be accurate, however, to give the impression that Sufism became a stagnant intellectual and religious movement after the classical period. Sufi fraternities, the emergence of popular Sufi poetry and devotional literature in a wide variety of languages, devotion to saints, and pil-

MYSTICISM, ISLAMIC

grimage all testify to the continued vibrancy of Islamic mysticism in its many forms.

Part of the success of Sufi fraternities and devotional piety is attributable to the highly intellectualist and esoteric tradition fostered by the school of Ibn ᶜArabī, which, it appears, did not adequately fulfill the religious needs of the wider Muslim population. However, the origins of the Sufi fraternities are considerably earlier. The oldest remains of a Sufi convent, on the island of Abādān in the Persian Gulf, date from the end of the eighth century.

Through the eleventh century the structure of Sufi groups remained somewhat fluid, often dependent on the charismatic personality of the individual Sufi master (*shaykh* or *pīr*), who attracted disciples and acted as the binding force of the group. With the death of the *shaykh,* the group often disbanded.

By the thirteenth century, however, the structure of the fraternities had become far more stable. The civil authority of the Sunni Seljuks, who took control of the Abbasid caliphate in the mid eleventh century, played an important role in this process. Community support of convents through the waqf system, which had begun before the Seljuk takeover, was substantially increased. Regular support for a particular convent or fraternity encouraged the orderly transition of authority from master to master. Consequently, by the thirteenth century self-perpetuating fraternities (*ṭarīqa*s) became the norm. These institutionalized groups preserved the spirit and teachings of the charismatic founder through a line of *shaykh*s who traced their initiation and training back to him.

Membership in many Sufi fraternities did not remain restricted to the inner circle of devotees who dedicated themselves completely to the spiritual Path in retirement from the world. Participation in orders like the Shādhilīyha, founded by Abu' Ḥasan al-Shādhilī (*d.* 1258), for example, did not necessitate the abandonment of one's secular life and profession. In fact, quite the opposite was encouraged. For the majority of adherents the focus of membership in a Sufi community is not to give oneself fully to the rigorous training of the Sufi Path; rather, the emphasis is on participation in ritual exercises, especially *dhikr* and *samāᶜ*.

Dhikr, derived from the Arabic root "to remember," is an individual or group exercise in which the name of God in one or more of its forms is repeated. *Dhikr* developed complex forms in the different fraternities, often involving rhythmic body movements, breathing techniques, chant forms, and the like—all leading to some form of ecstasy, either self-induced or granted by God.

The *samāᶜ* (hearing) is a musical recital of religious poetry, often accompanied by Koran recitals, involving ritual dance. The type of poetry, music, and dance varies dramatically from group to group, ranging from the meticulously choreographed and aesthetically inspiring dance of the *mevlevī*s, which is based on the poetry of Jalāl al-Dīn Rūmī, to the frenetic and emotionally charged *samāᶜ*s still encountered in many Muslim cities and villages, where the music and poetry are inspired by local mystic-poets and musicians whose creativity is channeled through the dialects and poetic forms of the particular region.

In addition to *dhikr* and *samāᶜ*, the founders and most notable *shaykh*s of the various fraternities gradually took on increased significance in the popular piety of the community. These spiritual giants were believed to possess *baraka,* a unique spiritual power that could be transmitted from saint to disciple and/or devotee. *Baraka* did not disappear with the death of the *walī* (saint); visits to the tombs of holy men and women became an important means of acquiring blessing. The power of a saint's *baraka* is not restricted to the realm of spiritual development; on the contrary, saints, both living and dead, are capable of performing *karamāt* (miracles) of various sorts: healings, psychological cures, or general spiritual blessings.

The impact of the *shaykh* of a fraternity thus becomes far more than that of a revered spiritual guide. The charismatic figure serves as the *quṭb* (pole), the unique exemplar of spiritual power and authority on earth, and the intercessor who mediates all religious experience for the members of the community. He is the perfect man.

The fourteenth century witnessed the increased indigenization of Sufism through the integration of local dialects into religious literature, in which Arabic and Persian had dominated. With creative geniuses like the Turkish poet-mystic Yūnus Emre (*d. ca.* 1321), the various languages of the Islamic world became vehicles for the inculcation of Sufi experience into the lives of increased numbers of Muslims. Central Asia, the Indian subcontinent, Africa, Indonesia—every corner of the Islamic world has produced its local poet-preacher-saint whose infectious spirit and power of *baraka* remain important catalysts for renewed religious fervor.

On a more practical level, these wandering Sufis have had a great impact on the continued spread of Islam, especially in Africa.

While it is true that the period from the ninth through the fifteenth centuries was an exceptionally creative one in the history of Islamic mysticism, the tradition of Sufism remains alive and vibrant. Doubtless it will continue to shape Islamic religious experience through the modern period of Islamic revival.

BIBLIOGRAPHY

Abul Ela Affifi, *The Mystical Philosophy of Muḥyid Dīn-Ibnul ᶜArabī* (1939, repr. 1974); Farīd al-Dīn ᶜAṭṭār, *The Conference of the Birds,* Afkham Darbandi and Dick Davis, trans. (1984), *Muslim Saints and Mystics,* A. J. Arberry, trans. (1966, repr. 1973), selections from the *Tadhkirat al-awliyāᵓ*, *The Ilāhīnāma; or, Book of God of Farīd al-Dīn ᶜAttār,* John Andrew Boyle, trans. (1976), and *Le livre de l'épreuve (Muṣībatnāma),* Isabelle de Gastines, trans. (1981); Gerhard Böwering, *The Mystical Vision of Existence in Classical Islam* (1980); Henry Corbin, *Creative Imagination in the Ṣūfism of Ibn ᶜArabī,* Ralph Manheim, trans. (1969); Joseph van Ess, *Die Gedankenwelt des Ḥāriṯ al-Muḥāsibī, anhand von Übersetzungen als seinen Schriften dargestellt und erläutert* (1961); ᶜAlī ibn ᶜUthmān al-Hujvīrī, *Kashf al-maḥjūb, Reynold A. Nicholson,* trans. (1911, repr. 1976); Muḥyī al-Dīn ibn ᶜArabī, *The Bezels of Wisdom,* R. W. J. Austin, trans. (1980); Ibn ᶜAṭāᵓillāh and ᶜAbdullāh Anṣārī, *The Book of Wisdom* and *Intimate Conversations,* Victor Danner and Wheeler M. Thackston, trans. (1978); Abū Bakr al-Kalābādhī, *The Doctrine of the Ṣūfis,* Arthur John Arberry, trans. (1935, repr. 1977); Serge de Laugier de Beaurecueil, *Khwādja ᶜAbdullāh Anṣārī (396–481 H./1006–1089)* (1965); Bruce Lawrence, *Notes from a Distant Flute: The Extant Literature of Pre-Mughal Indian Sufism* (1978).

Richard J. McCarthy, trans., *Freedom and Fulfillment* (1980), translation of al-Ghāzāli's *al-Munqidh min al-dalāl* and other works by him; Louis Massignon, *Essai sur les origines du lexique technique de la mystique musulmane,* rev. ed. (1954), and *The Passion of al-Hallāj,* Herbert Mason, trans., 4 vols. (1982); Menahem Milson, trans., *A Sufi Rule for Novices* (1975), a translation of the *Kitāb ādāb al-murīdīn* of Abū 'l-Najīb al-Suhrawardi; Reynold A. Nicholson, *Studies in Islamic Mysticism* (1921, repr. 1979), and *The Idea of Personality in Sufism* (1923, repr. 1970); Paul Nwyia, *Exégèse coranique et langage mystique* (1970), and *Ibn ᶜAtāᵓ Allāh et la naissance de la confrérie šāḏilite* (1972); Hellmut Ritter, *Das Meer der Seele* (1955, repr. 1978); Jalāl al-Dīn Rūmī, *The Mathnawī,* Reynold A. Nicholson, ed. and trans., 8 vols. (1925–1971), *Mystical Poems of Rūmī, First Selection, Poems 1–200,* A. J. Arberry, trans. (1968, repr. 1974), *Second Selection, Poems 201–400* (1979), and *Dīvāni Shamsi Tabrīz,* Reynold A. Nicholson, ed. and trans. (1973, repr. 1977); Annemarie Schimmel, *Mystical Dimensions of Islam* (1975), *The Triumphal Sun: A Study of the Works of Jalāloddin Rumi* (1978, rev. ed. 1980), and *As Through a Veil: Mystical Poetry in Islam* (1982); Margaret Smith, *Rābiᶜa the Mystic and Her Fellow-Saints in Islam* (1928, repr. 1984), and *An Early Mystic of Baghdad: A Study of the Life and Teaching of Ḥārith b. Asad al-Muḥāsibī (A.D. 781–A.D. 857)* (1935, repr. 1977); John Spencer Trimingham, *The Sufi Orders in Islam* (1971).

PETER J. AWN

[See also **Dervish; Egypt, Islamic; Ghazālī, al-Ghaznavids; Ḥallāj, al-; Iblis; Iranian Literature; Islam, Religion; Rūmī, Jālal al-Din.**]

MYSTICISM, JEWISH. See **Cabala.**

MYTHOLOGY, CELTIC. The study of Celtic mythology presents serious problems not only for the beginning student but for the seasoned scholar as well. Our earliest written information on religious and mythological aspects of the Celtic cultures comes from Greek and Roman writers, beginning about the sixth century B.C., and concerns the Celts (Greek: *Keltoi;* Latin: *Celtae*) of the Continent. Although Plato, Aristotle, and others mention the Celts, the most important of these early commentaries is that of Posidonios of Apamea (first century B.C.), whose writings survive in the works of such later writers as Diodorus Siculus, Strabo, and Athenaeus. From this Posidonian tradition we learn, among other things, that druids were the "philosophers and theologians" of the Celts, and that they sacrificed both animals and humans, divining the future from their death throes. The druids officiated at sacrifices as the only ones who could converse with the gods.

However much he owed to this tradition of Greek ethnography and to first-hand observation, Julius Caesar provides perhaps the most tantalizing information concerning the religion of the Celts. He states that the Celts of Gaul are much given to religious superstition, and in *De bello gallico* (VI, 17) he says that the Celts worship Mercury above the other gods as inventor of all arts, as patron of routes and roads, and as influential in commerce.

MYTHOLOGY, CELTIC

After him come Apollo, Mars, Jupiter, and Minerva; concerning these gods, Caesar says, the Celts hold almost the same notions that others do: Apollo averts disease, Minerva is the patron of arts and crafts, Mars receives the spoils of war, and Jupiter holds sway over the heavens. These names, of course, are the names of Roman divinities, and Caesar simply interpreted the facts of continental Celtic mythology in Roman terms (*interpretatio romana*). Still, it seems likely that the functions he associates with the gods and goddesses he names represent functions associated with their Celtic equivalents. Nevertheless, the *interpretatio romana* remains a serious obstacle for students of continental Celtic mythology. Later writers do occasionally provide Celtic names of divinities, as when the Roman poet Lucan (first century), in *De bello civili* (I, 444–446), names Teutates, Esus, and Taranis as gods to whom the Gauls sacrificed—by drowning, hanging and wounding, and burning, respectively, according to a later commentator on Lucan. And the Greek rhetorician Lucian (second century) states that Hercules was known to the Celts as Ogmios, since the Celts associated strength with eloquence.

Perhaps the most fertile source for our knowledge of local names of Celtic gods and goddesses is the large number of inscriptions on altars, statues, bas-reliefs, and monuments of other sorts, constructed largely during the period of the romanization of Gaul. These inscriptions often couple the name of a Roman god or goddess with that of a Celtic one. The great variety of the Celtic names (many of which occur only once) suggests an essentially local and tribal character for Celtic religion, although the names may only be various nicknames for the same Celtic god. For example, Mercury is nicknamed Moccus (Pig) and Artaius (Bear), and Apollo is called Toutiorix (King of the Tribe) and Maponos (Divine Youth).

The expansion of Celtic cultures in the middle of the first millennium B.C. is amply attested by the place-names of Western Europe. Some of these names, such as Nemetodurum (Nanterre), suggest places of worship (*nemeto,* sacred), while names such as those derived from Lugdunum or Lugudunum (Lyons, Liegnitz, Laon, Leiden) attest to the popularity of the god Lug, and names such as Matronae (Marne) and Danu (Danube) identify Celtic tutelary goddesses of rivers.

Finally, the archaeological record has provided supporting evidence for various aspects of Celtic religion and mythology, evidence of sanctuaries of various sorts, votive sacrifices and objects, and funerary furnishings reflecting Celtic concepts of the supernatural and the afterlife.

These fragmentary sources constitute our base of information on the mythology of the earliest Celts, the Celts of the continent of Europe. They date from various periods and relate to various tribes; and with the exception of place-name evidence and the archaeological record, they represent a culture viewed through the eyes of alien peoples. But whatever their shortcomings may be, they constitute an important part of the historical record and our earliest glimpses of Celtic cultures.

The most important sources are the writings of the Celtic peoples themselves. Regarding Gaul they are virtually nonexistent, for, as Caesar tells us, the Celtic learned class committed nothing to writing; traditional learning was handed on orally. Prior to the introduction of Christianity into the British Isles, the Celtic cultures of Britain and Ireland, like those of their predecessors on the Continent, preserved their traditions orally. There is considerable debate about when the Irish or British first began to write down their traditions, but it was certainly after the introduction of Christianity; and there is every reason to believe that written versions of native mythological tales existed by the early seventh century—if not earlier—in Ireland. These have not survived, however, and the earliest manuscripts preserving native secular materials date from the early twelfth century in Ireland and the mid thirteenth century in Wales (the major surviving Celtic region in Britain by that time). It is to these texts that students of Celtic mythology must turn for information on the religion and mythology of the Celts. Comparison of Irish and Welsh texts, supported by information gleaned from sources on the continental Celts, allows us to make certain deductions about Celtic mythology, although our conclusions must always be considered tentative.

From the surviving Irish and Welsh texts, it is clear that the Celts of Ireland and Britain preserved traditions about the creation of their world, the establishment of the social order, the origins of wisdom, and other etiological myths. These concerns are most evident in the surviving Irish material, which is far more voluminous than the Welsh, though the latter often complements and sometimes completes the former. In the *Leabhar Gabhála Éireann* (The book of the taking [or invasions] of Ireland) certain cosmogonic traditions

MYTHOLOGY, CELTIC

were "edited" by the medieval Irish literati to make Irish mythological tradition conform to biblical tradition. Hence, we find reference to a first occupation of Ireland in antediluvian times, then a succession of invaders, including the Partholonians, the Nemedians, the Fir Bolg, and the Túatha Dé Danann (Tribes of the Goddess Danu); and the coming of the historical Gaels, the so-called sons of Míl (Milesians). With the exception of the last, these inhabitants are credited with clearing plains, creating lakes, and in general shaping the land; inventing plowing, churning, and other agricultural activities; and establishing and perfecting the high office of kingship.

Welsh narrative tradition preserves no such systematic etiological myth or legend, but does credit the origins of certain features of the land to a sow named Henwen (the Ancient White One). This is quite significant, given the fact that swine were an important part not only of the domestic economy of the Celts but also of their mythology. In Gaul, the Roman god Mercury was known by the name Moccus (Irish: *mucc;* Welsh: *moch,* both meaning pig), among other names, and the pig figures prominently in early Irish and Welsh tales of shapeshifting and the otherworld. Henwen, while pregnant, is said to have been pursued by King Arthur; at various places she gave birth to wheat, barley, bees, a wolf, an eagle, and a kitten. The first three account for the origins and excellence of those commodities in the regions where they were brought forth by Henwen; the other three are associated with evil.

Two major texts belonging to the Leabhar Gabhála Éireann tradition are the first and second battles of Moytura. The second battle has attracted the most attention from scholars, for it appears to echo traditions recorded elsewhere in the Indo-European community—traditions about a battle between two classes (or functions) in society: agriculture, on the one hand, and sovereignty and force, on the other; the battle leads to concord and accommodation between them. In this case the Fomorians represent the chthonic and agricultural aspect; the Túatha Dé Danann, the functions of sovereignty and force. In Welsh the tale known as *Cyfranc Lludd a Lleuelys* (The adventure of Lludd and Lleuelys) has been seen to contain the kernel of the same myth.

In a society that valued eloquence and ranked its poets with its kings, it is not surprising to find traditions of the acquisition of wisdom prominently displayed. Wisdom is depicted as a divine commodity, residing in the otherworld, of which only the privileged are allowed to partake. The poet or initiate exposes himself to dangerous liminal states, between this world and the other, in the expectation of sharing in the divine wisdom that reveals the past and the future. In the process, the poet is reborn, or passes through other shapes, or is renamed as he becomes divinely inspired and acquires supernatural wisdom. The Irish traditions about Finn mac Cumhaill and Welsh traditions about Taliesin provide paradigms of the myth of the archetypal poet-seer.

In these tales, as in Irish and Welsh narratives about the remarkable births, youthful deeds, courtships, marriages, and deaths of divine heroes, the otherworld plays a very important part. While there is much ampler treatment of the otherworld in the early Irish material than in the Welsh, there is sufficient agreement between the two to point to an inherited Celtic idea of what might be called a parallel universe, since the otherworld in Celtic mythology is not a land of the dead. In Irish sources, the otherworld is known variously as Tír Tairngiri (Land of Promise), Mag Mell (Plain of Delight), Tír na n-Óg (Land of the Young), and simply *sídh* (fairy mound; pronounced as in *banshee,* woman of the fairy mound). In Welsh, the otherworld usually goes by the name of Annwfn or Annwn. It is often conceived of as a place out at sea, beyond the sea, on an island, or beneath the sea, but it is often enough coterminous with mortal domains. It is a place of perfection, where aging and pain have no place; life goes on there as in our world, with births, marriages, banqueting, even battles; its physical beauty and perfection, and that of its inhabitants, are remarkable; and often it is a place inhabited chiefly or solely by women. Mortals come into contact with the otherworld in various ways. Sometimes the encounter seems accidental: the hero is out hunting and becomes lost, is on a voyage, or travels to a distant and unknown land; at other times, it is the denizen of the otherworld who initiates the encounter: The mortal is lured to the otherworld by a beast that he unwittingly pursues, or the denizen assumes the shape of an animal and invades the mortal's world.

In the Celtic mythopoeic mind, there was a kind of elasticity of space that permitted the coexistence of these natural and supernatural worlds, and that permitted them to overlap and even intrude on each other almost randomly. It is a striking feature of

God with boar on torso, wearing a heavy torque around his neck. Gallo-Roman limestone sculpture from Euffigneix. MUSÉE DES ANTIQUITÉS NATIONALES, ST. GERMAINE-EN-LAYE. PHOTO: JEAN ROUBIER

medieval Irish and Welsh mythological narratives that mortals and immortals tread each other's domains with unselfconscious regularity. In the same way that space is mutable, so is shape. Shape-shifting occurs with the same regularity as the movement between worlds. Mortals turn into animals and back again, toadstools are changed into animals and weapons, gods and mortals exchange places, taking each other's shape, and so on. Sometimes the shape-shifting is done as a punishment, but often it is an expedient. Sometimes it bears a relationship to what might be called the zoomorphic element in Celtic mythology, whereby a god has both a human and an animal shape, but often it represents only a perceived continuity between human and animal and inanimate nature, a continuity in which each participates in the nature of the others. Thus did the early Celts overcome the naturally imposed barriers of space and form in their conceptions of the supernatural.

Finally, a word must be said about the gods and goddesses. The combined evidence from place-names and surviving Celtic literature shows that the god Lugus was worshiped widely. In Irish he is known as Lugh and is said to be master of all crafts; in Welsh he is called Lleu of the Skilled Hand, one of the three golden shoemakers of the Isle of Britain; his name is plural in form (Lugoves) in a dedication at a guild of shoemakers in Osma, Spain. Lugh belonged to the mythical Túatha Dé Danann, all of whose gods were craftsmen, though the other gods of that group are scarcely known outside of Ireland, a fact that testifies to the essentially local nature of Celtic mythology. Lugh was said to be reincarnated as Cú Chulainn, the divine hero of the Ulster Cycle.

In Gaul, goddesses often were depicted as consorts of gods. They also were associated with rivers as tutelary divinities, and were honored as Matres or Matronae (mothers). Earth and mother goddesses of this sort were known in Ireland, too, associated with various features of the landscape. The goddess for whom we have the most evidence on the Continent, however, is Epona (Divine Horse, Horse Goddess). This equine goddess has powerful counterparts in the literature of medieval Ireland and Wales. In Ireland the narratives about Macha are shaped by the myth of Epona, and in Wales we see reflections of it in the stories about Rhiannon. The equine goddess is essentially a sovereignty figure, and without her no man can be king. She is aggressive, choosing her mates. In Ireland she consummates the "wedding-feast of kingship" by proffering a draft of liquor to her husband/king, and so she is sometimes known as Medb (English: Maeve; the Intoxicating One or Intoxication). Other prominent goddesses in the well-attested Irish tradition are the warrior-goddesses, who preside over the battlefield, often in the shape of scaldcrows. Though the Mórrígan (perhaps Great Queen) is the best-known name of this type of goddess, other names occur, and the goddess is often depicted as triple—the three Mórrígans, or Badb (Crow), Nemain (Frenzy), and Mórrígan. Scáthach (Shadowy) was the name given the warrior goddess who trained the hero Cú Chulainn.

It is impossible to paint a clear picture of Celtic mythology. The evidence is distant in time, wide-

The goddess Epona. Gallo-Roman sculpture from Alesia in eastern France. MUSÉE ALESIA, ALISE-STE.-REINE. PHOTO: JEAN ROUBIER

ranging, and inconsistent. The Celts of Gaul must be studied from the writings of sometimes unsympathetic foreigners and from the archaeological record; information about the insular Celts must be gleaned from the surviving literary record, and our understanding of the mythological significance of those texts is still far from complete.

BIBLIOGRAPHY

Rachel Bromwich, ed. and trans., *Trioedd ynys Prydein: The Welsh Triads* (1961); Jan Filip, *Celtic Civilization and Its Heritage,* Roberta Finlayson Samsour, trans. (1962); Patrick K. Ford, *The Mabinogi and Other Medieval Welsh Tales* (1977); Elizabeth A. Gray, "Cath Maige Tuired: Myth and Structure (1–24)," in *Éigse,* **18** (1981); Proinsias Mac Cana, *Celtic Mythology* (1970); Alwyn Rees and Brinley Rees, *Celtic Heritage* (1961, repr. 1973); Anne Ross, *Everyday Life of the Pagan Celts* (1970); Marie-Louise Sjoestedt-Jonval, *Gods and Heroes of the Celts,* Myles Dillon, trans. (1949, repr. 1982); J. J. Tierney, "The Celtic Ethnography of Posidonius," in *Proceedings of the Royal Irish Academy,* sec. C, 60 (1960); Jan de Vries, *Keltische Religion* (1961).

PATRICK K. FORD

[See also **Irish Literature; Welsh Literature.**]

MYTHOLOGY, SCANDINAVIAN. See **Scandinavian Mythology.**

N-TOWN PLAYS, a largely fifteenth-century compilation of some forty religious plays or play sequences in about 11,400 lines, performed at "N-Town," which is preserved in the Cottonian collection. British Library, MS Cotton Vespasian D.VIII was titled "liber Ludus Coventriae sive ludus corporis Christi" by Richard James, Sir Robert Cotton's first librarian, who obtained it from Robert Hegge of Corpus Christi College, Oxford, in the early 1630's. The dates, authorship, and auspices of these plays are unknown. Thomas Sharp in 1825 distinguished them from the true Coventry cycle, and because the Cotton manuscript play banns advertise performance at "N. [or *nomen*] town" on a Sunday, the text may well not be Corpus Christi plays (this feast always falls on a Thursday). W. W. Greg used the name "N-town plays" when he analyzed their multiple strata by reference to manuscript features, handwriting, prosody, sources, staging, and a comparison of what the banns promise and what the texts contain. Numerous authors have shown that the N-town manuscript is a single scribe's compilation, written in a Norfolk dialect toward the end of the fifteenth century, of at least six groups of plays or play sequences.

The banns describe a cycle, of which we have the first seven plays (the Creation, Fall of Lucifer and Man, Cain and Abel, Noah, Abraham and Isaac, Moses, and the Tree of Jesse), two plays from a Marian sequence (Joseph's Trouble About Mary, and the Trial of Joseph and Mary), a Nativity sequence (the Birth of Christ, the Shepherds, the Magi, and the Slaughter of the Innocents), a Ministry group (Christ and the Doctors, the Baptism, the Temptation, the Woman Taken in Adultery, and Lazarus), a Passion, Harrowing of Hell, and Resurrection sequence of which only three plays remain (the Marys at the Sepulcher, the Appearance to Mary Magdalen, and the Appearance to

N-TOWN PLAYS

Cleophas and Luke, and to Thomas), and three "last" plays (Ascension, Pentecost, and a fragmentary Doomsday).

This cycle was played on a Sunday beginning at six o'clock in the morning in one town, arguably in a fixed location, a "locum interludij" (4:141), with scaffolds or wagons "in strete and stage" (3:188). Bann criers advertised the performance in neighboring communities. An itinerant troupe of performers is most unlikely. The plays' emphasis on preaching (as in the Woman Taken in Adultery), the learned texts (as in the Moses, the Tree of Jesse, Joseph's Trouble, and Christ and the Doctors), and the lack of craft guild allusions suggest the work of a religious guild or (in fourteenth-century terms) "a clerks' play," probably written by monks or friars.

To this basic cycle the scribe added, as he wrote the manuscript, five other plays or groups of plays. First are five plays about Anne and Mary (the Conception of Mary, Mary in the Temple, the Betrothal of Mary, the Parliament of Heaven and the Annunciation, and the Visit to Elizabeth), each introduced and concluded by an allegorical expositor, Contemplacio. Whereas the cycle has Latin stage directions and thirteen-line stanzas, and draws source material mainly from Matthew, the Marian plays (four of which are not in the banns) have English-Latin stage directions and long-lined octaves, and rely loosely on the Golden Legend, St. Bonaventure's *Meditationes*, the liturgy, and illuminated Books of Hours. This sequence also had stationary performance on one day (the feast of St. Anne, 26 July, is often suggested), but with frequent music and more elaborate scaffold stages.

The next addition is a Purification of Mary, similarly staged, absent from the banns, and dated 1468. The third addition, Passion Play I, covering the period from the conspiracy to the close of the betrayal, was a separate manuscript, and is not the Passion play described in the banns. This new sequence has rich English stage directions; uses quatrains, couplets, and octaves; and relies on the *Northern Passion*. The similar Passion Play II begins with Christ before Annas and Caiaphas, and ends indistinctly at the Resurrection, where a different Harrowing of Hell is split in two by a play on the Burial of Christ. The entire group evidently supplanted another Passion play in *rime couée* that is partly described in certain additions to the banns. Both Passion plays call for outdoors place-and-scaffold performance in the round in alternate years.

The last major addition is an Assumption of the Virgin, a long play (full of Latin music) that is missing from the banns and was written by a second scribe, perhaps from Bury St. Edmunds. The main scribe-compiler, whom some believe to have written the Passion plays, apparently added other learned episodes to the banns cycle (Lamech, the burning bush, and the cherry-tree miracle). His equally learned genealogical glosses imply that he worked in an ecclesiastical house. His dialect belongs to the vicinity of Harling, from which there is record in 1452 of an "original" of an interlude once played at the church gate. Later, two revisers worked on the manuscript. One added a quire to the Betrothal play. The second, in the early sixteenth century, made selective changes for acting versions of three play groups: a Nativity group (Shepherds, Magi, Slaughter, and Baptism) and a two-day Resurrection group, from the Harrowing to the appearance to Thomas. Despite instructive attempts to show dramatic unity in the N-town plays, the text remains a late medieval anthology of independent sequences, although the scribe-compiler's often transparent work reveals the artistic methods of fifteenth-century dramaturgy. The texts have been placed at Lincoln and at Bury St. Edmunds, but dialect firmly indicates Norfolk, not Lincolnshire or Suffolk. Scriptural plays are recorded in Norfolk at Great Yarmouth (1473–1508), Bishop's Lynn (1384–1484), and Norwich. The last, a cathedral city with a Benedictine monastery, four large friaries, an important library, and large religious guilds, had dramatic activity from about 1260 well into the sixteenth century, including an early Corpus Christi procession and scriptural pageants by a St. Luke's Guild and then by the craft guilds from about 1530 (for one of which a text survives).

BIBLIOGRAPHY

Katherine S. Block, ed., *Ludus Coventriae; or, The Plaie Called Corpus Christi, Cotton MS. Vespasian D. VIII,* Early English Text Society, e.s. **120** (1922, repr. 1960), the standard edition; Patrick J. Collins, *The N-town Plays and Medieval Picture Cycles* (1979); Hardin Craig, *English Religious Drama of the Middle Ages* (1955), 239–280; Reginald T. Davies, ed., *The Corpus Christi Play of the English Middle Ages* (1972), modern text of most of the N-town plays; Mark Eccles, "*Ludus Coventriae:* Lincoln or Norfolk?" in *Medium aevum,* **40** (1971); Frances A. Foster, ed., *The Northern Passion,* II, Early English Text Society, 147 (1916), 89–101; David Galloway and John Wasson, eds.,

Records of Plays and Players in Norfolk and Suffolk, 1330–1642 (1981); Claude Gauvin, *Un cycle du théâtre religieux anglais du moyen âge: Le jeu de la ville de "N"* (1973); Walter W. Greg, *Bibliographical and Textual Problems of the English Miracle Cycles* (1914), and *idem*, ed., *The Assumption of the Virgin: A Miracle Play from the N-town Cycle* (1915); Stanley J. Kahrl, ed., *Records of Plays and Players in Lincolnshire 1300–1585* (1974); Peter Meredith and Stanley J. Kahrl, intro., *The N-town Plays. A Facsimile of British Library MS Cotton Vespasian D VIII* (1977), the best introduction to the manuscript; Anna J. Mill, "The Miracle Plays and Mysteries," in *A Manual of the Writings in Middle English, 1050–1500*, V (1975); Stephen Spector, "The Composition and Development of an Eclectic Manuscript: Cotton Vespasian D VIII," in *Leeds Studies in English*, n.s. 9 (1977); Esther L. Swenson, *An Inquiry into the Composition and Structure of Ludus Coventriae* (1914); Rosemary Woolf, *The English Mystery Plays* (1972).

IAN LANCASHIRE

[See also **Drama, Liturgical; Drama, Western European; Mystery Plays.**]

NADĪM, IBN AL- (Abū 'l-Faraj Muḥammad) (*d.* 995 or 998). He was the most distinguished medieval Arab bibliographer and the author of the celebrated work *Kitāb al-Fihrist* (The index), an encyclopedia of medieval Islamic culture. The scanty information we possess about Ibn al-Nadīm is gathered mostly from *al-Fihrist.* Like his father, he was a copyist or a bookseller (*warrāq*) and lived mainly in Baghdad and Mosul. The epithet al-Nadīm (a court or boon companion) could be a reference to him, to his father, or to a more distant ancestor. He was a Shiite and a Muᶜtazilite, and it is assumed that his liberal and comprehensive outlook, his interest in various sciences, his admiration for philosophy, especially Aristotle, and his tolerance in religious matters were a direct influence of the prominent philosophers, logicians, grammarians, and philologists who were among his non-Sunni teachers.

Al-Fihrist, completed according to Ibn al-Nadīm himself in 987/988, was intended as a catalog of all books written in Arabic by Arabs and non-Arabs. It exists in two recensions: the larger contains ten discourses (*maqālāt*) and a preface; the smaller one, which was given the name *Fawz al-ᶜulūm* (The triumph of sciences) by the later encyclopedist Hājjī Khalīfa (*d.* 1657), comprises a preface and the last four discourses of the larger one. The first six discourses of the larger edition deal with books on the following Islamic subjects: (1) the holy scriptures of Muslims, Jews, and Christians, with emphasis on the Koran and koranic sciences. Ibn al-Nadīm also treats in this section languages and scripts of fourteen Arab and non-Arab peoples, their writing methods, and the writing pen and paper in their different varieties; (2) grammar and philology; (3) history, biography, genealogy, and kindred subjects; (4) poetry; (5) scholastic theology (kalam); and (6) law and tradition. The last four discourses deal with non-Islamic subjects such as the Arabic translations from Greek, Syriac, and other languages, together with Arabic books modeled on those translations. These subjects are: (7) philosophy and the "ancient sciences" of the great pre-Islamic civilizations, including mathematics, astronomy, medicine, metaphysics, philosophy, music, and so on; (8) legends, fables, magic, conjuring, and so forth; (9) the doctrines of the dualist creeds, such as the beliefs of the Sabaeans and the Manichaeans, and of Buddhism and the religions of India and China; and (10) alchemy.

Arabic literature of the first four centuries of Islam is presented in a bibliographic (not biographical) arrangement, since Ibn al-Nadīm's foremost interest as a bookseller was to catalog books and not authors. Books on classes of poets (*ṭabaqāt*) already existed, but Ibn al-Nadīm was the first to classify larger areas of knowledge in a bibliographic manner. His system in compiling the index was rigorous and quite elaborate. He would give the titles of those books that he had seen or the existence of which was attested to by reliable persons with a brief biography of their authors. He would often mention the size of a book and occasionally the number of pages, and he would refer to famous calligraphers, bibliophiles, and book auctions. At times Ibn al-Nadīm would venture his own opinions on topics such as sorcery, superstition, and alchemy. He also left blank spaces in his manuscript for additional data, but he died before obtaining all the information he desired. Ibn al-Nadīm's style in *al-Fihrist* is direct and unembellished because of the technical nature of its content. The language is unusually common, and represents, as Johann W. Fück pointed out, "the colloquial of the educated classes of the capital [Baghdad]."

In sum, Ibn al-Nadīm succeeded in faithfully recording the entire spectrum of medieval Arabic writing, belles lettres, scientific and popular literature, old and new poetry, anonymous light literature, love stories, fairy tales, books of adventure and good manners, cookery books, books on poison, hunting, sports, magic, and prophecy, collections of farces, and books on husbandry. Ibn al-Nadīm also wrote another book entitled *Kitāb al-awṣāf wa 'l-tashbīhāt* (The book of descriptions and comparisons), which has not survived.

The great distinctive value of *al-Fihrist* lies in the fact that it was more than a mere catalog of the material on the Baghdad book market in the tenth century. Indeed, it became a cultural history of the Arab world and a true record of medieval Islamic civilization. The book reveals to us at once the enormous output of Arabic literature and the paucity of the surviving material.

BIBLIOGRAPHY

The Arabic text of the *Kitāb al-Fihrist* was published in two volumes, together with annotations, by Gustav L. Flügel (1871–1872). A reprint of this edition appeared in Cairo in 1930. Two photographic reproductions of the same edition also appeared in Beirut by Dār Khayats in 1964 and 1966. An English translation of *The Fihrist of al-Nadīm* was executed by Bayard Dodge and published by Columbia University Press in two volumes (1970). Johann W. Fück translated the Tenth Discourse of *al-Fihrist* with introduction and commentary under the title "The Arabic Literature on Alchemy According to an-Nadīm (A.D. 987)," in *Ambix*, IV (1951). An English translation of the preface of the *Fihrist*, together with a summary of its contents, is given by Edward G. Browne in his *A Literary History of Persia*, I (1902, repr. 1977). A complementary article entitled "New Material on the *Kitāb al-Fihrist* of Ibn al-Nadīm" was published by Arthur J. Arberry in *Islamic Research Association Miscellany*, I (1948). For general works on Ibn al-Nadīm and his monumental book *al-Fihrist*, consult the old and new editions of the *Encyclopaedia of Islam* and Ḥājjī Khalīfa's *Kashf al-ẓunūn ʿan asāmī al-kutub wa 'l-funūn* (*Lexicum bibliographicum et encyclopaedicum*), Gustav L. Flügel, ed. and trans., 7 vols. (1835–1858, repr. 1964). A French translation of the tenth discourse of Flügel's edition of *al-Fihrist* was published in 1893 by O. Houdas in Marcellin Berthelot, *La chimie au moyen âge*, III (1893).

MANSOUR J. AJAMI

[See also **Arabic Literature; Arabic Numerals.**]

NAGID, a biblical royal title used by medieval Jews in the Islamic world to designate the leader of a provincial community. Officials exercising empire-wide authority were the gaons and the exilarch. Nagids were found in North Africa, Spain, Egypt, Syria, Palestine, and the Yemen. Most famous among them was Samuel "the Nagid" Ibn Nagrela (933–1056), the Spanish Hebrew poet, vizier of Granada, and head of Andalusian Jewry during the second quarter of the eleventh century.

Scholarly controversy surrounds the question of the origins of the nagidate as an institution. The popular theory, based on certain Hebrew stories about the first Egyptian nagid, holds that at the time of the breakup of the Abbasid empire Muslim rulers of the successor states appointed local nagids in order to sever Jewish contacts with the exilarch in Baghdad. The Fatimids are believed to have initiated this practice when they conquered Egypt in 969.

The other view states that the office of nagid, actually "head of the Jews" (*raʾīs al-Yahūd*), the Arabic title bestowed by the Fatimid government, originated a century later as a result of interacting internal and external forces. In the 1060's, the Fatimid empire entered a period of political and economic instability during which the Palestinian province was lost to the Seljuks. After security and order were restored in Egypt around 1074, the Fatimids abandoned their Shiite imperialistic ambitions and turned inward. As a by-product, the non-Muslim communities felt a centralizing pull on their own institutions of self-government. The Fatimid vizier pressed the Coptic patriarch to abandon his ancient seat in Alexandria and remain permanently in Cairo, from where the government could use his good offices to negotiate with the tributary kingdoms of Abyssinia and Nubia, whose Monophysite state churches fell under the ecumenical sway of the Coptic prelate.

During the same period of time, the gaonate of Palestine, long recognized by the Fatimids as the sovereign authority over Egyptian Jewry, declined in importance, and Jewish leaders in the Fatimid capital began to grope for a new basis of communal leadership. By the year 1100, following a gradual, organic evolution of power, this transformation had been completed, and the Egyptian nagid, or head of the Jews, had replaced the Jerusalem gaon as suzerain over Fatimid Jewish affairs.

The rights and duties of the head of the Jews, known from Jewish and Muslim sources alike, were several. He was first and foremost the chief judicial and administrative officer of the Jewish community. He appointed chief judges in the Egyptian capital and, either through them or directly, designated local judicial and administrative functionaries. As a judge himself, he exercised an appellate function. To enforce his authority he relied principally upon the prestige he derived from his position of influence with the Muslim court and from the respectful dread (*hayba*) that his subjects felt toward him. In the late Mamluk period, the nagid operated a prison and made extensive use of the ban (excommunication). Unlike the earlier years, when his jurisdiction was limited to Rabbinite Jews alone, in the late Mamluk period his authority extended to the Karaites and Samaritans as well.

As head of the community, the nagid was bombarded with requests for charity and other forms of assistance, including intercession with the government in order to obtain redress of grievances. As chief religious arbiter, he supervised the domain of family law. During the Mamluk period, when Jewish economic and demographic strength, as well as general security, declined, the office of nagid became increasingly autocratic. This development constituted a response to centrifugal forces threatening the integrity of the community. Upon the Ottoman conquest of Egypt in 1517, the institution was dissolved under circumstances that are somewhat unclear.

BIBLIOGRAPHY

Eliyahu Ashtor, "Some Features of the Jewish Communities in Medieval Egypt" (in Hebrew), in *Zion*, 30 (1965), and (also by the name of Eli Strauss), *Toledot ha-yehudim be-Miṣrayim we-Suria taḥat shilṭon ha-mamlukim* (The history of the Jews in Egypt and Syria under Mamluk rule), II (1951), 237–253; Mark R. Cohen, *Jewish Self-Government in Medieval Egypt: The Origins of the Head of the Jews, ca. 1065–1126* (1981); Solomon D. Goitein, *A Mediterranean Society: The Jewish Communities of the Arab World as Portrayed in the Documents of the Cairo Geniza*, II (1971), 23–40; Haim Z. Hirschberg, *A History of the Jews in North Africa*, M. Eichelberg, trans., I, 2nd rev. ed. (1974); David Neustadt (later David Ayalon), "Some Problems Concerning the 'Negidut' in Egypt During the Middle Ages" (in Hebrew), in *Zion*, n.s. 4 (1938–1939).

MARK R. COHEN

[See also **Exilarch; Gaonic Period; Jewish Communal Self-Government: Islamic World; Jews in Egypt.**]

NAḤMANIDES, MOSES (Moshe ben Nachman, or Ramban, the acronym for the Hebrew *Ra*bbi *M*oshe *b*en *N*achman) (*ca.* 1195–*ca.* 1270). Born in Gerona, Catalonia, Naḥmanides was widely renowned as a scholar, a defender of the faith, and a pioneer in reestablishing the Jewish community in Jerusalem.

As a Talmud scholar, Naḥmanides defended older authorities in his *Milchamoth Hashem, Sefer ha-Zekhut,* and *hasagoth* on the *Sefer ha-Mitzvot* of Maimonides. His commentary on the Pentateuch is noteworthy for its penetrating analysis of biblical themes and for its challenging many points in works of Rashi and Abraham ben Meir ibn Ezra. Naḥmanides also wrote the *Chidushim* on tractates of the Talmud, the *Torath ha-Adam* (The law of man; on inevitable aspects of human life, such as illness, death, judgment, and resurrection), and the *Sefer ha-Ge'ullah* (Book of redemption). He challenged Aristotelian rationalism, yet in a letter to French rabbis (1232) he defended Maimonides' works as completely authoritative. This opinion did not deter him from criticizing many points in Maimonides' *Guide of the Perplexed.* He also introduced mysticism (cabala) as an interpretive element of Scriptures.

In 1263 Naḥmanides was forced to participate in a public disputation at Barcelona with the apostate monk Pablo Christiani, in the presence of King James I and church officials. He asked for, and received, freedom of speech. The disputation was held in four sessions (20, 23, 26, and 27 July). At the request of the bishop of Gerona, Naḥmanides wrote a Hebrew account, for which he was later threatened by monks, although the king was for his complete acquittal. Finally he decided to go into exile. In the spring of 1267 he arrived in Acre, a Christian city that still had a substantial Jewish community, and on 1 September of that year he came to Jerusalem, where he reestablished the Jewish community. (The synagogue he founded is still in existence.) Naḥmanides emended his commentary on the Pentateuch as a result of actually seeing the geography of the land.

BIBLIOGRAPHY

Ramban (Nachmanides), *Commentary on the Torah*, 5 vols. (1971–1978), and *Writings and Discourses*, 2 vols. (1978), both trans. and annotated by Charles B. Chavel. See also E. Gottlieb, "Nahmanides," in *Encyclopedia judaica*, XII (1972), with bibliography.

CHARLES B. CHAVEL

[See also **Cabala; Jews in Christian Spain; Jews in the Middle East; Palestine; Maimonides, Moses; Palestine; Polemics, Christian-Jewish; Talmud, Exegesis and Study of.**]

NAJD, the great central plateau of Arabia, bounded by the sands of the Empty Quarter (al-Rubᶜ al-khālī) to the south and those of the Nafūd to the north. On its western flank it is separated from the Hejaz by a narrow strip of passable sands, and to the east the long sandy strips of the Dahnāᵓ mark the transition to the coastlands of the Persian Gulf. The vast interior region so delineated is Najd proper; it too contains some areas of sand desert, but for the most part consists of gravel steppeland. There are no permanent streams in Najd; most water supplies come from wells and springs, and settled life has thus focused throughout the area's history on the oases, where sedentary agriculture can best be maintained. Elsewhere, crops must be irrigated from wells. On the steppes, the periodic rains produce extensive pasturelands, which historically have supported a relatively high level of nomadic population.

The role of Najd in the history of the medieval Near East involved the interplay of several important factors: its size, the ties it provided between distant areas, and its large nonurban population. From ancient times Najd had been the focus of all interior Arabia, with numerous trade routes traversing it in many directions. By facilitating communications over vast ranges of territory, these highways helped to reduce the isolation of parts of Arabia from other areas and provided important links with Syria and Iraq.

The rather small towns of Najd played only a minor role in its history, for the social force of the region was its nonurban population, consisting of tribes which fluctuated between complete pastoralism and semisedentary agriculture depending on prevailing climatic and political conditions. Numerous tribal kingdoms arose in Najd in pre-Islamic times, and although these were usually only loose tribal confederacies, some, that of the chieftain Imruᵓ al-Qays in the fourth century and that of the tribe of Kinda in the fifth, managed to extend their influence over most of the interior. Such tribal combinations often posed serious threats along the inland frontiers and the vulnerable trade routes, and even when the Najd tribes were weak their feuds and other tribal disputes tended to spill over to involve the more sedentary tribes around them.

With the rise of Islam, the significance of Najd began to decline. Its tribes were gradually won over to Islam and provided manpower to the early armies of conquest, and the Umayyad caliphs of the seventh century continued to value the region for its pasturage and agricultural potential. But at the same time, all of the peninsula was gradually becoming a backwater; the shift of the imperial capital from Medina to Damascus, and later to Baghdad, marked the course of Arabia's increasing isolation from the affairs of the empire. Correspondingly less attention was thus paid to the region, and Najd gradually became a source of tribal unrest and a haven where ideological dissent could find refuge. The Kharijites were already a problem in Najd under the Umayyads, and under the Abbasids partisans of the Alids gave trouble. The movement of the Qarmaṭians, in particular, drew important sources of manpower and tribal influence from Najd in the tenth century. Even before this, autonomous petty states had begun to assert themselves in various parts of Arabia, and such principalities often tried to extend their authority into Najd.

BIBLIOGRAPHY

There is an enormous literature on Arabia, but comparatively little on the medieval history of the Najd. For an excellent description, see Alois Musil, *Northern Negd* (1928). Far more helpful on historical points are G. Rentz, "Djazīrat al-ᶜArab," in the *Encyclopaedia of Islam,* 2nd ed., and Kamal S. Salibi, *A History of Arabia* (1980), with an extensive bibliography. For further bibliographical references, see Eric Macro, *Bibliography of the Arabian Peninsula* (1958).

LAWRENCE I. CONRAD

[See also **Arabia.**]

NAJRĀN, an Arab city that played an important role in the history of the Arabian Peninsula and of Eastern Christianity in the century before the rise of Islam. Favored by nature with an impregnable position in mountainous northern Yemen and located in a most fertile valley, the city developed into one of the main urban centers of the Arabian Peninsula, a position of eminence enhanced by its location as a station on two caravan routes: one that started from Ḥaḍramawt in South Arabia and ran through Hejaz to the eastern Mediterranean, and another that crossed central and northeastern Arabia to Iraq. Thus Najrān developed into a major caravan city between South Arabia and the Fertile Crescent, an agricultural region celebrated for its fruits, vegetables, and cereals, and an industrial center well known for its leather and textiles.

Arab tribal groups inhabited the city, which was situated between the Arab and the Himyarite areas for centuries before the rise of Islam. Of these groups the most important was al-Ḥārith ibn-Kaʿb, which dominated the city and its history in the sixth century in much the same way that the Lakhmids dominated Al-Ḥīra. Its most prominent clan was the Banū ʿAbd al-Madān.

Although the city was far removed from the Mediterranean basin, it was brought within the range of Roman imperial designs in the reign of Augustus, when the emperor dispatched Aelius Gallus in 25 B.C. to reduce South Arabia. The latter failed to do so but succeeded in capturing Najrān.

It was, however, with the introduction of Christianity in the fifth century from Ḥīra that Najrān was drawn into the orbit of Mediterranean medieval history. In the sixth century, Christian missionaries converged on it from three directions: from the eastern Fertile Crescent (al-Ḥīra), from Syria through the Ghassanids, and from Ethiopia across the Red Sea. Monophysitism was the form of Christianity that prevailed in Najrān. Around 520 the Christians of South Arabia were persecuted and many of those in Najrān, together with their leader, al-Ḥārith, were martyred. These events convulsed the Christian Orient and shortly after led to a joint expedition by Ethiopia and Byzantium to avenge the martyred Christians of South Arabia. The expedition succeeded in restoring the fortunes of Christianity in South Arabia and in making it an Ethiopian dependency amenable to Byzantine influence.

This successful military expedition ushered in the golden period in the history of Najrān, which lasted for a century until the rise of Islam. The city, made holy by the blood of its martyrs and by their relics, became the Arabian martyropolis and a place of pilgrimage for the Christian Arabs of the peninsula. One of these martyrs, Arethas, was canonized; the feast of St. Arethas and his companions falls on October 24. Najrān was to the Arabs as, respectively, Edessa, Etchmiadzin, and Axum were to the Syrians, the Armenians, and the Ethiopians of the Christian Orient.

The fortunes of the city fluctuated with changes in the international scene and with new political configurations in the peninsula, of which the most important was the Persian occupation of South Arabia in 572, which exposed the region to political and religious currents hostile to Christianity. Nevertheless, the city maintained its dominant position, and it was only with the rise of Islam that it fell into a gradual but irreversible decline.

The attitude of Islam toward Christianity and its South Arabian version was friendly in the Meccan period of Muḥammad's mission (610–622). Around 630 a deputation of Najrānites, including their bishop, came to Muḥammad in Medina, which thus became the scene of the first Christian-Muslim confrontation. A *mubāhala,* an objurgation between the two parties suggested by Muḥammad, was averted when the Najrānites withdrew from the contest. Muḥammad then concluded a treaty with them, by the terms of which they were left free to practice their religion unmolested but they had to pay the annual tribute, the most important part of which was 2,000 robes. The second confrontation took place during the caliphate of ʿUmar (634–644), who ordered the Christians of Najrān to evacuate their city. They emigrated to Syria and Iraq. Most of them settled in al-Najrānīya, not far from Al-Kufa on the lower Euphrates, but some evidently stayed on, since Christians are attested in Najrān in the late Middle Ages.

In spite of the emigration of its enterprising inhabitants, Najran survived. The tribe of al-Ḥārith ibn-Kaʿb, or a part of it, had apparently adopted Islam and thus the Ḥārithids remained the lords of Najrān throughout the Muslim period. The converted Banū ʿAbd al-Madān became influential in early Abbasid times through the marriage of one of them, Rayṭa, to Muḥammad ibn ʿAli. Their son became the first Abbasid caliph, Abu 'l-ʿAbbās al-Suffāḥ (r. 750–754). Consequently the Najrānite clan of Banū ʿAbd al-Madān was referred to as "al-Akhwāl," the maternal uncles of the ruling Abbasid dynasty. Many of them attained high administrative positions.

Najrān itself, being a rich oasis, remained important in the economic life of South Arabia in medieval Islamic times. But with the transference of Islamic political power from the Arabian Peninsula to the Fertile Crescent, it was consigned politically, like many South Arabian cities, to a relatively insignificant and isolated provincial orbit. However, in the consciousness of medieval Christendom it survived as the city of the Christian Arab martyrs, and so it has till the present day in the churches of the Christian Orient.

BIBLIOGRAPHY
Muḥammad Hamīdullah, *Majmuᶜat al-watha 'iq al-siyāsiyah* (1969), originally published as *Documents sur la diplomatie musulmane á l'époque du prophète et des khalifes orthodoxes* (1935); Henri Lammens, "Le califat de Yazid Ier," in *Mélanges de la faculté orientale* of the Université Saint-Joseph, Beirut, **5** (1912), 648–688; Louis Massignon, *Opera minora,* I (1963), 550–572; Axel Moberg, ed. and trans., *The Book of the Himyarites* (1924); Ibn al-Mugawir, *Descriptio arabiae meridionalis (Ta'rīh al-Mustabsir)*, Oscar Löfgren, ed., II (1954), 208–217; Irfan Shahîd, *The Martyrs of Najrān* (1971), with extensive bibliographies on Christian Najrān, and "Byzantium in South Arabia," in *Dumbarton Oaks Papers,* **33** (1979); Strabo, *The Geography of Strabo,* Horace L. Jones, trans., VII (1930), 357–363; Ibn ᶜAbd Allāh al-Ḥamawī Yāqūt, *Muᶜjam al-Buldān,* II (1956), 538–539.

IRFAN SHAHÎD

[See also **Ghassanids; Ḥaḍramawt; Hejaz; Ḥīra, Al-; Lakhmids; Monophysites; Saffāh, Abū 'l-ᶜAbbās al-; Yemen.**]

NALOI. See **Analoi.**

NANNI DI BANCO (*ca.* 1384–1421), Florentine sculptor, was the son of Antonio di Banco. He matriculated in the guild of masons and carpenters in 1405 and worked with his father on the Duomo of Florence in 1406–1407. In 1407–1408 he executed a marble prophet for the Porta della Mandorla, for which Donatello produced a companion piece. Nanni received a commission for a marble seated St. Luke for the Duomo facade (now in the Museo dell'Opera) in 1408 and completed it in 1413. Concurrently with or immediately after this work he worked on statues of St. Eligius, St. Philip, and the four crowned saints for Or San Michele. His last work, a marble relief of the Assumption of the Virgin over the Porta della Mandorla, was done after 1414. Together with Donatello and Brunelleschi, he produced a model for the cupola of the Duomo in 1419. His heroic, fluid style reveals a personal interpretation of Ghiberti's and Donatello's work. His untimely death cut short a promising career.

BIBLIOGRAPHY
Luciano Bellosi, *Nanni di Banco* (1966); Jenö Lányi, "Il profeta Isia di Nanni di Banco," in *Rivista d' arte,* **18** (1936); Michael Phillips, "A New Interpretation of the Early Style of Nanni di Banco," in *Marsyas,* **11** (1962–1964); Leo Planiscig, *Nanni di Banco* (1946); John Pope-Hennessy, *Italian Gothic Sculpture* (1955); Charles Seymour, Jr., *Sculpture in Italy, 1400–1500* (1966, repr. 1968); Paolo Vaccarino, *Nanni* (1951); Manfred Wundram, *Donatello und Nanni di Banco* (1969).

ADELHEID M. GEALT

[See also **Brunelleschi; Donatello.**]

NANNI DI BARTOLO. See **Giovanni (Nanni) di Bartolo.**

NAOS. Architecturally and functionally, the naos was the core and the sanctuary of a Byzantine church, the area in which the liturgical service was performed. Normally a centrally planned space, it was extended to the east by an apsed bema containing the altar. This central area of the naos was usually covered by a dome.

BIBLIOGRAPHY
Richard Krautheimer, *Early Christian and Byzantine Architecture* (1965, 3rd ed. 1979).

ROBERT OUSTERHOUT

[See also **Bema; Early Christian and Byzantine Architecture.**]

NAPLES. Situated on the northern edge of the bay that bears its name, Naples was founded by the Greeks in the late seventh or early sixth century B.C. Conquered by Rome in the fourth century B.C., during the late empire it was a popular resort for wealthy Romans. During the sixth century of the present era, it suffered a severe population decline. Lombard invaders, whose kingdom extended from the Po Valley south to Capua and Salerno, attacked the city in 581, 592, and 599, but it remained subject to the imperial exarch in Ravenna. In 616 it severed its ties to the exarch and, after 661, when the Byzantine emperor Constans II named Basilios as the first duke and erected the duchy of Campa-

Assumption of the Virgin. Marble relief by Nanni di Banco from the Porta della Mandorla of S. Maria del Fiore, Florence, after 1414. ALINARI/ART RESOURCE

nia, its dukes depended directly on the Byzantine emperors of Constantinople.

Little is known of the early growth of Christianity in Naples. Archaeological evidence reveals a significant Christian population as early as the second century, attested by the catacombs of S. Gennaro, but much remains to be done to clarify its history prior to the sixth century. The clergy of the city was divided into Greek-speaking and Latin-speaking. According to one tradition, the earliest cathedral, built in the fourth century, was dedicated to the Savior. When the remains of S. Restituta were translated from Ischia, the church was rededicated to her. This cathedral served the Greek clergy and community. In the late fifth century a second cathedral, again dedicated to the Savior, was built for the Latins. The two cathedrals shared a common atrium, but each had its own apse. The Baptistery of St. John dates from the fifth century. By the seventh century the prestige of the bishops had increased in pace with the growing popularity of the cult of S. Gennaro, who emerged as the patron of the city.

Under Byzantine rule Naples controlled a large part of Campania. During the eighth century the dukes of Naples became more independent of Byzantium and began to develop closer ties to the papacy. Use of the Greek language declined, and the image of S. Gennaro replaced that of the emperor on the coinage. In 812, Muslim pirates attacked islands in the Bay of Naples and nearby Benevento threatened the city. The dukes turned to their Muslim enemies in the search for allies against Benevento. After the Carolingians' conquest of the Lombard kingdom and their intervention in Rome and southern Italy, Naples was forced into unstable alliances aimed at preserving its independence. This quasi equilibrium ended with the eleventh-century Norman conquest of Capua and the rising power of Robert Guiscard in Apulia. In 1139, Naples became part of the newly founded kingdom of Sicily of Roger II.

Norman rule did not end local administrative autonomy but subordinated the city administration to a royal official, the *compalazzo* (count of the palace), and to royal dukes. The strengthening of the Castel dell'Ovo in the harbor and the Castel Capuano to the northeast ensured royal control of the city, as well as protection against external enemies. Consolidation of Norman rule in the twelfth century ended the independence of Amalfi, which had developed important commercial relations with the East. Loss of political control by the local aristocracy weakened Amalfi's mercantile power, which may have produced some benefits for Naples; the city gradually attracted more foreign merchants to its harbor. Between 1191 and 1194, following the death of King William II, Naples supported the succession of Tancred against Constance of Sicily and Emperor Henry VI in return for his grant of extensive privileges, confirming its claims to local autonomy, and providing exemptions from taxes. The victory of Constance and Henry brought the city once more under strong royal control, but this was short-lived. Following the death of Henry in 1197, Constance granted the Neapolitans considerable autonomy. She died the following year, entrusting her minor son, Frederick, to the care of Pope Innocent III. This decision was contested by the Germans remaining in the kingdom under the leadership of Markward of Anweiler. With the imperial throne also disputed between Philip of Swabia, the uncle of Frederick, and Otto of Brunswick, Innocent III vacillated before lending his support to the latter. But Otto broke the promises made to Innocent and invaded Italy. This action posed a threat to the interests of the papacy as well as to the inheritance of young Frederick. The counts of Forlì and Capua seized the city in the name of Emperor Otto IV.

Not until 1220 was Frederick, now Holy Roman emperor as well as king of Sicily, able to restore royal administration. He enlarged the royal castles in Naples and appointed his own officials, but prior to the promulgation of the Constitutions of Melfi in 1231, he adhered to the policies set by his Norman predecessors. This legislation clearly reveals his intention to deal firmly with any effort by the cities of the kingdom to establish communal government. While they did not completely deprive the Neapolitans of local autonomy, the Constitutions foreshadowed the harsh measures he pursued during his war with the papacy and the Italian communes of the north. In 1246 revolts erupted throughout the kingdom. In Naples, Archbishop Peter supported an uprising by the aristocracy, which Frederick ruthlessly crushed.

The cultural life of Naples under the Normans and Swabians was strongly influenced by the great monastic houses of the region, particularly Monte Cassino, and by the papal reform movement, which had its beginnings in the second half of the eleventh century. The famed Beneventan script, which reached its greatest development at Monte Cassino under Abbot Desiderius, and the classical and Romano-Christian influences developing in art and architecture merged with Byzantine and local traditions. In literature and history, Petrus de Ebulo, author of *Carmen de rebus Siculis* and the *De balneis Puteolanis,* deserves special mention because of his ties with the region of Naples. In 1224, Emperor Frederick II founded the University of Naples to provide his subjects with an alternative to the University of Bologna. In addition to a law school, Naples had a medical school. In his later legislation regulating examination and licensing of physicians, Frederick placed the Naples faculty of medicine on a par with the great medical school of Salerno. Shortly after their arrival in 1231, the Dominicans inaugurated the teaching of theology at the university. Their most illustrious student was Thomas Aquinas. However, it was not until the Angevin period that the university began to gain a stable position in the educational life of the kingdom. The life of the university was disrupted by Frederick's conflict with the papacy, especially following his excommunication at the Council of Lyons in 1245, and the expulsion of the Dominicans and the Franciscans from the kingdom.

After Frederick's death in 1250, Naples once more became a center of turmoil during the papal-led struggle against Frederick's heirs. The city generally favored the papal cause against Manfred, in return for the promised restoration of its autonomy, but the victory of the Angevins in the Battle of Benevento (1266) brought the city under tight royal control. The wars of Frederick II and Manfred had seen increasing demands for taxes by the monarchy. The *collecta*, originally an extraordinary tax, came to be levied every year throughout the kingdom. Although Charles of Anjou had promised to abolish this and other burdens, he and his successors were forced to maintain and even increase them. Between 1310 and 1340, the farm of the customs (*dogana*) of Naples increased by almost 30 percent. Moreover, efforts to reform local administration and legislation provoked opposition, while dissatisfaction with the heavy taxes needed to pay the costs of the wars of the Angevins and the success of the Sicilian Vespers (1282) persuaded many Neapolitan nobles that the time had come to throw off the Angevin yoke. The rebellion of 1284 failed, however.

The difficult years of the fourteenth century, shadowed by the perils of the plague, were marked by continued political turmoil, with unsuccessful revolts in 1346–1347, 1348, 1378, and 1381. At the same time the Angevins were consolidating their position in southern Italy, with Naples as the capital of the kingdom. Under King Robert the Wise, Naples became a cosmopolitan center with strong ties to Florence and Tuscany. The Florentine banking houses of the Bardi, Acciaiuoli, and Bonaccorsi were important creditors of the crown and played a substantial role in trade. Special encouragement was given the wool guild (*arte della lana*), founded in 1308 but in decline by the end of the century. The Angevins made significant improvements in harbor facilities between 1320 and 1347.

The importance of northern Italians in the economic life of the kingdom of Naples was paralleled by their influence in cultural life. From Giotto on, numerous Tuscan artists and architects were employed in the beautification of the new capital and its churches, above all that of S. Chiara, the royal chapel, built for the Poor Clares. The charterhouse of St. Martin, begun by Charles, duke of Calabria, and completed by Giovanna I in 1368, was embellished with sculptures by Pacio da Firenze. The Angevin period also witnessed a substantial influx of noble French families into the city. By the middle of the fourteenth century, the population had reached approximately 60,000, but it fell, as a result of the Black Death and recurring plagues, to about 40,000 by the end of the century.

The late fourteenth and early fifteenth centuries witnessed conflicts over the royal succession among the various branches of the Angevin house, as well as the Sicilian house of Aragon. In 1442, Alfonso of Aragon conquered the kingdom and ushered in a period of Spanish dominance. He began the reconstruction of the capital, including the royal palace (the Castel Nuovo, begun in 1279 and completed by Charles II), and a triumphal arch. He initiated major improvements of the streets and aqueducts. He surrounded himself with humanists, including Lorenzo Valla, and founded the first learned academy in Italy, later named the Accademia Pontaniana. During the long reign of Ferrante I (1458–1494), despite his involvement in foreign wars and continued internal unrest, there was a considerable cultural flowering in Naples. Although there was not yet a strong local tradition of painting, numerous artists from northern Italy and Spain were attracted to the capital. Chairs of literary studies were established at the university. The second half of the fifteenth century was important for the development of local music and art. By the end of the century, the city's population had reached 120,000. Naples had undergone a gradual transformation from one of a group of south Italian coastal cities sharing a common heritage of commerce and culture to the capital of the Aragonese kingdom in the south.

BIBLIOGRAPHY

Archivio storico per le province napoletane (1876–); Bartolommeo Capasso, *Le fonti delle storia delle provincie napoletane dal 658 al 1500* (1902, repr. 1967); Gino Doria, *Storia di un capitale: Napoli dalle origine al 1860*, 5th ed., rev. (1968); Vittorio Gleijeses, *La storia di Napoli*, 3 vols. (1981); Cecil Headlam, *The Story of Naples* (1927, repr. 1971); *Storia di Napoli*, 11 vols. in 15 (1967–1978).

JAMES M. POWELL

Naqsh ḥadīda decoration in arcades of the al-ᶜAṭṭārīn Madrasa, Fēs, 1323–1325. PHOTO: JEAN MAZENOD, EDITIONS MAZENOD, PARIS

[See also **Angevins; Byzantine Empire: History (330–1025); Desiderius of Monte Cassino; Frederick II of the Holy Roman Empire; Hohenstaufen Dynasty; Innocent III, Pope; Italy, Byzantine Areas of; Lombards; Melfi, Constitutions of; Normans and Normandy; Ravenna; Sicily, Kingdom of.**]

NAQSH, an Arabic noun, used also in Persian and Turkish, with the basic meaning of something variegated through the application of color or embellished with carving. In Persian the equation of *naqsh* with a picture or painted image gradually superseded its association with carved or incised designs. By extension *naqsh* became the outward appearance of something in juxtaposition to its inner substance (*hafs*).

BIBLIOGRAPHY

ᶜAli Akbar Dehkhoda, *Loghatnama* (1972); Edward W. Lane, *An Arabic–English Lexicon* (repr. 1955–1956), 2840.

PRISCILLA P. SOUCEK

[See also **Islamic Art and Architecture.**]

NAQSH ḤADĪDA, an Arabic term for something engraved with an iron tool. Normally it is applied to the finely carved stucco widely used in the Islamic architecture of Spain and North Africa. The use of *naqsh ḥadīda* reached its zenith in the lacelike stuccoes of the Alhambra. Andalusian emigrants later carried the technique to Fēs, Marrakech, Tunis, and other North African cities.

BIBLIOGRAPHY

R. Dozy, *Supplément aux dictionnaires arabes*, 3rd ed., 2 vols. (1967), I, 256.

PRISCILLA P. SOUCEK

Valerian kneeling before Šābuhr I. Rock relief carving at Naqsh-i Rustam, Iran, after 260. PHOTO: PRUDENCE OLIVER HARPER

[See also **Alhambra; Islamic Art and Architecture; Muqarnas.**]

NAQSH-I RUSTAM, an archaeological site in southwestern Iran forty miles (about sixty kilometers) northeast of Shiraz, near the Isfahan road. Monumental reliefs carved in a sheer rock face at the base of a mountain and once thought to represent Rustam, a hero of the Persian national epic, are now attributed to several early kings of the Sasanian dynasty (226–651) who are shown in the company of nobles, receiving kingship from deities and triumphing over their enemies, domestic and foreign. Above these reliefs are the earlier rock-cut tombs of four Achaemenid kings. Each tomb has an enormous cruciform facade on which appears the image of a king standing before a fire altar on a throne platform supported by representatives of subject nations. On the tomb of Darius I (521–485 B.C.) the nations appear again in an inscription in Old Persian, Elamite, and Akkadian.

In front of the cliff and roughly contemporary with the tombs is a square tower traditionally called Kaᶜbah-i Zardusht (the Kaaba of Zoroaster). Built of dressed stone, it contains a small chamber reached by an external stairway. A long inscription in Middle Persian (Pahlavi), Parthian, and Greek, cut later in the base, describes the military campaigns of the Sasanian king Šābuhr I (241–272) against the Roman armies that in 260 culminated in the defeat and capture of Valerian in Syria. A list of nobles in order of rank provides vital information about the organization of the empire in the third century. A shorter inscription cites the honors bestowed by Šābuhr upon Kartir, founder and priest of the Sasanian state religion, who appears in relief on the adjacent cliff. Neither the original nor the secondary function of the tower is known. It has been variously interpreted as a tomb, a house for the sacred fire of Zoroastrian ritual, and as a repository for a text of the Avesta.

Although the precise function of Naqsh-i Rustam remains unclear, its proximity to Persepolis and to the important Sasanian city of Istakhr and the nature of its monuments, partially enclosed by a temenos wall during the Sasanian period, suggest it was highly venerated by Iran's two great pre-Islamic dynasties as a national shrine.

BIBLIOGRAPHY

For a detailed account of the monuments of Naqsh-i Rustam and excavations at the site, see Erich F. Schmidt, *Persepolis, III: The Royal Tombs and Other Monuments* (1970). On the Old Persian and Pahlavi inscriptions, see Marie-Louise Chaumont, "L'inscription de Kartir a la 'Ka^cbah de Zoroastre' (texte, traduction, commentaire)," in *Journal asiatique,* **248** (1960); Walter B. Henning, "The Great Inscription of Šāpūr I," in *Bulletin of the School of Oriental Studies,* **9** (1939); Roland G. Kent, *Old Persian Grammar, Texts, Lexicon* (1950). For bibliography, see Philippe Gignoux, *Glossaire des inscriptions pehlevies et parthes* (1972). An evaluation of the diverse opinions on the functions of the Ka^cbah-i Zardusht is in Klaus Schippmann, *Die iranischen Feuerheiligtümer* (1971), 185–199.

LIONEL BIER

[See also **Ka^cba of Zoroaster; Sasanian Art; Sasanians.**]

NARBONNE RITE. Although practiced from late patristic antiquity down to the twentieth century in southwest France and modern-day Catalonia, and designated by such alternative names as Catalan, Pirenean, and Languedocian, the Narbonne liturgical rite or use had to wait until the second half of the twentieth century before being investigated by such scholars as Miquel Gros, Aimé-Georges Martimort, and Brian Bethune.

In late patristic times the liturgical practices in the Roman provinces of Narbonensis Prima and Tarraconensis were probably not much different from those throughout Gallican-rite territories stretching from northern Italy to southern Spain; in fact, texts from the eighth-century Bobbio Missal (MS Paris, Bibl. Nat. lat. 13246), representing the liturgy of Pavia, are found in the oldest Spanish and Narbonne liturgical books.

With the establishment of the Visigothic capital at Toulouse in 419, there was an ecclesiastical reorganization of the region under Caesarius of Arles (*ca.* 470–542). Under him there was held in 506 a national council at Agde, not far from Narbonne, and a uniform liturgical rite was prescribed for the Visigothic realm of Toulouse.

After the defeat of the Visigoths by Clovis (507) and their descent south of the Pyrenees, where they established their capital at Toledo, Narbonne came under the influence of liturgical practices created in the Iberian Peninsula. In the mid sixth century there was significant liturgical creativity just south of Narbonne in the province of Tarraconensis, where such bishops as Justus of Urgel (*d.* after 546) and Peter of Lérida created psalter collects and series of Mass prayers. Bishops from Narbonne began to attend national councils at Toledo, where they participated in the liturgical unification of territories under Visigothic rule. It is highly probable that during the liturgical renaissance at the time of Julian of Toledo (*d.* 690), Toledan books with the Old Spanish (Mozarabic) rite were taken to Narbonne and used there.

When the Iberian Peninsula and southern France fell to the Muslims after 711, Narbonne continued to use the Hispanic liturgical rite, but when Pepin III the Short (*d.* 768) reconquered the city in 759 and the Spanish March was created in northeastern Spain by Charlemagne, liturgical practices took another turn. Narbonne became the metropolitan city over such sees as Urgel, Vic, Gerona, Barcelona, and La Roda that had been under Tarragona. As part of the Carolingian realm, however, Narbonne began to adopt Romano-Frankish liturgical uses. This came about in part because Charlemagne was an enthusiastic proponent of the Roman liturgy and in part because the Spanish rite was considered to be infected with the Adoptionist heresy, which both Charlemagne and the pope attempted to suppress. As a result the liturgy of Narbonne was modified, probably in large part by Benedict of Aniane and Bishop Nebridius of Narbonne.

Manuscript evidence for this modification is found in codices of the eleventh and twelfth centuries and later, but there are indications in them that substantial changes were taking place in the early ninth century in such rites as clerical ordination, the dedication of churches, the benediction of oils on Maundy Thursday, baptism, and marriage. Basically, there is in the rites a mixture of Romano-Frankish and ancient Spanish prayers and rubrical texts, and even the ecclesiastical hierarchy reflected in the ordination texts is a strange fusion of Spanish and Romano-Frankish usages.

NARDO DI CIONE

From the ninth century on, there was a progressive romanization (or Franco-romanization) of the rite of Narbonne, but elements of the rite persisted in Catalonia and elsewhere in Spain. Elements of the rite of ordination were taken to Toledo after its reconquest in 1085, and were used there and in Castile down to at least the fifteenth century. Moreover, bishops of Catalonia did not fully accept the Roman ritual of Paul V before 1925, and continued to use supplementary texts reflecting the ancient Spanish and Narbonne rites.

BIBLIOGRAPHY

Miquel S. Gros, "Las órdenes sagradas del pontifical ms. 104 (CV) de la Bib. cap. de Vic," in *Hispania sacra,* **17** (1964), "El ordo romano-hispánico de Narbona para la consagración de iglesias," *ibid.,* **19** (1966), "El 'missale parvum' de Vic," *ibid.,* **21** (1968), "L'ordo pour la dédicace des églises dans le sacramentaire de Nonantola," in *Revue bénédictine,* **79** (1969), "El antiguo ordo bautismal catalano-narbonense," in *Hispania sacra,* **28** (1975), "L'ordre catalano-narbonès per a la benedicció dels sants olis," in *Revista catalana de teologia,* **1** (1976), "La liturgie narbonnaise: Témoins d'un changement rapide de rites liturgiques," in *Liturgie de l'église particulière et liturgie de l'église universelle* (1976), 127–154, and "Le pontifical de Narbonne," in *Liturgie et musique (IXe –XIVe s.) Cahiers de Fanjeaux,* **17** (1982); Roger E. Reynolds, "The Ordination Rite in Medieval Spain: Hispanic, Roman, and Hybrid," in Bernard F. Reilly, ed., *Santiago, Saint-Denis, and Saint Peter: The Reception of the Roman Liturgy in León–Castile in 1080* (1985), and "The Ordination of Clerics in Toledo and Castile After the Reconquista According to the 'Romano-Catalan' Rite," in Ramón Gonzálvez-Ruiz, ed., *II. Congreso internacional de estudios mozárabes: IX. centenario de la reconquista de Toledo, 1085–1985* (1987).

ROGER E. REYNOLDS

[See also **Mass, Liturgy of.**]

NARDO DI CIONE (*fl. ca.* 1343–1365/1366), Florentine painter, was the brother of Andrea (Orcagna) and Jacopo. One of the most gifted painters of his generation, his style was based on an understanding of Giotto and an affinity for the works of Maso di Banco, Simone Martini, and the brothers Ambrogio and Pietro Lorenzetti. The key to his oeuvre is the *Last Judgment* fresco cycle (*ca.* 1354–1357) in the Strozzi chapel of S. Maria Novella. Numerous panels, including a standing Madonna and Child (Minneapolis Institute of

Detail from the *Last Judgment* fresco cycle of Nardo di Cione, Strozzi chapel, S. Maria Novella, Florence, *ca.* 1354–1357. The top row shows the Old Testament sinners Cain, Pharaoh, Korah, Dathan, and Abiram. Other sinners include Caiaphas tearing his robes and a pope discoursing with an emperor. UFFIZI, FLORENCE, SGF 66309

Arts), a *Madonna and Child Enthroned* (New York, Metropolitan Museum of Art), and a portable triptych of the *Madonna and Child with Saints* (Washington, D.C., National Gallery of Art), are ascribed to him. They all demonstrate a sense for monumental, yet graceful, forms that are both powerful and enigmatic, and reveal the interest in

Narthex of S. Ambrogio, Milan, 11th–12th centuries. PHOTO: WIM SWAAN

volume juxtaposed to flatness that characterizes much mid trecento painting.

BIBLIOGRAPHY
Adelheid M. Gealt, "Nardo di Cione's Standing Madonna with the Child," in *The Minneapolis Institute of Arts Bulletin,* **64** (1978–1980); Millard Meiss, *Painting in Florence and Siena After the Black Death* (1951, repr. 1964); Richard Offner, *A Critical and Historical Corpus of Florentine Painting,* sec. IV, vol. II (1960), and *Studies in Florentine Painting: The Fourteenth Century* (1927, repr. 1972).

ADELHEID M. GEALT

[See also **Giotto di Bondone; Gothic Art; Painting; Jacopo di Cione; Lorenzetti, Ambrogio; Lorenzetti, Pietro; Maso di Banco; Orcagna (Andrea di Cione); Simone Martini.**]

NARTHEX, in Roman basilicas and the early Christian churches modeled on them, a portico along the facade of the building, separated from the nave by a wall or screen and often continuing the colonnades of an atrium. In Byzantine and Western medieval churches, the narthex is frequently an enclosed porch or antenave and is sometimes preceded by an outer porch or exonarthex. It has been argued that in the early church the narthex was reserved for catechumens and penitents during the celebration of the Eucharist, but the evidence does not support this position. The narthex may have served as the site for the assembly of liturgical processions.

BIBLIOGRAPHY
Richard Krautheimer, *Early Christian and Byzantine Architecture* (1965; 2nd ed., rev., 1975, 3rd ed. 1979); Thomas F. Mathews, *The Early Churches of Constantinople: Architecture and Liturgy* (1971), 125–130.

GREGORY WHITTINGTON

[See also **Basilica; Church, Types of; Early Christian and Byzantine Architecture; Gothic Architecture; Romanesque Architecture.**]

NASHKI. See **Naskhī.**

NASI, in the Middle Ages an honorific title given to Jewish personages of the house of David. Beginning in the eleventh century, many such descendants of the Babylonian exilarch came to Jerusalem, Egypt, Damascus, Aleppo, Mosul, and Spain, where they achieved considerable power. Heads of the Karaites, from the founder, Anan ben David, through the eighteenth century, bore the same title. A medieval Jewish tradition about the arrival of a nasi in Narbonne, France, has given rise to a controversial historical theory about the establishment of a Jewish principality in Carolingian France.

BIBLIOGRAPHY
Salo W. Baron, *A Social and Religious History of the Jews,* V–VI, 2nd ed., rev. and enl. (1952–1969); Solomon D. Goitein, *A Mediterranean Society,* II (1971); Jacob Mann, *The Jews in Egypt and in Palestine Under the Fāṭimid Caliphs,* 2 vols. (1920–1922, repr. 1970), Samuel Poznański, *Babylonische Geonim im nachgaonäischen Zeitalter nach handschriftlichen und gedruckten Quellen* (1914); Arthur J. Zuckerman, *A Jewish Princedom in Feudal France, 768–900* (1972).

ELIEZER BASHAN

[See also **Exilarch; Karaites; Naxos.**]

Leaf from a Koran in *naskhī* script. Egyptian, 14th century. THE METROPOLITAN MUSEUM OF ART, NEW YORK, (1975.29.1)

NASKHĪ, the name of an Arabic script widely used for the transcription of books. Distinguished from *kūfī* (kufic) by the rounded forms of its letters, *naskhī* (from *nasakha*, "to copy") may have developed from a cursive script used for official correspondence during the seventh and eighth centuries. Literary sources document its growing popularity during the tenth and eleventh centuries. After the reforms of Ibn Muqla (*d.* 940) and Ibn al-Bawwāb (*d.* 1022) the script was regularized and often used to transcribe the Koran. Letters in *naskhī* style are written in their canonical form without exaggerated elongation or unusual ligatures.

BIBLIOGRAPHY

Nabia Abbott, *The Rise of the North Arabic Script and Its Ḳur$^{\supset}$ānic Development* (1939), 36–38, 42–44; David S. Rice, *The Unique Ibn al-Bawwāb Manuscript in the Chester Beatty Library* (1955), 7–9, 11–12; Annemarie Schimmel, *Islamic Calligraphy* (1970).

PRISCILLA P. SOUCEK

[See also **Bawwāb, Ibn al-; Calligraphy; Kūfī.**]

Leaf from *The Language of the Birds* with calligraphy by Sultan Alī al-Mashhad in *nasta^{c}liq* script. Iran, 1483. THE METROPOLITAN MUSEUM OF ART, NEW YORK, FLETCHER FUND, 1963 (63.210.53 verso)

NASTA^{c}LIQ, a script widely used in Iran from the fourteenth century onward, often said to have been invented by Mīr ^{c}Alī al-Tabrīzī around 1400. As the name suggests, it combines features of *naskhī*, a clear hand much used for books, and those of *ta^{c}līq*, a fluid and cursive script employed in official correspondence. Its letter forms are similar to those used in *naskhī*, but their selective elongation and diagonal placement on the page, giving the words a downward inclination, are closer to *ta^{c}līq*.

BIBLIOGRAPHY

C. I. Huart, *Les calligraphes et les miniaturistes de l'orient musulman* (1908), 36–43; Aḥmad ibn Mīr Munshī al-Husainī (Qāḍī Aḥmad), *Calligraphers and Painters*, Vladimir Minorsky, trans. (1959), chap. 3.

PRISCILLA P. SOUCEK

[See also **Calligraphy; Naskhī.**]

Nativity mosaic from the Kariye Djami, Constantinople, 14th century. COURTESY OF THE BYZANTINE PHOTOGRAPH COLLECTION, NEG. K.102.57.51, © 1986 Dumbarton Oaks, Trustees of Harvard University, Washington, DC

NATIVITY. Although Luke 2:1–20 and Matthew 2 emphasize the imagery of the birth of Jesus in Bethlehem, it was not until the fourth century that artists began to take an interest in depicting Christ's birth. The earliest surviving images of the Nativity are found on sarcophagi in Rome and Gaul. Early representations show the Christ Child in a trough or willow basket with no indication of place. Animals, such as the ox and ass, are always depicted, even though their presence has no textual validity. Sometimes even Mary is omitted. By the fifth century, Joseph is commonly present. Frequently, artists combined the adoration of the shepherds with that of the Magi; this, too, does not correspond to the biblical text. Artists perhaps were not interested in exact narrative illustration but in the overall visual expression of the importance of Christ's birth.

In the Western images the manger is generally large and contains the Christ Child wrapped in swaddling clothes. In the Eastern Orthodox Church of the sixth century, a new type of Nativity emerged, lasting throughout the Byzantine period. This Nativity is in a cave, and Mary is always depicted reclining on a couch (*kline*). The Nativity image in the East often includes a star, which in the West is usually found only in depictions of the Adoration of the Magi. The cave, described in apocryphal New Testament sources, most likely prefigures the tomb of Jesus' burial.

The Washing of the Christ Child is a common feature in Byzantine Nativity depictions. This incident is possibly also derived from the apocryphal gospels and is only rarely seen in later medieval images in the West.

BIBLIOGRAPHY

Ormonde M. Dalton, *Byzantine Art and Archaeology* (1911, repr. 1961); Ernst Kitzinger, *The Art of Byzantium and the Medieval West,* W. Eugene Kleinbauer, ed.

(1976), and *Byzantine Art in the Making* (1977); Gertrud Schiller, *Iconography of Christian Art*, Janet Seligman, trans., 2 vols. (1966).

JENNIFER E. JONES

[See also **Byzantine Art; Early Christian Art; Gothic Art: Painting.**]

NĀᶜŪRA (Arabic; whence Spanish and English *noria*), a vertical wheel driven by the current of a river or stream so that it lifts water into irrigation canals; smaller versions serve as mill wheels. The device was known to Vitruvius in the first century B.C., and al-Jazarī made use of its principles in his book on automata (*ca.* 1206).

Although no ancient example survives, the *nāᶜura* was in use in the ninth century on the Orontes, in the tenth on the Guadalquivir, and in the early eleventh on the Euphrates, suggesting technological continuity in former Roman territory in the Islamic period. According to al-Maqdisī (al-Muqaddasī), the Buyid ᶜAḍud al-Dawla introduced it to Fārs and Khūzistān in the late tenth century. *Nāᶜūra*s are depicted in a copy of *Bayāḍ wa Riyāḍ* (Vatican Ar. 368) illustrated in Almohad Spain at the turn of the thirteenth century and in the frontispiece to one volume of the *Kitāb al-aghānī* (Cairo, National Library, Adab 579), copied at Mosul in 1217.

Such water wheels have been used in the twentieth century in Iraq, Syria, Spain, and Morocco, and *nāᶜūra* builders were still active at Damascus about 1900.

BIBLIOGRAPHY

Miguel Asín Palacios, "Enmiendas a las etimologías árabes del 'Diccionario de la Lengua de la Real Academia Española,'" in *Al-Andalus*, 9 (1944), 35; J. C. Baroja, "Norias, azudas, aceñas," in *Revista de Dialectologia y tradiciones populares*, 10 (1954); Gertrude Bell, *Amurath to Amurath* (1911), fig. 60, p. 101; D. R. Hill, trans. and ed., *The Book of Knowledge of Ingenious Mechanical Devices by Ibn al-Razzāq al-Jazarī* (1974), 186–189, 275; Thorkild Schiøler, *Roman and Islamic Water-lifting Wheels* (1973); *Vitruvius on Architecture*, Frank S. Granger, ed. and trans., II (1962), 304–305; Andrew Watson, *Agricultural Innovation in the Early Islamic World* (1983), chap. 20, esp. notes; Jacques Weuleresse, *L'Oronte* (1940), 55–59.

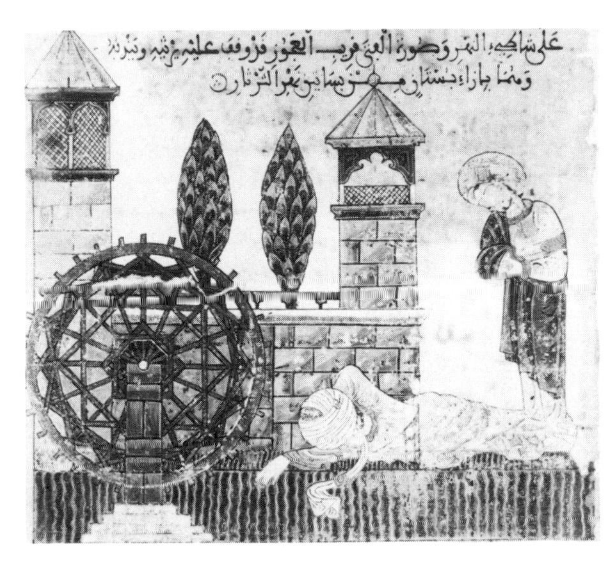

A *nāᶜūra* depicted in a miniature from the tragic love story *Bayāḍ wa Riyāḍ*. Almohad Spain, early 13th century. VATICAN, BIBLIOTECA APOSTOLICA MS ARAB 368, fol. 19r

ESTELLE WHELAN

[See also **Agriculture and Nutrition; Irrigation; Mills.**]

NAVARRE, KINGDOM OF. The kingdom of Navarre began to take its initial form in the early ninth century when a native Basque family, the Aristas, drove out the local Muslim garrison and established an independent principality around the town of Pamplona. From this nucleus grew a state that would enjoy the fruits of frontier expansion against Muslim Spain and ultimately become the victim of that expansion as well. The kingdom embraced at times nearly all Basque-speaking peoples in Álava, Guipúzcoa, Vizcaya, and parts of southern Gascony but was more commonly restricted to the Basques of the western Pyrenees and the upper Ebro Valley, positioned south of the strategic Roncesvalles pass in the Pyrenees. At the time of its formation, Navarre was populated by peoples not yet fully christianized who prized their independence and stoutly resisted the efforts of their neighbors to absorb them, as they had resisted similar efforts by the Romans and the Visigoths during the preceding centuries. The maintenance

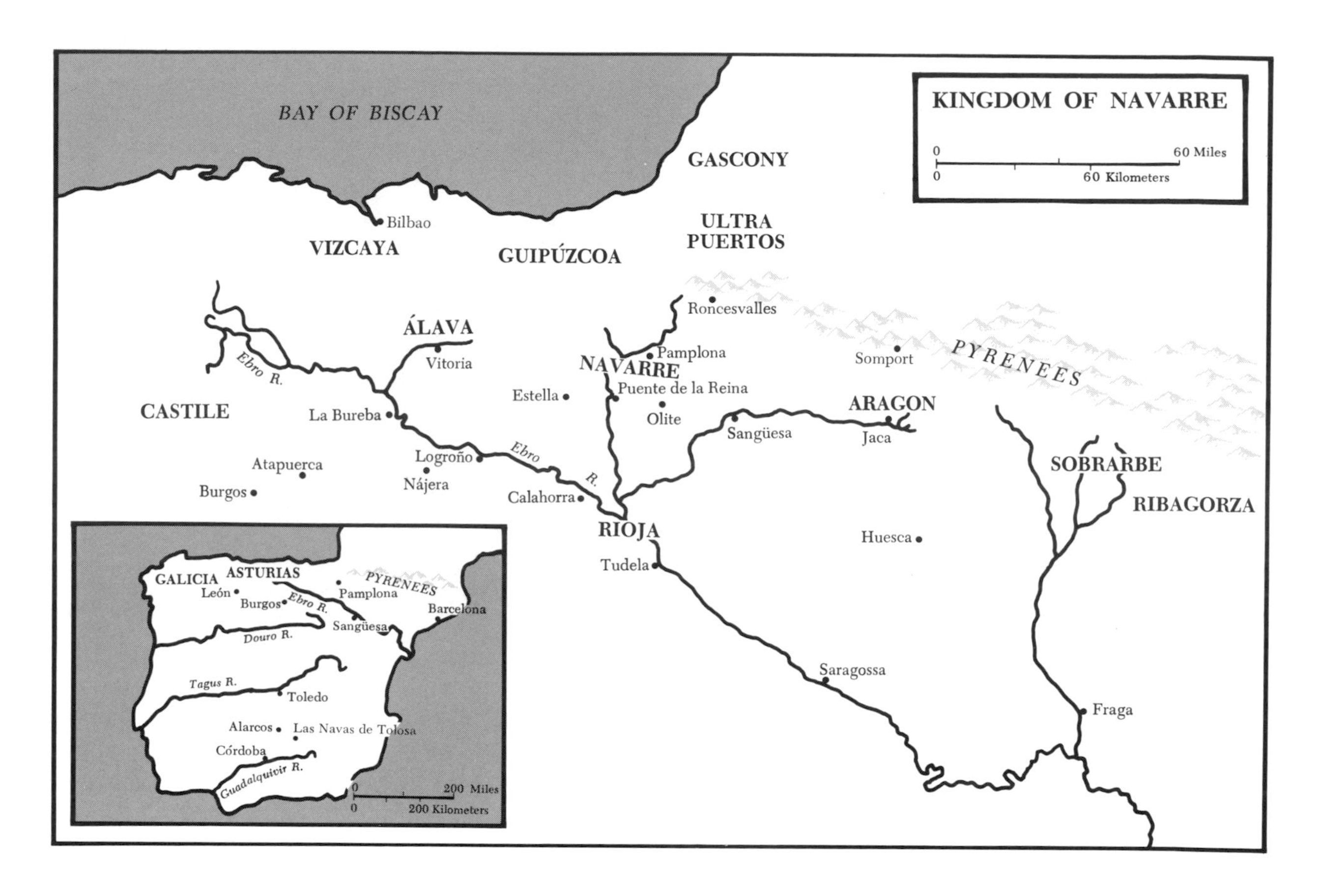

of their independence would prove a continuing challenge.

Their will to meet this challenge was first made clear as a result of the renowned expedition of Charlemagne to Spain in 778. After he failed to capture Saragossa, the Frankish monarch razed the fortifications of Pamplona on his homeward journey. According to contemporary Frankish sources, the Basques avenged themselves by ambushing his rear guard in the Roncesvalles pass, an event later forged into the epic *Song of Roland,* which substituted the Saracens for the Basques as the perpetrators. By the ninth century, Navarre found itself poised among several competing principalities. To the north, the Carolingian Empire and the dukes of Gascony controlled the far side of the Pyrenees. The east held the emerging state of Aragon under a native family of counts who were associated with the Carolingian marcher lords on the south flanks of the Pyrenees. To the south, the powerful Banu Qasi dynasty controlled Saragossa, Huesca, and Tudela, operating independently of the emirate at Córdoba. On the western frontier the nascent state of Asturias and its buffer county of Castile filled out a roster of warlike and expansive neighbors. With a careful balance of conflicts, truces, and marriage alliances, the Pamplonan principate maintained itself in the ninth century, survived a dynastic change to the Jimena family under Sancho I Garcés (905–925), and achieved expansion in the tenth century.

The kingship evolved from an elective to a hereditary monarchy in this period and absorbed the county of Aragon while establishing dynastic ties to the Asturo-Leonese state. The area known as the Rioja (the upper Ebro Valley) was jointly penetrated by the Navarrese and Leonese kings, although strong counterattacks by the caliphate of Córdoba reversed some of these gains. By the end of the tenth century, a relatively unstructured form of feudalism had penetrated the kingdom, useful in a land where military forces were required to garrison the numerous fortresses that dotted the Navarrese-Aragonese frontier. By 1000 Navarre included three episcopal sees, Aragon, Pamplona, and Nájera, and monasteries were increasing in number, especially in the Aragonese-Navarrese borderlands. Moreover, the rapidly developing pilgrimage routes to Santiago de Compostela entered Navarre through two passages: the Somport Pass to Aragonese Jaca and the Roncesvalles Pass to Pamplona. The two routes joined at Puente de la Reina in the southern part of Navarre. The pilgrimage route and the newly acquired lands in Aragon and the Rioja drew numerous non-Basques into Navarre and gave the kingdom a rich cultural mixture as the eleventh century opened.

The reign of Sancho III Garcés (known as the Great, 1000–1035) was a pivotal one for Navarre and for the whole of Christian Spain. For the only time in its history Navarre became the dominant state in Christian Spain. Commencing from a base in Navarre and Aragon, Sancho III added Sobrarbe and Ribagorza, the old Carolingian marcher counties to the east of Aragon. Holding out the possibility of an alliance against the Muslim central Ebro Basin, Sancho made the count of Barcelona his vassal, although little would result from this linkage for either party. The Navarrese monarch also attempted to press his rights to succession in the duchy of Gascony in southern France, but this attempt to link the two Basque-speaking regions into one political hegemony also proved abortive. Sancho enjoyed greater success to the west, where he was able to secure the county of Castile for his second son, Fernando, after the legitimate heir to Castile had been murdered. Sancho concluded his reign by marching westward to occupy the city of León in 1034, claiming the title of "Emperor of Hispania" while the Leonese king fled to Galicia. In addition, Sancho's reign was significant for the early "Europeanization" of Christian Spain.

The king modified and improved the Santiago pilgrimage routes through his lands, while the passage west became increasingly secure after the decline of the Muslim *taifa* states (small units that resulted from the breakdown of the caliphate). The Cluniac monastic reform and the Romanesque artistic style it favored became well established through Sancho's encouragement. Feudalism intensified its institutional grip within his monarchy. Indeed, it was French feudalism rather than any Hispanic imperial concept borrowed from León that determined his decision to treat his territorial acquisitions as patrimonial rather than imperial states. At his death in 1035 Sancho's empire was partitioned among his sons, with the eldest, García III Sánchez (1035–1054), receiving Navarre. While Navarrese dynasties were implanted on the thrones of León-Castile and Aragon in the persons of his younger sons, these territories rapidly developed their separate histories, which would later constrain the future development of Navarre itself.

García's portion included Navarre, Vizcaya, Álava, and Guipúzcoa, as well as land in Old Castile and the Rioja. He spent much of his reign contending with his brother Fernando I of Castile over disputed territories, although there was still time for resecuring Calahorra and the lands lost to the tenth-century counteroffensive of the caliphate. However, García was killed in battle against Fernando at Atapuerca in 1054, and the latter gained La Bureba in Old Castile as a result.

García was succeeded by his son Sancho IV Garcés (1054–1076). With the Castilian frontier temporarily stable, Sancho largely concerned himself with his aggressive cousins Ramiro I and Sancho I Ramírez of Aragon. This pressure upon his eastern frontier led Sancho Garcés to ally himself with the *taifa* chieftain Muqtadir of Saragossa, also a victim of Aragonese raiding. Feudal tenancies and honors increased in the hands of Sancho Garcés' nobles as the Navarrese king sought to garrison his troubled frontiers. In 1076 he was suddenly murdered in a conspiracy fomented by his brothers, neither of whom gained the throne despite their efforts. Rather, the kings of León-Castile and Aragon moved to seize the advantage.

As matters resolved themselves, Sancho I Ramírez (1063–1094) of Aragon took the title Sancho V in Navarre, which he retained (as the county of Navarre) as a vassal of Alfonso VI of Castile. Alfonso VI, in addition to Sancho's vassalage, gained the Rioja, the Basque provinces of Vizcaya and Álava, and much of Guipúzcoa. Navarre thus lost its status as an independent kingdom and was reduced to the frontiers it had held at the beginning of the century. As a county of Aragon, it would see the future of its expansion against Islam dramatically engulfed by the conquests of Castile and Aragon.

Navarre languished in this status under Sancho I Ramírez and two of his sons, Pedro I and Alfonso I the Battler. From 1076 to 1134, Aragon became a major power in the peninsula, capturing Huesca in 1096 and finally opening the central Ebro Valley for conquest by taking Saragossa from the Muslims in 1118. Since Navarre had no share in these gains, its potential for expansion in the Ebro Valley had been effectively foreclosed. Opportunities remained in the west and southwest. Alfonso I the Battler (1104–1134) took advantage of his marriage to Urraca, queen of León-Castile, to extend his holdings into Castile, regaining the Rioja and much of Vizcaya and Álava, lost earlier to Alfonso VI in 1076. While much of the Rioja was returned to Urraca's son Alfonso VII in the Peace of Támara (1127), Vizcaya, Álava, and Guipúzcoa were reunited with Navarre.

When Alfonso the Battler passed away after the disastrous battle of Fraga (1134), his will, which left Aragon-Navarre to the military orders of the Holy Sepulcher, the Hospital, and the Temple, provoked a revolt among the nobility and provided the opportunity for Navarre to break free from the Aragonese grip and become an independent kingdom once more. The great nobles of Navarre gathered at Pamplona and elected a descendant of García III, García IV Ramírez, as king. García IV, known as the Restorer, controlled essentially the same territory that Sancho III the Great had passed to his eldest son in 1035, except for the Rioja. However, he had inherited a vastly different strategic situation than his ancestor had.

The growth of Aragon had completely enclosed Navarre's southeastern frontier, and the revitalization of León-Castile under Alfonso VII had sealed off the southwest. Navarre was the first of the Christian monarchies in the peninsula to lose geographic contiguity with the territories of Muslim Spain. Any future expansion would come at the expense of neighboring Christian kings, an awkward situation in that the papacy had never recognized the restored Navarrese monarchy, insisting that Alfonso I's bequest to the military orders be fulfilled. The last three monarchs of the dynasty, García IV (1134–1150), Sancho VI the Learned (1150–1194), and Sancho VII the Strong (1194–1234), would strive to secure additional territories, especially the former holdings in the Rioja, in the face of alliances by Aragon and Castile to partition the kingdom of Navarre between themselves. In 1162–1163, Sancho VI seized the Rioja south of the Ebro River, taking advantage of the royal minorities in Castile (Alfonso VIII) and Aragon (Alfonso II). Between 1173 and 1176, Alfonso VIII directed a series of campaigns that won much of the Rioja back for Castile. Ultimately, Sancho VI and Alfonso VIII submitted their Riojan dispute to Alfonso's father-in-law, Henry II of England, who ruled in favor of Castile. The peace that ensued in 1179 was broken again in 1190 by an alliance of Sancho VI and Alfonso II of Aragon for mutual assistance against Castile. This fratricidal conflict of Christian Spanish monarchs so troubled the papacy that strong pressure was exerted through papal envoys to secure peace in order to deal with the growing menace of the Almohad Muslims.

After Castile's disastrous loss to the Almohads at Alarcos in 1195, Sancho VII renewed his pressure on the Rioja. This time even Pope Celestine III's recognition of the Navarrese kingdon in 1196 was insufficient to restrain Sancho's acquisitiveness. Alfonso VIII rebounded from his defeat at Alarcos, however, and turned on Navarre with a vengeance, not only retaking the Rioja but also conquering part of Vizcaya, Álava, and Guipúzcoa in 1199–1200, losses that would become permanent in the Treaty of Guadalajara in 1207. While Sancho joined Alfonso in the great victory over the Almohads at Las Navas de Tolosa in 1212, no important concessions were obtained as a result. On the other hand, Sancho was able to strengthen his grip on the French Pyreneean approaches to the Roncesvalles Pass, because after the death of his brother-in-law Richard the Lionhearted, Sancho seized some areas to which there were Plantagenet claims. Nonetheless, the concessions of 1207 broke the political unity of the Spanish Basques, blocked Navarre from access to the Bay of Biscay, and opened direct contact between Castile and Gascony, adding another factor to the complex diplomacy of southern France. Of greater significance, these losses to Castile were permanent. Navarre had been restricted to the boundaries in Iberia that it would have for the remainder of the Middle Ages.

In 1234 Sancho VII died without an heir. He had attempted to adopt James (Jaime) I and pass Navarre to the crown of Aragon. However, Sancho's nephew Thibaut, count of Champagne, came to Navarre to validate his claim. Navarrese support placed him on the throne in lieu of claimants, inaugurating the house of Champagne and bringing Navarre under much stronger French influence for the remainder of the medieval period. Thibaut I (1234–1253) spent little time in his kingdom. He did agree to the *fuero antiguo* in 1240, which acknowledged the people of Navarre as the source of law and the electors of their king, an act of considerable constitutional importance. When Thibaut II (1253–1270) succeeded to the throne, Alfonso X of Castile attempted to reduce the kingdom of Navarre to vassalage, an enterprise frustrated by the intervention of Jaime I of Aragon.

The male line of Champagne ended with Henry I (1270–1274), but Henry's daughter Joanna I succeeded to the throne. By her marriage to the future Philip IV, king of France, Navarre became a direct possession of the French crown down to the death of Philip's youngest son in 1328.

During this period, Navarre was frequently ruled by governors who found themselves confronted with tensions that had been building between French and nativist forces for decades. French settlers had been given exclusive rights to occupy and control trading rights in several towns, most especially Estella. In Pamplona an entire district populated by Frenchmen, San Cernin, had exclusive trading rights to the lucrative pilgrimage road traffic. The twelfth- and thirteenth-century Navarrese monarchs had vacillated in their support of the French quarter as against that of the native Navarrería quarter in Pamplona. The conflict was further complicated by the strong governmental role played by the bishops of the city, an authority renowned for its inability to keep order. In 1276 the Navarrería revolted over the right to fortify its sector, a revolt quashed brutally by French arms, which devastated the sector. The Navarrería was later repopulated, and the bishop relinquished his temporal power in 1319, but the revolt gave indications of some important internal tensions in the kingdom.

In 1328, the tradition of rule through the descent of the female line reasserted itself. The termination of the direct Capetian line that brought Philip VI of Valois to the French throne released Navarre from French royal control. Joanna II (1328–1349), daughter of King Louis X of France and granddaughter of Joanna I, gained control of the kingdom. While her marriage to Philip of Evreux kept Navarre involved in French territorial interests, the rulers returned to Navarrese residency. Philip and Joanna agreed to rule by the ancient *fuero general* of Navarre, although Philip did alter and update a number of these laws in the *amejoramiento* (improvement) of 1330. For the next 184 years Navarre's pivotal strategic position among Castile, Aragon, and France dominated its political life. During this turbulent age France and England waged the Hundred Years War while Castile and Aragon became involved in major civil wars—providing both hazards and opportunities for the rulers of Navarre. No king attempted to take greater advantage of this situation than Carlos II (1349-1387), nor encountered greater frustration. Initially seeking recovery and consolidation of lands in France claimed by Evreux and Navarre, Carlos enmeshed himself in the revolt of the nobles against the French crown (1356) and the suppression of the peasant *Jacquerie* (1358). Events in France gained him little except a growing reputation for mischief and treachery, however, and he returned to Navarre, where he quickly became entangled in the Castilian civil war between Pedro the Cruel and his half brother Henry of Trastámara. Carlos allied first with Pedro and then with Henry, failing to support either at crucial moments in the struggle. Once Henry II was crowned in Castile, Carlos joined a Portuguese-Aragonese alliance against him, seizing Logroño and Vitoria in 1369. After these had been returned in 1372, Carlos married his son to Henry's daughter, a prelude to the ultimate Trastámaran absorption of Navarre. When Carlos again plotted to seize Castilian land, Henry marched on Navarre and forced him to sign the Treaty of Briones in 1379, in which Navarre had to accept peace with France and Castile while yielding frontier fortresses as a guarantee.

The accession of Carlos III the Noble (1387–1425) brought a very different personality to the throne and a long period of stability to the kingdom. To the five *merindades* (provinces) that had been formed by the fourteenth century (Pamplona, Estella, Sangüesa, Tudela, and the trans-Pyreneean Ultrapuertos), Carlos added Olite (1407). He also contributed his own *amejoramiento* to the *fuero general* (1418) and formalized the position of heir apparent with the title prince of Viana (1423), a position he granted to his grandson Carlos. As so often in the past, Carlos III produced no male heir, and descent of the royal title passed to his daughter Blanche (1425–1441). Her marriage to Juan of Trastámara, a younger son of the king of Aragon, brought the Trastámara dynasty of Castile and Aragon that much closer to claiming its third peninsular kingship.

Navarre had long since stabilized its population at approximately 100,000, which it would retain throughout the later Middle Ages. The small Pyreneean kingdom was now thoroughly encompassed by its more populous and powerful neighbors, the monarchies of Castile, Aragon, and France. Increasingly a pawn in Trastámaran diplomacy, it clung desperately to its last decades of independence. For much of his reign, Juan of Trastámara concerned himself with the internal intrigues of Castile and Aragon, leaving Navarre to

NAVARRE, KINGDOM OF

be governed by Blanche and, after her death (1441), by their son Carlos, prince of Viana. Prince Carlos was a remarkable figure, a competent administrator and Renaissance humanist, entitled by Navarrese law to rule in his own right. Nevertheless, his father resisted naming him as heir. This was probably because Juan, who had remarried, was being pressed by his second wife, Juana Enríquez, to provide for the succession of their son, Ferdinand. Juan became king of Aragon when his older brother died in 1458, and Carlos was arrested on unfounded charges of treason in 1460. Juan was forced by popular demand in Aragon and Navarre to clear Carlos, free him, and name him as heir in 1461. However, in that same year Carlos died, a suspected victim of poisoning. Juan II and Louis XI of France then conspired to pass the kingship of Navarre to Carlos' sister Lenore and her husband, Gaston de Foix. The kingdom was placed in Gaston's hands, and at his death evolved into a brief queenship for Lenore; then it passed to Gaston's son Francisco (1479–1483), and finally to Gaston's daughter Catalina. When Juan died in 1479, his son Ferdinand the Catholic permitted Navarre to remain in the hands of his grandnephew and then his grandniece. Catalina de Foix's marriage to John of Albret suited Ferdinand's diplomacy at the time, but the end of an independent Navarre was in sight. Inside the kingdom active pro-French (Agramonte) and pro-Aragonese (Beaumonte) parties were seething. John of Albret and Catalina attempted to steer a middle course, but the growing hostility between France and the Spain of Isabel and Ferdinand made Navarre far too strategic a territory to remain free. Utilizing his extraordinary gift for diplomacy, Ferdinand arranged a confrontation with John of Albret, invading Navarre and annexing it to Castile in 1512. Ferdinand appropriated only the five *merindades* south of the Pyrenees, leaving Ultrapuertos as indefensible, an independent kingdom of Navarre in France. From this omission a final irony would arise. Navarre had given both Castile and Aragon their dynastic monarchies. The line of Albret, intermarrying with that of Bourbon in the sixteenth century, allowed Navarre to give Europe one more major dynastic line, the Bourbon house in France.

BIBLIOGRAPHY

Sources. Selections of documents are available in José Yanguas y Miranda, *Diccionario de antigüedades del reino de Navarra,* 3 vols. (1840–1843, repr. 1964), and *Diccionario de los fueros del reino de Navarra* (1828). The standard edition of the *fuero general* is Pablo Ilarregui and Segundo LaPuerta, eds., *Fuero general de Navarra* (1869). The documents for the reign of Sancho VII have been assembled in Carlos Marichalar, ed., *Colección diplomática del rey don Sancho VII (el fuerte) de Navarra* (1934). Indispensable for the study of municipal charters is José María Lacarra and Angel J. Martín Duque, eds., *Fueros de Navarra,* I, *Fueros derivados de Jaca,* 1. *Estella-San Sebastián*; 2. *Fueros de Jaca-Pamplona,* (1969–1975).

Studies. There are no general works in English on the medieval kingdom of Navarre. The history of Navarre is discussed in Joseph F. O'Callaghan, *A History of Medieval Spain* (1975); and J. N. Hillgarth, *The Spanish Kingdoms, 1250–1516,* 2 vols. (1976–1978). In Spanish, the most significant general study is José María Lacarra, *Historia política del reino de Navarra, desde sus orígenes hasta su incorporación á Castilla,* 3 vols. (1972–1973), and *Historia del reino de Navarra en la edad media* (1975). A general study that compares the various interpretations of Navarrese history from a French point of view is Pierre Narbaitz, *Nabarra, ou quand les Basques avaient des rois* (1978).

The origins and development of the early kingdom are examined in Joaquín Arbeloa, *Los orígenes del reino de Navarra (710–925),* 3 vols. (1969). Claudio Sánchez-Albornoz y Meduiña's articles covering the early stages of Navarre's history have been gathered in his *Vascos y navarros en su primera historia* (1974). For kingship in the later Middle Ages, see P. E. Schramm, "Der König von Navarra (1035–1512)," in *Zeitschrift der Savigny-stiftung für Rechtsgeschichte,* **68,** I (Germanistiche Abteilung, 1951). The history of the royal oath to govern by the *fueros* of Navarre has been studied by José María Lacarra, *El juramento de los reyes de Navarra (1234–1328)* (1972).

For later medieval administrative history, see Javier Zabalo Zabalegui, *La administración del reino de Navarra en el siglo XIV* (1973). The old but still indispensable study of the last years of the independent kingdom of Navarre is Prosper Boissonnade, *Histoire de la réunion de la Navarre à la Castille: Essai sur les relations des princes de Foix-Albret avec la France et l'Espagne* (1893). Biographies of several Navarrese monarchs are available: Justo Pérez de Urbel, *Sancho el Mayor de Navarra* (1950); Luis del Campo, *Sancho el Fuerte de Navarra* (1960); José Ramoń Castro, *Carlos III el Noble, rey de Navarra* (1967); Tomás Domínguez Arévalo, *Los Teobaldos de Navarra* (1909); Georges Desdevises du Dezert, *Don Carlos d'Aragon, prince de Viane* (1889).

For the history of Pamplona, the entire medieval period is surveyed in María Angeles Irurita Lusarreta, *El municipio de Pamplona en la edad media* (1959), while central and later medieval Pamplona is examined in J. J.

Naval battle between Byzantines and Muslims. Miniature (anachronistic) from a late-10th-century Byzantine MS of the *Cynegetica* of Oppian. VENICE, BIBLIOTECA NAZIONALE MARCIANA, COD. GR. 479, fol. 23r

Martínez Ruiz, *La Pamplona de los burgos y su evolución urbana, siglos XII–XVI* (1975). The standard work on medieval Navarrese art is José E. Uranga Galdiano and Francisco Iñigüez Almech, *Arte medieval navarro,* 5 vols. (1971–1973). For medieval music, see Higinio Anglés, *Historia de la música medieval en Navarra* (1970).

JAMES F. POWERS

[See also **Alfonso I of Aragon; Aragon** (800–1137); **Aragon, Crown of** (1137–1479); **Asturias–León; Basques; Castile; Cortes; Fuero; Pilgrimage, Western European; Roland, Song of.**]

NAVE, the main part or body of a church, from the facade to the choir or chancel, intended primarily for the laity. In a basilica or basilican-plan church, the nave is the high, central aisle and is flanked by lower side aisles. In a cruciform church the term also describes the western arm of the church between the facade and the crossing, taking the central and side aisles together as a unit distinct from the chancel and transepts. In Byzantine architecture the nave or main space of a central-plan church, together with the sanctuary, is called the *naos,* from the Greek for the sanctuary of a temple.

GREGORY WHITTINGTON

[See also **Basilica; Chancel; Choir; Naos.**]

NAVIES, BYZANTINE. See **Warfare, Byzantine.**

NAVIES, ISLAMIC. Navigation has been considered a novelty that remained alien to Islam; and early orientalists, such as Martin Hartmann, believed this was because Muslims were "afraid of the sea." Nevertheless, the early Muslims inherited naval traditions from the pre-Islamic Arabs, the Phoenicians (via the Syrians), and the Greeks and Romans (via the Byzantines), and by the ninth century were ready to challenge Byzantine supremacy of the Mediterranean. Although pre-Islamic Arabs were known to have sailed the Red Sea and Persian Gulf, little is known of their traditions and naval experience.

Islamic naval history in the Middle Ages divides itself into four periods: (1) an early Umayyad phase (to 750), when ships and arsenals were built, and successes against the Byzantines were scored; (2) a "golden age" under the early Abbasids (750–950); (3) a revival under the Fatimids (909–1171); and (4) a decline, beginning in the thirteenth century, when ports along the eastern Mediterranean were deliberately destroyed and European city-states ruled the "sea between the lands."

SUCCESSES UNDER THE UMAYYADS

In spite of the fact that the Arabs conquered the coastal towns of Aradus, Acre, Tyre, Sidon, and

Tripoli, they made little use of the famous Phoenician naval tradition because the majority of the local Christian population did not cooperate with the Muslim conquerors. Muᶜāwiya, the first Umayyad caliph (661–680), was keen to promote naval activity against the Byzantines, and an early decree of his ordered the importation in 662 of a large number of Persian (so say the historians) craftsmen to replace the uncooperative Christian workers in the dockyards. A repairing station was organized in Acre when Muᶜāwiya was still governor (it was later transferred to Tyre). Muᶜāwiya also offered land and houses to the fighters who settled in Acre, Tyre, and the rest of the coastal towns.

The Byzantines had maintained dockyards in Egypt, and when the Arabs took control of that province in 640–642, they found shipyards in Alexandria and Clysma (Al-Qulzum, a mile south of Al-Suways, modern Suez); Al-Fusṭāṭ, Rosetta (Rashīd), Damietta, and Tinnīs became naval centers. Egyptians, for the most part Christian, were drafted to work in the dockyards and to man the ships taken from the Byzantines. Severe penalties were inflicted on those who neglected their duties. Within a very short time the Muslims were able to assemble a navy from their shipyards (called *dār al-sināᶜa,* whence the English "arsenal") and to staff their ships with skilled professionals. Sea raids were now launched against the Byzantines, and Cyprus was attacked in 648/649 and 653/654; within a few years the Muslims imposed neutrality on the island, which until then had been a base of operations against them. Sicily was pillaged in 652, Rhodes in 654, and Crete in *ca.* 656. Naval raids now became a standard military operation, often carried out every year. A combined Syro-Egyptian fleet under the command of ᶜAbd Allāh ibn Saᶜd met the Byzantine fleet in 655/656 off the coast of southeastern Asia Minor, near Phoenix (modern Finike), and inflicted a humiliating defeat on the Byzantines. Muᶜāwiya, ᶜAbd Allāh ibn Saᶜd, and the Syrians Abū'l Aᶜward and Buṣr ibn Abī Arṭah (who were in charge of the Syrian squadron at Dhāt aṣ-Ṣawārī), along with ᶜAbd Allāh ibn Qays (who raided Crete in 674), were the first Muslim admirals. The battle of Dhāt aṣ-Ṣawārī (Battle of the Masts), resulted in large Muslim losses, preventing them from pressing the victory and advancing against Constantinople. Nineteen years later, in 674, the Muslims dared to lay siege to Constantinople and fought until 678, when they were forced to retreat after losing most of their fleet. A second, more formidable attack against the Byzantine capital was undertaken by Maslama in August 717, and after a year of futile siege the Muslims retreated, suffering a humiliating defeat.

Alexandria, still adorned with its famous lighthouse, whose torches guided boats safely to harbor, emerged as a great naval base and commercial center. On Egypt's Red Sea coast, Al-Qulzum became important, since the fleet of grain ships that once was sent to Constantinople was now sent to Al-Jār, the port of Medina, to feed the inhabitants of the holy cities. (Later, Jidda became the principal port for pilgrims going to the Hejaz.) Al-Qulzum remained a key port until the tenth century, when its trade went to ᶜAydhāb, further down the coast. In its heyday Al-Qulzum became the Muslim base of operations in the Red Sea, and in the early years of the caliphate attacks by Africans on Arabian coastal towns had to be repelled by its fleet. In 641 Caliph ᶜUmar ordered a raid to be carried out against Abyssinia, and Adulis, its chief port, was sacked. Later the Abyssinians defeated the Muslims on land, and Muslim ambitions in the Red Sea were momentarily curtailed.

On the other side of the peninsula, the Persian Gulf was the staging ground for a raid in 636 against Thana, a port near Bombay; although it failed, raids continued to be launched against India. Routes across the Indian Ocean to India and East Africa were monopolized by Persians and Omanis, who operated from the ports of Sīrāf, Qais, Sohar, and Hormuz.

THE GOLDEN AGE

By the first quarter of the ninth century, the Muslims had developed an impressive commercial fleet with experienced crews and a formidable naval armada. Crete fell into their hands about 824, and raids against Sicily were commenced soon after (culminating in conquest in 902). Operations against Crete had been undertaken by a crew of Spanish malcontents, but the ships were built in Egypt and equipped with Egyptian arms—indeed, the invaders sailed from Egypt.

As a result of this loss, the Byzantines reorganized their navy and began patrolling their coasts, setting up an elaborate warning system that linked islands and coastal towns. Suffering numerous raids, they reciprocated in kind and began attacking towns along the Syro-Palestinian coast and the Egyptian port of Damietta (in 800 and in 853).

Counterraids were mounted from Syria (especially Tarsus and Tripoli), Egypt, and even North Africa. Thessaloniki, the second largest Byzantine city, was sacked in 904 by a combined Syro-Egyptian fleet. From Crete, the Muslims ravaged the Byzantine coast and established footholds on numerous islands in the southern Aegean.

Under the direction of the Egyptian ruler, Aḥmad ibn Ṭūlūn (868–884), the Egyptian fleet was strengthened and the arsenal at Al-Fusṭāṭ rebuilt, becoming the most developed of the Muslim shipyards.

In the heyday of Muslim fleets in the eastern Mediterranean, the Muslims of Al-Andalus (the Iberian Peninsula) also developed a formidable navy, while their cargo ships crossed the Mediterranean, reaching even Constantinople. Especially during the reign of ᶜAbd al-Rahmān III (912–961), a large number of ships were constructed in Al-Andalus, and ᶜAbd al-Rahmān's navy often defeated the fleets of the Spanish Christian kingdoms of the peninsula. Simultaneously, the sea trade between Al-Andalus and these kingdoms, as well as with Amalfi and Constantinople, was intensified, and special treaties allowed the ships of both Christians and Muslims to visit freely each other's ports. After the eleventh century, when the pressure of the *Reconquista* brought an increasing weakness to Al-Andalus, its naval activities decreased rapidly.

Muslim naval superiority elsewhere in the Islamic world, however, began a brief decline as early as the mid tenth century. Crete was taken back by a formidable Byzantine armada in 961, and Cyprus, which had been neutralized for two centuries, was reunited with Byzantium in 965. The reasons for this decline have been attributed to intra-Muslim wars and, of less importance, to a depletion in supplies of timber and other materials necessary in shipbuilding.

FATIMID REVIVAL

Muslim naval fortunes revived under the Fatimids (909–1171), who reversed the policies of the Ikhshidids in Egypt and undertook intensive shipbuilding and marine training. The Fatimid naval base in North Africa had been at Mahdia, along the coast near Qayrawān (Tunisia); after their transfer to Egypt in 969, Alexandria, Damietta, and Al-Fusṭāṭ (which became "Old Cairo") once again became major shipbuilding centers.

The Fatimid naval achievements have been exaggerated in some Arabic sources, particularly by Ibn Khaldūn (1332–1402), who claimed that they were masters of the entire Mediterranean. In reality, their successes were restricted mainly to the western Mediterranean; elsewhere they suffered defeats.

The Fatimid navy captured fortified Reggio in Calabria in just one night's assault (August 918). A few years later (923–924), Sant Agata, a fortress near Reggio, was conquered by twenty Fatimid ships. More spectacular was the sack of Genoa by twenty Fatimid ships under the admiral Yaᶜ qūb ibn Ishaq al-Tamīmī (June 934).

After the second half of the tenth century, the Fatimid navy started declining. Thus, in spite of the pompous offers of assistance by the Fatimid ruler Muᶜizz to the Muslims of Crete, not a single Fatimid ship was dispatched to Crete when Nikephoros Phokas reconquered the island in 961. In 971–972 a Fatimid squadron of fifteen ships was destroyed by Byzantine ships in Jaffa. Above all, the withdrawal of the Fatimid navy and naval installation from the seacoast of Egypt to Cairo (described by the Persian traveler Nasir-i-Khusraw, writing in the mid eleventh century) manifests the Fatimids' weakness.

Muslims now faced new and dangerous foes in Western Europe. The Normans completed their conquest of Sicily in 1090, ending Muslim hegemony there and extinguishing an important naval base. Pisa, Genoa, and, later, Venice emerged as powerful maritime forces that preyed on Muslim shipping, particularly in the western Mediterranean. And, finally, the crusaders established footholds in Syria.

Under the Fatimids the commercial fleet prospered. The Cairo genizah documents relating to the activities of Jewish merchants evidence the vitality of trade along the Mediterranean—and from the Red Sea to India—well into the twelfth century. The decline of Sīrāf and then Qais (Kīsh), the preeminent Persian Gulf ports, benefited international traders operating from Egypt.

POST-TWELFTH-CENTURY DEVELOPMENTS

Acre and Tyre fell to the Crusaders in 1104 and 1124 respectively, severely affecting Muslim maritime fortunes. Saladin, however, understood the importance of naval power, and he painstakingly reestablished the navy by reviving the arsenal in Alexandria and by increasing the salaries of sailors. Acre and other coastal towns were retaken in 1187,

NAVIES, ISLAMIC

but the siege of Tyre failed and it remained in European hands. When the Mamluks came to power in 1250, they expelled the Europeans from Syria, and in order to render its coastal towns less attractive in the future, they were deliberately destroyed. The Mamluks also resorted to using convicts and prisoners of war for oarsmen, and the efficiency of the navy as a military force deteriorated rapidly. In later Mamluk times a permanent navy did not exist. The Italian city-states now ruled Mediterranean trade, and at the end of the Middle Ages the Muslims controlled only trade in the Red Sea and Indian Ocean. With the coming of the Portuguese, this, too, was taken away.

TYPES OF SHIPS

Arabic sources offer only snippets of information on ships and shipbuilding, and what evidence they do provide often comes in the form of word lists; rarely are functions of particular ships described. In this the later Muslim geographers and literati may have been unconsciously following the pre-Islamic poets, who preferred to mention the "beauty" of a ship but not how it was used or what purpose it served. Even naval battles were described in the barest detail. The extant naval manuals remain largely in manuscript form.

From the sources it is evident that warships and cargo vessels, though used for different purposes and of different designs, could, if necessary, perform either function. In time of peace, warships served as cargo vessels, with sails used instead of oars; in time of war, cargo vessels were converted into warships, with sails removed and oars installed. Cargo ships tended to be propelled by wind power, oars being used only when ships were entering or leaving harbors.

WARSHIPS

Muslim writers used a number of different terms for ships and were quite capable of applying the same word to different kinds of ships at different times. This has caused great confusion among naval historians. *Safīna* and *markab* were the general words for "ship"; they were modified to indicate special kinds of ships (thus *markab kabīr* for "big ship," *markab tawīl* for "long ship," *markab muṣattila* for "decked ship").

In the tenth century, Muslim ships hardly differed from Byzantine ships. The *dromon* and *pamphylos,* terms the Byzantines used interchangeably for "ship of the line," could be matched with the Muslim *shīnī* (*shīnīya* or *shānī*) and *shalandī,* terms used for "warship." The standard size of the man-of-war, whether *shīnī* or *shalandī,* cannot be determined precisely. According to the most reliable sources, the standard man-of-war was propelled by 100 oarsmen and sometimes by as many as 180 to 200 oarsmen and carried a contingent of not more than 150 marines. According to estimates made by Dolley and van Doorninck, based on the space needed to accommodate 200 oarsmen, the standard man-of-war averaged 120–135 feet in length. One Moorish fleet is recorded as comprising forty ships, twenty carrying Greek fire and twenty carrying soldiers. The entire complement of soldiers and marines numbered 3,000 men.

The medieval *shīnī* or *shalandī* was a two-banked vessel, its main characteristic being the forecastle. Marines, taking protection under it, threw various projectiles, such as heavy stones, or launched arrows from its cover. Earthen pots stuffed with combustibles were also hurled by special machines used by Arabs and Byzantines alike. Descriptions of such machines and of fire bombs appear in many Arabic manuscripts. Naval battles were duels of hand-propelled or machine-hurled missiles; battering rams were no longer used. Catapults, which the Greeks and Romans had devised, also were employed.

MERCHANT FLEETS

There was a close connection between the merchant and war fleets, and the experienced crews and technology (nautical instruments, charts, and the like) used by the merchant fleets were also used on the advanced warships. As far as their merchant marine was concerned, the Arabs classified ships mainly according to the shape of the hull. The generic terms for warships, such as *safina* and *markab,* were then applied, frequently modified to indicate whether the ship was a heavy cargo vessel or a light craft (*markab thaqīl, markab khafīf*). Some of these vessels were immense: literary sources mention one that had a seventy-five-foot mast and a cargo capacity of 300 tons.

The Mediterranean Muslim ships, cargo as well as warships, were originally modeled after the Byzantine tradition. Only a few elements were taken from Phoenician naval architecture: for example, the stern post which ended in a horse's head (no doubt transmitted via the peoples of the Syrian coast).

A marked difference in design existed between

Christ and St. Peter walking on the water. The Coptic MS of 1178–1180 depicts an Egyptian ship with axial stern rudder and double steering oars PARIS, BIBLIOTHÈQUE NATIONALE, MS COPTE 13, fol. 41v

boats used in the Mediterranean and boats used in the Indian Ocean. Indian Ocean vessels tended to be built without nails; instead, planks of the hull were sewn together. In due course, however, a single Muslim tradition of shipbuilding emerged. Caulked and nailed ships began to ply the Indian Ocean.

Literary and pictorial evidence shows that by the tenth century both Muslims and Byzantines were using lateen sails on one, two, or three masts. Islamic illuminated manuscripts depict merchant ships having special passenger compartments on their decks. (See illustration at "Navigation, Indian Ocean.")

Advances in rigging were matched by the development of sophisticated nautical instruments, detailed books of nautical instructions (*dafātir*), and nautical charts (*ṣuwār*). Muslim geographers, such as Ibn Ḥawqal and al-Idrisī, illustrated their treatises with elaborate maps, testimony to the knowledge of lands and seas that Muslims had accumulated.

Muslims may also have been responsible for inventing lateen sails, which eventually replaced square sails in the Mediterranean after the ninth century. The lateen, a unique triangular sail bound on a very long antenna connected to the main beam at an angle, proved to be the best for the Mediterranean vessels. Moreover, the use of the single stern rudder instead of the double steering oars, dating at least from the twelfth century, was again perhaps a Muslim invention. This and other naval technological advances were transmitted to the Europeans, especially the Italians, Spanish, and Portuguese, who in due course supplanted the Muslims' domination of the seas.

BIBLIOGRAPHY

Aḥmad Mukhtar al-ᶜAbbādī and al-Sayyid ᶜAbd al-ᶜAzīz Salim, *Taᵓrīkh al-baḥrīya al-Islamīya fi Miṣr wa 'l-Shām* (1972); Hélène Ahrweiler, *Byzance et la mer* (1966); R. Browning, "Byzantium and Islam in Cyprus in the Early Middle Ages," in *Epeteris Kentron Epistemonikon Ereunon (Cyprus)*, 9 (1977–1979); N. Chittick, "Sewn Boats in the Western Indian Ocean and Survivals in Somalia," in *International Journal of Nautical Archaeology*, 9 (1980); Vassilios Christides, "The Raids of the Moslems of Crete in the Aegean Sea: Piracy and Conquest," in *Byzantion*, 51 (1981), "Two Parallel Naval Guides of the Tenth Century: Qudāma's Document and Leo VI's *Naumachia*," in *Graeco-Arabica*, 1 (1982), and "Naval Warfare in the Eastern Mediterranean (6th–14th Centuries)," *ibid.*, 3 (1984), and "The Naval Engagement of Dhāt aṣ-Ṣawārī, A.H. 34/A.D. 655–656: A Classical Example of Naval Warfare Incompetence," in Βυζαντινα, 13 (1985); R. H. Dolley, "The Warships of the Later Roman Empire," in *Journal of Roman Studies*, 38 (1948); Ekkehard Eickhoff, *Seekrieg und Seepolitik zwischen Islam und Abendland* (1966);

Andrew S. Ehrenkreutz, "The Place of Saladin in the Naval History of the Mediterranean Sea in the Middle Ages," in *Journal of the American Oriental Society,* **75** (1955); Aly Mohamed Fahmy, *Muslim Naval Organisation in the Eastern Mediterranean,* 2nd ed. (1966), and *Muslim Sea-power in the Eastern Mediterranean* (1966); S. Qudratullah Fatimi, "In Search of a Methodology for the History of Muslim Navigation in the Indian Ocean," in *Islamic Quarterly,* **22** (1978).

Solomon D. Goitein, *A Mediterranean Society,* I, *The Economic Foundations* (1967), and *Letters of Medieval Jewish Traders* (1973); Hadi Hasan, *A History of Persian Navigation* (1928); George F. Hourani, *Arab Seafaring in the Indian Ocean* (1951, repr. 1963, 1975); T. Kollias, "The Taktika of Leo VI the Wise and the Arabs," in *Graeco-Arabica,* **3** (1984); Hilmar C. Krueger, "The Italian Cities and the Arabs Before 1095," in Kenneth M. Setton and Marshall W. Baldwin, eds., *A History of the Crusades,* 2nd ed., 2 vols. (1969), I, 40–53; Wladyslaw B. Kubiak, "The Byzantine Attack on Damietta in 853 and the Egyptian Navy in the 9th Century," in *Byzantion,* **40** (1970); Y. Lev, "The Fatimid Navy, Byzantium and the Mediterranean Sea 909–1036 C.E./297–427 A.H.," in *Byzantion,* **54** (1984); Tadeusz Lewicki, "Les voies maritimes de la Méditerranée dans le haut moyen âge d'après les sources arabes," in *La navigazione mediterranea nell'alto medioevo,* II (1978); Su^cād Mahir, *Al-baḥirīya fi Miṣr al-Islamīya* (1967); Darwish Nukhayli, *Al-sufun al-Islamīya* (1979); J. H. Pryor, "Transportation of Horses by Sea During the Era of the Crusades: Eighth Century to 1285 A.D.," in *Mariner's Mirror,* **64** (1982); J. R. Steffy, "The Reconstruction of the 11th-century Serce Liman Vessel," in *The International Journal of Nautical Archaeology and Underwater Exploration,* **11** (1982); Gerald R. Tibbetts, trans., *Arab Navigation in the Indian Ocean Before the Coming of the Portuguese* (1971), a translation of Aḥmad ibn Mājid al-Nadjī, *Kitāb al-fawāʾid . . .* ; Avram L. Udovitch, "Time, the Sea and Society," in *La navigazione mediterranea nell'alto medioevo,* II (1978); Frederick van Doorninck, "Byzantium, Mistress of the Sea, 360–641," in George F. Bass, ed., *A History of Seafaring Based on Underwater Archeology* (1972); David Whitehouse, "The Decline of Siraf," in *Proceedings of the Third Annual Symposium on Archaeological Research in Iran* (1975).

V. CHRISTIDES

[See also **Alexandria; Byzantine Empire: History (330–1025), (1025–1204), (1204–1453); Crete; Fatimids; Islam, Conquests of; Muʿāwiya; Navigation: Indian Ocean, Red Sea; Rhodes; Ships and Shipbuilding, Mediterranean; Ships and Shipbuilding, Red Sea and Persian Gulf; Sicily, Islamic; Thessaloniki; Tripoli; Warfare, Byzantine.**]

NAVIES, WESTERN. The disintegration of the navy and naval organization in Western Europe in the fifth century was part of the general decline of Roman government. When Rome was the only political authority in the West the navy was made up of light, fast coastal patrol vessels. The only threat to Roman hegemony after the battle of Actium in 31 B.C. had been piracy, but that problem was all but wiped out by the beginning of the Christian era. Naval forces played a minor role in the internal struggles of the third century; but the confusion of that period opened the way to piracy and led in turn to the development of naval defenses. In Britain the Saxon shore, a series of land forts complemented by ships, was set up in the closing years of Roman rule to protect the coasts from Pictish pirates. The German tribes living in Scandinavia and northern Germany at that time had no maritime forces and, at least in the fourth and fifth centuries, tended to stay away from the water, the exceptions being the Saxons and the Vandals.

To settle in North Africa the latter had to cross the Strait of Gibraltar. Local vessels and sailors ferried a total of some 80,000 people to North Africa in 429. The piratical fleets that operated from the newly established Vandal kingdom presumably relied upon indigenous skills and technology, since the Vandals brought no knowledge of the sea with them. They must have used the ships and mariners they found in Carthage and elsewhere along the North African coast. Those fleets made possible the successful Vandal attacks on and conquest of the islands of the western Mediterranean and even the sack of Rome in 455.

The East Roman emperor Justinian I destroyed the Vandal kingdom and its navy in 533 as part of his effort to reconquer the western part of the Roman Empire. The success of the Byzantine Empire was based in part on its superior naval organization; no other state in Europe could build, deploy, or maintain the ships and the men that the East Roman Empire could. While Justinian's reconquest had mixed success on land in Italy and Spain, it was completely successful at sea. Until the seventh century the navy of the Roman Empire dominated the Mediterranean. Then, the Byzantine Empire faced a new threat, this time from the Arabs, who took to the sea soon after conquering Syria and who proved to be more than the equal of any other enemy. Byzantine naval organization became more complex and efficient. The Byzantines and Muslims had the only standing naval forces in European waters. The Byzantines even had permanent bases, continuing officers, and methods for directing tax income directly to the ships and men of the navy. For peace at sea and protection from pirates, traders had to rely on the forces of the eastern Mediterranean.

In northern Europe there was no force at all to contain violence at sea. In the fourth through the eighth centuries German tribes were still largely confined to the land; their short excursions at sea presented no serious threat. The beginnings of the attacks by Vikings at the end of the eighth century, however, created the need for some type of naval defense.

The Viking raids proved very easy for the sailors from Scandinavia. Using a newly developed type of sailing ship, they made their way without problems or opposition to the undefended shores of Britain, France, and Spain. Monasteries, the favorite targets of the raiders, were often located near navigable bodies of water, which made the attacks even easier. Although Vikings organized their naval forces very simply, they were still more advanced than the Western Europeans they faced. The leader of a Norse clan would have a ship built and then enlist men for his voyage of trading and raiding. Apparently all crew members had an equal say in making decisions, and they shared in the profits of the voyages, however such profits might be gained. Ships could join together in raids, although such a coalition was only a temporary expedient. In the course of the ninth century Viking raiders gained greater cohesion. They traveled to Western Europe in larger groups, carried out campaigns through more than one season, and went further inland, even settling for a time. There was no permanent organization to these armies of amphibious raiders; groups broke up and reassembled from time to time. As the voyages proved lucrative and as the superiority of Viking ships and tactics became clear, the nascent royal authorities of Scandinavia tried to bring naval forces under their control. The Vikings did not have to worry about Western European naval forces, but they did face possible attack from other Vikings. For both offense and defense a unique regional militia system emerged in Scandinavia, which ultimately came under royal authority. The *ledung* system required each district to supply a certain number of ships and men. Typical vessels were similar to other Viking warships but larger, usually with about twenty-five rowers to a side and a total crew of more than sixty men. *Ledung* fleets were supposed to be massive, and in fact they were large enough to allow the kings of Norway and Denmark to pit hundreds of ships against each other in the tenth and eleventh centuries. The Vikings had virtually no form of artillery, so naval battles were fought hand to hand by the rowers, who doubled as soldiers. Exact maneuvering was critical, since how the ships met each other determined their ability to defend or attack. The presence of the ships and the availability of men interested in potential gain from violence made it possible for the kings to deploy large navies; it was not because these navies had a complex organization of their own.

In the ninth century the governments of England and France began to develop forces to defend themselves against the Vikings. The Anglo-Saxon kingdom of Alfred the Great (849–899) had ships built specially to meet the enemy at sea and a system for the support and maintenance of that naval force. The system may have been copied later in Scandinavia and was certainly not destroyed in England even after the conquest by Danish Vikings in the early eleventh century. King Cnut (1016–1035) relied on such organization to rule a naval empire bordering the North Sea that included England, Norway, and Denmark. His lands depended on naval forces for strength and cohesion.

In France local lords developed static defensive positions along the rivers and estuaries, but there was no navy set up to fight the Vikings at sea. The Carolingians rarely deployed naval forces; this was true both in the northern seas and in the Mediterranean. When naval forces were needed, either none was available or authorities turned to what talents and vessels were available locally. For example, in 1066, when William, duke of Normandy, needed a large naval force to transport an army across the English Channel, he called on all the available expertise to create a purely temporary navy. Despite Danish Viking ancestry the duchy of Normandy seems to have fallen into the pattern of disinterest in navies typical of the rest of Francia. With the rising power of central authority in Scandinavia in the eleventh century, the greater control of raiding voyages, and in general the end of the Viking age, the need for naval forces in the north declined. Although piracy was by no means eliminated, it was so much a part of shipping and fishing that no government perceived a need to maintain a standing navy to prevent it. In any case, it is highly unlikely that a navy could have stopped theft and reprisal at sea.

In the western Mediterranean in the tenth century sailors and ships from Italian towns took up profit-seeking naval action against Muslim ships and ports, with participants and investors sharing in the booty. Such groups disbanded on completion of a single voyage. In the eleventh century the ports of Pisa and Genoa, especially, enjoyed great success in what were little more than piratical attacks. The decline of the Byzantine Empire and its naval strength in the eleventh century increased the potential for piratical action both by Muslims and by sailors from the Italian ports. The oared galleys used to carry luxury goods were easily converted to naval use. Though they might or might not have rams and might even carry some devices for hurling heavy missiles, the principal armament was the crew and their hand weapons. Rowers doubled as fighting men when necessary. Because of the danger of piracy all vessels had to be defensible, carrying large crews and arms.

The crusades, starting in the last years of the eleventh century, served to bring northern European fighting ships into the Mediterranean and to bring fleets of warships organized by the Italian city-republics to the eastern shores of that sea. Northern Europeans usually arrived in large transports, leaving naval action against Muslim forces in the hands of the Italian maritime republics. In exchange for clearing the eastern Mediterranean of hostile forces, those towns received trading concessions in the crusader states, concessions that allowed them to enhance their naval power. Since it was the government that won the concessions it was also the government that organized the naval expeditions.

The pattern had already been established in 1082 when the Byzantine Empire made extensive trade concessions to Venice in exchange for naval support in the Adriatic. Venice, the Italian city closest politically and economically to the Byzantine Empire, imitated to a limited degree the Eastern Roman naval model. Nevertheless, naval forces typically remained temporary; individual noblemen, groups of investors, or governments still built, bought, or rented ships for the duration of a campaign with the expectation that after the fighting ended the ship, if it survived, would be turned over to commerce. By the thirteenth century that had changed, in large part because of changes in ship design.

Fighting ships became less useful or effective as commercial vessels as they became increasingly specialized. That was true of both transport and combat vessels. For example, for the crusades of King Louis IX of France (*d.* 1270) Italian ports constructed horse transports to specific and precise designs. After their short careers moving mounts for knights the ships needed extensive modification before they could be used commercially. Warships were transformed by changes in rowing practice. Instead of increasing the number of benches or levels of rowers to raise the number of oars as had been Byzantine practice, Italian shipbuilders simply added a third rower to each bench in the single level. Each rower pulled on his own oar. That gave the optimum angle for entry of the oars into the water and also allowed for an increase in crew size and in power, making the galleys faster without building them higher. The galleys had large crews and had little cargo space left. Missile launchers at the bow took up even more of what available stowage area was left. By the end of the thirteenth century only governments could afford to build and maintain such vessels, and in the course of that century they developed institutions for that purpose.

Conflict with Muslims or between Christian states often opened the door to pirates in the twelfth and thirteenth centuries. Cargo ships, whether powered by oars or sail, still had to be defensible; as they grew in the twelfth and thirteenth centuries their sheer size made them less likely to be attacked. The oared galleys had big crews and could maneuver when there was no wind, so they too were difficult targets. Governments in the Italian towns took steps to prevent attacks on their ships by requiring complements of fighting men on board or by organizing convoys. But no state was strong enough or committed enough to dominate the Mediterranean, and so no state could or would stamp out piracy. In addition, those same states also contributed to the high level of violence at sea through the wars they fought among themselves, which became common in the thirteenth and fourteenth centuries.

Permanent government institutions to look after naval forces—to build fighting galleys and maintain them between periods of hostilities—began to emerge in the Mediterranean in the thirteenth century. The office of admiral first appeared in the Latin West in the kingdom of Sicily; in the late eleventh century an admiral had oversight of a town or district. But the office soon became associated with fiscal administration and organization of the navy, which in wartime meant commanding naval forces. After a period when the admiral was perhaps the most important figure in the Norman government in Sicily, the office fell into disfavor; it was revived in the last quarter of the twelfth century, with an emphasis on the naval aspects of the post. The admiral was certainly the commander of the Sicilian fleet in wartime. In the years just after 1200, in part because of the fame of the Sicilian admiral Margaritus of Brindisi, the towns of northern Italy began to acquire their own admirals. From the mid thirteenth century the office found a place in the governments of northern Europe. The admiral was responsible for commanding naval forces, for naval affairs, and for the growing naval institutions of the Italian states. The navies in the Mediterranean even had their own buildings. The term arsenal originally referred to a place of work, but in the thirteenth century came to mean a building for the construction and maintenance of warships. The facilities started as small storage depots but expanded over the years to become bases holding interchangeable parts for different classes of warships built at the arsenals. The most famous was in Venice, although there were similar arsenals in Barcelona and Narbonne. In peacetime the arsenals were active, building new warships and keeping naval supplies in readiness. The admiral ran this department of the state with his subordinates, keeping records of stores, expenditures, and employment. In wartime the arsenals, directed by the admiral, rapidly assembled new warships from prefabricated parts. They also fitted out existing ships and did necessary repairs. Although it was only in the sixteenth century that the Venetian arsenal reached the height of its size, efficiency, and acclaim, many of the elements of its later success were apparent by the fourteenth century. The galley fleets produced by the arsenals were specialized fighting forces; their rowers were not slaves but paid citizens in the service of the republic or the king. Mediterranean navies were staffed by free men until the fourteenth century, when one after the other went over to using galley slaves. Navies then became institutions responsible for incarceration as well as defense.

Northern European kingdoms tried to copy the system of organization that was emerging in the Mediterranean, but with only mixed success. The office of admiral appeared in France in 1246 and in England a half century later. The admiral was responsible for deploying and commanding naval forces for the crown. These forces, however, were not permanent. Since before the Norman Conquest the English crown had had a special relationship with a group of harbors on the southeast coast to supply naval vessels for a fixed period. The warships of those Cinque Ports (originally Dover, Hastings, Hythe, Romney, and Sandwich), modeled on earlier Viking designs, proved effective in transporting troops and royal parties between England and the Continent and in preventing the worst of piratical acts in the Channel. At the beginning of the thirteenth century the royal government set about establishing an office for developing naval facilities. It was in that same period that the Cinque Ports reached the height of their importance. By the end of the century, however, they took on a minor role since they could no longer meet the increasing and special needs of the crown.

Edward I of England, in response to the establishment of an arsenal at Rouen in 1294 by Philip IV of France, ordered galleys to be built for him in different ports to precise specifications. He needed specialized warships to meet the French galleys, which presumably were modeled on Italian designs. They were very different from the vessels of the Cinque Ports. The new galleys had only limited uses in the rough Atlantic waters. The more valuable and important warships for the English crown and for other states in northern Europe were large cargo ships that also served as transports. In the fourteenth century the crown owned large ships for use in war but leased them to merchants in peacetime for carrying cargo. The crown also rented and even impressed merchants' ships when necessary. Naval administrators were to see to the maintenance of the king's ships, which included chartering them to get some return in peacetime, and to the proper fitting out of ships in wartime. Galleys required regular attention, needed large crews, and above all could not be used commercially. In the Hundred Years War between England and France, galleys proved effective in coastal waters and for amphibious operations, but the major naval vessels that decided the battles at sea were large cargo ships.

The cog was both the predominant cargo ship and the predominant warship in northern waters in the thirteenth century. It was larger and rode higher in the water than any other contemporary vessel.

French and English cogs at the Battle of Sluis (1340). Miniature by Loyset Liédet from Volume I of the *Chroniques de Jean Froissart,* mid 15th century. PARIS, BIBLIOTHÈQUE NATIONALE, MS FRANÇAIS 2643, fol. 72

Naval battles were fought like land battles; the ships were grappled together so that armed men could move back and forth across the decks as on a battlefield. The men carried the same arms that they would on land. Victory depended largely on the number of ships and men rather than on skill or technical superiority. The size of the cog meant it could carry large numbers of troops. That also made it the ideal transport. The high freeboard of the cog allowed fighting men to hurl missiles down on an enemy, an invaluable advantage. The addition of raised structures, castles, at both the bow and the stern gave archers and spear-throwers an even better position for firing. Little decks high up the single mast, fighting tops, provided another valuable location. For the fourteenth and much of the fifteenth century the major naval vessels of northern Europe were cargo ships when they were not being used in battle.

In the later Middle Ages navies were still raised when they were needed, largely from existing shipping. The Hanseatic League, for example, put together an overpowering naval force in a matter of months to destroy the threat to its naval hegemony in the Baltic from King Waldemar IV of Denmark in 1367–1368. It took longer for the league to mobilize sufficient naval and diplomatic force to suppress the pirates who called themselves the *Vitalienbrüder* in the last decade of the century. Without a standing naval force there was no authority responsible for keeping peace at sea. Governments could and did use pirates as a naval force. In the case of the *Vitalienbrüder,* the duke of Mecklenburg, faced with losing a war, resorted to

Battle between two cogs showing fore- and aftercastles. Miniature from the *Smithfield Decretals*, *ca.* 1330. BY PERMISSION OF THE BRITISH LIBRARY, LONDON, MS ROY 10 E. IV, fol. 19

informal and uncontrolled violence, unleashing pirates against his enemies. Royal governments beginning in the fourteenth century tried to gain control over such violence, claiming that they had a monopoly of coercion. As the kings worked to assert that principle at sea, admirals became their principal agents. The office of admiral came to be dominated by legal and juridical considerations. Admirals became lawyers, courtiers, and noblemen, who no longer commanded ships at sea. Looking after warships and fitting them out was left to lesser officials.

In early-fifteenth-century England, King Henry V marshaled a massive naval force (of ships either purchased or specially built) and launched a successful invasion of France. After Henry's death, however, the vessels were sold off, broken up, or simply left to rot—in part because England no longer faced a naval threat in the Channel from France or her Genoese allies and in part because of the high cost of maintaining the naval force. Henry V had a keeper of the king's ships, a special if minor official who looked after the naval vessels, but the job disappeared with the ships. As the navy was disbanded the admiral returned to juridical matters. It was not until the sixteenth century that the admiralty as a department of the government had a permanent board of officials responsible for maintaining naval forces. That change was dictated by the development of a new type of sailing ship and by the appearance of heavy guns on board warships.

Northern Europeans brought cogs into the Mediterranean in the thirteenth and fourteenth centuries. Cogs proved, after modification, to be effective cargo carriers. The same advantages of defensibility recommended cogs in the south as they had in the north. It proved easier to use the relatively new and powerful crossbow on board a cog than on a traditional Mediterranean cargo ship. Fewer armed men—that is, marines—were needed to defend the cogs, and Italian states were able to reduce the required ratio of fighting men to sailors. The cog even contributed to a decline in piracy in the Mediterranean since it was hard to capture. It also contributed to a rise in the importance of state navies. Among the modifications tried by Mediterranean shipwrights was the addition of a triangular lateen sail, fitted on a second mast, to the square rig of the cog. With both fore-and-aft as well as square sails the cog, or carrack, as the new type came to be called, was much more maneuverable. It could sail under more varied conditions, which increased its usefulness in wartime.

Guns had appeared on ships as early as the thirteenth century, but they were largely antipersonnel weapons that were used alongside crossbows until the sixteenth century. In the north, especially, guns were just for hurling missiles at enemy sailors. At the end of the fifteenth century heavy siege guns found their way to the main decks of the new type of full-rigged large cargo ship. Such armament made it possible to sink an enemy vessel, even if with difficulty. As the guns were improved and increased in number, warships became distinct from cargo ships. With all those guns warships could no longer function economically as cargo carriers in peacetime except possibly on the most dangerous routes, where freight rates were very high. Since merchants found it increasingly difficult to maintain warships, governments had to take on the full responsibility for supplying sailing fighting ships just as they had earlier with oared galleys. That process, which began in the closing years of the fifteenth century, came to fruition in the seventeenth.

The distinction between warships and cargo ships came much earlier in the south, and thus so did the establishment of permanent departments of state to look after the navy. Guns on galleys, located at the bow, combined with changes in rowing made those vessels into pure warships. The Italian maritime republics and, in imitation, the Iberian kingdoms had permanent if small naval forces. As in the north, those states had the problem of rapidly expanding their fleets when hostilities began. But they had the advantage of having larger merchant fleets on which to draw. Realizing the need for defensible naval ships, fifteenth-century states often subsidized the construction of vessels that could be used in wartime. The laws of the states helped admirals to impress such ships when needed. The long naval struggle between Genoa and Venice for dominance of Mediterranean trade, the attacks by pirates from the Barbary coast, and the incursions into the Atlantic by competing Iberian states created an almost unending need for navies in southern Europe in the closing years of the Middle Ages. The fall of Constantinople in 1453 to the Ottoman Turks introduced a new naval threat from the East.

Neither that threat nor the increasing use of guns on board made for sudden changes in navies, in tactics, or in naval organization. Admiralties and arsenals had existed for centuries and even had their origins in the naval institutions of the early medieval Byzantine Empire. The administrative structures continued to exist and to produce navies for the states of the Mediterranean. The copies of those institutions in Iberia and northern Europe supplied and maintained the heavily armed sailing fighting ships that in the course of the sixteenth century would ultimately sweep away established navies and naval powers in the Mediterranean and shift the center of maritime strength to northwest Europe.

BIBLIOGRAPHY

Hélène Ahrweiler, *Byzance et la mer* (1966); Hélène Antoniadis-Bibicou, *Études d'histoire maritime de Byzance* (1966); George F. Bass, ed., *A History of Seafaring Based on Underwater Archaeology* (1972); Anton Wilhelm Brøgger and Haakon Shetelig, *The Viking Ships: Their Ancestry and Evolution*, Katherine John, trans. (1951); Frederick W. Brooks, *The English Naval Forces, 1199–1272* (1932); Eugene H. Byrne, *Genoese Shipping in the Twelfth and Thirteenth Centuries* (1930); Fredric L. Cheyette, "The Sovereign and the Pirates, 1332," in *Speculum*, **45** (1970); Carlo M. Cipolla, *Guns and Sails in the Early Phase of European Expansion, 1400–1700* (1965); Philippe Dollinger, *The German Hansa*, D. S. Ault and S. H. Steinberg, trans. and ed. (1970); John E. Dotson, "Jal's *Nef X* and Genoese Naval Architecture in the Thirteenth Century," in *The Mariner's Mirror*, **59** (1973); John F. Guilmartin, *Gunpowder and Galleys* (1974); Evelyn Jamison, *Admiral Eugenius of Sicily: His Life and Work* (1957); Frederic C. Lane, *Navires et constructeurs à Venise pendant la Renaissance* (1965), "The Crossbow in the Nautical Revolution of the Middle Ages," in David Herlihy, Robert S. Lopez, and Vsevolod Slessarev, eds., *Economy, Society, and Government in Medieval Italy: Essays in Memory of Robert L. Reynolds* (1969), and *Venice: A Maritime Republic* (1973); Charles de La Roncière, *Histoire de la marine française*, 2nd ed. (1909–1932); Archibald R. Lewis, *Naval Power and Trade in the Mediterranean, A.D. 500–1100* (1951), and *The Northern Seas: Shipping and Commerce in Northern Europe, A.D. 300–1100* (1958); Archibald R. Lewis and Timothy J. Runyan, *European Naval and Maritime History, 300–1500* (1985); Michael E. Mallett, *The Florentine Galleys in the Fifteenth Century* (1967); Louis Nicolas, *Histoire de la marine française*, 2nd ed. (1961); Michael Prestwich, *War, Politics, and Finance Under Edward I* (1972); John H. Pryor, "Transportation of Horses by Sea During the Era of the Crusades," in *The Mariner's Mirror*, **68** (1982), and "The Naval Architecture of Crusader Transport Ships," in *The Mariner's Mirror*, **70** (1984); Timothy J. Runyan, "Ships and Mariners in Later Medieval England," in *The Journal of British Studies*, **16** (1977); Geoffrey V. Scammell, *The World Encompassed: The First European Maritime Empires, c. 800–1650* (1981); Richard W. Unger, *The Ship in the Medieval Economy, 600–1600* (1980), and "Warships and Cargo Ships in Medieval Europe," in *Technology and Culture*, **22** (1981).

RICHARD W. UNGER

[See also **Admiral; Bow and Arrow/Crossbow; Cannon; Hanseatic League; Hundred Years War; Ships and Shipbuilding, Mediterranean; Ships and Shipbuilding, Northern European; Sicily, Kingdom of; Venice; Warfare, Western European.**]

NAVIGATIO SANCTI BRENDANI. See **Irish Literature: Voyage Tales.**

NAVIGATION: INDIAN OCEAN, RED SEA. Navigation in the Indian Ocean is known to have connected China and the Malay Archipelago with the Near East and Africa from before the Christian era. Chinese navigators and merchants seem to have discovered the advantages of the transoceanic trade fairly early, sending their ships as far as the East African coast. The island of Ceylon played an important role on this route, with Sabaean traders using it as a way station for trade passing through the Strait of Malacca and Sumatra to the Persian Gulf. It is known that Nestorian Christian and Armenian merchants also participated in the trade with Southeast Asia, but there is much less known about who captained and manned the boats they traveled in. A notable decline in the trade exchange is recorded around the advent of Islam. In 651 an Arab embassy was sent to China, however, and in the same century the latter found its representation in the Muslim geographical view of the world as the head of the bird whose breast was in the Middle East (later, the bird image changed its direction, and its beak became the Red Sea). Under the Abbasids (750–1258) the trade picked up spectacularly. It is believed to have followed two main itineraries, one for China and her goods, for example, musk, porcelain, and silks, and the other for the west coasts of Sumatra and Malaya, for example, aromatic woods. In exchange the ships carried eastward ivory, metal goods, cloth, and African slaves. They also carried horses from Arabia and Iran to the Indian ports. The nature of the trade exchange remained fairly constant for centuries, and in time pepper, perfumes, and other luxury items were added to the list of goods traded.

The voyages of the Near Easterners who profited from the monsoons (earlier known to the Chinese) started either in Aden or in the harbors of Sīrāf (destroyed by an earthquake in 977), Sohar, or Hormuz in the Persian Gulf, and lasted about eighteen months, until the ships returned with the westbound monsoons. The same merchants often went south, along the East African coast, where a large number of ports handled the transfer of goods. Neither the trade nor the transportation were seemingly monopolized. By the appearance of the Portuguese in the 1490's, a multitude of small states or city-states around the whole of the Indian Ocean thrived on their maritime trade.

Navigation in the Red Sea is equally old and has been known through Greek and other pre-Muslim sources. It differed from the oceanic navigation, in that boats traveled only by day and stayed close to the shoreline. The travel distance of the sea was known to be thirty days. The traditional exchange included Egyptian wheat and copper, and regular items of the transoceanic trade. The advent of Islam added a considerable seasonal flow of passengers, which has been growing ever since. Pious Muslims performed their pilgrimage to the holy cities of Arabia, making Jidda a lively port. The latter was also the point of merchandise transfer to and from transpeninsular caravans.

From the navigational point of view, the Red Sea was tricky and demanded exceptional skills because of contrary winds, currents, and submerged reefs. The southern tip of the Sinai Peninsula was particularly feared because of the meeting of winds from the gulfs of Suez and Aqaba. According to a legend, the same area had a magnetic mountain, hence making local shipbuilders refrain from using iron parts, and in fact, ships plying the Indian Ocean were made of planks sewn together without being nailed.

The Arabic ships, or dhows, often two-masted, were at most about thirty meters long and four meters deep (underwater), and could carry perhaps up to 200 tons of cargo. The shape of the sail evolved from square to almost triangular (lateen), which was useful both close to the shore and in high seas. One more sail, the makeshift topsail or the Indian sail, may be assumed to be in use for the same time. The rigging was fairly developed but no detailed account exists now. Once the sail was hoisted, the yard was made firm to the mast by tightening a truss and parrel surrounding both mast and yard. The latter was always raised and lowered according to the strength of the wind; reefing was unknown. The rudder was lashed to the sternpost or, probably, attached to it, as in the

Muslim merchant ship on the Persian Gulf. Note the stern rudder, iron grapnel anchor, Arab passengers, and apparently Indian crew. Miniature by al-Wāsiṭī from the *Maqāmāt* of al-Ḥarīrī, 1237. PARIS, BIBLIOTHÈQUE NATIONALE, MS ARABE 5847, fol. 119v

Ḥarīrī miniature, making it a true stern one. Two types of anchor, of stone and of iron, were in use. A small boat was another piece of the ship's equipment, which also included a vessel for holding fresh water, a binnacle, a lead line, a latitude-measuring board, a compass box, and an astrolabe.

All this equipment was in the hands of the captain and his crew, which could be subdivided into as many as eleven categories. It was thought a captain ought to possess many nautical skills and to be well versed in astronomy; since he had to sail his ship day and night, he was expected to know the sky nomenclature by heart. The captain seems to have been a professional and a member of a kind of class of pilots, not being accepted into the merchant class. He would usually be contracted by the shipowner to perform numerous duties from the correct fitting of the ship and inspection of the gear to the supervision of the stores and loading. He would be responsible for anything missing as well as for the crew and passengers, including their physical safety, health, and personal rights. The contract ended only on his return with goods from the other end of the itinerary. In case of shipwreck he stayed with the ship, hoping only for God's mercy. His duties were formulated in the maritime laws of

 NAVIGATION: WESTERN EUROPE

Maḥmūd Shāh of Malacca (1488–1530) and hence preserved.

Maps and navigational aids and manuals were practical materials and hence in heavy use; only a few have been preserved. Three names of pilots survived, from the late fifteenth and sixteenth centuries: Aḥmad ibn Mājid, Sulaymān al-Mahrī, and Sidi ᶜAli Çelebi. The last was the commander of the ill-fated Turkish Indian Ocean fleet, attacked and scattered in 1553, and, being a latecomer, relied heavily on his Muslim predecessors. The former two were practical pilots in the Red Sea and Indian Ocean. Aḥmad ibn Mājid is thought by some to have guided Vasco da Gama from Africa to India; a nameless Gujarati Muslim is preferred for this role by others.

BIBLIOGRAPHY

Arabic texts have appeared in the facsimile editions of Gabriel Ferrand (in his unfinished series *Instructions nautiques et routiers arabes et portugais des XVᵉ et XVIᵉ siècles,* 3 vols. [1921–1928]) and those of T. A. Shumovsky, *Tri neizvestnye lotsii Akhmada ibn Madzhida, arabskogo lotsmana Vasko da Gamy* (1957) and in the printed edition of Ibrāhīm Khūrī (in his series *al-ᶜUlūm al-baḥrīya ᶜinda al-ᶜArab* [1970–1972]). Gerald R. Tibbetts translated one work by Aḥmad ibn Mājid and published it with copious commentaries as *Arab Navigation in the Indian Ocean Before the Coming of the Portuguese* (1971, repr. 1981), and a collection of excerpts from various works as *A Study of the Arabic Texts Containing Material on South-east Asia* (1979). Tibbetts' works complement and partially supersede the pioneering work by Gabriel Ferrand, *Introduction à l'astronomie nautique arabe* (1928), and may be contrasted with a survey by T. A. Shumovsky, "Arabskoe moreplavanie," in *Ocherki istorii arabskoi kultury V–XV vv.* (1982). See also reviews of Khūrī and Tibbetts by Paul Kunitzsch in *Der Islam,* **51** (1974) and **56** (1979).

S. A. SHUISKII

[See also **Astrolabe; Navies, Islamic; Ships and Shipbuilding, Red Sea and Persian Gulf; Trade, Islamic.**]

NAVIGATION: WESTERN EUROPEAN. European navigation often began where narrow coastal strips were bordered by mountains. This was true of the ancient Greeks, the Norwegians from the ninth century on, the Genoese and the inhabitants of Amalfi in the eleventh century, the Basque, Cantabrian, and Galician coasts in the twelfth century, and the Portuguese region in the fourteenth. The inhabitants of these narrow strips that were either infertile or overpopulated were forced to take to the sea. Navigation along these shores began with fishing and short voyages from one settlement to another. The sea routes, however, were also useful for carrying heavy products, such as grain, which had to be imported where the soil was not very fertile. Thus economic considerations affected the development of maritime trade routes. Prices, exchange rates, and opportunities for gain all played a role in determining the cargoes to be carried, and these cargoes varied with the economic and political situation. Capes, straits, and islands helped to determine the trade routes, and also the types of ships. The nature of the cargo to be carried also influenced ship design.

Navigation was at first coastal, for there was no way to determine the correct route when out of sight of land. Gradually sailors learned by experience something about the meteorology, the climate, and the hydrology of their region. This understanding of the signs given to the sailor by the sea and the sky made voyages on the high seas possible. By the eleventh century Norwegians knew enough about the winds and currents of the North Atlantic to reach North America, after having reached Iceland in the ninth century and Greenland in the tenth. In the fourteenth century Genoese navigators in the service of Portugal were able to use the trade winds to discover the Canaries, Madeira, and the Azores, and to return safely after these long voyages. It was only later that navigation by intelligent guesswork was replaced by scientific navigation through the use of specially designed instruments.

A regular network of sea routes was first established in the eastern Mediterranean. It was based on the many islands, peninsulas, and bays of the region, each of which offered shelter and indicated the ship's position. Down to the time of the crusades ships from the Greek, Syrian, and Egyptian coasts continued to follow these traditional routes. It was in the eastern Mediterranean that maritime customary law, codified later as the law of Rhodes, took form and spread to Rome, and later to Byzantium and the West. The Greeks and the Carthaginians reached Spain early, in the eighth century B.C., and the east and west coasts of the Mediterranean were closely connected by shipping under the Roman Empire. At the end of the empire, however, activity in the western part of the sea dwindled. Byzantium then controlled a network of eastern sea routes, while the Islamic sailors of

NAVIGATION: WESTERN EUROPE

Genoese merchant ships. Miniature (illustrating "salt water") from the *Tacuini sanitatis of Ibn Buṭlān*. Lombard, *ca.* 1390. VIENNA ÖSTERREICHISCHEN NATIONALBIBLIOTHEK CODEX SER. NOV. 2644, fol. 88

North Africa dominated the western routes until the time of the crusades. In the twelfth century, Amalfi, Genoa, and Venice renewed the connection between East and West, but this time the initiative came from the West. Alexandria and Beirut received many ships but sent out few. Fleets followed regular, seasonal routes. Convoys of galleys from Venice went to Egypt, Syria, Byzantium, and North Africa. At Genoa the galley was not the only type of ship used in Mediterranean trade. The cog—shorter, but deeper and better suited for cumbersome freight, kept up Genoese connections with trading posts in the Black and Aegean seas. The schedule of sailings was not as regular as that of Venice, because of differences in ship types, but on the whole there were more sailings than from Venice.

The shipping of these two Italian maritime republics connected with the caravan routes that brought silk, spices, and slaves across Asia and southern Russia, and with the North African routes that provided gold and slaves. Genoa and Venice thus controlled the distribution of Near Eastern and Oriental products in continental Europe. At first these products were landed in western Mediterranean ports, but by the end of the thirteenth century some ships went directly to Atlantic ports from Italy. Mediterranean sea routes are shown on the first marine charts (the portolanos). They followed the coasts, but at times had to cross the open sea.

In northwestern Europe, sailors from Frisia were engaged in the coastal trade from the ninth century on. They went from the estuaries of the Scheldt and the Rhine to the Baltic Sea, following the coast around Denmark. They crossed the English Channel to London and to York, where they found it easy to trade because their language was closely related to Anglo-Saxon. They also sailed up and down the Rhine and the Meuse, carrying millstones to Denmark and Flemish cloth to Sweden, Finland, and Russia. At times they went up the Rhine to Switzerland and up the Elbe to Bohemia. The Frisians stimulated long-distance Scandinavian trade. They visited Birka on Lake Mälaren and even reached Visby on the island of Gotland. Both were centers of Swedish trade, which in the tenth century reached the Caspian and Black seas by way of the Russian rivers.

The German Hanseatic League took over the Scandinavian trade after the foundation of Lübeck in 1143. By 1161 German merchants had reached Visby, and soon afterwards they were trading at Novgorod in Russia. Also, from 1188 on, large ships carried crusaders from Cologne to the Holy Land—a ship could take up to 375 passengers. This was a very large capacity for that period and shows how rapidly the quality of Hanseatic ships had improved. These ships were at first the *kiel* and the hulk. The first was a ship of a little more than twenty tons, the second somewhat less. The *kogge* (cog) soon became as large as 100 to 120 tons and was recognized as the typical transport ship of the North and Baltic seas. Tonnage grew thereafter, with a draft of three meters or so (ten–twelve feet) and a beam of eight meters (over twenty-five feet).

The Hanseatic ships were successors of those of the Vikings. The high bowsprits of the ships found at Gokstad and at Oseberg show the elegance and beauty of these ships. The first had sixteen pairs of

NAVIGATION: WESTERN EUROPE

oars and was under twenty-four meters long and over five meters wide. It drew less than one meter of water. The other was a vessel for state occasions. After the long ships of the Vikings came a ship with a broader beam, where the bridge was closer to the bow. It was still steered by a large oar on the side far aft, like its predecessors. The rear rudder appears only about the middle of the thirteenth century. As a result, the size of the ship could grow, for the manipulation of a rear rudder did not depend on the strength of one man, as did the manipulation of a side oar. The internal construction of the ship had also been modified, perhaps in imitation of the Irish coracles and the Anglo-Saxon curraghs (these were leather boats, built on the framework of the hull). This is the *kogge* of the north, the ancestor of the cog at Genoa. The Catalans also adopted this type of ship. The caravel (more like the northern ship because of its lightness) and the carrack (closer to the *kogge*) were both the result of a combination of northern and southern ship types. The hulk had become a ship with a flat bottom and a large hold. Its keel and bow were like those of the *kogge*. By 1400 these ships could carry up to 500 tons on routes going from the Baltic to the Bay of Biscay.

Genoese galleys went through the Straits of Gibraltar from 1278 on and began the regular Flemish convoy that also went to southern England. Portolano charts guided ships of various types along the routes that carried Spanish wool and salt from the bay of Bourgneuf (and later from Setúbal in Portugal). Portugal produced the ships used in the great voyages of discovery. They were all of the composite type, derived from the Italian *barinel* and the northern *kogge*, which had produced the caravel. The caravel was the kind of ship used by Columbus in his discovery of America. His navigation was based on observation of wind and water conditions and variations in the declination of the compass, and he calculated his position by observing the height of the sun at noon.

The compass was part of the nautical inheritance that Europe had received from the East, and began with the magnetized needle brought by the Arabs from China (twelfth century). This needle, floated on a thin reed placed in water, became the compass. About 1200 the needle was mounted on a pivot, and soon afterwards was attached to a card that indicated direction from north to east to south to west and back to north again. The apparatus was placed in a box mounted along the axis of the ship's keel, and thus it could indicate the course that was being followed. All these improvements were in use in the Mediterranean by about 1275.

From that time on it was possible to mark the course of the ship on a chart and so to determine its position. The charts then used showed the Mediterranean divided in half, with two circles precisely aligned. Sixteen lines radiated from the centers of these circles and represented different wind directions. At each point where a line touched the circle was an indicator of direction. This made it possible to fix the course to be followed in relation to the point of departure. These charts were called portolanos. They made no allowance for the curvature of the earth and had no indication of parallels or meridians. Even worse, on the earliest charts different regions were drawn to different scales. The general shape of the coasts of Europe represented on these charts from about 1400 on was nevertheless reproduced with little modification by cartographers clear into the eighteenth century. Since by the end of the Middle Ages the distances covered in a voyage had become much longer, tables were prepared that enabled pilots to observe how much they had deviated from the direction originally given by the compass, and thus to correct their course.

Besides these charts, which were in daily use at sea, there were much larger charts—world maps, or groups of maps combined in an atlas. These charts recorded new observations that had been noted on the portolanos by navigators. One can observe this process in the oldest edition of the atlas of the Alexandrian geographer Ptolemy (printed at Ulm in 1482). Here the different regions of the Mediterranean and the Baltic are shown much more accurately than in the original, thanks to information written down on portolanos by seamen. This combination of scholarly cartography with empirical cartography had begun long before. The discoveries of the islands of the Canaries, Madeira, and the Azores had been recorded on world maps since the middle of the fourteenth century and in the famous Catalan atlas of about 1375.

Nautical science also included the use of the astrolabe, which made it possible to determine latitude with a large degree of accuracy. Estimates of longitude were very inexact until the invention of the chronometer in the eighteenth century. For latitude, however, there were tables showing the changes in the altitude of the sun above the horizon at noon for every degree and every day of the year. Altitude could be determined by the use of the astrolabe. Both the instrument and the tables were of Arabic origin.

Thus the instruments available to Europeans when the great age of discovery began were of considerable importance. Nevertheless, one should not forget that these discoveries were made in tiny ships commanded by captains who combined the new elements of scientific navigation with a long tradition based on the experience of their predecessors.

BIBLIOGRAPHY

Anton W. Brøgger and Haakon Shetelig, *The Viking Ships: Their Ancestry and Evolution*, Katherine John, trans. (1951); Eugene H. Byrne, *Genoese Shipping in the Twelfth and Thirteenth Centuries* (1930); Abel Fontoura da Costa, *A marinharia dos descobrimentos*, 3rd ed. (1960); Gerald R. Crone, *Maps and Their Makers*, 2nd ed. (1962); Manuel Nunes Dias, *O capitalismo monárquico português (1415–1549)*, 2 vols. (1963–1964); Vitorino de Magalhaes Godinho, *L'economie de l'Empire portugais aux XVe et XVIe siècles* (1969); Jacques Heers, *Genes au XVe siècle: Activite economique et problèmes sociaux* (1961); Paul Heinsius, "Dimensions et caractéristiques des koggen hanséatiques dans le commerce baltique," in Colloque International d'Histoire Maritime, 3rd, 1958, *Le navire et l'économie maritime du nord de l'Europe du moyen âge au XVIIIe siècle* (1960); J. N. Hillgarth, *The Spanish Kingdoms, 1250–1410*, I, *1250–1410: Precarious Balance* (1976); Frederic C. Lane, *Venetian Ships and Shipbuilders of the Renaissance* (1934), and *Venice: A Maritime Republic* (1973); Erna Patzelt, *Schiffe machen Geschichte: Beiträge zur Kulturentwicklung im vorchristlichen Schweden* (1981); Geoffrey V. Scammell, *The World Encompassed: The First European Maritime Empires, c. 800–1650* (1981); Eva G. R. Taylor, *The Haven-finding Art* (1956); Richard W. Unger, *The Ship in the Medieval Economy, 600–1600* (1980).

CHARLES VERLINDEN

[See also **Astrolabe; Azores; Canary Islands and Béthencourt; Compass, Magnetic; Genoa; Gotland; Hanseatic League; Madeira Islands; Ships and Shipbuilding; Venice; Vikings.**]

NAXARAR (Parthian: **naχvadār;* Middle Iranian: *naχva;* Pahlavi: *naχust* + [Middle Iranian] *-dār*, "keeper"), a general term designating the first estate of the Armenian medieval nobility rather than a particular office. Despite some etymological difficulties, the term seems clearly derived from Iranian. It included all the members of an Armenian noble family, the *tanutēr* as well as the *sepuhs*. As members of the hereditary nobility, the *naχarar*s were autonomous dynasts and equal *de jure*. In the early Middle Ages they resisted all the efforts of the Armenian Arsacid kings to impose their authority over them. In later periods the *naχarar*s recognized the ultimate suzerainty of the crown, but their centrifugal tendencies manifested themselves unabated to the end of the medieval period.

BIBLIOGRAPHY

Hrač^c^eay Ačaryan, *Hayerēn armatakan baraṙan*, III, 2nd ed. (1977), 420–421; Nikolai Adonts, *Armenia in the Period of Justinian*, Nina G. Garsoïan, ed. and trans. (1970); Émile Benveniste, "Titres iraniens en arménien," in *Revue des études arméniennes*, 9 (1929); Cyril Toumanoff, *Studies in Christian Caucasian History* (1963), 115–116 n. 188, 130–131 n. 229.

NINA G. GARSOÏAN

[See also **Armenia, Social Structure; Arsacids.**]

NAXČAWAN (Greek: Naxuana; Arabic: Al-Nashawa; modern Naχiǰewan or Nakhichevan), city on the Araks River some 78 miles (125 kilometers) southeast of Dwin, known from antiquity through its inclusion in Ptolemy's *Geography* (V, xii, 5), although the Arab historian al-Balādhurī attributed its construction to Xusrō I Anōšarwān. It was usually considered to be part of the Armenian province of Vaspurakan, although it stood on the north bank of the Araks.

Naχčawan was an important trade center on the east–west highway crossing Armenia, and was probably a city of some importance by the fourth century, if the figures on the population deported from it at the time of its capture by the Sasanians in 364 are any indication. The main period of its importance, however, appears to have come after the Arab conquest, when its strategic position in the valley of the Araks made it both a garrison town and an administrative center. The Armenian Bagratid kings retook Naχčawan on occasion, and its grant alternately to the princes of Vaspurakan and of Siwnik^c^ by King Smbat I at the end of the ninth century aroused the antagonism of both. For the most part, however, the city remained a Muslim emirate and the seat of a deputy of the Arab *ostikan* of Armīniya residing in Azerbaijan. As such, it presented a perpetual threat to central Armenia. Thus, it was to Naχčawan that the Armenian *naχarar*s were summoned by its governor at the order of the *ostikan,* on the pretext of a muster, and exterminated in 705/706. Despite its overwhelmingly Muslim domination, however, the population of Naχčawan seems to have remained predominantly native, since the Arab geographer Ibn Ḥawqal relates that the language of the city was still Armenian in the tenth century. In the later medieval period, Naχčawan passed into the hands of various Muslim dynasties, though it withstood the attack of the Daylamites in 1021. The city benefited from the presence of the Shaddadids at nearby Dwin, and a final spate of building activity took place there during the early thirteenth century, in the period of Zakᶜarid rule.

BIBLIOGRAPHY

Al-Balādhurī, *The Origins of the Islamic State,* Philip K. Hitti, trans., I (1916, repr. 1968), 307, 315, 330; Heinrich Hübschmann, *Die altarmenischen Ortsnamen* (1904, repr. 1969), 455; Hakob Manandyan, *The Trade and Cities of Armenia,* Nina G. Garsoïan, trans., 2nd rev. ed. (1965), 86–87, 133, 184; Aram Ter Ghewondyan, *The Arab Emirates in Bagratid Armenia,* Nina G. Garsoïan, trans. (1976), 62, 67, 70, 72–73, 76, 78, 94, 100–103, 120–121, 131.

NINA G. GARSOÏAN

[See also **Araks River; Bagratids, Armenian; Balādhurī, al-; Dwin; Naχarar; Ostikan; Sasanians; Shaddadids; Siwnikᶜ; Smbat I; Vaspurakan; Xusrō I Anōšarwan; Zakᶜarids.**]

NAXOS, DUCHY OF. The duchy of Naxos was established in the wake of the Fourth Crusade, when the island was captured by the Venetian Marco Sanudo. He took a number of other Aegean islands and set up a duchy that he ruled from 1207 to 1227, keeping about eleven islands for himself and giving the rest in fief to other Venetians, who did homage to him. His descendants ruled the duchy until 1383, first as vassals of the Latin emperor of Constantinople, then of the Villehardouin princes of the Achaea, and finally of the Angevins of Naples and Taranto. In 1418 the islands were taken by the Ottomans, who deposed the last Christian duke in 1566 and set up the Jewish dynasty of the Nasi. The duchy was extremely prosperous during the thirteenth and much of the fourteenth century and attracted many Westerners, for whom a Latin cathedral was built.

BIBLIOGRAPHY

Kenneth M. Setton, "The Latins in Greece and the Aegean from the Fourth Crusade to the End of the Middle Ages," in *Cambridge Medieval History,* IV, pt 1 (1966).

LINDA C. ROSE

[See also **Latin Empire of Constantinople; Nasi.**]

NECHTAN (*d.* 732). Of the four Pictish kings of this name, the last, Nechtan, son of Derile (sometimes called Nechtan IV by historians), is the best known and apparently also the most important. Having succeeded his brother Brude (or Bridei) in 706, he was largely responsible, in the wake of the Synod of Whitby (*ca.* 664), for the introduction of the Roman Easter tables and the Roman tonsure into Pictland. Sometime after the war with the Northumbrians in 711, he wrote to Ceolfrid, abbot of Monkwearmouth and Jarrow, for learned advice on the matter, as well as for masons to build a stone church to be dedicated to St. Peter. After the Columban church at Iona had also accepted the Roman observance in 716, Nechtan, in the following year, expelled those of the Irish clergy who had presumably refused to join in this acceptance, across Drumalban (*dorsum brittanniae*) into Dalriada, according to the Annals of Ulster. This decision may have been influenced by the threat posed by an increasing number of incomers from Dalriada. Having (unwillingly?) retired into religious life in 724, Nechtan was, in 726, imprisoned by Drust; he briefly recovered the throne in 728 and was ultimately defeated by Óengus mac Fergus in 729. He died, probably an old man, in 732. While his name is most frequently quoted in its Gaelic form, Nechtan, its Pictish equivalent was Neiton.

BIBLIOGRAPHY

Marjorie O. Anderson, *Kings and Kingship in Early Scotland* (1973, 2nd rev. ed. 1980).

W. F. H. NICOLAISEN

[See also **Celtic Church; Picts; Scotland: History; Whitby, Synod of.**]

NECKHAM, ALEXANDER (1157–1217). The English scholar and educator Alexander Neckham (or Neckam) was born at St. Albans. He was probably educated in the abbey school of St. Albans, and then taught for a while in the local grammar school of Dunstable. In the late 1170's he went to Paris to complete his studies. He must have been a very eager student, for after completing the arts course he learned a good deal about law, theology, and medicine. He was teaching at Paris in 1180, but returned to England about 1186 and again taught at Dunstable. He became a canon of the Augustinian house at Cirencester and was elected abbot in 1213.

Neckham was in love with words, definitions, and lists of scholarly works. His *De nominibus utensilium* is concerned with ordinary utensils and the details of ordinary living. For example, he writes about mules, harnesses, saddles, horseshoes, and carts, the equipment needed for a scriptorium (a room where manuscripts were copied), the techniques of a goldsmith, the structure of a castle, the proper furnishing of a church, and the tools and equipment of a peasant household. His *De naturis rerum* is more encyclopedic. For example, he writes about strange animals (parrots, monkeys), the seven liberal arts, the game of chess, medicine (bathing is good for the health), the new type of plow, astrology, and Vergil as a magician, drawing a moral wherever he can.

Neckham also wrote a summary of Latin grammar and a verbal commentary on the Bible. Finally, he compiled a list of books that should be read by scholars in almost every field of study, a list that clearly reflects the interest of teachers in the late twelfth century. The classics still have a permanent place, while translations from the Arabic in science and mathematics are not as numerous as these would have been a century later. Altogether, however, the list shows a wide range of interests, as do Neckham's other works.

BIBLIOGRAPHY

Charles H. Haskins, *Studies in the History of Mediaeval Science,* 2nd ed. (1927), 356–376; Urban T. Holmes, *Daily Living in the Twelfth Century* (1952), which includes paraphrases and translations of most of the *De nominibus utensilium.*

JOSEPH R. STRAYER

[See also **Castles and Fortifications; Encyclopedias, European; Fables; Fables, French.**]

NEIDHART "VON REUENTAL" (*ca.* 1190–1240). The Middle High German court poet traditionally known as Neidhart von Reuental is not attested in the historical records of his time. Information about his life must therefore be culled from the sixty-five lyric poems (songs) that nineteenth-century editors determined to be his oeuvre. We have learned to read the Middle High German court lyric as literature no less fictional than, say, the courtly romance. Statements that used to strike scholars as autobiographical utterances must therefore be scrutinized in the light of the imaginary world of Neidhart's poetry. This world centers on the amorous adventures of a village knight, living among uncouth peasants, who is called "der von Reuental" after the country manor he owns. Finding the historical Neidhart is complicated by the fact that he became a figure of folklore, known as "Sir Neidhart Fuchs (Neidhart the Fox), the Peasant Foe." By the fourteenth century—when his remains were allegedly transferred to a tomb attached to St. Stephen's Cathedral in Vienna (actually built for a bishop named "Fuchs")—Neidhart's mythical life had evolved into a full-scale legend, storied enough to fill a comic novel.

The questions begin with his name. Scholars now believe that Reuental (vale of grief) was a fictitious place-name befitting the downtrodden manor that serves the knight of the poems as base of operation. Yet Reuental does occur in (later) historical records as a name for monastic retreats. One of these lay near Landshut in Bavaria, long held to be Neidhart's native province. Moreover, Reuental is not mentioned in the songs that Neidhart apparently wrote in Austria. This leads one to believe that Reuental was somehow attached to circumstances of the first half of Neidhart's life.

We know, at any rate, that the poet was known to his contemporaries as Sir Neidhart (Hêr Nîthart). Wolfram von Eschenbach calls him by this name in his William of Orange epic (*Willehalm*) of about 1220. Since Wolfram's bantering comments refer to a major topic of the so-called Winter Songs, constituting the bulk of Neidhart's work, we can assume that Neidhart had, by about 1220, emerged as a major and widely known poet.

Neidhart wrote two poems with references to events of campaigns of 1217–1219 during the Fifth Crusade. Speaking in "the stance of the crusader" (*kriuzliet*) was, by 1217, an established form of court poetry. We cannot be certain, therefore, that Neidhart himself traveled to the Near East (Egypt)

NEIDHART "VON REUENTAL"

as a member of those expeditions. Yet by dispatching "his messenger" to Landshut (*sage ze Landeshuote*) in one of the crusading songs, he does seem to be addressing a court in which he had an interest. Landshut castle was, in the 1220's, the main residence of Duke Ludwig I of Bavaria. It is therefore possible that Neidhart was attached to this court during the first decades of his career. It is unlikely that he spent his entire career at the Austrian court (as Olive Sayce has intimated). We would, in that case, expect the allusions to events affecting Lower Austria to have started earlier than 1234 and to have covered a longer time span (the last datable reference is 1237).

Frederick II, duke of Austria (1230–1246), had the reputation of being a big spender. A songsmith of sorts, he drew to his court (at Klosterneuburg and Wiener Neustadt) professional poets in search of patrons (Reinmar von Zweter, Tannhäuser, Bruder Wernher). Neidhart wrote a number of strophes in which he both asks and thanks Duke Frederick for gifts. It was likely Frederick's largess (*milte*), then, that attracted him to the Austrian court, causing him to leave an earlier patronage shortly after 1230 (most likely in Bavaria).

His appeals to the generous hand also suggest that Neidhart, like Walther von der Vogelweide, depended on his poetry to earn a living. Since we do not find persons of aristocratic birth becoming professional poets in his time, we can assume that Neidhart was not born to the landed gentry.

In the manuscript attestation of Middle High German poetry, Neidhart is second only to Walther (twenty-seven manuscripts, complete or partial). The textual transmission is more long-lived than Walther's, extending over three centuries, from the *Carmina Burana* codex (*ca.* 1230/1240) to the last edition of the chapbook *Neithart Fuchs* (1566), a narrative fashioned from mainly spurious song texts.

In contrast to minnesong, which has come down to us, anthology fashion, in collective codices, Neidhart's poems were mainly gathered and handed down in separate manuscripts. The compilers of the great collections of the southwest (manuscripts *A*, *B*, and *C*) had limited access to his work. We owe our knowledge of the "courtly Neidhart" to the first of such separate manuscripts, the Riedegg manuscript (Berlin-Dahlem, Staatsbibliothek Preussischer Kulturbesitz, MS Germ., fol. 1062). It was compiled about the same time (*ca.* 1300) as *A*, *B*, and *C*, but in the distant southeast, in Lower Austria, Neidhart's home in his last decade.

Hêr Nîthart depicted as the peasant foe of legend raising his arms in the oath of denial to protest his innocence (modeled on the capture of Christ in Gethsemane). Miniature from the Manesse Codex, Zurich, *ca.* 1300–1340. HEIDELBERG, UNIVERSITÄTSBIBLIOTHEK COD. PAL. GERM. 848, fol. 273r

Curiously new and dissonant, Neidhart's songs proved to be popular comic fare, widely augmented and imitated by nameless minstrels for at least a century after his death. This caused the corpus to be gathered in separate, "collected works" manuscripts. The largest of these, the "complete Neidhart" of around 1465 (MS *c*, probably Nuremberg), contains some 132 song texts. About eighty-three of these are considered imitations, known by the generic term *Neidharte*. The new Salzburg editorial project will reclaim some of these as authentic Neidhart.

Neidhart's poetry is essentially a parody of the kind of minnesong that had been in high fashion at the courts for two generations. To be appreciated, Neidhart must be read in the context of the Middle High German minnesong or love lyric.

Like most parodists, Neidhart works with inversion. He turns the world of the minne canzone (from the Romance canso) upside down, thus creating a counterform that appears to have quickly become popular as dancing songs at court. It is a counterform in two variations: the Summer Songs, introduced by the animated landscape of May (trees, grasses, flowers, songbirds), and the Winter Songs, beginning with briefer images of a countryside laid waste by winter's onslaught. These "nature introductions," of which Neidhart is the master in Middle High German, are based on the medieval Latin lyric.

In the Summer Songs, the lofty Lady of the canso—the embodiment of virtue, in beauty and expectations unapproachable—is replaced by an amorous peasant lass who is bent on putting on her finery in order to dance with the "Knight of Reuental" under the village linden. The guardians of court morality (*huote, merkaere*) are here turned into the girl's relentless mother or her equally coarse-spoken girl friend, whose chaperoning zeal extends to the physical. Envy plays a part because in other songs both mother and companion are themselves game to go frolicking with the handsome seducer, the Knight of Reuental.

The first two sections of a typical Winter Song (barren landscape, complaints about the cruel and fickle Lady) read like a minne canzone. Yet in the third (and main) section we find ourselves, suddenly, in the village, privy to the irregular affairs of boorish peasants (*dörper*), antipodes to the gentlemen-courtiers (*ritter*) of minnesong. The cultivated speaker (singer) of the canso—whose self-discipline is the very source of self-improvement—is turned by Neidhart into a rusticated squire, and a frustrated one to boot. For the "Lady" he desires is actually a lascivious country girl. Attentive to nature and kind, she prefers to bestow her affections on sturdy peasant lads, who in dress and arms pass themselves off as knights. It is a world gone topsy-turvy.

Much ink has been spilled trying to explain the origin of Neidhart's Summer and Winter Songs. It may be sufficient to regard them as parodistic inversions of traditional minnesong, popularized as dance tunes. If prototypes are needed, one might, with Olive Sayce, view the Summer Songs as "an individual refashioning of a native tradition of summer and dancing songs," and see the Winter Songs (more complex metrical forms, influenced by the didactic lyric) as "probably a new development, created as a deliberate counterpart to the summer songs" (p. 233). Neidhart may have derived the impetus for both forms from the pastourelle, a song type—often performed at dances—most popular in northern France. Framed by the bucolic setting of pastoral poetry, the pastourelle features a knight, charming but duplistic, who tries to seduce a witty and well-spoken shepherdess. More often than not, he does not succeed.

Neidhart is the first Middle High German poet for whose oeuvre a substantial number of melodies have survived. The manuscripts contain musical notations for some fifty-six songs. Yet most of these (thirty-nine) are imitative *Neidharte.* Only seventeen melodies belong to texts (two Summer Songs, fifteen Winter Songs) traditionally regarded as authentic Neidhart. Since more than a century passed before the extant notated manuscripts began to be compiled (the oldest, the Frankfurt fragment O, dates from about 1350), it is likely that the melodies had undergone considerable changes. Our transcriptions would seem to preserve little more than the outlines of the tunes conceived by Neidhart.

BIBLIOGRAPHY

Sources. The standard edition is Edmund Wiessner and Hanns Fischer, eds., *Die Lieder Neidharts,* 4th rev. ed. by Paul Sappler, and melodies ed. Helmut Lomnitzer (1984). See also Siegfried Beyschlag, ed., *Die Lieder Neidharts* (1975), including translations into modern German; Frederick Golden, trans., *German and Italian Lyrics of the Middle Ages* (1973), 151–173; Helmut Lomnitzer, ed. and trans., *Lieder von Neidhart von Reuenthal* (1966).

Studies. Olive Sayce, *The Medieval German Lyric, 1150–1300* (1982); Eckehard Simon, *Neidhart von Reuenthal* (1975), may serve as an introduction, with English translations of some of Neidhart's poems. There is also a record: *Lieder und Reigen des Mittelalters, Neidhart "von Reuenthal,"* sung by Eberhard Kummer, on Schallplatten der Fa. PAN-Ges., Wien, PAN 170 005 (1986).

ECKEHARD SIMON

[See also **Carmina Burana; German Literature: Lyric; Middle High German Literature; Minnesingers; Pastourelle; Walther von der Vogelweide; Wolfram von Eschenbach.**]

NENNIUS. A prologue found in five extant medieval manuscripts of the Welsh-Latin *Historia Brittonum* attributes the text to one Nennius, an otherwise unknown writer. None of these manuscripts antedates 1164, and the primary Harleian recension of the *Historia Brittonum* (compiled in 829–830 and best represented by British Library, MS Harley 3859) is anonymous. Despite the textual evidence, repeated efforts have been made to connect Nennius with the original compilation. The prologue in question, however, can now be shown to date from around 1050.

BIBLIOGRAPHY

David N. Dumville, "'Nennius' and the *Historia Brittonum*," in *Studia celtica*, **10–11** (1975–1976).

R. WILLIAM LECKIE, JR.

[See also **Arthurian Literature; Historia Brittonum.**]

NEOPLATONISM is a modern term employed to describe the form of Platonism that flourished from the time of Plotinus (205–270) until 642, when the Arab conquest brought an official end to the school of Alexandria (although it survived unofficially in some form for a number of decades afterward). In this specific sense, "Neoplatonism" is the expression used to distinguish this species of Platonism from other types, such as "the Old Academy," "the Middle Academy," "the New Academy," and "Middle Platonism." In relation to these characteristics of Neoplatonism in the strict sense one can then discover Neoplatonic sources, tendencies, and antecedents in earlier philosophers, and notice influences, followers, and disciples in later philosophers and theologians. Thus the term Neoplatonism can be expanded: Its broader definition includes elements of middle Platonism, Stoicism, Neo-Pythagoreanism, and Plato himself on the earlier side and Gemistos Plethon, Marsilio Ficino, Giovanni Pico della Mirandola, the Cambridge Platonists, and Thomas Taylor on the later side.

PLOTINUS AND HIS FOLLOWERS

The attempt to forge a more consistent form of Platonism, initiated by Plotinus, was an effort to go beyond the tensions of Middle Platonism, as its adherents strove to balance the establishment of an orthodox Platonism with eclectic tendencies to incorporate Aristotelian and Stoic thought into their world view. In relation to the Neoplatonism which succeeded them, the teachings of Middle Platonism were characterized by flux and a lack of a persuasive consistency, despite efforts at unification. Plotinus, the founder of what we call Neoplatonism, may have had predecessors for a number of his ideas in Antiochus of Ascalon (*ca.* 130–68 B.C.), the teacher of Cicero and Varro, or in the Stoic Posidonius (*ca.* 135–31 B.C.), or the neo-Pythagorean Numenius of Apamea (*ca.* 150–200), but none of these men pushed Platonism to the degree of unity we find in Plotinus himself, the most famous pagan student of Ammonius Saccas, an Alexandrian teacher (175–242).

Nevertheless, the efforts made toward a greater unity by Plotinus in the six books of nine treatises called the *Enneads* (*ennea* means *nine*) do not offer a pure Platonism. His is a masterful attempt to incorporate Aristotle (as interpreted by Alexander of Aphrodisias in the second century A.D.), as well as Middle Platonic, Stoic, and neo-Pythagorean elements, into a newly interpreted Platonic metaphysical and psychological structure. Just as the *Enneads* does not offer a pure Platonism, neither does it offer a formal system in a modern sense of the term. Reality for Plotinus is ultimately inexpressible in written or spoken words, although, as he treats particular philosophical questions, he attempts to come closer to what is ultimately ineffable, and to explain why it is not expressible. Read against the background of his Middle Platonic predecessors, he is, however, a more synthetic thinker, both in dealing with individual issues and in his overall view. The succeeding history of Neoplatonism, as well as a fair evaluation of the movement, together point to the many strings he left untied.

From a pedagogical viewpoint one may say that the study of reality for Plotinus begins with what appears to be most real, the sensible objects in the outside world. He then attempts to lift us from this lower life by showing us the unsubstantial aspects of these objects that seem most real and to lead us on the road to a fuller, simpler, and more unified understanding, as we search through different stages for the ultimate source and explanation of the reality we experience at each stage. The ultimate term or goal of the journey is the first hypostasis: the One.

From a metaphysical viewpoint the One or first hypostasis is also the starting point in Plotinus' philosophy (*Enneads* VI.9.1): "It is in virtue of unity that beings are beings." Yet the One itself is not a being: "Strictly no name is apt to it, but since name it we must there is a certain rough fitness in designating it as unity, with the understanding that it is not the unity of some other thing" (VI.9.5). Such negations as Plotinus applies to the One are not the normal negations we apply to things in our experience; they are denials of whatever is opposed to the One's perfection, especially a denial of all multiplicity.

From the One necessarily emanates, like an overflowing fountain or a bright light, a second substantial reality or second hypostasis which is not the One; this is Intelligence (*Nous*). The "world" of Intelligence is the domain of the Forms. Yet, Plotinus stresses the unity of this "intelligible world." Perhaps a good way of grasping the unity of the intelligible domain in contrast to the next lower level is in Plotinus' own comparisons of Intelligence and reason or eternity and time. Intelligence is akin to insight: We see something all at once. Reason follows a different pattern: We go from one step to another or reason from one object to another. Likewise, in the Plotinian contrast between eternity and time we find another indication of the contrast between Intelligence and the next lower hypostasis. Time is successive; knowing temporally is knowing objects in succession. The character of the world of Intelligence is not marked by this type of succession and distinction. The intelligible world is one in which the Intelligence grasps the Forms of species and individuals in a single timeless vision.

The third hypostasis, or Soul (*Psyché*), is also a necessary emanation, flowing forth from Intelligence. Some knowledge of Soul's nature has already been indicated: It is connected with succession and time. It is the connecting link between the intelligible world of Forms and the sense world of matter. For Plotinus there are, in a sense, two World Souls: (1) the higher Soul standing near to the intelligible world of the Forms and having no contact with the sense world; (2) the lower Soul, the real Soul of the world we perceive with our senses. Another name for the lower Soul is Nature.

Our individual human souls proceed from the World Soul and are likewise divided into two elements: (1) a higher soul, which is more akin to the world of Intelligence, and (2) a lower soul, connected with our body. In particular passages Plotinus at times might employ different tripartite divisions, but his general tendency seems to depend on viewing man as focusing either on the things above or on the things below. The great danger for the human soul is that it may "tend" or care too much for bodily things and so forget the pure Forms.

Thus the material world, which, in terms of Plotinus' overall image of light, is like the trailing off of light's radiation toward dimness and darkness, has the lowest reality. As darkness it is evil, but not as a positive force; rather it is *steresis*, sterility or poverty—a lack of light, true unity, and goodness. Just as the human soul can give too much attention to the material world, so also is it, in a sense, the source of moral evil.

Plotinus' philosophy is not only a metaphysics. It is also a discipline, a call to salvation, an invitation to a return to the divine or the One through mystical union. Plotinus holds that happiness is possible in this life, and that it is found in the assimilation of the individual human higher soul to the One through virtue (I.2). The expression "by virtue" underscores the discipline that purifies the lower soul from its attachment to the world of sense and turns the higher soul's attention toward the intelligible world. From the intelligible world the higher soul must climb ultimately to the source of both the Soul and Intelligence, to union with the One.

The immediate influence of Plotinus is found in three disciples. Eustochius made an edition of his master's works, which is now lost. Amelius Gentilianus' few innovations are noted by later Neoplatonists: In stressing the unity of all souls and their kinship with Intelligence, he attenuated the distinction between hypostases, while also introducing new distinctions within each hypostasis as well as new Forms. By far the most influential of Plotinus' immediate disciples, and his successor in Rome, was Porphyry of Tyre (*ca.* 232–*ca.* 304), who has provided us with most of our information about the master in his *Vita Plotini* and with the key to his philosophy in his edition of the *Enneads*. Besides providing sources, he also provided direction. His simplified version of Neoplatonism influenced both pagans and Christians and established the form of Neoplatonism the West would know until Pseudo-Dionysius the Areopagite was translated in the ninth century. Porphyry developed the moral and ascetic side of Neoplatonism, incorporating moral doctrine and discipline from neo-Pythagorean sources. His efforts to relate his philosopher to nonphilosophers led him to consider popular religions more seriously.

Like the Stoics, Porphyry interpreted the myths allegorically; but he limited theurgy, and this grudgingly, to the beginning stages of salvation for those unable to pursue philosophy straight off. His *Letter to Anebo* shows his critical attitude toward popular religion and his *Against Christians* attacks Christianity for its lack of rationality, its doctrines of the Incarnation and a suffering God, and its belief in Jesus' miracles. It is Porphyry who seems to have introduced the *Chaldean Oracles* (a late-second-century representation in mythical form of the active character of divine goodness, of the unifying power of love, and of the role of sacraments in the purification of the soul) into Neoplatonism, perhaps to compete with the Christian Bible as a sacred book. He likewise provided a commentary that reconciled the enigmatic *Oracles* with his philosophy. His most influential work in the West, however, was the *Isagoge* (Introduction) to Aristotle's *Categories*. It shows his openness to Aristotle, at least on the level of logic. The influence of this Neoplatonic interpretation of Aristotle's categories was extensive, especially in the Latin West before the twelfth- and thirteenth-century translations of the *Logica nova* (that part of the *Organon* which includes the *Prior Analytics*, the *Posterior Analytics*, the *Topics*, and the *Sophistical Refutations*) and Aristotle's nonlogical works. Through Boethius (*ca.* 480–524/526) it sparked the early medieval debate over the nature of universals between realists and nominalists.

Porphyry's principal student was Iamblichus (*d. ca.* 326), who founded his own school in his native Syria, and whose influence in the Greek-speaking world paralleled that of Porphyry in the West. He initiated some basic innovations that were developed in the schools of Athens and Alexandria.

Plotinus himself in the *Enneads* speaks of the divinity of the Soul in the phrase "raised to Godhead, or better, knowing its Godhead . . . " (VI.9.9). His early followers, Amelius Gentilianus, but less surely Porphyry, in removing the barriers between the different types of souls (such as divine, human, and animal) and stressing the kinship with Intelligence also pointed to the divine character of the Soul. Iamblichus went in a dramatically different direction: He stressed the distinction between the different types of souls. The human soul in its essence is, for Iamblichus, in a state of sin and misery and lacks the pretended perfection ascribed to it by Plotinus and his earlier followers. He stressed its intermediary character in order to point out its imperfect character. The human soul participates "at the same time in the higher and lower; it is neither permanent, nor completely changeable" (*De anima*). His interpretation of the earlier Neoplatonic principle that "everything is in everything" underscored the qualifying addition "but only according to its own level."

Parallel to his view of the human soul was his view of salvation. The *De mysteriis* challenged the earlier Neoplatonists who advanced the view that philosophy alone could save, or at best admitted theurgy only at the beginning stage of a process that depended essentially on philosophy. For Iamblichus, theurgy played a more important role in achieving the vital union of man with the gods. Ritual actions do not work magically, since the manipulation of the superior by the inferior is never possible, but they work because of the voluntary gift of divine power. Salvation ultimately comes not through the soul's own power but through the divine will.

These new directions initiated by Iamblichus demanded a different reading of the Platonic texts, the *Chaldean Oracles*, and the traditional myths. One of Iamblichus' most important contributions toward the systematization of Neoplatonism was his push for a consistent interpretation of these Neoplatonic sources. He developed an official curriculum for reading the dialogues of Plato, starting with the simpler *Alcibiades I*, *Gorgias*, and *Phaedo*, and working up to what he judged to be the more difficult and more important *Timaeus* and *Parmenides*. He also tried to establish exegetical principles for interpreting his Neoplatonic sources based on the purpose of the text (was it theurgic or philosophical?). If philosophical, he asked to what branch of philosophy it belonged (ethics, physics, and so on). In parallel ways he attempted to develop a more consistent reading of the traditional myths and thus to get beyond the more arbitrary interpretations of Plotinus and the moral interpretations of Porphyry.

Iamblichus was not very successful in his immediate students. His main disciple, Aedesius of Cappadocia, began a theurgic school at Pergamum, but contributed little that was new. Another pupil, Theodorus of Asine, became, at least to some degree, a rival, as he went back to Plotinus' position that there is an unfallen level of the soul. One of Aedesius' students, Maximus of Ephesus, became a counselor to the emperor Julian the Apostate (*r.* 360–363). He provided him with a theology of Neoplatonism via Iamblichus as an intellectual weapon in his war to reestablish ancient pagan religion. But this came to naught when Julian's other weapons failed. Iamblichus had to wait for the Platonic schools of Athens and, to a lesser degree, of Alexandria to have his efforts bear fruit.

When Plutarch of Athens (*d.* 433) became head of Plato's Academy, the Academy became Neoplatonic. Among his successors before it was closed by Justinian in 529, the most famous was Proclus (410–485). Besides his commentaries on such Platonic dialogues as the *Timaeus* and *Parmenides* Proclus also wrote the very influential and most tightly systematic of all Neoplatonic works on metaphysics, *The Elements of Theology,* and the likewise systematic *Platonic Theology.* For the most part he carried on the Iamblichean form of Neoplatonism, completing what Iamblichus had left unfinished. One Proclean contribution was the doctrine of henads (or unities), which were horizontal emanations within the first hypostasis. The Iamblichean inspiration for this innovation may be found in the role such a doctrine plays in the religious dimension of this type of Neoplatonism. It permitted Proclus to place the traditional polytheistic worship on a more philosophical basis as he set up his parallel between the henads on the level of the first hypostasis and the traditional gods in the mythical world. He could provide each god with a philosophical meaning.

In dealing with the Christian religion, he imitated Porphyry and attacked it vehemently. One of the principal forms of the attack was in opposition to the Christian view of creation: It consisted in a defense of the eternity of the world. It was answered by a sixth-century Christian Neoplatonist of Alexandria, John Philoponos.

The Alexandrian school of Neoplatonism had many close ties with the Athenian school, to a great extent because of Ammonius, son of Hermias—its head in the late fifth and early sixth centuries—who had studied with Proclus at Athens. Yet the circumstances of the schools differed. The Alexandrian school was less independent financially and politically. The students and teachers tended to study in a more uninvolved scholarly way, gave their efforts frequently to Aristotle's less disturbing works, and seemed willing to make necessary compromises. Both Christians and pagans were members of the school, and its eventual and smooth change to a Christian head after Olympiodorus (*fl.* sixth century) gave it a longer life than the Academy (closed in 529), which it outlasted by more than a century (until 642). The Alexandrian school counted among its leaders the famous Aristotelian commentators Ammonius, Philoponos, and Simplicius (*fl.* early sixth century), whose commentaries, under all their Aristotelian surface, bring with them a great deal of Neoplatonic substance.

CHRISTIANITY AND NEOPLATONISM IN THE PATRISTIC PERIOD

If we leave aside the late Neoplatonic school at Alexandria, strict Neoplatonism throughout its history was decidedly anti-Christian from beginning to end. Plotinus' attacks against the Gnostics (*Enneads* II.9) were meant for Christian Gnostics and on some points for all Christians. The attacks of Porphyry and Proclus are legendary; and Julian the Apostate's battle with Christianity was inspired enough by Maximus of Ephesus that it cost the latter his life. Even the more toned-down Neoplatonic school of Alexandria had its moments of eruption, as can be seen late in its history when Simplicius answered Philoponos' attack on Proclus' arguments for the eternity of the world. On this more technical level we can find numerous doctrinal conflicts, as when emanation is defended against creation, or Jesus' miracles are contested, or the crucifixion of God is ridiculed.

Yet despite this antagonism between Neoplatonism and Christianity, elements from each entered into the other's world. The adoption of the *Chaldean Oracles* by Neoplatonism and the growth of its religious system were positive responses to the appeal being exercised by Christianity. On the other hand, Neoplatonism had a strong influence on Christianity in both the Eastern and Western churches.

If we stay with our strict definition of Neoplatonism we must be careful in making precise claims for Neoplatonism in the early Christian East. Authors like Gregory of Nazianzus (*ca.* 330–389/390), Basil the Great (*ca.* 330–379), and Gregory of Nyssa (*ca.* 335–*ca.* 394)—known as the Cappadocian Fathers—are very strongly connected with Origen, the Christian contemporary of Plotinus who studied with him under Ammonius Saccas. Influences from Origen should more strictly be connected with Middle Platonism. However, Basil's probably authentic *On the Spirit* is inspired by Plotinus, and so are many of his later works. Nemesius (*fl. ca.* 390), the author of *On the Nature of Man,* who was for a long time confused with Gregory of Nyssa, likewise knew Plotinus, since he attacks his view of man in the opening chapter of this work.

In dealing with the Western church similar caution is needed in separating Middle Platonic and Neoplatonic influences. Gaius Marius Victorinus (*fl.* fourth century) translated a number of Neoplatonic treatises and also employed Porphyrian notions in his attempt to provide a systematic explanation of the Trinity through the triad of Being-Life-Thought (*esse, vivere, intellegere*), risking thereby a charge of modalism on the part of Christians and of a misuse of philosophy on the part of Neoplatonists.

St. Augustine himself informs us in his *Confessions* (VII.9.13) that he read "certain books of the Platonists translated from the Greek" (by Marius Victorinus). Scholars of the "Cassiciacum dialogues" conclude that these were a number of treatises of Plotinus and quite likely the *Sentences* of Porphyry. Certainly in many of his works he manifests a detailed knowledge of Porphyry; and no less certainly does he at times use certain treatises of Plotinus' *Enneads.*

Boethius likewise knew the Neoplatonists. This is evident from his commentary on the *Isagoge* of Porphyry (which Marius Victorinus had translated) and also by the numerous references to Porphyry in his commentary on Aristotle's *Categories* and his second more elaborate commentary for *On Interpretations*. The influence of Alexandrian Neoplatonism is present not only in his focus on the less contentious elements of logic, but also in his treatment of the divine knowledge of future contingents, which he borrowed from the reflections of the Alexandrian Neoplatonic commentator Ammonius concerning *On Interpretations,* found in *The Consolation of Philosophy.*

Since Boethius was the source (through translation and commentary) of much of the *Logica vetus* (that part of Aristotle's *Organon* containing the *Categories* and *On Interpretation*), which played an important part in the liberal arts curriculum of monastic, cathedral, and palace schools, and since Augustine was the chief teacher for studies going beyond that preparatory curriculum, the presence of Neoplatonism, especially, but not exclusively, of the Porphyrean variety, was guaranteed in the Christian West.

MEDIEVAL INFLUENCES

Although Justinian closed the anti-Christian Neoplatonic school of Athens in 529, its influence was still felt through a collection of four Greek works (*The Divine Names, Mystical Theology, The Celestial Hierarchy,* and *The Ecclesiastical Hierarchy*), which were purported to have been written by Dionysius, who was baptized after listening to St. Paul's sermon in the Areopagus (Acts 17:34). In fact these forged works, which contain a great deal of Proclean Neoplatonism, were written in the late fifth or early sixth century, though many in the East and West gave them almost apostolic respect. Their authenticity was challenged as early as 532 by Hypatius of Ephesus, and some of their teachings were contested and needed defense. The defenses of authenticity and teaching came in the commentary of John of Scythopolis in the sixth century and in the two books entitled *Ambigua* written about 630 by Maximus the Confessor. These works of Pseudo-Dionysius the Areopagite and the *Ambigua* of Maximus had their greatest influence in the Latin West, where they were translated by John Scottus Eriugena, under the commission of Charles the Bald, between 860 and 862. Eriugena knew he had a new kind of Platonism in these works, far different from the Platonism he had himself inherited from the West. In his own work, *De divisione naturae,* he attempted to bring together the new Proclean and old Porphyrean strains of Platonism bequeathed to him with the Middle Platonism he inherited from Origen. Through John Scottus Eriugena's translations and personal work Neoplatonism took on a new life in the Latin West.

Just as the influence of the Neoplatonic Academy at Athens continued beyond its closure through Pseudo-Dionysius, so the influence of the Alexandrian school of Neoplatonism survived the conquest by the Arabs. It did so in two ways. One of its late members, Stephanus, moved to Constantinople, where he became head of the Imperial Academy. Mainly through commentaries on Aristotle's works he fostered the development of a Neoplatonized Aristotelianism. Constantinople continued to be important in the propagation of Neoplatonic thought, especially in the work and thought of Michael Psellos (*d. ca.* 1078), Nikephoros Gregoras (*d.* 1360), and Georgios Gemisthos Plethon (*d.* 1452), who played such a vital role in the establishment of the Platonic restoration at the court of the Medici. The other means by which Alexandrian Neoplatonism survived was through the efforts of Christian teachers in Alexandria itself. The school of Alexandria endured in altered form until the early eighth century and then moved in turn to

Antioch; around 900 it journeyed again, this time to Baghdad, where al-Fārābī (*d.* 950) studied under Christian Neoplatonic scholars.

Neoplatonic influences in the Muslim world were especially strengthened by two further forgeries: the *Book Concerning the Pure Good (Liber de expositione bonitatis purae),* also called the *Book of Causes (Liber de causis),* and the *Theologia Aristotelis* (Theology of Aristotle). Both were attributed to Aristotle. In fact, the contents of the *Theologia Aristotelis* are borrowed from Plotinus' *Enneads,* IV–VI. The *Liber de causis* was discovered to be a non-Aristotelian work by Thomas Aquinas after he studied William of Moerbeke's 1268 translation of Proclus' *Elements of Theology.* He realized that the ultimate source of the forged work had to be Proclus. Following in the footsteps of many other thirteenth-century authors, however, he did not hesitate to write a commentary on it. Before their importance in the Latin world, and certainly before they were discovered to be forgeries, they had a very great influence on medieval Moslem thinkers. Such works seemed to give a religious dimension to Aristotle and thus made him more attractive to religious minds. They also, however, created many difficulties for those who tried to reconcile the two Aristotles (or rather, Aristotle with Plotinus and Proclus). One can imagine difficulties such as that raised in chapter 3 of the *Theologia Aristotelis,* which provides Plotinus' refutation of Aristotle's doctrine of the soul.

Muslim philosophers and theologians as broadly diverse in their thinking as Ibn Sīnā (Avicenna, *d.* 1037), al-Ghazālī (*d.* 1111), and Ibn Rushd (Averroës, *d.* 1198) all had to wrestle with this quagmire; when they tried to be Aristotelian they were still being Neoplatonic, and when they tried to escape Aristotle they were still held unknowingly by Plotinus and Proclus.

In the Jewish medieval world Neoplatonism showed up principally in the Spanish Arabic philosopher Solomon ben Judah ibn Gabirol (Avicebron, *d.* 1058). His principal work was translated into Latin as *Fons vitae* (Fountain of Life) about 1150. It is an avowedly Neoplatonic work, which gained some recognition through its interpretation of Plotinus' intelligible matter in the Latin West, but survived in the Hebrew world mainly through the *Zohar,* or the principal work of the cabala. Franciscan authors of the thirteenth century followed the position of Avicebron regarding intelligible matter and claimed to be following the tradition in the West. Was their appeal to tradition an appeal to the middle of the preceding century or was this most famous doctrine of Avicebron already in earlier forms of Neoplatonism? Answers to this and many other questions of the meaning of representing the traditional viewpoint depend on a close investigation of the stages of influence of Neoplatonic thought.

NEOPLATONISM AND THE LATIN WEST IN THE SCHOLASTIC PERIOD

The twelfth and thirteenth centuries in intellectual history are known for the "invasion of Aristotle." His *Logica nova* and all his nonlogical works were translated into Latin during this period. This dramatic situation can, however, be deceiving. For Aristotle's works entered a world that was, philosophically speaking, Middle Platonic and Neoplatonic. Boethius and Augustine, principally, were early guarantors of the Neoplatonic influence, which was of a Porphyrian form that was marked appreciably by Christian belief. Then the Proclean form of Neoplatonism entered with the translations of the works of Pseudo-Dionysius. Both forms were reinforced by John Scottus Eriugena and the school of Chartres, although John's influence was attenuated later by the condemnation of his two followers, David of Dinant and Amalric of Bène, in 1210. Twelfth-century translations, such as the one of Avicebron's *Fons vitae* and the *Liber de causis,* added another dimension of Neoplatonism. The translators of Aristotle's commentators, especially the strongly Neoplatonic Avicenna, and the gradual arrival of Greek Neoplatonic commentators from Alexandria and Constantinople brought not only Aristotle but new elements of Neoplatonism as well. All of these inheritances had to be assimilated along with Aristotle and his more Aristotelian commentators. It was, therefore, not only an Aristotelian invasion, but also a continually diversified Neoplatonic invasion. The Neoplatonic influence was not so new in the Latin West as that of Aristotle; it had been going on in stages since the time of Marius Victorinus, but it was nonetheless diversified at each stage. It also continued in the diverse Neoplatonic and Christian Neoplatonic influences on Meister Eckhart (*d. ca.* 1328), Heinrich Suso (*d.* 1366), Johannes Tauler (*d.* 1361), and Nicholas of Cusa (*d.* 1464).

Nor did it come to an end with the "rediscovery"

of Plato by the Renaissance. The translations of Marsilio Ficino's Platonic Academy included Plotinus, along with a commentary; and Giovanni Pico della Mirandola attempted to go beyond Ficino's aim of reconciling the Platonic and Chaldean traditions with Christianity. Pico added the Jewish cabala to the traditions he wished to reconcile in the list of 900 theses he proposed to demonstrate. Florentine Platonism was richly Neoplatonic, not pure Plato. Nor was Renaissance Platonism the only cultivator of new Neoplatonic sources during this period. Those who pursued Aristotle translated and employed commentaries with a strong Neoplatonic flavor, such as Simplicius' commentary on the *De anima* of Aristotle. Neoplatonism thus had a very complex history in the medieval and Renaissance West.

BIBLIOGRAPHY

Arthur H. Armstrong, ed., *Cambridge History of Later Greek and Early Medieval Philosophy* (1967, repr. 1970); Werner Beierwaltes, *Proklos: Grundzüge seiner Metaphysik* (1965); Émile Bréhier, *The Philosophy of Plotinus,* Joseph Thomas, trans. (1958); Eric R. Dodds, "Theurgy and Its Relation to Neoplatonism" in *Journal of Roman Studies,* 37 (1947); Ernest L. Fortin, *Christianisme et culture philosophique au cinquième siècle* (1959); Étienne H. Gilson, *History of Christian Philosophy in the Middle Ages* (1955); Pierre Hadot, *Plotin, ou la simplicité du regard* (1963), and "Ouranos, Kronos, and Zeus in Plotinus' Treatise Against the Gnostics," in H. J. Blumental and R. A. Markus, eds., *Neoplatonism and Early Christian Thought* (1981); Paul Henry, *Plotin et l'occident* (1934); Jean Pépin, *Théologie cosmique et théologie chrétienne* (1964); Plotinus, *The Enneads,* Stephen MacKenna; trans., 4th ed. rev. by Bertram S. Page (1969); H.-C. Puech, "Plotin et les Gnostiques," in *Les sources de Plotin* (1960); John M. Rist, *Plotinus: The Road to Reality* (1967); Laurence J. Rosán, *The Philosophy of Proclus* (1949); R. T. Wallis, *Neoplatonism* (1972); Thomas Whittaker, *The Neoplatonists,* 4th ed. (1928, repr. 1961).

STEPHEN F. BROWN

[See also **Aristotle in the Middle Ages; Augustine of Hippo, St.; Basil the Great, St.; Boethius; Eckhart, Meister; Gemistos Plethon, Georgios; Ghazālī, al-; Gregory of Nazianzus, St.; Gregory of Nyssa, St.; Nikephoros Gregoras; Origen; Philosophy and Theology; Plato in the Middle Ages; Psellos, Michael; Pseudo-Dionysius the Areopagite; Rushd, Ibn; Sīnā, Ibn; Solomon ben Judah ibn Gabirol; Suso, Heinrich; Victorinus.**]

NERI DI FIORAVANTI (*fl.* 1340–1384), Florentine architect and sculptor who vaulted the Sala del Consiglio Generale in the Bargello (1340–1346). In 1349 he worked with Benci di Cione in Or San Michele, and on the church now known as S. Carlo dei Lombardi. A document of 5 January 1351 places Neri and Francesco Talenti among subcontractors working on the campanile of the Duomo. Neri also took part in plans for completing the Duomo. A guild member, he sponsored Orcagna's application to join the Masons' Guild in 1352.

BIBLIOGRAPHY

Wolfgang Braunfels, *Mittelalterliche Stadtbaukunst in der Toskana* (1953), 212, 232; Walter Paatz, "Zur Baugeschichte des Palazzo del Podestà (Bargello)," in *Mitteilungen des kunsthistorisches Instituts in Florenz,* 3 (1931); Marvin Trachtenberg, *The Campanile of Florence Cathedral: "Giotto's Tower"* (1971), 78, 111, 113.

BRUCIA WITTHOFT

[See also **Florence; Orcagna; Talenti, Francesco.**]

NERSĒS I THE GREAT, ST. (*ca.* 310–*ca.* 373), great-great-grandson of St. Gregory the Illuminator and patriarch of Armenia. The dates of his pontificate have been confused by the irreconcilable claim of Armenian sources that it lasted thirty-four years, by the chronological inaccuracies of the *Epic Histories* attributed to P^{c}awstos Buzand, and by the occasional identification of Nersēs with his contemporary Basil of Caesarea. The dates most widely accepted at present are 353–373.

Like all the members of the Gregorid house, Nersēs was seen by his contemporaries as the hereditary heir to the patriarchal dignity, although this office had been declined by his father and his own early training had been military, leading to the office of *senekapet* (royal chamberlain). With the restoration of order in Armenia at the accession of Aršak II (*ca.* 350), however, the patriarchate returned to the Gregorid house, and Nersēs was consecrated at Caesarea in Cappadocia like his predecessors.

Throughout his pontificate Nersēs was the dominant figure in Armenia. He seems to have served as royal ambassador to the Byzantine court in 358, and as arbiter between the king and his *naχarars.* His main activity, however, was naturally devoted to the church, in which he introduced a number of Greek usages. A council called under his presidency at Aštišat formally regularized ecclesiastical doctrine and customs. Implementing its decisions, Nersēs is especially renowned for his creation of extensive monastic and charitable institutions, as well as schools, throughout Armenia. These were closely supervised by patriarchal deputies.

Following the tradition of his family, Nersēs opposed the growing Arianism of his time. This policy soon brought him into conflict with Aršak II, who followed the religious tendencies of the Constantinopolitan court, and led to Nersēs' long exile (359–364) along with other orthodox bishops, and eventually to his murder at the instigation of King Pap, whom he had helped restore to the Armenian throne after the deportation of Aršak in 364, but whose policies the patriarch also censured and opposed. According to the Armenian sources, the bishops assembled at Caesarea, outraged by Nersēs' murder, refused to consecrate the successor designated by Pap, breaking the link between the Armenian church and Caesarea. Nersēs' death came shortly before Pap's murder in 374; thus the persistent Armenian tradition that has Nersēs attending the Council of Constantinople in 381 has no foundation in fact.

BIBLIOGRAPHY

Norman Baynes, "Rome and Armenia in the Fourth Century," in *English Historical Review,* **25** (1910), repr. in his *Byzantine Studies and Other Essays* (1955); Gérard Garitte, *La Narratio de rebus armeniae* (1952), 57, 61–62, 74–75, 382, 402, 406, 417–418, 420; Nina G. Garsoïan, "Politique ou orthodoxie? L'Arménie au quatrième siècle," in *Revue des études arméniennes,* n.s. **4** (1967), "Quidam Narseus—A Note on the Mission of Saint Nersēs the Great," in *Armeniaca* (1969), and "Sur le titre de *protecteur des pauvres,*" in *Revue des études arméniennes,* n.s. **15** (1981); H. Gelzer, "Die Anfänge der armenischen Kirche," in *Bericht über die Verhandlungen der königlichen sachsischen Gesellschaft der Wissenschaften zu Leipzig,* Phil.-hist. Klasse (1895); Josef Markwart, *Die Entstehung der armenischen Bistümer* (1932), 152–233; Malachia Ormanean, *Azgapatum,* I (1912), 163–222.

NINA G. GARSOÏAN

[See also **Arianism; Aršak II; Gregorids; Katholikos; Naχarar; P^cawstos Buzand.**]

NERSĒS II AŠTARAKAC^cI (BAGREWANDAC^cI), *kat^cołikos* of Armenia (*ca.* 548–557). The increasing proselyting of the Nestorians in Armenia led him to an extensive correspondence with orthodox ecclesiastics in Syria and Persia in which he condemned the Council of Chalcedon and the *Tome* of Pope Leo I. The activity of the *kat^cołikos* culminated in the calling of one or two councils that met at Dwin between 551/552 and March 555 at which he presided, assisted by the bishops Meršapuh (or Neršapuh) Mamikonean and Peter of Siwnik^c. The Council of 555 anathematized the Nestorians, whom it identified with the local heresy of the Paulicians (although this has been questioned by some scholars), but not explicitly with the Council of Chalcedon, as has often been asserted. The council promulgated a number of canons and bound itself by an oath of union, all of which have been preserved. The "Canons of Nersēs and Neršapuh" were subsequently incorporated into the official *Canonbook* of the Armenian church.

BIBLIOGRAPHY

Paul Ananian, "Patmakan yišatakaran mə Duini II žołovk^ci masin," in *Pazmaveb,* **115** (1957) and **116** (1958); Gérard Garitte, *La Narratio de rebus armeniae* (1952), 154–175, 429; Nina G. Garsoïan, *The Paulician Heresy* (1967), 87–90, 132–133, 236–238; *Kanonagirk^c Hayots^c*, Vazgen Hakobyan, ed., I (1964), 475–490, 638–640; Malachia Ormanean, *Azgapatum,* I (1912), 535–555; Karekin Sarkissian, *The Council of Chalcedon and the Armenian Church* (1965), 6–8, 12–13, 15, 214–215.

NINA G. GARSOÏAN

[See also **Armenian Church, Doctrines and Councils; Katholikos; Leo I, Pope; Mamikonean; Nestorianism.**]

NERSĒS III IŠXANEC^cI (Šinoł) (Nerses the Builder), kat^cołikos of Armenia (641–661) at the time of the first Arab invasions who sought to maneuver between the Byzantine Empire and the newcomers. His Greek education seems to have turned his sympathies primarily toward Byzantium, and he was suspected of Chalcedonian sympathies by his contemporaries because of his support of Monothelitism. He attempted to placate Emperor Constans II and, perhaps against his will, he received Communion with the Greek bishops during Constans II's residence at Dwin in 652–653. Fearing possible retaliation, he then sought refuge in Tayk^c and did not return to Dwin until the administration of Hamazasp Mamikonean, named *curopalates* of Armenia in 658 at his request. Nevertheless, the Council of Dwin, at which he presided in 648, rejected the Byzantine religious position embodied in the *Type,* and Nersēs seems to have collaborated at least temporarily with Theodore Ṙštuni in negotiating the treaty between the Armenians and the Arabs in 652.

As is evidenced by the epithet *šinoł* (the builder) commonly given to him, Nersēs III was especially known for his building activities. He restored the martyrium of St. Sergios at Dwin, destroyed by the Arabs, and erected a number of other religious monuments, of which the most famous is the tetraconch Church of the Heavenly Host (Zwartᶜnocᶜ) near Ējmiacin, together with an adjoining residence for the *katᶜołikos,* parts of which are still visible.

BIBLIOGRAPHY

Gérard Garitte, *La Narratio de rebus armeniae* (1952), 338, 339, 432; René Grousset, *Histoire de l'Arménie* (1947), 296–304; Stepᶜan Kh. Mnatsᶜakanian, *Zvartnots* (1971); Malachia Ormanean, *Azgapatum,* I (1912), cols. 707–742; Joseph Strzygowsji, *Die Baukunst der Armenier und Europa,* I (1918), 108–119, 241.

NINA G. GARSOÏAN

[See also **Armenia: History of; Dwin; Katholikos; Monothelitism; Taykᶜ; Zwartᶜnocᶜ.**]

NERSĒS IV ŠNORHALI (the Graceful) (*ca.* 1100—15 August 1173), Armenian poet and *katᶜołikos,* belonged to the Pahlawuni feudal family, various members of which occupied the Armenian patriarchal see from about 1066 to 1203. Having lost their parents in their early youth, both Nersēs and his older brother Grigor were first placed under the guardianship of their grand uncle, the *katᶜołikos* Grigor II Vkayasēr, and after his death in 1105 under that of the *katᶜołikos* Barseł. In 1113 Nersēs' brother Grigor became *katᶜołikos,* while the young Nersēs continued his education in the Karmir [Red] Monastery near Kesun (modern Keysun, to the southwest of Besni), where he studied with Stepᶜanos Manuk. Among his schoolmates were Ignatios (*d.* 1160?) and Sargis (*d.* 1167?), who also bore the surname *Šnorhali,* which seems to have been an honorific given to the graduates of the Karmir Monastery. The school probably emphasized biblical exegesis, since Nersēs as well as Ignatios and Sargis were authors of commentaries.

Nersēs was probably ordained a priest in the early 1120's and thereafter spent the rest of his life in close association with his brother, Katᶜołikos Grigor III. He gradually rose to the rank of bishop and in 1166 became *katᶜołikos* himself and coadjutor of Grigor, after whose death in the same year he reigned for seven years.

Nersēs Šnorhali is especially renowned for his attempt to establish unity between the Armenian and the Byzantine churches. His correspondence with the Byzantine emperor Manuel I Komnenos (*r.* 1143–1180) and the patriarch Michael, his encyclicals and letters to the Armenian bishops of Greater Armenia and the patriarch Michael I, the Syrian, patriarch of Antioch (1126–1199) and author of the famous *Chronicle,* as well as the texts of the theological discussions with the Byzantine theologian Theorianos are still extant. All of these documents reveal a man endowed with a spirit of ecumenism. These discussions began in 1165 and were continued after Nersēs' death.

Nersēs Šnorhali is one of the major poets of medieval Armenian literature. He is well known for his skillful use of rhyme, multiple variations of metrical patterns, rhetorical devices, and new poetical forms and genres. The corpus of his poetical works includes epics, lyric poems, elegies, various types of hymns, and verses written for entertainment. Nersēs experimented with both poetical form and content, but also incorporated the rigid traditional patterns with those that he created or picked up from popular songs. His poems and hymns are among the best in the Armenian *Book of Hours* and the *Hymnal*

Among the literary accomplishments of Nersēs one must mention his role in editing the liturgical books of the Armenian church, translations of hagiographical works, and the *Lectionary.*

The theological and pastoral writings of Nersēs are distinguished by the author's ability to synthesize earlier doctrines and dogmas and to present complicated concepts in a simple but picturesque language. For centuries these works have served as textbooks and have occasionally been read from the pulpit.

According to the thirteenth-century sources, Nersēs was also an accomplished musician who wrote the music to the words that he composed. He composed hymns in the traditional tones, and songs whose rhythmic patterns suggest a popular source.

Nersēs was probably among the first writers to make use of such material.

Nersēs Šnorhali is commemorated as a saint by the Armenian church, and his name is listed with those of the holy translators.

BIBLIOGRAPHY

Sources. Works by Nersēs IV Šnorhali include: *Bank' čᶜapᶜaw* [Poems] (1928); *Jesus, Son Only-Begotten of the Father,* Jane S. Wingate, trans. (1947); *Ołb Edesioy* [Elegy on the capture of Edessa] (1973); *Vipasanut'iwn* [Epic] (1981). Other sources include: Nikoghos K. Tᶜahmizyan, *Nerses Šnorhalin ergahan ew eražišt* [Nerses Snorhali as a composer and musician] (1973); *Sancti Nersetis clajensis armeniorum catholici opera,* Joseph Cappelletti, ed., 2 vols. (1833).

Studies. Łevon Ališan, *Šnorhali ew paragay iwr* (1873); *Nersēs Šnorhali* (1977); Pōłos Ananean, "S. Nersēs Šnorhali Katᶜołikos Hayocᶜ [Saint Nersēs the Graceful, Katholikos of Armenia]," in *Bazmavep,* **131** (1973), nos. 3–4, **132** (1974), nos. 3–4, **133** (1975), nos. 3–4; H. S. Anasyan, "Nerses Šnorhalin ew 'Armat hawatoy' Žołovəcun [Nerses the Graceful and the collection called 'Root of Faith']," in *Ejmiacin* (1973), no. 12.

KRIKOR H. MAKSOUDIAN

[See also **Armenian Literature; Armenian Saints; Grigor II Vkayasēr; Manuel I Komnenos; Michael the Syrian; Music, Armenian; Pahlawuni.**]

NERSĒS LAMBRONACᶜI (Nersēs of Lambron) (1153/1154—1198), a father of the Armenian church and the archbishop of Tarsus. His father was Ōšin II (*d.* 1168), the Hetᶜumid prince of Lambron of Cilicia, and his mother was the niece of the *katᶜołikos* Nersēs IV Šnorhali. His baptismal name, Smbat, was changed to Nersēs at the time of his ordination in 1168/1169. A very serious childhood disease was the reason why the parents of Nersēs had promised to give their third child to the church. The young Nersēs received elementary education at the monastery of Skewṙa and continued his early education in the patriarchal seminary at Hṙomklay on the Euphrates. He later spent several years in the Armenian and Western monasteries on the Amanus (Nur) Mountains, where he was primarily preoccupied with scholarly pursuits, gathering materials for biblical commentaries and learning Greek and Latin.

In 1175 Nersēs became the archbishop of the prelacy of Tarsus. His academic interests, however, kept him away from his ecclesiastical post, and he continued to travel from one monastic institution to another, writing, translating, and doing research. In 1179 he participated in the Council of Hṙomklay, which had convened to discuss the question of unity with the Byzantine church. Nersēs himself, being an ardent believer in the cause, displayed an ecumenical spirit that was misinterpreted by those who opposed communion with the Chalcedonians. This as well as his own impetuous nature were responsible for his controversial reputation.

Nersēs remained in Hṙomklay until the early 1180's. After his return to Lambron he became the prior of the monastery of Skewṙa. In 1190 the Rubenid prince Lewon (Leo) II sent him to Seleucia to greet the emperor Frederick I Barbarossa. Nersēs could not meet the emperor, since the latter drowned before reaching his destination. Seven years later, Nersēs headed an embassy to Constantinople to discuss church unity with the emperor Alexios III Angelos (*r.* 1195–1203), but the dialogue with the Byzantines led to no concrete results. One of his last works in 1197 may have been signing with the other Armenian bishops the document that brought the Armenian church into union with Rome.

Nersēs is well known for his scholarship and numerous works. Among the latter there are important studies such as commentaries on the different books of the Bible; his commentary on the divine liturgy, translations of liturgical and legal texts, orations, homilies, theological treatises, poems, and hymns; and a compilation of the letters and documents exchanged between the Armenian *katᶜołikoi* and the Byzantine emperor Manuel Komnenos with editorial comments and historical information, and other authoritative editions such as the *Lives of the Egyptian Fathers* and the Holy Scriptures.

BIBLIOGRAPHY

For a complete bibliography of the works of Nersēs of Lambron and of studies about him see Nersēs Akinian, *Nersēs Lambronacᶜi* (1956).

KRIKOR H. MAKSOUDIAN

[See also **Armenian Church, Doctrines; Armenian Literature; Cilician Kingdom; Hetᶜumids; Hṙomklay; Nersēs IV Šnorhali; Rubenids; Skewṙa.**]

NESTORIANISM is the doctrine that Jesus Christ exists in two distinct, subsistent natures, one fully divine and one fully human, which are joined together without confusion in one person. The doctrine derives its name from Nestorius, the patriarch of Constantinople (428–431). Nestorius' condemnation at the Council of Ephesus (431) began the process by which, toward the end of the fifth century, Nestorianism had developed into an independent church localized within the borders of the Persian Empire. The definitive synthesis of Nestorian doctrine was achieved by Babai of Kashkar (Babai the Great) in the first half of the seventh century. Between 431 and the seventh century, Nestorianism underwent a gradual development largely in reaction to Monophysitism, its most potent rival in the Christian East.

The doctrinal tendencies that evolved into the Nestorian movement developed at the theological school of Antioch and were based on the teachings of Eustathius of Sebaste (*ca.* 300–*ca.* 377), Diodorus of Tarsus (*d. ca.* 390), and his pupil Theodore of Mopsuestia (*ca.* 350–428), who became the preeminent authority for subsequent Nestorian theologians. Theodore, following his predecessors, tended toward a literal interpretation of the Bible that was grounded in a historical, critical, and philological exegetical method. This interpretation was in contrast to, and a reaction against, the allegorical method developed by the theological school of Alexandria.

In Old Testament exegesis, this tendency made the Antiochenes reluctant to apply prophecies indiscriminately to Jesus. In the New Testament, they tended to take literally those texts that spoke of Jesus' human development and bodily sufferings. Since the Word of God, the Second Person of the Trinity, was defined as being consubstantial (*homoousios*) with the Father by the Council of Nicaea (325), the human traits mentioned in the Gospels could not be attributed to the divinity. Thus, the Antiochenes taught that there were two natures joined together in the person Jesus Christ, between which there could be no communication of attributes (*communicatio idiomatum*). It would be wrong to say that the Word of God grew in wisdom or suffered and died. Conversely, foreknowledge and miracles could not be attributed to the human nature of Jesus. The conjunction of the Word of God with human nature was not a metaphysical union but an indwelling. Only in this sense could one say that the Word became flesh. This Antiochene interpretation was taught and disseminated without arousing undue controversy. Theodore died in full communion with the church.

But controversy arose shortly, not on the level of theological speculation but in the forum of popular piety. At the end of 428, Nestorius, the patriarch of Constantinople, an Antiochene by training, began to preach that Mary should not be addressed by the title "Mother of God" (*Theotokos*). Instead, she should be called "Mother of Christ" since she bore the man but not the Word of God. The sermons drew immediate criticism and were resented especially by the ordinary believer, who had grown up revering Mary as *Theotokos.* When news of Nestorius' preaching reached Egypt, Cyril, the patriarch of Alexandria, entered the dispute, which quickly engaged the attention of the whole church. Cyril wrote to Nestorius warning him that his teaching on Mary implied heresy. Nestorius persisted in his position and attempted to win over Pope Celestine I. But Celestine was persuaded to support Cyril, whom he delegated to condemn and depose Nestorius. This action was accomplished at the Council of Ephesus in 431.

The christological disputes that began in the fifth century have often been characterized as mere quibblings over semantics, but in fact, genuine philosophical and theological differences lay behind the disputes. Grounded in Aristotelianism and a literal exegesis of the Bible, the Antiochenes tended to equate nature (*physis*) with concrete substance (*ousia*) and to distinguish it from person (*prosōpon*). For the Alexandrians, grounded in Platonism and an allegorical-mystical exegesis of the Bible, nature was an abstraction that only had meaning when the two natures were united in the subject or person Jesus Christ. Hence, Cyril could speak of "one nature of the incarnate Word," while allowing that the concrete subject was the result of a unification of two natures, human and divine, in the one person. He could then attribute all the actions of the incarnate word to this one divine-human subject. He would not allow a mere conjunction of two distinct, subsistent natures, as Nestorius seemed to be doing. As a result, for Cyril, Mary was indeed the mother of God. It appeared to him that Nestorius was positioning two persons in Christ and thus making the Trinity a quaternity. Later, Monophysites would take up this last charge and use it as a major anti-Nestorian slogan in their polemics.

Nevertheless, it would be simplistic to maintain that the christological dispute was confined to theological differences alone. Political considerations, both secular and ecclesiastical, and personal friendships and antipathies played a role. It was in the interest of Emperor Theodosius II (*r.* 408–450) to maintain the religious unity that was considered essential for preservation of unity in the empire. While satisfying both Rome and Alexandria, he was compelled to defend the prestige of the see of the capital, Constantinople. Cyril resented this prestige (as did Celestine of Rome), and he seems to have personally disliked Nestorius. His objective was the humiliation of Constantinople in the person of its patriarch. While Nestorius, reasonably secure at home, bungled his relationships with Celestine, Cyril managed to secure a virtual blank check from the pope to proceed against Nestorius. The council, convened by Theodosius II, met in June 431. Nestorius later lamented that Cyril accused and summoned him and acted as judge and bishop of Rome, in short, that he was everything (*Bazaar of Heraclides*).

With Nestorius' condemnation, the two-nature Christology seemed to be discredited. Nestorius was deposed and exiled. But the Antiochene position retained qualified support from some Syrian bishops, notably Theodoret of Cyr and Ibas of Edessa. Both men supported dialogue and reconciliation but detected Apollinarian tendencies in Cyril's one-nature Christology. Their suspicions seemed confirmed when Cyril's successor, Dioscorus, endorsed the radical Monophysitism of Eutyches at the "Robber Synod" of Ephesus in 449. This synod also condemned Theodoret and Ibas.

After the death of Theodosius II, Emperor Marcian and Empress Pulcheria, under pressure from Pope Leo I, convened another council at Chalcedon in 451. It attempted to reconcile the two-nature Christology espoused by Leo with Cyril's teachings, at the same time condemning both Nestorius and Eutyches. It also restored Theodoret and Ibas to their sees. The Nestorian party felt partially vindicated by the council's acceptance of a two-nature Christology but rejected the hypostatic union of the natures and the condemnation of Nestorius. They remained unwilling to accept the term *Theotokos* and the possibility of the mutual communication of divine and human attributes. They subsequently dubbed both Chalcedonians and Monophysites "Theopaschites" (those who say that God suffered).

After Chalcedon, attention within the empire was focused on the struggle between Chalcedonians and Monophysites. Nestorianism was outlawed and driven to the eastern frontier, with its center at Edessa. In 457, Emperor Zeno suppressed the Nestorian school of Edessa, and its faculty and students fled to Nisibis in Persian territory. In 543, an edict of Justinian I sought to definitively discredit Antiochene theology and conciliate the Monophysites by condemning the letter of Ibas to Mari, bishop of Hardashir, the works of Theodore of Mopsuestia, and the works of Theodoret of Cyr against Cyril. The Second Council of Constantinople (553) confirmed the edict and thus formally severed ties with the Nestorians.

With the founding of the school of Nisibis, Nestorianism became an essentially Syriac-speaking movement confined to the Persian Empire. The first director of the school, Narsai (*ca.* 399–*ca.* 503), was among the most illustrious of Syriac theologians. Beginning at Edessa as early as 440, he helped shape the pattern that Nestorian theology was to follow. His work consisted of biblical commentaries and hymns. He established the works of Theodore of Mopsuestia as criteria for orthodoxy. Theodore became known simply as "the Commentator." His works together with those of Nestorius and Diodorus of Tarsus were translated into Syriac. Narsai taught for about sixty years and was reputed to have had over 1,000 students. The school became a chief source of clergy for the Nestorian church. Narsai's principal supporter was Bar Sauma, bishop of Nisibis (*ca.* 420–*ca.* 490), the tireless Nestorian propagandist who succeeded in having a Nestorian, Akakios, made katholikos of Seleucia-Ctesiphon. At a synod of the Persian church (486) a Nestorian confession of faith was adopted and reaffirmed at subsequent synods.

The Nestorians never claimed that they were introducing novel doctrine. They appealed to the Fathers of Nicaea, who they said were correctly interpreted by Theodore and Nestorius. Consequently, their theology was innovative only in the sense that they sought to elucidate and simplify the thoughts of their forefathers, principally Theodore.

Narsai's contribution was to translate Nestorianism into the Syriac idiom. His hymns were a characteristically Semitic mode of expression stemming from the hymns of Bar Daisan and Ephraem. The traditions of his school were carried through the sixth century by his successors, Abraham of Bet Rabban and Paul of Nisibis. A similar school was founded in 541 at Seleucia by the katholikos Mar Aba. The synod of 585 under Katholikos Ishoᶜiabh

I officially made the teachings of Theodore the touchstone of orthodoxy. He "filled the ecclesiastical libraries with a shining treasure of doctrines" and "fought the seducers who . . . produce doctrines contrary to the true doctrine" (cited in Chabot). Whoever rejects him is excommunicated. A subsequent synod (596) reaffirmed this decree. In 612 a Nestorian profession of faith was presented to Xusrō II, probably under the supervision of Babai the Great (*ca.* 550–*ca.* 630).

Babai was the first synthesizer and systematizer of Nestorian doctrine. The necessity for such work arose as a result of his dispute with Ḥenānā, who became director of the school of Nisibis about 571. Ḥenānā rejected the exegetical method of Theodore of Mopsuestia in favor of an allegorical method based on those of Origen and John Chrysostom. He also taught that there was one nature and one hypostasis in the incarnate Word, which was the Monophysite position. To counteract such doctrines, Babai produced his principal work, the *Tractate on the Divinity and Humanity and on the Person of the Union,* and a shorter work, the *Tractate Against Those Who Say: As the Soul and the Body Are One Hypostasis, So God the Word and the Man Are One Hypostasis.* Here Babai synthesizes Nestorian belief by showing how it conforms to biblical and patristic tradition and how it best explains the divine economy of salvation, especially through the mediation of the sacraments. Babai refined Nestorian Christology down to its final definitive formula: two natures (Syriac: *kĕyānā*) and two hypostases (Syriac: *qĕnōmā*) in one person (Syriac: *parṣōpā*). His chief contribution lies in the uniquely Nestorian distinction between hypostases. In the influential *Exposition of the "Book of Centuries" of Evagrius of Pontus,* Babai interpreted spirituality and mysticism in the light of Nestorian theology. So successful was Babai's synthesis that it became the norm for subsequent Nestorian theologians. It is no exaggeration to say that the doctrine of his successors is virtually interchangeable with his own.

While Nestorian theology remained static after Babai the Great, it continued to be reexpressed to an ever-widening audience as the church's missionaries moved eastward to central Asia, India, and China. In the late eighth century, the most notable theologian was the katholikos Timothy I (780–823), who in two synods reaffirmed his church's adherence to Nestorian doctrine. The author of some 200 letters of instruction, he was also the first Nestorian on record to engage in dialogue with Islam when he expounded Christianity to the caliph al-Mahdī. His contemporary, Theodore bar Konai, whose book of *Scholia* is an important theological and philosophical source, provided valuable descriptions of heretical sects, especially Nestorianism's rival, Manichaeism. This period also marks the beginning of apologetic works produced in Arabic, culminating in the comprehensive *Conferences* (*Majālisu*) of Elias bar Shināyā of Nisibis (975–1046). In the ninth century, Īshōᶜdād of Merv produced extensive commentaries on the Bible. Without sacrificing Nestorian orthodoxy, he appears to have employed the exegetical method of Ḥenānā of Nisibis.

The last great exponent of Nestorianism was ᶜAbdhishoᶜ bar Berīkā (Ebedjesu) in the early fourteenth century. His output was vast, including biblical commentaries, works on philosophy and science, and antiheretical writings. A monumental catalog describes the works of Nestorian theologians who preceded him. He produced the last Nestorian dogmatic compendium, the *Book of the Pearl.* His death in 1318 marks the death of Syriac literature. The destruction of the Mongol khanate by Tamerlane at the end of the fourteenth century resulted in the destruction of the Nestorian centers of learning and the eventual reduction of the Nestorians themselves to a handful of refugees in the mountains of northern Iraq and Persia.

BIBLIOGRAPHY

Sources. The critical edition of the conciliar acts of Ephesus and Chalcedon, as well as related documents, including fragments of Nestorius' writing, is Eduard Schwartz, ed., *Acta conciliorum oecumenicorum,* 13 vols. (1914–1940). Jean Chabot, ed. and trans., *Synodicon orientale ou recueil des synodes nestoriens* (1902), gives the Syriac text and a translation of the extant acts of the Persian church synods, valuable sources for tracing doctrinal development. Luise Abramowski and Alan E. Goodman, eds. and trans., *A Nestorian Collection of Christological Texts,* 2 vols. (1972), contains selections from Nestorian theological texts.

Studies. For the context in which Nestorius' thought developed, see Johannes Quasten, *Patrology,* III (1960), 302–554; see also Christoph Schäublin, *Untersuchungen zu Methode und Herkunft der antiochenischen Exegese* (1974). The theological development of early Nestorianism is set forth in Jaroslav Pelikan, *The Christian Tradition,* I–II (1971–1974); and Robert V. Sellers, *Two Ancient Christologies* (1940). Arthur Vööbus, *History of the School of Nisibis* (1965), is based on much hitherto unpublished documentation. For an overview and bibliographies of the Nestorian theologians who wrote in Syriac, see Ignatius Ortiz de Urbina, *Patrologia syriaca,* 2nd ed. (1965); for authors who wrote in Arabic, see Georg Graf, *Geschichte der christlichen arabischen Literatur,* 5 vols. (1947).

D. W. JOHNSON

[See also **Byzantine Church; Chalcedon, Council of; Christian Church in Persia; Christology; Church, Early; Church Fathers; Councils, Ecumenical** (325–787); **Monophysitism; Nisibis; Syrian Christianity; Syrian Rites; Theodoret of Cyr; Theotokos.**]

NESTORIUS (*ca.* 381–*ca.* 452), patriarch of Constantinople, sometimes called the founder of Nestorianism, the movement that bears his name. He was born of Persian parents at Germanicia in northeast Cilicia. He entered the monastery of Eupreprios at Antioch, where he was ordained a priest and where he gained a reputation for preaching and writing.

Because of the rivalries that arose at Constantinople after the death of the patriarch Sisinnius, Nestorius was brought from Antioch and consecrated patriarch in April 428. He set the tone for his administration in his first sermon: "Give me, my prince, the earth purged of heretics and I will give you heaven as a recompense" (Socrates Scholasticus, *Ecclesiastical History* 7.39). He himself implemented this purging by harassing several small sects in the region of Constantinople and in Asia Minor.

Around Christmas of 428, Nestorius preached his first sermon against the use of the title *Theotokos,* Mother of God. The title of the Virgin Mary was deeply imbedded in the popular piety of the capital. But it offended Nestorius, with his background in Antiochene theology, which taught two distinct natures in Christ. The sermon aroused popular displeasure and caused Nestorius to be accused of teaching that Jesus was a mere man, in the manner of Paul of Samosata. Nestorius detected Apollinarianism in the popular piety and continued to reject the term *Theotokos.*

In 429, he compiled some of his sermons and sent them to Pope Celestine. These sermons also circulated in Egypt, where they disturbed the monks. They appealed to Cyril of Alexandria, the patriarch (412–444). He responded by defending the *Theotokos;* this letter, in turn, reached Constantinople, where it was used against Nestorius. After an initial polite exchange of letters between the principals during which neither yielded, the dispute turned ugly. For Pope Celestine, Cyril wrote *Five Books Against the Blasphemies of Nestorius* and later sent him his own sermons together with those of Nestorius, which he interpreted (or misinterpreted) in his own favor. At the same time Nestorius antagonized the pope by sheltering five Pelagian bishops whom Celestine had condemned and exiled. Celestine then condemned Nestorius and authorized Cyril to carry out the condemnation. In December 430, a synod at Alexandria condemned Nestorius, and the synodical letter to which Cyril attached twelve anathemas and the letter of Celestine were sent to Nestorius.

Neither Cyril nor Celestine operated from purely theological motives. The third canon of the Council of Constantinople (381) had granted honorary precedence to the see of Constantinople over all other sees, except Rome. This was a threat to the papacy and a humiliation for Alexandria. Cyril, with papal approval, was determined to humiliate Nestorius ecclesiastically as well as to neutralize him theologically. In the face of this, Emperor Theodosius II called a council to be held at Ephesus, which convened on 22 June 431. Without waiting for Nestorius' supporters to arrive, Cyril condemned him and ordered him deposed. On 27 June at a countercouncil, Nestorius' supporters condemned and deposed Cyril and his party. An impasse dragged on until August, when Theodosius summoned eight representatives from each side to Constantinople. As a result, Nestorius, deserted by his supporters, was condemned, deposed, and exiled to Antioch. He was subsequently moved to Petra in Arabia in 436 and finally to Egypt, first to the Khārga Oasis, then to Akhmīm, where he died sometime after 451.

During exile, Nestorius wrote two major works defending his teachings, the *Tragedy* and the *Bazaar of Heraclides.* The latter survives in an interpolated Syrian translation. The best contemporary characterization of Nestorius and his doctrine is found in Socrates Scholasticus' *Ecclesiastical History.* Some modern scholars have maintained that he did not hold the doctrines that bear his name, but two subsequent councils, Chalcedon (451) and Constantinople II (553), upheld his condemnation.

BIBLIOGRAPHY

Luise A. Abramowski, *Untersuchungen zum Liber Heraclides des Nestorius* (1963); James F. Bethune-

Baker, *Nestorius and His Teaching* (1908); Louis Duchesne, *Early History of the Christian Church*, Claude Jenkins, trans., III (1924), 313–388; Friedrich Loofs, *Nestorius and His Place in the History of Christian Doctrine* (1914); Johannes Quasten, *Patrology*, III (1960), 514–519, for extensive bibliography; Luigi Scipioni, *Nestorio e il concilio de Efeso: Storia, dogma, critica* (1974), includes updated bibliography.

D. W. JOHNSON

[See also **Byzantine Church; Celestine I, Pope; Councils (Ecumenical, 325–787); Cyril of Alexandria, St.; Socrates Scholasticus; Theotokos.**]

NET VAULT. See **Vault.**

NEUMA (neupma, pneuma; from the Greek *pneuma*, breath), an extended melisma, or unarticulated passage sung on one vowel. A considerable number of such melismas, although they were not usually sung as separate pieces, achieved a certain independence, for musical or symbolic reasons, and were inserted in, or appended to, chants other than those in which they began. The two main classes of neumae were (1) the melismas of the *echemata* and the Latin mnemonics, formulas used to demonstrate the characteristics of the eight musical modes, and (2) the melismas of the responsories and alleluias. (The term is also used for a sign indicating one or several notes in the notation used for ecclesiastical chant [probably from the Greek *neuma*, sign].)

The melismas of the demonstration melodies seem to be later additions to these formulas in both the Latin and the Byzantine churches. It is not clear whether the neumae were especially composed for the purpose in the ninth or tenth century, or whether they were borrowed from other chants. In any case, these melismas were also used very widely in the Middle Ages (and much later) to conclude certain antiphons, especially the Magnificat, the Benedictus, and the last antiphon of vespers and lauds on solemn occasions.

The use of borrowed melismas in the responsories and the custom of greatly extended neumae for the alleluias seem to date from the eighth century, and are perhaps an indication of Frankish taste and Byzantine influence. The extended neumae of the alleluias were neither borrowed melismas nor newly composed, but prolongations by means of repetitions of the usual jubili. The independence of these neumae resulted from their subsequent development, for the custom of providing words for these *longissimae melodiae* (as Hucbald called them) gave rise by the ninth century to the sequence, one of the most important poetical and musical forms of the Middle Ages; and the melismas, provided with text (and even when not), were soon sung in association with unrelated alleluias.

BIBLIOGRAPHY

Frank Harrison, *Music in Medieval Britain* (1958, 4th ed. 1980).

TERENCE BAILEY

[See also **Antiphon; Jubilus; Melisma; Musical Notation; Neume; Noeannoe; Sequence.**]

NEUME, a sign used in the notation of music, chiefly plainsong. Neumes represent one note (simple) or more (compound). Compound neumes never set more than one syllable of text. There are two further categories of neumes that indicate nuances of performance. Liquescent neumes (*semivocales*) are used for diphthongs (ae, au, eu) or consecutive consonants (re*gn*um, te*mp*lum), including those ending and beginning consecutive words (patru*m* *n*ostrorum). The liquescent note, appended to the neume, is sung for the second of the two vowels in a diphthong, or for the glottal articulation between two consonants. Ornamenting neumes represent figures as tremolos, trills, and turns, but for the most part their exact interpretations are unknown.

Four sources for the origin of neumes have been postulated, none of which has established clear superiority: (1) symbols of pronunciation in Byzantine musical notation, (2) synthetic signs in Jewish musical notation, (3) grammatical signs in Latin, (4) and Latin accentual signs.

The earliest neumes are unheighted; they are called chironomic, suggesting that they derive from hand signals used to direct a chorus. Since they show only the contour of the melody, they remind the singer of a chant already transmitted orally. The actual pitches of the melody can be determined only by comparing later versions. Sources from about 1000 use diastematic neumes, which indicate melodic intervals by the height of the neumes above

Gregorian Easter chant showing neumes with a tendency toward diastematic writing and the forms from which square notation developed. Northern France, late 11th century. BY PERMISSION OF THE BRITISH LIBRARY, LONDON, MS EGERTON 857

the text. With the addition of staff lines and clefs, later sources transmit intervals and pitches accurately. In the thirteenth century, square notation, which uses individual notes joined by lines to form ligatures, was developed. This type is used for modern chant notation. Manuscripts written before 1200 that contain polyphony use neumes borrowed from plainsong notation. The rhythmic significance of neumes is a vexed issue that has inspired great debate and is still unresolved.

BIBLIOGRAPHY

Sources. The facsimiles published by the monks at Solesmes in the series *Paléographie musicale* (1889–) and by Henry M. Bannister, *Monumenti vaticani di paleografia musicale latina,* 2 vols. (1913), are indispensable.

Studies. Valuable studies on notation are published in the introductions to the volumes of *Paléographie musicale,* particularly I, *Le Codex 339 de la bibliothèque de Saint-Gall* (1889), 96–160, and *La notation musicale des chants liturgiques latines* (1963). More recent research from Solesmes is contained in Eugène Cardine, "Sémiologie grégorienne," in *Études grégoriennes,* **11** (1970). See also Solange Corbin, *Die Neumen* (1977); *idem,* Miloš Velimirović, and Mireille Helffer, "Neumatic Notations," in *The New Grove Dictionary of Music and Musicians,* XIII (1980); Constantin Floros, *Universale Neumenkunde,* 3 vols. (1970), a detailed study of medieval Byzantine neumes; Ewald Jammers, *Tafeln zur Neumenschrift* (1965); Bruno Stäblein, *Schriftbild der einstimmigen Musik* (1975); Grégoire M. Suñol, *Introduction à la paléographie musicale grégorienne* (1935); Richard Rastall, *The Notation of Western Music* (1983);

Leo Treitler, "The Early History of Music Writing in the West," in *Journal of the American Musicological Society,* 35 (1982), and "Reading and Singing: On the Genesis of Occidental Music-Writing," in *Early Music History,* 4 (1984).

JAMES GRIER

[See also **Musical Notation; Musical Ornamentation; Neuma.**]

NEVSKY, ALEXANDER (*ca.* 1220–1263), prince of Novgorod in northwest Russia. He led that city-state's military forces in driving back the Swedes in 1240 and then the German Order of Swordbearers (the "Livonian Knights") in the famous "battle on the ice" of Lake Peipus in 1242. With northwest Russia thus threatened from the West, Nevsky counseled temporary acceptance of Tatar-Mongol rule over Russia following the Mongol invasion of 1240. Made grand prince of Vladimir in 1252, Nevsky often interceded successfully in favor of Russia with his Mongol overlords. Nevsky's military and political actions eventually brought him recognition as a national hero and a saint of the Orthodox church.

BIBLIOGRAPHY

John Fennell, *The Crisis of Medieval Russia: 1200–1304* (1983); A. E. Presniakov, *The Formation of the Great Russian State* (1970); George Vernadsky, *The Mongols and Russia* (1953). Soviet treatments tend to be panegyrical.

GEORGE P. MAJESKA

[See also **Chivalry, Orders of; Mongol Empire; Novgorod.**]

NEW CHRISTIANS (*marranos, conversos*), the term given to the Jewish mass converts to Christianity as an outcome of the 1391 pogroms and the Tortosa disputation (1413–1414). They were joined in 1497 by the forced mass conversion in Portugal. These converts constituted an intermediate society that had left Judaism but did not assimilate into Old Christian Spanish society. Most considered their conversions to be temporary and lived in hope of returning to the fold of their forefathers. Some conversos continued clandestinely to fulfill precepts of Mosaic law; others left their dwelling places and either joined a Jewish community far from their former home or joined a Jewish community outside Spain. There were, nevertheless, conversos who fully integrated into Christian society.

In 1449 Old Christians, headed by Pedro Sarmiento, rioted against New Christians in Toledo. The riots spread to Ciudad Real. Fourteen prominent New Christians were arrested and tried according to inquisitional procedure for having taken possession of offices in Toledo forbidden to them according to the ruling of the Fourth Council of Toledo (633), which declared that "no Jews nor those that are from the Jews" can have any jurisdiction over Christians.

A literary polemic ensued over whether the conversos should be admitted and accepted in Old Christian society and, if so, how. Besides this genre of literature there were satires in verse and other forms, which spread mostly in court circles and among the upper class. A "privilege given to an hidalgo," so that he might live and act like a New Christian, was circulated as a pattern of converso perfidy; so was the forged correspondence between Chamorro, head of the Jewish community of Toledo, and Yusuf, head of the Jewish community of Constantinople. The advice given by Yusuf to Chamorro is that Jews should convert and penetrate Christian society, to corrupt and destroy it from within.

The first to propagate the establishment of a Spanish National Inquisition was Alonso de Espina, in his work *Fortalitium fidei contra Judaeos.* He described in detail how conversos kept the precepts of Mosaic law. The educational measures within Christianity suggested by Alonso de Oropesa, head of the Order of St. Jerome, failed completely.

Isabel and Ferdinand, upon ascending the throne of Castile and Aragon (1474), were fully prepared to deal with the problem of Judaizing conversos. They were prevented for some years by the rising of the marquess of Villena, who favored the marriage of Juana la Beltraneja of Castile to her uncle Afonso V of Portugal, which would have united Castile and Portugal. Many conversos, especially of the La Mancha region, joined with the marquess, perhaps as an answer to the riots against them in 1467 and 1473–1474. When this rising was quelled, Alonso Carrillo, archbishop of Toledo, appointed an inquisitor to investigate the Judaizing practices in Ciudad Real (1475). The inquisitor, Tomás de Cuenca, tried many conversos, but it seems most probably that the crown stopped this Inquisition.

In 1477, while visiting Seville, the Catholic monarchs were approached by the friar Alonso de Hojeda, who complained about the state of religion in Seville and the Judaizing practices of the New Christians. The crown immediately appealed to Pope Sixtus IV, asking permission to found the Spanish National Inquisition. Permission was granted in 1478, and in 1480 two inquisitors, Miguel de Morillo and Juan de San Martín, were appointed for Seville and for the kingdom of Castile. Many conversos were arrested, tried, and burned at the stake. In 1482 another group of inquisitors was appointed, among them Tomás de Torquemada, who rose immediately to head the whole Inquisition. Year after year new courts were established, spreading throughout Spain and in 1484 incorporating the courts of the Papal Inquisition, which existed in Aragon, within the Spanish National Inquisition.

Jews were forced to testify against their former brethren on their Judaizing ways, but themselves were never put on trial by the Inquisition, since it had no jurisdiction over Jews. The Inquisition succeeded in proving Jewish complicity in the Judaizing practices of the conversos, which led to the order of expulsion against the Jews in 1492.

BIBLIOGRAPHY

Haim Beinart, "The *Converso* Community in 15th Century Spain," in Richard D. Barnett, ed., *The Sephardi Heritage* (1971), *Records of the Trials of the Spanish Inquisition in Ciudad Real,* 4 vols. (1974–1985), and *Conversos on Trial* (1981); Henry C. Lea, *A History of the Inquisition of Spain,* 4 vols. (1906–1907; repr. 1966); Bernardino Llorca, *Bulario pontificio de la inquisición española* (1949), and *La inquisición en España,* 3rd ed. (1954).

HAIM BEINART

[See also **Anti-Semitism; Aragon; Castile; Converso; Expulsion of Jews; Inquisition; Jews and the Catholic Church; Jews in Christian Spain.**]

NEW ROME. See **Constantinople.**

NIBELUNGENLIED. This poem is, if not the best, at least the best-known work of medieval German literature. It has something like the status of a national epic akin to *Beowulf* in England, the *Song of Roland* in France, and the *Poem of the Cid* in Spain. But it is later, longer, and more "courtly" than these. It was written around 1200, probably in what is now Bavaria, by an unknown poet, who combined two old heroic tales to form an unbroken epic sequence.

The first of these tales (stanzas 1–1,142 in redaction *B*) tells the story of Siegfried, Kriemhild, and Brünhild. Siegfried is a prince of the Netherlands, Kriemhild a princess of Burgundy residing at Worms with her brothers Gunther, Gernot, and Giselher, and their preeminent vassal Hagen. When Siegfried comes of age, he learns of Kriemhild's fabled beauty and sets out for Worms to woo her. After a brash challenge to Gunther, he is mollified, takes up residence with the Burgundians, and acquits himself with storybook prowess in a war against the Saxons and Danes. Ultimately, he is granted Kriemhild's hand in marriage, but the ceremony is delayed while he accompanies Gunther on his wooing expedition to Island, where the princess Brünhild stakes her hand on three athletic contests that can prove fatal for the suitor. Brünhild seems to be expecting Siegfried as her suitor, but he defers to Gunther, claiming to be only his vassal. The bridal games are arranged, to Gunther's considerable dismay. Siegfried comes to his rescue by donning a cloak of invisibility that allows him to perform the necessary feats unseen while Gunther goes through the ostensible motions. Having apparently won the day, Gunther brings his bride back to Worms, where both marriages are celebrated. The first night passes to the utter satisfaction of Siegfried and Kriemhild, but Brünhild repulses Gunther's advances, ties him hand and foot, and hangs him unceremoniously on the wall until daybreak. The next day a dejected Gunther again appeals to Siegfried, who once more resorts to his cloak of invisibility, takes Gunther's place in bed, and subdues Brünhild so that Gunther can consummate the marriage.

The two couples now live harmoniously for some time until one day the queens quarrel over their relative status and Kriemhild angrily reveals the wedding-night deception. Brünhild demands vindication, and although Gunther accepts Siegfried's offer of an oath to clear himself of any charge that he took Brünhild's virginity, she nonetheless appeals to Hagen to kill him. Gunther reluctantly gives in to Hagen's urging and allows him first to devise a scheme for exposing the vulnerable spot between Siegfried's shoulder blades (his "Achilles' heel") and then to stage a hunt for the purpose of committing the murder. During the hunt Hagen kills Siegfried with a spear thrust from behind as he lies drinking at a spring. This section concludes with bitter mourning and recriminations.

The second, once independent, tale recounts how Kriemhild avenged her husband (stanzas 1,143–2,379). Some years after his death, she agrees to marry Etzel, king of Hunland, because she foresees that this powerful alliance will provide the means for revenge. Having endeared herself to the Huns, she induces Etzel to invite her brothers to a banquet on the pretext that she yearns to see them. The invitation is greeted with apprehension by Hagen and other members of the Burgundian court, but carefree courage prevails and they set out from Worms. Their journey is described in considerable detail, including the dire prophecy of a mermaid near the Danube, an encounter with a detachment of Bavarians, and various stops along the way, notably a stay with Etzel's vassal Rüdeger at Bechelaren, where Kriemhild's youngest brother Giselher is betrothed to Rüdeger's daughter. The arrival at Etzel's court is marked by immediate expressions of hostility from Kriemhild, who tries, at first unsuccessfully, to instigate a Hunnish attack against the Burgundians. The following day, however, she is able to persuade Etzel's brother Blœdelin to lead the slaughter of nine thousand unarmed Burgundian attendants. When news of the slaughter reaches the banquet hall in which Huns and Burgundians are seated, Hagen reacts by beheading Etzel and Kriemhild's young son. General fighting then breaks out and continues for two days until innumerable Huns and every last Burgundian have fallen. Kriemhild's vengeance is accomplished, but she does not survive to rejoice: she is cut down by an outraged Meister Hildebrand. The epic concludes with general lamentations.

These lamentations are continued in a separate poem of 4,360 rhymed couplets called *Die Klage,* which is found in all the main *Nibelungenlied* manuscripts but one. This poem recapitulates the *Nibelungenlied,* relates the gathering and interment of the dead, and tells how the news of the catastrophe was brought to Bechelaren, Passau, and Worms. *Die Klage* was clearly based on the *Nibelungenlied,* but a number of discrepancies in detail have given rise to various speculations on the exact relationship between the two poems.

Despite a certain thematic grandeur, the *Nibelungenlied* often seems conceptually unsatisfactory. The motivation of several episodes is unclear. Why does Siegfried, who is intent on winning Kriemhild's hand, issue a hostile challenge to her brothers the moment he arrives in Worms? Does Brünhild and Siegfried's mutual recognition on Island indicate a prior relationship such as we find in the Norse sources? Why does Brünhild beset Gunther with tears and threats because of what she perceives as a mismatch between the princess Kriemhild and the alleged vassal Siegfried? What exactly is Siegfried charged with and what is the precise motivation for his murder? Why does Kriemhild change character so drastically in the second part of the poem and why, at the last moment, does her interest seem to shift from a desire for vengeance to a desire for Siegfried's treasure? There are no obvious answers to such questions despite repeated analyses of all of them. A reading of the Norse analogues suggests that the poet sometimes failed to blend his sources into his new conception, but critics have also argued that his version makes perfect sense provided we understand the text in its full complexity.

Whatever the conceptual and psychological difficulties may be, the poet succeeded in giving the story strong and dramatic colors. Many of the individual scenes are memorable, particularly the powerfully etched confrontations between Brünhild and Kriemhild, between Hagen and Kriemhild, or between Rüdeger and Etzel. These scenes are remarkable for their sharp focus and telling dialogue. No other Middle High German narrative projects personal antagonisms and quandaries with the same intensity. They are marked by a sense of dignity and ceremony and a strong underlying melancholy. The characters may be psychologically opaque on occasion, but they are highly individualized. Siegfried is the naive hero and athlete, uncomplicated to the point of culpability. Kriemhild, despite her unholy vengefulness, engages our sympathy for her shattered world. Nowhere else in the epic of the High Middle Ages is a female protagonist treated so fully. Hagen's motivations are shrouded, but his clenched fatalism once the die is cast equals or outdoes the mannered heroism of the older Germanic tradition. Even the peripheral characters are generously conceived: Gernot in his moderation, Etzel in his guilelessness, Volker in his loyalty. Only Gunther lacks firm definition, but that lack is in itself a fair statement of his character.

Epic poetry is in general notable for moments of high drama, but the quality of epic may also be judged by the interstices between such moments. In this area the *Nibelungenlied* is deficient. The dips in the action are filled with protracted and rather vapid court festivities, particularly in the first part. These festive digressions are sometimes viewed in the context of "modern" courtly literature, but it should be noted that the major courtly writers of the period (Hartmann von Aue, Wolfram von Eschenbach, and Gottfried von Strassburg) had no taste for such ceremonies. The discrepancy between our poet's interest in high drama on the one hand and tedious etiquette on the other remains something of a curiosity.

The stories told in the *Nibelungenlied* belong to an old and well-attested Germanic heroic cycle. The same stories are told in the Eddic Sigurd and Gudrun poems (*Sigurðarkviða in forna, Sigurðarkviða in meiri, Sigurðarkviða in skamma, Guðrúnarkviða,* I, II, III), *Atlakviða* and *Atlamál, Vǫlsunga saga, Þiðreks saga,* and the later *Lied vom Hürnen Seyfrid.* Such heroic tales often derive from or attach to documented history. Brünhild has been identified with the Merovingian queen Brunechildis and less convincing Merovingian models have been proposed for Siegfried. The fall of the Burgundians mirrors hostilities between Huns and Burgundians in the mid fifth century (Etzel is a reflex of Attila the Hun). The Burgundian laws from about 500 record the names of Gundicarius (Gunther), Gundomar (closer to the Norse Gotþormr than the German Gernot), and Gislaharius (Giselher).

By comparing the Norse and German variants, the Swiss scholar Andreas Heusler tried to reconstruct how the differing versions of the story evolved from the sixth to the twelfth century. Whatever the exact details of this evolution, it seems fairly clear that the *Nibelungenlied* poet's immediate sources were two separate poems. The first was perhaps a few hundred lines long, either written or oral, and was titled the "Brünhildenlied" by Heusler. The second was a written poem of more epic dimensions, perhaps a few thousand lines. Heusler labeled it the "Ältere Not." Both these lost poems were also available to the author of the German original of *Þiðreks saga,* and a comparison of the *Nibelungenlied* with the relevant sections of *Þiðreks saga* allows us to form some estimate of their content. More recent speculations on the evolution of the text have emphasized traces of oral diction (Bäuml).

The *Nibelungenlied* poet's chief concern was to combine these stories in a new and grander epic style. He achieved these new dimensions with an expanded cast of characters, ceremonial insertions, fuller dialogue, borrowings from literary sources, the differentiation of a single old scene into several new scenes, and the outright invention of new episodes. Some of his more important innovations are Siegfried's knightly service for Kriemhild's hand, the staging of a sham war to expose Siegfried's vulnerable spot, Siegfried's hunting exploits prior to his murder, the elaborate mourning of his death, personal confrontations between Hagen and Kriemhild and Hagen and the Huns in adventures 29–30, and adventure 37, in which Rüdeger faces a hopeless dilemma in deciding between his loyalties to his Burgundian kinsmen by marriage and his lord Etzel. This last scene by itself assures the poet a permanent place in medieval literature.

The poet is unknown and cannot even be identified by class. He has been variously identified as a minstrel of the better sort (a social category that may not have existed), a cleric, or a knight. The best that can be done is to circumscribe the time and place in which he worked. His language is Austro-Bavarian and he is topographically at home in the Danube valley. Mentions of Passau in the poem and in *Die Klage* point particularly in that direction. Chronologically he comes between Heinrich von Veldeke and Hartmann von Aue, who seem to have inspired two scenes in the *Nibelungenlied,* and Wolfram von Eschenbach, who in turn quotes the *Nibelungenlied.* The narrowest dating that has been proposed (Rosenfeld) is 1202–1204. The date can hardly be later and is not likely to be much earlier.

The prosodic form of the poem is anomalous. It is not in the four-beat rhymed couplets of the contemporary epic writers, but in stanzas of eight paired hemistichs. The first and second hemistichs of each pair are distinguished by cadence and the final hemistich is set apart by yet a third cadence. This stanzaic form is very close to Der von Kürenberg's lyric stanza, but opinions divide over whether the *Nibelungenlied* poet modeled himself on Der von Kürenberg, Der von Kürenberg on an earlier Nibelung epic, or both on a common antecedent form.

A further anomaly is the transmission of the *Nibelungenlied.* It has come down to us in a large number of whole or partial manuscripts, of which the most important are thirteenth-century manuscripts from Hohenems (now Munich) (*A*), St. Gall (*B*), and Hohenems (now Donaueschingen) (*C*). These three manuscripts represent three separate redactions differing in length, style, and even content. *A* is the shortest and least polished. *C* is the longest and most finished. In addition, it systematically rehabilitates Kriemhild at Hagen's expense. These three separate redactions form a text-critical impasse beyond which the editor cannot proceed. It is therefore not possible to establish precisely the poet's original version, and we must content ourselves with three variations on his work.

BIBLIOGRAPHY

Editions. Redaction A: Karl Lachmann, ed., *Der Nibelunge Not und die Klage* (1826, repr. 1960); redaction B: Helmut de Boor, ed., rev. by Roswitha Wisniewski, *Das Nibelungenlied,* 21st ed. (1979); redaction C: Ursula Hennig, ed., *Das Nibelungenlied nach der Handschrift C* (1977); synoptic edition: Michael S. Batts, ed., *Das Nibelungenlied: Paralleldruck der Handschriften A, B und C nebst Lesarten der übrigen Handschriften* (1971); *Die Klage:* Karl Bartsch, ed., *Die Klage, mit den Lesarten sämmtlicher Handschriften* (1875, repr. 1964).

Translation. Arthur T. Hatto, *The Nibelungenlied: A New Translation* (1965 and later printings).

Dictionary. Karl Bartsch, *Der Nibelunge Nôt,* II (1880, repr. 1966).

Concordance. Franz H. Bäuml and Eva-Maria Fallone, *A Concordance to the Nibelungenlied (Bartsch-de Boor Text)* (1976). Bäuml and collaborators have also published a series of studies on oral-formulaic traces in the *Nibelungenlied,* including: Franz H. Bäuml and Donald Ward, "Zur mündlichen Überlieferung des Nibelungenliedes," in *Deutsche Vierteljahrsschrift,* **41** (1967); Franz H. Bäuml and Agnes M. Bruno, "Weiteres zur mündlichen Überlieferung des Nibelungenliedes," *ibid.,* **46** (1972).

Manuscripts. Helmut Brackert, *Beiträge zur Handschriftenkritik des Nibelungenliedes* (1963).

Dating. Hellmut Rosenfeld, "Die Datierung des Nibelungenliedes Fassung *B und *C durch das Küchenmeisterhofamt und Wolfger von Passau," in *Beiträge zur Geschichte der deutschen Sprache und Literatur* (Tübingen), **91** (1969), but *cf.* Werner Hoffmann, *Das Nibelungenlied* (below), p. 98.

Bibliography. Willy Krogmann and Ulrich Pretzel, *Bibliographie zum Nibelungenlied und zur Klage,* 4th ed. (1966).

Survey of older research. Mary Thorp, *The Study of the Nibelungenlied: Being the History of the Study of the Epic and Legend from 1755 to 1937* (1940).

Legendary background. Theodore M. Andersson, "The Epic Source of *Niflunga saga* and the *Nibelungenlied,*" in *Arkiv för nordisk filologi,* **88** (1973), and *The Legend of Byrnhild* (1980); Andreas Heusler, *Nibelungensage und Nibelungenlied: Die Stoffgeschichte des deutschen Heldenepos* (1921 and later editions); Roswitha Wisniewski, *Die Darstellung des Niflungenunterganges in der Thidrekssaga: Eine quellenkritische Untersuchung* (1961).

General works. The most up-to-date survey of the relevant literature is Michael Curschmann, "'Nibelungenlied' und 'Klage,'" in Kurt Ruh, ed., *Die deutsche Literatur des Mittelalters: Verfasserlexikon,* VI (1986). The best introduction is Werner Hoffmann, *Das Nibelungenlied,* 5th ed. (1982). Introductions in English are Theodore M. Andersson, *A Preface to the Nibelungenlied* (1987), and Winder McConnell, *The Nibelungenlied* (1984). Other works include Karl Heinz Ihlenburg, *Das Nibelungenlied: Problem und Gehalt* (1969); Bert Nagel, *Das Nibelungenlied: Stoff, Form, Ethos* (1965); Friedrich Neumann, *Das Nibelungenlied in seiner Zeit* (1967); Friedrich Panzer, *Das Nibelungenlied: Entstehung und Gestalt* (1955); Werner Schröder, *Nibelungenlied-Studien* (1968); Gottfried Weber, *Das Nibelungenlied: Problem und Idee* (1963).

Die Klage. Michael Curschmann, "'Nibelungenlied' und 'Nibelungenklage': Über Mündlichkeit und Schriftlichkeit im Prozess der Episierung," in Christoph Cormeau, ed., *Deutsche Literatur im Mittelalter: Kontakte und Perspektiven. Hugo Kuhn zum Gedenken* (1979); Burghart Wachinger, "Die Klage und das Nibelungenlied," in "Hohenemser Studien zum Nibelungenlied," in *Montfort: Vierteljahresschrift für Geschichte und Gegenwart Vorarlbergs,* **32** (1980).

THEODORE M. ANDERSSON

[See also **Atlakviða; Atlamál; Brynhild; Burgundians; Der von Kürenberg; Guðrúnarkviða, I, II, III; Huns; Lied vom Hürnen Seyfrid, Das; Sigurd; Sigurðarkviða in Forna, in Meiri, in Skamma; Þiðreks Saga; Vǫlsunga Saga**.]

NICAEA, COUNCILS OF. See **Councils, Ecumenical.**

NICAEA, EMPIRE OF. The conquest of Constantinople by the Venetians and the soldiers of the Fourth Crusade in April 1204 temporarily destroyed the Byzantine Empire. In its place the Latin Empire of Constantinople was set up, though not without resistance from Greeks in various parts of the old Byzantine Empire. One of these centers of resistance was Nicaea, in northwestern Asia Minor. Theodore I Laskaris (1204–1221/1222), a son-in-law of a previous Byzantine emperor, Alexios III Angelos (1195–1203), escaped there at the turn of 1203 and had himself proclaimed emperor, probably in April 1206. He had two immediate tasks: to

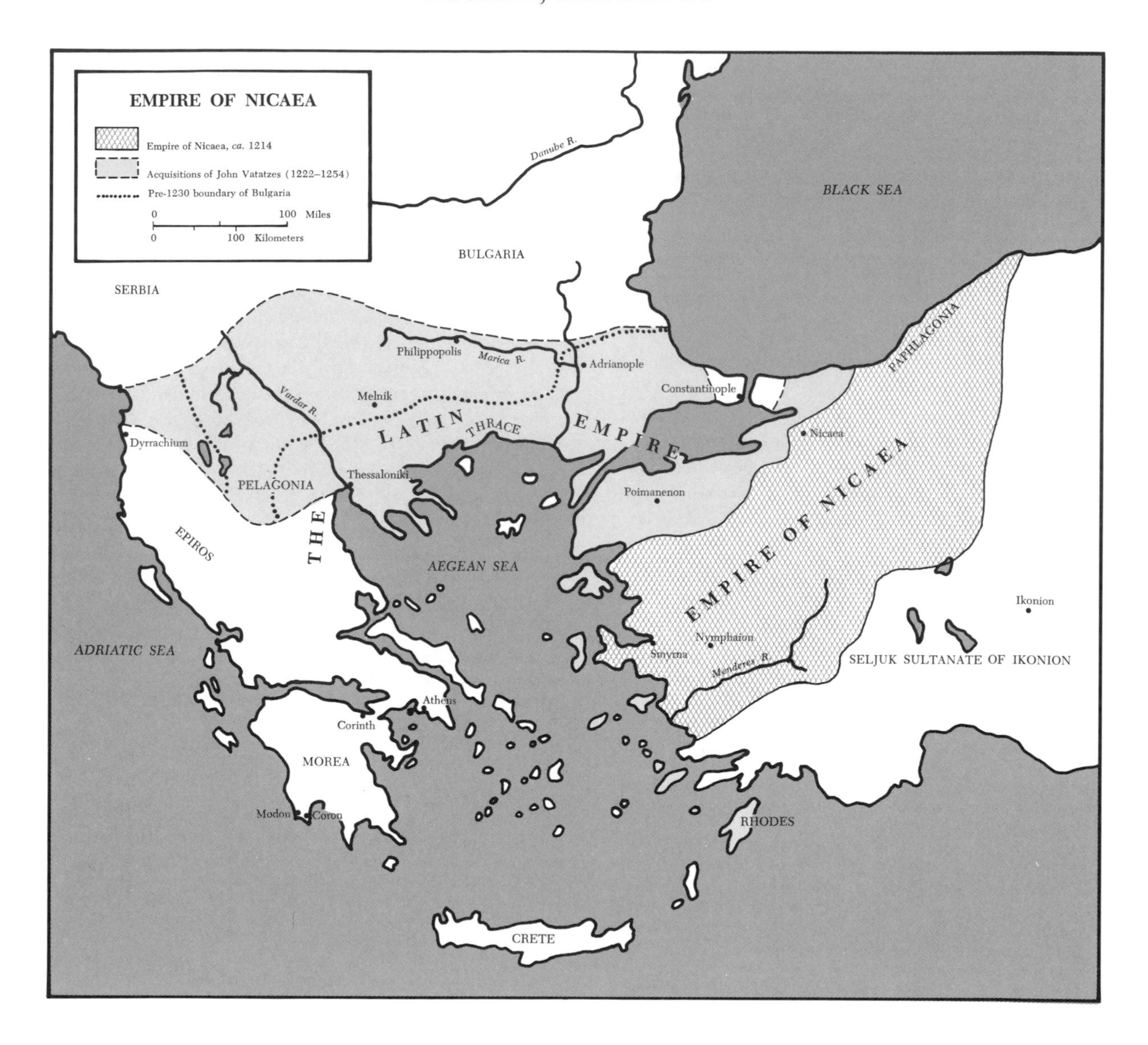

organize resistance to the Latin armies, which were endeavoring to conquer Asia Minor, and to assert his authority over various Greek lords who had taken advantage of the anarchy surrounding the Latin conquest of Constantinople to make themselves independent rulers. His task was eased in March 1205 when the Latin emperor Baldwin I (1204–1205) was defeated and killed by the Bulgarians at the Battle of Adrianople. The Latin armies were withdrawn from Asia Minor and Theodore I was able to bring most of the petty Greek rulers of western Asia Minor under his suzerainty. He also succeeded in beating off attacks from the most formidable of them, David Komnenos, the ruler of Paphlagonia.

Theodore's authority and his claim to be the true successor to the Byzantine emperors were enhanced in March 1208 when he had an Orthodox patriarch installed at Nicaea. The patriarch's first act was to crown Theodore emperor. Thus were the twin pillars of the Byzantine Empire symbolically restored in exile. At the same time, Theodore was able to establish a rudimentary government based upon his family and household and to restore provincial administration. He also set about refortifying his main towns. These measures enabled him to meet a new wave of attacks that came to a head in 1211. The Seljuk sultan attacked from the east, and was defeated and killed. Almost immediately the Latin emperor Henry of Flanders invaded from the north. Theodore had lost his best troops fighting the Seljuks, and his scratch army of levies was no match for the Latins. The Nicaeans were defeated and the Latin armies marched south toward the town of Nymphaion, encountering no resistance. The Greek population had been evacuated to the hills on Theodore's orders. These tactics produced a stalemate, and Henry came to terms. The Latins kept what they had conquered in the northwestern corner of Asia Minor, while Theodore held on to a cluster of towns around Nicaea and another nucleus of territory around Nymphaion.

Theodore's position improved slightly in 1214 when he was able to annex Paphlagonia after the death of David Komnenos, but any hopes he entertained of recovering Constantinople seemed doomed to disappointment. The best he could do was to put forward a scheme involving a series of marriage alliances that would unite the Nicene ruling house with that of the Latin emperors of Constantinople, in the hope that Constantinople might eventually return to the Greeks. This plan came to nothing because it required recognition of papal supremacy by the Orthodox church, a price that was considered much too high, given that one of the factors that had stiffened Greek resistance to the Latins was a desire to preserve their religious independence.

Theodore I Laskaris died in 1222 and was succeeded by his son-in-law John III Vatatzes (1222–1254). The Latins, hoping to exploit the discontent occasioned by this change of rulers, invaded the Nicene Empire, but were decisively defeated at the Battle of Poimanenon in 1224. John Vatatzes followed this up with the conquest of the Latin territories in northwestern Asia Minor, but avenues for further expansion appeared to be blocked.

An attempt to establish control over Thrace was thwarted by Theodore Angelos, the Greek ruler of Epiros, who had conquered Thessaloniki in 1224 and had been proclaimed emperor. This impasse was broken in 1233 when John Vatatzes was able to tempt the Bulgarians into an alliance against the Latins of Constantinople.

This alliance soon foundered, but it enabled the Nicaeans to establish a bridgehead in Thrace, which put them in a position to exploit the growing political instability of the southern Balkans. Their primary objective was the city of Thessaloniki. A first expedition in 1242 had to be called off because of news of the Mongol invasion of eastern Asia Minor, but a second one brought the Nicaeans not only Thessaloniki in the autumn of 1246 but also the Bulgarian territories in the southern Balkans. These were considerable conquests that had to be defended against repeated attacks by the Greeks of Epiros and by the Bulgarians. Nicene control of these regions was finally confirmed by their victory over the Epirotes and their Frankish allies at the Battle of Pelagonia in the late summer of 1259.

It was now only a matter of time before Constantinople fell to the Nicaeans. The actual conquest of the city on 25 July 1261 was largely a matter of luck. A small Nicaean force that had been sent to reconnoiter the Bulgarian frontier penetrated the walls of the city when the Latin garrison was absent. Constantinople was once more in the hands of the Greeks and the Byzantine Empire restored.

The Nicene Empire preserved the essentials of the Byzantine Empire in exile. Exile provided the perspective necessary for a new appreciation of Byzantine traditions. Great emphasis was placed by Nicene scholars on their classical heritage. They generalized the practice of referring to themselves as "Hellenes." These scholars, preeminently Nikephoros Blemmydes, sought to rescue the corpus of Byzantine learning. Emperor John III Vatatzes took an active part in this. Under his patronage a concerted effort was made to recover and to copy manuscripts.

For all this work of recovery, there were decisive changes. There was a weakening both at home and abroad of the traditional authority of the emperor and the patriarch. The Nicenes were forced to recognize the independence of the church in Serbia (1220), and patriarchal status was awarded to the Bulgarian church (1235). At home, the emperor had to condone the growth of aristocratic and municipal privilege. Grants of *pronoiai* and of immunities were made on a much larger scale than ever before. The price paid for the swift conquest of the southern Balkans was the grant of privileges to the towns and fortresses.

For all this, the Nicene Empire seems to have been a much healthier political organism than either the Byzantine Empire destroyed in 1204 or that restored in 1261. The agriculture of western Asia Minor prospered, and this prosperity was reflected in the considerable amount of building in its towns and fortresses during this period. The key to this newfound prosperity was a better balance between available resources and imperial expenditure. Government was comparatively simple and efficient. The bureaucratic incubus had been swept away in 1204 and replaced by a system of household government. Court life was simple and comparatively inexpensive. The dangers held in store by the recovery of Constantinople were foreseen at the time by one Nicene minister. His words were prophetic: "Oh, what is this I hear? Has this been saved up for our days? How have we sinned that we should live to see such a disaster? Let no one hope for further good fortune, now that the Byzantines have set foot in Constantinople once more" (George Pachymeres, *De Michaele et Andronico Paleologis,* I [1835]).

BIBLIOGRAPHY

Hélène Ahrweiler, "La politique agraire des empereurs de Nicée," in *Byzantion,* **28** (1958), "L'histoire et la géographie de la région de Smyrne entre les deux occupations turques (1081–1317), particulièrement au XIIIe siècle," in *Travaux et mémoires,* **1** (1965), and "L'expérience nicéenne," in *Dumbarton Oaks Papers,* **29** (1975); Michael J. Angold, *A Byzantine Government in Exile* (1975), and "Byzantine 'Nationalism' and the Nicaean Empire," in *Byzantine and Modern Greek Studies,* **1** (1975); E. Francès, "La féodalité et les villes byzantines au XIIIe et au XIVe siècles," in *Byzantinoslavica,* **16** (1955); Alice Gardner, *The Lascarids of Nicaea* (1912); Deno J. Geanakoplos, "Greco-Latin Relations on the Eve of the Byzantine Restoration: The Battle of Pelagonia—1259," in *Dumbarton Oaks Papers,* **7** (1953); Michael Hendy, *Coinage and Money in the Byzantine Empire, 1081–1261* (1969); Herbert Hunger, "Von Wissenschaft und Kunst der frühen Palaiologenzeit," in *Jahrbuch der österreichischen byzantinischen Gesellschaft,* **8** (1959); Apostolos Karpozilos, *The Ecclesiastical Controversy Between the Kingdom of Nicaea and the Principality of Epiros (1217–1233)* (1973); Donald M. Nicol, "Ecclesiastical Relations Between the Despotate of Epirus and the Kingdom of Nicaea in the Years 1215 to 1230," in *Byzantion,* **22** (1952); Nicolas Oikonomidès, "Cinq actes inédits du patriarche Michel Autôreianos," in *Revue des études byzantines,* **25** (1967), and "La décomposition de l'empire byzantin à la veille de 1204 et les origines de l'empire de Nicée: À propos de la *Partitio Romaniae,*" in *Rapports et co-rapports, 15th International Congress of Byzantine Studies, 1976* (1977).

MICHAEL ANGOLD

[See also **Anatolia; Baldwin I of the Latin Empire; Byzantine Church; Byzantine Empire; Constantinople; Crusades and Crusader States: Fourth; Epiros, Despotate of; John III Vatatzes; Latin Empire of Constantinople; Nymphaion; Patriarch; Pronoia; Seljuks of Rum; Serbia; Theodore I Laskaris; Thessaloniki.**]

NICCOLÒ DA BOLOGNA or Niccolò di Giacomo) (*d. ca.* 1400), the leading illuminator in Bologna during the second half of the fourteenth century. His numerous works, some of which are signed, in legal, liturgical, and other texts show active, strongly modeled figures, crowded compositions, bold colors, and a lively, concrete, and inventive treatment of the subjects.

BIBLIOGRAPHY

Erardo Aeschlimann, "Aggiunte a Nicolò da Bologna," in *Arte lombarda,* **14,** no. 2 (1969); Paolo d'Ancona, "Nicolò da Bologna miniaturista del secolo XIV," *ibid.;* Elly Cassee, *The Missal of Cardinal Bertrand de Deux: A Study in Fourteenth-century Bolognese Miniature Painting,* Michael Hoyle, trans. (1980); Francesco Filippini and Guido Zucchini, *Miniatori e pittori a Bologna: Documenti dei secoli XIII e XIV* (1947), 175–181; Mario Rotili, *La miniatura gotica in Italia,* I

The Crucifixion with Mary, John, and Mary Magdalen. Miniature by Niccolò da Bologna, early 1370's. THE CLEVELAND MUSEUM OF ART, GIFT OF J. H. WADE

(1968), 72–76; Mario Salmi, *Italian Miniatures,* Elisabeth Borgese-Mann. trans. (1954), 21–22.

MICHAEL JACOFF

[See also **Trecento Art.**]

NICCOLÒ DA VERONA. See **Nicholaus da Verona.**

NICCOLÒ DI BUONACCORSO (*ca.* 1348–1388), Sienese painter. A follower of Duccio and Simone Martini, Niccolò specialized in small-scale, private devotional paintings, for which his diminutive, decorative style was ideally suited. The key to his rather large extant oeuvre is the signed *Marriage of the Virgin* in the National Gallery, London. A prolific if somewhat minor artist, Niccolò maintained the Duccesque tradition well into the late fourteenth century.

BIBLIOGRAPHY

Kenneth Ames, "An *Annunciation* by Niccolò di Buonaccorso," in *Wadsworth Atheneum Bulletin,* **2** (1966); Bruce Cole and Adelheid M. Gealt, "A New Triptych by Niccolò di Buonaccorso," in *Burlington Magazine,* **119** (1977).

ADELHEID M. GEALT

[See also **Duccio di Buoninsegna; Gothic Art: Painting and Manuscript Illumination; Simone Martini.**]

NICCOLÒ DI GIACOMO. See **Niccolò da Bologna.**

NICCOLÒ DI PIETRO GERINI (*fl.* 1369–1415), Florentine painter. Most likely trained by Taddeo Gaddi, Gerini rigidly codified the stylistic precepts first stated by Orcagna. Stiff, symmetrical, and hieratic, his style found favor with the conservative elements in Tuscan society. His chief surviving panel paintings are the *Entombment* (*ca.* 1390, in S. Carlo dei Lombardi, Florence) and the *Baptism* (roughly the same date, in the National Gallery, London). Frescoes include the *Resurrection,* in the sacristy of S. Croce, and the *Life of St. Matthew,* in S. Francesco, Prato.

Marriage of the Virgin. Miniature by Niccolò di Buonaccorso, Siena, late 14th century. COURTESY OF THE TRUSTEES, THE NATIONAL GALLERY, LONDON, 1109

BIBLIOGRAPHY

Umberto Baldini, *La capella Migliorati nel S. Francesco di Prato* (1965); Bruce Cole, *Masaccio and the Painting of Early Rennaissance Florence* (1980); Richard Fremantle, *Florentine Gothic Painters* (1975).

ADELHEID M. GEALT

[See also **Gaddi, Taddeo; Gothic Art: Painting and Manuscript Illumination; Orcagna, Andrea;** and illustration overleaf.]

NICCOLÒ, LORENZO DI. See **Lorenzo di Niccolò di Martino.**

NICHE, a recess or hollow in a wall, pier, or buttress, generally shallow, often intended to house a statue or other ornament. Niches appear both

Baptism of Christ with Sts. Peter and Paul. Panel painting by Niccolò di Pietro Gerini, 1387. COURTESY OF THE TRUSTEES, THE NATIONAL GALLERY, LONDON, 579

singly and in groups, indoors and out. They are frequently semicircular, but may also be rectangular or polygonal; they may be topped by a lintel, a groin or rib vault, or a semidome, the latter often in the form of a conch shell in Roman and Renaissance architecture. Widely used by the Romans, niches were comparatively rare in the early Middle Ages and recurred in Gothic architecture from the beginning of the thirteenth century, often as a means of organizing large sculptural ensembles, as at the cathedrals of Wells, Rheims, and Florence.

GREGORY WHITTINGTON

[See also **Aedicula; Miḥrāb.**]

NICHOLAS I, POPE (*ca.* 820–867), was born in Rome, the son of a senior official in the papal government. He entered that government himself, becoming a subdeacon around 844 and a deacon around 850. He served as a principal adviser to Pope Benedict III from 855 to 858. Elected pope from the diaconate on 24 April 858, he spent the rest of his life attempting to impose upon the Christian world his strong conviction that the pope, as recipient of Christ's charges to Peter, was (as he put it several times) "princeps over all the earth." He continually acted on the assumption that the pope was the commander of all other churchmen, including those previously considered more or less autonomous. In his battles for papal monarchy and on behalf of individuals he deemed oppressed, he also assumed a position of command over temporal rulers.

Thus, in 861/862 Nicholas used his superior position and popularity to force the submission of Archbishop John VIII of Ravenna, who had tried to ignore his claim of temporal and spiritual rulership. Nicholas did this despite John's friendship with the Carolingian emperor Louis II, who had used his supporters in the Roman church to aid in the pope's election. When the Byzantine emperor Michael III deposed Ignatios, patriarch of Constantinople, Nicholas insisted on an unprecedented papal right to review the deposition. His legates were allowed to preside at a show trial of Ignatios in 861. Two years later, however, Nicholas was persuaded by friends of Ignatios that the sentence was unjust, and he then deposed and excommunicated Ignatios' successor, Photios, in a Roman council. His insistence on the efficacy of this sentence so exasperated the Byzantine government that it drove Michael III to bar the pope's legates in 866 and Photios to despose him, equally ineffectively, in a council of 867.

Nicholas also insisted on the pope's right to make the final decision in the divorce case of Louis II's brother, King Lothair II of Lorraine. At the end of 862, Lothair ignored Nicholas' claim to this right, and married his mistress after his two principal archbishops had given him the divorce he wanted from his hated queen; he then suborned the papal legates to agree to this at the Synod of Metz in June 863. Nicholas thereupon championed the queen, nullified this council, and in November 863 deposed the two archbishops purely by papal fiat, an extension of his power over distant sees. Louis II entered Rome with troops in the spring of 864 to force Nicholas to reinstate them, but Nicholas waged a successful passive resistance, and Lothair had to take back his original wife in the presence of Nicholas' legate in 865. This episode changed the initial concord of Nicholas and Louis to a coldness bordering on enmity that lasted until Nicholas' death. Nicholas also clashed twice with Hincmar of Rheims, who considered that he had rights as a metropolitan archbishop that the pope should not override. In 865 Nicholas reinstated Hincmar's suffragan bishop Rothad of Soissons, whom Hincmar had deposed for cause; and in 866 he forced Hincmar to hold a council to reinstate a group of illegally ordained clerics deposed by Hincmar in 853.

In these and many minor cases, Nicholas had the valuable help of the scholar and stylist Anastasius, the future papal *bibliothecarius*, who became his untitled assistant at the end of 862. He was also aided in furthering papal supremacy by the False Decretals, which were probably brought to his attention by Rothad of Soissons in 864; he avoided quoting these forgeries, but his references to them helped them gain acceptance in the Frankish West. His letter of elementary advice on the Christian life to the newly converted Bulgar nation in 866 is perhaps his single most interesting literary monument, though atypical in its relative lack of emphasis on papal primacy. Nicholas died after a long illness on 13 November 867. The unfinished matters of Ignatios and Lothair were resolved more or less according to his wishes under his successor, Adrian II. Adrian also asked the bishops of France to honor him as a saint just three months after his death, and he has been so regarded ever since.

The pontificate of Nicholas I was of prime importance in the history of the medieval papacy. For centuries before him, popes had asserted various rights in the church and carried out some of the functions of temporal sovereigns. Nicholas was the first to consolidate all the claims and powers that had thus accumulated, discern that they amounted to absolute monarchy in the church and paternal superiority in the world, and put them into practice. His ideas, prevailing over opposing views in his own day, influenced canon law and the actions of his successors; and, though it was eclipsed by political disintegration after his death, it was his conception of the papacy that came to fruition two centuries later in the Gregorian era.

BIBLIOGRAPHY

Nicholas' letters are edited by Ernst Perels in *Monumenta Germaniae historica: Epistolae*, VI (1925), 257–690. The most complete modern work about him is Jane Bishop, *Pope Nicholas I and the First Age of Papal Independence* (diss., Columbia, 1980). The best short introduction to his political significance is Frederick A. Norwood, "The Political Pretensions of Pope Nicholas I," in *Church History*, **15** (1946). Ernst Perels, *Papst Nikolaus I und Anastasius Bibliothecarius* (1920), corrects some previous misapprehensions on the subject; Francis Dvornik, *The Photian Schism: History and Legend* (1948), is vital for the truth about Nicholas' Byzantine policies.

JANE BISHOP

[See also **Anastasius Bibliothecarius; Bulgaria; Byzantine Church; Councils, Byzantine** (859–1368); **Cyril and Methodios, Sts.; Decretals, False; Papacy, Origins and Development of; Photios; Schism, Photian.**]

NICHOLAS OF AUTRECOURT (*ca.* 1300—after 1350), philosopher and theologian, was born at Autrecourt, near Verdun. After studying theology at Paris, he received a prebend at Metz (1338) but probably continued to teach theology at Paris. By 1340 he had gained a reputation for rather unconventional views in philosophy and theology. Furthermore, he was suspected of teaching erroneous doctrines and was summoned to the papal court at Avignon to answer for his errors. The death of Benedict XII in April 1342 interrupted the investigation, but Clement VI ordered it resumed. Nicholas was condemned in 1346 and forced to retract his errors, and to witness the burning of his writings in 1347. He took refuge in Germany at the court of Louis the Bavarian, but was not punished further, and in 1350 he became dean of the cathedral of Metz. This is the last time he is mentioned.

Nicholas' main offense was the exposition of his theory of knowledge. He argued that the logic of Aristotle and his commentators was based on false principles, in that causality cannot be demonstrated, that reason gives man very little certainty, that even the existence of an external world may be an illusion planted in the human mind by God. Some things are more probable than others, but "there can be little certitude from purely natural appearances. . . . Men should not waste their lives in logical discourses . . . but should explain the meaning of the divine law to the people."

Since Aristotelian logic had been firmly incorporated into medieval theology, such views seemed dangerous. Nicholas made matters worse by suggesting that the Greek (but certainly not Aristotelian) theory of a universe composed of combinations of atoms was correct, that these atoms are eternal, and that changes in their combinations could explain most apparent phenomena.

Nicholas had relatively little influence on the ideas of his contemporaries. He did, however, represent a growing dissatisfaction with Aristotelian thought and its application to theology.

BIBLIOGRAPHY

J. Reginald O'Donnell, "The Philosophy of Nicholas of Autrecourt and His Appraisal of Aristotle," in *Mediaeval Studies,* 4 (1942); Maurice De Wulf, *History of Mediaeval Philosophy,* Ernest C. Messenger, trans., II (1926), 238–241; Julius R. Weinberg, *Nicolaus of Autrecourt* (1948).

JOSEPH R. STRAYER

[See also **Aristotle in the Middle Ages; Philosophy and Theology, Western European: Late Medieval.**]

NICHOLAS OF CLAMANGES (Nicholas Poillevillain, *ca.* 1360–1432), curial official and reformer during the Avignon period. Born at Clamanges in Champagne, Nicholas took the name of his native village. He was a brilliant student at the University of Paris and became rector of the university in 1393. A friend of Pierre d'Ailly and John Gerson, he was attracted to the papal court at Avignon, as were many other scholars. He became secretary and librarian of Benedict XIII in 1394 and remained faithful to his patron until Benedict's final break with King Charles VI of France in 1408. Nicholas was suspected of having written the papal bull excommunicating the king and never held high office again. He returned to his old College of Navarre at Paris, where he died.

Nicholas' letters give a very favorable impression of Benedict and of the papal court at Avignon. On the other hand, no reformer was more vehement in denouncing the evil state of the church. In his *De ruina ecclesiae* he attacked papal provisions, the sale of benefices, the appointment of ignorant men to office, the encouragement of litigation at the papal curia, the abuse of power by bishops, and the immorality of all groups in the clergy. He admits that there are some good clergymen, "but scarcely one in a thousand does what his profession requires." All this had been said by others, but seldom by a papal secretary.

BIBLIOGRAPHY

Alfred Coville, ed., *Le traité de la ruine de l'église de Nicolas de Clomanges et la traduction française de 1564* (1936); Mandell Creighton, *A History of the Papacy from the Great Schism to the Sack of Rome,* I (1901), 152, 221, 301–302, 375.

JOSEPH R. STRAYER

[See also **Ailly, Pierre d'; Councils, Western (1311–1449); Gerson, John; Schism, Great.**]

NICHOLAS OF CUSA (1401–1464), philosopher, theologian, and mathematician. He was born in the German town of Kues, situated along the Moselle River across from Bernkastel (today one city, Bernkastel-Kues). His name, Niclas Krebs (in Latin:

Nicolaus Cancer), was gradually altered during his lifetime to Niclas von Cusse (Nicolaus de Cusa, Nicolaus Cusanus), thus reflecting his birthplace. Of Nicholas' early life almost nothing is known except that he was one of the four children of Johan Krebs (or Cryfftz), a prominent shipper, and Katharina Römer Krebs. The legend that he was a pupil of the Brothers of the Common Life at Deventer in central Holland remains without adequate historical support.

In 1416 Nicholas enrolled at the University of Heidelberg, where he studied the liberal arts. The following year he moved to the University of Padua, concentrating on canon law and receiving his *doctor decretorum* in 1423. There he was exposed to the latest developments in mathematical and astronomical thinking, as well as to the revitalizing influence of the Italian humanists and their reintroduction of the Greek language. Toward the beginning of 1425 Nicholas was back in Germany, enrolling during the spring at the University of Cologne; he is presumed both to have delivered and to have attended lectures in canon law. Through his friend Heimericus de Campo, he was influenced by the thought of Pseudo-Dionysius, Albertus Magnus, and Ramon Lull. During this Cologne period, the exact length of which is uncertain, Nicholas lived from ecclesiastical benefices given him by Otto of Ziegenhain, archbishop of Trier. (By September 1427 he was referring to himself as Otto's secretary.) Toward the end of 1428 he discovered twelve lost comedies of Plautus. In December of that year and again in 1435 he was offered a chair of canon law at the University of Louvain; both times he declined.

In 1430 a dispute broke out regarding the election to fill the vacant archbishopric of Trier. When the controversy was appealed to the Council of Basel in 1432, Nicholas pleaded the cause of his client, Ulrich of Manderscheid, by contesting the right of the pope to "impose" Raban of Helmstadt as archbishop. Though the appeal was lost (15 May 1434), Nicholas became prominent at the council by participating in its other affairs. Upon having taken the oath of the council on 29 February 1432, he had been made a member of the committee to examine matters of faith. His recommendations on how to draw the Hussites back to the Roman church date from 1433 and were the basis of the council's accommodation, as it was announced in 1436. This same year, 1436, he also presented to the council a memorandum regarding revision of the church calendar (*De reparatione kalendarii*).

Initially, Nicholas sided with the council, which claimed to be superior in authority to the pope. But by December 1436 his sympathies had changed to the extent that he voted with the minority faction in favor of letting Pope Eugenius IV determine the location of a projected ecumenical meeting with the Greeks. Nicholas was named by the minority party to the three-man delegation which, with the pope's blessing, sailed to Constantinople in August 1437. Their mission was to persuade the emperor and the patriarch to meet with the pope and the conciliar faction, in the hope of reuniting Eastern and Western Christendom. The agreement that was reached at Florence on 5 July 1439 brought only a short-lived "reunification." Nicholas' change of sympathies is to be attributed mainly to his belief that dissent within the Council of Basel was destroying the unity of the church. In his own day, however, many conciliarists ascribed his "sudden" support of the papacy to ambitious opportunism.

Between 1438 and 1448 Nicholas, as one of several papal envoys, sought to sway the German nation away from its neutrality; partly through his efforts Frederick III, king of Germany and archduke of Austria, signed the Concordat of Vienna on 17 February 1448, aligning the German nation with Pope Nicholas V and against the Council of Basel. In 1446 Pope Eugenius IV had named Nicholas cardinal as a reward for his labors; but Eugenius died (23 February 1447) before making the naming official. Nicholas V elevated him to cardinal on 20 December 1448, and on 3 January 1449 assigned him a titular church in Rome: St. Peter in Chains. (Nicholas had become a priest sometime between 1436 and 1440, although he had held benefices much earlier, as a cleric.)

During 1451 Nicholas traveled throughout Austria and Germany as a papal legate under instruction to reform the church. In April 1452 he assumed the active, personal administration of the bishopric of Bressanone (Brixen in Tirol), to which he had been named on 23 March 1450. His attempts to reform the diocese and to free it from domination by Sigismund, duke of Austria and count of Tirol, led to threats and clashes that twice caused him to seek consolation and refuge in Rome. He died on 11 August 1464, in the Italian town of Todi, while en route from Rome to Ancona. His body was reposited in his titular church but was lost sometime after its later relocation there. In accordance with his will, his heart was placed in the hospice which he commissioned to be built at Kues and which still serves its founder's aim: to shelter thirty-three—the number coinciding with the years of Christ's earthly life—impoverished men, each being no less than fifty years old. Already underway in 1453 and essentially completed by 1458, though not consecrated until 1465, the hospice also houses his personal library.

Nicholas wrote many works: *De maioritate auctoritatis sacrorum conciliorum supra auctoritatem papae* (1433), *Libellus inquisitionis veri et boni* (1433, lost), *De modo vero habilitandi ingenium ad discursum in dubiis* (1433, lost), *De concordantia catholica* (1433), *De auctoritate praesidendi in concilio generali* (1434), *De reparatione kalendarii* (1436), *De docta ignorantia* (1440), *De coniecturis* (1442–1443), *De deo abscondito* (1444), *De quaerendo deum* (1445), *De filiatione Dei* (1445), *De geometricis transmutationibus* (1445), *De arithmeticis complementis* (1445), *De dato patris luminum* (1445–1446), *Coniectura de ultimis diebus* (1446), *De genesi* (1447), *Apologia doctae ignorantiae* (1449), *Idiota de sapientia* (1450), *Idiota de mente* (1450), *Idiota de staticis experimentis* (1450), *De circuli quadratura* (1450), *Quadratura circuli* (1450, *Tres epistolae contra Bohemos* (1452), *De pace fidei* (1453), *De visione Dei* (1453), *De mathematicis complementis* (1453), *Complementum theologicum* (1453), *De mathematicis complementis* (second version 1454), *Declaratio rectilineationis curvae* (date uncertain), *De una recti curvique mensura* (date uncertain), *Dialogus de circuli quadratura* (1457), *De caesarea circuli quadratura* (1457), *De beryllo* (1458), *De mathematica perfectione* (1458), *De aequalitate* (1459), *De principio* (1459), *Aurea propositio in mathematicis* (1459), *De possest* (1460), *Cribratio alkorani* (1461), *De li non aliud* (1461), *De figura mundi* (1462, lost), *De ludo globi* (book I, 1462), *De venatione sapientiae* (1462), *De ludo globi* (book II, 1463), *Compendium* (1464), and *De apice theoriae* (1464).

In *De concordantia catholica* Nicholas distinguishes between a universal council (which is open to the bishops and select ecclesiastics of the whole church—that is, of the five patriarchates) and a patriarchal council (which is composed of the bishops and select ecclesiastics of a given patriarchate). Provided there is agreement, a universal council, which is superior to the pope, is more likely to be infallible than is the pope alone; the greater the consensus, the greater the assurance of infallibility. (The Council of Basel was considered a universal council even though bishops of the non-Roman patriarchates—which were in schism or captivity—were not present.) Yet in matters of faith, agreement between a Roman patriarchal council and the pope, to whom the council is subordinate, also guarantees infallibility; and in matters of faith even the decisions of a universal council require the consent of the pope, provided he is not a heretic. A universal council can depose a pope for heresy or for maladministration; a Roman patriarchal council can declare the pope heretical and separate itself from him, but it cannot depose him for merely administrative reasons. Nicholas modified his theory in his letter of 8 November 1439 (*Quamvis, pater colendissime*) and in his speech at Frankfurt between 21 and 23 June 1442. In both cases he inclined toward giving more authority to the pope.

Nicholas' most important philosophical work is *De docta ignorantia*. The title is drawn from the following consideration: When we learn that God cannot be known as he is, we will be more learned. Thus, the title deliberately employs "doctus" in a twofold sense. Strictly speaking, we can know neither what God is nor what he is like, for he is beyond all differentiation; and, as undifferentiated, he is not similar to anything finite. In him all things coincide—not only in the sense that he is undifferentiated being itself, but also in the sense that, ontologically prior to their creation, all finite things are in God and, qua in God, are God. *De docta ignorantia* emphasizes the *via negativa* but does not deny the practical need for analogical and symbolic representations of God—for example, that God is Cause. Furthermore, it minimizes argumentation for God's existence. And, through developing the notion of mathematical infinity, it attempts to elucidate the sense in which "God is the Essence of all things." This latter statement, however, has given rise to conflicting and highly controversial interpretations of Nicholas' metaphysics. Nonetheless, there is now general agreement that Nicholas is not a pantheist, something he explicitly denied being. *De docta ignorantia* also presents his cosmology, which diverges in several important respects from the Ptolemaic conception, although it cannot rightly be said to anticipate Copernicus' theory. Finally, the Christology presented in book 3 must be regarded as orthodox.

In *De pace fidei* Nicholas seeks to show that monotheist religions such as Islam and Judaism are compatible with Christianity, so that together they can be "una religio in rituum varietate." In his attempted harmonization he does not minimize the doctrine of Christ but, instead, stresses the doctrine of learned ignorance: "God as Creator is three and one; as infinite, however, he is neither three nor one nor any of those things which can be spoken of." Nicholas' most literary treatise is *De visione Dei*. It presents his speculative mysticism, and its dialectical reasoning testifies amply to his intellectual movement away from the Middle Ages and toward the modern age. Though his intellectual influence on his own times was minimal, both his prefiguring of certain ideas in Leibniz and his effect on Paul Tillich's theology are intellectually significant.

Among the many writers who contributed to Nicholas' philosophical and theological development are Albertus Magnus, Anselm of Canterbury, Aristotle, Augustine, Bonaventure, Pseudo-Dionysius, Meister Eckhart, John Scottus Eriugena, John Gerson, Heimericus de Campo, Hermes Trismegistus, Hugh of St. Victor, Maximus the Confessor, Plato, Proclus, Ramon Lull, Robert Grosseteste, Thierry of Chartres, Thomas Aquinas, and Thomas Gallus. Nicholas' writings are both extremely rich and extremely difficult to comprehend. Perhaps no other medieval or Renaissance thinker has so often been so widely misinterpreted.

BIBLIOGRAPHY

Works. A critical edition of Nicholas' works is being issued by the Heidelberg Academy of Letters under the series title *Nicolai de Cusa Opera Omnia* (1932–); many of these texts are reprinted, without the critical apparatus, in the series *Schriften des Nikolaus von Kues in deutscher Übersetzung*. Earlier editions include the one published by Martin Flach in Strassburg (1488) and the one published by Jacques Le Fèvre d'Étaples in Paris (1514); these editions were reprinted in Berlin (1967) and in Frankfurt (1962), respectively. Also essential is *Acta Cusana: Quellen zur Lebensgeschichte des Nikolaus von Kues*, Erich Meuthen and Hermann Hallauer, eds. (1976–).

English translations. Unity and Reform: Selected Writings of Nicholas of Cusa, John P. Dolan, ed. (1962), contains G. Heron's translation of Book 3 of *Learned Ignorance*, most of E. Salter's translation of *The Vision of God*, and Dolan's translation of *Idiota de sapientia, De pace fidei*, and *Idiota de staticis experimentis;* Jasper Hopkins, *A Concise Introduction to the Philosophy of Nicholas of Cusa* (1978, 3rd ed. 1986), contains a translation of *De possest; Nicholas of Cusa on God as Not-other: A Translation and an Appraisal of De Li Non Aliud* (1979, 2nd ed. 1983); *Nicholas of Cusa on Learned Ignorance: A Translation and an Appraisal of De Docta Ignorantia* (1981, 2nd ed. 1985); *Nicholas of Cusa's Debate with John Wenck: A Translation and an Appraisal of De Ignota Litteratura and Apologia Doctae Ignorantiae* (1981, 2nd ed. 1984); *Nicholas of Cusa's Metaphysic of Contraction* (1983), contains a translation of *De dato patris luminum;* and *Nicholas of Cusa's Dialectical Mysticism: Text, Translation, and Interpretive Study of De Visione Dei* (1985); *The Vision of God*, Emma G. Salter, trans. (1928); *Idiota de mente. The Layman: About Mind*, Clyde Lee Miller, trans. (1979); *De ludo globi (The Game of Spheres)*, Pauline M. Watts, trans. (1986).

Studies. Maurice de Gandillac, *Nikolaus von Cues: Studien zu seiner Philosophie und philosophischen Weltanschauung*, Karl Fleischmann, trans. (1953); Karsten Harries, "The Infinite Sphere: Comments on the History of a Metaphor," in *Journal of the History of Philosophy*, **13** (1975); Rudolf Haubst, *Das Bild des Einen und Dreieinen Gottes in der Welt nach Nikolaus von Kues* (1952), *Studien zu Nikolaus von Kues and Johannes Wenck, Beiträge zur Geschichte der Philosophie des Mittelalters*, XXXVIII (1955), *Die Christologie des Nikolaus von Kues* (1956), and, as editor, *Mitteilungen und Forschungsbeiträge der Cusanus-Gesellschaft* (1961–), with bibliographies in vols. I, III, VI, X, XV; Gerd Heinz-Mohr and Willehad P. Eckert, eds., *Das Werk des Nicolaus Cusanus: Eine bibliophile Einführung* (1962, 2nd ed. 1975); Klaus Jacobi, *Die Methode der cusanischen Philosophie* (1969); Tyrone Lai, "Nicholas of Cusa and the Finite Universe," in *Journal of the History of Philosophy*, **11** (1973); Erich Meuthen, *Die letzten Jahre des Nikolaus von Kues: Biographische Untersuchungen nach neuen Quellen* (1958), *Das Trierer Schisma von 1430 auf dem Basler Konzil* (1964), and *Nikolaus von Kues, 1401–1464: Skizze einer Biographie* (1964, 4th ed. 1979); Hermann Schnarr, *Modi essendi: Interpretationen zu den Schriften De docta ignorantia, De coniecturis und De venatione sapientiae von Nikolaus von Kues* (1973); Paul E. Sigmund, *Nicholas of Cusa and Medieval Political Thought* (1963); Edmond Vansteenberghe, *Le Cardinal Nicolas de Cues* (1920, repr. 1963); Morimichi Watanabe, *The Political Ideas of Nicholas of Cusa with Special Reference to His De Concordantia Catholica* (1963).

JASPER HOPKINS

[See also **Conciliar Theory; Councils, Western (1311–1449); Concordat; Papacy, Origins and Development; Philosophy and Theology, Western European; Schism, Great.**]

NICHOLAS OF ELY (*fl.* after 1230), sometimes seen as the designer of Salisbury Cathedral, begun in 1220. The evidence, however, reveals only that he was a mason on the site in 1230. It is more likely that he simply supervised construction of a design that he may have formulated together with Master Elias of Dereham.

BIBLIOGRAPHY

John Harvey, *English Medieval Architects* (1954), 83–84, 93–94; Historical Manuscripts Commission, *Report on Manuscripts in Various Collections,* I (1901), 382; Nikolaus Pevsner, *Wiltshire* (1963), 352.

STEPHEN GARDNER

[See also **Gothic Architecture; Masons and Builders; Salisbury Cathedral.**]

NICHOLAS OF LEIDEN. See **Gerhaert, Nicholas.**

NICHOLAS OF LYRA (*ca.* 1270–1349), Franciscan exegete, was born in Normandy, probably at Lyre (modern Neuve-Lyre). About 1300 he took the Franciscan habit at the convent of Verneuil near his home and soon was sent to Paris to study theology. He was a regent master in theology from 1309 to 1311. From 1319 to 1324 he was the Franciscan minister provincial for the order's province of Paris and from 1324 to 1330 for the province of Burgundy. By 1333 he was again teaching in Paris, where he remained until his death on 16 October 1349. Lyra was known as the "clear and useful doctor."

Lyra's lasting reputation stands on his biblical commentaries contained in the *Postillae perpetuae super totam Bibliam*. This work exists in hundreds of manuscripts and many printed editions. In printed texts, it is often accompanied by the *Additiones* of Paul, bishop of Burgos (*d.* 1435), and the *Replicae* of Matthew Doering (*d.* 1469). Lyra's commentaries were reprinted well into the seventeenth century.

Nicholas commented on both the canonical and deuterocanonical books of Scripture. He began with Genesis in 1322; by 1332 he had made his final revisions. In October 1333 he completed an abridgment known as the *Liber differentium*. In 1339 he added the *Postilla moralis*, drawing from selected texts a spiritual meaning which could be used in preaching and moral instruction. In general, his commentaries served as veritable encyclopedias of linguistic, historical, scientific, and canonical information for all the theologians of the later Middle Ages and for Martin Luther.

Nicholas also wrote Jewish-Christian polemics. He composed the *Probatio adventus Christi* in 1309 and revised it (*ca.* 1333) in response to "a little book written in Hebrew" that has since been lost. The second tract, *Responsio contra quendam Judaeum* (1334), is a point-by-point refutation of that book.

Although in these tracts Nicholas polemicizes against Jewish traditions and beliefs, his *Postillae* attest to his careful study not only of the Hebrew Bible, but also of the Midrash and Talmud, the works of Rashi, and those of Maimonides. Unlike the handful of twelfth-century Christian Hebraists who relied largely on personal conversations with rabbis for their knowledge of Hebrew traditions, Lyra was fully competent to work with the Hebrew texts on his own.

In addition to these works, Nicholas composed some 259 sermons, a commentary on the *Sentences* of Peter Lombard, and other opuscula.

Lyra is also known for his teaching of a double-literal sense, by which the citations of the Hebrew Scriptures that were found in the New Testament had two literal meanings. The primary and perfect literal meaning referred to Christ; the seondary and less perfect meaning referred to the facts of biblical history before Christ. Lyra is also among the first to disclaim formally any authority for his personal opinions and to measure the patristic tradition against Scripture, rather than the usual medieval approach of interpreting Scripture through the Fathers.

BIBLIOGRAPHY

Sources. Palémon Glorieux, *Répertoire des maîtres en théologie de Paris au XIIIe siècle* (1933). Johannes B. Schneyer, *Repertorium der lateinischen Sermones des Mittelalters* (1972), 338–357; Friedrich Stegmüller, *Repertorium biblicum medii aevi,* IV (1954) and IX (1977).

Studies. Herman Hailperin. *Rashi and the Christian Scholars* (1963), 137–246; James S. Preuss, *From Shadow to Promise* (1969), 61–71; Ceslaus Spicq, *Esquisse d'une histoire de l'exégèse latine moyen âge* (1944), 335–342.

MARK ZIER

[See also **Biblical Interpretation; Exegesis; Paris, University of; Rashi.**]

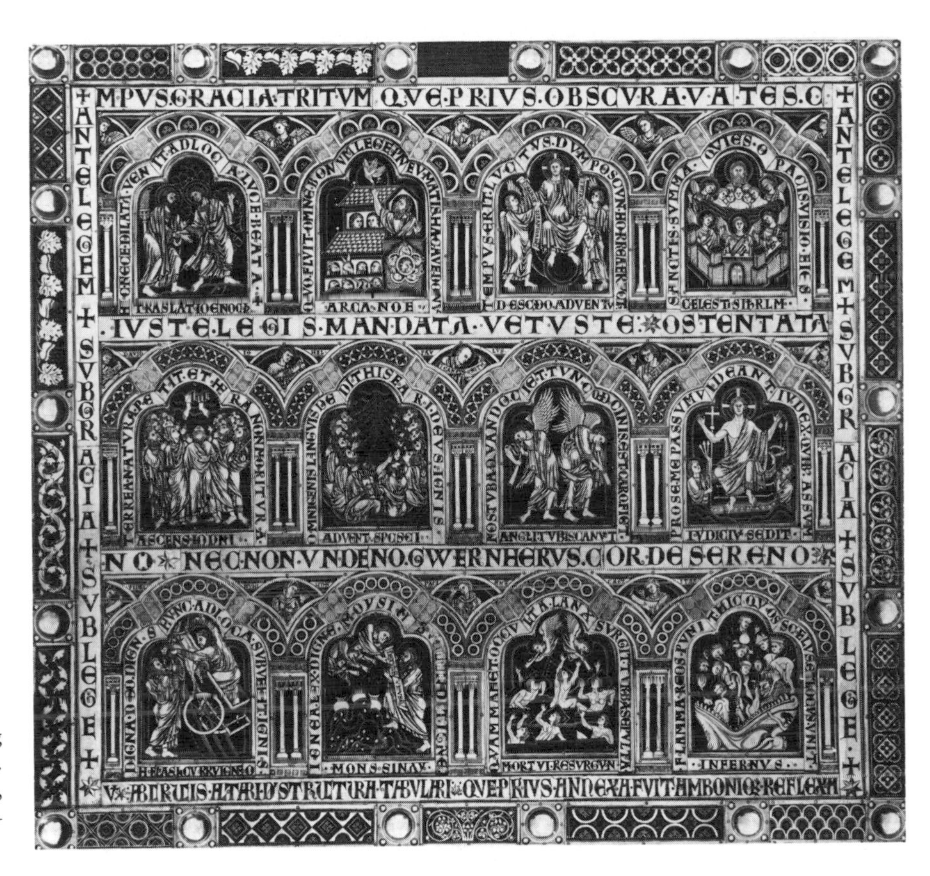

Panel from the Klosterneuburg ambo of Nicholas of Verdun. Champlevé enamel on copper, 1181. STIFT KLOSTERNEUBERG. PHOTO: BUNDESDENKMALAMT, VIENNA

NICHOLAS OF VERDUN (*fl.* 1181–1205) is named as the artist in the inscriptions found on two works of art, the Klosterneuburg ambo and the Mary Shrine at Tournai. The original inscription on the ambo, formerly attached to the choir screen of the Augustinian abbey of Klosterneuburg, specified that it was commissioned by Prior Wernher, that it was dedicated to the Virgin, and finally that it was completed in 1181: "Nicholaus opus Verdunensis fabricavit" (Nicholas of Verdun made this work). The original program comprised forty-five champlevé enamel scenes arranged in fifteen vertical rows of three scenes each: the New Testament "under grace" (*sub gratia*) in the center, an Old Testament scene "before the law" (*ante legem*) above, and another Old Testament scene "under the law" (*sub lege*) below, a systematic typological concordance based on Augustinian concepts concerning the three ages of history.

Restoration of the ambo in 1949–1951 revealed unfinished engravings on the reverse of several plaques that suggest that before completion of the work there was a change of program, that the artist did not provide preliminary drawings for the patron, and that Nicholas probably worked in situ at the abbey.

The Shrine of Mary in Notre Dame de Tournai had an inscription, since lost, which was transcribed in the seventeenth century: "Hoc opus fecit magister Nicolaus de Verdun . . . Anno ab Incarnatio Domini MCCV consummatum est hoc opus aurifabrum" (Master Nicholas of Verdun made this work . . . in 1205 this goldwork was finished). This shrine has been heavily restored since the sixteenth century, and at present reveals little of the artist's style.

Among the numerous objects attributed on stylistic grounds to Nicholas or to his workshop, the most convincing are the Shrine of the Magi and the Anno Shrine. The Shrine of the Magi at Cologne Cathedral was probably planned and partly executed by Nicholas (the architecture, the decorative work, and the prophets of the long sides are generally attributed to him) between 1181 and 1205. The Anno Shrine, at St. Michael's in Siegburg, was probably executed in 1183, the year in which Anno was canonized by Pope Lucius III.

Verona cathedral, west portal, detail of jamb with armed knight and prophets by Nicholaus da Verona, *ca.* 1139. FOTO MARBURG/ART RESOURCE

Nicholas' style exerted an immediate influence in the Rhine and Meuse regions, notably at Siegburg, Tournai, Oignies, Trier, Cologne, and Aachen. The repercussions of his style were also felt farther afield in northern France, as manuscript illumination and cathedral sculpture of the early thirteenth century testify.

BIBLIOGRAPHY

Helmut Buschhausen, "The Klosterneuburg Altar of Nicholas of Verdun: Art, Theology, and Politics," in *Journal of the Warburg and Courtauld Institutes,* **37** (1974); Erika Doberer, "Die ehemalige Kanzelbrüstung des Nikolaus von Verdun im Augustiner-Chorherren-Stift Klosterneuburg," in *Zeitschrift des Deutschen Vereins für Kunstwissenschaft,* **31** (1977); Rebecca Price Gowen, "The Shrine of the Virgin in Tournai, I: Its Restorations and State of Conservation," in *Aachener Kunstblätter,* **47** (1976–1977); Joseph Hoster, "Zur Form der Stirnseite des Dreikönigenschrein," in *Miscellanea pro arte: Hermann Schnitzer zur Vollendung des 60. Lebensjahres* (1965); Floridus Röhrig, *Der Verduner Altar* (1955, 3rd ed. 1964).

GRETEL CHAPMAN

[See also **Enamel, Champlevé (with color frontispiece); Gothic Art; Mosan Art.**]

NICHOLAS TREVET. See **Trevet, Nicholas.**

NICHOLAUS DA VERONA (Niccolò da Verona, *fl.* 1120–1140), a north Italian Romanesque sculptor known through inscriptions at S. Giorgio, the cathedral of Ferrara (*ca.* 1135); S. Maria Matricolare, the cathedral of Verona (*ca.* 1139); and S. Zeno, Verona (*ca.* 1138). Somewhat earlier sculpture at the cathedral of Piacenza (Assunta) and at the Sagra di S. Michele (Abbazia della Chiusa) is also attributed to him. Nicholaus is best known for his innovative portal designs.

BIBLIOGRAPHY

Christine Verzar Bornstein, *Portals and Politics in the Early Italian City-State: The Sculpture of Nicholaus in Context* (1986); Angiola Maria Romanini, ed., *Nicholaus e l'arte del suo tempo,* 3 vols. (1985).

DOROTHY F. GLASS

[See also **Romanesque Art.**]

NICOLA PISANO. See **Pisano, Nicola.**

NICOLAITISM. "Nicolaitans" were denounced in the Bible in Revelation 2:6 and described by patristic cataloguers of heresy (for example, Irenaeus in *Adversus haereses*) as a sect of sexually licentious Gnostics. Eleventh-century church reformers branded as "Nicolaites" all clerics who, while bound to celibacy, nevertheless kept wives or concubines. These reformers viewed clerical incontinence as a breach not merely of morals but of orthodoxy as well. The earliest example of the new usage of the term Nicolaites may be that of Humbert of Silva Candida (*Contra Nicetam,* 1054). He was speaking, however, only of the Byzantine practice of clerical marriage. Pope Nicholas II

(1059–1061) used the term in reference to the Western clergy in 1059. Peter Damian, in 1063, wrote "clerici uxorati Nicolaitae vocantur" (married clerics are called 'Nicolaites'). Émile Amann gives a full account of what patristic and early medieval authors said about Gnostic Nicolaitism, although there is no historical exposition of how the shift in the term's usage came about.

BIBLIOGRAPHY

Émile Amann, "Nicolaites," in *Dictionnaire de théologie catholique,* XI.1 (1931); Humbert of Silva Candida, *Contra Nicetam,* in *Patrologia latina,* CXLIII (1882), 996D; Pope Nicholas II, *Epistolae et diplomata, ibid.,* 1314B; Peter Damian, *Dissertatio secunda contra clericorum intemperantiam,* in *Patrologia latina,* CXLV (1867), 414B.

ELAINE GOLDEN ROBISON

[See also **Celibacy; Church Fathers; Reform, Idea of.**]

NICOLAUS DE TUDESCHIS (1386–1445), also known as Abbas Siculus and Panormitanus, was one of the most influential canonists of the later Middle Ages. Born in Catania, he became a Benedictine and studied at Bologna and Padua. After teaching law at Bologna and Siena, he became abbot of S. Maria de Maniaco in Messina (1425) and archbishop of Palermo (1434). He participated in the Council of Basel (1431–1449) and wrote *Consilia* and a commentary on the Decretals of Pope Gregory IX, among other works. As a conciliarist he took a mildly conservative line, insisting on the pope's divine right to exercise power in the church and on the supreme power of the church as a whole.

BIBLIOGRAPHY

John A. Clarence Smith, *Medieval Law Teachers and Writers, Civilian and Canonist* (1975), 94; "Panormitain," in *Dictionnaire de droit canonique;* Kurt W. Nörr, *Kirche und Konzil bei Nicolaus de Tudeschis* (1964); Hermann Schüssler, *Der Primat der heiligen Schrift als theologisches und kanonistisches Problem im Spätmittelalter* (1977), 172–224.

ANTHONY GRAFTON

[See also **Conciliar Theory; Councils, Western.**]

NICOLE BOZON (Nicholas Boson, Bozoun) (*fl.* late thirteenth–early fourteenth centuries), Franciscan friar, preacher, and prolific author. Perhaps a member of the distinguished Bozon family of Norfolk, he almost certainly belonged to the Nottingham friary and probably studied at Oxford. His works, all in Anglo-Norman French and in a variety of verse forms, are for the most part moralizing and didactic, stressing repentance and reform. He uses allegory and concrete examples frequently, and employs a simple, direct style that probably appealed to an educated lay audience.

Most famous of Nicole Bozon's works is his *Contes moralisés,* a collection of edifying exempla, tales, and anecdotes in prose that apparently served as a sourcebook for preachers. His other works include allegorical poems, social satires, glossed proverbs, devotional poems to Mary, verse sermons, and eleven saints' lives.

BIBLIOGRAPHY

Sources. Works of Nicole Bozon are found in Sister M. Amelia Klenke, ed. and trans., *Three Saints' Lives by Nicholas Bozon* (1947), and, ed., *Seven More Poems by Nicholas Bozon* (1951); Brian J. Levy, ed., *Nine Verse Sermons by Nicole Bozon: The Art of an Anglo-Norman Poet and Preacher* (1981); Lucy Toulmin Smith and Paul Meyer, eds., *Les contes moralisés de Nicole Bozon, frère mineur* (1889, repr. 1968); Anders Christopher Thorn, ed., *Les proverbes de bon enseignement de Nicole Bozon* (1921); Johan Vising, ed., *Deux poèmes de Nicholas Bozon: Le char d'orgueil; La lettre de l'empereur Orgueil* (1919, repr. 1974), and, ed., "La plainte d'amour," in *Göteborgs Högskolas Årsskrift,* **11** (1905), **13** (1907).

Study. Sister M. Amelia Klenke, "Nicholas Bozon," in *Modern Language Notes,* **69** (1954).

ELLEN WEHNER

[See also **Anglo-Norman Literature; Exemplum; Preaching and Sermon Literature.**]

NICOPOLIS, on the Danube River in Bulgaria, site of the biggest crusade of the fourteenth century, organized in response to Turkish domination of the Balkans. It was besieged in September 1396 by an army that included principally French, Burgundians, Hungarians, and Germans under John of Nevers and King Sigismund of Hungary. French knights impetuously attacked the Turkish relief force of Bāyazīd I, leading to calamitous defeat for the Christians, probably on 25 September.

The Last Supper, the Burning Bush, the Annunciation. Niello decoration on the Tremussen chalice, Poland, *ca.* 1180. FOTO MARBURG/ART RESOURCE 193.231

BIBLIOGRAPHY
Aziz Suryal Atiya, *The Crusade of Nicopolis* (1934); Joseph Delaville Le Roulx, *La France en Orient au XIVe siècle* (1885), 211–234; Kenneth M. Setton, *The Papacy and the Levant,* I (1976), 341–357.

SUSAN M. BABBITT

[See also **Bāyazīd I, Yildirim; Crusades of the Later Middle Ages.**]

NIELLO. The niello print is an intaglio impression from a silver or gold plate. Although executed much like a copperplate engraving, the niello plaque was intended not for printing but for decoration. To this end, the lines were eventually filled with a black compound of fused sulfur and borax called *nigellum,* hence the term niello. In some cases, the print was taken from a very fine sulfur cast rather than from the metal plate. During the fifteenth century, the production of nielli was centered in Florence and Bologna.

BIBLIOGRAPHY
André Blum, *Les nielles du quattrocento* (1950); Jean Duchesne, *Essai sur les nielles* (1826); Arthur M. Hind, *Nielli, Chiefly Italian of the Fifteenth Century: Plates, Sulphur Casts, and Prints Preserved in the British Museum* (1936); Jay A. Levenson, Konrad Oberhuber, and Jacquelyn L. Sheehan, *Early Italian Engravings from the National Gallery of Art* (1973); John Goldsmith Phillips, *Early Florentine Designers and Engravers* (1955).

R. S. FIELD

[See also **Engraving; Metalsmiths, Gold and Silver.**]

NIGEL OF LONGCHAMP (Nigel Wireker) (*fl.* twelfth century), Anglo-Latin satirist, author of the *Speculum stultorum* (The mirror for fools), the popular story of Brunellus the Ass. Little is known for certain of his life. He was probably born at Longchamp in Normandy around 1130 into a family that later settled in Canterbury. The surname "Wireker," long thought to associate him with Whitacre in Kent, is now regarded as spurious. Given his apparent familiarity with the schools and curriculum in Paris, it is likely that he studied there. Nigel boasts of his acquaintance with Thomas Becket ("whom I saw with my own eyes and touched with my hands, with whom I ate and drank"); he may have spent some time in the archbishop's service before entering the monastery of Christ Church, Canterbury, around 1170. He spent the remainder of his life as a Benedictine monk, a priest, and, possibly, precentor at Christ Church. A strong defender of the rights of monastic chapters, he was spokesman for his brethren in their dispute with Archbishop Baldwin (1186–1189), and he also actively protested the expulsion of the monks of Coventry Cathedral by Bishop Hugh (1191). No definite date has been established for his death; however, as he was already an old man when he completed the *Speculum stultorum* (*ca.* 1180), it is likely that he died sometime before 1200.

Written in Latin elegiac verse, the *Speculum stultorum* tells of the futile attempts of Brunellus, the ambitious but foolish ass, to procure a longer tail, acquire an education in Paris, and establish a new religious order. Although the character of Brunellus may be taken from a fable of Avianus ("The Ass and the Lion's Skin"), the story is largely original. Its intention, Nigel explains in a dedicatory letter to William of Longchamp, is to show the foolishness of the ambitions and vain pretensions of members of religious orders. Interwoven with the adventures of Brunellus are a number of other stories and fables, several of which became popular exempla in sermons and were later retold by such authors as Boccaccio, Chaucer, and Gower.

Nigel's other major work, a treatise *Contra curiales et officiales clericos* (Against courtiers and ecclesiastical administrators), is in prose with an elegiac verse prologue. Addressed to William of Longchamp, then (in 1193–1194) bishop of Ely, royal chancellor, and regent, the treatise forcefully criticizes the involvement of prelates in secular politics and government. Like the *Policraticus* of John of Salisbury, it warns of the dangers of court life, the evils of vain ambition, and the abuses of education; but, unlike John, Nigel was primarily concerned with the effects of such ills on the church. His satire is sharpest when he writes of the ignorance and corruption of the prelacy and clergy.

In addition to his satire, Nigel wrote at least one theological work, a commentary of the *Historia scholastica* of Peter Comestor. All his other extant works are in verse; they include a collection of seventeen Marian miracle legends, two saints' lives, and a variety of moral and religious poems. It is, however, for his skills as a satirist and storyteller that Nigel is known.

BIBLIOGRAPHY

Nigel of Longchamp, *The Book of Daun Burnel the Ass: Nigellus Wireker's Speculum stultorum*, Graydon W. Regenos, trans. (1959), *Speculum stultorum*, John H. Mozley and Robert R. Raymo, eds. (1960), and *A Mirror for Fools: The Book of Burnel the Ass*, John H. Mozley, trans. (1963). See also André Boutemy, *Nigellus de Longchamp dit Wireker* (1959); Max Manitius, *Geschichte der lateinischen Literatur des Mittelalters*, III (1931), 809–813; John H. Mozley, "The Unprinted Poems of Nigel Wireker," in *Speculum*, 7 (1932); Frederic J. E. Raby, *A History of Secular Latin Poetry in the Middle Ages*, II (2nd ed. 1957), 94–100.

S. C. FERRUOLO

[See also **Latin Literature; Latin Meter.**]

NIKEPHOROS, PATRIARCH (*ca.* 758–829), patriarch of Constantinople from 806 to 815, born to a noble family of the capital. Like his father (who had been banished by Constantine V Kopronymos for his iconodule beliefs), Nikephoros became an imperial secretary; in this capacity he served at the Seventh Ecumenical Council of Nicaea in 787. Upon the death of Tarasios I in 806, Emperor Nikephoros I (802–811) chose Nikephoros as the successor to the patriarchal throne. At first violently opposed by the Studites because of his lay background, Nikephoros became a potent political figure, especially during the reign of Michael I (811–813), and was to become, along with Theodore of Studios, a chief defender of orthodoxy in the struggle against Leo V's (813–820) revival of iconoclasm. Nikephoros, deposed and exiled by Leo in 815, never returned to Constantinople. He died in 829.

Nikephoros' literary output was considerable. His so-called *Breviarum* (Short history), written while he was still in the imperial service, treats of the period from the death of Emperor Maurice to the marriage of Leo IV (602–769). Along with the *Chronicle* of Theophanes Confessor, with whom Nikephoros shares a lost literary source, the *Breviarium*, abounding in curiosities, is of priceless historical worth. A shorter earlier version is also extant, affording us the rare opportunity to observe a Byzantine author revising his own text. Nikephoros also composed a chronographic list, reaching from Adam to the reign of Michael II (820–829). This work was widely read, to judge from the great number of manuscripts in which it is preserved, and was translated early on into Latin and Old Church Slavonic.

The last and most important of Nikephoros' theological works is the still unpublished *Refutatio et eversio*, in which he refutes the *Definition* of the Council of St. Sophia of 815. Here Nikephoros attempts to disprove the accusation of the revivers of the heresy that icons were counterfeit images. In his earlier *Apologeticus major* and three *Antirrhetici,* he denounces the false monks who had become the pawns of Leo V and had used the impious works of Constantine Kopronymos in their preparations for resuscitating the heresy. He refutes, with Aristotelian arguments among others, the doctrines set forth against icons during the first period of iconoclasm. From the *Antirrhetici,* it is possible to reconstruct the lost works of Constantine Kopronymos. In the first *Antirrheticus*, Nikephoros refutes the christological arguments against icons of Christ; in the second he proceeds to the icons of the Virgin and the saints; in the third he discusses the scriptural basis for icons. Of great interest to historians is Nikephoros' concluding description of the composition of the iconoclastic party. In two other works, *De magnete* and *Contra Eusebium et Epiphanidem,* Nikephoros accuses the Iconoclasts of using spurious patristic passages in support of their arguments. In these works, Nikephoros, not unlike a modern editor, discusses the manuscripts in which he found particular texts.

BIBLIOGRAPHY

Sources. Breviarium and Chronography, in Carl de Boor, ed., *Nicephori archiepiscopi Constantinopolitani opuscula historica* (1880), 1–77, 79–135; *Apologeticus major* and *Antirrhetici,* in *Patrologia graeca,* C (1865), 201–850; *De magnete* and *Contra Eusebium et Epiphanidem,* in Jean B. Pitra, ed., *Spicilegium solesmense,* I (1852–1858), 302–335, 371–503.

Studies. Paul J. Alexander, *The Patriarch Nicephorus of Constantinople* (1958); Marie-José Baudinet, "La relation iconique à Byzance au IXe siècle d'après Nicéphore le Patriarche: Un destin de l'aristotélisme," in *Les études philosophiques,* **1** (1978); Hans G. Beck, *Kirche und theologische Literatur im byzantinischen Reich* (1959), 489–491; Herbert Hunger, *Die hochsprachliche profane Literatur der Byzantinen,* I (1978), 343–347.

JEFFREY FEATHERSTONE

[See also **Byzantine Literature; Constantine V; Councils (Ecumenical, 325–787); Hiereia, Council of; Historiography, Byzantine; Icon, Theology of; Iconoclasm, Christian; Theodore of Studios.**]

NIKEPHOROS I (*r.* 802–811), Byzantine emperor. He served Empress Irene as general logothete (finance minister) before overthrowing her in a bloodless coup. His greatest achievement was to reform the Empire's financial machinery to assess and collect the taxes of the rich and the church more strictly. He also reestablished Byzantine control over the Peloponnesus, most of which had long been in the hands of the Slavs. Though Nikephoros made a determined attempt to curb the power of the Bulgarians under Khan Krum, in 811 they ambushed and defeated his army and killed him. Harshly criticized in the contemporary chronicle of Theophanes Confessor, Nikephoros has been rehabilitated by modern historians.

BIBLIOGRAPHY

John B. Bury, *History of the Eastern Roman Empire* (1912), 1–42, 212–218, 249–250, 317–325, 339–345 (partly outdated, but still the most detailed treatment); George Ostrogorsky, *History of the Byzantine State,* Joan Hussey, trans. (rev. ed., 1969), 186–200; Warren T. Treadgold, "The Revival of Byzantine Learning and the Revival of the Byzantine State," in *American Historical Review,* **84** (1979).

WARREN T. TREADGOLD

[See also **Byzantine History (330–1025); Krum; Theophanes Confessor.**]

NIKEPHOROS II PHOKAS (*r.* 963–969), Byzantine emperor and descendant of a wealthy Cappadocian family. A distinguished general, he recaptured Crete from the Arabs in 961. He seized power in 963, married Theophano, the widow of his predecessor, and reigned together with her two children, Basil II and Constantine VII. Nikephoros conquered Cilicia and Cyprus in 965 and campaigned repeatedly in Syria, capturing Antioch in 969. He launched an unsuccessful expedition against the Arabs of Sicily in 965 and vehemently opposed the Western imperial title of the German Otto the Great. In 968 he used his Russian allies to crush the Bulgarians.

In spite of his deep piety, he tried to check the expansion of church property. His onerous fiscal policy and the inflation resulting from military expenditure made him very unpopular. He was murdered in 969, victim of a plot of his wife and her lover, the young general John Tzimiskes (who succeeded Nikephoros as emperor).

BIBLIOGRAPHY

George Ostrogorsky, *History of the Byzantine State,* Joan Hussey, trans. (rev. ed. 1969), 284–293; Gustave Schlumberger, *Un empereur byzantin au dixième siècle: Nicéphore Phocas* (1890).

NICOLAS OIKONOMIDES

[See also **Athos, Mount; Byzantine History (330–1025); Encyclopedias, Byzantine; Eparch, Book of the; John I Tzimiskes.**]

NIKEPHOROS BRYENNIOS (*d.* 1137), a member of one of the great noble families of the Byzantine Empire and husband of Anna Komnena, the daughter of Emperor Alexios I. He was both an excellent general and a man of great cultivation, a writer and diplomat as well as a soldier. The empress Irene urged him to take the throne on the death of his father-in-law in 1118, but he hesitated because he believed Anna's brother John to be the rightful emperor. He wrote a history of Alexios I but died before he could complete it. Anna, who was devastated at his death, wrote her own history of her father's reign, which has come down to us as the *Alexiad.* In this work, she describes her husband Nikephoros as a man of exceptional qualities to whom she was devoted.

BIBLIOGRAPHY

Elizabeth A. S. Dawes, trans., *The Alexiad of the Princess Anna Comnena* (1928); Henri Grégoire, "Nicéphore Bryennios: Les quatres livres des Histoires," in *Byzantion,* **23, 25–27** (1953, 1955–1957); Edgar R. A. Sewter, trans., *The Alexiad of Anna Comnena* (1969).

LINDA C. ROSE

[See also **Alexios I Komnenos; Anna Komnena, Byzantine Empire; Byzantine Literature; Historiography, Byzantine.**]

NIKEPHOROS GREGORAS (1290/1291–1360), Byzantine historian and scholar, was born in Heraclea Pontica. After studying under Patriarch John Glykys and Theodore Metochites, who initiated him into the science of astronomy, he became a court favorite of the learned emperor Andronikos II Palaiologos. After the latter's downfall in 1328, Nikephoros left the court and continued to teach at the private school he had opened in Constantinople.

Nikephoros opposed the hesychast theology of Gregory Palamas and after 1346 became a leader of the anti-Palamite party, writing many polemical theological treatises. Condemned for this opposition at the synod of 1351, he suffered several years of imprisonment. Nevertheless, he completed his major work, the *Roman History,* which covers the years 1204–1359 and describes Nikephoros' participation in the hesychast controversy.

BIBLIOGRAPHY

Nikephoros' major work is available as *Byzantina historia,* Ludwig Schopen and Immanuel Bekker, eds., 3 vols. (1829–1855), Greek text and Latin trans., in the series Corpus Scriptorum Historiae Byzantinae; and *Nikephoros Gregoras Rhomäische Geschichte,* Jan Louis van Dieten, trans., 2 vols. in 3 pts. (1973–1979). A partial edition of his correspondence is *Correspondance de Nicéphore Grégoras,* Rodolphe J. Guilland, ed. and trans. (1927).

A study is Hans-Veit Beyer, "Eine Chronologie der Lebensgeschichte des Nikephoros Gregoras," in *Jahrbuch der österreichischen Byzantinistik,* 27 (1978).

FRANCES KIANKA

[See also **Andronikos II Palaiologos; Byzantine Literature; Gregory Palamas; Hesychasm; Historiography, Byzantine.**]

NIKETAS CHONIATES (*ca.* 1155/1157—*ca.* 1215/1216), Byzantine historian. He was born in Chonai, near ancient Collosae in Phrygia Pacatiana, to a family of the lesser nobility and completed his education in Constantinople under the supervision of his older brother Michael, who later became an eminent metropolitan of Athens. The designation of his surname as Acominatus is a misnomer and should be avoided.

Niketas began his career around 1180 as imperial secretary to the last of the Komnenian emperors, Andronikos I (*ca.* 1120–1185). He rose rapidly in the civil bureaucracy under their successors, the Angeloi, serving in such important posts as governor of the theme of Philippopolis, grand chamberlain of the public treasury, judge of the *Velum*, and, finally, grand logothete.

The usurpation of Alexios V Doukas in 1204 brought an end to Niketas' political fortunes, and with the fall of the capital to the Fourth Crusade in the same year he went into exile, having lost all his possessions. Remaining in Selymbria until 1026, he returned to Constantinople for six months and completed the draft of the last chapter of his history, dealing with the events that followed the fall. Migrating to the newly established empire of Nicaea, where his vast political experience was largely ignored, he died a disillusioned man.

A Byzantine polymath, Choniates instinctively infuses the events of his own times with the Homeric tradition and deftly interweaves classical and Christian skeins into a harmonious cloth. He is, nonetheless, weighed down by his cultural bias—Byzantium and everything Byzantine are the ultimate standard by which all else must be measured, and thus his field of vision is necessarily narrowed.

Niketas' history, a major document covering the years 1118–1206, continuing where Anna Komnena and John Zonaras end theirs and overlapping in part with that of John Kinnamos, is a necessary pendant to the Western accounts of the Fourth Crusade. As an eyewitness to much of what he writes, he provides an extremely valuable account; personally engulfed by the catastrophe of 1204, he writes with a deep and bitter passion.

Choniates authored other works as well. *The Thesaurus of Orthodoxy,* whose last five chapters deal with contemporary theological issues, has a certain significance; his eighteen orations and eleven letters are at best minor works, but his history remains a *monumentum aere perennius.*

BIBLIOGRAPHY

Sources. Michael Akominatos Choniates, *The Preserved Works* (in Greek), Spyridōn Lampros, ed., I and II (1879–1880); Niketas Choniates, *Historia,* in Immanuel Bekker, ed., *Corpus scriptorum historiae byzantinae,* XXIII (1835), in Jan Louis van Dieten, ed., *Corpus fontium historiae byzantinae,* XI.1 (1975), and in *Byzantinische Geschichtsschreiber,* Franz Grabler, trans. VII, VIII, IX (1958); *Orationes et epistulae,* in Jan Louis van Dieten, ed., *op. cit.,* III (1973), and *Thesaurus orthodoxae fidei,* in *Patrologia graeca,* CXXXIX–CXL (1865). See also *O City of Byzantium: Annals of Niketas Choniatēs,* Harry J. Magoulias, trans. (1984).

Studies. Robert Browning, *The Byzantine Empire* (1980); Marie E. Colonna, *Gli storici bizantini dal IV al XV secolo,* I (1956); Anthony Cutler, "The *De signis* of Nicetas Choniates: A Reappraisal," in *American Journal of Archaeology,* **72** (1968); Jan Louis van Dieten, "Noch einmal über Niketas Choniates," in *Byzantinische Zeitschrift,* **57** (1964), and *Niketas Choniates: Erläuterungen zu den Reden und Briefen nebst einer Biographie* (1971); Karl Krumbacher, *Geschichte der byzantinischen Litteratur* (1897), 285; Gyula Moravcsik, *Byzantinoturcica,* I (1942–1943, 2nd ed., 1958), 444–450; Georg Stadtmüller, "Zur Biographie des Niketas Choniates," in *Byzantinische Forschungen,* **1** (1966); Fedor Uspenskij, *Vizantiiskii pisatel' Nikita Akominat iz Khon* (1874).

HARRY J. MAGOULIAS

[See also **Byzantine Literature; Crusades and Crusader States: Fourth; Historiography, Byzantine; John Kinnamos.**]

NIKITIN, AFANASII (*d.* 1472), a Russian merchant of the town of Tver (now Kalinin) on the upper Volga, became famous for his trade voyage to Iran and India (1466–1472). On the Iranian portion of his voyage, he sailed down the Volga and along the western coast of the Caspian Sea; the journey was plagued with misfortunes from the start. The Indian part of Nikitin's travelogue is rich in socioeconomic and historical detail, while the rest is but an enumeration of toponyms. He may have converted to Islam at least temporarily, as his text, preserved as a part of a Russian chronicle of the late fourteenth–early fifteenth century, ends with an unparalleled evocation of God in Arab-Persian terms. Nikitin died in Smolensk.

BIBLIOGRAPHY

Khozhenie za tri moria (Journey beyond the three seas) exists in full or partially in seven MSS. It has been edited a number of times and translated into modern Russian at least four times, the preferred version being that by Varvara Pavlovna Adrianova-Peretts (1948, 2nd ed. 1958, repr. 1970); the 1960 edition (Moscow) includes an English translation.

Studies include I. S. Lure, "Podvig Afanasia Nikitina," in *Izvestia Vsesoyuznogo geograficheskogo obshchestva,* **99** (1967); A. M. Osipov, *Afanasy Nikitin i ego vremia* (1951); M. N. Vitashevskaya, *Stranstvia Afanasia Nikitina* (1972). Nikitin's travels have become the subject of many other Soviet studies and even a Soviet-Indian film production (1957).

SERGEI SHUISKII

NIKOLAOS KAVASILAS (Cabasilas) (1322/1323–*ca.* 1390), one of the most important late Byzantine writers, was born in Thessaloniki of a prominent Chamaëtos family. Emulating his uncle, the monk and metropolitan Neilos, he chose a career of letters (but not of the church). In 1347, in Constantinople, where he extended his training, Nikolaos identified himself with the faction of Emperor John VI Kantakouzenos and with the doctrines of Gregory Palamas. An expert in both civil and church law, he wrote extensively. Nikolaos' most important works are on mysticism, greatly admired then and since; he also composed theological, philosophical, and poetic essays. His treatise against secular abuse of church property is no longer regarded as a condemnation of the Zealot movement of Thessaloniki.

BIBLIOGRAPHY

Sources. Nikolaos' writings are in *Patrologia graeca,* CL (1865, repr. 1978), 368–772. Translations include *Sakramentalmystik der Ostkirche: Das Buch vom Leben in Christus,* Gerhard Hoch, trans., Endre von Ivánka, ed. (1958); *La vida en Cristo,* Luis Gutiérrez Vega and Buenaventura García Rodríguez, trans. (1958); *A Commentary on the Divine Liturgy,* Joan M. Hussey and P. A. McNulty, trans. (1960).

Studies. Rodolphe Guillaud, "La correspondence inedité de Nicolas Cabasilas," in *Byzantinische Zeitschrift,* **30** (1929–1930); Myrrha Borodine Lot, *Un maître de la spiritualité byzantine au XIVe siecle: Nicolas Cabasilas* (1958); Ihor Ševčenko, "Nicolas Cabasilas' 'Anti-Zealot' Discourse: A Reinterpretation," in *Dumbarton Oaks Papers,* **11** (1957).

JOHN W. BARKER

[See also **Gregory Palamas; Thessaloniki; Zealots.**]

NIKOLAOS I MYSTIKOS, PATRIARCH (852–925). Patriarch of Constantinople (901–907 and 912–925), ecclesiastically and politically one of the most prominent holders of the Constantinopolitan see. Of Italian origin, but also in some way related to Photios, he felt endangered by the latter's downfall in 886 (the year of the accession of Emperor Leo VI) and took the monastic habit. Later, Leo made him his personal secretary (*mystikos*) and in March 901 raised him to the patriarchal see. The most signal event of this first patriarchate was the conflict over Leo's fourth marriage (the so-called tetragamy), the validity of which involved also the legitimacy of Leo's long-awaited son and heir, the later Constantine VII. Unable or unwilling to grant a dispensation, Nikolaos was deposed in February 907 and replaced by Euthymios, with a schism as the result. When Leo died in May 912, his brother and successor Alexander reinstated Nikolaos. On his deathbed, just over a year later, Alexander appointed the patriarch head of a regency council. As such, Nikolaos was for eight months the virtual ruler of the empire, until ousted in February 914 by the empress dowager Zoë. His position as patriarch remained precarious until the coup d'etat of Romanos I in March 919, under whose leadership the schism was at least officially ended in July 920. After five more years of intense ecclesiastical and diplomatic activity, Nikolaos died in May 925.

The second patriarchate is especially well-documented by extant correspondence, totaling 190 letters, among which are many substantial pieces of great historical interest, such as those to Symeon of Bulgaria and other Christian princes, to some Muslim rulers, and to the popes Anastasius III and John X. In addition to the letters, there are some other chancery documents (in particular the *Tome of Union* of 920), a sermon on the fall of Thessaloniki in 904, and a few hymns.

BIBLIOGRAPHY

Sources. Venance Grumel, *Les regestes des actes du patriarcat de Constantinople,* I (1936), 133–271; Romilly J. H. Jenkins and L. G. Westerink, trans., with Greek text, *Nicholas I, Patriarch of Constantinople, Letters* (1973); Patricia Karlin-Hayter, trans. with Greek text and intro., *Vita Euthymii, Patriarchae CP* (1970); L. G. Westerink, trans., with Greek text, *Miscellaneous Writings* (1981).

Studies. Romilly J. H. Jenkins, *Studies on Byzantine History in the 9th and 10th Centuries* (1970); Patricia Karlin-Hayter, "Le synode à Constantinople de 886 à 912 et le rôle de Nicolas le Mystique dans l'affaire de la tétragamie," in *Jahrbuch der Österreichischen Byzantinistik,* **19** (1970); Io. Ch. Konstantinides, *Nikolaos A' ho Mystikos* (1967); Steven Runciman, *The Emperor Romanus Lecapenus and His Reign* (1963).

L. G. WESTERINK

The Transfiguration, with warrior saints. Gable relief from the east facade of the church of Nikorcᶜminda, 1010–1014. FROM WACHTANG BERIDSE/EDITH NEUBAUER, *DIE BAUKUNST DES MITTELALTERS IN GEORGIEN* © UNION VERLAG (VOB), BERLIN 1981. Foto Klaus G. Beyer, Weimar

[See also **Byzantine Church; Byzantine Empire; Constantine VII Porphyrogenitos; Leo VI the Wise, Emperor; Photios; Romanos I Lekapenos; Symeon of Bulgaria.**]

NIKOLAOS MESARITES (*fl.* early thirteenth century) was a Byzantine ecclesiastic who spent his earlier career in Constantinople and became metropolitan of Ephesus by 1212–1213. He wrote several works that are important sources for early-thirteenth-century Byzantine history, and a long description (*ekphrasis*) of the Church of the Holy Apostles in Constantinople that is of interest to historians of Byzantine art, architecture, and education.

BIBLIOGRAPHY

Source. August Heisenberg, *Nikolaos Mesarites: Die Palastrevolution des Johannes Komnenos* (1907), includes text and commentary.

Studies. Hans-Georg Beck, *Kirche und theologische Literatur im byzantinischen Reich* (1959, 1977), 666–667; Glanville Downey, "Nikolaos Mesarites: Description of the Church of the Holy Apostles at Constantinople," in *Transactions of the American Philosophical Society,* **47** (1957); Herbert Hunger, *Die hochsprachliche profane Literatur der Byzantiner,* I (1978), 181–182.

HENRY MAGUIRE

[See also **Historiography, Byzantine.**]

NIKORCᶜMINDA, a church located nine miles southwest of Ambroulauri, was built between 1010 and 1014. The southern and western porches, sumptuously decorated with reliefs, were added later in the first half of the eleventh century. Nikorcᶜminda is a rare example of the centrally planned hexagonal church surmounted by a massive dome. The eastern elongated portion is emphasized by a lofty presbytery and a semicircular apse. The walls of its cruciform exterior are exceptionally rich in ornamental decorations and reliefs having religious and secular themes, as well as articulated representations of animals on the window frames and their brows, on the tympana, on the lunettes of the porches, and on the lower cornice of the dome's drum. The interior of the church is covered with sixteenth- and seventeenth-century wall paintings.

BIBLIOGRAPHY

Natela Aleksandrovna Aldashvili, *Nikortsmindis reliephebi* (1957), in Georgian with Russian and German résumés; Adriano Alpago-Novello, Vahtang Beridze, and Jacqueline Lafontaine-Dosogne, *Art and Architecture in Medieval Georgia* (1980); Russudan Mepisashvili and Wachtang Tsintsadze, *Die Kunst des alten Georgien,* Barbara Donadt, trans. (1977); N. P. Severov and G. N. Chubinashvili, *Kumurdo i Nikortsminda* (1957), 17–26, pls. XVII–XXVIII.

WACHTANG DJOBADZE

[See also **Georgian Art and Architecture.**]

NIL SORSKY, ST. (1433–1508), one of the major personalities of Russian monasticism of the late medieval period, and spokesman of the "Nonpossessors," who defended the principle and practice of monastic poverty. Born into a peasant (*poselyanin*) family, he received the monastic tonsure early in his youth, traveled to Turkish-occupied Constantinople, and visited Mt. Athos, where he learned Greek. Upon his return to Russia, Nil settled north of the Volga, at the monastery founded by St. Cyril of Belozero. Soon he retired to a skete ten miles from Belozero, where, together with an older monk, Paisy Yaroslavov, he led a revival of the hesychastic way of life, following Egyptian, Syrian, and Byzantine models.

A copyist of manuscripts, a compiler of saints' lives, and the author of several ascetic and spiritual writings—including the *Ustav* (Rule) and *Predanie* (Instructions to disciples)—in which he profusely quotes Byzantine monastic literature, Nil appears as an extraordinarily sober and profound teacher of the continuous Jesus prayer ("Lord Jesus Christ, Son of God, have mercy on me").

In 1489–1490, as the heretics called Judaizers were being prosecuted in Novgorod, Nil expressed his opposition to the inquisitional measures being taken against them. At the Council of Moscow (1503), he opposed the secularization of monastic property as unnecessary and harmful to the spiritual life.

BIBLIOGRAPHY

Editions of Nil's writings include, M. A. Borovkova-Maikova, ed., *Nila Sorskago Predanie i Ustav* (St. Petersburg, 1912) (*Pamiatniki drevnei pis'mennosti*, CLXXIX), abridged trans. in G. P. Fedotov, *A Treasury of Russian Spirituality* (1948), 90–92. G. M. Prokhorov, "Poslania Nila Sorskogo," in *SSSR, Akademiya Nauk, Otdel drevne-russkoi literatury, Trudy*, **29** (1974), is a critical edition of Nil's letters showing that some unauthentic texts were used by earlier authors.

See also Aleksandr S. Arkhangelsky, *Nil Sorsky i Vassian Patrikeev* (1882, repr. 1966); Fairy von Lilienfeld, *Nil Sorskij und seine Schriften* (1963); George A. Maloney, *Russian Hesychasm: The Spirituality of Nil Sorski* (1973), includes translations of Nil's letters.

JOHN MEYENDORFF

[See also **Hesychasm; Russian Orthodox Church.**]

NILE (Greek: *Neilos*, probably from the Semitic root *naḥal* meaning "valley" or "river valley"). The medieval Nile existed as a font of literary allusion and of moral example; as a fundamental feature of cosmography; and, to some, as a real and familiar river. This diversity of views derived from the surviving knowledge of antiquity, the scriptures of Judaism, Christianity, and Islam, and the accumulation of practical experience.

On occasion the Nile set a suitable tone for an otherwise unrelated discourse. Thus, in the fifth century Sidonius Apollinaris alluded to the dangers of travel in general through reference to "the dull flood of the Nile with all its awful crocodiles," and Dante, with characteristic symmetry, used images of the river borrowed from Lucan once in each book of the *Divine Comedy*.

While debates raged about the shape of the earth and the possibility of habitable or inhabited land outside the known *oikoumene*, the place of the Nile within the latter was secure. Water separated the three familiar continents; the Nile divided Asia from Africa and the sons of Shem from the children of Ham. A conspicuous peculiarity of the Nile was its annual summer flood. The preferred medieval explanation attributed it to the southward-blowing Etesian wind, which was believed to impede the normal flow of the river except in summer.

After meeting the sea, the Nile, like other rivers, was believed to join the scriptural "waters under the earth," which were assumed to circulate through subterranean channels analogous to the blood vessels of the human body. The source of the Nile, by consensus, was a spring in the Terrestrial Paradise, usually said to be located at temperate latitudes in the extreme east and sufficiently elevated to have escaped the Flood. The Nile was said by Christians to be the biblical Gihon, one of the four rivers of Eden. In order to reconcile the inaccessibility of Paradise to living men with the observed course of the lower Nile through Egypt, it was necessary to postulate an underground channel running beneath the divinely established waste of thorns and into the inhabited world.

More problematic was the question of where the Nile emerged, a difficulty compounded by the confusion of Ethiopia with India and the incorrect assumption that Africa was a small continent symmetrically in balance with Europe. One theory, favored by Orosius (*Historiae adversum paganos*, ca. 417) and his followers, argued that the Nile emerged in Ethiopia near the Red Sea and that its entire course ran predominantly northward. More popular was the interpretation advanced by Isidore of Seville (*Etymologiae*) that the Nile appeared on the southern slopes of the Atlas Mountains in the far west of Mauretania and flowed eastward for a great distance through a desert tract, or possibly underground, before turning north to Egypt. This theory economically accounted for the very vague existing references to large West African rivers, possibly the Niger, Benue, and Senegal, by making them all a part of the Nile; even the eyewitness reports of medieval Mediterranean visitors to the region failed to clarify the situation. A final scheme, advanced by Ibn Khaldūn, sought to combine these versions by postulating a single Ethiopian Nile source but maintaining that the river divided into two streams, a northward-flowing "Nile of Egypt" and a westward-flowing "Nile of the Negroes."

Any of these theories could be combined with specific details derived from Ptolemy's *Geography:* the Mountains of the Moon, the Maeotic Swamp, the Island of Meroë, and the cataracts. All were assumed to lie not far south of Aswan, for the presumed uninhabitability of the torrid zone demanded a drastically foreshortened southward perspective. At the end of its course through Egypt, the Nile divided into a form resembling the letter *delta* and entered the sea via seven mouths.

Though the Nile was not commonly made to bear a heavy burden of moral or allegorical significance, it was sometimes said to represent one of the Evangelists or one of the cardinal virtues. That it could be made to serve such a purpose was demonstrated by Abelard in his ingenious sermon on Amos 9:5. He compared the descent of the Nile from Paradise to the emanation of divine power and wisdom, which brought life to the carnal world as the Nile waters did to Egypt. The Nile in winter represented the apostles immediately after the Resurrection, inhibited from spreading the Gospel by Etesian winds of local hostility and their own inertia.

Few who actually saw the Nile failed to note its impact upon Egypt, "in which the land is so burned and sterile," as William of Tyre (*d. ca.* 1185) put it, "that it supports no herb and no manner of tree, except where the River Nile waters the ground when it is in flood." Ibn Baṭṭūṭa (traveled 1325–1354) concluded that "the Egyptian Nile surpasses all rivers of the earth in sweetness of taste, length of course, and magnitude of utility." To the Egyptians, noted Benjamin of Tudela (traveled 1160–1173), the annual flood was no mystery, but the result of the Ethiopian rainy season. Visitors often commented upon the ancient but functional Nilometer, by means of which could be calculated the height of the flood, and thus the degree of prosperity or hardship to be anticipated in the year to come. Several Islamic historians recorded the various past attempts to link the Nile to the Red Sea by canals whose remains were still visible. Many visitors sensed the unusual character of the people who lived along the Nile; some noted the allegedly devious mentality of the peasants, and others, the apparent tyranny of their rulers. These observers perceived, if imperfectly, psychological traits indigenous to a medieval Egyptian society whose structure had been so definitively determined by its total dependence upon the great river.

BIBLIOGRAPHY

Charles G. M. de La Roncière, *La découverte de l'Afrique au moyen âge,* 2 vols. (1925); John Kirtland Wright, *The Geographical Lore of the Time of the Crusades* (1925, repr. 1965).

JAY L. SPAULDING

[See also **Baṭṭuṭa, Ibn; Benjamin of Tudela; Cairo; Egypt; Geography and Cartography; Roman Egypt, Late; Sudan; William of Tyre.**]

NIMBUS (from Latin meaning "cloud" or "mist"), also called halo, is a zone of light, in the shape of a disc or plate, placed vertically behind the head of a sacred or divine person. Generally the nimbus is golden, but it may also be red, blue, green, or in the hues of the rainbow. The nimbus was used in religious symbolism of the Hellenistic period to distinguish gods and demigods. Roman emperors were often portrayed with a crown of rays to assert their divine lineage. In Christian art of the third and fourth centuries, the use of the nimbus is restricted to Christ and the Lamb. From the fifth century on, it appears in the depiction of angels, saints, and the Virgin. In the eighth century the use of the square nimbus to designate living persons such as donors, bishops, or popes is first noted.

The cruciform nimbus, a cross within a circle, symbolizes the Trinity and redemption through the cross, and therefore is used only in representations of Christ. Its use occurred as early as the beginning of the fourth century and was prevalent by the sixth century in both Christian East and West. The triangular nimbus also represents the Trinity.

BIBLIOGRAPHY

Marthe Collinet-Guérin, *Histoire du nimbus* (1961); Ormonde M. Dalton, *Byzantine Art and Archaeology* (1911, new ed. 1961); George W. Ferguson, *Signs and*

Symbols in Christian Art (1954, repr. 1961, 1973); André Grabar, *Christian Iconography* (1968); Gertrud Schiller, *Iconography of Christian Art,* Janet Seligman, trans., 2 vols. (1971–1972).

JENNIFER E. JONES

[See also **Early Christian Art; Iconography; Mandorla.** Examples of the plain and cruciform nimbus are shown at **Noli Me Tangere,** this volume.]

NINIAN, ST. (*d. ca.* 432), is regarded as a founder of Christianity in Scotland. What little is known about him, however, is subject to much controversy. The evidence suggests that the saint, whose name may have had a British (Celtic) form, **Niniavos,* was a bishop consecrated to minister, probably in the first half of the fifth century, to a Roman or sub-Roman Christian community in southwest Scotland at Whithorn in Galloway.

Four written sources purport to provide evidence about him. In his *Ecclesiastical History* (731) Bede interpolates in his account of St. Columba a report about "Nynia(s)" (the form of the name is uncertain), who, he says, was a bishop instructed in Rome who had converted the southern Picts. The saint was buried in his episcopal church, which was dedicated to St. Martin. The place was called *Ad candidam casam* (White House), so named, as has been argued, because Ninian probably built the church out of dressed stone. (The place is generally agreed to be Whithorn, which in Bede's day fell within the borders of the Anglo-Saxon kingdom of Bernicia.)

A second source, an eighth-century Latin poem, *Miraculi Nynie episcopi,* claims that after consecration by the pope, the saint preached to a Pictish people in whose territory he founded many monasteries before returning to the British and building his church. The British were subject to a king called Tuduael (Thuuahel), who clashed with him. After Ninian's death and burial in his church, various miracles took place at his tomb, some of which the poem recounts. A hymn, probably by the same author, adds no further information.

A *Life* compiled by Ethelred of Rievaulx (*ca.* 1110–1167) is the first to call the saint "Ninianus." It claims that Ninian visited St. Martin of Tours (*d.* 397) on his return journey from Rome.

Tombstones with Latin inscriptions from Whithorn and nearby point to a Christian community in Galloway in the fifth century (though their dating is imprecise). Genealogical evidence indicates that in the first half of the fifth century there was a Tudwal who might have ruled the Isle of Man, less than twenty miles from Galloway. Most scholars hold it improbable that Ninian met Martin and doubt that he established monasteries; such references and the mention of his papal consecration could have arisen in the context of an eighth-century Anglo-Saxon cult.

A fifth-century consecration as a missionary bishop would be anachronistic, but Ninian may have preached to the Picts: archaeological evidence suggests their presence south of the Firth of Forth in that century. A letter of St. Patrick to the soldiers of Coroticus of Strathclyde(?), probably dating from the latter half of the fifth century, refers to "apostate Picts," who could conceivably have been converted by Ninian. If so, an area east of Glasgow would be a possible location of his endeavors. His name does appear in place-names and church dedications as far north as the Shetlands, but most of these could be interpreted, like Ethelred's *Life,* as evidence of an efflorescence of his cult in the twelfth century.

BIBLIOGRAPHY

Editions and translations of medieval sources include *Bede's Ecclesiastical History of the English People,* III.4, Bertram Colgrave and Roger A. B. Mynors, eds. (1969), 222–223, text and translation; Ethelred of Rievaulx, *Vita Niniani,* in *Lives of S. Ninian and S. Kentigern,* Alexander P. Forbes, ed. (1874), 3–26 (translation), 137–157 (text); *Miracula Nynie episcopi* and *Hymnus sancti Nynie episcopi,* Karl Strecker, ed., in *Monumenta Germaniae historica: Poetae latini medii aevi,* IV.3 (1923), 943–962 (text only); Winifred W. MacQueen, ed., "Miracula Nynie episcopi," in *Transactions of the Dumfriesshire and Galloway Natural History and Antiquarian Society,* 3rd ser., 38 (1959–1960), text, trans., and commentary.

Modern studies include John MacQueen, *St. Nynia: A Study of Literary and Linguistic Evidence* (1961); A. Charles Thomas, "The Evidence from North Britain," in M. W. Barley and R. P. C. Hanson, eds., *Christianity in Britain, 300–700* (1968), 93–121; Charles Thomas, *Christianity in Roman Britain to AD 500* (1981), 275–294.

DAVID PELTERET

[See also **Celtic Church; Missions and Missionaries, Christian.**]

St. George altarpiece by Pedro Nisart, 1468. MUSEO DIOCESANO, PALMA DE MALLORCA. FOTO MAS, BARCELONA

NINO, ST. (*d. ca.* 338). According to Rufinus (*ca.* 400), a Roman captive woman converted Bakur, the pagan king of Georgia, to Christianity. At the beginning of the sixth century, her name, Nino, appeared in the early versions of Agatᶜangełos' *History of the Armenians,* where she figures as one of the forty companions of St. Hṙipᶜsimē. In a tenth-century Georgian codex the extensive legend of St. Nino derives from seven letters by different witnesses. The complexity and the internal contradictions of that work suggest a long prehistory. Such features as the discovery of Christ's tunic in Mcᶜχetᶜa and the foundation of the celestial pillar tend to match Greek narratives of the conversion of Constantine.

BIBLIOGRAPHY
I. Abuladze, ed., *Jveli Kᶜartᶜuli agiograpᶜiuli jeglebi,* I (1963), 81–163, is a critical edition of *The Conversion of Iberia.*

See also Michael van Esbroeck, "Un nouveau témoin du livre d'Agathange," in *Revue des études arméniennes,* n.s. 8 (1971); David Marshall Lang, ed. and trans., *Lives and Legends of the Georgian Saints* (1956), 13–39; Josef Markwart, "Die Bekehrung Iberiens und die beide ältesten Dokumente der iberischen Kirche," in *Caucasica,* 7 (1931); Cyril Toumanoff, *Studies in Christian Caucasian History* (1963), 374–375.

MICHAEL VAN ESBROECK

[See also **Agatᶜangełos; Georgian Church and Saints.**]

NISART, PEDRO (*fl. ca.* 1468), painter (with Rafael Moguer) of a St. George altarpiece for the Confraternity of St. George in Palma de Mallorca, documented 1468. The central panel (Museo Diocesano, Palma) is unusually Eyckian in style for Mallorcan painting, which was then generally still in the International Style. Several aspects resemble details in van Eyck's Mystical Lamb altarpiece at St. Bavon, Ghent, but Nisart may have seen a (now lost) *St. George* by van Eyck, sold to Alfonso V of Aragon in 1444.

BIBLIOGRAPHY
José Gudiol Ricart, *Pintura gótica* (1955); Augusto L. Mayer, *Historia de la pintura española,* 2nd ed. (1942).

MARY GRIZZARD

[See also **Gothic Art: Painting.**]

NISHAPUR. Now a provincial city in northeastern Iran, Nishapur (or Neyshābūr; Arabic: Naisābūr) rivaled Baghdad and Cairo as a great metropolis of the medieval Islamic world. It was founded in the pre-Islamic period, probably by the Sasanian emperor Sābuhr II (310–379), as a small, fortified city protecting the caravan route from Central Asia to Sasanian Iran at a vulnerable point near the eastern extremity of the Elburz Mountains. Also known as Abarshahr, Nishapur was a district as well as a city, but the precise signification and geographical extent of either name are uncertain.

The Sasanian governor (*kanārang*) surrendered to Muslim Arab invaders in 644, and the city rapidly expanded after becoming an Arab administrative center. Villages surrounding the fortress and walled inner city were incorporated. The new population was both Arab and Iranian Muslim, with the latter component increasingly dominant as conversion to Islam rapidly accelerated in the late eighth and early ninth centuries. The congregational mosque, governor's offices, and main markets were located in the newly incorporated areas.

Nishapur served as a primary or secondary capital for various dynasties, including the Abbasids, Tahirids, Samanids, Ghaznavids, and Seljuks. It was the dominant city of Khorāsān, an eastern Iranian province of great commercial, political, and cultural importance. It appears to have attained a population well over 100,000, with the peak around the year 1000. After that date economic and demographic decline associated with, if not caused by, the influx of Turkish nomads brought a halt to the city's physical growth. Nevertheless, it flourished as an intellectual and educational center in the eleventh century. The educational institution known as the madrasa, later to become widespread in Islamic countries, had roots there; and Nishapur's poets, theologians, and mystics are legion. Among them are the poets ᶜUmar Khayyām and Farīd al-Dīn ᶜAṭṭār, the theologians Imām al-Ḥaramain al-Juwainī and al-Ghazzālī; and the mystics Abū 'l-Qāsim al-Qushairī and Abū ᶜAbd al-Raḥmān al-Sulamī.

The price of Nishapur's dynamism was the emergence in the tenth century of endemic factional feuding between groups representing different schools of legal thought. The destruction caused by their enmity increased during the eleventh century and seemed beyond the control of the Seljuk sultans after the initial force of that Turkish dynasty dwindled toward the end of the century. After Sultan Sanjar was defeated and taken prisoner by nomads in 1153, nomads and bandits plundered the city. Final destruction came at the hands of factions within the city that engaged in intraurban warfare instead of working for the city's recovery. By 1161–1162 the city had been largely abandoned and a smaller Nishapur refounded in the quarter of Shādyākh in the western suburbs.

The new Nishapur flourished before being destroyed by Genghis Khan's army in 1221, but it never was more than a shadow of its predecessor. After the Mongol period Nishapur continued to exist. Several severe earthquakes caused it to be moved to slightly different locations, the present city being the furthest west. It never again rose above the rank of a secondary provincial city.

BIBLIOGRAPHY

The most important primary sources in Arabic and Persian are in Richard N. Frye, ed., *The Histories of Nishapur* (1965).

Studies include Clifford E. Bosworth, *The Ghaznavids: Their Empire in Afghanistan and Eastern Iran* (1963), 145–202; Richard W. Bulliet, *The Patricians of Nishapur* (1972), and "Medieval Nishapur: A Topographic and Demographic Reconstruction," in *Studia iranica,* 5 (1976).

RICHARD W. BULLIET

[See also **Ghaznavids; Iran: History After 650; Saffarids; Samanids; Tahirids.**]

NISI PRIUS, a writ and action required by the writ, in English common law. As the central courts of the king of England settled in Westminster, suitors may have been pleased to have the major royal courts in a fixed place. But when a case came to an issue of fact that required the verdict of a local jury, much time and some expense were required to bring the jury before the king's justices in Westminster. After various experiments in the late twelfth and early thirteenth centuries, the crown instituted a new system in clause 30 of the Statute of Westminster II (1285). Recognizing that fact-finding was separable from the rest of legal procedure, the central government ordered sheriffs to bring the required jury to Westminster unless before (*nisi prius* in Latin) that date the king's assize justices had visited the county. If, as usual, these justices appeared in time, the case was said to be heard at nisi prius.

BIBLIOGRAPHY

Alan Harding, *A Social History of English Law* (1966, repr. 1973); Stroud F. C. Milsom, *Historical Foundations of the Common Law* (1969); Theodore F. T. Plucknett, *A Concise History of the Common Law,* 5th ed. (1956).

RICHARD W. KAEUPER

[See also **Assize, English; Justices, Itinerant; Law, English Common: After 1272; Petty Assizes, English; Westminster, Statutes of.**]

NISIBIS (Armenian: Mcᶜbin; Arabic: Naṣībīn; modern Nusaybin, Turkey), a city in Upper Mesopotamia on the Hirmas (Greek: Mygdonias) River (37°05′N. × 41°11′E.), first mentioned as Na-si-pi-na or Na-sib-i-na in ninth-century-B.C.

Assyrian sources and known in the Hellenistic period as Antioch of Mygdonia. It should not be confused with Nisibis al-Rūm/Nsepin on the Euphrates.

In late antiquity and the early Middle Ages, Nisibis was a center of major economic and strategic importance because of its position on the Roman-Iranian frontier. It was the seat of the duke of Mesopotamia and the site of diplomatic negotiations and the signing of peace treaties. Nisibis was actively disputed between Byzantium and the Sasanians, passing from one to the other. Roman in the early fourth century, the city was besieged by the Persians in 338, 346, and 350, and ceded to them by Emperor Jovian in 363. Thereafter, it remained mostly in Persian, and subsequently Arab, hands, although it was briefly retaken by the Byzantines in 942, during the eastward expansion of the Macedonian dynasty, and burned by them in 972.

From early Christian times the city was an important religious center boasting distinguished ecclesiastical figures such as Bishop James (Hakob) of Nisibis, who attended the First Council of Nicaea (325), and the renowned poet and theologian Ephraem the Syrian (later in the fourth century). The city was elevated to a metropolitan see in the Persian church at the Council of Ctesiphon (410). Its most famous institution was the "School of the Persians," a major center of learning that moved from the Byzantine city of Edessa in 489 because of its Nestorian orientation. In addition to its theological and didactic importance, the School of Nisibis was the major center for the translations through which Greek learning was preserved and transmitted to the East.

Nisibis was also an important center for the textile and silk industries, and a major market to which traders came from distant lands. In the sixth century it was designated one of the official customs posts between the Byzantine and Sasanian empires. The city continued to prosper in later Muslim times, and was noted as a market and gardening center by Arab geographers and travelers such as Yāqūt, Ibn Ḥawqal, and Ibn Jubayr, though most of it was in ruins by the fourteenth century, according to the traveler Ibn Baṭṭūṭā.

BIBLIOGRAPHY

Louis Dillemann, *Haute Mésopotamie orientale et pays adjacents* (1962); Ignazio Guidi, "I statuti della scuola di Nisibi," in *Giornale della Società asiatica italiana,* 4 (1890); Ernest Honigmann, *Die Ostgrenze des byzantinischen Reiches von 363 bis 1071*(1935), and *Le couvent de Barṣaumā et le patriarcat jacobite d'Antioche et de Syrie* (1954); Arnold H. M. Jones, *Cities of the Eastern Roman Empire,* 2nd ed. (1971); Nina V. Pigulevskaya, *Les villes de l'état iranien* (1963); Charles Renoux, "Nisibe face au Perses, dans les Mēmrē sur Nicomédie de saint Éphrem," in *Handes amsoriya,* 90 (1976); Guy le Strange, *The Lands of the Eastern Caliphate* (1905, repr. 1966); A. A. Vööbus, *History of the School of Nisibis* (1963).

NINA G. GARSOÏAN

[See also **Christian Church in Persia; Nestorianism.**]

NISIBIS, SCHOOL OF. See **Syrian Christianity.**

NITHARD (790/800—844/845) was the illegitimate son of Charlemagne's daughter Bertha and Charlemagne's minister of state, Angilbert, who was also a noted poet. He was a soldier and for some time held high public office; he was also a man of learning who is today chiefly remembered as the official historian of Charlemagne's youngest grandson (and therefore Nithard's cousin), Charles II the Bald. Nithard's *Historiarum libri quattuor* covers the period from his grandfather's death in 814 to the Treaty of Verdun in August 843. The *Histories* remains the most important source of information about the wars among the sons of Louis the Pious, although it was self-confessedly composed as a piece of propaganda on behalf of Charles the Bald. While Nithard's work is invaluable as an eyewitness account, it also contains a number of factual errors, a circumstance perhaps partly caused by the fact that some of it was written years after the events took place. Furthermore, Nithard's style and diction are relatively unsophisticated and the text is often obscure and faulty. The *Histories* clearly reflects a man of action who, either from ignorance or by intention, did not follow set literary models or bother to polish his narrative; this roughness may also be attributable to the *Histories'* having been written during, or immediately after, some of the last campaigns described in the work.

The four books fall into two quite distinct sections, the first book providing straightforward history and the last three focusing on contemporary events, such as political maneuvering, military campaigns, diplomatic missions, and changes in alliances among the brothers. Nithard is careful to omit mention of any facts unfavorable to Louis the Pious or Charles II. He portrays Lothair as indecisive, cowardly, overbearing, and treacherous, and Louis the German as noble and magnanimous. These are judgments that are generally confirmed by other contemporary sources. Nithard perceives the young Charles, however, quite differently from later interpretations: as a cautious diplomat, a resolute leader, a masterly strategist, humble, charitable, virtually a martyr. There is no doubt that Charles the Bald was gifted and well educated, but other accounts of his subsequent rule suggest that he was also spineless, cowardly, greedy, crafty, and ruthless. Janet L. Nelson has argued that the fourth book does not show any sympathy for Charles.

Particularly important are Nithard's verbatim accounts of the oaths made by Charles the Bald and Louis the German at Strasbourg on 16 February 842 in front of their respective armies, each using the language spoken in the other's territory. In these speeches they renewed their fealty to each other and against their brother Lothair. Nithard's is the only extant version of these famous *Strasbourg Oaths* (III.5) in Old High German and in Old French; the latter are the earliest written records of the French language. Their existence made it clear that the language of the western and eastern parts of the Carolingian empire had already diverged sharply and that members of the royal family spoke both languages.

Nithard's activities as statesman and soldier include being Charles's emissary in the fall of 840, together with a Count Adalgar, to make peace with Lothair. Both envoys were relieved of the fiefs they held from Louis the Pious, since they refused to defect from Charles. Nithard also participated in the fratricidal Battle of Fontenoy on 25 June 841. In 842 he was chosen as one of the twelve magnates of the western half of the empire to consult with the twelve nobles from the eastern half about dividing the empire between Louis and Charles.

Like his father, Nithard became abbot of St. Riquier (Centulum) and custodian of the paternal tomb near Amiens in Picardy (842/843, or perhaps as late as 845). He shared this office with his kinsman Abbot Richbod, another of Charlemagne's grandsons. Hariulf's eleventh-century history of the abbey recounts that he was buried there beside his father. When Angilbert's remains were translated in the eleventh century, Nithard's body was placed in his empty tomb, and it is said that the head wound that had killed him was still visible. An epitaph written by Mico, a monk and deacon of St. Riquier, describes his courage and wisdom, and mourns his premature death by the sword in a battle against the Normans in Pouthieu on 15 May 845. According to Janet L. Nelson, however, the more likely date of Nithard's death was 14 June 844, since he was killed in the battle of Angoumois in Aquitaine.

Nithard's *Histories* seems not to have had much of an audience during the following centuries. Indeed, his work remained obscure until it was rediscovered in the sixteenth century. We know of only one ninth/tenth-century manuscript written at the abbey of St. Médard in Soissons; it is now in Paris (Bibliothèque Nationale, fonds latin 9768; a fifteenth-century copy of this manuscript is numbered BN 14663).

BIBLIOGRAPHY

Sources. Nithardi Historiarum libri IV, K. Pertz, ed. (1839), 3rd ed. by Ernst Müller (1907, repr. 1965); *Nithard. Histoire des fils de Louis le Pieux,* Philippe Lauer, ed. and trans. (1926, repr. 1964); *Carolingian Chronicles: Royal Frankish Annals and Nithard's Histories,* Bernhard W. Scholz and Barbara Rogers, trans. (1970).

Studies. François L. Ganshof, "Note critique sur la biographie de Nithard," in *Mélanges Paul Thomas* (1930); Gerold Meyer von Knonau, *Über Nithards vier Bücher Geschichten* (1866); Janet L. Nelson, "Public *Histories* and Private History in the Work of Nithard," in *Speculum,* 60 (1985); Hans Patze, "*Justitia* bei Nithard," in *Festschrift für Hermann Heimpel* (1972); Hans Prümm, *Sprachliche Untersuchungen zu Nithardi Historiarum libri IV* (1910).

EVELYN SCHERABON FIRCHOW

[See also **Angilbert, St.; Carolingians and the Carolingian Empire; Hariulf.**]

NIVARDUS OF FLEURY (*fl. ca.* 1025), Lombard painter and sculptor called to work at St. Benoît-sur-Loire in 1026, when Abbot Gauzlin rebuilt the monastery and churches after a disastrous fire. Nivardus is documented as chasing the small columns of the *chorus psallentium* in Notre Dame de Fleury and as the painter of a monumental crucifix for the church of St. Pierre.

BIBLIOGRAPHY
Robert-Henri Bautier, "Le monastère et les églises de Fleury-sur-Loire sous les abbatiats d'Abbon, de Gauzlin et d'Arnaud (988–1032)," in *Mémoires de la Société nationale des antiquaires de France,* n.s. **4** (1969).

BRUCIA WITTHOFT

NIẒĀM AL-MULK (literally, Order of the Realm), the honorific of Abū ᶜAlī'l Ḥasan ibn ᶜAlī ibn Isḥāq al-Ṭūsī (1018–1092), grand vizier of the Seljuk sultans Alp Arslan (*r.* 1063–1072) and Malikshāh (*r.* 1072–1092). The son of a Ghaznavid official, he entered Seljuk service several years after the Ghaznavid debacle at Dandānqān (1040). In due course he became the principal adviser of Alp Arslan after having engineered the latter's succession to the sultanate. In an empire that was wracked by centrifugal forces, Niẓām al-Mulk, like many Iranian officials upon whom the Seljuk administration was based, consciously took as his models the centralizing monarchic traditions of the Sasanids and Ghaznavids. His ideas and aspirations for government are recorded in his *Siyāsatnāma* (Book of government), written for Malikshāh in 1091. This work remains one of the most important sources for the political institutions of the eastern Muslim world.

Hoping to bind the fiefholders (*iqṭādārs*) closer to the government, Niẓām al-Mulk expanded and extended governmental supervision of the *iqṭā*ᶜ system (originally an inheritable land grant, it had come to designate the allocation of revenue from lands or districts). In the furtherance of central authority, he revived the elaborate internal (and foreign) espionage network of earlier times. He also aided the educational system, founding madrasas (called in his honor *niẓāmīyas*) that would equal those of the Shiite and Fatimid opposition, and provide well-trained Sunni personnel for the state bureaucracy. Of these the Niẓāmīya of Baghdad was the most famous.

His personal authority was so great that Niẓām al-Mulk is said to have told Malikshāh that he was his "co-equal" in rule, and that the realm and monarchic power were dependent on the vizierate. These observations did not endear him to the sultan. He was murdered by an Ismaili, but many believed that Malikshāh was the ultimate instigator.

BIBLIOGRAPHY
Sources. Niẓām al-Mulk, Siyāsat-nāma, M. Qazvīnī and M. M. Chahārdihī, eds. (1956), trans. by Hubert Drake as *The Book of Government; or, Rules for Kings* (1960, 2nd ed. 1978).
Studies. Claude Cahen, "L'évolution de l'iqtaᶜ du IXᵉ au XIIIᵉ siècle," in *Annales: Économies, sociétés, civilisations,* **8** (1953), and "The Historiography of the Seljuqid Period," in *Historians of the Middle East,* Bernard Lewis and P. M. Holt, eds. (1962); Martijn T. Houtsma, "The Death of the Niẓām al-Mulk and Its Consequences," in *Journal of Indian History,* ser. 3, **7** (1924); I. Kafesoğlu, *Sultan Melikşah devrinde Büyük Selçuklu imparatorluğu* (1953); K. E. Schabinger, "Zur Geschichte des saldschuqischen Reichkanzlers Nizamu'l-Mulk," in *Historisches Jahrbuch,* **62** (1949).

PETER B. GOLDEN

[See also **Alp Arslan; Iran, History: After 650; Madrasa; Malikshāh; Seljuks.**]

NJÁLS SAGA is the longest, most broadly conceived, and most famous of the Icelandic family sagas. Set mainly in southern Iceland (and for brief periods in Norway, Orkney, Scotland, and Ireland) from about 960 to 1015, *Njála* (as it is often referred to in Icelandic scholarship) tells two related but distinct stories. The first (chaps. 1–81) concerns the three marriages of Hallgerðr, above all her last, to the hero, Gunnarr of Hlíðarendi. Once a model citizen, Gunnarr is driven, by Hallgerðr's malevolence and by his own failures of judgment, to commit deeds that bring him a sentence of outlawry. His death at the hands of attackers, preceded by a heroic self-defense and an act of paramount indifference on the part of his wife, is one of the most dramatic passages in saga literature. The saga's second half (chaps. 82–159) focuses on the lawyer and sage Njáll and his unruly sons. Community resentment of their high-handed dealings, coupled with outright malice, leads eventually to Flosi Þórðarson's assault with fire on Njáll's farm at Bergþórshváll. All the male members of Njáll's family are killed but one, his son-in-law Kári, who, after prosecuting the case and taking partial revenge, is eventually reconciled with Flosi in the saga's last chapter. Interspersed throughout these two main plots are four semi-independent subplots: the story of Unnr and Hrútr's marriage and divorce (chaps. 1–8), the account of Iceland's conversion to Christianity (chaps. 100–105), the comic tale of Bjǫrn of Mǫrk (chaps. 148–152), and the Clontarf episode (chaps. 154–157).

The structural unity of *Njáls saga,* in particular the question of whether it is an amalgam of two originally separate works, has long been a scholarly crux. As plots, the halves are only weakly connected, mainly by the presence of certain characters in both (notably Njáll, who serves as Gunnarr's adviser, and Njáll's wife, Bergþóra, whose extended feud with Hallgerðr is the structural backbone of chapters 35–45). Thematically, however, *Njáls saga* is all of a piece, at least in the form in which we now have it. From beginning to end it is informed by an opposition between legal, peaceful dealings (associated generally with Christianity) and illegal, violent ones (associated generally with paganism). Njáll is a man of the new order: a believer in law ("With laws shall our land be built up, with lawlessness, laid waste," he says in chapter 70) and, when the opportunity presents itself, a believer in Christ ("In my opinion the new faith is much better; happy the man who receives it. . . . I shall do all I can to further it," he claims in chapter 100). Throughout the saga he contends against those, including his wife and sons, who adhere to the old system of blood revenge. Gunnarr is a man in the middle: he holds to Njáll's principles as far as he is able, but under pressure he reverts to old-style heroic retaliations. Njáll, though not perfectly immune to vengeful feelings, remains true to his convictions to the end—indeed, the author suggests, to the point of acquiescing in his own death and that of his family rather than have any of them survive to prosecute revenge and so perpetuate the deadly cycle. In ethical terms, part I of *Njáls saga* is a failed version of part II; part II, despite the loss of life, marks the arrival of a new age.

Perhaps because of *Njála*'s preeminence, scholars and critics have tended to generalize its characteristics to saga literature as a whole. This is a mistake, for *Njáls saga* is in many respects an exceptional saga. Its length (some 400 pages in the modern edition) and its scope (some 600 named individuals) are unmatched by any other saga. Its bipartite structure is unprecedented (except possibly by *Ljósvetninga saga*), and its proportion of direct discourse to narrative text (40 percent) is unusually high. Especially remarkable is *Njála*'s articulation of its vast mass of events through a carefully planned and controlled system of forecasts and correspondences, as well as its elaborate and often gratuitous interweaving of plot lines—in these respects *Njáls saga* stands as the tour de force of early Icelandic prose. Also characteristic of *Njáls saga* is its use of personal leitmotifs—Hallgerðr's hair and eyes, Njáll's beardlessness, Skarpheðinn's grin—as indicators of character. *Njála*'s author is also more given than others to conspicuous contrasts (Gunnarr as *fortitudo,* Njáll as *sapientia*) and epic triads (the three slaps that Hallgerðr suffers at the hands of her three husbands, and the three deaths that inevitably follow).

The prolonged and elaborate vendettas of *Njáls saga* are singular in saga literature; nor does any other saga anatomize their causes and effects in such precise detail. In its preoccupation with women and marriage, *Njála* parallels and echoes *Laxdœla saga,* but in its studied misogyny it stands alone. Although many sagas concern themselves with the law and its failures, only *Njála* puts law and lawyers at center stage; its lengthy revelation of judicial procedures is unique. No other Icelandic family saga more consistently or patently poses Christian morality as an antidote to civil disorder, or draws so palpably on the conventions of medieval hagiography (the depiction of Njáll's death and burial). Finally, in its effort to apprehend two of the major historical developments in early Iceland—the adoption of Christianity and the institution of the Fifth Court—*Njáls saga* goes further than any other saga in transcending the local and achieving a national perspective.

Njáls saga is thought to have been written toward the end of the classical saga period (*ca.* 1280), and some scholars find in it signs of decline (tendency toward exaggeration, coarse humor, interest in finery). Like all of the family sagas, it is anonymous. Scholars of the so-called Icelandic school believe the author made extensive use of written sources, including other family sagas (mainly *Laxdœla saga* and *Eyrbyggja saga*), a lost *Kristni Þáttr* (source of the conversion episode), a lost *Brjáns Þáttr* (source of the Clontarf episode), and lost genealogical and legal records. Other scholars, particularly those influenced by modern research on oral literature, consider it unnecessary to assume all of these written sources, particularly unattested ones, choosing instead to regard the saga as a manifestation of traditional narrative art.

The question of *Njála*'s historicity, like that of all the sagas, is problematic. The main events (such as the slaying of Gunnarr at Hlíðarendi and the burning of Njáll at Bergþórshváll) are known or assumed to be true (by virtue of their mention in such historical sources as *Landnámabók* and the Icelandic annals); on the other hand, the author is sometimes mistaken on major points of fact (such as the attribution of the Fifth Court reform to Njáll) and the legal passages in particular contain anachronisms. In general it is assumed that *Njála*, like other sagas, is a somewhat imaginative rendering of a somewhat distorted historical tradition.

Njáls saga survives in more than fifty manuscripts, of which nineteen are of medieval date. These high numbers indicate the unusual popularity of *Njáls saga* in early as well as later periods. Another measure of the early impact of *Njála* is that the names of its "negative" characters (Hallgerðr, Mǫrðr, Hrappr) subsequently dropped out of Icelandic use.

BIBLIOGRAPHY

Sources. Einar Ólafur Sveinsson, ed., *Brennu-Njáls saga* (1954), translated by Magnus Magnusson and Herman Pálsson as *Njal's Saga* (1960); Carl F. Bayerschmidt and Lee M. Hollander, trans., *Njál's Saga* (1955).

Studies. Richard F. Allen, *Fire and Iron: Critical Approaches to Njáls Saga* (1971); Lars Lönnroth, *Njáls Saga: A Critical Introduction* (1976); Ian Maxwell, "Pattern in *Njáls saga*," in *Saga-Book of the Viking Society*, **15** (1957–1961); Einar Ólafur Sveinsson, *Njáls Saga: A Literary Masterpiece*, Paul Schach, ed. and trans. (1971).

CAROL J. CLOVER

[See also **Darraðadljoð; Eyrbyggja Saga; Family Sagas, Icelandic; Laxdœla Saga.**]

NJǪRÐR. Njǫrðr is the Norse god of the sea and fertility. According to Snorri's *Edda, Heimskringla,* and the *Poetic Edda,* he is the father of Freyr and Freyja; together the three deities are the only named members of a group known as the Vanir; their collective specialty is human and agricultural fertility. Njǫrðr's name is often associated with Freyr's in the sources: *Landnámabók* relates that, according to the law of Úlfljótr, all oaths made at the assembly should be in the name of Freyr and Njǫrðr and *hinn almáttki áss* (the almighty god); *Heimskringla* states that at the great sacrificial feasts held by Sigurðr Hlaðajarl, the first drink was dedicated to Odin and the next to Njǫrðr and Freyr; on two occasions in his poetry Egill Skallagrímsson mentions the gods together, once in his curse against King Eiríkr and once in his poem of praise for his friend Arinbjǫrn. Njǫrðr lives in Nóatún (Boat Enclosure), and his province, at least at the time of the major sources, seems to have been restricted to the sea.

The Old Icelandic mythological sources state that Njǫrðr originally came to the Æsir as a hostage from the Vanir in an attempt to end a stalemated war. When the truce was concluded, he was permanently admitted to the society of the Æsir. In the pseudo-historical *Ynglinga saga,* Snorri says that Odin became the first king of Sweden, and was succeeded by Njǫrðr and then Freyr. During the reigns of the latter two, there was peace and prosperity in the land. Njǫrðr is said to have been married twice, the first time to his sister (while he lived among the Vanir), a custom not permitted among the Æsir. Snorri relates the mythical tale of Njǫrðr's second marriage in his *Edda.* The giantess Skaði came to the gods to demand compensation for the slaying of her father, Þjazi. To satisfy one of her terms, she was allowed to choose a husband from among the gods, and she selected Njǫrðr. However, the pair could not live together, for Njǫrðr hated Skaði's home in the mountains and she detested his at the seashore.

A tantalizing piece of information about putative early cults of Njǫrðr is found in Tacitus' *Germania* (first century). Tacitus writes that a number of Germanic tribes worship a goddess named Nerthus, identified by him as *Terra mater,* whose cult center lies on an island in the ocean. Periodically, when the presence of the goddess is felt, she is carried in a procession in a wagon drawn by cows. During this time all weapons are put away, and peace and rejoicing prevail. The name Nerthus corresponds to the proto-Germanic form *Nerþuz, from which the Old Norse name Njǫrðr is derived. But how can we explain the difference in sex? This problem has never been satisfactorily resolved. Because of the references to Njǫrðr's incestuous marriage with his sister and the existence of the twins Freyr and Freyja, it is commonly held by scholars that Njǫrðr and Nerthus may originally have been a similar set of male and female twin deities. De Vries mentions the possibility that both Nerthus and Njǫrðr may have developed as female and male in their respective cultures from an original hermaphrodite fertility deity.

The abundant place-name evidence indicates that the cult of Njǫrðr and the Vanir was strong along the west coast and in the Oslo region of

NOBILITY AND NOBLES

Norway, and in the area of Uppsala and Sigtuna in eastern Sweden.

BIBLIOGRAPHY

Sources. Gustav Neckel and Hans Kuhn, eds., *Edda: Die Lieder des Codex Regius,* 4th ed., I (1962), 69–77; Snorri Sturluson, *The Poetic Edda,* Henry A. Bellows, trans. (1923, 1957), 107–120, *Ynglinga Saga,* in *Heimskringla,* II, Samuel Laing, trans. (1961), 8–15, and *The Prose Edda,* Jean I. Young, trans. (1966), 10–62.

Studies. Ó. Briem, "Vanir og Æsir," in *Studia islandica,* **21** (1963); Georges Dumézil, *Gods of the Ancient Northmen,* Einar Haugen, trans. (1973), 73–79; Edward O. G. Turville-Petre, *Myth and Religion of the North* (1964, repr. 1975), 162–165; Jan de Vries, *Altgermanische Religionsgeschichte,* II (1957, 1970), 163–177.

KAAREN GRIMSTAD

[See also **Æsir; Egill Skallagrímsson; Freyr; Landnámabók; Skaði; Snorra Edda; Vanir.**]

NOBILITY AND NOBLES. Medieval writers identified nobles by a variety of terms (*nobiles, proceres, primates, optimates, illustres, maiores, magnates, barones, domini*), but failed to explain precisely what constituted nobility. Hagiographers and chroniclers associated noble standing primarily with birth and assumed that the well-born possessed inherently superior physical and moral qualities that destined them to positions of leadership. The belief in such a "noble culture" persisted through the Middle Ages.

What contemporaries omitted to note—because it was self-evident or perhaps not in good form to mention—was the enormous landed wealth of noble families, which assured them the domination of the countryside in an age when the rural economy was primary. Birth, wealth, and service to the prince went hand in hand as aspects of nobility, but the weight of modern scholarship suggests that landed proprietorship was the crucial element, as it gave the power (*potestas*) to dispose freely of all human and physical resources on the land. The fact that nobles preferred to marry among themselves and served in high offices, both secular and religious, was a consequence of their being the landed elite.

THE EARLY MIDDLE AGES

Before the arrival of Germanic tribes in the western provinces of the Roman Empire, imperial government had been supplanted by the senatorial aristocracy, the great landed families that monopolized public offices and supplied virtually the entire episcopacy of the late empire. An admixture of very old and recently promoted families, this aristocratic "cousinhood" survived the Germanic conquest of Gaul to become a pillar of the new Frankish state. The leading Germanic families of the conquest became great proprietors in their own right through a form of expropriation known as "hospitality," by which they took half or more of the largest Roman estates. After the conversion of Clovis (*ca.* 500) had removed the chief obstacle to intermarriage, Roman and Germanic families began to merge and by the seventh century a single network of families provided kings with their governors and the church with its bishops, abbots, and missionaries. The Frankish-Roman nobility, in fact, formed a number of regional nobilities characterized by distinct law codes and dialects within the Frankish subkingdoms (Austrasia, Neustria, Burgundy) and provinces (Aquitaine, Alemania, Bavaria). The few who served the king directly, for which they were amply rewarded with lands, privileges, and exemptions, became an elite within the nobility.

Roman landlords survived the Visigothic occupation of Spain, but in considerably reduced circumstances, as the Visigothic hospitality claimed two-thirds of their estates. Moreover, the Visigoths deliberately resisted assimilation by retaining their personal law code and Arianism, and thus in Spain two separate societies—and two landed elites—coexisted through the sixth century. King Recared's conversion to orthodoxy (589) opened the way to intermarriage, but apparently little mixing occurred before the formulation of a single law code for Romans and Visigoths (654). Since the Visigothic church remained largely in the hands of Visigoths even after 589, it appears that families of Roman descent constituted de facto a secondary layer of late Visigothic nobility. Both nobilities disappeared in 711, when the Muslim conquest of Spain destroyed Visigothic society altogether. Northern Italy shared a somewhat similar experience: an Ostrogothic nobility tolerated, but did not assimilate, the old Roman landlords. In 568 both were displaced by the Lombards, who, after their own defeat by Charlemagne (774), were in turn replaced by Frankish, Burgundian, and Bavarian nobles loyal to Charlemagne.

The most thorough destruction of a Roman

provincial society occurred in Britain after the Anglo-Saxon conquest. Anglo-Saxon nobles (gesiths) cooperated closely with their kings in founding several new kingdoms: they shared in governance, represented the kingdom in the absence of the monarch, and chose his successor from the royal family. As in other Germanic societies, the nobles were protected by large wergelds, the legal recognition of their social and economic importance. The Viking occupation of the ninth century, however, destroyed all the Anglo-Saxon kingdoms except that of Wessex. With the reconquest of the lost lands under the king of Wessex, his nobles became the sole nobility (the thanes) of late Saxon England.

On the Continent the demise of the first Frankish dynasty (Merovingian), in large part due to the excessive rewards and immunities granted to the nobles, was accelerated by the ambitious Arnulfingian family of Austrasia. The military successes of its most prominent member, Charles Martel, mayor of the palace, led to his son Pepin's usurpation of the throne in 751. The new dynasty of Carolingians, having co-opted their fellow Austrasian nobles during their rise to power, appointed Austrasians as governors and bishops throughout the Frankish realm. Austrasian nobles became in effect a royal nobility, whose loyalty and service were vital to Charlemagne's (*r.* 768–814) territorial expansion and unification of his diverse peoples. Although the regional nobilities are difficult to detect in the sparse sources, they seem to have remained in place, great proprietors that they were, and to have held local offices below the royal nobles, for their cooperation was essential to the good order of society in the absence of a civil service. Only the nobility of Bavaria, for which there are exceptionally rich sources, has been studied in some detail. A relatively small number of families with enormous estates, the Bavarian nobles were virtually autonomous. They actively developed their resources, mostly through land clearing, and aggressively sought offices and marriage alliances to aggrandize their families. With origins to the eighth century, and extending to the twelfth, they exhibited remarkable longevity. If their energy and initiative were typical of the Carolingian nobility, we would have to conclude that the accomplishments of Charlemagne rested on an exceptionally vigorous landed elite.

The fate of the Carolingian nobility has been much debated since Paul Guilhiermoz proposed, in his *Essai sur l'origine de la noblesse en France au moyen âge* (1902), that the collapse of the Carolingian state and the devastations of the Vikings from the ninth century effectively destroyed the nobility. Marc Bloch's *Feudal Society* (1939) extended that argument into a general explanation for the rise of feudal institutions: by the eleventh century, he claimed, a new nobility of arms (essentially self-made men) had replaced the old nobility. Recent research, however, has demonstrated conclusively that the greatest Carolingian families did survive the tenth-century hiatus: they became the ducal and comital families of the High Middle Ages. The Herbertian family from Neustria, for example, whose roots almost certainly dated to the eighth century, emerged as the counts of Vermandois. Indeed, the premier Neustrian family, the Robertians, attested at least as early as the first half of the eighth century, was chosen by its colleagues in 987 as a new royal dynasty (Capetian) in France. The dukes of Saxony, who had acquired similar prestige through their military exploits, established the Ottonian dynasty in Germany (936). In southern France and Catalonia, as well, the old families survived but were less successful in forming the territoral states that characterized northern France and Germany.

The fate of the less prominent regional nobilities is not entirely clear. In those provinces of the German empire where Carolingian institutions and regional identities remained strong, such as in Bavaria, noble families apparently survived to the eleventh century and beyond. In the more disrupted western areas, the lack of solid information on the origins of the eleventh-century castellans and viscounts leaves the issue open. It has been claimed that those without demonstrable lineages were ipso facto "new men," although obviously not all men of unknown origin had to be non-noble; some might have belonged to distant or less prominent noble families that cannot be detected in the extant sources. Moreover, since even minor Carolingian offices were the preserve of nobles, the later possessors of those and similar offices, who often shared the same names but whose exact genealogies cannot be reconstructed, most likely were of noble descent.

Yet there do exist well-documented cases attesting to the rise of new men into the nobility in the tenth, eleventh, and twelfth centuries. The Erembalds of Flanders are perhaps the best known. A certain Erembald became castellan of Bruges

NOBILITY AND NOBLES

(1067) through perfidy, murder of the castellan, and marriage to the castellan's widow. In 1089 the Erembalds were already referred to as *nobiles* and within two generations they controlled the very household and administration of the count of Flanders. When their characteristic and unseemly haughtiness drew a legal challenge and a reminder of their ignoble origin, they responded by murdering Count Charles the Good (1127). According to Galbert of Bruges, the count's notary who observed the events, those parvenus were unworthy of their offices, in a word, of nobility. Had they observed the norms of noble behavior they, like most other non-nobles, would have passed silently into the nobility, as they had acquired noble blood through a female line. Modern historians of Flanders regard the Erembalds as a rare example of non-nobles penetrating the relatively closed Flemish nobility, and it may be that usurpations of that sort attracted the attention of contemporary chroniclers as noteworthy cases.

THE HIGH MIDDLE AGES

From the twelfth century on, the volume of written materials—especially legal documents, administrative registers, and chronicles—is sufficiently large to permit detailed family histories. Prosopographical studies indicate that noble families everywhere faced serious problems of survival: 25 to 50 percent of them failed each century. Infant mortality and infertility accounted for some failures: the Dabo family of Lorraine, for example, a powerful lineage since the tenth century, succumbed to the infertility of its last heiress in the 1220's, and saw its lands dispersed. The consequences of warfare and the crusades varied by region. Whereas the English baronage escaped the perils of crusading, the nobility of Champagne was permanently scarred by that experience: the count of Bar-sur-Seine, to take one example, perished with his only son at Damietta (1219) on the Fifth Crusade; not only did his lineage disappear, but his county was partitioned into four parts, all of which soon passed into the Champagne domain.

The most serious threat to the nobility was not biological failure but rather derogation resulting from the partible inheritance practices common throughout Europe. Although the eldest son usually was favored with his father's title and the largest share of the paternal estate, all siblings were entitled to equitable distributions—in accordance with the family's standing—that in specific cases turned out to approximate equal shares of the inheritance. The least wealthy were at greatest risk, since patrimonies systematically dismantled with each generation rarely could be restored by a dowry or princely grant. Indebted nobles became a recurring theme from the late twelfth century. Mortgages for extraordinary expenses—a marriage, a knighting, a crusade—often led to further alienations of property and revenues. Alarmed by the flood of sales in mortmain, the kings of England and France, among others, attempted to curb those transfers, but they acted too late and were unsuccessful. Inevitable social slippage followed the hemorrhage of resources, and some families suffered *déclassement.* The downward movement could last several generations, but ultimately, those unable to live like nobles were no longer regarded as nobles, no matter what their family origins. The average "life" of a noble family has been estimated at three to six generations.

Despite the tendency of nobilities to dwindle in size and to lose their overwhelming domination of the rural economy and society, some families countered that trend. Through marriage, collateral inheritance, and princely favor (especially in the form of new fiefs), enterprising families could amass new landed fortunes. Moreover, the highest nobility, like the princes and monarchs, possessed the strongest sense of lineage and patrimony, and actively sought to stave off the consequences of partition. They found ecclesiastical placements for younger children while limiting their traditional largesse to the church. They increased their revenues by founding new villages, clearing lands, and converting customary exactions from their tenants into income-based taxes whenever possible. They constructed mills, imposed new banalities (taxes, in effect, on agrarian production), and sold off distant resources (often dowries) in order to invest in closer ones. And they gradually began to circumvent partible inheritance, despite the strong force of custom; by the end of the thirteenth century, daughters and younger sons increasingly saw their settlements reduced in favor of the eldest son, and in England the practice of entail triumphed in the next century. Ultimately, however, these were policies of conservation adopted in the face of shrinking landed resources; only in Reconquest Spain and eastern Germany could the nobles carve out vast new estates reminiscent of the early Frankish period.

The emergence of knights as a lower nobility

NOBILITY AND NOBLES

was one of the most significant social events of the Middle Ages. Originally low-born military retainers, they experienced an extraordinary rise in prestige in the course of the twelfth century, partly due to the crusades, and by the end of the century came to enjoy the titles and privileges reserved for the old nobility only a few generations earlier. The concept of nobility, in short, was enlarged to include all those who held a fief. The knights soon aped the old families by acquiring seals and coats of arms; they submitted to formal ceremonies of dubbing, previously restricted to the old nobles, and they counted themselves among the "gentlemen," whose status was guaranteed by tenure.

Despite their formal attainments, most knights enjoyed quite modest resources, often barely adequate to support a family, and produced generally short lineages. Their incapacity to absorb temporary financial reverses left the fate of each generation in balance. Alienations of entire fiefs were common, even in the presence of living heirs; often a local monastery would take a whole patrimony in return for a life annuity to the knight and his wife. Knighting, which was widely restricted to the sons of knights, became less appealing to them because of the heavy costs of war-horses, armor, and weapons. Often only the eldest son would be knighted, then by the late thirteenth century frequently all the sons of a former knight would forgo knighting. The king of England attempted to distrain everyone enjoying £20 annual income to become a knight and to be enrolled as such on his military lists, but with limited success. As long as noble status was assured by tenure, knighting was unnecessary. Dubbing became rare even among the old nobles in the next century.

Since knights commonly married townswomen and even peasants, the pool of noble-born persons steadily increased, but in France, at least, there developed some confusion as to just who was a noble. The Parlement of Paris investigated a number of cases but found that definitions of nobility varied by province. In some areas, only those born of two noble parents possessed nobility, whereas in others a single noble parent sufficed. Moreover, other tests were posed, such as military service and style of life (some were said not to live like nobles because they engaged in a trade). Confusion was averted in Germany, where the nobility was stratified into several precise levels. Knights occupied the fifth level, just above *ministeriales*, another new category of noble. Formerly low-born estate administrators, the *ministeriales* had become a hereditary class that acquired noble standing and became a powerful force in German society during the fourteenth and fifteenth centuries.

Only in England did the earlier baron-knight distinction continue into the thirteenth century, for two reasons: the king set standard reliefs for baronies (£100) and knights' fiefs (£20), and Parliament institutionalized the separation of the two levels of feudal tenants. Intermarriage did of course occur; indeed, the royal abuse of the wardship and marriage rights of high-born minors brought the rebuke in Magna Carta against the disparagement of heirs. A prime example of newcomers rising through royal favor into the baronage is William Marshal. The fourth son of a minor royal official, and without an inheritance, William became a knight-adventurer who developed considerable skill at tournaments, where he collected ransoms from the vanquished; but his fortune turned with his appointment as royal tutor, in which role his moral qualities as well as professional expertise were admired. He was rewarded with a barony, an appropriate marriage, and finally the regency of England after the death of King John in 1216.

We know relatively little about the formation of entirely new nobilities in the High Middle Ages. The dukes of Normandy apparently purged their baronage in the early eleventh century to form a more trustworthy elite, whom they rewarded with confiscated lands. The subsequent installation of that new nobility in England after the conquest of 1066 was an exceptional case of the transplant of an entire existing nobility to a new land. Quite different nobilities emerged in the Levant after the First and Fourth Crusades. Although nobles led those expeditions, they returned home early, leaving to their knights the task of occupying the countryside. In the Kingdom of Jerusalem, the barons who sat on the High Court all descended from knights of obscure origins who had acquired noble status by virtue of their military service. The Ibelins, for example, who descended from Italian Norman knights, grew into a distinguished family of military leaders, jurists, and prelates, whose influence pervaded the Levant. After the fall of Jerusalem (1187) many Latin barons and knights resettled in Cyprus, where the Lusignan kings granted them fiefs in accordance with their recently acquired ranks.

Of the Latin states created on Byzantine lands after the conquest of Constantinople (1204), only the Principality of the Morea (the Greek Peloponnese) proved viable. There selected knights became a crusader baronage that within two generations was contracting marriages with other illustrious *outre-mer* families of equally modest origins. The crusader princes, like the Norman kings of England, created their nobilities by assigning them the requisite fiefs and responsibilities; but the Latin nobles of the Levant, unlike those of England, constituted truly new nobilities.

THE LATE MIDDLE AGES

Although the failure of noble families continued unabated through the later Middle Ages, the fate of nobility as a whole depended increasingly on the availability of new land and royal service. In Castile, for example, extinct families were replaced by cadet lines, and the size of the nobility—excluding knights—increased slightly. But the Castilian nobles had the run of the land and developed unrivaled new sources of wealth from their sheep herds with absolute rights of transhumance. The contemporary expansion of German landlords east of the Elbe produced similar vast new estates over which they exercised full authority. In both areas powerful landed elites continued to dominate the countryside.

In the more settled areas of England, France, and western Germany, the nobles no longer controlled the major economic resources of their societies; therefore they turned to royal service to augment their incomes and maintain their social standing. The rise of the Habsburg state provided careers for nobles and knights who together formed a new nobility of service. In England the Hundred Years War offered nobles the rewards of military service, although it is still debated whether that war improved their fortunes over the long term. For the French nobles, the war was a disaster: not only did they suffer heavy casualties at the outbreak of hostilities, but they saw their lands ravaged by English expeditions and later by the Free Companies. Their misfortune, however, created opportunities for the lesser nobles to acquire some of the vacated offices and lands.

It has been suggested that the noble style of life, firmly rooted in the land but increasingly dependent on fixed rents of declining real value, became incompatible with the market-driven economy of the later Middle Ages. Not only were the main sources of new wealth located in the towns and cities rather than the countryside, but in some areas peasant farmers were even able to dominate the grain market to the detriment of the landlords. No longer the wealthiest families with virtual autonomy in the countryside, the landed nobility had become a rentier class subjected to forces beyond their control. No longer the companions of kings enjoying extensive delegated authority, they had become the willing servants of late medieval monarchs. Although medieval nobilities were never entirely closed to outsiders, the nobilities of the early Middle Ages appear more uniform and stable than those of the later centuries, when extinction, the loss of patrimonies, and the rise of newcomers are clearly visible.

BIBLIOGRAPHY

Recent general essays, with extensive bibliographies, include Frederic L. Cheyette, ed., *Lordship and Community in Medieval Europe: Selected Readings* (1968); Philippe Contamine, ed., *La noblesse au moyen âge, XIe–XVe siècle* (1976); Georges Duby, *The Chivalrous Society*, Cynthia Postan, trans. (1977); Léopold Genicot, "La noblesse médiévale: Pans de lumière et zones obscures," in *Tijdschrift voor Geschiedenis*, **93** (1980); Timothy Reuter, ed., *The Medieval Nobility: Studies on the Ruling Classes of France and Germany from the Sixth to the Twelfth Century* (1979).

Selected studies. Michael Altschul, *A Baronial Family in Medieval England: The Clares, 1217–1314* (1965); M. T. W. Arnheim, *The Senatorial Aristocracy in the Later Roman Empire* (1972); Constance Bouchard, "The Origins of the French Nobility: A Reassessment," in *The American Historical Review*, **86** (1981); Dietrich Claude, *Adel, Kirche and Königtum im Westgotenreich* (1971); David C. Douglas, *William the Conqueror: The Norman Impact upon England* (1964); John B. Freed, "The Origins of the European Nobility: The Problem of the Ministeriales," in *Viator*, 7 (1976); Frank D. Gilliard, "The Senators of Sixth-century Gaul," in *Speculum*, **54** (1979); Franz Irsigler, *Untersuchungen zur Geschichte des frühfränkischen Adels* (1969); Andrew W. Lewis, *Royal Succession in Capetian France: Studies on Familial Order and the State* (1981); K. Leyser, "The German Aristocracy from the Ninth to the Early Twelfth Century," in *Past and Present*, **41** (1968).

Henry R. Loyn, *Anglo-Saxon England and the Norman Conquest* (1962); Jane Martindale, "The French Aristocracy in the Early Middle Ages: A Reappraisal," in *Past and Present*, **75** (1977); Sidney Painter, *William Marshal: Knight-Errant, Baron, and Regent of England* (1933); Édouard Perroy, "Social Nobility Among the French *Noblesse* in the Later Middle Ages," in *Past and Present*, **21** (1962); Joshua Prawer, *Crusader Institutions* (1980); Jonathan Riley-Smith, *The Feudal Nobility and the Kingdom of Jerusalem, 1174–1277*

(1973); Joel T. Rosenthal, *Nobles and the Noble Life, 1295–1500* (1976); Roger Sablonier, *Adel im Wandel: Eine Untersuchung zur sozialen Situation des ostschweizerischen Adels um 1300* (1979); Wilhelm Störmer, *Früher Adel: Studien zur politischen Führungsschicht im fränkisch-deutschen Reich von 8. bis 11. Jahrhundert,* 2 vols. (1973); Edward A. Thompson, *The Goths in Spain* (1969); E. Warlop, *The Flemish Nobility Before 1300,* J. B. Ross and H. Vandermoere, trans., 2 vols. in 4 (1975–1976).

THEODORE EVERGATES

[See also **Baron; Castellan; Castles and Fortifications; Chivalry; Class Structure, Western; Feudalism; Fief; Inheritance, Western European; Kingship, Theories of; Knights and Knight Service; Mayor; Mortmain; William Marshal.**]

NOEANNOE, one of the words, or collections of syllables, accompanying melodies that represented the ecclesiastical modes. In the West, at least, these words were not stable either with respect to their form and spelling or their association with particular modes and melodies. Among others found in Western manuscripts of the ninth through eleventh centuries are *noeonoeane, nonannoeane, noeane, noeagis, noeais, anne,* and *aianeoeane.*

The earliest mention of the formulas occurs about the middle of the ninth century in the *Musica disciplina* of Aurelian of Réôme, where it is stated that the meaning of the words is unknown. Aurelian also says that *noeannoe* and the rest were Byzantine in origin; indeed, similar formulas (*hagia, anes, neanes, aneanes, ananeanes*) are found in later Byzantine books. These *echemata* (*enechemata, apochemata*), or vocalizations, were used in teaching to illustrate the modality; were copied at the beginning of chants (although usually only the last few notes) as *martyriai* (witnesses) of the mode (*echos*) of the chant; and were sung by the cantor to establish the main intervals of the *echos* for the hymns to follow. *Echemata* were also sung as median formulas, perhaps as a check that the mode had not been lost (the Byzantine musical notation, like those of the West, was not entirely self-sufficient), and in some instances, evidently, as indications of modal transposition.

It is hard to imagine that the *noeannoe* tropes were ever much more than curiosities in the West. There is some evidence that they were used in teaching, but although their concluding melismas were occasionally sung as cadential flourishes to certain chants, they were never, as in the East, incorporated regularly into the chants of the liturgy. Without the melismas the formulas are very brief and do not seem particularly representative of the modes they are intended to typify. Contemporary comparisons are impossible—the earliest Byzantine examples are centuries younger—but it seems clear enough that the Western formulas are versions of the Eastern melodies current in the eighth and ninth centuries, and it is hardly to be expected that they would have served well for the Gregorian repertory. It is almost certainly for this reason that the melismas were added. These additions, found with all but the earliest examples of the formulas, are much more typical of the Gregorian *melos,* particularly of the antiphons (for which modal decisions governing the psalmody were particularly important); but it is obvious that no single formula could ever hope to represent the vast number of chants, varying in style from the starkly simple to the luxuriantly melismatic, that are classified as belonging to the same mode.

There were, nevertheless, further attempts. Other modal formulas began to appear in the tenth century. These were of Western origin and had Latin texts, most of them mnemonics such as *Primum querite regnum Dei, Secundum autem simile est huic,* and so on. Although the *noeannoe* tropes can be found in books of the twelfth century and later, these formulas were generally supplanted by such newer compositions. In any case, improvements in notation, the emergence of a modal classification based entirely on *finalis,* and the rapid rise of polyphony, which effectively put an end to chant composition, made the formulas irrelevant.

BIBLIOGRAPHY

Terence Bailey, *The Intonation Formulas of Western Chant* (1974); Jørgen Raasted, *Intonation Formulas and Modal Signatures in Byzantine Musical Manuscripts* (1966); Oliver Strunk, "Intonations and Signatures of the Byzantine Modes," in *Musical Quarterly,* **31** (1945).

TERENCE BAILEY

[See also **Gregorian Chant; Melisma; Mode; Neuma; Solmization.**]

NOGARET, GUILLAUME DE (*ca.* 1260–1313), the most prominent of the lawyers who served

Philip IV the Fair (1285–1314) as governmental administrators and counselors. Some writers have thought that these men, influenced by the principles of Roman law, contributed to the building of a strong, centralized French monarchy under Philip.

Nogaret was probably a native of the region around Toulouse, although nothing of his early life or family background is known with certainty. He may have been a practicing lawyer as early as 1282, and he was certainly a professor of law at the University of Montpellier in 1292, if not earlier. Having acquired a reputation as a lawyer and performed provincial service as the *juge mage* of Beaucaire, in 1295 he was summoned by the king to Paris, where he was soon a member of the royal council and of the Parlement of Paris.

This was a rapid rise to a position of such power, and Nogaret received almost immediately a royal commission to carry out a sweeping investigation and reform of the administration in Champagne. The king used such commissions to reestablish and strengthen his royal rights and to tie the provinces more closely to the crown.

After Pierre Flote, the king's primary adviser, was killed in the Battle of Courtrai (1302), Nogaret emerged as the king's chief lawyer in the continuing struggle with Pope Boniface VIII. He conceived of the strategy whereby the pope was accused of heresy and summoned to a future council to answer for his conduct. To accomplish this plan, Nogaret went to Italy and in the late summer of 1303 confronted Boniface in the papal residence at Anagni, intending to take him to France to stand trial. Although backed by armed force, at the last moment Nogaret abandoned this plan as too risky. Boniface died a few weeks later, and within two years the cardinals elected a Frenchman as Clement V. He settled the papacy at Avignon, where it remained for seventy years, largely under the control of the French kings. Nogaret must be considered an important force in these developments.

Although the struggle with Boniface VIII was the outstanding event in his career, and in the reign of Philip the Fair, Nogaret played a leading role in many other royal projects. He was primarily responsible for the confiscation of Jewish wealth in 1306 and for the decision in 1307 to arrest and try the Templars on charges of heresy. To strengthen Nogaret in the latter endeavor, the king made him keeper of the seals, a position equivalent to that of chancellor.

Like many of the lawyers who served Philip the Fair, Nogaret accumulated landed estates through royal favor and through his own enterprise. The size of his property, which lay between Nîmes and Montpellier, has been estimated at 400 square miles. It included some 40 or 50 villages, with close to 10,500 inhabitants, and made him a great landed seigneur.

Much is known of what Nogaret did, but almost nothing of what he thought or said. Whether he was guided by the principles of Roman law or not, his conduct as a royal agent served to strengthen Philip's position as a king.

BIBLIOGRAPHY

The most original and informative study of Nogaret is by Louis Thomas, "La vie privée de Guillaume de Nogaret," in *Annales du Midi,* **16** (1904). Franklin J. Pegues, *The Lawyers of the Last Capetians* (1962), covers his career and compares him with the other lawyers of Philip the Fair. Joseph R. Strayer, *The Reign of Philip the Fair* (1980), studies Nogaret within the government and bureaucracy of the king. See also Joseph R. Strayer, *Les gens de justice du Languedoc sous Philippe le Bel* (1970). For an older but still valuable study, see Robert Holtzmann, *Wilhelm von Nogaret* (1898).

FRANKLIN J. PEGUES

[See also **Boniface VIII, Pope; Chivalry, Orders of; France; Jews in Europe; Parlement of Paris; Philip IV the Fair.**]

NOLI ME TANGERE is Latin for "Touch me not." After Christ had arisen, the first person he is said to have appeared to was Mary Magdalene, whom he met outside the tomb. Initially, she did not recognize him as the Son of God. Upon recognizing this "stranger" as Christ, Mary Magdalene reached out to touch him, calling him *rabbuni* (Hebrew for "my master"). To this, Christ replied, "Touch me not for I am not yet ascended to my Father" (John 20:16–17). The scene depicting this meeting of Christ and Mary outside the tomb is commonly referred to as the *Noli me tangere* and is frequently found in pictorial representations of the life of Christ. Notable examples are a mosaic in S. Apollinare Nuovo (Ravenna, early sixth century) and Giotto's fresco cycle of the Life of Christ in the Arena Chapel (Padua, 1305).

Noli me tangere. Detail from the Life of Christ fresco cycle by Giotto di Bondone in the Arena Chapel, Padua, 1305. ALINARI/ART RESOURCE

BIBLIOGRAPHY
C. R. Dodwell, *Painting in Europe 800–1200* (1971); André Grabar, *Christian Iconography: A Study of Its Origins* (1968).

JENNIFER E. JONES

[See also **Resurrection Cycle.**]

NOMEN SACRUM (holy name). *Nomina sacra* are certain frequently found, standard abbreviations for the names and attributes of the Christian divinity—for instance, $\overline{\text{ds}}$ for deus. The Christian use of *nomina sacra* during the Middle Ages may have been derived from the Jewish reluctance to write the full name of God, although some scholars believe *nomina sacra* are simply a medieval continuation of a common Greek orthographical practice of abbreviation.

BIBLIOGRAPHY
José O'Callaghan, "*Nomina sacra*" *in papyris graecis saeculi III neotestamentariis* (1970); A. H. R. E. Paap, *Nomina Sacra in the Greek Papyri of the First Five Centuries A.D.* (1959); Ludwig Traube, *Nomina sacra* (1907).

WILLIAM J. DIEBOLD

[See also **Codex; Codicology; Manuscript Books, Production of; Paleography; Papyrus; Scriptorium.**]

NOMINALISM, in the strict sense, is a term used to describe the philosophical position that only individuals really exist and that universal concepts, such as genera and species, are not real things but mental constructs derived from our experience with individuals. For a nominalist, things of the same species are not similar because they share a common nature that inheres in them; rather the coincidence of individual characteristics allows us to form a universal concept. In the broad sense, nominalism refers to a range of philosophical and theological opinions associated with or compatible with the above position.

Nominalism first appeared in the late eleventh century and became an intensely discussed issue in the early twelfth century. Support for nominalism waned in the next century and a half. In the early fourteenth century, however, as part of a reaction against Platonism and certain versions of Aristotelian thought, nominalism reappeared, and it became an influential force in late medieval philosophy.

The term *nominales* (nominalists) was used in the late twelfth and early thirteenth centuries to identify those who defended the unity of the noun (*nomen*) and who applied the grammatical-logical theory "that a proposition once true is always true" to defend the immutability of divine knowledge. Nominalism in the sense of a theory of language and universal concepts, however, is more closely associated with Roscelin and Abelard. Roscelin of Compiègne (*ca.* 1050–1125) is said to have taught that only individuals exist and that universal concepts are simply names, words, or mere sounds (*flatus vocis*). The controversy as it developed in the late eleventh and early twelfth centuries was essentially ontological: What degree of reality is possessed by the universal concept, and from where does it come? Many of the leading figures of the age took sides on the issue: William of Champeaux (*ca.* 1070–1121), an extreme realist; Peter Abelard (*ca.* 1079–1142), a moderate nominalist; and Gilbert of Poitiers (*ca.* 1075–1154), a moderate realist. The problem had theological as well as philosophical significance because the relation of universals and individuals was used as a way of understanding the doctrine of the Trinity.

Among the twelfth-century opinions, that of Abelard remains the most important. Before Abelard, most philosophers were essentially Platonists; they assumed that there were ideal forms that inhered in things and made them similar. Moreover, the standard mode of analysis was through grammar rather than logic.

Abelard found both the ultrarealism of William of Champeaux and the ultranominalism of Roscelin unsatisfactory. Logic, for Abelard, was the study of verbal signs, which are predicable of more than one individual in a class. Moreover, only verbal and written signs, linguistic terms are predicable of many individuals. Abelard, however, could not entirely shake off the Platonic heritage. He continued to accept the idea of a common nature inhering in things of the same species that made them similar.

The strong current of Platonism in Abelard's thought prevented him from applying his moderate nominalism (or, better, "nonrealism") to problems in theology and in natural philosophy. Nominalism stressed individuality and could, when applied to the problem of the Trinity, overemphasize the distinction of persons at the expense of the single divine essence. Despite charges against him in his own day, Abelard's teaching on the Trinity was orthodox, and he did not undermine the unity of God by applying conclusions based on grammar and logic. Nor was Abelard's natural philosophy or ethics relativistic, as is often suggested of nominalists. Abelard tended to regard the natural and moral orders as absolute, based on absolute norms and laws that God implemented because they were right and good. While Abelard made an important distinction between outward act and inner intention, he considered ethical and moral norms, against which intentions and acts were to be judged, as absolute. Moreover, Abelard denied God's freedom to act otherwise than he did; in this he differed from most of his contemporaries and also from those late medieval theologians who are generally called nominalists.

From the second half of the twelfth century to the end of the thirteenth, nominalism attracted little support. Most thinkers in that period can be characterized as moderate realists—that is, they ascribed some measure of actual existence to universals. In this group were Albertus Magnus (*ca.* 1200–1280), Bonaventure (*ca.* 1217–1274), Thomas Aquinas (1224–1274), and John Duns Scotus (*ca.* 1266–1308). The term *nominales* appeared in thirteenth century writings, but only as a description of an early-twelfth-century position that was no longer maintained. At the beginning of the fourteenth century, nominalism was reintroduced, this time in the company of compatible positions in natural philosophy and theology that made it far more influential.

Dissatisfaction with a realist explanation of concepts and human knowledge began to appear by the second decade of the fourteenth century in the work of Durand of St. Pourçain (*ca.* 1275–1334) and Peter Aureoli (*ca.* 1280–1322) at Paris and, independently, in William of Ockham (*ca.* 1285–1347) at Oxford. Ockham revived the view that external reality is composed of individuals, although universals as linguistic terms can be predicated of many things.

Ockham found no basis for realism in epistemology: We identify things as belonging to the same species not because we recognize their similarity to a universal concept already within us but because we slowly create that concept through our experience with individuals.

Ockham went beyond earlier forms of nominalism by rejecting the idea of common nature. For Ockham, the universal has no existence in external reality, either independently or as "attached to" individual things. According to him, things in external nature may, in fact, be similar, but not because they share a common nature nor even because they share similarity. Initially Ockham maintained the view that the universal was a purely mental creation, a *fictum,* but he later modified this in the direction of conceptualism, eventually holding that the concept was a mental act, an intention of the soul. Consequently his position has been described as modified nominalism or as realistic conceptualism.

In contrast to Abelard, Ockham's nominalism was part of a larger body of compatible ideas that were interrelated. Already in the last decades of the thirteenth century, Peter Olivi (*ca.* 1248–1297), a Franciscan from southern France, had argued that several of the Aristotelian categories, specifically quantity and relation, were not things in themselves but descriptions of substances and qualities. For example, quantity was not a distinct, separately existing entity (*res extra*) but simply a means of expressing the fact that a body has part separate from part and is extended in space. Similar views began to be put forward at Oxford by Henry of Harclay (*ca.* 1270–1317) while he was regent in theology. Ockham shared these views and built them into a new and controversial natural philosophy. According to Ockham, quantity, relation, place, motion, and time are not *res extrae animam* (things existing outside the soul or mind) but rather descriptions of the way in which substances and qualities act or interact. Things are related, but they do not "share" relation as if it were some third entity. Just as Ockham reinterpreted propositions containing universal terms, analyzing them as logical shorthand for many propositions containing equivalent individual terms, so too, he found statements about time, motion, quantity, and relation to be useful shorthand terms that described states of affairs, not entities. In Ockham's views, external reality is composed solely of substances and qualities.

This "reductive" technique, so common in Ockham, is reflective of one of his fundamental principles, which he adopted from earlier writers (mainly Aristotle) and frequently employed. This is the principle of parsimony or economy: Never posit pluralities without necessity. This principle has become so associated with Ockham that it is known as Ockham's razor.

Ockham's sparse ontological world was paralleled by a similar reductionism in theology. In his teachings on justification and on sacramental causality, Ockham rejected the notion of virtues inherent in things that directly cause grace or the reward of eternal life. All causal relationships, whether in the order of nature or in the order of grace, operate only because God has so ordered or arranged them to act. In the physical world of nature, the causal relationship operates through ordained secondary causes; in the realm of grace and the church, causality operates through a value that God ascribes to human acts, when they are properly performed (in the case of the sacraments) or intended (in the case of meritorious acts and the reception of the sacraments).

Ockham's theology was ultimately grounded in his perception of God's relationship with his creation. In order to underscore the contingent but dependable nature of that relationship, Ockham distinguished between what God might have done and still theoretically can do (*de potentia Dei absoluta*) and what he in fact has done and promises to do (*de potentia Dei ordinata*). That perception was highly compatible with salient aspects of his philosophical nominalism, such as his reduction of metaphysical categories and distinctions, his distaste for inherent natures or virtues, and his emphasis on the conventual nature of spoken and written language.

Although it is difficult to find anyone who accepted all or even most of Ockham's philosophy and theology, several aspects of his thought, particularly his nominalism, did attract a following in subsequent decades and centuries. Adam Wodeham (*ca.* 1298–1358) at Oxford shared Ockham's views on the problem of universals and on quantity, time, motion, and relation, even as he modified or rejected some of Ockham's opinions in epistemology and on the object of knowledge. A similar reaction can be found in Gregory of Rimini (*ca.* 1300–1358) at Paris in the early 1340's. Robert Holcot (*ca.* 1298–1349) at Oxford in the early 1330's, although only indirectly influenced by Ockham, did adopt a more thoroughgoing nominalism in logic.

In the second half of the fourteenth century at Paris the nominalist solution to the problem of universals as well as to issues in natural philosophy found many supporters, most notably Henry Totting von Oyta (*ca.* 1330–1397), Marsilius von Inghen (*ca.* 1330–1396), and Pierre d'Ailly (ca. 1350–1420). One must be careful, however, not to assume that these authors were followers of Ockham or shared his views on most issues. There was not in the fourteenth century any school of thought that could appropriately be termed either Ockhamism or Nominalism.

In the early fifteenth century, with a revival of the thought of Thomas Aquinas and Albertus Magnus, divisions arose within the arts faculties of several universities about the way to teach logic and, secondarily, natural philosophy. Some masters urged a return to the sources and approaches taken in the third quarter of the thirteenth century, particularly at Paris. These included the logic of Aristotle (*logica antiquorum*), Averroës (Ibn Rushd), and the commentators of the late thirteenth century, which followed the approach of the speculative grammarians that had remained active in the fourteenth century, particularly in teaching centers in Germany. This approach to teaching logic became known as the *via antiqua;* its supporters were called "realists" *(reales).* Other masters wanted to continue the approach of the fourteenth-century terminists (logicians who emphasized the meaning and reference of terms), whose sources went back not only to Aristotle but also to the additional treatises of the twelfth and early thirteenth centuries on the properties of terms (*logica modernorum*). As "updated" textbooks they preferred Ockham's *Summa logicae* or the commentaries of Jean Buridan (*ca.* 1295–*ca.* 1358) and Marsilius von Inghen. This approach came to be known as the *via moderna;* its supporters were called "nominalists" *(nominales).*

The association of the Wycliffite and Hussite "heresies" with realism in the years immediately following the Council of Constance (1414–1418) led the majority of the German electors to favor the adoption of a nominalist approach to the exclusion of realism at the University of Cologne (1425). Supporters of the *via antiqua* at Cologne responded in defense of realism, and in 1427 their colleagues at the University of Louvain actually prohibited the teaching of Ockham, Buridan, Marsilius, and their followers.

Throughout most of the fifteenth century both approaches were viable in most universities. Even Cologne, traditionally associated with the *via antiqua,* possessed both traditions, and it was while studying at Cologne that Gabriel Biel (*ca.* 1412–1495) acquired his first texts of Ockham's works. One of the most heated moments in the conflict of the two approaches came in 1474 at Paris, when the nominalists were temporarily driven out of the university by royal decree (they were reinstated in 1481). In the documents produced by that conflict, both sides gave their own versions of the history and development of the two ways. The nominalists defined themselves as those who do not reify terms—that is, posit the existence of things corresponding to every grammatical term—but who concentrate their logic around the properties of terms (the *logica modernorum*).

Nominalism remained a viable and strong alternative in the two generations before the Reformation. Gabriel Biel, an influential teacher in Germany in the last decades of the fifteenth century, was one of the principal defenders of Ockham's thought in a wide variety of areas. He also became the figure whose name was most closely associated with nominalist philosophy and theology in the polemical literature of the sixteenth century.

BIBLIOGRAPHY

Philotheus Boehner, *Collected Articles on Ockham* (1958); Stephen F. Brown, "A Modern Prologue to Ockham's Natural Philosophy," in Jan P. Beckmann *et al.*, eds., *Sprache und Erkenntnis im Mittelalter* (1981); M.-D. Chenu, "Grammaire et théologie aux XIIe et XIIIe siècles," in *Archives d'histoire doctrinale et littéraire du moyen âge,* 10–11 (1935–1936); William J. Courtenay, "Nominalism and Late Medieval Thought: A Bibliographical Essay," in *Theological Studies,* 33 (1972), "Nominalism and Late Medieval Religion," in Charles Trinkaus and Heiko A. Oberman, eds., *The Pursuit of*

Holiness in Late Medieval and Renaissance Religion (1974), and "Late Medieval Nominalism Revisited: 1972–1982," in *Journal of the History of Ideas,* **44** (1983); Astrik L. Gabriel, "'Via Antiqua' and 'Via Moderna' and the Migration of Paris Students and Masters to the German Universities in the Fifteenth Century," in Albert Zimmerman, ed., *Antiqui und Moderni* (1974); G. Gál, "Gualteri de Chatton et Guillelmi de Ockham controversia de natura conceptus universalis," in *Franciscan Studies,* **27** (1967); Neal W. Gilbert, "Ockham, Wyclif, and the 'Via Moderna,'" in Albert Zimmermann, ed., *Antiqui und Moderni* (1974); Helmar Junghans, *Ockham im Lichte der neueren Forschung* (1968); Heiko A. Oberman, *The Harvest of Medieval Theology* (1963), and *Masters of the Reformation,* Dennis Martin, trans. (1981); Franz Pelster, "Nominales und reales im 13. Jahrhundert," in *Sophia,* **12–14** (1944–1946); Gerhard Ritter, *Studien zur Spätscholastik,* II, *Via antiqua und via moderna auf den deutschen Universitäten des XV. Jahrhunderts* (1922); Martin M. Tweedale, *Abailard on Universals* (1976); Paul Vignaux, *Nominalisme au XIVe siècle* (1948).

WILLIAM J. COURTENAY

[See also **Abelard, Peter; Ailly, Pierre d'; Albertus Magnus; Aquinas, St. Thomas; Aristotle in the Middle Ages; Biel, Gabriel; Bonaventure, St.; Buridan, Jean; Councils, Western; Duns Scotus, John; Durand of St. Pourçain; Gilbert of Poitiers; Gregory of Rimini; Holcot, Robert; Hussites; John of Salisbury; Ockham, William of; Paris, University of; Philosophy and Theology, Western European; Rushd, Ibn (Averroës); Terminism; Universals; Universities; Via Moderna; Wyclif, John.**]

NOMISMA, the customary term for the Byzantine gold coin (full form: *nomisma chrysoun;* Latin: *solidus aureus*). Following the monetary system established by Constantine the Great in the fourth century, it was struck at seventy-two to the pound (weight: *ca.* 4.5 grams). Its fineness of twenty-four carats was maintained until the 1030's, when the first signs of gradual debasement appeared.

BIBLIOGRAPHY

Philip Grierson, ed., *Catalogue of the Byzantine Coins in the Dumbarton Oaks Collection and the Whittemore Collection,* III, pt. 1 (1973), 14–44.

JOHN W. NESBITT

[See also **Ducat; Mints and Money, Byzantine.**]

NOMOCANON. A term used in Byzantine canon law to designate a collection presenting synoptically both ecclesiastical canons (*kanones*) and civil laws (*nomoi*) on ecclesiastical subjects. Earliest was the *Nomocanon in Fifty Titles,* assembled by an unknown compiler toward the end of the sixth century from two works by the lawyer-patriarch of Constantinople, John III Scholastikos (*r.* 565–577): (1) the *Synagoge in Fifty Titles,* a topical arrangement of conciliar canons to which John added the so-called apostolic canons, the African Code, and diverse excerpts from the letters of Basil the Great; and (2) a collection of civil laws in eighty-seven chapters.

More influential was the *Nomocanon in Fourteen Titles,* assembled between 629 and 640 by the anonymous jurist usually known as Enantiophanes. Civil laws are drawn from a collection known as the *Tripartita,* while canons and overall arrangement derive from the *Syntagma in Fourteen Titles,* which appeared in Constantinople in the later sixth century. More comprehensive than the *Synagoge in Fifty Titles,* particularly in its selection of excerpts from Basil and other patristic sources, the *Syntagma* is also more conservative in format: Canonical texts are presented in their traditional, roughly chronological order, with the "titles" serving simply as a topical index.

The *Nomocanon in Fourteen Titles* as well as the *Syntagma* went through several later recensions, these serving chiefly to incorporate new canonical texts. Most famous is the 883 recension of the *Nomocanon,* often ascribed to Patriarch Photios, which enjoyed wide circulation not only in the Byzantine Empire but also, in Slavonic translation, in the Balkans and Russia. Also noteworthy is the recension of Theodore Bestes (in 1090), which gives an improved text for the imperial laws, and the extensive commentary of Theodore Balsamon (about 1170–1178).

In late Byzantium the term *nomocanon* also came to be applied to manuals on penitential matters intended for the use of confessors. Such manuals circulated from the ninth century, often under the name of John the Faster (patriarch of Constantinople, 582–595). Their wide diffusion in the Slavic world, particularly in Russia, stems above all from the monastic communities of Mount Athos.

BIBLIOGRAPHY

Hans-Georg Beck, *Kirche und theologische Literatur im byzantinischen Reich* (1959), 145–147, 422–425.

JOHN H. ERICKSON

[See also **Athos, Mount; Basil the Great of Caesarea, St.; Byzantine Church; Councils, Ecumenical; John IV the**

Faster, Patriarch; Law, Byzantine; Photios; Theodore Balsamon.]

NORAVANKᶜ AT AMAŁU, an Armenian monastery at the episcopal seat of Siwnikᶜ, was constructed during the thirteenth and fourteenth centuries by the Orbelean princes. The surviving monuments include the domed hall church of S. Karapet erected by Prince Liparit between 1221 and 1227; its vaulted, columnless *gawitᶜ*, commissioned by Prince Smbat in 1261, with two tympana, one a unique and complex composition; S. Lusaworičᶜ, erected in 1285 by Prince Tarsaitch as the Orbelean mausoleum; and the two-level mausoleum-church of S. Astuacacin commissioned by Prince Burtᶜel and completed by the architect-sculptor-painter Momik, a monk, in 1339. S. Astuacacin is richly decorated with elegant blind arcades and figured tympana.

BIBLIOGRAPHY

Sirarpie Der Nersessian, "Deux tympans sculptés arméniens datant de 1321," in *Cahiers archéologiques,* **25** (1976), and *Armenian Art* (1977).

LUCY DER MANUELIAN

[See also **Armenian Art; Gawitᶜ.**]

NORBERT OF IBURG (*d. ca.* 1117), a Benedictine monk. He was born in Brabant and entered the monastery at Iburg, which had been founded by Benno II of Osnabrück. He became abbot in 1084. Norbert's *Vita Bennonis II episcopi Osnabrugensis* provides important information about eleventh-century history.

BIBLIOGRAPHY

Norbert of Iburg, *Vita Bennonis II episcopi Osnabrugensis,* Henricus Bresslau, ed. (1902), is the modern edition. Edgar N. Johnson, "Bishop Benno II of Osnabrück," in *Speculum,* **16** (1941), discusses Norbert at some length.

EDWARD FRUEH

[See also **Benno of Osnabrück.**]

NORMANS AND NORMANDY. Normandy, the duchy and later province in the medieval kingdom of France, was formed as the result of a Scandinavian settlement in the lower Seine Valley, in and around Rouen, in the early tenth century. It came to occupy the territory bounded by the English Channel, by the rivers Bresle and Epte through most of their course, and by stretches of the Eure, Avre, Sarthe, and Couesnon. Only a relatively small part of this territory was settled at all intensively by Scandinavian people (Vikings, Northmen, Normans, Normands); apart from its aristocracy, much of the indigenous Frankish-Gallo-Roman population survived, to transmit its ethnic ingredient, its law, and some of its institutions to the later duchy. The word "Norman," however, came to be applied to all the people living in this territory, even though the Scandinavian element may have been quite small, consisting of the descendants of ex-Vikings who had taken over the estates of dispossessed Frankish landowners, leaving the peasantry largely undisturbed.

Nothing in the earlier history of this territory prefigured the duchy, neither the Carolingian partitions nor any of the marches or duchies created in the ninth century, nor the Merovingian partitions and subdivisions before them; and though the later Normandy corresponded in general terms to the late Roman province of *Lugdunensis secunda,* perpetuated in the ecclesiastical province of Rouen, it is difficult to see how this could have determined the territorial formation of the duchy. Moreover, Normandy has no geographical unity. The west, which belongs to Brittany, has always been relatively remote and undeveloped. The east belongs to the Paris Basin. It has always been near to the political and cultural centers (save, perhaps, while the Carolingian empire was a reality); Rouen and Paris are interdependent and indissolubly linked by the great artery of the Seine. It is even difficult to find a boundary between these two regions, for there is a middle territory which belongs properly to neither. These fundamental ethnic and geographical facts have profoundly affected the structure and the history of Normandy from the tenth century to the twentieth.

FOUNDATION OF THE DUCHY

The river Seine had been one of the principal routes by which Viking raiders had penetrated Carolingian Francia. Their earliest appearance in the valley, so far as is known, was in the year 820; they first wintered in the lower Seine in 851; and by the end of the century they had devastated all the country within reach. The Carolingian kings of West Francia had been unable to organize an effective defense until King Charles the Simple resorted to a device which had already been em-

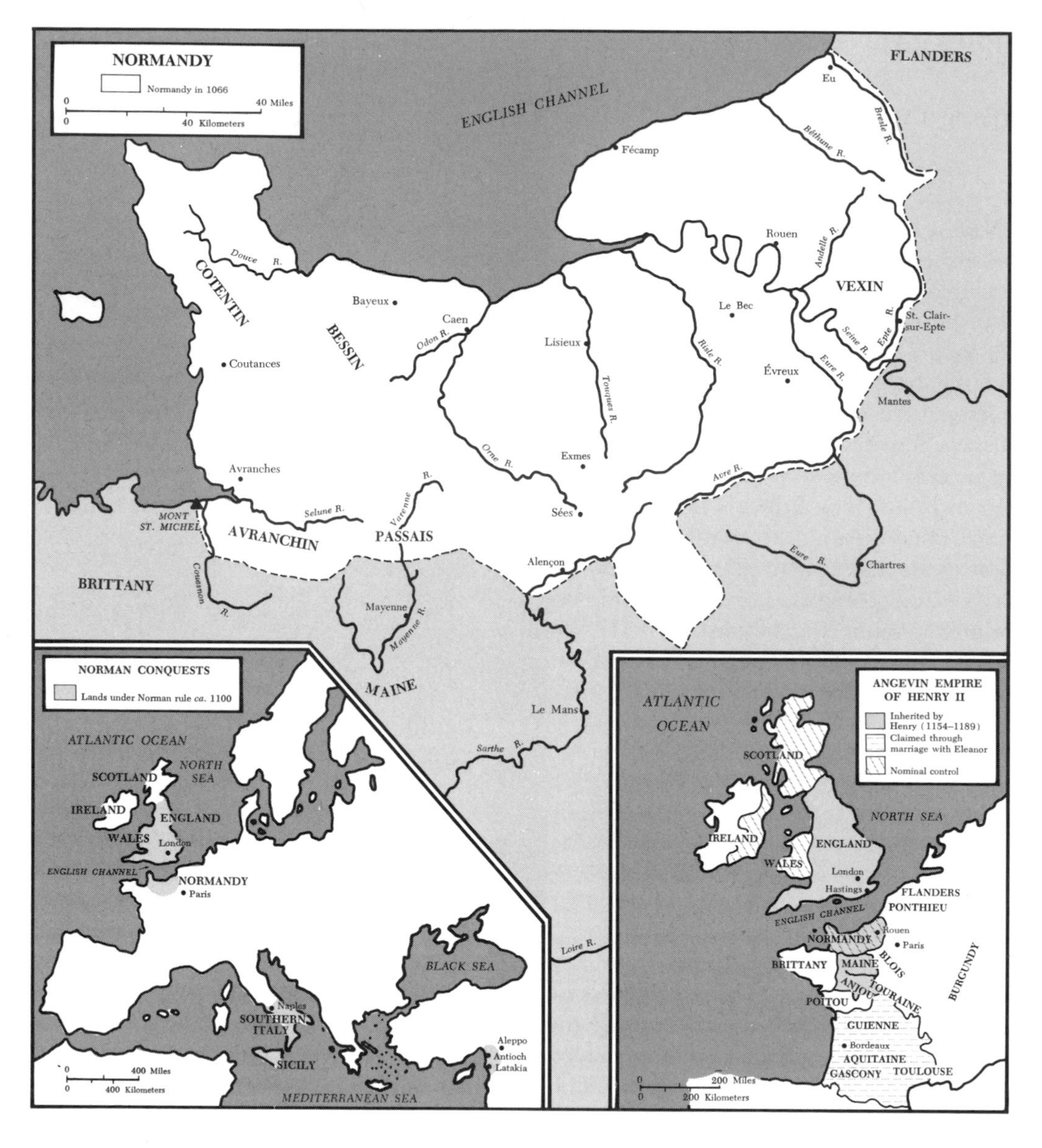

ployed by his predecessors against invading Bretons in the west and against the Vikings themselves in northeastern Francia, as well as by the Anglo-Saxon kings of Wessex. Choosing the moment when the leader of the principal band of Vikings operating from the Seine, one known to history as Rollo, had suffered a defeat near Chartres, King Charles came to an agreement with him whereby he and his followers should be allowed to settle in and around Rouen in return for their conversion to Christianity. This agreement has been generally known as the Treaty of St. Clair-sur-Epte, made in the year 911 at a place on what was to be the boundary between Normandy and France. As no text of this treaty has survived, if one was ever made, its terms in any detail can only be inferred; but it is clear from later developments that the king's permission to settle on the designated lands involved making Rollo a Carolingian count. With this office would have gone the rights and lands that attached to that office within the territory he had conquered; he would also have received the virtual autonomy that other Carolingian counts possessed at that date. In addition, Rollo got the lands of pillaged or destroyed religious institutions and of the dispossessed native aristocracy, whether these were formally granted or not. In return, the king hoped that with land of their own to defend, these Northmen would protect at least those parts of Francia accessible from the Seine Valley, and, with the conversion of Rollo and his chief men, that they would tolerate what survived of Christianity in the lands assigned to them. This would facilitate the Northmen's relations with the native Frankish people, and also their ultimate assimilation.

There has been much debate on the juridical

NORMANS AND NORMANDY

nature of the treaty: whether or not it created a fief to be held of the king by Rollo and his successors. No doubt the Viking leaders were required to give the same promise of loyalty as was required of the other "princes" of West Francia; but the question is unreal, for the fief as a form of tenure was still in an early stage of development, and the Viking leaders would certainly not have understood it in any sophisticated form. The relationship between the ruler of Normandy and the king, like the political organization of the duchy and even its territorial definition, were all of slow growth and development over the century and a half following the year 911.

There were further cessions of territory, with repeated undertakings of fidelity, in 924 (the Bessin and probably the Hiémois) and 933 (probably the Cotentin and the Avranchin); but these two grants, together with the original grant of 911, can hardly be thought of as defining Normandy territorially or in any other respect. Though there were no further raids using the Seine as their way into the country, the Northmen "settled" by the agreement of 911 endeavored, for half a century at least, to extend their possessions by violence in all landward directions, and the "grants" of 924 and 933 may have been no more than a recognition and "ratification" of forcible occupation. The limits of Normandy were eventually settled partly by a military balance of forces among the Normans and the count of Flanders to the east, the duke of the Franks to the south, and the Bretons to the west, and partly by the limits of effective government and administration exercised by the duke, as that developed. The process cannot be said to have been completed until after William the Conqueror had annexed the Passais in 1051; and even then the dukes were striving to extend their frontier in the Seine Valley from the Epte to the Oise until well into the twelfth century, while the kings of France were trying to push them back to the Andelle.

DUCAL ADMINISTRATION

The duchy of Normandy was made by its dukes. There is unfortunately almost no direct evidence that would enable us to define the nature of their powers and authority during the greater part of the tenth century, but many features in the government of Normandy during the eleventh century can only be explained by postulating some such origin and development as follows. Rollo and his early successors were Viking leaders who had been invested with the powers and position of a Carolingian count. In their first capacity they retained a form of military authority; in their second capacity they were given authority over the Frankish population they dominated. It is unlikely that nice distinctions were made; the warlord aspect must have been more in evidence at first, gradually superseded by the Frankish inheritance, which had much more to contribute to the making of a state.

There was one noteworthy survival of Viking military authority, the power to impose instant banishment for disobedience or opposition, a power exercised by the dukes to the time of William the Conqueror and beyond. It was a valuable complement to the powers of a count, and its use may go some way to explain how it was that the early dukes disposed of or subdued other Viking leaders, as they must have had to do, not only among those in the army of 911 but also among the leaders of the independent bands of Northmen that established themselves in Normandy from time to time during the next half century. Banishment was, however, a negative power; many more positive qualities were needed to build the Normandy that could conquer England while sending out men to found principalities in southern Italy and in Palestine during the eleventh century. Those powers came from the Frankish element in the ducal office.

Several titles are attributed to the rulers of Normandy in documents of the tenth and eleventh centuries, though the most usual was "count" (for convenience "duke" will be used here throughout). This must mean that they were regarded as succeeding to the position of the Carolingian counts in the counties *(pagi)* and parts of counties included in Normandy. To that extent they were fitted into the political structure of the kingdom. Moreover, with the conversion, however superficially, of Rollo and his chief men to Christianity, the return of the archbishop of Rouen to his city and of some monks of St. Ouen de Rouen to their monastery, and the possibility that the structure of Carolingian administration had not been entirely destroyed in some of the counties included in Normandy (a Frankish count is recorded in Rouen as late as the year 905), the means were given to the rulers of Normandy to continue to reconstruct something of Carolingian administration.

This they did only slowly. Yet, when the outlines of a scheme of local government emerge around the beginning of the eleventh century, it becomes apparent that the dukes had appointed counts or

NORMANS AND NORMANDY

vicomtes in most of the old counties, and these counties had retained their territorial outlines. Both counts and *vicomtes* held office on a revocable basis, which recalls Carolingian practice, and they were rewarded for their service with a portion of the ducal lands, as their Carolingian predecessors had been; yet they also had more contemporary characteristics in that the counts were all drawn from the ducal family, and both they and the *vicomtes* were given custody of ducal castles. Rollo and his successors were also able to preserve some of the profitable rights of a Frankish count (certain tolls and direct taxes such as *graverie* and *bernage)*. The law and custom of Normandy, when it becomes possible to know anything about it, was almost wholly Frankish in content. The few exceptions were mostly in maritime matters. Yet, though the Carolingian counties, or *pagi,* survived as governmental units, their former social coherence and their institutions for the administration of justice had been disrupted; and though the dukes preserved some overriding judicial rights and exclusivities derived from Carolingian royalty, their justice by the middle of the eleventh century was more like a bundle of *consuetudines* than a general judicial authority. This practice was also true of other seigneurs and princes in contemporary France, even the king himself.

OTHER BASES OF POWER

The relatively great power and authority which the dukes of the eleventh century exercised within their duchy, and their prestige and influence beyond it, were derived also from other sources. One was the extraordinary vitality of the ducal family itself. The long and evidently competent reigns of Richard I (942–996) and Richard II (996–1026) gave stability; the family was remarkably free from the rivalries and ambitions which have so often torn apart not only a ruling family but the country which it ruled, and this was so even though the early dukes provided themselves with consorts by Danish pagan custom and rite as well as Frankish wives in accordance with Christian usage. The mode of succession seems to have been settled quite early: designation within the family by the reigning duke with the approval of the magnates. Before 1100 there were only three critical moments. After the assassination of William Longsword in 942, it was at least possible that the king or the duke of the Franks might have reoccupied Normandy as the Danish states in England were just then being conquered by the kings of Wessex. The succession of Robert I to his brother Richard III in 1027 may have been by violence; and after the disturbances of William the Conqueror's minority there was a determined attempt to replace him in 1047 by his cousin Guy of Brionne. In the conditions of the tenth and early eleventh centuries the Norman principality showed remarkable durability.

Another source of power was the great wealth of the early dukes. Either as an element in the royal "grants" of 911, 924, and 933, or otherwise, the royal lands (including lands that had been assigned to the counts) had come into the hands of the dukes, along with royal rights over bishoprics and monasteries. In addition, the dukes had the opportunity to possess themselves of a great deal more than the old royal and comital lands. The greater Frankish landowners were unlikely to find a place in the new regime; the monasteries had mostly been destroyed; and there were considerable gaps during the tenth century in the succession of bishops at Lisieux, Avranches, Sées, and probably Bayeux (those of Coutances deserted their diocese and lived in Rouen for more than a century). Certainly what is known of the history of the monastic lands suggests very strongly that they were in the duke's hands until the monasteries could be reestablished. Moreover, other forms of wealth were available. Throughout the tenth century there was a great deal of more or less lawful trade among Normandy, the British Isles, and Scandinavia, and a quantity of Viking loot also found its way to the duchy. The duke had income through tolls, taxes, and other dues, and of course he had the product of the lands that he kept for himself and his family. (This may have been substantial from an early date; there is no reason to suppose that the cultivation of the land of Normandy did not rapidly recover as soon as the raiding stopped.)

This unusually great wealth, together with the circumstances of their establishment in Normandy, provided the dukes around the beginning of the eleventh century with an opportunity that was given to few contemporary rulers. Unlike their neighbors, the dukes of Normandy were in a position to create their own aristocracy; and all the evidence suggests that that is what they did. It seems that few Norman families were prominent before the duke made them so. What is more significant is the evidence of men receiving land from the ducal demesne or the possessions of the church, and of men from outside the duchy, from Brittany, Maine,

NORMANS AND NORMANDY

France, even Germany, receiving land within the duchy, and it is hard to imagine any of this happening save by ducal act or consent. Most significant of all is that so many of the greater families of the mid eleventh century, those which eventually gained most from the conquest of England, claimed kinship with the duke. For the counts, some of the bishops, and some others, this relationship was real enough. In some cases it may have been remote or even fictitious, but the fact that the claim was so often made shows that rank and consequence were deemed to come from the duke rather than from otherwise eminent ancestry. The duke could build up a family, and he could also dispossess and virtually destroy it.

Since few if any of the greater magnates in Normandy could impose themselves on the duke or even challenge him, since his aristocracy was so very largely of his own creation and, moreover, so recently established that the terms on which it had obtained its possessions must have been generally and exactly known, duke and magnates could work in partnership, at least in normal times; and a foreign adventure like the conquest of England would be a genuinely joint enterprise in which their interests coincided. Within the duchy, the duke's relationship with his nobles enabled him to maintain a high degree of control over the building and keeping of castles, preventing the formation of quasi-independent *châtellenies,* which were a real problem for many of the duke's neighbors.

A very important element in the power of the duke was derived from his relationship with the church. The Vikings had arrived in Normandy as pagans, and ecclesiastical institutions and property were easy prey. Since the early dukes had the wealth and the power, only they could take the initiative in restoring the church in Normandy. Rollo's baptism made revival possible, but little was achieved during the tenth century.

The great reform and expansion came later, beginning when Richard II, in 1001, persuaded William of Volpiano, a Cluniac monk who was then abbot of St. Bénigne of Dijon and a great reformer with ideas of his own, to establish monks at Fécamp and to be their abbot. William also reformed, in a generally Cluniac sense, the few houses already reestablished, and subsequent foundations drew their original nucleus of monks from one or another of these houses. Until the 1030's new foundations were made, wholly or in large part, by the ducal family; thereafter the Norman baronage took a vigorous hand in them. By 1066 there were at least thirty-five monasteries and nunneries in the duchy, though only four in the two western dioceses, and nearly all were under direct ducal authority.

The secular church in Normandy took longer to reorganize and to bring into line with the more advanced ideas of the day It is likely that the dukes had had a considerable part in reestablishing the bishoprics. Until the end of the eleventh century at least, the bishops were drawn predominantly from Norman aristocratic families, even the ducal family itself, and they shared the interests and outlook of the class from which they came. But what they may have lacked in spirituality, they made up in organizing ability. The structure of diocesan administration—cathedral chapters, archdeaconries, and diocesan synods—was largely formed toward the middle of the eleventh century. Also, around this time, an indigenous program of reform in discipline was set on foot, largely through a series of provincial councils in which the duke certainly had a predominant part and in which, also, the relationship between the ecclesiastical and governmental spheres of activity was defined in a way that left the duke at the head of both.

At the time, then, when William the Conqueror had overcome the troubles of his minority, Normandy emerges as a very compact principality. The ducal family, the aristocracy, and the ecclesiastical hierarchy were bound up together; for the most part their families had achieved wealth and prominence quite recently. The monasteries, likewise, had been founded or refounded within the last half century, most of them very recently, and had drawn their initial nucleus of monks and their customs from a common source. They too were bound up with the duke and the aristocracy; and with the distinction of Fécamp and Le Bec and of men like Lanfranc and Anselm, and the continuing spate of new foundations, the monks of Normandy could well feel a sense of community and of mission—as well as an enthusiasm—which would not be opposed to the ambitions of the ruling class.

EXTERNAL RELATIONS

In the establishment of the ducal family, the new aristocracy, and the new or renewed church, Normandy had been fitted into the political structure of Capetian France. The objective of King Charles the Simple had at length been realized. Normandy in the early tenth century had been a

NORMANS AND NORMANDY

Viking state, living largely by plunder. It had gradually been assimilated. The point of change has been dated to the early years of the eleventh century, when trading and other external relations ceased to be predominantly with the Scandinavian north and turned more to France. In any case, the fact that the Scandinavian settlers in Normandy had always been a minority, though a dominant minority, meant that they had to come to an accommodation sooner or later with the milieu in which they had settled. They came to adopt, almost wholly, the law of the Franks, their language, their religion, and their ecclesiastical organization.

This process of integration showed itself in other ways. The relationship between the duke and the king of France was the normal relationship between a great prince of the kingdom and the king. Normandy was regarded as part of the kingdom; the duke was a *fidelis* of the king; the expression of that relationship varied with circumstances and personalities, but it was not the full feudal relationship of the late twelfth or thirteenth centuries, and the duke was autonomous in practice. Within the duchy, relations between the duke and the magnates, and between the magnates and their principal tenants, were taking on feudal form, as they were in northern France generally; but feudal institutions were not so fully developed by 1066 as has often been thought. The terms "fief" and "vassal" hardly occur as yet in contemporary Norman documents, knights did not yet have the social status they later acquired, and though the duke's military forces may have been organized in a way approaching feudal form, it is doubtful if they were yet based on definite quotas of knight service from the duke's direct tenants.

What can be termed the extension of ducal power and influence into neighboring lands also took on the quasi-feudal form that other successful princes of the time were employing. In the tenth century, raids from Normandy into Flanders or Brittany, and the use of Normandy as a base for raids into England, had all been characteristic of Viking activity. But when, around the beginning of the eleventh century, a double marriage was arranged in the ruling families of Normandy and Brittany, and magnates from eastern Brittany were permitted, or perhaps encouraged, to take lands in western Normandy, the duke of Normandy assumed a form of lordship over the duke of Brittany as well as over some Breton nobles. When William the Conqueror seized the *comté* of Maine in 1063, it was primarily to resist what he regarded as the aggression of the count of Anjou, in which the great cross-border family of Bellême was deeply involved. William also established a feudal superiority over the counts of Ponthieu and Boulogne, and even the count of Flanders may have been his pensioner.

All these actions were entirely characteristic of the politics of the princes of France in the eleventh century, and of the manner in which other "feudal empires" were being built up. The process extended the area from which a ducal army could be recruited by a mixture of obligation, volunteering, and mercenary hire. But though Normandy was wealthy, and the duke evidently had the means to mobilize that wealth for his purposes, we know little of the mechanics of his government before 1066, save that the counts and *vicomtes* seem more like ducal officers and less like barons than elsewhere. His court, his household, the means of producing charters in his name, do not seem much more developed or sophisticated than elsewhere.

Yet Normandy had its particularities, due as much to the circumstances of its foundation as to any possible "Viking inheritance." The most important was the power of the duke, his relationship with his aristocracy (particularly in his control of castles and private war) and with the church (at this point the relatively close coincidence of the ecclesiastical province and the limits of the duchy must have been a great asset to the duke), and the widespread community of interests and outlook among all the notables of Normandy. Another particularity was the restlessness which the Normans certainly showed in the elevent h century. This restlessness may reflect their partly Viking ancestry or at least their recent attachment to the land of Normandy. Men from Normandy joined the Christian forces in Spain, went adventuring as freebooters or mercenaries in southern Italy, made pilgrimages to distant lands, and joined the First Crusade in some force. But some had been exiled by the duke and were seeking to repair their fortunes abroad; some may already have found it difficult to find a living according to their ambitions in Normandy. All this wandering was Norman expansion of a kind; and, along with the extension of ducal authority beyond the duchy, it brought ideas and still more wealth into Normandy, as is shown by the intellectual and artistic distinction of its monasteries and the number and scale of the churches that were being built even before 1066.

NORMANS AND NORMANDY

CONQUEST OF ENGLAND

The greatest adventure by far, though still only a part of this "expansion," was the conquest of the kingdom of England. It had been long prepared. Even during the tenth century Viking raiders in England found a base, sometimes a refuge, and often a market for their booty in Normandy; but the origin of the Norman interests in England that led to the Conquest lay in the agreement between King Ethelred II the Unready and Duke Richard I in 991, which resulted in King Ethelred's marriage in 1002 to Emma, Duke Richard's daughter. A small group of Normans came to England in her entourage looking for places and property; and when Emma and Ethelred's elder son, Edward the Confessor, succeeded to the throne in 1042, being half Norman by ancestry and having spent a large part of his early life in Normandy, he brought with him a much larger band of Normans, as chaplains or bodyguards; and these men acquired bishoprics, churches, and lands in England. During Edward's reign, and before, Norman churches acquired lands in the kingdom, and the merchants of Rouen acquired privileges in London. The scale of this influx is difficult to measure, but it was sufficient, with all the traffic between England and Normandy which it necessarily engendered, to indicate to the Normans the possibilities which England might hold for them. It also provided Duke William with all the intelligence he would need if he and his magnates decided to enforce the claim which they believed he had to the throne of England.

The Battle of Hastings, in October 1066, was probably decisive, for it destroyed the English royal family and most of the aristocracy, and it enabled William to secure London and the southeast and to be crowned before further English resistance could be organized. He even felt able to spend most of the year 1067 celebrating his triumph in Normandy; but the conquest, in the military sense, was not entirely secure until he had overcome resistance in the north, dealt with a Danish invasion, and settled his relations with the king of Scots in 1072.

We should like to know more than we do about the mounting of the invasion of 1066. It was said that the magnates of Normandy, on whom its success would largely depend, had to be persuaded of its feasibility; it is certain that the invasion army, though largely raised in Normandy, also included men from Brittany, Maine, Flanders, even Poitou, the countries into which ducal authority and influence had been penetrating in the preceding decades. We know that the political situation was unusually favorable, with most of the powers in France that were capable of interfering with the enterprise temporarily unable to do so. Also, the record of the dukes as leaders and patrons of the regeneration of the church in their lands helped to persuade the pope, and so public opinion as it then existed, of the rightness of William's cause. In the end William was lucky even with the weather during the autumn of 1066. The building of the necessary transports, itself a formidable operation, was achieved, it seems, by assigning quotas to the chief magnates, though behind this assignment there may still have been some relics of a Viking chieftain's maritime authority among the constituents of ducal power. In any case the whole operation would have been quite impossible without the exceptional position of the duke in his duchy and the relationship the dukes had built up with the artistocracy and the church of Normandy during the preceding half century.

The subject of the conquest was not simply England in the geographical sense but the whole bundle of rights and authority exercised by King Harold and King Edward, and this included a superiority, hard to define in modern terms, over the rulers of the Welsh and the Scots. Military conquest was followed by colonization. King William took for himself the royal lands which Harold and Edward had held, and a good deal more besides; most of the remainder of the land of England he distributed very unevenly among his principal followers. Norman ecclesiastics were appointed to English bishoprics and made abbots of the more important English monasteries. Religious houses in Normandy received lands in England, and colonies of Norman merchants appeared in English towns. There was soon a Norman element in the cathedral chapters, among the monks of some English monasteries, and even among the ordinary folk of the countryside. This colonizing process was extended to Wales and eventually to parts of Scotland.

THE ANGLO-NORMAN REALM

The result was the formation of an Anglo-Norman realm, a "regnum Norman-Anglorum," as the Hyde chronicler called it. Neither William nor Henry I elected to settle in one country and govern the other by some form of deputy. Instead they governed both directly by moving constantly

NORMANS AND NORMANDY

from one to the other and from place to place within each, though they generally appointed regents, if possible from the royal family, to supply a royal presence during their absence from either. Centralized rule meant that all the central institutions of government—king, household, seal, embryonic chancery, and court—were common to the two countries; and though the king was never called "king of the Normans" he certainly acted with royal authority in Normandy.

Similarly, those Normans and others who received lands in England did not give up their patrimonies and emigrate from Normandy, as those who settled in southern Italy or beyond more or less had to do. These Anglo-Normans therefore built up cross-Channel estates, often very extensive, and generated a great deal of traffic between the two countries. In some families there were partitions, leading to the formation of a Norman branch and an English branch, and though this often separated the Norman from the English estates it did not necessarily do so. In any case estates straddling the Channel could be formed or reformed at any time by the usual means—marriage, inheritance, grant, purchase, or exchange. The churchmen, and the merchants, naturally, also maintained close relations with Normandy.

The Norman Conquest of England, therefore, made Normandy far more a part of a larger political complex than it had been hitherto, for the earlier dukes, though they acknowledged that their duchy was a part of the realm of France, were to all intents and purposes independent.

In this expanded realm, the Norman kings soon found it necessary to delegate some of the powers, chiefly financial and judicial. By the end of Henry's reign there was a nonroyal, ministerial regent in each country seeing to the execution of the king's commands when the king was absent, coordinating the work of the delegated institutions, and acting on his own authority when necessary.

In Normandy, institutional development was not quite so precocious nor taken so far as in England, where the preconditions were more favorable; but the Exchequer and the administration of justice were organized on the same lines as in the kingdom, and a beginning was made in the development of a law of the king's court which, so long as the relationship with England endured, would be much the same as in the kingdom.

It is now generally thought, moreover, that the quite exceptional opportunity given to King William to define his tenurial relations with his aristocracy in England also enabled him to perfect feudal institutions in Normandy, leaving him in a very strong position. So far as the more important barons were concerned, he was dealing with the same individuals in both countries.

There was, however, a strong element of insecurity in this Anglo-Norman realm—the succession. In all probability William the Conqueror intended his eldest son, Robert, to succeed him in all his lands; Henry I designated his only legitimate son, William, to succeed likewise. The Conqueror was thwarted by his son Robert's rebellion, Henry by his own son's premature death in 1120.

The first incident led to the rule of William Rufus and then Henry in England, with Robert Curthose in Normandy, from 1087 to 1106. During this time the brother ruling in England always had a substantial foothold in Normandy; Rufus actually held the duchy from 1096 to 1100 while Robert was on crusade. In addition, the baronage, though divided, was anxious for a settlement that would allow them to keep their estates in both countries. Still, it was not inconceivable then that England and Normandy might have been separated permanently. In fact Henry defeated his brother and reunited kingdom and duchy, and the integration of their government and institutions could continue, though during most of his reign he was haunted by the claims of his nephew, William Clito, Robert's son.

The succession crisis at Henry's death in 1135 was more serious. After his son William's death he had designated his daughter, the widowed empress Matilda, as his heir in both countries and married her to Geoffrey Plantagenet, who, soon after the marriage, succeeded to the lands of the counts of Anjou. Matilda and Geoffrey could not prevent Stephen of Blois (son of Henry's sister) from seizing England and Normandy on Henry's death, and though Geoffrey succeeded in conquering Normandy, Matilda could not drive Stephen from England. From 1144 (when Geoffrey effectively completed his drive on Normandy) to 1153 (when Stephen accepted Henry II as his heir in England) England and Normandy were ruled by men of different and rival families; and though there were still conditions that could have facilitated reunion, it must have seemed to any political observer of the time that Normandy and England were separated forever. Although, therefore, the Norman Conquest of England meant that Normandy had been

NORMANS AND NORMANDY

bound up with the kingdom, and that there had been a progressive assimilation and union of the two countries as a practical solution to the problem of governing them together, these achievements were still at risk.

THE ANGEVIN EMPIRE

Geoffrey "gave" Normandy to his eldest son, Henry, in 1150; and Henry's military campaign in England three years later induced Stephen (whose own eldest son had just died) to accept him as his heir. At the end of 1154, Henry, already duke of the Normans and of the people of Aquitaine and count of the Angevins, was crowned king of the English. This act reestablished the relationship between Normandy and England as it had been in the time of Henry I. Families which had held lands on both sides of the Channel could and did reconstruct their cross-Channel estates, and new ones could be and were formed; for though the change of dynasty was the result of a military conquest of the Anglo-Norman realm by the counts of Anjou, there was no Angevin colonization of England and Normandy in any way comparable with the Norman colonization of England after 1066. Ecclesiastics could move from positions in one country to the other, though Normans no longer had the near-monopoly of the higher positions in the English church that they had had earlier. It is still a question how far the institutions created by the Norman kings, the delegated jurisdictions and the exchequers, had collapsed during the period of separation. At all events they were soon reestablished. Henry claimed to be the lawful heir of his grandfather Henry I, and he set about the reconstruction of the earlier Henry's government in all respects.

But he was doing so under different conditions. As king of England, Henry acted in the Norman tradition. He reestablished the old Norman lordship over the kings of Scots and the Welsh princes and continued an ongoing attempt to conquer Ireland. On the Continent, however, he was count of Anjou and duke of Aquitaine as well as duke of Normandy. He also achieved direct rule in Brittany and some degree of lordship over the counts of Toulouse, Ponthieu, Boulogne, and Flanders, among others.

This expanded role on the Continent had various effects. While Henry's father, Geoffrey, had been ruling Anjou and Normandy together, he ruled by moving constantly from one to the other. Henry did the same in his vastly extended dominions. This action meant again that king, household, and court were common to all the countries directly ruled. But it also meant that they would be absent longer and more often from any one of them than the Norman kings had been, and the result was a powerful stimulant to delegation. It is true that the Angevin kings, from 1154 to 1204, spent more time in Normandy than in any one of their other lands, even England, and to that extent Normandy was the political center of the "Angevin Empire," as it was geographically; but even in Normandy the king was more absent than present.

In Normandy as in England there were solid foundations on which to build, foundations laid by the Anglo-Norman kings; indeed the structures erected in the two countries were remarkably similar at the end of the twelfth century. In both countries a group of royal justices sat with the king when he was available, or without him, often "at the Exchequer" if he was away; in both the same justices presided over royal courts and performed other administrative work in different parts of the country, though apparently in less regular circuits in Normandy than in England; in both, the king's courts were beginning to keep regular written records. In both new procedures of writ and inquest were being devised to protect property and repress violence, on exactly the same principles, if with differences in detail. In both the Exchequer was developed as a commission of the king's court for the auditing of accounts as well as the administration of justice and was improving its procedures on the same lines if, again, with differences in detail. In both countries the head of this judicial and financial administration was a nonroyal regent, the seneschal in Normandy and the justiciar in England, who put into execution the king's commands when he was abroad but could also act on his own authority even as a military commander. Both these ministers had a body of clerks, probably a fluctuating detachment from the itinerant chancery, for producing judicial and administrative writs in the king's name. In sum, each country was developing a relatively sophisticated administration quite capable of functioning on its own for several years at a time.

The Angevin kings observed the principle that each land should be governed according to its own laws and customs, but the principle did not exclude uniform solutions to new problems as they arose, and while lawyers spoke of a "custom of England"

NORMANS AND NORMANDY

and "a custom of Normandy," yet there was great interdependence. The personnel of administration moved freely from one to another. (The great seneschal of Normandy William fitzRalph, who virtually made the office during his long tenure from 1178 to 1200, was English by birth, upbringing, legal formation, and administrative experience, and at one point the archbishop of Rouen was at the same time justiciar of England.) Cases begun in one country could be adjourned *coram rege* (before the king) in the other, and the two exchequers worked together. Moreover, there were administrative connections between Normandy and the countries to the south, Anjou and Poitou, a further suggestion that if the Angevin Empire had endured in its twelfth-century form Normandy might well have been its political center.

PHILIP AUGUSTUS SEIZES NORMANDY

During the Angevin rule, the relationship with the king of France was very much closer than it had been under the Norman kings. This closeness was in the Angevin tradition, going back almost to the formation of the county. The Angevin kings did not resist the feudal overlordship of the king of France. They performed homage, even liege homage, specifically for Normandy and their other lands within the kingdom of France, and they accepted the implications of this homage as they were gradually worked out. This relationship made Normandy far more certainly a parcel of the kingdom of France; it gave the king of France a reason, even a duty, to intervene in Angevin affairs, and the quarrels within Henry II's family provided abundant occasion for such intervention.

It is in this context, then, that King Philip Augustus summoned King John to his court in 1202, to answer charges in a matrimonial dispute. When John failed to appear, Philip proceeded to occupy Normandy, completing the task in 1204.

There are several possible explanations for the relative ease with which Philip Augustus seized Normandy. First of all, there was a fairly general assumption in feudal law that confiscation of a vassal's lands for breach of feudal duties would not be more than temporary. Second, feudal custom admitted occasions for transferring allegiance from one lord to another; such acts, done properly, did not carry in the thirteenth century the aura of treason that they would carry in the twentieth. Third, the material and moral power of the French kings had increased substantially during the twelfth century, whereas the Angevin dynasty had been in disorder for some time.

It seems that John did not put a great deal of persistence into his defense of Normandy, possibly because he too thought that it would be recovered in the course of time, as he is reported to have said. It was John, however, who refused to allow men in his allegiance to hold lands of the king of France. When Philip took retaliatory action in France, so that those who remained loyal to John could hold nothing in Normandy and those who persisted in their allegiance to Philip could hold nothing in England, the breach in political terms was complete.

These actions form an important landmark in the development of national monarchy in France and England, but their full significance was not understood for some time. The king of France was taking into his hand the land of a contumacious vassal; though he did not take the title, he was now duke as well as king and behaved as such, and since Normandy was a wealthy land from which he might derive considerable strength, he would not disturb its administration or economic structure unnecessarily.

Some changes he had to make, however. There was inevitably a considerable redistribution of lands. He suppressed the office of seneschal, since he and his court would be near at hand. The exchequer of pleas and the exchequer of audit were now more clearly distinguished, and both were staffed with officers from the royal court. Certain cases would now go from the Norman courts to the French king's court, much as they had been adjourned *coram rege* under the Angevin kings. In finance the real work came to be done in Paris. The *baillis* were retained, reorganized, much strengthened, and, for some time, drawn from the king's service outside Normandy. Local officers at lower levels survived and were mostly Norman but correspondingly weakened.

Most important, no change was consciously or deliberately made in the *coutume de Normandie* (custom of Normandy). The *Grand coutoumier* itself, which became the authoritative exposition of Norman law, was compiled some forty or fifty years after the French conquest; and the "laws and customs of the country" became the rallying cry in any Norman resistance to French royal centralization.

NORMANS AND NORMANDY

FROM DUCHY TO PROVINCE

Yet Normandy could not escape changes due to the development of the French monarchy during the thirteenth century, just as it had been involved in the development of government and administration in the lands of the Norman and Angevin kings. The French monarchy developed a specialized law court, which came to be known as the Parlement of Paris. An important part of this court's jurisdiction was appeals from princely and seigneurial courts throughout the kingdom. The Exechequer in Normandy was particularly defenseless against this insidious erosion of the judicial sovereignty it still had, and since Norman seigneurs and churchmen regularly attended the Exchequer's sessions and participated in its judgments, they could see what was happening and naturally came to fear for the integrity of their *coutume*. In matters of procedure, likewise, the Norman courts, having developed in parallel with those of England until 1204, now tended to look to France, which was far more open to the influence of Roman and canon law than England was to be. Norman discontent was brought to a head by the taxation of King Philip IV the Fair (*r.* 1285–1314) and by his manipulation of the currency, though it was assuaged for a time by the *Charte aux Normands* (Norman Charter) of 1315. By this act King Louis X (*r.* 1314–1316) gave an undertaking that no cause arising in Normandy should be judged elsewhere and no taxation should be levied without consent. By the first provision, judicial sovereignty was restored to the Exchequer; the second, though it was greatly weakened by making an exception of "urgent necessity," provided the opportunity for the Estates of Normandy, already in embryo, to grow as an institution.

These concessions would seem to have given Normandy the chance to develop a regional consciousness and a degree of regional autonomy in the territory, very precisely defined, within which the *coutume de Normandie* was applied. In fact they mark, as clearly as any other incident, the point at which Normandy became a province of France. For the grievances that produced the *Charte aux Normands* were shared by other regions, and the charter was accompanied by similar charters for other provinces, and all were ultimately ineffective. Though Normandy retained a number of particularities which were the product of its history and gave it its character, so did other principalities as they came under royal government, one by one, to become provinces.

The people and the land of Normandy were inevitably involved in the Hundred Years War. At the very outset, in 1339, an extraordinary plan was drawn up for a new Norman Conquest of England, with forces from Normandy under the king's son, for whom the title "duke of Normandy" had been revived six years earlier. This plan came to nothing. During the fourteenth-century phase of the war discontented or ambitious elements in the Norman nobility allied themselves from time to time with the English, and during the 1350's quite considerable areas of the duchy were occupied by English troops in alliance with King Charles the Bad of Navarre and his followers. Documents were even produced, in Edward III's name, in which the title "duke of Normandy" was attributed to him and the claim advanced that he was ruling the occupied territories "according to the laws and customs of the country." But these actions were mostly a matter of noble factions; with the confused loyalties of the time similar restiveness was happening in many other parts of France, and there was certainly no general move to take any opportunity the war might offer to establish an autonomous Normandy.

Henry V's conquest of Normandy in the years 1417–1419 produced a somewhat different situation, for it seemed to be thought that the king was recovering an essential part of his inheritance. Certain traditional institutions were revived, at least in name—the seneschal, the Exchequer in its dual form of a judicial exchequer at Rouen and an exchequer of accounts at Caen—and, a novelty, the University of Caen was founded, to survive the French reconquest in 1450 and material destruction in 1944 as well. Yet English rule in Normandy from 1419 to 1450, though a great deal was said of respect for Norman liberties, was never much more than a military occupation; and such support as it ever secured from some elements in the population was only given to it when they felt that the presence of the English was preferable to continuing warfare.

Adjustments after the French reconquest were conservative. The judicial exchequer continued, though the exchequer of accounts, which had already been abolished, was not revived; the office of seneschal continued for a while and then lapsed; the ducal title was revived momentarily for the king's brother and then abolished definitively. Normandy emerged from the troubles of the later fifteenth century as a diversified administrative unit that had little ability to resist developing royal absolutism, and in this inability it showed no difference from other provinces.

In the last resort the individuality of Normandy remained in its *coutume,* the customary law which, on a Frankish basis, had been molded by the Norman and Angevin kings and which provided the cherished modes of inheritance and tenure of property and therefore much of the framework of social organization. The king could respect it at no cost to his authority. When the ancient judicial Exchequer was transformed into the *Parlement* of Rouen in 1515, it was being brought into line with other provincial *parlements;* but it provided the instrument for the conservation and development of the *coutume* within the territorial limits that had been fixed in the eleventh and twelfth centuries and which have remained the best definition, in territorial terms, of Normandy and the Normans. For Normandy was never a natural geographical unit. Medieval Normandy was made by its dukes and the "king-dukes" of the years before 1204, and by the law and the justice that they and their ministers formed and provided.

BIBLIOGRAPHY

The primary work is Michel de Boüard, ed., *Histoire de la Normandie* (1970), by several contributors and with critical notes on bibliographies of Norman history and all the principal general and specialized studies to the date of publication. Note particularly the publications of Lucien Musset and Jean Yver, which have transformed the early history of the duchy.

On Norman law, Robert Besnier, *La coutume de Normandie: Histoire externe* (1935), is a useful introduction.

Among recent works in English, see R. H. C. Davis, *The Normans and Their Myth* (1976); David C. Douglas, *The Norman Achievement, 1050–1100* (1969), and *The Norman Fate, 1100–1154* (1976); J. C. Holt, "The End of the Anglo-Norman Realm," in *Proceedings of the British Academy,* **61** (1975); John Le Patourel, *The Norman Empire* (1976), and *Feudal Empires, Norman and Plantagenet* (1984); Joseph R. Strayer, *Medieval Statecraft and the Perspectives of History* (1971).

Among regional periodicals, see *Normannia* (1928–1939) and the *Annales de Normandie* (1951–), particularly for bibliography; the *Bulletin* and the *Mémoires* of the Société des Antiquaires de Normandie should also be noted.

JOHN LE PATOUREL

[See also **Angevins; Anselm of Canterbury; Aquitaine; Bailli; Ban, Banalité; Brittany, Duchy; Capetian Family Origins; Carolingians and the Carolingian Empire; Castellan; Class Structure, Western; Cluny, Order of; County; Crusades and Crusader States; Custumals of Normandy; Duchy; Edward the Confessor, St.; Edward III of England; Eleanor of Aquitaine; England: Norman-Angevin; Ethelred the Unready; Exchequer; Feudalism; Flanders and the Low Countries; France; Hastings, Battle of; Henry I, II, III, V of England; Hundred Years War; Inquest; John, King of England; Jury; Justiciar; Kingship, Theories of; Knights and Knight Service; Lanfranc of Bec; Law, English Common: To 1272; Law, French: In North; Nobility and Nobles; Parlement of Paris; Philip II Augustus; Political Theory; Richard I the Lionhearted; Seneschal; Tenure of Land; Vikings; William I of England; William of Volpiano.**]

NORNA-GESTS ÞÁTTR. Part of *Óláfs saga Tryggvasonar en mesta* in two closely related versions, this artistically constructed, self-contained episode is usually dated about 1300. The frame story tells how a vigorous old man named Gest (guest) visits King Olaf in 998. On a wager, Gest produces part of a golden saddle buckle that had belonged to Sigurd Fáfnisbani; pressed for an explanation, Gest begins his reminiscences of the heroic age with the story of Sigurd's youth, including a minor incident in which Gest, then his servant, acquired the buckle, and the story of Sigurd's death at the hands of his brothers-in-law. The next day Gest's saga telling continues with an account of Brynhild's death and Gest's experience with the sons of Ragnar Loðbrók on their abortive expedition against Rome. The reminiscences conclude with the virtues of six kings from the fifth to the ninth centuries. Now Gest volunteers the explanation of his destiny: when he was an infant, spae-wives (*nornir, völur, spákonur*) came to his home; the first two prophesied good, but the third said he should live no longer than the candle beside him would burn. He now carries the candle with him. After a life of 300 years he has come to Olaf to be baptized. After his baptism he quietly lights his candle and expires in Olaf's presence.

The prominent folklore motif that associates a man's life with an object is best known from the Greek story of Meleager; the *þáttr* has combined this motif with native ideas about fate and the Norns. The name of the pilgrim from Rome whose ruse turned back the sons of Loðbrók is borrowed from a French source, but the incident itself must be from a version of *Ragnars saga Loðbrókar.* Friedrich Panzer connects Gest with French and Italian references to the long-lived Johannes a Temporibus and similar figures, arguing that Gest's career as sword-bearer and other characteristics derive from these models. However, the genre of the *þáttr* and the character of Gest seem to have deep roots in Germanic culture. The fictional poet Widsith and the seventh- or eighth-century poem bearing his name can be extensively compared with *Norna-Gests þáttr*, and both wanderers have some coloring from the god Odin. In Old Norse literature there are many episodes that offer definite analogies to *Norna-Gests þáttr*.

For the heroic reminiscences of Gest the author drew on a collection of poems very similar to the Codex Regius of the *Poetic Edda*, but the exact relationship of the *þáttr* to *Vǫlsunga saga*, the *Poetic Edda*, and Snorri's *Edda* is still disputed. Many scholars believe that the "Saga of Sigurd Fáfnisbani" cited in the *þáttr* was a written source that also served *Vǫlsunga saga* and the *Poetic Edda*. Some of the author's sources were oral and some incidents invented. Genuine old traditions seem to be represented by the allusion to the poem *Guðrúnarbrǫgð* and by the war of Sigurd and the sons of Gjúki against the sons of Gandálf, missing from the Eddas but having an analogue in the *Nibelungenlied*. In the late Middle Ages the story was made the subject of a Faroese ballad.

BIBLIOGRAPHY

Sources. Sophus Bugge, ed., *Norrøne skrifter af sagnhistorisk indhold*, I (1864), 45–80, from MS Arnamagnaean 62 fol.; *Fornaldar sögur Norðrlanda*, I (1829), 312–342, from Codex 2845, 4°, Old Royal Collection, Copenhagen; Guðbrandur Vigfusson and Carl R. Unger, eds., *Flateyjarbók: En samling af norske konge-sagaer . . .*, I (1860), 346–359, from Codex Regius no. 1005 fol.; critical edition of *Norna-Gests þáttr* based on *Flateyjarbók* in Ernst H. Wilken ed., *Die prosaische Edda im Auszuge nebst Vǫlsunga-saga und Nornagests-tháttr*, I (1877, rev. ed. 1912), 235–261. An English translation is in Nora Kershaw Chadwick, ed. and trans., *Stories and Ballads of the Far Past* (1921); "Nornagests ríma," in Napoleon Djurhuus and Christian Matras, eds., *Føroya kvæði: Corpus carminum færoensium*, I (1941), 248–253 (no. 4), English trans. in Chadwick.

Studies. Rolf W. Brednich, *Volkserzählungen und Volksglaube von den Schickalsfrauen* (1964), esp. 28–31, 205–220; Sophus Bugge, *The Home of the Eddic Poems . . .*, William H. Schofield, trans., rev. ed. (1899, repr. 1972), 96–107, and, as editor, *Norrøne skrifter*, I (1864), 80, and *Norrœn fornkvæði . . .* (1867), XLI–XLIV, Nora Chadwick, ed. and trans., *Stories and Ballads of the Far Past* (1921), 11–14, 220–228; Friedrich von der Hagen, trans., *Volsunga- und Ragnars-saga nebst der Geschichte von Nornagest*, 2nd ed., rev. by Anton Edzardi (1880), LXII–LXX, 343–397; Joseph Harris, "*Guðrúnarbrögð* and the Saxon Lay of Grimhild's Perfidy," in *Mediaeval Scandinavia*, **9** (1976); Lee M. Hollander, "Notes on the *Nornagests þattr*," in *Scandinavian Studies*, **3** (1916); Kemp Malone, ed., *Widsith* (1962), 77–79; Friedrich Panzer, "Zur Erzählung von Nornagest," in Paul Merker and Wolfgang Stammler, eds., *Vom Werden des deutschen Geistes: Festgabe Gustav Ehrismann* (1925); Margaret Schlauch, "Wīdsīth, Víthförull, and Some Other Analogues," in *Publications of the Modern Language Association*, **46** (1931); Barend Sijmons and Hugo Gering, eds., *Die Lieder der Edda*, I (1888, 1906), LXIX–LXXVII; Ernst H. Wilken ed., *Die prosaische Edda*, I (1877, rev. ed. 1912), LXXXV–CIII.

JOSEPH HARRIS

[See also **Eddic Poetry; Faroese Ballads; Nibelungenlied; Norns; Óláfs Saga Tryggvasonar; Ragnars Saga Loðbrókar; Vǫlsunga Saga.**]

NORNS. The Norns are the spinners of the thread, the weavers of the web, of fate. In earliest Nordic tradition there was only one, Urðr, while in later writing the Norns numbered three. Only *Vǫluspá* 20 and Snorri's *Gylfaginning* 15 expressly mention three Norns.

The name *Urðr* has among its cognates the Latin *vertere* (turn), the Sanskrit *vartulā* (spindle), the Latvian *audi* (web), the Old Icelandic *auðinn* (fated), the Old High German *wurt*, the Old Saxon *uurd*, and the Old English *wyrd* (modern *weird*), all meaning "fate."

The triad of Norns seems to be associated with the fertility cult of Freyja and with the Valkyries and *dísir*. The Norns, Valkyries, and *dísir* are all called upon at births to "loosen the children from women," as is said in *Sigrdrífumál* 9, where the Valkyrie offers helpful runes and the presence of *dísir* at birth. The Norns are called upon in *Fáfnismál* 12 for help in need and to deliver ("choose") sons from the mother. In *Vǫluspá* 20 it is the "three maidens much knowing" who number among them Urðr and who "laid laws, chose lives for the children of men, [chose] the fates of men."

The other two Norns are Verðandi, who is mentioned only in *Vǫluspá* 20 among the older writings, and Skuld, which name appears in *Vǫluspá* 31 as that of a Valkyrie. These names can be viewed as a scholarly innovation based on the association of Urðr with the verb *verða* (become; past plural, *urðu*) and then with the verb *skulu* (should) to form a semantic sequence Urðr, Verðandi, Skuld (something like Happened, Impending, Obligated or Fate, Being, and Necessity).

Urðr's association with spinning and weaving the *ørlǫg seggja* (fates of men, *Vǫluspá* 20) is matched elsewhere in the literature by the frequently occurring compounds *ørlǫgþáttr* and *ørlǫgsíma* (thread of fate). If the Norns are weavers of fate, then so are the Valkyries. In *Darraðarljóð*, a recounting of the Battle of Clontarf, which took place in 1014, the Valkyries set up a loom with men's heads as weights, human entrails as the woof and warp, and an arrow as the shuttle. In their song they describe the fate of the heroes in battle. The Valkyries can thus be viewed as the Norns of battle, in that they fulfill the same function of weaving life and death. Indeed, the word *valkyrja* (Valkyrie) means "chooser of the slain." The Norns are the dreaded casters of the "judgment [doom] of the Norns" in *Fáfnismál* 11. They are referred to in this function in the Christian *Sólarljóð*, where the protagonist sits in the (judgment?) seat of the Norns for nine days before being put on a horse and transported to the realm of death. In another context the compound *urðarmáni* (Urðr's moon) is understood as foreboding death.

The Norns thus come at birth to forecast life, and later to rule death. At the birth of Helgi in *Helgi Hundingsbani* I the Norns appear in the courtyard to twist the *ørlǫgþáttu* and make them fast *und mána sal miðjan* (under the middle of the moon's hall). They hide the ends to the east and west; the prince (Helgi) is to have all the land between. The sister of Neri, Loki's daughter Hel, fastened one strand on the northern way (the direction of the realm of the dead) and bade it ever hold. In *Helgi Hundingsbani* II, 18, when Helgi tells Sigrún that he has killed her father and brother, he attributes their falling in battle to the Norns. Here the Norns and Valkyries are the same.

In *Gylfaginning* 15, Snorri says: "There stands a fair hall under the ash [world tree] by the well, and from that hall come three maidens who are called Urðr, Verðandi, and Skuld. These maidens shape the destiny of men. We call them Norns. Still there are more Norns who come to each man who is born to shape [his] destiny, and these are related to the gods, and others to the elves, a third group to the dwarves." We learn further that "good Norns from noble stock shape good destinies. But those men who meet misfortune owe their fate to evil Norns." Snorri relied on *Vǫluspá* 19, which tells of the world tree, Yggdrasil, standing ever green over the well of Urðr. The next verse states that the three Norns come "from that sea" (the well). The Norns are thus identified with the tree and the well, which perhaps can also be related to the worship of the *dísir* at Uppsala, Sweden, with its temple, evergreen tree, and well.

Continental analogues are perhaps found in the veneration of the *matres* in the Rhineland, where statuettes dating from romanized Germanic settlements show three seated female figures with names like Gabiae (Givers), Alagabiae (All-Givers), and Afliae (Powerful Ones). With respect to the latter example, at the birth of Helgi the Norns spun the threads of fate *af afli* (with [their] power).

BIBLIOGRAPHY

Corpus poeticum boreale, Gudbrand Vigfusson and F. York Powell, eds. and trans. (1883, repr. 1965): *Darraðarljóð,* 281–283, and *Sólarljóð,* 201–211; Hilda R. E. Davidson, *Gods and Myths of Northern Europe* (1964), 26, 61, 112; R. L. M. Derolez, *Götter und Mythen der Germanen* (1973), 173–176; Sigurður Nordal, *Vǫluspá,* B. S. Benedikz and John McKinnell, trans. (1978), 39–41, a commentary; *The Poetic Edda,* Henry Adams Bellows, trans. (1923, 1957): *Fáfnismál, Helgakvitha Hundingsbana* I and II, *Sigrdrífumál, Vǫluspá;* Snorri Sturluson, *The Prose Edda,* Arthur G. Brodeur, trans. (1960), 28–29; Folke Ström, *Diser, nornor, valkyrjor* (1954), 44–89; Jan de Vries, *Altgermanische Religionsgeschichte,* I (1956), 267–272.

JAMES E. CATHEY

[See also **Darraðarljóð; Gylfaginning; Helgi Poems; Reginsmál and Fáfnismál; Sigrdrífumál; Sólarljóð; Valkyrie; Vǫluspá.**]

NORSE FLYTING. "Flyting" is the word commonly used in English scholarship to refer to the stylized boast-insult contests found throughout Norse literature. Prominent examples include *Lokasenna, Hárbarðsljóð,* the Helgi lays, *Qrvar-Odds saga* (chap. 27), *Magnússona saga* in *Heimskringla* (chap. 21), *Bandamanna saga* (chap. 10), *Njáls saga* (chaps. 119–120), and those in Saxo Grammaticus' *Gesta Danorum* (especially in books I, V, and VI). Both the number of examples and their representation over the literary range

NORSE FLYTING

(Eddic and skaldic poetry; Saxo's Latin history; and the kings', Icelandic family, and legendary sagas) suggest the popularity of the form in early Scandinavia and justify its consideration as a coherent literary genre.

The use, in non-English scholarship, of the Norse words *senna* and *mannjafnaðr* in reference to this genre requires clarification. *Senna,* related to *sannr* (true), appears to mean "quarrel" (compare *sverða senna,* quarrel of swords, a skaldic kenning for battle). It may once have referred to a legal procedure in which the plaintiff argued the guilt of a defendant by enumerating his negative character qualities as well as the points of evidence. *Mannjafnaðr* (man-comparison) refers to an early social practice in which two people match personal reputations by a process of escalating boasts. It also has been associated with the legal practice of citing a slain man's virtues in an effort to secure the highest possible compensation. Whether either term was used in medieval Scandinavia to designate a category of literary entertainment (as the Eddic title *Lokasenna* might suggest) is unclear. What is clear, however, is that the modern use of the terms suggests a distinction not reflected in the literary examples, which in every case freely combine boasts with insults (as well as threats and vows) in such a way as to indicate not two categories but one, itself well defined and easily identifiable even when it is embedded in a longer context. The English word "flyting" (Old English: *flītan,* to strive, contend, dispute, rebel; Scottish: *flyte,* scold) is used here to avoid that confusion.

The Norse flyting has two standard settings: one outdoors, with a body of water separating the contenders, and one indoors, in the hall. The quarrel sometimes arises spontaneously, but at other times is introduced as an entertainment. In *Magnússona saga,* verbal contesting is said to be a drinking custom (*ölsiðr, ölteiti*). In *Qrvar-Odds saga* the verbal contest is combined with a drinking contest. Flytings prompted by the arrival of a newcomer to the shore or hall take the form of an interrogation. The contestants are usually men, less often a man and a woman (in the latter case the woman always loses). Flytings between women argue not their own merits and demerits, but those of their menfolk (this includes the "quarrel of the queens" in the Brynhild tradition, reflected in *Vǫlsunga saga, Snorra Edda, Þiðreks saga,* and *Njáls saga,* as well as the *Nibelungenlied*).

Two contestants is the rule, although some of the most colorful examples involve one person addressing several others in sequence: Loki versus the gods and goddesses in *Lokasenna,* Ófeigr versus the chieftains in *Bandamanna saga,* and Skarpheðinn versus the chieftains in *Njáls saga.* Another variation involves the use of delegates, whereby a younger man of lesser status speaks on behalf of an older man of greater status (for instance, Guðmundr for Helgi in the Helgi lays; compare Unferþ's role in *Beowulf*). The contenders are credited with unusual eloquence—"smooth of tongue," "superior in words," "rich in rejoinders," "able to converse with kings,"—Saxo's flyting master Ericus has the cognomen Disertus (Eric the Eloquent).

In accordance with the tendency in heroic societies to cast all human endeavors in competitive terms, the flyting is conceived and presented as an oral battle or "voice war," and the disputants as "word warriors" or "speech champions." (The hostile use of eloquence and of early poetry in general is suggested in the cognomina of several Norse skalds—*illskálda, hornklofi, hnúfa, vandræðaskáld, skáldaspillir, ormstunga*—and in the word *skáld* itself, which may originally have meant "scorn" or "insult" (compare the English "scold"). As a form of combat, the flyting has clear rules and clear winners and losers. The loser typically retreats into silence, while the winner continues with a victory coda. Although flytings often contain threats of violence, they seldom have a violent outcome.

The content and, to a certain extent, the phrasing of the flytings are highly traditional. Boasts are always about martial exploits and the conquest of women. Insults are more varied and more imaginative in expression. Many are simply boasts in reverse (that is, they claim that the opponent deserted or lost a battle, or failed to master a woman), but others have to do with pointless adventures, trivial or lazy behavior, alimentary taboos (eating corpses, drinking urine), and personal appearance. Crimes of kinship form a significant insult category. For men these entail the failure to avenge a slain relative, incest, and fratricide and parricide; for women, incest and sex with the slayer of her father or brother. Sexual irregularity is a common theme. Men are said to be castrated and are charged with bestiality and passive homosexuality. This last, being a "female" in the sexual act, probably lies behind the charge that a man has milked cows or carded wool (women's chores), or

NORSE FLYTING

been held captive (used sexually by the captors). Open charges of sexual inversion (*níð*) were punishable by law in early Scandinavia, but they seem to have flourished in the literary context of the flyting. It is worth noting that women are not charged with inversion but with promiscuity. Flyting threats, when they occur, promise physical violence to men and sexual degradation to women.

Bizarre sexual threats notwithstanding, the flytings concern themselves on the whole with real past events. This is clear from the texts, where the facts are not disputed, not even by the offended party. *B* may defend or justify the ignominious deed *A* has attributed to him, but he does not deny it. In the same way, he does not challenge the facts of *A*'s boast, but rather tries, in his response, to diminish their importance. In many cases the preliminary incidents that form the basis of the flyting can be documented in other sources (for instance, the cryptic claim in the Helgi lays that Sinfjǫtli was a fratricide is substantiated in some detail in *Vǫlsunga saga*). Flytings thus argue interpretations, not facts. The obviously fantastic sexual insults would seem to be an exception to this rule, although it is possible that even here there is a "real" reference, to sexual deviance, and that its metaphoric form is the function of the taboo nature of the subject and/or legal injunctions against direct accusation. But such claims are in any case relatively few in number; they are far outnumbered by plausible allusions to events accepted by both parties as essentially true. These mutually acknowledged allusions thus provide a rich source of information about the Norse gods and legendary heroes, and they associate flyting with more directly didactic forms such as the wisdom dialogues (for instance, *Vafþrúðnismál* and *Grímnismál*).

Both its content and its tone and stylized quality set the flyting apart not only from its immediate context but also from similar traditions (such as the Latin debates). The speeches have an evenly blocked, "stanzaic" quality, even when the flyting is in prose, and are characterized by syntactic parallelism and verbal repetition. Tag lines using proper names are an integral feature of the form: "What were you doing in the meantime, Thor (Odin)?" occurs nine times in *Hárbarðsljóð;* "You weren't there, Oddr (Sjólfr, Sigurðr)" occurs twelve times in *Ǫrvar-Odds saga.*

One of the longest (twelve pages in modern edition) and most flamboyant flytings is the one in chapter 27 of *Ǫrvar-Odds saga.* Although it is not typical of the genre in every respect, its unusual length and wealth of procedural detail make it a useful example. It begins when two retainers of King Hárekr, the brothers Sjólfr and Sigurðr, challenge the visiting hero, Oddr, who is in a disguise and whose true identity is unknown to them, to a match in which each man must drink a horn (in Oddr's case two) of beer before reciting a boast-insult stanza. Oddr agrees, and the contest begins. Each proceeds, in turn, to brag in verse of his own adventures and to impugn the masculinity of the other. At first the brothers hold their own, but as the drink begins to affect them, Oddr gains the upper hand.

To the last stanza Sjólfr manages to recite ("Oddr, you weren't on Atalsfell when we took the bright gold; we bound the berserks and boldly slaughtered the king's army"), Oddr responds with two stanzas, one directed at Sjólfr and the other at Sigurðr, each consisting of a boast in the first helming and an insult in the second. It is now the brothers' turn, but they fail to respond, so Oddr adds another set of stanzas: "Sjólfr, you weren't there when we reddened our sharp swords on the earl of Læsö—while you, lascivious talker, were at home wavering between the calf and the slave girl" and "Sigurðr, you weren't there on Zealand when I felled the battle-hard brothers Brandr and Agnarr, Ásmundr and Ingjaldr, and Álfr the fifth—while you were lying at home in the king's hall, full of tall stories, a gelded captive." Again the brothers fail to respond, and Oddr continues with three more sets of stanzas in the same vein. At this point the two brothers fall into a wordless stupor and the audience breaks into applause for Oddr. He brings his performance to a grandiose close with a six-stanza summary of his career, concluding: "Now I have recounted all the exploits we performed so long ago; laden with victories we returned home to the high seat." The following day Oddr's true identity is revealed and he is invited to occupy the seat of honor in Hárekr's court.

Characteristic of the genre are the hall setting and the situation, in which the newcomer Oddr is put through his verbal paces. The flyting is introduced as a familiar contest. The speeches, verse stanzas embedded in a prose context, have a common structure (twelve begin with the tag line) and play on previous formulations and rhetorical oppositions. They make use of insults and boasts in roughly equal proportions. The boasts enumerate specific past events (which in this case recapitulate the earlier action of the saga) and aggrandize the role of the speaker. The insults charge womanish behavior and sexual deviance. The losers are silenced, and the winner concludes with a victory coda. Less typical of the genre as a whole are the hidden-identity motif (which, although it has a parallel in *Hárbarðsljóð*, is otherwise associated with the wisdom-dialogue tradition), the monothematically sexual content of the insults, and the drinking contest (which is not elsewhere programmatically linked with the flyting). The boisterous and generally crude tone is typical of the legendary saga flytings and, to a certain degree, of the Eddic examples, but it is in marked contrast with the thoughtful quality of the classical saga examples—a disparity that points up the adaptability of the form.

Detailed correspondences with the Norse flytings are found in the English tradition in *Maldon* and in the Unferþ episode in *Beowulf;* in German in the *Nibelungenlied* (especially adventures 14, 25, and 29), the Walter cycle, and the *Hildebrandslied;* and in the Middle Latin histories of Gregory of Tours (especially book VII), Widukind of Corvei, and Paul the Deacon (especially books I and V). From this it may be concluded that the flyting was once current in the wider Germanic tradition. It occupies a place in the near-universal phenomenon of blame literature attested in living traditions (for instance, among Turkish youths and Eskimos, and in Black English vernacular) as well as earlier ones (such as Sumerian, Indic, Irish, and Greek).

BIBLIOGRAPHY

Carol J. Clover, "The Germanic Context of the Unferþ Episode," in *Speculum,* 55 (1980); Joseph Harris, "The *Senna:* From Description to Literary Theory," in *Michigan Germanic Studies,* 5 (1979), and "Eddic Poetry as Oral Poetry: The Evidence of Parallel Passages in the Helgi Poems for Questions of Composition and Performance," in Robert J. Glendinning and Haraldur Bessason, eds., *Edda: A Collection of Essays* (1983); Paul Herrmann, *Erläuterungen zu den ersten neun Büchern der dänischen Geschichte des Saxo Grammaticus,* II, *Die Heldensagen des Saxo Grammaticus* (1922); Andreas Heusler, *Die altgermanische Dichtung,* 2nd ed., rev. (1941, repr. 1957), 105–108; Johan Huizinga, *Homo ludens* (1955, 1970), 65–71; Bertha S. Phillpotts, *The Elder Edda and Ancient Scandinavian Drama* (1920), 156–159.

CAROL J. CLOVER

[See also **Bandamanna Saga; Beowulf; Eddic Poetry; Grímnismál; Hárbarðsljód; Helgi Poems; Hildebrandslied; Lokasenna; Njáls Saga; Nibelungenlied; Ǫrvar-OddsSaga; Saga; Saxo Grammaticus; Scandinavian Literature; Skaldic Poetry; Snorra Edda; Vafþrúðnismál; Vǫlsunga Saga.**]

NORSE KINGS' SAGAS. The writing of history began very early in Iceland and antedates the classical age of saga writing by a century. The first writing of any kind appears to be a recording of Icelandic law carried out in the winter of 1117–1118. Ten or fifteen years later Ari Þorgilsson (1067/1068–1148) wrote a brief epitome of Icelandic history entitled *Íslendingabók* (Book of the Icelanders). This sober little survey covers the settlement of Iceland (traditionally dated 870–930) and Greenland (traditional date, 985), the creation of Iceland's legal institutions, the conversion of Iceland to Christianity in 999 or 1000, and a review of the earliest Icelandic bishops. Ari's prologue states that the book is a second version that omits the genealogies and lives of kings included in an earlier version. The lost genealogies may be the original form of *Landnámabók* (Book of the settlements), a family-by-family account of the colonization of Iceland extant in various redactions from the thirteenth century and later. The lost kings' lives presumably dealt chiefly with the Norwegian kings at least from the time of Harald I Fairhair (*ca.* 870–*ca.* 930) down to Ari's own day (King Sigurd Jerusalem Farer, *d.* 1130). Later references make it clear that Ari's slightly older contemporary Sæmundr Sigfússon (1056–1133) also wrote a history of the Norwegian kings from Harald Fairhair to Magnus I the Good (*d.* 1047). There is no trace of either history. Estimates of their size have varied greatly, but the assiduousness with which later writers cite the authority of these pioneer historians makes it clear that their work was of great importance.

The first efforts to write history in Norway date from half a century later and are sometimes referred to as the "Norwegian synoptics." They include three short works, each of which fills about fifty pages in a modern edition. The *Historia de antiquitate regum Norwagiensium,* by an unidentified Theodoricus, was written about 1180 and, like Ari's lost kings' lives, covers the period from Harald Fairhair to Sigurd Jerusalem Farer. The anonymous *Historia Norwegiae* has been dated as early as about 1170 and as late as about 1220. It

NORSE KINGS' SAGAS

includes a fairly detailed geographical preface, reviews the legendary kings of Scandinavian prehistory, and treats the historical period from Harald Fairhair, breaking off with the return of St. Olaf to Norway in 1015. A vernacular work entitled *Ágrip af Nóregs knounga sǫgum* (Synopsis of the sagas of the kings of Norway) is extant in a single manuscript defective at both the beginning and the end, but in its original form it covered the period from Harald Fairhair to 1177. It is commonly dated about 1190. The relationship of the synoptics to one another and to the lost Icelandic works is complicated and much disputed. There is some agreement that *Ágrip* made use of Theodoricus' history, and that *Ágrip* and *Historia Norwegiae* borrow from a common source. Connections among all three synoptics and both Sæmundr and Ari have been argued by various scholars. Though difficult to decide, the matter is of some importance because it determines whether Norwegian history writing is an independent phenomenon or entirely derivative from Icelandic models.

While Norway produced epitomes in the second half of the twelfth century, Iceland embarked on the writing of full-scale kings' sagas. The first of these (perhaps as early as 1150–1160) is Eiríkr Oddsson's *Hryggjarstykki* (meaning uncertain). It is difficult to calculate the contents of this book because it survives only as it was reworked in the later *Morkinskinna, Fagrskinna*, and *Heimskringla.* The most recent investigation suggests that it was a biography of the pretender to the Norwegian throne Sigurðr Slembidjákn and covered only the years from 1136, when Sigurðr killed the Norwegian king Harald Gilli, to 1139, when Sigurðr was killed by Harald's sons. Another lost text is *Skjǫldunga saga* (*ca.* 1180–1200), the story of the legendary Danish Scylding dynasty. It is preserved only in a Latin synopsis by the sixteenth-century Icelandic humanist Arngrímur Jónsson and in extracts in a few saga texts.

In 1185 the abbot of the northern Icelandic Benedictine monastery at Þingeyrar, Karl Jónsson, went to Norway and undertook to write the life of the reigning king, Sverrir (*d.* 1202), under the king's own direction. He wrote the first part of this saga before returning to Iceland; the biography was completed perhaps by Karl himself and perhaps by a continuator. There is little agreement on the extent of Karl's initial composition or the date of the completion, estimates ranging from 1204 to 1230. However these details are to be resolved, Karl Jónsson was perhaps the first to conceive a book-length biography of a Norwegian king. Though he appears not to have finished his project, two other monks at Þingeyrar, Oddr Snorrason and Gunnlaugr Leifsson (*d.* 1218/1219), were perhaps inspired by his example and wrote biographies of King Óláfr Tryggvason (*r.* 995–1000). Both wrote in Latin, Oddr about 1190 and Gunnlaugr a little later. Oddr's book survives in three somewhat differing Icelandic translations; Gunnlaugr's book survives only to the extent that parts of it were incorporated into later redactions of the kings' sagas.

The same period saw the composition of the first saga of St. Olaf (*r.* 1015–1028), which is extant in six short fragments. This text was once believed to be the oldest of the kings' sagas, but has been recently redated to about 1200. It was reworked by Styrmir Kárason (*d.* 1245)—his version is extant only in late extracts—and Snorri Sturluson (*d.* 1241), first in a *Separate Saga of St. Olaf* and then in *Heimskringla.* It was also reworked by the anonymous author of the *Legendary Saga of St. Olaf* sometime before the middle of the century. The transmissions on the two Olafs, whose reputations rested chiefly on their conversion of Norway and Iceland to Christianity, are thus more abundant than in the case of any other Norwegian kings.

The Icelanders were, however, not exclusively interested in royal biography. At the same time they were at work on the lives of Sverrir and the two Olafs, they were engaged in the writing of provincial histories, a history of the Orkney Islands (*Orkneyinga saga*) and the Faroe Islands (*Færeyinga saga*). It has been suggested that *Orkneyinga saga* was begun as early as 1165, but the extant redaction is from the early thirteenth century. It covers the period from Harald Fairhair down to the twelfth century. *Færeyinga saga* (composed *ca.* 1200–1220) is less historical in orientation and more akin to the Icelandic family sagas of the thirteenth century. It is centered on the political career of the Faroese chieftain Þrándr í Gǫtu in the late tenth and early eleventh centuries.

Somewhat similar to *Orkneyinga saga* and *Færeyinga saga* in their regional concerns are two other sagas from around 1200, *Jómsvíkinga saga* and *Hlaðajarla saga. Jómsvíkinga saga* tells the adventurous story of the Jómsvíkings, who formed a warrior community, established a fortress somewhere along the southern Baltic, and challenged the

NORSE KINGS' SAGAS

rulers of both Denmark and Norway. Their ambitions culminate in the Battle of Hjǫrungavágr (974–985) against Earl Hákon of Norway, an encounter in which they suffer a flamboyant defeat. The original form of the saga is difficult to judge because it survives in five differing redactions. Though some of the events described are in some manner historical, the style of the tale has much in common with the legendary sagas. *Hlaðajarla saga* is still more difficult to judge, because it comes down to us only to the extent it was absorbed by the later histories in *Fagrskinna* and *Heimskringla.* It was presumably a history of the earls of Hlaðir located on the central coast of Norway (Trondheim), but the exact coverage of the saga is uncertain. The earls of Hlaðir were the greatest chieftains of Norway during much of the Middle Ages and the chief rivals of the king.

The lost works of Ari and Sæmundr, the Norwegian synoptics, and the first Icelandic biographies and regional histories were a prelude to the better-known and more compendious histories of the Norwegian kings written about 1220–1230: *Morkinskinna, Fagrskinna,* and Snorri Sturluson's *Heimskringla. Morkinskinna* (Rotten parchment) and *Fagrskinna* (Fair parchment) are the popular names for the manuscripts in which these kings' sagas are preserved, and are used by extension to designate the texts (the parchment *Fagrskinna* no longer exists and the text is preserved only in copies). *Heimskringla* (Circle of the world) is a modern title taken from the first two words of the section called *Ynglinga saga* (History of the Yngling dynasty). The original version of *Morkinskinna* was probably composed about 1220, but we have only a reworking from the latter part of the century. It covers Norwegian history from the death of St. Olaf (1030) and breaks off in 1157, but the original probably extended to 1177. A particular feature of *Morkinskinna* is a series of interlarded episodes often dealing with the adventures of Icelanders at the Norwegian court, so-called *þættir* (plural of *þáttr*). *Morkinskinna* is fullest on the lives of the kings Magnus I the Good (*d.* 1047) and Harald Hardrule (*d.* 1066).

Whereas *Morkinskinna* is an Icelandic work, *Fagrskinna* is more likely Norwegian, or at least written in Norway. It is based to a large extent on *Morkinskinna,* but covers the whole period from Halfdan the Black down to 1177. The date of composition is thought to be around 1225. Both *Morkinskinna* and *Fagrskinna,* as well as a number of the sagas already mentioned, were used by Snorri Sturluson in his great compilation *Heimskringla* (*ca.* 1230). Snorri is mentioned as author only in two sixteenth-century Norwegian translations of *Heimskringla,* but its attribution to him seems fairly secure. He begins with the legendary prehistory of the Yngling dynasty and brings the story down to 1177, that is, the point where *Sverris saga* takes over. Snorri's analytical and narrative powers make *Heimskringla* the highpoint of the Norse kings' saga and the only work of medieval Scandinavian historiography known outside the narrow circle of Norse scholars (with the exception of the Danish history of Saxo Grammaticus). Snorri's reputation is fully deserved, but tends to obscure the fact that the writing in *Morkinskinna,* for example, is no less vivid. Neither of these works has its narrative equal elsewhere in medieval historiography.

Snorri caps the development of the kings' saga, and the history written later in the century does not attain his level. The most important of the later kings' sagas are the anonymous *Knýtlinga saga,* a history of the Danish kings (especially St. Cnut, *r.* 1080–1086) from the late tenth century to 1187, written in the middle of the century, and *Hákonar saga Hákonarsonar,* a biography of King Hákon the Old of Norway (*r.* 1217–1263) written at his son's behest by Snorri Sturluson's nephew Sturla Þórðarson (*d.* 1284). Sturla's *Hákonar saga* is fuller, more documentary, and far less dramatic than his uncle's *Heimskringla.* Toward the end of the thirteenth century and in the fourteenth century, various compilations of kings' sagas were made, combining the available redactions with relevant material from Icelandic family sagas and *þættir.* The saga of Olaf Tryggvason in particular was expanded in this way, and an encyclopedic final form is contained in the late-fourteenth-century redaction known as *Flateyjarbók.*

The reconstruction of medieval Scandinavian history rests to a large extent on the Icelandic kings' sagas. Nineteenth century historians retained considerable faith in their accuracy and tended to rehearse their accounts in great detail. Modern historians have increasingly looked under the surface of the medieval narratives to find the political and economic causes of the events they describe, but the stories told by twelfth- and thirteenth-century Icelandic saga writers are still the basis for any historical speculation.

BIBLIOGRAPHY

Sources. Ágrip and *Fagrskinna: Ágrip af Nóregskonunga sǫgum; Fagrskinna—Nóregs konunga tal,* Bjarni Einarsson, ed. (1985); *Flateyjarbók: Flateyjarbók,* Guðbrandur Vigfússon and Carl R. Unger, eds., 3 vols. (1860–1868), and *Flateyjarbók,* Vilhjálmur Bjarnar, Finnbogi Guðmundsson, and Sigurður Nordal, eds., 4 vols. (1944–1945).

Færeyinga saga: *Færeyinga saga,* Ólafur Halldórsson, ed. (1967), trans. by Muriel A. C. Press as *The Saga of the Faroe Islanders* (1934) and by George Johnston as *The Faroe Islanders' Saga* (1975).

Hákonar saga Hákonarsonar: Hakonar Saga and a Fragment of Magnus Saga, Guðbrandur Vigfússon, ed., George W. Dasent, trans. (1887, repr. 1964), and *Hákonar saga Hákonarsonar: Etter Sth. 8 fol., AM 325 VIII, 4°,* Marina Mundt, ed. (1977).

Heimskringla: Heimskringla, Bjarni Aðalbjarnarson, ed., 3 vols. (1941–1951), trans. by Lee M. Hollander as *Heimskringla: History of the Kings of Norway* (1964); *Historia de antiquitate regum Norwagiensium,* in *Monumenta historica Norvegiae,* Gustav Storm, ed. (1880, repr. 1973), 3–68; *Historia Norwegiae,* in *Monumenta historica Norvegiae,* Gustav Storm, ed. (1880, repr. 1973), 69–124.

Íslendingabók: Íslendingabók; Landnámabók, Jakob Benediktsson, ed. (1968), translation by Halldór Hermannsson as *The Book of the Icelanders (Íslendingabók)* (1930, repr. 1966).

Jómsvíkinga saga: Jómsvíkinga saga efter Arnamagnaeanska handskriften n:o 291 4:to i diplomatariskt aftryck, Carl af Petersens, ed. (1882), normalized ed. *Jómsvíkinga saga,* Ólafur Halldórsson, ed. (1969), *Jómsvíkinga saga (efter Cod. AM 510 4:to) samt Jómsvíkinga drápa,* Carl af Petersens, ed. (1879), *Jómsvíkinga saga efter skinnboken no. 7 4to å Kungl. Biblioteket i Stockholm,* Gustaf Cederschiöld, ed. (1874), Stockholm 7 4° translation by Lee M. Hollander as *The Saga of the Jómsvíkings* (1955), and by N. F. Blake as *The Saga of the Jomsvikings* (1962).

Knýtlinga saga: Sǫgur Danakonunga, Carl af Petersens and Emil Olsen, eds. (1919–1925), 27–294, and *Danakonunga sǫgur,* Bjarni Guðnason, ed. (1982), 93–321.

Landnámabók: Íslendingabók; Landnámabók, Jakob Benediktsson, ed. (1968), trans. by Hermann Pálsson and Paul Edwards, *The Book of Settlements: Landnámabók* (1972); *Legendary Saga of St. Olaf: Olafs saga hins helga,* Oscar Albert Johnsen, ed. (1922), and *Olafs saga hins helga,* Anne Heinrichs, Doris Janshen, Elke Radicke, and Hartmut Röhn, eds. (1982).

Morkinskinna: Morkinskinna, Carl R. Unger, ed. (1867), and *Morkinskinna,* Finnur Jónsson, ed. (1932).

The Oldest Saga of St. Olaf: Otte brudstykker af den ældste saga om Olav den hellige, Gustav Storm, ed. (1893); *The Separate Saga of St. Olaf: Saga Olafs konungs hins helga,* Oscar Albert Johnsen and Jón Helgason, eds., 2 vols. (1930–1933).

Oddr Snorrason's *Óláfs saga Tryggvasonar: Saga Óláfs Tryggvasonar af Oddr Snorrason munk,* Finnur Jónsson, ed. (1932).

The Longest Saga of Olaf Tryggvason: Óláfs saga Tryggvasonar en mest, Ólafur Halldórsson, ed., 2 vols. (1958–1961).

Orkneyinga saga: Orkneyinga saga, Sigurður Nordal, ed. (1913–1916), and *Orkneyinga saga,* Finnbogi Guðmundsson, ed. (1965), trans. by Alexander B. Taylor as *The Orkneyinga Saga* (1938) and by Hermann Pálsson and Paul Edwards as *Orkneyinga Saga* (1978, reiss. 1981).

Sverris saga: Sverris saga etter Cod. AM 327 4°, Gustav Indrebø, ed. (1920).

In addition, *Hákonar saga Hákonarsonar,* the *Legendary Saga of St. Olaf,* Oddr Snorrason's *Óláfs saga Tryggvasonar,* the fragments of the *Oldest Saga of St. Olaf,* and *Sverris saga* are in Guðni Jónsson's popular edition *Konunga sögur,* 3 vols. (1957).

Studies. A brief introduction in English with bibliography is Theodore M. Andersson, "Kings' Sagas *(Konungasögur),*" in *Old Norse-Icelandic Literature: A Critical Guide,* Carol J. Clover and John Lindow, eds. (1985), 197–238. See also Edward O. G. Turville-Petre, *Origins of Icelandic Literature* (1953, repr. 1967). On *Hryggjarstykki* see Bjarni Guðnason, *Fyrsta sagan* (1978); on *Skjǫldunga saga,* Jakob Benediktsson, "Icelandic Traditions of the Scyldings," in *Saga-Book of the Viking Society,* **15** (1957–1961), and Bjarni Guðnason, *Um Skjöldungasögu* (1963); on the *Legendary Saga of St. Olaf,* Jónas Kristjánsson, "The Legendary Saga," in Bjarni Vilhjálmsson, Jónas Kristjánsson, Þór Magnússon, and Guðni Kolbeinsson, eds., *Minjar og menntir* (1976); on *Sverris saga,* Geoffrey M. Gathorne-Hardy, *A Royal Impostor: King Sverre of Norway* (1956), and Lárus H. Blöndal, *Um uppruna Sverrissögu* (1982). The best study of Snorri Sturluson's narrative art is Hallvard Lie, *Studier i Heimskringlas stil: Dialogene og talene* (1937).

THEODORE M. ANDERSSON

[See also **Eiríkr Oddsson; Færeyinga Saga; Hákonar Saga Hákonarsonar; Iceland; Jómsvíkinga Saga; Landnámabók; Oddr Snorrason; Óláfs Saga Tryggvasonar; Orkneyinga Saga; Skjǫldunga Saga; Snorri Sturluson; Sverris Saga.**]

NORSE LITERATURE. See **Scandinavian Literature.**

NORSEMEN. See **Vikings.**

NORSE SAGAS. See **Bishops' Sagas; Family Sagas, Icelandic; Fornaldarsögur; Norse Kings' Sagas; Riddarasögur.**

NORTH AFRICA. See **Maghrib, Al-.**

NORWAY. Some time near 890 the Norwegian Ottar (Othere) visited King Alfred in England. He told the king "that he lived northernmost of all Northmen." From his home in northern Norway he sailed southward along "the land of the Northmen." According to the carefully recorded Old English account of his narrative in Alfred's translation of Paulus Orosius' *Universal History* (fifth century), he also called his country *Norðweg*, the northern way. Quite possibly the name alludes to the long and mostly protected coastal sailing route that united Norwegian territory at a time when land, with its mountains and forests, tended to divide.

This is the first more elaborate mention of Norway and its inhabitants in extant sources. Ottar depicts Norway as a long and narrow stretch of territory extending from the land of the Finns or Lapps in the north (present-day Finnmark) to *Denamearc* (Denmark) in the south. East of Norway, Ottar knew of *Swéoland*, the land of the Swedes. Norway thus enters history in a clear Scandinavian context. The country obviously comprised most of its present territory, and was inhabited by a separate ethnic group, the Northmen or Norwegians.

At that time the political unification of Norway under a single monarch had as yet barely started, so the ethnic identity of its inhabitants must have been due to more general sociocultural features, such as the common Old Norse language, which had by now started to develop traits of its own as compared with Danish and Swedish dialects, and the cult of the same Nordic deities. Communications at sea brought people from various parts of the country together. From the fjords cutting inland, traffic and settlement would follow river valleys and lakes toward higher ground, and people would traverse high plateaus and use mountain passes between the main regions. This network of communications favored barter between areas of different natural and economic conditions and helped to forge social links between various regions.

More distinct Norwegian boundaries were a consequence of the long medieval process of political unification coming to an end in the thirteenth century. The Old Norse kingdom now included present Norway and the later Swedish provinces of Jämtland to the east and Bohuslän to the south. South of Bohuslän the three medieval kingdoms of Scandinavia converged at the mouth of the Göta River. In the early 1260's the Norse-speaking inhabitants of Iceland and Greenland placed themselves under the Norwegian crown. Further south the Western Isles from the Faroe Islands to the Hebrides and Isle of Man had, like Iceland and Greenland, been settled from Norway in the Viking Age and had later been made tributary territories under Norway. The Hebrides and Isle of Man were ceded to Scotland in 1266, while further north, Norwegian dominion over the Orkney, Shetland, and Faroe islands was now more effective than before. This was the total extension of the Norwegian realm until the Orkneys and Shetlands were pledged to the Scottish king in 1468–1469. Formally the rest of the "tributary islands" to the west belonged to Norway until the end of the Middle Ages.

SETTLEMENT AND POPULATION

Medieval Norway was a predominantly agrarian society in which towns were few and small and in which the agricultural population was settled on individual farms. Over the years these farms were divided into varying numbers of holdings, that is to say, units of production run by individual households, usually families. Regular villages in the common European sense did not exist in medieval Norway. No more fundamental socioeconomic dividing line can be drawn through preindustrial Scandinavia than the one between the area of individual farms to the north and the west—in Norway, Iceland, and peripheral parts of Sweden—and the best agricultural regions with their village settlement to the south and east—in central and southern Sweden and most of Denmark. In the first area large and at the same time compact estates were never feasible and society in general was less aristocratic than in the village regions.

From the Viking age to the first half of the fourteenth century there was a considerable extension of agrarian settlement. In the oldest and best agricultural areas settlement became denser through the increasing division of farms and the exploitation of less accessible resources. At the same time new farms and whole farm districts were cleared in less favorable or central areas; there was a general expansion of settlement toward the interior, higher up, and further north. This process can only be explained as connected with a rapid increase of population. The evidence suggests that the increase was greatest in eastern Norway, where the reserves of agricultural land were most extensive. In the southern and western coastal districts the growing population found an outlet through the Viking colonization of the Atlantic isles to the west and even parts of the British Isles. When this outlet had been closed, a particularly extensive division of farms took place in those districts.

At the so-called "high-medieval maximum" in the first half of the fourteenth century the total number of farms in Norway has been estimated at about 36,500. Unfortunately, it cannot be ascertained how far the division of those farms into holdings had progressed by this time. Nor do contemporary sources provide a solid basis for estimating the average number of persons per holding. These and other uncertainties make it difficult to produce a reliable estimate of Norway's total population at the end of the High Middle Ages more precise than between 300,000 and 500,000.

At the time when the population reached its maximum, life must have been hard in the many new small holdings. There is evidence to suggest that the soil was being exploited to the greatest possible extent and that the standard of living had fallen to subsistence levels in many places. It is possible that the standard of living for those who were worst placed in peasant society was so low that their powers of resistance to food shortage in years of crop failure and to epidemics were gradually undermined. At the same time there is some evidence that the climate became somewhat cooler and more damp from the twelfth century on. It is therefore possible that the catastrophic decline in the size of population and the contraction of settlement that occurred during the Black Death of 1349–1350 and the following cycle of epidemics were the result in part of conditions that began to appear in the High Middle Ages.

As a consequence of the population crisis of the latter half of the fourteenth century the number of farms in Norway may have been reduced by one-half to two-thirds. The number of holdings may have gone down to one-third. This would suggest a loss of at least half of the high-medieval population. The consequent contraction of agrarian settlement was, to a large extent, the reversed process of the earlier expansion. Gradually the population was concentrated in the best and most central agricultural districts and, within each district, on the best farms. At the same time there was a marked tendency for the coastal districts of western and northern Norway to keep their population more successfully than the best agricultural areas inland. And there was even a clear expansion of Norwegian settlement northward and eastward along the coast of Troms and Finnmark, the northernmost areas of present-day Norway. The increased economic importance of fishing is the obvious explanation for the last development. In general, agrarian settlement and population do not show any signs of renewed growth until the second half of the fifteenth century or, over large parts of the country, the first half of the sixteenth century.

ECONOMY AND SOCIAL STRUCTURE

Arable land was scarcer in mountainous Norway than it was in Denmark and Sweden. Still, it was relatively ample in east Norway and Trøndelag, further north. In the coastal districts of western and northern Norway and in the mountain valleys the restricted strips and patches of farming land were supplemented by extensive pastures. Thus, even in Norway agriculture in the form of mixed farming was the completely dominant means of subsistence, although it must be stressed that supporting economic activities like fishing, hunting, forestry, and the extraction of bog iron were important for most farmers. Fishing, above all, made an indispensable contribution to the daily diet in the coastal districts to the north and west.

The growing of grain, mainly oats and barley, played a predominant role in eastern Norway, Trøndelag, and the fertile southwestern province of Rogaland. In the rest of the country natural conditions generally imposed limits on grain growing, and animal husbandry was relatively more important, based on the keeping of cattle, sheep, and goats. Agricultural production increased during the early and High Middle Ages—through the extension of the area under cultivation, through an increase in the amount of labor devoted to each unit of land, and possibly also through minor improvements in agricultural methods. But agricultural production hardly kept pace with the growth of population, and this might have accounted for the

NORWAY

reduced standard of living of many peasants at the end of the High Middle Ages.

Some exchange of goods between Norway and foreign areas had gone on since prehistoric times. Such exchange was stimulated by the closer contact with Europe in the Viking age. International trade was still restricted in quantities, however, and tended to favor luxuries over necessities. This changed when the growth of European population from the eleventh century on, together with the fasting rules of the church, created a market for dried fish or stockfish, the first product ever exported from Norway on a large scale. In the course of the twelfth century, when the Norwegians seized the opportunity of exchanging fish for whatever foreign produce they needed, the cod fisheries of Lofoten and Vesterålen in northern Norway developed into a major industry. But cod and other fish suited for drying were also caught along the rest of the northern and western coasts. The town of Bergen, conveniently situated on the western shore of the country, became the emporium of the new foreign trade, which helped to activate other branches of Norwegian production as well. Still, stockfish alone may have accounted for as much as 80 to 90 percent of the total value of Norwegian exports in the High and most of the late Middle Ages. Other fish products like fish oil and herring came next, together with lumber, hides, and furs. In the course of the late Middle Ages lumber became the second bulk commodity of Norwegian export trade.

Up to the fifteenth century Norway enjoyed constantly rising prices on her stockfish. The exchange of fish for grain and malt, the most important imports, was increasingly favorable from a Norwegian point of view. Such terms of trade go a long way to explain why the peasants of the northern and western coastal districts tended to reduce their strenuous grain growing, poor in yields, to concentrate on animal husbandry for their own subsistence and fishing that would bring them both food in itself and, in return, imported cereals, textiles, beer, salt, and other products. Together with wine and other luxurious commodities such imports were also in demand in the higher strata of society and in the towns and their surrounding countryside.

Up to the fourteenth century it appears that most of the stockfish went to east English ports. English wheat and flour dominated the early importation of cereals, but from the middle of the thirteenth century Baltic rye from Lübeck and other German ports played an increasingly dominant role. When the English after 1400 started to obtain their fish directly from Iceland, the European continent and especially the Rhine area took over as the main market for Norwegian stockfish.

Since agricultural land was by far the most important means of production, the ownership of such land and the right to use it were decisive in shaping the structure of medieval Norwegian society. By the early fourteenth century the majority of Norwegian peasants were obviously tenants or part tenants of clerical or lay landowners. The distribution of land in terms of value has been roughly estimated as follows: 7 percent for the crown, 20 percent for the lay aristocracy, 40 percent for the church, and 33 percent for freeholding peasants and burghers.

The traditional hypothesis concerning the socioeconomic structure of medieval Norway maintained that the tenancy system was well developed as early as the prehistoric period or at the latest in the early Christian era, before the middle of the twelfth century. Recent research has strengthened this hypothesis. A solid core of the tenancy system appears to have existed already in the Viking age and the early Christian period. Nor is there any empirical basis for the belief that the great mass of Norwegian peasants were freeholders and that society was generally less aristocratic in an earlier period. In the Viking age great landed families commanded the support of peasants not only by means of traditional and personal loyalties and wealth to pay followers, but probably also in part by means of the control landlords could exercise over tenants.

There is no doubt that the tenancy system became increasingly important in the following period. It was, however, not the only source of wealth and power for the magnates. The centralization of church and monarchy produced a development away from an old clan aristocracy, whose power base was overwhelmingly local, toward a service aristocracy that based its social position mainly on its participation in the government of state and church. Still, high-medieval Norway was not a particularly aristocratic society compared with Denmark, Sweden, and most of the rest of Europe. Since the agricultural resources of the country were scarce and scattered, there were few really great landowners. The clergy and the royal service aristocracy were certainly placed above ordinary people in wealth and status, but the boundary between these two groups and peasant society was a fluid one, and both were recruited from the peasantry. In general, the clerical and lay aristocracy lacked the private economic power base that would have made it strong enough in number and influence to strive for independent control of society.

On the other hand, the situation of the Norwegian tenant of the Middle Ages was, in European terms, quite favorable. Not only would tenants of crown, church, and aristocracy farm the best land of the country—so that they would not rarely be better off than many freeholders—but the tenant was also, in legal terms, a free man who cultivated the soil he leased on a contract basis. The landowner exercised no private jurisdiction over him; he was not obliged to perform labor services; and he was not tied to the soil. In other words, there was no serfdom or villenage in Norway. Regular slavery had ebbed away in the early Christian period.

The evidence suggests that land rent was a relatively heavy burden at the end of the High Middle Ages, constituting perhaps one-fifth to one-sixth of the yield. Moreover, in some districts the demand for land made it possible to extract additional payments over and above the rent. Still, the tenants enjoyed a relatively great measure of security of tenure. The law codes of the twelfth and thirteenth centuries refer to short leases (one to three years), but they also open the way for longer contracts. Most of the written contracts that have survived from before 1350 are leases for life, and some of them even provide for the right of the son to inherit the lease from the father. It can be argued that leases of this type represent normal practice.

As a consequence of the catastrophic decline of population in the late Middle Ages land became plentiful. Land rents dropped to one-fourth or one-fifth of what they had been before the Black Death. At this low rent there was more and better land for each tenant. Thus, when the terror and sufferings of the plague and the following epidemics had subsided, the standard of living of the average peasant household must have been considerably higher than it had been before the middle of the fourteenth century. In economic terms the crisis of the late Middle Ages was a crisis for the recipients of land rents, taxes, and other dues from the agrarian population, that is, the crown, the church, and the private landowners. The high aristocracy of the country was strongly reduced in number and became more clearly separated from the rest of the population. This had partly to do with the fact that royal service could no longer sustain an important low aristocracy. Society below a handful of great families thus became more egalitarian than before.

THE LONG PROCESS OF UNIFICATION

In Ottar's days there was as yet no social and political organization for more than parts of the country. Territorial unification under one monarchy started seriously with King Harald I Fairhair in the decades around 900. It was achieved by two main stages of military struggle with a more peaceful period in between.

The first stage came to an end shortly after the middle of the eleventh century. Throughout most of this phase a monarchy with its chief power base in the coastal region of western Norway tried to gain a more permanent foothold in other parts of the country as well. A king like Olaf II Haraldsson (*r.* 1015/1016–1028), the later St. Olaf, managed to make his power felt over most of Norwegian territory. Still, his reign was only an episode in a period when Danish power was paramount in southeastern Norway. Not until the disintegration of the Danish North Sea empire after the death of Cnut the Great in 1035 did it become possible for Norwegian monarchs to control the whole of Norway more permanently. Norwegian territory was now secured southward through Bohuslän to the mouth of the Göta River. And the inland agricultural regions of eastern Norway, called the Uplands, and Trøndelag were brought under more effective royal rule.

Now followed a phase of comparative stability and peace. But frequent reigns of two or three joint rulers, commanding support from different regions and interest groups, indicate that political unity was far from achieved.

In the 1130's began a century of wars of succession, termed the civil wars by posterity. This was the second stage of the unification struggle, ending in victory and hereditary single rule for the kings of the line of Sverre Sigurdsson (1177–1202). The civil wars ebbed in the 1220's under Sverre's grandson, Håkon IV Håkonsson (*r.* 1217–1263). The territorial divisions and social tensions that had for so long provided support for rival pretenders and their parties were now finally overcome by a national system of government.

One cornerstone of this system was the incorporation of the magnates of the country in the royal *hirð* or body of retainers, as the leading members of a royal service aristocracy. The *hirð* originally functioned as the bodyguard and household of an itinerant king, constituting the core of his military power. Over the years it came to function as a corps of administrative personnel as well, comprising royal officials and helpers in the local districts. The termination of the first phase of the unification struggle in the eleventh century was connected with the downfall of the last of the more independent local chieftains of the land and the subordination of other magnates under the king as "landed men" or barons; they were granted royal land in return for fealty and service and constituted the leading rank of the *hirð*. In the following period royal service in the *hirð* attracted magnates and leading peasants all over the country, so that, finally, *hirð* membership became the criterion of lay aristocratic status. During the civil wars the *hirð* aristocracy was as yet divided between rival kings and pretenders. The wars ended when it was united under one king.

Another cornerstone of the national system of government was the collaboration of the church and the clergy with the monarchy. Christianity had started to seep in to the coastal regions of western and southern Norway in the Viking age, mainly from the British Isles. But it was through the help of missionary kings, above all Olaf Haraldsson, that it was legally established as the one and only permitted religion of Norway. The oldest Norwegian church was a national church, led by the king and incorporated into peasant society by his help. By the establishment of a separate Norwegian church province in 1152 or 1153, governed from the metropolitan see of Nidaros (Trondheim), and covering also the six dioceses of the western isles from Greenland to the Hebrides and Isle of Man, the Norwegian church broke away from its heavy dependence on monarchy and peasant society and became more firmly incorporated in the universal church under papal leadership. By means of its national hierarchic organization it developed into an almost statelike public authority at the side of the monarchy, contributing greatly to the unification of Norwegian society, not least in the wider, cultural sense.

The more independent church continued to collaborate with the monarchy, although there were also passing clashes between the two parties, developing into bitter conflicts in the days of King Sverre and again in the early 1280's. The consolidated monarchy of the thirteenth century would not accept a politically autonomous church. But it was, by and large, prepared to grant the church internal autonomy, judicial powers in spiritual matters, and financial privileges.

All the time, the clergy furnished the king with able, literate helpers in the government of state. After the civil wars the bishops generally acted as counselors and political guarantors for the monarchy. Clerics of lower rank served the king in embassies and administrative tasks, particularly members of the mendicant orders and cathedral chapters. Still, the church used most of its personnel and considerable revenue for its own purposes. This explains why Håkon Håkonsson and his successors worked more systematically to create a clergy of their own within the framework of the royal chapel.

The clerical helpers of the king must have contributed essentially to the formulation of royal political ideology. The most important work of medieval political theory in Norway, the *King's Mirror,* from the 1250's, emphasizes the king's likeness to God and his function as God's chosen representative on earth. The position of the king is presented as so elevated and superior in relation to other temporal authorities that the work must be said to defend an absolutist ideology. A related ideology pervades the extensive royal legislation of the following period, culminating in the great law codes of King Magnus VI Håkonsson, the Law Mender (*r.* 1263–1280). Both in this legislation and in the official saga biographies of King Sverre and his successors, the position of the king as the heir of St. Olaf, the national patron, is stressed.

Even if the *hirð* aristocracy and the clergy played key roles in the state-building process of the High Middle Ages, they were in themselves too slender a basis on which to build national royal power. Norwegian society was predominantly a peasant society, and no public authority of importance could be established and maintained without positive support from the agrarian population. Fundamentally important for the political unification of the country and the development of a nationwide political system was the need of peasant society for a minimum of peace and order, internally and externally. From this stemmed the two main functions of monarchy in society: the king as the enforcer of justice and the king as military leader.

Centrally placed in the relations between king and peasants were the popular assemblies or "things." In the form of universal gatherings of the freemen of local districts they went back to prehistoric times. As such they continued to function locally in judicial and, partly, also political matters in the Middle Ages. Politically, some of them acquired special importance by the "taking" or acclamation of a new king. From the days of Harald I Fairhair (Haraldr hárfagri, *r.* 850–930, *d.* 933) the monarchy was active in promoting the so-called law-things as representative assemblies of larger regions or law-provinces and supreme instances of legislation and judicial decisions. The provincial law codes regulated the king's role in the enforcement of justice with the right to legal fines and confiscations and his role as military leader commanding the important naval levy of the *leiðangr,* which was supplied by the peasantry.

The national monarchy of the High Middle Ages reduced the judicial and political influence of peasant society through the things. In the law codes of Magnus the Law Mender the king assumes the role of the highest judge and legislator in the land. The participation of the law-things in legislation had by now been reduced to more formal assent to royal enactments, which would in advance have been sanctioned by central royal assemblies or parliaments. Although freemen representing local districts were summoned to such central assemblies at the side of prelates and magnates, their participation was hardly decisive for the outcome of discussions and negotiations; it was intended more to bind the rest of the population.

Still, the monarchy attached importance to the preservation of the legal basis and support it had acquired from the agrarian population at an early stage of the unification process. The relationship between monarchy and peasants was never free from tension because of the economic and military burdens placed on the people and infringements by royal representatives. But the royal taxation of the population in the form of a partial conversion of the *leiðangr* was less heavy in Norway than in the neighboring kingdoms, at the same time as the peasantry kept its military function. Royal legislation also reveals that the monarchy tried to protect its subjects from abuses on the part of royal officials and private landowners. It is debatable how far this policy was carried out in practice, but it is hard to see how the monarchy, on a comparatively weak financial basis, could have been built up to its strength and influence at the end of the High Middle Ages without some form of positive functional relationship with the great majority of the population.

The establishment of a national system of government required more solid points of support than the royal estates visited by an itinerant king and his *hirð* at the first stage of the unification process. In this light must be viewed the role of kings as town promoters. In the rise and development of Norwegian towns from the eleventh century on, attention should be drawn not least to their function as administrative and fiscal centers of monarchy and church in which were gathered, increasingly, revenues in kind from the agrarian countryside. Such revenues not only supported royal and ecclesiastical personnel in the towns but also contributed to their role as centers for the exchange of goods and the production of craftsmen.

Norwegian towns remained few and small throughout the Middle Ages. The only exception was the international commercial center of Bergen, which may have reached a permanent population of 5,000 to 10,000. In the thirteenth century Bergen became the first town to deserve the name of a national capital of Norway. Beside Bergen only fourteen other Norwegian centers, at the most, reached the status of formal towns. Only three others may have counted their inhabitants in the low thousands—the archiepiscopal town of Nidaros and the eastern towns of Oslo and Tønsberg. Still, in their role as royal, ecclesiastical, economic, and cultural centers Norwegian medieval towns were of far greater importance than their number of inhabitants would seem to indicate.

In the days of the last of the Old Norse kings, Håkon V Magnusson (*r.* 1299–1319), the royal machinery of government consisted of a local administration that fairly systematically covered the whole country: about fifty local officials (Old Norse: *sýslumenn*) corresponding to the English sheriffs, representing the king in fiscal, legal-administrative, and military matters; ten "lawmen" acting as judges and administrating justice on the king's behalf in as many law-provinces; and four regional treasurers in the royal castles or estates of the largest towns. The king and his daily *hirð* retinue were still to some extent itinerant, but they would only stay for longer periods in the largest towns, most frequently in Bergen. In the thirteenth century Bergen was the rallying point of the agencies of central government—a royal chancery, a permanent royal council, and, more irregularly, national political assemblies. In Håkon V's days Oslo started to develop into a rival political center for the increasingly important eastern part of the country, while Bergen kept its position as the center of northern and western Norway and the tributary islands to the west.

It appears that toward the end of the High Middle Ages the crown exerted a greater political influence than its power apparatus and revenues by themselves would suggest. The cause of this may well have been that there was a certain balance between the main sociopolitical groups of the country in the sense that none of them was strong enough to dominate the others and to act against the interests of the kingdom as a whole; they were all to some extent dependent on the crown. But this equilibrium proved fragile. When the consolidated monarchy of the thirteenth century directed its newfound strength into an active and at times aggressive foreign policy, it was shown after some time to have insufficient resources in open confrontations with the more populous and economically stronger neighboring kingdoms and with the north German seaports that were later united in the Hanseatic League.

From the latter half of the thirteenth century, Hanseatic merchants expanded and dominated Norwegian foreign trade. They started to entrench themselves as "winter-sitters" in Bergen in the 1250's and thereby laid the foundations for the later settlement or *Kontor* there, established around 1360. The *Kontor* acquired a near monopoly of the Norwegian stockfish trade.

POLITICAL DEVELOPMENT IN THE LATE MIDDLE AGES

When Håkon V died in 1319 Magnus VII Eriksson (1319–1355), the son of his daughter and a brother of the Swedish king, inherited the Norwegian crown. In the same year his election to the throne of Sweden (as Magnus II) led Norway into a little more than personal union with that kingdom. The union lasted until the second son of Magnus, Håkon VI (*r.* 1355–1380), became Norwegian king. This was the period when Norway suffered most acutely from the population and production crises of the late Middle Ages. The already weak financial basis of the crown was now reduced to the degree that one may well ask whether the preconditions of a fairly effective and independent Norwegian state authority any longer existed.

Håkon VI married Margaret, the daughter of the Danish king Waldemar IV, and was drawn into Waldemar's ill-fated struggle with the Hanseatic League. His son with Margaret, Olaf IV (*r.* 1380–1387), was accepted as Danish king before he inherited his father's throne. This was the origin of a Danish-Norwegian union that was to last for more than four centuries; for some periods of the late Middle Ages it also included Sweden.

Norway entered the union with Denmark as a kingdom in its own right, represented by a "council of the realm," an aristocratic representative and sanctioning body that derived from the consultative and executive royal council of the High Middle Ages. This was a particular Scandinavian institution, combining the role of a permanent royal council with that of parliaments or estates in other European kingdoms. However, the weak Norwegian aristocracy was not capable in the long run of defending its own and other Norwegian interests in relation to the Danish-Norwegian monarchs, governing from Denmark, and the strong conciliar aristocracy of that country.

In 1536, on the eve of the Lutheran reformation and after an unsuccessful revolt by the last Catholic archbishop of Norway, Olaf Engelbrektsson, the much-reduced council of which he had been the leader ceased to function. Norway was now formally, albeit never fully in practice, incorporated into the Danish realm, ruled by the Danish king and his Danish council.

BIBLIOGRAPHY

Recent studies of medieval Norwegian history are catalogued in great detail in the annual *Bibliography of Old Norse-Icelandic Studies* (1963–). Bibliographies of sources and more important literature are found in Per Sveaas Andersen, *Samlingen av Norge og kristningen av landet 800–1130* (1977), and Knut Helle, *Norge blir en stat, 1130–1319,* 2nd ed. (1974). Other recent comprehensive works are Andreas Holmsen, *Nye studier i gammel historie* (1976), and *Norges historie fra de eldste tider til 1660,* 4th ed. (1977); Knut Mykland, ed., *Norges historie,* vols. 1–5 (1976–1977). An encyclopedic work of great importance for medieval Scandinavian history and culture is the series *Kulturhistorisk leksikon for nordisk middelalder,* 22 vols. (1956–1978).

Comprehensive treatments in non-Scandinavian languages are extremely scarce and brief, as is the case with Karen Larsen, *A History of Norway* (1948), and John Midgaard, *A Brief History of Norway,* 8th ed. (1982). A more up-to-date survey of early medieval Scandinavian history and culture is to be found in Peter Foote and David Wilson, *The Viking Achievement* (1970). Two historiographical surveys for the High and late Middle Ages are Knut Helle, "Norway in the High Middle Ages: Recent Views on the Structure of Society," in *Scandinavian Journal of History,* 6 (1981), and Helge Salvesen, "The Strength of Tradition: A Historiographical Analysis of Research into Norwegian Agrarian History During the Late Middle Ages and the Early Modern Period," *ibid.*, 7 (1982). See also Svend Gissel *et al., Desertion and Land Colonization in the Nordic Countries c. 1300–1600* (1981).

Articles in major European languages appear in *Mediaeval Scandinavia, Scandinavian Economic History Review,* and *Scandinavian Journal of History.*

KNUT HELLE

[See also **Black Death; Class Structure; Denmark; Feudalism; Fisheries, Marine; Hanseatic League; Scandinavia; Serf, Serfdom; Sweden; Tenure of Land; Trade; Urbanism; Vikings.**]

NOTGER OF LIÈGE (*ca.* 940–1008), perhaps educated at St. Gall, became bishop of Liège in 972. He encouraged learning and so promoted building in his diocese that he is often called Liège's second founder. A nephew of Otto I, Notger also served the Ottonian emperors in various capacities. He died on 10 April 1008.

BIBLIOGRAPHY

Sources. Notger's commentary on Boethius' *Arithmetica* is in Nikolai M. Bubnov, ed., *Gerberti postea Silvestri II papae opera mathematica* (1899, repr. 1963), 297ff. The lives of saints once attributed to Notger were probably written by his associate Heriger of Lobbes, perhaps with Notger's active collaboration. Notger's correspondence, pieces of which survive, has not been published in a comprehensive edition.

Studies. Godefroid Kurth, *Notger de Liège et la civilisation au Xe siècle,* 2 vols. (1905); Cora E. Lutz, *Schoolmasters of the Tenth Century* (1977), 92–99; Max Manitius, *Geschichte der lateinischen Literatur des Mittelalters,* II (1923), 219–223.

CHARLES R. SHRADER

[See also **Otto I, the Great, Emperor.**]

NOTITIA DIGNITATUM, a semiofficial handlist of the ranks and offices, both military and civilian, of the late Roman Empire, for the use of the *primicerius notariorum.* The respective lists for East and West may vary somewhat in date, but they reflect conditions between the last decade of the fourth century and approximately 420. The *notitia* contains important illustrations of insignia of office. Although it is one of the most important descriptions of the division of provinces and military commands, one should avoid assuming that its rank order and nomenclature remained unchanged throughout the late Roman Empire.

BIBLIOGRAPHY

The standard edition is by Otto Seeck, *Notitia dignitatum* (1876; repr. 1962). See also Roger Goodburn and Philip Bartholomew, eds., *Aspects of the Notitia Dignitatum,* in BAR Supplementary Series, **15** (Oxford, 1976).

WALTER EMIL KAEGI, JR.

[See also **Byzantine Empire, Bureaucracy; Roman Empire, Late.**]

NOTKE, BERNT (*fl.* 1463–1509), leading wood sculptor of north Germany in the late fifteenth century and a noted painter. He is known for naturalistic figures in expressive poses that are sculpted in the round from several pieces of wood. Notke's main works are the *Dance of Death* murals for the Marienkirche in Lübeck (1463), now in St. Nicholas in Tallinn; the Aarhus altarpiece in Denmark (1478/1479); the altarpiece in the Holy Ghost Hospital, Tallinn (1483); and the statue of St.

Detail from the Aarhus Cathedral altarpiece showing life-size figures of Pope Clement I, St. Anne, and St. John the Baptist. Oak carving by Bernt Notke, 1478/1479 (restored). PHOTO: LENNART LARSEN, NATIONALMUSEET, COPENHAGEN

George in the Church of St. Nicholas, Stockholm (1483–1489).

BIBLIOGRAPHY
Max Hasse, *Das Triumphkreuz des Bernt Notke im Lübecker Dom* (1952); Walter Paatz, *Bernt Notke und sein Kreis,* 2 vols. (1939), and *Bernt Notke* (1944); Alfred Stange, *Deutsche Malerei der Gotik,* VI (1954), 103–112.

LARRY SILVER

NOTKER BALBULUS (Notker the Stammerer, *ca.* 840–912), monk of the Benedictine abbey of St. Gall, poet, and author of prose works. The son of a wealthy Swiss landowner from Thurgau, Notker joined the St. Gall monastery as a child, and he lived there throughout the rest of his life. On the basis of those works of his that have survived, he seems to have enjoyed the monastery's international flavor and the fellowship of Irish, Byzantine, and West Frankish monks. His fame rests on two achievements: the *Gesta Caroli* (Life of Charlemagne), which was one of the most popular works in the early Middle Ages, and which has only in modern times been identified as his; and the texts of musical sequences (chants that are sung after the Alleluia of the Latin Mass), which marked a great advance in medieval music.

Unlike Einhard's *Vita Caroli Magni,* Notker's *Gesta* was based chiefly on oral traditions, and it reflected the "mythical" and popular—rather than historical or personal—portrait of the great Frankish ruler. The work, which was inspired by the visit in 883 of Charles III the Fat to St. Gall and probably written around 884–887, lacks the whole of its third part and a section of its second; it shows an acquaintance with Einhard's earlier *Vita.* Already, Charlemagne had become a figure of fascination for the common people, and popular traditions and stories about him had sprung up. Notker's work includes many of the anecdotes that circulated at that time. Although the *Gesta* mixes historical fact with legend and allegory, and contains amusing stories of rascally monks, profligate courtiers, and shrewd ambassadors, the figure of Charlemagne that emerges is of an outstanding and wise ruler, a protector of the honest and humble, and an enemy of Christian immorality. He is the pious but iron-willed monarch, an exemplar for the whole world.

Notker also wrote a prosometric *Vita S. Galli* (Life of St. Gall, extant in fragments only) and a sermon ("Sermo S. Galli") which has been preserved only in a seventeenth-century published edition. Both works display his poetic qualities (which figured strongly in his sequences). A collection of specimen letters (the *Formulae Sangallenses miscellaneae*) survives; it includes illustrative biographies of Christian writers (a popular form in his time), models for royal diplomas and ecclesiastical letters, and a correspondence with a former pupil, Solomon, later bishop of Constance, and with his brother Waldo. Around 881, Notker wrote *Breviarium regum Francorum,* a continuation of Erchanbert's work.

Notker's lasting fame rests on his contribution to the new hymn form, the sequence. His hymnological interest was generated by the congenial atmosphere of St. Gall, where the innovative spirit created two hymn forms, the trope and the processional *(versus).* His association with Ratpert of St. Gall, his master, and with Tutilo, his friend and the poet of tropes, must have been particularly beneficial. In the preface to his *Liber hymnorum,* Notker states that the model for his sequences came from a monk who arrived at St. Gall with an antiphoner, having fled the West Frankish monastery of Jumièges, which had been ravaged by the Normans (*ca.* 860). Notker composed new texts for the elongated Alleluia melodies, allowing one syllable to each musical note. The language of his sequences was full of poetic insight and imagery, considerably above the West Frankish models. He is thus credited with transforming the West Frankish sequence into a full-fledged and powerful musico-poetic form, thus greatly affecting subsequent musical and hymnic developments.

Notker's collection was dedicated to Liutward, bishop of Vercelli and chancellor of Charles the Fat, and was compiled around 884. He seems to have begun the composition of sequences as early as 860 and continued writing them until his death. Calling it *Liber hymnorum,* Notker would appear to be emphasizing their "hymn character," and modern musicologists should be encouraged not to separate sequences from the general history of hymnody. Few of Notker's sequences can be safely identified, and only forty are ascribed to him with certainty. The sequences for Good Friday, the Dedication of Church (*Psallat ecclesia*), and Pentecost (*Sancti spiritus assit nobis gratia*) are probably his earliest. Notker also wrote four inferior St.

Stephen hymns and a chant for Louis the German or Charles the Fat. Notker was beatified in 1512.

BIBLIOGRAPHY

Sources. Notker Balbulus, *Gesta Caroli,* in *Two Lives of Charlemagne,* Lewis G. Thorpe, trans. (1969), *Taten Kaiser Karls des Grossen,* Hans F. Haefele, ed. (1959), and *Notkeri poetae—Balbuli—Liber ymnorum,* Wolfram von den Steinen, ed. (1960).

Studies. Walther Bulst, "Susceptacula regum," in *Corona Quernea: Festgabe Karl Strecker* (1941); Richard L. Crocker, "The Early Frankish Sequence: A New Musical Form," in *Viator,* **6** (1975), and *The Early Medieval Sequence* (1977); Wolfgang Eggert, "Zu Kaiser- und Reichsgedanken des Notker Balbulus," in *Philologus,* **115** (1971); Hans Haefele, "Zum Aufbau der *Casus Sancti Galli* Ekkehards IV," in *Typologia litterarum: Festschrift für Max Wehrli* (1969); Heinrich Husmann, "Die St. Galler Sequenzentradition bei Notker und Ekkehard," in *Acta Musicologica,* **26** (1954); Karl Langosch, "Notker Balbulus," in *Die deutsche Literaturs des Mittelalters: Verfasserlexikon,* V (1955), and "Komposition und Zahlensymbolik in der mittellateinischen Dichtung," in *Miscellanea mediaevalia,* VII (1970); Theodor Siegrist, *Herrscherbild und Weltsicht bei Notker Balbulus* (1963); Bruno Stäblein, "Hymnus: B. Der lateinische Hymnus," in *Musik in Geschichte und Gegenwart,* VI (1957), 993–1018; Wolfram von den Steinen, *Notker der Dichter und seine geistige Welt,* 2 vols. (1948), and *Menschen im Mittelalter* (1967), esp. 88–113; Hans Spanke, *Deutsche und französische Dichtung des Mittelalters* (1943), 16–32.

JOSEPH SZÖVÉRFFY

[See also **Carolingian Latin Poetry; Charlemagne; Einhard; Music, Western European; Musical Treatises; Ratpert of St. Gall; Sequence; Tutilo.**]

NOTKER LABEO. See **Notker Teutonicus.**

NOTKER OF ST. GALL. See **Notker Teutonicus.**

NOTKER TEUTONICUS (also known as Notker Labeo, *ca.* 950–1022) was born into a noble family from Thurgau in northern Switzerland. He entered the Benedictine monastery of St. Gall, where he became a monk and one of the most learned and beloved teachers. Notker died there in 1022. His fame rests on his masterful translations into his native Alemannic, done about 1000, of several books that figured prominently in the curriculum of monastic education. He also wrote some small Latin treatises. We know much about his teaching and his writings because of a letter he wrote to Hugo, bishop of Sitten from 998 to 1017.

Notker considers the seven liberal arts (the trivium and the quadrivium) as necessary means and instruments to achieve an optimal understanding of the religious and theological books. He undertook the arduous task of translating several schoolbooks in order to facilitate his students' access to these religious books. Some clear-cut hierarchies emerge: vernacular leading to Latin, books of the "wordly" liberal arts leading to theology.

Notker's normal method is first to divide the original Latin text into syntactic units of manageable length (whereby he often simplifies difficult Latin syntax), then to translate each unit as accurately as possible into his Alemannic dialect, and finally to add, if necessary, an explanation mainly in the vernacular but with Latin phrases and key words under discussion (*Mischprosa* or reversed barbarolexis). Notker also adds in-line Latin glosses to his basic text. Such explanations and glosses are taken from the standard scholarly or exegetical commentaries, as well as from many other books. The following works by Notker are extant:

(1) A translation-explanation of Boethius' *De consolatione Philosophiae* in five books. Boethius' work was a basic schoolbook during the Middle Ages. In it the author, who is in prison, condemned to death, and desperate, is comforted by Lady Philosophy and, by her logical and rhetorical arguments, is led to a truly philosophical attitude toward himself, his former life and misfortune, his destiny, God's providence, his own free will, and other issues.

(2) A translation-explanation of Martianus Capella's *De nuptiis Philologiae et Mercurii.* This fifth-century work consists of nine books: I and II depict the allegorical wedding of Lady Philology (the human soul that strives for knowledge) and Mercury (divine wisdom). As a wedding gift Philology receives seven servants, the seven liberal arts; these "ladies" are treated in books III–IX of Martianus' work. The work was extremely popular during the Middle Ages, although its language and style are very complex and difficult to understand.

NOTKER TEUTONICUS

Notker's rendering encompasses books I and II only.

(3) Works on logic. Translations-explanations of Boethius' *Categoriae* and *De interpretatione,* which themselves are translations of Aristotles' *Kategoriai* and *Peri hermeneias.* Both works were fundamental for the teaching of logic in monastic schools. In addition, Notker has been credited with two small works on logic, *De syllogismis* and *De partibus logicae* (mostly in Latin but with German examples); similar to *De partibus logicae* is a fragment, *De definitione,* mainly in Latin but with explanations in German, that is also attributed to him.

(4) Similar to *De partibus logicae* and *De definitione* is Notker's *De arte rhetorica,* in Latin with examples in German.

(5) Entirely in Latin are Notker's *Computus,* a small treatise designed mainly to be used to compute the Easter cycle within the church year, and his letter to Bishop Hugo.

(6) Almost entirely in German is Notker's *De musica,* the five chapters of which treat some basic musical concepts.

(7) Notker's most extensive work is his translation-explanation of the Psalter: all 150 psalms, the *Cantica veteris et novi testamenti,* and three catechetical texts (the Lord's Prayer, the Apostles' Creed, and the Athanasian Creed). In it he draws not only upon the standard commentaries by St. Augustine, Cassiodorus, and St. Jerome, but also uses many minor sources, carefully selecting his explanations and often joining or even combining different exegetical positions. The Latin phrases that Notker inserted or simply took over from his sources, mainly Bible quotations, are frequently translated into German by a later glossator and appear as interlinear glosses in the only complete manuscript (St. Gall 21); several scholars consider Ekkehard IV, Notker's favorite student, a likely candidate. Besides the one complete manuscript, there are about twenty incomplete versions and fragments of his Psalter. Unlike Notker's other works, which have been preserved in few manuscripts, the Psalter appears to have found a wide circulation in medieval Germany.

Several works by Notker have been lost: a treatise titled *Principia arithmeticae* (perhaps based on Boethius); perhaps a treatise on the Trinity (based on Boethius' *De trinitate*); and certainly (and most regrettably) his translation-explanation of the Book of Job, very probably based upon the standard commentaries, especially the *Moralia in Job* of Gregory the Great. Whether Notker ever translated Cato's *Distichs,* Vergil's *Bucolics,* and Terence's *Andria* is uncertain; in his letter to Bishop Hugo he mentions that he was asked to translate these three works.

Besides being a prolific, diligent, and creative translator, Notker was a very good stylist: his prose exhibits great clarity; it flows with strongly rhythmic impulses and can easily become poetic; he likes to enliven its harmonious flow with pithy phrases and proverbs, and its elevated level of scholarliness by references to realistic details taken from daily life (animals, navigation, the mountains, the stars). On the whole, his varied and flexible use of the vernacular in all of these areas of very scholarly and abstract expression is quite astonishing.

Notker also had a keen ear for the sounds of his own language. He writes according to a carefully observed orthographic system, the most salient feature of which is the *Anlautgesetz,* the devoicing of the voiced consonants *b, d, g* at the beginning of a word that follows a word ending in a voiceless consonant (for example, not *daz du* but *daz tu*). Notker also insisted that German words normally should be written with accents: the acute on stressed short vowels and on the diphthongs *ei, ou, iu;* the circumflex on all long vowels and on the diphthongs *ie, uo, io, ia.* This accentuation system is most clearly evident in his *Consolation of Philosophy.* Finally, Notker observed a uniform system of punctuation, an adaptation and application, also to German, of a division *per cola et commata.* Unfortunately, Notker had no immediate successors. A new religious prose in the German vernacular developed in the sermons and mystical works of the thirteenth and later centuries; a new worldly prose took, with a few exceptions, even longer. It appears that Notker's achievement, with the exception of his Psalter, failed to inspire imitation (except perhaps by Williram von Ebersberg), and almost all of his writings were quickly forgotten.

BIBLIOGRAPHY

Editions. Die Schriften Notkers und seiner Schule, Paul Piper, ed., 3 vols. (1882–1883, repr. 1895); *Notkers des Deutschen Werke,* E. H. Sehrt and Taylor Starck, eds., 7 vols. (1933–1955); *Die Werke Notkers des Deutschen,* James C. King and Petrus W. Tax, eds., 11 vols. to date (1972–).

A good bibliography is in Evelyn S. Firchow [Coleman], "Bibliographie zu Notker III. von St. Gallen: Zweiter Teil," in William C. McDonald *et al.,* eds.,

Notre Dame de Paris, three-story interior elevation of the nave, modified before 1250. PHOTO: JEAN ROUBIER, PARIS

Spectrum medii aevi: Essays in Early German Literature in Honor of George Fenwick Jones (1983).

Studies. Herbert Backes, *Die Hochzeit Merkurs und der Philologie* (1982); Helmut de Boor, *Die deutsche Literatur von Karl dem Grossen bis zum Beginn der höfischen Dichtung, 770–1170,* 8th ed. (1971), 109–119, 131, 278; Dieter Furrer, *Modusprobleme bei Notker* (1971); Jürgen Jaehrling, *Die philosophische Terminologie Notkers des Deutschen in seiner Übersetzung der Aristotelischen Kategorien* (1969); Dietlinde Klein, *Der caritas-minna-Begriff im Psalmenkommentar Notkers des Deutschen* (diss., Freiburg, 1963); Horst D. Schlosser, "Formwille in Notkers *Consolatio*-Bearbeitung," in Heinz Otto Burger and Klaus von See, eds., *Festschrift Gottfried Weber* (1967); Ingeborg Schröbler, *Notker III. von St. Gallen als Übersetzer und Kommentator von Boethius' De consolatione Philosophiae* (1953); Stefan Sonderegger, *Althochdeutsch in Sankt Gallen* (1970), esp. 97–123, 182–183; Benedikt Vollmann, "*Simplicitas divinae providentiae:* Zur Entwicklung des Begriffs in der antiken Philosophie und seiner Eindeutschung in Notkers *Consolatio*-Übersetzung," in *Literaturwissenschaftliches Jahrbuch der Görres-Gesellschaft,* n.s. 8 (1967).

PETRUS W. TAX

[See also **Boethius; Ekkehard of St. Gall; German Language; Martianus Capella; Psalter; Quadrivium; Translation and Translators, Western European; Trivium; Williram von Ebersberg.**]

NOTRE DAME DE PARIS, CATHEDRAL OF. The Cathedral of Notre Dame is one of the most famous churches in the world, ranking in this respect with St. Peter's in Rome and Westminister Abbey in London. Notre Dame owes its fame mainly to its location in the heart of Paris and its literary associations, most especially with Victor Hugo's *The Hunchback of Notre Dame* (1831).

The present Gothic cathedral replaced what originally (sixth century?) was a three-church complex on the Île de la Cité: the church of the bishop (St. Étienne), a parish church (Notre Dame), and a baptistery (St. Jean-le-Rond). The last mention in documents of St. Étienne as the episcopal church is in 1130, and subsequent gifts to the Church of Notre Dame indicate it had replaced the former as the city cathedral by the 1140's/1150's.

The Gothic cathedral was begun by Maurice de Sully, who became bishop of Paris in 1160. The official *fundatio* of the building is traditionally recorded as 1163, when Pope Alexander III laid a cornerstone for the choir, but when construction was actually begun is unknown. The chevet was consecrated on 19 May 1182 and was in use in 1185 when a sermon was preached ex cathedra.

By the 1180's the nave had been begun, most probably by a different designer; it must have been nearly complete in 1196 when Sully died and left 200 livres for construction of its roof. To the casual observer the nave looks like the choir. There was until the nineteenth century, however, a fundamental difference in the nave: the earliest exposed flying buttresses in Gothic architecture.

About 1200 there was a change in the concept of the west facade, and new sculpture was cut for the three portals by about 1225/1230, when the west rose was installed. The western towers, whose spires were never built, were completed about 1250. Even before this date the original design was radically modified in two ways: the four-story interior elevation of the main arcade, vaulted gallery, oculi,

NOTRE DAME SCHOOL

and clerestory was altered into a three-story design by replacing the upper two elements with tall clerestory windows. Chapels were built, beginning in 1234, between the *culées,* giving a continuous plane to the periphery of the building. Between the 1240's and the 1260's, each arm of the transept was extended outward, the north by Jehan de Chelles, the south by Pierre de Montreuil, and they were given the great rayonnant wheel windows for which the building is justly famous.

Notre Dame is an imposing (its high vaults are 115 feet [35 meters] above the floor) example of the "thin wall" design of the second generation of French Gothic architecture. Its five-aisle plan without projecting transept and radiating chapels, recalling early Christian design, influenced Bourges Cathedral and other later buildings.

Notre Dame was radically restored by Jean-Baptiste Lassus and Eugène Viollet-le-Duc between 1845 and 1864. It has lost most of its original stained glass and sculpture (significant examples of which were accidentally discovered in 1977). Nonetheless, the building is impressive and remains a significant example of French Gothic architecture of the twelfth century.

BIBLIOGRAPHY

The bibliography on Notre Dame is enormous. Popular works include Yves Bottineau, *Notre-Dame de Paris and the Sainte-Chapelle,* Lovett Edwards, trans. (1967), with many illustrations; Allan Temko, *Notre Dame of Paris* (1956). The standard monograph on the building is Marcel Aubert, *Notre-Dame de Paris, sa place dans l'architecture du XIIe au XIVe siècle* (1928). More accessible is Denise Jalabert, *Notre-Dame de Paris,* 5th ed. (1963).

CARL F. BARNES, JR.

[See also **Ambulatory; Apse; Buttress; Cathedral; Chapel; Chevet; Construction; Gothic Architecture; Nave; Paris; Rose Window; Transept.**]

NOTRE DAME SCHOOL. While Anonymus IV did not specifically associate Leoninus with the Parisian cathedral of Notre Dame, the context and circumstantial evidence compel the conclusion that the latter was Perotinus' predecessor and that both presumably functioned as precentors or in a similar role at the cathedral. Thus, there are two known composers (and presumably others) with a combined active period from about 1165 to 1225 with whom a Notre Dame school can be and has been connected. Nevertheless, the terminal point of that school (or of the Notre Dame period) is generally set about a quarter of a century later, at a time when the decisive innovations of Johannes de Garlandia (John of Garland), preceding the ultimately enduring notational reforms of Franco of Cologne, began to supplant the conventions of modal notation.

Moreover, several compositions in styles characteristic of the Notre Dame school originated elsewhere—for example, England (perhaps Worcester), Beauvais, Sens, St. Germain-l'Auxerrois, and the abbey of St. Victor. A source associated with the latter contains compositions written in the 1240's, and the three manuscripts that are the chief sources of the Notre Dame repertoire—Wolfenbüttel, Herzog August Bibliothek, Helmstedt 628 (Heinemann Catalog 677 [W_1]); Florence, Biblioteca Mediceo Laurenziana, MS Pluteus 29.1 [F]; Wolfenbüttel, Herzog August Bibliothek, Helmstedt MS 1099 (Heinemann Catalog 1206 [W_2])—can all be dated from the mid thirteenth century (1240's to 1260's). Thus, the three Notre Dame generations that can be said to have been active must be associated, respectively, with Leoninus and his *Magnus liber organi,* which was clearly intended for the liturgy as celebrated at Notre Dame; with Perotinus and his organa tripla and quadrupla, his abbreviation of the *Magnus liber,* and the composition of clausulas; and with the development of the motet to about mid century by unknown composers active in Paris.

The genres cultivated by the Notre Dame composers are conductus; organa for two voices; organa for three and four voices; clausula, and motet. The evolution of the conductus in terms of style, form, and contrapuntal technique remains to be thoroughly investigated (for reasons exceeding the scope of this article), in contrast with the other genres, which have been, and continue to be, explored in considerable detail. The changes in the styles and contrapuntal techniques found in the three known versions of the *Magnus liber* and in the remaining genres—all of them rooted in Leoninus' comprehensive work—convincingly demonstrate the emergence of what may be called a new Gothic style from the declining Romanesque. In his organa (settings of the solo portions of festal responsorial chants constituting the *Magnus liber*) Leoninus, "*optimus organista,*" had favored the organal style.

Discant style, usually from two to four rhythmically precise notes in the upper voice *(duplum)* set against each note of the cantus firmus sung by the lower voice (tenor), is, in contrast with organal style, generally applied to melismatic portions of the chant melody. While the notation also indicates that many of the long melismas in the *dupla* of the organal sections should be read in modal or premodal rhythm, there are quite a few passages whose ligature notation is so unpatterned as to require a rhythmically free and flexible performance (as in earlier twelfth-century organa) which seems to have had characteristics evocative of the fast virtuoso rendition of vocal cadenzas in later musical traditions. It was this relatively rapid and unbridled motion of the presumably Leoninian organal idiom that Perotinus seems to have reined in and to which he applied order and measure. The extant versions of the *Magnus liber*—the one preserved in W_1 being the oldest—demonstrate stages in this process; none of the three can be said to preserve the Leoninian original. The redactions that Perotinus (and perhaps others) lavished on the *Magnus liber* reflect the changing concepts of musical style, whose benefit such an excellent work was deemed worthy of receiving; increasingly, passages written with the rationally ordered precision and concision of discant style replaced originally organal settings.

Discant passages became the models for and progenitors of motets. The increasing vogue of composing motets with French texts—a development whose beginnings Perotinus may have witnessed, but which he evidently did not cultivate—demonstrates the urbanization of polyphony in France and its centralization in Paris. Just as the polyphonic setting (conductus and motet) of the new rhymed Latin lyric poetry, such as the poems of Philip the Chancellor, was decreasingly practiced in the provincial monasteries, so the poetic and, to some extent, the musical heritage of the trouvères at the various French courts was gradually taken up and assimilated by the composers associated with the cathedral, the cathedral school, and the University of Paris, and incorporated in various ways in numerous motets. The new patrons of this new sacred and secular music, created by clerical and university composers, were the clerical and secular nobility of the Parisian cathedral and court.

BIBLIOGRAPHY

Julian Brown, Sonia Patterson, and David Hiley, "Further Observations on W_1," in *Journal of the Plainsong & Mediaeval Music Society,* **4** (1981); Heinrich Husmann, "Notre Dame Epoche," in *Die Musik in Geschichte und Gegenwart,* IX (1949); Frederick W. Sternfeld, ed., *Music from the Middle Ages to the Renaissance* (1973), 103–139.

ERNEST H. SANDERS

[See also **Anonymous IV; Ars Antiqua; Florence, Biblioteca Mediceo-Laurenziana, MS Pluteus 29.1; Franco of Cologne; Leoninus; Motet; Organum; Perotinus; Wolfenbüttel, Helmstedt MS 628.**]

NOUVELLE, a genre of short French narrative that evolved from such earlier verse compositions as the lai and the fabliau under the influence of the Italian novella. It took definitive form in the fifteenth-century *Cent nouvelles nouvelles* (1456–1462), a collection of one hundred comic tales in prose emanating from the Burgundian court and presumably told by the duke and members of his entourage.

BIBLIOGRAPHY

Roger Dubuis, *Les cent nouvelles nouvelles et la tradition de la nouvelle en France au moyen âge* (1973); Werner Söderhjelm, *La nouvelle française au XVe siècle* (1910, repr. 1973); Franklin P. Sweetser, ed., *Les cent nouvelles nouvelles* (1966).

RICHARD O'GORMAN

[See also **Cent Nouvelles Nouvelles; Fabliau and Comic Tale; Lai, Lay.**]

NOVELLAE. See **Corpus Iuris Civilis.**

NOVGOROD, a contraction for *novyi gorod* (new town), was the most important settlement in the early history of the north Russian plain. Though the *Russian Primary Chronicle* speaks of the existence of Novgorod in the middle of the ninth century, extensive archaeological excavations conducted since the end of World War II have found no evidence of artifacts datable prior to the mid tenth century. The name of "new town" has persuaded historians to believe in an earlier establishment, an "old town," but no consensus exists for the location of the earlier foundation.

Individual settlements on both sides of the river Volkhov joined together to become the city of Novgorod. River networks facilitated trade both near and far. Two major arteries gave access to distant markets. The Dnieper, reached via portages, flowed south to the Black Sea; and the majestic but sluggish Volga wound its way to the Caspian Sea, allowing access to entrepôts in Constantinople and the Near East. Moreover, proximity to the Baltic gave Novgorod an initial trading advantage and later contributed greatly to its prosperity when trade revived in northern Europe.

Novgorod had evolved into a city-state of huge proportions. It embraced an area of more than 320,000 square kilometers, which stretched from a vertical line in the west marked by Lake Peipus to the Ural Mountains in the east. A portion of the northern frontier reached the shores of the White Sea, and in the south the boundary stopped at the edge of the principalities of Tver and Muscovy. Most of that vast land was unsuitable for agriculture and unattractive to settlers. Population figures for the early centuries are a matter of speculation. A late-fifteenth-century cadastral survey, though somewhat incomplete, established a population of at least 520,000 for all the Novgorodian territories. The capital contained 32,130 residents, and eight smaller towns embraced another 16,233 inhabitants. Most of the populace lived in the southwest, with the capital at the hub. Here the calculated density was three persons per square kilometer, whereas the north was almost empty. (The overall average was 1.8 persons for each square kilometer.) The capital's population, with 6.18 percent of the total for the state, exceeded that of any other city on the Russian scene, except Moscow, and testified to its economic vitality.

DEVELOPMENT OF REPUBLICAN INSTITUTIONS

Novgorod's political and social evolution mirrored its commercial interests. It was the only Russian polity (aside from several of its offshoots) to develop a republican form of government. The early mercantile activities and the indifference of its overlords favored the shift. The Viking adventurers, who initially penetrated the area where the Novgorodians settled, located their capital at Kiev, some 500 miles to the south. Advantageously situated on the edge of the steppe and on the lower Dnieper River, Kiev stood below the funnel of the major tributaries, which allowed the ruling princes better access to the tribute-paying tribes, as well as to the collection of natural products and slaves for trade with Byzantium. Yet the Kievan princes did not abandon their suzerainty over Novgorod and their demands for tribute. The northern town's importance may be deduced by the assignment of viceroys, who ruled in the name of the senior prince. Each delegated a son, usually his eldest, as prince of Novgorod and required that two-thirds of his income be sent to the Kievan treasury.

Disillusioned by their subordinate status, the drain upon their taxes, and the lack of interest in their affairs, the inhabitants of Novgorod resolved to alter relations with their overlords. The Kievan princes were primarily interested in steppe politics and trade with Constantinople. Subsequently, dynastic struggles developed for the senior princely throne, and Asiatic invaders began to threaten the east European steppe. The weakening of the suzerains' position encouraged the Novgorodians to strike out on their own. Their commercial interests favored a broader governing structure. Martial prowess was not esteemed by the upper classes, an attitude that played some role in the republic's ultimate demise.

The Novgorodians began the disengagement from their Kievan overlords in the late eleventh century, when they decided to select their prince from the reservoir of Rurikid descendants who sprouted in the divided land. The Novgorodians' attitude was best expressed in the speech attributed to the envoys sent to Svyatopolk II of Kiev in 1102: "We are sent to you, oh Prince, with positive instructions that our city does not want either you or your son. If your son has two heads, you might send him."

Once the Novgorodians succeeded in the hiring of their princes, they sought to erode their authority. Traditionally, the prince-viceroy had resided inside the city and had his "court" on the right bank of the Volkhov River near the marketplace. He named his own officials, made law, dispensed justice and collected the fines for himself, guarded the frontiers, protected the trade routes, and maintained domestic tranquillity. There was little the inhabitants could do about a corrupt or uncooperative viceroy, other than complain to Kiev.

Under the new system, the invited princes became hired agents, and their tenure was generally short. Required to guard Novgorod's freedoms and to respect its laws, the princes were carefully supervised. As a precaution against interference or a coup, princes were to reside in their own abode outside the town walls and could recruit no more than fifty military retainers. They were forbidden to hold land or to engage in trade or even to make loans to Novgorodians and could take no action without the approval of the elected senior official. And while they could not make laws without popular consent, the town assembly did not require their concurrence to pass legislation. The princes' income came from an annual stipend, a portion of the taxes, tolls, and judicial fines. Audits were made of their income to guard against illegal activities.

The desired diminution in princely authority could not be fully implemented for some time. Rival financial interests within Novgorod sought to use the princes to best their opponents. Each side sought a prince who would advance its own selfish aims. Election or the deposition of a prince often led to popular divisions and sometimes erupted into large-scale violence. Polarized politics favored the hired princes and allowed them considerable latitude. When the great families finally determined to settle commercial rivalries among themselves at the end of the thirteenth century, the prince's position declined in importance. For example, treaties with other commercial powers were written in the name of the prince prior to 1302; after that date they contained the names of the *posadniki* and the *tysyatskii* (elected officials) and all Novgorod, meaning the assembly, but the prince's name disappeared.

The Novgorodians set about developing their own institutions. An ancient tribal institution, the *veche* (an assembly of freemen), became the sovereign political power. While all freemen in the realm were able to participate, in practice only those within range of the sound of the great bell's summons could assemble. For all practical purposes, the *veche* became a city institution. Any freeman had the right to convene it, but most often the responsibility rested with the prince or a senior elected official. The assembly voted on all issues concerned with the general welfare. These included declarations of war, the endorsement of military and commercial treaties, the deposition or selection of princes, the election of senior officeholders, and the nomination of the ecclesiastical primate. The major officials elected by the *veche* were the *posadniki* (the heads of the civil administration), the *tysyatskii* (literally the commander of a unit of a thousand men, and initially the republic's militia leader), as well as the candidates for the senior ecclesiastical position. In 1156, upon the death of their bishop, the assembly decided to select a Novgorodian as their candidate. Their success persuaded them, in 1165, to demand archiepiscopal rank for their religious leader. Once selected, the local candidate required investiture by the metropolitan of all Rus, the ranking Russian primate, who resided in the capital of the senior prince (in Kiev until the end of the thirteenth century and in Moscow from early in the fourteenth). The Novgorodians found in their archbishops willing ecclesiastical supporters of their secular aspirations. The archbishop's influence gave him an unusual say in the republic's affairs. He played a pivotal role in defusing domestic conflicts and often represented Novgorod in tempering demands made by suzerain princes.

Growth as well as politics affected Novgorod's political organization. Economic prosperity and population increase created pressure for administrative reorganization of the city's districts. In 1291 the number of *kontsy* (literally: ends) was increased to five. The hinterland mirrored these divisions. Five *pyatiny* (fifths) embraced the remaining lands, each radiating from the capital to the outer limits of the state. These largely superseded the older "hundreds," the administrative and military subdivisions of the *kontsy.* In time of danger each had raised its own militia under an elected commander. This pattern remained, but now the senior *posadnik* rather than the *tysyatskii* led the combined militia of Novgorod. The latter assumed the duties of a chief constable, responsible for the protection of the marketplace, the foreign merchants, and domestic tranquillity. He also participated in economic negotiations and treaty formulation.

Sectional interests were not neglected in the 1291 reforms, for local autonomy remained in force. Each *konets* retained its assembly and elected its own *posadnik* as chief executive, while a senior *posadnik* headed the combined city administration. Local issues were left to the requisite units, while general concerns were voiced in the city *veche.* Wealth and status determined eligibility for high office. The great landlords and financiers formed the highest class of boyars. In practice only they held the offices of the *posadniki* and *tysyatskii.* Beneath them came the more important merchants and middling landholders. The majority of the merchants formed the third echelon. The lowest class of freemen were the "black people": the laborers, artisans, peasants, and sharecroppers. Beneath them stood the unfree—the slaves and the indentured. Differentiation developed within each class, including the highest. In Novgorod's later history some few boyar families contributed the greatest number of *posadniki.*

Structure often belies substance. An elite dominated Novgorodian politics despite the sovereignty of the *veche.* This situation had to have the formal support of the upper orders and the acquiescence of the lower. Economic coercion by landlords, workshop owners, and other employers probably played a role in obtaining desirable voting blocs in the elections; nevertheless, individual self-interest had to make compromises and accommodations with various borough and class interests.

The factional violence engendered by upper-class groups, which had allowed the prince significant leeway to maneuver and conditioned Novgorodian politics in the later twelfth and thirteenth centuries, evaporated after the creation of a supreme council in the 1291 reforms. This *soviet gospod* (council of lords) included the archbishop, the prince's representative, and the *tysyatskii* and *posadniki* then in office. In time the membership expanded to almost fifty, indicating the inclusion of previous major officeholders of the *kontsy* and the central administration. While this allowed the leading families a voice in the management of affairs, it also permitted them to settle their differences in private. The internal process is unknown, but it is noticeable that the issues that had earlier led to violence declined sharply after the creation of the council. Henceforth the prince was removed from the center of politics. Future agitation at the *veche* reflected the growing economic disparity between the wealthy and the impoverished, not the issues that had divided them earlier.

ECONOMIC ACTIVITIES

Novgorod's prosperity derived from its favorable location and the development of regional and international commerce. In the eleventh century the Gotland merchants created a trading base in the city. The development of the Hansa by the thirteenth century increased the Baltic traffic, and the Hanseatic traders superseded the Gotlanders. They desired the luxurious furs, walrus tusks, wax, and flax brought from the Novgorodian hinterland as much as they did the silks, spices, and luxury goods imported from the Near East via the Volga route. In exchange they sold the fine woolen cloths of Flanders and England, wines, linens, and arms.

A city the size of Novgorod required provisioning and promoted specialization. Fish, meat, mead, flour, and dairy products came from the rural areas. Since Novgorod was situated in a marshy area and could not grow sufficient grain, the city depended on imports. Finished goods supplied the urban population and found their way into the rural settlements. Excavations have established the existence of a variety of workshops for copper, iron, and silver and for work in leather, wood, and bone. There were also workshops of carpenters, clothmakers, and masons. Products made of iron appeared in the form of kitchen utensils, scythes, axes, and plowshares. Since rural Russia contained isolated hamlets and villages, with few able to support blacksmiths, agricultural implements manufactured by town artisans, such as axe heads and scythe bars, were needed to fill the void.

The waterlogged soil on which Novgorod stands has aided in the preservation of types of medieval remains that have disappeared in other areas. Wood, leather, cloth, and iron survived in the layers of the city's growth. The Novgorodians paved their streets with small-diameter logs. Twenty-eight levels of wooden causeways have been uncovered. Soviet scientists have dated the layers through a study of the tree rings and the creation of a continuous growth-rate chart. They were aided in their quest by drawing upon chroniclers' accounts of fires, which were frequent and well reported, and they correlated them with the blackened remains in the burnt layers. Coin finds, also simple to date, aided in the process. Many specimens from Byzantium, Persia, and the West aid in the verification of trade relations.

Among the many discoveries are more than 400 documents written on birch bark. These strips of bark, often two to three inches wide and generally less than a foot long, contain scratched Russian letters. The soft inner bark was better for use with a pointed piece of wood or metal, but sometimes a longer message carried over to the reverse side. The document was then rolled for transmission or storage. While the contents were generally brief, they covered a wide range of use. These included petitions, orders, instructions, letters, agreements, and even a proposal of marriage. The existence of the birch bark documents has altered previous notions about prevalent illiteracy in medieval Russia, although the Novgorod experience may not have been typical of nonmercantile settings.

SUBJECTION TO MOSCOW

The republic had to depend upon grain imported from Suzdal, a finger of fertile soil in the forest zone to the northeast of Moscow. This allowed the grand princes, with their pretensions to suzerainty over "all Rus," to exploit Novgorod's weakness whenever differences arose. Interdiction of the grain supplies led to hardship and even famine. The de jure suzerains invariably won the day and demanded lucrative indemnities. Ever mindful of the potential danger to their independence, the Novgorodians embarked upon a policy of weakening the position of the grand prince whenever possible. The senior Moscow princes had wrested permanent possession of the grand princely dignity in the fourteenth century and thereby became the object of Novgorod's suspicion. Matters came to a head in the fifteenth century when a family successional crisis developed in Moscow. It began in 1425 and dragged on for about a quarter century. The Novgorodians gave sanctuary to the momentary loser, which at one time even included Grand Prince Vasilii II himself. A weaker Muscovy gave added insurance to the republic. In the final stage of the struggle Novgorod sheltered the defeated pretender and even allowed him to use its territory as a base of operations against Moscow.

Retribution was not long in coming. In 1456 Vasilii turned his anger and army against Novgorod, which in his view had committed treason against its overlord. He spurned overtures of peace in order to teach his enemy a lesson, his forces inflicting a bloody defeat upon the more numerous but less martial Novgorodians. He demanded an indemnity of 8,500 rubles and forbade them ever again to harbor his enemies. He also required that all future charters and treaties be submitted for his approval and seal. The message that they were shackled to Muscovite overlordship was not lost upon the vanquished, although they prudently postponed a response until Vasilii II died.

The succession of Vasilii's son, Ivan III (1462–1505), encouraged them to test Moscow's resolve. Since the Lithuanian government had expressed anxiety over Muscovite penetration into what it considered its sphere of influence, the Novgorodian leadership hoped that Lithuania would counter Muscovite aspirations. Lithuania, which had once desired to expand eastward, had shifted its principal orientation to central Europe once its grand princes were also elected as kings of Poland. *Veche* endorsement allowed the leadership to form an alliance in 1471 with Casimir, grand prince of Lithuania (who was also king of Poland). Casimir accepted Novgorod's conditions: His nominee as prince of Novgorod had to be Orthodox, and no Catholic churches were to be allowed. Given the religious animosities between Roman Catholicism and Orthodoxy in the aftermath of the Council of Ferrara-Florence and the aggressive Latin campaign to obtain control over the Eastern church, the Novgorodians feared that religious issues would further inflame the Muscovite ruler.

Ivan III confirmed their apprehensions. He enlisted the aid of the metropolitan, who vigorously warned the Novgorodians against apostasy. Meanwhile the grand prince collected every available contingent to counter the expected Lithuanian involvement. The Lithuanians never appeared—the Polish involvement in central European politics had aborted Casimir's plan. Once again the Novgorodians stood alone, and the fiasco of 1456 was repeated but at greater cost. The chroniclers, who are not reliable for correct estimates, claimed that 12,000 Novgordians fell in one battle and did not bother to record the carnage in a second. Even then, the city remained defiant until reduced by hunger.

Uncertainty about Casimir's reaction prompted Ivan to reimpose the earlier conditions. The two bloody battlefield defeats sapped much of Novgorod's resistance, although some still determined to oppose the demeaning settlement. Ivan had executed some of the boyars and had jailed others in 1471, yet he suspected that clandestine opposition would continue. In 1475 he reappeared in Novgorod, determined to undermine resistance and to drive a wedge between the affluent and the oppressed. He won popularity with the lower classes by siding with the weak and punishing their alleged oppressors. His primary purpose was to seek out political dissidents. He arrested several boyars for voicing a pro-Lithuanian point of view. His actions so unnerved the boyars and the affluent merchants that they showered Ivan with costly gifts. Ivan willingly fleeced them and planned for more. He tightened the noose in a series of calculated moves, aided unwittingly by intimidated Novgorodians, who believed that they could appease him. The grand prince decided in 1477 to press for recognition as sovereign and demanded full judicial authority in Novgorodian affairs. As the unhappy republicans scrambled to protect their remaining liberties, Ivan had his forces ring the capital with his troops. While prepared for the possibility of Lithuanian involvement, he pressed forward with the annexation of Novgorod in 1478. This time the men in the city avoided military action and relied vainly upon persuasion. The annexed land became a viceroyalty of Muscovy, administered by one of Ivan's boyars. The *veche* disappeared, as did the elected officials. By the end of the century Ivan had forcibly removed the Novgorodian upper classes to the Muscovite interior and had given their lands in conditional service tenure to his own men-at-arms.

Novgorod may have paid a price for its hostility to Moscow, but its disappearance was inevitable. Muscovy had embarked upon a program of annexation by which even docility did not ensure toleration. Pskov had accepted Muscovite suzerainty and grand princely dictates, yet it suffered a similar fate. In 1510 Vasilii III imposed the same solution upon that docile republican offspring that his father had designed for Novgorod.

BIBLIOGRAPHY

The Chronicle of Novgorod, 1016–1471, Robert Michell and Nevill Forbes, trans. (1914, repr. 1970); Carsten Goehrke, "Gross-Novgorod und Pskov/Pleskau," in Manfred Hellman, ed., *Handbuch des Geschichte Russlands,* I (1981); Valentin L. Ianin, *Novgorodskie posadniki* (1962); Vasilii O. Klyuchevskii, *A History of Russia,* C. J. Hogarth, trans. (1960); Jorg Leuschner, *Novgorod: Untersuchungen zu einigen Fragen seiner Verfassungs- und Befölkerungsstruktur* (1980); *The Russian Primary Chronicle: Laurentian Text,* Samuel H. Cross and Olgerd P. Sherbowitz-Wetzor, eds. and trans. (1953); M. W. Thompson, *Novgorod the Great* (1967); George Vernadsky and Michael Karpovich, *A History of Russia,* II and IV (rev. ed. 1961); Wladimir Vodoff, "Les documents sur écorces de bouleau de Novgorod," in *Journal des savants* (1966), and "Les documents sur écorce de bouleau de Novgorod: Découvertes et travaux récents," in *Journal des savants* (1981).

GUSTAVE ALEF

[See also **Boyar; Fairs; Hanseatic League; Ivan III of Muscovy; Kievan Rus; Muscovy, Rise of; Russian and Slavic Art; Russian Architecture; Russian Orthodox Church; Trade, European; Vladimir-Suzdal.**]

NUBIA, the name given in medieval times to a section of the Nile Valley lying immediately south of Egypt. It extended approximately from Aswan, in southern Egypt, to the site of modern Khartoum, in the modern-day Republic of Sudan, where the Blue and the White Nile converge. The land of Nubia, although watered by the Nile, lacked the legendary fertility of Egypt, and the river itself was impeded by cataracts which made travel difficult. For these reasons Nubia never attracted Egyptian settlers. Its native inhabitants were African in racial origin and in speech, although their cultures were always strongly influenced by those of neighboring Egypt.

In ancient times the peoples of Nubia were the subjects as well as the rulers of the great empire of Kush, whose political and religious institutions were modeled on those of pharaonic Egypt. The empire of Kush broke up in the fourth century, but many Egyptian traditions and beliefs lingered on in the petty kingdoms that succeeded it. By the sixth century there were three such kingdoms: Nobadia in the north, Makuria (Arabic: Muqurra) in the region roughly between the second and fifth Nile cataracts (today the nothern Sudan), and Alodia (Arabic: ʿAlwa) in the region around the confluence of the Blue and White Niles.

Egypt became Christian, along with the rest of the Roman Empire, in the fourth century, but the Christian faith did not penetrate into Nubia until two centuries later. In the sixth century, however, the rivalry between Monophysite and Melchite (Byzantine) sects in Egypt had become so intense that each sought to strengthen its cause by enlisting the support of the Nubians, whose warlike prowess was legendary. According to tradition the emperor Justinian dispatched a Melchite mission to convert the Nubians in 542, while at the same time his wife Theodora secretly commissioned a rival Monophysite mission. The course of subsequent events is not entirely clear, but it is evident that the conversion of the Nubians was fairly rapid, and that the cause of the Monophysites was ultimately triumphant. By the end of the sixth century all of the Nubian kingdoms had embraced Christianity, and by the end of the seventh century all of them formed an extension of the Egyptian Coptic church (which was Monophysite).

The Islamic conquest of Egypt (642) followed less than a century after the christianization of Nubia, but it did not affect the lands to the south of Aswan. Muslim armies made two attempts to invade Nubia, in 642–643 and 652–653, but both were successfully resisted. After the second invasion a treaty of peace, the *baqṭ*, was concluded, which assured the political and religious independence of Nubia in exchange for an annual payment of slaves and other tribute. The *baqṭ* treaty remained in effect for over six hundred years, and it laid the foundations for a flourishing trade between Nubia and Egypt which was the cornerstone of medieval Nubian prosperity. In addition, the Nubians were allowed to continue their allegiance to the Coptic Christian church without disturbance until the end of the Middle Ages.

ADMINISTRATIVE ORGANIZATION

Sometime after 700 the two northern kingdoms of Nobadia and Makuria were merged into a single polity, under the rule of the king of Makuria. The principal capital was at Dongola, a city about halfway between the third and fourth Nile cataracts, but there were evidently royal residences elsewhere as well. The king was assisted by various court functionaries who bore Byzantine titles, although little is known about their actual functions. One medieval traveler reported that there were also local vassal kings under the rule of the Great King at Dongola. At least in the later Middle Ages, succession to the throne of Makuria was sometimes matrilineal; that is, it passed from the ruler to his sister's son rather than to his own son.

Although it was annexed by Makuria in the eighth century, the northern district of Nobadia always retained its own name and a separate administrative status. It was governed by an appointed viceroy called the eparch of Nobadia, who resided sometimes at Faras (Pachoras) and sometimes at Qasr Ibrim (Phrim). Nobadia was a free trade zone in which Egyptian and other foreign merchants were allowed to trade and to settle, and where Egyptian currency was in circulation. Conduct of commercial relations with the Egyptians was one of the chief duties of the eparch of Nobadia. In Makuria proper, on the other hand, all foreign trade was a royal monopoly, and the entry of foreign merchants was forbidden on pain of death.

Both Nobadia and Makuria were nevertheless visited about 975 by the Egyptian Fatimid envoy Ibn Sulaym al-Aswānī, and much of our information about medieval Nubia is derived from his account. He was impressed by the peaceful and prosperous conditions in the land of Makuria. However, he provided only scanty information about the kingdom of ᶜAlwa, and we remain largely ignorant of conditions in this most southerly of Nubian kingdoms. Although Makuria and ᶜAlwa shared a common faith and cultural heritage, it appears that they were often at political odds.

THE LATE MIDDLE AGES

The advent of Mamluk rule in Egypt (1250) had immediate repercussions in Nubia. The Mamluks demanded a resumption of the *baqṭ* payment of slaves, which had been in arrears for a long time, and they sent military expeditions to Nubia when the tribute was not forthcoming. They also began intervening in the dynastic quarrels that were now weakening the kingdom of Makuria. Most importantly, the Mamluks expelled from Egypt a number of Bedouin Arab tribes that had settled on the flanks of the Nile Valley. These peoples were mostly driven south into the Sudan, where in time they overran much of the territory of the medieval kingdoms. In 1323 the throne of Makuria passed into the hands of a Muslim claimant, and not long afterward the kingdom disintegrated into warring principalities. In the far north, a shadowy remnant kingdom called Dotawo kept up a semblance of independence and of the Christian faith until the end of the fifteenth century, while in the far south a remnant of the kingdom of ᶜAlwa survived until about the same time. In the sixteenth century all of the old territory of Nobadia came under Ottoman control, while the remainder of Nubia was annexed by the Muslim sultanate of Sennar, in the central part of present-day Sudan. At this point all traces of the Christian faith and of Nubia's medieval civilization came to an end.

THE NUBIAN CHURCH

In the early years after conversion, there was continuing rivalry between Monophysites and Melchites for the allegiance of the Nubian Christians. The Arab conquest of Egypt in (642), however, assured the final ascendency of the anti-Byzantine Monophysites (henceforth to be known as Copts), both in Egypt and in Nubia. The Nubian church became, organizationally, an extension of the Egyptian Coptic church, and its bishops were appointed by the Coptic patriarch of Alexandria. According to one church history there were seven bishoprics in the kingdom of Makuria, and six in ᶜAlwa. All of the bishops were apparently Egyptians, as were some of the other clergy.

In spite of the dominant influence of Egypt, the Coptic language was never used in the Nubian liturgy as it was in Egypt. Greek, the language of the original missionaries, always remained the liturgical language of the Nubians. In the later Middle Ages the native Nubian language, written in Greek characters, was also used both for sacred and for secular texts. All surviving documents from the kingdom of Dotawo are in the Nubian language.

There were also architectural and artistic differences between the Nubian and Egyptian churches. The Nubian church building was relatively long and narrow, with entrances on the north and south sides, quite unlike the medieval Coptic churches of Egypt. The largest Nubian churches were the cathedrals at Qasr Ibrim, Faras, and Dongola, each of which had a wide central nave flanked by two aisles on either side (rather than the more usual single flanking aisles). Church painting in the beginning was closely similar to that of Egypt, but later the Nubians developed their own distinctive school of mural painting, in which local kings, princes, and bishops were depicted along with the traditional holy figures. Nubian personages were always shown with African coloring and features, in contrast to the Holy Family, archangels, and apostles. The finest of the Nubian murals, excavated in the cathedral of Faras in the 1960's, may today be seen in the National Museum of Antiquities in Khartoum and in the Polish National Museum in Warsaw.

Monasteries did not play the important role in Nubian religious life that they did in Egypt. They were relatively small and few in number, and it appears also that a large number of the monks were Egyptian rather than Nubian. For some reason—perhaps because of their vulnerability to attack—all of the Nubian monasteries appear to have been abandoned after the twelfth century.

TOWN AND VILLAGE LIFE

Medieval Nubia, like modern Nubia, was preeminently a land of small villages. The overwhelming majority of the people were peasant farmers, raising cereal crops and dates along with a few cattle and sheep. The rather scanty arable land was divided into tiny plots irrigated by the ox-driven waterwheel, or sakieh. Dates were the only important cash crop; they were harvested in the early fall and were floated down to Egypt at the peak of the Nile flood in October.

Artisans resided mainly in the few towns of Nubia. They included woodworkers, leather workers, metalsmiths, weavers, and potters. Unlike their Egyptian neighbors the Nubian weavers made almost no use of flax, but wove entirely in cotton and wool. They produced brightly colored patterns of stripes and checks, but nothing comparable to the elaborate embroidery of the Egyptian Copts. The finest textiles, including silks, were always imported from abroad; commercial documents indicate that they were in great demand among the Nubian elite. The medieval Nubians also made brightly colored pottery, decorated with free-flowing designs borrowed from Coptic manuscript illumination. This was perhaps the most distinctive of indigenous Nubian arts, for the Egyptian potters attempted nothing comparable.

Nearly all Nubian house architecture was of sun-dried mud brick. However, a few churches were of roughly dressed stone, especially in the earlier Middle Ages, and the finest cathedrals were of cut and dressed stone. Most villages had at least one church, and many of them had two, three, or even four. The larger towns always had several churches, and the major administrative centers had a cathedral as well. Cathedrals were usually at the town center, while ordinary churches were more often at the outskirts, where there was room for an adjoining cemetery. Apart from churches, very few monumental or public buildings have been retrieved by archaeologists. It appears that manufacturing and commerce were conducted in private homes, or in outdoor marketplaces, while administrative business may have been carried on partly in the churches and cathedrals. Even the most important towns were relatively small compared to those of Egypt; the largest of them (Dongola) probably counted no more than 10,000 inhabitants.

In the late Middle Ages the character of Nubian towns began to change. Many small and outlying villages were abandoned, and the population drew together into defensible locations that were often provided with fortification walls. Islands in the Nile were especially favored for refuge settlements. In the thirteenth century miniature castles of mud brick began to appear, and by the fifteenth century they had supplanted the church as the dominant architectural expression of Nubian civilization. Militarism, however, is a feature not so much of medieval as of post-medieval Nubia. The High Middle Ages, as described by Ibn Sulaym al-Aswānī, was a time of peace, prosperity, and piety in the lands south of Aswan.

BIBLIOGRAPHY
William Y. Adams, *Nubia: Corridor to Africa* (1977), 433–546; Yusuf Fadl Hasan, *The Arabs and the Sudan* (1967), 17–134; Kazimierz Michałowski, *Faras* (1974); Ugo Monneret de Villard, *Storia della Nubia cristiana* (1938); Giovanni Vantini, *Christianity in the Sudan* (1981).

WILLIAM Y. ADAMS

[See also **Blacks; Christianity, Nubian; Copts and Coptic Church; Egypt, Islamic; Melchites; Monophysites; Nile; Sudan.**]

NUMBERS, NUMERALS. See **Arabic Numerals; Roman Numerals.**

NUMISMATICS. See **Mints and Money.**

NUNCIO, PAPAL. Throughout the Middle Ages the papacy's role in the church necessitated extensive diplomatic activity. In this the *nuncius* (or *nuntius*) played a major role. Contemporaries and later historians have often confused the functions of nuncios and papal legates, but the papacy maintained a rigid distinction between them. Initially the *nuncius*—in both papal and secular diplomacy—had no capacity for independent activity; he was merely a messenger appointed for a specific task, and could do no more than carry out instructions. In time, however, the role of the papal *nuncius* altered, especially from the fourteenth century on, and by the end of the fifteenth century the nuncio was clearly becoming a permanently resident papal ambassador (although this process, with the establishment of the permanent nunciatures, was not completed until much later). Moreover, as the diplomatic vocabulary developed, the term "nuncio" was gradually restricted to papal envoys, and possibly also to diplomatic agents of other ecclesiastical princes, such as the episcopal electors in Germany.

As papal administration developed during the later Middle Ages, the roles of various types of *nuncii* gained stricter definition, the most important being the *nuncius et collector,* who conducted papal fiscal business, and the *nuncius et orator* or solemn nuncio, with more specifically diplomatic duties that included representing the papacy in its dealings with local churches. However, functions could, and did, overlap for any individual nuncio. From the mid fourteenth century, for reasons not yet clearly elucidated, the diplomatic role of the nuncios increased; they generally replaced the former chief agents of papal diplomacy, the *legati missi.* This process was virtually completed by 1400, so much so that later nuncios often were granted legatine powers, even those of a legate *a latere.*

In the fifteenth century general developments in European diplomacy led to the rise of resident ambassadors. The papacy was rather slow in following this trend; but from the pontificate of Sixtus IV (1471–1484) some nuncios were appointed at papal pleasure rather than for specific purposes, and they took up residence at courts. By the end of the century at least some had become virtually resident ambassadors accredited to governments, a foundation from which the permanent nunciatures arose in due course.

BIBLIOGRAPHY
Clifford I. Kyer, "*Legatus* and *Nuntius* as Used to Denote Papal Envoys: 1245–1378," in *Mediaeval Studies,* 40 (1978); Georges-L. Lesage, "La titulature des envoyés pontificaux sous Pie II (1458–1464)," in *Mélanges d'archéologie et d'histoire,* 58 (1941–1946); Gino Paro, *The Right of Papal Legation* (1947), 111–120; Donald E. Queller, "Thirteenth Century Diplomatic Envoys: 'Nuncii' and 'Procuratores,'" in *Speculum,* 35 (1960), repr. in his *Medieval Diplomacy and the Fourth Crusade* (1980); P. Richard, "Origines des nonciatures permanentes: La représentation pontificale au XVe siècle (1450–1513)," in *Revue d'histoire ecclésiastique,* 7 (1906); Richard A. Schmutz, "Medieval Papal Representatives: Legates, Nuncios, and Judges-delegate," in *Studia gratiana,* 15 (1972); John A. F. Thomson, *Popes and Princes, 1417–1517* (1981), 102–105.

R. N. SWANSON

[See also **Diplomacy, Western European; Legate, Papal; Papacy, Origins and Development of.**]

NUNS. See **Women's Religious Orders.**

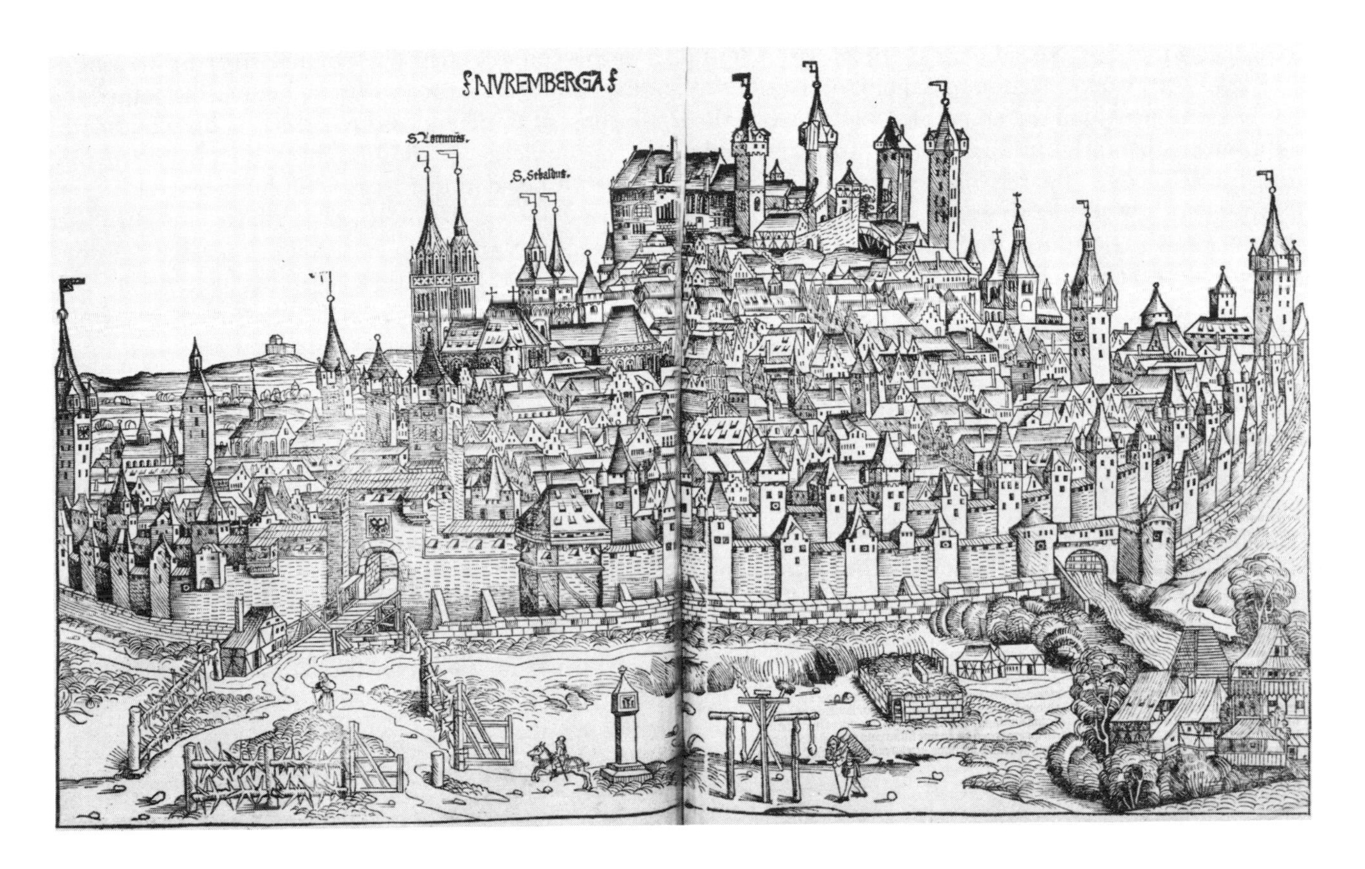

Nuremberg. Woodcut by Michael Wolgemut. Reproduced from Hartmann Schedel, *Liber chronicarum* (1493). THE NEW YORK PUBLIC LIBRARY, RARE BOOKS & MANUSCRIPTS DIVISION, ASTOR, LENOX & TILDEN FOUNDATIONS

NUREMBERG, immortalized in Richard Wagner's *Die Meistersinger von Nürnberg* as the archetypal imperial city, was the creation of the Salian and Hohenstaufen kings. About 1040, Henry III (1039–1056) built a castle on the hill north of the Pegnitz from which the city derives its name, and granted market rights to the settlement that formed at the base of the fortress, near the site of the later Church of St. Sebald (built 1225–1273). Conrad III's (*d.* 1152) development of the extensive imperial domains around Nuremberg, a crucial link in the Hohenstaufen holdings, provided the major impetus for the city's growth. Around 1140 he appointed a burgrave to command the castle and the ministerial garrison. The Hohenzollern obtained this office from the counts of Raabs around 1190. To administer justice in the fortified community around St. Sebald, Frederick I Barbarossa selected an imperial bailiff or magistrate *(Schultheiss)* from the ranks of the imperial ministerials. The Hohenstaufen founded a new settlement, the Lorenzstadt, south of the Pegnitz in the middle of the twelfth century; it grew so rapidly that it obtained its own parish church, St. Lawrence, in the thirteenth century. The two parts of the city were linked by a single wall only in the 1320's. Frederick II's (*d.* 1250) 1219 privilege granted the city exemption from various imperial tolls and established the king as the burghers' advocate. The latter privilege was a device to bring the townspeople, many of whom were dependents of the bishop of Bamberg, under direct royal control.

During the interregnum (1250–1273) the burghers became conscious of their common identity and assumed control of the city government. The council (*Rat*), largely composed of merchants of ministerial origin, is first mentioned in 1256. At the same time the citizens successfully resisted the attempts by the burgraves and the dukes of Bavaria to incorporate the city into their own principalities. In the course of the fourteenth century, the council gradually deprived the *Schultheiss* of his authority, until it finally bought the office in 1385. The construction of Nuremberg's first city hall (1332–1340) symbolized its emancipation.

The city provided the emperor, Louis the Bavarian, with substantial tax payments and loans, and in turn he pledged the regalian rights in the city to Nuremberg's wealthiest burgher, Konrad Gross, the founder in 1332 of the still-standing Hospital of the Holy Ghost. The council's decision to recognize Louis's opponent Charles IV of Luxemburg led to the only "guild revolution" in Nuremberg's history (1348–1349). It was in reality a pro-Bavarian uprising and was quickly suppressed with the king's assistance. The guilds never exercised any real political influence within the city.

This revolt and the city's subsequent alliance with the Luxemburg dynasty had, however, several important consequences. First, membership in the council was open to new families until 1521, when the so-called Dance Statute closed the ranks of the patriciate to those families who were permitted to dance in the city hall. Second, to provide greater security in the countryside, the council started to develop the city's territory by forcing burghers who owned castles to put them at the city's disposal. By 1500 Nuremberg governed a rural hinterland of 25 square miles, the largest territory controlled by an imperial city in Franconia. Third, the city procured Charles's permission to expel the Jews and to construct a bigger market, today's Hauptmarkt, in place of the ghetto. An aroused mob killed 562 Jews, and in 1349 Charles built the still-standing Church of Our Lady on the site of the synagogue. Finally, Charles IV stipulated in the Golden Bull of 1356 that each newly elected German king was required to hold his first diet in Nuremberg, a privilege that brought the city prestige and profit.

The city adhered to its pro-Luxemburg policy in the following decades. In the 1420's it became a staging area for German crusades against the Hussites in Bohemia. To protect itself, the city completed (in 1452) the walls that still encircle it. In 1423 the council persuaded Sigismund that the imperial regalia would be safer in Nuremberg than in Prague, in the center of heretical Bohemia. The city served as the depository of the crown jewels until 1796. In 1427 the city bought the burgrave's castle from Frederick VI, whom Sigismund had enfeoffed with Brandenburg in 1415. This ended the Hohenzollern rights within Nuremberg, but the city was often at war with the Hohenzollern margraves of Ansbach over their respective rights in the countryside. The council strove throughout the fifteenth century to limit the jurisdiction of the bishop of Bamberg and to assert its own authority over the clergy. It attained these objectives in 1525, when it decided in favor of Luther's teachings.

Its role as a major royal residence was the chief cause of Nuremberg's initial economic development. It is not situated in a rich agricultural area, and the Pegnitz is not a navigable stream. The court and the castle garrison attracted the first merchants, and the city's close ties to the monarchy remained an important factor in its late medieval prosperity. The merchants took advantage of the decline in the fairs of Champagne in the fourteenth century and Nuremberg's central location to establish commercial ties with the Low Countries, the Baltic, Eastern Europe, and Italy. After 1370 many of them also became involved in international banking. Nuremberg was the foremost producer of metalware in Europe, including weapons, household utensils, and technical instruments. The abundance of timber in the surrounding forests, the waterpower of the Pegnitz, and ready access to the iron ore deposits of the Upper Palatinate led to the development of this industry. By 1450 Nuremberg was the third largest city in Germany, with a population of more than 20,000.

The lifetime of Nuremberg's most famous son, Albrecht Dürer (1471–1528), was the city's golden age. Other major figures in Nuremberg's renaissance, which was a by-product of its wealth and its contacts with Italy, were the humanists Johann Pirckheimer (1440–1501) and his son Willibald (1470–1530), the poet Konrad Celtis (1459–1508), the historian Hartmann Schedel (1440–1514), and the meistersinger Hans Sachs (1494–1576). Nuremberg became, after 1470, a major center for the printing of books, but the city's economy was hurt by the opening of the Atlantic trade routes, religious conflict, most notably the Thirty Years War, and the hostility of the margraves of Ansbach. The romantic image of Nuremberg as the quintessential German city was the result of the three centuries of stagnation that followed its golden age and, thanks to Adolf Hitler, a major cause of its destruction in 1945.

BIBLIOGRAPHY

Gerhard Pfeiffer, ed., *Geschichte Nürnberg in Bilddokumenten* (1970), and *Nürnberg—Geschichte einer europäischen Stadt* (1971); Max Spindler, *Handbuch der bayerischen Geschichte,* II, pt. 1 (1971), 324;

Gerald Strauss, *Nuremberg in the Sixteenth Century* (1966, repr. 1976).

JOHN B. FREED

[See also **Arms and Armor; German Towns; Germany; Patrician, Urban.**]

NYMPHAEUM, from the Greek *nymphaion,* a shrine of the nymphs. In Roman and medieval times the word came to signify a fountain enclosure, often in a formalized architectural setting. The fountain in the atrium of a church was occasionally known by this name.

ROBERT OUSTERHOUT

NYMPHAION (modern Kemal Pasha) lies some fourteen miles (twenty-two kilometers) east of İzmir (Smyrna). It was chosen by the Nicene emperor John III Vatatzes (*r.* 1221/1222–1254) as his principal residence. The remains of his palace stand on the edge of the modern village. It resembles the slightly later palace of Tekfur Saray at Constantinople. Two treaties were concluded at Nymphaion. The first, in December 1212, recognized Latin control of northwestern Asia Minor. The second, 13 March 1261, purchased Genoese naval support for a projected attack on Constantinople against exemption from customs duties and the cession of quarters in various cities.

Members of the Nicene court aristocracy established their residences at Nymphaion, but after the recovery of Constantinople in 1261 they left for the capital. Nymphaion then lost much of its importance. Emperor Andronikos II Palaiologos (*r.* 1282–1328) resided there from 1290 to 1293, and it was a center for operations against the Turks. It finally fell to the Turks in 1315.

BIBLIOGRAPHY

H. Ahrweiler, "L'histoire et la géographie de la région de Smyrne entre les deux occupations turques (1081–1317), particulièrement au XIIIe siècle," in Centre des Recherches Byzantines, *Travaux et mémoires,* **1** (1965); S. Eyice, "Le palais byzantin de Nymphaion près d'Izmir," in *Akten des XI: Internationalen Byzantinisten-Kongresses* (1958); Edwin Freshfield, "The Palace of the Greek Emperors of Nicaea at Nymphio," in *Archaeologia,* **49** (1886).

MICHAEL ANGOLD

[See also **Anatolia; Andronikos II Palaeologos; John III Vatatzes; Nicaea, Empire of.**]

Ó BROLCHÁIN, MAOL ÍOSA (*d.* 1086), poet and eminent cleric of the church of Armagh. His death at Lismore in the south of Ireland is noted with suitable eulogistic phrases by all the Irish annals. The Martyrology of Oengus and the Martyrology of Donegal commemorate him on 16 January and list some of his works.

The poet was closely related to the Clann Sínaigh, the controlling family of the abbacy of Armagh, and received his early education at Both Chonais. His writings can serve as a good illustration of the monastic culture of the period between the flowering of Irish monasticism in the previous centuries and the religious reform of the twelfth century, which was underway at the time of his death.

Ó Brolcháin is famed principally as a religious vernacular poet. Many works attributed to him have survived in later manuscripts. These are all personal prayers of the type current in continental sources like the Book of Cerne, for which Celtic origins have been claimed. The techniques are traditionally Irish, with lorica and litany forms predominating. He shows a consistent interest in aligning the separate features of the lorica form with the Seven Deadly Sins and their antidotes. His vernacular hymn to St. Michael has been justly praised. Less certain—though current scholarship seems to favor his authorship—is the attribution to him of several other pieces. Most famous of these is the poem addressed to Crínóc, an old female companion, a clever allegory for his psalter. The corpus of his work is suffused with a spirit of ardent piety. It is a link in an unbroken tradition of Irish vernacular devotional poetry that looks back to the productions of an earlier monastic age and also anticipates in many respects the new ornate religious bardic verse of the thirteenth century.

BIBLIOGRAPHY

Muireann Ní Bhrolcháin, "Maol Íosa Ó Brolcháin agus a chine," in Pádraig O'Fiannachta, ed., *Léachtaí Cholm chille* (1985); David Greene and Frank O'Connor, eds. and trans., *A Golden Treasury of Irish Poetry: A.D. 600 to 1200* (1967); Mairtín Mac Conmara, MSC, ed., *An Léann Eaglasta 1000–1200* (1983); Gerard Murphy, ed., *Early Irish Lyrics* (1956, rev. 1963).

ANN DOOLEY

[See also **Armagh; Irish Literature.**]

Ó DÁLAIGH, DONNCHADH MÓR (*d.* 1244), Irish poet. Nothing is known of the life of this poet save his place in the family genealogy and the date of his death, which is listed in all the Irish annals. Later tradition and the western annals link him with the Cistercian Abbey of Boyle, an abbey founded and patronized by the Uí Conchobhair (O'Connor) kings of eastern Connacht. Since his brother Muiredhach also composed poems for Cathal Crobhderg O Conchobhair, this may well be an authentic tradition.

An immense number of poems are attributed to Donnchadh Mór in later modern paper manuscripts, and the religious revival of the Irish Counter-Reformation seems to have used his name as a way of asserting the Gaelic-Catholic (Irish-Roman) orthodoxy of their verse. Some secular verse is also attributed to him, but the only authentic material may be three poems in the Book of Uí Mhaine (or Uí Maine, late fourteenth century). These are in the strict versification of the bardic schools; nevertheless, the poems succeed in conveying a sense of sincere piety. They look back to the earlier religious tradition of the Irish church for much of their material: descriptions of heaven and hell, the Seven Deadly Sins and their antidotes, litanies of all the saints, lore on the life and death of Christ and the apostles, and the general treatment of fate and the last things. What is new is the detailed contemplation of the Passion of Christ, increased devotion to Mary, self-consciousness about the process of contemplation, and the use of native concepts of the relation of poet and patron to describe the relationship between man and God.

BIBLIOGRAPHY

Lambert McKenna, ed., *Dán Dé* (1922).

ANN DOOLEY

[See also **Irish Literature.**]

Ó DÁLAIGH, GOFRAIDH FIONN (*d.* 1387), Irish poet whose career spanned some sixty years. Later generations of bardic poets held him in highest regard as one of the greatest poets and teachers in the entire bardic tradition. He probably belonged to the Duhallow branch of the Ó Dálaigh poetic family. From internal evidence in his poems we know he attended a bardic school of the MacCraith family, who supplied poets to the chiefs of Thomond, and a poem of his on the rules of poetry survives. His principal patrons were the MacCarthy and Desmond lords, but it is a remarkable feature of his career that many of his poems are written for other chieftains, not just in south Munster but also in Thomond and east Connacht. For example, he was present at, and provided a commemorative poem for, the famous feast for poets given by Ó Ceallaigh of Uí Mhaine (Uí Mhaine) in 1380.

Gofraidh Fionn is quoted extensively in the later fifteenth-century Irish grammatical tracts as a model of correct diction. A favorite device of his is the use of apologue, or exemplary tale. His most often quoted verses are those addressed to the earl of Desmond, in which he speaks of offering the sovereignty of Ireland to Anglo-Norman lords while at the same time urging Irish lords to expel the foreigners totally from Ireland. This has been seen as extreme bardic cynicism vis-à-vis their ancient role as upholders of the political and even cosmic order. But the lines are rather an index of the refinement, sophistication, and courtly elegance of Irish literary culture of the period, a culture embracing both Irish and Anglo-Norman aristocracy and of which the oeuvre of Gofraidh Fionn is such an eloquent testimony.

BIBLIOGRAPHY

Lambert McKenna, ed. and trans., *Dioghluim Dána,* 2 vols. (1938), and *Aithdioghluim Dána: A Miscellany of Irish Bardic Poetry,* 2 vols. (1939–1940).

ANN DOOLEY

[See also **Bard; Bardic Grammars; Irish Literature.**]

Ó DÁLAIGH, MUIREADHACH ALBANACH (*ca.* 1180–1250). This early-thirteenth-century Irish poet is of significance to Irish literary history as one of the first poets of the hereditary families who presided over the transformation of Gaelic learning in the late twelfth and early thirteenth centuries. The genealogical evidence makes him brother to Donnchadh Mór of the Westmeath family of Ó Dálaighs, and this is not unreasonable. Some twenty poems of his survive, of which most are addresses to princes. One, a lament for his wife, is deeply personal, and there are a few religious poems whose transmission is mainly through the Scottish manuscript tradition. Although doubts have been cast on the reliability of this information, the *Annals of Ireland* provide, under the year 1213, several biographical facts, such as that he was poet to O'Donnell but killed his patron's tax collector in anger, thus incurring the wrath of that prince, who pursued him to his several places of refuge with the O'Briens and the Anglo-Norman family of de Burgo, and in the city of Dublin. He is also reputed to have lived for a time in Scotland, hence the nickname *Alban ach*—"Scottish"—and the Scottish tradition which assigns to him the role of founder of the bardic order there and the headship of the bardic family of Mac Vuirrich. There are also a number of pilgrim poems ascribed to him, which indicates that he might have in fact traveled to Jerusalem. Insofar as one can ascertain from his extant and published poems, he was a master craftsman, both of the art of composition in the strict *dán díreach* style and of more simple forms as shown in some of his religious verse. His personality is one of the most vivid in the whole corpus of Irish bardic verse.

BIBLIOGRAPHY

William Gillies, "A Religious Poem Ascribed to Muireadhach Ó Dálaigh," in *Studia celtica,* **14–15** (1979–1980); David Greene and Fergus Kelly, comps. and eds., *Irish Bardic Poetry,* Osborn Bergin, trans. (1970, repr. 1971), Lambert McKenna, ed., *Dioghluim Dána* (1938), and McKenna, ed. and trans., *Aithdioghluim Dána,* 2 vols. (1939–1940); Brian Ó Cuív, "Eachtra Mhuireadhaigh Í Dálaigh," in *Studia hibernica,* **1** (1961).

ANN DOOLEY

[See also **Bard; Irish Literature; Irish Literature: Bardic Poetry.**]

Ó HUIGINN, TADHG DALL (*ca.* 1550–1591). A member of a great bardic family, the Connacht Ó hUiginns, Tadhg Dall (Blind Tadhg) is regarded as sixteenth-century Ireland's greatest court poet. Contemporary documents offer limited biographical information; notices of his fairly substantial property holdings confirm that he had a very successful career, as might be deduced from the status and number of his aristocratic patrons. A 1617 legal memorandum states that he was murdered by some members of the O'Hara family—according to seventeenth-century manuscript tradition, in revenge for a satire.

Like his ancestor Tadhg Óg, Tadhg Dall uses the persona of the *ollamh* (master poet) as a principal element in his work. He handles the traditional materials of bardic verse—conventional epithets and images, units of narrative drawn from history, legend, and genealogy—with the assurance that their significance must be revealed in the present through poetry. The *ollamh* commemorates the events of aristocratic life by offering images of what that life should be. One of Tadhg Dall's favorite devices, the addition of verses of exegesis to the illustrative anecdotes (*uirsgeala*) conventionally inserted in praise poetry, functions as a paradigm of the court poet's role. He is interpreter of the present in terms of the entire cultural tradition.

Technically, Tadhg Dall handles a wide range of strict meters (*dán díreach*) with complete mastery. Some of his poems in less rigorous forms, possibly evidence of an interest in experimentation, are also preserved. A modern reading of his work is inevitably colored by the knowledge that he was composing at the end of a tradition. Tadhg Dall in fact plays with the contemporary poetic topos of the neglect of bardic poetry in favor of vulgar forms: in one poem he praises an aristocratic patron as a "good merchant" who settles accounts by trading transitory wealth for the permanent glory of a poem. With the passing of the bardic order, Tadhg Dall remained the type of the court poet, his fame surviving in the oral tradition until the early twentieth century.

BIBLIOGRAPHY

The Bardic Poems of Tadhg Dall O Huiginn, Eleanor Knott, ed. and trans., 2 vols. (1922–1926).

HEATHER HENDERSON

[See also **Irish Literature: Bardic Poetry; Ó hUiginn, Tadhg Óg.**]

Ó HUIGINN, TADHG ÓG (*d.* 1448). Tadhg Óg (Young Tadhg) Ó hUiginn was born into one of the great bardic families of medieval Ireland, the Connacht Ó hUiginns. Aside from genealogical material, little biographical information is available for Tadhg Óg. Both his father and his brother were working poets. The latter is commemorated in Tadhg Óg's best-known poem, "Anocht sgaoilid na sgola" (Tonight the schools scatter). Among members of the profession, Tadhg was accorded the status of "archpoet." In his obituary in the *Annals of Loch Cé* (1448) he is called "the master teacher of the poets of Ireland and Scotland." The sixteenth-century bardic grammarians frequently cite him as an authority on crucial points of style and usage. Many of his poems are preserved in *duanaireadha* (poem books) that seem to have been assembled as anthologies of the best of bardic poetry, such as the *duanaire* in the Yellow Book of Lecan (written in 1473), which is largely devoted to Tadhg's work.

More than forty poems on religious and secular topics can be attributed to Tadhg Óg. His court poetry is addressed to members of the most prominent aristocratic families of his time throughout the Gaelic cultural area in Ireland and Scotland. He refers to himself as *ollamh* (master poet), and in his verse assumes the role of interpreter of the Irish historical and cultural tradition. The *ollamh* persona thus explains and sanctions events in the present by placing them in the context of the past.

Tadhg Óg's religious verse is characterized by a similar sense of connection between past and present forged through the energy of poetic language. Typically, the speaker prays for mercy with an urgency heightened by constant reference to the approach of death and judgment. Like earlier bardic religious poets, Tadhg Óg draws on both native and European topoi in developing the central image of the divine as all-powerful ruler.

Tadhg Óg's assured handling of the formal and conventional demands of his craft places him among the great practitioners of bardic verse.

BIBLIOGRAPHY

Sources. Poems by Tadhg Óg are found in David Greene and Fergus Kelly, comps. and eds., *Irish Bardic Poetry,* Osborn J. Bergin, ed. and trans. (1970), 61–63, 147–150; Lambert A. J. McKenna, ed., *Dán Dé* (1922), *Dioghluim Dána* (1938), and *Aithdioghluim dána: A Miscellany of Irish Bardic Poetry,* 2 vols. (1939–1940).

Studies. The Bardic Poems of Tadhg Dall Ó Huiginn, Eleanor Knott, ed. and trans., 2 vols. (1922–1926); E. C. Quiggin, "Prolegomena to the Study of the Later Irish Bards, 1200–1500," in *Proceedings of the British Academy,* 5 (1911–1912).

HEATHER HENDERSON

[See also **Irish Literature: Bardic Poetry; Ó hUiginn, Tadhg Dall.**]

O ROMA NOBILIS, an eleventh-century poem in praise of the city of Rome that is often characterized as a "pilgrim song" without any real justification. Its function is difficult to determine because it does not appear in context in any liturgical manuscript. In one manuscript it appears with the text of the love song "O admirabile Veneris idolum," together with a melody in heightened neumes. Another manuscript preserves what appears to be the same melody in a kind of staff notation with solmization letters. Both in form and in style, the melody seems to anticipate many features of later vernacular song.

BIBLIOGRAPHY

Bernard M. Peebles, "O Roma nobilis," in *American Benedictine Revue,* **1** (1950).

ROBERT FALCK

[See also **Neume; Solmization.**]

O'SINAICH, CELLACH (1080–1129), became abbot of Armagh in August 1105, after the death of his great uncle Domnall. Cellach was ordained a bishop in September 1106. Though he became abbot by hereditary succession, Cellach proved to be a vigorous prelate and an active reformer. As such, he is a transitional figure between the old monastic form of the Irish church and the reforms of the twelfth century. He traveled throughout Ireland to expand the influence of Armagh and to use its prestige to curb the violence of contemporary political struggles. Cellach was instrumental in arranging the Synod of Uisnech (1111), which supported the introduction of a diocesan system. Before his death he deliberately attempted to break his family's control of the abbacy by naming St. Malachy as his successor. Upon Cellach's death his family tried to retain their hold on Armagh, but eventually his plan succeeded. Malachy entered Armagh formally as its archbishop in 1134.

BIBLIOGRAPHY
Annals of the Kingdom of Ireland, by the Four Masters, John O'Donovan, ed. and trans., 7 vols. (1856, repr. 1966); *The Annals of Ulster,* William M. Hennessy and Bartholomew MacCarthy, eds. and trans., 4 vols. (1887–1901); Bernard of Clairvaux, *The Life and Death of St. Malachy the Irishman,* Robert T. Meyer, trans. (1978); Tomás Ó Fiaich, "The Church of Armagh Under Lay Control," in *Seanchas Ardmacha,* 5 (1967–1970), pt. 1; Hugh J. Lawlor and Richard I. Best, "The Ancient List of the Coarbs of Patrick," in *Proceedings of the Royal Irish Academy,* 35 (1919).

DOROTHY AFRICA

[See also **Armagh; Celtic Church; Malachy, St.**]

OATH, the invocation of the divine name in witness to the truth. Three Latin terms were used to designate the oath: *iusiurandum, iuramentum,* and *sacramentum.* The first two, deriving from *ius* (a right or a law), indicate its legal character, and *sacramentum,* from *sacrum* (sacred), its religious nature. In Roman law the oath as a form of proof played a much more significant role than it does in modern times.

After some initial hesitation canon law came to consider the oath so important that without it testimony prejudicial to another's interest was not to be believed. Even clerics had to testify under oath.

The Germanic form of trial procedure exerted a strong influence on both canon and civil law. Ecclesiastical authorities more or less consistently resisted *compurgatio vulgaris* (trial by ordeal); finally the Fourth Lateran Council (1215) prohibited clerics from participating in judicial tests or ordeals. The *compurgatio canonica,* on the other hand, involved the accused's taking an oath supported by several of his relatives or kinsmen. The oath helpers, known as *eideshelfer, consacramentales,* or *coniuratores,* swore not to the facts of the case but to the good character of an individual. An oath taker was often referred to as a "hand," perhaps from the practice of raising one's hand while swearing. Thus, in the proof known as the witness of the seventh hand *(testimonium septimae manus)* seven oath helpers took part.

In a unique way the oath secured the bonds of medieval society. The ceremony of homage by which one became a vassal or "commended man" of a lord was sealed with an oath of fealty. The vassal, laying his hand on the Scriptures or on relics of the saints, swore to be faithful to his master. As knights were dubbed, they often took an oath defining their obligations. The commune or autonomous urban community arose as an association of burgesses sworn to maintain and extend their liberties.

BIBLIOGRAPHY
St. Thomas Aquinas, *Summa theologiae,* II–II, q. 89, aa. 1–10; François L. Ganshof, "Charlemagne et le serment," in *Mélanges Louis Halphen* (1961); Bernard Guindon, *Le serment, son histoire, son caractère sacré* (1957); Theodor Körner, *Iuramentum und frühe Friedensbewegung 10–11 Jh.* (1977); Frederick Pollock and Frederic W. Maitland, *The History of English Law,* 2nd ed. (repr. 1968).

JOHN E. LYNCH

[See also **Commendation; Compurgation; Law, German; Ordeals.**]

OATH, MORE JUDAICO (Jewry oath, also known as *juramentum judaeorum*), the oath that Jews were required to take in lawsuits that involved Christians. The oath, which dates back to the fifth century, reflects both the Christian suspicion of the Jews' trustworthiness and the inadmissibility of Jewish testimony against Christians.

The oath contained an invocation of the name of God, followed by curses intended to discourage perjury. These curses eventually became so characteristic that in some regions the oath was named for them. There is evidence that several oath formulas from the early Middle Ages served as prototypes in a number of European countries. In most of them the curses and plagues were taken from the Pentateuch, undoubtedly in order to arouse awe and reverence in the Jew. The one who lied was spared no calamity.

The ceremonial accompanying the oath, generally degrading, differed from land to land and from period to period. The oath was often taken while the Jew, standing, held or touched the Torah. Sometimes a tablet of the Decalogue, kept in the Christian court, replaced the Torah. The Jew either repeated the formula recited to him or simply answered "amen." In Germany the judge or plaintiff held a staff that the Jew touched while pronouncing the oath. He had to stand on a sow's skin and wear his mantle and special hat. In Aragon the Jew knelt in a darkened room lit by a candle while the oath was administered. In tenth-century Byzantium, Jews, standing in water, swore with girdles of thorns around their loins. Other laws demanded that the Jew stand, barefooted or bareheaded, on a bloody lamb's hide or a three-legged stool.

The oath was administered either in court or in the synagogue. In Barcelona it was done in the central square. In Spain, however, in return for a payment, Jews could obtain a partial alleviation or a total exemption. In Aragon entire communities were permitted to take an annual oath in the synagogue on matters necessitating an oath. Privileged Jews enjoyed various advantages, such as upper-class Jewish women in Tortosa, who took the oath at home.

In the Emancipation era opposition was voiced against the oath. Despite certain changes subsequently introduced in the text of the oath and its conditions, the oath persisted long after the formal abrogation of the Jews' disabilities in Europe. In France it was finally annulled in 1846, and in Romania it was administered until 1912.

BIBLIOGRAPHY

H. Beinart, "Jewish Witnesses for the Prosecution of the Spanish Inquisition," in *Essays in Honour of Ben Beinart, Acta judaica* (1978); Guido Kisch, "The Landshut Jewry Oath," in *Historia judaica,* 1 (1938–1939), and *The Jews in Medieval Germany* (1970), 275–287; Bertil Maler, "À propos de quelques formulaires mediévaux du 'sacramentum more judaico,'" in *Stockholm Studies in Modern Philology,* n.s. 5 (1976); A. Scheiber, "The *More Judaico* Oath of Pressburg," in *Zion,* 37 (1972), in Hebrew; Zosa Szajkowski, *Franco-Judaica* (1962), 43–44.

YOM TOV ASSIS

[See also **Jews in Christian Spain; Jews in Europe: After 900; Law, Jewry.**]

OATS. See **Agriculture and Nutrition; Grain Crops.**

OBECO, the painter and scribe of a copy of Beatus of Liébana's *Commentary on the Apocalypse* made at the monastery of Valcavado (León, Spain) in 970 for Abbot Sempronius (Valladolid, University Library, cod. 433). It exhibits an exuberant version of the Mozarabic style.

BIBLIOGRAPHY

Wilhelm Neuss, *Die Apokalypse des hl. Johannes in der altspanischen und alt christlichen Bibel-illustration,* 2 vols. (1931), I, 16–18.

JOHN WILLIAMS

[See also **Apocalypse, Illustration of; Beatus Manuscripts; Mozarabic Art; Pre-Romanesque Art.**]

OCCITAN. See **Provençal Language.**

OCCITANIA. See **Languedoc.**

OCHRID (**Ohrid, Ochrida**), city on the northeastern shore of Lake Ochrid in southwest Macedonia, (modern Yugoslavia), located on the Via Aegnatia and known as Lychnidos in the third century. Ochrid emerged as an important center of Christianity and Slavic letters in the late ninth century when Clement and Naum, two followers of Cyril and Methodios, worked there during the rule of the Bulgarian czar Symeon (*r.* 893–927). In the late tenth and early eleventh centuries Ochrid was Czar Samuil's (*r.* 976–1014) capital and the seat of the revived Bulgarian patriarchate. Conquered in 1018 by the Byzantine emperor Basil II (*r.* 976–1025), Ochrid became an autocephalous archbishopric under Byzantium and controlled the Orthodox churches in southern Slavic lands. Slavic texts, important for the preservation and expansion of the Slavic language and culture, were copied prolifically in Ochrid.

After the creation of the Second Bulgarian Empire (1187), a separate Bulgarian archbishopric was established in Trnovo. In 1219, when the Serbian church was elevated to the status of an autocephalous archbishopric, the archbishop of Ochrid lost his jurisdiction over it. In 1334 Ochrid was conquered by the Serbian king (later czar) Stefan Dušan (*r.* 1331–1355). After the Ottoman conquest Ochrid's ecclesiastical jurisdiction was expanded into Serbian and Bulgarian lands, which lost their own patriarchates. With the reestablishment of the Serbian patriarchate at Peć (1557), Ochrid lost ground, but the archbishopric continued until 1767, when it was abolished by the Ottomans.

Notable preserved medieval churches in Ochrid are St. Panteleimon, built in the second half of the ninth century by Clement, who was buried there; St. Sofia, built in the middle of the ninth century and adorned with numerous frescoes from the eleventh through the fourteenth centuries; and Perivleptos, from the late thirteenth century, containing icons, frescoes, and manuscripts.

BIBLIOGRAPHY

G. Bošković and K. Tomovski, *L'architecture médiévale d'Ochrid* (1957); S. Ćirković, "Pravoslavna crkva u srednjovekovnoj srpskoj državi," in *Srpska pravoslavna crkva,* I (1969); Ferdinando Forlati, Cesare Brandi, and Yves Froidevaux, *Saint Sophia of Ochrida* (1953); B. Granić, "Kirchenrechtliche Glossen zu den vom Kaiser Basileios II dem autokephalen Erzbistum von Achrida verliehenen Privilegien," in *Byzantion,* **12** (1937); S. Novaković, "Ohridska arhiepiskopija u početku XI veka," in *Glas Srp. Kr. Akad.,* **76** (1908); N. L. Okunev, "Fragments de peintures de l'église Sainte-Sophie d'Ohrida," in *Mélanges Charles Diehl,* II (1930); Ivan Snegarov, *Istoria na Ohridskata arkhiepiskopia,* 2 vols. (1924–1931).

BARIŠA KREKIĆ

[See also **Bulgaria; Samuil of Bulgaria; Symeon of Bulgaria.**]

OCKHAM, WILLIAM OF (*ca.* 1285–1347), a Franciscan theologian generally recognized as one of the greatest philosophical minds of the Middle Ages. His thought was particularly influential from the late fourteenth to the early sixteenth century. He has been viewed as the first of the late medieval nominalists.

Ockham was born around 1285, probably in the village of Ockham, southwest of London. His early education would have been received in the neighborhood of his village, perhaps through the village priest or at some nearby religious house. He entered the Franciscan order at an unusually early age, certainly before fourteen, and was probably sent for his philosophical education to the school of the London custody (a subdivision of the Franciscan province of England) maintained at the London convent. There at Southwark in 1306 he was ordained subdeacon by Robert Winchelsey, archbishop of Canterbury. Subsequently, he went to Oxford to study theology, and around 1317–1319 he lectured on the *Sentences* of Peter Lombard as Franciscan bachelor of theology. His *Reportatio* on books II–IV of the *Sentences* dates from this period of his life.

After completing his residency at Oxford, Ockham was sent to a custodial school as lector in philosophy, probably at the Franciscan convent in London; at this time he was in close association with Walter Chatton and Adam Wodeham. This was the most productive period in Ockham's life. During these years he revised his commentary on the first book of the *Sentences* (which became known as his *Ordinatio*), lectured on Aristotle's logic and physics (these lectures are contained in the *Expositio aurea,* the *Expositio super libros Elenchorum,* and the *Expositio in libros physicorum*), and wrote his massive *Summa logicae* and at least the first five of his *Quodlibeta septem* and possibly also his treatises on the Eucharist (*De quantitate* and *De corpore Christi,* the first or both sometimes referred to as *De sacramento altaris*). Attacks on his teaching, especially as occasioned by his natural philosophy in relation to his understanding of transubstantiation, precipitated a summons to the papal court in Avignon to answer charges of heretical teaching. This event, which came only a few months before Ockham was probably to have become regent master at Oxford, brought to an end his academic career.

In the summer of 1324 Ockham crossed the English Channel and traveled south to Avignon. There, in the Franciscan convent, he remained for four years while his case was investigated and his orthodoxy judged. The papal commission charged with his case drew up two lists of suspect propositions by 1327, but no formal action was taken. While at Avignon, Ockham met Michael of Cesena, the minister general of the Franciscans, who was summoned to Avignon in 1327 because of his views on apostolic poverty. At the insistence of Cesena, Ockham studied the papal constitutions on apostolic poverty and became convinced that the pope, John XXII (*r.* 1316–1334), had fallen into heresy.

During the night of 26 May 1328, Ockham, Cesena, and Bonagratia of Bergamo fled to Aigues-Mortes, took a boat to Genoa, and thence traveled to Tuscany, where they joined the entourage and received the protection of Emperor Louis IV of Bavaria, the political opponent of the pope in Italy and Germany. Ockham returned to Bavaria with Louis and remained at the Franciscan convent in Munich for the last two decades of his life. During this period almost all of his writings were political, many of them aimed at what he took to be the false teachings of John XXII and his successors. The most significant of these were his *Opus nonaginta dierum* and his *Dialogus*. Ockham died on 10 April 1347 and was buried in the choir of the Franciscan church at Munich.

The most important fact in understanding Ockham's thought is that he was first and foremost a Franciscan theologian. Although deeply interested in logic and natural philosophy, Ockham rarely concerned himself with a philosophical issue that did not have some theological application. Even his major work in logic, the *Summa logicae,* was written for those who would become theologians. Moreover, while he was thoroughly conversant with the Bible and the major writers of the Christian theological tradition, particularly the scholastic theologians of the previous generation, he was mostly concerned with the thought of his fellow Franciscans, above all John Duns Scotus.

Ockham's attitude toward Scotus was mixed. On the one hand, large sections of Ockham's theology were derived from Scotus or influenced by his thought—for example, Ockham's view of divine omnipotence, his view of grace and justification, much of his sacramental theology, and his ethical system. Even Ockham's epistemology, with its stress on intuitive cognition, must to some degree be understood as developing out of Scotus' epistemology. On the other hand, many aspects of Ockham's thought departed from or specifically rejected Scotistic ideas and approaches. This can be seen most clearly in Ockham's rejection of the formal distinction *ex parte rei* (that is, as applied to created things), his view of predestination and penance, his understanding of universals, and his application of the rule of parsimony or "sufficient reason" to simplify explanations.

GUIDING PRINCIPLES

There were a number of principles or rules that Ockham adopted from his predecessors and applied repeatedly. The first was his firm belief in the total transcendence of God and the utter contingency of all aspects of creation: nothing other than God is absolutely necessary, including the physical and moral laws of our world. This view, basic to Christian theology, had recently found new expression in Scotus, and Ockham's reaffirmation followed that lead.

A second principle was closely related to the first and also derived from Scotus and thirteenth-century thought. This was the distinction between God's power considered by itself (*potentia absoluta*) and that same power considered from the standpoint of his decrees (*potentia ordinata*). Ockham constantly reaffirmed God's omnipotence and the contingent, non-necessary character of things, relationships, and states of affairs. In Ockham's view, God's power, considered absolutely, is the ability to do anything that does not include a contradiction. However, Ockham noted that God, although free, has bound himself to uphold and work within the natural and spiritual orders he has established. Thus God's created order represents only the willed and realized possibilities out of numerous others. This distinction between God's power viewed absolutely or according to his ordinations was an important methodological device that ran throughout Ockham's thought.

The third principle was Ockham's belief that individual substances and qualities are the fundamental physical realities in human experience. Our world is composed of individually existing things. Consequently, it is similarity and universality that need to be explained, not individuation.

By combining these three principles, two subprinciples were derived. First, God can produce or conserve directly one reality or entity without requiring the presence or existence of any other, as long as those entities are distinct. Second, God can produce or conserve directly any effect that is normally produced or conserved through secondary causality. These principles had been reaffirmed in the Parisian Articles of 1277.

A final and fourth principle, frequently invoked, became known subsequently as Ockham's razor. This was the principle of economy, or "sufficient reason": plurality ought not to be posited without necessity. Through this principle Ockham rejected what he saw as unnecessary assumptions or unwarranted inferences in the argumentation of others.

OCKHAM'S NOMINALISM

Many different aspects of Ockham's thought have been referred to under the term "nominalism." By Ockham's nominalism most scholars mean his opinion on the origin and ontological status of the universal concepts around which we organize our thoughts and with which we make propositional statements about external reality. For instance, in the proposition "man is a rational animal," whence come the concepts "man" and "animal" in the human mind, what are they, and what is their relationship to individual things in the observed world of sense experience?

Ockham began with the assumption that individuals are the fundamental reality and that even the mental concept is an individual that is universal only in the sense that it can be predicated of many individuals in external reality. The similarity on which that universality is based is not a figment of the human imagination, but a valid inference from experience. Ockham acknowledged that individuals of the same species were similar. Although in external reality we only encounter particular individuals and never any entity equivalent to species, category, or archetype, our inference that a rose bears a greater resemblance to other flowers and especially to other roses than to any animal is not a misimpression created in the mind but a valid inference grounded in experience.

It was on the issue of the ontological status of similarity that Ockham separated himself from most of his contemporaries and from previous thinkers. Ockham rejected the view, common until his day, that similarity among things of the same species is produced by a common nature that inheres in all things of the same species and makes them alike. For Ockham there are no common natures. Socrates is a rational animal, as is Plato. But they do not "share" rationality as a common nature or possession that makes them rational.

Thus in answer to the ontological question regarding universals, Ockham disallowed both the view of a universal or common nature existing apart from things and the view of a universal or common nature existing in things. He also addressed the epistemological question of universals—that is, how we arrive at a general concept. Ockham affirmed that we do not begin with a universal in mind through which we recognize individual examples in external reality; we begin with our experience of individuals and slowly build up our idea of similarity.

Ockham's position on the nature of the universal concept in the mind changed in the years immediately after 1319. Initially Ockham had held that the universal concept was a mental object, a *fictum* or image created by the mind but possessing no reality other than logical being. Eventually Ockham maintained that the concept was a psychic entity identical with the act of knowing, specifically the act of abstractive cognition. This latter position may be termed modified nominalism or realistic conceptualism.

It is impossible to know whether Ockham's belief in the primacy of the individual and his view of the origin and nature of the universal concept led him to a number of related positions in logic and natural philosophy, or whether his understanding of the relation of language and reality led him to that particular formulation. In his thought they are of one piece, and there is a remarkably high degree of consistency in Ockham's philosophy, particularly between his logic and his natural philosophy. Ockham was opposed to any logic that assigned ontological status to parts of speech, linguistic expressions, or abstract nouns. For him, propositions containing general terms are simplified equivalents for multiple propositions containing singular terms. The only realities for Ockham were substances and qualities, and the other categories, such as quantity, relation, place, motion, and time, were simply descriptions or ways of speaking about substances and qualities.

OCKHAM'S NATURAL PHILOSOPHY

Ockham's understanding of motion, time, place, causality, and relation is integrally related to his logic and his nominalism. His revisionary understanding of nature, which anticipated and perhaps stimulated some developments in subsequent physics, disturbed many of his contemporaries as much as any aspect of his thought.

External reality for Ockham was composed of individually existing things, or substances, and their qualities. The other Aristotelian categories were not separately existing realities, *res extra animam*, but descriptions of substances and qualities in various states. For example, motion was not a *res extra* distinct from things in motion but a way of describing that some thing, present at point *a*, is subsequently present at point *b*. That did not mean for Ockham that motion was broken down into atoms of time, for *continua* were infinitely divisible. Similarly, time was not an entity separate from things in time. Without existing things, time, in our sense, would not exist. Likewise, relations were not entities distinct from the things related or the causes of their being related.

Ockham accepted the reality of natural causation. He added, however, two cautionary observations. The first was that natural causality was not a necessary relationship inherent in the nature of things but rather a relationship established by God that could, in miraculous acts, be suspended. The second was that we do not directly experience the causal connection but instead we make the valid inference, based on past experience, that when *a* is present, under certain conditions *b* will occur.

OCKHAM'S EPISTEMOLOGY AND EMPIRICISM

Ockham's natural philosophy is sometimes characterized as "scientific empiricism," by which two things are usually meant. First, Ockham restricted demonstration in the strict sense (*demonstratio*) to a proposition whose conclusion is certain because its premises are self-evident or derived from propositions that are self-evident. Second, Ockham stressed intuitive cognition: the existential, sensible, direct confrontation between the knowing mind and the existing object.

In the first of these contributions Ockham removed from Aristotelian philosophy the need to support a "scientific" natural theology. In contrast to what is often asserted, Ockham had an ontology and a metaphysics, nor did he fully separate the spheres of faith and reason. But the number of theological truths that could be proved by reason as well as Scripture and church teaching were fewer than for most thirteenth-century thinkers. Christian theology was, for Ockham, unquestionably true, but most of its doctrines could be known only through revelation. In Ockham's system, Aristotelian logic and physics, having been freed from the need to support a "scientific" theology, could proceed to fulfill their proper functions in philosophy and in understanding the physical world surrounding man.

Ockham's contribution to epistemology was more controversial. Building upon Scotus' formulation of intuitive cognition, Ockham defined the latter as the existential knowledge by which we judge an object to exist when it is present to our senses and not to exist or be present when it is not present to our senses. This was in contrast to Aristotelian epistemology, according to which the agent intellect abstracted a composite of intelligible species from the sensible species emanating from an object. They were, in turn, implanted upon the passive intellect. For Ockham, intuitive cognition stressed immediate, existential knowledge by which the mind came into direct contact with the known object.

Several features of Ockham's formulation of intuitive cognition proved difficult or unacceptable to most of his contemporaries. One of these was his complete rejection of sensible and intelligible species, which he felt were unnecessary to an adequate explanation of either knowing or seeing an object. Most contemporaries, including his student and editor, Adam Wodeham, felt that species were necessary in order to explain the physical process of vision. Another feature was Ockham's belief that intuitive cognition informed one of what was not present as well as what was present to the senses, information that others felt was the result of abstractive rather than intuitive cognition. Finally, as theologian, Ockham acknowledged the possiblity of an intuitive cognition of a nonexistent. This could happen, *de potentia Dei absoluta,* because God, as principal sustaining cause of all that happens, could cause directly what he normally causes through a secondary agent. Ockham attempted to protect the certitude of our knowledge by arguing that God could create the intuitive cognition of a nonexistent but could not cause our assent to that cognition or experience. Nonetheless, many of his contemporaries felt that his formulation undermined the certainty of scientific knowledge.

OCKHAM'S THEOLOGY

Ockham's theology was Franciscan, derived in large measure from John Duns Scotus. It was also nominalistic and, in that sense, compatible with his philosophical presuppositions. Most prominent among the parallels between Ockham's philosophy and his theology are his understanding of the contingent, covenantal character of both the physical universe and the theological order of salvation established by God; his use of linguistic analysis as a major tool for the decipherment of philosophical as well as theological problems; his belief that transubstantiation could not be explained by hypothesizing quantity to be a thing distinct from substance and quality; and his grounding of most theological doctrines in revelation and probable arguments based on inference from experience, which parallels his restricted metaphysics.

In general, however, the Scotistic elements of his theology are more prominent than the nominalistic, although they are compatible with it. The central idea that Ockham took from Scotus and from the larger body of earlier theology, particularly from Augustine, was the absolute omnipotence of God, who stands above and outside the categories of our universe and, in this life, is ultimately hidden from our full knowledge. Both the physical universe and the sacramental system of salvation within the church are contingent on God's will, which is one with his reason. At the same time Ockham wished to preserve the integrity and freedom of man, the reliable functioning of the physical and sacramental worlds, and the Franciscan emphasis that God rewards human effort in attaining salvation.

The seeming incompatibility of these two approaches is resolved through Ockham's use of the thirteenth-century distinction between viewing things according to absolute or ordained power. Apart from the plan God has established and actualized for his creation, God is free, limited only by the principle of noncontradiction. God could have arranged things differently; there is no necessity that stands over and above God, determining his actions from without. Yet God has bound himself, and from the area of absolute possibility (*de potentia Dei absoluta*) God has chosen to implement a certain number of possibilities, which he has put into operation in time through his ordinances (*de potentia ordinata*). This solution to the problem of God's freedom and the certitude of the orders of nature and grace, developed in the twelfth and thirteenth centuries and used extensively by Scotus, became a principal tool in Ockham's theology.

Alongside his extensive use of the distinction between the absolute and ordained power of God, Ockham adopted a number of theological teachings fundamental to Scotus, particularly in the area of grace and justification. Ockham retained Scotus' differentiation between a good act and a meritorious act, the latter being based not on the quality of the act or its conformity with the commandments of God, but on God's acceptation (*acceptatio divina*) of that act as worthy of eternal life. Ockham also accepted Scotus' teaching, derived from earlier Franciscan thought, that God had of his own free will committed himself to reward with the gift of grace those who, on the basis of what remained of their natural powers after the Fall (*ex puris naturalibus*), did their best to fulfill the commandments of God (*facientibus quod in se est Deus non denegat gratiam*). If one continued to use that grace to the best of one's ability, God would ultimately reward that person with eternal life.

Ockham altered Scotus' teaching on grace and justification in two important respects. The first change concerned the doctrine of predestination. Scotus had maintained that God's election of those to be saved is based on God's inscrutable will, not on foreseen merits. Predestination occurred for Scotus, in contrast to almost all his contemporaries, before foreseen merits (*ante praevisa merita*). Ockham, in keeping with the majority opinion of the thirteenth century, considered predestination to be based on foreseen merits (*post praevisa merita*).

Ockham's second modification of Scotus' teaching on grace and justification was in the area of penance. Scotus had argued that in order to initiate the return to God, only the barest attrition for one's sins was necessary (*parum attritus*). In this matter as well Ockham sided with the majority opinion of the thirteenth century in holding that a higher level of sorrow and regret was required by God.

At the heart of Scotus' and Ockham's teaching on grace and justification lies the concept that the meritorious quality of a good act is not inherent in the act but is ascribed to it by God, both because the definition of what is good lies in the will of God and because merit is based on acceptation, not acceptation on merit. That same idea was applied by Scotus and Ockham to the sacraments. In contrast to the realm of nature, in which God has implanted certain forces that cause their effects through their own agency as well as the sustaining power of God, the sacraments, de facto, do not operate by inherent virtue for Ockham but by an ascribed virtue or power. For example, it is not some inherent power in the water of baptism, the words of consecration, or the oil of ordination that causes the sacramental effect. Instead, God has established a system whereby he will directly cause the effect when the sacrament is properly performed both in word and in symbol. The only sacrament in which the signs or symbols receive their own inherent virtue is in the Eucharist, where, after consecration, the body and blood of Christ are really present.

A more controversial aspect of Ockham's sacramental teaching was contained in his views on transubstantiation. Ockham believed that the substance of the body and blood of Christ was not produced out of the substance of bread and wine but succeeded to the place previously occupied by the bread and wine. Moreover, the accidental qualities of bread and wine, such as size, shape, color, texture, taste, and odor, which did remain, did not inhere in the quantity (*quantitas*) of bread and wine but inhered in nothing, upheld by the power of God. This last position was based on Ockham's view that quantity cannot be a *res extra*, separate from substance or quality, but is rather a description of a substance with parts extended in space. Ockham's position contradicted Aristotle's view that substance and accidents are always found together in nature, and it was attacked by both Thomists and Scotists.

In keeping with Ockham's general convenantal view, the ethical norms (that is, the laws established by God) are not absolute ethical norms but ones freely chosen by God from a far larger number of possibilities. God could have so arranged things that murder, theft, and adultery would be acceptable acts. He did not, however. Nevertheless, the system chosen by God is not arbitrary, inasmuch as in God his will and reason are one. God's ordained moral system is not only revealed in Scripture; it is written in our hearts in terms of natural law, which we know through the dictates of right reason.

On the practical level Ockham's ethics did not differ greatly from earlier, thirteenth-century views, save in the issue of the degree to which the Ten Commandments are a direct expression of natural law. On the theoretical level, however, Ockham's ethical system is contingent and its content not absolutely necessary. Ethical norms are good because God has chosen them; God did not choose them because they were good.

In the generation following Ockham's departure from England, the general body of his thought remained controversial and attracted only a handful of followers, although individual elements were more influential. The second half of the fourteenth century, however, saw an increasing number of thinkers who shared many of the views of Ockham, principally Pierre d'Ailly. By the fifteenth century Ockham had become one of the principal authorities for a major school within late medieval thought, the nominalists.

BIBLIOGRAPHY

Sources. William of Ockham, *Opera philosophica et theologica* (1967–), and *Opera politica* (1940–). Selected translations may be found in William of Ockham, *Philosophical Writings: A Selection,* Philotheus Boehner, ed. and trans. (1957).

Studies. Léon Baudry, *Guillaume d'Occam: Sa vie, ses oeuvres, ses idées sociales et politiques,* I, *L'homme et les oeuvres* (1949); Philotheus Boehner, *Collected Articles on Ockham* (1958); André Goddu, *The Physics of William of Ockham* (1984); Erich Hochstetter, *Studien zur Metaphysik und Erkenntnislehre Wilhelms von Ockham* (1927); Gordon Leff, *William of Ockham: The Metamorphosis of Scholastic Discourse* (1975); Jürgen Miethke, *Ockhams Weg zur Sozialphilosophie* (1969); Ernest A. Moody, *The Logic of William of Ockham* (1935).

For additional bibliography see Valens Heynck, "Ockham-Literatur 1919–1949," in *Franziskanische Studien,* **32** (1950); James P. Reilly, "Ockham Bibliography: 1950–1967," in *Franciscan Studies,* **28** (1968); Alessandro Ghisalberti, "Bibliografia su Guglielmo di Occam dal 1950 al 1968," in *Rivista di filosofia neoscolastica,* **61** (1969); William J. Courtenay, "Nominalism and Late Medieval Thought: A Bibliographical Essay," in *Theological Studies,* **33** (1972), and "Late Medieval Nominalism Revisited: 1972–1982," in *Journal of the History of Ideas,* **44** (1983).

William J. Courtenay

[See also **Aristotle in the Middle Ages; Duns Scotus, John; Franciscans; Nominalism; Peter Lombard; Philosophy and Theology, Western European; Rushd, Ibn (Averroës); Scholasticism, Scholastic Method; Theology, Schools of; Thomism and Its Opponents; Universals; Via Moderna.**]

OCTATEUCH, the first eight books of the Old Testament (Genesis through Ruth), combined as a textual unit in Byzantium. Though a few earlier fragments are preserved, Octateuchs did not become popular until after the iconoclasm controversy. Six Octateuchs from the eleventh, twelfth, and thirteenth centuries contain illustrations: Vaticanus Graecus 747; Florence, Biblioteca Mediceo-Laurenziana, MS Pluteus 5.38; Vaticanus Graecus 746; Smyrna, Evangelical School, Codex A. I (destroyed 1922); Istanbul, Seraglio, Codex 8; and Mt. Athos, Vatopedi, Codex 602. All but the Florence manuscript have extensive, related picture cycles that illustrate the biblical narrative in great detail. It has been argued that the Octateuch pictorial sequence was invented during the pre-iconoclastic period; but while there is evidence that some parts of this sequence date from at least the sixth century, the actual compilation of the full cycle and most of its imagery must be placed in the tenth century.

BIBLIOGRAPHY

Leslie Brubaker, "The Tabernacle Miniatures of the Byzantine Octateuchs," in *Actes du XVe Congrès international d'études byzantines,* II (1981); Dirk C. Hesseling, *Miniatures de L'Octateuque grec de Smyrne* (1909); Fedor Uspensky, *L'Octateuque de la Bibliothèque du*

Sérail à Constantinople (1907); Kurt Weitzmann, "The Octateuch of the Seraglio and the History of Its Picture Recension," in *Actes du Xe Congrès international d'études byzantines* (1957).

LESLIE BRUBAKER

[See also **Iconoclasm, Christian; Pentateuch.**]

OCTOECHOS is a term used in two different senses. In the first it designates a collection of Byzantine liturgical texts that are chanted from Saturday evening through Sunday, arranged in an eight-week cycle; each week one mode dominates and is used for chanting. This arrangement of texts according to cycles dominated by a single mode spread among the Slavs and a few other neighboring churches. It was a long-standing belief that Severus of Antioch (*d.* 538) deserved credit for this organization, but recent research has established that the ordering of the eight modes is of a later date. A church book containing the texts for the whole week, arranged in eight weekly cycles dominated by a ruling tone in each week—that is, an expanded *octoechos*—is known as a *parakletike.*

In the second sense it is a technical term for a system of eight modes of music. All indications point to Byzantium as the place of origin of this system, though some Syrian roots are likely to have existed at one time. From Byzantium the system spread to the West, into the Gregorian chant (undergoing modifications in the process), and to the Slavic, Armenian, and Georgian churches. Western Syrian Christians also use such a system.

The system consists of eight modes known as *echoi* (singular, *echos:* sound), each of which, definitely not a scale, contains a set of melodic formulas for the openings and endings of chants. While some melodies are characteristic for a single mode, others migrate into other modes. Most chants sung in a single mode use a stock of melodic formulas that are distinctly similar, yet simultaneously flexible and subject to interpretations of individual singers.

Western European and American scholars studying the origin and evolution of the modal system of the *octoechos* are convinced of the system's use of diatonic sequences of tones, avoiding (or using sparsely) chromatic alterations of tones. Eastern Europeans, particularly Greeks, convinced of the stability of oral tradition, accept chromatic alterations and nondiatonic intervals (which Western scholars view as Turkish and Arabic influences).

BIBLIOGRAPHY

Heinrich Husmann, "Modulation und Transposition in den bi- und trimodalen Stichera," in *Archiv für Musikwissenschaft,* 27 (1970), "Die oktomodalen Stichera und die Entwicklung des byzantinischen Oktoëchos," *ibid.*, and "Oktoechos," in *The New Grove Dictionary of Music and Musicians,* XIII (1980); Kenneth Levy, "The Byzantine Sanctus and Its Modal Tradition in East and West," in *Annales musicologiques,* 6 (1958–1963); Jørgen Raasted, *Intonation Formulas and Modal Signatures in Byzantine Musical Manuscripts* (1966); William Oliver Strunk, *Essays on Music in the Byzantine World* (1977); Henry J. W. Tillyard, *The Hymns of the Octoechus,* 2 vols. (1940–1949); Egon Wellesz, *Byzantine Music and Hymnography,* 2nd ed., rev. and enl. (1961).

MILOŠ VELIMIROVIĆ
NICOLAS SCHIDLOVSKY

[See also **Hymns, Byzantine; Liturgy, Byzantine Church; Mode; Music, Byzantine.**]

ODA OF CANTERBURY (*ca.* 890–958), born to pagan Danish parents, was converted to Christianity during his youth. Appointed bishop of Ramsbury by King Athelstan in 927, he was subsequently an ambassador to Hugh Capet, duke of the Franks. In 942 King Edmund offered Oda the archbishopric of Canterbury. He accepted the post, but first received the Benedictine habit from Fleury. As archbishop he instituted numerous reforms, including mandatory annual visits by bishops to their dioceses. Oda also commissioned ten chapters dealing with ecclesiastical discipline and morals; their content was drawn largely from the Legatine Councils of 786. In addition, he asked Frithegod to compose a metrical life of St. Wilfrid of York.

Oda played an important role in the education of his nephew Oswald (later archbishop of York). After being tutored by Frithegod, Oswald was sent to Fleury. Oda died 2 June 958. His designated successor, Ælfrige, died before receiving the pallium. Byrhthelon was then nominated, but he was subsequently asked to return to Wells, his former see. Finally, Dunstan was consecrated archbishop of Canterbury in 960.

The life of Oda "the Good," incorrectly attributed to the monk Osbern, is now ascribed to

Eadmer, who provides further information concerning Oda's life in his *Vita sancti Oswaldi.*

BIBLIOGRAPHY

Oda's writings are in *Patrologia latina,* CXXXIII (1881) 945–952.

The *Vita Sancti Odonis* by "Osbern" is in *Patrologia latina,* CXXXIII (1881), 933–944. See also R. R. Darlington, "Ecclesiastical Reform in the Late Old English Period." in *English Historical Review,* **51** (1936); Max Manitius, *Geshichte der lateinischen Literatur des Mittelalters,* II (1923), 497; G. Schoebe, "The Chapters of Archbishop Oda (942/6) and the Canons of Legatine Councils of 786," in *Bulletin of the Institute of Historical Research,* **35** (1962); Frank M. Stenton, *Anglo-Saxon England* (1943, 2nd ed. 1947, 3rd ed. 1971).

NATHALIE HANLET

[See also **Eadmer of Canterbury; England: Anglo-Saxon; Frithegod.**]

ODDR SNORRASON (*fl.* second half of the twelfth century), a monk in the Icelandic monastery of Þingeyrar, mentioned in Old Norse manuscripts as the author of a Latin biography of King Olaf Tryggvason. This biography is now lost, but a free Icelandic translation of it has been preserved in two rather different versions, often referred to as "Odd's *Óláfs saga Tryggvasonar.*" This work, one of the main sources for Snorri Sturluson's *Heimskringla,* was probably written in the early thirteenth century; its Latin original is believed to have been written at Þingeyrar around 1190. It represents one of the earliest attempts to record oral saga tradition about the Norwegian kings in a large literary composition, and thus is of particular interest to students of saga origins.

It appears from Oddr Snorrason's preface, which has been preserved in one of the Icelandic versions, that he wrote the saga for a clerical audience ("Christian brothers and fathers") in order to promote Olaf Tryggvason's reputation as a missionary and a champion of the Christian faith in Scandinavia. For this reason he sternly rejects the evidence of what he calls "stepmother tales told by shepherds," that is, secular folk tales about the king, and instead tries to structure the biography according to the conventional pattern of Latin saints' lives. It is nevertheless obvious that his narrative is largely based on the very kind of oral saga tradition he officially rejects, even though he tries to make the "stepmother tales" more Christian than they were originally.

Later versions of the *Óláfs saga Tryggvasonar* are largely built on Oddr Snorrason's work, but some of them, especially Snorri Sturluson's version, omitted the hagiographic elements as well as the most obvious elements of pagan folk belief, in an attempt to make the saga seem rational and realistic.

A fantastic *fornaldarsaga, Yngvars saga víðförla*—dealing with a Swedish expedition to Russia in the early eleventh century—is also attributed to Oddr Snorrason, but this attribution is somewhat more doubtful.

BIBLIOGRAPHY

Sources. Saga Óláfs Tryggvasonar af Oddr Munk, Finnur Jónsson, ed. (1932); *Yngvars saga víðfǫrla,* Emil Olson, ed. (1912).

Studies. Bjarni Aðalbjarnarson, *Om de norske kongers sagaer* (1937); Erma Gordon, *Die Olafssaga Tryggvasonar des Odd Snorrason* (1938); Dietrich Hofmann, "Die *Yngvars saga víðfǫrla* und Oddr munkr inn fróði," in Ursula Dronke, *et al.,* eds., *Speculum Norroenum* (1981); Lars Lönnroth, "Studier i Olaf Tryggvasons saga," *Samlaren,* **84** (1963).

LARS LÖNNROTH

[See also **Fornaldarsögur; Iceland; Óláfs Saga Tryggvasonar; Saga; Snorri Sturluson; Yngvars Saga Víðförla.**]

ODDRÚNARGRÁTR, preserved only in Codex Regius 2365, 4°, is one of the Eddic elegies that attach to the legend of Sigurd and Brynhild. It introduces the new figures of Oddrún (Brynhild's sister and Gunnarr's lover after Brynhild's death), her friend Borgný (daughter of King Heiðrekr), and Borgný's lover Vilmundr (referred to as the killer of Hǫgni, Gunnarr's brother). Oddrún learns of Borgný's difficulty in giving birth and comes to her assistance with magic charms. She then launches into a recital of her tragic life. Her father (Buðli) wished her to marry Gunnarr while Brynhild remained a shield maiden (Valkyrie), but Sigurd broke into Brynhild's fortress and deceived her (a cryptic reference to Brynhild's betrothal to Sigurd, the potion that caused Sigurd to forget her, and her subsequent marriage to Gunnarr—all related elsewhere in the legend). Brynhild took revenge and committed suicide, leaving the way open for Oddrún to become Gunnarr's lover. Gunnarr's family offered Oddrún's brother Atli compensation for Brynhild's death in order to make it possible for the lovers to marry, but Atli refused. He then sent spies to expose their love affair and avenged it by casting Gunnarr into a snake pit and cutting out Hǫgni's heart. Gunnarr summoned Oddrún to his aid by striking his harp, but she arrived too late. She concludes her lament with a declaration of her love for Gunnarr.

Oddrúnargrátr has been dated anywhere between the eleventh and thirteenth centuries, but is more likely to be late than early. The new characters (Oddrún, Borgný, and Vilmundr) appear to be apocryphal, and the rehearsal of woes is reminiscent of *Guðrúnarkviða I* and *Helreið Brynhildar*. There are also verbal reminiscences of *Guðrúnarkviða II*. The form of the legend underlying *Oddrúnargrátr* appears to be the version found in *Sigurðarkviða in meiri,* the latest of the Eddic Sigurd poems. Only in this version do we learn the full story of Sigurd's prior betrothal to Brynhild, his abandonment of her in favor of Gudrun, and her revenge. The idea that Sigurd breaks into Brynhild's fortress is found elsewhere only in *Þiðrekssaga* (chap. 168) and appears to originate in a German variant of the tale. This evidence of late composition is, however, contradicted by *Sigurðarkviða in skamma,* which (in stanzas 58–59) summarizes the content of *Oddrúnargrátr* and has verbal reminiscences of *Oddrúnargrátr* (stanzas 20, 28). *Sigurðarkviða in skamma* is generally believed to be slightly older than *Sigurðarkviða in meiri.* The textual relationships are thus unresolved.

BIBLIOGRAPHY

Sources. An edition is Gustav Neckel, ed., *Edda: Die Lieder des Codex Regius nebst verwandten Denkmälern,* 4th ed. rev. by Hans Kuhn (1962). English translations are by Henry A. Bellows, *The Poetic Edda* (1923, repr. 1957, 1969); Lee M. Hollander, *The Poetic Edda* (2nd rev. ed. 1962, repr. 1977).

Studies. Theodore M. Andersson, *The Legend of Brynhild* (1980); Wilhelm Jordan, "Oddruns Klage," in *Germania,* **13** (1868); Wolfgang Mohr, "Entstehungsgeschichte und Heimat der jüngeren Eddalieder südgermanischen Stoffes," in *Zeitschrift für deutsches Altertum und deutsche Literatur,* **75** (1938), and "Wortschatz und Motive der jüngeren Eddalieder mit südgermanischem Stoff," *ibid.,* **76** (1939); Gustav Neckel, *Beiträge zur Eddaforschung mit Exkursen zur Heldensage* (1908); Einar Ól. Sveinsson, *Íslenzkar bókmenntir í fornöld* (1962).

THEODORE M. ANDERSSON

[See also **Brynhild; Eddic Poetry; Guðrúnarkviða I; Guðrúnarkviða II; Helreið Brynhildar; Sigurd; Sigurðarkviða in Meiri; Sigurðarkviða in Skamma; Þiðreks Saga.**]

ODERICUS. See **Oderisi, Pietro.**

ODERISI, PIETRO (Pietro di Oderisio, *fl. ca.* 1267–1274), an Italian sculptor and marbleworker to whom the tomb of Clement IV (sculpted 1271–1274) in S. Francesco alla Rocca, Viterbo, is attributed on the basis of a lost inscription. Scholars have both asserted and denied that Pietro Oderisi is to be identified with either the "Petrus" or the "Odericus" known to have worked in Westminster Abbey, London, from about 1267 to about 1272.

BIBLIOGRAPHY

Julian Gardner, "Arnolfo di Cambio and Roman Tomb Design," in *Burlington Magazine* **115** (1973); John White, *Art and Architecture in Italy, 1250–1400* (1966).

DOROTHY F. GLASS

ODILO OF CLUNY, ST. (962–1049). Born of the Auvergnat nobility, Odilo became fifth abbot of Cluny in 994. Under his vigorous leadership Cluniac usages and daughter houses increased throughout France, Italy, and Spain. Popes granted Cluny temporal immunities and exemptions from episcopal control. Odilo and German emperors provided mutual assistance. He mediated disputes among princes, and helped to extend the Peace of God and Truce of God. He established All Souls' Day and a Cluniac customary. His feast day is 29 April.

BIBLIOGRAPHY

Odilo's writings are in *Patrologia latina,* CXLII (1853), 831–1038. See also Jacques Hourlier, *Saint Odilon, abbé de Cluny* (1964).

THOMAS RENNA

[See also **All Souls' Day; Church, Latin: To 1054; Cluny, Order of; Peace of God, Truce of God.**]

ODIN (Old Norse: Óðinn; Old Germanic: *Wōþanaz, probably leader of the slain) is a major god of Scandinavian mythology. According to *Snorra Edda* (*Gylfaginning,* 4 and 11), he was the All-father: father of all the gods, creator of the cosmos and man. Snorri may have based this Odin theology on his conception of the natural religion of his pagan forebears; the other sources offer a less systematic picture of the mythology and make no god the head of the pantheon. Certainly, however, Odin plays an extremely important role. He was indeed involved in creation; he endowed the first human couple with breath or spirit (Old Norse: *ǫnd*) and, according to Snorri, he and his brothers Vili and Vé killed the protogiant Ymir and created the cosmos from his corpse (*Gylfaginning,* 5). *Vǫluspá* 4 says only that the sons of Bórr—Odin's father—lifted up the earth.

Central to Odin is his thirst for wisdom. To this end he awakens dead seeresses to learn mythic history (*Vǫluspá*) and the fate of Baldr (*Baldrs draumar*); in *Hávamál* 157 he boasts of knowing a charm to make corpses of hanged men talk with him, and other sources note that he consults with the head of Mímir, killed by the Vanir after the war between them and the Æsir. Odin has only one eye. The other is hidden in Mímir's well, apparently as a pledge (*Vǫluspá* 27–28; *Gylfaginning,* 8), and scholars have suggested that Odin obtained additional wisdom from this pledge, maiming his sensory equipment to obtain inner vision.

Important manifestations of wisdom are poetry, magic, and the runic writing system; and Odin sought out each. Poetry and wisdom are associated because the Norsemen transmitted their history in verse form, and perhaps also because skaldic poetry must have required some practice to understand and training to produce; further, it may have promoted group bonds within a chieftain's retinue. Odin obtained the mead of poetry for gods and men in a story alluded to in many kennings of pagan poets and recounted in differing versions in *Hávamál* (104–110) and *Snorra Edda* (*Skáldskaparmál,* 4–6). The versions agree that Odin obtained the mead from the giant Suttungr with the aid of his daughter Gunnloð, whom Odin seduced, and that Odin entered or left the giant's rocky dwelling through a hole drilled for the purpose. Snorri has many additional details on the origin of the mead, Odin's employment with Suttungr's brother Baugi, and his escape from Suttungr in the form of an eagle. The euhemeristic *Ynglinga saga* (7) reports that men held as true everything Odin said; he spoke only in verse, and his priests (*hofgoðar*) were called songsmiths.

His acquisition of runes and magic spells encompasses one of the most emblematic myths of Odin (*Hávamál* 138–145). "I know," he says, "that I hung on the windswept tree for nine full nights, wounded with a spear, given to Odin, myself to myself . . . " (*Hávamál* 138). Hanging and marking with the spear are thought to have characterized the cult of Odin, for which this myth might once have been paradigmatic. After his ordeal, intensified by deprivation of food and drink (*Hávamál* 139), Odin received nine powerful spells and a drink of the mead of poetry, and he could carve, color, and understand runes.

Odin used his wisdom on several occasions. In *Vafþrúðnismál* he overcame Vafþrúðnir, wisest of the giants, in a contest of wisdom. The questions and answers deal with cosmogony, cosmology, and eschatology. Odin's final question, which gives him victory and the giant's head, asks what Odin whispered in the ear of Baldr before the latter mounted the funeral pyre. In *Grímnismál* Odin recites mainly cosmological name lore to the human king Geirrøðr, who, in a scene reminiscent of Odin's self-sacrifice, has set the disguised god between two fires for eight nights. The poem ends with a terrifying epiphany, and the prose coda has Geirrøðr fall on his sword and die.

Odin can use his magic powers to dull his enemies' weapons and blind them with panic; his own warriors fight with supernatural strength, and although they wear no armor, they feel no wounds (*Ynglinga saga,* 6). These are the berserks, whose frenzy recalls that of Odin. Another group of warriors associated with Odin is the *einherjar,* the dead champions who inhabit Valhalla, Odin's hall. There they fight each day but are reconciled by night (*Vafþrúðnismál,* 41; *Gylfaginning,* 25). They await Ragnarǫk, when Odin will lead them in the final battle with the forces of evil. There he will be killed by the Fenris wolf.

Odin's connection with wisdom and ecstasy, and his self-sacrifice on a tree—perhaps Yggdrasill, the world tree—have led many observers to consider a relationship to shamanism, particularly in its Siberian manifestations. The shaman enters a trance, usually induced by rhythmic dance and sometimes with the aid of narcotics. In this state of ecstasy the shaman makes contact with the world of the spirits, sometimes by traveling there. *Ynglinga saga* (6–7) adds additional elements of shamanism to Odin's dossier: he sent his ravens about the world to gather news for him. A shape-changer, he lay as though dead or asleep, and in the form of an animal traveled to distant lands. He also practiced *seiðr*, a form of magic reminiscent of shamanistic practices and better suited to priestesses.

Cognates of Odin in other Germanic areas include Woden in England and Wotan in Germany. The former gave his name to the day of the week Wednesday and was thus equated with Mercury, who, perhaps as god of trade, was imported to Germania during late antiquity. Tacitus reported that the Germans worshiped Mercury, and many other sources indicate worship of this god, presumably called Wotan in the vernacular. Some scholars have argued that the cult of Woden/Odin spread from south to north and replaced that of *Tīwaz (Týr). The relative lack of ancient place-names indicating worship of Odin in western Norway and Iceland may support this hypothesis and suggest that such worship expanded during the Viking age, perhaps amid changing social circumstances. However, Georges Dumézil has adduced Indo-European parallels of an awesome, magico-religious sovereign god and regards Odin as fulfilling this function.

BIBLIOGRAPHY

Georges Dumézil, *Gods of the Ancient Northmen* (1973); Karl Helm, *Wodan: Ausbreitung und Wanderung seines Kultes* (1946); Otto Höfler, *Kultische Geheimbünde der Germanen* (1934); Finnur Jónsson, ed., *Edda Snorra Sturlusonar* (1931); Åke Ström and Haralds Biezais, *Germanische und baltische Religion* (1975); Folke Ström, *Den döendes makt och Oden i trädet* (1947); Edward O. G. Turville-Petre, *Myth and Religion of the North* (1964, repr. 1975), and *Nine Norse Studies* (1972); Jan de Vries, *Contributions to the Study of Othin, Especially in His Relation to Agricultural Practices in Modern Popular Lore* (1931), and *Altgermanische Religionsgeschichte,* II (1957, 3rd ed. 1970).

JOHN LINDOW

[See also **Æsir; Baldrs Draumar; Eddic Poetry; Fenris Wolf; Frigg; Grímnismál; Hávamál; Scandinavian Mythology; Snorra Edda; Snorri Sturluson; Vafþrúðnismál; Vanir; Vǫluspá.**]

ODINGTON, WALTER (Walter of Evesham) (*fl.* 1280–1320), English scientist and musician, monk of St. Mary's, Evesham. In 1298 he was an administrator of Gloucester College, a Benedictine college in Oxford, and about 1316 he gave his deliberations (that is, made his initial public disputation) at Oxford.

Odington's works include treatises on alchemy (*Icocedron*), music (*Summa de speculatione musicae*), astronomy (*Declaratio motus octavae spherae*), geometry (translation of book V of Euclid's *Elements*), and arithmetic (*Ars metrica*), an almanac for Evesham, and *De multiplicatione specierum.* His best-known works are the *Icocedron,* in which his thinking presages that of Richard Swineshead, and the *Summa,* a comprehensive and systematic exposition of music theory and practice. Part VI of the *Summa* presents the only contemporary guide to English mensural polyphony, explaining the notation of rhythm by notes of differing lengths (mensuration) and outlining the various polyphonic musical forms of the day.

BIBLIOGRAPHY

Sources. The *Summa* has been published twice: Edmond de Coussemaker, ed., in *Scriptorium de musica medii aevi,* I (1864, repr. 1963); Frederick F. Hammond, ed., *Walteri Odington Summa de speculatione musicae* (1970). Part VI was translated by Jay A. Huff as *Walter Odington: De speculatione musicae Part VI* (1973).

Studies. Frederick F. Hammond, "Odington, Walter," in *The New Grove Dictionary of Music and Musicians,* XIII (1980); Donald Skabelund and Phillip D. Thomas, "Walter of Odington's Mathematical Treatment of the Primary Qualities," in *Isis,* 60 (1969); Phillip D. Thomas, "The Alchemical Thought of Walter of Odington," in *Actes du XIIIe Congrès international d'histoire des sciences* (1968), and *idem,* ed., "David Ragor's Transcription of Walter of Odington's *Icocedron,*" in *Wichita State University Studies,* 76 (1968); Lynn Thorndike, *A History of Magic and Experimental Science,* III (1934), 127–132, 682–684.

ALEJANDRO ENRIQUE PLANCHART
ELAINE GOLDEN ROBISON

[See also **Alchemy; Musical Notation, Western; Swineshead.**]

ODO OF CLUNY, ST. (*ca.* 879–944), was the second abbot of Cluny. Born of noble parents, he was raised at the court of William of Aquitaine. He rejected the knightly life, however, and became a canon at Tours. He turned from the study of classical letters to the Scriptures. Following a stay at Baume as a monk, Odo succeeded Berno as abbot of Cluny in 927, and made Cluny the center of monastic reform throughout Gaul and Italy. He restored the Benedictine Rule and the autonomy of monasteries. Rudolf II of Burgundy, king of the Franks, gave Cluny a charter. Pope John XI granted Cluny exemptions and the right to receive monks from unreformed houses. Odo arbitrated disputes, received many donations of land, and did much to extend the influence of monastic ideals. He wrote a *Life* of Gerald of Aurillac as a model for the secular nobility. His *Collations* and *Moralia in Job* reflect early Cluniac spirituality and humanistic culture. After naming a successor, Odo died at Tours.

BIBLIOGRAPHY

Odo's writings are in *Patrologia latina,* CXXXIII (1881), 9–816. Studies include Barbara Rosenwein, *Rhinoceros Bound: Cluny in the Tenth Century* (1982); Gerard Sitwell, ed. and trans., *St. Odo of Cluny* (1953).

THOMAS RENNA

[See also **Benedictine Rule; Benedictines; Cluniac Rite; Cluny, Order of; Monasticism.**]

ODO OF METZ (*fl.* late eighth century), architect. A lost inscription, allegedly recorded in situ but not corroborated by other medieval sources, names Odo as builder of Charlemagne's chapel at Aachen: "Emperor Charles the Great ordered this distinguished hall of state; the excellent *magister* Odo executed it; he lies beloved in the city of Metz."

BIBLIOGRAPHY

Wolfgang Braunfels, ed., *Karl der Grosse,* III (1965), 532–533; Ludwig Falkenstein, *Der "Lateran" der karolingischen Pfalz zu Aachen* (1966), 7; Oswald Holder-Egger, ed., *Einhardi Vita Karoli Magni* (1911), vii; Julius von Schlosser, *Schriftquellen zur Geschichte der karolingischen Kunst* (1892), 28.

DALE KINNEY

[See also **Aachen, Palace Chapel; Pre-Romanesque Architecture.**]

ODO OF MEUN (also called Odo Mugdunensis, *fl.* early eleventh century) was a practicing doctor who wrote a very popular poem on the use of herbs, often ascribed to a pseudonymous "Macer." *De viribus herbarum* (On the power of herbs) consists of 2,269 Latin hexameters. Of its seventy-seven sections, sixty-five list individual herbs and their uses, while the last twelve describe twelve spices. The work draws on ancient sources and folk medicine and has little poetical merit.

BIBLIOGRAPHY

Macer Floridus, *De viribus herbarum,* Ludwig Choulant, ed. (1832), and *A Middle English Translation of Macer Floridus' De viribus herbarum,* Gösta Frisk, ed. (1949). See also Max Manitius, *Geschichte der lateinischen Literatur des Mittelalters,* II (1923).

W. T. H. JACKSON

[See also **Botany; Herbals, Western European; Medicine, History of.**]

ODOACER (*ca.* 433–493), a Germanic barbarian, either Scirian or Rugian, son of Edeco, one of Attila's generals. Odoacer made his way to Italy, where he joined the Roman army and rose to a position of command. He was involved in a rebellion of troops against Orestes, who had become commander *(magister militum)* in 475, demanding distribution of lands, as had been provided for federates *(foederati)* in southwest and southeast Gaul. On Orestes' refusal to meet this demand, the troops elected Odoacer king. Orestes was captured and killed, and the emperor he had created, his son Romulus Augustulus, was deposed and exiled to Campania.

Odoacer named no new emperor but asked that the Eastern emperor Zeno regularize his position. The title of patrician may have been granted, but he normally styled himself "king." He distributed the land (principally in the Po Valley) promised to the troops, maintained the old Roman administration, worked closely with the Senate, and cooperated with the Catholic church (he himself was an Arian). Odoacer's dominions were at first limited to Italy and parts of Raetia and southern Noricum (Alpine areas north of Italy); but during his "reign" he secured Sicily from the Vandals in return for an annual tribute, and in a series of successful campaigns he defeated the barbarians living in Dalmatia and northern Noricum, although he did not attempt to extend his control over these two territories.

Odoacer's successes evidently aroused the fear of the Eastern emperor, and this fear, coupled with a need to settle the problem of the troublesome Ostrogoths, led Zeno to commission the Ostrogoths, under their king, Theodoric, to go west to Italy and restore it to imperial control.

The Ostrogoths crossed the Julian Alps in 488–489. Odoacer, defeated twice in the field, retired to Ravenna, from which he came forth several times, only to be defeated. Between 489 and 493 Theodoric gradually secured the submission of most of Italy, working with the Catholic clergy. (Theodoric, rather than Odoacer, was regarded as the official representative of the empire.) In February 493, Odoacer was induced to accept an agreement with Theodoric that would allow the two kings to share the government of Italy. At a banquet celebrating this event, Theodoric killed Odoacer and his followers massacred the followers of Odoacer.

There is little contemporary information for the period of Odoacer, and it is difficult to evaluate the success of his reign. Although his position did not differ markedly from that of earlier emperor-makers, circumstances did not support his efforts to establish a legitimate rule in Italy. Since his kingdom did not rest on leadership of a single Germanic tribe but, rather, upon a heterogeneous group of German soldiers who were technically serving in the Roman army, Odoacer's Italy is not regarded as one of the Germanic kingdoms. In many ways, however, Theodoric copied his policies but was much more effective in getting public support.

BIBLIOGRAPHY

John B. Bury, *History of the Later Roman Empire,* I (1923); Pierre P. Courcelle, *Histoire littéraire des grandes invasions germaniques,* 3rd ed. (1964); Walter A. Goffart, *Barbarians and Romans A.D. 418–585* (1980); Ludwig M. Hartmann, *Geschichte Italiens im Mittelalter,* I (1897, repr. 1969); Thomas Hodgkin, *Italy and Her Invaders,* 2nd ed., II (1892) and III (1896, both repr. 1931); Arnold H. M. Jones, *The Later Roman Empire, 284–602,* I (1964); Joseph Vogt, *The Decline of Rome,* Janet Sondheimer, trans. (1967).

KATHERINE FISCHER DREW

[See also **Barbarians, Invasion of; Ostrogoths; Roman Empire, Late; Theodoric the Ostrogoth.**]

ODOFREDUS (*fl.* mid thirteenth century), professor of law at the University of Bologna and, in the opinion of the Carlyles, the most important scholar of the period in that subject. His *Commentary on the Digest* and *Commentary on the Code* were standard textbooks throughout the later Middle Ages. He was a supporter of imperial authority and believed that the pope had no power over the emperor in temporal affairs (although following a vacancy, the pope confirmed the new emperor). In theory, according to Odofredus, all men should be subject to the emperor; in an age of independent principalities, however, that was not possible. On the problem of the relationship of custom and law, Odofredus maintained, against Placentinus, that the Roman people could continue to make law (and that their customs might abrogate certain laws) even though, as a general matter, they ceded the right to make law to the emperor when they gave him his power. He, in turn, was bound by the law and had no right to the property of his subjects.

Odofredus is the source of much of our information about the early history of the law school of Bologna. He also left a sort of prospectus of his own method of teaching the *Digest,* one of the few statements of this kind from a medieval professor.

BIBLIOGRAPHY

Robert W. Carlyle and A. J. Carlyle, *A History of Mediaeval Political Theory in the West,* V (1928), 48–49, 66–67, 97, 102, 141, 355–356; Charles H. Haskins, *The Renaissance of the Twelfth Century* (1927), 203–204; Hastings Rashdall, *The Universities of Europe in the Middle Ages,* I, new ed. by F. M. Powicke and A. B. Emden (1936), 105–114.

JOSEPH R. STRAYER

[See also **Corpus Iuris Civilis; Law, Schools of; Placentinus; Political Theory, Western European: After 1100.**]

OECUMENICAL COUNCILS. See **Councils, Ecumenical.**

OECUMENICAL PATRIARCH. See **Ecumenical Patriarch; Patriarch.**

OFFERTORY (Latin: *offertorium, offerenda*), a chant of the proper of the Mass, sung as the offerings of the faithful are received. At one time the offerings were brought to the altar in a procession (and since the Second Vatican Council this custom has been revived). The texts of the offertories are most often drawn from the Book of Psalms. They are set to music in such a way that there are frequently several notes to a syllable, sometimes only one note, and occasionally many notes (a melisma). In manuscripts of the tenth through twelfth centuries, there are verses for this chant. Their style is in general like that of the first section, known as the antiphon (though in function it is more like a respond); the last part returns after each of the verses as a refrain. Later sources omit the verses; this seems to have resulted from the discontinuing of the offertory procession.

Although one might expect offertory texts to include references to offering or sacrifice, such is not often the case; they may be prayers, songs of praise, or even narratives—descriptions of scenes or events. One distinctive feature is the repetition of phrases and sometimes of individual words. If the phrase is repeated immediately, the music is varied, made more elaborate. If the phrase returns after other material has intervened, the music accompanying it does not change.

There is a different offertory for nearly every Sunday in the year and for major feasts and saints' days. One eleventh-century manuscript, Montpellier, Bibliothèque de l'École de Médecine, H. 159, includes 104 offertories, distributed among the ecclesiastical modes as follows: modes 1 and 2, twenty-eight; 3 and 4, twenty-nine; 5 and 6, sixteen; and 7 and 8, thirty-one. In some other manuscripts the number is slightly larger; but the repertory is not much subject to change. To some writers, the style of the verses seems to differ significantly from that of the opening parts of these chants, particularly in the long melismas in which some of them end, but also in other ways. There are hints in some medieval works on music that verses for the offertory may at one time have been sung to formulas rather than having had independent melodies; but these hints are difficult to interpret and there is no longer a consensus concerning them.

BIBLIOGRAPHY

Willi Apel, *Gregorian Chant* (1958), 363–375; J. Dyer, "The Offertory Chant of the Roman Liturgy and Its Musical Form," in *Studi musicali,* **11** (1982); Helmut Hucke, "Die Texte der Offertorien," in Heinz Becker and Reinhard Gerlach, eds., *Speculum musicae artis* (1970); Josef Jungmann, *The Mass of the Roman Rite,* Francis A. Brunner, trans., II (1959), 26–31; *Liber usualis,* ed. by the Benedictines of Solesmes (1962); Carolus Ott, *Offertoriale sive versus offertorium* (1935).

RUTH STEINER

[See also **Antiphonal; Gregorian Chant; Mass; Psalm Tones.**]

OFFICE. See **Divine Office; Rhymed Office.**

OGEE ARCH. See **Arch.**

OGHAM, a special alphabet for writing Irish, attested from Ireland and those parts of Britain (Wales, Cornwall, the Isle of Man, Scotland) colonized by Irish settlers. The word "ogham" (earlier: *ogom, ogum*) is apparently related etymologically to Gaulish Ogmios, a god of eloquence. The surviving examples of ogham are almost all confined to inscriptions on stones dating from an undefined period probably before the seventh century. About 375 such inscriptions have survived; they are most heavily concentrated in the southwest of Ireland, spreading eastward and then north from there in a pattern that may reflect the progress of the Érainn tribe. The great majority of these inscriptions consist of a proper name in the genitive case, followed by a patronymic: for example, *Corbagni maqi Biviti* (of Corbagnas son of Bivitas). References to the writing of ogham on stone pillars and wooden staves in early Irish heroic literature suggest that many of them had a funerary purpose, while others carried cryptic messages and incantations; they may also have served to prove title to property and to define boundaries.

The original ogham alphabet consisted of twenty letters made of straight grooves and notches cut on a central vertical line (Irish: *druim*)—that line being the angle formed by the face and an adjacent side of a stone slab. The twenty letters fall into four groups (Irish: *aicme*) of five letters, the first letter in each group consisting of one mark, the second of two, and so on. All letters carry the Irish names of trees and shrubs and each group is called after its first (one-mark) letter. (A chart of ogham accompanies the article "Alphabets" in this *Dictionary*.) Letters in the B-group are formed by grooves cut on the face of the stone, at right angles to the central line; those of the H-group consist of grooves cut on the side of the stone, again at right angles to the central line; the M-group cuts diagonally across the central line; the A-group (the five vowels) consists of notches cut into the central line. Later, in the historical period, other letters were added, apparently to the form of ogham written into manuscripts: *p* (a sound originally absent from the Goidelic branch of Celtic) and various diphthongs. Occasionally a second symbol for *c* (perhaps for *cc*) occurs as a cross intersected by the central line. The symbol for *f* denotes a *w* or *v* in the earlier inscriptions; that for *h* occurs only in later inscriptions (perhaps influenced by Irish use of *h* from the Latin alphabet), while that for *z* is not reliably attested.

The origins of the ogham alphabet remain uncertain. The theory that it is based on the runic alphabet has not won much approval. Most scholars prefer the explanation that ogham derives from the Latin alphabet as taught by late Latin grammarians such as Donatus in the fourth century. But since some of the inscriptions have been dated to the early fifth century this explanation presupposes an extraordinarily rapid diffusion of the new alphabet. For this and other reasons some scholars (especially archaeologists) believe that ogham was introduced into Ireland by a Goidelic people centuries before the proposed fourth-century date. Whatever the immediate origins of the alphabet, the form and organization of its letters probably go back much earlier, to a primitive system of counting that marked notches on a tally stick and reckoned up to twenty units on the basis of the twenty digits of the human body.

Even after the introduction of the Latin alphabet in Ireland, ogham continued to be used and studied among the learned classes, as evidenced by its occasional presence in medieval Irish manuscripts, for example, a ninth-century copy of Priscian (St. Gallen, Stiftsbibliothek MS. 904) and a tract on ogham in the fourteenth-century Book of Ballymote (Dublin, Royal Irish Academy MS. 23 P 12).

BIBLIOGRAPHY

Sources. The most comprehensive (though neither complete nor entirely accurate) edition of the ogham inscriptions is R. A. S. Macalister, *Corpus inscriptionum insularum celticarum*, I (1945). See also A. A. Korolev, *Drevneishie pamiatniki irlandskogo iazyka* (1984).

Studies. For bibliography up to 1941, see R. I. Best, *Bibliography of Irish Philology and of Printed Irish Literature* (1913), 54–55, and *Bibliography of Irish Philology and Manuscript Literature* (1942), 52–53. See also James Carney, "The Invention of the Ogom Cipher," in *Ériu*, **26** (1975); Kenneth Jackson, *Language and History in Early Britain* (1953), 149–153; Maud Joynt, ed., *Contributions to a Dictionary of the Irish Language: N-O-P* (1940); Wolfgang Keller, "Die Entstehung des Ogom," in *Beiträge zur Geschichte der deutschen Sprache und Literatur*, **62** (1938); Éoin MacWhite, "Contributions to a Study of Ogam Memorial Stones," in *Zeitschrift für celtische Philologie*, **28** (1960–1961); Rudolf Thurneysen, *A Grammar of Old Irish*, D. A. Binchy and O. Bergin, trans. (1946); J. Vendryes, "L'écriture ogamique et ses origines," in *Études celtiques*, **4** (1940).

PÁDRAIG P. Ó NÉILL

[See also **Alphabets; Auraicept Na nÉces; Celtic Languages.**]

OGIVE ARCH. See **Arch.**

OIL PAINTING. Traditionally credited as the invention of the great Flemish painter Jan van Eyck (*d.* 1441), this technique is already recorded in fourteenth-century handbooks, such as that of Cennino Cennini. It used oil, especially linseed oil, rather than egg yolk or water as a binding medium for paint pigments and offered the advantages of greater flexibility, richness of color, and adherence to a support. Combined with translucent glazes, oil pigments could be built up in layers to suggest effects of luster and reflected lights in depth. The technique won fame for fifteenth-century Flemish painters like van Eyck and later became the glory of sixteenth-century Venetian painting.

BIBLIOGRAPHY

Paul Coremans, *L'agneau mystique au laboratoire* (1953); Elisabeth Dhanens, *Hubert and Jan van Eyck* (1980), 68–70; Charles Eastlake, *Materials for a History of Oil Painting* (1847); Erwin Panofsky, *Early Netherlandish Painting* (1953), 151–153; Alexandre Ziloty, *La découverte de Jean van Eyck* (1947).

LARRY SILVER

[See also **Cennini, Cennino; Flemish Painting.**]

Twin stelae from Ōjun, 7th century. FROM SIRARPIE DER NERSESSIAN, *ARMENIAN ART* © 1977 Arts et Métiers Graphiques, Paris

ŌJUN. The Armenian church of Ōjun is a large-domed basilica with vaulted porticoes on three sides. It was constructed in northern Armenia during the sixth or seventh century; according to the historian Kirakos Ganjakec^{c}i (thirteenth century) some additions were made by Bishop Yovhan of Ōjun in the eighth century.

Ōjun is notable for its reliefs of Christ and angels on the south and east facades, among the earliest known figural sculpture in stone on the exterior of a Christian church. Nearby are tall obelisk-shaped twin stelae set on a stepped platform. They date from the sixth or seventh century and are carved with panels of figured reliefs about the story of Armenia's conversion to Christianity.

BIBLIOGRAPHY

Architettura medievale armena (Roma-Palazzo Venezia, 10–30 Giugno 1968) (1968); L. Azarian, "Ōjuni ew Brdajori Kot'ołnerė," in *Patma-banasirakan Handes,* no. 4 (31) (1965); Sirarpie Der Nersessian, *The Armenians* (1970), and *Armenian Art,* Sheila Bourne and Angela O'Shea, trans. (1977 and 1978); V. Harouthiounian and M. Hasratian, *Monuments of Armenia* (1975); G. Hovsepian, "Sepulchral Steles and Their Archaeological Value for the History of Armenian Art" (in Armenian), in *Materials for the Study of Armenian Art and*

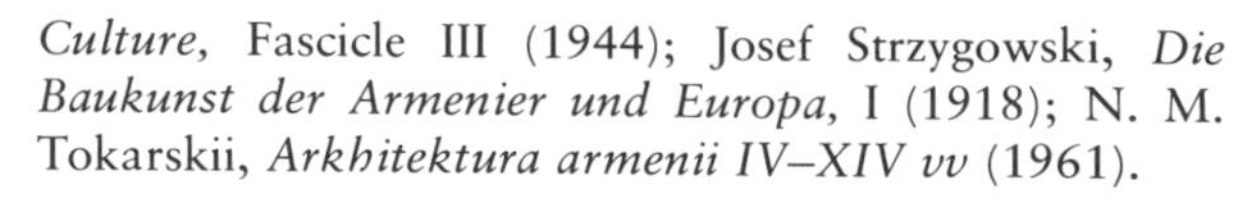

Culture, Fascicle III (1944); Josef Strzygowski, *Die Baukunst der Armenier und Europa,* I (1918); N. M. Tokarskii, *Arkhitektura armenii IV–XIV vv* (1961).

LUCY DER MANUELIAN

[See also **Armenian Art.**]

OKOL'NICHIE. See **Duma.**

OKTOECHOS. See **Octoechos.**

ÓLÁFS SAGA HELGA (The saga of St. Olaf), an Old Norse saga, preserved in several different versions, about King Olaf Haraldsson of Norway, saint and martyr (*b. ca.* 995, ruled from 1015, *d.* 29 July 1030 in the Battle of Stiklestad). The saga is based partly on skaldic poetry, partly on popular oral tales, and partly on the official church legend of his martyrdom and miracles. It is possibly the oldest and certainly the longest and most important of the early *konunga sǫgur* (sagas of the kings) written in Norway and Iceland from about 1170 to about 1300.

The earliest version is the so-called *Oldest Saga,* of which only a few fragments remain. It is believed to have been written in Iceland, possibly in the monastery of Þingeyrar, before 1180, although Louis-Jensen has recently shown that it may have been written somewhat later. It appears to have been a loosely structured collection of tales and anecdotes about the king, built largely on skaldic tradition.

The next version is the *Legendary Saga,* which is represented by a Norwegian manuscript (Uppsala, University Library, *De la Gardie 8*) from about 1250. It combines the material from the *Oldest Saga* with material from the official church legend about the martyrdom and miracles of St. Olaf. The secular stories about the Viking king and his skalds have been placed in a hagiographic framework to serve the interests of the Norwegian church. Another hagiographic version, also based on the *Oldest Saga* in combination with the saint's life, was written by the Icelandic priest Styrmir Kárason, probably in the 1220's. It is now lost, apart from some fragments that show it to have had a more amplified and rhetorical style than *Legendary Saga* or *Oldest Saga.*

Shortly afterward, about 1230, the Icelandic chieftain Snorri Sturluson composed the version that has ever since been regarded as the "classical" one. In it the various tales and anecdotes are subordinated to an overall plan that is not hagiographic, but is inspired by Icelandic saga tradition as well as by secular biographics in the Latin tradition. The rise and fall of Olaf's power in Norway is presented as a logical sequence of events, a function of the king's character and of the political conflicts in which he became involved. Olaf himself is pictured primarily as a shrewd and pragmatic ruler and military leader. He acquires the qualities of a saint only toward the end of the saga, and the hagiographic tone is present only in the reports of miracles occurring after his death. This saga was first composed as an independent work, but it was later incorporated into Snorri's *Heimskringla.*

In later Norse redactions of *Óláfs saga helga,* Snorri's version was used as the basic text, but it was expanded with material from the older versions and from family sagas.

BIBLIOGRAPHY

Sources. Otte brudstykker af den ældste saga om Olav den hellige, Gustav Storm, ed. (1893); *Óláfs saga hins helga,* Oscar A. Johnsen, ed. (1922); *Den store saga om Olav den hellige,* Jón Helgason and Oscar A. Johnsen, eds. (1930–1941); Snorri Sturluson, *Heimskringla,* Bjarni Aðalbjarnarson, ed., II (1945).

Studies. Theodore M. Andersson, "Kings' Sagas (*Konungasögur*)," in *Old Norse-Icelandic Literature: A Critical Guide* (1985); Anne Holtsmark, "Óláfs saga helga," in *Kulturhistorisk leksikon for nordisk middelalder,* XII (1967); Oscar A. Johnsen, "Olavs-sagaens genesis," in *Edda,* 6 (1916); Jónas Kristjánsson, "The Legendary Saga," in *Minjar og menntir* (1976); Jonna Louis-Jensen, "Syvende og ottende brudstykke," in *Bibliotheca Arnamagnæana,* 30 (1970); Sigurður J. Nordal, *Om Olav den helliges saga* (1914); Fredrik Paasche, "Heimskringlas Olavssaga," in *Edda,* 6 (1916); Johan Schreiner, "Studier i Olav den helliges saga," in *Arkiv för nordisk filologi,* 43 (1927).

LARS LÖNNROTH

[See also **Norse Kings' Sagas; Skaldic Poetry; Snorri Sturluson.**]

ÓLÁFS SAGA TRYGGVASONAR, an Old Norse saga that exists in several quite different versions, about King Olaf Tryggvason, an obscure and short-lived Viking leader who died in the year 1000 and is said to have been the first king to support the Christianization of Norway and Iceland. Early sources, such as Adam of Bremen's *Gesta hammaburgensis ecclesiae pontificum,* picture him neither as saintly nor as heroic, but by the latter half of the twelfth century several chronicles praise him as "the Apostle of the North" and as a major saga hero. Many of the oral tales on which the *Óláfs saga Tryggvasonar* was based were evidently circulating at this time in Iceland and in the Trondheim area of Norway.

The first major biography, a collection of such tales, was written in Latin around 1190 by Oddr Snorrason, a monk in the Icelandic monastery of Þingeyrar. Another monk in the same monastery, Gunnlaugr Leifsson, expanded this version around 1200. Both works are now lost, but they are believed to have formed the ultimate basis for the later written sagas about Olaf Tryggvason. Of these the best known and most admired is the one attributed to Snorri Sturluson (around 1230) and incorporated into his *Heimskringla* (History of the Norwegian kings). Other versions are included in the manuscript *Fagrskinna,* in a free translation of Oddr Snorrason's lost work, and in the so-called *Longest Saga of Olaf Tryggvason,* a compilation found in fourteenth-century manuscripts.

Although these versions are widely divergent—some are "clerical" and stress Olaf's Christian virtues while others are "secular" and stress his qualities as a Viking leader—the basic structure is always the same, a curious mixture of saint's life and saga. Olaf is portrayed as a noble heathen chosen by God to convert the Norsemen. Like Christ, he suffers persecution as a child, and his mother has to take him away to Sweden. As a young boy he is abducted by pirates, sold as a slave, miraculously rescued, and brought to the Russian court, where he becomes the king's foster son. Later he leads Viking expeditions against England and other Western European countries, until one day he is converted to Christianity. He decides to return to Norway and claim the throne as the first Christian ruler. He must fight the heathen forces of Earl Hákon the Great, but he eventually succeeds to the throne and then sets about converting his subjects, often by force and sometimes, when they resist, with considerable brutality. In the course of this crusade he incurs the enmity of the heathen kings of Denmark and Sweden, who finally attack him in the famous sea battle of Svǫldr, where he is said to have drowned after a magnificent defense. According to some versions, however, he escaped from the battle and decided to spend the rest of his life anonymously as a holy monk or hermit in Palestine.

Although one of the least trustworthy of the Norse sagas, *Óláfs saga Tryggvasonar* was of considerable importance for later saga writing and for the Romantic poets and historians of nineteenth-century Scandinavia. Heroes of family sagas are often said to have visited the court of Olaf Tryggvason. His death in the Battle of Svǫldr, as told in *Heimskringla,* is the Scandinavian equivalent of Caesar's death in Rome or Roland's at Roncevaux. In the twentieth century the critical reaction against national romanticism has led to a considerable depreciation of *Óláfs saga Tryggvasonar* as a historical source. As a literary work, however, it remains a classic.

BIBLIOGRAPHY

Sources. Óláfs saga Tryggvasonar en mesta, Ólafur Halldórsson, ed., 2 vols. (1958–1961); *Saga Óláfs Tryggvasonar af Oddr Snorrason Munk,* Finnur Jónsson, ed. (1932); Snorri Sturluson, *Heimskringla,* Bjarni Aðalbjarnarson, ed., I (1941), 225–372.

Studies. Bjarni Aðalbjarnarson, *Om de Norske Kongers Sagaer* (1937); Walter Baetke, "Das Svoldr-Problem," in *Berichte über die Verhandlungen der sächsischen Akademie der Wissenschaften zu Leipzig, Philologisch-historische Klasse,* **98** (1951); Ólafur Halldórsson, "Óláfs saga Tryggvasonar," in *Kulturhistorisk leksikon for nordisk middelalder,* XII (1967); Gwyn Jones, *The Legendary History of Olaf Tryggvason* (1968); Lars Lönnroth, "Studier i Olaf Tryggvasons saga," in *Samlaren,* **84** (1963).

LARS LÖNNROTH

[See also **Norse Kings' Sagas; Snorri Sturluson.**]

OLD ENGLISH LANGUAGE. Old English, or Anglo-Saxon, as it is sometimes called, is the oldest stage of the English language. It is traditionally placed (along with Afrikaans, Dutch, Flemish, Frisian, Low German, modern standard German, and Yiddish) in the West Germanic group of the Germanic branch of the Indo-European family of languages. English is usefully but somewhat artificially divided into three periods: Old English (450–1100), Middle English (1100–1500), and Modern English (1500–). The opening date of the Old English period is one traditionally assigned to the first waves of Germanic invasions of Britain from the coastal areas of northern Europe, especially from what is now northern Germany, the Netherlands, and Denmark. The closing date is more arbitrarily placed soon after the Norman invasion in 1066, though many of the characteristics that differentiate Old and Middle English begin to appear earlier.

The precise identity and homeland of the invaders who brought their Germanic language to Britain is somewhat uncertain. The traditional view derives from Bede's *Ecclesiastical History of the English People,* completed in 731, some 300 years after the events recounted. It identifies three groups: Jutes, Angles, and Saxons. Following Bede, the traditional view places the homelands of both the Jutes and Angles on the Danish peninsula—the Jutes at the northern end and the Angles farther south; it places the homeland of the Saxons along the northern German coast, perhaps as far southwest as the Rhine.

The specific details of this view now seem unlikely. Bede himself abandons the name Jute in the rest of his history and often seems to equate the Angles and Saxons; other Old English chroniclers do not distinguish these same groups among the invading peoples. Further, there is no evidence (for example, place-names) to show that Jutes were ever present in England. It also seems quite doubtful that the invading groups were monolithic tribal groups as Bede suggests; it is much more likely that they settled in mixed groups in various areas of Britain. Archaeological evidence confirms a mixture of cultures among the invading tribes. At the same time, it suggests that Bede's and the Anglo-Saxon Chronicle's claim of a common Saxon origin for the peoples of Essex, Wessex, and Sussex is not true (although the names are combinations of the obvious directions and "Saxon"). Finally, the dialects of Old English, which could be seen as providing evidence for the migration of groups with somewhat different dialects, may be more reasonably explained as arising after the invasions. Whatever the details of the Germanic invasions, however, it is clear that they began shortly before 450 with plundering raids and were followed by large-scale colonization lasting until about 500. As a result, a group of closely related West Germanic dialects eventually replaced the native Celtic language in much of Britain.

Just how much variation existed among the

OLD ENGLISH LANGUAGE

dialects of the various invading groups is uncertain, although it could not have been very great. It seems likely that some of the differences were smoothed away with the mixing of cultures and peoples after the migration (though some undoubtedly remained). On the other hand, new differences between the dialects of the relatively isolated parts of Britain immediately arose. These native dialects were confused and altered by influences from the coastal areas of northern Europe (especially Frisia), which maintained close trading ties with Britain, and especially with Kent and the southeast in general.

THE FOUR MAJOR DIALECTS

Although the origin of the Old English dialects, like the origin of the invaders themselves, is controversial, its results are a fairly clear division of early Old English into four major dialects: Northumbrian (north of the Humber), Mercian (roughly from the Thames to the Humber), Kentish (the extreme southeast below the Thames), and West Saxon (the rest of the area below the Thames to Cornwall in the west). In addition, Northumbrian and Mercian share enough features to be grouped together as Anglian dialects. The dialects are distinguished primarily on the basis of phonological characteristics (especially changes in the accented vowels of West Germanic) that are too complex to be discussed here. The dearth of texts, especially of texts before 1000 that can be localized with reasonable certainty, severely limits our knowledge of their precise boundaries and characteristics. After 1000, texts are plentiful, but by that time West Saxon had become the standard written dialect, so that very few texts exemplifying the other dialects can be found. Because Late West Saxon, as this dialect is called, is thus the first dialect for which reasonably full documentation exists, it is the form of Old English whose characteristics will be described below. This situation continues until the Middle English period, when large numbers of texts in various dialects appear; these are often valuable in providing clues about the Old English dialects from which they presumably developed.

Political events following the Germanic invasions shed additional light on the importance of the major dialects of Old English. Consolidation of power in local centers began almost immediately, and by the early 500's resulted in seven major political divisions (traditionally called the Anglo-Saxon heptarchy): Northumbria, Mercia, East Anglia, Essex, Sussex, Wessex, and Kent. These divisions partly reflect the Old English dialects, with Kent and Northumbria in particular being roughly coextensive with the Kentish and Northumbrian dialects. Wessex and Sussex together occupied the West Saxon dialect area, and Mercia, East Anglia, and Essex, the Mercian.

The first area to achieve political and cultural ascendancy was Kent—partly because of its earlier importance under Roman rule, but mainly because of its close commercial ties with the Continent. Soon after 600, this position was taken over by Northumbria, then by Mercia in the 700's. In the 800's Wessex became dominant, and when King Egbert overthrew the Mercian king in 825 the kings of Wessex could claim lordship over all of England. It was this political and social event that resulted in the temporary establishment of the West Saxon dialect as a literary standard, a position it held until it was replaced by French for a time following the Norman Conquest. By the time English reemerged and the London dialect became the standard, the language was no longer Old English but Middle English.

Yet the West Saxon hegemony did not go completely unchallenged. Another Germanic invasion from outside the country was to have important consequences for the English language. According to the Anglo-Saxon Chronicle, Viking raids had begun in 787 in the north and east, continuing intermittently until the end of the century. The raids resumed in 834 and spread to the south, becoming an organized invasion followed by general plundering and the establishment of large settlements after 850. Only the heroic efforts of King Alfred in Wessex (871–899) prevented the complete conquest of England. A treaty signed by Alfred and Guthrum, the Danish king, in 878 established the Danelaw, an area north and east of a line running northwest from London to north of Chester, in which the Danes were free to live under Danish law. More important for the history of English, however, is the fact that they continued to speak their native language.

After a period of relative peace under Alfred and his successors, the invasions resumed late in the century, led this time by Olaf Tryggvason (later king of Norway) and Svend (Sweyn) Forkbeard, king of Denmark. Svend drove King Ethelred into exile in 1014, crowning himself king and establishing a Danish rule that lasted until Edward the

OLD ENGLISH LANGUAGE

Confessor became king in 1042. After Edward's death in 1066, Harold, earl of Wessex, was chosen as king, but later in that same year, Harold III Hardråda, king of Norway, and William, duke of Normandy, almost simultaneously invaded the country in attempts to establish their own claims to the throne. William's eventual triumph established French as the official language of England, and resulted in the huge influx of French words that makes Modern English seem almost as much a Romance language as a Germanic one.

PRONUNCIATION

Old English, as it appears in Late West Saxon texts of about 1000, was written with the following characters derived primarily from the Latin alphabet:

a æ b c d e f g h i k l m
n o p r s t u w x y z þ ð

The letters *k, x,* and *z* were rare, and *g, r,* and *w* were rather different in shape from their modern counterparts. The consonants *b, d, k, l, m, n, p, r, t, x,* and *z* were pronounced with approximately their modern values, though *r* was probably trilled. The letters *f* and *s* and the interchangeable pair *þ/ð* stood for both voiceless (*f, s, th* as in *thin*) and voiced (*v, z, th* as in *then*) sounds, depending on their phonetic contexts. The voiced sounds were pronounced when the consonants appeared between other voiced sounds, for example, *wise* (wise), *suþern* (southern), and the voiceless sounds otherwise, for example, *wæs* (was), *suð* (south). It is this characteristic of Old English that is responsible for Modern English pairs like *bath/bathe* and *wolf/wolves*, in which, as the spelling suggests, the *th* or *f* was at one time between two voiced sounds in the second word of the pair. When *h* appeared before a vowel, it was pronounced as in Modern English, but in other positions it had the sound of Modern German *ch* as in *ich* or *ach*, depending on the surrounding sounds. The pronunciations of *c* and *g* were even more complicated, with *c* pronounced as Modern English *k* or *ch*, depending on the surrounding sounds, and *g* as Modern English *g* or *y*, again depending on the surrounding sounds. In addition, the clusters *sc* and *cg* were pronounced as Modern English *sh* and *j*. Unlike Modern English, which has many "silent" consonants, all Old English consonant letters are pronounced, including double consonants (except in word-final position).

There are seven Old English vowel letters, each with a long and a short value. The sounds can best be described by presenting each Old English vowel along with a representative Old English word in which it appears and an indication of the approximate Modern English equivalent (Table 1). In addition, there were three important long and short diphthongs: *ea, eo,* and *ie*. Long and short *ea* began with long or short *æ, eo* with long or short *e*, and *ie* with long or short *i*. The second part of all of these diphthongs was the neutral vowel schwa (as in the first syllable of Modern English *about*). (This is the traditional view; there is considerable disagreement about the exact character of the short dipthongs especially.)

Old English clearly had a strong stress accent, usually on the first syllable of each word or compound, except for a group of well-defined unstressed prefixes. Many words, notably self-explaining compounds, for example, *boccræft* (bookcraft), *deaðbedd* (deathbed), contained a second strong accent on a following meaningful element. Although evidence for sentence stress is almost entirely lacking, it seems very likely that verbs and adverbs were generally less heavily stressed than nouns and adjectives.

GRAMMAR

The most important grammatical difference between Old English and Modern English is the presence of many inflections in Old English.

Table 1. Vowel Sounds

Short Vowels		Long Vowels	
a in OE *sacu* (strife)	as in MnE *pot*	*a* in OE *bat* (boat)	as in MnE *bond*
æ in OE *fæst* (fast)	as in MnE *bat*	*æ* in OE *dæd* (deed)	as in MnE *bad*
e in OE *bedd* (bed)	as in MnE *bet*	*e* in OE *fet* (feet)	as in MnE *bait*
i in OE *dim* (dim)	as in MnE *bit*	*i* in OE *win* (wine)	as in MnE *beat*
o in OE *god* (God)	as in MnE *bought*	*o* in OE *god* (good)	as in MnE *boat*
u in OE *sunu* (son)	as in MnE *put*	*u* in OE *hus* (house)	as in MnE *boot*
y in OE *synn* (sin)	as in MnGerman *fülle*	*y* in OE *fyr* (fire)	as in MnGerman *grün*

OLD ENGLISH LANGUAGE

Whereas Modern English indicates the functions of words in the sentence and their relationships to each other by word order, prepositional phrases, and separate function words, these tasks are accomplished in Old English largely by the addition of inflectional suffixes. A complete description of the inflections of Old English is beyond the scope of this article, but a simplified look at the inflections of the definite article, the noun, and the verb will help to clarify the basic character of Old English.

The Modern English definite article, *the,* has a single, invariable form, but in Old English the definite article is inflected to indicate the gender, number, and case of the noun with which it is associated; we find *se fot* (the foot), but *seo scinu* (the shin), and *þæt cneow* (the knee). Adjectives are also marked for gender, case, and number and also agree with the noun they modify. In addition, personal pronouns are also more finely differentiated in Old English than in Modern English. The category of number in Old English is quite similar to our current system (except that Old English had a special set of dual pronouns used for just two people, for example, *wit* [we two], *git* [you two]), but gender and case have changed so radically that a brief explanation seems appropriate.

Modern English has a system of natural gender, in which the sex of the object determines the gender of the noun that refers to it, except in a few exceptional cases (ships, for example, are still often referred to as "she"). But in Old English, as in other Germanic languages, genders are essentially arbitrary grammatical or inflexional classes that have no relation to biological gender or meaning. All Old English nouns fall into three large groups, or genders: "masculine," "feminine," and "neuter." The nouns in each of these groups display similar sets of inflections for case and number, and each group is also preceded by a distinct set of forms of the definite article. The arbitrary and classificatory nature of grammatical gender is more readily apparent in languages with more than three genders (some have as many as seven), but the selection of nouns in Table 2 demonstrates clearly the difference between Old English grammatical gender and Modern English natural gender.

Case is a still more difficult concept for speakers of Modern English because only a rudimentary case system remains in English, and even that is restricted mainly to pronouns. The four major Old English cases—nominative, accusative, dative, and genitive—are, like the three genders, grammatical

Table 2. Gender

Masculine	Feminine	Neuter
wifman (woman)	*mægð* (maiden)	*wif* (wife)
fot (foot)	*scinu* (shin)	*cneow* (knee)
muþ (mouth)	*nosu* (nose)	*eage* (eye)
mece (sword)	*secg* (sword)	*sweord* (sword)

or inflectional classes. Unlike genders, however, cases perform important organizational and semantic functions in Old English, marking the functions of nouns in sentences and their relationships to surrounding words. The subject of a verb is marked by nominative endings, the direct object and some objects of prepositions by accusative endings, and the indirect object and most other objects of prepositions by dative endings. The functions marked by genitive endings are more complex: the most important are possession, which remains in Modern English as *'s,* and the partitive genitive, which may be seen in *fiftig wintra* (fifty [of] winters), in which *winters* appears in the genitive case.

Table 3 presents the inflections of the definite article and three common kinds of nouns for number, gender, and case.

Like nouns, verbs in Old English were much more fully inflected than in Modern English, in which present-tense verbs have an inflectional ending only in the third-person singular (*he/she/it walks*). In contrast, Old English verbs had additional distinctive endings, as shown in Table 4. The table also shows the distinction between strong (irregular) and weak (regular) verbs that is characteristic of all the Germanic languages. This distinction remains in Modern English, though fewer than seventy of the Old English strong verbs survive; the others have been lost or have become weak.

Old English word order, like that of Latin and other inflected languages, is much freer than that of Modern English, largely because of the full set of inflections available for nouns and pronouns. Since the functions of nouns are usually distinguishable by a case ending or a distinctive article or adjective, almost any order is comprehensible. But the freedom should not be overstated. In fact, the normal word order for a simple declarative sentence is the same in Old English as in Modern English: subject-verb object (*He geseah þone mann,* "He saw the man"). Following an introductory adverb, however, the normal order is verb-subject-object (*Þa geseah he þone mann,* "Then he saw the man").

OLD ENGLISH LANGUAGE

Table 3. Noun and Article Inflection

Case	Gender		
	Masculine	Feminine	Neuter
		Singular	
Nom.	*se stan*	*seo lar*	*þæt hus*
Acc.	*þone stan*	*þa lare*	*þæt hus*
Dat.	*þæm stane*	*þære lare*	*þæm huse*
Gen.	*þæs stanes*	*þære lare*	*þæs huses*
		Plural	
Nom.	*þa stanas*	*þa lara*	*þa hus*
Acc.	*þa stanas*	*þa lara*	*þa hus*
Dat.	*þæm stanum*	*þæm larum*	*þæm husum*
Gen.	*þara stana*	*þara lara*	*þara husa*

The third major word order, subject-object-verb, is found following the conjunction of a subordinate clause (*Þæt cild hloh for þam þe he þone mann geseah,* "The child laughed because he saw the man.").

VOCABULARY

The vocabulary of Old English is very heavily Germanic. Because of the tremendous influx of French and Latin borrowings in the Middle English period, and because most of the Old English vocabulary has not survived, Old English must be learned as a foreign language. Nevertheless, the earliest stages of the language already contain significant numbers of borrowed words. Some Latin words, especially agricultural, military, and trade words, were borrowed into the various continental Germanic dialects before the speakers of those dialects invaded England. A few more were indirectly borrowed through Celtic languages shortly after the invasion, along with an even smaller number of native Celtic words. The greatest Latin influence came, however, as an indirect effect of the Christianization of Britain that began in 597 and was essentially complete by 700. Early borrowings were mostly religious terms learned from Latin services and the schools set up by the church, but some names for household artifacts, foods, clothing, and plants were also borrowed early. Later borrowings tended to be of a more learned nature and were largely a result of the increase in interest in learning that is associated with the Benedictine reforms of the late 900's. As important as some of the words may seem, all of the Latin borrowings before and during the Old English period amount to only a few hundred words—not enough to have a great effect on the overall Germanic character of the vocabulary.

The only other significant foreign element in the Old English vocabulary is Scandinavian. However, because the Scandinavian settlements come rather late in the Old English period, and because few late Old English texts from the Danelaw have survived, most of the borrowings do not show up in texts until the Middle English period, when they become quite numerous. These Scandinavian borrowings tend to be of a more intimate and everyday character than the Latin, and, by the Middle English period, remarkably include the pronouns *they, their,* and *them,* some other function words, and even a form of the verb "to be" (*are*).

BIBLIOGRAPHY

Grammars. Karl Brunner, *Altenglische Grammatik,* 3rd ed. (1965); Alistair Campbell, *Old English Grammar* (1959); Karl Luick, *Historische Grammatik der englischen Sprache* (1949); Randolph Quirk and C. L. Wrenn, *An Old English Grammar,* 2nd ed. (1973); Frederic T. Visser, *An Historical Syntax of the English Language,* 3 pts. in 4 vols. (1963–1973); Joseph and Elizabeth M. Wright, *Old English Grammar* (1925, 3rd ed. 1982).

Table 4. Verb Inflection

Number	Present Tense Type: Strong	Present Tense Type: Weak	Past Tense Type: Strong	Past Tense Type: Weak
Singular				
1st person *ich* (I)	*bind-e*	*frem-me*	*band*	*frem-ede*
2nd person *þu* (you)	*bind-est*	*frem-est*	*bund-e*	*frem-edest*
3rd person *he/heo/hit* (he/she/it)	*bind-eþ*	*frem-eþ*	*band*	*frem-ede*
Plural				
All persons *we/eow/hie* (we/you/they)	*bind-aþ*	*frem-maþ*	*bundon*	*frem-edon*

Dictionaries. Joseph Bosworth and T. N. Toller, *An Anglo-Saxon Dictionary* (with supplements) (1921); John R. Clark Hall, *A Concise Anglo-Saxon Dictionary,* 4th ed. (1960); Ferdinand Holthausen, *Altenglisches etymologisches Wörterbuch* (1963); University of Toronto, Dictionary of Old English Project, a computer-assisted dictionary (in progress).

Bibliographies. Stanley Greenfield and Fred C. Robinson, *A Bibliography of Publications on Old English Literature to the End of 1972* (1980); "Old English Bibliography," in *The Old English Newsletter,* annual (1967–).

Studies. Albert C. Baugh and Thomas Cable, *A History of the English Language,* 3rd ed. (1978); Morton W. Bloomfield and Leonard Newmark, *A Linguistic Introduction to the History of English* (1963, repr. 1979); Otto Jespersen, *Growth and Structure of the English Language* (1923, 9th ed. 1956); George P. Krapp, *Modern English: Its Growth and Present Use* (1909, rev. 1969 by Albert H. Marckwardt); Robert A. Peters, *A Linguistic History of English* (1968); Thomas Pyles, *The Origins and Development of the English Language,* 2nd ed. (1971); Joseph M. Williams, *Origins of the English Language* (1975); Henry C. Wyld, *A History of Modern Colloquial English,* 3rd ed. (1937).

DAVID L. HOOVER

[See also **Anglo-Saxon Literature; Anglo-Saxons, Origins and Migration; England: Anglo-Saxon; Indo-European Languages, Development of; Middle English Language.**]

OLD ENGLISH LITERATURE. See **Anglo-Saxon Literature.**

OLD FRENCH. See **French Language; French Literature.**

OLD HALL MS, a musical manuscript of major importance containing English sacred polyphony composed during the period from about 1370 to 1425. Now the property of the British Museum (MS Add. 57950), it is named after its former location at St. Edmund's College, Old Hall Green, near Ware. The present contents, preserved in 112 of the original 137 folios, comprise 147 complete and fragmentary works, of which some 95 have been securely attributed to twenty-three English and two foreign composers. The manuscript preserves the first substantial collection of English polyphony after the Winchester Troper of around 1000, and is the first such collection to identify many of its contributors.

The process of compilation took place in two stages. Current opinion favors the early part of 1421 as the terminus ante quem for the first layer rather than the previously accepted dating of 1410–1415. The initial effort was made by a single scribe who assembled all of the works destined for inclusion and copied some four-fifths of the surviving contents. This first scribe imposed a clearly discernible twofold arrangement upon the music, first by grouping the pieces by liturgical function, then by arranging the works within each group according to musical notation. An opening gathering of Kyries is presumed lost, so that the first of the six extant sections consists of Glorias. This is followed by compositions on Marian texts, settings of the Credo, Sanctus, and Agnus Dei, and, finally, isorhythmic motets as replacements for the *Deo gratias.* In the four sections devoted to Ordinary texts, score notation precedes notation in separate parts (also known as choirbook format or *cantus collateralis*). The Marian pieces use the method of score notation exclusively, the concluding motets notation in separate parts.

The second layer, copied after the cessation of work on the part of the original scribe and the first illuminator, can be attributed to at least seven copyists, some of whom may have been the composers of the newer pieces. This layer consists of thirty compositions, entered either on unused or on newly added folios and interspersed throughout the main body of the manuscript.

While a good deal of information may be adduced as to the general social and political factors underlying the collection, conclusions regarding its original commission and early history remain speculative. The period from 1390 to 1425 witnessed a reaffirmation of elaborate service music as part of the reaction against the musical abstemiousness of the Lollard heresy. In the political sphere, the texts of three of the motets suggest links with the Battle of Agincourt in October 1415, and with the preceding and subsequent negotiations between the combatants.

A more detailed understanding of Old Hall's history is furnished by manuscript concordances and biographical data on the composers. The identity of Roy Henry, contributor of a Gloria and a Sanctus, has not been conclusively determined, although current opinion favors Henry V over Henry IV. The view that the main body of the collection was drawn from numerous English localities is supported by available information on the remaining composers in the first layer, as well as by the existence of sixteen English concordances (of a total of twenty-six) for this layer. The later career of Leonel Power (*d.* 1445), whose twenty-four works make him the most substantially represented composer in Old Hall, may link the collection with Christ Church, Canterbury; but from as early as 1411, Power's service under Thomas, duke of Clarence and heir apparent to the throne, points to the duke's chapel as the collection's original destination.

The simultaneous membership of four of the second layer composers in the royal household chapel of Henry V is indicative not only of the manuscript's association with that institution in the years following the compilation of the first layer, but also of a shift to a more localized repertory. At the same time, the presence in continental sources of eleven of the fifteen concordances for the later pieces argues for substantial musical interaction between the royal court and various European centers.

The music of Old Hall embodies a broad range of styles and compositional procedures. The fundamental distinction among these is drawn between English descant on the one hand, and a number of continental practices on the other. The English descant pieces are notated exclusively in score, setting the plainsong in the middle voice in note-against-note fashion against prominent contrary motion in the other two strands. Later pieces in this category are rhythmically more complex and show increasing sophistication in their handling of the cantus firmus, which migrates from one part to another and is sometimes dropped altogether.

The continental styles, reflecting musical contacts with Avignon and northern Italy, show a concentration of rhythmic and melodic interest in the upper part or parts over a supportive texture supplied by one or two slower voices. Included in this group are seven canonic works, a large number of isorhythmic pieces, and pieces in chanson style that, because they employ up to three texted upper parts above a structural duo, are frequently similar in sound to isorhythmic motets. The isorhythmic works embody various approaches to the handling of *color* and *talea,* including changes of mensuration and the imposition of the durational scheme upon the upper voices. In addition to these two general groups, there are a few compositions where the English descant style assumes the rhythmically freer texture of the chanson pieces.

The manuscript demonstrates the leading role of English composers in the pairing of Mass movements. Although the priority granted liturgical ordering normally obscures links based upon purely musical factors, such relationships can frequently be defended through an examination of physical placement, clef combinations, mensuration schemes, modal identity, and general musical similarities. The presence of paired movements, coupled with early examples of double canon, mensuration canon, and canonic materials derived from plainsong, contribute to Old Hall's historical importance. But an overriding consideration remains the value of the manuscript as a gathering, from a wide chronological and geographical range, of most of the styles current at the time, and of the adaptation of these styles to the musical and textual demands of the Mass.

BIBLIOGRAPHY

Sources. Andrew Hughes and Margaret Bent, eds., *The Old Hall Manuscript,* 3 vols. (1969).

Studies. Margaret Bent, "Initial Letters in the Old Hall Manuscript," in *Music and Letters,* **47** (1966), "Sources of the Old Hall Music," in *Proceedings of the Royal Musical Association,* **94** (1967–1968), "The Old Hall Manuscript," in *Early Music,* **2** (1974), and "The Progeny of Old Hall: More Leaves from a Royal English Choirbook," in *Gordon Athol Anderson (1929–1981): In Memoriam,* I (1984); Roger Bowers, "Some Observations on the Life and Career of Lionel Power," in *Proceedings of the Royal Musical Association,* **102** (1975–1976); Manfred Bukofzer, *Studies in Medieval and Renaissance Music* (1950); Frank L. Harrison, *Music in Medieval Britain,* 2nd ed. (1963); Andrew Hughes, "Mensuration and Proportion in Early Fifteenth-century English Music," in *Acta musicologica,* **37** (1965), "Mass Pairs in the Old Hall and Other English Manuscripts," in *Revue belge de musicologie,* **19** (1965), "Mensural Polyphony for Choir in Fifteenth-century England," in *Journal of the American Musicological Society,* **19** (1966), and "The Old Hall Manuscript: A Reappraisal," in *Musica disciplina,* **21** (1967); Andrew Hughes and Margaret Bent, "The Old Hall Manuscript: An Inventory," in *Musica disciplina,* **21** (1967); Ann B. Scott, "The Performance of the Old Hall Descant Settings," in *Musical Quarterly,* **56** (1970).

ARTHUR LEVINE

[See also **Agincourt, Battle of; Agnus Dei (music); Gloria; Isorhythm; Mass Cycles, Plainsong; Music; Winchester Troper.**]

OLD HIGH GERMAN LITERATURE. "Old High German" is a linguistic term denoting the dialects of southern and central Germany (Upper German, comprising Bavarian and Alemannic, and Middle German, comprising East, Rhenish, and Middle Franconian) to the mid eleventh century and first recorded in writing in the mid eighth. In descriptions of the vernacular literature of this period it is customary to include also texts written in Old Saxon, the language of northern Germany, and Old Low Franconian, the language of the Low Countries, even though these are linguistically not High German (since they are unaffected by the consonantal changes known as the High German consonant shift). Old High German literature must be taken to include every text written in the vernacular before about 1050.

Germany at this time had a copious literature written in Latin; it also had a rich tradition of vernacular oral poetry, but of this hardly any was committed to writing, save a few charms and one heroic lay. Most of the writings in Old High German had a utilitarian purpose, as an adjunct to clerical learning or a means of propagating the Christian faith. The earliest texts from the second half of the eighth century and the early ninth, for example, are Latin-German glossaries, arranged either alphabetically, like the great *Abrogans* glossary (preserved in manuscripts in Paris, Karlsruhe, and St. Gall), or according to subjects, like the *Vocabularius Sancti Galli.*

From this early period there are also interlinear glosses of biblical, liturgical, and ecclesiastical texts, among the earliest of these being the Benedictine Rule, the Lord's Prayer, the Creeds, and a collection of Ambrosian hymns. The most extensive interlinear gloss, that of the *Diatessaron* of Tatian, was made around 830. In the main these early translations adhere closely to the originals; a notable exception is the skillful rendering of Isidore's *De fide catholica contra Judaeos* from the late eighth century. Glosses and translations continued to be made throughout the period, culminating in the masterly German renderings that Notker III (Teutonicus) of St. Gall (*d.* 1022) made of the Psalms and various secular texts, notably Boethius' *Consolation of Philosophy.* Notker was the first to evolve a German prose style that made free use of imitations of Latin constructions. However, even Notker's translations were intended simply as aids to the understanding of the original works, as he himself stated in a letter to his bishop.

During Charlemagne's Saxon wars the Saxons were converted to Christianity. A product of such missionary activity was the Old Saxon baptismal vow, which includes mention of the pagan gods whom the baptized individual was to abjure. The *Wessobrunner Gebet* (Wessobrunn Prayer) from the late eighth to early ninth century is thought by some scholars, on account of its echoes of Germanic cosmological poetry, to have been a piece of conversion literature, harmonizing Christian and pre-Christian conceptions of the beginning of the world. This text employs alliterative verse, which is also the medium of the two ninth-century biblical epics in Old Saxon, the *Heliand* (Savior), based on the Gospels, and the fragmentarily preserved *Genesis.* Both works adapt the biblical narrative to the native taste and ways of thought. Moreover, the biblical epic in alliterative verse was probably a literary import from England. (One manuscript of the *Heliand* was probably written in England, and most of the *Genesis* is preserved only in an Old English translation.)

A quite different work, composed in rhyming verse and apparently directed to a more learned public, is the *Evangelienbuch* (Gospelbook) of Otfrid von Weissenburg (*d. ca.* 870). This work is a discursive and interpretative account of the life of Christ and draws extensively on contemporary theological learning. It seems to have been the author's intention to provide his countrymen with a worthy national literature that compared favorably with the works of Latin Christendom. A somewhat degenerate form of alliterative verse, interspersed with rhyming lines, is used in *Muspilli,* an eschatological poem of the ninth century in which early scholars thought they discerned traces of pre-Christian notions of the end of the world. All the other religious poems employ rhyme. The *Petruslied* (Song to St. Peter) is a short hymn with the refrain "Kyrie eleison"; the *Georgslied* (Song of St. George), an account of the saint's life and miracles, employing frequent refrains in German; and *Christus und die Samariterin,* an accomplished strophic rendering of the conversation between Christ and the woman of Samaria.

Among the secular texts of the period the most archaic is a fragment of a German translation of the *Lex salica* (Law of the Salian Franks) made around 830. The meeting between Charles II the Bald and Louis the German in 842 gave rise to the *Strasbourg Oaths,* of which a French and a German version are recorded. From the tenth century there is a piece of macaronic verse known as *De Heinrico,* which commemorates an unidentifiable political event and has been called the first political poem in German. The most notable celebration of contemporary history in German is the *Ludwigslied,* a poem in praise of Louis III of France composed between his victory over the Danes at Saucourt in August 881 and his death in August 882. Some scholars regard it, despite its Christian veneer, as a late representative of the ancient genre of encomiastic poetry known as the "Preislied," while others see in it a forerunner of the chansons de geste.

The most outstanding poetic text of the period is undoubtedly the *Hildebrandslied,* recorded on the first and last pages of a German manuscript from the second quarter of the ninth century but deriving, according to some scholars, from a Langobardic original of the eighth century or even earlier. This unique masterpiece, which consists of a dramatic conversation between a father and son who meet between two opposing armies and finally do battle, is the earliest heroic lay preserved in any Germanic language.

There were undoubtedly other heroic lays current in oral form; some of these were transmitted to Scandinavia and supplied subjects for some of the lays of the Old Norse *Edda,* and some formed the basis of the German heroic epics of the thirteenth century, but there is no continuity between the other literary works of the period and those that came after it. Alliterative verse died out on the Continent after the ninth century, and the biblical epics and the short religious poems of the eleventh and twelfth centuries owe nothing to their forerunners of the ninth. Otfrid's achievement was soon forgotten, and Notker had no imitators as a writer of German prose. Even within the period few links can be discerned between the individual vernacular works. Old High German literature thus consists of a number of isolated monuments that the literary historian can at best arrange in chronological order and attempt to see against the ecclesiastical and intellectual background of the period.

BIBLIOGRAPHY

Charles C. Barber, *An Old High German Reader* (1951); Helmut de Boor and Richard Newald, *Geschichte der deutschen Literatur von den Anfängen bis zur Gegenwart,* I, 4th ed. (1960); John Knight Bostock, *A Handbook on Old High German Literature,* 2nd ed., rev. by Kenneth C. King and David R. McLintock (1976); Theodor Wilhelm Braune, *Althochdeutsches Lesebuch,* 16th ed., rev. by Ernst A. Ebbinghaus (1979); Gustav Ehrismann, *Geschichte der deutschen Literatur bis zum Ausgang des Mittelalters,* I, 2nd ed. (1932); J. Sidney Groseclose and Brian O. Murdoch, *Die althochdeutschen poetischen Denkmäler* (1976); Brian O. Murdoch, *Old High German Literature* (1983); Horst Dieter Schlosser, *Althochdeutsche Literatur: Mit Proben aus dem Altniederdeutschen: Ausgewählte Texte mit Übertragungen* (1970).

DAVID R. MCLINTOCK

[See also **Baptismal Vow, Old High German/Old Saxon; Charms, Old High German; Christus und die Samariterin; Georgslied; German Language; German Literature: Allegory; Heinrico, De; Heliand; Hildebrandslied; Lai, Lay; Ludwigslied; Muspilli; Notker Teutonicus; Otfrid von Weissenburg; Petruslied; Tatian; Vocabularius Sancti Galli; Wessobrunner Gebet.**]

OLD ROMAN CHANT, a body of liturgical melodies found in five manuscripts of the eleventh, twelfth, and thirteenth centuries. They are all of Roman origin and contain essentially the same liturgy and texts (though with some clear differences) as the manuscripts of the far more widely disseminated Gregorian chant. The complex relationship of these two forms of chant is in fact one of the chief issues of modern musicology and liturgical studies. Three of the manuscripts are graduals: Cologny-Geneva, Bodmer Library, MS 74 (incomplete, containing tropes and sequences as well, and copied in 1071 at S. Cecilia in Trastevere); Vat. lat. 5319 (probably from the Lateran or a satellite church, dated about 1100); Vat. Arch. di S. Pietro, MS F. 22 (thirteenth century, from St. Peter's). The remaining two sources are office antiphoners: London, British Library, Add. MS 29988 (twelfth century, perhaps from the Lateran); Vat. Arch. di S. Pietro, MS B 79 (twelfth century, from St. Peter's). With these is associated a large and diverse group of other manuscripts, some of which reflect Roman liturgical texts and customs but contain little or no music, while others that are definitely not Roman contain material that may be Old Roman in origin.

At the heart of the problem is the melodic similarity of Old Roman to Gregorian chant. Liturgy and texts are essentially the same in the two traditions, and the melodies for the same text, though distinct, often resemble one another in their underlying skeletal structure. The question, then, is

OLD ROMAN CHANT

one of origins, that is, how did this state of affairs come about? The pioneer researchers of the nineteenth century paid little attention to these few and peculiar sources. André Mocquereau recognized the melodic relationship of the two repertories but dismissed the Old Roman as late and corrupt while asserting that the tradition of Gregory the Great himself was enshrined in the innumerable "Gregorian" manuscripts. Only Raphael Andoyer disagreed, detecting signs of greater archaism in the Old Roman chant but holding nonetheless that the traditional repertory was Gregorian in the strict sense while labeling the Old Roman "pre-Gregorian." Thus matters rested until the modern debate was ignited by Bruno Stäblein in 1950 with a hypothesis that Gregorian chant developed out of a late-seventh-century revision in Rome of the Old Roman. Though he later abandoned the details of this hypothesis, he had defined the terms for all future debate. Some scholars were aware that the oldest Gregorian manuscripts of Roman provenance were from the thirteenth century (and thus later than the Old Roman sources) and that there was a profusion of earlier non-Roman Gregorian books from as early as the beginning of the tenth century. They suggested that the Gregorian chant had not developed in Rome at all but was a Frankish reworking of the *cantus romanus* brought north by the Carolingians in the eighth and ninth centuries. Attention was thus concentrated on the Gregorian chant. Was it Frankish or Roman? If Frankish, how did it develop? If Roman, how did two related forms of chant come to exist side-by-side in the same city?

This Frankish theory was first proposed by Helmut Hucke, who attributed the development of the Gregorian chant to the deep cultural differences between Rome and the barbarian north. More recently Leo Treitler, pointing out that early chant was an oral tradition and drawing parallels with the hypotheses of Milman Parry and Albert Lord concerning oral tradition and epic poetry, seems to attribute the development to the functioning of memory in such a tradition. Supporters of a Roman theory (Stäblein, Smits van Waesberghe, Gajard, Jammers, van Dijk) have offered several explanations for the growth of two kinds of chant within the city. It has been attributed, for instance, to the division of regular and secular clergy, or, more convincingly, to the distinction between papal and urban rites. This latter opinion has been most effectively argued by van Dijk. Basing himself on sound historical and liturgical evidence, he sees the Gregorian as a special chant developed for the byzantinized papal court of the late seventh century and the Old Roman as belonging to a continuing nonpapal tradition in the city churches.

Treitler apart, little has been added recently to the now stagnant debate. Neither theory has been in any sense proved. While the Romanists have advanced solid historical evidence for twofold rites in medieval Rome, for a byzantinized papal custom, for papal musical activity in the seventh and eighth centuries, the evidence is all circumstantial regarding the main issue: Was a second form of chant developed for the papal court as part of that activity? Advocates of the Frankish theory, on the other hand, gloss over fundamental difficulties: If cultural differences induced Frankish cantors to make deep revisions of Roman chant, how does one explain the rapid dissemination of a unified, extensive Gregorian repertory to such disparate cultures as those of England, southern Italy, Spain, and so forth? And in spite of Treitler's frequently brilliant insights, his claims for the influence of oral tradition have been vastly overstated. He draws unwarranted parallels with the Parry-Lord hypotheses, which are founded on data regarding the dissemination of a secular textual tradition among largely illiterate Balkan folksingers who had few constraints not to alter their material from one audience to another. It is assuming too much to apply conclusions about the way memory functions in such a milieu to its role in the dissemination of a sacred musical tradition among literate and highly trained medieval cantors for whom the text and the melody were a matter of rigid constraint. On the contrary, the "folk" tradition of Parry and Lord is the opposite of the "court" tradition of medieval liturgical chant. Indeed, in his latest work Treitler has noted obliquely the overstatement of his earlier identification of formulaic melody as "oral" and therefore unstable; he cites Larry Benson's demonstration that formula was frequently only a matter of medieval style and does not necessarily indicate "oral" composition.

That chant was an oral tradition down to about the tenth century is undeniable, but it was an oral tradition of a very distinct and as yet not understood kind. Certainly there is no ground yet for accepting a view that it could not have been disseminated throughout Europe in a fairly stable and fixed state, and it is ultimately for this reason that

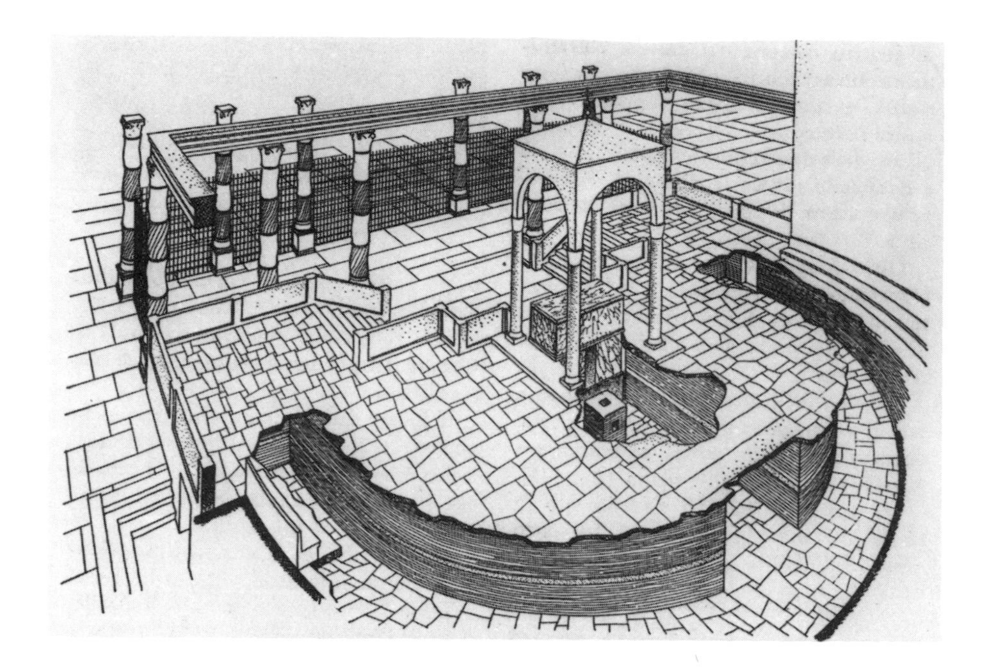

Old St. Peter's, showing annular crypt. Rome, late 6th century. FROM *ESPLORAZIONI SOTTO LA CONFESSIONE DI SAN PIETRO IN VATICANO* © 1951 Letteraria e Artistica alla Santa Sede, Vatican City

one must still declare the Old Roman problem to be very much an open question.

BIBLIOGRAPHY

Raphael Andoyer, "Le chant romain antégrégorien," in *Revue du chant grégorien,* **20** (1911–1912); Thomas H. Connolly, "Introits and Archetypes: Some Archaisms of the Old Roman Chant," in *Journal of the American Musicological Society,* **25** (1972); S. J. P. van Dijk, "The Urban and Papal Rites in Seventh- and Eighth-century Rome," in *Sacris erudiri,* **12** (1961), "The Old-Roman Rite," in *Studia patristica,* **5,** Texte und Untersuchungen, **80** (1962), and "Recent Developments in the Study of the Old-Roman Rite," in *Studia patristica,* **8,** Texte und Untersuchungen, **93** (1966); Georges Frénaud, "Les témoins indirects du chant liturgique en usage à Rome aux IXe et Xe siècles," in *Études grégoriennes,* **3** (1959); Jacques Hourlier and Michel Huglo, "Un important témoin du chant 'vieux-romain': Le graduel de Sainte-Cécile du Transtévère," in *Revue grégorienne,* **31** (1952); Helmut Hucke, "Gregorian and Old Roman Chant," in *The New Grove Dictionary of Music and Musicians,* VII (1980), and "Toward a New Historical View of Gregorian Chant," in *Journal of the American Musicological Society,* **33** (1980); Michel Huglo, "Le chant 'vieux-romain': Liste des manuscrits et témoins indirects," in *Sacris erudiri,* **6** (1954); Ewald Jammers, *Musik in Byzanz, im päpstlichen Rom und im Frankenreich: Der Choral als Musik der Textaussprache* (1962); Margaretha Landwehr-Melnicki, *Die Gesänge des altrömischen Graduale: Vat. lat. 5319* (1970); André Mocquereau, *Paléographie musicale,* II (1891–1892), 4; Robert J. Snow, "The Old Roman Chant," in Willi Apel, ed., *Gregorian Chant* (1958); Bruno Stäblein, "Alt- und neurómischer Choral," in Hans Albrecht *et al.,* eds., *Kongress-Bericht Gesellschaft für Musikforschung, Luneburg 1950* (n.d.), "Zür Entstehung der gregorianischen Melodien," in *Kirchenmusicalisches Jahrbuch,* **35** (1951), "Kann der gregorianische Choral im Frankenreich entstanden sein?" in *Archiv für Musikwissenschaft,* **24** (1967), and "Nochmals zur angeblichen Entstehung des gregorianischen Chorals im Frankenreich," *ibid.,* **27** (1970); Leo Treitler, "Homer and Gregory: The Transmission of Epic Poetry and Plainchant," in *Musical Quarterly,* **60** (1974), and "Oral, Written, and Literate Process in the Transmission of Medieval Music," in *Speculum,* **56** (1981).

THOMAS H. CONNOLLY

[See also **Antiphonal; Gradual; Gregorian Chant; Plainsong, Sources of.**]

OLD ST. PETER'S, ROME. The church of St. Peter, *princeps apostolorum* and founder of the see of Rome, was one of the most prestigious, best known, and most widely emulated buildings of the Middle Ages. It was systematically demolished during 1506–1618; knowledge of it depends on visual and verbal records, and modern excavations.

The church was built by the emperor Constantine the Great in a cemetery on the slope of the

Mons vaticanus, adjoining the Circus of Nero, where it was believed that Peter was martyred. The building enveloped the shrine *(tropaion)* thought to mark the apostle's grave. Begun after 319 and completed by 329, this was the largest of Constantine's Roman church foundations (length, including apse, about 119 meters or 390 feet; width across transept about 91 meters or 299 feet; height to apex of nave roof about 37 meters or 121 feet). Like the Lateran Cathedral, it had a nave, four aisles, and a western apse, but it differed in having also a transept—the first Christian building, apparently, to have it. The transept was a feature both pragmatic—providing an architecturally distinctive space for the apostle's shrine—and symbolic, giving the building as a whole a *T* or crosslike shape.

The shrine originally stood free, in front of the apse, under a baldachin on precious twisted marble columns decorated with vine scrolls. A late-sixth-century remodeling (perhaps by Pope Gregory I) raised the floor level around the shrine so that an altar could be placed above it; access to the shrine was then (as now) via a configuration of corridors ("annular crypt") under the apse floor. This ingenious scheme was both a response and a stimulation to the increasing demand that every altar be associated with relics. Like the transept, the annular crypt appears in many later churches, especially in the eighth- and twelfth-century milieux of reform and revival, and then frequently as an explicit allusion to the authoritative paradigm of St. Peter's.

The pictorial decoration, added after Constantine, was likewise influential. It included a facade mosaic showing the apocalyptic Elders and Lamb (sponsored by Marianus, ex-prefect and consul, at the request of Pope Leo I, 440–461); remade under Pope Gregory IX (1227–1241); forty-six narrative paintings on the nave walls under the windows, representing Old Testament scenes on the right and the life of Christ on the left (sponsored by Pope Leo I; repainted under Pope Formosus, 891–896, and again by Pietro Cavallini in the thirteenth century); western apse mosaic showing Christ with Peter and Paul (Pope Innocent III, 1198–1216; replacing a fourth[?]-century subject, possibly the *Traditio legis*); and Giotto's mosaic of the *Navicella* (1298) on the east inner wall of the atrium.

Before the millennium, no Christian site in Western Europe was more visited or venerated than St. Peter's, and pilgrims continued to stream there throughout the twelfth century. It contained many relics, including the *sudarium* of Veronica, and countless notable tombs, including (according to medieval guide books) Bede's. At St. Peter's were kept the pallia, with which archbishops were invested, and many came to Rome to receive them. Beginning with Charlemagne in 800, St. Peter's also was the site of imperial coronations. In the twelfth century, it explicitly rivaled the Lateran as *fundamentum et caput omnium aliarum ecclesiarum* (the foundation and head of all of the other churches); in the fifteenth century, St. Peter's took undisputed precedence as the seat of the Roman church.

BIBLIOGRAPHY

Peter Franke, "Traditio legis und Petrusprimat," in *Virgiliae Christianae,* **26** (1972); Richard Krautheimer, "The Carolingian Revival of Early Christian Architecture," in *Art Bulletin,* **24** (1942), and *idem,* Spencer Corbett, and Alfred K. Frazer, *Corpus basilicarum christianarum Romae,* V (1977), 165–286; P. Mallius, "Descriptio Basilicae Vaticanae," in Roberto Valentini and Giuseppe Zucchetti, eds., *Codice topografico della città di Roma,* III (1946), 375–442; Stephan Waetzoldt, *Die Kopien des 17. Jahrhunderts nach Mosaiken und Wandmalereien in Rom* (1964), 65–72.

DALE KINNEY

[See also **Basilica (with illustration); Coronation, Papal; Early Christian Architecture; Pilgrimage, Western European.**]

OLD SARUM. Originally an Iron Age hill fort and subsequently a Roman, Saxon, and Norman stronghold, Old Sarum became a cathedral town in 1075. The site of a Romanesque cathedral and castle, it was abandoned after 1219, when the episcopal seat was transferred to the new lowland town of Salisbury, 1.5 miles (2.4 km) to the south.

BIBLIOGRAPHY

Thomas S. R. Boase, *English Art, 1100–1216* (1953), 116–119; Peter H. Brieger, *English Art, 1216–1307* (1957, 2nd ed. 1968), 1–2; Jocelyn P. Bushe-Fox, *Old Sarum* (1937); D. H. Montgomerie and Alfred Clapham, "Old Sarum," in *Archaeological Journal,* **104** (1947); Hugh de Sausmarez Shortt, *Old Sarum* (1965).

STEPHEN GARDNER

[See also **Salisbury Cathedral.**]

OLD TESTAMENT TRINITY. See **Trinity, Old Testament.**

OLEG (*d.* 912/913) succeeded Rurik as the leader of the early Russian state. Between 880 and 882 he extended his power southward from Novgorod, capturing Smolensk and Kiev. Making the latter his capital, he expanded his dominion over the tribes east and west of the Dnieper River, much of the course of which he controlled. In 907 Oleg mounted a combined naval and cavalry attack on Constantinople and compelled the Byzantines to grant the young Russian state extensive trading rights; the treaty was expanded in 911, and Russo-Byzantine trade flourished. Popularly considered a wizard, Oleg "the Seer" may perhaps be identified with Odd of the Norse sagas.

BIBLIOGRAPHY

Samuel H. Cross and Olgerd P. Sherbowitz-Wetzor, eds. and trans., *The Russian Primary Chronicle* (1953); Dmitrii S. Likhachev, ed., *Povest vremennykh let*, 2 vols. (1950); George Vernadsky, *Ancient Russia* (1943), *Kievan Russia* (1948), and *The Origins of Russia* (1959).

GEORGE P. MAJESKA

[See also **Kievan Rus; Novgorod; Rurik.**]

OLGA/HELEN (*d.* 968). Probably of Slavic background, Olga was the wife of Grand Prince Igor of Kiev. While regent for their young son Svyatoslav after Igor's death in 945, she reformed the administration of the realm significantly. She adopted Byzantine Christianity privately in 955, taking the Christian name Helen, and two years later was received at the imperial court of Constantinople. She was revered as a saint after her death in 968, particularly after her grandson Vladimir adopted Christianity as Russia's official faith.

BIBLIOGRAPHY

Samuel H. Cross and Olgerd P. Sherbowitz-Wetzor, eds. and trans., *The Russian Primary Chronicle* (1953); Dmitri S. Likhachev, ed., *Povest vremennykh let*, 2 vols. (1950); George Vernadsky, *Kievan Russia* (1948).

GEORGE P. MAJESKA

[See also **Kievan Rus; Vladimir, St.**]

OLIBA (also Oliva, *ca.* 971–1046) was a member of the ruling family of Catalonia, the house of Barcelona. His father, Oliba Cabreta, count of Cerdanya–Besalú, retired to the monastery of Monte Cassino in 988, two years before his death, and Oliba succeeded him as count, sharing the title with two brothers. In 1002 or 1003, Oliba entered Ripoll as an ordinary Benedictine monk and ceased calling himself "count." He was elected abbot in 1008, and in the same year the monks of Cuixà made him their abbot as well. Oliba exerted a loose form of rule over a number of other Catalan monasteries and is credited with founding the shrine of Montserrat by creating a separate nucleus, dedicated to the Virgin Mary, apart from the established community of S. Cecilia.

In 1017 Oliba became bishop of Vic (Vich) while remaining abbot of Ripoll and Cuixà. His nearly thirty-year episcopacy is most notable for the Truce of God, a movement he is generally considered to have initiated. The Truce, which prohibited warfare on certain days of the week and at certain times of the year, was closely associated with the southern French Peace of God that protected the goods and property of clergy and other noncombatants. Oliba presided at the Synod of Tuluges, in the diocese of Elne (1027), at which the first known truce proclamation was issued. Additional regulations were enacted at a council held at Vic in 1033 (or 1043, according to Poly), and the Truce was renewed and elaborated at successive Catalan and southern French councils.

As bishop of Vic, Oliba mediated his family's numerous quarrels, encouraged settlement on the Islamic frontier to the west, and rebuilt many of the churches and monasteries of the diocese. The campanile of Vic is the best-known monument to his architectural supervision.

BIBLIOGRAPHY

Sources. Oliba's extant works are few, and there is some dispute over what may confidently be considered genuine. Letters, sermons, and poems attributed to him are in *Patrologia latina*, CXLII (1880), 591–604. The poems are not by the abbot Oliba but by another monk of Ripoll with the same name. The sermon on St. Narcissus also is probably the work of someone else. The letters are Oliba's, and to those in *Patrologia* may be added one to Sancho the Great, king of Navarre, in Rudolf Beer, ed., *Die Handschriften des Klosters Santa Maria de Ripoll*, I (1908), 79; and one to the monks of Ripoll in Jaime Villanueva, *Viaje literario a las iglesias de España*, VI (1821), 308–309.

The horn of Ulph (length: 71 cm / 28 in). Oliphant from Salerno (?) presented to York Minster before 1042. CHAPTER HOUSE OF YORK MINSTER

Studies. The two most important books about Oliba are Ramon d'Abadal i de Vinyals, *L'abat Oliba, bisbe de Vic, i la seva època* (1948, 3rd ed. 1962); and Anselmo M. Albareda, *L'abat Oliba, fundador de Monserrat* (1931, repr. 1972). A brief, more recent account is Eduard Juneyent, *Esbós biogràfic: Commemoració mil.lenaria del naixement de l'abat–bisbe Oliba* (1971). On Oliba and the Truce of God, see Hartmut Hoffmann, *Gottesfriede und Treuga Dei* (1964), 73–79; Eduard Juneyent, *La pau i treva* (1975), 29–39; Karen Kennelly, "Catalan Peace and Truce Assemblies," in *Studies in Medieval Culture,* 5 (1975); Pierre Ponsich, "Oliba et la trêve de Dieu," in *Les cahiers de Saint-Michel de Cuxa,* 3 (1972). On problems connected with dating the truce councils and some doubts regarding their Catalan origin, see Jean-Pierre Poly, *La Provence et la société féodale, 879–1166* (1976), 191–204.

PAUL FREEDMAN

[See also **Catalonia; Peace of God, Truce of God.**]

OLIPHANT, a medieval end-blown ivory horn, often beautifully carved. Examples from the tenth and eleventh centuries were largely produced by Islamic artisans in Sicily and southern Italy. The oliphant could be hung by a chain from two metal bands, one attached toward each end. It was used less as a musical instrument than as a token of land tenure or even as a reliquary in churches. A good extant example is the "horn of Ulph" in York Minster.

BIBLIOGRAPHY

Frederick Crane, *Extant Musical Instruments* (1972); Otton von Falke, "Elfenbeinhorner. I. Ägypten und Italien. II. Byzanz," in *Pantheon,* **4** (1929), and **5** (1930).

MARY GRIZZARD

[See also **Ivory Carving, Islamic; Musical Instruments, Middle Eastern; Musical Instruments, European.**]

OLIVI, PETER JOHN. See **Peter John Olivi.**

ÖLJEITÜ. See **Uljaytu Khudabānda.**

OMAR I. See **ᶜUmar I ibn al-Khaṭṭāb.**

OMAR II. See **ᶜUmar II ibn ᶜAbd al-Azīz.**

OMAR KHAYYAM. See **ᶜUmar Khayyām.**

OMOPHORION (Russian: *omofor*), the long, broad stole worn by a bishop in the Byzantine church. It is normally worn so that it encircles the neck completely and falls loose front and back, although iconographically it sometimes appears as a circle of material with centered strips hanging front and back. It is related to the Western pallium.

GEORGE P. MAJESKA

[See also **Vestments, Liturgical.**]

ONION DOME. See **Dome.**

ONULF OF SPEYER (*fl. ca.* 1050), a teacher at the school of Speyer. He wrote the *Rethorici colores,* intended as an instructional manual but remarkable for its blending of old pagan rhetorical figures with distinctly Christian content. Onulf sought to further a Christlike ethic for clerics through rhetoric.

BIBLIOGRAPHY

Max Manitius, *Geschichte der lateinischen Literatur des Mittelalters,* II (1923), 715.

EDWARD FRUEH

OPSIKION, THEME OF. The elite mobile expeditionary and praesental army of the Byzantine emperor, called the *obsequium* (Greek: *opsikion*), emerged in the early seventh century under its count. By the early eighth century it had become a theme with a territorial jurisdiction that extended over the Asian shores of the Hellespont and Sea of Marmara and included Bithynia, Paphlagonia, and parts of Phrygia; its capital was Nicaea. Its elite forces were often stationed in and dispatched to widely scattered areas. Constantine V (741–775) reduced its power by subdividing it, parts of it becoming the Optimaton and Bucellarian themes.

BIBLIOGRAPHY

John F. Haldon, *Byzantine Praetorians: An Administrative, Institutional, and Social Survey of the Opsikion and Tagmata, ca. 580–900,* in Rudolf Habelt, ed., *Poikila Byzantina,* III (1984).

WALTER EMIL KAEGI, JR.

[See also **Themes; Warfare, Byzantine.**]

OPTICS, ISLAMIC. Greek works bearing the title *Optika,* such as the treatise written by Euclid around 300 B.C. and the one by Ptolemy in the second century A.D., presented a theory of vision in terms of "visual rays" issuing from a point inside the eye of the observer in the form of divergent discrete lines (Euclid) or a continuous cone of radiation (Ptolemy). The geometrical approach of these works allowed the explanation of a number of visual appearances, such as the variable shapes and sizes of physical objects, in terms of mathematical lines and angles. Euclid probably also wrote a *Catoptrics,* which may be reflected in the late compilation attributed to him under this title, and in which mirror images are investigated with reference to a fixed viewpoint. The subject of specular images was taken up in a book on *Catoptrics* by Hero of Alexandria (first century A.D.), and it was included in the *Optics* of Ptolemy (second century A.D.), who added a separate treatment of refraction, or the bending suffered by the rays as they pass from one transparent medium into another. The Greeks also wrote treatises on the reflection of solar rays from burning mirrors of various shapes; they investigated the projection of images, such as those of the eclipsed sun or moon, through openings; they endeavored to explain the shape and size of the rainbow; and medical writers like Galen (second century A.D.) described the anatomy of the eye and the uses of its various parts. But there was no attempt to combine all these inquiries into a unified science of "optical" phenomena in our general sense of the word. And while optics as a restricted geometrical treatment of vision was generally considered a mathematical science, it was not a prominent member of the mathematical disciplines, and its standing among the sciences remained somewhat uncertain. Aristotle described it as one of "the more physical of the mathematical disciplines," a position that it shared with the important science of astronomy; but it never achieved the prestige of astronomy, although astronomers would turn to it for occasional help, as when they puzzled over the apparent magnification of celestial magnitudes when they approach the horizon.

A similar situation to the one described above prevailed in the Islamic world for a long time after the great movement of translation of Greek scientific and philosophical works into Arabic during the eighth and ninth centuries. Islamic mathematicians, natural philosophers, and physicians tended on the whole to study different aspects of light and vision, and they wrote about them in the different styles and terminologies already adopted in the various Greek disciplines. Mathematicians, for example, composed separate works on the geometrical properties of burning mirrors, on the formation of shadows, and on vision; and for their treatment of the last subject they employed the Euclidean-Ptolemaic language of visual rays. Philosophers, such as Ibn Sīnā (Avicenna, eleventh century) and Ibn Rushd (Averroës, twelfth century), treated vision as a subject essentially belonging to natural philosophy, and they followed Aristotle and his commentators in explaining vision in terms of "forms" received into the eye from the visible object. And physicians, like Ḥunayn ibn Isḥāq (809–873) and those who came after him, generally adhered to a Galenic version of the visual ray theory, according to which the air was transformed into an instrument of vision when it was struck by the visual spirit as it rushed out of the eye. As for treatises on the science of *manāẓir* (the Arabic word for the Greek *optika*), they continued for the most part to be limited in scope. Even the advanced *Kitāb al-manāẓir* (Book on optics), which al-Ḥasan ibn al-Haytham (Alhazen, 965–*ca.* 1040) wrote in the eleventh century, was intentionally restricted to problems of vision, while other writings by the same author included a large number of substantial treatises on practically every aspect of optical inquiry that received attention in antiquity or in the Middle Ages. It was not until much later that an author expressly argued for widening the concept of "optics" so as to include subjects other than those traditionally discussed in works on *manāẓir*.

At the beginning of the fourteenth century a Persian mathematician named Kamāl al-Dīn al-Fārisī wrote a commentary on Ibn al-Haytham's *Kitāb al-manāẓir,* to which he appended recensions of a number of treatises by his predecessor, among them treatises on the rainbow, on the physical properties of shadows, and on the shape of projected solar and lunar images, his stated reason for making these additions being that they naturally belonged to the subject. And yet there was no discussion of burning mirrors, although Kamāl al-Dīn gave a lengthy analysis of Ibn al-Haytham's work on the burning sphere, for use in his own new explanation of the rainbow.

One of the first serious students of optics in the Islamic world was a Muslim Arab scholar associated with the Abbasid court in Baghdad. Abū Yūsuf Yaʿqūb ibn Isḥāq al-Kindī (*d. ca.* 870), recognized as the first important philosopher to write in Arabic, was a forceful champion of Greek learning (to which he had access only in Arabic translations), and a prolific writer on almost every branch of Greek science and philosophy. His writings included many works on light and vision, most of which have perished; the most important among the few that have survived is found only in a Latin translation made in the twelfth century and known as the *De aspectibus* (On optics). Though apparently composed as part of a compendious exposition of the mathematical sciences (*scientiae doctrinales,* the Latin translation of *al-ʿulūm al-taʿlīmīya*), it is distinctly individual in character. It is clearly influenced by the form and content of Euclid's *Optics,* but, unlike Euclid's book, it is not purely geometrical or solely concerned with rectilinear vision. It is frequently polemical against unnamed authors who obviously included Euclid, and at times it strays into philosophical discussions. In the opening paragraph al-Kindī declares that in his treatment of the subject he will aim at satisfying the requirements of both natural science and mathematics, a clear indication of a tendency already apparent in late Greek thought.

The *De aspectibus* then begins with a discussion of shadows (a subject left out of Euclid's *Optics*), for the purpose of establishing the rectilinear extension of external light, of which the author later asserts that it proceeds from each part, however small, of the shining object. Having discussed and

OPTICS, ISLAMIC

rejected explanations of vision in terms of received "forms" of any kind, al-Kindī takes the view that vision is brought about through a luminous power that emanates from the eye to the visible object in the form of a solid cone of radiation. Thus he accepts the "extramission" hypothesis of vision in the version adopted by Ptolemy, in preference to the Euclidean picture of discrete rays, against which he argues at length. Al-Kindī further maintains the widely held view that vision occurs instantaneously, and not through a successive process. To account for the superior clarity of vision at the center of the visual field, he resorts to an idea, apparently an ancient one, according to which we see, not from a unique point (as in the Euclidean and Ptolemaic model), but from an area on the surface of the eye. Treating every point on this area as a source of visual radiation, al-Kindī succeeds in showing that the middle of the visual field would receive more "illumination" than any other part of it. Finally, in addition to formulating the law of equal angles for reflection from plane and spherical mirrors, al-Kindī struggles with the difficult problem of how we see images in mirrors. As well as expounding the author's own views, the *De aspectibus* undoubtedly reflects discussions that had taken place in late antiquity after the time of Euclid, a fact that should enhance, not diminish, its historical significance.

Nothing of what has come down to us from the tenth century compares in scope and competence with al-Kindī's *De aspectibus*. But we know that works continued to be written on the problem of vision, for instance, by the famous physician and philosopher al Rāzī (Rhazes, *d.* 923/924), and on burning mirrors and shadows, the last subject being approached, however, principally as a branch of astronomy, not of optics. An account of *manāẓir* in *Iḥṣā᾽ al-ᶜulūm* (Enumeration of the sciences), prepared by the philosopher al-Fārābī (*d.* 950), does not indicate that the subject had made much progress, but the impression given by al-Fārābī's book may be misleading. Probably toward the end of the century, a mathematician named Abū Saᶜd al-ᶜAlā᾽ ibn Sahl was engaged in studying Ptolemy's *Optics*, but only a short fragment of his study has survived.

A dramatic change happened in the first half of the eleventh century with the appearance of two major works: Ibn Sīnā's *Kitāb al-shifā᾽* (Book of healing) and Ibn al-Haytham's *Kitāb al-manāẓir*, the first in Iran and the second in Egypt, where Ibn al-Haytham had moved from his native Iraq. The two works differed greatly in their treatment of light and vision, with regard to both doctrine and approach, and it is instructive to see how they contrast with one another. Both were destined to exert profound influence on medieval Latin writers. Ibn Sīnā's great summa of Peripatetic philosophy contained a section, "On the Soul," which paralleled Aristotle's *De anima* without being either a commentary on or a faithful rendering of the Aristotelian work. In a long section devoted to vision, Ibn Sīnā formulates views and arguments that are not found in Aristotle, but he accepts the Aristotelian doctrine of light as the actualization of the potentially transparent medium, and of vision as the occurrence in the eye of the object's visible form when the intermediate air is actualized by the presence of a light source. In a characteristically dialectical mode of argumentation he goes through what he takes to be a complete list of visual ray hypotheses, and having disposed of all of them he is left with the only viable explanation: Aristotle's "intromission" theory.

Ibn Sīnā appears in a different vein in another part of *Kitāb al-shifā᾽*, which corresponds to Aristotle's *Meteorology*. Here he shows himself a critic of Aristotle's remarks on the rainbow and an independent observer of the phenomenon. He expressly states that he was "not satisfied with what our friends the Peripatetics have to say about the rainbow." A number of observations that he personally made (and that he reports in some detail) convinced him that the rainbow phenomenon was not produced by parts of the "dark cloud" itself, but rather by clear water droplets hanging in the air in front of it. Even the presence of a cloud as a background was not necessary, he said, as when he observed the rainbow depicted in a cloudless but moist air against a high mountain, and as evidenced in the formation of rainbows by fountain sprays and the like. He reports with approval the generally accepted description of the shape and size of the bow (a full semicircle when the sun is on the horizon, gradually decreasing in size as the sun goes up). But he found no satisfactory explanation of the rainbow colors, saying plainly that the Peripatetics had not proposed anything on this subject that he could comprehend, and candidly confessing that he himself had nothing new to add, except to suggest that the cause of these colors might perhaps be sought in the eye of the observer.

The *Optics* of Ibn al-Haytham was a mathematician's book written in the style of Ptolemy's

OPTICS, ISLAMIC

Optics, not a philosophical essay in the style of Aristotle's *De anima.* Ibn al-Haytham was, however, convinced that natural philosophers were right in their belief that visual perception consisted in the reception of forms, rather than in sending out rays to the objects seen. He therefore saw his task as that of providing a theory of vision that had the advantages of the mathematical mode of inquiry while being in agreement with physical truth. That is the meaning of his statement at the beginning of the *Optics* that his investigation combined the physical and the mathematical sciences. The result of this synthesis was not an eclectic account, but a new approach to the study of vision. Thus he tried to show, for the first time, how a representation of the visible object is produced in the eye by considering the paths of *light* rays proceeding from points on the object's surface; and he saw that his problem involved regarding the eye as an optical system. More than that, he realized that a theory of the psychology of visual perception was fundamental to any intromissionist explanation.

These statements should now be elaborated. According to Ibn al-Haytham, it is a property of light and color that they rectilinearly "radiate" from each point on the surface of a visible object in all directions, regardless of whether they inhere naturally in such a body or are temporarily acquired by it from an outside source. It follows that every point on the surface of the eye will receive the light and color of every point on the object facing it. Some of these light and color rays will pass through the cornea in straight lines, while others will be bent or refracted before they strike the surface of the crystalline humor (eye-lens), where, again, their behavior will depend on the shape of that surface. To ensure a perfect match between the arrangement of light and color in the crystalline (which, following Galen, he considers to be the organ where visual sensation is first registered) and their array on the object's surface, Ibn al Haytham introduces certain "necessary" assumptions. One is that the cornea's surface and the front surface of the crystalline must be spherical and concentric, with their common center located behind the body of the crystalline. This means that rays traveling from points on the visible object along lines drawn from the common center will be perpendicular to both surfaces. A second crucial assumption is that, owing to the directional sensitivity of the crystalline, only rays along these perpendicular lines can be effective in producing vision. Thus, in each plane that cuts

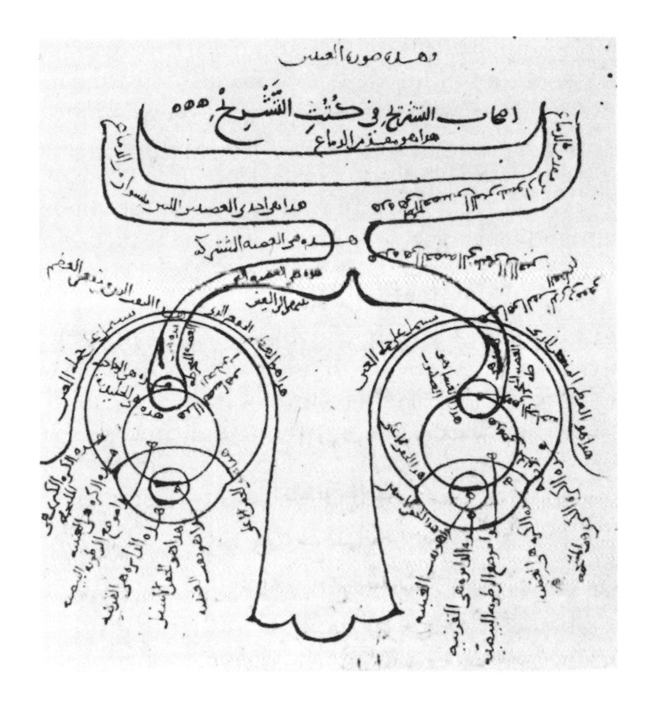

The visual system according to Ibn al-Haytham. Miniature from a copy of the *Kitāb al-manāẓir* executed by the author's son-in-law, Aḥmad ibn Ja^{c}far, at Basra, 1083. İSTANBUL, SÜLEYMANIYE LIBRARY, MS FATIH 3212, fol. 81b

the visual axis inside the crystalline, there is a one-to-one correspondence between all sensitive points in that plane and all points on the visible object. This is equivalent to asserting that throughout the crystalline there is a distinct sensation (or sensed image) of the light and color array facing the eye. The perceiver does not, however, become aware of this sensation until this configuration of light and color (what Ibn al-Haytham calls a "form") has been transmitted as a whole, first through the vitreous humor (placed immediately behind the crystalline) then through the optic nerves, to the optic chiasma, where it is finally perceived by the "last sentient power" that resides in the front of the brain. It is to be noticed that in this explanation the eye functions neither as a pin-hole camera nor as a lens-camera, and the transmission in question is the transmission of sensation (albeit a unique one that preserves shape and order as well as illumination and color) and not one according to the laws of geometrical optics

Ibn al-Haytham clearly asserts that all visual perception, even when not accompanied by a conscious effort at discrimination, is perception of objects in external three-dimensional space. How, then, do we arrive at such a perception from an

OPTICS, ISLAMIC

impression inside the eye after it has been presented to the brain? In his view no intromissionist theory of vision could be maintained without a complete answer to this question. And his answer, to which he devotes the whole of book II (the *Optics* consists of seven books), constitutes in fact his most important and most original contribution to the theory of straight-line vision. In general the answer is that perception of all visible properties, with the exception of light and color, involves acts of inference performed by a faculty of judgment on the basis of what is received in the brain through the optic nerve. Implied in this answer is a distinction between "pure sensation," which, according to Ibn al-Haytham, can only be of light and color as such, and perception, which is always inferential, even though he applies the same name (*idrāk/comprehensio*) to both. Book II accordingly presents a detailed account of the modes of inference involved in the perception of such visible properties as distance, size, shape, solidity, transparency, opacity, smoothness, roughness, beauty, and so on. Ibn al-Haytham is careful to point out that even identifying a color as red or green involves an act of "recognition" based on past experience and memory, and therefore goes beyond mere sensation. Book III complements these accounts with an extended treatment of errors of rectilinear vision.

The rest of the *Optics* deals with reflection (books IV–VI) and refraction (book VII). Here also the presence of a viewing eye frequently determines the formulations of problems and complicates their solutions. The famous "Alhazen's problem," as it was called by seventeenth-century mathematicians in Europe, who gave it much attention, was formulated as that of finding the point or points of reflection on the surface of a plane, spherical, cylindrical, or conical mirror, convex or concave, given the positions of the two points related to one another as object and eye. The problem, which is solved by the intersection of a circle and a hyperbola, occupies a considerable part of book V. In book VII an attempt is made for the first time in the history of optics to consider refraction as a factor in direct vision. And in the same book an explanation is given of the illusory enlargement of celestial bodies near the horizon, which has been mistakenly ascribed to Ptolemy.

And yet, it would be wrong to regard the *Optics* as a book exclusively concerned with problems of vision. The first three chapters in book I (missing from the medieval Latin translation) are an experimental examination of the behavior of light and color. And in books IV and VII Ibn al-Haytham offers remarkable explanations of the reflection and refraction of external light, using dynamical concepts borrowed from the Muslim theologians of his time, and in which he applies the geometry of the parallelogram to what he considers to be an analogical mechanical situation. In these explanations the "motion" of the light impinging on a reflecting or refracting surface is analyzed into two components, one parallel and the other perpendicular to the surface; then the effect of the surface on each component is examined separately. In this manner Ibn al-Haytham deduces the equality of angles in reflection, and in his treatment of refraction he associates the bending of light toward the normal in a dense medium with a decrease in the "speed" of the impinging light as a result of meeting greater "resistance." Whatever the subjects discussed in the *Optics*, the book has an unmistakable "modern" flavor, and it cannot fail to impress the reader with its commitment to the methods of observation and experiment, and the application of mathematics whenever appropriate.

Among the extant optical writings of Ibn al-Haytham are treatises *On the Light of the Moon, On the Light of the Stars, On the Rainbow and the Halo, On Spherical Burning Mirrors, On Parabolic Burning Mirrors, On the Burning Sphere, On the Form of the Eclipse, On the Quality of Shadows,* and *Discourse on Light.* In the first of these Ibn al-Haytham argues in support of the view that the moon derives its light from the sun, and against the view that it reflects solar rays like a mirror. In a skillful combination of experimental and mathematical arguments he shows that the moon emits its borrowed light in the same way as a self-luminous body does: that is, from each point on its surface in all directions. The unsuccessful explanation of the rainbow departs significantly from the equally unsuccessful explanation in Aristotle's *Meteorology,* and draws closer to the treatment of images in spherical concave mirrors in Ptolemy's *Optics* and in book V of Ibn al-Haytham's own *Optics.* The treatises on burning mirrors and the burning sphere all treat solar rays as agents of combustion (not of vision) and all are impressive by their show of mathematical skill. The treatise *On Parabolic Burning Mirrors* is the only optical writing of Ibn al-Haytham, other than the *Optics,* that was rendered into Latin in the Middle Ages, probably by Gerard of Cremona in the twelfth century. In a brief introduction, the author tells us what he knew about earlier achievements in this field. The "ancients," he says, knew and were able to prove that solar rays could be gathered in a single point from a single circle on the surface of a concave spherical mirror. To increase burning power, some "famous" mathematicians, among them Archimedes and Anthemius of Tralles (*fl.* sixth century), used systems of plane or spherical mirrors. The ancients also became aware of the fact that solar rays could be focused in a point from the whole concave surface of a paraboloid of revolution. But, according to Ibn al-Haytham, no one had provided a satisfactory proof of this fact until he was able to do so in his own treatise. His statement seems to be supported by the historical evidence that has come down to us. The treatise *On the Form of the Eclipse* deals with the problem: why does the partially eclipsed sun cast a crescent-shaped image while the crescent moon casts a circular image, when both images are projected through the same narrow circular opening? By considering, separately, the light that emanates from each point on the luminous object through all points on the opening, then that which emanates from all points on the object through each point on the opening, Ibn al-Haytham is led to formulate and apply two principles of the working of the pin-hole camera. But the general problem of the camera remains unsolved. The *Discourse on Light* is in part a summary of arguments more fully developed in the *Optics,* after which it was written; it further expounds a doctrine of light in Aristotelian terms which are absent from the earlier work.

It is remarkable that no one in late antiquity or in the Islamic world seems to have made any effective use of Ptolemy's *Optics* until Ibn al-Haytham, starting from the work of his Greek predecessor, wrote the book which actually superseded it. It is even more remarkable that no one in the Islamic world seems to have made effective use of Ibn al Haytham's *Optics* until the end of the thirteenth century. Medical writers on anatomy and ophthalmology ignored Ibn al-Haytham's account of the construction of the eye and of the physiology of vision; and mathematicians acquainted with at least some of Ibn al-Haytham's astronomical and mathematical writings appear not to have had access to the *Optics.* Naṣīr al-Dīn al-Ṭūsī (*d.* 1274), for example, prepared a recension of Euclid's *Optics* which later enjoyed a wide circulation, while a treatise of his on

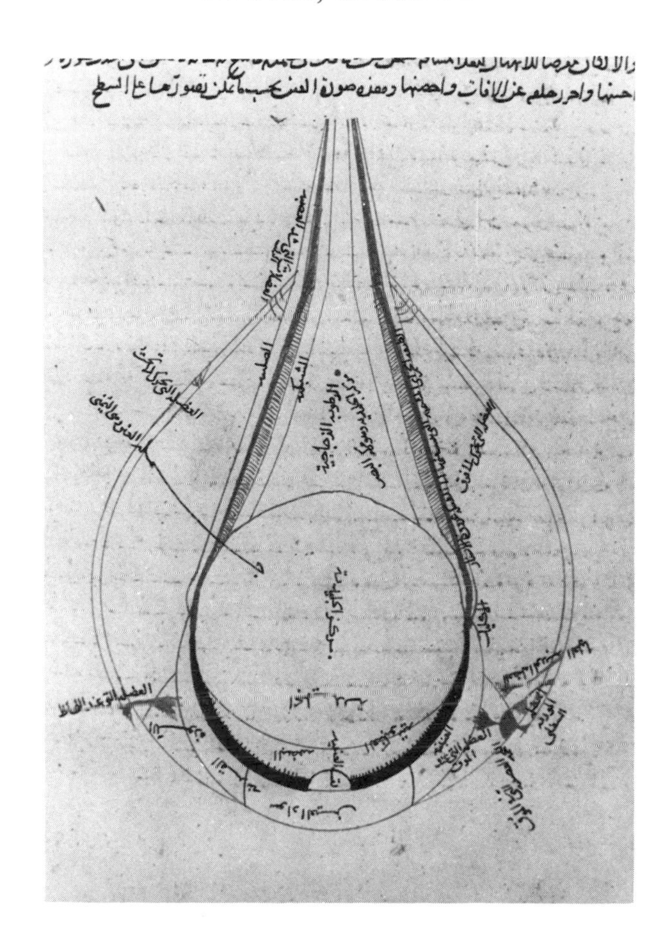

Diagram of the eye from a 1316 MS of the *Tanqīḥ al-manāẓir*, representing Kamāl al-Dīn's understanding of the structure of the eye. TOPKAPI PALACE MUSEUM, İSTANBUL, MS AHMET III 3340, fol. 25b

refraction clearly shows that he was ignorant of Ibn al-Haytham's (and Ptolemy's) ideas on the subject. Finally a copy of Ibn al-Haytham's *Optics* was brought "from a distant land" (Egypt?) to Tabriz in northwestern Iran for Kamāl al-Dīn al-Fārisī to write a commentary on it, as suggested to him by his teacher, Quṭb al-Dīn al-Shīrāzī, who had seen the book "in his youth" but had not read it. This commentary, known as *Tanqīḥ al-manāẓir* (Revision of the *Optics*), is a landmark in the history of Islamic optics. It is a large book that deals, competently and with much insight, with all the subjects discussed in Ibn al-Haytham's book and in his other writings referred to above; and it subsequently became the main vehicle for disseminating Ibn al-Haytham's ideas in the Islamic world. But, although he was an avowed admirer, Kamāl al-Dīn was no mere follower of Ibn al-Haytham, and his "commentary" is frequently supplemented by

OPTICS, ISLAMIC

criticisms and new ideas, the most far-reaching among them being his new theory of the rainbow, which he thus arrived at about the same time that Theodoric of Freiberg (*d. ca.* 1310) offered a somewhat similar explanation.

Kamāl al-Dīn tells us that he was guided in his investigation of the rainbow by Ibn Sīnā's remarks in the *al-Shifāᵓ* summarized above. It would seem that it was Ibn Sīnā's reference to water sprays that inspired Kamāl al-Dīn to disregard the idea of a cloud acting as a huge concave mirror and to concentrate on individual drops. This was a radical departure from the approach of both Aristotle and Ibn al-Haytham; but in his study of the path of light through the drop Kamāl al-Dīn had to rely on the rules of refraction as set out by Ibn al-Haytham in book VII of the *Optics* and on his detailed study of the passage of light through glass spheres. Another major departure from all earlier treatments was Kamāl al-Dīn's successful attempt to duplicate the natural phenomenon by an artificial object, a spherical globe filled with water representing the water drop, which could then itself be made subject to direct experimental investigation. This was no easy task: Kamāl al-Dīn's arguments, though competent and even sophisticated, are frequently tortuous and not always free from error. But they achieve a correct explanation of the appearance of the primary and secondary bows, including their shape and the reversed order of colors in them. Kamāl al-Dīn concludes in fact that the primary lower rainbow is produced when solar rays reach the eye after two refractions (upon entering and leaving the water drop) and one reflection inside the drop; while the secondary bow appears when two internal reflections occur between the two refractions. As might be expected, Kamāl al-Dīn's explanation of the generation of the rainbow colors is not successful, though he relates them in part to refraction in a vague way.

When Kamāl al-Dīn completed his *Tanqīḥ* about the year 1300, the *Optics* of Ibn al-Haytham had already been known and extensively studied in Europe for at least three quarters of a century (together with al-Kindī's *De aspectibus*, Ibn Sīnā's *On the Soul*, and Ptolemy's *Optics*, the last having been translated from the Arabic version in Sicily in the twelfth century). Thanks to the *Tanqīḥ*, however, Ibn al-Haytham's doctrines came to be known to mathematicians, philosophers, and theologians in the Muslim world all the way down to the sixteenth century. But there were no breakthroughs in the study of light and vision. The substantial work on optics, *Nūr ḥadaqat al-abṣār*, composed for the Ottoman Sultan Murād III (1574–1595) by the Damascus-born engineer and astronomer Taqī al-Dīn ibn Maᶜrūf, is an intelligent summary and discussion of the main topics in the *Tanqīḥ*, but it does not go beyond the stage already reached in the work of Ibn al-Haytham and Kamāl al-Dīn.

BIBLIOGRAPHY

Sources (translated). Al-Kindī: *De aspectibus*, in Axel Anthon Björnbo and S. Vogl, eds., "Alkindi, Tideus und Pseudo-Euklid: Drei optische Werke," in *Abhandlungen zur Geschichte der mathematischen Wissenschaften*, **26:3** (1912); Ḥunayn ibn Isḥāq: *The Ten Treatises on the Eye, Ascribed to . . .*, Max Meyerhof, ed. and trans. (1928); Ibn Sīnā (Avicenna): *Liber de anima* (critical ed. of medieval Latin text), S. van Riet, ed., intro. by G. Verbeke, 5 vols. in 2 (1968–1972); *Psychologie d'Ibn Sīnā*, Ján Bakoš, trans. 2 vols. (1956); *Avicenna's De anima*, F. Rahman, ed. (1959); *Avicenna's Psychology*, R. Rahman, trans. (1952, repr. 1981), trans. of bk. II, ch. 6, of *Kitāb al-najāt*, a summary of *Kitāb al-shifāᵓ*; Ibn al-Haytham (Alhazen): *Opticae thesaurus*, Friedrich Risner, ed. (1572, repr. 1972); *Rasāᵓil* (1938–1939), in Arabic; H. J. J. Winter and W. ᶜArafāt, "A Statement on Optical Reflection and 'Refraction' Attributed to Naṣīr ud-Dīn aṭ-Ṭūsī," in *Isis*, **42** (1951).

Sources (Arabic). Ibn al-Haytham, *Kitāb al-manāẓir*, Books I–III, Abdelhamid I. Sabra, ed. (1983); Kamāl al-Dīn al-Fārisī, *Tanqīḥ al-manāẓir*, 2 vols. (1929–1930).

Studies. David C. Lindberg, *Theories of Vision from Al-Kindī to Kepler* (1976); Max Meyerhof, "Die Optik der Araber," in *Zeitschrift für ophthalmologische Optik*, **8** (1920); M. Naẓīf, "Kamāl al-Dīn al-Fārisī: Some Researches in Optics" (in Arabic), in *Risālat al-ᶜIlm*, **25** (December 1958); S. B. Omar, *Ibn al-Haytham's Optics: A Study of the Origins of Experimental Science* (1977); Roshdi Rashed, "Optique géometrique et doctrine optique chez Ibn al-Haytham," in *Archive for History of Exact Sciences*, **6** (1969–1970), "Le modèle de la sphere transparente et l'explication de l'arc-en-ciel: Ibn al-Haytham, al-Fārisī," in *Revue d'histoire des sciences et de leurs applications*, **23** (1970), and "Kamāl al-Dīn," in *Dictionary of Scientific Biography;* Abdelhamid I. Sabra, "Explanation of Optical Reflection and Refraction: Ibn al-Haytham, Descartes, Newton," in *Proceedings of the Tenth International Congress on the History of Science*, 2 vols., I (1964), "Ibn al-Haytham," in *Dictionary of Scientific Biography*, VII (1973), "The Physical and the Mathematical in Ibn al-Haytham's Theory of Light and Vision," in *Bīrūnī International Congress*, Tehran, 1973 (1976), "Sensation and Inference in Alhazen's Theory of Visual Perception," in P. Machamer and R. G. Turnbull,

OPTICS, WESTERN EUROPEAN

eds., *Studies in Perception* (1978), and "Ibn al-Haytham's Lemmas for Solving 'Alhazen's Problem,'" in *Archive for History of Exact Sciences,* **26** (1982); Matthias Schramm, "Zur Entwicklung der physiologischen Optik in der arabischen Literatur," in *Sudhoffs Archiv für Geschichte der Medizin und der Naturwissenschaften,* **43** (1959), and *Ibn al-Haytham's Weg zur Physik* (1963); Eilhard Wiedemann, *Aufzätze zur arabischen Wissenschaftsgeschichte,* 2 vols. (1970), and *Gesammelte Schriften zur arabisch-islamischen Wissenschaftsgeschichte,* 3 vols. (1984). (These last two include collections of Wiedemann's translations [in German] and paraphrases of works by Ibn al-Haytham and Kamāl al-Dīn al-Fārisī.)

A. I. SABRA

[See also **Archimedes in the Middle Ages; Astrology/Astronomy; Bacon, Roger; Fārābī, al-; Kindī, al-; Rāzī, al-; Sīnā, Ibn.**]

OPTICS, WESTERN EUROPEAN

SOURCES, TRADITIONS, AND METHODS

During the early Middle Ages, knowledge of matters that we would now consider optical was extremely limited. Roman encyclopedias, such as Seneca the Younger's *Natural Questions* and Pliny the Elder's *Natural History,* had touched upon vision, mirrors, and meteorological phenomena involving light; and this knowledge was available in the Middle Ages. However, the only source that provided anything even approaching a systematic account of light, color, and vision was the first half of Plato's *Timaeus,* translated into Latin by Chalcidius (perhaps early fourth century) and supplemented by Chalcidius' weighty commentary. In the *Timaeus* Plato argued that visual fire emanating from the observer's eye coalesces with daylight to form an optical medium capable of transmitting the motions of external bodies to the soul, where they result in visual sensation. The only other significant writer on optics during the early Middle Ages was St. Augustine, who touched upon light and vision in several of his works and generally lent support to the Platonic theory. With these meager sources to build upon and very little reason for studying optical phenomena, scholars in the early Middle Ages (that is, prior to the eleventh century) contributed little to the science of optics. Their thought remained largely Platonic and, in comparison with the Greek achievement, exceedingly primitive.

This state of affairs was dramatically altered by the translations of the eleventh, twelfth, and thirteenth centuries, which supplied medieval Christendom with the best optical literature of Greek antiquity and medieval Islam. One of the earliest optical sources rendered into Latin was the *Ten Treatises on the Eye* of Ḥunayn ibn Isḥāq (the ninth-century translator of scientific works from Greek and Syriac into Arabic, who also wrote a number of treatises of his own in Arabic), translated late in the eleventh century by Constantine the African. In this work Ḥunayn nicely summarized Galen's views on the anatomy and physiology of the eye, and through Constantine's translation they were widely disseminated in the West. Other optical works soon followed. Euclid's *Optics* and *Catoptrics* were translated, probably about the middle of the twelfth century. Ptolemy's great optical text (*Optics* or *On Vision*) and al-Kindī's small but influential one (*On Vision*) appeared in the second half of the twelfth century. About the same time a number of philosophical works touching upon optical phenomena were translated: Aristotle's *On the Soul, On Sensation,* and *Meteorology;* and Ibn Sīnā's *On the Soul,* a section of his *Book of Healing* (of the soul). These were followed, near the end of the twelfth century or the beginning of the thirteenth, by the most original Arabic source on optics, Ibn al-Haytham's *Book on Optics,* and early in the thirteenth century by Ibn Rushd's commentaries on Aristotle. Finally, there were translations of a large quantity of medical literature dealing with the anatomy and physiology of the eye and the treatment of eye diseases.

These translations transformed the study of optics. Whereas the West had heretofore had only a scanty collection of optical materials, principally Platonic, it now possessed an impressive corpus of highly sophisticated treatises representing a variety of scientific and philosophical traditions. The pressing problem was to assimilate this body of diverse literature, reconcile conflicting ideas where possible, and choose among alternatives where necessary. This task was eagerly taken up in the thirteenth century by Robert Grosseteste, Albertus Magnus, Roger Bacon, and others.

The first impact of the newly translated material is perceptible in the writings of Robert Grosseteste (*d.* 1253), lecturer and chancellor at the University of Oxford and later bishop of Lincoln. Under the influence of Neoplatonic writings, such as those of Pseudo-Dionysius and St. Augustine, Grosseteste

OPTICS, WESTERN EUROPEAN

became convinced that light held the key to an understanding not only of the natural world but also of divine creative and redemptive activity. He developed a philosophy of light in which (1) creation of the material universe was seen as the result of the self-propagation of a point of light, (2) all causation within the material world was conceived as analogous to the radiation of light, (3) knowledge of the eternal truths was explained by analogy with corporeal vision through the eye, and (4) theological and moral truths were elucidated by means of light metaphors. Grosseteste had thus legitimized the study of optics for himself and for a coterie of followers. He also confronted some of the more technical problems of the optical tradition: vision, reflection, refraction, and the rainbow. Grosseteste's achievement, based on a knowledge of some but not all of the new sources, was intelligent but unspectacular. His theory of vision, for example, while taking some account of newly translated works by Euclid, al-Kindī, Aristotle, and Ibn Sīnā, was nevertheless basically a restatement of the traditional Platonic view.

A fuller command of the new materials is evident about mid century in the work of Albertus Magnus (*d.* 1280) and Roger Bacon (*d. ca.* 1292). Albertus dedicated himself to promoting Aristotle's theory of vision at the expense of its competitors, while Bacon attempted to establish the mathematical tradition in optics (of Euclid, Ptolemy, al-Kindī, and Ibn al-Haytham) and to reconcile it with the philosophical tradition of Aristotle, Ibn Sīnā, and Ibn Rushd.

The outcome of these thirteenth-century efforts was not a final resolution of the difficult issues and problems facing the science of optics, but the creation of a set of traditions within which these problems would be pursued for the next 400 years. We can discern four such traditions—frequently overlapping, sometimes merging, yet distinguishable. The largest, in terms of the number of adherents, was undoubtedly the Aristotelian, inspired by the work of Albertus Magnus and found in commentaries and questions on Aristotle's *On the Soul* and *On Sensation.* Within this tradition the dominant problems were, of course, those raised in the Aristotelian text—mainly physical, ontological, and psychological in nature, with little if any attention to mathematical analysis. The second tradition was that of *perspectiva,* built upon the mathematical and physical analysis of optical phenomena by Ptolemy and Ibn al-Haytham (combined with certain Aristotelian, Platonic, and Galenic elements), and vigorously promoted by Roger Bacon, John Peckham (*d.* 1292), and Witelo (*d.* 1277). Although *perspectiva* did not adopt an exclusively mathematical approach, it soon came to be viewed as the home of mathematical optics. A third loosely organized tradition can be characterized as theological; pursued principally by theological masters on the basis of theological sources, it was concerned with the role of light in creation, problems of cognition, and the application of light metaphors to various theological issues. Finally, within the medical tradition Galen's teachings on ocular anatomy and physiology were preserved, and remedies for diseases of the eye and visual system continued to be sought. It must be emphasized that medieval optics was not a unified body of doctrine taught by a single community of scholars, but a diverse collection of theories viewed in a variety of ways and studied for a variety of reasons by the members of different communities.

Who populated these different communities, and what methods did they employ in the study of optics? The first question can easily be answered in general terms. Optics entered the curriculum of the medieval university in a number of ways: under the heading of *perspectiva* (sometimes to fulfill degree requirements in mathematics), through lectures on the works of Aristotle, through theological works that raised questions of an optical nature, and through the study of Galenic medicine; its practitioners were therefore the professorial staff responsible for preparing and delivering the lectures, and the student audience obliged to listen to them. It seems that few masters or students pursued optical studies at an advanced level, but at an elementary level knowledge of optical theory must have been quite widespread.

What methods were employed by the master or student who wished to press forward to what we might call "research" in optics? This is an important question because of the tendency of some historians to see the beginnings of experimental science in the optical work of Robert Grosseteste, Roger Bacon, or Theodoric of Freiberg (*d. ca.* 1310). It is also a very difficult question that must be approached with great caution. First, medieval optics was not devoid of observation and experimentation. It is doubtful that medieval scholars in any discipline having empirical consequences ever feared to put theory to observational test, and if we see little experimentation during the Middle Ages,

 OPTICS, WESTERN EUROPEAN

one of the reasons is that readily testable consequences were not numerous. In any case, there is no reason to doubt Theodoric of Freiberg's claim to have experimented with prisms and transparent spheres when investigating the rainbow; nor should we suppose that Roger Bacon and his fellow perspectivists, in trying to understand image formation in mirrors, never examined one, or that visual theorists failed to gather empirical data on the facts of sight whenever they could.

Nonetheless, the activities of the optical "researcher" were principally literary and intellectual. His energy was devoted largely to mastering the literature of the optical tradition going back to Greek antiquity, to discussing and (if possible) resolving its many contradictions and difficulties, and to thinking through its implications. Even Roger Bacon, with a reputation for experimental prowess, did not in fact expend much time or effort in observation and experimentation. Bacon frequently appealed to observations, but they were generally not his own. He could also acknowledge the importance of empirical foundations for optical knowledge. But his own achievement was to work out an intellectual compromise between differing optical traditions. He and his fellow students of optics were not applied or experimental scientists, but philosophers of nature.

THE NATURE OF LIGHT AND COLOR

One of the most discussed issues within medieval optics was the nature of light and color. These discussions were exceedingly intricate, and can only be summarized here. The dominant early medieval view was that of the Platonic tradition: that light issuing from flame or the fiery body of the sun is itself a kind of fire. Indeed, it was maintained that even the "light" issuing from the eye and cooperating with external light in the act of vision is a "fiery virtue" having the same nature as fire.

This picture was changed by the coming of Aristotelian philosophy. Aristotle had argued that light is not fire or some other substance, but a quality or characteristic of the medium. It is, to be specific, the actualization of the transparent medium—the realization by the medium of full transparency, so that bodies separated from the observer by the medium become visible. Color, Aristotle maintained, is a quality of visible objects that is able to produce qualitative changes in a medium that has already achieved the full actuality associated with light; these qualitative changes can be communicated to the transparent humors of the eye, thereby giving rise to visual perception of the colored object. It was one variant or another of this Aristotelian theory that prevailed in the West from the thirteenth century on.

One of the most influential of the variants was developed in the Islamic world. Ibn Sīnā accepted Aristotle's distinction between light and color, but further subdivided light into (1) brightness or *lux* (in the Latin translation of Ibn Sīnā's work), the quality of fiery objects by which they are perceived; (2) the splendor or *lumen* shining from luminous bodies, which falls on nonluminous objects and makes them visible; and (3) the ray or radiance that surrounds luminous bodies "as though it were something emanating from them." Another variant was proposed by Ibn Sīnā's contemporary Ibn al-Haytham, who argued that both light and color send their forms through the medium to the observer's eye (rather than color alone, as in Aristotle's theory). Ibn al-Haytham thus defended the novel position that both color and light are objects of visual perception.

We find similar themes endlessly repeated in the West. Ibn Sīnā's distinction between *lux* and *lumen* was widely (but not universally) employed, *lux* being viewed as the luminous quality of the fiery body and *lumen* as its effect propagated through the surrounding transparent medium. *Lux* was light in the body; *lumen* was light in the medium. A somewhat different and highly influential view, first presented by Grosseteste and brought to a high state of refinement by Bacon, held that a visible object multiplies from itself a likeness, called a "species," that comes into being in each successive part of the medium out of the potentiality of the medium, through the action of the species in the immediately preceding part of the medium. This is the doctrine that has come to be known as "the multiplication of species."

THE GEOMETRY OF PROPAGATION

Discussions of the nature of light and color, and the physical processes involved in their propagation, were central to medieval optics. But it was also widely recognized that the propagation of light could be described mathematically. If the path of light can be represented by a geometrical line proceeding according to well-defined mathematical rules, then the propagation of light is reducible to ray geometry. To illustrate the level of medieval knowledge, let us look at the work of Roger Bacon.

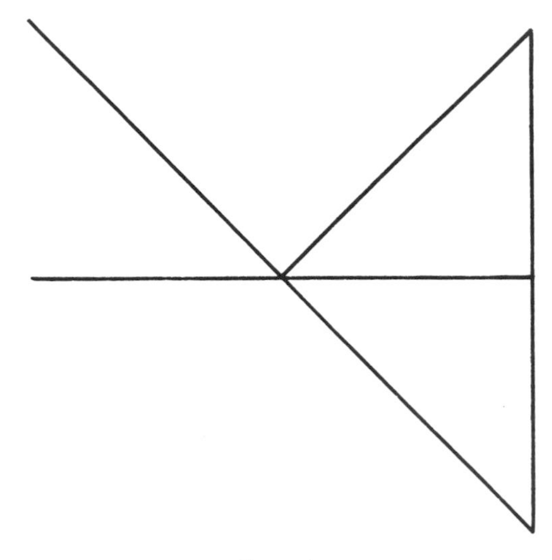

Figure 1

But as we do so, we must recognize that, except for several very minor details, all medieval Western knowledge of the geometry of propagation was inherited from ancient Greece and the medieval Islamic world. Bacon and his fellow perspectivists did not contribute significantly to the creation of geometrical optics, but faithfully transmitted to later generations what they had learned from the Greek and Islamic optical traditions.

In several of his works, Bacon defined five geometrical modes of propagation. The first is direct radiation in a straight line, which occurs whenever light passes through a homogeneous medium. The principle of rectilinear propagation had been variously defended in antiquity, and the medieval commitment to it was virtually unshakable. Second, if light traversing one medium falls obliquely on a medium of different density, it is refracted and assumes a new orientation in the second medium; we thus have two straight lines joined to form an angle. It was understood that if light is perpendicularly incident on the interface separating these two media, no refraction occurs. Third, when light encounters a smooth body of density too great to permit penetration, it is reflected in such a way that the angle of reflection equals the angle of incidence. Fourth, each point of a ray of primary light (emanating from the sun, for example) is the source of secondary light; thus the corner of a room that receives no primary light is nevertheless weakly illuminated by secondary light. This is not a matter of the bending of light, but of two different lights (primary and secondary), the one generated by the other but each proceeding along straight lines unless reflected or refracted. Fifth, there is the special case of light in an "animated medium," by which Bacon meant the spirits filling the optic nerve; light entering the eye proceeds into and through the optic nerve to its junction with the other optic nerve, and in so doing is able to follow the twisting course of the nerve without reflection or refraction. "And this takes place," Bacon states, "by the power of the mind directing the passage of the species. . . . "

Knowledge of the principles of reflection and refraction was quite advanced. In the case of reflection, it was known not only that the angles of incidence and reflection are equal, but also that the incident and reflected rays define a plane perpendicular to the plane of the mirror (or, if the mirror is curved, perpendicular to its tangent plane at the point of reflection). The principles of image formation were also well understood. In the simple case of a plane mirror, it was known that the image is located as far behind the mirror as the object is before it, and that a straight line connecting any point of the object to the corresponding point of the image is perpendicular to the reflecting surface. Thus, in Figure 1, *ABC* is the reflecting surface, *E* the object, *D* the eye, and *F* the image; *ECF* is perpendicular to the mirror, and *EC* = *CF*. For curved reflecting surfaces, it was concluded that the image is located at the intersection of the ray entering the observer's eye (the reflected ray) and the perpendicular dropped from the visible object to the reflecting surface. Medieval scholars were able to apply such rules to exceedingly difficult cases involving mirrors that were spherically concave or convex, the object being variously located with respect to the center of curvature; moreover, there was an implicit understanding of the concept of focal point.

Knowledge of refraction was at approximately the same level. It was known that light passing from a less dense to a more dense medium is refracted toward the perpendicular to the refracting interface, and that light passing from a more dense to a less dense medium is refracted away from the perpendicular. It was also recognized that the image of an object seen by refraction is located at the intersection of the rectilinear extension of the ray entering the eye (the refracted ray) and the perpendicular dropped from the visible object to the refracting interface; thus, in Figure 2, if *A* is the observer's eye and *CD* the refracting interface, an

OPTICS, WESTERN EUROPEAN

object at *B* will appear at *L*. This knowledge was applied to refraction at interfaces of curved, as well as plane, figures. It must be noted, however, that the principles of refraction were rarely applied to refraction at more than a single interface; that is, no theory of thin lenses was developed, although the principles from which such a theory could have been built were at hand. An exception was the transparent burning sphere, in the analysis of which it was recognized that rays emanating from a given point on one side of the sphere are brought to a focus on the other side.

Relatively good quantitative data on refraction were also available. In antiquity, Ptolemy had measured corresponding angles of incidence and refraction at 10° intervals for various pairs of media and had attempted to generalize these into a mathematical law of refraction. Ptolemy's data were known in the West, but they were rarely reported—the only known instance was by Witelo, a thirteenth-century Silesian scholar.

THEORIES OF VISION

No understanding of medieval visual theory is possible without some knowledge of the ancient and Islamic background. Three Greek traditions had a significant impact on medieval visual theory. The first was that of Euclid and Ptolemy, who developed a mathematical theory of perspective based on the idea that radiation issues conically from the observer's eye and gives rise to visual experience when intercepted by an opaque object; we can call this an "extramission" theory. It should be remembered that although the theory is not devoid of physical content, its goals were largely mathematical. The second theory was that of Aristotle, having as its principal goal the explanation of physical contact between object and observer (with no concern for the mathematics of the process); according to this "intromission" theory, the visible object alters the transparent medium, and this alteration is propagated instantaneously to the observer's eye to produce sensation. The third theory was that of Galen, who argued that visual spirit emerging from the observer's eye transforms the medium and endows it with sensitivity, enabling it to function as an extension of the optic nerve; the transformed medium then directly perceives objects with which it is in contact. Galen's theory also contained an extensive account of the anatomy and physiology of the eye.

All three of these theories were known in the Islamic world, where they were defended and extended. But the most significant event in Islamic visual theory (and probably the most significant event in visual theory between antiquity and Kepler's theory of the retinal image) was the attempt by Ibn al-Haytham (965–*ca.* 1040) to produce a synthesis of the three ancient theories—to take what he considered the essential achievements of each and to construct from them a new intromission theory. In broad outline, what Ibn al-Haytham did was to combine Aristotle's account of the nature of light with the mathematics of Euclid and Ptolemy, and the ocular anatomy and physiology of Galen. He produced a theory that was to be enormously influential in the West and that would serve as the foundation for Johannes Kepler's work in the seventeenth century.

All of the visual theories that have been mentioned became known in the West through translations. Because of the strength of Aristotelianism in the medieval university, it was inevitable that the Aristotelian theory of vision should receive wide acceptance. Albertus Magnus gave it a forceful defense in the middle of the thirteenth century, and thereafter it never lacked supporters. But the theory

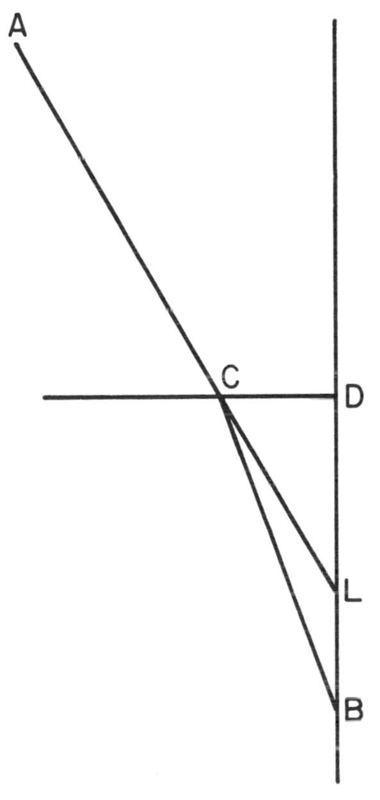

Figure 2

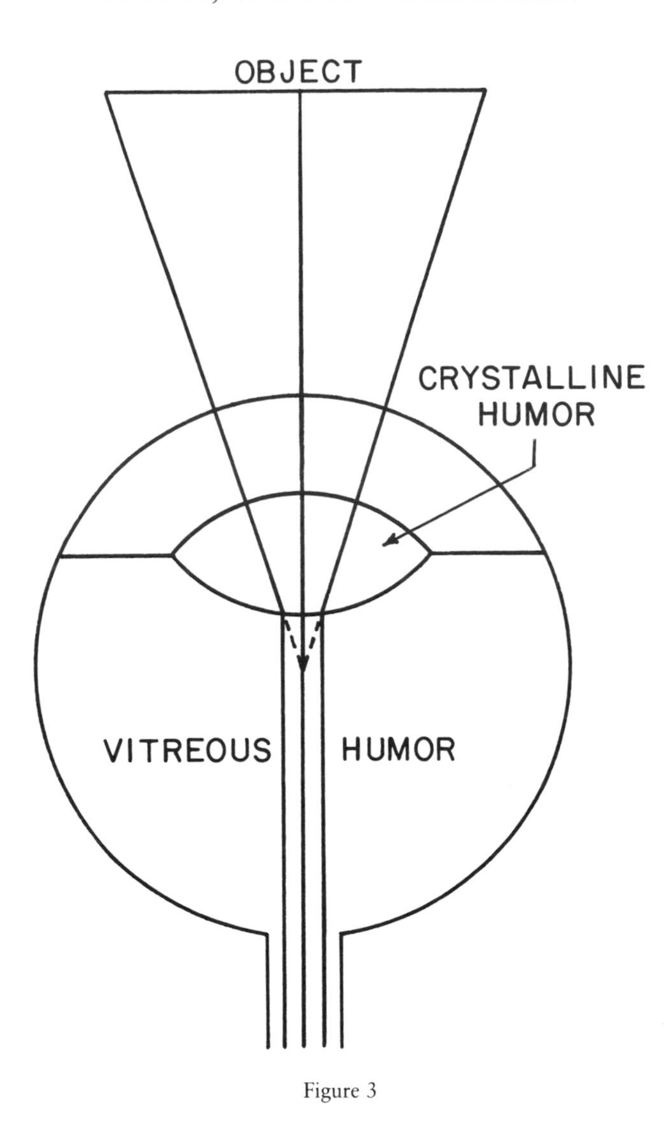

Figure 3

of Ibn al-Haytham was also widely known and held. Roger Bacon was its earliest proponent, and through his influence it passed to the later Middle Ages and the Renaissance. Let us briefly sketch this theory as presented by Bacon.

Radiation (the "species" discussed above) issues in all unobstructed directions from each point in the visual field, some radiation from every point entering the eye of an observer. But a problem is thus posed: If radiation from every point in the visual field enters the observer's eye (indeed, reaches virtually every point of the observer's eye), the result should be mixing and confusion. How could the observer then distinguish different objects in their various places? For clear perception, each point in the visual field must influence a single point in the eye; a one-to-one correspondence must be established. The solution to the difficulty is found in the phenomenon of refraction. A given point in the visual field sends many rays (a virtual infinity) into the eye, but only one of these falls perpendicularly on its spherical surface. All others are refracted and thereby sufficiently weakened (since bending weakens) to fall below the threshold of sensibility; consequently, for the purposes of visual theory, they can be ignored. Each point in the visual field, then, sends one ray to the eye perpendicularly, and the collection of all such perpendiculars (all of them directed toward the center of curvature of the eye) constitutes a visual cone. The visual cone of the extramission theory is thus incorporated into an intromission theory, bringing with it all of the mathematical capabilities of the extramission theory (Fig. 3). The rays of this cone pass into the crystalline humor (the front surface of which is concentric with the outer surface of the eye) without refraction and are perceived by it. At the rear surface of the crystalline humor, they are refracted in such a way as to avoid intersection and inversion; they then proceed, maintaining their arrangement, through one optic nerve to its junction with the other optic nerve; here the species from the two eyes are joined, and a final visual judgment is made.

THE RAINBOW

Aristotle had discussed a number of meteorological phenomena involving light, and one of them in particular, the rainbow, became the object of intense discussion and debate during the Middle Ages. The basic geometry of the rainbow had been adequately worked out by Aristotle: the sun, the observer, and the center of the rainbow fall on a straight line; the observer is situated in the middle and can be thought of as the pivot about which this line turns as the sun rises or sets; the rainbow is circular and is situated symmetrically about the line passing from the sun, through the observer, to the center of curvature of the rainbow. This much was known and accepted by all medieval scholars who considered the matter.

The main point of debate was the physical means by which the colors of the rainbow were produced. Aristotle's position had been that visual rays are reflected to the sun from droplets of mist in a concave cloud. Because of the extreme minuteness of these reflecting surfaces, the sun's color is visible, but not its true shape; differential weakening of the rays is responsible for the various colors. Alternatives to this theory were presented during the Middle Ages. Grosseteste suggested that refraction of light must be involved. Bacon responded by demonstrating that refraction (employed macroscopically in the cloud as a whole, as Grosseteste had employed it) would not work, and returned to an explanation based exclusively on reflection. Witelo argued that the rainbow resulted from a combination of reflected and refracted rays. Finally, early in the fourteenth century, Theodoric of Freiberg presented a theory, involving both reflection and refraction in the individual raindrop, that embodied the basic principles of the formation of the rainbow as understood today. Light, according to Theodoric, enters individual raindrops (Fig. 4), experiencing refraction upon entrance and exit, and internal reflection at the back of the drop. Theodoric also understood the production of the secondary rainbow by a double internal reflection (Fig. 5). He understood, moreover, how the observer could see the same colors in circular bands symmetrically arranged with respect to the line connecting the sun, the observer, and the center of the rainbow—and how different colors were seen in different circular bands. However, Theodoric's theory did not attract much notice from his or succeeding generations (either because it was never presented to them or because it did not appeal to them), and it did not reappear until the seventeenth century, in the work of Descartes—whether independently or on the basis of a knowledge of medieval sources, we cannot say.

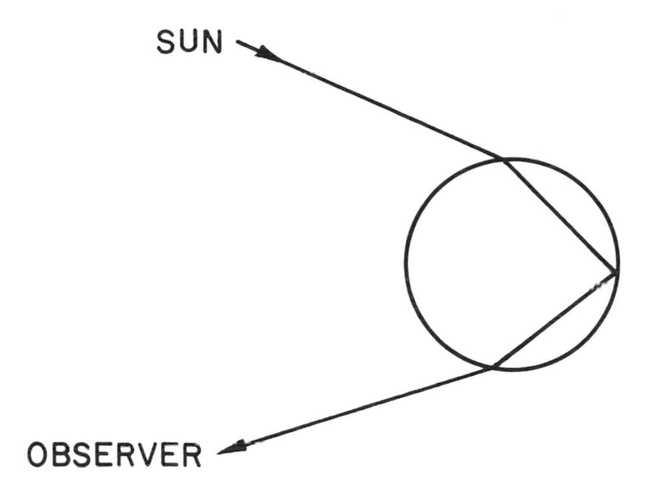

Figure 4

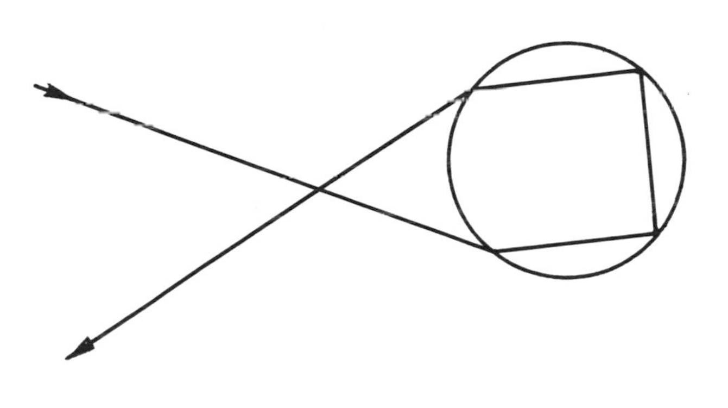

Figure 5

BIBLIOGRAPHY

The essential primary sources, both printed and manuscript, are listed in David C. Lindberg, *A Catalog of Medieval and Renaissance Optical Manuscripts* (1975). For a handy translation of a medieval optical text, see *John Pecham and the Science of Optics: Perspectiva communis*, David C. Lindberg, ed. and trans. (1970). Further primary sources in translation are in Edward Grant, ed., *A Source Book in Medieval Science* (1974), 376–441.

Secondary literature that provides analyses of most of the topics discussed in this article are Carl B. Boyer, *The Rainbow: From Myth to Mathematics* (1959); Alistair C. Crombie, *Robert Grosseteste and the Origins of Experimental Science, 1100–1700* (1953, 3rd ed. 1971); David C. Lindberg, *Theories of Vision from al-Kindī to Kepler* (1976), and "The Genesis of Kepler's Theory of Light: Light Metaphysics from Plotinus to Kepler," in *Osiris*, n.s. 2 (1986). For another introductory account of medieval optics, see David C. Lindberg ed., *Science in the Middle Ages* (1978), chap. 10.

DAVID C. LINDBERG

[See also **Albertus Magnus; Aristotle in the Middle Ages; Bacon, Roger; Grosseteste, Robert; Kindī, al-; Lenses and Eyeglasses; Optics, Islamic; Plato in the Middle Ages; Peckham, John; Rushd, Ibn; Sīnā, Ibn; Theodoric of Freiberg.**]

OPUS ALEXANDRINUM, a very rich variety of opus sectile combining relatively large pieces of marble or stone with mosaic in a guilloche design. This technique characterizes the work of the medieval Roman marble workers known as the Cosmati.

GREGORY WHITTINGTON

[See also **Cosmati Work; Opus Sectile;** and illustration overleaf.]

Altar front from S. Prassede, Rome, showing Cosmati work in opus alexandrinum. 12th–13th century. ALINARI/ART RESOURCE

OPUS ANGLICANUM, elaborate English embroidery of the tenth to sixteenth centuries, particularly prized in the thirteenth and fourteenth centuries (the 1295 Vatican inventory, for example, describes 113 examples). From the middle of the thirteenth century, production centered in London. The embroidery was often done on velvet with a lavish use of gold thread (made by wrapping tin strips coated with gold leaf around silk) and applied jewels, especially pearls. It was time-consuming work: four women worked for nearly four years on a single altar frontal at Westminster (completed around 1271). Pattern books, one of which survives at Magdalene College, Cambridge (MS 1916), apparently were used, but little else is known about the manufacturing methods.

BIBLIOGRAPHY

Grace Christie, *English Medieval Embroidery* (1938); C. R. Dodwell, *Anglo-Saxon Art: A New Perspective* (1982), 175–187; Janet Mayo, *A History of Ecclesiastical Dress* (1984), 50–61.

LESLIE BRUBAKER

[See also **Textiles.**]

OPUS FRANCIGENUM. The term *opus Francigenum* (Frankish work) appears in the *Chronicle* of Burchard von Hall (*ca.* 1280) in the form *opere Francigeno.* It is the earliest recorded term for what is now called Gothic architecture, and indicates that the French origins of the Gothic style were known to Burchard and his contemporaries.

BIBLIOGRAPHY

Paul Frankl, *The Gothic: Literary Sources and Interpretations* (1960), 55–57.

GREGORY WHITTINGTON

[See also **Gothic Architecture.**]

OPUS MIXTUM. In Roman rubble construction (*opus caementicium*), a type of wall covering composed of bands of tufa introduced at intervals in a brick facing. The term is also applied to mixed reticulate, a wall facing combining brickwork and *opus reticulatum.*

GREGORY WHITTINGTON

[See also **Brick; Construction and Building.**]

The Chichester-Constable chasuble, showing the Coronation of the Virgin, Adoration of the Magi, and Annunciation. Opus anglicanum embroidery of gold and silk on velvet with applied pearls, 1330–1350. THE METROPOLITAN MUSEUM OF ART, FLETCHER FUND, 27.162.1

Virgin Orant (with *platytera* depiction of the infant Jesus). Egg tempera icon ("The Great Panagia") from the Monastery of the Savior, Yaroslavl, sometimes attributed to Alimpi, *d.* 1114. STATE TRETYAKOV GALLERY, MOSCOW. PHOTO: BELYAKOV/SOVFOTO

OPUS RETICULATUM (from the Latin *reticulum,* net). In Roman construction, a decorative wall facing composed of small pyramidal blocks with their points embedded in the mortared rubblework core and their exposed square bases set diagonally, creating a netlike pattern. In Byzantine and Western medieval architecture, the term is applied to any similar reticulated revetment, regardless of the composition of the wall.

GREGORY WHITTINGTON

[See also **Brick; Construction and Building.**]

OPUS SECTILE, or sextile, is an ornamental pavement or wall revetment made up of large pieces or slabs of marble, glass, or other material arranged in various patterns, usually geometrical but occasionally figural. The component pieces are larger than the tesserae of ordinary mosaic.

GREGORY WHITTINGTON

[See also **Cosmati Work; Mosaic and Mosaic Making; Opus Alexandrinum.**]

ORANT, a standing, frontal figure with both arms raised symmetrically in a gesture of prayer, popular in the early Christian period. The orant originated in the Roman period as an allegorical figure representing piety, the afterlife, or the soul of a believer. By the early third century, both the type and its meanings had been adopted by the Christians. During this century the significance and appearance changed; the orant pose was used for portraits of deceased Christians, as an indication of individual piety. By around 400 the position was reserved for those of special holiness, such as the Virgin, saints, and martyrs, and the type became one of intercession.

BIBLIOGRAPHY

André Grabar, *Christian Iconography: A Study of Its Origins* (1968); Theodore Klauser, "Studien zur Entstehungsgeschichte der christlichen Kunst I," in *Jahrbuch für Antike und Christentum,* I (1958).

LESLIE BRUBAKER

[See also **Early Christian Art.**]

ORARION (Russian: *orar*), the long, narrow stole of a deacon in the Byzantine church. Embroidered three times with the word "holy" (or with three crosses), the orarion is worn over the left shoulder and reaches to the floor. Sometimes it is arranged to form an *X* on the deacon's back and leave his hands free.

GEORGE P. MAJESKA

ORATORY, a small chapel for private devotion and prayer, usually not intended for the celebration of the liturgy. The name applies to chapels attached to private dwellings, or in fortresses or abbeys, as well as small edifices erected to commemorate the site of a miraculous occurrence or the residence of a holy person.

ROBERT OUSTERHOUT

[See also **Chasovnya.**]

ORBAIS, JEAN D'. See **Jean d'Orbais.**

ORBĒLEAN, STEPᶜANOS (*ca.* 1255–1303/1304). Stepᶜanos Orbēlean, metropolitan of the district of Siwnikᶜ in eastern Armenia between 1285/1286 and 1303/1304, was the house historian of the illustrious Orbēlean family. While the date of his birth is uncertain (1250–1260), his extant tombstone suggests 1303/1304 as the year of his death. Stepᶜanos received a clerical education and became successively a scribe, deacon, and priest of the Armenian church. In 1285/1286 his father sent him to Cilicia, where, on Easter day, he was ordained the metropolitan of Siwnikᶜ. Back in Siwnikᶜ, Stepᶜanos engaged in a protracted struggle with rebellious bishops, after which he asserted his full control and began renovating the ruined and dilapidated churches and monasteries under his jurisdiction.

Stepᶜanos' *History of the State of Sisakan* (Siwnikᶜ), which was completed in 1299, is an important source for Caucasian and Middle Eastern history. Written in the fashion of earlier Armenian histories (regarding the activities of the Mamikonean, Bagratid, and Arcrunid families), Stepᶜanos' work focuses on the role played in Armenian affairs by the Orbēleans and their predecessors, the Sisakans. When writing about early Armenian history, Stepᶜanos cites documents, inscriptions, and colophons unavailable in other sources. Indeed, many inscriptions that have survived in a damaged state both from Stepᶜanos' time and from earlier periods have been reconstructed thanks to this historian, who frequently incorporated their complete texts into his *History.* The great importance of this work is further confirmed when Stepᶜanos speaks about his own times. As the educated son of the former secular lord of Siwnikᶜ and the brother of the ruling lord, Stepᶜanos was in a position to know intimately all the important noble personalities of that state and in Armenia generally. His knowledge of Georgian and the existence of a powerful Georgian branch of his own family doubtlessly made him privy to information unavailable to many Armenian historians regarding events in Georgia. As metropolitan of Siwnikᶜ he had jurisdiction over all churches and monasteries located there. Furthermore, he had numerous highly placed acquaintances and enjoyed their respect. He was also personally acquainted with three Mongol khans, Arghun, Gaykhatu, and Ghāzān, all of whom esteemed this important dignitary and quickly granted his requests.

BIBLIOGRAPHY

Robert G. Bedrosian, "Turco-Mongol Invasions and the Lords of Armenia in the 13–14th Centuries" (diss., Columbia Univ., 1979); Marii Brosset, *Histoire de la*

The Strozzi altarpiece, depicting Christ with Sts. Michael and Catherine, the Virgin Mary, and St. Thomas Aquinas (left) and Sts. Peter, John the Baptist, Paul, and Lawrence (right). Panel painting by Orcagna, 1354–1357, S. Maria Novella, Florence. ALINARI/ART RESOURCE

Siounie, par Stéphannos Orbélian, 2 vols. (1864–1866); G. M. Grigoryan, "Stepʿannos Orbelyan," in *Patma banasirakan Handes,* 4 (1976); Tʿadewos X. Hakobyan, Stepʿan T. Melikʿ-Baxšyan, *Stepʿanos Orbēlean* (1960); Cyril Toumanoff, "The Mamikonids and the Liparitids," in *Armeniaca* (1969).

ROBERT BEDROSIAN

[See also **Armenia, History of; Armenian Church; Armenian Literature; Cilician-Roman Church Union; Ēǰmiacin; Historiography, Armenian; Metropolitan; Siwnikʿ.**]

ORCAGNA, ANDREA (Andrea di Cione) (*fl.* 1330–1368), Florentine painter, sculptor, and architect, the brother of Nardo di Cione. Orcagna is considered the foremost practitioner of a severe, hieratic style that emerged in mid trecento Tuscany.

Documents record wide-ranging activities. In 1343 or 1344 Orcanga's name appears in the records of the Florentine painters guild, the Arte dei Medici e Speziali. In 1347 he and Nardo are listed as candidates for a commission in Pistoia. Five years later his name appears in the register of the Florentine sculptors' guild. In 1355 Orcagna was *capomaestro* of Orsanmichele, Florence. Between 1359 and 1360 he was the chief architect of Orvieto Cathedral. Little survives from what must have been a prolific career.

Orcagna's chief surviving painting is the signed and dated (1357) altarpiece, executed between

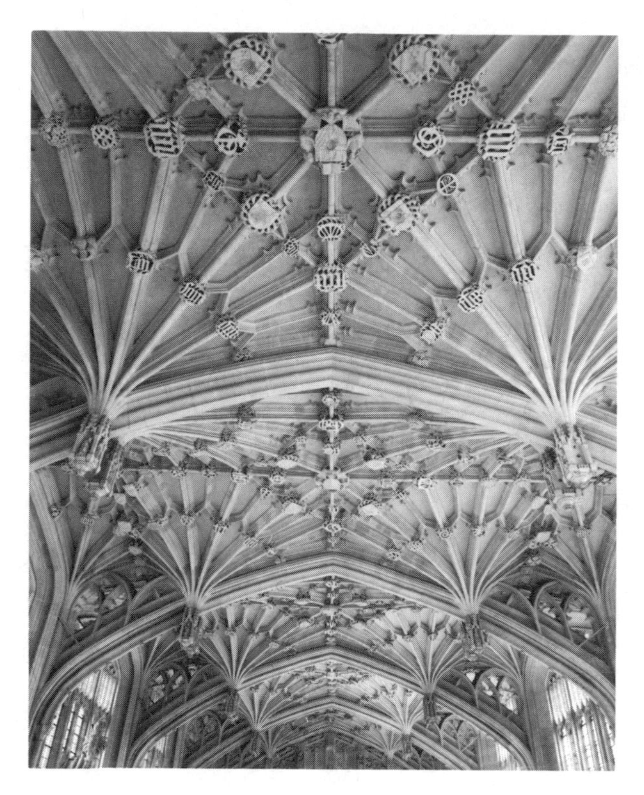

Oxford Divinity School, stone pendant vaults by William Orchard, 1479–1480. PHOTO: WIM SWAAN

1354 and 1357, for the Strozzi Chapel of S. Maria Novella. This chapel was decorated by Nardo with frescoes depicting the Last Judgment. Aside from the Strozzi altarpiece, only fragments from a large *Triumph of Death* fresco cycle in S. Croce attributed to Orcagna have come down to us.

Between 1354 and 1357, Orcagna designed and carved the marble tabernacle to enshrine Bernardo Daddi's *Virgin and Child* of 1347. Carved with scenes depicting the life of the Virgin, this sumptuous fusion of tectonic and sculpted forms is the major sculptural monument to survive from mid trecento Florence.

With its high-key colors, hieratic central image, and deliberate ambiguities, Orcagna's Strozzi altarpiece is the chief example used by scholars to point out the changes in art that took place after the Black Death of 1348. For this reason, Orcagna's stylistic origins are critical to our understanding of his role in trecento painting.

Orcagna's ideas exhibit the stylistic tendencies found in Tuscan paintings of the 1320's and 1330's. Giotto's Bardi Chapel frescoes (*ca.* 1325, in S. Croce, Florence) demonstrate a tension between dimensionality and flatness. Orcagna's deepest affinity lies with Sienese painters, notably Simone Martini. Martini's 1333 *Annunciation* panel posits all of the solutions that Orcagna carried further. Ambiguity, tension, emphatic linearity, and a language based on solids juxtaposed against voids, as well as on psychological remoteness, are all present in Martini's watershed image.

BIBLIOGRAPHY

Hans D. Gronau, *Andrea Orcagna und Nardo di Cione* (1937); Millard Meiss, *Painting in Florence and Siena After the Black Death* (1951); Richard Offner, *Critical and Historical Corpus of Florentine Painting,* sec. 4, I (1962); John Pope-Hennessy, *Italian Gothic Sculpture* (1955); Klara Steinweg, *Andrea Orcagna* (1929).

ADELHEID M. GEALT

[See also **Daddi, Bernardo; Gaddi, Agnolo; Giotto di Bondone; Jacopo di Cione; Lorenzo Monaco; Mariotto di Nardo; Nardo di Cione; Niccolò di Pietro Gerini; Simone Martini; Trecento Art.**]

ORCHARD, WILLIAM (*d.* 1504). From 1468 until his death, William Orchard was the most important builder-architect in Oxford. One of the few notable masters of the period who did not work for the crown, he was involved throughout his career with the erection of Magdalen College, especially its hall, cloisters, and chapel. He built also for Balliol and St. John's colleges, perhaps undertook private commissions, and owned and operated his own stone quarry. The most spectacular of Orchard's achievements are the sumptuous pendant vaults of the Divinity School at Oxford, and the vault of St. Frideswide Cathedral (now the older Oxford Cathedral), where he is buried.

BIBLIOGRAPHY

Eric Gee, "Oxford Masons, 1370–1530," in *Archaeological Journal,* **109** (1952); John Hooper Harvey, *English Medieval Architects* (1954), 199–201; Douglas Knoop and G. P. Jones, *An Introduction to Freemasonry: Some Medieval Masons* (1937), 88–90; Geoffrey Webb, "The Universities of Oxford and Cambridge: The Divinity School, Oxford. I," in *Country Life,* **65** (1929).

STEPHEN GARDNER

[See also **Oxford University.**]

The ordeal of cold-water submersion. 12th-century miniature. GMUNDEN, KLOSTER LAMBACH COD. LAMBACENSIS 73, fol. 64

ORDEALS. The word "ordeal" derives from the Germanic word for judgment (modern form: *Urteil*) and describes a variety of methods of judicial proof known in the early Middle Ages as "judgments of God" *(judicia Dei)*. Ordeal became common in the centuries after the Germanic invasions and continued to be widely used by both ecclesiastic and secular courts until the twelfth century. Participation of priests in ordeals was banned by the Fourth Lateran Council in 1215, and the use of ordeals declined sharply in the following decades, but traces of the custom remained for some centuries.

Ordeals could take many forms. In the ordeals of boiling water and glowing iron, burns were inflicted on a proband who might be either the person whose case was at issue or a substitute. The burned areas were sealed for three days, and the case was lost if there were signs of infection when the bandages were removed. The ordeals of cold water required the proband to be immersed, usually while bound; if the water rejected the proband—that is, if he or she floated—the case was lost. All these ordeals had their roots in Germanic custom. Also of Germanic origin were compurgatory oaths, which were complicated verbal formulas that the swearer had to repeat correctly, and judicial duels. These too were ordeals because they were based on the belief that their results revealed a divine judgment on the question at issue.

Despite the pagan origin of many ordeals, the early medieval church was far from opposed to their employment, and priests often presided at their administration. One formulary has the iron heat up in the fire for as long as it takes the priest to say Mass. The priest is then to take communion and give it to the proband, sprinkle the iron with holy water, invoke the blessing of the Trinity on the judgment, and place the iron in the proband's hand for him to carry nine feet. Other ordeals also distinctly show their origins in Christian theology. In the Carolingian ordeal of the cross, the litigants held their arms out from their shoulders to form the shape of the cross; the first one whose arms fell lost the case. During the Gregorian reform movement of the eleventh century, suspected simoniacs were often required to prove their innocence by taking the Eucharist (inability to swallow it proved guilt) or recite the Lord's Prayer.

Judgments of God were not the only proofs admissible in early medieval courts, but whenever documentary evidence or testimony of witnesses was lacking (and these cases may have been in the majority) courts generally accepted the verdict of some form of ordeal. Property disputes, adultery, treason, and heresy were among the cases settled by ordeals without, as far as we know, any participant complaining that the procedure was untrustworthy.

The widespread use of ordeals in the early Middle Ages was possible only because no one doubted that God frequently intervened in worldly affairs to reward the good and punish the wicked. The ordeal differed from other miracles worked on behalf of justice, however, in that people could use the ritual to focus God's attention on a specific issue. This confidence in the power of the ritual made it possible not only to single out a single dispute for resolution but also to substitute a third party for the litigants, sometimes without the knowledge or consent of the principals. A story from the time of the investiture controversy reports that an Italian abbot, Piero Igneo, who was a partisan of Gregory VII, performed an ordeal in secret to determine the justice of the pope's dispute with the emperor; he decided that the results had to be hushed up when they favored the imperial side.

Confidence in ordeals was slow to decline, but in the twelfth century doubts began to multiply. In England, Henry II's distrust of ordeals is apparent in his legal reforms: he punished those accused of breaking the peace by exile even if they succeeded at the water ordeal (if they failed he had them executed), and he denied "notorious" individuals any right at all to prove their innocence by ordeal. He also made it possible for any person in possession of land to avoid having to defend his right at trial by battle by having a jury of the neighborhood render a verdict. Several legists, notably Peter of Blois and Huguccio, denounced all forms of ordeals, but the leading scholarly critic of ordeals was the Parisian theologian Peter the Chanter (*d.* 1197). Peter collected evidence of ordeals that had failed and cautioned his clerical readers that just because the Bible contains many stories of God's intervention on behalf of the just they should not believe that the blessing of water or iron is certain to result in a miracle.

Peter's writings against ordeal belong to a trend that looked much more critically upon all claims to miracles, and this increased skepticism led, in 1215, to the Fourth Lateran Council's ban on priestly participation in ordeals. Except in England, which was under papal regency during the minority of Henry III, the ban did not result in an immediate end to ordeals, but the rituals disappeared in most parts of Europe in the course of the thirteenth century. Settlement of disputes by duel remained legally possible for centuries, however, and the early modern custom of "swimming a witch" might also be considered a late survival of ordeals.

BIBLIOGRAPHY

John W. Baldwin, "The Intellectual Preparation for the Canon of 1215 Against Ordeals," in *Speculum,* **36** (1961); Charles M. Radding, "Superstition to Science: Nature, Fortune, and the Passing of the Medieval Ordeal," in *American Historical Review,* **84** (1979).

CHARLES M. RADDING

[See also **Henry II of England; Huguccio; Law, German; Law, Procedure of; Peter of Blois; Peter the Chanter.**]

ORDERICUS VITALIS (1075–*ca.* 1142), one of the most remarkable medieval historians. He was born of mixed Anglo-French parentage near Shrewsbury on 16 February 1075, and baptized in St. Eata's church at Atcham on the following Holy Saturday. His father, Odelerius of Orléans, a learned clerk in the household of Roger of Montgomery, earl of Shrewsbury, sent him as a boy of ten to become an oblate monk in the Benedictine abbey of St. Evroult on the southern frontier of Normandy; there he spent the remainder of his life. He was educated in the monastic school under John of Rheims and became a skilled calligrapher. His life work, the *Ecclesiastical History,* in thirteen books, was begun before 1114 and completed in 1141. He died probably on 13 July in a year not earlier than 1142.

The *History* begins with a life of Christ based on gospel harmonies and chronological tables. Up to the eleventh century it is a short chronicle derived from other sources, notably Bede, for whom he had a great admiration; from about 1050 it becomes increasingly important as a record of oral tradition. Because Ordericus copied extensively from the lost parts of the *Gesta guillelmi* of William of Poitiers, his work has the value of a contemporary account of the first stages of the Norman conquest of England from 1066 to 1070; thereafter he was able to make use of eyewitness reports of important events. He owed much to the epic traditions of secular Norman society, as well as to monastic culture. Vivid accounts of battles often combine detailed information on tactics with heroic passages more important for what they reveal of the knightly culture of the twelfth century than the actual course of events.

Many leading magnates visited his monastery, and their families were involved in enterprises all over the Norman world, from Scotland to Spain, southern Italy, and the Crusader States. In describing their exploits he left a record of evolving custom and feudal law. For the period from 1087 to 1141 his work is the most important early source for events in Normandy and Maine; and it also contains firsthand information on English affairs, particularly events in Shropshire. It includes a detailed, eyewitness account of the Council of Rheims in 1119 and copies of the canons of many Norman synods. It is a mine of information on monasticism in Normandy.

Ordericus was an accomplished stylist who wrote in rhythmic, rhymed prose, making free use of dramatic dialogues. He had a rich vocabulary of over 8,000 words, which owed much to Carolingian writings and glossaries as well as to the Vulgate and the early Fathers. Some passages, notably his accounts of the death of William the Conqueror, the vision by a country priest of "Hellequin's hunt," the new monastic orders, and the wreck of the White Ship, are distinguished literary compositions as well as historically important. Because of its length, the *History* was little copied in the Middle Ages, but it has been used extensively since the sixteenth century.

BIBLIOGRAPHY

Marjorie Chibnall, ed. and trans., *The Ecclesiastical History of Orderic Vitalis,* 6 vols. (1969–1980), and *The World of Orderic Vitalis* (1984). Augustus Le Prévost, ed., *Orderici Vitalis ecclesiasticae historiae libri tredecim,* 5 vols. (1838–1855); Hans Wolter, *Ordericus Vitalis* (1955).

MARJORIE CHIBNALL

[See also **Benedictines; Councils, Western (869–1179); Historiography, Western European; Normans and Normandy.**]

ORDINALE. Although in postmedieval times, particularly in Anglican usage, "ordinale" referred to a book containing ordination formulas, in medieval parlance it referred to a book of liturgical directions, especially for priests. Like the *liber ordinarius,* an *ordinale* contained a calendar, general rubrics (especially for the Mass and Office), and incipits of texts arranged according to the liturgical year and followed by the specific church, monastery, or order for which it was created.

The term "Ordinal of Christ," as used by Roger Reynolds, refers to a variety of short medieval texts in which each ecclesiastical grade is sanctioned or justified by words or deeds of Christ. These texts reflect a current in clerical spirituality that attempted to show how each ecclesiastical officer, especially in his liturgical functions, imitated Christ.

BIBLIOGRAPHY

Peter F. Bradshaw, *The Anglican Ordinal: Its History and Development from the Reformation to the Present Day* (1971); Virgil Fiala and Wolfgang Irtenkauf, "Versuch einer liturgischen Nomenklatur," in Clemens Köttelwesch, *Zur Katalogisierung mittelalterlicher und neuerer Handschriften* (1963); Roger E. Reynolds, *The Ordinals of Christ from Their Origins to the Twelfth Century* (1978).

ROGER E. REYNOLDS

[See also **Divine Office; Liturgy, Treatises on.**]

ORDINANCE (FRENCH AND ENGLISH), from the French *ordonnance,* was a legal pronouncement of varying force.

In English usage the word applies to an order or rule laid down by the king in council, though not necessarily in the formal council (*magnum concilium*) or in the afforced council (Parliament). A statute, on the other hand, would have required the formal assent of the great council in the mid thirteenth century and the formal assent of Parliament in the later thirteenth century and afterward. An ordinance might be passed or enunciated in such formal settings, but this was not regarded as a requirement. An ordinance would affect legal usages, but it would not under normal conditions change the substance of the law in a major fashion. Statutes supposedly would. The difficulty of precisely defining what was major and what was minor is at the root of differentiating a statute from an ordinance. Some statutes seem to deal with trivia in comparison with some ordinances (such as the Ordinances of 1311), which reorganize the very basis of government. Perhaps it is more accurate to say that ordinances dealt either with minor matters, or with matters purely of procedure (no matter how important), or with prescriptions that the issuers of ordinances wished people to regard as traditional even if they were not (the Ordinances of 1311). The word "provisions," as in the Provisions of Oxford (1258), served the same propagandistic purpose at times. Statutes addressed issues that were regarded as substantive even if their substance was trivial and even if the substantive issue may strike modern readers as procedural (for example, the issuance of writs). Even in the Middle Ages a certain confusion reigned: the first formal pronouncement on praemunire (1353) both "ordains" (the word that would indicate an ordinance) and "establishes" (the word that would suggest a statute). Other pronouncements are similarly worded.

In the later Middle Ages the distinction between ordinances and statutes was further complicated by the legal doctrines that grew up around the use of the king's personal seal as opposed to the great seal. Orders issued under the small seal or under the signet could have far-reaching implications; and though they cannot be called statutes, they often dealt with matters more important substantively and procedurally than many statutes passed in formal parliaments. Consequently, the use of the seals was closely regulated whenever baronial factions seized the reins of government.

In France the royal government issued *constituciones, statuta,* and *établissements,* terms that connote a kind of formality and elegance. These were sometimes collected by legists in the thirteenth century. The most famous example is the private compilation known as the *Établissements de Saint Louis* (*ca.* 1270). But there is no strong evidence that an *ordonnance* was less important than an *établissement.* This does not mean that it is impossible to identify clear phases in the history of royal legislation in France, especially the beginning of the so-called "établissement pour le commun profit." It was in the early thirteenth century, perhaps as early as 1230 with the Ordonnance of Melun concerning the Jews, that *ordonnances* for the common good began to take on a "national" character. But they remained, at least in name, *ordonnances.*

The role of the king's council in stating *ordonnances* underscores the kind of rule-of-thumb classification of *ordonnances* that French scholars have identified at least for the thirteenth century. The first sort of *ordonnance* (or *établissement*) was comparable to the English statute. It was assented to in a solemn great council and dealt with matters of importance or of high ceremony. The second kind of *ordonnance* was an outgrowth of the king's council as a court (*parlement*). The judgment of the court (*arrêt*) became a rule of law. Even if the decision was intended to be limited to the case before the judges of the Parlement, the presence of provincial administrative officials in the court who took knowledge of the judgment back to the provinces often transformed an *arrêt* into an informal *ordonnance.* Indeed, any order emanating from the king might be interpreted as an *ordonnance.* For example, some scholars see the restriction of private war in the diocese of Le Puy in 1258 as the first step in the informal application of the rule to the entire kingdom. The third type of *ordonnance* was composed of rules, regulations, and proscriptions sent to the king's men in the field. They correspond to the commissions or articles of justices in eyre in England and to numerous orders sent by letters patent to the sheriffs. *Ordonnances* were also issued by the various governing bodies of royal provinces (such as the Echiquier of Normandy and the Parlement of Toulouse) and by various members of the feudal nobility for their domains.

BIBLIOGRAPHY

Raymond Cazelles, "La reglementation royale de la guerre privée de Saint Louis à Charles V et la précarité des ordonnances," in *Revue historique de droit français et étranger,* 4th ser., **38** (1960); Quentin Griffiths, "New Men Among the Lay Counselors of Saint Louis' Parlement," in *Mediaeval Studies,* **32** (1970); Gavin Langmuir, "*Judaei nostri* and Capetian Legislation," in *Traditio,* **16** (1960); Achille Luchaire, *Manuel des institutions françaises* (1892, repr. 1964), 487–504; Bryce Lyon, *A Constitutional and Legal History of Medieval England,* 2nd ed. (1980); Charles Petit-Dutaillis, "L' 'Établissement pour le commun profit' au temps de St. Louis," in *Anuario de historia del derecho español,* **10** (1933); Frederick Pollock and Frederic William Maitland, *The History of English Law,* 2 vols., 2nd ed. (repr. 1968), I, 181.

WILLIAM CHESTER JORDAN

[See also **Établissements de St. Louis; Law, English Common; Law, French; Parlement of Paris; Parliament; Praemunire; Statute.**]

ORDINARIUS, LIBER. Sometimes called *breviarium, ordinale, consuetudinarium,* or *ordo officiorum,* the *liber ordinarius* was a book of directions governing liturgical services in secular or monastic churches. The volume usually began with a calendar and group of general rubics for the Mass, the Divine Office, or both. Thereafter, incipits referring to full texts in other liturgical books were given for the various parts of the Mass or Office, such as antiphons, psalms, readings, responsories, prayers, and hymns. These were arranged according to the ecclesiastical year followed in the particular church, monastery, or order for which the *liber ordinarius* was compiled. The golden age for the creation of these books was the thirteenth century, although many churches thereafter codified their liturgical usage in these books.

BIBLIOGRAPHY

Virgil Fiala and Wolfgang Irtenkauf, "Versuch einer liturgischen Nomenklatur," in Clemens Köttelwesch, *Zur Katalogisierung mittelalterlicher und neuerer Handschriften* (1963); Anton Hänggi, *Die Rheinauer Liber ordinarius* (1957); Franz Kohlschein, *Der Paderborner liber ordinarius von 1324: Textausgabe mit einer strukturgeschichtlichen Untersuchung der antiphonalen Psalmodie* (1971); Adalbert Kurzeja, *Der älteste liber ordinarius der Trierer Domkirche* (1970); Placide F. Lefèvre, ed., *Les ordinaires des collégiales Saint-Pierre à Louvain et Saints-Pierre-et-Paul à Anderlecht d'après des manuscrits due xive siècle* (1960), and *L'ordinaire de la collégiale, autrefois cathédrale, de Tongres d'après un manuscrit du xve siècle,* 2 vols. (1967–1968).

ROGER E. REYNOLDS

[See also **Divine Office; Liturgy, Treatises on.**]

ORDINATION, CLERICAL. Among the rites of initiation in the Middle Ages, two were held preeminent: baptism and clerical ordination. The former was generally recognized as the more important because it was seen as the gateway to redemption and membership in the church. Ordination, on the other hand, was seen as admission to a special status within the church that gave one the power to perform and effectuate certain of the duties and sacraments not allowed to others. As such, ordination was seen as the basis for many other liturgical actions, including the Eucharist.

When one was ordained or consecrated (the Middle Ages scarcely recognized the difference between the two terms), he entered into both "orders" and an "order." What orders and an order were was a subject of constant debate among medieval theologians, canonists, and liturgiologists, but it was generally the case that orders was the special status conferred on one entering any of the grades of the clerical state, and an order was the individual step, grade, or status within the clerical state. One could, of course, enter orders of different sorts—regal or imperial orders, monastic or religious orders, and the like—but these were not usually viewed as conferring the status of orders in the clerical sense. Hence, the term "ordination" usually refers to clerical ordination.

TEXTUAL SOURCES

The earliest ordination texts were almost certainly kept apart from other liturgical books within *libelli* or gatherings of folios. This would be the case not only for the prayer texts of ordination, but also for the directions.

Prayer libelli. The earliest "sacramentary," the *Sacramentarium Veronense* (or Leonine Sacramentary) of around 600, was actually a collection of earlier texts from *libelli* arranged according to a monthly cycle of liturgical feasts. One of the components of this sacramentary is a group of ordination prayers. They are now neatly embedded into other texts, but their existence in independent *libelli* in the Roman church is almost certain because in later sacramentaries, including the Gregorian Sacramentary of Pope Adrian I (*r.* 772–795), the *Hadrianum,* they are "pasted" onto the beginning of the Sacramentary together with the canon of the Mass.

Libelli with ordination directions. The earliest evidence for collections with these directions comes in two forms. First, there is the canonical collection called the *Statuta ecclesiae antiqua,* written about 475, probably by Gennadius of Marseilles, on the basis of earlier canonistic and liturgical materials. Directions for the Gallican rite of ordination are gathered together in one part of the small collection and describe the ordination of the bishop, presbyter, deacon, subdeacon, acolyte, exorcist, lector, doorkeeper, psalmist, virgin, and widow. That these directions were thought of as a separable *libellus* from the remainder of the canons in the collection is clear in that they have their own rubric and there were in the Middle Ages several traditions of the *Statuta* presenting the ordination directions as a whole in various positions in the text. The second piece of evidence for *libelli* with ordination directions comes in the *Ordines romani.* The *ordines* that described ordination, particularly *Ordines XXXIV–XXXVI,* are often found in manuscripts floating independently among other materials, suggesting that they had an independence of their own before being incorporated into the protopontificals and pontificals of the late eighth century and beyond.

Sacramentaries. Sacramentaries contained pri-

ORDINATION, CLERICAL

marily eucharist prayers, but could also contain prayers for other sacraments, including ordination. Hence, in the earliest sacramentaries of all the rites there are ordination prayers. Often, not only the prayers themselves would be incorporated into the sacramentaries, but also ceremonial directions for the conferral of orders.

Lectionaries and antiphonalia. Because the orders were usually conferred within the context of the Mass, the other Mass books contained appropriate texts for ordination. Hence, the special readings for ordination were included in the lectionaries, and the musical sections were kept in the *antiphonalia.*

Allocution libelli. Closely related to the *libelli* earlier described and to the lectionaries were groups of texts used in the exhortations, admonitions, and allocutions to the ordinands in the first part of the ordination ceremonies. These texts could be in a variety of forms, and there is little rhyme or reason to their groupings in medieval manuscripts. They are often in the form of florilegia. Among the texts included to be read to the ordinand were snippets from Isidore of Seville's *De ecclesiasticis officiis* (*ca.* 620) and *Origines,* the Pseudo-Jeromian *De septem ordinibus ecclesiae,* the Pseudo-Isidorian *De officiis septem graduum* and *Epistula ad Leudefredum,* the Pseudo-Alcuinian *Liber de divinis officiis,* the Ordinals of Christ, and a variety of sermons, including *Sermo II,* attributed to Ivo of Chartres (*ca.* 1040–1115).

Pontificals. All of the above texts were gathered together into one volume, variously called *ordines, ritualia,* and the like, but because the ordination ceremony was reserved to the bishop or pontiff, they came to be known by the thirteenth century as pontificals. The pontificals generally did not contain complete lections or music for ordination Masses since these parts were performed by other clerics, but they did have canon-law material relating to ordination, ceremonial directions, and prayers and benedictions. By the time pontificals came into existence, the Gallican rite had been submerged into other rites, but there are clearly other families of pontificals in the Middle Ages: the Old Spanish found in the *Liber ordinum;* the Insular found in Anglo-Saxon pontificals from the Pontifical of Egbert of York (Paris BN lat. 10575 [s. x, York]) down to the twelfth century, when Anglo-Norman forms were combined; and the Roman pontificals. These last pontificals were widely diffused from the tenth century on, and include the tenth-century *Pontificale romano-germanicum* (a hybrid pontifical containing both Gallican and Roman ordination rites); the *Pontificale romanum XII saeculi* (an offshoot of the *Pontificale romano-germanicum* developed during the Gregorian Reform period), the *Pontificale romanae curiae* (a further refinement of the *Pontificale romanum XII saeculi* compiled at the time of Pope Innocent III [*r.* 1198–1216]); and the *Pontificale Guilelmi Durandi* (a magnificent true pontifical compiled by Guillaume Durand (*ca.* 1230–1296), on the basis of earlier Roman pontificals and local, especially Gallican, ordination practices he knew). It was basically this modified Roman rite of ordination that was used in the Roman church down to 1972.

Liturgical commentaries. From at least the third century, liturgical treatises often described the ceremony of ordination. Not only did they contain the texts already described, but they also presented the rationale behind the ceremonies of ordination.

SYSTEMS OF CLERICAL ORDERS

In the Western church of the Middle Ages there were three or perhaps four systems of clerical orders represented in the texts of ordination ceremonies. In each system there was considerable variation regarding the exact number and names of the grades, and there was contamination from one system or rite to another, but the basic configurations are fairly clear.

Spanish. In the Old Spanish *Liber ordinum* the ordination rites include those for tonsure and cutting of the beard and for ordination to the clerical state and to the orders of sacristan, overseer of books and scribes, subdeacon, deacon, archdeacon, *primiclericus* (overseer of lower clergy and liturgy), presbyter, archpresbyter, and abbot. There was almost certainly an ordination ceremony for the bishop, but it has been lost. This Old Spanish system of orders in the *Liber ordinum* was maintained into the eleventh century, when it was replaced by Roman and the Romano-Catalan rites of ordination.

Despite this system of clerical orders represented in the ordination rites of the *Liber ordinum,* there were clearly other systems and grades known in Visigothic and Mozarabic Spain. Isidore of Seville (*ca.* 560–636), in his *De ecclesiasticis officiis* and *Origines,* has a list resembling the Gallican and Roman systems, including doorkeeper, exorcist, acolyte, lector, psalmist, cantor, precentor, succentor, subdeacon, *custos* (keeper of liturgical

ORDINATION, CLERICAL

vessels), deacon, presbyter, chorbishop (chorepiscopus), bishop, and the higher episcopal dignities. In the Pseudo-Isidorian *Epistula ad Leudefredum* most of these orders appear as well as the archdeacon, *primicerius,* thesaurarius (treasurer), *economus,* and *pater monasterii.* In the Pseudo-Jeromian *De Septem ordinibus,* probably written in Catalonia or the Roussillon, there is a hierarchy of gravedigger, doorkeeper (*hostiarius*), lector, subdeacon, deacon, presbyter, and bishop.

Gallican. The hierarchy of eight grades plus psalmist in the Gallican rite was early laid out in the *Statuta ecclesiae antiqua.* It was probably based on an earlier Roman one, and when Roman ordination texts came to northern Europe in the eighth century it was this Romano-Gallican system that gradually supplanted the hierarchy as reflected in the Roman ordination texts and became the system of orders used in the Roman church until 1972.

Roman. Debate continues over the number of orders in the early medieval Roman hierarchy, with several different texts supporting different opinions. One of the earliest texts describing the Roman hierarchy, that of Eusebius of Caesarea (*ca.* 263–*ca.* 340) discussing the Roman clergy at the time of the mid-third-century Pope Cornelius, mentions the eight male grades found in the *Statuta ecclesiae antiqua,* but with the psalmist missing. There are also the Roman interstices texts spelling out the time necessary between advances from one grade to another; these texts present different traditions.

In addition, there are the early Roman ordination texts themselves in *Ordo romanus XXXIV,* where there are only the grades of acolyte, subdeacon, deacon, presbyter, and bishop, to which *Ordo XXXV* adds the lector. That there were doorkeepers and exorcists in Rome from the seventh and eighth centuries on is beyond question, since they are mentioned in several documents. But there is a question as to whether they were ordained or ordered, since there is no early Roman text for them.

As the *Ordines romani* were taken north of the Alps, they were quickly contaminated by the texts of the *Statuta ecclesiae antiqua* and Gallican-rite sacramentaries. Hence, by the mid eighth century, the Roman sacramentaries had ordination directions for the Gallican hierarchy of orders. These same Gallican orders were included in the *Supplemented Gregorian Sacramentary* with its additions by Benedict of Aniane (early ninth century) and eventually in the Roman pontificals.

COMPONENTS OF ORDINATION RITES

General instructions. Liturgical commentators and formulae often laid out instructions of a general nature for ordinands to observe. For example, the *Pontificale Guilelmi Durandi* stresses that ordinands should be certain their tonsures are well trimmed, their clothing fittingly kept and maintained, and the *instrumenta* or symbols they received in perfect condition.

Time of ordination. Almost from the beginning of the church it was recognized that some days were more appropriate than others for ordination. Especially fitting were Pentecost, the feast of Peter and Paul, and days following fasting. Because it was felt that ordinands should be prepared for ordination by fasting, the last day of ember days was thought to be especially appropriate, and thus, in both the Roman and Frankish rites, the Saturday of ember days was chosen for ordination. Particularly fitting were the ember days of Pentecost. For the bishop, the ordination rite was split into two days: the examination and preconsecratory rites on Saturday and the ordination rites proper on Sunday.

Although ordination of some of the lower orders, for which there are very general or hazy instructions, may have been given on days other than Saturday or Sunday and at times other than the Mass, ordinations were usually connected with the Mass. Depending on the season and the grade itself, the order might be conferred at different times during the Mass. For example, tonsure could be given after the introit or, in seasons when the Gloria was sung, after the Kyrie. In the Old Spanish ordination rite the cutting of the beard came at the end of Mass, before the *Missa acta est.* For the grades from doorkeeper through bishop, however, the general practice was to begin the ordination rites themselves so that the newly ordained cleric could subsequently exercise his newly given power. For most grades the ordination rite began after the response or alleluia, although for the presbyter it was after the Gospel. In the ordination rites for the presbyter and bishop the ceremony was carried on throughout the Mass and beyond, even going to the reception of the title church of the new presbyter in Rome. During these extended ceremonies the new ordinands would exercise their new functions. For example, the subdeacon read the Epistle, the deacon the Gospel, and so forth.

Place of ordination. Because the bishop was the chief consecrator or dispenser of orders, the actual ceremony was performed in one of the chief basil

ORDINATION, CLERICAL

icas of a city, preferably where the bishop had his cathedra (although in Rome the basilica of St. Peter was preferred). The ordination itself took place near the altar. The ordinands could be arranged in rows or circles, and if several grades were to be ordained they might take up different places in the presbytery. The *Pontificale Guilelmi Durandi,* for example, says that when subdeacons, deacons, and presbyters are to be ordained, the subdeacons stand on the north side, the deacons on the south, and the presbyters in the middle. In the case of the bishop, there was a great deal of moving about from the sacristy, where vesting and washing took place, to the presbytery, and in the presbytery from front to back of the altar and to the cathedra.

Presentation and nomination of ordinands. In almost all initiation ceremonies from baptism to the consecration of religious, the candidate was presented to the bishop and people and was named. So in ordination the ordinands were called forth and were involved in a ceremony of reception. Usually it was the archdeacon who called on the ordinands to present themselves. Sometimes, as in the *Pontificale romano-germanicum,* the individuals were named by the archdeacon and the church from which they came was specified. In the ordination of a bishop the clerics of his own church presented him to his consecrators, and the bishop-to-be presented his decretum from his electors.

Examination and oath of ordinands. The *Pontificale Guilelmi Durandi* lays down the general rule that all ordinands be examined and approved before ordination. In the ordination rite the examination continued—sometimes in a very cursory way, sometimes at length, depending on the order—even though it might have begun before the ceremony. For the lower grades there seems to have been some chance for the people to object to an unfit candidate. In the *Statuta ecclesiae antiqua,* for example, the bishop was given permission to speak on the life and morals of the lector-to-be, and presumably the assembled people were able to object. The people's role in the examination was far more obvious for the higher grades. In the *Pontificale romano-germanicum* the people were asked specifically if they had objections to the candidates for subdeacon, deacon, and presbyter.

For the higher or sacred orders there was an oral examination. For example, all ordinands from subdeacon up were asked about and were required to swear that they had not been guilty of the four capital crimes of sodomy, bestiality, adultery, and violation of nuns. The bishop especially was examined at length as to his prior ordinations (particularly to the presbyterate), his election, his morals, the books necessary for his church, his knowledge of the canons and doctrine, and the like.

Either in the examination itself or toward the end of the Mass an oath of obedience and reverence was taken by a presbyter to his bishop or by a bishop to his metropolitan.

Prayers and benedictions. The heart of the ordination ceremonies was in the prayers and benedictions, and in the liturgical books these take up the majority of space. The prayers may be called *praefationes, orationes,* and *benedictiones,* and they are said not only over the ordinands, but also over the instruments to be given to them. In content they usually call down a blessing on a person or thing, referring often to the Old Testament, and occasionally to the New. Sometimes, the prayers may be very general, even banal. In the ordination rites the number of prayers and blessings varies considerably from order to order, ranging from as few as one to as many as thirty for some of the higher orders.

Musical portions of ordinations. Inserted into the ordination prayers and ceremonies were a variety of antiphons. Sometimes these seem to have been used to fill in time as certain ceremonies were taking place. For example, there was in the Old Spanish rite an antiphon during tonsure and cutting of the beard, and in the *Pontificale Guilelmi Durandi* the responsory *Iam non dicam* was sung while many presbyters were being ordained. But there could also be musical pieces specifically appropriate to the ordination itself: for example, the *Veni sancte spiritus* or *Veni creator spiritus* after the alleluia in the ordination of a presbyter, or the *Te Deum* at the conclusion of the ordination Mass for the bishop.

Allocutions and admonitions. From the fifth century on the common practice was to give allocutions and admonitions during the ordination rites. These were directed both to the ordinand himself and to the people. They could range in length from one sentence to several paragraphs, again depending on the order itself. Some of these admonitions were given to the ordinand as he received his instruments or symbols, but there were other admonitions and allocutions given at other times, especially at the beginning of the ceremonies. These allocutions usually were florilegia of texts chosen by the bishop and delivered seated with

Bishop Landulf of Benevento presents subdeacons with paten and chalice while an archdeacon presents a pitcher and basin (after 969). ROME, BIBLIOTECA CASANATENSE 724 (B.I. 13)

miter on. The texts, often pseudonymous, generally dealt with the origins of the order, the duties of the cleric, and his morality and life.

Tradition of instruments. Next to the prayers, the tradition of porrection, or the extending, of instruments or symbols to the ordinand by the bishop or archdeacon was the most important component of the ordination rites, and many theologians argued that the *traditio instrumentorum* was the essential part or matter of the rite. The instruments given were the books, utensils, and vestments used in the liturgical performance of the cleric's duties. Hence, the psalmist received an antiphonary. The cleric in the Old Spanish rite was given a tunic and alb; the sacristan a key ring as chief doorkeeper; and the overseer of books and scribes a key to the *scrinium* (case or chest for books and documents). The doorkeeper received keys from the archdeacon, and on "receiving" a bell rope from the archdeacon rang the church bell. The lector was given a lectionary by the bishop, and the *Pontificale romanae curiae* specifies that it be a book of the prophetic lessons. The exorcist was given a *libellus* of exorcisms, which might be in the form of a rotulus. The acolyte received from the archdeacon a candlestick with candle and an empty *urceolum*. *Ordo romanus XXXIV* states that the acolyte received a linen bag from the bishop, in which he would carry the *Sancta* or consecrated bread. Over the course of the Middle Ages the number of *instrumenta* received by the subdeacon varied greatly and grew from a few items to as many as nine, signifying the change of his status after the late eleventh century from a minor order to a sacred or major order. In the Old Spanish rite the subdeacon received a paten, a chalice, and a "codicem Pauli apostoli." According to *Ordo romanus XXXIV* he received from the bishop or archdeacon a chalice, and in *Ordo romanus XXXV* a chalice and paten. In the Gallican *Statuta ecclesiae antiqua* he was given an empty paten and chalice by the bishop and a vessel, basin, and towel by the archdeacon. By the twelfth century all of these Gallican symbols were given to the subdeacon together with a maniple and tunic, and by the thirteenth century an amice and epistolary as well. In *Ordo romanus XXXIV* the deacon received a dalmatic, but his major *instrumenta* were a stole (placed over the left shoulder) and a Gospelbook. The archdeacon in the Old Spanish rite received a rod, as did the *primicerius*. Like the deacon, the presbyter received appropriate vestments: the chasuble and stole (either over the right shoulder or crossed over the breast). As symbols of his liturgical duties he was given a chalice with wine (and sometimes water) and paten with *oblata*. The Old Spanish rite adds a *manuale* (book from which he adminsters the sacraments). Other *instrumenta* and gifts could also be given, such as a ring (for a cardinal presbyter), gold and silver vessels, wine, fruit, and oil. In the Old Spanish rite the archpresbyter was given a *liber orationum.* The bishop was vested before the Mass with sandals, dalmatic, and chasuble; during the ordination rite itself Gospels were laid over his neck and shoulder; after his unction he was given a staff, ring, and Gospelbook; and after the communion he was presented with a miter and gloves. Finally, if he were an archbishop, an archpresbyter of the Roman church gave him a pallium.

Actions and gestures during ordination. During the entire ordination ceremony there was a flurry of activity, and each gesture was usually assigned some symbolic significance. Among the various actions and gestures there might be the following. When one entered the clerical state, he might be tonsured and shaved of his beard. The Old Spanish rite provided for the waxing of the beard. Before each of the prayers and benedictions, the deacon would call out, "Flectamus genua," and there would be a genuflection. In the Roman tradition it was generally the practice for the ordinand to kneel when receiving the *instrumenta.* Kneeling, especially by the pope on his faldstool, might also be done during the litany. Other ordinands prostrated themselves on a carpet during the singing of the litany, and several grades prostrated themselves before kissing his feet. Several types of kisses might be given, from a simple exchange of peace before, during, and after the ordination of a bishop or other clerics to a kissing of the hands or feet of the consecrator as a sign of respect. Before ordination to the higher orders, one took off some of the vestments, which were then replaced during the ceremony. Also there was a constant putting on and off of the miter by the bishop. For prayers, the hands could be held in the orantes position or folded on the breast. There was a multiple laying-on of hands for the higher orders. This might be done by the bishop alone, by bishops and presbyters, and by metropolitans and other bishops. There could also be a second laying-on of hands over presbyters to signify a reception of the power of the keys. Several types of unction were used in ordination ceremonies, depending upon the order. The hands of deacons, presbyters, and the bishop were anointed, the thumb of presbyters and bishops, and the head of bishops. Especially in connection with unction there could be several washings and dryings, first of the excess from the ordinand and second of the hands of the consecrator. Finally, there was the crowning conclusion of an episcopal consecration, the enthronement.

Presentation of offerings. The offering of symbolic gifts was a minor but highly significant part of the Roman ordination rite for the higher orders. Subdeacon, deacon, and presbyter presented their oblations to the bishop.

A final component of the ordination rite, the final credo, is found in the presbyteral ordination in the *Pontificale Guilelmi Durandi.* After communion the presbyter said the Creed, perhaps thereby showing his competence to exercise the keys given to him in the second laying-on of hands.

BIBLIOGRAPHY

Richard W. Pfaff, *Medieval Latin Liturgy: A Select Bibliography* (1982), 36, 38–39, 72–82; Roger E. Reynolds, "A Florilegium on the Ecclesiastical Grades in *Clm 19414:* Testimony to Ninth-century Clerical Instruction," in *Harvard Theological Review,* **63** (1970), "The Pseudo-Hieronymian *De septem ordinibus ecclesiae:* Notes on Its Origins, Abridgments, and Use in Early Medieval Canonical Collections," in *Revue bénédictine,* **80** (1970), "The Portrait of the Ecclesiastical Officers in the *Raganaldus Sacramentary* and Its Liturgico-canonical Significance," in *Speculum,* **46** (1971), "The *De officiis vii graduum:* Its Origins and Early Medieval Development," in *Mediaeval Studies,* **34** (1972), "A Ninth-century Treatise on the Origins, Office, and Ordination of the Bishop," in *Revue bénédictine,* **85** (1975), "Isidore's Texts on the Clerical," in *Classical Folia,* **29** (1975), "Ivonian Opuscula on the Ecclesiastical Officers," in *Mélanges Gérard Fransen (Studia gratiana,* **20**) (1976), "Marginalia on a Tenth-century Text on the Ecclesiastical Officers," in *Law, Church, and Society: Essays in Honor of Stephan Kuttner,* Kenneth Pennington and Robert Somerville, eds. (1977), 115–129, *The Ordinals of Christ from Their Origins to the Twelfth Century (Beiträge zur Geschichte und Quellenkunde des Mittelalters,* VII, H. Fuhrmann, ed., 1978), "'At Sixes and Sevens'—and Eights and Nines: The Sacred Mathematics of Sacred Orders in the Early Middle Ages," in *Speculum,* **54** (1979), "An Early Medieval Tract on the Diaconate," in *Harvard Theological Review,* **72** (1979), "The 'Isidorian' *Epistula ad Leudefredum:* An Early Medieval Epitome of the Clerical Duties," in *Mediaeval Studies,* **41** (1979), "The 'Isidorian' *Epistula ad Leudefredum:* Its Origins, Early Manuscript Tradition, and Editions," in *Visigothic Spain: New Approaches,* Edward James, ed. (1980), "Patristic 'Presbyterianism' in the Early Medieval Theology of Sacred Orders," in *Mediaeval Studies,* **45** (1983), "Image and Text: The Liturgy of Clerical Ordination in Early Medieval Art," in *Gesta,* **22** (1983), "A South Italian Ordination Allocution," in *Mediaeval Studies,* **47** (1985), "The Ordination

Rite in Medieval Spain: Hispanic, Roman, and Hybrid," in *Santiago, Saint-Denis, and Saint Peter: The Reception of the Roman Liturgy in León-Castile in 1080,* Bernard F. Reilly, ed. (1985), and "The Ordination of Clerics in Toledo and Castile After the Reconquista According to the 'Romano-Catalan' Rite," in *II Congreso Internacional de Estudios Mozarabes: IX. Centenario de la Reconquista de Toledo, 1085–1985,* R. Gonzálvez-Ruiz, ed. (1987).

ROGER E. REYNOLDS

[See also **Alcuin of York; Church, Latin: Organization; Clergy; Durand, Guillaume; Gallican Rite; Isidore of Seville, St.; Lectionary; Mozarabic Rite; Pontificals; Sacramentary.**]

ORDINES ROMANI (ordinals). An *ordo* is a book of ceremonial directions or rubrics made to supplement other liturgical books containing the texts of prayers, music, lessons, and the like. From the twelfth century *ordines* were often mixed with extraliturgical material, and from the thirteenth century the term *ordo* virtually disappeared, to be replaced by such terms as *ordinarium* or *ceremoniale.* Hence, liturgiologists generally restrict the term *ordo* to ceremonial directories of the eleventh century and before. *Ordines* were made throughout Europe on local initiative, and where *ordines* from other locations were useful they could be copied and modified to conform to local practice. The *Ordines romani* were such texts made for use by the churches of Rome, and when they were taken elsewhere in Europe they were copied and modified for use there.

Most of the *Ordines romani* are fairly brief and originally were probably kept in *libelli* of only a few folios. But by the eighth century they were gathered into more extensive collections. The twentieth-century scholar Michel Andrieu designated as *Collection A* the *Ordines romani* compiled before 750, perhaps in France, and widely diffused in the Carolingian Empire due to the Romanizing tendencies in liturgical practice fostered by Pepin the Short (*d.* 768) and Charlemagne (*d.* 814). This collection contains ceremonial directions for Mass, baptism, Holy Week, the deposition of relics in a church, ordination, readings during the liturgical year, and burial. *Collection A* has Roman texts that have been modified with Gallican and Frankish texts; but even more Gallicanized is Andrieu's *Collection B,* designating texts compiled sometime between 750 and 814/820. This collection contains many of the items in *Collection A* in the same or modified form, but with ceremonial descriptions for the dedication of churches, liturgical practice on ember days, and ordination according to the Gallican rite. Other major early collections of the *Ordines romani* made during the Carolingian period were the so-called *Collection of St. Amand* (*Ordo romanus* IV) compiled in Ravenna or more likely France, and the *Capitulare ecclesiasticis ordinis,* the former adding directions for the major litany and the feast of the Purification, and the latter adding monastic ceremonial and material for the Divine Office celebrated in Rome. Beyond these four major collections of *Ordines romani* were several minor ones that contained directions for such things as nonpapal masses and the use of vestments.

In copying these collecions of *Ordines romani* into manuscripts, scribes often thought it appropriate to add related didactic material such as liturgical treatises and extracts from canon-law collections and capitularies. Particularly frequent among these additions were baptismal tracts occasioned by Charlemagne's letter of inquiry (812) and Carolingian explanations of the Mass. These mixed compilations of *Ordines romani* and didactic material served as protopontificals and protorituals. By the ninth century, true pontificals and rituals were being created, and by the tenth century these new types of books had incorporated many of the previously independent *ordines* or collections of *ordines.*

BIBLIOGRAPHY

Michel Andrieu, *Les ordines romani du haut moyen âge,* 5 vols. (1931–1961); Roger E. Reynolds, "Image and Text: A Carolingian Illustration of Modifications in the Early Roman Eucharistic *Ordines,*" in *Viator,* **14** (1983), and "Image and Text: The Liturgy of Clerical Ordination in Early Medieval Art," in *Gesta,* **22** (1983); Cyrille Vogel, *Introduction aux sources de l'histoire du culte chrétien au moyen âge* (1975).

ROGER E. REYNOLDS

[See also **Baptism; Carolingians; Ordination, Clerical.**]

ORDO. See **Ordines Romani.**

ORENDEL, the Middle High German version of the epic story of Christ's holy, seamless gray tunic

(*Grauer Rock*) and how it was brought to Trier. (The Virgin Mary was supposed to have spun the fabric of the tunic from wool, while Helena, born in Trier, finished it without seams; Christ then supposedly wore it during his fast of forty days in the desert.) The tale is the rather shallow retelling of the popular Hellenistic romance *Apollonius of Tyre* and its French imitator's *Jourdain de Blaivis.* "Graurock" is also the name by which its latest possessor, Orendel, is addressed in the course of this story.

Of all the German minstrel epic poems (*Spielmannsepik*), *Orendel,* of 3,937 lines with end rhymes, is the least well preserved and, in terms of literary quality, the least well written. The manuscript was lost in the bombardment of Strasbourg in 1870; a copy of it (from 1818) is kept in Berlin at the Staatsbibliothek der Stiftung Preussischer Kulturbesitz (formerly MS Germ. 4° 817a). However, the lost version was not an original Middle High German manuscript, but one that was printed at Strasbourg in 1477. *Orendel* was also recast into more modern verse and prose versions, both of which appeared at Augsburg in 1512. They have been reedited by Ludwig Denecke.

Orendel may date back to the very late twelfth century, but it more likely originated at Trier early in the thirteenth. Historically Christ's tunic was reported to have been kept in the cathedral of Trier, where it was reburied in 1196.

The narrative concerns the liberation of the Holy Sepulcher in Jerusalem, which is ruled by the Valkyrian Queen. Orendel sets out to win her and is later crowned by her as a successor to King David. But the couple may not make love during nine long years of marriage. They then travel to Trier to liberate it from the pagans and to deposit the tunic. They are called back to Jerusalem, where they again liberate the Holy Sepulcher. However, their love must remain unconsummated, and they die in an unnamed monastery.

Scholars agree that this story lacks a substantial narrative structure. The author simply adds one twist after another in order to prove Trier's claim to the gray tunic.

BIBLIOGRAPHY

Sources. Karl Simrock, trans., *Orendel* (1845); Arnold E. Berger, ed., *Orendel* (1888, repr. 1974); Hans Steinger, ed., *Orendel* (1935); Ludwig Denecke, ed., *Orendel: Der graue Rock* (1972), facs. of 1512 edition.

Studies. Michael Curschmann, "'Spielmannsepik': Wege und Ergebnisse der Forschung von 1907–1965" (2 parts), in *Deutsche Vierteljahrsschrift für Literaturwissenschaft und Geistesgeschichte,* **40** (1966); Uwe Meves, *Studien zu König Rother, Herzog Ernst und Grauer Rock (Orendel)* (1976); Walter J. Schröder, ed., *Spielmannsepik,* 2nd ed. (1967), 63ff, and *Spielmannsepik* (1977), 145–167.

CHRISTIAN GELLINEK

[See also **Middle High German Literature.**]

ORESME, NICOLE (*ca.* 1320–1382), French philosopher, mathematician, and theologian. The little that is known of Oresme's life is derived from the records of the University of Paris. He was born near Caen in Normandy and during the 1340's entered the University of Paris, where he probably studied with the celebrated arts master John Buridan. He became a master of arts prior to 1348; that year he is mentioned as a theology student at the College of Navarre. In 1355 or 1356, Oresme received the mastership in theology and in 1356 became grand master of the College of Navarre. Thereafter, his rise was steady as he became canon of Rouen (23 November 1362); canon of Ste. Chapelle, Paris (10 February 1363); dean of the cathedral of Rouen (18 March 1364); and finally bishop of Lisieux (1377). Oresme's ecclesiastical career was undoubtedly enhanced by faithful service to the French court, first to John II and then to his son, Charles V, whom Oresme had taught when he was dauphin. Charles rewarded Oresme with the bishopric of Lisieux for services rendered between 1369 and 1377, when Oresme translated four of Aristotle's treatises from Latin into French (*Ethics, Politics, Economics,* and *On the Heavens*) and furnished each with a commentary. Perhaps he also translated into French a Latin version of Ptolemy's *Tetrabiblos,* although the translation is actually attributed to G. Oresme.

Oresme was a scholar of enormous range. Not only was he a commentator on quite a few of Aristotle's works, but he also wrote independent treatises on theology, mathematics, physics, cosmology, magic, money, and the evils of astrology. Moreover, he was probably the first author to write anything of scientific significance in the French language, which he helped fashion into an instrument for the expression of scientific ideas.

Few, if any, medieval natural philosophers and scientists can equal Oresme's contributions in

ORESME, NICOLE

range and originality. While there is no single key to unite his varied interests, there is evidence that theological preconceptions influenced his interpretation of the role that science and natural philosophy played in the acquisition of knowledge. Although he did not explicitly discuss the relations of faith and reason in the works that have survived, there are indications that Oresme emphasized the absolute truths of faith over the often uncertain "truths" of natural philosophy or science and sought to demonstrate that experience and natural reason could not determine physical truth precisely and unambiguously. To achieve this, Oresme frequently proposed and defended equally plausible alternatives to widely accepted opinions. Two well-known examples involving basic beliefs about the Aristotelian cosmos illustrate his approach. Where Aristotle had argued against the possibility that more than one world could exist and had even denied that body, place, void, or time could exist beyond our finite world (*De caelo,* or, *On the Heavens*), Oresme demonstrated that a plurality of simultaneously existing worlds was in no sense demonstratively impossible. Each world would be just like ours with its own center and circumference, within which heavy and light bodies would behave as in ours. According to Oresme, no scientific arguments could decide the issue.

The diurnal rotation of the earth was treated in much the same manner in his *Livre du ciel et du monde* (1377). By a brilliant use of the principle of relativity of motion, Oresme demonstrated that the assumption of the earth's daily rotation could account for the astronomical phenomena just as well as the traditional explanation. Moreover, on the assumption that bodies hurled above the earth's surface would share the earth's rotation, Oresme could easily explain why such bodies would fall approximately to the place from whence they had been launched. Once again, no demonstrative argument could decide the issue. Satisfied that neither reason nor experience could decide these two great problems, Oresme retained the traditional interpretation: there is only one world and the earth lies immobile at its center. Oresme the theologian had thus shown that if the principles of natural philosophy were incapable of deciding between alternatives in a physical problem, they could aid even less in the comprehension of the truths of faith. Thus did Oresme seek to protect his faith from the probing analysis of natural philosophy. And yet, whenever possible, he sought rational and causal explanations for natural phenomena. Indeed, he made a determined effort to subvert confidence in magical, supernatural, and demonic explanations for allegedly marvelous phenomena (in his *De causis mirabilium*). Such events were better explained by natural causes.

As a mathematician Oresme was much concerned with the Euclidean theory of proportionality. In *De proportionibus proportionum* he developed original theorems and concepts within the context of a doctrine which he, and others before him, called "ratios of ratios" (*proportiones proportionum*). Here he showed how one could relate any two rational or irrational ratios by means of a rational or irrational exponent, the latter conceived as a "ratio of ratios." Eventually he devised a quasi-proof, based on probabilities, in which he inferred that any two proposed unknown ratios are probably incommensurable (he calculated the odds) and extended his reasoning to ratios representing physical magnitudes such as motion and time. Oresme was thus prepared to argue that any two celestial or terrestrial motions or magnitudes are probably incommensurable and form an irrational ratio from which a devastating consequence must follow: If most relationships between continuous physical magnitudes are probably incommensurable, exact knowledge about the physical world would be unattainable. Oresme thus concluded that precise astrological prediction would be impossible.

Oresme was also a major contributor to the doctrine of intension and remission of forms or qualities. In his *Tractatus de configurationibus qualitatum et motuum,* written in the 1350's, he sought to represent variations in qualities by means of two- and three-dimensional geometric figures. Despite Oresme's awareness that intensities are not spatial and that their geometric representations are fictional, the figures were meant to reflect varying internal arrangements of qualities in a subject, each somehow productive of a different effect. He discussed representations of a multiplicity of effects generated by internal configurations in natural powers and qualities such as sounds, music, the magical arts, pains, and joys. His graphic geometric representations of the distributions of uniform and nonuniform qualities in subjects, which included uniform velocities and uniformly and nonuniformly accelerated motions as particular cases, were of profound importance. It was here that Oresme anticipated Galileo's famous mean-speed theorem, usually represented as $S = \frac{1}{2}at^2$, where S is the distance traversed, *a* the uniform acceleration, and *t* is the time of acceleration.

As modern scholarship has probed more deeply into Oresme's works and thought, his stature has only increased. He ranks as perhaps the greatest scholastic product of the University of Paris in the fourteenth century. His yet unedited works are not likely to alter that perception.

BIBLIOGRAPHY

Sources. Recent editions of Oresme's works are Bert Hansen, *Nicole Oresme and the Marvels of Nature* (1985), ed. and trans. of *De causis mirabilium,* with commentary; Stephen C. McCluskey, Jr., "Nicole Oresme on Light, Color, and the Rainbow" (diss., Univ. of Wisconsin, 1975), ed. and trans. of part of *Questiones super quatuor libros meteororum;* Nicole Oresme, "Quaestio contra divinatores horoscopios," Stefano Caroti, ed., in *Archives d'histoire doctrinale et littéraire du moyen-âge,* **51** (1976).

Studies. H. L. L. Busard, "Die Quellen von Nicole Oresme," in *Janus,* **58** (1971); Stefano Caroti, "Nicole Oresme precursore di Galileo e di Descartes?" in *Rivista critica di storia della filosofia,* **32** (1977); Marshall Clagett, "Oresme, Nicole," in *Dictionary of Scientific Biography,* X (1974), which contains an excellent bibliography; Edward Grant, "Scientific Thought in Fourteenth-century Paris: Jean Buridan and Nicole Oresme," in Madeleine Pelner Cosman and Bruce Chandler, eds., *Machaut's World: Science and Art in the Fourteenth Century* (1978); Claudia Kren, "The Rolling Device of Nasir al-Dīn al-Tūsi in the *De sphera* of Nicole Oresme?" in *Isis,* **62** (1971); George A. Molland, "Nicole Oresme and Scientific Progress," in Albert Zimmermann, ed., *Miscellanea mediaevalia,* IX, *Antiqui und Moderni: Traditionbewusstsein und Fortschrittbewusstsein im späten Mittelalter* (1974).

EDWARD GRANT

[See also **Aristotle in the Middle Ages; Astrology/Astronomy; Buridan, Jean; Mathematics; Physics.**]

ORFEO, SIR. See **Sir Orfeo.**

ORGAN. Invented in Hellenistic Alexandria by the third century B.C., the organ was known throughout the Roman world. The ingenious use of water pressure to assure a steady supply of wind accounts for its name, *hydraulis.* The instrument was appropriated by the Byzantine court, where it was played in the imperial liturgy during ceremonial acclamations of the emperor. By the time the organ had been reintroduced into Western Europe around the eighth century, the hydraulic mechanism had been replaced by a pneumatic system of bellows to supply the air. Primitive hand pulls connected directly to the pipes acted as valves. The loud, clumsy mechanism and weak tone, however, made the instrument unsuitable for extended musical performance.

During the "Carolingian renaissance" both ceremonial and iconographical elements, including the use of the organ in imperial and religious contexts, were borrowed from Byzantium. In 757 Emperor Constantine V sent an organ to Pepin. According to some sources, Charlemagne was given an instrument, perhaps by the caliph Hārūn al-Rashīd in 812, along with musicians who set it up in Aachen and then taught Frankish monks how to play it. Louis I the Pious (*r.* 813–833, 834–840) had an organ built by a Venetian monk named Gregorius fourteen years later. Instruments were built for the monastic churches in Freising and Strassburg, the former so esteemed that in 872 Pope John VIII summoned an organ builder from Freising to construct a similar instrument in Rome.

Many writers, such as Notker Labeo, refer to organ building in German monasteries. The rise of monasteries led to their expansion as centers and disseminators of culture, and as focal points for the development of liturgical chant. The organ was used as an adjunct to this growing pomp. In 953 the organ in Cologne was played for the installation of Archbishop Bruno I, brother of the future emperor Otto I. Sometime later, a certain Guglielmo donated an organ to the Basilica of S. Salvatore in Turin, so that choristers at Easter and other high holidays could sing "with [both] the organ and the boys" (*de organo cum pueris*). The English abbeys of Abingdon, Winchester (*ca.* 980), Malmesbury (*ca.* 985), and Glastonbury also figured in this new wave of organ building. Archbishop Gerbert of Rheims, the future Pope Sylvester II, gave an instrument to the cloister at Aurillac around 991–995 for use in its liturgical observances. The cloisters of Halberstadt (tenth century) and Augsburg (1060) installed large instruments, and in 1092 the monastery of La Cava near Salerno resounded on high feast days (*in summa festivitate*) with the sounds of its new organ.

Whether or not the organ was used to accompany the various Mass sections at this early period is open to question; it may have been limited to preludes, interludes, and postludes. However, there was a growth of special pomp on ceremonial occasions. Newly composed pieces, such as tropes and sequences, served as embellishments to introduce liturgical action and extend processional music. Considering their function of adding color to the Mass, organ accompaniment of these interpolations was likely. For example, an eleventh-century manuscript from Douai contains a sequence along with the notation *cum organa.*

The organ gained admission to the Mass gradually, its use restricted to high feast days and to certain Mass texts. Theophilus wrote in his *Diversarum artium schedula* (first half of the eleventh century) that actual practice had established the use of the organ in the liturgy. Honorius of Autun (early twelfth century) stated emphatically that the organ alone might be used as an instrument of praise. Likewise, Honorius of Canterbury wrote that the organ and bells were the instruments used in liturgical worship. According to Abbot Hildebrand, the Mass in the cloister at Hildesheim took three or four hours to celebrate, owing to the extensive ritual and drawn-out chanting and organ music. Even by 1107, however, when Bishop Baudri of Dôle documented the organ in the abbey of Fécamp, its use could still be characterized as rare.

In his *Roman de Brut* (*ca.* 1155), the Norman trouvère Robert Wace observed that "Quant li messe fu commensie / Qui durement fu essaucie / Mout oïssiés orgues sonner / Et clercs chanter et orguener" (When Mass had begun / Which was sung with jubilation / One could hear organs playing loudly / And clerics singing in unison and in harmony). And the *Lancelot* (*ca.* 1177–1181) of Chrétien de Troyes associated the organ with high holidays: "Por oïr les ogres / Vont au mostier a feste annuel / A Pantecoste ou a Noel" (To hear the organs / They went to the abbey or church on the annual holy days / At Whitsuntide or Christmas). Although the larger cathedral music schools (*maîtrises*), such as those at Paris and Rheims, possessed instruments somewhat earlier, it was the fourteenth century that saw a widespread surge in organ building. This is reflected in numerous contemporary literary references. For example, the historian Froissart records that in 1388, at a festive Mass in the royal chapel, the service was as solemnly celebrated as if it were Christmas or Easter, with a large group of singers and an organ playing "melodiously." Chaucer referred in The Nun's Priest's Tale to "the murie organ, / On messe-dayes that in the chirche gon." And John Lydgate wrote (*ca.* 1430) of "Thi organys so hihe begynne to syng ther messe."

Numerous fifteenth-century sources describe the role of the organ in the liturgical service. In Paris, a St. Valentine's Day Mass was celebrated (1401) "à note, à son d'orgues, chant et déchant" (from the [written] score, to the sounds of organs, plainchant and discant [that is, polyphony]). In 1413, "uns orguens qui servesquen al a solemnitat dels officis divinals" (an organ that serves for the solemnity of the Divine Office) was purchased for the royal chapel of King Alfonso I of Aragon in Barcelona. The sacristy book of the Church of St. Severin in Speyer records that during the masses for Christmas Eve, Epiphany, the purification of the Virgin, Septuagesima Sunday, and Corpus Christi, "man singet uf der Orgel" (people sing with the organ).

During the upsurge of Gothic organ building, specific evidence shows the repeated use of the instrument on important feast days during certain services, especially at Mass and vespers. The Benedictines, particularly the Cluniac order, pioneered in new attempts to enrich the liturgical service. And according to the customary of St. Augustine's Church at Canterbury, the organ was used to adorn the liturgy at Christmas and on the feast days of St. John and St. Thomas, Epiphany (at high Mass), the feast of St. Adrian and its octave, the purification of the Virgin (if not in Lent, also at high Mass), the Annunciation (if not in Easter week), Easter Day, the translation of St. Augustine (at both vespers and in the sequence of the Mass), and on the feast of St. Michael (in the sequence only). As something new and special, polyphony was used to lend distinction to high points in the liturgy on these special holidays, and here the organ's role was important. For example, it accompanied the voices in organum (a type of early medieval polyphony), performing the slower-moving Gregorian cantus firmus (a preexistent melody). Giles of Zamora (thirteenth century) wrote that the church used only the organ for various chants, as well as in proses, sequences, and hymns. The conductus was presumably a song or processional sung as the clergy moved about the church, performing their liturgical functions. It lent itself particularly to organ accompaniment. The motet, a short polyphonic composition based upon a "borrowed" melody from Gregorian chant,

Nave organ in the cathedral of Basel. Detail from the *Holy Family (Sacred Conversation)* by Konrad Witz, 15th century. GALLERIA NAZIONALE DI CAPODIMONTE, NAPLES. ALINARI/ART RESOURCE

was ceremonial in nature, and here, too, the organ duplicated or reinforced the vocal line on occasion.

By the mid fourteenth century most major churches possessed both large and small organs, the former usually hanging on the wall of the nave or transept and the latter in a gallery near the choir and the singers. The larger instrument was used for the twenty-three high feast days, while the smaller "positive" or "chamber" one (an organ with one or more ranks of pipes, a range of at least two octaves [including some chromatic notes], and uniform tone color) was used on minor holidays. By the mid fifteenth century the organ both accompanied and substituted for voices, and was played solo in all important liturgical services.

The ordinary of the Mass included chants featuring the alternation of soloists and choir. Polyphonic settings developed in the fourteenth century, a further impetus to the organ's use. A contemporary document states that at Notre Dame de Paris the organist played during the four movements of the ordinary. In addition, he played during the gradual, alleluia, and sequences. Succeeding verses of the Gloria and creed were often separated by textless intermediate passages; and here the organ's use was also suggested.

The proper included ornate chants sung in both responsorial and antiphonal fashion. Generally, the organ was played for double feasts except during Advent, Lent, and the six Sundays following Epiphany. According to the Statutes of Bourges (1407), in all masses, whatever the feast, the introit, responses, alleluia, offertory, and post-Communion, as well as the Kyrie, Gloria, Sanctus, and Agnus Dei, were either sung alone or along with the organ. A noteworthy feature was the alternation between chorus and soloist, which was carried over to the use of the organ: between instrument and plainsong; between polyphonic singing and the organ; and among all three. Thus, by this time the organ both accompanied and substituted for voices in the various Mass sections on most feast days, generally observing the principle of alternation, especially in movements of the ordinary. The requiem Mass was unaccompanied during the Middle Ages.

The organ was also played in designated sections of the canonical hours, or Office. One of the earliest references, the *Life of St. Oswald* (*ca.* 992), cites the organ's use at Turin in both the Mass and canonical hours. Referring perhaps to the vespers service, Guido of Arezzo mentions in his *Micrologus* (after 1026) that the organ was used for "hymns, antiphons, and other offices as well." The *Annales de Saint Louis* describes how the king devoutly "fit chanter la messe et solempnement glorieuses vespres et matines et toute le service à chant et à deschant, à ogre et treble" (ordered sung the Mass and solemn, glorious vespers, matins, and the entire service in plainchant, discant [polyphony], organ, and in three parts). A document of 1365 states that at the abbey of St. Stephen in Vienna the whole Office was performed with organ accompaniment during great festivals.

On the evenings preceding major feast days the vespers service began with a solemn procession, officials and celebrant entering the church as the organ was played. At S. Maria del Fiore in Florence, the choristers were expected to sing at all Sunday vespers services for major feast days, at which time the organist also had to play.

The Magnificat, always a musical high point, also featured the organ, which quite possibly accompanied the even-numbered verses only. The Te Deum, used in the celebration of both offices and festive occasions outside the church proper, was a song of special rejoicing. Often both organs were played, as, for example, at Metz (". . . grand solemn Mass, with the large church bells, and the large and small organs"). Contemporary records indicate that as a general rule the chorus and organ alternated in rendering the verses.

The sliding levers or knobs that controlled

access of air into the organ pipes were often so bulky that they had to be depressed by fist or elbow. The wheezing bellows, clanking mechanism, and wind pressure, too, were unreliable. Aelred of Rievaulx (twelfth century) objected to this state of affairs, calling the new instrument at Canterbury more like thunder than sweet music. During the Gothic period, organ building came to match the growing requirements of liturgical music more closely. Instruments usually had a single manual with a range of from one to three octaves and from twenty to forty pipes, combined in ranks to produce different qualities of sound by means of various stops. Starting with B-flat, accidentals were introduced, and by the fifteenth century the entire chromatic scale was available. The primitive levers had been replaced (in the thirteenth century) by the modern keyboard with mechanical linkages (tracker action) to control the access of air. The sound was thus much improved. Magister Lambertus (*fl.* 1260) wrote in his *Tractatus de musica* about the organ's "marvelous" utility and its music that "penetrates beyond the church doors." Bellows, too, were improved, and by the fourteenth century a more uniform wind pressure was achieved through the introduction of the *conflatorium,* a refinement wherein air was not blown by the bellows directly into the pipes but first passed through a reservoir, or wind-chest. The pedal board was invented by the Fleming Louis van Valbecke (*d.* 1318), but its widespread use in conjunction with an independent series of pipes came later, along with springs and catches enabling the pedal to be held in a depressed position.

With the impetus from polyphonic music played on (and in some cases written for) keyboard instruments, organ construction and technique developed more rapidly during the fifteenth century: the instruments became larger; their range increased at both ends of the scale; new stops were introduced; the number of pipes and their respective sizes grew; and bellows were multiplied to furnish a greater wind supply. A new conception of organ registration evolved, starting with several manuals (keyboards) and including various arrangements of separate and unique groups of pipes, each providing entirely new tone colors. Foundation stops (sounding the written note) were joined by mutations (sounding a harmonic such as the fourth, fifth, or octave) and mixtures (a combination of pipes of different types or tone colors).

Organ in the transept of a Gothic church. Detail from a Life of Christ triptych attributed to Louis Alimbrot, mid 15th century. MUSEO DEL PRADO, MADRID. INV. NO. 2538. Foto MAS, Barcelona

BIBLIOGRAPHY

Willi Apel, "Early History of the Organ," in *Speculum,* 23 (1948); H. Avenary-Loewenstein "The Mixture Principle in the Medieval Organ," in *Musica disciplina,* 4 (1950); Edmund A. Bowles, "The Organ in the Medieval Liturgical Service," in *Revue belge de musicologie,* 16 (1962), and "The Symbolism of The Organ in the Middle Ages," in Jan LaRue, ed., *Aspects of Medieval and Renaissance Music* (1966); John Caldwell, "The Organ in the Medieval Latin Liturgy," in *Proceedings of the Royal Musical Association,* 18 (1966–1967), and "The Organ in the British Isles Until 1600," in *Organ Yearbook,* 2 (1971); Hermann Degering, *Die Orgel: Ihre Erfindung und ihre Geschichte bis zur Karolingerzeit* (1905); Norbert Dufourcq, *Esquisse d'une histoire de l'orgue en France du xiiie au xviiie siècle*

(1935); Ernst Flade, "Literarische Zeugnisse zur Empfindung der 'Farbe' und 'Farbigkeit' bei der Orgel und beim Orgelspiel," in *Acta musicologica,* **22** (1951); Gotthold Frotscher, *Geschichte des Orgelspiels und der Orgelkomposition,* 2 vols. (1935–1936, 2nd ed. 1959); Otto Gombosi, "About Organ Playing in the Divine Service, Circa 1500," in Harvard University, *Essays on Music in Honor of Archibald Thompson Davison* (1957); Pierre Hardouin, "De l'orgue de Pépin à l'orgue médiévale," in *Revue de musicologie,* **52** (1966); Hans Klotz, *Über die Orgelkunst der Gotik, der Renaissance und des Barock* (1934); J. Madurell, "Documentos para la historia del órgano en España," in *Anuario musical,* **2** (1947); E. Meyer-Hermann, "Beitrag zur kirchenmusikalischen Praxis im Ausgang des Mittelalters," in *Zeitschrift für Musikwissenschaft,* **12** (1930).

Jean Perrot, *The Organ from Its Invention in the Hellenistic Period to the End of the Thirteenth Century,* Norma Deane, trans. (1971); Gerhard Pietzsch, "Orgelbauer, Organisten und Orgelspiel in Deutschland," in *Die Musikforschung,* **11** (1958); Rudolf Quoika, *Die Altösterreichische Orgel der späten Gotik* (1953); Rudolf Reuter, *Bibliographie der Orgel* (1973); A. Schering, "Zur Frage der Orgelmitwirkung in der Kirchenmusik des 15. Jahrhunderts," in Willibald Gurlitt, ed., *Bericht über die Freiburger Tagung für deutsche Orgelkunst* (1926); Leo Schrade, "Organ Music in the Mass of the Fifteenth Century—Part II," in *Musical Quarterly,* **28** (1942); Leo Söhner, *Die Orgelbegleitung zum gregorianischen Gesang* (1936); Peter F. Williams, *The European Organ, 1450–1850* (1978), "How Did the Organ Become a Church Instrument?" in A. Dunning, ed., *Visitatio organum* (1980), and *A New History of the Organ from the Greeks to the Present Day* (1980); Franz Zehrer, *Die Orgel als Begleitinstrument des liturgischen Gesanges* (1943). For illustrations of medieval organs, see Edmund A. Bowles, "A Preliminary Checklist of 15th-century Representations of Organs in Paintings and Manuscript Illuminations," in *The Organ Yearbook,* **13** (1982).

EDMUND A. BOWLES

[See also **Conductus; Mass Cycles; Mass, Liturgy of the; Motet; Music, Western European; Musical Instruments, European.**]

ORGANUM. The word has been used in a variety of musical contexts, which range from references to musical instruments of all kinds to specific aspects of polyphonic composition or performance. While a vestige of the former usage remains in the modern word for the organ, the special meanings expressed by the latter disappeared from the active vocabulary of music after the thirteenth century. When the Latin form *organum* is used in contemporary musicography, it normally refers only to a particular kind of medieval polyphony, or to analogous styles in more recent or non-Western music. It would be misleading to infer any direct connection between the sound and musical capabilities of the organ and the sound and style of medieval organum, though some scholars persist in claiming such a connection.

In Latin translations of the Bible and in the patristic literature, the word stands for any kind of musical instrument, either "artificial" or "natural" (that is, the voice), and, by extension, for that which is sung. As an adjective, it can refer either to instrumental music, or to singing that is precise and mathematically regulated (*organicum melos*), derived from the older Greek tradition for *organon* as a precise scientific instrument. We cannot be certain which of these traditions was the determining one for the early association of the word with polyphonic music. In the early phase from the ninth to the twelfth centuries, the word refers not to a musical form or genre, but to either the individual tone or the entire voice set against a preexistent melody. It can also refer to the whole complex of voices, and is thus a name for polyphony in general, which is virtually synonymous with *diaphonia* during the same period.

Eventually most of these older meanings were forgotten, and the word was restricted to that genre of polyphonic music in which one to three florid voices are added to a slow-moving tenor voice, usually derived from the responsorial chants of the Mass and the Office. As such, the term *organum* became part of the complex taxonomy of polyphonic genera associated with the Notre Dame school. It is this meaning which is the primary one for the student of medieval music, though both the word and the musical genre died out almost completely after the thirteenth century.

BIBLIOGRAPHY

Fritz Reckow, "Organum," in *Handwörterbuch der musikalischen Terminologie,* (1972), *idem* and Rudolf Flotzinger, "Organum," in *New Grove Dictionary of Music and Musicians,* XIII (1980).

ROBERT FALCK

[See also **Ars Antiqua; Consonance/Dissonance; Diaphonia; Notre Dame School.**]

ORIEL WINDOW, a bay window projecting outward from a wall, normally at some distance above the ground level and supported on corbels, oversailing courses, or, occasionally, supports built up from the ground. The term defines the projecting bay or construction rather than the tracery or design pattern of the window itself. Oriel windows were found throughout medieval Europe but were especially common in Britain.

CARL F. BARNES, JR.

ORIENTIUS (*fl.* first half of the fifth century), the Christian poet who composed the extant *Commonitorium* (Letter of instruction) about 430, in two books totaling 518 elegaic couplets. He generally is thought to be the St. Orientius who was bishop of Auch about 430–440 and was said to have been of Spanish origin. In 439 this latter Orientius served, unsuccessfully, as mediator between the Visigothic king Theodoric I and his attacker, the Roman commander of Hun mercenaries Litorius, who subsequently was captured and killed.

The skillfully composed *Commonitorium* describes the devastation of Gaul caused by the barbarian invasions, laments human faults and immortality, and advises preparation for the world to come. Such statements appear in other works of this period, such as those by Salvian of Marseilles.

Also (rather doubtfully) attributed to Orientius are the poems *On the Birth of the Lord,* in 7 hexameters; *On the Names of Our Savior,* in 5 elegaic couplets; *On the Trinity,* in 95 hexameters; *Explanation of the Names of the Lord,* in 146 hexameters; a *Laudation,* in 33 hexameters; and 24 *Orationes,* of which a pair survive in 65 iambic hexameters.

BIBLIOGRAPHY

The texts of the *Commonitorium* and other poems are in *Patrologia latina,* LXI (1847), 977–1006; and, edited by Robinson Ellis, in *Poetae christiani minores,* pt. 1 (1888, repr. 1972), 205–253 (*Poetae . . .* is vol. XVI in the series Corpus Scriptorum Ecclesiasticorum Latinorum). Louis Bellanger, *Le poème d'Orientius* (1903), has the text and a French translation. Mildred D. Tobin, *Orientii Commonitorium* (1945), provides the text and an English translation.

Bibliographies and discussions are in Eligius Dekkers, comp., Emil Gaar, ed., *Clavis patrum latinorum,* 2nd ed. (1961), nos. 1465–1467; Martin Schanz, Carl Hosius, and Gustav Krüger, *Geschichte der römischen Literatur,* IV, pt. 2 (1920, repr. 1959), 365–367. For a discussion of Orientius and his work, see Eleanor S. Duckett, *Latin Writers of the Fifth Century* (1930).

RALPH W. MATHISEN

[See also **Latin Literature; Salvian of Marseilles.**]

ORIGEN (*ca.* 185–*ca.* 254), teacher, exegete, philosopher, and theologian, was born in Alexandria, Egypt, and died in Caesarea, Palestine. The scope of Origen's career and the influence of his literary works are unique in the history of Christianity. He is known as the first great theologian of the early church, the originator of a widely used allegorical approach to the interpretation of the Bible, and the figure who made the most successful bridge between Platonic philosophy and the Christian theological enterprise. His lasting influence is all the more remarkable since his writings were condemned as heretical in 553 at the Second Council of Constantinople, called by the emperor Justinian I.

Origen was born to a Christian family and educated in both Christian and Hellenistic literature. The earliest account of Origen's life, Book VI of the *Ecclesiastical History* of Eusebius of Caesarea, relates that his father, Leonides, was martyred in the persecutions of Septimius Severus in 202. Origen showed an early enthusiasm for ascetic spirituality and is said to have castrated himself in response to the admonition in Matthew 19:12 to become a eunuch for the sake of the Kingdom of God. If true, this shows a literal understanding of the Gospel quite at odds with his usual allegorical approach. He was a brilliant student, probably in the school of Ammonius Saccas, where the founder of Neoplatonism, Plotinus, studied a bit later. Around 204, Bishop Demetrius of Alexandria appointed Origen the head of his catechetical school. Origen traveled to Rome and to Palestine and became known to many important secular and ecclesiastical personages. He was ordained in Caesarea in 230, an event which Bishop Demetrius took as an affront to the Alexandrian church. Consequently, Origen spent most of his remaining years in Palestine. During the persecutions of Decius, which began in 250, he was arrested and tortured. He died a few years after his release from prison.

ORIGEN

Origen's Platonism, like that of Plotinus, was marked by a hierarchical understanding of reality along the lines of the "great chain of being." He used this concept to explain the trinitarian deity of Christianity, and he used the revealed truths of the Christian "rule of faith" to show the ultimate rationality of a scheme of mediation between the uncreated, eternal God and the created world. The defense of Christianity in *Contra Celsum* (after 245) shows his encounter with Hellenism; and the *De principiis* (*Peri archon*, before 230) elaborates the connections between Christian revelation and the Platonic conception of a First Principle.

Platonism may have predisposed Origen to allegory, but his understanding of the Bible was equally rooted in the developing rabbinical tradition. In Alexandria, he was exposed to the Hebrew language and the writings of Philo; and in Caesarea, he may well have had contact with the important school of Rabbi Hosheya. The *Hexapla,* Origen's sixfold comparison of Greek translations of the Hebrew Bible, was begun in Alexandria and completed in Caesarea. No complete copies of this text are extant, but many fragments (some with additional Latin material or transliteration into the Roman alphabet) circulated in the Middle Ages. Latin authors who cite Hebrew Bible texts often refer to some version of this text. More generally, Origen's knowledge of Jewish exegesis taught him to approach Scripture as a multifaceted vehicle of divine truth, each verse existing on many levels of signification. In Book IV of *De principiis,* in what is itself an allegorical interpretation of the Wedding at Cana, Origen shows that the historical sense of Scripture gives rise to christological and spiritual, or mystical, understandings. There is nothing ironclad about these categories; rather, they suggest the multiplicity of divine revelation in a system that is complex, sophisticated, and flexible.

Origen's breakthrough into allegorical exposition of Scripture laid the cornerstone of a vast edifice of medieval Christian exegesis. In the Latin West during the Middle Ages, the *De principiis* (in a loose translation of Rufinus) and his biblical commentaries (especially on the Song of Songs, Jeremiah, Luke, and Matthew, translated by Jerome, Rufinus, and anonymous authors) were widely read and greatly influential. This is especially striking in the case of the Song of Songs, for which Origen's commentary and homilies shaped a fervent outpouring of exegesis. The Song of Songs commentary of Gregory of Nyssa popularized Origen's interpretation in the Byzantine church, even though the Greek original was lost. In the West, partial translations of the commentary by Rufinus and the homilies by Jerome were available in a great many monastic libraries. Origen's understanding of the text as the love between God and the church, or God and the soul, was the basis for such famous Song of Songs commentaries as that of Haimo of Auxerre (ninth century) and many twelfth-century authors, notably Bernard of Clairvaux. However, few medieval exegetes cite Origen by name, and it is not until the Scholastic period that authors such as Peter Riga and Nicholas of Lyra credit him with the basic Christian understanding of the text.

Clearly, the condemnation of Origen in 553 changed the nature of his influence on medieval Christianity. However, the reason for this condemnation is difficult to reconstruct. It seems to be an outgrowth of the fourth-century struggles over the coherent, universal definition of Christian theological premises. Origen, who lived well before these disputes, was invoked by both sides of the Arian heresy, to take one example; but his Platonized hierarchy fell a bit too much on the side of what was declared heresy than on the side of the newly defined orthodoxy. Other aspects of the "Origenist heresy" involved political disputes among monastic factions in fourth-century Egypt. These aspects had little to do with the medieval reception of Origen except insofar as they contributed to his condemnation. That Origen's ideas were possibly too complex for the post-Hellenistic world may be evident in the alacrity with which both Rufinus and Jerome, once his ardent admirers, openly laundered their Latin translations of excessive Platonism and even of excessive subtleties. But Origen's genius is evident in the flourishing transmission of his works, in however fragmentary a form, for well over a millennium after his death.

BIBLIOGRAPHY

Sources. Texts of Origen's works comprise twelve volumes (1899–1955) in *Die griechischen christlichen Schriftsteller der ersten drei Jahrhunderts.* Translations are Origen, *Contra Celsum,* Henry Chadwick, ed. and trans. (1953), *An Exhortation to Martyrdom, Prayer, and Other Selected Works,* Rowan A. Greer, trans. (1979), and *The Song of Songs Commentary and Homilies,* R. P. Lawson, trans. (1957).

Studies. Henri Crouzel, *Bibliographie critique d'Ori-*

ORKNEYINGA SAGA

gène (1971); Jean Daniélou, *Origène* (1948), trans. by Walter Mitchell as *Origen* (1955); Richard C. P. Hanson, *Allegory and Event* (1959); Henri de Lubac, *Histoire et esprit* (1950); Joseph W. Trigg, *Origen: The Bible and Philosophy in the Third-century Church* (1983).

E. ANN MATTER

[See also **Arianism; Bernard of Clairvaux, St., Christology; Councils (Ecumenical, 325–787); Eusebius of Caesarea; Haimo of Auxerre; Jerome, St.; Neoplatonism; Plato in the Middle Ages; Philosophy/Theology.**]

ORKNEYINGA SAGA traces the history of the earls of the Orkneys from about 900 to the early thirteenth century. It was originally written in the late twelfth century, but is only preserved in a revised version from about 1230. The oldest manuscripts of the saga are three fragments; the largest (AM 325 I 4°), dating from about 1300, consists of eighteen leaves. In its entirety the saga is preserved in *Flateyjarbók,* where it is incorporated into *Óláfs saga Tryggvasonar* and *Óláfs saga helga.*

The most important paper manuscripts are Cod. Isl. Paper 39 fol. in the Royal Library, Stockholm, and AM 332 4°. The first is a translation into Danish made in the west of Norway about or shortly after 1570 from a very old Icelandic manuscript that later, in an incomplete state, reached Copenhagen, where it was destroyed in the great fire of 1728. The other is Ásgeir Jónsson's copy of the fragments of this manuscript found in Copenhagen before the fire. The text of *Flateyjarbók* can often be amended by variants from these manuscripts.

The translation shows that the original version ended with the slaying of Sveinn Ásleifarson around 1171. The last chapters of the *Flateyjarbók* version, ending with accounts of Earl Jón Haraldsson (*d.* 1231), are later additions. The legendary opening chapters are also likely to be later additions.

Orkneyinga saga was evidently known to Snorri Sturluson, who, in his *Óláfs saga helga,* refers to it as *Jarla saga* or *Jarla sögur.* Most likely the name *Orkneyinga saga* is an abbreviation of *Orkneyinga jarla saga.* It also seems obvious that Snorri Sturluson was in some way or other involved in the revision of *Orkneyinga saga.* The present writer has (in 1965) gone so far as to suggest that Snorri himself was responsible for the opening chapters. However that may be, his influence can be indisputably seen by the fact that chapters 13–19 of *Orkneyinga saga* have been taken directly from his *Óláfs saga helga,* with the result that the corresponding part of the original version is now completely lost. Finally, there is a definite connection between Snorri Sturluson's writing of *Heimskringla,* especially of the first third of it, and the revision of *Orkneyinga saga.* Snorri makes changes that can be traced to *Orkneyinga saga,* and the reviser of *Orkneyinga saga* in turn adapts his work in a few places to *Heimskringla.*

Another important result of the revision was the adding of miracles to the section dealing with Earl Magnús Erlendsson. The main source for the miracles is the *Vita Sancti Magni* by Master Roðbert, although *Orkneyinga saga* does not accept the vita's adverse judgment on Earl Hákon Pálsson (who had Earl Magnus killed) and Hávarðr Gunnason, who was married to the earl's niece, Bergljót. On the contrary, they are defended so strongly that it looks as if the author of the revised version was being influenced by some descendants of Hákon Pálsson, presumably his grandson, Earl Haraldr Maddaðarson, and Eiríkr, whose father, Hákon kló (Hákon Claw, a son of Hávarðr Gunnason), is often mentioned in *Orkneyinga saga* together with his brothers. Eiríkr Hákonarson's wife was of the Hvassafell family, in the north of Iceland, members of which were known for their interest in books and learning.

Orkneyinga saga covers a period of more than three centuries, and it is clear that the author depended on Icelandic traditions for the first two centuries, including Arnórr Jarlaskáld's *Þorfinnsdrápa.* Accounts of events toward the end of the saga are supported by oral tradition from Orkney. It is most likely that the author had himself visited the islands and Scotland.

It is probable that the accounts of Earl Rögnvaldr's crusade in 1151–1153 and his slaying in 1158 were written down shortly after the event, the writer following the example set by Eiríkr Oddsson in his *Hryggjarstykki.* A close connection between *Orkneyinga saga* and *Ágrip,* for instance in chronology, may indicate that the Icelandic author of *Orkneyinga saga* completed his work in Norway. Nothing really speaks against the original *Orkneyinga saga* having been written before 1190. The mention of Earl Rögnvaldr's sainthood (he was canonized in 1192) may just as well have been added to the saga later.

BIBLIOGRAPHY
Editions are Finnbogi Guðmundsson, ed., *Orkneyinga saga* (1965); Sigurður J. Nordal, ed., *Orkneyinga saga* (1913–1916); Gudbrandr Vigfusson, ed., *Orkneyinga Saga and Magnus Saga, with Appendices* (1887). Translations are Alexander B. Taylor, ed. and trans., *The Orkneyinga Saga* (1938); Hermann Pálsson and Paul Edwards, *Orkneyinga Saga* (1978). Bibliography is in *Islandica,* **3** (1910) and **26** (1937).

Studies. Einar Ól. Sveinsson, *Sagnaritun Oddaverja* (1937); Rudolf Meissner, "Ermengarde, Vicegräfin von Narbonne, und Jarl Rögnvald," in *Arkiv för nordisk filologi,* **37** (**41**) (1925); Sigurður J. Nordal, *Om Orkneyingasaga* (1913); Alexander B. Taylor, "Orkneyinga Saga—Patronage and Authorship," in International Saga Conference, 1st, University of Edinburgh, 1971, *Proceedings* (1973).

FINNBOGI GUÐMUNDSSON

[See also **Háttalykill; Óláfs Saga Helga; Óláfs Saga Tryggvasonar; Snorri Sturluson.**]

ORLÉANS, CHARLES OF. See **Charles of Orléans.**

ORMULUM. The text of this collection of metrical English sermons survives in a single manuscript, Bodleian MS Junius 1. The work was composed, it is believed, late in the twelfth century in Lincoln or nearby by an Augustinian canon named Orm (which he himself spelled Orrm) or Ormin (spelled Orrmin). The bold hand in which the manuscript is written, the numerous corrections, some by the main scribe himself and others by later hands, and the strict economy with which the text is crowded into the available space, together with other features, suggest that it was a "workshop" draft which the author intended to have recopied by a professional scribe, as was commonly done in medieval times. The text of the sermons is entered on the main leaves of the manuscript, and a large number of irregularly shaped leaves containing additional or revised material have been inserted in many places. The main text itself has been revised and corrected several times and in many ways, almost certainly at the author's behest or by the author himself, and the new readings are awkwardly and untidily squeezed into the narrow margins. No other surviving medieval manuscript with comparable subject matter (whether in Latin or English) is written on such poor parchment and with so little regard for its appearance.

The surviving manuscript contains 20,000 lines of verse; to judge from the table of contents and from other evidence, it almost certainly ran once to 160,000 lines. The remainder has been lost or destroyed, some unfortunately during or since the seventeenth century, when the manuscript was owned in turn by the Dutch scholars Franz Junius and Jan van Vliet.

The sermons are of little literary or theological value. The work is of primary interest, however, to lexicographers and grammarians because, nearly two hundred years before Chaucer, it illustrates at considerable length the regional form of English that later emerged as Received Standard English. Moreover the numerous corrections in the manuscript, which were mainly based on a desire to eliminate one of a pair of apparently equally current variants (such as *kaserr/keȝȝse* [emperor] reduced to *kaserr, ȝho/ho* [she] normalized to *ȝho,* and the diphthong *eo* in words like *freond* [friend] reduced throughout to *e*), provide scholars with an unparalleled opportunity to judge the linguistic changes occurring at the time in the East Midlands in England. The most celebrated scribal feature was Orm's use of a doubled consonant after a short vowel in closed syllables (*himm* [him], *senndenn* [to send]) and a single one after a long vowel (*stan* [stone], *win* [wine]). The work is one of three main texts (the others being the *Ancrene Riwle* and the *Ayenbite of Inwyt*) used by Middle English scholars as a triangular base for surveying and mapping the English language in the early Middle English period.

BIBLIOGRAPHY
An edition is Robert M. White and Robert Holt, eds., *The Ormulum,* 2 vols. (1878). See also Robert W. Burchfield, "The Language and Orthography of the Ormulum MS," in *Transactions of the Philological Society* (1956), and "*Ormulum*: Words Copied by Jan van Vliet from Parts Now Lost," in Norman Davis and C. L. Wrenn, eds., *English and Medieval Studies Presented to J. R. R. Tolkien* (1962); Martin Lehnert, *Sprachform und Sprachfunktion im* "Orrmulum" (*um 1200*) (1953); H. C. Matthes, *Die Einheitlichkeit des Orrmulum* (1933).

ROBERT W. BURCHFIELD

[See also **Ancrene Riwle; Exegesis, Middle English; Middle English Language; Middle English Literature.**]

ORNEMENT DES DAMES (Ornatus Mulierum), an anonymous thirteenth-century beauty manual for women composed of such things as recipes for hair dyes and treatments for wrinkles, freckles, and parasites. Written in Anglo-Norman French prose and extant in only one manuscript, the text makes fictitious references to Galen and other medical authorities, and most frequently cites "Dame Trote"—that is, the *Trotula minor,* which the *Ornement* resembles.

BIBLIOGRAPHY

Pierre Ruelle, ed., *L'Ornement des dames (Ornatus mulierum)* (1967), is the edition. A critical review by Mary Dominica Legge is in *French Studies,* **24** (1970).

ELLEN WEHNER

[See also **Beauty Aids, Cosmetics; Trota and Trotula.**]

OROSIUS (Paulus Orosius, *fl.* early fifth century), early Christian historian. A native of Braga in Spain (now in Portugal), Orosius was forced by the Vandal invasion (414) to flee to Africa, where he discussed the problem of Priscillianism with Augustine at Hippo. Sent by Augustine to Jerome at Bethlehem, Orosius denounced Pelagianism at the Council of Jerusalem in 415 but was himself condemned. His involvement in these controversies resulted in his extant works *Instruction on the Error of the Priscillianists and Origenists* and *Apologetic Book Against the Pelagians.*

After his return to Augustine in 416, Orosius declined to go back to Spain because of the continued barbarian presence. He was then encouraged by Augustine to compose his most important work, the *History Against the Pagans* (completed by 418), the first Christian history. The work was intended to be a response to pagan claims that the recent Roman misfortunes had been caused by the Christian rejection of Rome's pagan past. Orosius argued that all human history had been guided by God and that, in point of fact, the Romans always had suffered setbacks—and more of them before Christian times. His work, therefore, tends to be a list of calamities, mostly culled from such earlier pagan authors as Livy, Justin, Tacitus, and Eutropius. Although the work was hastily written and contains many errors, it is nonetheless very useful as an independent source for the period 378–417. Even though the *History* merely served as a prelude to Augustine's much more powerful *City of God,* it was very popular in the Middle Ages; it was translated, for example, by Alfred the Great into Anglo-Saxon, and nearly 200 manuscripts of it survive.

BIBLIOGRAPHY

Sources. The texts of *Historiarum adversum paganos* and *Liber apologeticus,* ed. by Karl Zangenmeister, are in vol. V of the series Corpus Scriptorum Ecclesiasticorum Latinorum (1882, repr. 1966); the text of *Commonitorium de errore priscillianistarum et origenistarum,* ed. by Georg Schepss, is in vol. XVIII (1889), 151–157, of the same series. See also *Patrologia latina,* XXXI (1846), 635–1216.

Studies. Eligius Dekkers, comp., Emil Gaar, ed., *Clavis patrum latinorum,* 2nd ed. (1961), nos. 571–573; J. R. Martindale, *Prosopography of the Later Roman Empire,* II (1980), 813; Martin Schanz, Carl Hosius, and Gustav Krüger, *Geschichte der römischen Literatur,* IV, pt. 2 (1920, repr. 1959), 483–491.

RALPH W. MATHISEN

[See also **Alfred the Great and Translations; Augustine of Hippo, St.; Heresy; Pelagius; Priscillian.**]

ORPHANOTROPHOS. In the Byzantine Empire, *orphanotrophos* (literally, rearer of orphans) was the title given to the director of an orphanage. The concern of both church and state, orphans received legal and moral protection. Some were given to relatives, some were placed under the aegis of monasteries, others were placed in foster homes, and the rest were put in orphanages. We know of three such institutions in Constantinople and of others in provincial cities such as Thessaloniki, Nicaea, and Neapolis (Naples). Imperial legislation provided annual contributions, and pious individuals gave generously.

The most important *orphanotrophos* was that of the Great or Imperial Orphanage, named after St. Paul, in Constantinople. He was appointed by the emperor, held patrician rank within the eleventh ministry, and was the fiftieth on the list of government officials. Usually a clergyman, a monk, or a public official, an *orphanotrophos* could exert great influence. John Orphanotrophos, brother of Emperor Michael IV (*r.* 1034–1041), ruled the empire from behind the throne. Others became bishops and even patriarchs (Andrew of Crete, Akakios,

Euphemios). Directors of orphanages in the provinces were appointed by the local bishops.

The office of *orphanotrophos* in Constantinople was defunct by the middle of the fourteenth century, but the title survived and was bestowed as an honor upon persons in imperial favor.

BIBLIOGRAPHY

John B. Bury, *The Imperial Administrative Sytem in the Ninth Century, with a Revised Text of the Kletorologion of Philotheos* (1911, repr. 1958), 103–104; Demetrios J. Constantelos, *Byzantine Philanthropy and Social Welfare,* 2nd rev. ed. (1986); Rodolphe J. Guilland, "Études sur l'histoire administrative de l'empire byzantin: L'orphanotrophe," in *Revue des études byzantines,* **23** (1965), and *Recherches sur les institutions byzantines,* 2 vols. (1967); Phaidon I. Koukoules, *Byzantinon bios kai politismos,* II, pt. 1 (1948), 156–174; Jean Verpeaux, *Pseudo-Kodinos, Traité des offices* (1966).

DEMETRIOS J. CONSTANTELOS

[See also **Byzantine Empire: Bureaucracy.**]

ORPHREY refers to a richly embroidered cloth in which gold threads are employed (from the Latin: *aurum phrygium,* "Phrygian gold"). The term is also used in a more general sense for any richly embroidered cloth, especially one employed as a decorative band or border on a larger cloth, such as an altar hanging, or on an ecclesiastical garment, such as a chasuble.

CARL F. BARNES, JR.

[See also **Opus Anglicanum; Plaschanitsa** (both with illustrations).]

ORTHODOX EASTERN CHURCH. See **Byzantine Church; Russian Orthodox Church.**

ORTHOGRAPHIA GALLICA, a late-thirteenth- or early-fourteenth-century treatise of English origin composed in Latin, containing some thirty rules for the spelling of French. An earlier orthographical treatise, the *Tractatus orthographiae* (late thirteenth century), also of English origin, was written by a student who had studied in Paris; he signed only his initials, T. H. This work was revised in the fourteenth century by an Orléans cleric named Coyfurelly.

BIBLIOGRAPHY

Mildred K. Pope, "The 'Tractatus Orthographiae' of T. H., Parisii Studentis," in *Modern Language Review,* **5** (1910); Jakob Stürzinger, ed., *Orthographia gallica* (1884).

BRIAN MERRILEES

[See also **Anglo-Norman Literature; French Language.**]

ORTNIT. *Ortnit* and *Wolfdietrich,* to which it is closely related, are part of the late medieval Middle High German narrative tradition. *Ortnit,* possibly first circulated around 1225 in a form resembling surviving versions, survives in numerous manuscripts and early printed versions that date from the early fourteenth to the early sixteenth century. All versions are composed in the four-line *Hildebrandston* strophe, but individual versions vary considerably in the order, number, and wording of the strophes, the names of the characters, and the details of the plot. Such variation is typical of narrative freely (that is, without regard to a printed text) transmitted for casual entertainment.

The story is much the same in all versions. Ortnit, king of Lombardy in northern Italy, is advised to marry. From his uncle, Ilja of Russia, he hears of the daughter of Machorel of Tyre, heathen king of Jerusalem. Despite the fact that Machorel has his daughter's suitors killed because he wants to marry her himself, Ortnit decides to seek her hand in marriage. Ortnit's vassal Zacharias, a noble heathen from Sicily, provides boats for the army. Ortnit's magic ring enables him to see Alberich, a dwarf who is otherwise invisible; he reveals that he is Ortnit's father. Ortnit, Ilja, Alberich, and the army sail to Tyre. Alberich presents Ortnit's proposal to Machorel, who has a tantrum. Ortnit's army defeats Machorel's in battle and besieges Muntabur, his palace. Alberich persuades the princess to marry Ortnit, and on the way home she is baptized. In revenge Machorel sends Ortnit two dragon's eggs. The dragons soon begin to devastate Lombardy. In some versions Ortnit falls asleep and is devoured. In others he is to be devoured in the future.

The variations at the end of the plot are conditioned by the relationship of *Ortnit* to different versions of *Wolfdietrich*. The first variant corresponds to *Wolfdietrich A*, in which Ortnit is dead when Wolfdietrich appears. One example of this variant is found with *Wolfdietrich A* in the Ambras manuscript of about 1516. The same poet, probably a Bavarian, is thought to have written the Ambras *Ortnit* and the first 505 strophes of *Wolfdietrich A*. The second variant fits logically with *Wolfdietrich B* and *Wolfdietrich D*, in which Wolfdietrich encounters the living Ortnit, although no two texts correspond in all other details.

As part of the late medieval tradition, *Ortnit* is a compound of popular literary elements. Ortnit's courtship and the depiction of Machorel are characteristic of the *Spielmannsepik* (minstrel narrative poetry). Zacharias, the noble heathen, is a figure from courtly literature. Alberich's role is like that of Auberon in the French chanson de geste *Huon de Bordeaux*, as well as of dwarfs in the fairy-tale Dietrich epics. Loose similarity to tales of Hertnid in the *Þiðreks saga*, as well as to tales of Ilja in Russian byliny, suggests some contact with Low German, if not Russian, popular narrative.

Ortnit as we know it might have appeared around 1225, the year of the marriage of the Hohenstaufen emperor Frederick II to Isabella, queen of Jerusalem.

BIBLIOGRAPHY

Sources. Kaspar von der Rhön, *Dresdener Heldenbuch* of 1472, in Friedrich H. von der Hagen and Alois Primisser, eds., *Der Helden Buch in der Ursprache*, pt. 2, in Friedrich H. von der Hagen and Johann G. Büsching, eds., *Deutsche Gedichte des Mittelalters*, II (1820), 1–26; Adelbert von Keller, ed., *Das deutsche Heldenbuch: Nach dem muthmasslich ältesten Drucke* (1867), 16–125; Arthur Amelung, ed., *Deutsches Heldenbuch*, III (1871, repr. 1968), 3–77, based upon the Ambras and Windhagen MSS; Justus Lunzer, ed., *Orneit und Wolfdietrich nach der Wiener Piaristenhandschrift* (1906), 1–57.

Studies. Amelung, *op. cit.*, V–VIII, lists texts; Helmut de Boor, *Die höfische Literatur: Vorbereitung, Blüte, Ausklang* (1979), 196–199, 461–462; Wolfgang Dinkelacker, *Ortnit-Studien: Vergleichende Interpretation der Fassungen* (1972), 9–56, 387–395; Ruth H. Firestone, "A New Look at the Transmission of Ortnit," in *Amsterdamer Beiträge zur älteren Germanistik*, 18 (1982); Norbert Voorwinden, "Zur Überlieferung des Ortnit," in *Amsterdamer Beiträge zur älteren Germanistik*, 6 (1974).

RUTH H. FIRESTONE

[See also **Ambraser Heldenbuch; Dresdener Heldenbuch; Middle High German Literature; Wolfdietrich.**]

ORTUQIDS (preferably Artuqids), a Turkish dynasty descended from Artuq ibn Aksab (*d.* 1091), a follower of the Saljūqids (Seljuks). Artuq and several members of his family were active in the military politics of the Fertile Crescent, at one point controlling Palestine (*ca.* 1086–1098); the two longest-lived branches of the dynasty were, however, established in the province of Diyār Bakr in northern Mesopotamia. One of Artuq's grandsons, Dā˒ūd ibn Sukmān (*d. ca.* 1144), established his capital at Ḥiṣn Kayfā (modern Hasankeyf) on the upper reaches of the Tigris; after Saladin captured Āmid (modern Diyarbakir) in 1183, Dā˒ūd's own grandson Muḥammad ibn Qarā Arslān was named governor and transferred his seat there. Two of Muḥammad's sons divided his realm, ruling from Āmid and Kharpūt (modern Harput), respectively, until the Ayyubids retook their territory in 1232–1234.

Dā˒ūd's uncle Īlghāzī I (*d.* 1122) had established a second branch of the family at Mardin, with a lesser center at Mayyāfarqīn (modern Silvan). His descendants were usually in a relation of vassalage to more powerful neighbors: the Zankids (dominant in Mosul), then the Ayyubids, to whom they lost Mayyāfarqīn in 1185, and finally the Mongols. This branch survived until 1409, when it was brought to an end by the Qarā Qoyunlu.

Although the Artuqids were thus relatively minor princes, they had disproportionate importance as patrons of material culture. In 1147 Timurtāsh ibn Īlghāzī introduced to Mesopotamia the practice of striking copper coinage with figural imagery, a practice that spread almost immediately throughout the region. Many of these coins were copies or adaptations of Greek imperial models; the period has therefore been characterized as one of "classical revival," but it is unlikely that the Artuqids or their contemporaries had any comprehensive grasp of classical civilization. Indeed, as the models also included Sasanian and Byzantine coins and seals, manuscript illustrations, and portable objects from Europe, it is likely that these princes were engaged in a broader search for suitable sovereign imagery.

This view is borne out by their architectural monuments. The dynasty sponsored a number of caravansaries and bridges, as well as major reno-

ÖRVAR-ODDS SAGA

vations to the fortifications at Āmid and Mayyāfarqīn. Most of these constructions were adorned with relief sculptures of human beings, animals, and preternatural creatures, reflecting deeply rooted regional traditions adapted to dynastic aims. The accompanying inscriptions, largely political in content, range in style from an ornate cursive closely related to the Kufic script that had long been characteristic of the region to a more fully developed type written in multiple levels with strong diagonals.

Artuqid patronage extended to literature and the arts of the book. Alpī ibn Timurtāsh (1152–1176) commissioned a new translation from the Syriac of Dioscorides' *De materia medica;* a beautifully illustrated contemporary copy is preserved at the shrine of Imam ᶜAlī al-Riḍāᵓ in Mashhad. Alpī's cousin Maḥmud ibn Muḥammad asked al-Jazarī to write his famous *Automata,* which was completed at Āmid in 1206. No Artuqid illustrated copy of this text survives, but several elegantly written unillustrated manuscripts of various texts attest to the richness of dynastic libraries.

BIBLIOGRAPHY

Max van Berchem and Josef Strzygowski, *Amida* (1910); Claude Cahen, "Le Diyār Bakr au temps des premiers urtukides," in *Journal asiatique,* **227** (1935); Florence E. Day, "Mesopotamian Manuscripts of Dioscorides," in *Bulletin of the Metropolitan Museum of Art,* n.s. **8** (May 1950); Albert Gabriel, *Voyages archéologiques dans la Turquie orientale,* 2 vols. (1940); Donald R. Hill, trans and ed., *The Book of Knowledge of Ingenious Mechanical Devices* (*Kitāb fī Maᶜrifāt al-Ḥiyāl al-Handasiyya) by ibn al-Razzaq al-Jazarī* (1974); Carole Hillenbrand, "The Establishment of Artuqid Power in Diyār Bakr in the Twelfth Century," in *Studia islamica,* **54** (1981); Stanley Lane Poole, *Coins of the Urtūki Turkumāns* (1875); A. S. Ünver, "Quelques nouveaux exemples du service rendu par les Artoukides de l'empire Seldjuk à l'histoire des sciences," in *Archives internationales d'histoire des sciences,* **4** (**1**) (1948).

ESTELLE WHELAN

[See also **Ayyubids; Islamic Art and Architecture; Mints and Money, Islamic; Seljuks.**]

ÖRVAR-ODDS SAGA. The story of Örvar-Oddr, which belongs to the Halogaland cycle of adventure tales (the others being *Ketils saga hængs, Gríms saga loðinkinna,* and *Áns saga bogsveigis*), was written in Iceland in the thirteenth century. The earliest extant manuscript, on vellum, dates from the fourteenth century, but there are later manuscripts in which the tale has been drastically revised and augmented with material borrowed from folktales and other models.

Örvar-Oddr—the name means literally "an arrowpoint"—is born far away from his ancestral home in northern Norway and brought up by his father's friend, Ingjaldr, in the south. Oddr and Ingjaldr's son, Ásmundr, become blood brothers as well as foster brothers. When Oddr insults a certain sorceress, she makes a prophecy that he will live for three hundred years, wandering from land to land, and ultimately be killed by the skull of the stallion Faxi. The blood brothers kill the horse and bury him in a deep pit, piling huge boulders on top. Having taken these precautions, Oddr sets off with his blood brother, vowing never to come back. After visiting his family, his first major adventure takes him north to Permia; on his way back he encounters Lappish sorcerers and giants. He undertakes one perilous journey after another, acquiring the nickname *inn víðförli* (the far-traveled; compare *Yngvars saga víðförla* and *Eiríks saga víðförla*). He fights with many Vikings, usually making friends with them, only to lose them later in battle. With the death of his erstwhile opponent and now blood brother, Hjálmarr (who figures also in *Hervarar saga ok Heiðreks konungs*), a tragic note is struck, which then recurs throughout the rest of the narrative. In contrast to all the other adventure tales among the *fornaldarsögur,* Oddr faces an indestructible enemy, Ögmundr Eyþjófr's-Killer, who kills off Oddr's blood brothers one after another and also his son by a giantess, Vignir, but all Oddr's efforts to avenge them are in vain and ultimately he is forced to make peace with his adversary.

This Ögmundr is no ordinary mortal. After Oddr's visit to Permia, where he had done a lot of damage, the Permians "took an ogress living under this great waterfall, packed her full of magic and sorcery, and put her in bed beside King Harek," and Ögmundr was their son. "When [Ögmundr] was three he was sent over to Lappland, where he learned all sorts of magic and sorcery." Before meeting Oddr, Ögmundr had murdered his best friend in his sleep. Combining thorough wickedness with witchcraft and sorcery, he proves too powerful for Oddr.

After many other adventures, set in Ireland,

France, the Holy Land, and elsewhere, Oddr becomes king of Greece, ruling it for a time. Then he travels to Norway and, arriving at his place of birth, he finds the old farm in ruins and the soil eroded away. A horse's skull is lying on the ground, and from under it a venomous snake wriggles out to give him his death wound and complete the prophecy, ending his life at the place where it began.

The story contains many verses, including those attributed to the hero and two challengers confronted by him in a combined drinking and verse-making contest. As Oddr lies dying he declaims a poem, probably composed in the twelfth century, about his life and adventures.

Örvar-Oddr figures also in Saxo Grammaticus' *Gesta Danorum.*

BIBLIOGRAPHY

Editions are Richard C. Boer, ed., *Örvar-Odds saga* (1888), and *idem, Örvar-Odds saga* (1892). Translation is Hermann Pálsson and Paul Edwards, trans., *Seven Viking Romances* (1985).

See also Richard C. Boer, "Über die *Örvar-Odds saga,*" in *Arkiv för nordisk filologi,* 8 (1892), and "Weiteres zur *Örvar-Odds saga,*" *ibid.;* Nora K. Chadwick, *The Beginnings of Russian History* (1946); Knut Liestl, *Norske trollvisor og norrne sogor* (1915), 93–106; Alan S. C. Ross, *The Terfinnas and Beormas of Ohthere* (1940).

HERMANN PÁLSSON

[See also **Áns Saga Bogsveigis; Fornaldarsögur; Gríms Saga Loðinkinna; Hervarar Saga ok Heiðreks Konungs; Ketils Saga Hængs; Yngvars Saga Víðförla.**]

OSEBERG FIND. The name refers to a wooden ship unearthed from a burial mound in the Vestfold district of Norway, originally on the shores of the Oslofjord. The Oseberg ship and its contents, the greatest archaeological treasure of medieval Norway, were discoverd at Oseberg farm near Tønsberg in August 1903, and excavated over a nine-week period beginning the following June. The ship was in fragments but nonetheless remarkably well preserved by a blue clay that lay beneath the sod used in the mound's construction. The wealth of gifts for the deceased included a wagon, four sleds, beds, kitchen utensils, riding accessories, and agricultural implements. The ship was probably built around 800 and placed in the mound some fifty years later.

"Academician's" animal-head post in carved oak from the Oseberg find, 9th century. UNIVERSITETETS OLDSAKSAMLING, OSLO

As reconstructed by Norwegian archaeologists, the Oseberg ship measures about 71 feet (21.44 meters) in length, 17 feet (5.10 meters) at its extreme width, and (amidships) approximately 5 feet (1.58 meters) from rails to keel. The builders made the vessel almost entirely of oak, and supplied it with fifteen pairs of oars (apparently made specifically for the interment, as some are too short to have been used at sea). The ship's construction indicates that it was a pleasure craft used principally for travel along the protected waterways of the coast or upon the tranquil waters of a fjord.

The deceased for whom the ship was a tomb was a young woman of twenty-five or thirty, who was buried with another female, aged sixty or seventy, who is thought to have been the younger woman's servant. The ladies were well supplied for their journey. They lay in a burial chamber on a large bed, wider than it is long, furnished with feather pillows, blankets, and quilts. There were two other

Front panel of the Oseberg wagon. Carved oak, 9th century. UNIVERSITETETS OLDSAKSAMLING, OSLO

beds, as well as nail-studded, iron-bound wooden chests containing personal effects (the remnants of clothing and toilet articles such as combs). Domestic animals were present, including thirteen horses (perhaps associated with the Nordic pantheon of Odin and twelve lesser gods), two oxen, and three dogs. There were also about fifty wild apples, hazelnuts, grains, and seeds. The women may once have been adorned with jewelry, but as the grave was broken into shortly after the interment, virtually nothing remains of what may have been a splendid hoard of silver and bronze.

In their eagerness to plunder the grave, the robbers neglected the most significant part of the Oseberg treasure: the glorious wood carvings that adorn the ship; the wagon and sleds, whose sides are covered with carved designs; and the "animal-head" posts, with their fearsome countenances.

A number of styles are visible in the Oseberg woodcarving; they have been attributed to various masters over a period of about fifty years. As in all Viking art, the carving that is purely ornamental or decorative predominates over pictorial art, which is limited to a few representations on the Oseberg wagon. Animal ornament is the principal feature of Oseberg's decorative art, in patterns so complex that the original features of the animal—perhaps a gripping beast that has seized upon itself—have been subordinated by the woodcarver to the effect or impression of constant, ceaseless motion.

Among the other grave goods found at Oseberg are a significant number of kitchen utensils, including the "Buddha bucket"—a pail of yew wood with bronze bands and a bronze handle attached to the body of the pail by two metal pieces in the forms of seated male figures. The body of each little man, in an attitude of repose not unlike that associated with Buddha, is decorated with colored enamel. Although it has affinities to Oriental art, the "Buddha" is more likely to be a divinity of Celtic origin.

Another kind of domestic equipment found in the Oseberg burial are looms and other implements for making textiles. There were also pieces of a woolen tapestry (or tapestries) that apparently once lined the walls of the burial chamber, depicting a religious procession or other scenes of daily life. This tapestry is virtually unique in the early medieval art of northern Europe.

The Oseberg ship burial has considerable importance for historians because it provides a substantial view of the material culture of Scandinavia in the ninth century. The Oseberg discoveries demonstrate the high level of achievement of Viking craftsmen, whose skill in shipbuilding and woodcarving is unmatched elsewhere in medieval Europe. Oseberg, together with other ship finds (principally at Gokstad and Tune, also on the shores of the Oslofjord), enables one to understand how the Vikings accomplished their long journeys overseas.

BIBLIOGRAPHY

The fundamental work on the Oseberg ship burial is Anton W. Brøgger, Hj. Falk, and Haakon Shetelig, eds., *Osebergfunnet, Utgitt av den norske stat,* 4 vols. (1917–1928). See also Brøgger and Shetelig, *The Viking Ships: Their Ancestry and Evolution,* Katherine John,

Deesis relief from the south pastophory at Oški, 963–973. Christ is flanked by the Virgin and John the Baptist, with Bagrat, duke of dukes, at far left and David of Tao at far right. PHOTO: WACHTANG DJOBADZE

trans. (1951, 2nd ed. 1971); Aslak Liestøl, ed., *Osebergfunnet* (1958); Thorleif Sjøvold, *The Oseberg Find and the Other Viking Ship Finds*, Mary Fjeld, trans. (1959).

SIDNEY L. COHEN

[See also **Ships and Shipbuilding, Northern European; Viking Art.**]

OŠKI. Formerly an important medieval monastic center in the southern Georgian province of Tao-Klarjetᶜi (now in northeastern Turkey). It contains the remains of a bishop's palace, a seminary, a refectory (*trapeza*), and a scriptorium where numerous manuscripts were copied and illustrated, including a Bible copied in 978 that is preserved in the monastery of Iviron on Mt. Athos. Among the churches, the most outstanding is the cathedral built from 963 to 973 by the Georgian kings Bagrat, duke of dukes (*d.* 966), and his brother David of Tao (*d.* 1001). The church is a central-plan domed triconch in which the dome is supported by four free-standing piers. The cathedral is unusually large (interior: length, 133.5 feet [40.7 meters]; width, 88.6 feet [27 meters]; height, 112.2 feet [34.2 meters]; diameter of the dome, 29.5 feet [9 meters]) and contains such innovations as arcades, triangular niches, and a variety of sculptures and decorative vegetal motifs. The cathedral abounds with historical inscriptions. One of them, on the tympanum of the southern porch, discloses unique information pertaining to the cost of its construction and the donors' names.

BIBLIOGRAPHY

Wachtang Djobadze, "The Donor Reliefs and the Date of the Church at Oški," in *Byzantinische Zeitschrift*, **69** (1976), and "The Georgian Churches of Tao-Klarjetᶜi: Construction Methods and Materials," in *Oriens christianus*, **62** (1978); Euthynius Takaishvili, *Arkheologicheskaia ekspeditsia 1917 go goda v iuzhnye provintsii Gruzii* (1952), 45–67, and (Georgian ed., 1960) 32–58.

WACHTANG DJOBADZE

[See also **David of Tao; Georgian Art and Architecture.**]

OSMAN I (*ca.* 1254–*ca.* 1326), Turkoman chieftain and founder of the Ottoman (Osmanli) dynasty. Little is certain concerning the origins of the Ottoman house; in particular, the coming of Osman's forebears to Anatolia is lost in the chaos of Turkoman migrations from Central Asia. In the initial years after the Byzantine defeat at Manzikert (1071), Turkoman nomads occupied almost all of Anatolia. The border was subsequently restored to central Anatolia, and the loss of their European holdings and their capital during the Fourth Crusade (1204) made the Byzantines more solicitous of their Asian territories. The centralized state of the Seljuks of Rum at Ikonion (Konya), seeking to preserve stable relations with Byzantium, worked to check the migratory and predatory habits of the pastoralists. In the mid thirteenth century, however, the Mongols invaded Anatolia, damaging Seljuk power and prestige and forcing many Turkomans of eastern and central Anatolia to flee westward. By 1300, Seljuk rule in Anatolia had been replaced by that of some dozen independent Turkoman principalities (*beyliks*), while the Byzantines, having regained Constantinople, began again to neglect their Anatolian provinces. Osman's *beylik,* the most northwesterly, was on the frontier of Bithynia, and it was from his base, at Söğüt, that he and his followers began raiding in Byzantine territory around 1299.

Still the most common explanation of these initial raids is that from the very first Osman and his followers saw themselves as *ghāzī*s—warriors for the faith—and that, as essentially a *ghāzī* state, they attracted to their camp adventurers from other beyliks that, lacking a common border with an infidel enemy, offered few opportunities for glory and booty. A recent alternative explanation sees Osman's role in the context of Turkish nomadism: the breakdown of Byzantine control in Bithynia, along with an influx of Turkomans fleeing the Mongols, led to raids that typify the eternal confrontation between pastoralists and farmers. In this scheme, religious hostilities count for little; many local Christians, impressed with the dynamism and success of Osman's enterprise, threw in with him.

Whatever the motive, Osman's raids gradually developed into territorial conquest, as he enjoyed steady, if limited, success in the power vacuum of Anatolia. The battle of Baphaeon (1301), showed him to be the most powerful ruler in the area and perhaps sealed the fate of Byzantine Anatolia. From this point on, his forces swelled with Turkomans, while more Greeks, impatient with Byzantine incompetence or indifference, either fled westward to Constantinople or went over to the Turks. One by one the cities of Bithynia, grown isolated and defenseless, capitulated, including Yenişehir, which Osman made his capital. By his death (*ca.* 1326), only the strongest and best defended of western Anatolian cities remained in Greek hands: Brusa (Turkish: Bursa), already isolated, held out until April 1326, while Nicaea (İznik) and Nicomedia (İzmit) fell in 1331 and 1337, respectively.

What Osman founded was a dynasty, not a state. It was left to his son Orkhan (*r. ca.* 1326–1362) to develop the structures of sedentary rule that were to transform the realm from a nomad principality into an established Islamic polity. Nonetheless, by harnessing for himself and his family the energies of the disparate Turkish and non-Turkish elements in chaotic western Anatolia in the early fourteenth century, Osman contributed significantly to the latter successes of his descendants.

BIBLIOGRAPHY

Scholarship on the early Ottoman period has for the last half century been dominated by the theories put forward by Paul Wittek in his monograph, *The Rise of the Ottoman Empire* (1938, repr. 1971). Rudi Paul Lindner has offered an intriguing reinterpretation in his *Nomads and Ottomans in Medieval Anatolia* (1983), which challenges, rather convincingly, some of Wittek's essential arguments. More general outlines may be found in Halil Inalcik's *The Ottoman Empire: The Classical Age 1300–1600,* Norman Itzkowitz and Colin Imber, trans. (1973), and Stanford J. Shaw's *History of the Ottoman Empire and Modern Turkey,* I (1976). In French, Mehmet Fuat Köprülü's *Les origines de l'empire ottoman* (1935) is quite useful; *Osmanli imporatorlugunun Kurulugu* (1972), is a revised edition in Turkish. A good account of Anatolia before the Ottomans is Claude Cahen's *Pre-Ottoman Turkey,* J. Jones-Williams, trans. (1968), although the translation is somewhat unwieldy.

RALPH S. HATTOX

[See also **Anatolia; Brusa; Byzantine Empire: History; Ghāzī; Ottomans; Seljuks of Rum; Turkomans.**]

OSONA, RODRIGO DE. See **Rodrigo de Osona.**

OSTIKAN (Pahlavi: *ōstīgān*). Title given by the Armenian sources of the Arsacid period to the keeper of the royal fortresses. Subsequently this title was applied to the governors appointed by the caliphate for the province of Armīniya, which included portions of Iberia and Azerbaijan as well as Armenia proper. The creation of this province and of the office of ostikan probably dates from the turn of the seventh to the eighth century. The office was normally granted by the caliph and held in rapid rotation among different families. Exceptionally, however, the Shaybānī house held the ostikanate in hereditary succession, so that thirteen members of the family were ostikans within one century, some on several occasions. The residence of the ostikan was first divided between Dwin in Greater Armenia and Bardhaᶜa (Partaw) in Azerbaijan. After 789, Bardhaᶜa became the normal residence, and the control of the ostikan over Armenia decreased, although it still manifested itself strongly under the Turkish Sājids in the tenth century and the palace of the ostikan at Dwin was still an active center in the middle of the century, according to the historian Ibn Ḥawqal. After the consolidation of Bagratid power in Armenia, however, the ostikan ceased to have direct authority over the country.

BIBLIOGRAPHY

Nikolay G. Adontz (Adonts), *Armenia in the Period of Justinian,* Nina G. Garsoïan, trans. (1970); Heinrich Hübschmann, *Armenische Grammatik* (1897, repr. 1962, 1971), 215–216; Aram Ter Ghewondyan, *The Arab Emirates in Bagratid Armenia,* Nina G. Garsoïan, trans. (1976); Cyril Toumanoff, *Studies in Christian Caucasian History* (1963).

NINA G. GARSOÏAN

[See also **Armenia: History of; Armenian Muslim Emirates; Bagratids (Bagratuni), Armenian; Bardhaᶜa; Dwin.**]

OSTROGOTHS. The Ostrogoths emerged as an organized confederacy of related east Gothic kin groups during the fourth century while living in the region north of the Black Sea and east of the Dniester River (the related Visigoths lived west of the Dniester). This consolidation had probably been influenced by contacts with Rome, contacts which had been close for over a hundred years. In the third century, the Goths had penetrated the Danube frontier during the Roman civil wars and had raided extensively in the Balkan peninsula and Asia Minor before returning north of the Black Sea. Thereafter, the Romans maintained basically friendly relations with the Goths, who now broke into eastern (Ostrogothic) and western (Visigothic) groups. By the late fourth century there were Ostrogothic kings who had emerged as more powerful than the other nobles and these kings now negotiated with Rome in the name of the entire nation.

In 375, the Ostrogoths under their king, Ermanaric, were defeated by the Huns, and thereafter for seventy-five years most of the Ostrogoths were part of a loosely coordinated Hunnish empire that eventually stretched from the Urals to the eastern Alps; during this period the Ostrogoths fought in the Hunnish army. Following the death of Attila, king of the Huns, in 453, the Ostrogoths revolted against Attila's sons (battle of Nedao, 454) and regained their independence. The bulk of the Ostrogoths under King Valamir (of the royal Amal family) received permission from the Eastern Roman emperor Marcian to settle as federates in Pannonia. Another group of Ostrogoths under Theodoric (Theodoric Strabo), son of Triarius, were also allowed to enter as federates and settled further to the east.

Friction between these Ostrogothic groups as well as with other Germanic settlers in the Eastern Empire led the Eastern imperial court to demand hostages from the Valamir Ostrogoths. Accordingly, the seven-year-old Theodoric, son of Thiudmir, a nephew of King Valamir, was sent to Constantinople. For approximately ten years, the young Theodoric lived at the court of the emperor Leo, learning much about Graeco-Roman culture and the Roman administrative system, although he presumably did not learn to write. During this interval Theodoric's father, Thiudmir, succeeded his brother Valamir as king of the Goths in Pannonia. In 471, just before his death, Thiudmir designated his son Theodoric to be his successor. Under Theodoric, who commanded a strong loyalty based on the union of his own personal following with that of his father, the Ostrogoths moved southward into Illyria and by continuing to exert pressure on the empire were finally granted lands in Macedonia, where they came into renewed conflict with the other Ostrogoths under Theodoric Strabo, who were now living as federates in Thrace. Imperial policy tended to play the two groups of Goths off against one another and as a result neither was very strong. In 481, Theodoric Strabo was killed in battle, and thereafter his followers and some of his people joined Theodoric the Amal, son of Thiudmir, and gradually a larger and stronger Ostrogothic grouping developed. During this interval, the Ostrogothic king Theodoric enjoyed many concessions from the Eastern Roman ruler, including the grant of the title patrician, elevation to the consulship, and adoption as Emperor Zeno's son.

But as the Ostrogothic power grew, it became a more serious threat to Zeno (*r.* 474–491), who, to solve that problem and an Italian problem at the same time, commissioned Theodoric and his Ostrogoths to go to Italy to overthrow Odoacer, who had been ruling there since his deposition of Romulus Augustulus in 476.

The entire Ostrogothic nation headed west in 488–489. Odoacer was defeated twice by the Ostrogothic army and retired to Ravenna, from which he emerged several times only to be defeated again. Meanwhile, Theodoric concentrated on reducing the rest of Italy, while continuing to blockade Odoacer in Ravenna. The conquest of Italy was practically achieved between 490 and 493—a conquest in which Theodoric enjoyed the cooperation of the Catholic hierarchy and the Roman senate, a cooperation made possible by the official commission that Theodoric held from the Eastern emperor. In 493, Theodoric concluded an agreement with Odoacer whereby the government of Italy would be shared between the two "kings," and Theodoric then entered Ravenna. At a banquet celebrating the new regime, Theodoric killed Odoacer and his son, and his followers killed the followers of Odoacer.

In spite of the means whereby he had made himself ruler of all the Ostrogoths, Theodoric thereafter proved himself to be an able and conscientious ruler. He was now again designated king by the Ostrogoths and requested recognition by the Eastern emperor. But, although Theodoric was finally in 497 sent the imperial regalia by the emperor Anastasius (*r.* 491–518), he was not recognized as king of Italy, and his imperial title remained that of patrician. In theory, therefore, Theodoric ruled Italy in the name of the Eastern emperor, although in fact he enjoyed virtual independence and was regularly addressed as king.

Theodoric reigned from 493 until 526. Having become ruler of Italy, he did his best to conciliate his Italian subjects and strove to maintain peace with his neighbors. During his reign, Ostrogothic Italy established a kind of protectorate over the Germanic peoples who were neighbors of the Ostrogoths. Theodoric arranged a series of dynastic marriages with the ruling families of the Franks in northern Gaul, of the Burgundians in the Rhône Valley, of the Visigoths in southwestern Gaul and Spain, and of the Vandals in Africa. Although Theodoric could not prevent the Franks from attacking and defeating the Visigoths at Vouille in 507, he did ensure that the Visigoths would retain at least a part of their lands in Gaul in addition to their territory in Spain. Theodoric's own Ostrogothic territory included all of Italy, Sicily, Noricum, Dalmatia, and part of Rhaetia. After the Frankish defeat of the Visigoths, he also held Provence as well as a formal protectorate over the kingdom of the Visigoths, where his grandson Amalaric became king (511–531).

In Italy, Theodoric continued the Roman administrative system that had been maintained under Odoacer and continued the method of distributing land that had been followed by Odoacer. The exact nature of this distribution in not known, but it was supervised by the Roman Liberius, praetorian prefect of Italy. In theory, perhaps a third of the larger (senatorial?) estates throughout Italy were available for distribution, but the Ostrogoths were not nearly numerous enough to necessitate the distribution of all of this. Those landholders who were not required to share with a Goth were liable to a payment called the *tertia* for the third of their lands that they were not required to distribute. For the most part, the Gothic settlement was confined to the central Po area (the region from Lake Como south through Milan and Pavia to Tortona), the region around Verona and Ravenna, and the central part of Tuscia et Umbria down into Samnium. Evidently this distribution of land raised no serious protest from the Romans, so the assignment of lots must have been done fairly.

As governor of Italy, Theodoric maintained the administrative system as well as its personnel, cooperated with the Senate (which played a more active role in the government under Odoacer and Theodoric than it had in the late empire), maintained a good working relationship with the Catholic church (although he and his people were Arians), was careful that food supplies were imported in sufficient amounts, encouraged games and circuses, and patronized a revival of learning (Ennodius, Boethius, Cassiodorus, and Venantius Fortunatus are the best-known writers of this period). His own Ostrogoths were also cared for by the provision of land, the establishment of Arian bishoprics in the areas most densely settled by the Ostrogoths, and by the creation of an army for defense that was predominantly Gothic and that received regular payments as well as special annual donatives. A building program benefited both peoples: cities were rebuilt, monuments restored, and new buildings appeared in Verona and Ravenna, the cities preferred as residences by Theodoric. Ravenna especially benefited from the royal favor: there a number of churches, including S. Apollinare Nuovo (which still stands), an elaborate royal palace, and a mausoleum for Theodoric were constructed.

We have a great deal of information about the reign of Theodoric from a series of minor chroniclers as well as from the early part of Procopius' work on the Byzantine-Gothic wars. But most important are the works of Cassiodorus, one of the Romans appointed to office by Theodoric, who continued to serve the Ostrogoths after Theodoric's death. From the official memoranda kept by Cassiodorus while he was in office, from his numerous letters, and from the history of the Goths (which survives only in Jordanes' epitome) that he produced after his retirement, we are familiar with many aspects of Theodoric's reign. The legal regime was based on the concept of personality of law, that is, Roman law continued to be the law of the Roman part of the population and Ostrogothic custom that of the Gothic population. Unfortunately, we do not have the legal edicts issued by Theodoric and, consequently, do not know what modifications of Roman and Gothic legal rules were issued to enable the two different legal regimes to live side by side. We do know that the Goths took their cases to courts presided over by a Gothic count, the Romans to one presided over by a Roman magistrate, and that in cases involving the two peoples, the case went to a court presided over by the Gothic count joined by a Roman learned in Roman law.

The reign of Theodoric thus saw much of the prosperity and splendor of imperial Italy restored, and, although Ostrogoth and Roman remained distinct, there was a considerable accommodation occurring, especially on the part of the Gothic nobility, which held large landed estates and tended to imitate its aristocratic Roman neighbors. It seemed that Theodoric's policy would soon see a final resolution of the problem of barbarians and Romans living peacefully together under a beneficent king.

But the latter part of Theodoric's reign was marred by increasing unrest in Italy. On the Gothic side there may have been some resistance occasioned by Theodoric's too great concessions to the Roman part of the population. On the Roman side, the problem was associated with religion. For the greater part of Theodoric's reign, the Arianism of the Goths aroused no great resistance from the Romans because there was at that time no sympathetic Catholic power to which they could appeal since the court at Constantinople was inclined toward schismatic Monophysitism. Furthermore, Theodoric had extended his protection to the Catholic church and in 498 had played an important role in bringing the Laurentian schism to an end. Theodoric himself is credited with saying that religion was not a matter that could be dictated to an individual, and under his rule the royal protection was even extended to the Jews.

But the peace of the reign came to an end in 523 when the orthodox emperor Justin (*r.* 518–527) proscribed Arianism throughout the empire. If the decree had been applied in Italy, it would have completely undermined Theodoric's government, and, not surprisingly, Theodoric became very sensitive about suspected treasonable activities in his kingdom. In addition, the Franks, recently converted to Catholicism, used defense of the faith as a way to get support from the Gallo-Roman bishops of Visigothic Gaul in their campaign against the "heretical" Visigoths, which culminated at Vouille in 507. Theodoric, an Arian, feared they might be invited to intervene in Italy. In this disturbed situation, a distinguished Roman senator, Boethius, seemed to be implicated in treasonable correspondence with Constantinople. Theodoric had him thrown into prison (where he wrote his famous *De consolatione Philosophiae*); he and his father-in-law Symmachus were eventually executed. The position of the Senate in this matter was ambivalent, to say the least.

Theodoric's increasing problems with internal dissension were intensified by dynastic problems. He had no sons and had planned that his son-in-law, Eutharic, married to his well-educated daughter, Amalasuntha, should succeed him. But Eutharic predeceased Theodoric, and accordingly just prior to his death Theodoric recommended that the Goths accept his grandson Athalaric, under the guardianship of his mother, Amalasuntha.

After Theodoric's death, the Goths accepted his choice of rulers, but the problems of the kingdom increased rapidly. The religious problem faded in importance as internal dissension rent the Ostrogothic kingdom. While Theodoric lived, he had been able to keep the Gothic nobles under control, but after his death they again asserted their old claims to a share in shaping the policies of the state. They found adequate excuse in the regency of a woman—a woman whose rule was doubly unacceptable because her education had been Roman rather than Gothic, and because she was suspected of being pro-Roman in her policies. The rebellious Gothic nobles insisted that the young king should be separated from his mother and educated in the

Gothic tradition. Athalaric had come completely under Gothic domination by the time of his premature death in 534.

To get the support for her own rule, Amalasuntha now married Theodahad, a nephew of Theodoric, and made him joint ruler. Although Theodahad had received much the same education as Amalasuntha, he now joined the Gothic party, imprisoned Amalasuntha, and shortly thereafter (when he learned that she had sought help from the Eastern emperor Justinian) had her murdered.

The removal of Amalasuntha gave Justinian the excuse he needed to attack Ostrogothic Italy, a move that he had been planning for some time in order to extirpate the Arian heresy in Italy as well as to bring Italy back under direct imperial control. In 534, the Byzantine armies under the general Belisarios had just defeated the Vandals in Africa. Belisarios then proceeded to Sicily (which he occupied without difficulty), moved north through Naples, and occupied the city of Rome. In the meantime, Theodahad proved to be a most unworthy king; he was deposed by the Ostrogoths, who elected a new king, the noble Witigis. Witigis laid siege to Rome for an entire year before withdrawing his troops to go to the aid of Milan, which had been occupied by another Byzantine army operating in northern Italy. The situation seemed desperate for the Goths, but was somewhat relieved when Justinian sent yet another Byzantine army to Italy under the command of the eunuch Narses. Jealous friction between Narses and Belisarios (Narses had probably been commissioned by Justinian to spy on Belisarios, who had been too successful for the comfort of his enemies at the Byzantine court) allowed the Goths to reoccupy Milan (and to destroy much of the city). In 539, Narses was recalled, however, and thereafter Belisarios alone pressed the Ostrogoths so hard that by May 540 they were ready to negotiate. Justinian, distracted by renewed difficulties with Persia, agreed to allow the Goths to retain the territory north of the Po River, but Belisarios refused to accept this compromise, hoping to overthrow the Ostrogothic kingdom as completely as he had overthrown the North African Vandal kingdom earlier. At this point, a curious episode occurred: The Goths proposed secretly to Belisarios that he declare himself emperor and that they become his loyal subjects. Belisarios seemingly agreed; the Goths surrendered Ravenna and turned over the Gothic treasury. Then Justinian recalled Belisarios, and the Goths saw him leave Italy carrying with him King Witigis, some of the Gothic nobles, and the Gothic treasury.

The disillusioned Goths now elected a new king and resumed the struggle. The war dragged on for another twenty years. That the Byzantines had so much difficulty in overcoming Gothic resistance was due partly to the fact that Justinian had already overstrained his treasury by his campaigns in Africa and Italy; now war resumed with Persia, and the major Byzantine effort turned in that direction. The Italian campaign received inadequate support, although the Goths could never drive the Byzantines out entirely.

After several short reigns, the Goths in 541 elected Totila, who proved to be a very able and effective leader. So successful was he in pressing back the Byzantine armies that in 544 Belisarios was sent back to Italy to resume the command. Although the arrival of Belisarios revived the Byzantine offensive, the Byzantine position suffered from continued inadequate support from Constantinople and from Justinian's insistence that the exhausted estates of Italy support the Italian war through taxation, which alienated the Roman population. The Goths moved south through the peninsula and from 545 to 546 Totila besieged Rome, occupying it in December 546. This siege very nearly completed the decimation of Rome's civilian population that had begun during the siege by Witigis during 535 and 536. But the Ostrogoths were now too closely pressed by Belisarios to retain the city. Almost as soon as the Gothic army left, the Byzantine army occupied Rome and refortified the city. But the Byzantine forces were inadequate to take further offensives against the Ostrogoths, and when his requests for reinforcements were not met, Belisarios requested recall in 548. In 550, Totila recaptured Rome and then invaded Sicily. The renewed Ostrogothic threat aroused Justinian, who now appointed Narses to the Italian command. Before accepting the appointment, Narses insisted on adequate forces, and, as a result, he commanded a very large army (including many Lombards and Heruls). In 552, the Ostrogothic and Byzantine armies met at Taginae (Busta Gallorum) in the Appenines. Narses won the victory; Totila was killed. This was the end of organized Gothic resistance, although the Byzantines had to take the Ostrogothic cities one by one. The last of these did not fall until 561.

The Byzantine-Gothic wars were disastrous for Italy. Rome ceased to be a populous city, and her abandoned monuments rapidly decayed; the city of Milan was destroyed. Heavy Byzantine taxation dismayed the surviving population of the countryside, and the church resented Byzantine interference. Continued Byzantine problems in other parts of the empire, especially on the Persian border, kept the Italian garrisons undermanned. Italy had become nearly a political vacuum, and into that vacuum poured the Germanic Lombards in 568, rapidly conquering the Po Valley and much of the central part of the peninsula.

And what of the Ostrogoths? The Ostrogothic resistance had revived so many times during the course of the wars, one must conclude that, in spite of the Ostrogothic dissension during the regency of Amalasuntha, there nevertheless survived a strong feeling of Ostrogothic identity and great loyalty to continue the struggle for so long. It is also clear that there was no serious cleavage between the Ostrogoths and the Roman population in spite of the difference in religion. (This difference was in fact soon diminished, probably because Catholicism was spreading rapidly among the Ostrogoths.) And although the bulk of the Roman population took no sides during the struggle, a number of Romans did fight for the Goths—they already feared control (religious and financial) from Constantinople.

Following the decisive defeat by Narses in 552 and the final capitulation of the last Ostrogothic city in 561, however, the Ostrogoths rapidly faded from history. The Gothic language left few traces in the vernacular dialects of Italy, and there is no record of Gothic resistance to the Lombard invasion in 568. In the long run, it was as if the Goths had been completely wiped out, although it is certain not all were since some charters survive from the seventh century in which one or more parties to the document sign themselves as living by Ostrogothic law. But aside from some continued Ostrogothic possession of land, the Ostrogoths were gone, and the Germanic content of medieval Italian civilization would be provided primarily by the Lombards and (later) the Franks.

BIBLIOGRAPHY

For primary material dealing with the Ostrogoths see Cassiodorus, *Opera* (1958); Thomas Hodgkin, *The Letters of Cassiodorus* (1886); Charles C. Mierow, *The Gothic History of Jordanes* (1960); Procopius, *History of the Wars*, H. B. Dewing, trans., 7 vols. (1914, repr. 1979); Norbert Wagner, *Getica: Untersuchungen zum Leben des Jordanes und zur frühen Geschichte der Goten* (1967).

For more general works see John B. Bury, *History of the Later Roman Empire,* II (1923); H. M. Gwatkin and J. D. Whitney, eds., *Cambridge Medieval History,* I and II (1957–1967); Walter Goffart, *Barbarians and Romans A.D. 418–585* (1980); Ludwig M. Hartmann, *Geschichte Italiens in Mittelalter,* I (1897); Thomas Hodgkin, *Italy and Her Invaders,* 2nd ed., III and IV (1928), and *Theodoric the Goth* (1923); Arnold H. M. Jones, *The Late Roman Empire,* 2 vols. (1964); James J. O'Donnell, *Cassiodorus* (1979); Gabriele Pepe, *Le moyen âge barbare en Italie* (1956); Giacinto Romano, *Le dominazioni barbariche in Italia (395–888),* 3rd rev. ed. (1940); Settimane di Studio del Centro Italiano di Studi sull'alto Medioevo, III: *I Goti in occidente* (1956); Herwig Wolfram, *Geschichte der Goten* (1979).

For specialized studies dealing with archaeological and linguistic evidence see Nils Åberg, *Die Goten und Langobarden in Italien* (1923); Thomas Burns, *The Ostrogoths: Kingship and Society* (1980); Rolf Hachmann, *Die Goten und Skandinavien* (1970).

KATHERINE FISCHER DREW

[See also **Belisarios; Boethius; Byzantine Empire; Cassiodorus; Ennodius; Italy, Byzantine Areas of; Justinian I; Odoacer; Ravenna; Theodoric the Ostrogoth; Visigoths; Zeno the Isaurian.**]

OSWALD, ST.: GERMAN EPICS, two medieval German verse epics generally classified under the heading *Spielmannsepik* (literally, "minstrel's epic"), and devoted to St. Oswald: *Der Münchner Oswald* (*MO*) and *Der Wiener Oswald* (*WO*). They share the same form (four-stress rhymed couplets) and the same narrative core—a realization of the *Brautwerbungsschema* (courtship pattern), a widespread narrative structure, especially productive in Germany (for example, *Tristan, Nibelungenlied, König Rother,* and many others). Both versions of the story begin when King Oswald decides to marry. He hears from a pilgrim of a suitable candidate, a heathen princess; but it is dangerous to woo her, since her father kills all suitors. Oswald dispatches a messenger, a talking raven, who establishes contact with the princess and returns with her consent to marry. Oswald sets out with an army, but instead wins his bride through a ruse—her father is tricked into hunting a golden stag, and during his absence she escapes. Her father pursues them with an army, is defeated, and converts to Christianity. To this narrative core have been added many elements typical of saints' legends: God aids the raven in his mission and the princess in her escape; Oswald's prayers change the weather and raise the heathen army from the dead; Oswald and his wife abstain from all sexual contact.

MO differs from *WO* in its length (it is two and a half times as long), in the greater definition of its characters (especially of the clever but very touchy raven), in the presence of crusade *topoi* (Oswald's soldiers wear crosses and are promised salvation if they fall in battle), and in its conclusion. In *MO*, after Oswald returns home, Christ appears as a beggar and the king, who has sworn to give whatever is asked in God's name, hands over his wife and his kingdom. These are restored by the beggar, who enjoins Oswald and his wife to lead chaste lives. *WO* tends to avoid the inconsistencies and digressions of *MO*. Oswald's piety and continence are stressed from the outset; prayers, the baptism of the heathen army, and a vision of heaven and hell dominate the conclusion.

The German works about Oswald have their origin in the life of the seventh-century Northumbrian king St. Oswald, although his life, as reported by Bede, shares only a few elements with the Middle High German epics (Oswald warred against the heathen and married the daughter of a converted neighbor king). Veneration of the saint, whose cult had reached the Continent by the eighth century, flourished in southern Germany in the eleventh and twelfth centuries and again in the fourteenth century. These dates, coupled with the way in which the author treats love (like Hartmann and Wolfram, he raises the question of how earthly love can be justified before God), his answer (marriage without sex), and the presence (in *MO*) of crusade motives, lead one to suppose that the original Middle High German Oswald epic was composed late in the twelfth century. Whether *MO* (as seems more likely) or *WO* represents this original more faithfully is still a matter of controversy. *MO*, in which artisans (goldsmiths) are prominent and in which a Regensburg cult (fourteenth century) reflecting Oswald's popularity in that city is mentioned (verse 3,513), seems to owe its present form to a later, urban (Regensburg?) interest in the saint. The present form, perhaps the original, of *WO* was composed in Silesia in the fourteenth century.

The four manuscripts of *MO* (as well as those of three differing prose descendants) and the three manuscripts of *WO* all date from the fifteenth century. There exists as well a fragment of a fourteenth-century verse epic (*Sant Oswald von Norwegen*) that is not directly related either to *MO* or to *WO*.

BIBLIOGRAPHY

Sources. Georg Baesecke, ed., *Der Münchner Oswald* (1907), repr. in Walter J. Schröder, ed., *Spielmannsepik*, II (1977), and *Der Wiener Oswald* (1912); Michael Curschmann, "'Sant Oswald von Norwegen': Ein Fragment eines Legendenepos," in *Zeitschrift für deutsches Altertum und deutsche Literatur*, **102** (1973), and *Der Münchner Oswald* (1974); A. Edzardi, ed., "Die Stuttgarter Oswaltprosa," in *Germania*, **20** and **21** (1875–1876); Gertrud Fuchs, ed., *Der Wiener Oswald* (1920); Moriz Haupt, ed., "Oswalt," in *Zeitschrift für deutsches Altertum*, **13** (1876); Ignaz Zingerle, ed., *Die Oswaldlegende und ihre Beziehung zur deutschen Mythologie* (1856), 43–66.

Studies. Rolf Bräuer, *Das Problem des "Spielmännischen" aus der Sicht der St.-Oswald-Überlieferung* (1969); Michael Curschmann, *Der Münchner Oswald und die deutsche spielmännische Epik* (1964), and *Spielmannsepik: Wege und Ergebnisse der Forschung von 1907–1965* (1968); Josef Dünninger, "St. Oswald und Regensburg: Zur Datierung des Münchner Oswald," in Erlangen, Universität, Seminar für romanische Philologie, *Gedächtnisschrift für Adalbert Hämel* (1953); Walter Haug, "Struktur und Geschichte: Ein literaturtheoretisches Experiment an mittelalterlichen Texten," in *Germanisch-romanische Monatsschrift*, n.s. **23** (1973).

JAMES A. SCHULTZ

[See also **König Rother; Middle High German Literature; Nibelungenlied; Tristan, Roman de.**]

OSWALD OF RAMSEY (925–992), bishop of Worcester, archbishop of York, and one of the moving forces of the late-tenth-century monastic revival in England. After studying Benedictine monasticism at Fleury, Oswald, with the political blessing of King Edgar (959–975), established or reformed many monasteries (including Worcester, Ramsey, and York) which had been destroyed or had decayed during the Viking invasions.

BIBLIOGRAPHY

John Godfrey, *The Church in Anglo-Saxon England* (1962), 294–309; Eric John, "St. Oswald and the Tenth-century Reformation," in *Journal of Ecclesiastical History*, **9** (1958), "The King of the Monks in the Tenth-century Reformation," in *The Bulletin of the John Rylands Library*, **42** (1959–1960), and "The Sources of the English Monastic Reformation: A Comment," in *Revue bénédictine*, **69** (1960); David Knowles, *Saints* *and Scholars: Twenty-five Medieval Portraits* (1962); J. Armitage Robinson, *St. Oswald and the Church of Worcester* (1919), 5–15, and *The Times of Saint Dunstan* (1923, repr. 1969), 127–134.

THOMAS H. OHLGREN

[See also **England: Anglo-Saxon; Ethelwold and the Benedictine Rule.**]

OSWALD VON WOLKENSTEIN (*ca.* 1377–1445), south Tyrolean composer-poet, the second son of Frederick von Wolkenstein and Katharina von Vilanders, was born at Schöneck Castle in the Puster valley. Of his early life we know only what he relates in his retrospective song *Es fügt sich*, which he composed at the Council of Constance in his fortieth year. This song tells how he ran away at the age of ten; lived in hardship; learned ten languages; mastered several musical instruments; visited Prussia, Russia, the Holy Land, and North Africa; fought under two emperors; and was honored by four queens. Recent critics have proved that this song cannot be taken at face value, because Oswald stylized his adventures to conform to accepted literary stereotypes. Nevertheless, the basic events are true, even if misinterpreted and exaggerated; they corroborate each other and concur with the numerous official documents concerning Oswald.

Although he was born into a noble family, as a second son who had two brothers and four sisters Oswald received little inheritance. He had to make his own way in the world, and he did this successfully. While residing at Neustift Cloister after his pilgrimage to the Holy Land, he ruthlessly misappropriated Hauenstein Castle, of which he had inherited only a third part from the Jäger family, who had inherited the other two-thirds. In 1415 he accompanied his liege, the bishop of Brixen, to Constance, where Emperor Sigismund had convened a council to end the Great Schism. There he entered the service of Sigismund, who was trying to persuade all three popes to abdicate so that a candidate acceptable to all factions might be elected.

Oswald's stay at Constance was interrupted by a mission probably via England and possibly also via Scotland or Ireland to Portugal, where he joined an expedition against Ceuta in North Africa. After that victory, apparently the only one in his military career, he hurried to Perpignan, where Sigismund was negotiating with the recalcitrant Pope Benedict. The sojourn in Perpignan and the triumphant return via Narbonne, Avignon, and Paris furnished material for a rambling autobiographical song, *Es ist ain altgesprochner rat*, which ignored the historical events of the time and stressed only humorous trivia, as did Oswald's songs from Constance. Returning to Constance, Oswald married the Swabian heiress Margaret von Schwangau, for whom he composed some tender love songs.

Oswald von Wolkenstein, after a portrait attributed to Pisanello, *ca.* 1432. INNSBRUCK, UNIVERSITÄTSBIBLIOTHEK: OSWALD VON WOLKENSTEIN SONGBOOK, MS B, PORTRAIT PAGE

From Constance, Oswald returned to Tyrol, presumably in Sigismund's service, to help organize the free lords against the policies of their new duke, the Habsburg prince Frederick IV "with the Empty Purse." Although recently married, Oswald allowed a former sweetheart, Anna Hausmann, to lead him into an ambush, where he was seized and thrown into prison by the wronged owners of

Hauenstein. Fearing for his life and soul, he composed some of his most heartrending songs. Later, after his transfer to Duke Frederick's custody, his prison songs became less obsequious and more sarcastic.

Freed on bail by his brothers, Oswald sought aid from Sigismund, who was in Hungary, and participated in a disastrous crusade against the Hussites, against whom he composed a virulent diatribe that likened them to geese, the name Hus meaning "goose" in Czech. Despairing of help from Sigismund, Oswald finally followed his brothers and the other Tyrolean magnates in submitting to Duke Frederick, who had imprisoned him again for failing to appear at court to settle the Hauenstein affair. Pardoned by the duke after minimal concessions, Oswald journeyed down the Rhine to Westphalia to join the *Femegericht,* a secret court (which centuries later, via Goethe and Walter Scott, would furnish the mystique for the Ku Klux Klan). This connection helped him in his subsequent feuds with his liege, the bishop of Brixen. After spending the winter of 1432 with Sigismund in Italy, Oswald returned to Tyrol. He remained politically aggressive almost until the day of his death, despite the songs of his old age that preached the vanity of this world and the need of preparing for the next.

Although Oswald's songs often follow literary conventions, they nearly all reveal his personal stamp. The old forms hold new contents: he inherited the form of the alba from the courtly minnesingers, but his lovers, sometimes married, wake only to join the May dance. He pays lip service to *Frauendienst* (service to one's lady), yet he sings more convincingly of the prostitutes in Constance. He also follows the tradition of Neidhart von Reuental in composing "rustic" court poetry, and his rustics seem very much at home in his Tyrolean setting. His most original songs result from his travel, captivity, and financial woes. His Palestinian pilgrimage, for example, inspired a song full of foreign words that were first thought to be gibberish but are now recognized as well-recorded nautical commands spoken by the crews recruited from various Italian ports.

Oswald's songs run the gamut from piety to pornography and furnish the most varied anthology of his century. Many of them are the oldest examples of their genres, a fact that may show his originality or only that he was the first person vain enough and wealthy enough to record for posterity what other singers left unrecorded. Some of his songs, being occasional songs, are difficult to understand, as his "beard songs" were until Ulrich Müller showed that his "beard" was a humorous metaphor for his purse.

As a man of means, Oswald was independent of patrons; yet he did strive to please his public, whose attention he craved even if he had to play the fool to win it, as he did in his Perpignan song. His need for acceptance and adulation was aggravated by his empty eye socket (he had lost an eye while still a youth), about which he was very sensitive and which he mentioned in several songs to and about women. Exceedingly proud of his voice, he boasted of the honors he had won by entertaining at court; and, as an inveterate name dropper, he often mentioned royalty and other dignitaries in familiar terms. Oswald was the first German-language poet to leave us his picture—he left a total of five likenesses, the most famous being a realistic portrait putatively by Pisanello, who painted one of Sigismund at the same time. His desire for posthumous fame is further indicated by the chapel he dedicated to his patron saint with a bas-relief of himself, and by his two handsome illuminated songbooks, each with a portrait.

Despite his desire for posthumous fame, Oswald was forgotten by all but his family until the mid nineteenth century, when his statue was unearthed and his songbook published; but even then he was celebrated only as a quaint adventurer and local political leader who dabbled in poetry. His genius has been recognized only recently, and now he has an enthusiastic following. On the occasion of his six hundredth anniversary in 1977, his popularity was attested by an international symposium at Seis in south Tryol and the publication of its transactions, as well as by three biographies and a handsome facsimile of MS *A*. At the same time Trostburg Castle was restored as a monument to him, and his Pisanello portrait graced an Austrian postage stamp. His music has also been made known through several new musicological studies and songbooks with modernized notations of his melodies, as well as through many recordings of both his oral and instrumental works. He is now generally recognized as the greatest German poet between Walther von der Vogelweide (*d. ca.* 1230) and Goethe.

BIBLIOGRAPHY

Sources. Die Lieder Oswalds von Wolkenstein, Karl K. Klein, ed. (1962, rev. ed. 1975); *Oswald von*

Wolkenstein: Abbildungen zur Überlieferung, Hans Moser and Ulrich Müller, eds. (1972), MS *B;* George F. Jones, *et al.,* eds., *Verskonkordanz zu den Liedern Oswalds von Wolkenstein* (1973); *Oswald von Wolkenstein,* Francesco Delbono, ed. (1977), MS *A.*

Studies. George F. Jones, *Oswald von Wolkenstein* (1973), and "Oswald von Wolkenstein 1377–1977: Present State of Research," in *Monatshefte,* 70 (1978); Egon Kühebacher, ed., *Oswald von Wolkenstein: Beiträge der philologisch-musikwissenschaftlichen Tagung in Neustift bei Brixen 1973* (1974), with bibliography to 1974; Dieter Kühn, *Ich Wolkenstein: Eine Biographie* (1977); Hans-Dieter Mück and Ulrich Müller, *Gesammelte Vorträge der 600-Jahrfeier Oswalds von Wolkenstein: Seis am Schlern 1977* (1978); Ulrich Müller, ed., *Oswald von Wolkenstein* (1980); Alan Robertshaw, *Oswald von Wolkenstein: The Myth and the Man* (1977); Anton Schwob, *Oswald von Wolkenstein: Eine Biographie* (1977).

GEORGE FENWICK JONES

[See also **German Literature: Lyric; Germany; Middle High German Literature.**]

OTAQ (Turkish) is a large, round tent, particularly the tent erected for the commanders, including the sultan, and high officials of the Ottoman Empire during campaigns. The *otaq-i humayun* is the imperial tent. Ottoman miniatures depicting historical scenes show several round tents at army camps. The largest tent, which belonged to the sultan, was highly decorated and furnished with chairs, cushions, and rugs. Since the members of the Ottoman government followed the sultan even to the battlefield, the imperial *otaqs* were large enough to serve as audience rooms and retained furnishings worthy of royalty. The outside of the *otaq* was covered with brightly colored materials and appliquéd work. The flattened central part of the domical roofs was covered wtih a separate flap that, when opened, could let in light and air. The skirt of the dome and edge of the central opening were decorated with colorful bands.

Often, a flat, rectangular sheet would be pitched on four poles in front of an *otaq* to serve as an umbrella or porch. A number of *otaqs* set up in the battlefield would be surrounded with white canvas, which served presumably as a protective "wall" and ensured some privacy. Several Turkish *otaqs* from the sixteenth and seventeenth centuries have been preserved in Europe and are quite impressive in workmanship and size. Among speakers of eastern Turkic dialects the term used to mean simply "a room." In Turkey a derivation, *oda,* means room.

Sultan Süleyman I and his advisers in an *otaq* during the campaign against Hungary. Miniature by Nakkas Osman, 1588. İSTANBUL, TOPKAPI SARAY MUSEUM, HAZINE 1524, fol. 279b

BIBLIOGRAPHY

C. Cürük and E. Çiçekciler. eds., *Ornekleriyie Türk Çadirlari* [Illustrated Turkish Tents] (1983).

ÜLKÜ Ü. BATES

OTFRID VON WEISSENBURG (*d.* 870's). Otfrid, a monk of Weissenburg (Wissembourg) in Alsace, was the author of the *Liber evangeliorum,* or *Evangelienbuch* (Gospelbook), a work of little poetic merit but of great importance in the early history of German literature. It is prefaced by a dedication in German rhyming verse to Louis the German, a letter in Latin to Liutbert, archbishop of Mainz, and another verse dedication to Salomo, bishop of Constance. It ends with a verse epistle to the author's friends Hartmuat and Werinbert, monks of St. Gall. Since Liutbert became archbishop in 863 and Salomo died in 871, we conclude that Otfrid completed his work between these dates. To Liutbert he writes that he was educated by Hrabanus Maurus; from this we infer that he attended the monastery school at Fulda, of which Hrabanus was master before becoming abbot.

The *Evangelienbuch* runs to over 7,000 lines of German rhyming verse, a form which Otfrid is widely believed to have been the first to use, taking as his model the rhymed Latin hymn. However, although he expatiates to Liutbert on the problems of German versification, he does not discuss the origin of his verse form. As models he mentions the Christian Latin poets Juvencus, Arator, and Prudentius, as well as the pagans Vergil, Ovid, and Lucan. Some chapters employ refrains, no doubt in imitation of hymns, and his verse dedications have acrostics and telestichs. He tells Liutbert that he was encouraged to write his work by certain brothers and a lady called Judith and that he hopes it will supplant the vulgar songs of the laity. In the first chapter (*Cur scriptor hunc librum theotisce dictaverit;* or, Why the writer composed this book in German) he says he wants to provide the Franks with a worthy medium in their own tongue by which they too, like the Romans and Greeks (to whom they are in no other way inferior), may praise God. This statement, together with his dedication to the king—a "noble Frank" whom he compares with David—makes it clear that his endeavor was inspired by both religious piety and patriotic zeal.

Otfrid's work was not intended for the illiterate but, rather, for educated men like Hartmuat and Werinbert, whom he reminds of the benefits of reading. Repeatedly he urges the reader to consult the books of Scripture directly. He tells Liutbert that for the beginning and the end of the work he carefully selected his material from the Gospels, but that in the middle he reluctantly omitted many of Christ's parables and miracles and much of his teaching. The work is divided into five books. Its contents may have been chosen with reference to a lectionary, and Otfrid probably consulted Augustine's *De consensu evangelistarum* for the chronology of the biblical events. Being deeply versed in theology and well acquainted with the standard commentaries, he provides an exegesis of the texts he renders according to contemporary categories of interpretation. This material appears in separate chapters headed *Spiritaliter, Mystice,* and *Moraliter.*

Otfrid's work is preserved in two manuscripts of the ninth century. One of these, now in Vienna (*V*), was perhaps corrected by Otfrid himself, and one chapter may be in his hand. The other, in Heidelberg (*P*), has neums added in one chapter, indicating that at least parts of the work were for singing. A third manuscript, from Freising (*F*) and now in Munich, was copied before 906 and has Bavarian features. Fragments of a fourth, the "Codex Discissus" (*D*), exist in Berlin, Wolfenbüttel, and Bonn. Otfrid's work seems to have been rapidly forgotten and was not rediscovered until the sixteenth century.

BIBLIOGRAPHY

J. Knight Bostock, *A Handbook on Old High German Literature,* K. C. King and David R. McLintock, eds., 2nd ed. (1976), 190–211; Ulrich Ernst, *Der Liber Evangeliorum Otfrids von Weissenburg: Literarästhetik und Verstechnik im Lichte der Tradition* (1975); Rainer Patzlaff, *Otfrid von Weissenburg und die mittelalterliche versus-Tradition* (1975).

DAVID R. MCLINTOCK

[See also **Biblical Poetry, German; Gospelbook; Old High German Literature.**]

OTHMAN. See **Osman I.**

OTLOH OF ST. EMMERAM (*ca.* 1010–*ca.* 1070), religious and ecclesiastical writer and monk, born in Bavaria. After studies in the Benedictine monasteries of Tegernsee and Hersfeld, and in Würzburg, he moved to the famous abbey and school of St. Emmeram at Regensburg (Ratisbon), where about 1032, after a psychological crisis, he became a Benedictine monk. Here he spent (with some interruptions) a very active life as a scribe, librarian, editor, and teacher, and especially as a writer. He was appointed dean of St. Emmeram in 1055. Because of disagreements with the bishop of

OTLOH OF ST. EMMERAM

Regensburg he spent the years 1062 to 1066 in Fulda.

This monk is a fascinating personality because of his autobiographical works, notably *Libellus de suis temptationibus, Liber visionum* (*ca.* 1065), and *Liber de cursu spiritali* (*ca.* 1068), in which one finds surprisingly personal accounts of his psyche, inner struggles, temptations, dreams, feverish visions, and divine warnings, as well as a new acceptance of God's grace and purpose. Such self-analytical writing, which ultimately goes back to St. Augustine's *Confessions,* is unique in its time and place. Otloh's *Libellus de suis temptationibus* also contains a survey of his own writings and of the manuscripts he himself wrote and copied for St. Emmeram and other monasteries, as well as several versions of two personal prayers, one in prose, one in hexameters; one of the Latin prose versions appears in a vernacular rendering (Bavarian dialect) as *Otlohs Gebet.*

Otloh often externalizes his own subjective struggles in works in which he comes to grips with theological issues: problems of good and evil, divine providence, and God's justice and mercy, for example in *Dialogus de tribus quaestionibus* (*ca.* 1055; also important for number symbolism) and in *Epistola de permissionis bonorum et malorum causis.* He also conveys messages of a didactic-pastoral nature, encouraging and urging priests as well as laymen to live a truly religious and Christian life by studying Holy Scripture, particularly the Psalter, and (in the case of the *illiterati*) by meditating on the created world as a mirror of God's goodness, for example in his poem *De doctrina spiritali* (*ca.* 1035), *Liber de admonitione clericorum et laicorum* (*ca.* 1065), *Amorbach Sermon* (*ca.* 1067), and *Liber de cursu spiritali.* In conjunction with such didactic purposes Otloh collected religious and moral sayings in verse and prose from the Bible, particularly the Old Testament, and other sources, adding several of his own making, and published them in alphabetical order in *Liber proverbiorum.*

Otloh composed new versions of several saints' lives: *Vita S. Wolfkangi* (*ca.* 1052; Wolfgang was bishop of Regensburg, *d.* 994), *Vita S. Nicolai* (before 1062), *Vita S. Altonis* (before 1062; Alto was the patron saint of Altomünster in Bavaria), *Vita S. Bonifatii* (*ca.* 1065), and *Vita S. Magni* (*ca.* 1068; Magnus or Mang was the patron saint of Füssen, Bavaria). Otloh also wrote several Latin hymns and one trope in Latin (on the Kyrie of the Mass, before 1049). St. Emmeram monastery often had to defend its independence, especially against attacks by the bishop of Regensburg. In order to "prove" its old rights, Otloh helped to forge a document, called *Translatio I* (or *Translatio S. Dionysii*), about the rediscovery of St. Dionysius' body in St. Emmeram after it had been carried off from St. Denis in France. Otloh left numerous autographs of his works, most of which are now in the Bayerische Staatsbibliothek in Munich.

BIBLIOGRAPHY

Sources. Otloh's works can be found in *Patrologia latina,* CXLVI (1884), 27–434, LXXXIX (1863), 633–664, XCIII (1850), 1103–1128, and CXXII (1853), xv–xvii. Editions of *Otloh's Gebet* are: Theodor Wilhelm Braune and Ernst A. Ebbinghaus, eds., *Althochdeutsche Lesebuch,* 15th ed. (1969), 80–82; Emil Elias von Steinmeyer, ed., *Die kleineren althochdeutschen Sprachdenkmäler* (1916, repr. 1963, 1971), 182–189, German and Latin texts; Friedrich Wilhelm, ed., *Denkmäler deutscher Prosa des 11. und 12. Jahrhunderts,* 2 vols. (1914–1918, repr. in 1 vol. in 1960), I, 1–3, II, 1–13, German and Latin texts; Karl V. Müllenhoff and Wilhelm Scherer, eds., *Denkmäler deutscher Poesie und Prosa aus dem VIII.–XII. Jahrhunderts,* 3rd ed., 2 vols. (1892, repr. 1964), I, 267–269, II, 411–416.

Editions of other works are: *Othloni libellus proverbiorum,* William Charles Korfmacher, ed. (1936); *Translatio I,* A. Hofmeister, ed., *Monumenta Germaniae historica, Scriptores,* XXX, 2 (1934, repr. 1964), 823–837; *Vita S. Altonis,* G. Waitz, ed., *ibid.,* XV, 2 (1888, repr. 1963), 843–846; *Vita S. Bonifatii,* Wilhelm Levison, ed. (1905, repr. 1977), 111–217; *Vita Wolfkangi Episcopi,* G. Waitz, ed., *Monumenta Germaniae historica, Scriptores,* IV (1841, repr. 1981), 521–542; *Vita Wolfkangi Episcopi, Acta sanctorum,* Nov., II, 1 (1894), 565–583. Otloh's hymns and trope are in *Analecta hymnica medii aevi,* **50** (1907), 320–328, and **47** (1905), 98–99. A facsimile with Otloh's handwriting appears in Erich Petzet and Otto Glauning, eds., *Deutsche Schrifttafeln des IX. bis XVI. Jahrhunderts aus Handschriften der Bayerischen Staatsbibliothek in München* (1975, repr. of 1910–1930 ed.), plate I, 13.

Studies. Bernhard Bischoff, "Literarisches und künstlerisches Leben in St. Emmeram in frühen und hohen Mittelalter," in *Studien und Mitteilungen zur Geschichte des Benedektiner Ordens und seiner Zweige,* **51** (1933), and "Über unbekannte Handschriften und Werke Otlohs von St. Emmeram (Regensburg)," *ibid.,* **54** (1936); Gillian R. Evans, "'Studium discendi': Otloh of St. Emmeram and the Seven Liberal Arts," in *Recherches de théologie ancienne et médiévale,* **44** (1977); Otto Meyer, "Regensburg: Otloh," in Wilhelm Wattenbach, Robert Holtzmann, and Franz-Josef Schmale, eds.,

Deutschlands Geschichtsquellen im Mittelalter, I, *Das Zeitalter des Ottonischen Staates (900–1050)* (1967); Georg Misch, *Geschichte der Autobiographie,* III, 2nd part, 1st half (1959), 57–107; Helga E. Schauwecker, *Otloh von St. Emmeram: Ein Beitrag zur Bildungs- und Frömmigkeitsgeschichte des 11. Jahrhunderts* (1964), containing plates with Otloh's handwriting; Werner Schröder, "Der Geist von Cluny und die Anfänge des frühmhd. Schrifttums," in *Beiträge zur Geschichte der deutschen Sprache und Literatur,* 72 (1950), esp. 371–382; Josef Szöverty, *Die Annalen der lateinischen Hymnendichtung: Ein Handbuch,* I (1964), 240, 402–405.

PETRUS W. TAX

[See also **Carmina Burana.**]

OTTO OF BAMBERG, ST. (1060/1062–1139), known as the Apostle of Pomerania, attracted the notice of his secular superiors and after a trip to Poland in 1080 was made supervisor of the building of Speyer Cathedral by Emperor Henry IV. He became bishop of Bamberg in 1102, although he was suspended for a time because of his support for Henry V when the latter was in exile. He was instrumental in bringing about the Concordat of Worms and played a large role in the Christianization of Pomerania. The large rewards he received enabled him to found many religious houses.

BIBLIOGRAPHY

Lexikon für Theologie und Kirche, Josef Höfer and Karl Rahner, eds., VII (1962), 1302–1303.

W. T. H. JACKSON

[See also **Henry IV of Germany; Investiture and Investiture Conflict; Worms, Concordat of.**]

OTTO I THE GREAT, EMPEROR (*r.* 936–973), the real founder of the medieval German kingdom and the ruler who did the most to make Germany the strongest state in Europe in the tenth and eleventh centuries. Practically nothing is known of his physical appearance or personality, but he clearly was endowed with enormous strength, energy, and determination. At the onset of his reign he was faced with extremely grave internal and external challenges, but by extraordinary perseverance he managed to overcome almost all of these. He was the only medieval German king to be called "the Great," and there is little doubt that he deserved that appellation.

Internally, Otto's greatest problem was maintaining control over the German dukes. The dukes of the five main political units of medieval Germany—Saxony, Franconia, Swabia, Bavaria, and Lorraine—were military leaders of independent German tribes. In 919, faced with attacks from Danes, Slavs, and Hungarians, which threatened their own ability to rule, the dukes of the first four territories had agreed to recognize the overlordship of the duke of Saxony, Otto's father, Henry I. Henry took the title of king and reigned as such until his death in 936, but for practical purposes he was little more than a military chief of staff. Throughout his reign the dukes ruled in their own duchies more or less as they pleased. But Otto I was determined to make Germany something more than a military confederacy. After his accession he put down numerous ducal rebellions and then embarked on a firm policy of royal domination. He did away with the duchy of Franconia and reserved that territory entirely for himself. Since Otto already ruled Saxony by inheritance, the addition of neighboring Franconia—the centralmost part of Germany—gave him a very strong power base. Otto allowed the other duchies their continued existence, but he eliminated their tribal dynasties and replaced them with new rulers who usually came from his own family. This was no absolute guarantee of loyalty because some of the new dukes were quick to identify with the traditions and interests of their newly acquired territories. Nonetheless, in the second half of his reign Otto was able to keep an upper hand over his dukes.

Otto's subordination of the dukes was aided by the alliance he forged with the German bishops, a second main governmental accomplishment of his reign. Since Otto ruled at a time when literacy was extremely rare (Otto himself only learned to read haltingly when he was a grown man), he could by no means hope to build up his own independent administrative staff. Therefore, he relied primarily on the German bishops—the best-educated men of the day—to provide basic administrative services. Of course the bishops did not serve as administrators out of mere admiration for Otto; in effect they were paid for their work by large grants of land and governmental privileges over the territories they were granted. To make sure he was not giving away land and rights to potential enemies, Otto kept appointments to bishoprics entirely under his own control. Ruling as much as possible through his own family, he appointed his brother and most trusted aide, Bruno, as archbishop of Cologne. (For a time, while Bruno was archbishop of Cologne, Otto's bastard son was archbishop of Mainz and another close relative archbishop of Trier.) Otto and subsequent German kings were able to count on the loyalties of the bishops because the episcopal office, unlike the ducal one, was not hereditary; thus, the king could put in his own new men whenever there were vacancies. Loyal bishops provided troops from their lands when the king needed them and thus helped to keep the dukes in check as well as fight Germany's external enemies. All in all, alliance between the crown and the bishops helped make Germany the most stable and best-governed country of continental Europe for well over a century.

Externally, Otto was threatened at the beginning of his reign by the might of the Hungarians, as well as by the fact that other enemies on almost every border were poised for attack whenever Otto was occupied elsewhere. To make matters worse, foreign enemies in the first years of Otto's reign often struck alliances with rebellious German dukes. Thus, until 955, Otto was engaged in seemingly interminable warfare. Frequently he could only make progress on one front by giving up ground on another, but by dint of extraordinary determination he finally forced all his major foreign enemies into submission. Otto's first major triumphs were in the West. There he ensured continued German rule over Lorraine and predominance on the West Frankish frontier by a victory in 939 over several dukes who had allied with the king of the West Franks, and by a campaign deep into France in 940 during which he received the homage of many leading West Frankish magnates. Also in 940 Otto began to bring the kingdom of Burgundy under German influence, thus preparing the way for Burgundy's full acquisition by Germany in 1033.

In the East, Otto gained dominance over the Slavic Wends after numerous campaigns and in 950 gained recognition of German suzerainty over Bohemia. Otto's greatest military victory was over the Hungarians in 955 at the battle of the Lechfeld, near Augsburg. Thereafter the Hungarians were no longer a threat to the security of Western Europe. After 955 Otto was able to take the offensive and he began to threaten Poland, but in 966 the pagan Polish ruler Mieszko converted to Christianity, probably to deprive the Germans of any excuse for aggression. (Otto's new archbishopric of Magdeburg, established in 968, subsequently served as a point of departure for further German missionary work in the northeast.)

The symbolic culmination of Otto's reign came in 962, when he was crowned emperor by the pope in Rome. There is much disagreement about the causes and intrinsic significance of this event, but two points are clear. One is that every medieval German ruler after Otto continued to regard it as part of his office to seek imperial coronation by the pope. This locked medieval Germany into a close relationship with the medieval papacy that would prove extremely fateful for both sides. There is also no doubt that Otto was fully determined to extend his own direct rule into Italy; in the last twelve years of his reign he spent close to ten years fighting to assert his power south of the Alps. Virtually all of his successors followed him in this policy, but none was able to eliminate Italian resistance, and their frequent absence from Germany usually created severe difficulties for them back home. But these problems only became fully evident later on. Within Otto's own lifetime, and until about 1075, he appeared to have built up the foundations of German kingship extremely well.

BIBLIOGRAPHY

Geoffrey Barraclough, *The Origins of Modern Germany,* 2nd rev. ed. (1947, repr. 1984), and *The Crucible of Europe* (1976), 106–121; Josef Fleckenstein, "Otto der Grosse in seinem Jahrhundert," in *Frühmittelalterliche Studien,* 9 (1975); Boyd H. Hill, Jr., ed., *The Rise of the First Reich* (1969); Karl Leyser, "The Battle at the Lech, 955," in *History,* 50 (1965), and *Rule and Conflict in an Early Medieval Society: Ottonian Saxony* (1979); Martin Lintzel, *Die Kaiserpolitik Ottos des Grossen* (1943); Gerd Tellenback, *Die Entstehung des deutschen Reiches* (1943), and "Otto der Grosse," in Hermann Heimpel, ed., *Die Grossen Deutschen,* I (1956); Harald Zimmermann, ed., *Otto der Grosse* (1976).

ROBERT E. LERNER

[See also **Germany; Germany: Idea of Empire; Liutprand of Cremona; Widukind of Corvei.**]

OTTO III, EMPEROR (980–1002). The career of Otto III, the son of Otto II and the Byzantine princess Theophano, was haunted by the memory of ancient and early Christian Rome. Immediately after the three-year-old child was crowned king of Germany in Aachen on 25 December 983, it was learned that his father had died. Otto's closest male relative, Henry the Wrangler, the deposed duke of Bavaria, claimed the guardianship. When it became apparent that Henry was seeking the crown for himself, Theophano obtained the regency. Although she was forced to reinstate Henry as duke and was unable to reestablish German hegemony east of the Elbe, she used the Carolingian-Capetian rivalry in France to strengthen imperial control over Lorraine. After her death in 991, Otto's grandmother Adelaide assumed the guardianship until he attained his majority in 994.

While on his way to Rome for his imperial coronation in 996, Otto learned of the pope's death; he selected his cousin Bruno as the first German pope, Gregory V. At the synod that was convened after his coronation, Otto met the two men who were to be most influential in his life: Archbishop Gerbert of Rheims and Adalbert of Prague. Gerbert, the foremost scholar of the tenth century, became his teacher. Adalbert, along with Nilus, Romuald of Camaldoli, and Brun of Querfurt, aroused Otto's ascetic yearnings and convinced him that his chief responsibility as emperor was the conversion of the pagan peoples of Eastern Europe.

After Otto returned to Rome in 998 to suppress a revolt, he built a palace on the Aventine and revived the imperial court offices. These actions were part of a larger program that was summarized in the formula "Renovatio imperii Romanorum" (the renewal of the Roman Empire). The pope and emperor were to be the corulers of this revived Roman Empire, which was perceived as coterminous with Christendom. Gregory, who had adopted the traditional curial views on imperial-papal relations, opposed Otto's plans.

Gregory's sudden death in 999 enabled Otto to appoint Gerbert, who shared his views, as Pope Sylvester II. They dealt with the problem of incorporating Poland and Hungary into Western Christendom. In 1000 Otto went to Gniezno, the newly designated metropolitan see of Poland, where the martyred Adalbert had been buried, to elevate Boleslav the Brave from the rank of tributary prince to the status of an ally and friend of the Roman Empire. The next year the pope and emperor authorized the establishment of the archbishopric of Esztergom and the coronation of Stephen as king of Hungary. Otto's right to participate in these ecclesiastical decisions was expressed in his titles "servant of Christ" and "servant of the Apostles." Although Rome was in open rebellion by the time of Otto's premature death, and although his Eastern and Roman policies were severely criticized both by his contemporaries and by nationalistic German historians of a later era, there is little doubt that he had a more profound perception of his office than any other medieval emperor, save possibly Frederick II.

BIBLIOGRAPHY

Bruno Gebhardt, *Handbuch der deutschen Geschichte,* 9th ed., Herbert Grundmann, ed., I (1970), 265–279; Percy Ernst Schramm, *Kaiser, Rom und Renovatio,* 3rd ed. (1962), 87–187; Theodor Sickel, ed., *Die Urkunden Otto des III* (1893, repr. 1957); Mathilde Uhlirz, *Jahrbücher des deutschen Reiches unter Otto II. und Otto III.,* II, *Otto III. 983–1002* (1954).

JOHN B. FREED

[See also **Germany: 843–1137; Sylvester II, Pope.**]

OTTO OF FREISING (*ca.* 1114–1158), author of *The History of the Two Cities* and *The Deeds of Frederick Barbarossa,* is widely regarded as the greatest medieval historical thinker. He came from the highest ranks of the German aristocracy. His grandfather was Emperor Henry IV; his uncle, Henry V; his half brother, Conrad III; and his nephew, Frederick I Barbarossa. The fifth of eighteen children born to Henry IV's daughter Agnes and Margrave Leopold III of Austria (of the Babenberg family), Otto was destined from birth for an ecclesiastical career. He spent his school years in Paris, where he studied under Hugh of St. Victor and, possibly, Peter Abelard. Returning from France to Germany around 1133, Otto suddenly decided to join the Cistercian order while he was staying in the Cistercian cloister of Morimund in Burgundy. For about five years he remained as a monk in Morimund, becoming abbot around 1137. Shortly thereafter, he became bishop of Freising, near Munich, an office he held until his death. As bishop of Freising, Otto accompanied his half brother Conrad and his nephew Frederick on the Second Crusade (1147–1149) and played an active role in the ecclesiastical affairs of his diocese.

Otto's fame as a philosopher of history rests primarily on his *History of the Two Cities,* a world

OTTO OF FREISING

chronicle composed between 1143 and 1146. The original version does not survive, but we have the second, revised version that Otto sent to Emperor Frederick I Barbarossa in 1157. The *History of the Two Cities* treats the entire course of human events from the perspective of the relations between two "cities"—the communities of the faithful (the "City of God" or the "City of Christ") and the damned (the "City of the Earth" or the "City of the Devil"). It is indebted for some of its organizational principles to the work of Orosius, and for much of its historical information to the world chronicle of Frutolf of Michelsberg. Since the version of Frutolf's chronicle he used stopped in 1106, Otto wrote the history of his own time until 1146 (the terminal historical date of the *Two Cities*) primarily on the basis of oral reports and personal observations. For the bulk of his work he also drew on a remarkably wide variety of other historical, philosophical, and poetic sources. His primary inspiration was unquestionably the dualistic scheme of "two cities" advanced in St. Augustine's *City of God.* Otto was the only medieval thinker to use Augustine's polarities to construct a fully developed interpretation of events in world history.

Otto's main originality lay in setting forth a scheme of three phases for the community of believers, the "City of God." In the first the believers are in a minority, living under heathen princes; in the second the community is freed from oppression and reaches the zenith of its earthly existence; in the third it will be entirely freed from its earthly bonds. This development is one of progress: the first phase is "lowly," the second is "fortunate," and the third is "blessed."

The first phase began with men like Abel and Noah, who had a glimmering knowledge of the truth; it gained strength with the emergence of the Jewish state; and it reached its culmination during the Incarnation, when Christ extended the City of God from the Jews to the whole world and gave the City visible form by founding the universal church. Nonetheless, for three centuries after Christ, the City of God still suffered from heathen oppression.

The second phase began not with Christ but with the Roman emperors Constantine I and Theodosius I, who together freed the City of God from its earthly distress. These two emperors began the time of the *civitas permixta* (mixed city), when the City of Earth was subordinated to the City of God and became "as if numb." This time lasted until the outbreak of the investiture controversy, when the *civitas permixta* began to fall apart because of the struggle between pope and emperor. Convinced that the second phase was nearing completion, Otto was certain that the world was about to end and the third phase, the time of otherworldly eternal peace for the City of God, about to begin. Therefore, his last book describes the imminent Last Judgment, the resurrection of the dead, and the exaltation of the heavenly city as if these future events were an integral part of history.

The *Two Cities* sets forth a number of other historical theories, of which only a few can be mentioned here. Otto believed that in his own time the City of God was breaking through more gloriously than ever in the activity of the monastic orders. He also believed that history progressed geographically from East to West: thus monasticism was founded in Egypt and in Otto's day had reached its peak in France and Germany; similarly, learning was founded in Babylon, spread via Abraham to Egypt, then was taken by philosophers to Greece, from there to Rome, and finally in Otto's day was flourishing in the farthest western areas of France and Spain. The fact that history was currently reaching its western limits was another sign that the world was about to end. The history of the City of the Earth was characterized by unceasing instability, but it also went through three phases: the time before grace (up to Christ); the time of grace; and the time after the Last Judgment. Of these the first was "miserable," the second was "more miserable," and the third was "most miserable." All of history is determined by Providence, whose plan is unique and linear (not cyclical), and entirely predetermined. Men should study history to learn of God's ways, to learn how to scorn transitory earthly affairs over which they have no control, and to know how to prepare for the end.

Otto worked on *The Deeds of Frederick Barbarossa* from 1157 to 1158. By the time of his death he had written only two books, and the narrative was continued by his secretary, Rahewin, who added two more books. Otto's part treats the history of Barbarossa's Hohenstaufen family from 1079 to Frederick's accession in 1152, and his reign until 1156; Rahewin's brings the story down to 1160. Although there is less explicit speculation about the meaning of history in *Deeds* than in the *Two Cities,* the view that Otto abandoned his earlier theoretical framework in the *Deeds* and "stepped down to the position of a mere chronicler" must be rejected. Rather, Otto became con-

OTTO VON BOTENLAUBEN

vinced by Barbarossa's early accomplishments that the phase of the *civitas permixta* was not going to end soon after all. The reason for this change of mind lay in his conviction that Frederick had created a new security for the community of believers by establishing peace in Germany and by forming a new harmony between the priesthood and the state. Thus Otto conceived of the *Deeds* as a "joyous history" instead of his previous "tragedy" and emphasized the charismatic greatness of the Hohenstaufen family, culminating in the deeds of Barbarossa. The *Deeds* is therefore not at all an exhaustive and impartial "reporting of facts" but a very tendentious account. Nonetheless, in addition to being an excellent expression of a particular point of view, it is full of unique information on a wide range of subjects, and is without a doubt the most valuable surviving source for the early years of Barbarossa's reign.

BIBLIOGRAPHY

Sources. Otto of Freising, *Chronik, oder die Geschichte der zwei Staaten,* Adolf Schmidt, trans., Walther Lammers, ed. (1960), German translation of *Two Cities* with facing page in Latin, also in English, *The Two Cities,* Charles C. Mierow, trans. (1928); *Die Taten Friedrichs, oder richtiger Cronica,* Adolf Schmidt, trans., Franz Schmale, ed. (1965), German translation of *Deeds* with facing page in Latin, also in English, *The Deeds of Frederick Barbarossa,* Charles C. Mierow, trans. (1953).

Studies. Charles C. Mierow, "Otto of Freising and His Two Cities Theory," in *Philological Quarterly,* 24 (1945), and "Bishop Otto of Freising, Historian and Man," in *Proceedings of the American Philological Association,* 80 (1949).

ROBERT E. LERNER

[See also **Frederick I Barbarossa; Germany: 843–1137; Germany: 1138–1254; Historiography, Western European; Hohenstaufen Dynasty.**]

OTTO VON BOTENLAUBEN (1170/1180–1244), Franconian poet. He was a son of Count Poppo VI of Henneberg, who accompanied Emperor Frederick I Barbarossa on the Third Crusade (1189–1192), from which neither returned. Otto himself joined the crusade of Frederick's son, Emperor Henry VI, in 1197. It is on the basis of these circumstances that Botenlauben is assumed to have been born during the decade of the 1170's.

Botenlauben's trip to the Holy Land resulted in a twenty-year residence in that area. During his stay he married Beatrice, a daughter of Joscelin III, seneschal of the kingdom of Jerusalem. Otto left the Holy Land permanently in 1220, returning to his Franconian homeland as a wealthy man and taking up residence in his castle Botenlauben. Not many years later, this situation was changed drastically by a series of religiously motivated acts that culminated in the sale by Otto and Beatrice in 1234 of all their earthly possessions. Otto devoted the latter part of his life to the church and church establishments around Würzburg.

It is generally agreed that Botenlauben's poems were composed early in his life, perhaps between 1197 and 1207. According to such a dating, Botenlauben would have been active as a poet at about the same time as Walther von der Vogelweide, Wolfram von Eschenbach, and Reinmar der Alte, all of whom Botenlauben outranked socially, but who were and are considered superior poets. Thirteen poems of Botenlauben have been preserved according to Carl von Kraus, fifteen according to Klaus Dieter Jaehrling, Botenlauben's editors.

These poems are quite varied, both in metrical structure and subject matter. Four (III, IX:IV, XIII, and XIV) treat the situation of the dawn song (*Tagelied*), one of which focuses not on the parting of lovers but on their meeting. Poem VIII is a monostrophic woman's song (*Frauenlied*) that reminds one of the older Danubian minnesong and especially of Dietmar von Aist. Poem XII is a crusade poem in the form of a *Wechsel* (man's stanza plus woman's stanza) that seems to echo Hausen. In other poems a male speaker utters familiar plaints about unrequited love, but in subtle formulations tending toward the allegorical and making use of lore reminiscent of the earlier *Physiologus* texts while anticipating the pretentious scholarliness of later thirteenth-century poets.

BIBLIOGRAPHY

Georg Drummer, "Otto von Botenlauben," in *Bayerische Literaturgeschichte,* I, Eberhard Dünninger and Dorothee Kiesselbach, eds. (1965); Klaus Dieter Jaehrling, *Die Lieder Ottos von Bodenlouben* (1970); Carl von Kraus, ed., *Deutsche Liederdichter des 13. Jahrhunderts,* I (1952), 307–316; Ernst G. Krenig, "Otto von Botenlauben," in *Fränkische Lebensbilder,* I, Gerhard Pfeiffer, ed. (1967); Joachim Kröll, "Otto von Botenlauben," in *Fränkische Klassiker,* Wolfgang Buhl, ed.

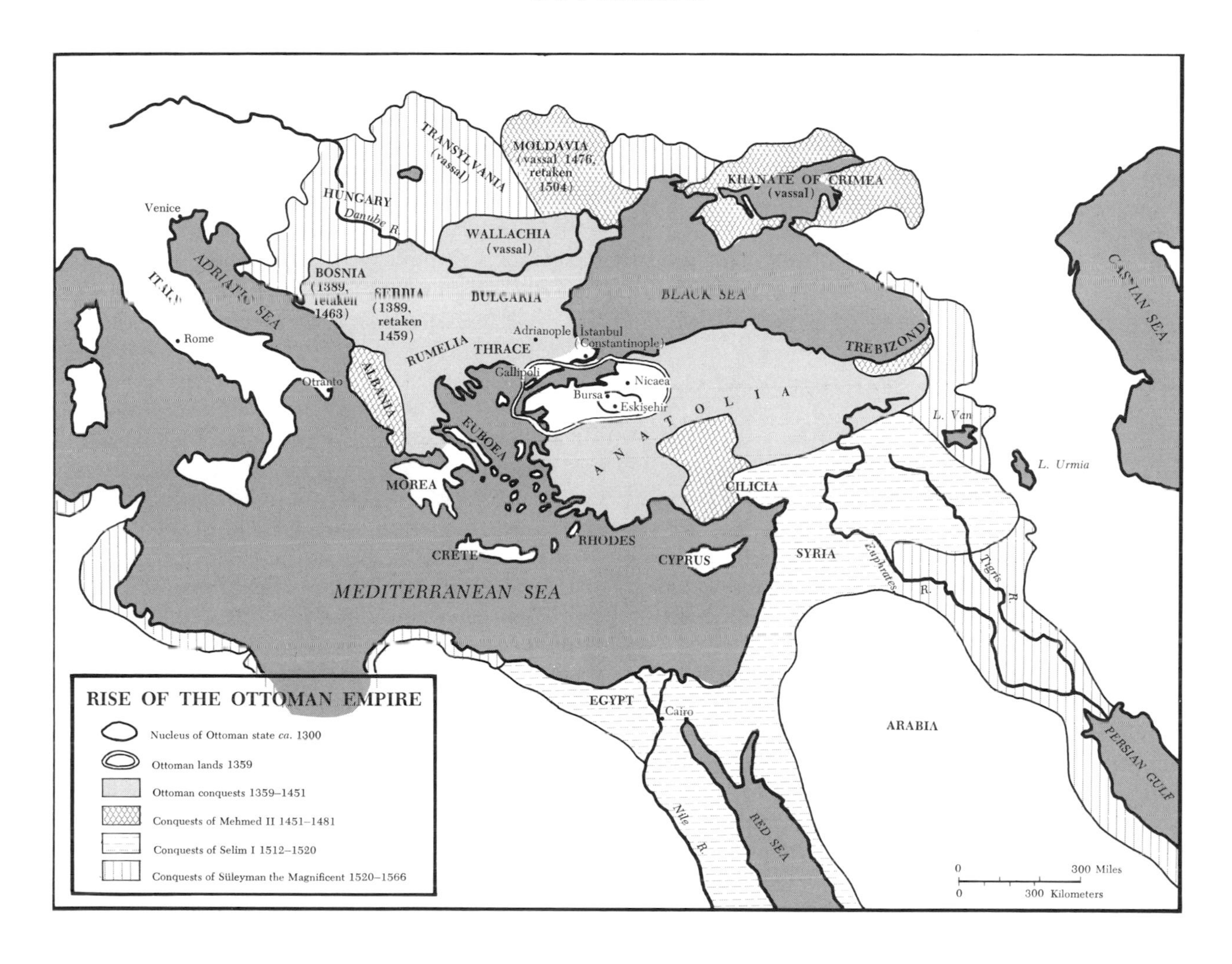

(1971); Hans-Karl Schuchard, *Der Minnesänger Otto von Botenlauben* (1940).

WILLIAM E. JACKSON

[See also **Crusades and Crusader States: To 1192; Dietmar von Aist; Frederick I Barbarossa; Minnesingers; Reinmar der Alte; Seneschal; Walther von der Vogelweide; Wolfram von Eschenbach.**]

OTTOMANS. In origin the Ottomans were a group of Anatolian Turks who inhabited the area between Eskişehir (Dorylaeum) and Nicaea before 1300 and founded the Ottoman principality, which in later centuries developed into an Islamic empire ruling over Asia Minor, the Balkans, the Crimea, Hungary, and parts of Syria, Arabia, and North Africa. The name Ottoman is derived from the name of Osman I (*d.* 1324), a chieftain who brought together under his command on the Seljuk-Byzantine frontier zone the *ghāzīs*, Muslim volunteers fighting for Islam, and established a dynamic principality. There were thirty-six rulers in the Ottoman dynasty between 1300 and 1922.

ORIGINS AND FOUNDATION OF THE OTTOMAN PRINCIPALITY

The zeal for *ghazā*, Islamic Holy War, became once more heightened in the Islamic world as a matter of survival when in the second half of the thirteenth century independent Islam, then reduced to Syria and North Africa, was threatened in its existence by the Mongols from the east and the crusaders from the west. It was this situation that led to the rise of the so-called military "empires," first in Egypt, where the Mamluks took over in 1250, and later in Asia Minor, where the Ottomans prevailed. In Egypt a professional army organized similarly to the traditional mercenary-slave armies of the Middle East simply seized the sultanate; in Asia Minor military leaders of various origins, by organizing warlike Turkoman forces in the marches, established dynamic centers of power, some of which developed into full-fledged principalities. After the Mongol Ilkhanids of Iran had reduced the Seljuk sultanate in Asia Minor to a vassal state in 1243, the Turkomans made common cause with the Mamluk sultan Baybars I al-Bundugdārī (1260–1277), who defeated the Mongols in Syria and challenged Mongol rule in Asia Minor. When in the period from 1291 to 1334 the Mongol governors of Asia Minor espoused the native Islamic cause in their rebellion against the Ilkhanids of Iran and attempted to take control of the marches, the Turkoman leaders in turn intensified the Holy War against the neighboring Christian lands in Byzantine western Anatolia and Lesser Armenia in Cilicia. The most active of the Turkoman centers at that time was the Ottoman principality in northwest Anatolia.

The raids into the "infidel land," or Abode of War (*Dar al-Ḥarb*), were motivated by the Holy War ideology, but perhaps even more urgently by the need for acquiring booty. Furthermore, population pressure on the marches grew because of constant immigration of mobile population from central Anatolia during the Mongol thrust.

The original core of the early Ottoman ruling elite consisted of the *ghazā* leader's slaves or clients (*yoldash*s or *nöker*s), who came, often from far away, to join him in the raids. Throughout their history, the Ottoman sultans encouraged by rewards and promises strangers with some useful skills to serve them. The frequently used word *kul* (slave) in this context also meant client, comrade, as it did in the beginning of the Ottomans. In the *ghāzī* period, these mounted warriors emerged as a privileged group within the Turkish tribal society. They were handsomely rewarded from the booty and were extolled by dervishes as fighters on the path of Allah. The *ghāzī* leader who by his successes could attract the greatest number of clients also drew in or forced other neighboring leaders, including Byzantine frontier lords, to join him. These first allies or war companions of Osman *ghāzī* established influential families whose members held leadership positions in the army, in particular on the Balkan frontiers, for more than a century (for example the Mihal family on the lower Danube, descended from a Greek frontier lord who had accepted Islam, or the Timur-tash family, which provided governors and commanders of the cavalry in Anatolia and Rumelia). In a few decades the original personal war band of the *ghāzī* leader evolved into an elite corps of standing infantry, the so-called Janissaries.

The hypothesis of population pressure on the frontier as the major condition of Turkish conquest and expansion toward the west has been supported by the data in the early Ottoman population and tax registers (*tahrir defteri*s). The internal disorders in Asia Minor and periodic Mongol repressions, as well as replacement of Turkoman nomads by Mongol tribal army groups in central Anatolian pasturelands, resulted in an exodus of population to western Anatolia. From 1250 onward, a massive population movement and settlement coincided with the formation of Turkoman principalities in the lands taken over from the Byzantines in western Anatolia in the 1290's as well as the Ottoman expansion in the eastern Balkans in the fourteenth century. A number of new Turkish villages mushroomed on the lands abandoned by the indigenous population as a result of Byzantine civil wars, the *ghāzī* raids, or epidemics (for instance, the plague of 1348). Usually dervishes were pioneers in this settlement process and a great number of villages came into existence around hospices (*zaviyes*) that had tax franchises which were readily granted by the Ottoman rulers. Motivated in acquiring "fiefs" (*timar*s) on the newly conquered lands, members of the military elite or volunteer raiders (*akinci*) on the frontiers were relentlessly pushing the conquests in a westerly direction.

EXPANSION OF THE OTTOMANS INTO EUROPE

It is equally true that the collapse or weakening of central powers in Iran, Byzantium, and the Balkans (partitioning of the powerful Greek-Serbian empire of Stefan Dušan after his death in 1355) facilitated the Ottoman expansion. The Ottomans first occupied a bridgehead on European soil in 1352 (Tzympe) as allies of Emperor John VI Kantakouzenos, and under the leadership of Süleyman Pasha they vigorously pushed forward by establishing marches for raiders and encouraging Turkish settlement. With the fall of Adrianople (Edirne) in 1361, Ottoman possession of Thrace became an established fact. Now Constantinople itself was threatened by the Turks. The crusade plans in the West gave priority to saving the imperial city from the Turkish threat over the deliverance of the Holy Land. When the Turkish raiders reached the Adriatic coast, Pope Gregory XI (1370–1378) declared that Italy itself was under threat and admitted that the first task of any crusaders' army was to push the Turks back to Asia Minor. The pope's failure in organizing a crusade, together with the defeat of a Serbian army that marched on Edirne in 1371 while the Byzantines threatened the rear of Sultan Murad I (1362–1389) in Pegae on the Sea of Marmara, made the sultan master of the Balkans. Thereupon the Serbian and Bulgarian princes as well as the Byzantine emperor John V Palaiologos (1341–1391) recognized him as their suzerain. This is the decisive moment for the transformation of the Ottoman frontier principality into an empire.

The success in the Balkans made Murad I predominant also in Asia Minor. The only powers that were still able to challenge the Ottomans were the Hungarian monarchy and Venice, the former in the northern Balkans (Danubian Bulgaria, Serbia, and Bosnia) and the latter in Albania, the Morea, and the Aegean. Under Bāyazīd I (1389–1402) the Ottomans defeated Hungary (the Crusade of Nicopolis, 1396), established their control over Albania, and successfully fought Venetian influence in the Morea. Bāyazīd I created a threatening sea power against Venice when he annexed the western Anatolian principalities (1389–1392) and took over and reorganized their navies. He also turned Gallipoli in a powerful naval base, which the Venetians attempted to destroy in 1416, 1429, and 1444. The growth of the Ottoman navy is of decisive importance for the rise of the Ottoman Empire, but the navy could challenge Venetian power on the open sea only by the end of the fifteenth century.

THE OTTOMAN ARMY

By 1400 the Ottoman army consisted of two components: the first included recruits from the peasant population or Muslim *azaps* (*azebs*), who succeeded the early voluntary Turkoman fighters, and when need arose also included Christian *cerehors* (hired soldiers) as well as the *reaya* peasant groups organized for temporary military service (Muslim *yaya* and *müsellems*, Christian *voyniks*). Organized in units of a certain number of households, these groups had to equip fighters for the imperial army in return for tax exemptions. Turkomans and *azebs* were known as formidable archers with their double compound long-range bows, which were employed as late as the sixteenth century until the musket made them obsolete.

The second component included the standing army in the capital and the provincial *sipahis*, cavalrymen who were granted by the sultan a kind of fief (*timar*) in the provinces. During campaigns they joined the sultan's army under *beylerbeyi*, governor-generals. The standing army was under the direct command of the sultan. In addition to the Janissary corps or infantry, the standing army included cavalry and artillery divisions, an armory corps, and a corps of war (canon) wagons. The standing army divisions received salaries directly from the central treasury. The provincial *sipāhīs* and standing army made up a professional military group as distinct from the soldiers of the *reaya* origin in the first category. As *kapikulu*, that is "the Sultan's slaves," these military men formed a privileged elite above all the *reaya* groups. The sultan chose the agents of executive power exclusively from among the *kapikulu*. Slaves, war captives, and periodic levies of Christian boys (or *devshirme*) from the *reaya* were the source of manpower for the *kapikulu*, whose number was over twenty thousand under Mehmed II (1444–1446 and 1451–1481).

THE OTTOMAN DYNASTY

The Ottoman family had a key importance in the whole Ottoman system. The Ottoman state was a dynastic state, that is, a political structure which originally owed its formation to the initiative of a leader and in which the charismatic founder succeeded in establishing for his offspring an absolute control over political power. Succeeding members of the family were successful in consolidating this control so that the ruling elite and the state itself identified themselves with this dynasty. Later, the Ottoman government came to be referred to as the "Sublime Porte," which originally meant the place where the sultan heard suits and conducted government business.

As in the Eurasian Turko-Mongol khanates, the sons of an Ottoman sultan all had the same and equal right to succeed their father to the throne. Because it was an old custom and belief that God arranged and determined who is to ultimately gain sovereignty, no human law or arrangement was allowed to interfere with divine will. Wills and particular arrangements for succession of an Ottoman sultan were always ignored after his death. If one of the brothers of a new sultan succeeded in overpowering him, he was recognized as the legitimate sultan. Islamic *bayᶜa*, a formal contractual agreement of a group on behalf of the Islamic community in electing the caliph, did not replace this Turko-Mongol practice. Consequently, at the death of each sultan, or even before his death, the struggle for succession began among the brothers, often degenerating into a civil war. The transition period was always the most dangerous time for the whole society. The Ottoman Empire experienced civil war and the danger of dismemberment at the deaths of Bāyazīd I, Mehmed I, and Mehmed II; war between brothers broke out under Bāyazīd II and Süleyman I. Enemies of the Ottomans, Venice, Hungary, and the papacy, exploited this critical situation in the Ottoman Empire. An Ottoman pretender, Prince Orhan, fought against Mehmed II at the walls of Constantinople in 1453. Popes Innocent VIII and Alexander VI made plans to use Jem Sultan in a crusade against his brother Bāyazīd II. Thus, the practice by the sultan of killing his brothers in order to "secure the good order of the world" was regarded as something "permissible," and the provision was inserted into the law code of the Conqueror. Under Murad III (1574–1595), the practice of sending the princes out to the provinces as governors was modified and only the eldest son, Mehmed, enjoyed this privilege, which made him an heir apparent. But when on his accession to the throne Mehmed III (1595–1603) murdered his nineteen brothers, including infants, it shocked the people of the empire. By this time, the old Turko-Mongol customs and beliefs had long lost their power and influence. Under the sultans after Mehmed III, brothers were still killed, but some of them—minors or those who were not considered to be potential rivals—were spared. Gradually, the seniority principle began to be followed.

THE GROWTH OF THE EMPIRE

In official language the state was called *Devlet-i Osmaniyye,* the Ottoman state, or *Devlet-i Aliyye,* the empire. As an entity separate from the state itself, the lands and population under the Ottoman dynasty were referred to as *memalik-i mahruse,* "well-protected lands," that is, against tyranny and exploitation of local lords and attack of foreign enemies. From the beginning the state was thus identified with the Ottoman dynasty or the sovereignty of the reigning Ottoman sultan. At the death of a sultan, all titles to office, land possession or privilege became null and void and renewal by a diploma of the new sultan was necessary. This concept of the Ottoman state was later formulated as *Osmanlîlîk* (Ottomanism). Ottomanism was shaped by the Islamic ideology, which considered the absolute power of the ruler simply an instrument for realizing the prescriptions of Islamic law and made him responsible for the good and prosperity of the whole community.

The self-image of the Ottoman sultans and their concept of state evolved as their empire grew. Osman, the founder of the dynasty, had the title of *ghāzī,* warrior for Islam, while from Orkhan's time (1324–1362) all the Ottoman rulers used the Islamic title of sultan, which denoted an independent ruler within the Islamic world (independence was symbolized by minting coins with the sultan's name and by mention of the sultan's name by the preacher in the ceremonial prayers in the mosques on Fridays). The idea of supreme ruler appeared with Murad I with the title of *hüdavendigar,* which was soon replaced by more popular title of padishah. Aspiring to be an heir to the Seljuk sultanate in Asia Minor, Bāyazīd I (1389–1402) asked the caliph in Cairo to confer on him the title of *Sultan al-Rūm,* which had been used by the Seljuk sultans and meant the ruler of the lands of Eastern Roman Empire.

It took half a century of struggle to restore Bāyazīd's empire in Asia Minor and the Balkans following his defeat at the hands of Tamerlane and the dismemberment of his empire in 1402. Mehmet II the Conqueror (1444–1446 and 1451–1481) realized Bāyazīd's aspirations by conquering Constantinople (29 May 1453), Serbia (1454–1459), the Morea (1458–1460), Trebizond (1461), Bosnia (1463), Euboea (1470), and Moldavia (1476), and putting an end to the Turkish principalities in Asia Minor. It was he, a prototype of an Ottoman padishah, who created in its ultimate form the centralized Ottoman Empire, with the most powerful families monopolizing the high posts in the government and the frontier commanders leaving their places to the sultan's *kul*s. Mehmed II styled himself *Fatih,* the conqueror of the seat of the Eastern Roman Empire, the sultan of two lands (Asia Minor and the Balkans) and two seas (the Aegean and the Black Sea). He and his followers included among their titles the title of *kayser* (Caesar). Claiming to be the heir to the Roman Empire, he gained a bridgehead in Italy by conquering Otranto in 1480 and was prepared to conquer Rome. He is also the first Muslim sultan to codify secular laws concerning public administration side by side with the Islamic law. Being an open-minded ruler, he borrowed and considerably improved Western war technology, created a powerful navy by using Western and Greek experts, and reconstructed the ruined city of Constantinople as a new Ottoman-Turkish city. A city of 30,000 or 40,000 before the conquest, İstanbul developed into a large metropolis of about 200,000 people by 1500.

The Conqueror also aspired to primacy in the Islamic world as the victor over Christendom. This led him to challenge the Mamluk sultan of Egypt, whose primacy in Islam as the protector of Mecca and Medina had hitherto been effectively uncontested.

It was his grandson Selim I (1512–1520) who put an end to Mamluk rule in Syria and Egypt (1516–1517) and took the title of the servant of the two sacred cities (of Mecca and Medina). His son Süleyman (Suleiman) the Law-giver, or Magnificent (1520–1566), could claim the worldwide protection of Islam's lands and fight against the *Shīᶜa* heterodoxy in Islam. He employed in this sense the title of the caliph of all Muslims. From this time on the Ottoman state was transformed gradually into a classical Islamic caliphate in its policies and institutions; frontier traditions and Mehmed II's secular public laws gave way over time to Islamic law, applied more strictly than ever before. Ottoman power and influence in the Islamic world continued to rest, however, on the Ottoman frontier tradition, that is, on the defense and expansion of Islam. The sultans of Gujarat in India and Atche in Sumatra and the khans of Turkestan appealed to the Ottoman sultan for aid against the Portuguese and Russians, respectively, in the second half of the sixteenth century. The original Islamic idea of one caliphate over the whole Islamic world was fully resurrected by the Ottoman sultans only in the eighteenth century as a diplomatic instrument against Iran and Russia.

SOCIAL STRUCTURE

Combining a Turko-Mongol, Middle Eastern–Islamic, and Byzantine-Balkan heritage, Ottoman society was molded primarily by the existense of a militaristic, authoritarian, and centralized power. A major factor in the emergence of this power was the frontier tradition and constant necessity to fight against Western Christendom, but later, the heavy financial burden and pressure that this military might brought upon the economy and the society became the cause of its decline.

At the top of the Ottoman social pyramid was the ruling military-bureaucratic group, the *askeri,* which not only had political power but also controlled the most important economic resources—land and agriculture, mines and interregional trade. The most widespread form of capitalization of wealth was turning land and cash into *waqf*s, or pious foundations, and maintaining family control over them.

The function of the *reaya,* the productive and tax-paying subjects, was to support the power of the state. In return, the sovereign was considered responsible before God for protecting the *reaya* against injustices and for guiding them in the path of the true faith. The *reaya* were divided hierarchically into merchants, farmers, and artisans. The good order and prosperity of the world, it was believed, depended on the ruler's success in keeping every class or estate in its own compartment.

Although it was a fundamental principle that the *askeri* and *reaya* remained distinct, there was quite a high degree of social mobility. The state's need for manpower and skills kept the ranks of the ruling elite open to people of any origin, since the sultan's decision made it possible for the members of the *reaya* groups to move to the higher echelons in the social structure. By a simple decree the sultan could bestow the highest privileges on a humble person—as he could also abolish all the privileges of another person.

Even during its decline the Ottoman state was able substantially to preserve its control over agricultural lands and maintain its agrarian system based on small agricultural units cultivated by peasant families. The state's resistance to the changes in the system of land tenure in the countryside and in that of the guilds in the towns kept the Ottoman social structure, particularly in the Balkans and Asia Minor, almost intact in its medieval backwardness until the nineteenth century.

NON-MUSLIMS UNDER THE OTTOMANS

In general, the non-Muslims (Christians and Jews) under the Ottomans enjoyed the dhimmi status as prescribed by Islamic law. In other words, as subjects of the Islamic state, they were free in the exercise of their religion and had protection from the state for their lives and properties. They could freely circulate in the Ottoman territories. As dhimmis, however, they had to pay an extra poll tax or *jizya* and were subjected to certain restrictions in their way of life. Following the Hanafīyya school of law and originating from a frontier society, the Ottoman state proved to be one of the most tolerant in Islamic history. In the cities each non-Muslim community lived in its own quarter organized around its district church or synagogue. While segregation was in force in the residential part of the city, people of every religion worked and traded together without discrimination in the commercial sector. Non-Muslim and Muslim artisans or traders were members of the same guilds. Religious-social outbursts of the Muslim population against non-Muslims occasionally occurred, but the state attempted to prevent such situations by stationing Janissary garrisons in the cities in order to protect the non-Muslims.

As under the Abbasid caliphate before it, the Ottomans recognized church organizations under their religious heads as autonomous entities in the Islamic state. The practice was that the synod first elected a patriarch and then the sultan recognized and appointed him by a special diploma (*berat*) as the religious head of the community. In his diploma the sultan ordered the congregation to recognize and obey the patriarch as their religious head. The members of the community were considered first as the dhimmi subjects of the sultan and the sultan empowered the head of the community in his religious authority and responsibilities over it. The patriarch could be deposed and punished by the sultan upon a complaint of the community or upon committing a criminal act, however, as could any appointee of the sultan.

The Ottomans recognized and protected the Greek Orthodox church from the beginning as a part of the state organization. Official records show the appointment of Orthodox metropolitans under Murad II (1421–1444, 1446–1451). They were even granted *timars* (fiefs) as state appointees. This systematic Ottoman policy facilitated Ottoman expansion no less than other factors. Mehmed the Conqueror reestablished the Greek Orthodox patriarchate (which had lapsed after the conquest in May 1453) by appointing Gennadius II patriarch on January 6, 1454, "with all the privileges" enjoyed by the patriarchs under the Byzantine emperors. He also appointed an Armenian patriarch for his Armenian subjects and is supposed to have organized the Jews under a chief rabbi as well. Under state protocol, the Orthodox church took precedence over other Christian groups or churches. No such organization was recognized for the Latins in the empire.

BIBLIOGRAPHY

Franz C. H. Babinger, *Mehmed the Conqueror and His Time,* Ralph Manheim, trans., William C. Hickman, ed. (1978); Joseph von Hammer-Purgstall, *Geschichte des osmanischen Reiches,* 10 vols. (1827–1835), the most detailed treatment of the subject, but superseded in many parts; Halil Inalcik, *The Ottoman Empire: The Classical Age, 1300–1600* (1973), and *The Ottoman Empire: Conquest, Organization, and Economy* (1978); Kenneth M. Setton, *The Papacy and the Levant (1204–1571),* I (1976), II (1978).

HALIL INALCIK

[See also **Abode of Islam—Abode of War; Anatolia; Bāyāzid I; Bāyāzid II; Ghāzī; Ilkhanids; Janissary; John VI Kantakouzenos; Mehmed I; Mehmed II; Minorities; Murad I; Murad II; Osman I; Selim I; Seljuks; Seljuks of Rūm; Sultan; Tamerlane; Waqf.**]

OTTONIAN ARCHITECTURE. See **Pre-Romanesque Architecture.**

OTTONIAN ART. See **Pre-Romanesque Art.**

OTTONIANS. See **Saxon Dynasty.**

OUNCE, a unit of weight in the British Isles used in the apothecary, avoirdupois, mercantile, tower, and English and Scots troy systems. The apothecary ounce contained 24 scruples, or 8 drams, or 480 troy grains (31.103 grams), and was equal to 1/12 apothecary pound of 5,760 grains. The avoirdupois ounce contained 437.5 grains (28.350 grams) and was equal to 1/16 avoirdupois pound of 7,000 grains. The mercantile and tower ounces contained 450 grains (29.160 grams), but the mercantile ounce equaled 1/15 mercantile pound of 6,750 grains, while the tower ounce equaled 1/12 tower pound of 5,400 grains. Both ounces were determined as 20 pennyweights, the pennyweight being 32 wheat grains (equal to 22.5 troy grains or barleycorns); hence, each mercantile or tower ounce equaled 640 wheat grains or 450 troy grains or barleycorns. The Scots troy ounce contained 475.5 grains (30.812 grams) or 16 drops of 29.72 grains each, and was equal to 1/16 Scots troy pound of 7,609 grains. The English troy ounce contained 480 grains (31.103 grams) and was equal to 1/12 troy pound of 5,760 grains. Consisting of 20 pennyweights of 24 grains each, the English troy ounce was 30 grains heavier than the mercantile and tower ounces and 42.5 grains heavier than the avoirdupois ounce. It was also the standard for the apothecary ounce of 480 grains, the only difference being that the apothecary ounce was divided into 8 drams of 60 grains each or 24 scruples of 20 grains each, while the troy ounce was divided into 20 pennyweights of 24 grains each. Etymologically, it was derived ultimately from Latin *uncia*, a twelfth, the twelfth part, ounce, inch.

RONALD EDWARD ZUPKO

[See also **Weights and Measures, Western European**.]

OUTER CRYPT. See **Crypt.**

OUTLAWRY (English law). In law, outlawry (*utlagaria*) is the act of placing a person outside the law. Outlawry is frequently found in archaic legal systems. It is characteristic of those systems with a weak central authority and little or no policing power. Outlawry is thought to be the most ancient of all legal penalties.

In English law the earliest references to outlaws that indicate some judicial process date from the early tenth century. It is likely that the use of outlawry was introduced to Anglo-Saxon law by way of contact with Scandinavian invaders. Until well after the Norman Conquest outlawry was used only against those who by fleeing refused to stand trial for felonies, the most serious criminal offenses. The process began in the county court. There the victim or injured party launched a personal appeal against the accused. If the "appelle" was not in court, the sheriff then exacted or demanded him at the four successive county court sessions in a prolonged attempt to force the suspect to answer his accuser. If he failed to appear after the fourth exaction the dread sentence of outlawry was pronounced upon him. He must "bear the wolf's head" in the picturesque but ominous words of a thirteenth-century plea roll.

The declaration of outlawry in Anglo-Saxon law was a sentence of death. The accused defied the community by flight: the community went to war against him. It was no more a crime to kill an outlaw than to kill an wolf; indeed, it was everyman's duty to do so. To knowingly harbor an outlaw was a capital crime. As the growth of royal power in England made the king a more effective guarantor of peace and justice, the outlaw's flight was seen as defiance of the king as well as the community. Therefore the king should have the outlaw's chattels and a year and a day waste of his land.

In English law only adult males could be outlawed, because only males twelve years of age or more put themselves within the law by an oath when they enrolled in a tithing. A similar but little used procedure for women was called waiver.

By the end of the twelfth century two new procedures were being used which led to outlawry. First, the king, in addition to injured parties, was instituting appeals against suspected criminals. Second, the juries created by the Assize of Clarendon in 1166 were being sworn to present the names of men suspected of serious crimes to the justices. Both procedures resulted in a writ *exigi facias* being sent to the sheriff, and this began the process of exaction already described. The result was a large increase in the number of outlaws.

Inevitably there were instances where men were outlawed but guilty of no crime or intentional contumacy, as for example when a supposed victim turned up alive and well or when the exaction went unheeded because it took place in a county distant from the home of the accused. This gave rise to royal writs which inlawed outlaws. Henry de Bracton, writing in the first half of the thirteenth century, discussed these writs and their effects. An inlawed man was not restored to his former status, but, in Bracton's words, "he is, as it were a child newly born and a man newly created" (*f.* 132b).

In addition to its role as a punishment, outlawry was a procedure designed to encourage appearance in court. The four successive exactions gave the accused time to ponder his chances in court. How successful outlawry was in this respect is not known. The county court was not a court of written record in the Middle Ages, and there is no sure way to determine how many accused appeared before the sheriff's final exaction. We do know, however, that the procedure was much used. Maitland estimated that in the king's eyres ten men were outlawed for each man hanged.

But whether or not the procedure was successful in bringing accused felons to court, outlawry was bound to be considered as a way of combating contumacy in other litigation. As is well known, medieval law was most reluctant to convict in the absence of the defendant. Therefore, plaintiffs eagerly sought any process that could put pressure on the defendant. Moreover, the threat of outlawry could be expected to have better results in nonfelonious litigation. An accused felon might well consider flight a desirable alternative, but plaintiffs in suits whose loss had less serious consequences were less likely to do so.

During the first half of the thirteenth century the courts began to recognize outlawry as an appropriate remedy in trespass cases. Nearly always the trespass was alleged to have been committed *vi et armis* (by force of arms). This gave the suit at least an appearance of peace-breaking, and that may have been the original argument for extending outlawry to trespass. In the late thirteenth century the use of outlawry was further extended by statute. In 1285 it was deemed appropriate in actions of account. The fourteenth century saw its use extended to actions of debt, detinue, and replevin. The statute of Praemunire of 1353 prescribed as punishment for those suing in the Roman curia for matters cognizable in the king's courts that they should be outlawed, lose lands and goods, and be imprisoned. This strange conjunction of outlawry and imprisonment is found again in 1382, when two commissions of the peace were ordered to imprison outlaws. Perhaps this was due to the large number of them in the wake of the Peasants' Revolt (1381).

Of course the more frequent use of outlawry meant that its harsher aspects were limited. According to Bracton, outlaws might not be slain unless they resisted arrest. Nonetheless it is somewhat surprising to find that by the fourteenth century imprisonment was thought suitable for outlaws. Outlawry, once equivalent to a sentence of death, became but one of a large number of procedures whose major aim was to combat contumacy. In the later medieval courts its use was the subject of much clever argument among the attorneys and judges of the king's courts. Outlawry lingered on in English law until 1879 in civil cases and was only abolished in criminal proceedings in 1938.

BIBLIOGRAPHY

Henry de Bracton, *On the Laws and Customs of England,* Samuel E. Thorne, trans., 4 vols. (1968–1977); Julius Goebel, *Felony and Misdemeanor* (1937); F. Liebermann, "Die Friedlosigkeit bei den Angelsachsen," in F. Liebermann, ed., *Festschrift Heinrich Brunner* (1910); Frederick Pollock and Frederic W. Maitland, *The History of English Law,* 2nd ed., 2 vols. (repr. 1985); Ralph B. Pugh, "Early Registers of English Outlaws," in *The American Journal of Legal History,* 27 (1983), and *Imprisonment in Medieval England* (1968).

T. A. SANDQUIST

[See also **Bracton, Henry de; Clarendon, Assize of; Jury; Justices, Itinerant; Law: English Common; Tithes; Trespass.**]

OUWATER, ALBERT VAN (*fl. ca.* 1445–1480), according to tradition, the founder of the early Haarlem school of painting. Little is known of his life, and only one painting, *Raising of Lazarus* (Berlin, *ca.* 1445–1450), is a certain attribution. Ouwater's figures closely resemble those of Dirk Bouts, another early Haarlem painter, and he is said to have excelled in landscape painting, but none survives. According to the early-seventeenth-century Dutch art historian Carel van Mander, Ouwater was the master of Geertgen tot Sint Jans, but this association is today questioned by many scholars.

BIBLIOGRAPHY

Carel van Mander, *Het Schilderboeck* (1604), translated by Constant Van de Wall as *Dutch and Flemish Painters* (1936).

JAMES SNYDER

[See also **Bouts, Dirk; Geertgen tot Sint Jans.**]

OVID IN THE MIDDLE AGES. Ovid (Publius Ovidius Naso, 43 B.C. – A.D. 17), the most sophis-

OVID IN THE MIDDLE AGES

ticated Roman poet of the Augustan age, composed works that were extensively copied, imitated, translated, and allegorized during the Middle Ages. Although his tragedy *Medaea* and perhaps an exercise in the Gothic language are lost, Ovid's writings have been well preserved by monastic copyists. The surviving text of the largely mythological miracles narrated in the *Metamorphoses* is based on three eleventh-century manuscripts. The brilliant early erotic elegiacs of the *Amores, Ars amatoria,* and the *Remedia amoris* are preserved in copies from the ninth and tenth centuries. For the romantic heroines' legends of the *Heroides,* there are texts from the ninth and twelfth centuries and a fragment from the eleventh. The catalog of Roman festivals in the *Fasti* is attested by two copies of the tenth and eleventh centuries. Ovid's poetical complaints from exile appear in the *Tristia,* for which there exists a tenth-century fragment and an eleventh-century copy, and in the *Epistulae ex Ponto,* preserved in a fragment of the sixth century and three manuscripts of the twelfth. Finally, Ovid's minor works, *De medicamine faciei,* the *Nux, Ibis, Halieuticon,* and the *Consolatio ad Liviam,* are witnessed by copies from the ninth to the fifteenth centuries.

For his rhetorical employment of the elegiac couplet and mythological subject matter in the service of love, Ovid served as the model par excellence for Latin verse throughout the Middle Ages. Among the scholars who came from all over Western Europe to the court and royal school of Charlemagne were such poets as Modoin, bishop of Autun (815, *d.* 840/843), who took the name "Naso" and celebrated Charles as the new Augustus. Modoin was in turn complimented by Florus, deacon of Lyon (*d. ca.* 860), in a long epistle borrowing from most of Ovid's works. This court devotion to Ovid was continued in the French cathedral schools by such poets as Godfrey of Rheims (*d.* 1095), who composed a long elegiac and allusive description of a beautiful lady. Such elegiac matter is combined with biblical learning in the work of Hildebert of Lavardin (*d.* 1133), but the peak of secularization can be seen in the poems of Baudri of Bourgueil, archbishop of Dol from 1107 to 1130, whose two epistles—"Florus to Ovid" and "Ovid to Florus"—are sophisticated school exercises based on the *Tristia.*

In the twelfth century—called the *aetas Ovidiana*—a new literary genus, the *comoedia* or versified tale, appears in the cathedral schools. The best

Jupiter, Mars, and Venus (with Cupid, doves, nymphs, and husband Vulcan fashioning the net to snare Mars and the unfaithful Venus). Miniature from a 15th-century Chaucerian MS of tales in the Ovidian tradition. COURTESY OF THE BODLEIAN LIBRARY, OXFORD, MS FAIRFAX 16, fol. 14v

example of these plain elegiac Latin narratives with happy endings is the *Pamphilus,* in which Venus instructs a youth in the craft of Love and a repulsive crone acts as go-between. In the twelfth-century poetical debate *The Love-Council of Remiremont,* Ovid becomes simply a name to conjure with. There, nuns assemble to decide whether knights or clerks are better lovers; first the gospel of Ovid is read, and then the presiding lady, *cardinalis domina,* puts the question to the assembly, which debates the issue and finds for the clerks and anathematizes all others. Ovid also influenced the goliardic poets of the late twelfth and thirteenth centuries, being linked with Hugh Primas of Orléans as one of the champions of Grammar. One of their poems typically urges the medieval Ovid's moral usefulness:

OVID IN THE MIDDLE AGES

> Auctoris intentio restat condemnare
> amores illicitos, fatuos culpare
> et recte ferventium mentes commendare:
> utilitas nostra sit iustum pignis amare.

Similarly, the lyrics of the *Carmina burana* (thirteenth century), while certainly not rhetorical exercises in elegiacs, reveal in their easy use of mythology in behalf of love their own mastery of Ovid. Another work from this period is the pseudo-Ovidian tale *De vetula* (between 1222 and 1266/1268), which presents Ovid as a Christian convert.

Western vernacular poetry also reveals Ovid's prodigious influence. The complex medieval conception of romantic love, for example, contains a heavy Ovidian component, centering on the mutuality and transforming power of the erotic experience. Such stories as those of Echo and Narcissus, Philomela, and Pyramus and Thisbe appear in Old French, German, and Netherlandish versions, and later in such works as the *L'amorosa Fiammetta* of Boccaccio, *The Legend of Good Women* of Chaucer, for whom Ovid was "Venus' Clerk," and the *Confessio Amantis* of John Gower. This vernacular Ovidian vogue passed undiminished into Renaissance poetry and art.

Although the Latin elegiac comedies were not translated, they do appear in the same contexts as the vernacular adaptations, along with the fabliaux. Chrétien de Troyes translated the *Ars amatoria,* and, though the work is lost, its influence is apparent in his Arthurian romances. Four other French translations of the *Ars* do survive from the thirteenth and fourteenth centuries; three versions of the *Remedia,* one from the early thirteenth century, a second one *ca.* 1300, and the third *ca.* 1380; and two of the *Heroides,* from the fifteenth century. Lactantius Placidus made a prose paraphrase of the *Metamorphoses* in the pre-Carolingian period. Albert von Halberstadt translated the *Metamorphoses* into German (probably 1210–1220), the first complete translation into German, and perhaps into any European vernacular, of one of the major works of classical literature. The *Metamorphoses* also appears in two anonymous French translations and was elaborated into the *Ovide moralisé*'s 70,000 verses of Christianizing moralization, reflecting the vigor of Latin commentary on the poem throughout the Middle Ages.

The medieval allegorical tradition of exegesis is indebted to Ovid, beginning with a lost poetic-mystical commentary of Manegold of Lautenbach (eleventh century) and extending through the glosses of John of Garland, Arnulf of Orleans (perhaps himself the author of *comoediae*), Pierre Bersuire, and Giovanni del Virgilio, to such late uses as John Calderia's *Concordances* in the fifteenth century. This stable tradition consists of narrative summaries that tend to become more realistic as the commentaries based on them become more explicitly Christian with the passage of time. Such glosses both influenced the vernacular poets and allowed friars like John Ridevall (*fl.* early 1300's) to provide, in his *Fulgentius metaphoralis,* a handbook for preachers that made exempla of virtue and vice out of the erotic urbanity of Ovid's verse. Thus, by the end of the Middle Ages, Ovid was available in varieties ranging from faithful transcriptions of his elegiac distichs, through vernacular adaptations that placed him in the courtly company of loyal lovers, to pious glosses of his bare plots.

BIBLIOGRAPHY

E. H. Alton, "Ovid in the Medieval Schoolroom," in *Hermathena,* **94** (1960); Lester K. Born, "Ovid and Allegory," in *Speculum,* **9** (1934); Paule Demats, *Fabula* (1973); John M. Fyler, *Chaucer and Ovid* (1979); Thomas J. Garbaty, "*Pamphilus, de Amore:* An Introduction and Translation," in *Chaucer Review,* **2** (1967); Fausto Ghisalberti, "Mediaeval Biographies of Ovid," in *Journal of the Warburg and Courtauld Institutes,* **9** (1946); Foster E. Guyer, "The Influence of Ovid on Crestien de Troyes," in *Romanic Review,* **12** (1921); Robert H. Lucas, "Medieval French Translations of the Latin Classics to 1500," in *Speculum,* **45** (1970), 241–244; Franco Munari, *Ovid im Mittelalter* (1960); Ettore Paratore, *Bibliografia Ovidiana* (1958); Frederic J. E. Raby, *A History of Secular Latin Poetry in the Middle Ages,* 2 vols., rev. ed. (1957); Edward K. Rand, *Ovid and His Influence* (1925); Dorothy M. Robathan, *The Pseudo-Ovidian "De Vetula"* (1968); C. A. Robson, "Dante's Use in the *Divina Commedia* of the Medieval Allegories on Ovid," in Colin G. Hardie, ed., *Centenary Essays on Dante* (1965); Bruno Roy, "Arnulf of Orléans and the Latin 'Comedy,'" in *Speculum,* **49** (1974); Jean Seznec, *The Survival of the Pagan Gods* (1953).

RICHARD A. DWYER

[See also **Albrecht von Halberstadt; Allegory; Baudri of Bourgueil; Carmina Burana; Courtly Love; Exegesis, Latin; Godfrey of Rheims; Goliards; Manegold of Lautenbach.**]

OVIDE MORALISÉ. This anonymous 72,000-line French poem from the early fourteenth century reconciles Ovid's *Metamorphoses* with Christian doctrine through allegorical interpretation. Evenly divided between fables and moralization, the text presents many expansions of Ovid's tales and some fables not in Ovid but provided by the copious marginalia in thirteenth-century "editions" of Ovid. Pierre Bersuire began an independent Latin version around 1340. The tradition continues in a fifteenth-century prose summary of the French version, Mansion's *Ovide moralisé,* and Vérard's *Bible des poètes.* The French metrical version preserves Chrétien de Troyes's *Philomena* and was used extensively by Machaut, Chaucer, and Christine de Pizan.

BIBLIOGRAPHY

Paule Demats, *Fabula: Trois études de mythographie antique et médiévale* (1973); *"Ovide moralisé": Poème du commencement du quatorzième siècle,* C. De Boer, ed., 5 vols. (1915–1938).

DANIEL RUSSELL

[See also **Allegory, French; Chaucer, Geoffrey; Chrétien de Troyes; Christine de Pizan; French Literature; Machaut, Guillaume de.**]

OWAIN GWYNEDD (Owain Fawr) (*r.* 1137–1170), king of Gwynedd, in northern Wales. Upon the death of his father, Gruffudd ap Cynan, in 1137, Owain succeeded to the throne of Gwynedd. Known as Owain Gwynedd to distinguish him from Owain (ap Gruffudd) or Cyfeiliog, he also gained for himself the richly deserved title of Owain Fawr (the Great). A man of excellent character and a ruler of outstanding ability, his leadership provided the strength to foil further Anglo-Norman ambitions in Wales.

Even before his father's death, Owain had shown his mettle by winning Rhos and Rhufoniog in 1118, Dyffryn Clwyd in 1124, and Meirionydd in 1123, aided by his brothers, Cadwallon (*d.* 1132) and the troublesome Cadwaladr (*d.* 1172). After his accession he extended and consolidated his territories even more to include Tegeingl, which stretched to the River Dee. This he did despite Cadwaladr's alliances against him and the wars waged by Henry II.

Owain's greatest triumph came in 1164. Ever since Henry II's campaign of 1157, fought with the aid of Madog ap Maredudd of Powys (*d.* 1160), Owain had been biding his time. Rhys ap Gruffudd's rebellion in 1164 against Henry II gave Owain his chance to fight again. Owain's alliance with Rhys prompted all the lesser Welsh princes to join "with one accord" against Henry, who had decided to crush Welsh resistance once and for all. But faced with Owain's united front, Henry abandoned totally his conquest without even engaging the Welsh in battle. Although the alliance was shortlived, Welsh independence was saved.

Owain also faced conflict from another quarter, the church. By stubbornly maintaining the independence of Gwynedd's see of Bangor, he incurred the wrath not only of Henry, but of the archbishop of Canterbury, Thomas Becket, and the pope as well.

After Bishop Meurig of Bangor's death in 1161, Owain had his own candidate, Arthur of Bardsey, consecrated bishop in Ireland (1166) against the express commands of all concerned. Owain's stubborness regarding the church also extended to his personal life. Although his marriage to his first cousin, Cristin, was within the forbidden degrees of kinship, he would not repudiate her. Both matters led to his excommunication. Despite this, he was buried in Bangor Cathedral after his death on 23 November 1170.

BIBLIOGRAPHY

Paul Barbier, *The Age of Owain Gwynedd* (1908); James Conway Davies, ed., *Episcopal Acts and Cognate Documents Relating to Welsh Dioceses, 1066–1272,* II (1948), 415–443; John E. Lloyd, *A History of Wales from the Earliest Times to the Edwardian Conquest,* II (1911, repr. 1948), 487–535; Albert Hughes Williams, *An Introduction to the History of Wales,* II, *The Middle Ages,* pt. 1 (1948), 1–10, 28–61.

MARILYN KAY KENNEY

[See also **Bangor (Wales); Becket, Thomas, St.; Cynnddelw Brydydd Mawr; Gruffudd ap Cynan; Wales: History.**]

OWL AND THE NIGHTINGALE, THE, a Middle English *débat* poem contained in two of the Petit Plet manuscripts (British Library and Jesus College, Oxford). The importance of this medieval

OWL AND THE NIGHTINGALE

English poem depends on an undemonstrable literary judgment universally held by medievalists in the field of English studies: that it is a work of rare and balanced humor of a quality not found elsewhere before the age of Chaucer and *Sir Gawain and the Green Knight* (*ca.* 1375–1400). It makes use of fabliau material, yet achieves refinement beyond that of the fabliaux, which are not well represented in English. It also makes use of the material of the beast fable, combining in the characters of the two birds avian characteristics and habits of life with human morality and intellectual aspirations; but it is more expansive than the fable.

In form it is a debate. It was recognized as such in the Middle Ages, for one of the two extant manuscripts, Oxford MS Jesus College 29, calls it *Altercatio inter filomenam et bubonem,* and a now lost manuscript (once belonging to Titchfield Abbey, Hampshire) had in it a work, presumably *The Owl and the Nightingale,* to which the early-fifteenth-century catalog refers as *De conflictu inter philomenam et bubonem in anglicis.* The poem shares with some Latin specimens of this literary kind—for example, the debates of Wine and Water and of Summer and Winter—a general assumption of a Christian morality together with a refusal to pass judgment at the end. Debates, too, are a literary kind not well represented in English.

Assessments of the poem often turn on its date of composition, which, like its provenance, is not a matter of certainty. The poem survives in two manuscripts (London, British Library, MS Cotton Caligula A9; Oxford, Jesus College MS 29 [since 1886 deposited in the Bodleian Library]). The manuscripts are closely related in content. Both contain most of the extant poetry of the Anglo-Norman poet Chardri (perhaps *ri-Chard* inverted, *fl.* early thirteenth century), which has affinities with our poem. Both are the products of professional scribes working in the Southwest Midlands at about the same time in the second half of the thirteenth century. It used to be thought that the Caligula MS was of the early thirteenth century, and that dating influenced the scholarly dating of the composition of the poem. Paleographical dating was, rightly, regarded as more secure than linguistic or literary dating.

The subject of the poem is, especially for most of the first 1,290 of a total of 1,794 lines, much concerned with the art of song and what it is best to sing about. Even when the primary concern at some point seems to be with theological matter—sins and woman's special proclivity to sin, for example—the argument begins with and returns to the birds' treatment of such themes in song. The Nightingale and the Owl are both night birds, and their song goes out to lovers in the night. They both make excuses for and show sympathy with aspects of love outside wedlock. These sympathies are with the woman in love, but sexual relations are seen from the point of view of both the woman and the man. This is especially so in the Nightingale's long speech (lines 1,298–1,510) toward the end of which the man is addressed directly and his pleasure or dissatisfaction seen in terms of his sexual power. The Nightingale encourages and urges for pity's sake, and must not be blamed when, alas, such love teaching is misunderstood. According to the Owl, the Nightingale—who visits only when the sensual heat of summer is here—ceases the song when lust has been sated (497–522, compare line 1,470) and seeks to entice people to the lusts of the flesh (895–899). Both birds claim to have the confidence of ill-used wives, and by song and prayer encourage them to find consolation at least in the hope of the husband's death, for which the Owl offers fervent prayers to Christ (1,565–1,570). The Nightingale claims to hate adultery, and the Owl reminds us that a Nightingale was punished in life and limb for encouraging a wife's adultery in story (1,045–1,066)—which we know, as the poet may have known it, in Marie de France's *Laüstic.*

The birds are actors in the created world, of which mankind is highest under God and service to mankind the best duty of lower creatures, especially when they help man in the veneration of God. The bird's song is in tune with man's to God: doleful chanting in the Owl's and joyous hymning in the Nightingale's. The Owl's ululation bewails our lot in this vale of tears; the Nightingale's song anticipates and glorifies the joys of heaven.

> Wenest þu hi bringe so liȝtliche
> To Godes riche al singinge?

"Do you expect to bring them [mankind] so easily just with song to the kingdom of God?" the Owl asks the Nightingale (lines 854–855), and offers instead a regimen of wailing fitter for sinners: the subject of the debate is, in the first place, about who serves mankind best in the highest exercise of human talent, and how to fulfill our hope of salvation.

The emphasis in the poem on the joyfulness of song and its role in the Christian hope of salvation

OWL AND THE NIGHTINGALE

reminds the modern reader of Franciscan attitudes to worship. The Nightingale's joyful communication of the arrival of spring and the connection made between that and the joy of love strikes a note not much heard before in English poetry; yet, fresh though it may seem, it is interwoven with rebukes and vindications from rebukes in which a Christian devotion appears uppermost. The Franciscans came to England at the end of the first quarter of the thirteenth century. When the Caligula MS was dated to the first quarter of the thirteenth century, it seemed impossible that our poem might have been influenced by the Franciscans in England, all the more so since it is demonstrable that the Caligula MS (like the Jesus MS) is not the author's own, and almost certainly was copied from at least one intermediate copy. The revised paleographical dating of the manuscript, to the later thirteenth century, makes it possible that the poem is the product of the middle third of the century; it could therefore show a Nightingale directly influenced by Franciscan notions and an Owl rigorous in rejecting them.

Only two place-names are mentioned in the poem in a way to make it possible to connect them with the provenance of the poem, Guildford in Surrey and Portisham in Dorset. Both are referred to in connection with one Nicholas of Guildford who lives in Portisham, and who is to be the judge between the birds when they repeat their debate before him. In the thirteenth century both places were in the diocese of Salisbury; Nicholas is a common name, and there are men of that name to be found in the diocese at that time. Portisham, now a little village and then perhaps even smaller, was important: the monastery of Abbotsbury, then a Benedictine house, was close to Portisham both geographically and in landholding; and in an important early charter of the monastery, in English, Portisham is made to sound as if it might be a geographical name for the monastic site. The topography of Portisham and the coast a few miles away is described in some detail at the end of the poem; it seems a pretty accurate description of the location as it is now and does not require the assumption, in itself not impossible, that there may have been change in the last seven or eight centuries.

The birds' dispute ranges widely, and they agree on nothing except that they at once agree on the merits of Master Nicholas and, without argument, choose him to be their judge (189–214); the wisdom of that choice is confirmed by the Wren (1,751–1,768), who is renowned for wisdom. It is a shame, we learn, that Master Nicholas, who is wise, too, has not been preferred as his wisdom and learning deserve. Such unanimous praise, unique in the poem, has been regarded as evidence that Nicholas himself wrote the poem in an attempt to call attention urbanely to his neglected merits—but with a tinge of sharpness, because others less deserving but more nearly, too nearly, kin to those in power have fared better.

If he was the author writing in the dialect of either Surrey or Dorset of about the middle of the thirteenth century (or somewhat earlier), that would fit well with what we know of early Middle English dialectology, for which the rhymes and the vocabulary are among the better sources of information. But rhyme evidence presupposes a standard of exactness that may not have been attempted by the poet; and in the extant manuscripts of early Middle English, rhyming verse is not attained. Where we have the evidence for assuming dialectal distinctions, rhyme evidence is often reinforced by the evidence of dialectally limited words and forms of words. For our poem the evidence points to the southeast, an area that includes Guildford but probably not Dorset. Even so, a Guildford man writing in Portisham might be driven by the need to find a rhyme to avail himself in Portisham of what would have fitted in better with the language of Guildford. As regards dialect words, we know only where they in fact occur in extant texts, not the limits within which they might have been used and understood when used.

If we translate the forms we find in the rhymes of the poem into the language of the southeast, we get exact rhymes: for example, *kunne/h(e)onne*, Kentish *kenne/henne* (kin, hence); *wise/ire*, Kentish *wise/ise* (manner, iron); *worse/mershe*, Kentish *werse/merse* (worse, marsh). The word *tobuneþ* (beats severely) is only once found elsewhere, in a Middle Kentish poem; *clut* (lump of earth in a ploughed field) is not found elsewhere until it turns up in nineteenth-century Kentish. Nevertheless, Sherman Kuhn, with the evidence of the poem before him and with the evidence of Middle English garnered in the files of his *Middle English Dictionary,* advised tentatively that we should look away from the southeast and investigate instead the evidence of names in Gloucestershire and Oxfordshire—not far from the home of the two extant manuscripts.

The poem is written in rhyming verse, in lines of four stresses each, often with an unstressed syllable

OWL AND THE NIGHTINGALE

at the end. Not infrequently there is more than one unstressed syllable instead of the regular one between the stresses; most lines begin with an unstressed syllable. There is in the poem, as we have it, considerable freedom in the handling of the verse. As a result, monotony of rhythm is avoided; even the mechanics of versification show a sense of ease to match the urbanity in the handling of the subject matter. Here, with some indication of the likely scansion, is the Nightingale's first speech:

> ′ x x ′ x x ′ x ′
> 'Vnwiʒt!' ho sede, 'awei þu flo!
> [Monster!' she said, 'fly off!
>
> x ′ x ′ x ′ x ′
> Me is þe vvrs þat ich þe so.
> I feel worse for seeing you.
>
> x ′ x ′ x ′ x ′ x
> Iwis for þine vvle lete
> Truly, because of your foul uproar
>
> x ′ x ′ x ′ x ′ x
> Wel oft ich mine song forlete.
> I very often neglect my song.
>
> x ′ x ′ x ′ x ′ x
> Min horte atfliþ & falt mi tonge
> My heart flees away and my tongue breaks down
>
> ′ ′ x x ′ x ′ x
> Wonnė þu art to me iþrunge.
> whenever you press close to me.
>
> x ′ x ′ x ′ x ′ x
> Me lustė bet speten þane singe
> I would rather spit than sing
>
> x ′ x ′ x ′ x ′ x
> Of þine fule ʒoʒelinge.'
> because of your hideous hooting.]
>
> (Caligula MS, 33–40)

One other early Middle English (and partly Anglo-Norman) poem has the same meter, *Les vnze peynes de enfern les queus Seynt Pool vist* (The eleven pains of hell that St. Paul saw).

Debates were common in medieval law schools, and they parody the rhetoric of pleading. Master Nicholas holds a master's degree and has the standing to judge the art of debating. At times the poem makes use of the vocabulary of the law, often going back to older and English terminology for what in the written documents of the period is more usually expressed in Anglo-Norman or Latin. The background allows metaphorical use to be made of trial by battle. Though *griþbruche* (breach of the peace) as expressed in the Wren's words (1,730–1,734) is an offense to the king, appeal seems to lie ultimately to the pope in Rome (745–746), so that there are overtones of canon law as if we were dealing with a clerical dispute. Not too much should, however, be read into such superficial lawyers' talk; it is not well distributed throughout the poem.

It is in the nature of debating to proceed from charge to reply and countercharge. Thus, the Nightingale's initial accusation that the Owl utters hideous *ʒoʒelinge* "hooting" (line 40) is answered by the Owl with the defense that it must not be thought that whoever is incapable of *writelinge* (chirping) is incapable of song (46–48). The Owl's claim to help mankind by means of song at Christmas, when they sing carols (481–484), is answered by the Nightingale's claim, in much the same words, that the singing of the canonical hours is fittingly accompanied by the Nightingale at midnight and dawn (721–735). The Nightingale's charge that the young of the Owl defile their own nest (96) is answered by the Owl with the reminder that human children, like the young of other creatures, do in their cradle what they later leave off (628–634), and by drawing attention to the Nightingale's insalubrious nesting site by the privy (588–594).

The debate is, however, not conducted with great forensic neatness. We are dealing with a clever and skillful poet, and it has been suggested that the disputants' lack of skill in pleading is deliberately introduced by the poet to lend force to the parody, and that his control of the arts of discourse is sufficient for him to mock the birds' lack of control.

In subject matter the birds range widely. Not only their song but also their appearance and habits are contrasted. The Owl, hateful to all other creatures and mobbed by little birds, is in owlish eyes splendidly hawklike—and no wonder: owls can claim kinship with these grand birds of prey. But the Nightingale is of undistinguished stature and unsightly coloring. The Owl, accused of eating snails and mice, can claim at least true service to man, cleansing his churches and barns of mice, to the enhancement of spiritual and bodily comfort (603–610). Besides, the Nightingale's diet of spiders, insects, and worms seems worse rather than better (597–602). The birds' service to mankind encompasses the Owl's skill and wisdom in prophecy, especially the foretelling of disasters and the concomitant experience that the prophet is blamed for disasters foretold, not thanked for the warning (1,145–1,290). In the disputants' order of operation astrology, cursing, and interdict have their place. The Nightingale, in an elaborate account of the sins, makes light—perhaps too much, but it is all relative—of the sins of the flesh (1407–1412), and the boast that the Nightingale's one great talent, song, is worth more than all the talents of the Owl (707–836) may contain feeble echoes of the scholastic debate concerning the all-embracing nature of one virtue when exercised fully.

The poem involves an intellectual world. It uses the fables of Marie de France as well as her lays. Among further sources, Alexander Neckam (Neckham or "Nequam," 1157–1217) has been suggested, and ultimately Pliny may have contributed to some of the natural history. Yet, though highly literary, *The Owl and the Nightingale* does not seem a bookish poem. The poet makes what he may have derived from books arise easily from the disputants' matter as they present it. There is some symbolism, especially in the birds' habitations: the Owl's nest in the hollow tree stump overgrown with ivy, in all seasons, and the Nightingale's blossom-covered dwelling. It is possible to trace the wild landscape, to which the sensible Nightingale refuses to travel as a missionary (lines 955–1,042), to authorities as varied as Gerald of Wales (1146–1223), Ohthere in the Old English Orosius, or even the Icelandic *Hákonar saga*. What matters is that it is introduced without heaviness. The poet refers to only one authority: King Alfred. In the part of the poem concerned with song (lines, 1–1,290) more than twenty proverbs are introduced, and over half of them are ascribed to Alfred, whose reputation for proverbial wisdom stood high in the twelfth and thirteenth centuries, when a collection of proverbs, demonstrably no earlier than the twelfth century, was ascribed to him.

The debate takes place at night and ceases with the dawn song. The little birds gather around, and to the Owl it seems that the Nightingale has *ibanned ferde* (called up the militia); indeed, they thought that the Nightingale had won the debate. So it seemed to the Nightingale, for the debate is about which is the better creature of the two, and the measure is the value to mankind of their existence. The Owl had boasted of service to mankind even when dead—as a scarecrow. On a technicality the Owl lost: Existence ceases with death.

The debate is over; the disputants go forward all alone to rehearse their pleas before Master Nicholas of Guildford at Portisham:

> Ah hu heo spedde of heore dome
> Ne can ich eu na more telle.
> Her nis na more of þis spelle.

[But how they fared at judgment I cannot say further. There is nothing more here of this tale.]

BIBLIOGRAPHY

Sources. Facsimiles of the manuscripts are in Neil R. Ker, ed., *The Owl and the Nightingale, Reproduced in Facsimile from the Surviving Manuscripts* (1963). For references to a lost manuscript, see R. M. Wilson, "The Medieval Library of Titchfield Abbey," in *Proceedings of the Leeds Philosophical and Literary Society,* 5, pts. 3 and 4 (1940–1941).

Editions include John W. H. Atkins, trans. and ed., *The Owl and the Nightingale* (1922, repr. 1971); Wilhelm Gadow, ed., *Das mittelenglische Streitgedicht Eule und Nachtigall . . .* (1909, repr. 1970); Eric Gerald Stanley, ed., *The Owl and the Nightingale* (1972). Besides the Atkins, translations include a somewhat free rendering by Graydon Eggers (1955); John C. Gardner, ed., *The Alliterative Morte Arthure, The Owl and the Nightingale . . .* (1971); Brian Stone, *The Owl and the Nightingale . . .* (1971).

Studies. Willi Breier, *Eule und Nachtigall* (1910), chiefly a linguistic study; H. Hässler, *The Owl and the Nightingale und die literarischen Bestrebungen des 12. und 13. Jahrhunderts* (Ph.D. diss., Frankfurt, 1942); Kathryn Hume, *The Owl and the Nightingale: The Poem and Its Critics* (1975); Bertil Sundby, *The Dialect and Provenance of the Middle English Poem The Owl and the Nightingale* (1950).

E. G. STANLEY

[See also **Anglo-Norman Literature; Antifeminism; Chardri; Débat; Middle English Literature.**]

OXFORD PSALTER. The Oxford Psalter is considered by some scholars to be the oldest surviving Anglo-Norman French text, and it may date from as early as 1100. The Oxford Psalter, which is a translation of the Gallican version of the Psalms, survives in several manuscripts, among which are the Montebourg Psalter (Oxford, Bodleian Library, MS Douce 320) and the Psautier de Corbie (Paris, Bibliothèque Nationale, MS fonds latin 768). Most French psalters down to the sixteenth century follow the Gallican rather than the Hebrew version.

BIBLIOGRAPHY

A. Beyer, "Die Londoner Psalterhandschrift Arundel 230 (31. 10.87)," in *Zeitschrift für romanische Philologie,* **11** (1887), **12** (1888); Francisque X. Michel, ed.,

OXFORD UNIVERSITY

Libri Psalmorum versio antiqua gallica e cod. ms. in Bibl. Bodleiana . . . (1860).

BRIAN MERRILEES

[See also **Anglo-Norman Literature; Cambridge Psalter; Psalter.**]

OXFORD UNIVERSITY, the older and larger of the two medieval English universities, is situated between the upper Thames (Isis) and Cherwell rivers at a crossroads about fifty-two miles northwest of London.

The town of Oxford, a Saxon settlement at the "ford of oxen," dates from the eighth century. The town was fortified by 912, and in the 1070's the Normans built a castle and walls, which partially survive. Although not a bishopric, Oxford grew into an important city in the High Middle Ages, due in part to its accessibility and proximity to the royal palace at Woodstock and the abbeys of Oseney and Godstow.

The origins of the university are shrouded in obscurity. Unlike Paris, Oxford did not develop from a monastic or cathedral school, a felicitous circumstance which, combined with its distance from the bishop of Lincoln, allowed the university to enjoy an unusual degree of independence. Oxford probably developed in the twelfth century out of an informal group of masters teaching near St. Mary's Church. Among the first known masters was Theobald of Étampes, who was lecturing before 1100 (*ca.* 1095) and continued until about 1125. This group of scholars seems to have increased markedly following Henry II's prohibition of foreign study in 1170, and by 1185 Gerald of Wales (Giraldus Cambrensis) recorded that they were organized into several faculties (*doctores diversarum facultatum*), which, although likely an exaggeration, indicates there was a varied group of scholars. This development is implied by several other late-twelfth-century authorities as well.

The university was first recognized as a legal corporation by a legatine ordinance of 1214, ending a dispersal of the university following a riot with the townsmen in 1209. The trouble originated when a scholar killed a woman and two scholars were hanged in response. Such violent quarrels occurred frequently in medieval Oxford, and since the university owned no real estate, the masters and

New College, Oxford, with the warden masters, bachelors, and choristers. 15th century. Miniature by Thomas Chaundler. FROM THE CHAUNDLER MS. BY PERMISSION OF THE WARDEN AND FELLOWS OF NEW COLLEGE, OXFORD

scholars simply left and reassembled elsewhere. These dispersals were usually ended by either royal or papal reconfirmation or augmentation of the university's immunities.

Oxford possessed an elected "master of the schools" (*magister scholarum Oxonide*) by at least 1201, a position which evolved into the chancellorship in 1214. Thus, the chancellor originated as the representative of the masters rather than of the bishop of Lincoln and, after long struggles with the bishop over the next two centuries, came eventually to exercise complete independence of diocesan control. By a succession of royal grants beginning with that of Henry III in 1231, the chancellor enjoyed spiritual and temporal jurisdiction over all matters pertaining to the university, its members, and its employees. The chancellor's executives were the two proctors, elected from the northern and south-

OXFORD UNIVERSITY

ern "nations," based on the geographical origins of the students.

The university was organized into the faculties of arts (*litterae humaniores*), theology, medicine, and civil and canon law, and was governed by two deliberative bodies. The congregation of regents (those currently teaching) and nonregents of all faculties (*congregatio magna,* later *convocatio*) decided on matters of great importance. The congregation of regent masters (*congregatio minor*) governed the ordinary business of the university.

The average student began in the faculty of arts. The bachelor's degree normally required four years of study in lectures and disputations, with another three years for the master's degree, and the *magisterium* carried with it the statutory obligation of giving two years of regent lectures. The curriculum included the seven liberal arts (grammar, rhetoric, dialectic, music, arithmetic, geometry, and astronomy) and the three philosophies (natural philosophy, moral philosophy, and metaphysics), with special emphasis placed on logic and natural philosophy. A degree in arts was required for entry into theology and medicine but not law. Degrees in the superior faculties demanded another long program, and the attrition rate was high; over half of the students in arts left before taking any degree.

Thirteenth-century Oxford was second only to Paris in its contributions to scholastic philosophy and theology, particularly after the arrival of the mendicant orders. In addition to the great secular master Robert Grosseteste (*d.* 1253), the university's celebrated masters included the Dominican Robert Kilwardby (*d.* 1279) and the Franciscan John Peckham (or Pecham, *d.* 1292), and later the great realist John Duns Scotus (*d.* 1307) and the nominalist William of Ockham (*d. ca.* 1350). The mendicants lived and taught in their own houses of study, and they came into conflict with the secular masters of the university in 1253, principally over the mendicants' right to take degrees in theology without first serving a regency in arts. This was the first of several bitter quarrels, which were not conclusively ended until the 1320's, after royal and papal intervention that only partially vindicated the friars.

The thirteenth century also saw the beginnings of the distinctly English collegiate system. Colleges were endowed foundations for secular students, usually in theology. Originally providing only their few fellows with lodging and meals, they developed in the fifteenth century into centers of instruction, taking in undergraduates and sponsoring their own lectures and disputations which, by 1500, largely supplanted the university-controlled regent lectures. The greatest of the early colleges was Merton, whose fourteenth-century fellows Thomas Bradwardine, Walter Burley, and others were noted for their interest in natural philosophy. However, most medieval students lived in halls, unendowed residences that offered few amenities.

The later Middle Ages was a difficult time for Oxford. The plagues after 1349 helped reduce the university to perhaps as few as 1,300 members. The heretical teaching of John Wyclif attracted unfavorable attention that culminated in Archbishop Thomas Arundel's forced visitation in 1411. But these years were also marked by some signs of growth. Merton and Queen's colleges between 1380 and 1410 produced men who wrote many realist works of logic and natural philosophy and compiled the collections of terminist *logica oxoniensis* (*logica terminorum*) that established England's international pre-eminence in that field.

Of more enduring importance were the foundations of New College (1379), Lincoln (1429), All Souls (1438), and Magdalen (1448). The last of these included a free grammar school that was instrumental in popularizing Renaissance style in late-fifteenth-century England. This was a time when collegiate instruction allowed for the flexible adaptation of new studies, such as Greek. Given the changing needs of the time, the congregation used its powers of dispensation to require regent lectures from only selected graduates on specific texts. Thus the scholastic curriculum was gradually modified to meet different needs, resulting in the eclectic culture of the old and new learning that was to be the hallmark of Tudor Oxford.

BIBLIOGRAPHY

The general histories of medieval Oxford include T. H. Aston, "Oxford's Medieval Alumni," in *Past and Present,* 74 (1977); Gordon Leff, *Paris and Oxford Universities in the Thirteenth and Fourteenth Centuries* (1968); Charles Edward Mallet, *A History of the University of Oxford,* 3 vols. (1924–1927, repr. 1968); Hastings Rashdall, *The Universities of Europe in the Middle Ages,* rev. ed., 3 vols., F. M. Powicke and A. B. Emden, eds. (1936), esp. III; *Statuta antiqua Universitatis Oxoniensis,* Strickland Gibson, ed. (1931); James A. Weisheipl, "Curriculum of the Faculty of Arts at Oxford in the Early Fourteenth Century," in *Mediaeval Studies,* 26 (1964).

Most of the medieval archival material has been

published in Oxford Historical Society Publications, vols. 1–101 (1885–1936), and the new series, vols. 1–28 (1939–).

Useful reference works include T. H. Aston, ed., *The History of the University of Oxford,* I: *The Early Oxford Schools,* J. I. Catto, ed. (1984); Edward Harold Cordeaux and Denis H. Merry, *A Bibliography of Printed Works Relating to the University of Oxford* (1968); Alfred B. Emden, *A Biographical Register of the University of Oxford to A.D. 1500,* 3 vols. (1957–1959).

DAMIAN RIEHL LEADER

[See also **Aristotle in the Middle Ages; Arts, Seven Liberal; Bradwardine, Thomas; Burley, Walter; Cambridge, University of; Duns Scotus, John; Grosseteste, Robert; Kilwardby, Robert; Lollards; Ockham, William of; Peckham, John; Universities; Wyclif, John.**]

OYER AND TERMINER, TRAILBASTON. The phrase "oyer and terminer" (from French) or *audiendum et terminandum* (Latin) refers to the powers given by the king to a panel of justices commissioned "to hear and determine" some alleged wrongdoing, that is, to take an inquest and render judgment. Oyer and terminer proceedings characteristically combined charges brought by private complaints (*querelae*) with charges made by inquest jurors (presentments); they were ad hoc rather than periodic, and they were utterly flexible, being issued for a wide range of causes. Some oyer and terminer commissions empowered justices to investigate a single complaint of trespass brought by one victim; some dealt with one type of offense or a related body of offenses in one or more counties; some were given virtually all the criminal justice of the general eyre as part of an inquest covering the entire realm. But we can roughly divide this entire oyer and terminer spectrum into the special, ad hoc commissions (usually dealing with the complaint of a single person), and the general commissions given a much wider jurisdictional and geographical scope.

The special oyer and terminers were a major feature of the concern for public order during the reigns of the first three Edwards (1272–1377). By this period the king's courts had developed a sizable jurisdiction in trespass, in effect bringing the endless feuds of the countryside into royal courts, and they had encouraged subjects to present complaints against the king's own officials. This new business proved too massive an addition to the heavy load already carried by the old general eyre; in the 1290's the eyre collapsed under the strain.

As the eyre faltered, increasing numbers of special oyer and terminers were issued to deal with the pressing volume of trespass litigation. Rather than bring suit by a formal writ before one of the central courts or the justices in eyre, a plaintiff could send his informal charges to Westminster and ask for an ad hoc panel of justices. If a commission was issued, the justices would come to his locality, take an inquest to collect a full story and a full slate of defendants, preside over a jury trial, and award damages to the plaintiff from guilty defendants; all this could often be accomplished within a matter of months. Thus speed, efficiency, and awards of heavy damages recommended oyer and terminer to the plaintiff. To the crown, the special commissions offered relief for the hard-pressed court system. Constant demand for oyer and terminers led to the issue of more than 100 commissions a year in the last years of the reign of Edward I, and more than 200 in some busy years of Edward II.

Yet if the special commissions were often used, an unending stream of complaint also came to the crown and shows that the oyer and terminers produced consequences that must have been unexpected in their scale if not in their very nature. Private and common petitions to the king and council charged bitterly that the special commissions were used for malicious prosecution in which the plaintiff's wrong was imaginary or his damages awarded out of all proportion to the real injury he had sustained. In fact the evidence does show that special oyer and terminers were susceptible to a degree of influence unusual even in the easygoing context of medieval English litigation. Plaintiffs might exercise their influence primarily by naming their own justices in their complaints. If the crown granted the justices they named (as it seems regularly to have done), the plaintiff's hand-picked nominees could select the dates and sites of all sessions and guide the process in his favor at every turn. The complaints of convicted defendants are believable: They had not been informed of the sessions, or had feared bodily injury if they appeared; the local officials and the jurors had been intimidated or prejudiced; the justices were relatives, friends, lords, or retainers of the plaintiff, and the defendant could not obtain justice.

Throughout the period, statutes promised strict regulation over the issue of commissions, the types of offenses given to their charge, and the personnel who might sit on the panel of justices. But the continuing, parallel stream of complaint to king and council, often in time of parliament, shows how little effect the pious statutory clauses had in practice. A device intended to promote order had in effect been given over to the control of local men and had become a powerful adjunct to countryside feuding. The experiment with special oyer and terminers seems to have been a significant source of disillusionment with royal justice. During the second half of the fourteenth century the special commissions slowly declined, not because of effective royal regulation but rather because of competition from other courts, especially that of the emerging justices of the peace, who were themselves given considerable powers of hearing and determining.

Yet the second main type of oyer and terminer, the general commissions, continued to flourish throughout the medieval period as a favorite crown weapon against lawlessness and disorder. This continued crown use reflects the very different quality of the general commissions, for whereas special oyer and terminers came to be virtually controlled by the powerful men in the counties, general oyer and terminer commissions were controlled from Westminster and carried on the criminal side of the old general eyre. Thus the history of general oyer and terminers begins a generation later than that of the special commissions, but it is a longer history.

In 1305 the crown issued the first general oyer and terminer, which soon became known popularly and even officially as a trailbaston commission. Derived from staves (trailbastons) used by the thugs whom the justices were to clear out of the highways, fairs, and localities of England, the name would stick to general oyer and terminers for about their first century of existence, even though the particular purposes of the commissions might vary. In the initial commission of 1305 Edward I acted vigorously against the organized violence, protection rackets, and conspiracies that flourished in an atmosphere of great stress brought about by wartime pressures compounding long-range economic and demographic dislocations. An earlier set of commissions to arrest vagabonds in 1304 (once confused by historians with the slightly later trailbaston) seems to have crammed the prisons so full and produced so much evidence of widespread terrorism and corruption of legal process that these initial commissions formed simply to investigate were transformed into commissions to investigate and do justice, to hear and determine. Later trailbastons show different emphases: the commissions sent out by Edward II in 1314, or that of Edward III in 1341, for example, were launched as investigations of complaints against local government officials. Trailbaston justices visited the whole country in 1305–1307, and 1314–1316; they visited most counties in 1321, 1326, 1328–1329, 1331–1332, 1336, and 1341–1342. After this period, in the second half of the fourteenth century, the nickname largely disappeared.

BIBLIOGRAPHY

Judith B. Avrutick, "Commissions of Oyer and Terminer in Fifteenth Century England" (diss., Univ. of London, 1967); Alan Harding, *The Law Courts of Medieval England* (1973), "Plaints and Bills in the History of English Law, Mainly in the Period 1250–1350," in Dafydd Jenkins, ed., *Legal History Studies 1972* (1975), and "Early Trailbaston Proceedings from the Lincoln Roll of 1305," in R. F. Hunnisett and J. B. Post, eds., *Medieval Legal Records Edited in Memory of C. A. F. Meekings,* (1978); Richard W. Kaeuper, "Law and Order in Fourteenth-century England: The Evidence of Special Commissions of Oyer and Terminer," in *Speculum,* **54** (1979); Ralph B. Pugh, ed., *Calendar of London Trailbaston Trials Under Commissions of 1305 and 1306* (1975).

RICHARD W. KAEUPER

[See also **Admiralty, Court of; Edward I; Edward II; Edward III; England: 1216–1485; Justices Itinerant (In Eyre); Justices of the King's Bench; Law, English Common; Trespass.**]

PACHER, MICHAEL (*fl.* 1467–1498), German painter and sculptor active in an outlying Alpine region in the South Tyrol. Pacher forged a distinctive personal style by fusing Italianate elements onto his Germanic training as both a painter and a sculptor. His masterwork is the St. Wolfgang Altarpiece (1471–1481, in the parish church of St. Wolfgang am Ambersee, Austria), an impeccably preserved abbey retable for which Pacher provided both gilded and polychromed sculptures and painted wings. His paintings were dependent on Mantegna's Paduan work for their low viewpoints and encompassing architectural perspectives. Simplified massive figures in both paint and wood characterize Pacher's work. His sculptures, further, contain the deep carving, generous draperies, and

St. Wolfgang Altarpiece. Carving and paintings by Michael Pacher, 1481. The central shrine depicts Christ blessing the kneeling Virgin, with Sts. Wolfgang and Benedict. PHOTO: BUNDESDENKMALAMT, VIENNA

descriptive details reminiscent of work by the Dutch sculptor Nikolaus Gerhaert (*fl. ca.* 1460–1473).

Other major works by Pacher include the Gries Coronation of the Virgin Altarpiece (Bolzano, 1471–1475); the Salzburg Franciscan Altarpiece (1484–1498, panels in Vienna, Österreichische Galerie); and the painted Neustift Church Fathers Altarpiece in Munich (Alte Pinakothek, *ca.* 1483).

BIBLIOGRAPHY

Michael Baxandall, *The Limewood Sculptors of Renaissance Germany* (1980), 252–254; Peter Halm, *Michael Pacher: Der Kirchenväter-Altar* (1957); Eberhard Hempel, *Michael Pacher* (1931); Theodor Müller, *Sculpture in the Netherlands, Germany, France, and Spain: 1400–1500* (1966), 120–123, plates 132–133; Nicolò Rasmo, *Michael Pacher*, Philip Waley, trans. (1971); Robert Stiassny, *Michael Pachers St. Wolfgang Altar* (1919).

LARRY SILVER

[See also **Gerhaert, Nikolaus; Gothic Art: Painting** .]

PACHOMIUS, ST. See **Monasticism, Origins.**

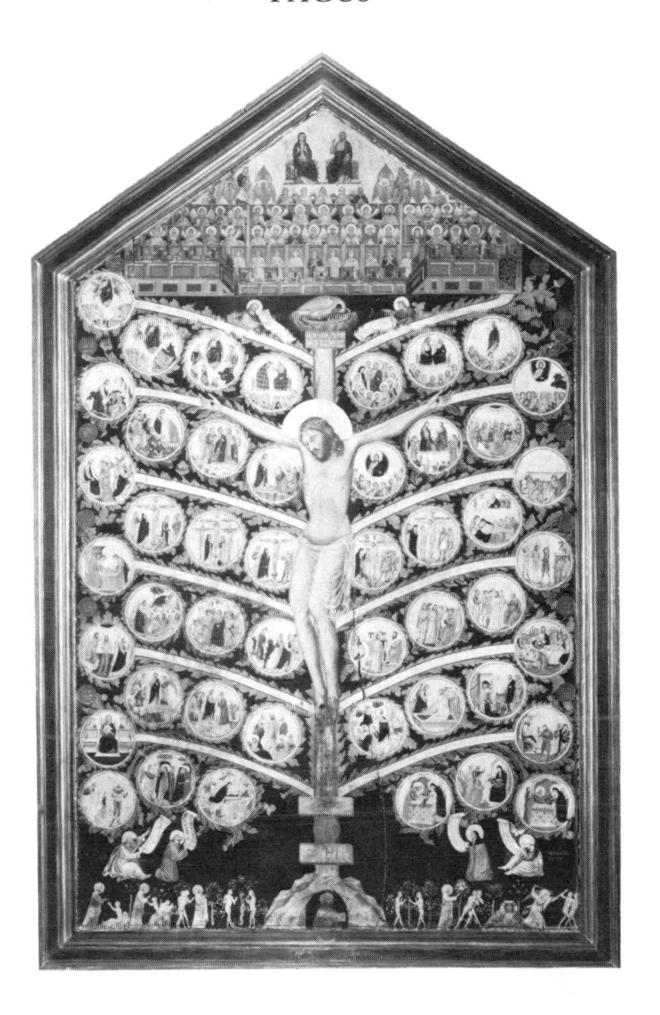

The *Tree of Life*. Panel painting by Pacino di Bonaguida, fourteenth century. ACCADEMIA DELLE BELLE ARTI, FLORENCE, NO. 8459. SCALA/ART RESOURCE

PACINO DI BONAGUIDA (*fl.* first half of the fourteenth century), Florentine painter and illuminator. Pacino was a leading figure among the more conservative contemporaries of Giotto. His works include a signed polyptych of the Crucifixion with four saints, the *Tree of Life* (both Florence, Accademia), and miniatures, mainly depicting the life of Christ, in New York (Morgan Library, MS 643).

BIBLIOGRAPHY

Richard Fremantle, *Florentine Gothic Painters from Giotto to Masaccio* (1975); Richard Offner, *A Critical and Historical Corpus of Florentine Painting*, sect. III, vol. II, pt. 1 (1930); Mario Rotili, *La miniatura gotica in Italia*, I (1968).

MICHAEL JACOFF

[See also **Gothic Art: Painting and Manuscript Illumination.**]

PAGUS, a word of many meanings in early medieval Latin, was often used to denote a territory or region under the domination of an ethnically distinct people or under the sway of an important city. This political or jurisdictional meaning derived immediately from the sense of *pagus* as a constituent subunit of a Roman *civitas* and more remotely from the tradition that the constituent elements of the Roman *populus* were originally *pagi* (ethnic units or clans). In the Middle Ages, *pagus* was used especially for a polity of sometimes vague territorial dimensions representing the historic center of domination of a barbarian people in Gaul. Eventually *comitatus* displaced *pagus* in this sense. In the Merovingian period *comitatus* still perhaps was limited in meaning to "the office of a count," but at least from the time of Charlemagne it took on the territorial signification "county."

The word *pagus* was also employed more loosely for a rural area (compare modern French *pays*), for the rural hinterland of a city, or for the countryside in general. Arguably, these significations, attested already in the Roman Imperial period, explain the meaning "unbeliever," attached to *paganus* (pagan, peasant; compare also paynim), because inhabitants of the *pagus* were perceived to be less molded by civilization and Christianity than the inhabitants of cities in the late antique and early medieval period. But *paganus* in the sense of unbeliever is also said to derive from the late antique usage of the word as a synonym for "civilian." Christians were soldiers of Christ. Their Roman Imperial adversaries were civilians (pagans).

In ecclesiastical usage, *pagus* (reflecting the antique meaning as a constituent part of a *civitas*) was used to denote a subdivision of an episcopal see, since in ecclesiastical Latin the latter was often expressed by the word *civitas*.

BIBLIOGRAPHY

The polemical study by Jacques Zeiller, *Paganus: Étude de terminologie historique* (1917), with criticisms of earlier views, is fundamental but should be used with caution. See also Adolf Berger, *Encyclopedic Dictionary of Roman Law* (1953), esp. "Paganus," "Pagus"; Arthur Giry, *Manuel de diplomatique* (1894), 424. Jan F. Niermeyer, *Mediae latinitatis lexicon minus* (1976).

WILLIAM CHESTER JORDAN

[See also **County.**]

PAHLAVI LITERATURE. The term "Pahlavi" (probably with the sense "ancient") is used of Zoroastrian literature in the Middle Persian language of Sasanian and early post-Sasanian Iran (third to ninth centuries). Much of this had already existed for centuries in oral transmission; and, once written down, these texts retained the characteristics of oral composition (anonymity, a common style, traditional subject matter, and free plagiarism). Their Pahlavi versions thus simply represent the final form in which they happen to have become fixed. By the late Sasanian period independent literary authorship was developing, with individuality appearing in style and matter. Traditional works continued to be recorded, however, down to the tenth century.

The script used, also called "Pahlavi," is a difficult one, with only fourteen letters (giving rise to ambiguities) and fossilized Aramaic ideograms; and the scribal standard is uneven. The oldest extant manuscripts date from the fourteenth century and were copied privately by practicing priests. Many books perished or were deliberately destroyed under Islamic domination, and allusions show that the surviving Pahlavi literature is only a small remnant of what once existed.

This literature was mostly composed and transmitted by priests, the scholars of their age; and the fundamental work on which they engaged was a complete Middle Persian translation of the Avesta, with glosses and commentaries, for example, the Pahlavi *Zand* (Interpretation). Here faithfulness to the original was all important, and little literary merit can be claimed for the translation. The exegesis is dryly scholastic and at its most detailed for the *Vendīdād* (The law against the demons) and *Nērangestān* (Book of incantations), two strictly traditional works concerned with observance and ritual. In other parts of the *Zand,* scholar-priests, commenting on matters such as astronomy, medicine, botany, and the like, drew on foreign works, notably Babylonian, Indian, and Greek (through Syriac translations), thus accumulating a wide store of learning that was eventually inherited by Islamic Iran.

Selections of texts on particular themes (such as creation, the nature of man and the physical world, and the end of time, with the last judgment and the resurrection) were then made from the *Zand* for more general enlightenment. Notable works of this kind are the *Bundahishn* (Original creation), and the *Wizīdagīhā* (Selections of Zādspram, a leading Persian priest of the ninth century). Much material from the *Zand* is contained also in the huge ninth-century compilation the *Dēnkard* (*Dēnkart*). There are a number of shorter didactic religious works of a traditional nature; and one, the *Shkand-gumānīg Wizār* (Doubt-dispelling exposition), embodies a philosophical inquiry into the tenets of other faiths (Christianity, Manichaeism, Islam), and a well-argued defense of Zoroastrian theology. This work was written by a layman, Mardān-farrox, also in the ninth century.

Zoroastrianism has an ancient apocalyptic tradition, going back to Zoroaster himself (if we accept the definition of "apocalyptic" as concerning a revelation of the history of the world and of mankind, the origin of evil, its course and inevitable overthrow, and the final consummation of all things); and remnants exist of a fine Avestan apocalyptic literature in verse. The chief Pahlavi texts are the *Zand ī Vahman Yasht* (in which the revelation is received by Zoroaster from Ohrmazd) and the *Jāmāsp Nāmag* (in which the seer is the wise minister of the prophet's royal patron). It is widely accepted that the forerunners of such works had a powerful influence on the development of Jewish apocalyptic writings. Another influential text is the *Ardā Wirāz Nāmag* (Book of the just Wirāz). Its subject is the visions of heaven and hell seen by Wirāz after he has drugged himself to release his spirit and discover for his community the fate of the dead. He travels the path of the departed, crosses the dreaded bridge where souls are judged, and is shown the joys of paradise and the tortures of hell. After seven days his soul returns to his body, and he tells what he has seen to those who have watched by it. The text has been shown to be the probable remote source of Dante's *Divine Comedy.*

A relatively large wisdom literature is based on gnomes (brief apothegms relating to universals). There is a long series of these in Book VI of the *Dēnkard,* and others in the *Dādestān ī Mēnōg ī Khrad* (Judgments of the spirit of wisdom), a sixth-century compilation which also contains basic doctrine and antiquarian learning simply expressed for the laity. Another branch of wisdom literature consists of collections of riddles. This ancient literary genre is represented in the *Book of Jōisht ī Fryān,* in which a pious Zoroastrian of old enters into a riddle contest with a sorcerer; and in *Drakht asūrīg* (The Babylonian tree), in which a date palm and goat strive in a riddling vein for precedence in usefulness. In a more sophisticated work, *Khosrow ud rēdag* (Xusrō and his page), a boy earns a place at court by a dazzling display of learning and accomplishments. This essentially worldly text has gained a place in religious literature because these accomplishments include a good knowledge of the Avesta and its *Zand,* and a training in religious observances.

A massive work compiled by Persian priests for the glory of the Sasanian dynasty was the *Khwadāy Nāmag* (Book of kings). In this work an artificial link was forged between the Sasanians and the remote Kayanian king Vishtāspa (Gushtasp), Zoroaster's patron. The huge chronicle survives almost solely through Arabic renderings and its derivative, the great Persian verse epic, Firdawsī's *Shāhnāma.* In these works of Islamic times the Zoroastrian element is much reduced, as is shown by two short Pahlavi texts which contain matter that was embodied in the *Khwadāy Nāmag.* One is the *Ayādgār ī Zarērān,* an epic fragment which celebrates a famous battle fought to establish the faith in the beginning; the other, the *Kārnāmag ī Ardashīr,* is a romantic tale about the founder of the Sasanian dynasty. For the later Sasanian reigns the chronicle is in the main historically accurate. The whole work furnished Persia with a history on the grand scale, stretching back (and through the incorporation of ancient myths, euhemerized) to creation and the origins of man; and it provided a foundation on which Muslim historiography was largely based. In general, Muslim scholars of the Abbasid period owed much to Pahlavi literature, from which many works were translated into Arabic, thus fertilizing the new culture.

BIBLIOGRAPHY

Mary Boyce, "Middle Persian Literature," in *Handbuch der Orientalistik,* Bertold Spuler, ed., I: IV, pt. 2 (1968), 31–66; Jean P. de Menasce, "Zoroastrian Literature After the Muslim Conquest," in *Cambridge History of Iran,* IV (1975), R. N. Frye, ed., and "Zoroastrian Pahlavī Writing," in *Cambridge History of Iran,* III, pt. 2 (1983), Ehsan Yarshater, ed.; Jehangir C. Tavadia, *Die mittelpersische Sprache und Literatur der Zarathustrier* (1956); Edward William West, "Pahlavi Literature," in *Grundriss der iranischen Philologie,* Wilhelm Geiger and Ernst W. A. Kuhn, eds., 4 vols. (1895–1904), esp. II, 74–129.

MARY BOYCE

[See also **Avesta; Bundahishn; Dēnkard; Iranian Languages; Iranian Literature; Sasanians; Shāhnāma; Zoroastrianism.**]

PAHLAWUNI, an Armenian noble family of the late Bagratid and post-Bagratid period (eleventh and twelfth centuries), presumably descended from the earlier Kamsarakan house. The domains of the Pahlawuni were in the province of Nig north of Ayrarat (east-central Armenia), with the fortress of Bǰni, and members of the family were repeatedly honored with the imperial titles of duke, *anthypatos* (proconsul), *curopalates,* and especially *magistros.*

The Pahlawuni also provided most of the Armenian *katᶜołikoi* of the eleventh and twelfth centuries.

The most distinguished secular members of the family include Vahram Pahlawuni, who led an anti-Byzantine party that brought the last Bagratid heir, Gagik II (*r.* to 1045, *d.* 1079), to the throne of Ani in 1041/1042. Vahram opposed the Byzantine annexation of the Armenian kingdom, but after its fall he served in the Byzantine armies against the Shaddadid emirs and was killed in the unsuccessful imperial siege of Dwin in 1049. His son, Grigor (*d. ca.* 1058), first followed his father's pro-Bagratid policy, but in 1045/1046 he withdrew to Constantinople, where he received the title of *magistros* and spent the rest of his life as governor of the newly created Byzantine themes in Armenia with the title of duke of Mesopotamian Vaspurakan (Basprakania) and Tarōn. Grigor Magistros, who had received a thorough Hellenic education, is especially known for his numerous translations of Greek philosophical works into Armenian and for his elaborately rhetorical *Letters,* which are a major source for the history and religious problems of the period. His son Vasak, the imperial duke of Antioch, was murdered there in 1078/1079, but members of the family continued to play a role in Armenian affairs under the Zakᶜarid viceroys and in Cilicia.

No less distinguished were the Pahlawuni *katᶜołikoi,* who ruled the Armenian church during the turbulent period following the fall of the Bagratid kingdom and carried on extensive dogmatic negotiations with both Constantinople and Rome.

The first of these *katᶜołikoi* was the eldest son of Grigor Magistros, the ascetic and learned Grigor II Vkayasēr (the Martyrophile, 1065/1066–1105). Grigor II moved the seat of the *katᶜołikos* to Tsamendav near Melitene, in the domain of the former king Gagik of Kars (*r.* until 1065) and corresponded with Pope Gregory VII. Because of the confused political situation, his pontificate inaugurated a period of internal struggle with antipatriarchs. The second *katᶜołikos* was his nephew and coadjutor, Barseł/Basil Anecᶜi (Barsegh I of Ani, 1105–1113).

The great grandson of Grigor Magistros, Grigor III Pahlawuni (1113–1166), was elected patriarch despite his youth because of his family connections and reputation for wisdom. He participated in the Latin council of Jerusalem in 1140, negotiated with Popes Lucius II and Eugenius III, and established the residence of the *katᶜołikosate* at Hṙomklay on the mid Euphrates, where it remained for more than a century. His pontificate was also troubled by the creation of an anti-*katᶜołikosate* at Ałtᶜamar that eventually became reconciled but survived to modern times.

The fourth *katᶜołikos* was Grigor's even more distinguished brother, the great theologian and poet Nersēs IV Klayecᶜi, commonly known as Šnorhali (the Graceful, 1166–1173), who achieved a temporary rapprochement with Byzantium in the reign of Manuel I Komnenos. Their nephew Grigor IV Tłay (the Youth, 1173–1193), under whom the Byzantine negotiations came to an end and who turned once more to Rome in the pontificate of Lucius III, was the fifth *katᶜołikos* of note.

The less successful careers of the last *katᶜołikoi* of the Pahlawuni family reflected the sharp disagreements within the Armenian church between the proponents of a union with the Latin church and their opponents. These include Grigor V Kᶜaravēž (Hurled from a cliff, 1193–1194), his predecessor's nephew, who was imprisoned and died under mysterious circumstances, and Grigor VI Apirat (1194–1203), who continued a pro-Latin policy and crowned the first king of Cilicia, Lewon (Leo I). Grigor VI consequently suffered rejection by the bishops of Greater Armenia, who opposed a union with Rome and elected Grigor's kinsman Barseł II Anecᶜi antipatriarch (1195–1206). He was the eighth Pahlawuni *katᶜołikos,* with whom the line finally came to an end.

BIBLIOGRAPHY

René Grousset, *L'empire du Levant: Histoire de la question d'Orient* (1949); Alexander Kazhdan, *Armiane v sostave gospodstvuiushchego klassa Vizantiĭskoĭ Imperii v. XI–XII vv.* (1975); Victor Langlois, "Mémoire sur la vie et les écrits du prince Grégoire Magistros, duc de Mésopotamie, auteur arménien du XIᵉ siècle," in *Journal asiatique,* 6th ser., **13** (1869); M. Leroy, "Grégoire Magistros et les traductions arméniennes d'auteurs grecs," in *Annuaire de l'Institut de Philologie et d'Histoire orientale* (1935); Malachia Ormanean, *Azgapatum,* I (1912), 1273–1558; Cyril Toumanoff, *Studies in Christian Caucasian History* (1963), and *Manuel de généalogie et de chronologie pour l'histoire de la Caucasie chrétienne* (1976); François Tournebize, *Histoire politique et religieuse de l'Arménie* (1910), 153–168, 235–279.

NINA G. GARSOÏAN

[See also **Armenia: Geography; Armenia: History of;**

Bagratids, Armenian; Gagik II; Grigor Magistros; Grigor II Vkayasēr; Kamsarakan; Nersēs IV Šnorhali; Tarōn; Vaspurakan; Zakᶜarids.]

PAIKULI, a commemorative monument of the Sasanian period and, by extension, its locality, about thirty kilometers (nineteen miles) south of Sulaimaniya in present-day Iraqi Kurdistan. The monument, known locally as Butkhana (idol temple) or Budakha, is today a mound of debris consisting of a mortar and rubble core surrounded by the dressed stone blocks and architectural fragments of its fallen revetment. Ernst Herzfeld, who made the first systematic study of the ruins, reconstructed the monument as a solid tower about nine meters (thirty feet) square crowned by a cornice of loopholes and stepped merlons. Stone busts, apparently representing the royal patron, decorated the four sides.

More than a hundred blocks bear portions of a long bilingual inscription in Middle Persian and Parthian in which Narseh (293–303), the youngest and last surviving son of Šabuhr (Shapur) I (240/241–272), justifies his usurpation of the Sasanian throne from his nephew, the young crown prince Bahram III. At the death of Bahram's father, Narseh was called home to Ērānšahr from Greater Armenia, where he was king, by a faction of nobles and officers of state who sought to end the civil war resulting from the power vacuum by installing a strong personality at Ctesiphon (in present-day Iraq). On his march to the capital, Narseh's supporters met him below one of the three passes that cross the last of the mountain chains separating the Iranian plateau from the Tigris and Euphrates valleys, and proclaimed him King of Kings. The Paikuli monument, which marks this spot, is vital for a political geography of the Sasanian Empire; the enumeration of kings, governors, high officials, and members of the clergy in its inscription permits the establishment of a hierarchical order of state functionaries and fixes their geographical spheres of influence and their roles in the Sasanian administration.

The Paikuli monument (reconstruction). Kurdistan, Iraq, late 3rd century. FROM E. HERZFELD, *PAIKULI* (1924)

BIBLIOGRAPHY

The basic study of the Paikuli monument is Ernst Herzfeld's *Paikuli: Monument and Inscription of the Early History of the Sasanian Empire*, 2 vols. (1924). The meaning of the monument is discussed by W. B. Henning, "A Farewell to the Khagan of the Aq-Aqatārān," in *Bulletin of the School of Oriental and African Studies*, **14** (1952). For portions of the inscription not included in Herzfeld's publication, and for a bibliography, see Volker Popp and Helmut Humbach, "Die Paikuli-Inschrift im Jahre 1971," in *Baghdader Mitteilungen* (*Deutsches archäologisches Institut*), **6** (1973), and Helmut Humbach and Prods O. Skjaervø, *The Sasanian Inscription of Paikuli*, 3 pts. in 4 vols. (1978–1983).

LIONEL BIER

[See also **Armenia: History of; Ctesiphon; Sasanian Art and Architecture; Sasanians.]**

PAINTING, SCHOOLS. See **Early Christian Art; Gothic Art: Painting; Migration and Hiberno-Saxon Art; Pre-Romanesque Art; Renaissances and Revivals in Medieval Art; Romanesque Art;** and the national and tribal schools.

Pala d'Oro (detail showing the *Majestas Domini* with four Evangelists). Byzantine cloisonné enamels from Constantinople (1105), reconstructed for S. Marco, Venice, 1342–1345. ALINARI/ART RESOURCE

PAINTING, TECHNIQUES. See **Fresco Painting; Manuscript Illumination; Oil Painting; Panel Painting; Tempera Painting.**

PAKUDA, IBN. See **Baḥya ben Joseph ibn Paquda.**

PALA D'ORO, a gold altarpiece decorated with jewels, and Byzantine and Venetian enamels, in S. Marco, Venice. Doge Pietro I Orseolo (*r.* 976–978) ordered the original, no longer extant, which probably consisted of silver plaques attached to a wooden panel, from Constantinople in 976–978. A second version, part of which survives, was sent from Constantinople in 1105 at the request of Doge Ordelaffo Falier (*r.* 1102–1118). Falier's gold and enamel antependium is now arranged as the lowest three registers of the present Pala d'Oro. Doge Pietro Ziani converted the antependium to a retable in 1209 and added the six enamels portraying the twelve great feasts of the Byzantine church (from the Entry into Jerusalem to the Koimesis, or Dormition of the Virgin) that now form the uppermost register of the Pala d'Oro. These plaques were part of the vast collection of booty extracted from Constantinople during the Latin occupation of the city (1204–1261).

The current disposition of the Pala d'Oro dates from 1342 to 1345, when Doge Andrea Dandolo (*r.* 1343–1354) had the retable reconstructed; the enamels, supplemented by Gothic and miscellaneous Byzantine plaques, were placed in a Gothic gemmed framework.

BIBLIOGRAPHY

Sergio Bettini, "Venice, the Pala d'Oro, and Constantinople," in *The Treasury of San Marco, Venice,* David Buckton, ed. (1984), 35–64; H. R. Hahnloser, ed., *Il tesoro di San Marco: La pala d'oro* (1965). For a brief discussion, see also John Beckwith, *Early Christian and Byzantine Art,* 2nd ed. (1979), 248–250.

LESLIE BRUBAKER

[See also **Antependium; Byzantine Art; Paliotto of S. Ambrogio; Pre-Romanesque Art; Twelve Great Feasts.**]

PALAIOLOGOI, the last Byzantine imperial family, ruling in Constantinople from 1261 to 1453. The first known member of the family is Nikephoros Palaiologos, a soldier in the late eleventh century; his son, George, married Anna Doukas. The family intermarried with the various imperial families of the eleventh and twelfth centuries: the Komnenoi, Doukai, and Angeloi. Although no very illustrious member is known from the twelfth century, there was a Palaiologos who was governor of Thessaloniki in the middle of the century. The despot Alexios Komnenos Palaiologos married Irene, eldest daughter of Alexios III Angelos (1195–1203), and was expected to succeed him on the throne. Alexios' daughter was the mother of Michael VIII (*r.* 1259–1282), who was thus a Palaiologos on both sides of his family.

The Palaiologoi came to power in September 1258, as a result of a palace revolution undertaken by some of the most powerful aristocrats against the brothers Muzalon (especially George Muzalon), who were regents for the young John IV Laskaris and continuators of the antiaristocratic policies of Theodore II Laskaris (1254–1258). Michael rewarded the aristocracy with grants of *pronoiai,* which for the first time were allowed to become hereditary. The economic, social, and political dominance of the landed aristocracy is a basic characteristic of the Palaiologan period.

In 1261 Michael VIII took Constantinople from the Westerners and made it once again the capital of the Byzantine Empire. The capture of the city created problems as various Western rulers claimed the imperial throne in Constantinople, starting with Charles of Anjou (1226–1285), and planned campaigns of reconquest. This factor played an important role in Byzantine foreign policy until approximately 1311. Subsequently, Byzantine relations with the West centered on the question of Western aid against the Turks; this was intimately connected to the problem of church union, which for the papacy was a condition for aid, while for the Byzantines the priorities were reversed. Union was achieved twice, in 1274 (Council of Lyons) and in 1439 (Council of Ferrara-Florence), but neither the Byzantine church in its totality nor the people of the empire accepted it.

The move of the capital to Constantinople entailed a shift of interest to the Balkan provinces and Western Europe, so that Asia Minor was neglected and its population alienated during the reign of Michael VIII. Despite the efforts of Andronikos II (*r.* 1282–1328, *d.* 1332), the province was overrun by the Turks in the late thirteenth century, and its conquest was completed in the 1330's. From Asia Minor the Turks crossed into Europe in the 1340's and established a stronghold in Gallipoli in 1354. The conquest of the Balkans followed rapidly; after 1371 the Byzantine Empire became a vassal state of the Ottomans, and by the end of the fourteenth century virtually all its territories had been conquered, with the exception of Constantinople itself and the Despotate of the Morea, which survived the fall of Constantinople by seven years (1460).

Internally, the Palaiologan period is marked by the decline of the power of the state and the assumption of power by such groups as the aristocracy, the towns (to a lesser extent), and the church. The decentralization of authority is evident at every level. Byzantine emperors gave their sons, or other people, appanages, which eroded the power of the state. The agricultural economy was in the hands of the landed aristocracy, while the economy of exchange, active until the end, was controlled by Italian merchants. There was a Byzantine merchant element, concentrated in a few cities, but its activities were limited. There were also grave social tensions, which resulted in two civil wars (1321–1328, 1341–1347). On the other hand, learning and the arts flourished in the Palaiologan period, in both Constantinople and Thessaloniki, and in the Despotate of the Morea, so that it is possible to speak of a "Palaiologan renaissance."

BIBLIOGRAPHY

Art et société à Byzance sous les Paléologues (*Actes du colloque organisé par l'association internationale des études byzantines à Venise en septembre 1968*) (1971); Peter Charanis, *Social, Economic, and Political Life in the Byzantine Empire* (1973); Victor Laurent, "La généalogie des premiers Paléologues," in *Byzantion,* 8 (1933); Donald M. Nicol, *The Last Centuries of Byzantium, 1261–1453* (1972); Averkios Th. Papadopoulos, *Versuch einer Genealogie der Palaiologen, 1259–1453* (1938); Steven Runciman, *The Last Byzantine Renaissance* (1970).

ANGELIKI LAIOU

[See also **Andronikos II Palaiologos; Andronikos III Palaiologos; Byzantine History; Constantine XI Palaiologos; Constantinople; Epiros, Despotate of; John V Palaiologos; John VIII Palaiologos; Manuel II Palaiologos; Mehmed (Muḥammad) II; Michael VIII Palaiologos; Nicaea, Empire of; Ottomans; Pronoia.**]

PALATINATES, areas ruled by a count of the palace who exercised semiroyal powers delegated by the crown, are found in several European countries. In Germany, where the development is perhaps clearest, the German rulers found it convenient to invest the counts palatine of Lotharingia, whose office was attached to the royal palace at Aachen, with a semiroyal authority from which developed the Rhenish Palatinate. During the course of the twelfth century the count palatine of the Rhine became one of the most powerful of the German princes. In France the title attached itself in the twelfth century to certain of the great feudatories, notably the counts of Champagne. In England, by way of contrast, the office of the count of the palace never existed. The term palatinate was used to describe certain of the great franchises as they had evolved by the end of the thirteenth century. The expression as it first emerged in England, therefore, was not so much a precise statement of specific rights as a general description indicating areas of alienated regalia.

The three great palatinates in medieval England were Chester, the bishopric of Durham, and Lancaster. With the exception of Lancaster, which was a later creation modeled on Chester, the palatinates developed on the basis of earlier liberties. In Chester, these liberties included the fiscal independence of the county and its special position regarding military service. The liberties of the franchise of Durham derived from the special position of the Northumbrian earls in relation to the West Saxon rulers.

Although they possessed powers normally enjoyed by the crown, the three great palatinates did not conform to a standard pattern. Lancaster regularly sent representatives to parliament, while Durham and Chester—which evolved on the basis of separate and individual liberties—did not obtain representation in the national parliament until the sixteenth and seventeenth centuries.

The creation of the English palatinate in no way implied any real diminution in royal power. Although palatinate jurisdiction was particularly suited to those regions where government from the center was difficult to sustain, such areas were by no means independent of royal authority. Chester and Lancaster were united to the crown during the later Middle Ages, while Durham was held within the framework of royal control. In the three great English palatinates, therefore, power was vested ultimately in the king, and a development that might have led to national fragmentation was turned to the political advantage of the crown.

In both England and its colonies, palatinate jurisdiction outlasted the Middle Ages. In certain of the North American colonies, notably Maryland and Carolina, palatinate rights were granted in the seventeenth century, while in England itself the last vestiges of palatinate rights at Durham and Lancaster disappeared only during the Victorian age.

BIBLIOGRAPHY

Geoffrey Barraclough, *The Earldom and County Palatine of Chester* (1953); Helen M. Cam, "The Decline and Fall of English Feudalism" in *History*, n.s., **25** (1940); Gaillard Lapsley, *The County Palatine of Durham* (1900); H. Metteis, *Der Staat des hohen Mittelalters,* 2nd ed. (1944); Jean Scammell, "The Origin and Limitations of the Liberty of Durham," in *English Historical Review*, **81** (1966); Sir Robert Somerville, *History of the Duchy of Lancaster* (published by the Chancellor and Council of the Duchy of Lancaster) (1953).

JOHN TAYLOR

[See also **County; Feudalism.**]

PALATINE COURT. See **Charlemagne.**

PALEAE. See **Gratian.**

PALEOGRAPHY, ARABIC AND PERSIAN. The Arabic alphabet consists of twenty-eight consonants, of which three, *alif, wāw,* and *yāʾ*, function also as long vowels. These twenty-eight consonants are, however, expressed with only fourteen or, at most, seventeen different letter shapes, so that a supplementary system of letter differentiation had to be devised.

PALEOGRAPHY, ARABIC

In recording only consonants and long vowels, and in writing them from right to left, Arabic follows a pattern devised originally for Phoenician and adapted later to the use of other Semitic languages, such as Hebrew and Aramaic. Arabic was also influenced by these previously used scripts in the names by which the various letters were designated and in the ordering of letters within the alphabet. An archaic alphabetical order used in North African Arabic had an even closer resemblance to that of earlier Semitic scripts than did the letter order used in other regions.

Arabic script is most directly related to those of two branches of Aramaic: Nabatean and Syriac. The earliest known inscription in the Arabic language, dated to A.D. 328, uses Nabatean script. A number of letter shapes used in Arabic script probably derive from Nabatean, as does a tendency to link the letters of a word.

An inscription of 512 is the first documented appearance of the Arabic script. In it letters are arranged along an ideal base line and linked together in a smoother fashion than in Nabatean script. Both the more fluid execution and base line of Arabic are probably attributable to the influence of cursive varieties of Syriac, the Aramaic of Syrian Christians. In Syriac both a cursive execution and extensive use of ligatures between letters tended to reduce differences in the shapes of individual letters, and two of them came to have an identical form. In Arabic this process was carried even further, and several sounds were equated with one letter shape. Thus the second and third letters of the Phoenician, Hebrew, and Syriac alphabets, *bet/beth* and *gimal/gamal*, are used in Arabic to designate three letters each: *bāʾ*, *tāʾ*, *thāʾ*, and *jīm*, *ḥāʾ*, *khāʾ*. During the second century A.D., Syriac scribes had begun to distinguish between letters of identical shape by placing dots above or below them. This method of letter differentiation was applied to Arabic from the seventh century.

The advent of Islam in the seventh century stimulated the development of new scripts suited to particular purposes as well as the creation of a system of vocalization. The debates among Muslims over the proper reading of the Koranic text and the adoption of Islam in regions where Arabic was not spoken dramatized the need for a method of recording the exact pronunciation of words. A technique for indicating short vowels, adapted from one used in Syriac, was devised during the late seventh or eighth century, probably in southern Iraq. In it dots, usually red, were placed above, below, or alongside a consonant indicating a reading with *a*, *i*, or *u* respectively. Paired dots were used to indicate the hamza or the presence of doubled consonants. Despite its obvious practicality this system aroused strong opposition in some religious circles, where an unadorned Koranic text was preferred. By the ninth century this method of vocalization gained acceptance and its use in Koranic manuscripts became customary. In it consonants were normally differentiated by the use of parallel strokes above or below the letters.

In a second method of vocalization, also said to have been invented in Iraq, short vowels were designated by writing miniature versions of the letters *alif*, *wāw*, and *yāʾ* above or below the consonants. Later the *alif* and *yāʾ* were stylized as diagonal strokes. Abbreviated letters were also used for the hamza and to indicate when a consonant should be doubled. Despite claims that it was invented in the eighth century, this system came into widespread use only after the eleventh century. Aside from its use in Koranic manuscripts, full vocalization of Arabic is rare, but consonant differentiation, especially by means of dots, became customary. In certain chancery scripts, however, even these aids to the reader are often missing.

Although Persian began to be written in the Arabic script during the ninth century, the first surviving examples are from the eleventh century. Four new consonants, *pe*, *se*, *čim*, and *že*, were created by adding dots or strokes to letters already found in Arabic, but medieval manuscripts show considerable variation in their use.

In Arabic as well as Persian both practical and aesthetic considerations prompted the development of numerous scripts which contained formal or stylistic variants of the same basic letters. In the *kūfī* script, letters were given a more geometrically regular shape than those of the pre-Islamic period. In monumental epigraphy and Koranic manuscripts this angular script was widely used until the twelfth century, when a new formulation of the alphabet gained popularity. Known as "measured writing," it featured a system of proportional measurement to harmonize the shape and scale of the letters. Invented in Iraq during the tenth century, this system was developed by Ibn al-Bawwāb (*d.* 1022), who stressed the curvilinear portions of letters. In this system visual harmony is achieved by stressing similarities between the forms of different letters, a technique that tended to regularize their

PALEOGRAPHY

shapes. Often applied to rounded scripts such as *naskhī* and *thuluth,* this method may have given them new importance. Certainly *naskhī* and *thuluth* predominate in Korans and monumental inscriptions of the twelfth to fourteenth centuries. Later, this proportional system was applied to even more cursive scripts and new hands were created, such as *nastaᶜlīq,* in which some letters follow the proportional system but others can be selectively lengthened for variety. *Nastaᶜlīq* was especially popular for poetic texts, where the visual stress could counterpoint that of the sound.

BIBLIOGRAPHY

Nabia Abbott, *The Rise of the North Arabic Script and Its Kurᵓānic Development* (1939); Régis Blachère, *Introduction au Coran,* 2nd ed. (1959); Adolf Grohmann, *Arabische Paläographie,* 2 vols. (1967–1971).

PRISCILLA P. SOUCEK

[See also **Alphabets; Arabic Language; Bawwāb, Ibn al-; Calligraphy, Islamic; Iranian Languages; Kūfī; Naskhī; Nastaᶜlīq; Thuluth.**]

PALEOGRAPHY, WESTERN EUROPEAN. Etymologically paleography simply means old writing (from Greek *palaios,* old, and *graphe,* writing), but commonly it means the knowledge or study of old writing, and more specifically the history of writing from its origins up to the present. Paleography deals with the classification, origin, development, persistence, dissemination, modification, dilution, and disintegration of specific types of script. Although it studies writing in all alphabets, and does not necessarily even limit itself to alphabetic writing, it is, in fact, usually and most fruitfully pursued within the limits of one alphabet at a time. Here attention will be devoted almost exclusively to the Latin alphabet, which was used, of course, for all the medieval Western European vernacular languages as well as for Latin and was the alphabet on which paleography got its start as a learned discipline. And attention here will also concentrate on the Latin alphabet as found in manuscripts and documents more than in inscriptions on stones, coins, seals, and stained glass windows. The predominance of book scripts in paleographical literature is due in part to the strong philological and literary interests of so many twentieth-century paleographers but it also reflects the fact that manuscript books preserve more medieval paleographical evidence than other kinds of texts.

HISTORY

As an organized body of knowledge about handwriting, paleography is not a medieval but a modern invention, though the handwriting that served as the original subject matter for this invention was medieval and paleography continues to preoccupy itself more with the medieval period than with any other. Scripts from the ancient world have since received intensive paleographical attention, but at the time the discipline was established the surviving ancient papyri that preserved a good part of ancient writing had not yet been uncovered. Modern scripts have still not received the systematic treatment they need and deserve and for a number of reasons, the main one being simply the massiveness of the task they present.

Medieval scholars were not without some of the knowledge of scripts that would later come under the aegis of paleography. If these scholars were going to correctly transcribe texts from much older manuscripts, for example, and this was not infrequently a task that they set themselves, they needed to have practical expertise in recognizing the letter forms of a variety of older Latin scripts. In the later Middle Ages writing masters were capable of making and detecting very refined distinctions between an almost bewildering variety of scripts. The culmination of this refinement came between 1510 and 1520, when Leonhard Wagner, a Benedictine monk at Augsburg, produced his *Proba centum scripturarum,* which supplied names for, as well as samples of, a hundred different Latin scripts. At various times master scribes, whether for aesthetic reasons or in order to make forgery of documents more difficult, had devised new scripts that consciously departed from the received tradition. Medieval scholars were aware that some scripts were older than others. In many parts of Europe they could still see Latin inscriptions from the Roman period. They occasionally called special attention to manuscripts copied in "littera antiqua." As for placing scripts, a ninth-century library cataloger at the monastery of St. Gall in Switzerland could recognize certain books as "scottice scripti," that is, copied in the Insular script that had developed in Ireland. The characteristic scripts of the papal curia were undoubtedly recognized over most of Europe, as were the scripts used by the professional copyists at the universities of Paris and Bologna. But in general the ability of medieval scholars to date and place with proximity to the truth scripts that were far removed from their own time and place was very limited. Their historical conceptions were vague and groping and offered little protection against egregious errors of judgment. Thus several medieval English librarians could anachronistically credit the Venerable Bede with copying manuscripts in types of handwriting not used until centuries after his death. In the fourteenth century Emperor Charles IV and his scholarly advisers believed that a famous Gospelbook, probably produced in the sixth century, had been copied by the hand of St. Mark himself (even though it contained the Latin Vulgate translation!). And it was the humanists who revived the Caroline minuscule, at least in part because they regarded it as a script from classical antiquity. For perspective's sake, however, it should perhaps be noted that a blunder of similar magnitude could still be committed by an eminent scholar of the nineteenth century.

The assembling of scattered fragments of medieval and early modern knowledge about handwriting history into a coherent body of knowledge, together with purging a large admixture of error and filling in huge lacunae, would have to await the beginnings of the Enlightenment, though the scholars responsible for this development would not be agnostic *philosophes* but rather very orthodox Benedictine monks with at least one foot still in the Middle Ages. In an effort to enucleate convincing tests for determining the genuineness of what purported to be the oldest extant medieval Latin charters, which often happened to contain royal grants to Benedictine houses and the authenticity of which was often under severe attack from the Jesuit Bollandists who were editing the *Acta sanctorum,* the Benedictine Maurist scholar Jean Mabillon realized that scripts, if properly studied, might serve as one of the more reliable criteria. The systematic treatment that he consequently accorded to scripts in his *De re diplomatica,* published at Paris in 1681, is the first study to which the name paleography might have been fitly applied, if it were not for the fact that the name itself does not seem to have been invented until 1708, when Mabillon's younger confrere, Bernard de Montfaucon, published a groundbreaking study of Greek scripts that he entitled *Palaeographia graeca.* For Mabillon, knowledge of script history served primarily as a means to corroborate or invalidate conclusions in diplomatics, along with enabling the diplomatist to read his documents more expeditiously and correctly. Paleography was only an auxiliary science, not something pursued for its own sake.

In the centuries since Mabillon, paleography has gradually assumed, for most of its practitioners, the status of an independent historical discipline. This development has not eliminated all disagreement over what its primary purposes should be, nor has it eliminated the auxiliary role that paleography has played for general history as well as for the more specialized disciplines of diplomatics, epigraphy, papyrology, philology, and codicology to which its own progress has been so closely tied. The reason it can continue to serve as an auxiliary science, and perhaps more effectively than ever, while assuming independent status is simply, apart from the possibility of greater objectivity, that the questions addressed to it by other disciplines are among the questions to which its own well-being demands answers. Paleography is asked for help in reading—sometimes deciphering would be a more appropriate term—strange and unfamiliar scripts. Unless it can provide this help, which involves recognition and at least a rough classification of scripts as well as the ability to transcribe individual letters into our present alphabet, it can hardly pursue its own proper tasks with any hope of success. It is also asked for approximate dates and places of origin of individual examples of script. Unless it can supply such dates and places, the examples in question lose much of their potential value as evidence for the history of handwriting. Some of the problems raised by the role paleography plays as an auxiliary science will be central to the discussion of methodology below.

Progress in paleography during the last century and a half has been closely tied to advances in technology. Because minute comparisons of scripts, as will be seen below, are an essential feature of paleographical argumentation, the invention of photography made possible a quantum leap forward. Photographic reproductions are not a completely satisfactory substitute for original manuscripts, but they have vast advantages over hand-drawn copies and tracings, to say nothing of the unaided human memory. Scholars could henceforth assemble in one place for leisurely and simultaneous comparison materials that were previously, because scattered far and wide, available only for serial consideration at disadvantageous intervals of time. The application of fluorescent light to manuscript photography starting in the second decade of the twentieth century resurrected many early palimpsested scripts for paleographical consideration. The manifest advantages of photography were naturally multiplied many times over as soon as photographs began to be reproduced in books, and these advantages, in turn, have been more than doubled by the development of xerography. Any scholar can now easily and economically acquire a private collection of the basic materials for paleographical study. Although paleography has only begun to exploit the graphic and manipulative capabilities of the computer, there seems a good chance that the eventual impact of computer technology may rival that of photography.

Apart from the contributions of technology, the most significant recent development in paleography has been the more efficient coordination of scholarly efforts through the establishment of the Comité International de Paléographie Latine at Paris in 1953. Besides holding periodic international conferences, the Comité, now consisting of elected members from most European and North American nations, has emphasized two objectives: (1) the creation of a polyglot lexicon of technical terms used in paleography together with a uniform nomenclature for Latin scripts, and (2) the publication of illustrated national catalogs of dated manuscripts in Latin scripts from the beginning up to the end of the sixteenth century. While much preliminary work has been done on the lexicon and nomenclature projects, the dated-manuscript project has made extraordinary progress. Thousands of facsimiles of dated manuscripts in Latin script have already been published and many more are in an advanced state of preparation. The impetus given to paleographical studies by this more organized approach has already borne much fruit, evident especially in the number of vigorous journals that have recently come into existence, and there is every reason to believe that the harvest has only begun.

NOMENCLATURE AND METHODOLOGY

Paleography's ability to trace and explain the various phases in the history of scripts naturally presupposes an ability to distinguish and classify scripts. But this in turn requires a uniform vocabulary to describe both scripts as a whole and the elements out of which they are composed. Until the nomenclature project of the Comité International de Paléographie Latine is completed and has won general acceptance, therefore, paleography's progress will be somewhat hampered. Nevertheless, because most of paleography's technical terms are taken from ordinary language and retain their original meanings, the disadvantage is less than it might be, and only a few terms to be used below need explanation here.

With regard to the elements that combine to form individual letters, the basic *i*-stroke (without dot) is often called a "minim," so named from the fact that in Gothic script this word was composed of ten *i*-strokes. The extension of a minim above or below the level of the shortest letters is called an "ascender" or "descender" respectively. The minim, with or without an ascender or descender, that supports another part of a letter is called a "stem." The "body" of a letter designates either the whole letter or that part that is not an ascender or descender. The lead-in or finishing stroke at the beginning or end of a letter is called a "finial" or "serif." The connective stroke between letters is sometimes called a "ligature," but this term is better used for two or more letters united in a way that changes the form of at least one of them or that eliminates a stroke by sharing.

Although the paleographer as such, unlike the calligrapher, is not interested in understanding how writing strokes are made and put together in order to make and put them together himself, he is nevertheless very interested in the process or dynamics of stroke formation, not only because differences here may help to distinguish and date and localize scripts but more importantly because the sequence and the direction of strokes, particularly in rapid writing, where they are easier to recognize, may help to explain the changes in appearance that letters undergo over the course of time. The name that has been given to express this idea of the sequence and direction, as well as the number, of the strokes used to form each letter of a script's alphabet is "ductus." But while ductus can often explain a change in the appearance of a letter, it is important to remember that a change in appearance can in turn generate a new ductus. "Shading" designates the presence of regularly contrasting thick and thin strokes, resulting usually from directional changes in the path of a broad-nibbed writing instrument held at a constant angle with respect to the horizontal writing line. Shaded scripts can be characterized by the angle their thickest strokes form with the writing line. This angle should not be confused with a script's "slant," that is, the angle of departure from the vertical of its upright strokes.

In the classification and naming of entire scripts, in contrast to the elements that compose them, both the dynamic process of letter formation and the static appearance of letters may come into play. Scripts have been divided into lettering and writing, and writing in turn has been subdivided into noncursive and cursive, formal and informal, majuscule and minuscule, and literary and documentary. "Lettering" uses more than one stroke to form each part of a letter, by building up or filling in or chiseling out its outline. "Writing" uses no more than one stroke for each part of a letter. "Noncursive" writing makes each part of each letter in a separate stroke. "Cursive" writing usually makes more than one part of a letter in one stroke and tends to make more than one letter without the writing instrument being removed from the writing surface. Consistent cursive calls for loops or doubled strokes on ascenders and descenders and favors ligatures. Naturally there is room for many intermediate scripts. Because even loops and ligatures can be written in noncursive fashion, the term "current" has been proposed for scripts that are actually written with the writing instrument remaining in contact with the writing surface through one or more letters, while "cursive" would designate scripts of which the appearance, with loops and ligatures, was originally generated by current writing but which may actually no longer be written currently. "Formal" scripts have a calligraphic objective and are written with regularity and deliberation and therefore noncurrently. "Informal" scripts tend to be written currently. Varying degrees of semiformality are of course possible in between. "Majuscule" scripts have letters all, or nearly all, of the same height, while "minuscule" scripts have some letters with ascenders and descenders, thus corresponding to the printer's uppercase and lowercase type fonts, respectively. "Literary" or "book" scripts tend to be formal and noncursive, while "documentary" or "charter" ones tend to be more current and to develop individualities that help protect against forgery. Both are named from their usual content, but literary scripts have sometimes been used for charters and documentary ones for books. The foregoing generic names and classifications, though by no means universally accepted, are relatively unproblematic; there is considerable disagreement, however, over the names for the species and subspecies that come under them.

In terms of its methodology and the reliability of its results or conclusions, paleography is like general history in being able to ascertain facts better than it can explain them. Although factors intrinsic to the act of writing—in particular various combinations of ductus and speed—can and do generate changes in scripts, factors well beyond the world of script—political, religious, educational, economic, technological, aesthetic—can also affect both the very existence of scripts and the kinds of changes they undergo. The very multiplicity of potential causal factors can make certainty in paleographical explanation difficult to achieve. But even in the descriptive generalizations that paleography makes about scribal behavior, as well as in the paleographical argumentation that uses these generalizations to put particular examples of script into their proper historical context, there are problems in achieving certainty or exactness. Because these problems have a direct bearing on the reliability of paleography's answers to the questions most frequently addressed to it, that is to say, questions about the date and place of origin of individual samples of script, something more must be said about them, for the benefit both of those who consult paleography from the outside and of those who are just beginning its study. The dating and localizing of individual examples of scripts, what might be called applied paleography, usually cannot be carried out without a historical framework, the creation of which might be called theoretical paleography. Both kinds of paleography have their problems that need to be discussed.

Applied paleography. The dating and placing objectives of applied paleography are not concerned simply with a script in the abstract but with a concrete example of it (let it be called MS *A*). However, while applied paleography may came to conclusions about the origin of MS *A* that are sometimes almost absolutely certain, the more dependable side of applied paleography operates on the abstract level. The problem to be solved is the identification of the species of script to which MS *A* belongs (this species, which is of course a factual and not an organic one, will have geographical and temporal limits) and then of the stage of development and the local variety to which it belongs within that species. If these problems can be solved, the supposition is that whatever is true of the species at its given stage of development is also true of MS *A*. If the species is a minuscule script and in the stage of development characteristic of early-ninth-century France, then MS *A* must have originated in early-ninth-century France. It may have happened, however, that the scribe of MS *A*, having mastered his craft in early-ninth-century France, actually copied MS *A* while visiting Rome. Or he may have copied it in the late ninth century, having continued to use the very same script learned in his youth well into his old age. Or, in a scenario perhaps harder to realize with perfection, MS *A* may have been written in fifteenth-century Florence by a scribe who took it upon himself to revive a mastery of the script of early-ninth-century France. These real possibilities lead to the making of a distinction between the stylistic date and place of origin on the one hand and the actual date and place of origin on the other. The stylistic date and place of origin of MS *A* are early-ninth-century France, even though the actual date and place in the hypothetical examples would be early-ninth-century Rome, late-ninth-century France, or fifteenth-century Florence. The scholar appealing to the paleographer for advice usually wants to know the actual dates and places of origin, but the paleographer's method is ideally suited to supply only the stylistic ones.

Although in most cases the two origins are identical, the processes by which they are established are quite different. To establish the stylistic origin of a manuscript, if one recognizes the species to which its script belongs, one can consult the appropriate bibliography and find both the theoretical studies in which the script is defined, its characteristic features delineated, its stages of development traced and dated, its geographic diffusion mapped, and the works in which facsimiles, particularly dated and placed ones, may be found. A close comparison must then be made both of general script features and of particular letters in terms of both their form and their ductus. In the most fortunate case the resemblance to one of the facsimiles may be so exact that one can conclude to an identity of scribe. Much more frequently, however, there will be divergences. Usually they are such as can be fitted between the stages of development or into a regional variation to which the theoretical studies have called attention or they can reasonably be regarded simply as idiosyncrasies of the individual scribe. Sometimes, however, the divergences are such as to bring into question the initial assumption about species or even genus. Reliability of judgments about the meaning of deviations improves with experience and is ever subject to further refinement. If, as is still all too often the case, no satisfactory theoretical study yet exists, the applied paleographer may have to become his own theoretician.

The comparison of a manuscript's script ought to be followed by similar comparisons of its abbreviations, punctuation, and various codicological elements with the theoretical studies on these subjects. Although the most essential knowledge that anyone can have about abbreviations is how to expand them correctly, it remains true that the various methods of abbreviation as well as individual abbreviations have a history that, if known, may be able to throw light on the date and place of origin of the manuscript in which they occur. Much of the history of abbreviations, however, still remains to be written. Punctuation methods and individual punctuation marks offer the same kinds of possibilities as abbreviations do, but even more still remains to be done on the history of punctuation. Writing materials (chiefly papyrus, parchment, and paper) and the ways in which they were prepared to receive script as rolls or codices, with measurable external dimensions and column sizes, with countable numbers of columns and lines per column, and with exactly specifiable methods of pricking, ruling, quire formation, and binding, are not matters that paleography studies for their own sakes nor need these matters directly affect the nature of scripts. Nevertheless some of these codicological features may have steady factual associations with scripts of certain times and places, and certain combinations of these exactly quantifiable features may point exclusively to one scriptorium during a short period of its history. Philological and art historical comparisons of a similar sort might also be undertaken. If the results of all these further comparisons argue for the same conclusion as the script does, or at least do not argue for any other, the paleographical conclusion about the manuscript's stylistic origin may be considered well established. If they do argue for another conclusion, the paleographical conclusion is not necessarily undermined, but at the least a question is raised as to whether the actual origin does not differ from the stylistic one.

As for establishing the actual date and place of origin of a manuscript, the working assumption of the applied paleographer, in the absence of contrary evidence, is that they do not differ from the stylistic, and as often as not he may be unable to go beyond the stylistic results. The most obvious kind of evidence that can prove a difference between actual and stylistic origins is a scribe's subscription saying that he copied the manuscript at a time and a place that disagree with the stylistic conclusion. (It should be noted that a stylistic conclusion can hardly ever be as exact with regard to date as a subscription can be, though it may be as exact with regard to place.) Thus a subscription entered in an Italian type of Gothic script by an Italian scribe in MS 214 of the Bibliothèque Municipale in Toulouse says that the manuscript was copied in Paris in 1465. Since there are reasons, to be discussed below, why even subscriptions are not absolutely convincing evidence, one may doubt that the Toulouse manuscript was actually written in Paris, but it would take more than the problem created by a difference between stylistic and actual origins to prove that it was not actually written in Paris. It should be noted that because manuscripts were sometimes copied in one place and then decorated, possibly much later, in another place, both the script and the decoration in the same manuscript but of differing geographical and chronological styles could each have actually been produced in its own stylistic home. It should also be noted that the assumed identity of stylistic and actual origin can be corroborated by the collaboration either of multiple scribes writing the same type of script or of multiple scribes, craftsmen, and artists whose respective styles of work all share the same geographical and chronological limits. It is easy for a scribe or two to travel away from home, but each additional scribe makes the assumption of travel less and less likely. Determining how many scribes actually collaborated on a manuscript, however, can be a difficult task. A change in the species of script need not mean a change of scribe, since scribes often mastered a variety of scripts. The objection to the same scribe using more than one species of script for the text of a work is a matter of aesthetics rather than of intrinsic difficulty. The more usual problem, however, is how to identify different scribes trying to write the same type of script. On the one hand, in a well-disciplined scriptorium of high standards, differences between scribes may be hard to detect. On the other hand, the performance of one and the same scribe can be noticeably modified by a change in his writing instrument or its nib cut or in writing speed or in the scribe's own physical or mental well-being. Where, within the same species of script, a minor but consistent change in appearance is introduced, but some doubt nevertheless remains whether the change implies a different scribe, one may have to leave the question open by speaking simply of a changed hand.

Of many other conceivable kinds of evidence bearing on the actual origin of a manuscript mention should finally be made of contents and provenance. The contents may be appropriate only to a place or time outside the stylistic boundaries. Examples might be a manuscript in an Italian type of script but containing a liturgical calendar usable only in an English monastery, or a manuscript in Caroline script containing works of Petrarch. If the earliest documented place of preservation of a manuscript, what may be called its provenance, is close in time to its presumed date of origin, provenance may be said to offer probable evidence for place of origin, but the degree of probability declines as the time between the date of origin and the date of attested provenance increases.

Theoretical paleography. Knowing something of the methodology of theoretical paleography may not seem essential to the nonpaleographical scholar or to the beginner in this subject, but in fact such knowledge is needed by anyone trying to judge the validity of paleographic conclusions. Both the outside scholar and the beginner may find that they cannot proceed very far even with their applied interests without becoming their own theoreticians. The incentive for most theoretical advances in paleography has come from a desire to solve an applied problem, and the number of such problems for which an adequate historical framework still does not exist is vast. Theoretical paleography, because it advances the discipline by establishing new criteria for dating and placing the origins of individual manuscripts, deserves the name of paleography in a more proper sense than does the applied branch. Ideally the method calls first for assembling a list of all the manuscripts apparently showing a given species or type of script, and then on the basis of direct examination as well as the study of photographs ascertaining the characteristic general features and individual letter forms that set the script off from other scripts. Some manuscripts tentatively considered part of the group may be eliminated at this stage. Then on the basis of those members of the group that are dated and placed by nonpaleographical evidence—in particular by scribal subscriptions—not only are chronological and geographical limits established for the script as a whole but the stages of development within the group are also both defined and dated and the regional variations are noted. The assembling of the manuscripts needed for this purpose has been greatly facilitated by the various national projects, referred to above, for the publication of facsimile specimens of dated and placed manuscripts.

This brief description of the ideal procedure overlooks a number of difficulties to be mentioned shortly. But first it should be noted that conditions are rarely as ideal as just pictured, either because the extant book and documentary script materials may not be fully representative, which is the case with the earlier Middle Ages, or because the extant materials are simply too numerous for exhaustive paleographic cataloging, which is the case with the later Middle Ages. Generalizations about scribal behavior, therefore, whether the generalizations are affirmative or negative, are not entirely trustworthy. However, although ideal conditions seem beyond hope of realization, significant improvement in the situation can nevertheless be achieved through fuller exploitation of the facsimile material being published in the various national dated manuscript projects.

But even when it is possible to make, if not a complete, at least a sufficient, enumeration of the extant examples of any given species or type of script, there may still be limitations on the validity of paleography's general conclusions. The basic weakness, of course, is that the rules enunciated in theoretical paleography have only a factual, not a necessary, character. Tradition weighs very heavily on scribes and for them to treat it with cavalier disregard would defeat their own communicative purpose. Nevertheless, scribes could and did depart from their tradition and not simply unconsciously or out of incompetence. Neither tradition nor the rules detected ex post facto by the theoretical paleographer absolutely determined how things were going to be.

This loophole in almost all paleographical generalizations can give rise to difficulties in the classification of scripts into species and types. The behavior of scribes, even when they seemingly try to write the same script, can eventually become so various that one finds it hard to say whether the results all belong to the same species or type. The answer will change from yes to no at some point along a continuum that cannot avoid appearing somewhat arbitrary.

Still other difficulties accompany the scribes' subscriptions telling when and where they did their work. The theoretical paleographer's working assumption is that these subscriptions are authentic and truthful. But it is of course possible that they may be forged or unwittingly taken over unchanged from the scribe's exemplar. The famous Echternach Gospelbook (Paris, Bibliothèque Nationale, MS lat. 9389), for example, which is copied in Insular script, has a subscription saying it was corrected in the year 558. If this information were true, the Echternach Gospelbook would antedate any other dated example of Insular script by several generations, even though the stage of development within Insular script represented by the Echternach Gospelbook is not otherwise attested until almost a century and a half after 558. A lone subscription is, alas, almost always subject to challenge. But even if there were no reason to suspect the genuineness and accuracy of a subscription with respect to the actual date and place of a manuscript's origin, there is no absolute assurance that these facts apply to other manuscripts copied in identical or similar script. The actual origin, as was pointed out above, may differ from the stylistic origin. As a result, real safety in theoretical paleography is to be found only in numbers. If a significant proportion of manuscripts in a stylistically related group and copied by different scribes contains subscriptions that almost all speak for approximately the same time and place of origin, this actual time and place may confidently be taken as the stylistic time and place of origin. In such a case, if a manuscript like Toulouse 214, referred to above, is said in a subscription to have been copied in Paris instead of Italy, one can explain it away with equanimity as the work of a traveling Italian scribe. But if this were the only localized example of the script, one might wrongly conclude that the style of this script was Parisian. In fact, this is the type of error that is more likely to occur as one goes further back in time and encounters fewer and fewer subscriptions. Many groups of stylistically related manuscripts simply have no subscriptions at all on the basis of which they can be tied down to an actual date and place of origin. A deficiency of reliable subscriptions can sometimes be compensated for by other evidence. Contents or other aspects of a manuscript, for example, may enable one to establish a date before or after which it could not have been copied. Further help in both localizing and dating may be available through provenance. The provenance of a single manuscript is not very persuasive evidence, but if most manuscripts in a given stylistic group were preserved from the earliest recorded time in the same region, this region is very likely the stylistic home of the group.

It follows as a corollary of scribal freedom that when a species of script is widely used in many different scriptoria or is even an international script, there is no reason why it should not be either in different stages of development at the same time or in the same stage of development at different times. Another corollary, recognized already by Mabillon, is that the use of one script at a given time and place does not exclude the use of another script for the same purpose at the same time and place.

In view of all the limitations under which theoretical paleography labors, it would seem that its conclusions, and a fortiori those of applied paleography, are shaky. By comparison with a geometrical proof they undoubtedly are shaky. Theoretical paleography is not an exact science and applied paleography is at best a delicate and somewhat imprecise art. But by comparison with intuition or pure guesswork, the conclusions of paleography possess an enviable solidity.

MEDIEVAL SCRIPTS

The survey that follows of the main kinds of writing used in the Middle Ages must limit itself largely to reporting a few, brief results of many, often extended, paleographical investigations. Accounts of the actual investigations and studies on which the survey is based can be found through the bibliography. For reasons already stated, the survey will concentrate on scripts used in books and documents to the relative neglect of those used in other contexts. A small facsimile will be provided of some of the scripts.

Roman scripts. The Latin scripts used in Western Europe at the beginning of the Middle Ages were all inherited from Roman antiquity. The medieval fates of these Roman scripts would include transformations into other types of script, dissolutions or disappearances, and revivals. And the Roman scripts, in whatever kind of afterlife they enjoyed, would also be brought, thanks to the geographical expansion of Western European medieval civilization, into many parts of Europe that had never known them in Roman times.

The most stately of these Roman scripts, representing a formalization of a very early stage of the

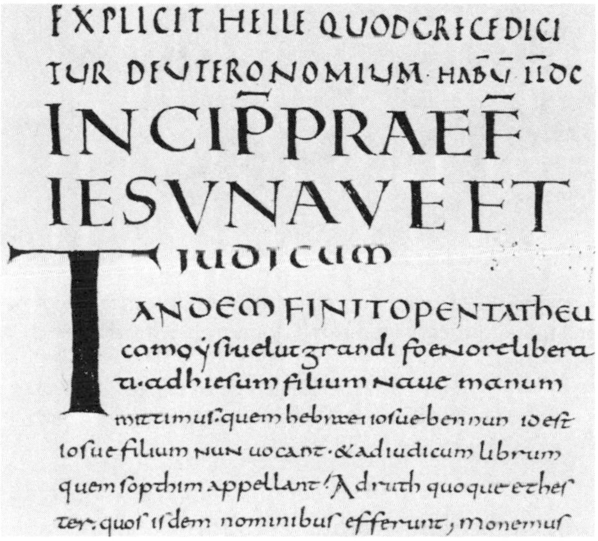

EXPLICIT HELLE QUOD GRECE DICI/TUR DEUTERONOMIUM. HAB(ET) V(ERSUS) MMDC. / INCIP(IT) PRAEF(ATIO) / IESU NAVE ET / IUDICUM / TANDEM FINITO PENTATHEU / *co moysi velut grandi foenore libera / ti ad hiesum filium nave manum* / mittimus, quem hebraei iosue ben nun id est / iosue filium nun vocant, et ad iudicum librum / quem sopthim appellant. Ad ruth quoque et hes / ter, quos isdem nominibus efferunt. Monemus

Fig. 1. Rustic capital (lines 1–2), square capital (3–4), uncial (5–6), half-uncial (7–8), Caroline minuscule (9–12). Tours, early 9th century. Old Testament (preface to Joshua and Judges). Paris, Bibliothèque Nationale, MS Lat. 11514, fol. 74r. REPRODUCED FROM E. K. RAND, *A SURVEY OF THE MANUSCRIPTS OF TOURS* (1929)

Latin alphabet, is traditionally known as square capital, easily recognized as the script used for the running heads on each page of this *Dictionary*. A majuscule script, it was used by the Romans mostly for inscriptions on stone. In manuscripts it served mainly for titles and colophons. As a text script it survives in only three fragmentary copies of Vergil from the fourth and fifth centuries. Square capital degenerated in the seventh century, was revived in the Carolingian period (Fig. 1), and after another period of eclipse was permanently revived by the humanists in the fifteenth century as a script for inscriptions and titles.

The most formal of the Roman bookscripts in frequent use was rustic capital. Its easily recognized form reflects regular and pronounced shading and consistent use of thick and almost horizontal finials at the foot of its thin vertical strokes. Rustic capital achieved canonical status in the first century after Christ and remained in use for copying texts

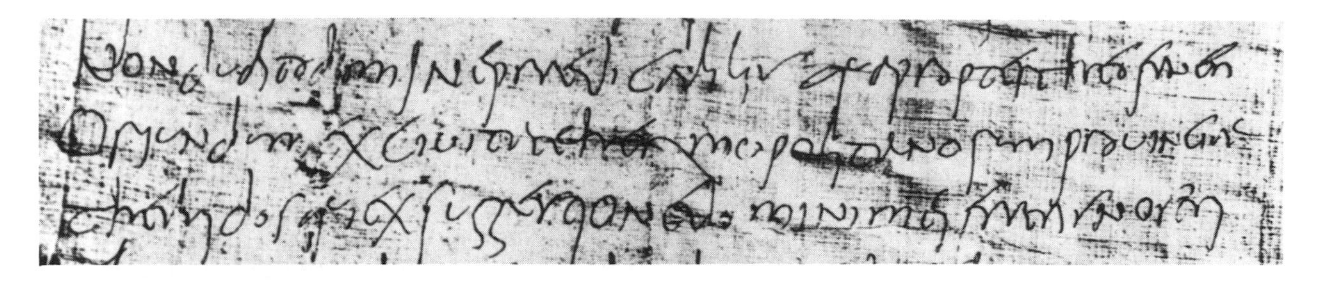

non dubito, domine praedicabilis, quapropter theofanen / oriundum ex civitate hermupolitanorum provinciae / thebaidos, qui ex suggestione domini mei fratris nostri

Fig. 2. Later Roman cursive. Egypt, 317–324. Letter of recommendation. Strasbourg, Bibliothèque Nationale et Universitaire, Pap. Lat. 1B. REPRODUCED FROM ZACARÍAS GARCÍA VILLADA, *PALEOGRAFÍA ESPAÑOLA* (1923)

through the sixth century. For centuries thereafter, and particularly in Spain, it was used for titles and other special purposes, sometimes in diluted or decorative or slightly deviant forms (see Fig. 8 below). It was introduced into England for prefatory texts in the early eighth century and in Carolingian France (Fig. 1) it was even used for the text of the famous Utrecht Psalter. Various rustic letters survived through most of the Middle Ages as capitals at the beginning of sentences.

The most frequently preserved bookscript from the Roman period was uncial, distinguishable from rustic capital by the form of its *A, D, E, G, H, M,* and *Q* and by the absence of regular finials at the foot of vertical strokes (Figs. 1, 8). The oldest dated example comes from the second half of the fourth century, but it may have developed a century earlier. Uncial's preeminent popularity, at least for the copying of books, continued into the eighth century and it was still used for this purpose in the ninth and tenth centuries. For titles and capitals at the beginning of sentences it was used even several centuries later. In the course of its history the bodies of its letters became rounder and its ascenders and descenders longer.

The next most popular bookscript, at least from the fifth to the seventh century, was half-uncial, the nearest approach yet to the modern Roman lowercase printing font. It differs from uncial in its *a, b, d, g, m, r,* and *s.* Its thickest strokes are almost vertical. Half-uncial in its fully developed form probably goes back to around the year 400—a more primitive version may share a common ancestor with uncial—and it continued in use, at least for special purposes, into the ninth century (Fig. 1).

Of the less formal, nonbookscripts of the Romans, the one that would overlap into the Middle Ages and also serve as an immediate or remote ancestor for several new medieval scripts was the later or newer Roman cursive, also called the new Roman common or everyday script. Usually two or more parts of one letter and sometimes even two or more whole letters were made in one continuous motion of the pen. Loops appear on many ascenders and ligatures are frequent. This newer cursive took shape no later than the second half of the third century and continued in use in some regions into the eighth century and occasionally even later. Early examples retained a form of *b* with the bow on the left side of the stem (Fig. 2).

Early medieval scripts. The breakdown of centralized political authority in the western half of the Roman Empire in the second half of the fifth century did not have an immediately visible impact on the history of scripts. The Roman scripts, as already seen, continued in use. What disappeared in the political decentralization, however, was the frequency or kinds of contacts that previously kept different provinces from unconsciously drifting apart from others in their writing habits, and possibly this also loosened the traditional restraints on experimentation. In addition, the public educational system, which had helped to preserve continuity by providing new generations of students with instruction in the art of handwriting, also went into a decline. Vividly visible effects of these new conditions, however, would be slow and uneven in appearing. Interestingly enough, some of the earliest noteworthy changes would show up in Ireland.

Literacy in Latin came to Ireland not in the wake of Roman conquest but through Christian conver-

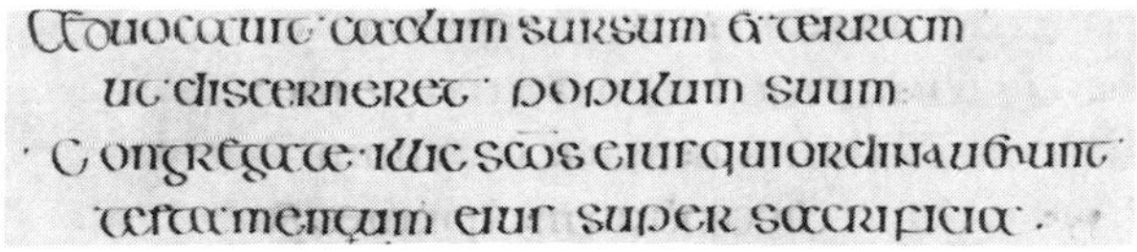

Advocavit caelum sursum et terram / ut discerneret populum suum / Congregate illic s(an)c(t)os eius qui ordinaverunt / testamentum eius super sacrificia

Fig. 3. Insular round or half-uncial. England, mid 8th century. Psalter. NEW YORK, PIERPONT MORGAN LIBRARY, MS M. 776, fol. 15r

sion. Although no extant Latin writing samples from Ireland can be dated with certainty before the early seventh century, Irish monks were certainly writing in Latin in the sixth century and there seems no reason why Latin could not have already been written in Ireland in the fifth century under St. Patrick. The Irish eventually developed two types of what are called Insular scripts because of their long dominance in the British Isles. One is the round or half-uncial (Fig. 3), used for the famous Book of Kells and Lindisfarne Gospel. It is broad, its thickest strokes are almost vertical, and its curved strokes tend to circular fullness. Upright strokes have wedge-shaped finials at the top. Characteristic is its *a* looking like contiguous *oc*. Because ascenders and descenders are short, the script is sometimes called Insular majuscule. Although this round script made use in modified form of all the letters of the Roman half-uncial alphabet, because it also used uncial forms of *D, R,* and *S* and a cursive form of *n,* it source material must have been a precanonical or uncanonical type of half-uncial.

The other Insular script, called pointed or minuscule (Fig. 4), is laterally compressed and its thickest strokes run at an angle only about 30 degrees below horizontal, so vertical strokes tend to end in a point at the bottom. Descenders and ascenders are fairly long. Typical is an angular, somewhat squeezed form of *a,* used along with an open *cc* form. There are often also two forms of *d.* The oldest surviving dated example of this pointed script is from the 680's.

The round script was taken to Great Britain probably before the middle, and the pointed script probably before the end, of the seventh century, and from both England and Ireland missionaries took them to the Continent. The popularity of the round script was declining by the ninth century, but examples of its use from as late as the fifteenth

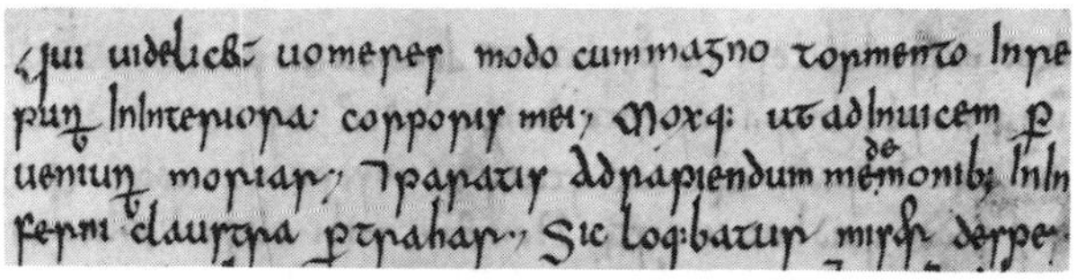

PALEOGRAPHY

qui videlicet vomeres modo cum magno tormento inre / punt in interiora corporis mei. Moxq(ue) ut ad invicem p(er) / veniunt moriar, (et) paratis ad rapiendum me \de/monib(us) in in / ferni claustra p(er)trahar. Sic loq(ue)batur miser despe[rans]

Fig. 4. Insular pointed, or minuscule. Probably England, early 9th century. Bede, *Ecclesiastical History.* BLOOMINGTON, INDIANA UNIVERSITY, LILLY LIBRARY, RICKETTS MS 177

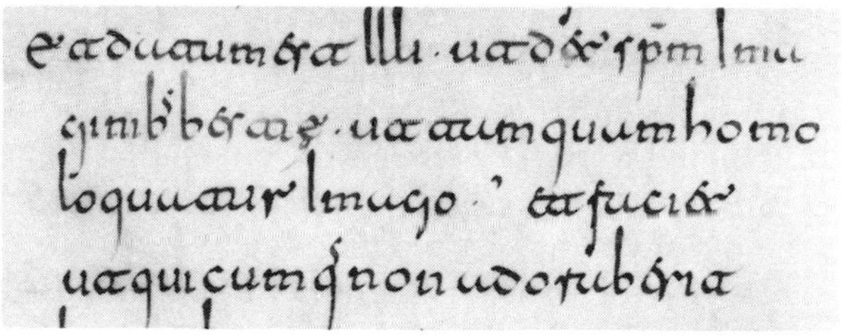

Et datum est illi, ut det sp(iritu)m ima / ginib(us) bestiæ, ut tamquam homo / loquatur imago. et faciet / ut quicumq(ue) non adoraberit

Fig. 5. Visigothic minuscule. Spain, 926. Beatus of Liébana, *Commentary on the Apocalypse.* NEW YORK, PIERPONT MORGAN LIBRARY, MS M. 644, fol. 172r

survive in titles in Gaelic manuscripts. The Anglo-Saxon missionary districts in Germany ceased to use the pointed script in the mid ninth century. In England this script died out for Latin texts in the tenth and eleventh centuries and for vernacular texts by the thirteenth century. In Ireland it was given up for Latin texts by the thirteenth century, but it has never wholly ceased to be used for Gaelic texts.

Another early medieval script that made extensive use of Roman half-uncial was Visigothic minuscule (Fig. 5). Even its characteristic uncial form of *g* may have come from a variant kind of half-uncial. The script is also like half-uncial in its relative breadth, but its thickest stroke is oblique rather than vertical and the foot of vertical strokes tends to be pointed rather than flat. And unlike the Insular half-uncial, Visigothic minuscule incorporated many elements from the later Roman cursive as well, in particular ligatures of *e* with a following *c, m, n, r, s,* and *x* and of *t* with a following *e, i,* and

PALEOGRAPHY

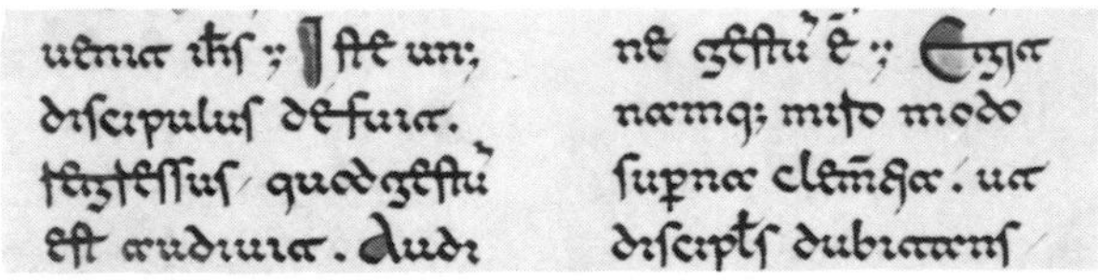

venit Ie(su)s. Iste un(us) / discipulus defuit, / regressus, quod gestu(m) / est audivit, audi[ta] / . . . [dispensatio]ne gestu(m) est. Egit / namq(ue) miro modo / sup(er)na clem(en)tia, ut / discip(u)l(u)s dubitans

Fig. 6. Beneventan minuscule. South Italy, *ca.* 1100. Lectionary. NEW YORK, PIERPONT MORGAN LIBRARY, MS M. 642, fol. 135r

r. Other features include an open *cc*-like *a* easily confusable with *u*, a tall *i* at the beginning of words and in mid word for the semiconsonantal sound (as in *eius*), a tall, thin *y*, and, in the later stages of the script, a *t* with its top bending down on the left to the foot of the stem. Visigothic minuscule developed in the Iberian Peninsula and the southernmost regions of France shortly before the Visigothic kingdom was invaded by the Muslims in 711. It was in a state of decline by the late eleventh century but nevertheless endured well into the thirteenth.

Beneventan minuscule was an important early medieval script that at least indirectly derived entirely from later Roman cursive. Although it would never abandon the letter forms it inherited from cursive and although it even made certain ligatures obligatory, particularly of *i* with various preceding letters, in the course of its long history it became extremely formal and deliberate, taking on strong shading, with the thickest stroke running 45 degrees or less below the horizontal, breaking its minim or *i*-stroke into two angles, and observing rules for the touching of letters with facing bows. Characteristic forms of *a* and *t* would be distinguishable from each other, once the top of *t* curved down on the left to the foot of the stem, only by their final strokes at the upper right (Fig. 6). The Benedictine abbey of Monte Cassino was the main center for this script, but it was used widely in south Italy from the mid eighth to the thirteenth century, with straggling examples surviving even from the sixteenth. From the tenth to the twelfth century it was also used in Dalmatia across the Adriatic, mostly in a variant version known as the Bari type.

Conscious or unconscious modifications and

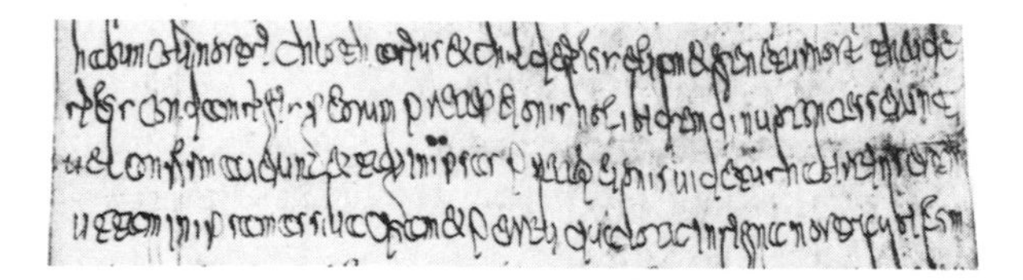

habuncoli nostri Chlotharius et Chyldericus, eciam et genetur nost(er) Theude / ricus, condam rigis, p(er) eorum precepcionis hoc ibidem dinuo concesserunt / vel confirmaverunt, et tal(iter) in ipsas precepcionis videtur habire insertum / ut, tam in ipsa Massilia quam et per reliqua loca in rigna nostra, ubicum[que]

Fig. 7. Merovingian cursive. Nogent-sur-Marne, France, 691. Privilege of Clovis III. Paris, Archives Nationales K 3, no. 5. REPRODUCED FROM PHILIPPE LAUER AND CHARLES SAMARAN, *LES DIPLÔMES ORIGINAUX DES MÉROVINGIENS* (1908)

mixings of inherited Roman scripts similar to those in south Italy and the Iberian Peninsula were also taking place in France and then in the neighboring Low Countries and the western parts of Germany and Switzerland, but here the long-term results were quite different. The only new script of long duration was a Merovingian cursive that gets its name from the fact that nearly all the oldest extant examples are found in charters issued by Merovingian kings (Fig. 7). This script, which clearly derived at least indirectly from the later Roman cursive and no later than the beginning of the seventh century, lasted through the Carolingian period and was still being used with recognizable continuity in Capetian royal documents of the early eleventh century. But calligraphic stylizations of this Merovingian cursive into new bookscripts—there were at least several of them in the seventh and eighth centuries—as well as more direct modifications of the inherited Roman scripts had a much shorter fate. Special mention should be made of the Luxeuil minuscule, originating in the second half of the seventh century and probably at the abbey that has given it its name (Fig. 8). Stylizations made in the eighth century, named from their probable places of origin and characteristic letter forms, included the Laon *az*, the *b* (possibly from Chelles near Paris), and the Corbie *ab* scripts. There were, in addition, numerous other deviations from, or eclectic combinations of, the prototypical Roman scripts that are less distinctive than the ones just mentioned or that survive in only one or two examples. One of these many competing types might have eventually achieved domination, but before this could happen

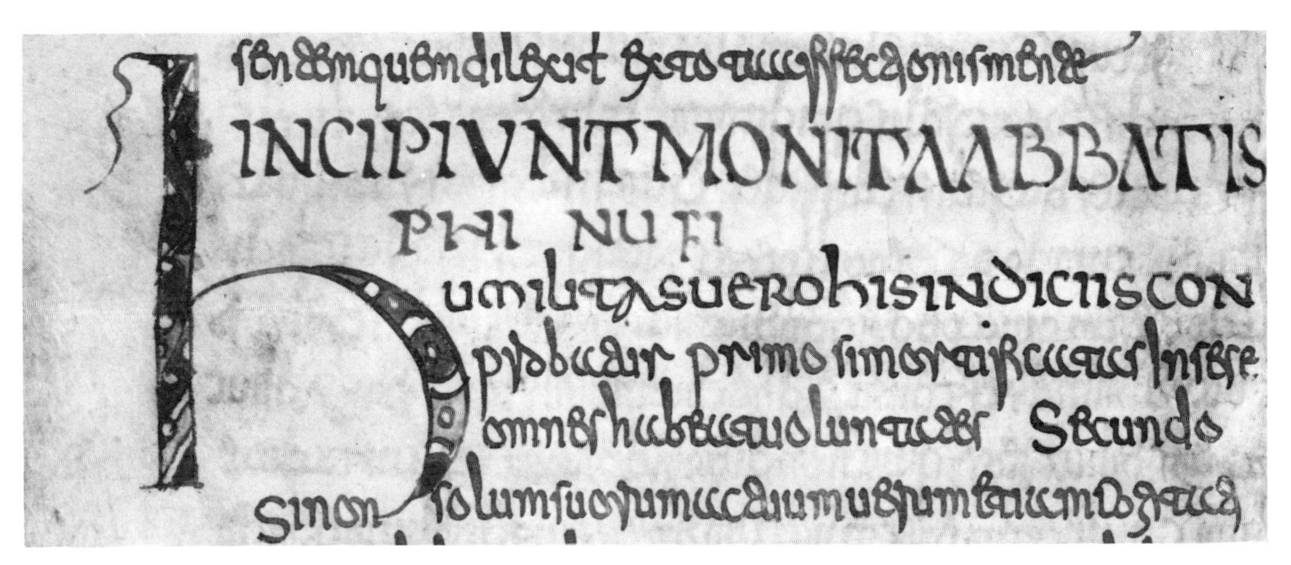

[ab]sentem quem dilexit ex tota affectionis mente. / INCIPIUNT MONITA ABBATIS / PHINUFI / **HUMILITAS VERO IIS INDICIIS CON** / probatur primo si mortificatas in sese / omnes habeat voluntates, secundo / si non solum suorum actuum verum etiam cogitati[onum]

Fig. 8. Luxeuil minuscule (lines 1, 5–7), rustic capital (2–3), uncial (4). France, probably Luxeuil, early 8th century. Caesarius of Arles, *Homilies*. NEW YORK, PIERPONT MORGAN LIBRARY, MS M. 17, fol. 37v

they were all either swept away or transformed by the Caroline minuscule.

Carolingian scripts. The Caroline minuscule is probably the most widely used script ever developed. Originating in the late eighth century in north France or the neighboring areas of Germany, it lasted for about four centuries until it was transformed into Gothic minuscule. Then, at the beginning of the fifteenth century, it was revived by Italian humanists and from them it was taken over in the 1460's by printers who turned it into the still widely dominant Roman type font. By the mid ninth century Caroline minuscule was being used for copying books in all of the Carolingian Empire except its southernmost fringes. It began to supplant the Anglo-Saxon scripts in England for Latin texts in the second half of the tenth century and the Visigothic minuscule in Spain in the late eleventh century. During these same centuries it was introduced into northeastern Germany, Poland, Bohemia, Hungary, and Scandinavia as these areas were brought within the bounds of Western Christendom. And it was being increasingly employed for the copying of charters. Although the spread of the new script may have been encouraged by royal and other patronage, its nearly universal triumph seems to have been due mainly to its intrinsic merits of economy, gracefulness, and legibility (Fig. 1).

The Caroline minuscule alphabet that prevailed during most of its long history differs basically from the modern Roman type font only in its long *s*. The forms of all its letters except *a*, *g*, and *n* could have come from Roman half-uncial, but in fact the model of most of them may actually have been provided more directly by one or another Merovingian or pre-Caroline script still being used in the second half of the eighth century. Many of its other qualities (for example, its grace and proportions) certainly came from a source of this kind. However, in eliminating most ligatures, Caroline minuscule consciously rejected a prominent feature of its Merovingian inheritance. While devising this new script, the Carolingians also revived the Roman capital scripts for special purposes and continued the use of uncial and half-uncial (Fig. 1).

Gothic scripts. Although Caroline minuscule is the handwriting legacy that the modern world has mainly appropriated from the Middle Ages, because Caroline minuscule seems so "modern," it is Gothic minuscule that is popularly regarded as the typical medieval script. This popular view also happens to be the true one, since far more medieval books and documentary texts are preserved in n(on) ambigat. Erit aut(em) ei (et) g(r)ande solatiu(m), si didic(er)it q(uo)d p(os)t me n(on) imp(er)it(us) vir aliq(u)is / aut indoct(us) atq(ue) ignorans divini minist(er)iu(m) v(er)bi (et) æccl(esi)astici ordinis, disciplinæ (ve)l / doct(r)inæ suscep(er)it cathedra(m) mea(m). Scit enim q(uia) si indoct(us) (et) inscius officiu(m) doc[toris]

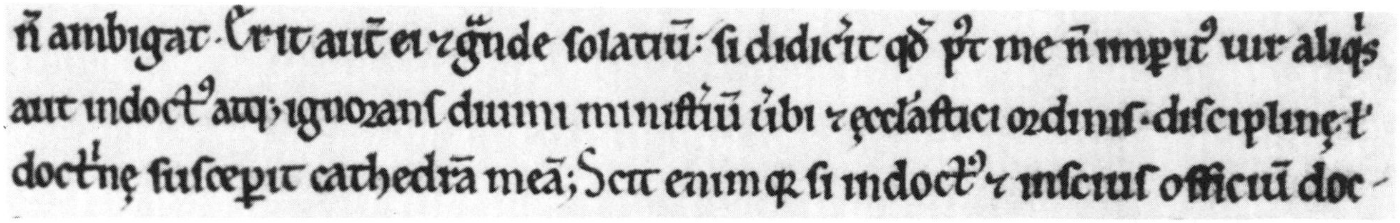

Fig. 9. Early Gothic textual. Villers, Belgium, late 12th century. Pseudo-Clement of Rome, *Epistle to James*. Louvain, Bibliothèque de l'Université, MS 186 (destroyed). REPRODUCED FROM EDMOND REUSENS, *ÉLÉMENTS DE PALÉOGRAPHIE* (1899)

Gothic writing than in any other. It must be remembered, however, that the name "Gothic" designates a whole complex of scripts that became increasingly differentiated as the Middle Ages came to an end. Several characteristic features tie this complex of scripts together, though not all the features are found in all the members of the complex. Included among these features are preferences for angularity over curves, for angular finials at the top and bottom of minims, for lateral compression that emphasizes height in short letters, and for considerable shading, with the perpendicular strokes fairly thick. Another feature was to have facing bows of adjacent letters (within the same word) overlap or share a common stroke, for example, the bows of *b* or *p* followed by those of *e* or *o*. Still another was an extension of an old habit of using a capital form of *R* in ligature with a preceding *o*. In Gothic this *R* was more and more regularly ligated with any preceding letter ending in a bow, for example, *b*, uncial *d*, and *p*. (By the end of the thirteenth century the part of the *R* that did not share a common stroke with the preceding bow, that is, the part that somewhat resembles an Arabic numeral 2, was beginning to be considered *r* all by itself and therefore used independently of a preceding bow.) Because these characteristic features were already starting to appear in Caroline minuscule in the twelfth century and some even in the late eleventh, the dividing line between Gothic and Caroline may seem arbitrary. What Gothic did to these characteristics, which seem to have originated as the result of gradual and perhaps unconscious changes in Caroline, was not only to use them with greater regularity but to tie at least several of them together in a deliberately comprehensive aesthetic system.

The original Gothic that developed out of Caroline in the twelfth century for the copying of book texts is often called textual, to distinguish it from other kinds, including cursive, originally used for charters, and hybrid, a later compromise that will be discussed below. Apart from being earlier, the textual more fully realized the Gothic aesthetic ideal. It possessed all the characteristic features mentioned above and in addition it manifested an awareness of the new aesthetic principle it was obeying by systematically treating alike the feet of all upright strokes standing on the line, giving each of them an angular finial. Specifically included in this treatment were the feet of *f* and tall *s*, which had usually descended below the line in late Caroline minuscule. Textual scripts that show this uniform treatment of feet but not yet the regular overlapping of facing bows are called early or primitive Gothic (Fig. 9).

Textual Gothic gradually came to be written with differing degrees of formality and speed. The more formal kind of textual, used especially for luxurious liturgical books, carried the Gothic principles to their ultimate in consistency. The angular finial on the feet of all upright strokes standing on the line became *v*-like, with the left branch of the *v* thick because of the direction of the pen nib and the right branch a hairline. In time the hairline stroke sometimes atrophied or was shortened and the finial took on the appearance of a rectangle balanced on its lower left corner. A corresponding upside-down version of this *v*-like finial was used at the top of minim strokes, but with the left branch a hairline and the right one thick. At the extreme of systematic symmetry achieved by the formal Gothic textual script, the finial system for minims was extended to curved strokes. At the bottom all

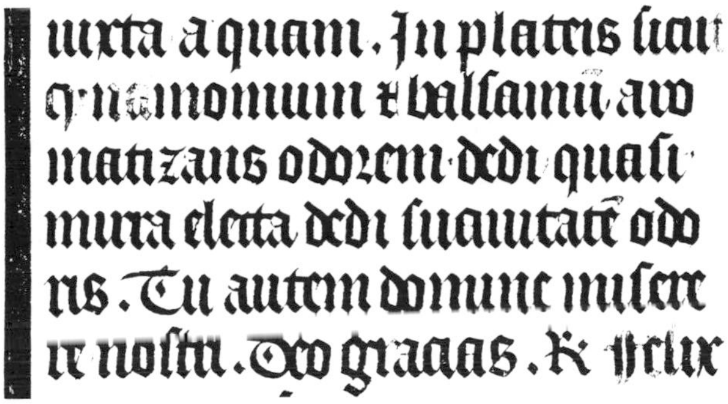

PALEOGRAPHY

iuxta aquam. In plateis sicut / cynamomum (et) balsamu(m) aro matizans odorem dedi quasi / mirra electa dedi suavitate(m) odo / ris. Tu autem domine misere / re nostri. Deo gracias. R(esponsorium). Felix

Fig. 10. Formal Gothic textual. Flanders, probably the Ghent-Bruges School, early 16th century. Book of Hours. FROM THE AUTHOR'S COLLECTION

leftward bulging bows or curves (for example, in *a*, *c*, *d*, and *e*) look like the lower finial of a minim stroke and at the top all rightward bulging bows or curves (for example, in *b*, *f*, *h*, and *p*) look like the upper finial of a minim stroke. Thus the letter *o* was reduced to two joined minims, the first lacking its top finial and the second lacking its bottom one (Fig. 10).

This exceedingly symmetricalized Gothic textual, which is the kind conjured up in one's imagination at the very mention of the word Gothic, had a number of less formal counterparts that were written with less care and deliberation or with less consistency in observing the Gothic rules. One kind of ordinary Gothic textual, called pearl script and used especially in France in the thirteenth and fourteenth centuries for pocket editions of the Bible, was written on so miniature a scale that it was difficult to break all curved strokes into Gothic angles. Another textual, called the Parisian script because it was used by the professional scribes who copied books in the thirteenth and fourteenth centuries for the university scholars in Paris, also left many curved strokes unbroken, did not emphasize lateral compression, and was far from regular in treating the feet of minims. Sometimes the angular finials were entirely lacking, often they were merely suggested, and hardly ever did they have the elaborate *v*-like shape of the formal textual (Fig. 11). Fancy finials were simply forbidden by the pressing need these professional scribes had for speed, a need reflected also in their enormously increased use of

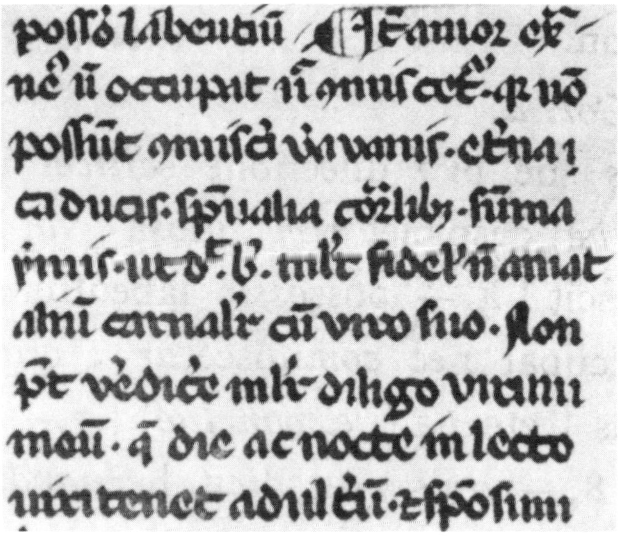

poss(essi)o labentiu(m). ¶ It(em) amor ex(tr)a- / ne(us) n(on) occupat n(e)c (com)miscet(ur), q(uia) no(n) / possu(n)t (com)misc(er)i v(er)a vanis, et(er)na i [*expunctuated as a space filler*] / caducis, sp(irit)ualia cor(por)alib(us), su(m)ma / ymis, ut d(ici)t b(ernardus). m(u)l(ie)r fidel(is) n(on) amat / aliu(m) carnal(ite)r cu(m) viro suo. Non / p(otes)t vere dic(er)e m(u)l(ie)r, diligo virum / meu(m), q(ue) die ac nocte in lecto / viri tenet adult(er)u(m), (et) spo(n)sum

Fig. 11. Gothic textual Parisian script. Probably Paris, 1293. Vulgaria. Louvain, Bibliothèque de l'Université, MS 46 (destroyed). REPRODUCED FROM EDMOND REUSENS, *ÉLÉMENTS DE PALÉOGRAPHIE* (1899)

abbreviations. Nonprofessional scribes copying for their personal uses could write the textual script even more rapidly. Eventually many of these ordinary or rapid textual scripts would be replaced by Gothic cursives.

The Gothic textuals described so far are the types that spread through most of France, the British Isles, the Low Countries, and Germanic, Slavic, and Scandinavian lands. In Italy, the southern coastal region of France, and the Iberian Peninsula, another kind of Gothic prevailed that is called rotunda or round. This southern Gothic does not lack angles, but because its letters are rather broad in relation to their height, its angles are obtuse enough to give a roundish impression. It observed the rules for overlapping facing bows and for ligating *R* with preceding bows, but even at its most formal it did not treat the feet of all minims alike, most of them being flat rather than having an angular finial. Its most characteristic letter is an

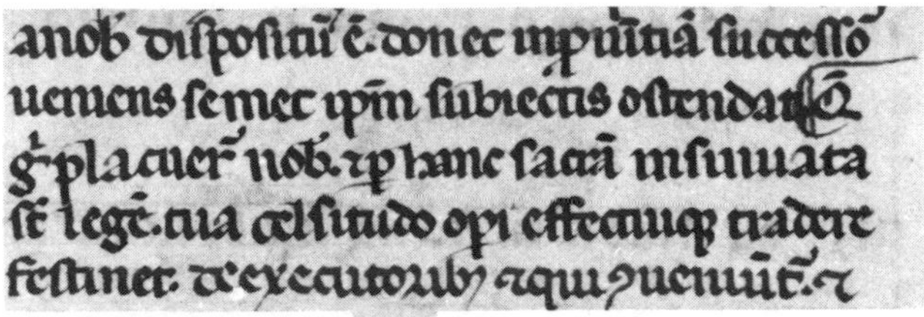

PALEOGRAPHY

[secundum quod] a nob(is) dispositu(m)ʸ e(st), donec in p(ro)vi(n)tia(m) successo(r) / veniens semet ip(su)m subiectis ostendat. ¶ Q(ue) / ig(itur) placuer(unt) nob(is), (et) p(er) hanc sacra(m) insinuata / s(un)t lege(m), tua celsitudo op(er)i effectuiq(ue) tradere / festinet. De executorib(us) (et) qui (con)veniu(n)t(ur), (et)

Fig. 12. Round Gothic textual Bolognese script. Probably Bologna, *ca.* 1300. *Corpus iuris civilis: Novellae.* PRINCETON, PRINCETON UNIVERSITY LIBRARY, COLLECTION OF FRAGMENTS OF MEDIEVAL AND RENAISSANCE CALLIGRAPHY, AM 21140

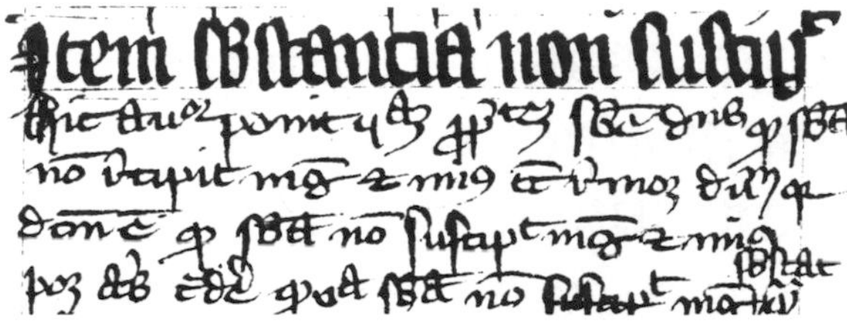

Item s(ub)stancia non suscip(i)t. / Hic au(ct)or ponit quintam p(ro)p(r)i(eta)te(m) s(u)b(stanci)e d(ice)ns q(uod) s(u)b(stanci)a / no(n) r(e)cipit m(a)g(is) (et) mi(nus). T(un)c r(e)mo(vet) du(biu)m. Q(uia) / d(i)c(tu)m e(st) q(uod) s(u)b(stanci)a no(n) suscip(i)t m(a)g(is) (et) mi(nus), / po(sset) a(l)i(qui)s c(re)d(er)e q(uod) u(n)a s(u)b(stanci)a no(n) suscip(i)t [cancelled] m(a)g(is) \s(u)bstat/ q(uam)

Fig. 13. Gothic textual (line 1) and current cursive (2–9). Germany, 14th century. Anonymous commentary on Aristotle's *Categories.* FROM THE AUTHOR'S COLLECTION

uncial form of *d* in which the bow is ample and the ascender short and almost horizontal. The best-known version of this script, which developed directly out of Italian Caroline minuscule in the late twelfth century, is called *littera Bononiensis* or the Bolognese script, because professional scribes used it for copying the legal texts studied at the University of Bologna (Fig. 12). A formal version of the script continued in use for liturgical texts into the sixteenth century and beyond.

In the course of the thirteenth century a significant new development occurred. The Caroline minuscule that had been taken over for the copying of documents was being transformed into a new Gothic cursive script quite independent of the long extinct later Roman cursive. Loops began to appear on the ascenders of *b, d, h,* and *l* and sometimes on the descenders of *f, p, q,* and long *s.* Several adjacent letters might be written without the pen being lifted from the writing surface, and from the late fourteenth century even signs for abbreviation began to be entered with a stroke continuing uninterruptedly from one of the letters. The ductus of several letters was simplified or basically changed. Although this new cursive script is clearly no longer Caroline, its claim to being Gothic has to be somewhat qualified. It did use some Gothic shading, it overlapped some facing bows, it used the *R* in ligature with a preceding bow, and it clearly permitted the angular breaking of curved strokes. But when it was written rapidly many angles inevitably tended to be rounded, and it was quite incompatible with the use of angular finials at the feet of all minims.

Various versions of this Gothic cursive, originally developed for copying documents, were eventually used for copying books (Fig. 13). An English type called *Anglicana* preserves a book of sermons copied as early as 1291. In the fourteenth and fifteenth centuries the new cursive increasingly took the place of Gothic textual for copying books, and as it did so it assumed more calligraphic pretensions. Without abandoning the loops and simplified letter shapes that a need for rapid writing had generated, Gothic cursive formed these loops and shapes with more and more regularity and deliberateness. The result was a formal Gothic cursive used even for deluxe books and particularly for ones in the vernacular languages (Fig. 14). A type of formal cursive that shortly before the mid fifteenth century began to deprive its ascending strokes of their loops has been given the name of Burgundian script.

The move from a Gothic cursive base toward textual that Burgundian script represents was matched by another, slightly earlier, move from a Gothic textual base toward cursive. The compromise, now called Gothic hybrid, included the cursive forms of *a* and *g* and of *f* and long *s,* but it followed textual models in avoiding loops on ascenders and descenders, and at least in the more formal versions it observed the textual rule with respect to finials on the feet of minims (Fig. 15).

PALEOGRAPHY

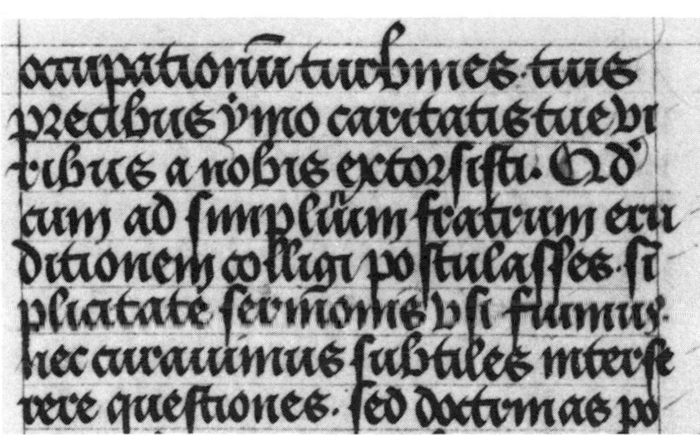

occupationu(m) turbines tuis / precibus ymo caritatis tue vi- / ribus a nobis extorsisti. Q(uo)d / cum ad simpli\ci/um fratrum eru- / ditionem colligi postulasses, si(m)- / plicitate sermonis usi fuimus, / nec curavimus subtiles interse- / rere questiones, sed doctrinas po- [tius]

Fig. 14. Formal Gothic cursive. Clairvaux, France, 1485. John of Turrecremata, *Exposition of the Rule of St. Benedict.* PRINCETON UNIVERSITY LIBRARY, MS GARRETT 91, fol. 178v

The hybrid was especially cultivated in the lower Rhineland and it spread to the Low Countries, France, and other parts of Germany, but its geographical limits have not yet been fully circumscribed. From the 1420's it lasted into the sixteenth century.

Humanistic scripts. The successive differentiations that Gothic scripts underwent reached something of a symbolic climax in Leonhard Wagner's *Proba centum scripturarum.* Actually, not even Wagner's tour de force could stop the further differentiation of Gothic—fancier and fancier versions continued to appear throughout the sixteenth century and beyond—but what is especially interesting about the work of this Augsburg Benedictine calligrapher is the appreciation it shows among the Germans for Italianate scripts, including a humanistic type that was introduced at least partially out of hostility to Gothic.

There were two main scripts popularized by the Italian humanists. One has been called the humanistic round or textual script or the formal humanistic. The humanists themselves called it the *antiqua* or the new *antiqua,* because it was a conscious revival of an old script that they themselves thought was used in ancient times, whereas it was really the Caroline minuscule in the form it had assumed in eleventh- and twelfth-century Italy. Poggio Bracciolini (1380–1459), a Florentine notary who became a papal secretary, was using the revived Caroline minuscule script in the very first years of the fifteenth century. The importance of the revival was vastly increased as a result of the adoption of the humanistic round as a type font by the Germans who brought the printing industry to Italy in 1464/1465. It became the widely familiar Roman font that was referred to above under Caroline minuscule. Although it is sometimes difficult to distinguish the humanistic round from its Caroline prototypes, usually a difference in proportions and the presence of features that suggest some Gothic ancestry on the part of the scribe (for example, dotted *i*'s or the 2-like part of *R* used independently as the whole letter) suffice for the recognition of the humanistic script (Fig. 16). Further assurance can come from the presence of Roman square capitals, another humanistic revival, in titles and colophons, and from the use of some later codicological innovations.

The other main script associated with the humanists is called humanistic cursive. Because it does not actually show some of the features normally considered an essential part of a cursive script (loops on ascenders and descenders or ligatures of

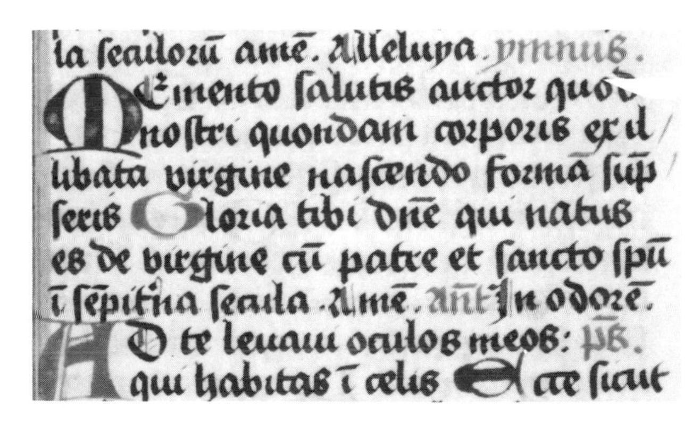

[secu]la seculoru(m) ame(n). Alleluya. *Ymnus.* / Memento falutis auctor quod / nostri quondam corporis ex il- / libata virgine nascendo forma(m) su(m)p- / seris. Gloria tibi, domine, qui natus / es de virgine cu(m) patre et sancto sp(irit)u / i(n) se(m)pit(er)na secula. Ame(n). *Ant(iphona).* In odore(m). / Ad te levavi oculos meos, *Ps(almus).* / qui habitas i(n) celis. Ecce sicut

Fig. 15. Formal Gothic hybrid. Probably Flanders, 1528. Book of Hours. ITHACA, CORNELL UNIVERSITY LIBRARY, MS BX C36 H848, fol. 30r

PALEOGRAPHY

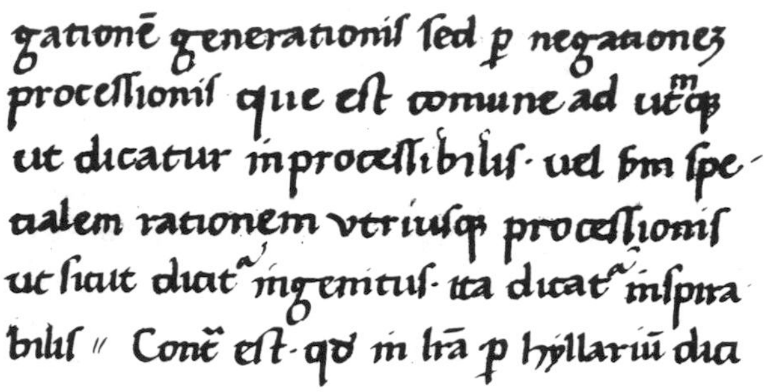

[ne]gatione(m) generationis sed p(er) negatione(m) / processionis que est comune ad ut(ru)mq(ue) / ut dicatur inprocessibilis, vel s(ecundu)m spe- / tialem rationem utriusq(ue) processionis / ut sicut dicit(ur) ingenitus, ita dicat(ur) inspira- / bilis. Cont(r)a est q(uo)d in l(itte)ra p(er) hyllariu(m) dici[tur]

Fig. 16. Humanistic round or textual. Italy, 15th century. Thomas Aquinas, *Commentary on the Sentences of Peter Lombard.* FROM THE AUTHOR'S COLLECTION

many adjoining pairs of letters, though it does use a few common ones), some scholars would prefer to call it italic, the name given to the permanently successful type font that was made of it in 1501. Although it can and would be written with deliberate formality, the forms of its letters clearly reflect its designers' need for speed. It has little shading, it leans to the right, its minims usually have no finials at the foot, many adjacent letters may be connected (though not ligated), and it tends to be more angular than the humanistic round script. Clearly it has links with some form of Italian Gothic cursive or hybrid. Such links, beyond the general ones just noted, are particularly evident in the simple *a*, the currently written *m* and *n*, and the *f* and tall *s* going below the line (Fig. 17). The origins of the script go back at least to the 1420's and the handwriting of Niccolò Niccoli. Possibly intended at the start mainly for scholars' correspondence and personal writing, it was soon employed in increasingly calligraphic fashion for copying books and was eventually enshrined in print.

The twilight of the Middle Ages marked a historic transition, not without its ironies, for both scripts and scribes. Although the history of handwriting obviously did not end with the development of the Gothic and humanistic scripts and the revival of the ancient square capital, it is these scripts, nevertheless, that seem to have set the guidelines for much of the further development of the next half millennium. These scripts were able to play this enduring role in part because their translation into printed type fonts gave them a more definitive status than they might otherwise have enjoyed. The fate of scripts, however, did not exactly parallel the fate of scribes. Somewhat ironically, the very centrality of books to medieval civilization that had exalted the status of scribes eventually contributed to the humbling of their role. For it was the medieval appetite for books that provided the inducement in the mid fifteenth century for the invention of printing with movable type. Although the new technology had a very limited effect on the scriveners and notaries who copied documents, it rendered thousands of book scribes obsolete. Books did continue to be copied by hand, particularly deluxe books, through the sixteenth century and even beyond, but in ever decreasing numbers. Book scribes became more and more marginalized. Strangely enough, however, within their shrunken margins the scribes who persisted found a certain liberation. They were more free to indulge their creativity and to cultivate variety that was beyond the capacity of printers. And if they chose to disseminate their results, they had at their disposal from the early sixteenth century onward an instrument of previ-

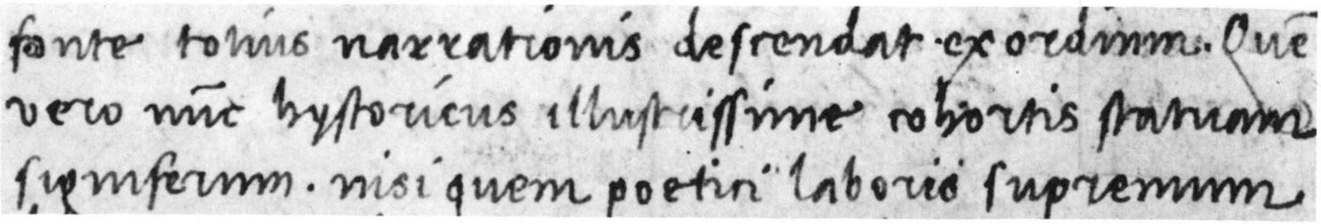

fonte totius narrationis descendat exordium. Que(m) / vero nu(n)c hystoricus illustrissime cohortis statuam / signiferum, nisi quem poetici laboris supremum

Fig. 17. Humanistic cursive. Italy, *ca.* 1500. Petrarch, *Of Memorable Things.* ITHACA, CORNELL UNIVERSITY LIBRARY, MS PETRARCH P P49 R4++, fol. 2r

ously unimagined effectiveness, the printed calligraphy book.

BIBLIOGRAPHY

The most comprehensive bibliographical guide is Leonard E. Boyle, *Medieval Latin Palaeography: A Bibliographical Introduction* (1984), covering publications through 1981, with occasional later references and frequent annotations. On current publications, see: *Codices manuscripti: Zeitschrift für Handschriftenkunde* (1975–), *Gazette du livre médiéval* (1982–), an informal clearinghouse for the exchange of ideas as well as a source for announcing new publications, conferences, seminars, exhibitions, research projects, and library and university personnel changes; the "Bulletin codicologique" in *Scriptorium: International Review of Manuscript Studies* (1946–); *Scrittura e civiltà* (1977–); and Jan-Olof Tjäder's extremely useful annotated English surveys in *Eranos: Acta philologica Suecana*, 75 (1977), 78 (1980), 80 (1982), and 82 (1984).

Sources. General collections of facsimiles: Franz Ehrle and Paul Liebaert, *Specimina codicum latinorum vaticanorum*, 3rd ed. (1932); Joachim Kirchner, *Scriptura gothica libraria a saeculo XII usque ad finem medii aevi* (1966), and *Scriptura latina libraria a saeculo primo usque ad finem medii aevi*, 2nd ed. (1970); Elias Avery Lowe, *Handwriting: Our Medieval Legacy* (1969), transcribed by W. Braxton Ross, Jr.; Franz Steffens, *Lateinische Paläographie*, 2nd ed. (1909, repr. 1929, 1964), still the best collection; Edward Maunde Thompson, *An Introduction to Greek and Latin Palaeography* (1912, repr. 1973), text antiquated; S. Harrison Thomson, *Latin Bookhands of the Later Middle Ages, 1100–1500* (1969).

Dated manuscripts series with sample facsimiles: Boyle, *Medieval Latin Palaeography*, numbers 313–340, for a listing of twenty volumes; *Les manuscrits datés: Premier bilan et perspectives, Neuchâtel 1983* (1985), for a listing of twenty-five volumes and a critical evaluation of the whole series by its editors.

Other large collections: Albert Bruckner and Robert Marichal, eds., *Chartae latinae antiquiores: Facsimile Edition of the Latin Charters Prior to the Ninth Century* (1954–); Elias Avery Lowe, ed., *Codices latini antiquiores: A Palaeographical Guide to Latin Manuscripts Prior to the Ninth Century*, 11 vols. plus Supplement (1934–1971; 2nd ed. of vol. II, 1972); Bernhard Bischoff and Virginia Brown, "Addenda to *Codices latini antiquiores*, in *Mediaeval Studies*, 47 (1985), adding fifty-four new items.

A guide to complete or partial facsimile editions: Hans Zotter, *Bibliographie faksimilierter Handschriften* (1976).

Studies. General introductions: Bernhard Bischoff, *Paläographie des römischen Altertums und des abendländischen Mittelalters* (1979), also in French, *Paléographie de l'antiquité romaine et du moyen âge occidental* (1985), the best work available; James J. John, "Latin Paleography," in James M. Powell, ed., *Medieval Studies: An Introduction* (1976); Berthold L. Ullman, *Ancient Writing and Its Influence* (1932, repr. with introduction and supplementary bibliography by Julian Brown, 1969, 1980).

Methodological and programmatic contributions: Colloque international de paléographie latine, *Nomenclature des écritures livresques du IXe au XVIe siècle, 1953* (1954); Léon Gilissen, *L'expertise des écritures médiévales: Recherche d'une méthode avec application à un manuscrit du XIe siècle* (1973); François Masai, "Paléographie et codicologie," in *Scriptorium*, 4 (1950), and "La paléographie gréco-latine, ses tâches, ses méthodes," *ibid.*, 10 (1956); Denis Muzerelle, *Vocabulaire codicologique: Répertoire méthodique des termes français relatifs aux manuscrits* (1985).

Other monographs and studies: Bernhard Bischoff, *Mittelalterliche Studien: Ausgewählte Aufsätze zur Schriftkunde und Literaturgeschichte*, 3 vols. (1966–1981); Elias Avery Loew [Lowe], *The Beneventan Script: A History of the South Italian Minuscule*, 2nd ed., Virginia Brown, ed., 2 vols. (1980), and *Palaeographical Papers, 1907–1965*, Ludwig Bieler, ed., 2 vols. (1972); Malcolm B. Parkes, *English Cursive Book Hands, 1250–1500* (1969, repr. 1980); Berthold L. Ullman, *The Origin and Development of Humanistic Script* (1960), groundbreaking; Wilhelm Wattenbach, *Das Schriftwesen im Mittelalter*, 4th ed. (1958).

On abbreviations: Adriano Cappelli, *Lexicon abbreviaturarum: Dizionario di abbreviature latine ed italiane*, 6th ed. (1979), and *The Elements of Abbreviation in Medieval Latin Paleography*, David Heimann and Richard Kay, trans. (1982), a translation of Cappelli's introduction; Charles Trice Martin, *The Record Interpreter: A Collection of Abbreviations, Latin Words, and Names Used in English Historical Manuscripts and Records*, 2nd ed. (1910, repr. 1969); Auguste Pelzer, *Abbréviations latines médiévales: Supplément au Dizionario di abbreviature latine, ed. italiana, di Adriano Cappelli*, 2nd ed. (1966).

JAMES J. JOHN

[See also **Alphabets; Codicology; Gospelbook; Kells, Book of; Lindisfarne Gospels; Manuscript Books, Production of; Manuscript Illumination; Monte Cassino; Paper, Introduction of; Scriptorium; Utrecht Psalter; Writing Materials.**]

PALERMO, the chief city of Sicily, was founded by the Phoenicians sometime before the seventh century B.C. The Romans captured the city in 254 B.C., during the First Punic War (264–241 B.C.), and it remained in their hands until its conquest by the Vandals under Genseric in A.D. 440. Thereafter it passed to the Ostrogoths and was captured in 535 by the Byzantine general Belisarios, acting for Emperor Justinian. In 831 Arabs from North Africa conquered Palermo, then the second largest city in Sicily, and it became the capital of a flourishing Islamic civilization. In the early eleventh century, the Italian cities of Genoa and Pisa expelled the Muslims from Sardinia, and, in the 1060's, the Normans of southern Italy, under Robert Guiscard and his brother Roger, began the conquest of Sicily. Palermo fell in 1072 and was divided between the two brothers. Roger (*d.* 1101) eventually emerged as the dominant Norman in Sicily, bearing the title "great count." His son Roger II, who succeeded him in 1101, created the Norman kingdom of Sicily in 1130; Palermo was its capital, a position it retained until King Charles I of Anjou transferred his chief residence to Naples. In 1282 the citizens of Palermo rose against the Angevins in the Sicilian Vespers and a group of Sicilian nobles, meeting in the Church of the Martorana, offered the crown of Sicily to King Peter of Aragon. Under the Aragonese the political importance of Palermo continued to decline and, for a considerable period, it fell under the control of a baronial family, the Chiaramonte.

The artistic and cultural life of Palermo shows little evidence of the 200 years of Muslim rule. The Arab geographer Ibn Ḥawqal, writing in 872–873, describes a populous city, divided into five sections and having an enormous number of mosques. It was the gathering place for many races and nationalities, he says, but had few scholars or men of talent. Though the latter statement may have been exaggerated, Palermo never reached first rank as a cultural center even during its most flourishing period under the Norman and Hohenstaufen kings of Sicily. Among the most important monuments of this period are the church of the Martorana, founded by Roger II's emir George of Antioch in 1143, and the palatine chapel in the royal palace, established by Roger II in 1132 and consecrated in 1140. The present cathedral, begun in 1185 by Archbishop Walter Ophamil, contains the tombs of the Norman-Hohenstaufen rulers of Sicily. On the outskirts of the city are the royal monastery and cathedral of Monreale, founded by William II in 1174.

The economic life of Palermo was based in part on its fishing industry and in part on its agricultural wealth, including the famous citrus-rich Conca d'Oro south of the city. To these factors may be added its excellent port and position as the administrative center of the island. Its major competitor was Messina, a city that generally took a more aggressive role in the struggle for local autonomy.

BIBLIOGRAPHY

Giuseppe Agnello, *Palermo bizantina* (1969); Ahmad Aziz, *A History of Islamic Sicily* (1975); Giorgio Arcoleo, *Palerme et la civilisation en Sicile* (1898).

JAMES M. POWELL

[See also **Roger I of Sicily; Roger II of Sicily; Sicily, Islamic; Sicily, Kingdom of; Sicilian Vespers.**]

PALESTINE. In the early Middle Ages Palestine was ruled from Byzantium, which had inherited control of the land from Rome, and its administration was appointed and directed by Greek-speaking Byzantines. Palestine was at this time divided into three provinces: Palaestina Prima, which encompassed the central part of the country, from slightly east of the Jordan River to the Mediterranean coast, having its capital at Caesarea; Palaestina Secunda, which encompassed the northern part of the country and was centered on the Sea of Galilee and included the Esdraelon Valley, Galilee, the northern segment of the Jordan Valley, and some cities of the old Decapolis, having its capital at Scythopolis (Bet She'an); and Palaestina Tertia or Salutaris, which included the Negev, Nabataea, and part of the Sinai, with its capital at Petra. After the Arab conquest (634–640), the first two became the *junds* (administrative and military districts) of Filasṭīn and al-Urdunn, respectively; the capital of the former was eventually transferred to Ramle and the latter to Tiberias. The boundaries of Urdunn, as defined by Arab historians and geographers, varied widely. Palaestina Tertia did not survive, but was divided between Filasṭīn and the *jund* of Damascus.

In the fifth century the population seems still to have consisted mainly of Jews, Samaritans, and pagans, the Christians remaining in a minority. Evidence for this may be found in the biography of the monk Bar Ṣauma, who allegedly led a force of monks to destroy several Jewish synagogues and pagan shrines in Palestine. Echoes of anti-Jewish persecutions by Byzantine authorities are preserved in talmudic sources, mainly in the Palestinian Talmud and in midrashim written in Palestine. The authorities also persecuted nonorthodox Christians, such as Monophysites and Nestorians.

But aside from an occasional upheaval, the Byzantine period was in general one of security and prosperity. There is archaeological evidence of a very considerable increase in population, and the number of Palestinian localities seems to have been three times greater than during the biblical period. The country's prosperity was due in no small measure to the special attention devoted to it by the Byzantines, spurred by religious reasons and by the desire to develop commercial relations with the east. To this end, they used Palestine and its southern port of Aelana (Aila, Elath, today's ᶜAqaba) as a main transit area. The construction of churches and monasteries, as well as of city walls and fortifications, certainly provided work and income to builders and other workers. The revenues from pilgrims and donations given by others to the holy places were so large that Justinian was compelled to enact a special law in 535 to bring order into the administration of the extensive properties of the Holy Sepulcher in Jerusalem.

Palestine was invaded in 614 by the Sasanids, who found they could rely on Jewish support within the country. Nevertheless, the part played by the Jews and the rewards they were to be given for their assistance was exaggerated by later (Christian) sources to bring added discredit to the Jews, and it is not at all clear what role the Jews had in the massacre of the Christian population of Jerusalem once it had been captured. It is significant that one of the oldest sources describing the taking of Jerusalem, the *Paschale chronicon,* does not mention Jews at all. The Sasanids soon changed their attitude toward Christians, and beginning in 617 they permitted an intensive reconstruction of monuments in Jerusalem, mainly of the Holy Sepulcher, carried out by Modestus, who replaced the exiled patriach, Zacharias.

Fourteen years later, Palestine reverted to Byzantine rule (628), after the successful offensive initiated by Emperor Heraklios (*r.* 610–641). He visited Jerusalem with Empress Martina in 630, and took part in the ceremony of the reinstallment of the Holy Cross, returned from Ctesiphon by virtue of a peace treaty.

The first Muslim incursion into Palestine occurred during Muḥammad's lifetime. Muᵓta, possibly in southern Palestine, was attacked in September 629, and a year later an expedition led by the Prophet himself came to Tabūk, near the southern border. It stayed only two weeks, due to the Byzantines' numerical superiority, which forced him to withdraw, but during that time Muḥammad concluded treaties with several localities in southern Palestine, including Aelana. Letters of security were granted in exchange for weapons, riding beasts, and the payment of annual tribute. The terms of these agreements served for generations as legal precedents for the treatment of conquered non-Muslim peoples.

The conquest of Palestine was carried out during the reigns of the first two caliphs and was accomplished in four phases. The first was inspired by the wish to take advantage of the weakness of the Byzantines, whose strength had been sapped by the protracted Sasanid conflict. The Muslims made two incursions in the spring of 634, one into the Gaza region, and the other toward Petra. Arab tribes living in the border area disregarded their commitments to the Byzantine suzerains and joined the Muslim invaders. A second phase was opened at the same time when a Muslim force under Khālid ibn al-Walīd abandoned the campaign against the Sasanids, under orders from the caliph Abū Bakr, and marched from the Euphrates straight across the Syrian Desert and over the Golan Heights to attack the Byzantine army at Ajnadain (Ijnādayn), on 30 July 634. The march, which was unprecedented in military history, took the Byzantines by surprise, and they were forced to retreat. In a third phase, a new and powerful Byzantine army was assembled in the region of Antioch to counterattack, and the Muslims moved to meet it in July or August 636 at the river Yarmuk. The Byzantines were defeated, and Syria fell into Muslim hands.

In the last phase, the Muslims consolidated their grip on Palestine. Jerusalem was captured in 638 after a long siege lasting eight months, and the fortified port cities of Caesarea and Ascalon fell in the early 640's. The terms worked out for the peaceful surrender of Jerusalem by the caliph ᶜUmar ibn al-Khaṭṭāb (who succeeded Abū Bakr in 634) guaranteed the Christian population its right to life, properties, churches, monasteries, and freedom of worship; these were given in exchange for payment of a poll tax. Males who had served in the Byzantine army or who were military auxiliaries were permitted to stay in the city under the same terms or to leave in safety and join the Byzantine forces. Rural refugees were given safe conduct out of the city so that they might return to their villages, and no taxes would be imposed upon them before the harvest. Finally, the ban on Jewish settlement in Jerusalem was continued. (Nevertheless, one of the first steps taken by the new rulers, perhaps a few years later, was to allow Jews to return to Jerusalem.)

Muslim sources describing Caliph ᶜUmar's visit to Jerusalem in 638 and the founding of the first mosque on Temple Mount (later known as Ḥaram al-Sharīf, the Noble Sanctuary) say that he consulted a Yemenite Jewish convert to Islam, Kaᶜb al-Aḥbār, as to the best site for erecting the mosque. He was advised to build north of the Ṣakhra (the Rock), which was venerated by the Jews, so as to unite the two *qibla*s (directions of prayer): that of Moses and that of Muḥammad. The obvious meaning was that by facing Mecca a person would also face the Rock. ᶜUmar refused to accept this advice, describing it as an imitation of Jewish practice, and the mosque was built south of the Rock. This is one of the proofs that in its earliest period Islam attributed no special holiness to Jerusalem.

It was only some two generations later, toward the end of the seventh century, that the Umayyad caliph ᶜAbd al-Malik and his son al-Walīd built (respectively) the Dome of the Rock (completed 691/692) and al-Aqṣā Mosque (begun 705). The building of these two most remarkable edifices was intended, according to the geographer al-Muqaddasī (a native of Jerusalem), to compete with the splendor of the numerous Christian monuments. The two new imposing buildings soon became an attraction for Muslim pilgrims bound for Mecca. As a result, a whole literature of Muslim traditions gradually developed that stressed the religious importance of Jerusalem. This centered around a Koranic verse, "The Night Journey" (sura 17), which mentions the miraculous journey made by the Prophet from the "Holy Mosque" to the "Remotest Mosque" (*masjid al-ḥarām, masjid al-aqṣā*). Muslim oral tradition in time connected these terms with the great mosque in Mecca and al-Aqṣā Mosque in Jerusalem, where the "Remotest Mosque" was thought to be. The ascension of the Prophet to heaven (*miᶜrāj*) was supposed to have taken place there as well. In fact, there is no unanimity on the matter, and there are traditions locating that mosque in Al-Kufa, for instance.

Under the Umayyads, Palestine benefited from a few public works—irrigation channels and roads—but with the removal of the Muslim capital eastward to Baghdad in 750, Palestine became a remote and neglected province. Internal strife and feuds led to destruction, dilapidation, and a decrease in population. During this period, two revolts broke out, one in 800, led by the Jew Yaḥyā ibn Irmiyā, the more serious in 842, led by the tribesman Abū Ḥarb Tamīm, nicknamed "al-Mubarqaᶜ" (the veiled one).

Palestine was conquered in 878 by Aḥmad ibn Ṭūlūn, the Turkish ruler of Egypt, who established an independent line. The Tulunid period, which lasted only thirty years, was one of peace and security. Bernard, a Frankish monk who visited Palestine at this time, reported that the inhabitants of Jerusalem could leave their belongings in the street without fear of theft.

In the tenth century, control of Palestine was briefly regained by the Abbasids, who then lost it in 935 to the Turkish commander Muḥammad ibn Tughj, founder of the Ikhshidids, the new rulers of Egypt, and then in 970 to the Fatimids. Thereafter, a long period of warfare ensued, lasting sixty years. The Holy Sepulcher was destroyed twice during those years, first in 966 and then again in 1009. The people of Palestine were now constantly disturbed by warring Turks, Arabs, Qarmatians (a Shiite sect), and even Byzantines, who, under Nikephoros II Phokas and John I Tzimiskes, managed, during 968 and 969 and again in 975, to capture the northern part of the region.

Palestine was overrun by the Turkomans in 1070, and under Alp Arslan's general Atsīz Jerusalem was captured in 1073. Then, in short succession, it was retaken by the Fatimids in 1098 and a year later by the crusaders, who retained control for nearly a century.

This first period of Muslim rule, lasting little more than four and a half centuries, was a period of decline for Palestine, due mainly to the continuous warfare conducted on its soil. Archaeological and geographical surveys reveal a sharp decline in population. For instance, out of ninety-three villages on the Sharon plain in the Roman-Byzantine period only fifty-two survived under the Muslims. In the central *ḥamrā*ᵓ area of hills and the adjacent littoral the number of towns dropped from fifty-eight to seventeen. A survey carried out by Guy in 1938 showed that in the Rehovot-Ramle-Lydda (Lod)-Ramallah area northwest of Jerusalem, 193 out of 293 villages had been abandoned, mainly due to soil erosion.

Under the crusaders, Palestine was ruled by the kings of Jerusalem, beginnning with Baldwin I

(1100–1118). After the capture of Jerusalem in 1187 by Saladin, the northern part of Palestine, specially Acre, became the center of crusader power; following the peace of Ramle in September 1192, the crusader state was established in the area between Tyre and Jaffa, while all the remaining parts of Palestine were returned to the Muslims. The Franks were finally expelled from Acre in 1291.

During the remaining centuries of the Middle Ages, Palestine's destiny continued to be linked with Egypt's: her overlords were the Egyptian Ayyubids (until 1250) and thereafter the Mamluks (until 1516, when Palestine was absorbed into the Ottoman Empire). It was the Mamluk sultan Baybars who in 1260 defeated the Mongols at the battle of ᶜAyn Jālūt. The Mamluks were responsible for the building of a large number of magnificent structures in Palestine, some of which are still standing. They also built many buildings of public utility, such as madrasas and mosques.

The accounts of Muslim geographers (from the tenth century onward) and merchants' letters (preserved in the Cairo genizah) show that Palestine's main export product was olive oil and its derivatives, especially soap. Fruits and fruit products, as well as glass produced in the region of Acre, were also important, and Palestine had a well-developed textile industry. The main market for Palestinian exports was Egypt, and in this trade Palestinian Jews, some of them of Maghribi extraction, were the main entrepreneurs. Imports included spices and various luxury articles and jewelry intended chiefly for pilgrims of all faiths, who came to Jerusalem and Hebron from all over the world.

BIBLIOGRAPHY

Michael Avi-Yonah, *The Jews of Palestine: A Political History from the Bar Kochba War to the Arab Conquest* (1976); Alphonse Couret, *La Palestine sous les empereurs grecs* (1869); J. Drory, "Palestine in the Mamluk State," in Joel Rappel, ed., *The History of Eretz-Israel*, II (1979), in Hebrew; Moshe Gil, *Palestine During the First Muslim Period (634–1099)*, 3 vols. (1983), in Hebrew; Michael J. de Goeje, *Mémoire sur la conquête de la Syrie* (1900); P. L. O. Guy, "Archaeological Evidence of Soil Erosion and Sedimentation in Wadi Musrara," in *Israel Exploration Journal*, 4 (1954); M. J. Kister, "You Shall Only Set Out for Three Mosques," in *Le muséon*, 82 (1969); Guy Le Strange, *Palestine Under the Moslems* (1890, repr. 1975); J. T. Milik, "La topographie de Jérusalem vers la fin de l'époque byzantine," in *Mélanges de l'Université Saint Joseph*, 37 (1961); Joshua Prawer, *The Latin Kingdom of Jerusalem* (1972); Steven Runciman, "The Pilgrimages to Palestine Before 1095," in Kenneth M. Setton, ed., *A History of the Crusades*, I (1969); Joshua Starr, "Notes on the Byzantine Incursions into Syria and Palestine(?)," in *Archiv Orientalni*, 8 (1936).

MOSHE GIL

[See also **Byzantine Empire: History; Cairo Genizah; Crusades and Crusader States; Fatimids; Ikhshidids; Jerusalem; Jews in the Middle East; ᶜUmar I Ibn al-Khaṭṭāb; Yarmuk River.**]

PALIMPSEST, a work or surface with a second text or image superimposed over an effaced original. Because of the scarcity and expense of parchment in the Middle Ages, older texts were sometimes scraped off the surface of the hide so that contemporary writings could be accommodated. In time, the original often shows through or can be revealed by special photographic techniques.

In painting, palimpsests indicate either reworking of the image by the original artist or, more often, the repainting of the image at a later date. As the more recent painting flakes, vestiges of the earlier image emerge. A famous example is the so-called palimpsest wall at S. Maria Antiqua in Rome, on which four painting campaigns are now visible: Maria Regina (540–550) peers through an Annunciation of about 600, on which are layered church fathers dating from 649 and, on top of them, a saint from about 705/707.

BIBLIOGRAPHY

Pietro Romanelli and Per J. Nordhagen, *S. Maria Antiqua* (1964).

LESLIE BRUBAKER

[See also **Fresco Painting; Parchment;** and illustration overleaf.]

PALIOTTO OF S. AMBROGIO, a reliquary altar of the ninth century, the so-called Golden Altar, in the Basilica of S. Ambrogio, Milan. Decorated with three panels of embossed gold relief on the front and panels of silver relief on the sides and back, it was commissioned by Angilbert II, archbishop of Milan (824–859), and designed and fashioned by the Carolingian artist Wolvinus for placement over

Palimpsest wall from the S. Maria Antiqua presbytery, Rome, 6th–8th centuries. FOTO DELL'I.C.C.D.—ROMA

the tombs of Sts. Ambrose, Gervase, and Protase. The paliotto is a lavishly decorated structure, with straps of gold covered with cloisonné enamels and gems around the panels. The panels themselves contain, on the front, representations from the life of Christ around a central panel depicting Christ in Majesty, and, on the back, scenes from the life of St. Ambrose, and portraits of Angilbert and Wolvinius.

Paliotto, meaning "little cloth" (from *palio*), originally referred to decorated cloth frontals or antependiums used to cover the fronts of altars, but became the popular term for the Golden Altar of S. Ambrogio, possibly as early as the ninth century. Although still used with its original meaning, the word can also refer to similar large gold and enamel altars. The Paliotto of S. Ambrogio belongs to a type of antependium found not only in Italy and Spain, but especially in northern Europe (the golden antependiums donated by Emperor Henry II to Basel Cathedral and to the palace chapel in Aachen, both early eleventh century).

BIBLIOGRAPHY
Arthur Kingsley Porter, *Lombard Architecture,* II (1916), 545–546; Peter Lasko, *Ars Sacra: 800–1200* (1972), 50–56, 129–130; George Bishop Tatum, "The Paliotto of Sant 'Ambrogio at Milan," in *Art Bulletin,* **26** (1944).

ROBERT K. HAYCRAFT

[See also **Antependium; Metalsmiths, Gold and Silver** (with illustration); **Pala d'Oro; Pre-Romanesque Art; Wolvinus.**]

PALLADIOS (*ca.* 363–*ca.* 431), an Egyptian monk born in Galatia and the author of two works: *Dialogus,* on the life of John Chrysostom, and the more important *Lausiac History.* The latter, a history of famous ascetics, was recounted to Lausos, a chamberlain of the court of Emperor Theodosius II, and was written around 420. In it Palladios gives an account of Egyptian monasticism at what was probably its high point, along with some glimpses of Palestinian monasticism. There are two versions of the history, a short and a long edition. While bishop of Helenopolis, Paladios fell from imperial favor when John Chrysostom was exiled; he was sent to Egypt from 406 to 412. He was made bishop of Asporina (Aspuna) in Galatia around 417 and died sometime before 431.

BIBLIOGRAPHY
Palladios, *The Lausiac History,* Edward Cuthbert Butler, ed., 2 vols. (1898–1904), the Greek text. See also Palladios, *The Lausiac History,* Robert T. Meyer, trans. (1965), and *Dialogus,* P. R. Coleman-Norton, ed. (1928).

LINDA C. ROSE

[See also **Hagiography, Byzantine; John Chrysostom, St.; Monasticism.**]

PALLIUM, worn by the patriarchs and, later, the metropolitans of the Christian church, is a thin band of white wool placed on the shoulders in the manner of a collar, with two long pendants that either fall in front and back or are gathered together in the middle of the back and chest. Derived ultimately from the Greek himation and akin in its amplitude to the toga, the pallium was also worn as a sash in official Roman dress, such as consular costume. The pallium was in widespread use by the sixth century as a symbol to underline the ties between provincial bishops and the pope. During the Carolingian period in the West, the pallium

Two figures wearing the pallium. Miniature from the Psalter of Henry of Blois, 1140–1160. BY PERMISSION OF THE BRITISH LIBRARY, LONDON, COTTON MS NERO C. IV, fol. 37

Palmette decorations (in circles) from a Byzantine Bible commentary, *ca.* 11th century. PARIS, BIBLIOTHÈQUE NATIONALE, MS COISLIN 193, fol 40v

became a common insignia of episcopal dignity and privileges.

BIBLIOGRAPHY

Joseph Braun, *Die liturgische Gewandung im Occident und Orient* (1907), 620–676; Henri Leclerq, "Pallium," in *Dictionnaire d'archéologie chrétienne et de liturgie,* XIII, 1 (1937), 931–940; Janet Mayo, *A History of Ecclesiastical Dress* (1984).

MICHAEL T. DAVIS

[See also **Coronation, Papal; Vestments.**]

PALMETTE, a decorative motif generally resembling a palm leaf, derived from the Greco-Roman acanthus leaf ornament. The stylized and pointed lobes of the leaf emerge fanlike and are usually in a curved teardrop form, with the point at the top. The palmette is characteristic of Sasanian art and Islamic art, from which it entered Byzantium by the ninth century; it is a typical feature of Greek manuscript decoration from the eleventh century on.

BIBLIOGRAPHY

Keppel A. C. Creswell, *Early Muslim Architecture,* I: *Umayyads, A.D. 622–750* (1932), 211–212; Alison M. Frantz, "Byzantine Illuminated Ornament," in *Art Bulletin,* **16** (1934).

LESLIE BRUBAKER

[See also **Islamic Art and Architecture; Manuscript Illumination: Byzantine; Sasanian Art and Architecture.**]

PÁLS SAGA BISKUPS, one of the so-called bishops' sagas, is an Icelandic life of Páll Jónsson, bishop of Skálholt, Iceland (1195–1211), written about 1215 by an anonymous author who probably also wrote *Hungrvaka.* The earliest manuscripts date from the seventeenth century.

For his portrait of the bishop, the author draws on his personal knowledge of Páll Jónsson and the see of Skálholt, to whose clergy he obviously belonged. The saga tells of a man of excellent descent and solid education who suddenly became bishop-elect when his maternal uncle, Bishop Þorlákr Þórhallsson, died in 1193. At that time Páll Jónsson had little or no intention of following a clerical career, although he was a deacon and had studied in England. He was a wise administrator, and the author clearly admires the bishop's levelheadedness in dealing with unruly elements in the Icelandic church, such as Guðmundr Arason. During Bishop Páll's reign, Þorlákr's sanctity was revealed and his feast day instituted in 1199.

Justinian and his retinue. The emperor and three of his followers are depicted wearing the paludamentum. Mosaic from S. Vitale, Ravenna, *ca.* 525–550. ALINARI/ART RESOURCE

Páls saga biskups is regarded as a sober and accurate record of the daily life at Skálholt during the term of office of a bishop who was less interested in ecclesiastical politics than in the orderly administration of his diocese, his pastoral duties, and the architectural improvements of the see. A stone coffin made for the bishop and mentioned in the saga was found during an excavation at Skálholt in 1954.

BIBLIOGRAPHY

An edition is Jón Sigurðsson and Guðbrandur Vigfússon, eds., *Biskupa sögur,* 2 vols. (1858–1878). A translation into English is Guðbrandur Vigfússon and F. York Powell, eds. and trans., "Páls Saga," in *Origines islandicae,* I (1905), 502–534. Other editions are Guðni Jónsson, ed., *Byskupa sögur,* 3 vols. (1948); Einar Ólafur Sveinsson, ed., *Páls saga biskups* (1954).

Studies include Magnús Már Lárusson, "Páls saga biskups," in *Kulturhistorisk leksikon for nordisk middelalder,* XIII (1968); Edward O. G. Turville Petre, *Origins of Icelandic Literature* (1953), 211–212; Chr. Westergård-Nielsen, in *Edda og saga* (1965), 14–16, with Danish translation on 33–58.

HANS BEKKER-NIELSEN

[See also **Bishops' Sagas; Guðmundr Arason; Hungrvaka.**]

PALUDAMENTUM, the long, ample mantle or cape, pinned at the neck or right shoulder, originally worn by the upper echelon of the Roman army, especially generals, but later adopted by rulers, aristocrats, and high government officials. Merged with the Greek chlamys (*chlamúdos*) during the Roman imperial period, it was decorated frequently with costly embroidery, pearls, precious stones, and blocks of color, or *tabulae.* The purple paludamentum was reserved for imperial wear, and it was with such a garment that Christ was robed prior to his Crucifixion.

BIBLIOGRAPHY

Henry Leclercq, "Chlamyde," in Fernand Cabrol, ed., *Dictionnaire d'archéologie chrétienne et de liturgie,* III, pt. 1 (1913), 1402–1406; Hertha Sauer, "Paludamentum," in *Paulys Real-Encyclopädie der classischen Altertumswissenschaft,* XVIII (1949), 281–286.

MICHAEL T. DAVIS

[See also **Costume, Byzantine; Costume, Western European.**]

PANEL PAINTING. Panel paintings produced outside Western Europe before the thirteenth century survive in very small numbers. We know that the Greeks and Romans practiced painting on panel, and we know that panel painting continued in various regions. The best-known early panels are the portrait heads produced primarily in Fayoum (Fayum), Egypt, between the first and third century A.D. Panel painting also played an important role in the Byzantine Empire, although the survival rate is very low owing to periods of iconoclasm. Sometime in the late twelfth century, panel painting experienced a revival in Western Europe. This development can be associated with new liturgical practices which placed priest and congregation on the same side of the altar, leaving the opposite side free for a holy image. Altar decoration was the chief form for early panel painting.

Though in use throughout Europe, panel painting flourished most abundantly in Italy. There, generations of craftsmen perfected a painstaking technique for preparing the panel and laying on the pigment, which ensured that the finished product would endure for centuries. The technique went relatively unchanged for nearly 300 years, although the introduction of oil paint in the fifteenth century gradually superseded the original medium of tempera. The use of canvas as a support for paint did not emerge as a frequently used medium until the sixteenth century.

The technique employed for panel painting is well known to us through Cennino Cennini's treatise *Il libro dell' arte* (1390, published in English as *The Craftsman's Handbook*), which set down the process then in use and passed it on to other generations of painters. His handbook describes in detail the laborious process of constructing the panel, its preparation, and the preparation and laying on of colors.

Each step in the process was painstaking, and it began with the construction of the panel. A carpenter would take seasoned wood, usually poplar, linden, or willow, which he planed and joined with other planks to obtain the desired size and shape of the final panel.

This panel would then be coated with size—a mixture of animal-skin glues and resins—and then covered with linen. Over this size, the painter would apply layer after layer of fine gesso. Each layer was sanded down before another layer was applied, and the final layer (sometimes the fifteenth) was scraped and polished until it had the smoothness and hardness of ivory.

Then the panel was ready for the design. Usually working in charcoal, the shop master would lay out a design, correcting it until it suited him and then fixing it with brush and ink. For the gold backgrounds, sheets of moistened gold leaf were applied, preferably on a damp day. Colors were laid in by the master, often assisted by the shop members. It was a tedious process. Working with small brushes dipped in mixtures of pigment and egg-yolk binder (tempera), the artist must paint slowly and carefully, applying one minute brushstroke at a time. Tempera dries fast and is not conducive to corrections, so each stroke has to be a premeditated part of the overall process. Tempera demands a fine hand and is ideal for detailed work. Historically, tempera's nonviscous nature helped shape the linear, precise style of dugento, trecento, and early quattrocento painters.

The early history of Italian panel painting remains obscure owing to the low survival rate. Some scholars even point to a 99.9 percent loss of the overall production of panel paintings made between 1200 and 1400. From what remains of early panel painting, it seems that the Tuscan towns of Arezzo, Lucca, Pisa, and Siena produced some of the earliest paintings, while Florence joined in a bit later. Umbria, Lombardy, Piedmont, Rome, and Venice all had practicing schools by the fourteenth century, since churches everywhere required altar painting. Some other types of panels, notably book covers, were painted, but the vast majority of the output was devoted to altar painting.

The earliest forms of altar paintings were dossals (horizontal rectangular panels decorating the backs of altars), altar frontals (similarly shaped panels placed along the front of the altar), and crucifixes, which generally hung above the altar. Small tabernacles, with movable shutters, for use in private devotions in homes or family chapels, also

PANEL PAINTING

came into use. All were painted with sacred images; most common were the Virgin and Child or Christ in Majesty on the altarpieces and Christus Triumphans on crucifixes. Saints surrounded by scenes of their lives were also common, and all subjects were treated in a symbolic, nonrealistic manner.

By the late dugento, there was a gradual shift in cultural and religious ideas, best expressed by and no doubt influenced by St. Francis of Assisi (*d.* 1226). St. Francis brought worshiper and deity into a closer relationship, and Franciscan influence on religious worship helped change the subject, style, and, to some extent, form of panel painting. Images of St. Francis proliferated; also at this time crucifixes depicted a suffering Christ to underscore his humanity. In general, images grew to enormous sizes, perhaps a reflection of society's need to come closer to the object of its devotions. Large, often gabled panels were the common form of altarpiece.

Guido da Siena's (*fl.* 1260's–*ca.* 1290) Palazzo Pubblico *Madonna and Child Enthroned,* Coppo di Marcovaldo's *Madonna and Child* (1261) in the church of S. Maria dei Servi, Siena, and Duccio's *Ruccelai Madonna* and Cimabue's *St. Trinita Madonna,* both in the Uffizi in Florence, demonstrate this development, while Giotto's S. Maria Novella *Crucifix* was a revolutionary reinterpretation of the crucified Christ.

Private devotions were performed before the numerous small folding tabernacles that were painted. The portable triptych was the most common form in Tuscany.

During the early trecento, there was a great deal of experimentation with the size, shape, and subject matter of large altar panels. Siena witnessed the greatest innovation. Duccio fashioned his revolutionary *Maestà* (1308–1311) for the Siena Duomo, and this work enlarged and expanded the *Maestà* subject and panel shape far beyond what had been known previously. Simone Martini (*ca.* 1284–1344) executed his *Annunciation* (Uffizi) in 1333, which is the earliest known representation of the *Annunciation* as the subject of the main field of an altarpiece. Pietro Lorenzetti's (*fl. ca.* 1315–1348) *Birth of the Virgin,* now in the Museo del Opera del'Duomo, set the same precedent for this subject. Ambrogio Lorenzetti's (*fl. ca.* 1317–1348) Massa Marittima *Maestà* and his Uffizi *Presentation in the Temple* are further explorations of the narrative and spatial possibilities of panel paintings. All of the panels discussed are remarkably diversified handlings of the fictive space within the panel, relative to the shape of the panel itself. None of these panels repeat their shapes, demonstrating how imaginative the Sienese were in panel design.

In Florence during the same decades, large and compartmentalized triptychs and polyptychs gained favor. Pacino da Bonaguida's (*fl.* 1303–*ca.* 1350) Ognissanti triptych, Bernardo Daddi's (*ca.* 1290–*ca.* 1348) Uffizi polyptych, Taddeo Gaddi's (*ca.* 1300–*ca.* 1366) S. Giovanni Fuorcivitas polyptych in Pistoia, with their predellas, lunettes, and pinnacles, are all typical examples of Florentine panel shapes during the early to mid trecento. All of these examples treat each element of the panel as a distinct entity, giving Florentine panel paintings an additive, rigidly segmented quality which is quite different from the fluid, more cohesive treatment of panel painting in Siena at roughly the same time.

These compartmentalized, additive triptychs and polyptychs remained popular in Florence throughout the trecento. Nardo di Cione's (*fl.* 1343–*ca.* 1365) Accademia triptychs depicting the *Trinity* and *Madonna and Child Enthroned* or Giovanni del Biondo's (*fl.* 1356–1392) altarpiece for the Rinuccini chapel in S. Croce, dated 1379, are typical examples of panel painting which flourished in Florence after the mid century.

That this type of panel painting gained favor in Siena after the mid century is demonstrated by the polyptychs of the *Madonna and Child,* and *Madonna and Child and St. Anne* by Luca di Tommè (*fl. ca.* 1356–1389), in the Siena Pinacoteca.

Several new panel types gained currency in Tuscany after the mid century. Single wingless panels, devoted to an isolated image, such as a seated saint or a standing Virgin and Child, became relatively common. Notable examples of seated saints include works by Giovanni del Biondo, Niccolò di Pietro Gerini, and Rosello di Jacopo Franchi.

Examples of the standing Virgin and child include Nardo di Cione's Minneapolis *Madonna,* as well as several examples by Niccolò di Tommaso (*fl.* 1343–1376).

By the mid trecento, Florence saw a new image type emerging which gradually appears to have superseded the portable triptych for use in private devotions. The single panel, showing the Madonna and Child Enthroned surrounded by saints, but without wings, and slightly larger than that found in a portable triptych, is found in great numbers after roughly 1350. Examples include Lorenzo di

Bicci's *Madonna and Child Enthroned,* in Villore, Cappella di S. Giusto; an image of the same subject attributed to the Master of the Arte della Lana in Christ Church at Oxford; and Giovanni del Ponte's version, which was formerly in Perugia, but whose whereabouts are presently unknown.

The half-length Madonna, often in polyptych form with saints, was the common format since the early trecento in Tuscany. By the late trecento, single images devoted only to the Madonna and Child emerged. One of Giovanni del Biondo's works, signed and dated 1377, is now in the Siena Pinacoteca; a second, signed and dated 1377, is now in the Siena Pinacoteca; while another example by him, 1387, is now in S. Felice in Florence. Numerous later examples survive, including works by Pseudo Ambrogio Baldese (Worchester Art Museum) and Mariotto di Nardo (Empoli, S. Christina). These images later emerged as the most popular form of private religious imagery in the fifteenth century, as examples by Lippi, Bellini, Matteo di Giovanni, Neroccio dei Landi, and many other painters demonstrate.

Sometime during the early fifteenth century, the taste for a single-field altar, often a square or closely related shape, joined the types of altar panels made by Italian painters. One of the earliest examples is Bartolo di Fredi's *Adoration of the Magi,* now in the Siena Pinacoteca, done before 1410.

The painted crucifix also changed. No longer a cruciform shape upon which a figure of Christ was painted, the crucifix actually took the shape of Christ's body hanging and supported by a cross, emulating sculpture rather than painting. This innovation of a "cutout" crucifix is generally given to Lorenzo Monaco (*ca.* 1370/1371–*ca.* 1424).

Changes in the conception of man, the nature of patronage, and the function of art affected the direction of panel painting in the fifteenth century and resulted in new types. The single biggest factor was the rise of secular art, which saw the appearance of a whole new series of panel types: chests (*cassone*), painted beds, birth trays (*deschi del parto*), and other furniture. The new awareness of the individual gave rise to another new type, the painted portrait.

BIBLIOGRAPHY

Ferdinando Bologna, *Early Italian Painting* (1964); Monika Cämmerer-George, *Die Rahmung der toskanischen Altarbilder im Trecento* (1966); Cennino Cennini, *The Craftsman's Handbook,* Daniel W. Thompson, Jr., trans. (1933); Bruce Cole, *Masaccio and the Art of Early Renaissance Florence* (1980), and *The Renaissance Artist at Work* (1983); Richard Fremantle, *Florentine Gothic Painters from Giotto to Masaccio* (1975); Edward Garrison, *Italian Romanesque Panel Painting* (1949); Hellmut Hager, *Die Anfänge des italienischen Altarbildes* (1962); Millard Meiss, *Painting in Florence and Siena After the Black Death* (1951, repr. 1973); Evelyn Sandberg Vavalà, *La croce dipinta italiana e l'iconografia della passione* (1929); John White, *Art and Architecture in Italy: 1250 to 1400* (1966).

Adelheid M. Gealt

[See also the artists named and **Altarpiece; Antependium; Cennini, Cennino; Diptych; Dugento Art; Gothic Art: Painting; Maestà; Polyptych; Retable; Trecento Art; Triptych.**]

PANORMITANUS. See **Nicolaus de Tudeschis.**

PANTOKRATOR, an epithet for Christ meaning "all-powerful." Though older images seem likely, the earliest preserved representations of Christ Pantokrator date from the sixth century, notable examples being an icon at St. Catherine's Monastery on Mt. Sinai (Sinai B.1) and a silver cross from the reign of Justin II (565–578) now in the treasury of St. Peter's in Rome. After the period of Byzantine iconoclasm, Christ Pantokrator appears as a standard component of Byzantine church decoration, usually in the dome.

As Pantokrator, Christ is shown as a frontal elongated bust, with at least portions of both arms included. His right hand is raised in blessing before his chest; his left holds a jeweled book. Normally the Pantokrator is bearded and has long brown hair, two strands of which escape over his forehead. A cruciform nimbus is also standard. The Pantokrator type may appear as a component of larger compositions such as the *majestas domini.*

BIBLIOGRAPHY

James Breckenridge, *The Numismatic Iconography of Justinian II* (1959), 46ff; Otto Demus, *Byzantine Mosaic Decoration* (1948), 17ff; André Grabar, *L'iconoclasme byzantin* (1957), 16ff; Kurt Weitzmann, *The Monastery of St. Catherine at Mount Sinai: The Icons,* I (1976), 13ff.

Leslie Brubaker

[See also **Early Christian Art** (with illustration).]

PAOLO DI GIOVANNI FEI (*fl.* 1372–1410), Sienese painter. Considered a pupil of Bartolo di Fredi and Andrea Vanni, Fei was a prolific painter who produced charming and fanciful reinterpretations of traditional Sienese images. His most important works include a copy of Pietro Lorenzetti's *Birth of the Virgin* (Siena, Pinacoteca Nazionale) and a copy of Ambrogio Lorenzetti's *Presentation of the Virgin* (Washington, D.C., National Gallery). Full of imagination, Fei's works demonstrate how fruitful the Sienese tradition was to succeeding generations of Sienese painters.

BIBLIOGRAPHY

Bernard Berenson, *Italian Pictures of the Renaissance, Central Italian and North Italian Schools,* 3 vols. (1968); Bruce Cole, *Sienese Painting in the Age of the Renaissance* (1985); Michael Mallory, *The Sienese Painter Paolo di Giovanni Fei* (1976); John Pope-Hennessy, *Sienese Quattrocento Painting* (1947).

ADELHEID M. GEALT

[See also **Bartolo di Fredi, Vanni, Andrea;** and illustration overleaf.]

PAOLO VENEZIANO (*fl.* 1333–1358; *d. ca.* 1367), Venetian painter. A gifted and important master whose style was based on Byzantine traditions of linearity and decorativeness, Paolo created numerous altarpieces that are remarkable for their mastery of color, and their dynamic and original composition. Important surviving works include the *Death of the Virgin* (1333), in the Museo Civico, Vicenza; the *Madonna and Child Enthroned* (1347), in Carpineta (near Cesena); and the *Coronation of the Virgin* (1358), in the Frick Collection, New York, on which his son Giovanni is thought to have collaborated.

BIBLIOGRAPHY

Bernard Berenson, *Italian Pictures of the Renaissance, the Venetian School,* 2 vols. (1957); Michelangelo Muraro, *Paolo da Venezia* (1970).

ADELHEID M. GEALT

[See also **Trecento Art** and illustration overleaf.]

PAPACY, ORIGINS AND DEVELOPMENT OF. The papacy, or the office of the bishop of Rome, emerged early in Christian history as the central institution of Latin Christianity. Since the medieval popes came to assert and exercise some measure of authority in all areas of ecclesiastical and religious life, one might take the theme of papal history as an occasion for discussing the entire history of the church. This article, however, will abstract from many specific matters in which the popes involved themselves and will focus on (1) the general development of papal claims to power within the church and over Christian society, (2) the actual enforcement of those claims, and (3) relations between the popes and secular rulers (especially the emperors).

The special role of the pope within the church rests upon a particular conception of Peter, the apostle to whom the popes claim succession. Peter's prominence in the Gospels and Acts of the apostles is clear: he is mentioned by name more than 190 times, while the next most frequently named apostle (John) occurs only 29 times by name. The Gospel according to Matthew refers to Peter as the first among the apostles (10:2); he is clearly not only the first of the apostles to have been chosen, but the most prominent among them. The key texts for later papal theory, however, are three. First is Matthew 16:18f, in which Christ addresses him, "You are Peter, and on this rock I will build my church. . . . I will give you the keys of the kingdom of heaven, and whatever you bind on earth shall be bound in heaven, and whatever you loose on earth shall be loosed in heaven." Second is Luke 22:31ff, where Christ tells Peter, "I have prayed for you that your faith may not fail; and when you have turned again, strengthen your brethren." Third is John 21:15–17, in which Christ, having had Peter assure him of his love, enjoins him, "Feed my lambs. . . . Feed my sheep. . . ."

Interpretation of these passages was diverse even among the fathers of the church. For example, while Ambrose recognized that the "rock" on which Christ founded his church might stand for Peter, he also interpreted it as referring to the faith in Christ that Peter had manifested, or to Christ himself. While other Fathers interpreted the rock as Peter, they more often took it as standing for the faith, and at times for Christ or even for all the apostles. In any case, Peter's prominence is restricted to the years of Christ's ministry and the period shortly after Christ's death. In the later sections of Acts he recedes in significance, and the leading figures in the church are James (at Jerusalem) and Paul (in the broader missionary field).

The theory of papal primacy within the church rests upon a double foundation: (1) the notion that

Presentation of the Virgin. Panel painting by Paolo di Giovanni Fei for the chapel of S. Pietro, Siena, *ca.* 1400. NATIONAL GALLERY OF ART, WASHINGTON, SAMUEL H. KRESS COLLECTION, 1961.9.4

Death of the Virgin, with Sts. Anthony and Francis. Polyptych by Paolo Veneziano, 1333. MUSEO CIVICO, VICENZA, INV. NO. A157

PAPACY

Peter enjoyed a divinely mandated primacy among the apostles, and (2) the postulate that the popes, as bishops of Rome, were successors to Peter in his putative role as the first bishop of that city. The second of these claims is a specific version of the broader thesis, forcefully argued in the second century by Irenaeus of Lyons, that the bishops generally are successors to the apostles. From a Roman Catholic theological viewpoint, it has been argued that this double claim is implicit in the New Testament texts even if it took many generations for the church to formulate an explicit theory of papal primacy. Historical research may not be able to pass judgment on this theological claim. What it can do is trace the gradual evolution in the popes' explicit assertions of power, their practical efforts to secure power, and reactions within the church to the growth of papal authority.

The periods covered here will be (1) the ante-Nicene era, from the first century until the toleration of Christianity and its establishment as an official imperial religion in the fourth century; (2) the post-Nicene era, from the fourth century to the eighth, when popes struggled with the Byzantine emperors and developed their own position as religious and political leaders in the Latin West; (3) the Carolingian and Ottonian periods, from the eighth century through the tenth, when a new alliance arose between the papacy and the new Western emperors; and (4) the rise of the reform papacy in the eleventh century. The chronological boundaries, however, serve more for convenience than as demarcations of absolute turning points.

THE ANTE-NICENE ERA (FIRST TO FOURTH CENTURIES)

The papacy arose in early Christianity through the elevation of the bishop of Rome to a position of special dignity and power. The first step in this development was the establishment of bishops in the early Christian communities. The office of bishop (*episkopos* in Greek, meaning "overseer" or "superintendent") is seldom cited in the New Testament, and mainly in books of relatively late composition (1 Tim. and Titus in particular). It is not clear from these texts that the bishop held a position clearly distinct from that of other officers (especially *presbyteres,* or elders), or even that there could only be one bishop in a city. By the early second century these developments had certainly occurred in Eastern Christendom: Ignatius of Antioch insisted on the rule of a single bishop in each diocese as normative. But while the "monarchical" episcopacy became established throughout the Eastern church by this time, there is scant evidence for its spread to the West (including Rome) until about the mid second century. Until that time the churches in the West may have been governed in collegial fashion by multiple officers.

There is evidence for Christians at Rome from the middle of the first century. The role that Peter and Paul played in this community is less clear, but it is generally accepted that they visited Rome, where they would both have been received as honored dignitaries, if not as bishops or holders of any other formal office. The tradition that they were both martyred there is at least plausible, if not certain. When the first extant lists of Roman bishops were drawn up, in the late second century, none of them included Peter as the first bishop of the city.

What is clear is that the Christian community at Rome quickly rose to a position of prominence within the broader Christian church. There were various reasons for this development. The city itself, as mother-city of the empire, held special political and cultural significance even when the emperors resided elsewhere. The persecutions, which befell Rome with special virulence, left that city with the honor of having provided an exceptionally large number of martyrs, including possibly both Peter and Paul. While there were important heretics among the Roman Christians, for instance Marcion (*d. ca.* 160), the Christian community as a whole established a reputation for orthodoxy. One of the strongest statements of Roman superiority from the second century, a text of Irenaeus from about 180, takes the church at Rome, founded by Peter and Paul, as an authoritative touchstone for Christian tradition: "With this church, because of its more influential preeminence, it is necessary that every church should agree." The special dignity of the bishop at Rome thus seems to have derived in large part from the prominence of the church that he served.

Throughout the church there were early signs of incipient central power by the third century. When the Council of Nicaea in 325 referred to metropolitans (or archbishops) as having authority over all the bishops in their vicinities, it claimed to be reasserting "ancient custom." The extent of this authority is unclear, though approbation of episcopal selection was one function of the archbishops. The church was thus already borrowing its organizational concepts and vocabulary from the Roman

Empire: the "diocese" of a bishop and the "province" of a metropolitan or archbishop corresponded to Roman imperial territories.

Three individuals who at this time played major roles in the establishment of Roman claims and Roman power were Victor I (189–199), Calixtus I (217–222), and Stephen I (254–257). Each of these bishops of Rome helped to refine the theory and practice of Roman authority by asserting his own power over the broader church in specific controversies.

The issue during the term of office of Victor I was the dating of Easter. Whereas the original custom was to celebrate Christ's resurrection on the same day as the Jewish Passover, the custom that arose in Alexandria and spread to Rome was to celebrate this feast on the Sunday following Passover. Coming at a time when Christians were still laboring to define the relationship between the Jewish tradition and their own, this controversy aroused intense passion. Rome was a focal point, in part because both usages were apparently practiced there by the diverse Christian groups. Victor, assuming that the Alexandrian system had been introduced into Rome by Peter and Paul, insisted around 190 that other churches comply with this tradition. The churches of Asia Minor resisted; he severed ties with them, and attempted to excommunicate them from the broader Christian church, though his sentence was generally ignored by churchmen outside of Rome. The earlier system for dating survived for several centuries in parts of Asia Minor, but eventually most local churches adopted the Alexandrian-Roman usage. What is most significant about the dispute from the viewpoint of the history of the papacy is that Victor could claim authority to dictate such policy to the church at large, even if his excommunication of the Asian Christians was not universally accepted.

Soon afterward, Calixtus I was again asserting widespread authority, this time with regard to penitential practice. During a time when major sins (such as adultery and murder) were treated with considerable severity, and offenders were readmitted to the church only after undertaking rigorous public penance, Calixtus was accused of advocating relative leniency, and his position gave rise to widespread controversy. It is probably he (if not Bishop Zephyrinus) who provoked Tertullian around 220 in his *De pudicitia* to the sarcasm about the "sovereign pontiff, that is the bishop of bishops," who dared to issue an edict remitting the offenses of adultery and fornication for those who had done penance. (Tertullian's comment: "O edict on which cannot be inscribed: Well done!") The edict in question seems to have appealed to Matthew 16:19; but Tertullian suggested that Christ gave the keys only to Peter, not to his successors.

It was under Stephen I that assertion of Roman power was most clearly linked with theoretical arguments based on the foundation of the Roman church by Peter. Shortly before Stephen's accession, the Novatian schism had arisen because a Roman presbyter named Novatian insisted on rigorous treatment of Christians who had made accommodations with paganism during the persecutions. The specific controversy that now arose, giving Stephen occasion for assertion of claims to power, was whether schismatic or heretical bishops could administer baptism. Cyprian of Carthage (*d.* 258), and the bishops of North Africa generally, adopted the rigorist position that baptisms by such bishops were invalid. Stephen, whose stance ultimately prevailed throughout the church, maintained that the validity of baptism did not depend on the status within the church of the person administering it. In upholding this position, Stephen explictly claimed primacy within the church based on his succession to the office of Peter. In 256 Bishop Firmilian of Caesarea in Cappadocia sent Cyprian a letter roundly condemning Stephen and his claims, thus indicating how a prominent Eastern bishop reacted to these assertions of authority: The Roman appeal to apostolic authority was in vain, since in many particulars (celebration of Easter and sacramental usage, for example) Rome differs from Jerusalem; there is indeed much diversity in the church on such matters, but this plurality has not disrupted peace and unity until Stephen, defaming the names of Peter and Paul, began to assert that heretics could validly baptize; Stephen was inviting further disunion by his encouragement of heretics (for though he boasted that "he holds his succession from Peter, on whom the foundations of the church were laid," he was "introducing many other rocks" and preparing "many new churches" with this encouragement); he claimed authority to excommunicate other churches, but in fact excommunicated only himself.

Many of Cyprian's own writings survive, and they afford more temperate testimony to the reception of Roman claims. In his letters he emphasized the unity of the church but conceived it as a unity attained through the cohesion of bishops. His notion of the church was that of "one episcopate, diffused throughout a harmonious multitude of many bishops." He recognized the bishop of Rome as successor to Peter, and he was among the first to speak of this bishop as occupying the "chair of Peter" (*cathedra Petri*), but he questioned the implications that Stephen drew from this notion. Peter himself, "whom the Lord chose first, and on whom he built his church, did not claim anything insolently and arrogantly for himself when Paul later disputed with him about circumcision." In short, Peter did not claim a primacy that would have required the obedience of all. While one version of Cyprian's treatise *On the Unity of the Catholic Church* does speak of primacy accorded to Peter and to the chair on which his successors sit, these passages are generally regarded as interpolations, consistent neither with Cyprian's own statements elsewhere nor with his stance in the baptismal controversy. What he was willing to grant the bishop of Rome was a "precedency" based on special honor. Before his rupture with Stephen, he thought of the Roman bishop as one whose initiative in controversies might usefully ensure unity within the church, though not through jurisdictional intervention so much as through persuasion.

By the end of the ante-Nicene era, then, the bishop of Rome had clearly established a precedent for a claim to moral prominence within the church. We know of such claims, however, largely from their numerous opponents. Thus it is difficult to ascertain precisely how much real jurisdictional power the bishops of Rome were claiming, or to comment extensively on the grounds for their claims.

THE POST-NICENE ERA (FOURTH TO EIGHTH CENTURIES)

The Council of Nicaea (325) was the first effort to attain consensus in the church through an assembly that claimed to represent all of Christendom. It played a major role in early church history also because the main theological issue it addressed, the Arian heresy, was the first major occasion for development of technical Christology. Furthermore, the role of Emperor Constantine in convoking and presiding over the council signaled a strong measure of imperial control over the church. The council occurred at a time of numerous changes in both church and empire. Constantine ended the era of persecutions and inaugurated a policy of close ties between church and empire. Shortly before the council he had moved his capital to Byzantium (Constantinople). This policy continued under most of Constantine's successors. Yet the empire itself was under strain, and imperial rule in the western part dissolved when Germanic peoples invaded in the fifth century.

One innovation at roughly this time deserves note, though its significance should not be exaggerated: it was in the fourth century that the title "pope" (*papa*), which had long been used for the bishops of Alexandria and Carthage, now came into regular use for other bishops, including the bishop of Rome. It retained its broader use for centuries (some Eastern churches still use the title in this broader sense), though in the eleventh century Gregory VII declared that it was to be used only for the bishop of Rome.

Of the popes who reigned during this period, the ones most significant for advancement of papal claims and papal power were Damasus I (366–384), Innocent I (401–417), Leo I (440–461), Gelasius I (492–496), and Gregory I (590–604).

The pontificate of Damasus I marked in some ways an enhancement of papal power unprecedented in the church's history. The emperor Gratian in 378 lent his support to Damasus' claim to exercise authority over the bishops of Western (Latin) Christendom. Two years later Theodosius I recognized the bishop of Rome as a special guardian of the faith—though he was mentioned alongside the bishop of Alexandria, and the emperor was favoring the orthodox faith of these men rather than the individuals or their offices.

Circumstances were in other respects favorable for Damasus. The African bishop Optatus of Mileve (Milevis), writing in 370–385 against the schismatic Donatists (*De schismate Donatistorum*), recognized papal authority far more than had Cyprian. The Donatists had cut themselves off from the Catholic church, "which is diffused throughout the world," and over which Peter presided: ". . . upon Peter first in the city of Rome was conferred the episcopal chair, on which sat Peter, the head of all the apostles, . . . that in this one chair unity should be preserved by all, lest the other apostles might uphold each for himself separate chairs. . . ." Optatus then gives a list of the bishops of Rome, which, though incomplete, extends back to Peter. Last on the list is Damasus, who "with the whole world agrees with us in one bond of communion." Clearly Optatus recognized the bishop of Rome as

THE POPES TO 1503

The following list, adapted from the *New Catholic Encyclopedia* (1967), notes the regnal dates of the popes and antipopes (in brackets) down to the end of the Middle Ages. Information concerning many of the early reigns is based on scholarly conjecture. Where two initial dates are given, the first is the date of election and the second is the date of coronation. The final date represents death, deposition, or resignation.

St. Peter, . . . 67
St. Linus, 67—76
St. Anacletus, 76—88
St. Clement I, 88—97
St. Evaristus, 97—105
St. Alexander I, 105—115
St. Sixtus I, 115—125
St. Telesphorus, 125—136
St. Hyginus, 136—140
St. Pius I, 140—155
St. Anicetus, 155—166
St. Soter, 166—175
St. Eleutherius, 175—189
St. Victor I, 189—199
St. Zephyrinus, 199—217
St. Calixtus I, 217—222
[St. Hippolytus, 217—235]
St. Urban I, 222—230
St. Pontianus, 21 July 230—28 Sept. 235
St. Anterus, 21 Nov. 235—3 Jan. 236
St. Fabian, 10 Jan. 236—20 Jan. 250
St. Cornelius, March 251—June 253
[Novatian, 251]
St. Lucius I, 25 June 253—5 March 254
St. Stephen I, 12 May 254—2 Aug. 257
St. Sixtus II, 30 Aug. 257—6 Aug. 258
St. Dionysius, 22 July 259—26 Dec. 268
St. Felix I, 5 Jan. 269—30 Dec. 274
St. Eutychian, 4 Jan. 275—7 Dec. 283
St. Gaius (Caius), 17 Dec. 283—22 April 296
St. Marcellinus, 30 June 296—25 Oct. 304
St. Marcellus I, 27 May 308—16 Jan. 309
St. Eusebius, 18 April 309—17 Aug. 309
St. Miltiades, 2 July 311—11 Jan. 314
St. Sylvester I, 31 Jan. 314—31 Dec. 335
St. Mark, 18 Jan. 336—7 Oct. 336
St. Julius I, 6 Feb. 337—12 April 352
Liberius, 17 May 352—24 Sept. 366
[Felix II, . . . 355—22 Nov. 365]
St. Damasus I, 1 Oct. 366—11 Dec. 384
[Ursinus, 366—367]
St. Siricius, 15, 22, or 29 Dec. 384—26 Nov. 399
St. Anastasius I, 27 Nov. 399—19 Dec. 401
St. Innocent I, 22 Dec. 401—12 March 417
St. Zosimus, 18 March 417—26 Dec. 418
St. Boniface I, 28 or 29 Dec. 418—4 Sept. 422
[Eulalius, 27 or 29 Dec. 418—419]
St. Celestine I, 10 Sept. 422—27 July 432
St. Sixtus III, 31 July 432—19 Aug. 440
St. Leo I, 29 Sept. 440—10 Nov. 461
St. Hilary, 19 Nov. 461—29 Feb. 468
St. Simplicius, 3 March 468—10 March 483
St. Felix III (II), 13 March 483—1 March 492
St. Gelasius I, 1 March 492—21 Nov. 496
Anastasius II, 24 Nov. 496—19 Nov. 498
St. Symmachus, 22 Nov. 498—19 July 514
[Lawrence, 498; 501—505]
St. Hormisdas, 20 July 514—6 Aug. 523
St. John I, 13 Aug. 523—18 May 526
St. Felix IV (III), 12 July 526—22 Sept. 530
Boniface II, 22 Sept. 530—17 Oct. 532
[Dioscorus, 22 Sept. 530—14 Oct. 530]
John II, 2 Jan. 533—8 May 535
St. Agapetus I, 13 May 535—22 April 536
St. Silverius, 1 June 536—11 Nov. 537
Vigilius, 29 March 537—7 June 555
Pelagius I, 16 April 556—4 March 561
John III, 17 July 561—13 July 574
Benedict I, 2 June 575—30 July 579
Pelagius II, 26 Nov. 579—7 Feb. 590
St. Gregory I, 3 Sept. 590—12 March 604
Sabinian, 13 Sept. 604—22 Feb. 606
Boniface III, 19 Feb. 607—12 Nov. 607
St. Boniface IV, 25 Aug. 608—8 May 615
St. Deusdedit I, 19 Oct. 615—8 Nov. 618
Boniface V, 23 Dec. 619—25 Oct. 625
Honorius I, 27 Oct. 625—12 Oct. 638
Severinus, 28 May 640—2 Aug. 640
John IV, 24 Dec. 640—12 Oct. 642
Theodore I, 24 Nov. 642—14 May 649
St. Martin I, . . . July 649—16 Sept. 655
St. Eugenius I, 10 Aug. 654—2 June 657
St. Vitalian, 30 July 657—27 Jan. 672
Deusdedit II, 11 April 672—17 June 676
Donus, 2 Nov. 676—11 April 678
St. Agatho, 27 June 678—10 Jan. 681
St. Leo II, 17 Aug. 682—3 July 683
St. Benedict II, 26 June 684—8 May 685
John V, 23 July 685—2 Aug. 686
Conon, 21 Oct. 686—21 Sept. 687
[Theodore, . . . 687]
[Paschal, . . . 687]
St. Sergius I, 15 Dec. 687—8 Sept. 701
John VI, 30 Oct. 701—11 Jan. 705
John VII, 1 March 705—18 Oct. 707
Sisinnius, 15 Jan. 708—4 Feb. 708
Constantine, 25 March 708—9 April 715
St. Gregory II, 19 May 715—11 Feb. 731
St. Gregory III, 18 March 731—Nov. 741
St. Zacharias, 10 Dec. 741—22 March 752
Stephen, 22 (23?)—26(25?) March 752
Stephen II (III), 26 March 752—26 April 757
St. Paul I, . . . 29 April, May 757—28 June 767
[Constantine, 28 June, 5 July 767—769]
[Philip 31 July 768]
Stephen III (IV), 1 Aug., 7 Aug. 768—24 Jan. 772
Adrian I, 1 Feb., 9 Feb. 772—25 Dec. 795
St. Leo III, 26 Dec., 27 Dec. 795—12 June 816
Stephen IV (V), 22 June 816—24 Jan. 817
St. Paschal I, 25 Jan. 817—11 Feb. 824
Eugenius II, . . . Feb./May 824— . . . Aug. 827
Valentine, . . . Aug. 827— . . . Sept. 827
Gregory IV, . . . 827— . . . Jan. 844
[John, . . . Jan. 844]
Sergius II, . . . Jan. 844—27 Jan. 847
St. Leo IV, . . . Jan., 10 April 847—17 July 855
Benedict III, . . . 29 July, Sept. 855—17 April 858
[Anastasius, . . . Aug. 855— . . . Sept. 855]
St. Nicholas I, 24 April 858—13 Nov. 867
Adrian II, 14 Dec. 867—14 Dec. 872
John VIII, 14 Dec. 872—16 Dec. 882
Marinus I, 16 Dec. 882—15 May 884
St. Adrian III, 17 May 884— . . . Sept. 885
Stephen V (VI), . . . Sept. 885—14 Sept. 891

Formosus, 6 Oct. 891—4 April 896
Boniface VI, . . . April 896— . . . April 896
Stephen VI (VII), . . . May 896— . . . Aug. 897
Romanus, . . . Aug. 897— . . . Nov. 897
Theodore II, . . . Dec. 897— . . . Dec. 897
John IX, . . . Jan. 898— . . . Jan. 900
Benedict IV, . . . Jan. or Feb. 900— . . . July 903
Leo V, . . . July 903— . . . Sept. 903
[Christopher, . . . July or . . . Sept. 903— . . . Jan 904]
Sergius III, 29 Jan. 904—14 April 911
Anastasius III, . . . April 911— . . . June 913
Lando, . . . July 913— . . . Feb. 914
John X, . . . March 914— . . . May 928
Leo VI, . . . May 928— . . . Dec. 928
Stephen VII (VIII), . . . Dec. 928— . . . Feb. 931
John XI, . . . Feb. or March 931— . . . Dec. 935
Leo VII, 3 Jan. 936—13 July 939
Stephen VIII (IX), 14 July 939— . . . Oct. 942
Marinus II, 30 Oct. 942— . . . May 946
Agapetus II, 10 May 946— . . . Dec. 955
John XII, 16 Dec. 955—14 May 964
Leo VIII, 4, 6 Dec. 963—1 March 965
Benedict V, 22 May 964—4 July 966
John XIII, 1 Oct. 965—6 Sept. 672
Benedict VI, 19 Jan. 973— . . . June 974
[Boniface VII, . . . June 974—July 974; then Aug. 984—July 985]
Benedict VII, . . . Oct. 974—10 July 983
John XIV, . . . Dec. 983—20 Aug. 984
John XV, . . . Aug. 985— . . . March 996
Greogry V, 3 May 996—18 Feb. 999
[John XVI, . . . April 997— . . . Feb. 998]
Sylvester II, 2 April 999—12 May 1003
John XVII, . . . June 1003— . . . Dec. 1003
John XVIII, . . . Jan. 1004— . . . July 1009
Sergius IV, 31 July 1009—12 May 1012
Benedict VIII, 18 May 1012—9 April 1024
[Gregory, . . . 1012]
John XIX, . . . April or May 1024— . . . 1032
Benedict IX, . . . 1032— . . . 1044
Sylvester III, 20 Jan. 1045—10 Feb. 1045
Benedict IX, 10 April 1045—1 May 1045
Gregory VI, 5 May 1045—20 Dec. 1046
Clement II, 24, 25 Dec. 1046—9 Oct. 1047
Benedict IX, 8 Nov. 1047—17 July 1048
Damasus II, 17 July 1048—9 Aug. 1048
St. Leo IX, 12 Feb. 1049—19 April 1054
Victor II, 16 April 1055—28 July 1057
Stephen IX (X), 3 Aug. 1057—29 March 1058
[Benedict X, 5 April 1058—24 Jan. 1059]
Nicholas II, 24 Jan. 1059—27 July 1061
Alexander II, 1 Oct. 1061—21 April 1073
[Honorius II, 28 Oct. 1061— . . . 1072]
St. Gregory VII, 22 April, 30 June 1073—25 May 1085
[Clement III, 26 June 1080; 24 March 1084—8 Sept. 1100]
Bl. Victor III, 24 May 1086—16 Sept. 1087
Bl. Urban II, 12 March 1088—29 July 1099
Pascal II, 13, 14 Aug. 1099—21 Jan. 1118
[Theodoric, . . . 1100]
[Albert, . . . 1102]
[Sylvester IV, 18 Nov. 1105— . . . 1111]
Gelasius II, 24 Jan., 10 March 1118—28 Jan. 1119
[Gregory VIII, 8 March 1118— . . . 1121]
Calixtus II, 2, 9 Feb. 1119—13 Dec. 1124
Honorius II, 15, 21 Dec. 1124—13 Feb. 1130
[Celestine II, . . . Dec. 1124]
Innocent II, 14, 23 Feb. 1130—25 Jan. 1143
[Anacletus II, 14, 23 Feb. 1130—25 Jan. 1138]
[Victor IV, . . . March 1138—29 May 1138]
Celestine II, 26 Sept., 3 Oct. 1143—8 March 1144
Lucius II, 12 March 1144—15 Feb. 1145
Bl. Eugenius III, 15, 18 Feb. 1145—8 July 1153
Anastasius IV, 12 July 1153—3 Dec. 1154
Adrian IV, 4, 5 Dec. 1154—1 Sept. 1159
Alexander III, 7, 20 Sept. 1159—30 Aug. 1181
[Victor IV, 7 Sept., 4 Oct. 1159—20 April 1164]
[Pascal III, 22, 26 April 1164—20 Sept. 1168]
[Calixtus III, . . . Sept. 1168—29 Aug. 1178]
[Innocent III, 29 Sept. 1179— . . . 1180]
Lucius III, 1, 6 Sept. 1181—25 Sept. 1185
Urban III, 25 Nov., 1 Dec. 1185—20 Oct. 1187
Gregory VIII, 21, 25 Oct. 1187—17 Dec. 1187
Clement III, 19, 20 Dec. 1187— . . . March 1191
Celestine III, 30 March, 14 April 1191—8 Jan. 1198
Innocent III, 8 Jan., 22 Feb. 1198—16 July 1216
Honorius III, 18, 24 July 1216—18 March 1227
Gregory IX, 19, 21 March 1227—22 Aug. 1241
Celestine IV, 25, 28 Oct. 1241—10 Nov. 1241
Innocent IV, 25, 28 June 1243—7 Dec. 1254
Alexander IV, 12, 20 Dec. 1254—25 May 1261
Urban IV, 29 Aug., 4 Sept. 1261—2 Oct. 1264
Clement IV, 5, 15 Feb. 1265—29 Nov. 1268
Bl. Gregory X, 1 Sept. 1271, 27 March 1272—10 Jan. 1276
Bl. Innocent V, 21 Jan., 22 Feb. 1276—22 June 1276
Adrian V, 11 July 1276—18 Aug. 1276
John XXI, 8, 20 Sept. 1276—20 May 1277
Nicholas III, 25 Nov., 26 Dec. 1277—22 Aug. 1280
Martin IV, 22 Feb., 23 March 1281—28 March 1285
Honorius IV, 2 April, 20 May 1285—3 April 1287
Nicholas IV, 22 Feb. 1288—4 April 1292
St. Celestine V, 5 July, 29 Aug. 1294—13 Dec. 1294
Boniface VIII, 24 Dec. 1294, 23 Jan. 1295—11 Oct. 1303
Bl. Benedict XI, 22, 27 Oct. 1303—7 July 1304
Clement V, 5 June, 14 Nov. 1305—20 April 1314
John XXII, 7 Aug., 5 Sept. 1316—4 Dec. 1334
[Nicholas V, 12, 22 May 1328—25 Aug. 1330]
Benedict XII, 20 Dec. 1334, 8 Jan. 1335—25 April 1342
Clement VI, 7, 19 May 1342—6 Dec. 1352
Innocent VI, 18, 30 Dec. 1352—12 Sept. 1362
Bl. Urban V, 28 Sept., 6 Nov. 1362—19 Dec. 1370
Gregory XI, 30 Dec. 1370, 5 Jan. 1371—26 March 1378
Urban VI, 8, 18 April 1378—15 Oct. 1389
Boniface IX, 2, 9 Nov. 1389—1 Oct. 1404
Innocent VII, 17 Oct., 11 Nov. 1404—6 Nov. 1406
Gregory XII, 30 Nov., 19 Dec. 1406—4 July 1415
[Clement VII, 20 Sept., 31 Oct. 1378—16 Sept. 1394]
[Benedict XIII, 28 Sept., 11 Oct. 1394—23 May 1423]
[Alexander V, 26 June, 7 July 1409—3 May 1410]
[John XXIII, 17, 25 May 1410—29 May 1415]
Martin V, 11, 21 Nov. 1417—20 Feb. 1431
Eugenius IV, 3, 11 March 1431—23 Feb. 1447
[Felix V, 5 Nov. 1439, 24 July 1440—7 April 1449]
Nicholas V, 6, 19 March 1447—24 March 1455
Calixtus III, 8, 20 April 1455—6 Aug. 1458
Pius II, 19 Aug., 3 Sept. 1458—15 Aug. 1464
Paul II, 30 Aug., 16 Sept. 1464—26 July 1471
Sixtus IV, 9, 25 Aug. 1471—12 Aug. 1484
Innocent VIII, 29 Aug., 12 Sept. 1484—25 July 1492
Alexander VI, 11, 26 Aug. 1492—18 Aug. 1503
Pius III, 22 Sept., 1, 8 Oct. 1503—18 Oct. 1503

having special dignity, though the extent of his authority is unclear. When Optatus speaks of Peter as the one apostle who received the keys, it is uncertain how he conceives Peter's relations with the other apostles—or the pope's relations with other bishops—in matters of practical jurisdiction.

In 381, Damasus was not invited to the council held at Constantinople, at which it was determined that "the bishop of Constantinople shall have the privileges of honor after the bishop of Rome, because it is the new Rome." The following year, a council at Rome declared that the Roman church "has been set before the rest by no conciliar decrees, but has obtained the primacy by the voice of our Lord . . . ," in the classic text from Matthew. Thus Damasus countered the implication that ranking within the church was subject to conciliar enactment.

Innocent I was pontiff when the Visigoths attacked Rome in 410; it has been suggested that the disruptions of this time gave him special opportunity to exert his own leadership, and that he did so in ways that contributed greatly to the development of the papacy. On the other hand, it is possible to represent him simply as a more effective advocate of traditional claims. He asserted authority in all major issues (*causae maiores*) throughout the church. In a letter of 417 he congratulated the bishops assembled at Carthage for referring local matters to him, in accordance with the divine decree "that whatever is done, even though it be in distant provinces, should not be ended until it comes to the knowledge of this see." He intervened in affairs of Eastern as well as Western dioceses and effectively secured an imperial edict against heresy. Nonetheless, even after his pontificate the practical power wielded by popes remained limited, and in 431 the Council of Ephesus still repudiated the Roman bishops' claim that Peter represented the "head of the entire faith."

The decline of imperial authority in the West left a power vacuum that was eventually filled by churchmen, and particularly by the pope. Thus Leo I was able to take advantage of the political situation by enhancing his position within the church and adopting the trappings and titles of monarchy. In 445 he obtained a declaration from the emperor Valentinian III giving him binding authority over the church in the West: it was to be unlawful for the bishops of Gaul or any other province to do anything without papal sanction; whatever the pope decreed should be "law for all"; if any bishop was summoned to trial before the pope and neglected to appear, he would be compelled by the provincial governor. Valentinian added that these rights were inherent in the papal office and were not granted but only confirmed by imperial rescript—"for what is not allowed in the church to the authority of so great a pontiff?"

Taking for himself the title *pontifex maximus* that the emperors had abandoned, Leo conceived his role as a combined one: with "plentitude of power" (*plenitudo potestatis*), he represented monarchical authority as well as supreme sacerdotal dignity. His numerous extant sermons and letters make clear that he built upon earlier papal theory and claimed unique authority as sole heir to Peter. Repeatedly he wrote of Peter as a channel of power: "In Peter the strength of all is fortified, and the help of divine grace is so ordered that the stability which through Christ is given to Peter, through Peter is conveyed to the apostles." Addressing his fellow bishop in Alexandria, which claimed Mark as the founder of its Christian community, he reminded this bishop that Mark was a disciple of Peter. He exercised close scrutiny over the Western church, ordering Sicilian bishops to send representatives to a synod at Rome, instructing other bishops how to deal with heretics, deposing insubordinate churchmen, and otherwise demonstrating the possibilities for papal power. Like Innocent I, he was able to exert himself at a time of civil strife. When Attila the Hun marched into Italy in 452, the pope joined a delegation that induced him to spare Rome; tradition ascribes the major role in this diplomatic venture to Leo.

Leo's greatest opportunity for dominance within the church came in 451, when the Council of Chalcedon accepted his position on the christological controversies then rampant. As the council fathers more than once observed, Leo had spoken as a mouthpiece for Peter. The same council, however, went beyond the Council of Ephesus by declaring that the church of Constantinople, rather than holding second place below that of Rome, held a position of equal dignity. Hence, whatever honors the pope may have held, and whatever authority he commanded in the West, there were still limits to his power within the church at large.

Relations between pope and emperor were not always so cordial as they were under Innocent and Leo. Indeed, uneasy papal-imperial relations became typical as the emperors grew more and more isolated from developments in the West. In the late fifth century, controversy in the East regarding christological questions led the emperor Zeno in 482 to issue a compromise formulation (the *Henotikon,* or Edict of Union), which the pope repudiated. While the pope was concerned about orthodoxy in doctrine, he was likewise troubled by imperial meddling in ecclesiastical affairs. The issue persisted after the deaths of this emperor and pope. Thus, in 494 Pope Gelasius I sent a letter to Emperor Anastasius in which he asserted, "There are two things, august emperor, by which this world is chiefly ruled: the sacred authority of bishops and the royal power." This famous text has been interpreted in various ways. It has been pointed out, for example, that in Roman legal parlance *auctoritas* was superior to *potestas,* the latter being derived from a higher figure who held the former. Two years later, however, in a treatise *On the Bond of Anathema,* Gelasius carefully specified that Christ (himself both true king and true priest) had distinguished ecclesiastical from secular offices, "so that Christian emperors would need priests for attaining eternal life, and priests would avail themselves of imperial regulations in the conduct of temporal affairs," neither encroaching on the other's rights. This separation of powers would, Gelasius continued, ensure proper humility: neither churchman nor ruler would be "exalted by the subservience of the other," and each office would be left to its own functions. In his insistence on the distinction between papal and imperial authority, Gelasius was reasserting a traditional demand of the Roman see.

The tension between the Eastern and Western portions of the Roman Empire was aggravated by the descent of further Germanic peoples into the Mediterranean region. Though the Huns had spared Rome, the Ostrogoths were consolidating their power in Italy as Gelasius quarreled with the emperor. In 533 the emperor Justinian I responded with a program of reconquest that was substantially successful. Yet by 568 a new wave of attack began, this time by the Lombards, who established themselves in northern Italy and for the next two centuries threatened central Italy, including Rome. While Constantinople did little to aid in the continuing struggle against the Lombards, the emperor maintained certain kinds of control over the papacy. From the mid sixth to the mid eighth century, popes had to obtain imperial confirmation of their elections; request for confirmation was accompanied by substantial payment to the imperial government. From 678 until the mid eighth century, a majority of the popes were either Greek or Syrian.

Of the popes who ruled during this period of Germanic invasions and Byzantine control, the one whom tradition has most honored is Gregory I the Great (*ca.* 540–604), also known as the "Father of the Medieval Papacy." Scion of a wealthy aristocratic family, he had served in the government of Rome and had been a papal envoy to Constantinople before withdrawing to a monastery. Elected pope in 590, he served Rome and its environs through secular as well as spiritual leadership. He reorganized the administration of the city, secured the municipal defenses, negotiated independently with the Lombard king, and attended in other ways to secular business that fell to him by default. He managed to retain courteous relations with Emperor Phokas, but his relations with the patriarch (or archbishop) of Constantinople were less cordial. The patriarchs had (at least since about 518) been styling themselves "ecumenical patriarchs," a title that impressed Gregory as dangerous and presumptuous. Gregory, who preferred to call himself "servant of the servants of God" (*servus servorum Dei*), repeatedly castigated this usage and other indications of what he took to be Byzantine pretension. As the first monk to become pope, he fostered monasticism by insisting on the independence of monasteries and by placing monks in several important episcopal sees, as well as by writing works (such as the earliest biography of Benedict of Nursia) that promoted the monastic ideal. Over the church in central Italy he exercised detailed control—naming pastors to churches, ordering shoes for deacons in one locality, providing warm clothes for a bishop who was suffering from cold weather, and so forth. He enhanced his prestige throughout the broader church by helping to settle controversies in Africa, Spain, Gaul, and elsewhere. He furthered missionary work in various parts of Europe, most notably England, to which he sent Augustine of Canterbury and companions in 596.

The significance of Gregory has been challenged by some historians. Johannes Haller, in particular, argued that Gregory was a petty despot within a small portion of central Italy, and that his efforts to extend his power and thwart the pretensions of Constantinople were futile and small-minded. What Haller saw as Gregory's lasting contribution to Western Christendom was the long-range impact of his missionary interest in England. To be sure, Haller insisted, it was not the Roman missionaries so much as the Celts and the Franks who were responsible for converting the English to Christianity. Yet the English themselves, thanks in part to Bede (672/673–735) and his *Ecclesiastical History,* acknowledged a profound debt to Gregory. It was from Gregory and Augustine of Canterbury that they had acquired a special devotion to St. Peter (manifested, for example, in church dedications and in a fondness for visiting Rome on pilgrimage). As the English themselves became leading missionaries to northern Europe in the eighth century, they took with them a fervent dedication to the papacy in general, to St. Peter, and to Gregory the Great, which they implanted in the areas that they converted. Haller perceived this English cult of the popes as substantially responsible for the development of the medieval papacy as a moral force in Europe.

Later missionaries (such as Boniface, *ca.* 675–754) did indeed maintain close ties with Rome as a source of legitimacy and support for their international missionary work. Thus, as the monk-missionaries of the early Middle Ages were helping to bring European Christendom into existence (as opposed to the earlier Mediterranean Christendom), they fostered a sense of affiliation with the pope that had important long-range influence. It was not until later, however, that the papacy began to reap the political fruit of these efforts—particularly in the age of the reform papacy.

The uneasy relations with Constantinople that characterized much of this era reached a head in 726, when Emperor Leo III gave imperial sanction to the iconoclast position that was popular among certain circles in the East. The pope at the time was Gregory II (715–731), one of the few Westerners on the papal throne during this period, who in typically Western fashion sought to protect the role of religious images in the church. He sent Leo a rebuke in 727: "You know that the dogmas of holy church are not the concern of emperors but of pontiffs," and that neither should intervene in the responsibilities of the other. Gregory complained that the emperor, in his "imprudence and stupidity," was unable to help defend Italy from the Lombards. Nonetheless, this same emperor threatened to march on Rome and seize the pope, and then carry him away to Constantinople. In fact, however, the popes have been the ones to maintain peace at Rome, and have gained support from the people: "The whole of the West faithfully offers its fruits to the holy prince of the apostles," and if the emperor attacks his image he will be responsible for the violence he provokes. To this the emperor sent a reply in which he proclaimed, "I am emperor and priest." Because the patriarch of Constantinople was allied with the emperor in this controversy, the pope (now Gregory III, a Syrian who continued his predecessor's policies) excommunicated the patriarch. Leo retaliated by stripping the pope of lucrative lands in southern Italy and Sicily, and by having several dioceses transferred from Roman to Byzantine jurisdiction.

Thus, while the beginning of the post-Nicene era saw the rise of papal aspirations and a general policy of imperial support for the popes, the lasting and growing rift between Eastern and Western interests brought about tension in imperial-papal relations that could remain acute even when the pope himself was of Eastern cultural background.

THE CAROLINGIAN AND OTTONIAN PERIODS (EIGHTH TO TENTH CENTURIES)

The continued threat of the Lombards and the rift between Rome and Constantinople led in the mid eighth century to a new alliance. Having risen to power in the post-Nicene era sometimes in cooperation and sometimes in competition with the emperors at Constantinople, the popes now established themselves as moral and political leaders through alliance with the new emperors, Carolingian and Ottonian, who in the early Middle Ages claimed valid succession to the ancient imperial dignity.

The first clear sign of this new policy came in 739, when Gregory III requested the aid of Charles Martel (ruler in the kingdom of Gaul) for defense against the Lombards. For political reasons of his own, Charles refused. When the Lombards renewed their assault in mid century, however, Pope Zacharias (741–752) supported the accession of the first Carolingian king of Gaul, Pepin the Short, to ensure that Pepin would support papal interests. Zacharias even had the missionary Boniface anoint Pepin in 751 as the new king, thus conveying the message that this royal office was dispensed by the pope. (Zacharias also ended the custom of obtaining ratification of papal elections by the emperor in Constantinople; indeed, he repeated his predecessor's condemnation of the emperor's iconoclasm.) The confrontation with the Lombards, and the correlative alliance with the Carolingian monarchs, was further solidified under Stephen II (752–757), who crossed the Alps and met Pepin in 754, begging

The Donation of Constantine. The emperor is depicted as bestowing tiara, crown, Lateran Palace, and the rank of imperial cavalry commander on Pope Sylvester I, who offers his blessing. Fresco in the chapel of St. Sylvester, Santi Quattro Coronati, Rome, 1246. PHOTO: WIM SWAAN

him on his knees to aid in the defense against the Lombard assault. Later that year, Stephen secured Pepin's support by various favors, including new consecration as king and bestowal of lands in Italy; in addition, Stephen forbade Pepin's subjects ever to select a king who was not descended from him. In that year, and again two years later, Pepin invaded Italy and defeated the Lombards, thus securing at least temporarily both the papal position and the papal Carolingian alliance.

One significant feature of this early bond with the Carolingians was the appeal that Stephen II made to his Petrine office. When the pope met Pepin in 754, both of these rulers acknowledged their responsibility to St. Peter, meaning to the office of the papacy. In asking Pepin to come a second time to his aid, Stephen presented to the king's mind the image of Peter "standing before you, living, in the flesh." And when in 756 an embassy from Constantinople claimed lands in northern Italy as imperial holdings, the answer (in the so-called Donation of Pepin) was that this territory had been reconquered for St. Peter from the Lombards. The biography of Stephen says that Pepin "was faithful to God and loved St. Peter," and when faced with an imperial demand he refused to relinquish the land in question "from the power of St. Peter and the jurisdiction of the Roman church. . . ." He swore that he had fought not for human favor but "for the love of St. Peter and for the remission of his sins."

In the wake of these developments, sometime in the second half of the eighth century, the political authority of the pope received expression in the so-called Donation of Constantine, a document forged to support widespread assumptions about what must have been historical fact. The actual powers gained by the popes were twofold: they now ruled over territories in central Italy as their own kingdom (the "Republic of St. Peter," later called the Papal States), and to a limited extent they had established their right (mainly through the Carolingian alliance) to consecrate secular monarchs. Assuming that such powers could only proceed from a historical transfer of imperial authority to the papacy, but perceiving that there was no extant document recording that transfer, an anonymous proponent of papal claims made up for the deficiency by drafting the Donation of Constantine. Purportedly a decree from the fourth-century emperor, this document granted rule over the Western Roman Empire to the papacy. The document first bestows the Lateran palace, the imperial crown and miter, the stole and cloak, and the rank of imperial cavalry commander upon the pope. So as not to demean the dignity of the crown, Constantine is supposed to have further granted the pope and his successors "all provinces, palaces, and districts of the city of Rome and Italy and of the regions of the West," all "placed at his disposal . . . as a permanent possession of the holy Roman Church." To avoid the impropriety of the emperor and the pope living as rulers in the same city, Constantine determined to transfer his own court to Byzantium. On the basis of this Donation, popes from the later eighth century onward could claim that the rulers (and specifically the emperors) of Western Europe owed their power to papal concession; the popes were intermediaries between the old Roman emperors and the medieval heirs to imperial authority.

The Carolingian alliance assumed far greater significance under the reign of Charles the Great (or Charlemagne). In 773–774, Adrian I (772–795) induced Charles to renew Pepin's commitment to support the papacy, to invade Lombardy, and to depose the Lombard king—whereupon Charles assumed rule over northern Italy for himself. Having thus become neighbors within the Italian Peninsula, Adrian and Charles quarreled about the extent of power claimed by each. Yet the papal territories remained secure and were even extended during this period, and Charles further aided Adrian by lending his support to the cause of unity in doctrine, liturgy, and canon law.

Adrian's successor, Leo III (795–816), was almost from the outset of his pontificate more submissive to Charles. His sense of linkage with the Carolingian throne was suggested by his custom of dating papal documents by Charles's regnal year as king in Italy. This bond was much enhanced in a crisis that befell Leo in 799. Seized and imprisoned by members of a rival faction, he escaped and took refuge with Charles. His enemies accused him of adultery, perjury, and other offenses; rather than submitting himself to judgment, he voluntarily took an oath asserting his innocence, and thus he asserted the principle that the papacy "is judged by no one." The danger he then faced was that his adversaries might refer the case to the emperor in Constantinople, who would have been a dangerous judge from the pope's viewpoint. Evidently to forestall this move, Leo approached Charles on Christmas Day in the year 800 and placed an imperial crown on his head. Though Charles is supposed to have suspected nothing, and to have protested afterward that he would not have cooperated if he had known of this plan in advance, he did not refuse the honor. Thus, the pope was now allied with a new, Western emperor of his own making, whose protection could guard him against threats from the Eastern emperor. The ongoing relationship between Leo and Charlemagne was essentially one of distant cooperation. (At the emperor's urging, for example, Leo took action against the Adoptionist heresy.)

The Carolingian line retained at least nominal power in Western Europe through most of the ninth century. While there was occasional friction and animosity, for the most part the ties with Rome persisted and were symbolized by the custom of papal coronation for each emperor, as a reminder that imperial power came through the pope. Charles the Great's successor, Louis the Pious, was crowned the first time without papal involvement, but the reigning pope (Stephen IV) insisted on crossing the Alps to repeat the coronation (in 816 at Rheims), to maintain his own claim as mediator of imperial authority. Repeatedly in the course of the century the popes asserted the right to anoint and crown heirs to the Carolingian throne, and in 875 John VIII made the point inescapably clear by extending the imperial crown to Charles the Bald as a "benefice of God" bestowed by "the privilege of the apostolic see."

The pope who most clearly established papal prerogatives within the church during this period was Nicholas I (858–867), a Roman nobleman who had served under previous popes and was well familiar with papal government. Asserting his superiority over the emperor, Nicholas claimed that the empire itself existed essentially for the sake of the church. In specific controversies he opposed important archbishops of the Western church. The False Decretals (or Pseudo-Isidorian Decretals) that were set forth in the mid ninth century, probably under Nicholas I, envisaged an alliance between pope and bishops at the expense of the archbishops. Nicholas likewise asserted papal prerogatives in opposition to the emperor and patriarch at Constantinople—most importantly, by competing with the Eastern church in missionary work among the Bulgars.

After Nicholas, the authority and prestige of the papacy declined markedly; popes came to power and were removed from power as pawns in the factional strife among central Italian aristocrats. Between 882 and 984, eight popes died violently (including one who died in prison). Whereas it was common for popes before this time to be venerated as saints, the pope-saints from 885 onward (up to the twentieth century, but for varying reasons) have been the rare exceptions. Having been accustomed to view the heir of Peter as a moral leader of Christendom, and having come to recognize the pope as the channel of imperial authority, Christendom, especially in northern Europe, viewed this decay of papal dignity as a major scandal. In the end, the popes were rescued from this situation by the intervention of emperors.

During the tenth century, the dukes of Saxony rose to power in Germany as successors to the Carolingians, in the sense that they not only were chosen as kings of Germany but obtained recognition as emperors. The Saxon dynasty (or Ottonian, since three of its members were Otto I, Otto II, and Otto III) began toward the end of the century to establish its own candidates on the papal throne. The purpose was not merely to ensure that the spiritual leader who nominally ruled the Western church would be favorable to the dynasty, but also to overcome the dependence of the popes on the aristocratic factions into whose hands the office had fallen. This effort met with mixed success. Sylvester II (999–1003) was a renowned scholar who had served as tutor to the young Otto III, and who was placed on the papal throne by Otto. Having acceded to the papacy, he asserted papal powers over the Western church that he himself had earlier resisted in his capacity as archbishop of Rheims. His years as pope were few, however, and his importance for the history of the papacy lies more in the fact that he represented a new alliance between papacy and empire than in any specific measures to enhance papal power.

If the Carolingian and Ottonian eras are not the most illustrious in the history of the papacy, they at least were years through which the papal ideal survived. In a period of severe economic contraction, repeated assault by various peoples from the periphery of Europe, and general political fragmentation, the survival of the popes even as figureheads representing unity within the church was a remarkable accomplishment. Anglo-Saxon England was divided into as many as twelve separate kingdoms; the Carolingian empire was repeatedly splintered and reconstituted, and in the best of times there were strong centrifugal tendencies at work. The staying power of papacy and empire throughout these times suggests the lasting hold that these ideals had in the European consciousness. Before long, both of these institutions would regain their strength—indeed, the papacy would rise to unprecedented power—and the consequences would be fateful for both.

THE RISE OF THE REFORM PAPACY (ELEVENTH CENTURY)

In various ways the eleventh century brought a resurgence of vitality to Europe. New governmental methods made for stronger monarchies in parts of Western Europe, and commerce and town life began to revive. One force for renewal that had already come into play in the tenth century was monastic reform: begun on a relatively small scale around 800, reform of the monasteries became widespread and far-reaching in the Cluniac and other movements of the tenth century. The effort eventually led to the formation of other monastic orders, such as the Cistercians and Carthusians, in the eleventh century. It soon occurred to many Christians that not only the monasteries but the papacy and the church generally needed reform. The role of the papacy in this movement was vital: quickly recognized as leaders in the campaign for reform, the popes of the High Middle Ages established their practical authority over the church far more effectively than they ever had before. Churchmen might have resisted unvarnished political aggrandizement, but they could not resist as effectively a pope who intervened in local affairs in the name of reform. The rise of the papal monarchy of the High Middle Ages thus rested squarely on the reform movement that emerged in the eleventh century.

The popes set on the papal throne by the Ottonians were in certain ways reform popes: Sylvester II, for example, took measures against simony and clerical concubinage. These offenses nonetheless continued on a wide scale. Indeed, simony in the form of payment for ecclesiastical offices was rampant, and some observers found clerical concubinage virtually universal. A deeper problem was the degree of control that lay rulers had come to exercise over the church during the early Middle Ages. The control of the papacy by aristocratic factions or by emperors had demonstrated that, while secular interference in church government could be helpful in setting matters aright, it could also turn the popes into political tools who had neither interest in nor effective control over the spiritual functions of the church. The problem was, however, more pervasive. It was not only the papacy, but countless individual churches, monasteries, and bishoprics throughout the Western church that had come under secular influence or control. Proprietary churches, in which the clergy were controlled as well as supported by laymen who owned the church buildings and lands, arose in Germanic lands before the Carolingian era, and became a dominant feature of the Western church during that period. Likewise, proprietary monasteries became common. Episcopal elections were theoretically made by the clergy and people in the episcopal cities, but in practice they were often in the hands of local rulers or political factions. The spiritual purposes of the church were ill maintained when the church itself fell under the control of secular authorities whose interests were more political than religious. There was reason to believe that the political situation of the church was in large part responsible for its moral plight: the lack of effective supervision of clerical morals, by individuals who saw this as their chief concern, meant that corruption would inevitably proliferate.

The moral and political morass in which the church found itself reached its clearest expression in the 1040's, when three claimants to the papal throne, each supported by his own faction, held out in fortified churches at Rome. One, Benedict IX, had been placed on the papal throne as the choice of one faction, only to be driven temporarily from Rome by a rival faction with its own pope, Sylvester III. To make matters more complex, Benedict accepted money to renounce his claim in favor of the third claimant, Gregory VI, who wanted the office to carry out a program of reform. But having in effect sold the papacy in the interests of this would-be reformer, Benedict nonetheless continued to uphold his own claims to it. The schism came to an end when Emperor Henry III came from Germany, deposed all three rivals, and established Clement II as the first of four German popes who reigned from 1046 to 1057 (Damasus II, Leo IX, and Victor II).

These early reform popes, like such earlier figures as Sylvester II, concentrated more on the moral problems facing the church (especially simony and clerical concubinage) than on the political problem of lay control. Leo IX (1048–1054), an Alsatian and a cousin of the emperor, fostered the goal of moral reform through various means. He traveled extensively, spending more time out of Rome than in it, crossing three times into France and Germany, and exercising close personal supervision over the church. In 1049, for example, he met with French clergy at Rheims and compelled them to tell under oath whether they had received their offices in exchange for monetary payment. Those who refused to attend, Leo excommunicated. The canons issued at the Rheims council covered numerous aspects of clerical discipline and morality. Likewise, Leo made use of Roman synods to enforce his reformist policy. Thus, the Easter Synod of 1049 required celibacy for all clergy from the rank of subdeacon upward. He brought reform-minded advisers from outside of Rome and made them cardinals; during this time, the cardinals, who had previously been little more than liturgical dignitaries, took on greater significance as aides in the project of reform.

Among the figures assembled at Rome under Leo were Hildebrand (the future Gregory VII), a zealous reformer who had been associated with Gregory VI; Humbert of Silva Candida, a well-known monk and scholar; and Peter Damian, one of the leaders of an ascetic revival in northern Italy. They did not always agree among themselves on matters of policy; while Peter Damian conceded that a simoniac could perform valid rituals, for example, Humbert denied this. On the whole, however, they were united in their quest for moral purity within the church. A further means toward this goal and toward the enhancement of papal power was the refinement of canon law. In 1050, a *Collection in 74 Titles* was drawn up, based largely on previous Roman enactments, as part of an ongoing effort to provide repositories of canon law that would lend authority to Rome as well as meeting the needs of the church.

Three popes in particular, while continuing the efforts of their predecessors, carried reform to its highest level of fervor: Nicholas II (1059–1061), Alexander II (1061–1073), and Gregory VII (1073–1085).

Under Nicholas II, two important measures were taken at Rome. First, to keep papal elections out of the hands of aristocratic factions, a new electoral procedure enacted in 1059 specified that cardinals alone should choose each new pope. (The result was the reverse of the intention: the cardinals themselves gave in to factional strife, and for more than a century, until another electoral reform, schisms proliferated.) Second, Nicholas issued a series of reform canons. These touched on many matters: the decree on papal elections was repeated in summary form; the faithful were exhorted not to attend masses celebrated by priests who were known to be keeping concubines; those clerics who had remained chaste were to eat and sleep together, holding their revenues in common and striving "to attain the apostolic life, which is a life in common"; no cleric was to receive a church from a layman, either gratis or for a price; no priest should hold two churches simultaneously; no one was to be ordained or promoted to any office in the church if that person was guilty of simony. The encouragement of clerics to live in common was an effort to curb concubinage. Peter Damian, who was particularly interested in this aspect of reform, had been associated with experimental types of monastic life in northern Italy; the revived interest in asceticism helped to encourage the communal life of the clergy in houses that would resemble monasteries in their discipline if not in their function and organizational structure.

Alexander II was significant as the pope under whom the cause of reform became separate and even alienated from the imperial government. Elected without imperial support, he had to establish himself against an antipope (Honorius II) whom the imperial court fostered. He repeated many of the reformist measures of his predecessors, for example by reissuing decrees against simony and clerical concubinage. He held four synods at Rome and sent legates to other lands to support the cause of reform. He intensified the effort and attempted to arouse popular fervor by specifying again that people should not attend masses celebrated by priests who were not celibate. He attempted to address the political difficulties in the church by removing episcopal elections from lay control and by forbidding laymen to invest clerics with their insignia of ecclesiastical office. And he lent force to his legislation by summoning important churchmen to Rome to account for their behavior, or by deposing as significant a figure as the archbishop of Milan for practicing simony. When the archdiocese of Milan needed in 1072 to elect a new archbishop, two claimants emerged, one of them chosen by a coalition of nobility and clergy and invested by the emperor, the other elected by a popular reformist group and consecrated by Alexander II. (A third eventually gained the office.) In addressing the political issues thus forthrightly, rather than restricting himself to moral reform, Alexander set the stage for intense conflict between papacy and empire.

Hildebrand, the cardinal who had already established a reputation for reforming zeal under Gregory VI, became pope as Gregory VII in 1073. Like his predecessors, he was eager to uproot simony and clerical concubinage; his concern for these issues is clear, for example, in his correspondence. But more importantly, his essential goal was a political one: to free the papacy and the church from lay control. In this project he saw continuity with the Cluniac movement of monastic reform, which emphasized freedom from both lay and episcopal control as a monastic ideal. While Gregory himself had not been a Cluniac monk, as was once believed, he was aware of the movement and had much sympathy for its quest of independence.

Two sources, apart from Gregory's letters, furnish important information regarding his program and his general conception of the papacy. The *Dictatus papae,* a kind of papal manifesto entered 1075 in Gregory's register, sets forth twenty-seven fundamental claims to power: that only the pope can depose bishops; that he alone can establish and divide bishoprics; that only he can convoke ecumenical councils or promulgate canon law; that only he can revise his own judgments; that only he is authorized to use the imperial insignia; that he can depose emperors; and so forth. These statements have sometimes been interpreted as rubrics for a collection of canon law; but while Gregory claimed to be asserting traditional norms, many of his specific claims are novel, and some are contradicted rather than confirmed by the established canon-law texts. Second, there is a series of decrees against lay investiture, which Gregory issued be-

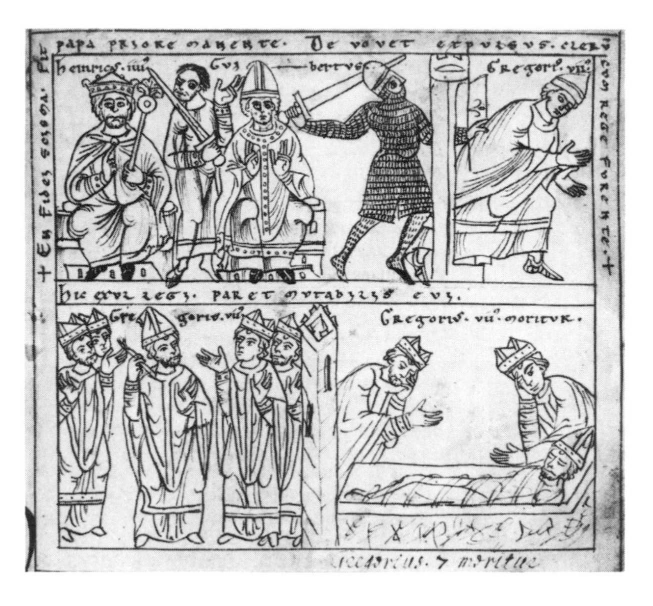

Scenes from the life of Pope Gregory VII: Emperor and antipope expel Gregory from Rome; the pope excommunicates emperor and clergy; death of Gregory. Miniature from the *Chronicon* of Otto von Freising, illuminated *ca.* 1170. JENA, UNIVERSITÄTSBIBLIOTHEK, MS BOS. Q.6, fol. 79r

tween 1075 and 1080. While it was appointment to ecclesiastical office rather than investiture that was the primary issue among reformers, investiture was an important symbolic concern, and an increasingly important area of debate as the century continued. The heart of the prohibition read, "We decree that no one of the clergy shall receive the investiture with a bishopric or abbey or church from the hand of an emperor or king or of any lay person, male or female."

The political background to these documents is the conflict that erupted between Gregory and Emperor Henry IV. The year 1075 was a significant one, in which yet another archepiscopal election in Milan resulted in the choice of an archbishop from the coalition supported by the emperor, whereupon Henry had a deputy perform the ceremony of investiture. Gregory threatened to depose Henry. A German diet of 1076 declared that Gregory himself was no longer to be recognized as pope (whereupon Henry sent Gregory a letter with the famous salutation to "Hildebrand, now not pope, but false monk"). Gregory retaliated in the same year by deposing and excommunicating Henry. Though an assembly of German bishops then declared Gregory to be excommunicated, some bishops and many of the German nobility began to desert Henry. To forestall further loss of support, the emperor obtained papal absolution by approaching Gregory barefoot as a penitent in the snow at Canossa in early 1077.

There was, however, no lasting settlement. Rather, Henry's opponents elected an antiking and Henry's supporters elected an antipope, thus intensifying the alienation. In a letter of 1081 to Bishop Hermann of Metz, Gregory argued that kingship is inherently inferior to priesthood because it is based on greed, arrogance, and diabolical inspiration, and that because kings are included in Peter's "flock" they should be subject to the pope. Theoretical postures were developed in greater detail by propagandists on both sides, such as the imperialist Wenrich of Trier and the papalist Manegold of Lautenbach. But the conflict was fought with swords as well as with pens. Between 1081 and 1084, Henry besieged the city of Rome; when he succeeded in capturing the city, Robert Guiscard (Gregory's principal secular ally) and his Norman troops responded by driving the Germans out amid looting and widespread destruction. Gregory, forced southward to Salerno, died in 1085 uttering an adaptation of the psalm text (Vulgate Psalm 44): "I have loved justice and hated iniquity; therefore I die in exile." His successors continued his efforts for reform, but proceeded with essentially different strategy and in the end effected a series of compromises that preserved Gregory's essential goals.

With the pontificate of Gregory, the development of the papacy reached a turning point. Earlier popes had been pitted against emperors in conflicts over various issues, but in the late eleventh century the most fundamental issues of papal versus imperial power were raised. Whereas Gelasius and Gregory II had been content to meet emperors' encroachment by insisting on a dualism in which priesthood and kingship respected each other's integrity and made no claims to subjugation, Gregory VII defiantly proposed that all princes should kiss the feet of the pope, and that the pope is entitled not only to crown (and thus sanction) emperors but also to depose them.

These developments may seem to follow as practical implications of the Donation of Constantine. Yet the social and political context of the eleventh century was entirely different from that of the eighth, and the effects of Gregory's program were far more wide-ranging than could have been imagined three centuries earlier. With the benefit of that prestige already gained from his predecessors' efforts at reform, Gregory could command attention and arouse support as no eighth-century pope could have hoped to do. Furthermore, the Gregorian era saw the beginnings of significant lay piety; with a relatively large number of people concerned about reform throughout Europe, there was an audience waiting to be addressed. This combination of circumstances—the presence of an eager audience and the arrival of a personality with principles and zeal that commanded respect—made for striking impact.

When the movement of reform gained momentum, however, the results could not be controlled. No doubt Gregory was delighted that his excommunication of Henry provoked rebellion among the emperor's subjects. But he could scarcely have been pleased when large numbers of laypeople, frustrated with apparently futile efforts at reform, opted for more radical reform through one or another form of heresy.

Thus Gregory's pontificate was a watershed: On the one hand, the papacy had gained enough power to command a hearing (the kind which, a few years later, would inspire the crusades). Furthermore, he brought to a high point the papal claims to power. Yet he did not see these claims put into effect, and he surely did not realize the full implications of his measures (such as encouraging people not to attend masses of sinful priests) when they reached the laity. In any case, he set forth a program which, adapted to the emerging circumstances of later centuries, committed the high medieval papacy to a quest for far-reaching powers over secular rulers as well as over the church. Later popes, following Gregory in his use of excommunication (and supplementing that sanction with interdict), would use such means to win the actual power that Gregory sought but never attained.

BIBLIOGRAPHY

The bibliography on this topic is immense; the following list covers only a few of the important works. Key sources for the history of the papacy are given in English translation in Edward Giles, ed., *Documents Illustrating Papal Authority, A.D. 96–454* (1952), and Brian Tierney, *The Crisis of Church and State: 1050–1300* (1964); Tierney's book includes several documents from before 1050. Most of the texts cited in this article are included in these books. Translations have generally been taken or adapted from those given by Giles and Tierney.

Among the useful surveys are Geoffrey Barraclough, *The Medieval Papacy,* rev. ed. (1979), which has a good annotated bibliography; Johannes Haller, *Das Papsttum: Idee und Wirklichkeit,* 5 vols. (1965); Trevor G. Jalland, *The Church and the Papacy* (1944); Beresford J. Kidd, *The Roman Primacy to A.D. 461* (1936); Horace K. Mann, *The Lives of the Popes in the Middle Ages,* 18 vols. (1906–1932), a survey extending to 1304; Karl F. Morrison, *Tradition and Authority in the Western Church, 300–1140* (1969); Richard W. Southern, *Western Society and the Church in the Middle Ages* (1970); Walter Ullmann, *The Growth of Papal Government in the Middle Ages,* 2nd ed. (1962), and *A Short History of the Papacy in the Middle Ages* (1972).

RICHARD KIECKHEFER

[See also **Alexander II, Pope; Apostolic Succession; Canossa; Cardinals, College of; Church, Early; Church, Latin; Clergy; Councils (Ecumenical); Councils (Western); Curia, Papal; Cyprian, St.; Decretals, False; Dictatus Papae; Donation of Constantine; Ecumenical Patriarch; Gelasius I, Pope; Gregory I the Great, Pope; Gregory VII, Pope; Henotikon; Henry IV of Germany; Investiture and Investiture Conflict; Leo I, Pope; Leo IX, Pope; Missions and Missionaries; Nicholas I, Pope; Papal States; Patriarch; Plenitudo Potestatis; Pope; Reform, Idea of; Roman Empire, Late; Rome; Schism, Eastern-Western Church; Simony; Stephen II, Pope; Sylvester II, Pope.**]

PAPAL CURIA, LITURGY OF. In the twelfth century, along with the term *curia romana,* a liturgy of the papal court appeared, differing both in place of celebration (the *basilica palatii* of the Lateran) and in form from the liturgy celebrated by the canons of the Church of St. John Lateran. Abelard, writing to St. Bernard on the subject, says: "Only the Church of the Lateran, the mother of all, preserves the ancient office; none of her daughters follow her in this, not even the basilica of the Roman palace" (Epistle 10). One must, however, regard Abelard's text with caution, since it reproduces the opinion of the canons of the Lateran. From other Roman evidence it appears that the Basilica of St. Peter was in general, at this time, more faithful to the ancient Roman liturgy than was the Lateran. The canons of the Lateran (who came from S. Frediano in Lucca), protecting themselves by reasserting the tradition of mother church, formed their *ordo officii* by combining the ordinary of Lucca with Roman practices, especially those for feast days when the pope and his court came for the liturgy of the Lateran.

At the beginning of the twentieth century, nothing was known of the liturgy of the Roman curia, the Office and daily Mass celebrated by the pope and his court in the papal chapel (in the medieval sense of the term). Since then, many essential texts have been published, permitting us to follow the history of this liturgy from the last quarter of the twelfth century. We know the calendar of the papal court from this period and can trace its development, which is characterized by the addition of a large number of martyr-popes (Bernold of Constance attributes this to Gregory VII). Possibly the popes of the mid thirteenth century added the feasts of newly canonized saints (or it may have been Giovanni Gaetano Cardinal Orsini, the future Nicholas III). The ordo of the papal Mass was fixed before the pontificate of Innocent III, since he comments on it, before becoming pope, in his *De sacro altaris mysterio*. Innocent III did not modify the Mass books, but the text of the pontifical edited by Michel Andrieu must be attributed to his reign (*ca.* 1200), as must the ordinal of the curia (1212–1213) that incorporates the changes adopted after the beginning of his reign. This ordinal is known through a single manuscript whose text contains the additions made throughout the thirteenth century. In editing it Stephen J. P. Van Dijk was forced to decide (largely by conjecture) what were the added elements. It is a complete ordinal giving, for the Office at least, the incipits of all the liturgical texts and detailed rubrics (*ordines*) for the principal days of the year. In general, Innocent III did not make significant changes in the liturgy of the papal court.

In the thirteenth century the Franciscans adopted the liturgy of the papal court, especially in their breviary and missal of 1230, revised in the ordinal (1243–1244) of Minister General Haymo of Faversham. It is possible, but not certain, that Nicholas III prescribed the use of the liturgy of the curia by all the churches of Rome; in any event this liturgy is no longer the liturgy of just the papal court but of the Roman church. Until the end of the Middle Ages, the number of dioceses that adopted the liturgy of the Roman curia was not great, but they accepted at least some of the new feasts prescribed by the papacy (for instance, Corpus Christi, 1264), and bishops frequently adopted the pontifical of the Roman curia, either directly or by way of the pontifical of Guillaume Durand (1293–1295).

In the fourteenth century the Roman curia, which had frequently sojourned outside Rome during the previous century, installed itself at Avignon. During the Avignon period, the liturgy of the papal court lost its Roman roots and developed a ceremonial aspect. The principal liturgical documents known from this period are ceremonials, including those of Jacques Cardinal Stefaneschi (*d.* 1341) and of Pierre Ameil (*d.* 1401). The ceremonies for which the pope was present took on increasing importance, but their number decreased. It is not known when the Office ceased to be celebrated regularly by the court, but the liturgy of the curia began to evolve in the direction of exceptional, rather than daily, ceremonies—the characteristic mark of the Renaissance.

BIBLIOGRAPHY

Michel Andrieu, ed., *Le pontifical romain au moyen âge*, III: *Le pontifical de Guillaume Durand* (1940); Marc Dykmans, "L'ordinaire d'Innocent III," in *Gregorianum*, 59 (1978), and (ed.) *Le cérémonial papal de la fin du moyen âge à la Renaissance*, 4 vols. (1977–1985); Ludwig Fischer, ed., *Bernhardi, cardinalis et Lateranensis ecclesiae prioris, ordo officiorum ecclesiae Lateranensis* (1916); J.-M. Gy, "L'influence des chanoines de Lucques sur la liturgie du Lateran," in *Mélanges Chavasse* (1984); Bernhard Schimmelpfennig, *Die Zeremonienbücher der römischen Kurie im Mittelalter* (1973); Stephen J. P. Van Dijk, ed., *Sources of the Modern Roman Liturgy*, 2 vols. (1963), and *The Ordinal of the Papal Court from Innocent III to Boniface VIII and Related Documents* (1975); *idem* and Joan Hazelden Walker, *The Origins of the Modern Roman Liturgy: The Liturgy of the Papal Court and the Franciscan Order in the Thirteenth Century* (1960).

JEAN-MARIE GY

[See also **Curia, Papal; Divine Office; Durand, Guillaume; Franciscans; Innocent III, Pope; Mass, Liturgy of the; Pontificals.**]

PAPAL STATES. The patrimony over which the bishops of Rome exercised control came into being in the mid eighth century. Its origins were mixed: elements of property rights which had formerly existed in private law over landed estates were present in it; so were elements of sovereign power usurped from the Byzantine Empire and elements of protection and dominion exercised by Frankish and German rulers. From the beginning the patrimony of St. Peter was closely associated with the interests of the Roman governing classes, whose institutional and social involvement with the Roman church was always close. For four and a half centuries, until the final weakening of the Holy

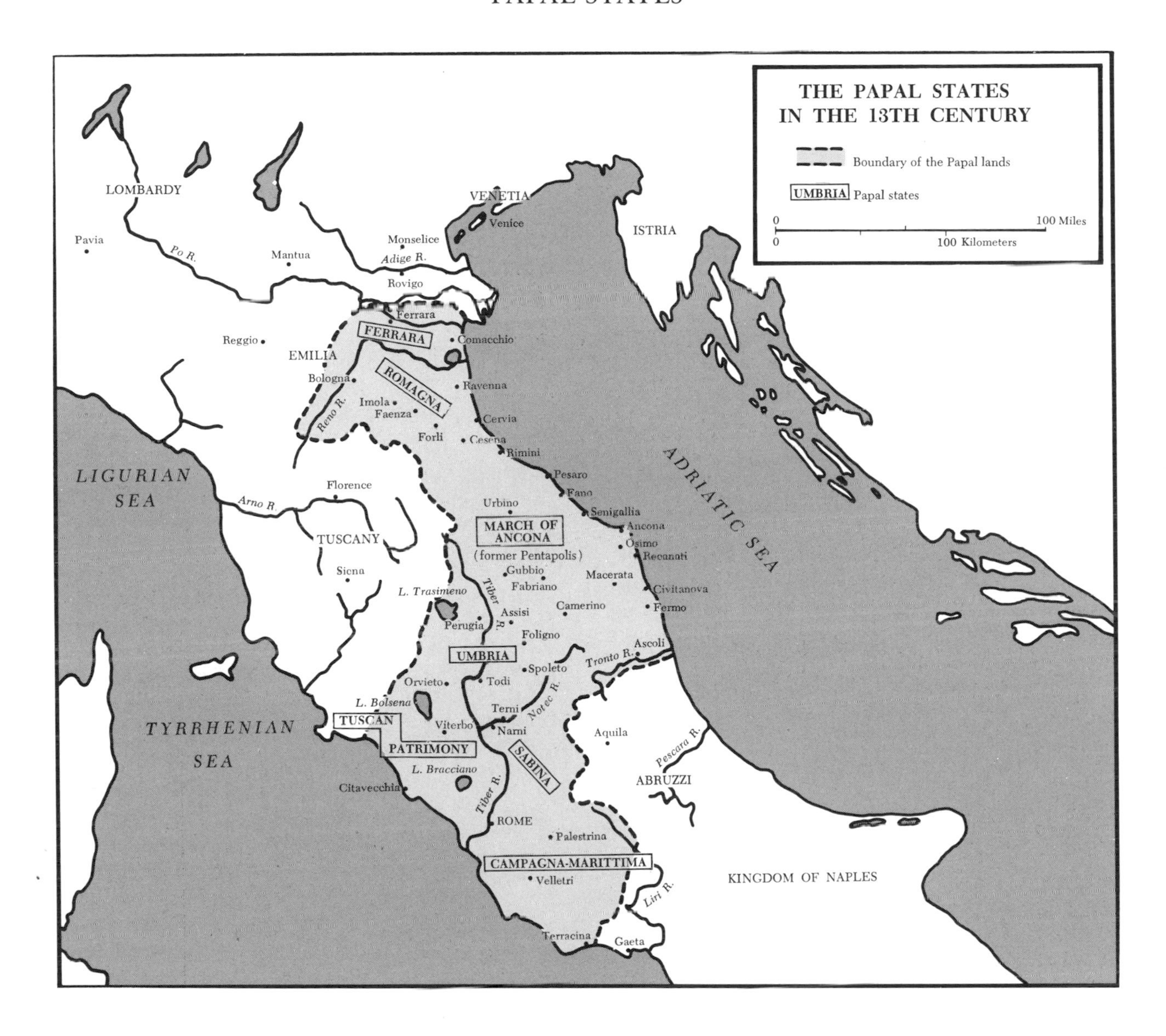

Roman Empire in the early thirteenth century, the status of the papal lands remained in some respects unclear or disputed. New imperial grants, and a new political situation very unfavorable to the empire, enabled the papal dominion to assume a new legal and political form, which it retained until the end of the Middle Ages. The watershed in the history of the papal states occurred under Innocent III (*r.* 1198–1216).

ORIGINS OF PAPAL TEMPORAL RULE

Although the church assumed some civic and local government responsibilities in seventh-century Byzantine Italy, it neither sought nor acquired overt political power. The pontificate of Gregory the Great (*r.* 590–604) saw no move in the direction of papal territorial authority. But during the seventh century the growing regionalism of the land-owning classes of the duchy of Rome and the exarchate of Ravenna provided a soil in which the claims of church authorities could grow. The huge estates documented in Gregory's letters attest to a landed power which made the church into a major political factor. The crux of the matter was Byzantine political and military weakness in Italy and the inability of Constantinople to defend the Latin provincials from Lombard aggression. The conversion of the Lombards to Catholicism provided no shield against Lombard greed. Their usurpations in imperial territory were recognized in a major peace settlement of about 681, but even this frontier proved hard to defend.

The armed power of the indigenous provincials protected Pope Sergius I (*r.* 687–701) from the displeasure of the Byzantine government after the pope had challenged the Quinisext Council decrees of 692. Not until the Byzantine government supported the "heretical" iconoclast doctrines in the 720's, however, did Rome openly defy imperial power. Significantly, the first clash occurred not over the iconoclast question but over papal sponsoring of resistance to imperial tax demands in Italy on the part of the Latin provincials (725–727). Pope Gregory II (*r.* 715–731) had the support of the provincial nobility, and he successfully resisted Byzantine attempts to arrest and depose him. But at the same time (727–732) the Lombard king Liutprand (*r.* 712–744) exerted new pressures on the Roman duchy, and although he could be bought off for the time being, it was clear that the provincials of the duchy and exarchate could not for long stave off barbarian occupation unless they found some kind of outside help.

If the Byzantine Empire, still the legitimate ruler of central and south Italy, was a rejected and broken reed, then the only option open to the Latin provincials was appeal to the Frankish kingdom. An abortive offer of friendship and of the office of "patrician of the Romans" was made by Pope Gregory III (*r.* 731–741) to Charles Martel. But the turning point in Frankish-papal relations came when Pepin III the Short (714–768), who had ruled the Frankish kingdom for four years without formal authority, sent an embassy to Pope Zacharias (*r.* 741–752) to ask for help in legitimizing his rule. Papal support was granted, and in 751 the Roman-influenced bishops of Francia anointed Pepin to the kingship.

Roman-Lombard relations were then at a critical point. In 752 the new Lombard ruler Aistulf (*r.* 749–756) denounced the treaties made with the Romans by Liutprand and demanded a poll tax, the symbol of political subjection, from the Romans. In 753, Pope Stephen II (*r.* 752–757) sought to stave off disaster by going in person to the hostile Lombard capital of Pavia; his security was assured by the presence with the Roman embassy of two envoys from Francia and one from Byzantium. Stephen failed to win any political concessions from Aistulf, but the Lombard king was powerless to stop the pope from continuing his journey to the Frankish kingdom. On 6 January 754, Pope Stephen met King Pepin III at Ponthion in Champagne. The pope fell before the king in sackcloth and ashes, and asked him if he would support the suit of St. Peter and of the "republic of the Romans." The king paid the pope the courtesies due to an imperial representative and swore to restore the exarchate of Ravenna and the rights and territories of the "republic." The promise was confirmed by a gathering of Frankish magnates at Quierzy-sur-Oise. In this way began the links of friendship (*amicitia*) and protective treaty-obligation which bound the Frankish monarchy and its successors to the Roman church for the rest of the Middle Ages.

How far the popes were pressed by immediate political necessity arising from the Lombard threat, and how far they were motivated by long-term political and ecclesiastical ambitions, must remain a matter for speculation. It has been conjectured that the forged Donation of Constantine was already in existence at this time, and that it was an influence on papal and Frankish policy. Others (notably Horst Fuhrmann) have contested this conjecture. Irrespective of the "Donation" in its final form, some elements in it (notably the claim of the Roman clergy to share in senatorial privileges) were already present in papal circles of the eighth century. The subtlety of papal diplomats, notably in their use of such ambiguous phrases as "republic of the Romans" (*res publica romanorum*), continues to obscure their true motives.

The immediate result of the 754 pacts was a Frankish invasion of Italy in 755, which forced Aistulf to "restore" Ravenna and other cities. He broke his oath to do so, and in 756 he appeared with a hostile army before Rome, closing the pilgrim roads and destroying the pilgrim shrines outside the city. Later in the same year the Franks forced him to withdraw, and to "restore" to St. Peter towns in the exarchate, Pentapolis (Rimini, Ancona, Fano, Pesaro, and Senigallia), and the duchy. The keys of these towns were placed on the altar of St. Peter's in Rome by the Frankish envoy. From this moment the papal states may be said to have existed.

THE PAPAL LANDS, 756–1046

From the beginnings of the temporal power there were fierce struggles in Rome between factions of the Roman nobles and clergy. The influence of external powers, notably of the Franks and of the nobles of Spoleto, was also always evident. Others had irons in this fire: for some time the Lombards exerted influence spasmodically in Rome, and so for a long period did the Byzantine government. One early effect of the power struggles was the Roman synod of 769, which ordained that the Roman bishop should henceforth be elected by all the clergy of Rome, the Roman nobles and people being allowed only an approbatory voice in the election. Though subsequently modified by a decree of 824, the decisions of the 769 synod were of fundamental importance, at least in theory, in protecting the Roman bishopric against noble control.

Desiderius, the last Lombard king, attacked Rome in 773, when he thought the young Frankish ruler, Charlemagne, to be too weak to intervene. The attack brought down on Desiderius the final invasion of the Frankish army and the dissolution of his kingdom, which was henceforth absorbed in the Frankish Empire. Charlemagne marched to Rome at Easter 774 and renewed the treaty and the obligation of friendship and protection between his dynasty and the Roman church. According to the papal account Charles promised to hand over or confirm to Pope Adrian I (*r.* 772–795) a very large territory which may perhaps correspond to the area defined in the treaty of 681 between the Byzantines and the Lombards. The border went from Luni on the Ligurian coast through Monte Bardone in the Appenines to Mantua on the Lombard plain and northeast to Monselice. The grant was also said to include Venetia and Istria, places which were never subsequently part of the papal state.

It is unlikely that the papal account of this act is complete. The "restitutions" of territory which Charlemagne in fact caused to be made to the pope were of a much smaller area, which with some exceptions corresponded to the lands which had been under discussion among Lombards, Franks, and Romans during the critical years of 753–756: the exarchate of Ravenna and Pentapolis; the towns on the Via Flaminia and the Via Amerina which connected the Roman duchy with Ravenna; the small hilly zone of Sabina; and Lombard Tuscia or Tuscany, an area in south Etruria. Papal claims in the south were successful only as far as the river Liri.

Frankish overlordship of the papal states was an acknowledged fact from their beginnings. The advent of the Holy Roman Empire in 800 made little change in their legal or territorial position, which was defined in a series of treaties of protection and friendship issued by Frankish and German emperors. Their texts were based on eighth-century prototypes (now lost) of 754, 774, and 787, but each successive treaty contained modifications which reflected the territorial and political situation of that time. Our only complete text of an early treaty is that of 817 (the "Ludovicianum" issued by Louis the Pious). Other treaties were issued in 850, 876, 883, and 892. The text of Lothar's Roman decree, the *constitutio romana* of 824, has survived. It was an energetic assertion of Frankish overlordship in Rome, which provided for the permanent presence there of an imperial envoy and judge (*missus*), and made a number of regulations which favored the noble as opposed to the clerical order in Rome, especially as regards the election of future popes.

Other treaties of the same nature as the 817 grant and its successors were issued by Otto I (*r.* 962–973) in 962 and by Henry II (*r.* 1014–1024) in 1020; both texts have survived. Otto III (*r.* 996–1002) issued no such treaty, but a document of his, making over eight counties in Pentapolis to Pope Sylvester II (*r.* 999–1003) in 1001, complained that the popes had granted away many of their possessions improperly, and claimed that to make up for these losses certain popes had fabricated false claims (in the forged Donation of Constantine) to imperial property. By implication Otto III denied that the pope could claim the lands in Pentapolis by right.

Otto III's claim that many lands and possessions of the Roman church had been granted away in feudal and other grants was substantially true. These concessions had been the tendency since the late ninth century, and they continued far into the eleventh. The insecure conditions of the ninth and tenth centuries had caused a regrouping of the rural population in new, fortified *castra,* or vills, most of which tended to fall under the direct control of the local aristocracy. Many of the enormous church estates of the earlier Middle Ages, including the papal *domuscultae,* which formed a ring of great papal *latifundia* round Rome, were fragmented and partly alienated. These huge church estates had always aroused opposition among the nobility. In the period 816–824 they had occasioned a minor civil war between the nobles and the papal tenants; in the insecure conditions of the later ninth and tenth centuries clerical control of the estates collapsed.

The nobles thus assumed an increasingly tight hold over the church. In the early tenth century the Roman family of Theophylact came to control the papacy itself; the zenith of the direct descendants of Theophylact was reached when Alberic, "senator of all the Romans," ruled Rome and the papal states from 932 to 954. Ottonian rule in Italy only temporarily modified the stranglehold of the great Roman families over the papacy, in spite of the deposition of Alberic's son, Pope John XII (*r.* 955–964), in 963, and of the purges of Roman officials and nobles carried out by all three Ottonian rulers. In 1012 the princely Roman family named for their seat at Tuscolo, near Frascati, assumed a control of the papacy which they did not relinquish until 1046. Recent research has modified the harsh judgments made by the old scholarship both against the house of Theophylact and against the Tusculans, who have both been shown to have been more careful of the spiritual and temporal interests of the Roman church than was once supposed. The Tusculans, in particular, are credited with a gradual if partial resumption of papal temporal rights in the early eleventh century.

THE EMPERORS AND THE LIBERTY OF THE CHURCH, 1046–1198

Opposition to the policies of the reform movement in the eleventh-century papacy came from two forces which were powerful in the politics of the papal states: the Roman nobles allied to the Tusculans (known to the reform propagandists as "the tyranny of the captains"), and the imperial court. But the reform movement was far from indifferent to temporal power. It is significant that his enemies charged Hildebrand, as archdeacon of the Roman church, with tyrannical and extortionate policies in the papal states. The most important act of the reform popes for the temporal power was their enfeoffment of the Norman princes with Capua, Apulia, and Calabria, and the promise of a future investiture of Sicily if this was taken from the Muslims. With the Norman feudal investitures of 1059 and 1080 the reform popes bound southern Italy to the papacy in a political system which was to last in one form or another until 1860. The feudal form of the investitures betrayed the pervasive influence of feudal law, which was to be a strong element in papal-state policies for the rest of the Middle Ages. The *regalia* (or tax and territorial rights claimed by St. Peter) of St. Peter are first referred to in 1059, and are subsequently an important element in the definition of papal temporal right. The 1059 definition of the south Italian lands as forming part of the "land of St. Peter" was also of permanent importance.

Apart from the Norman enfeoffment, the reform papacy was not much more effective in the assertion of papal temporal right than its predecessors. The former exarchate of Ravenna remained largely outside Roman influence, and the popes were at times hard put to defend papal lands on the Norman borders, or the southern papal enclave of Benevento. One addition to papal claims arose from the testamentary disposition of her allodial lands made in favor of the papacy by the countess Matilda of Tuscany, who died in 1115. The Matildine lands were spread through imperial Tuscany and Lombardy but also extended into parts of the former exarchate, such as the county of Ferrara. In 1133, Pope Innocent II feudally invested Emperor Lothair II (*r.* 1133–1137) with these lands, agreeing also to a further investment of the lands to the emperor's son-in-law, Henry of Bavaria. The Matildine lands occasioned disagreement between the popes and the empire; Emperor Frederick I Barbarossa (*r.* 1155–1190) was asked by Adrian IV (*r.* 1154–1159) to restore them to the papacy in 1159, but the emperor succeeded in excluding them from the Treaty of Venice in 1177. In the event neither pope nor emperor gained much profit from the Matildine lands, which were mostly usurped by the communes. The precedent of the Matildine bequest was, however, a factor in papal territorial claims in Emilia from the late thirteenth century on.

The temporal rule of the Roman church was prominent in the negotiations which took place at various points of the twelfth century between the Roman church and the empire. The emperors were naturally anxious to guarantee the papal lands only on terms which reserved imperial rights. In 1111, 1122, and 1133 the emperors took oaths to protect papal rights; the terms used to describe them were the "possessions," "patrimonies," and "regalia" of St. Peter. Frederick I Barbarossa also agreed at Constance (1153), while king of Germany (crowned 1152), to restore the "regalia of St. Peter," and similar expressions were used in the treaties of Anagni (1176) and Venice (1177). Imperial administration in papal lands was far from extinct, as was shown by the collection of the *fodrum,* or army supply tax, by imperial officials in the papal lands; by the presence of imperial residences in Ravenna, Rome, and some other towns, including Viterbo; by the numerous grants of impe-

PAPAL STATES

rial privileges to monasteries, churches, and towns in the papal states; and by the acceptance of oaths of obedience to the empire from others. After 1177 there was some negotiation directed on the imperial side toward obtaining the renunciation of temporal power in Italy by the popes, in return for a large annual cash payment raised from imperial lands. But these negotiations failed.

The rise of the communes was the most important Italian development of the twelfth century. For the popes the most important new commune was that of Rome, which from its foundation in 1143/1144 posed grave problems for the papal government. The papal curia and consistory had always shared some of their authority and temporal profits with the more powerful Roman laymen, but the emergence of a permanent and well organized secular government in Rome was a grave blow to clerical power, which led to disputes and intermittent conflicts throughout the rest of the twelfth century. Pope Clement III (*r.* 1187–1191) concluded a settlement with the Roman commune in 1188 which tacitly conceded that the Romans should choose their own senators and guaranteed substantial cash payments annually to the Romans in return for the restoration of the papal regalia.

FOUNDATION AND DEVELOPMENT OF THE PAPAL STATE, 1198–1307

The premature death of the emperor Henry VI in 1197 and the subsequent imperial interregnum gave the popes political opportunities which they seized with both hands, and which allowed them to put the papal lands on a legal and administrative basis which at last justifies the use of the expression "papal state." Otto of Brunswick (Otto IV, crowned emperor, 1209; *d.* 1218) made important new treaties with the pope at Neuss in 1201 and at Speyer in 1209, which in effect abandoned the old position of imperial legal domination of the papal lands and recognized them as independently governed by the popes. Substantially the same promises were made by the then papal ward, Frederick II, at Eger in 1213 and at Hagenau in 1219. These guarantees also recognized papal power in large areas which, while named in the early medieval treaties, had not been effectively under papal rule for centuries, or in some cases had never been ruled by the popes before. Not all imperial legal rights over papal patrimonies were abandoned; Pope Innocent III (*r.* 1198–1216) himself, for example, recognized the imperial right to tax for the *collecta* in the papal city of Perugia, and the emperor Frederick II later in the thirteenth century made strenuous, if eventually ineffective, efforts to assert governmental rights in the papal state. But between 1201 and 1219 a new legal framework had been erected for the papal state, and it was later strengthened by the renewal of the imperial guarantees by Rudolf of Habsburg in 1274 and by Henry VII in 1310. The particular effect of Rudolf's grant was to facilitate papal recovery of the area known as Romagna.

The area administered by the popes expanded dramatically in the thirteenth century. The duchy of Spoleto came for the first time under papal rule in the first decade of the century. The march of Ancona (formerly Picenum or Pentapolis) was brought into closer contact with papal officials than had ever before existed. Romagna (the designation for a part of the former exarchate of Ravenna) was slower in submitting to papal government, but had nominally done so by 1278. The "Patrimony of St. Peter in Tuscany" and the southern province of Campagna-Maritime saw an improvement in the machinery of papal government. The popes began to enjoy cash revenues from the papal state which were more substantial than any earlier popes had seen.

In the second half of the thirteenth century the decisive political factors were the invasion of Italy by Charles of Anjou in 1265–1266, and his sweeping military victories. Charles invaded with the political and financial support of the popes. His new kingdom of Naples (or of "Sicily") was feudally subject to the papacy, and he used his armies to install a "Guelph" Franco-papal regime which until 1282 was virtually supreme in the Italian peninsula. Guelph successes gave considerable impetus to papal temporal rule, and these gains were not wholly reversed by the costly War of the Sicilian Vespers after 1282. But the popes had to pay a heavy price for Angevin support, in the form of submission to the policy requirements of the French princes. For more than a century after 1266 the popes were shackled, sometimes closely and sometimes less so, to the royal house of France. In 1303 the disadvantages of this subordination were dramatically revealed when Pope Boniface VIII (*r.* 1294–1303) tried to end it and was instead humiliated and broken by the agents of the king of France at Anagni.

In Italy the main political development of the latter half of the thirteenth century was the decay of the free communal regime and the growth in north and central Italian cities of the rule of the absolute lord, or *signore*. This new form of government was not necessarily an obstacle to papal overlordship, but it proved so in some areas, particularly in the Romagna.

FROM AVIGNONESE RULE TO RENAISSANCE PRINCIPATE, 1307–1447

For seventy years the popes were absent from their see and located at Avignon in Provence, partly on the rather unconvincing grounds that security in the papal state was too poor to allow them to return to Rome. Historians have perhaps allowed this failure of nerve to pass with too little comment; security in the papal state in the fourteenth century was not notably worse than in the periods which preceded and followed it.

The policies of administrative centralization which were pursued by the Avignonese popes in church government were applied to the rule of the temporal power in Italy with very fair success. Most agents of these policies in the papal state were French clerics, but the most successful papal administrator in Italy was a Castilian, Cardinal Gil Albornoz, who ruled the papal state in the course of two "legations," from 1353 to 1357 and from 1358 to 1364. Albornoz pursued a vigorous policy of military aggression and administrative reform, and although his policies were less original and radical than they were once represented to be, he certainly brought a new atmosphere of thoroughness to papal temporal administration. Most historians have praised his political achievement, although this writer has suggested that the cardinal's accomplishments were more modest than is usually thought.

The return of Pope Gregory XI to Italy in 1376 took place at the time of a general papal-state rebellion which had been organized by Florence, the erstwhile "Guelph" ally of the papacy. After Gregory's death in 1378 the general conditions of insecurity in the papal state were a factor in encouraging the double papal election of that year, which led to the so-called Great Schism of the West.

The weak papal government of the Great Schism (1378–1417) helped the spread of the regionalism and the petty tyrannies which were endemic in the papal state of this period. Although Boniface IX (*r.* 1389–1404) could still achieve a short-term answer to his temporal power problems, by the time Pope John XXIII (*r.* 1410–1415) fled to Constance in 1414 government in the papal state had virtually collapsed. The return of a united papacy once more resident in Rome under Martin V (*r.* 1417–1431; he returned to Rome in 1420) allowed a new pacification of the papal state and the resumption of efforts to control it in a more uniform and centralized way. But the difficulties were still great, and Martin's achievements were clouded over by the long political crisis under his successor Eugenius IV (*r.* 1431–1447). The underlying trend of papal government was toward a more coherent and effective fiscal policy in the papal state; the popes were coming to depend increasingly on the temporal power for their cash income. But as Mario Caravale has observed (1978), rather than write the history of the papal state by reference to an imagined standard of institutional centralization, historians would do better to examine the relations of each region of the state with the Holy See.

INSTITUTIONS OF GOVERNMENT IN THE PAPAL STATES

In the early period, apart from administrators of the papal patrimonies, papal officials were not specifically charged with public administrative duties outside Rome. The judges were either those customary under Byzantine administration, or Carolingian *missi.* In Rome the Palatine judges, the *iudices de clero* and the *iudices dativi,* sat in the Lateran Palace. Great papal officials such as the *vestiarius, nomenclator,* and *primicerius defensorum* were important in temporal administration. Papal patrimonial estates were administered by *defensores* and *actionarii;* there were special administrative arrangements for the *domuscultae.* Important for the administration of the lands of the Roman churches were the deaconries (*diaconiae*) with their *dispensatores* which drew on the resources of church lands to finance social assistance in Rome.

In the tenth century, feudal trends produced a new administrative order. In Campagna papal counts (*comites*), drawn from the nobility, exercised judicial powers. Other "counts," unaccountable to the pope, appeared in the exarchate, and similar counts appeared north of Rome at Galeria and elsewhere. Some towns were conceded by the popes in feudal tenure (for example, Terracina and Palestrina). In the little province of Sabina there were papal "rectors," but this office too came under the control of the feudal nobles.

After 962 the exercise of imperial jurisdiction

recommenced in the papal states: imperial privileges were renewed to great monasteries and to bishoprics, and imperial tax obligations such as the *fodrum* and the *fodrum de castellis* were imposed.

The reform popes did not systematically reorganize the temporal power. Some earlier feudal grants were withdrawn by these popes (for example, Pesaro), and the monastery of Farfa complained of Hildebrand's harsh administration when he was archdeacon of the Roman church. Feudal law came to penetrate papal administration more and more. In the Maritime province the obligation of military service was feudal by 1065. The popes made feudal grants (*in feudum* or *in fegum*) even to monasteries. They also began to issue privileges to the new communes, both to rural communes (as in Sabina) and to civic communes (for example, Velletri). Feudal principles were vigorously applied in temporal administration under Pope Adrian IV (*r.* 1154–1159) and his chamberlain, Boso. At this time the household office of apostolic chamberlain became important for the administration of the papal states, listing and enforcing feudal, patrimonial, and other taxation rights. Cenci Savelli (later Pope Honorius III, 1216–1227) began to compile in 1192 the collection of papal land titles known as the *Liber censuum* while he was apostolic chamberlain.

The principles on which provincial government of the papal state was based were derived partly from canon law, partly from feudal law, partly from customary law. Military service, carriage service (providing carriage for the lord's goods and crops), attendance at assemblies, and the duty of defending the high roads were feudal obligations in most places, but the widely imposed and fiscally important *census* (patrimonial rent) payments were derived from canon law.

Innocent III began a new system of division into "provinces," which was continued and developed by his successors. Each province was ruled by a papal rector who in the thirteenth century was more frequently a cleric than a layman; after the thirteenth century he was almost invariably a cleric. But single provinces or groups of provinces were also frequently subordinate to the overall control of papal legates.

The rectors' courts claimed jurisdiction over all provincials and tried to make good the claim to hear appeals from the courts of communes and feudatories. The rectors held provincial assemblies in the thirteenth century, at first very occasionally, later (after 1278) more regularly. The rector was assisted by a provincial treasurer who was responsible directly to the apostolic chamber (the main papal financial office); in the thirteenth century the treasurer was usually a layman-banker, but later he was a cleric. The most important new tax was the *tallia militum* (or military service tax), which at first had to be voted by the provincials in parliament, but later was collected without such authority.

By the end of the thirteenth century the apostolic chamberlain was not only responsible for the direction of papal-state finances, but was also empowered to nominate many papal-state officials, and to conduct his own correspondence for the direction of routine matters of papal-state government. The college of cardinals was recognized under Gregory IX (1234) and Nicholas IV (1289) as having special rights in the administration of the temporal power, besides the duty to direct it *sede vacante*. The cardinals in the late thirteenth century set up their own financial office in order to share papal temporal and spiritual revenues.

Under the Avignonese popes there was a major reform of public law in the various papal-state provinces through the issue by papal legates of "constitutions" which were redactions of earlier provincial legislation. The effect was to strengthen the courts of provincial rectors, to regulate papal relations with the communes, and to reform the administration of finance. The first major reform was that of the legate Bertrand de Déaulx in 1355–1336; the second was that of the better-known Cardinal Gil Albornoz, in a collection which subsequently became known as the *Constitutiones aegidianae,* originally issued in 1357.

To try to deal with the problem of the tyrants, or *signori,* the church borrowed a legal device from the empire, that of the "vicariate." The "apostolic vicariate" was the legal delegation by the pope of wide judicial powers to a specified ruler for a specified period. The first important rulers to secure this concession were the Este of Ferrrara in 1339, and by the end of the century it became the standard means of securing recognition of papal rule from a *signore.* The cash payments due under the concessions of vicariate were substantial, but hard to collect. Under Martin V (*r.* 1417–1431), as a result of a decision of the Council of Constance, grants of vicariate were normally limited to periods of three years.

The regionalism and particularism characteristic of central Italy were too strong in the late medieval papal state to allow more than limited opportunities for the assertion of government power. The Avignonese popes had attempted to apply the kind of administrative measures typical of other great lordships, but the peculiarly foreign nature of their rule robbed it of much of its effectiveness. Papal administration was innovative and venturesome in public credit methods and central fiscal techniques rather than in local government.

BIBLIOGRAPHY

The basic work for the papal states in this period is Peter Partner, *The Lands of St. Peter: The Papal State in the Middle Ages and the Early Renaissance* (1972). See also Walter Ullmann, *The Growth of Papal Government in the Middle Ages,* 3rd ed. (1970).

For the early period, see Anna Marie Drabek, *Die Verträge der fränkischen und deutschen Herrscher mit dem Papsttum von 754 bis 1020* (1976); Horst Fuhrmann, "Konstantinische Schenkung und abendländisches Kaisertum," in *Deutsches Archiv für Erforschung des Mittelalters,* **22** (1966); André Guillou, *Régionalisme et indépendance dans l'empire byzantin au VIIe siècle: L'example de l'exarchat et de la Pentapole d'Italie* (1969); Adelheid Hahn, "Das Hludowicianum: die Urkunde Ludwigs der Fromme für die römische Kirche von 817," in *Archiv für Diplomatik,* **21** (1975); Jan T. Hallenbeck, "The Lombard Party in Eighth Century Rome: A Case of Mistaken Identity," in *Studi medievali,* 3rd ser., **15** (1974), and "Rome Under Attack: An Estimation of King Aistulf's Motives for the Lombard Siege of 756," in *Medieval Studies,* **36** (1974); Jörg Jarnut, "Quierzy und Rom: Bermerkungen zu den 'Promissiones Donationis' Pippins und Karls," in *Historische Zeitschrift,* **220** (1975); Peter Llewellyn, *Rome in the Dark Ages* (1971); David H. Miller, "The Roman Revolution of the Eighth Century," in *Medieval Studies,* **36** (1974); Thomas F. X. Noble, *The Republic of St. Peter: The Birth of the Papal State, 680–825* (1984); Pierre Toubert, *Les structures du Latium mediéval: Le Latium méridional et la Sabine du IXe siècle à la fin du XIIe siècle,* 2 vols. (1973).

For the middle period, see Uta-Renate Blumenthal, "*Patrimonia* and *Regalia* in 1111," in *Law, Church, and Society: Essays in Honor of Stephan Kuttner,* Kenneth Pennington and Robert Somerville, eds. (1977); József Déer, *Papsttum und Normannen: Untersuchungen zu ihren lehnsrechtlichen und kirchenpolitischen Beziehungen* (1972); Johannes Fried, "Der Regalienbegriff im 11. und 12. Jahrhundert," in *Deutsches Archiv für Erforschung des Mittelalters* **29** (1973); Klaus J. Herrmann, *Das Tuskulanerpapsttum (1012–1046)* (1973); Hartmut Hoffmann, "Petrus Diaconus, die Herren von Tusculum und der Sturz Oderisius' II. von Montecassino," in *Deutsches Archiv für Erforschung des Mittelalters,* **27** (1971); Daniel Y. Waley, *The Papal State in the Thirteenth Century* (1961); Katherine Walsh, "Papsttum, Kurie und Kirchenstaat im späteren Mittelalter," in *Römische historische Mitteilungen,* **16** (1974), and "Zum Patrimonium Beati Petri im Mittelalter," *ibid.,* **17** (1975).

For the later Middle Ages, see Mario Caravale and Alberto Caracciolo, *Lo stato pontificio da Martino V a Pio IX* (1978); Paolo Colliva, *Il cardinale Albornoz, lo stato della chiesa, le constitutiones aegidianae (1353–1357)* (1977); Maria Cristofari Mancia, *Il primo registro della tesoreria di Ascoli (20 agosto 1426–30 aprile 1427)* (1974); Arnold Esch, *Bonifaz IX. und der Kirchenstaat* (1969), and "Das Papsttum unter der Herrschaft der Neapolitaner," in *Festschrift für Hermann Heimpel,* II (1972); John Larner, *The Lords of Romagna* (1965); Peter Partner, *The Papal State Under Martin V* (1958); E. Pásztor, "Per la storia dell'amministrazione dello stato pontificio sotto Martino IV," in *Miscellanea giusti* (pub. by the Vatican), **2** (1978); Chantal Reydellet-Guttinger, *L'administration pontificale dans le duché de Spolete (1305–1352)* (1975); Evelio Verdera y Tuells, ed., *El cardenal Albornoz y el colegio de España,* 4 vols. (1972–1973), deals directly with Albornoz.

PETER PARTNER

[See also **Albornoz, Gil; Babylonian Captivity; Boniface VIII, Pope; Cardinals, College of; Church, Latin; Crusades, Political; Curia, Papal; Donation of Constantine; Gregory VII, Pope; Guelphs and Ghibellines; Holy Roman Empire; Innocent III, Pope; Italy; Jews in the Papal States; Lombards, Kingdom of; Matilda of Tuscany; Missi Dominici; Papacy, Origins and Development of; Pepin III and the Donation of Pepin; Ravenna; Schism, Great; Sicilian Vespers; Sicily, Kingdom of; Stephen II, Pope.**]

PAPER, INTRODUCTION OF. The use of paper, which was a Chinese invention, spread slowly westward. In the eastern Mediterranean world, the oldest examples of paper are fragments found in the caves of the Judaean desert; they date from the seventh century; the oldest Greek books of paper (end of the eighth century) were copied in Palestine. The technique of papermaking, acquired by the Muslims in 751, spread steadily throughout the Islamic world, from Bukhara in Central Asia to Morocco, and from there to Muslim Spain.

One can determine the origin of paper (before the invention of watermarks) by identifying the

PAPER, INTRODUCTION OF

material from which it was made and by examining the marks left on a sheet by the procedures used in producing it. In this way it has been established that the paper imported from the tenth century on by the Byzantines and by their neighbors, such as the Armenians, was made in Muslim countries. The oldest known specimens of paper in the imperial chancery of Constantinople date from the mid eleventh century. In the West the early use of paper—in Sicily and Spain—is related to the fact that both had been occupied by Muslims, who brought paper with them.

The use of paper on the Iberian Peninsula is attested from the tenth century on. It was locally produced from the eleventh century according to methods adopted by Maghribi craftsmen and was characterized by a zigzag mark that does not appear in paper made in the Muslim East. The export of paper from Muslim Spain, where the industry was centered in Játiva (Valencia), is mentioned by the beginning of the twelfth century. After the reconquest of most of the peninsula (early thirteenth century), the production of paper was continued, often by Jews, who used the same techniques as the Muslims but changed the size of the sheet to suit their own units of measure. By the middle of the thirteenth century Spanish-made paper was again being exported to southern France, Sicily, southern Italy, and maybe the Byzantine Empire. But a decline in production soon followed: Italian-made paper made its appearance in Spain by the beginning of the fourteenth century and fifty years later supplanted the local products. In the fifteenth century, the import of French paper began. Spanish production did not revive until the modern era.

Italy. In Sicily, paper was in use by the middle of the eleventh century. The oldest surviving dated specimen is a writ made out in the name of Countess Adelaide, the widow of Roger I, dated 1109. Paper was imported from Muslim countries, as was the paper used from 1154 to 1166 by Giovanni Scriba, a Genoese notary. In the first half of the thirteenth century two centers of Italian papermaking developed, one in the region of Genoa, the other at Fabriano. Unlike the Spaniards, the Italians did not inherit an earlier technological tradition, and consequently the early Italian papermakers had to invent new production methods—hammers with pointed nails to tear up rags, a rigid frame with metal wires that made it possible to produce watermarks, a new way of drying, and (from the end of the thirteenth century) sizing with animal gelatin so that ink would not run.

In less than fifty years Italian paper had acquired those qualities that would guarantee markets for its rapid expansion. The few countries that had exported paper until then were forced to fall back on their traditional outlets, and in time their industries were ruined. Countries that had only used parchment now bought paper. One can speak of an "explosion" of Italian paper, whose manufacture rapidly extended to central (Umbria, Tuscany) and northern (from Piedmont to Venice) Italy. In the east, Italian paper was exported across the Adriatric to the Dalmatian coast and Epiros (northwest Greece) by the middle of the thirteenth century, reaching Constantinople a few years after 1300. Toward the south, Italian paper was imported by North African countries during the first half of the fourteenth century, by Egypt at the end of the century, and by Syria soon afterward. In the west, Spanish production collapsed in the face of Italian competition, and in the north, the vast and rich markets from Western Europe to Russia were opened. The success of the Italians, however, led to the founding of paper mills in many European countries, first in France, which by the mid fifteenth century began to rival Italy as a paper exporter.

France. Paper was used in France by the beginning of the thirteenth century. It was at first imported from Spain, but by the second half of the century Italian paper imports grew rapidly. French papermaking began in Champagne (at Troyes) about 1330 and experienced a quick expansion. Many paper mills were soon set up in other regions—Auvergne, Périgord, Angoumois, Normandy—and French paper was exported throughout Western Europe, to many parts of Central Europe, and to Russia.

Germany and Central Europe. In Germany, paper (first Italian and then French) was in use a century before the first paper mill was founded, at Nuremberg in 1390. Mills then multiplied rapidly throughout southern Germany and the Rhine Valley. In Switzerland paper was used as early as 1275 (the Swiss, like the Germans, relied first on Italian imports, then on French), but the first mills were built at Basel in 1433, and at Bern in 1465. The diffusion of printing with movable type in Europe, in the second half of the fifteenth century, encouraged a rapid expansion of the industry, especially at Basel.

Through the fifteenth century, Central and

Pulp about to be pressed into a sheet. Woodcut by Jost Amman (the earliest picture of papermaking) in *Eygentliche Beschreibung* (1568). FROM *A TRUE DESCRIPTION OF ALL TRADES* ©1930 Mergenthaler Linotype Co.

Northern Europe imported Italian and French papers; it was not until 1469 that paper mills were founded at St. Pölten (Austria). Other mills were built in Pradnick Czerwony (now Kraków, Poland) in 1491 and at Wiener Neustadt (Austria) before 1498.

England, Netherlands, Russia. England, however, remained an importer of Italian- and French-made paper. The mill founded in 1495 in Hertfordshire was active for only a short period, in spite of the excellent quality of its product. New mills were built only after half a century had passed. In the Netherlands paper was in use from the early fourteenth century on, but mills were not constructed until the sixteenth century. Russia, too, was an importer of paper—chiefly from Italy via the Black Sea and the Crimea—from the fourteenth century; its paper mills also date from the sixteenth century.

Medieval names for paper. To find a name for this new writing material, Europeans often looked to its geographic origin. In the Byzantine Empire a paper book was called *bagdatikos* or *bambukinos,* signifying paper from Baghdad on Manbij (ancient Bambyke, on the Syrian border). This latter name was often confused with adjectives describing textile materials: *bambakinos* (cottony) or *bombukinos* (silken, "bombazine"). In the West the terms *pergamena graeca* and *charta damascena* referred to the region where it was first used or through which it transited (Byzantium), or to the city where it was supposed to have been made (Damascus, which was an important supplier of paper). As for *charta cuttanea,* the adjective is certainly a translation of the *bambakinos* of Byzantine Greek.

BIBLIOGRAPHY

General. André Blum, *On the Origin of Paper,* Harry M. Lydenberg, trans. (1934), and *La route du papier* (1946); Anne Basanoff, *Itinerario della carta dall'Oriente all'Occidente e sua diffusione in Europa* (1965); Charles-Moïse Briquet, "Recherches sur les premiers papiers employés en Orient et en Occident du Xe au XIVe siècle," in his *Opuscula* (1955), 129–161; Jean Irigoin, "Papiers orientaux et papiers occidentaux," in Jacques Bompaire and Jean Irigoin, *La paléographie grecque et byzantine* (1977).

Studies. Henri Alibaux, *Les premières papeteries françaises* (1926); Georg Eineder, *The Ancient Paper-Mills of the Former Austro-Hungarian Empire and Their Watermarks* (1960); Johann Lindt, *The Paper-Mills of Bern and Their Watermarks, 1465–1859* (1964); Nicolas Oikonomidès, "Le support matériel des documents byzantins," in Bompaire and Irigoin, *op. cit.;* Gerhard Piccard, "Über die Anfänge des Gebrauchs des Papiers in deutschen Kanzleien," in *Studi in onore di Amintore Fanfani,* III (1962); Wolfgang Schlieder, "Zur Geschichte der Papierherstellung in Deutschland von den Anfängen der Papiermacherei bis zum 17. Jahrhundert," in *Beiträge zur Geschichte des Buchwesens,* **2** (1966); Alfred Schulte, "Die ältesten Papiermühlen der Rheinlande," in *Gutenberg-Jahrbuch* (1932); Alfred F. Shorter, *Paper Mills and Paper Makers in England, 1495–1800* (1957); Walter Tschudin, *The Ancient Paper-Mills of Basle and Their Marks* (1958); Oriol Valls i Subira, *The History of Paper in Spain,* Sarah Nicolson, trans., 3 vols. (1978–1982).

JEAN IRIGOIN

[See also **Parchment; Watermarks; Writing Materials.**]

PAPERT (plural, *paperti*), a covered or, more often, enclosed exterior gallery or porch, such as was often built onto the nonsanctuary sides of medieval Russian churches. *Paperti* served as vestibules and sometimes as sleeping and eating areas (*trapeznye*) for worshipers who had traveled far to attend services.

BIBLIOGRAPHY

Hubert Faensen and Vladimir Ivanov, *Early Russian Architecture* (1975), 40, 46–47, 304; Arthur Voyce, *Art and Architecture of Medieval Russia* (1967), 114–115.

GEORGE P. MAJESKA

[See also **Russian Architecture.**]

PAPIAS (*fl. ca.* 1050), a lexicographer and grammarian. According to a tradition from the thirteenth century, he was a Lombard, and possibly even a citizen of the town of Pavia because of the similarity between his name and that of the town. The only evidence of his personal life derives from the letter accompanying his major work, the *Elementarium doctrinae rudimentum,* which reveals him to have been a married cleric in a community of clerics. He had two sons, but was separated from them on account of some sin, which, however, remains unspecified. He wrote the *Elementarium* in order to educate his sons through the written word since he was not able to educate them in person. He also compiled a grammar consisting of excerpts from Priscian.

The title of *Elementarium* was given by Papias himself. Internal evidence suggests that it was written in the mid eleventh century: the entry *Aetas,* a list of kings, ends with "Henricus minor XIII"; it was made in the thirteenth year after Henry III's coronation, that is, in 1040 or 1041. It is not clear whether the work was begun or completed at that date; and since it took Papias ten years to write the lexicon, it was most probably finished between 1040 and 1051. Papias is also mentioned in a prologue to a commentary on the Psalms written by a Bishop Bruno of Würzburg. This bishop died in 1045, and unless he referred to a different work of Papias or knew an earlier version, the *Elementarium* must have been known before the bishop's death.

The term "lexicon" does not do full justice to the *Elementarium.* It is partly a dictionary containing alphabetically arranged lemmata and their definitions, and etymologies for many words. It is also an encyclopedia, in that many entries (for example, *aetas, carmen, lapis, regnum*) go far beyond a simple definition of the term. Moreover, it contains many geographical, geological, medical, botanical, historical, theological, and even mythological names or terms, for which encyclopedic information is provided. In addition, the *Elementarium* is partly a grammar, not only in its explanations of grammatical terminology, but also in its inclusion of *differentiae* (definitions of words which resemble each other either in meaning or in spelling, that is, words which can easily be confused) and its arrangement of words in word families. Papias' work thus provides introductions to the basic concepts of most branches of medieval learning.

The *Elementarium* became very important in the later Middle Ages. Some ninety manuscripts of it are still extant, of which almost seventy date from the thirteenth and fourteenth centuries. Later lexicographers, such as Huguccio of Pisa, used the *Elementarium* in their own works. It was first printed in Milan in 1476.

Modern scholarship has somewhat discounted the importance of the *Elementarium.* In his letter, Papias mentions twenty-nine different sources from which he drew his material. Goetz, however, has shown that "the appearance of all-embracing knowledge, which Papias was able to give," disappears on closer examination. The largest part of the material as well as many references to the sources are taken from the *Liber glossarum* (written probably between 690 and 750, by an unknown author). Papias is therefore more important as a transmitter of knowledge than as an original contributor or compiler. Despite articles by such scholars as Manitius and Klinck, who find minor innovations in the *Elementarium,* Goetz's verdict on Papias is still the authoritative one.

BIBLIOGRAPHY

Sources. Lloyd W. Daly and B. A. Daly, "Some Techniques in Medieval Latin Lexicography," in *Speculum,* 39 (1964), which contains a translation of the "Preface" to the *Elementarium; Papiae Elementarium,* V. de Angelis, ed. (1977–); *Papias vocabulista,* Bonimus Mombritius, ed. (1496).

Studies. Georg Goetz, "Papias und seine Quellen," in *Sitzungsberichte der Bayerischen Akademie der Wissenschaften* (1903); Roswitha Klinck, *Die lateinische Etymologie des Mittelalters* (1970); Max Manitius, *Geschichte der lateinischen Literatur des Mittelalters,* II (1923).

GERNOT WIELAND

[See also **Encyclopedias and Dictionaries; Huguccio.**]

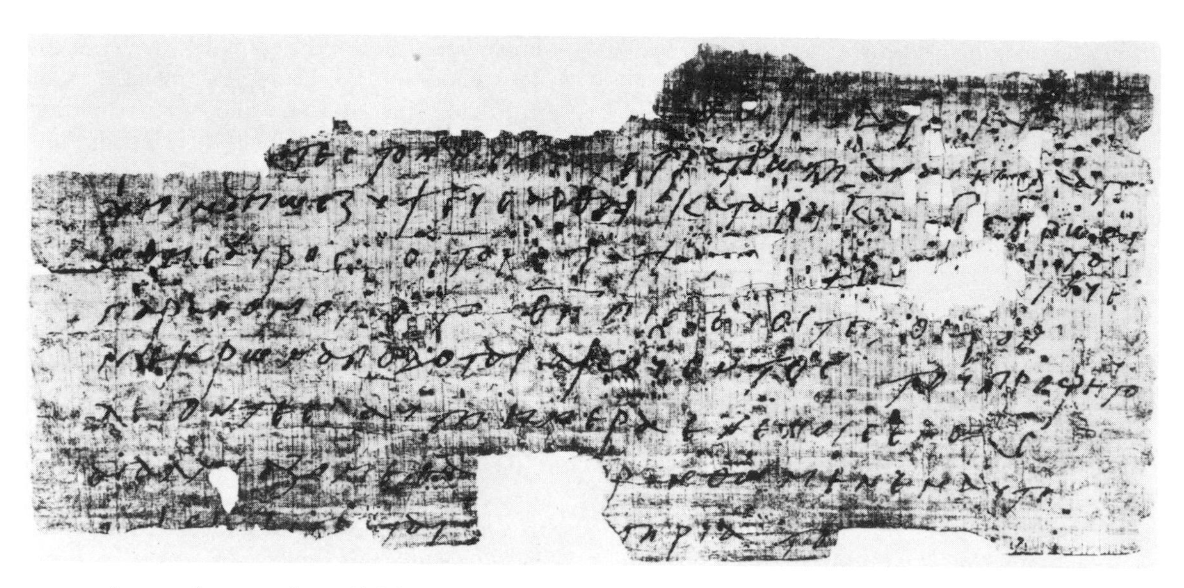

Papyrus fragment from Al-Ashmūnein in Middle Egypt, 6th–7th century. BY PERMISSION OF THE BRITISH LIBRARY, LONDON, INV. NO. 2906

PAPYRUS (from Greek *papyros*, papyrus plant) was the basic writing material of classical antiquity; it was produced in great quantities in Egypt. Wet strips sliced from the papyrus plant were superimposed, pressed, and then dried in the sun. The best-quality papyrus—ancient authorities distinguish seven grades—was white, thin, smooth, flexible, and more durable than many writing papers used today. Excavation in Egypt has uncovered thousands of whole or fragmentary papyrus documents and literary texts that have survived thanks to the dry climate. Far fewer specimens have been continuously preserved above ground in European archives and libraries since the early Middle Ages. The Muslim conquest of Egypt in the seventh century and the collapse of ancient commercial networks led to the gradual disappearance of papyrus and its replacement by parchment in the medieval West and Byzantium, a process that was largely completed by the ninth century and that has figured prominently in debate on the birth of the medieval economy. Nonetheless, isolated examples of papyrus books and documents continued to occur for another two centuries; in particular, the traditionally minded papal chancellery issued papyrus bulls into the eleventh century.

BIBLIOGRAPHY

Naphtali Lewis, *Papyrus in Classical Antiquity* (1974).

MICHAEL MCCORMICK

[See also **Paper, Introduction of; Parchment; Writing Materials.**]

PAQUDA, IBN. See **Baḥya ben Joseph ibn Paquda.**

PARADISE, ISLAMIC. According to the Koran (25:15), paradise is "the garden of eternity" (*jannat al-khuld*), and the garden has been the dominant symbol of paradise in Islamic belief and tradition. The Arabic word for garden, *al-janna,* is the usual term for paradise, and appears in the Koran in various combinations, such as "garden of paradise" (*jannat al-firdaws*), "garden of refuge" (*jannat al-maʾwā*), and "garden of felicity" (*jannat al-naʿīm*). Paradise was often identified with the Garden of Eden (*jannat ʿAdn*) as well, although most theologians held that Eden was only one part of paradise. The Koran and *ḥadīth* abound in vivid and evocative descriptions of paradise; later theologians, traditionists, preachers, and poets elaborated these descriptions to create a remarkably detailed literature on the joys of the hereafter. Iranian poets especially delighted in ingenious and subtle imagery derived from the allusive Koranic descriptions and epithets for paradise. However, the most impressive cultural creation inspired by the image of paradise has been the traditional Islamic garden, magnificent

Muḥammad, riding Buraq and guided by the angel Gabriel, sees the houris in paradise. Timurid miniature from a copy of the *Miʿraj-nāmeh,* Herāt, Khorāsān, 1436. PARIS, BIBLIOTHÈQUE NATIONALE, MS SUPPL. TURC 190, fol. 49

examples of which flourished throughout the Muslim world from Mughal India to Moorish Spain.

In the Koran, descriptions of paradise are usually linked in dramatic parallelism with harsh evocations of the torments of hell. Paradise is the place of ease, comfort, and refreshment, and its pleasures, both spiritual and physical, gain heightened power and allure in contrast with the grim agonies of hell (*jahannam*). Thus, while the damned are shackled or given boiling water to drink, the blessed enjoy a garden, or series of gardens, nurtured by pure, flowing streams; shade trees, thick with ever ripe fruit, help create an eternally clement springtime.

Springs and rivers course throughout paradise, and the prominence of cool, running water in Islamic conceptions of the hereafter is splendidly reflected in the many exquisite fountains of the classical Islamic garden. Among the innumerable rivers of paradise, there are rivers of milk, wine, and honey (47:15). The pristine waters of the spring of Tasnīm and the fountain of Salsabīl are mixed with invigorating wine for the refreshment of the elect (76:18).

Paradise is a place of unimaginable opulence and magnificence, but it is also a place where simple earthly pleasures abound, though often in transfigured form. This is well illustrated by the following *ḥadīth:*

> A bedouin asked the Prophet: "O Prophet! I love horses. Are there horses in paradise?" The Prophet replied: "When you enter paradise, you will receive a winged horse made of ruby, upon which you will be carried, and it will fly with you wherever you wish to go."

In paradise, the blessed wear dazzling raiment of green silk with gold embroidery, and they sport silver bracelets. They recline on raised couches lined with silk brocade. Immortal youths circulate among them and offer silver crystal goblets filled with a wine that delights without intoxication (76:5–6, 12–22).

Such sensual luxuries were usually explained as the just reward for deprivation or renunciation in earthly life; paradise also represents a reversal of earthly life. Thus, according to the Hanbalite theologian Ibn Qayyim al-Jawzīya (*d.* 1350):

> Whoever drinks wine in this life does not drink it in the hereafter; whoever wears silk in this life does not wear it in the hereafter; whoever eats from plates of gold and silver in this life does not eat from them in the hereafter. . . . As the Prophet said: "In this world, it belongs to them [the affluent], but in the next world, it belongs to you." (al-Jawzīya, *Ḥādī al-arwāḥ,* p. 191)

The blessed will also enjoy the favors of houris. These exquisite women, guarded in cloistered pavilions, are endowed with virginity that is perpetually renewed. "Houri" derives from the Arabic *ḥawrāʾ* (plural: *ḥūr*), denoting large and beautiful dark eyes, in which there is a marked contrast between the white of the eye and the pupil.

Amid sumptuous food, elegant clothing, and other pleasures of the senses, the blessed will enjoy all the familiar comforts of home. They will live forever surrounded by members of their families who have followed them into Islam (52:21). They will need no guides, for the paths of the celestial garden will be as familiar to them as those of their native towns.

This combination of the fabulous and the familiar in the life of paradise is well suggested in a *ḥadīth* reported by the traditionist Ibn Mājah (*d.* 886):

> Paradise is a brilliant light, a piercing perfume, a well-built castle, a flowing stream, ripe fruit, a lovely wife, plentiful clothing, in an eternal abode and peaceful haven of delights, greenery, joy and coolness.

While there is persistent emphasis on the sensual delights of paradise, the highest bliss was held to be the vision of God (*ruʾyat Allāh*). Though strenuously contested, especially by Mutazilite theologians, the doctrine prevailed and became an article of faith. In his treatise on paradise, Ibn Qayyim al-Jawzīya cites verses in which this belief is quite literally presented:

> The Lord of the heavens manifests himself openly to them;
> He laughs upon his seat, and then he speaks:
> "Peace be upon you!" And when he greets them, all hear his greeting with their own ears.
> (*Ḥādī al-arwāḥ,* p. 24)

The beatific vision and the divine approval (*riḍwān*) were deemed the highest rewards of paradise. The elect bask in God's approval, which makes their faces "shine like the moon" (83:24). In later accounts the divine approval is personified, and Riḍwān is the chief gatekeeper of paradise.

The structure and topography of paradise aroused great interest. Paradise is inconceivably vast in extent, "as large as the heavens and the earth," according to the Koran (3:133), but it is enclosed by walls set with splendid gates. Its exact location was unclear. It was usually said to be beyond the "Lotus tree of the utmost limit" (*sidrat al-muntahā*); only God's throne and seat are higher. Paradise comprises seven levels, or seven gardens, although sometimes eight, or as many as a hundred, are listed. Each garden was said to be composed of a different precious substance. The first garden is of white pearl, the second of ruby, the third of green chrysolite, the fourth of yellow coral, the fifth of white silver, the sixth of red gold, and the highest, the Garden of Eden, of red pearl.

Pious writers delighted in fabulous extrapolations on the features of paradise. For example, the houris have bodies formed of saffron; they grant their favors unstintingly and even seek the embraces of their appointed consorts with unflagging enthusiasm. They have the ability to renew the sexual vigor of their partners inexhaustibly. Paradise has its own market (*sūq al-janna*), a transfigured institution where one neither buys nor sells, but receives instantaneously whatever one wishes. In this market all class distinctions vanish: the rich and the poor, the high and the low, rub shoulders as equals. In addition to the *rafraf,* the winged mounts made of ruby, the blessed will ride upon shining white camels. The inhabitants of paradise all will conform to a spiritualized physical type: they will all be sixty cubits tall, the size of Adam; they will have neither beards nor pubic hair; they will all be thirty-three years old, the age of Jesus when he went to paradise. They will never need sleep; their sweat will be musk. Muslims will form the majority of the elect, and Arabic will be the only language spoken in paradise.

Predictably, various questions on the nature of paradise exercised the theologians. For example, does paradise now exist, or will it be created only at the end of time? If it is created, will it also be destroyed, together with the heavens and the earth, at the Last Judgment? There were more mundane questions as well: if there is sexual activity in paradise, will there also be childbearing?

The consensus held that God created paradise when he created the heavens and the earth, and that while these would be destroyed, paradise would endure forever. The blessed will enter paradise only at the end of time, after the Day of Judgment. Then the throng of the faithful, led by the prophet Muḥammad, will knock at the gates of paradise and be admitted triumphantly, to the strains of exquisite music. The poor will enter before the rich, Muslims before the pious of other faiths.

The longing for paradise, the predestined reward promised to "those who believe and perform good works," inspired Islamic poets, mystics, and theologians to produce an eschatological literature striking in its intensity and specificity of vision. This longing is well exemplified in the following *ḥadīth,* in which paradise itself cries out for fulfillment:

> O my God, my fruits have ripened and my rivers have grown abundant. I want to see my beloved ones. Will you hold them back?

BIBLIOGRAPHY

The best discussion is Ṣubḥī Sāliḥ (Ṣoubḥī al-Saleh) *La vie future selon le Coran* (1971). The fullest traditional Islamic treatment is Ibn Qayyim al-Jawzīyay, *Ḥādī al arwāḥ ilā bilād al-afrāḥ* (1962). On the soul's ascent to God's presence, see al-Ghazālī, *The Precious Pearl/al-Durra al-Fakhira,* Jane I. Smith trans. (1979), 25–27. For *ḥadīth* and traditional descriptions, see Arthur Jeffery, ed., *A Reader on Islam* (1962, repr. 1980), 84, 172–175, 239–248. A superb discussion of paradise in Islamic mysticism and poetry is Annemarie Schimmel, "The Celestial Garden in Islam," in Elisabeth B. MacDougall and Richard Ettinghausen, eds., *The Islamic Garden* (1976). On the Islamic garden in general, Jonas Lehrman, *Earthly Paradise: Garden and Courtyard in Islam* (1980).

ERIC L. ORMSBY

[See also **Purgatory, Islamic; Rauḍa; Resurrection, Islamic.**]

PARADISE, WESTERN CONCEPT OF.

PARADISE, WESTERN CONCEPT OF. The word "paradise" (*paradeisos*), as the Greek form of an Eastern word for "pleasure ground," was used in the Greek translation of Genesis for the Garden of Eden. By the New Testament era paradise had extended its meaning to include heaven, and this was its principal connotation in the Middle Ages. The primary sense of the word, however, was not lost, and the two meanings were looked on as complementary. Together they represented the symmetry of God's activity toward man. God's goodness moved outward in creation when he placed Adam in the first Eden; but a greater goodness was manifested in redemption when he brought Adam's descendants back to himself in the heavenly paradise. Dante (1265–1321) used this idea by locating the Garden of Eden at the summit of the mount of purgatory to represent the belief that in Christ man attained the original state of Adam and then surpassed it by moving into heaven.

Primitive Christianity taught that Jesus Christ would return to lead his followers into paradise, where the just would reign with him forever in glory. In the lengthening wait for his return, Christians had time to speculate about the heavenly existence of the angels and the saints. Here, as was so often the case, Augustine (354–430) provided the basis for medieval theology. Drawing upon the Bible and earlier Christian authors, he not infrequently wrote about heaven, most extensively in book 22 of the *City of God.* He described heaven as both the ultimate abode of the saints and their recompense. Their joy will consist in the beatific vision, that is, in seeing God face to face, and loving and praising him forever. This beatific vision will be accompanied by immeasurable and inexhaustible happiness. Augustine taught that the dead could experience God only incompletely until the final resurrection. The place of temporary beatitude, which he called "paradise" or the "bosom of Abraham" (Luke 16:23), differs from the highest heaven, not because the dead are unaware of, or are denied, God's presence, but because their vision of God is not yet that of the angels. Augustine did not specify the difference further. Similarly, although he depicted heaven in materialistic terms, Augustine said that its actual physical location cannot be known because divine mysteries are beyond human comprehension.

The writings of Pope Gregory I (590–604) acted as a channel that conveyed to the Middle Ages the theology of Augustine in a popularized form. Only one change was introduced. Gregory, following other Fathers, taught that the souls of the just enter immediately into the fullness of God's presence, the resurrection of the body at the end of time merely enhancing their beatitude. The vision of God constitutes the essential joy of heaven and is the source of the attributes of the blessed, which Gregory described as immutability, immortality, wisdom, and sanctity. Following Augustine's lead, he described, particularly in book 4 of the *Dialogues,* the psychology of the beatific vision in some detail. Saints are perfectly free because their wills are fixed on God, and so they are beyond the power of sin; desire is ever active and yet always completely satisfied; all things and persons are known because everything is visible in God; knowledge of evil, even of the state of the damned, does not disturb because the justice of God's sentence is recognized; there is no envy even though there are different states among the blessed, because love delights in the excellence of another.

The primary source of medieval conceptions of the afterlife was the liturgy, which was accepted unquestioningly as an authoritative presentation of Christian belief. The images of the prayers are specific and concrete: the souls of the just will climb toward heaven under the guidance of the angels, be welcomed by the martyrs and other saints, and stand in the presence of God in a place of refreshment, light, and peace, where they will rejoice forever with Christ and his faithful followers. Liturgical prayers also refer to the presence of the heavenly court around the altar on which Jesus was believed to be physically present under the signs of bread and wine. In attending Mass, therefore, the believer was joined to the sublime liturgy of heaven itself, where Christ is always interceding with his Father for the church (Rom. 8:34).

The very construction of the churches expressed a vivid belief in the reality of heaven. The biblical symbolism that compares the people of God to a building (for example, Eph. 2: 19–22) inspired the architecture and decoration of the house of God. The numerous statues of angels and saints, the gorgeous and highly colored decoration, the biblical scenes from the creation to the final judgment, the powerful image of Christ in glory, were all indications to the worshiper that the church entrance was a veritable portal to paradise.

A characteristic of the Middle Ages that influenced the popular understanding of paradise was the widespread devotion to the saints. Their all-powerful and widely dispersed relics and shrines provided sites for the church triumphant in heaven to aid the church militant on earth. Pilgrimage to a shrine was itself a symbolic journey toward heaven. That the goal of the earliest pilgrimages was Jerusalem suggests the parallel to heaven. The difficult journey, often part of a penance imposed for sins, was seen as being rewarded at the shrine by contact with the heavenly court, just as the goal of human life, with all its hardships, was entrance into paradise. The crusaders were, in theory at least, primarily pilgrims to the Holy Land, and a great part of the motivation of these military pilgrimages came from the special indulgences that were believed to assure an immediate entry into heaven for those who died in battle.

Heaven was also thought to be partially attainable on earth by the interior journey of monastic life. The closing words of the supremely influential *Rule of St. Benedict* (*ca.* 540) depict the monk as hastening to his heavenly country under the guidance of the rule. Bernard of Clairvaux (1090–1153) described mystical prayer, the goal of the monastic vocation, as a foretaste of heaven in which God's very essence could be glimpsed. The medieval ascetical spirituality, of both the monastery and the whole church, was essentially a turning away from the present world toward the next. Even the mendicant orders of the thirteenth century (mainly Franciscans and Dominicans), although more pastoral than the monastic orders had been, continued to honor the traditional commitment to asceticism and mystical prayer, as the life of Francis of Assisi (*d.* 1226) shows.

With the rise of Scholasticism in the thirteenth century, a new attention was directed to specula-

PARADISE, WESTERN CONCEPT OF

tion about heaven, the intuitive vision of God, and the state of the risen body. There was no doubt of, and hence no need to demonstrate, the existence of heaven as a place where the elect will be united in the common enjoyment of God. Speculations thus rather centered on the location of heaven, its nature, and its relation to the rest of the universe.

Heaven, it was universally believed, was beyond the universe, but not unrelated to it. Thomas Aquinas (1224–1274) accepted the traditional physical placement of heaven, but not uncritically. He connected this teaching to the ultimate purpose of creation. Since God has determined both a spiritual and corporeal glory for human beings, it is fitting that he should prepare a glorious and special place for them. And since spiritual and material creation form a single universe, it is fitting again that angels preside over all movement of the material, and rightly inhabit the supreme empyrean, which dominates all the world and where the elect will be reunited in Christ. All subsequent medieval thought concerning paradise drew upon that of Thomas Aquinas.

Once the existence of a special locale was admitted, its corporeality had necessarily to follow. Alexander of Hales (*ca.* 1185–1245) stated that the empyreal heaven was material, and Bonaventure (*ca.* 1217–1274) added that it was the largest body since it contains all the others. Theologians generally considered heaven to be made of fire as the most subtle and brilliant of the elements, but Aquinas denied that heaven was made of one of the four elements, postulating a fifth element that was "the most luminous and noblest material" or, in terms of his philosophy, "more act than form."

Derived from the perfection of its material were the physical properties of heaven: immobility, incorruptibility, universal homogeneity, uniform luminosity. Aquinas saw these properties as a result of the harmony that must exist between the glorious state of the elect and their abode. A changeless, splendidly luminous dwelling place is required for those who look directly on God, the uncreated source of all light.

Far more important than physical descriptions of heaven was the long-standing conviction that heaven consisted in the vision of God. In Thomas Aquinas this concept took on a new precision. He combined a philosophy of human beatitude, which came from Aristotle, with the traditional Christian description of the beatific vision, especially as it is found in Augustine and Boethius. From philosophy he accepted the idea of beatitude as a final cause, that is, the ultimate purpose for which a man acts and which therefore specifies in a fundamental manner each of his actions. Clearly, only God—who is neither partial nor limited—can be this all-embracing cause. This was derived both from Scripture (for example, 1 John 3:2) and from an analysis of the human intellect, which by its nature desires to know the cause when it sees an effect. Man is also possessed of a certain transcendence that prevents his being satisfied with only knowing created beings and their finite ("secondary") causes. But this transcendence is not to be taken as proof that the beatific vision can be naturally desired; knowledge of it, as well as the possibility of attaining it, comes gratuitously from God.

Medieval theologians disagreed about the fundamental characteristic of the beatific vision. Bonaventure and the Franciscan tradition thought that love is the initial impulse. Aquinas claimed that the intellectual knowledge of God's essence constitutes beatitude, but this knowledge is preceded and attended by love. Also essentially attendant on beatitude are delight and permanence. The latter is necessary, not only because what is temporary cannot be final beatitude, but also because the vision of God must always preserve wonder for a finite intellect which, therefore, could experience no desire to turn away.

That God's grace is necessary to receive beatitude did not for Aquinas indicate any deficiency because, as he stated, even in human affairs it is better to receive with the help of a friend a good that one could not acquire on one's own than to be limited to one's own resources and so not receive the good at all. Aquinas accepted the traditional teaching that there are different degrees of beatitude. These arise not from any variation in the object (which is God), but from the various dispositions of the souls entering God's presence.

The resurrection of the body was another truth of faith that Aquinas justified not by a logical deduction, but by reasons of fittingness. The body is part of the definition of being human, and as such, is required for the full human participation in the vision of God. Furthermore, as the instrument of good works, there is an obvious reason for the body's sharing the rewards of the just. In speculating on the relative numbers of the just and sinners, medieval theologians usually followed Augustine's somber opinion that although many would be saved, their number was small compared to the number of those who would be damned.

These abstract formulations received confirmation in the official teachings of the church, especially in the general councils of Lyons (1274) and Florence (1439) and in the decree "Benedictus Deus" of Pope Benedict XII (1336).

It was the genius of Dante to translate these theological formulations into poetry without sacrificing their precision. Heaven is portrayed in the *Divine Comedy* as the simultaneous experience of all created things seen in their cause, God himself. He is the inexhaustible source of love, which is shared by participants in the divine vision: "Pure intellectual light filled full with love" (*Paradiso,* XXX, 40).

BIBLIOGRAPHY

Augustine's and Thomas Aquinas' doctrines on paradise are in book 22 of *The City of God,* Henry Bettenson, trans. (1972), Thomas Aquinas, *Summa theologiae,* Thomas Gilby, ed. and trans., XVI (1969), and *Summa Theologica of St. Thomas Aquinas,* III (*Supplementum*), Dominican Fathers, ed. and trans. (1948), 91–96. See also P. Bernard, "Ciel," in *Dictionnaire de théologie catholique,* II (1910); Reginald Garrigou-Lagrange, *Life Everlasting,* Patrick Cummins, trans. (1952); Édouard Hugon, "De l'état des âmes séparées," in *Revue thomiste,* **14** (1906); Dorothy L. Sayers, "The Meaning of Heaven and Hell," in her *Introductory Papers on Dante* (1954); Peter Stockmeier, "'Models' of Heaven in Christian Religious Feeling," in Bastiaan M. F. van Iersel and Edward Schillebeeckx, eds., *Heaven* (1979).

DANIEL CALLAM

[See also **Angel/Angelology; Aquinas, St. Thomas; Augustine of Hippo, St.; Benedict of Nursia, St.; Dante Alighieri; Pilgrimage, Western European; Purgatory, Western Concept of.**]

PARAPHONISTA, one of the designated roles in the Roman schola cantorum. Of the seven adult *cantores* in the schola, the first three are titled simply *primus, secundus,* and *tertius,* but the fourth is called *archiparaphonista* and the remaining three are named *paraphonistae* (*Ordo romanus* I, 39–43). The term also appears in the description of the Roman Easter Vespers (*Ordo* XXVII, 70–71). Although all details of liturgical roles are not specified, the first three *cantores* seem to function as soloists, while the *paraphonistae* provide support for the boy singers (*infantes*) and lead the schola in responding.

The *paraphonista* is cited, in an account of Charlemagne's travels by an anonymous monk from St. Gall (*ca.* ninth/tenth century), as the leader of a group of singers, who wields a baton (*peniculus*), trying to maintain a degree of discipline. The word is also found in sequence texts in some eleventh-century Aquitainian manuscripts. The composers of these *prosae* (*Alle coeleste, Alme Deus, nunc parce tuis, Exsultet nunc omnis chorus*) obviously found the word useful to supply at least five notes with syllables and give the text a certain technical tone. A more specific function of the *paraphonista* cannot be determined from these usages.

There has been a dispute in musicological literature concerning the role of the *paraphonista* in singing polyphony. Peter Wagner suggests that *paraphonista* was related to *paraphonia,* a term used by certain Greek theorists to designate consonances of the fourth and fifth. Wagner concludes that the *paraphonista*'s role was that of singing polyphony or organum at the fourth or fifth. Jacques Handschin argues that the role is that of supporting cantor. He relates *paraphonista,* a term of Greek root that is not found in Greek treatises, to the Latin *succentor,* or subcantor. A degree of suspended judgment should be maintained, however, for Martianus Capella translated *paraphonia* as *succentus,* and Remigius' commentary on Martianus equates *succentus* with organum at the fourth or fifth.

BIBLIOGRAPHY

Sources. Monachus Sangallensis De Carolo Magno, in *Bibliotheca rerum Germanicarum, Monumenta Carolina,* IV, Philipp Jaffé, ed. (1867), 638; *Les Ordines Romani du haut moyen âge,* Michel Andrieu, ed., 5 vols. (1931–1961); *Prosarium Lemovicense,* in *Analecta hymnica medii aevi,* VII (1889), 98, 164, 173; *Remigii Autissiodorensis Commentum in Martianum Capellam,* Cora E. Lutz, ed., 2 vols. (1962–1965).

Studies. A. Gastoué, "Paraphonie et paraphonistes," in *Revue de musicologie,* **9** (1928); Jacques Handschin, *Musikgeschichte im Überblick* (1948, 2nd ed. rev. and enl. by Franz Brenn, 1964); Carl-Allan Moberg, "Ein vergessene Pseudo-Longius-Stelle über die Musik," in *Zeitschrift für Musikwissenschaft,* **12** (1929–1930); Richard Sherr, "Paraphonia," in *The New Grove Dictionary of Music and Musicians,* XIV (1980); Peter Wagner, "Über die Anfänge des mehrstimmigen Gesanges," in *Zeitschrift für Musikwissenschaft,* **9**

(1926–1927), "La paraphonie," in *Revue de musicologie,* 9 (1928), and "À propos de la paraphonie," *ibid.,* 10 (1929).

CALVIN M. BOWER

[See also **Cantor; Music, Western European; Ordines Romani; Sequence (Prosa).**]

PARCEVALS SAGA. Chrétien de Troyes's incomplete romance *Perceval* or *Le conte du graal* is represented in Scandinavia by *Parcevals saga* and *Valvens þáttr.* The French romance presumably was translated into Norwegian in the thirteenth century, perhaps during the reign of King Hákon Hákonarson of Norway (1217–1263), who was responsible for the translation of a number of French works. The translation of verses 1–6,513 of *Perceval* is entitled *Parcevals saga;* verses 6,514 to the end, *Valvens þáttr.* In the past the title *Valvers þáttr* was used, but the oldest fragment of the *þáttr* (Copenhagen, Det Arnamagnæanske Institut, AM 573 4to, second half of the fourteenth century) attests that the name was Valven (Gawain), a form known from other Arthurian *riddarasögur.*

Parcevals saga is in some respects inferior to other translated *riddarasögur.* Its imperfection is hardly the fault of the translator, however; he had to contend with an obscure and incomplete text. The odd and puzzling verses in Chrétien's *Perceval* regarding the nature and function of the *graal,* (3,000–3,003; 3,220–3,229; 3,234–3,439; 3,245–3,253, 3,290–3,293), which have been a source of conjecture and disagreement among Romance scholars, are telescoped in the saga into a single description of the object. A maiden enters the hall *ok bar í höndum sér því líkast sem textus væri; en þeir í völsku máli kalla braull; en vér megum kalla ganganda greiða* (She bore in her hands something just as if it were a *textus* [Gospelbook], and they call it *braull* in the French language, but we may call it *ganganda greiða* [*gangandi* is the present participle of *ganga,* to walk; *greiði* connotes acts of hospitality]). Although the preceding gives every appearance of being an explanatory text, the explication of *braull* (presumably a scribal corruption of an original *graal*) only serves to obfuscate further the significance of the *graal.* The phrase *gangandi greiði* is otherwise unattested in Icelandic literature. Varied interpretations of the above passage have been proffered, but the evidence is inconclusive. The grail passage in *Parcevals saga* remains enigmatic.

Like its French source, *Parcevals saga* is incomplete—the translator did not attempt to devise an ending for *Valvens þáttr.* The portion of *Perceval* devoted primarily to the fortunes of the eponymous hero becomes in the saga a self-contained entity framed by a short prologue and epilogue. *Parcevals saga* opens with a brief account concerning the hero's parents. This prologue—which diverges from the French—takes the form of an apologia for Parceval's solitary upbringing. His parents withdrew into solitude because Parceval's father, a knight, had abducted Parceval's mother, the daughter of a king, as his share of war booty. The saga concludes with an epilogue at the point where Chrétien de Troyes turns his attention to Gawain—that is, at the conclusion of the Good Friday episode. We learn that Parceval returned to Blankiflúr, married her, became an outstanding ruler, and defeated all knights who challenged him. Both prologue and epilogue are in the best tradition of saga writing. Whether they are the work of the translator or of a later Icelandic redactor cannot be determined.

Parcevals saga is written in the ornate, rhythmical prose that characterizes the thirteenth-century *riddarasögur.* The saga contains many synonymous and antithetic collocations (not infrequently alliterating) and participial clusters. The euphonious language generated by alliteration at times creates nuances that differ considerably from those in *Perceval. Parcevals saga* is unique among the translated *riddarasögur* in that two rhyming couplets occasionally are interwoven into the prose. Chapters 4–8 and 11–16 end with double rhyming couplets (they occur only once within a chapter—chapter 5). Although the content of the verses derives from *Perceval,* the rhymes are not attempts to emulate the French verse form; the couplets evolve out of the general context. Since all but one of the double rhymes occur at the ends of chapters, they presumably are the work of an Icelandic redactor rather than the translator.

Parcevals saga is transmitted in two Icelandic redactions, one represented only by a damaged vellum leaf from around 1350 (Copenhagen, Royal Library, NKS 1794b 4to) and the other by a slightly defective text in a large codex of romances from about 1400 (Stockholm, Royal Library, Holm perg. 6 4to). Comparison of corresponding passages in the fragment and in Holm perg. 6 4to with *Perceval* attests substantial corruption and attrition of the text by about 1400. The translation had transmitted more of the substance of *Perceval* than editions of the saga (based on the text Holm perg. 6 4to) suggest.

BIBLIOGRAPHY

Editions include Eugen Kölbing, ed., "Parcevals saga, Valvers þáttr," in *Riddarasögur* (1872); Bjarni Vilhjálmsson, ed., "Parcevals saga," in *Riddarasögur,* IV (1954); Helen Susan Maclean, ed., "A Critical Edition, Complete with Introduction, Notes, and Select Glossary, of *Parcevals saga* from the Stockholm Manuscript Codex Holmiensis Pergament no. 6, Quarto" (thesis, University of Leeds, 1968).

Studies include Peter G. Foote, "*Gangandi greiði,*" in Bjarni Guðnason, Halldór Halldórsson, Jónas Kristjánsson, eds., *Einarsbók: Afmæliskveðja til Einars Ól. Sveinssonar* (1969); Ann Broady Gardiner, "Narrative Technique and Verbal Style in *Parcevals saga ok Valvers þáttr*" (diss., Univ. of Pennsylvania, 1977); Eyvind Fjeld Halvorsen, "Parcevals saga," in *Kulturhistorisk leksikon for nordisk middelalder,* XIII (1968); Eugen Kölbing, "Die nordische Parzivalsaga und ihre Quelle," in *Germania,* **14** [n.s. **2**] (1869); Henry Kratz, "The *Parcevals saga* and *Li contes del Graal,*" in *Scandinavian Studies,* **49** (1977), and "*Textus, Braull,* and *Gangandi Greiði,*" in *Saga-Book of the Viking Society for Northern Research,* **19** (1977); Roger Sherman Loomis, "The Grail in the *Parcevals Saga,*" in *Germanic Review,* **39** (1964); P. M. Mitchell, "The Grail in the *Parcevals saga,*" in *Modern Language Notes,* **73** (1958).

MARIANNE E. KALINKE

[See also **Arthurian Literature; Chrétien de Troyes; Grail, Legend of; Riddarasögur.**]

PARCHMENT (French: *parchemin;* Late Latin: *pergamina*) is a term derived from Pergamum, where parchment was supposedly first produced. The preparation of parchment, a durable writing material produced from hides (as of goats, sheep, or cattle), differs from that of leather essentially in that the soaked hide is stretched during drying. This procedure produces a transformation in the hide's fiber network and lends parchment its unique characteristics of flexibility and durability. Except in the very highest grades of parchment, it is usually possible to distinguish the original hide's hair side (marked by follicles) from its flesh side. To judge by surviving books, technical mastery of the parchment-making process was achieved no later than the fourth or fifth century. For deluxe books, parchment was sometimes dyed purple. In the seventh and eighth centuries, Arab control of Egypt limited European access to that country's papyrus production, so that book producers of the Latin West and Byzantium turned increasingly to locally manufactured parchment. Parchment remained the predominant material support for permanent books and records until, from about 1000 on, it began to be replaced by a new, seemingly cheaper writing material: paper. By the sixteenth century, parchment had become the exception and paper the rule.

BIBLIOGRAPHY

R. Reed, *Ancient Skins, Parchments, and Leathers* (1972); Anna Di Majo, Carlo Federici, and Marco Palma, "La pergamena dei codici altomedievali italiani," in *Scriptorium,* **39** (1985).

MICHAEL MCCORMICK

[See also **Paper, Introduction of; Papyrus; Writing Materials.**]

PAREKKLESION, a term used in the Greek church to distinguish a side chapel from the cathedral or from the principal church (*katholikon*) of a monastery. Parekklesia could be small and intimate in scale or could match the dimensions of the principal church, and they could be annexed to or separate from it; their uses also varied widely. At the famous twelfth-century Pantokrator Monastery (Zeyrek Čamii) in Constantinople, one parekklesion, dedicated to St. Michael, served as burial place of the imperial family; another, dedicated to the Mother of God, served as a semipublic shrine for the veneration of an important icon of the Virgin. In other situations parekklesia seem to have had a kind of stational use for special feasts or commemorations. The design and decoration varied with the use and importance of the chapel.

BIBLIOGRAPHY

Gordana Babić, *Les chapelles annexes des églises byzantines: Fonction liturgique et programmes iconographiques* (1969); Richard Krautheimer, *Early Christian Architecture* (1965), 258–261, 295–296, 307–309.

THOMAS F. MATHEWS

[See also **Early Christian and Byzantine Architecture (with illustration); Katholikon; Monastery; Pastophory** (with illustration).]

PARES, JOHN (*fl.* 1531–1539), also known as Parrys, was a wood carver of North Lew, Devon, who, in 1531, contracted jointly with John Daw of Lawhitton to make a rood loft, rood screen, and other fittings for the church in Stratton, Cornwall. The elaborate contract survives, although the woodwork, finished and paid for in 1539, does not. After the Stratton job, he is thought to have begun the screen that survives at Atherington, Devon.

BIBLIOGRAPHY

Richard W. Goulding, *Records of the Charity Known as Blanchminster's Charity* (1898); Lawrence Stone, *Sculpture in Britain: The Middle Ages* (1955, 2nd ed. 1972).

BARRIE SINGLETON

PARIS

FIFTH TO TWELFTH CENTURY

In 451, Attila and his Huns surrounded the city of Paris on their ravaging expedition through the West. The terrified Parisians prepared for Judgment Day when, as the legend goes, a young woman named Geneviève (*ca.* 422–*ca.* 500) went out of the city to meet the army. Shortly thereafter Attila and his hordes turned and headed south toward Orléans. Whether Geneviève's prayers and supplications affected Attila does not really matter; he spared Paris and Geneviève became the patroness of the city. She would deliver Paris on other occasions; as late as 1129 her relics carried in procession saved the populace from an epidemic of "burning sickness" (ergot poisoning).

When Geneviève met Attila in the mid fifth century, Paris was not worth a major pillage. For nearly half a millennium the city had been a minor Roman outpost named Lutetia and subordinate to the larger province of Sens (Senones). The Romans established Paris in 52 B.C. on an island, formerly inhabited by the Parisii tribe of ancient Gaul, in the Seine River in a basin near the convergence of the Seine, Marne, Oise, Yonne, and Loire rivers. During this period Paris was a small town, a garrison primarily used for military and administrative matters. Of primary importance to the early settlers of the Cité, as the island became known, was the defensive value of the location. From the Cité, the Romans extended the town of Lutetia to the Left Bank of the Seine and to the hill that was later named after Ste. Geneviève. On the marshy Right Bank stood only a few villas on the hill of Montmartre (named for Christians martyred there). Before Attila, Germanic tribes attacked the Left Bank of the city in 258, 273, 275, and 355, when the Roman Julian the Apostate came to its defense, and his troops named him emperor there in 360. Defenders built the first wall around the Cité during these early Germanic invasions.

At the time of Attila's march through the West, Paris had few administrative functions left. But the city's history as a capital began in this age of disarray and collapse. The fifth century saw a new wave of Germanic invaders, and by the end of the century the pagan Franks emerged as dominant in Gaul. Clovis (*r.* 481–511), leader of the tribe, received baptism into orthodox Christianity in 496 and thus forged an important alliance for the history of Western civilization. With the help of the church Clovis had all of northern France under his dominion when he died in 511. Nominated consul by the Roman ruler of the Eastern Roman Empire, the king of the Franks chose Paris as his capital, where he could watch over the lands of the Loire, Rhine, Elbe, and Pyrenees. Paris had other advantages as a capital. It was the city of Ste. Geneviève and also the apparent site of the grave of St. Denis, a third-century martyr who became the patron saint of France and the object of a fervent religious cult. Clovis's identification with St. Denis emphasized his role as a Christian champion in the conquering of Gaul.

The reign of Clovis's son Childebert I (*r.* 511–558) is notable for the foundation of the abbey of St. Germain-des-Prés, which, along with the abbey of Ste. Geneviève, dominated the Left Bank of Paris for most of the Middle Ages. Childebert also transferred the episcopal seat of Paris to the Cité from the suburb of St. Marcel. During the entire Middle Ages, the bishopric of Paris was subordinate to the archdiocese of Sens.

Except for a brief period under Dagobert I (*r.* 629–639), who founded the fair of Lendit, which would take on international significance in the later Middle Ages, Paris played a minor role during the remainder of the Merovingian and all of the Carolingian dynasties. These were centuries of disorder, violence, and turbulence as various lords fought for dominance in the emerging feudal system that developed after the collapse of central authority in the West. The little economic life and activity that existed in Paris took place in and around the great abbeys—St. Germain-des-Prés, Ste. Geneviève, St. Marcel, and St. Victor on the Left Bank, and St. Germain-l'Auxerrois and St. Martin-des-Champs on the Right Bank. The Cité contained the old Merovingian cathedral and the bishop's palace on one end of the island, and the king's residence on the westernmost point. Paris at the time was little more than an administrative center, a fortress, and a symbolic religious capital.

The city reached its nadir at the end of the ninth century, when a new series of marauders invaded Western Europe. The Normans from Scandinavia appeared and laid waste the coasts of England, France, and the Iberian Peninsula and finally went inland, for the Seine was easily navigable for these expert seamen. From November 885 to November 886, the raiders besieged Paris. Tradition claims that the body of Ste. Geneviève, transferred to the Cité in 885, protected the city once again from hostile forces. Be that as it may, the actual defense of the city was conducted by Eudes (Odo), count of Paris (later king, *r.* 888–898). The Carolingian Empire, united for the last time under Charles II the Fat (king, 884–887), was largely ineffectual in its defense of Paris. Eudes, his men, and the populace retreated to the Cité as the Normans surrounded the city. For an entire year the invaders unsuccessfully attempted to broach the defenses. When Charles the Fat finally arrived, he did not fight but bribed the Normans to go away and even gave them leave to spend the winter upstream in Burgundy.

The poor showing of the Carolingians in their contest with the Scandinavians led to a century of struggles for the French throne. The feudal magnates deposed Charles the Fat for his incompetence, but his successors were little better. The local French lords rewarded Eudes, count of Paris and descendant of Robert the Strong, for his heroic defense of Paris by choosing him as king. The crown then seesawed back and forth between Robertinians and Carolingians. The Carolingian kings weakened central authority even more by granting extensive lands to local lords for their support against the Robertinians. The French crown came to the Robertinians permanently in 987 with Hugh Capet (*r.* 987–996), founder of the Capetian dynasty that reigned in France for over three centuries.

The center of the Capetian family lands, Paris was only a shell of its former self at the end of the tenth century. Both the Left and Right banks were almost devoid of life after centuries of fighting and violence. However, with local lords as the ruling family, Paris once again became a political, economic, and administrative capital as political stability returned and the economy experienced revival.

During the reign of Henry I (1031–1060), the principal abbey on the Right Bank, St. Martin-des-Champs, was restored. Situated on the main road to the north, the abbey became not only a center of rural economy but also a way station for travelers and pilgrims. It was also on the Right Bank that Paris saw the formation of its first concentration of merchants. A market existed for years on the Cité and a small contingent of merchants clustered on the Left Bank near the bridge known as the Petit Pont to serve the modest settlements around the abbeys. But in the eleventh century a suburb on the Right Bank consisting largely of merchants began to form between the churches of St. Gervais and St. Merry. There, boats could bank on the Place de Grève, and a market developed that would eclipse the one on the Cité. Also on the Right Bank, the eleventh century saw small settlements around the churches of St. Germain-l'Auxerrois and St. Gervais. Commercial activity revived to the extent that in 1060 the king created the post of city provost to be in charge of urban policy and security.

Paris experienced its first renaissance under King Louis VI (*r.* 1108–1137). Population multiplied, spreading from the Cité, home of king, bishop, and clergy, first to the Right Bank and then to the Left. The economy revived and injected new life into the commercial quarter. Schools began sprouting up on the Left Bank and attracted the multitude of students who turned the area into a university quarter.

Before any urban and intellectual renaissance could take place, political order was necessary. Louis VI, "the Fat," was noted for his outstanding fighting abilities that brought some stability to the Île-de-France. Louis VI was a hardy warrior who beat into subjection the many feudal bandits who infested his lands and laid the groundwork for the great building of Paris during the late twelfth and early thirteenth centuries under his grandson, Philip II Augustus. Under Louis VI, the fair of St. Lazare was inaugurated in 1131 and construction of the abbey of Montmartre began in 1134. Louis was also a patron of Suger, abbot of St. Denis. The career of Suger, born of humble parents, is a prime example of the successful Capetian policy of cooperation with the church and the effective use of talent regardless of birth. Suger helped Louis VI administer his lands and was later appointed regent when Louis VII left on the Second Crusade.

Suger is best known, however, for his building of the church of St. Denis in the new Gothic style. The great prestige of the abbey, identified with the patron saint of France, made the architecture and especially the great use of light with stained-glass windows a model for other churches in Europe. The west facade of the church went up between 1137 and 1144, and the dedication of the new choir took place in 1144.

The reign of Louis VII (1137–1180) was largely unproductive. He spent much of his tenure losing territory to his English rival, Henry II Plantagenet (*r.* 1154–1189). Louis drained the marshes in Paris and put the land under cultivation. What marked his term most of all, however, was the building of another church—Notre Dame (from initial construction, 1163, to completion of the chancel)—the city's best-known medieval landmark. Notre Dame's progenitor was the bishop of Paris, Maurice de Sully, who, like Suger, was of humble origins. Early in his episcopacy Maurice began planning for a cathedral worthy of the capital city of the kingdom. Located on the eastern end of the Cité on the site of a former church of the same name, Notre Dame's vast foundation was consecrated in 1163 by Pope Alexander III. Taking more than a century to complete, the cathedral is 427 feet (130 m) long and 157 feet (47.85 m) wide, with towers rising 230 feet (70 m) above the ground, and the foundations 30 feet (9 m) below. Maurice was able to see the chancel (1163–1180) completed. During the reign of Philip II Augustus (*r.* 1180–1223), the transept and the nave were finished. By 1250 the west front had risen, and the south and north facades were completed by 1270. Begun in the incipient period of the Gothic, Notre Dame embodies the changes that occurred in architecture over the century and is a virtual textbook of early and high Gothic styles.

PHILIP II AUGUSTUS (*r.* 1180–1223)

Under Philip II Augustus, Paris developed into a royal capital on the grand scale. Philip was primarily an administrator and not a warrior. His great feat was to extend the royal domain from its feudal center, the Île-de-France, far into the rest of the kingdom, which he accomplished through cunning, warfare, and shrewd marriage alliances.

The king was then faced with the task of extending government services and functions into the great expanse of additional territory. Until Philip's time the French governmental bureaucracy was peripatetic. Most of the accoutrements of government traveled with the king from castle to castle and from campaign to campaign. In the Battle of Fréteval (1194), the king lost all of his baggage, which included the royal archives. This unfortunate occurrence led Philip to decide to centralize archival administration at the royal palace in Paris. He also deposited the treasury in the capital at the Temple, the fortress of the crusading order of the Knights Templar, and placed six burghers of Paris in charge of finances when he left on the Third Crusade in 1190. The government became much more sedentary, and records show that Philip made seventy-five stays in Paris, more than any other French monarch before him.

The royal capital needed defense, and early in Philip's reign, in 1190, he began building a wall around the Right Bank of the city. Since this was for the protection of the commercial section of Paris, the merchants partially funded the construction. The king showed himself to be one of the first urban planners in French history with his orders in 1210 and 1211 to build the walls on the more sparsely populated Left Bank. The Right Bank walls surrounded already inhabited quarters, but the Left Bank was still in its infancy, rural in character, and peopled mostly by peasants cultivating the vine and working the fields. Several burgs indeed existed, especially those surrounding the monasteries of St. Germain-des-Prés and Ste. Geneviève. Like rural municipalities, these abbeys even had mayors of their own. This area was slowly being populated. Urbanization accelerated only with Philip Augustus' building of the walls: the expanding economy and university hastened the process of renting and building. When the city became enclosed, it contained an area of 252 hectares.

Although population figures for the Middle Ages are notoriously unreliable, we know that within two decades of the circumvallation of Paris, the number of people living on the Left Bank increased dramatically. For example, in 1222 the old parish church of Ste. Geneviève was no longer able to accommodate its parishioners, so Pope Honorius III authorized the building of a new church, St. Étienne-du-Mont, and attributed the need to the great population increase. The total population of Paris at the end of Philip's reign was perhaps 60,000.

Philip did not concentrate only on the military defense of Paris. Pestilential stench rose from fetid streets that featured pigs running loose devouring the garbage that littered the city. The king caused these marshy streets to be drained and was responsible for introducing paving stones into Paris. He had the principal streets paved by 1186.

Philip's other contributions included the building of a hospital and the central market of Les Halles. The market of Champeaux on the Right Bank, instituted by Louis VI, was open air. In 1182, Philip expanded the market through the confiscation and demolition of the houses of the Jews, whom he had expelled from the city in the same year. The next year he had two large buildings put up on this location, and this remained the central market and food quarter of Paris until it was transferred out of the city in the 1960's.

THE UNIVERSITY

The final element that made Paris the great capital city of the High Middle Ages was the university. Beginning in the early twelfth century, Paris had a reputation as a center of liberal arts learning, and the city steadily drew students, scholars, and others from all parts of Europe. By the thirteenth century, we can conceive of the university as a primary "industry" that drew secondary or ancillary population segments as suppliers of services to the primary population of students and scholars.

Early in the twelfth century most learning in Paris took place in the cathedral school of Notre Dame on the Cité. There, famous masters such as William of Champeaux and Peter Abelard reigned. On the Left Bank the monastic schools of Ste. Geneviève and St. Victor were largely dormant, caring for a few young students. Following a quarrel with his old teacher William of Champeaux, Peter Abelard withdrew from the Cité and set up a school on the Left Bank on the north side of the Mont Ste. Geneviève. Abelard took his students with him and his fame attracted others from all over Europe. Other schools sprung up in rented rooms and halls on the Left Bank. By the second half of the twelfth century the number of teachers or masters increased greatly. It was at this time that the scholars began to form associations and societies for mutual protection from the authorities, and to decide who could be admitted to their ranks. The actual creation of the university was the outcome of a series of conflicts with the king's provost and the bishop's chancellor that resulted in the exemption of the students and masters from civil jurisdiction through the recognition of the scholars' clerical status, and the confirmation of the masters' authority to promulgate statutes and to exclude unqualified men from membership.

The university comprised the four faculties of theology, law, medicine, and arts, and the four nations of France, Picardy, Normandy, and England. The nations, reflecting the international character of the university and the very city itself, developed out of voluntary organizations of students from the same country. Of the four faculties, Paris was most renowned for theology, the "queen of the sciences." Law meant canon law, and civil law was not taught in Paris until the fifteenth century (it was forbidden by Pope Honorius III in 1219). Canon law was taught in the clos Bruneau. The faculty of medicine is mentioned as early as 1213 and was housed in the rue de la Bûcherie. The lower faculty of arts had students ranging in age from thirteen to twenty, and they were a very mixed breed indeed. Most arts courses were taught in the rue de Fouarre (named for the straw students sat on while attending lectures).

Paris was the birthplace of the collegiate system of student lodging. Students began living together in hostels in the late twelfth century, and each college was basically an endowed hostel. The earliest known college was the Collège des Dix-Huit (College of Eighteen), founded in 1118 by a certain Jocius of London, in which eighteen students were gathered to live in the Hôtel Dieu on the Cité. The most important of the numerous colleges that sprang up thereafter (twenty colleges alone were founded between 1300 and 1336) was that endowed in 1257 by Louis IX's chaplain, Robert de Sorbon, for sixteen poor masters of arts entering into the long study of theology. Eventually the college's name applied to the faculty of theology and then to the whole university.

With the centralization of the court and the development of the university, the character of land ownership in Paris changed. The importance of the university to the growth of the city is evident in the great number of clerics and university-related institutions owning property on the Left Bank.

Philip II Augustus' son, Louis VIII, reigned for only three years (1223–1226) and spent most of his time out of Paris fighting in the Albigensian Crusade. His heir was St. Louis, Louis IX (*r.* 1226–1270), who left a permanent mark on the city. Under Louis IX France knew its longest period of internal peace; and it was also under Louis that the great cultural flourishing of Paris took place.

Louis was an avid patron of the arts. The increasing centralization of his government drew men to his court, and from 1235 Paris was the cultural center of Europe. Nobles from all over France found it necessary to build grand *hôtels* in the city to be near king and court, just as the clerics needed to be near the university. It is during this period that the university reached its height, that the great Gothic cathedrals rose, and that medieval thought achieved its highest point with Alexander of Hales, Bonaventure, Albertus Magnus, and Thomas Aquinas (who all taught at Paris).

The artisans and tradesmen took on even more importance in the city during Louis's reign. Approximately one hundred different crafts and trades were practiced in the city in the thirteenth century. Most of the artisans clustered in their own quarters, giving them distinctive neighborhood characteristics.

Louis's major change to the face of Paris came with his additions to the Cité palace and the Louvre, and especially his construction of the Ste. Chapelle, a Gothic masterpiece erected between 1243/1245 and 1248.

The final years of the Capetian dynasty saw few changes for the better in Paris. Perhaps the most important occurrence during this period was Philip IV's (*r.* 1285–1314) suppression of the Knights Templar. The Templars, a former crusading order, grew rich as bankers to kings and popes. They had a large fortress in Paris. Philip accused them of a multitude of crimes, including sorcery. With the acquiescence of the pope, he brought the leaders to trial, had them convicted, and confiscated their funds. The Temple itself later became a prison.

FOURTEENTH AND FIFTEENTH CENTURIES

The fourteenth and fifteenth centuries were primarily a period of misery for Paris and the Parisians. It was a time of pestilence, famine, and war, scourges that did not subside until the dawn of the Renaissance.

Beginning in the early fourteenth century, a series of severe political, economic, and natural crises hit northern Europe and drastically affected Parisian life. Until the fourteenth century the rural sector expanded greatly, reached its limits, and then stopped. The high population density and the lack of new lands for cultivation caused hopeless fragmentation of many rural plots into smaller and smaller tenures that could not offer subsistence. This development helped create a class of rural landless peasants who became day laborers in order to survive. One of the consequences of this movement was the flood into the cities of many of the rural destitute and poor, thereby enlarging the urban population. Urban expansion continued as rural growth ceased. And even the onset of the crises of the fourteenth century caused only lapses in the cities' population growth, as it was constantly infused with new rural blood. At the beginning of the fourteenth century Paris had perhaps from 100,000 to 120,000 people.

The first natural catastrophe struck in 1314 with a poor wheat harvest brought about by heavy rains and unusually cold weather. The resulting rise in grain prices and a severe famine that lasted until 1317 were responsible for the deaths of many people. Contemporary chroniclers describe the streets of Paris being littered with the dead during these years of scarcity.

Compounding the economic difficulties of food prices was the French monarchy's policy, started by Philip IV, of debasing the currency and thereby causing severe inflation and monetary instability throughout the century. Concurrent with monetary destabilization was the placement of the kingdom on a war economy. Beginning with Philip VI de Valois (*r.* 1328–1350), and continuing until the fifteenth century, France was involved in the Hundred Years War with England.

Then in 1348 the Black Death epidemic struck Paris and the rest of Western Europe. The mortality was great in the city. One chronicler placed the deaths at over 50 percent of the population. Although we cannot determine exactly the number of deaths, it is obvious from all contemporary evidence that a great many died. The Black Death lasted until 1350, but periodic outbursts of plague occurred throughout the century.

Not long after the first wave of plague subsided, Paris experienced its first revolution. In 1356, King John II (*r.* 1350–1364) and his French army were almost annihilated by the English at the Battle of Poitiers. The English caught and imprisoned the king. His son Charles, the dauphin, became regent of the kingdom during his father's imprisonment. During the regency, the Estates General, composed of representatives of the clergy, nobility, and towns, played an important role in the kingdom. The spokesman for the urban craftsmen and merchants was the provost of Paris, Étienne Marcel, a wool draper. Marcel, allied with Charles II the Bad, king of Navarre (*r.* 1349–1387) and a claimant to the French throne, effectively took control of Paris in 1358 and posed a threat to the monarchy itself. For a time, Marcel allied his cause with the peasant uprising, the Jacquerie, that took place in the countryside around Paris and caused much carnage among both peasants and nobles alike. Then, from 1360 to 1365, the English ravaged the countryside, forcing thousands of inhabitants into the city. It was not until the truce of 1365 between Charles V and Charles the Bad, king of Navarre, that the Parisians could once again be at peace. This period of stability coincided with the reign of Charles V (1364–1380), who was the first monarch since Philip II Augustus to substantially change the face of Paris. Charles destroyed the old walls on the Right Bank and built new ones that greatly increased the area of the city. Both the Temple and the monastery of St. Martin-des-Champs were brought within the enclosure, and much of this rampart remained until the time of Louis XIV. Beginning in 1370, Charles erected the fortress St. Antoine, known to history as the Bastille, to protect the eastern approaches to the city. He almost entirely rebuilt the Louvre to house his magnificent library, and he built the sumptuous Hôtel de St. Pol.

When Charles V died in 1380, his eleven-year-old son Charles VI (*r.* 1380–1422) began his sorry reign, which saw his uncles, the dukes of Burgundy, Bourbon, and Berry, vie for control of the throne. In 1382 discontent with tax policies caused the Maillotin uprising in Paris, which resulted in the death or beating of many of the state's tax collectors.

Charles VI had his first bout with madness in 1392, and he became less and less lucid as his reign progressed. The king's uncle, Philip the Bold, duke of Burgundy (*d.* 1404), and his brother, Louis, duke of Orléans (*d.* 1407), fought for power as leaders of the Burgundian and Armagnac parties, respectively. To complicate matters, Henry V (*r.* 1413–1422) came to the throne in England, and the Hundred Years War flared anew after several years of relative peace. The Treaty of Troyes (1420) resulted in the English and the Burgundians occupying Paris for seventeen years. These were unhappy years for Paris, years of warfare, brigandage, famine, and hunger. During this period population fell dramatically. In a few months in the 1420's, 1,200 people left the city in search of food. The chronicler known as the Bourgeois of Paris reported in 1433 that wolves roamed the deserted city streets at night. Paris had indeed fallen from the heights of the High Middle Ages.

The dauphin, who became Charles VII, was able to return to Paris in 1437 and end the English occupation after years of fighting. Within two decades Paris was thriving and prosperous once again, although the French kings made few stays in the capital throughout the remainder of the fifteenth century. Charles VII (*r.* 1422–1461), Louis XI (*r.* 1461–1483), and Charles VIII (*r.* 1483–1498) spent much more time outside Paris than within, and the courtly life and culture moved with the monarchs.

Little remains of fifteenth-century Paris. The last phase of Gothic architecture, the "flamboyant," survives in the churches of St. Germain-l'Auxerrois, St. Séverin, and St. Médard. François Villon's poetry, reflecting the nether side of Paris life, is the major cultural product of the fifteenth-century city. Although the movement of the richer inhabitants to the Marais section of the city on the Right Bank resulted in the development of a district of fifteenth-century mansions (some restored during the latter twentieth century), artistic patronage went with the kings out of the city. Nevertheless, in 1470 a new invention was introduced into Paris—the printing press. The printed book became the harbinger of a new age and a different Paris—the Paris of the Renaissance.

BIBLIOGRAPHY

John W. Baldwin, *The Government of Philip Augustus* (1986); Amédée Boinet, *Les églises parisiennes,* 3 vols. (1958–1964); Robert Branner, *St. Louis and the Court Style in Gothic Architecture* (1965), and *Manuscript Painting in Paris During the Reign of Saint Louis* (1977); Raymond Cazelles, "Quelques réflexions à propos des mutations de la monnaie royale française (1295–1360)," in *Le moyen âge,* **72** (1966), "La population de Paris devant la Peste Noire," in *Académie des inscriptions et belles-lettres: Comptes rendus* (1966), and *Nouvelle histoire de Paris, de la fin du règne de Philippe Auguste à la mort de Charles V, 1223–1380* (1972); Pierre Champion, *François Villon: Sa vie et son temps,* 2 vols. (1913); André Chedéville, Jacques le Goff, and Jacques Rossiaud, *Histoire de la France urbaine: La ville médiévale des Carolingiens à la Renaissance* (1980); Esther Cohen, "Le vagabondage à Paris à la fin du XIVe siècle," in *Le moyen âge,* **88** (1982); Philippe Dollinger, "Le chiffre de population de Paris au XIVe siècle: 210,000 ou 80,000 habitants?" in *Révue historique,* **216**

(1956); Gustave Fagniez, *Études sur l'industrie et la classe industrielle à Paris au XIIIe et au XIVe siècle* (1877); Jean Favier, *Nouvelle histoire de Paris: Paris au XVe siècle* (1974), and *La Guerre de Cent Ans* (1980), 301–306; Guy Fourquin, *Les campagnes de la région parisienne à la fin du moyen âge: Du milieu du XIIIe siècle au début du XVIe siècle* (1964).

Adrien Friedmann, *Paris: Ses rues, ses paroisses du moyen âge à la revolution* (1959); Bronislaw Geremek, *Le salariat dans l'artisanat parisien aux XIIIe–XVe siècles* (1968), and *Les marginaux parisiens aux XIVe et XVe siècles* (1976); Louis Halphen, *Paris sous les premiers Capétiens (987–1223): Étude de topographie historique* (1909); Jacques Hillairet (André Auguste Coussillan), *Connaissance du vieux Paris,* 3 vols. (1954), also published as *Évocation du vieux-Paris,* 3 vols. (1952); Anna Jourdan, *Paris: Genèse de la "Ville." La rive droite de la Seine, des origines à 1223* (1976); Thérèse Kleindienst, "La topographie et l'exploitation des "Marais de Paris" du XIIe au XVIIe siècle," in *Mémoires de la Fédération des sociétés historiques et archéologiques de Paris et de l'Île-de France,* **14** (1963); Robert de Lasteyrie, ed., *Cartularie générale de Paris* (1887); Pierre Lavedan, *Nouvelle histoire de Paris: Histoire de l'urbanisme à Paris* (1975); Gordon Leff, *Paris and Oxford Universities in the Thirteenth and Fourteenth Centuries* (1968); Françoise Leohoux, *Le Bourg Saint-Germain-des-Près depuis les origines jusqu'à la fin de la Guerre de Cent Ans* (1951); René de Lespinasse, *Les métiers et corporations de la ville de Paris,* 3 vols. (1886–1897).

Henry S. Lucas, "The Great European Famine of 1315, 1316, and 1317," in *Speculum,* **5** (1930); Jean Martineau, *Les Halles de Paris: Des origines à 1789* (1960); François Olivier-Martin, *Histoire de la coutume de la prévôté et vicomté de Paris,* 2 vols. (1922–1930); *Paris: Croissance d'une capitale* (1961); *Paris: Fonctions d'une capitale* (1962); Édouard Perroy, "À l'origine d'une économie contractée. Les crises du XIVe siècle," in *Annales,* **4** (1949); Marcel Poëte, *Une vie de cité: Paris de naissance à nos jours,* 4 vols. (1924–1931); Hastings Rashdall, *The Universities of Europe in the Middle Ages,* F. M. Powicke and A. B. Emden, eds., 3 vols. (1936); Michel Roblin, *Les juifs de Paris: Démographie, économie, culture* (1952); Simone Roux, "L'habitat urbain au moyen âge: Le quartier de l'Université à Paris," in *Annales,* **24** (1969); Larry E. Sullivan, "The Exploitation of Land in Medieval Paris: The Abbey of Sainte-Geneviève," in *Mediaevalia* (1987); Louis Tanon, *Histoire des justices des anciennes églises et communautés monastiques de Paris* (1883); Alexandre Tuetey, ed., *Journal d'un bourgeois de Paris, 1405–1449* (1881).

LARRY E. SULLIVAN

[See also **Abelard, Peter; Albertus Magnus; Albigensians; Alexander III, Pope; Alexander of Hales; Angevins, Aquinas, St. Thomas; Black Death; Bonaventure, St.; Burgundy, Duchy of; Burgundy, Kingdom of; Capetian Family Origins; Carolingians and the Carolingian Empire; Charles V of France; Charles VII of France; Châtelet; Clovis; Dauphin; Dominicans; Expulsion of Jews; Fairs; France; Franciscans; Gothic, Flamboyant; Gothic Architecture; Hundred Years War; Huns; Jacquerie; Louis VI of France; Louis IX of France; Louis XI of France; Merovingians; Notre Dame de Paris, Cathedral of; Notre Dame School; Parlement of Paris; Philip IV the Fair; Philip VI de Valois; Plantagenets; Roman Empire, Late; St. Denis, Abbey Church; Ste. Chapelle, Paris; Suger of St. Denis; Villon, François; William of Champeaux.**]

PARIS, MATTHEW. See **Matthew Paris.**

PARIS PSALTER, the most famous illustrated Byzantine manuscript, dating probably from the tenth century and now located at the Bibliothèque Nationale in Paris (MS gr. 139). Its apparent classicism—most notably the personifications—made it the key document for the notion of a "Macedonian renaissance." It contains fourteen full-page miniatures, eight of which depict scenes from David's life and the other six accompany Old Testament odes. The large number of full-page illustrations also gave rise to the theory of an "aristocratic" system of psalter illuminations. This manuscript is a product of the most traditional forms of court art. The classical formulas together with the Old Testament figures, such as David, Moses, and prophets, display a paradigm of the ideal Byzantine emperor.

BIBLIOGRAPHY

Hugo Buchthal, *The Miniatures of the Paris Psalter* (1938), and "The Exaltation of David," in *Journal of the Warburg and Courtauld Institutes,* **37** (1974); Ioli Kalavrezou-Maxeiner, "The Paris Psalter," in *Eighth Annual Byzantine Studies Conference: Abstracts of Papers* (1982); Henri Omont, *Facsimilés des miniatures des plus anciens manuscripts grecs de la Bibliothèque Nationale* (1902); Kurt Weitzmann, "Der Pariser Psalter Ms. Grec. 139 und die mittelbyzantinische Renaissance," in *Jahrbuch für Kunstwissenschaft,* **6** (1929).

IOLI KALAVREZOU-MAXEINER

[See also **Byzantine Art; Macedonian Renaissance;** and frontispiece to this volume.]

PARIS, UNIVERSITY OF. With the development of the royal court and the emergence of the communal movement, the city of Paris became a pleasant, organized urban center in the eleventh and twelfth centuries, and as its schools developed, it became one of the great student cities of the medieval period. The school of Notre Dame Cathedral on the Cité and the abbey of St. Victor and the collegiate church of Ste. Geneviève on the Left Bank of the Seine had already by the end of the twelfth century attracted such famous masters as Hugh of St. Victor, Peter Abelard, Stephen of Tournai, and Peter Lombard. In 1180 Alexander Neckham was able to write of an "honorable society of masters" who were teaching arts, theology, canon law, and medicine, disciplines that would later form the four faculties of the university. At this time, the right to teach (*licentia docendi*) and therefore to become a master was given out by the chancellor of the cathedral chapter of Notre Dame.

The masters organized themselves into an association between 1180 and 1210, later called *universitas magistorum et discipulorum,* and both kings and popes granted it protective privileges. In 1200, Philip II Augustus bestowed a charter of privileges granting exemptions and immunity from civil and criminal jurisdiction to the students and masters, subject only to their own elected officials and the bishop of Paris. The popes also offered assistance to the new corporation.

In the beginning, Paris church officials opposed the formation of this independent society, which claimed legal status and its own seal. The papacy, however, sided with the university. Rules regulating its operation, called "statutes," were granted in 1215 by Robert of Courson, papal legate, and these dealt specifically with curriculum and textbooks. The university soon had its own elected officers, headed by a rector, and proctors who were put in charge of four "nations" of scholars: French, Picard, Norman, and English. (Other European students in the arts were made members of one of these four: for example, the German students belonged to the English nation and those from Eastern Europe to the French nation.) The elected "receptor" inscribed the accounts in the *Liber receptorum.* All the officers were assisted by the beadles.

One of the methods employed to protect university privileges was the suspension of classes and university sermons. It was used, for instance, following the student disturbances of 1229, when the provost and his cohorts injured and killed several students. Not receiving satisfaction from the authorities for this "affront," the corporation of university masters threatened to disperse, and scholars left for other places, including Oxford, Cambridge, Toulouse, Orléans, and Angers. Pope Gregory IX came to the rescue and aided the return of the students. On 13 April 1231 he issued a bull, *Parens scientiarum,* which is considered the quasi-foundation charter of the University of Paris. Masters were confirmed in their right to teach anywhere (*ius ubique docendi*). They were also permitted to teach from all the books of Aristotle, including those dealing with the natural sciences.

The coming of the mendicant Dominicans and Franciscans in 1217 strengthened the young university, but not without friction. During the dispersion of 1229–1231, the mendicants failed to join hands with the university masters, and they continued to teach their theology classes. By 1254 they controlled twelve of the fifteen theology chairs. When they refused to take the oath of obedience to the statutes as requested by the university in 1253, they were asked to cease teaching. When the mendicants refused, they were expelled (1254). Pope Alexander IV nevertheless ordered their readmittance. In 1255 he issued a much-disputed bull, *Quasi lignum vitae* (Like the tree of life)—ironically termed "Like the tree of death" by the secular masters, since it restricted their right to suspend classes. William of St. Amour (*d.* 1272), a secular master, led the opposition to the bull by writing *De periculis novissimorum temporum* in 1255, but the pope silenced him and ordered his exile from France. The dispute continued for eight years, and in 1261 the mendicants were finally readmitted, though the Dominicans were limited to two chairs in theology. The conflict strengthened the cohesion of the university, gave power to the faculty of arts, obtained reconfirmation of university privileges, and led to improved financial administration.

These controversies did not dim the university's reputation among scholars, and during the years 1245–1265, the mendicants provided a notable number of brilliant teachers and writers of great summae: Roger Bacon (*ca.* 1239–1247), St. Bonaventure (1248–1257), and St. Thomas Aquinas (during three periods, *ca.* 1245–1248, 1252–1259, 1269–1272).

The problem of Averroism (the study of Aristotle with the help of the commentaries of Averroës [Ibn Rushd]) was heralded by Siger of Brabant and preoccupied the faculty of arts between 1260 and 1275. The supposed transgression of the limits of philosophy by the masters of the faculty of arts was looked upon with suspicion by the old school of Augustinian theologians. In 1270 Étienne Tempier, bishop of Paris, censured thirteen philosophical treatises; a hurriedly composed second condemnation followed in 1277. The latter included 219 erroneous propositions and signaled the end of active scholasticism that attempted to harmonize reason and faith. Consequently, theologians toward the end of the century and the beginning of the fourteenth—Henry of Ghent, John Duns Scotus, and Meister Eckhart—turned toward Ibn Sīnā (Avicenna) and Neoplatonism.

Under Louis IX (1226–1270) and his son and grandson, important colleges were founded. These were residence halls for poor students, where scholastic disputations and limited teaching were conducted. At the end of the fifteenth and in the sixteenth century they became teaching centers. The Sorbonne (founded by Louis' chaplain, Robert de Sorbon) became in later centuries so prestigious that it often spoke for the whole university and especially for the faculty of theology. The College of Navarre, founded by Jeanne de Navarre, wife of Philip IV, was almost as influential. This system of colleges also grew up at Oxford and Cambridge about the same time.

In the first part of the fourteenth century intellectual leadership returned to the secular masters and to such orders as the Cistercians and Augustinians. Of the outstanding masters, Marsilius of Padua (*ca.* 1275–1342) criticized the contemporary ecclesiastical structures in his *Defensor pacis* (1324). William of Ockham (*d.* 1347), who never actually taught at Paris but whose works became available there during 1325–1335, advocated the separation of natural reason and faith, and his doctrine was censured in 1339 by the faculty of arts. Jean Buridan, rector of the university in 1328 and again in 1340, was a logician whose theory of impetus opposed Aristotle's theory of motion.

Upon the outbreak of the Great Schism in 1378, the university was divided. The English (English-German) and Picard nations remained faithful to Urban VI (*r.* 1378–1389, the pope in Rome), while the French and Norman nations, together with the three higher faculties, supported the Avignon pope, Clement VII (*r.* 1378–1394). In early 1379 the university adopted a policy of neutrality. Leading masters like Conrad Gelnhausen and Henry of Langenstein favored the convocation of a general council, but when the university, after a long debate, definitively accepted the Avignon pope in 1381, Urbanist scholars suffered in the distribution of benefices. The famous German masters—Henry of Langenstein, Henry of Oyta, and Marsilius of Inghen—left Paris during 1381–1383 to become vital forces in the newly founded German universities. At the Council of Constance (1414–1418), which was attended by 200 delegates from the university, John Gerson emerged as the leading spokesman, with Pierre d'Ailly a close second.

During the later years of the Middle Ages, the period of the Hundred Years War (1337–1453), the university suffered from the animosities between the political factions of Armagnacs, which supported the dauphin Charles, and the Burgundians. In 1418 John the Fearless, duke of Burgundy, recaptured Paris. His sympathizers avenged the Armagnacs and ransacked the College of Navarre; several masters were killed or injured. In 1420, upon the signing of the Treaty of Troyes, the university accepted the idea of "double monarchy," thereby recognizing the king of England as also the king of France, and threw its support behind the Burgundian cause. Paris masters, although acting in good faith, endorsed the condemnation of Joan of Arc in 1431.

The consequences of the Hundred Years War, particularly the years 1433–1438, were miserable for the university, already plagued by the absence of students. The English-German nation became almost extinct. After the reconciliation of the Burgundians with Charles VII in the Peace of Arras in 1435, the king kept his distance from Paris. Epidemics raged during 1438–1440, only after which foreign students once again returned to Paris.

Because of repeated suspensions of classes and interruptions of lectures, the university aroused the ire of Charles VII, and in 1446 he abolished its jurisdictional privileges and referred all civil cases to Parlement. Further reforms were mandated by a 1452 statute issued by the papal legate, William Cardinal d'Estouteville.

During the third decade of the fifteenth century, humanism penetrated the university, and Hebrew and Greek studies flourished. The centers of teaching also increasingly shifted from schools in the rue de Fouarre to the colleges. German printers set up in 1470 the first printshop established in France in a building of the Sorbonne, thanks to John of

Lapide (Heynlin) and William Fichet, fellows of the Sorbonne.

Louis XI (1461–1483) exhibited no more goodwill toward the university than did his predecessor, and upon the outbreak of war with the Burgundians in 1471, he requested oaths of allegiance from all Burgundian scholars. He then expelled some 400 of them for refusing to take the oath, thereby inflicting irreparable damage to the international character of the university, and ordered that in the future the rector had to be a subject of the king of France. Louis XI even interfered with the freedom of lecturing. In 1474 he forbade the teaching of nominalism at the university and ordered the books of the nominalists—William of Ockham, Buridan, Marsilius of Inghen, Albert of Saxony, and others—to be handed over to the president of Parlement. The lifting of the interdiction in 1481 was due to the intercession of Martinus Lemaître and Berenger Marchand. Louis XI's death in 1483 caused no regrets at the university.

The accession of Charles VIII in 1483 brought on a period of royal noninterference and goodwill. During the last quarter of the fifteenth century, the university attracted such great masters as the Swiss Petrus Tataret, the philosopher John Mair, Hector Boèce, Giles of Delft, James Ulfonis (Ulvsson) of Sweden (founder of the University of Uppsala in 1477), and the French humanists Robert Gaguin and Jacques Lefèvre d'Étaples.

With a greater number of students living in colleges, the last years of the fifteenth century were marked by increased disorder among those living in private housing. In 1498, Louis XII announced a series of reforms to remedy abuses committed in the name of university privileges, among them the fraudulent import of tax-exempt goods. He decreed that in the future only gifts from fathers to sons or from uncles to nephews could be covered by the privilege. Six months' residency at the university was required before the rector could give students testimonial letters. Students registered for the arts course were now required to stay four years to complete their studies; law students, seven years; medical students, eight; and theology students, fourteen. University privileges were to be withdrawn from students once these time periods lapsed. In another ordinance, dated 1499, the king sought to reform the tribunal of apostolic conservators, where abuses were also noted.

The university, misjudging his mood, ordered a suspension of classes, beginning May 29. The king, however, was highly offended by the tone of sermons directed against him, through George d'Amboise, archbishop of Rouen, and reprimanded the masters by reminding them that their principal task was the teaching of wisdom. He threatened to charge those who continued to participate in the suspension of classes with high treason. The university hurriedly lifted its sanctions. But Louis XII could no longer tolerate the university's independence, and in 1499 he abolished the masters' right to suspend classes and the masters' and students' immunity from civil and criminal jurisdiction because of their "clerical" status. Thus he transformed the university into a national institution. The fifteenth century ended with the loss of autonomy for the university that had once been the most privileged in Western Europe.

BIBLIOGRAPHY

Sources. The basic sources are *Chartularium universitatis parisiensis,* 4 vols. (1889–1897, repr. 1964), and *Auctarium chartularii universitatis parisiensis,* 6 vols. (1894–1964). Lynn Thorndike, *University Records and Life in the Middle Ages* (1944), provides English translations of many important Paris documents.

Studies. Gary C. Boyce, *The English-German Nation in the University of Paris During the Middle Ages* (1927); Alan B. Cobban, *The Medieval Universities* (1975); Astrik L. Gabriel, *Student Life in Ave Maria College, Mediaeval Paris* (1955), *Skara House at the Mediaeval University of Paris* (1960), and "The College System in the Fourteenth-century Universities," in Francis Lee Utley, ed. *The Forward Movement of the Fourteenth Century* (1961, repr. 1962); Louis Halphen *et al., Aspects de l'Université de Paris* (1949); Pearl Kibre, *The Nations in the Mediaeval Universities* (1948); Gaines Post, "Parisian Masters as a Corporation, 1200–1246," in *Speculum,* 9 (1934); Hastings Rashdall, *The Universities of the European Middle Ages,* F. M. Powicke and A. B. Emden, eds., 3 vols. (1936).

ASTRIK L. GABRIEL

[See also **Ailly, Pierre d'; Albertus Magnus; Alexander of Hales; Antiquarianism and Archaeology; Aquinas, St. Thomas; Aristotle in the Middle Ages; Arts, Seven Liberal; Bacon, Roger; Bologna, University of; Bonaventure, St.; Buridan, Jean; Cambridge, University of; Châtelet; Classical Literary Studies; Courson, Robert of; Gerson, John; Gilbert of Poitiers; Hugh of St. Victor; Joan of Arc, St.; Medicine, Schools of; Mendicant Orders; Neoplatonism; Oxford University; Parlement of Paris; Peter Lombard; Philosophy and Theology, Western European; Schism, Great; Scholasticism; Schools, Cathedral; Stephen of Tournai; Universities.**]

PARISH, the basic unit of ecclesiastical organization through which the medieval church carried out the prime activities in the care of souls. The parish system developed slowly throughout the Middle Ages, with considerable local differences in the pace of development and in the specific structure of its organization.

Historically, the medieval parish represented a second stage in the development of the basic organization of the Christian community. Christianity had begun as a city religion; the entire body of the faithful in each city formed a single community led by a bishop, the pastor responsible for providing the total range of necessary activities. Although the bishop was assisted by priests (presbyters), deacons, and minor clerics, he remained the one pastor of the entire city and the single head of the developing clerical hierarchy. This city community was often called a parish (Greek: *paroikia*; Latin: *parochia*). By the fourth century the term "diocese," borrowed from Roman civil administration, began to be applied to the same city-based community directed by a bishop. It was centuries before a distinction was recognized between these two terms as designations of different elements of church organization.

THE EARLY RURAL CHURCH

The first step in the development of the medieval parish system came in the fourth century, in response to problems caused by the spread of Christianity beyond its city base into the rural areas of the Roman Empire. The solution involved both the extension of the bishop's sphere of authority to include the episcopal city and the surrounding countryside, and the creation within this enlarged territory of rural subunits having the personnel, the resources, and the authority to carry out the required functions in the full sense that the bishop had previously done.

Bishops took the lead in building rural churches to meet new pastoral responsibilities. Typically, such churches were located in a *vicus,* a village with at least a modest concentration of population. To these churches the bishop assigned a clerical staff of priests, deacons, and minor clerics. In some larger rural churches these clergymen lived a semicommunal life under the supervision of an archpriest; smaller rural churches were often served by a single priest and one or two minor clerics. These churches steadily expanded the range of their religious activities until they had acquired the right to perform all the vital Christian services: baptism, celebration of Mass, administration of Communion and the last rites, burial of the dead, and preaching. In legal terms, these rights were delegated to the rural clergy by the bishop, but in practice they were increasingly associated with the church itself, possession of which gave the resident clergy the right to perform these services.

The expanding autonomy of rural churches was reinforced by the development of a patrimony specifically linked to each church. That patrimony consisted of an endowment of land provided when the church was built (and later supplemented by gifts), of the income from this land, and of the offerings of the faithful. Since the parish was initially considered part of the bishop's patrimony and was under his control, it was he who assigned the use of all or part of it to the clergy serving the rural church. Gradually in practice and in law, limits were placed on episcopal authority over resources attached to a particular rural church, especially over gifts given specifically to that church. The usage developed that each church had its own patrimony, which the clergy in possession of the church could dispose of as they saw fit.

Thus, between the fourth and the seventh centuries there developed across much of Christendom a considerable number of rural churches that possessed the right and the necessary resources to provide the full care of souls. This development by no means effaced episcopal authority, however. During these same centuries the episcopal structure was extended geographically and solidified internally. Within his episcopal city the bishop retained his traditional role. He also established crucial rights over the emerging rural churches: to consecrate church buildings; to ordain and confirm; to bless the holy oil required to assure the efficacy of baptism and last rites administered by the rural clergy; to appoint clergy to rural churches; to visit those churches; and to require the rural clergy to attend episcopal synods. These episcopal rights assured that the embryonic rural parishes would remain an organic part of a larger ecclesiastical entity.

THE SPREAD OF PRIVATE CHURCHES

While bishops were active in most parts of the early medieval world creating rural centers of pastoral care located in the *vici,* another development was underway, particularly in the German-dominated West, that was destined to have a major effect on the medieval parish system. This was the emergence of the private church, an institution from which many parishes eventually developed. As early as the fifth century, individual landowners, moved chiefly by a desire to provide a place of worship for themselves, their households, and their laborers, took the initiative in building chapels on their estates (villae). The founding of these local churches was powerfully abetted by the rapid spread of the cult of saints, which created a demand for shrines where the remains of local holy persons could be venerated and their aid invoked in gaining divine help to solve local problems.

The founding landowner—sometimes a bishop or an abbot, but most often a layman—provided both the resources to build the new church and an endowment to support religious services. Many early private churches depended on clergymen from a parish church in a neighboring *vicus* to perform such religious services as baptism or burial. There were, however, compelling reasons for such churches to have their own clergy to fulfill these needs, and their founders usually discovered ways to assure their presence.

Of no less significance than the spread of private churches was the development of a law governing their existence. In briefest terms that law came to define these establishments as proprietary churches (*Eigenkirche*) that were the private property of the owner of the land on which they stood. The evolution of the law governing proprietary churches is shrouded in obscurity and has been the subject of considerable debate. Without entering that debate, perhaps it is fair to say that the assumption of rights of private ownership over churches was a part of a larger phenomenon that was transforming society—the increasing lordship of landowners over all that was associated with land. In short, the emergence of the private church was a part of the feudalization of early medieval society.

As early as the sixth century the private churches located on villae were causing stresses within the ecclesiastical organization. Episcopal synods laid down a succession of regulations that reflected the bishops' efforts to contain private churches within the emerging parish structure centered in the *vici* churches. The bishops, however, increasingly failed in this effort. Not only did the number of private churches increase, but many of them gained the right to provide the full range of religious services for those they served; they became parishes in the same sense that the *vici* churches were parishes. But these new parishes had a distinctive character by virtue of the control exercised over them by landlords who considered them to be their private property.

THE AGE OF CAROLINGIAN REFORM

The Carolingian age (750–900) marked an important stage in the definition of the medieval parish system. The impetus to this development was the Carolingian reform effort, at the heart of which was an attempt to improve the practice of Christianity throughout the Frankish realm. In order to make the full range of religious services available to all Christians in locations convenient to their place of residence, parish churches were established on villae, where most people lived and worked—and where the private church system was entrenched. The Carolingian reformers also wished to improve the quality of pastoral services, which required the reassertion of the bishop's authority to define the norms of correct religious practice. As a consequence, Carolingian legislation in this area attempted to reconcile two opposing forces relating to the parish: the right of ownership held by the owner of the villa where the church was located and the right of direction of religious life held by the bishop in whose diocese the church was located.

Carolingian reforming legislation clearly established in public law the rights of private ownership over churches, permitting proprietors to dispose of churches as they would any other property, to select whomever they wished as priests who would "use" their property, and to define the terms under which the priest would serve. But the proprietor's rights were not unlimited. The legislation vigorously reaffirmed the bishop's authority over the practice of religion in every church in his diocese and over the priests installed in those churches. That same legislation set forth a broad range of directives defining the religious norms that bishops required priests to apply. Particular attention was given to assuring that each local church had sufficient material resources to permit the proper practice of religion, a matter that was not always certain with so many churches in private hands. The chief step taken in this direction was the imposition on all Christians of the tithe, defined as a tax of one-tenth on all produce of the land or on earnings from trade or handicraft work. Three-fourths of the income from the tithe was reserved for support of the parish, with the remainder allocated to the bishop. An effort was also made to define the minimum size of the grant (benefice) given to a parish priest: each priest was to be granted the returns from the tithe and at least one *mansus* of land (the amount of land required to support a household) with three serfs, for all of which the priest owed no service except pastoral activities. At least in theory, parish churches were assigned some material resources that could not be controlled by the landowners who owned the churches.

This is not the place to assess the outcome of the Carolingian reform in terms of strengthening Christian life. But the legislation did decisively affect the parish system. With its legalization, the private church system became more widespread. Most private churches acquired parish status with rights to perform the full range of necessary religious services. With the spread of the private church (usually attached to the villa), the number of parishes increased. These parishes were smaller than the early ones associated with the *vici*. Increasingly the parish included an area and a population sufficiently small to be served by a single priest and his assistants. Parish boundaries were more precisely defined, especially after the tithe was assigned to a parish church, making it imperative that each priest know exactly who owed the tithe to his church. Increasingly, each parish sought to exclude outsiders from participation in its religious services and to require that those belonging to the parish depend on its priest and his church for those services. In general terms, the system taking shape in the Carolingian age contained the basic elements that would govern the parish system for the remainder of the Middle Ages.

In practice, the Carolingian effort to make the private parish church an effective instrument for carrying out pastoral work directed by the episcopacy was not entirely successful. Even during the ninth century, a time of vigorous legislative effort to solidify the new system, private owners of parish churches whose rights had been recognized by Carolingian law were gaining the upper hand in determining the destiny of the parish. By the late ninth century and during the succeeding two centuries, their victory was complete. The proprietors of parish churches absorbed their ecclesiastical properties into the emerging feudal-seigneurial system in such a way as to establish the landowner's complete control over religious affairs. Since the majority of landowners were laymen, control of religion therefore passed from clerical to lay hands.

SECULARIZATION AND FEUDALIZATION

The processes involved in the secularization of parish churches through the feudalization of church property were extremely complex. The church and its appurtenances were treated as a fief to be granted in return for services, including religious services, rendered to the landowner and his dependents. Thus, the proprietor chose a clergyman and invested him with the fief—and sufficient material resources to serve that end. That clergyman in turn became the grantor's vassal, obliged to serve his lord in a variety of ways customary to the institution of vassalage.

Since the proprietor was usually interested in realizing the greatest profit from his ecclesiastical property, he selected as his priest-vassal whoever would take the office with the smallest benefice or would pay the most for the office. That part of the wealth pertaining to the church not required to provide support for the priest was diverted to the use of the proprietor; often this included not only land but also tithes and the offerings of the faithful. The proprietor tried to exact the maximum return from these sources by imposing charges for religious services and was frequently abetted in this traffic by his vassal-priest. Worst of all, the proprietor often put church property and income into the hands of others through gift, grant, sale, or any other means of conveyance utilized in feudal practice. The effect was the gradual distribution of the parish patrimony into many hands and the imposition on the parish community of a variety of jurisdictions defined by who possessed rights over pieces of parish land or parts of parish income.

As the feudalization of parish churches proceeded, episcopal authority was greatly reduced and the quality of pastoral care deteriorated. Responsibility for religious services fell into the hands of priests chosen for reasons other than their pastoral capabilities. The feudalization of their offices imposed on them obligations to their secular lords that distracted them from religious responsibilities. Usually married (despite church law forbidding clerical marriage), these priests necessarily sought ways to assure that their fiefs were passed to their children, a desperate game that increased their dependence on the lord. The dissolution of the patrimony led to the neglect of the physical facilities of the parish and impoverished the clergy to the point where they were forced to find other means of support, especially the selling of church services (simony). It has often been said that the absorption of the parish church into the feudal-seigneurial system during the tenth and eleventh centuries produced the darkest age in Christian history.

ECONOMIC REVIVAL AND RELIGIOUS REFORM

The medieval parish structure was given its final form as a result of two powerful movements affecting society in general between the late tenth and the early fourteenth centuries. The first involved a vigorous revival of economic, political, and intellectual life; the second, a major religious reform.

The powerful upsurge of society after about 1000 led to a substantial increase in the number of parishes. Population growth, the settling of new lands, the revival of cities, and the extension of Europe's boundaries by warfare, colonization, and missionary activity combined to create pressure for new churches almost everywhere. Old parishes were divided and new ones established to serve newly conquered, colonized, or converted areas. Especially significant was the introduction of the parish system into the rapidly growing cities. The building of churches to serve new parishes, the provision of material support for them, and the recruitment of clergy to serve them represented a major aspect of religious life during the High Middle Ages. By the end of the thirteenth century the effort had produced a parish geography that would change little until at least the Industrial Revolution of the late eighteenth century.

While parish geography was being reshaped, parish structure was being more precisely defined by forces emanating from a powerful reform movement aimed at freeing the entire church from the feudal-seigneurial system. From the perspective of parish history, this reform movement was not revolutionary. It sought to solidify the basic parish structure defined in the Carolingian age, to subject the parish unit to higher ecclesiastical authority, and to eliminate abuses besetting the system, especially lay control and simony. The broad framework of parish reform was defined by papal directives and conciliar legislation, and was eventually distilled into canon law. The details of reform were usually worked out at the episcopal level. As a consequence parish life between 1000 and 1350 was shaped according to general principles that could be applied to the entire Roman Catholic world—although with great variety from place to place. Not until the Council of Trent (1545–1563) was a detailed, uniform, universally applicable delineation of the parish system set forth in canon law.

One outcome of the reform movement was a major modification of the proprietary church system that greatly reduced lay control over parish churches. The change took two major forms. On the one hand, many laymen, caught up in the spirit of reform, surrendered their ownership of churches—often conveying their rights to monasteries, cathedral chapters, or even bishops—in return for pious favors. On the other hand, the canon lawyers worked out legal concepts that transformed proprietorship into patronage, by which the church conceded to the lay possessor of a parish church certain rights derived from the original endowment of the church. But these rights were limited to three areas: the rights to oversee the administration of parish property, to present to the bishop a candidate for the office of parish priest, and to enjoy various extra considerations, such as special seating or burial in the parish church. Although the patronage system presented its own problems, its widespread acceptance greatly reduced the domination of parish life by landowners.

As the parish system was being partially extricated from lay control and feudal practices, its internal structure was being given more precise shape. Parish boundaries were fixed, and the definition of the parish as a territorial entity became generally accepted. By 1300 the principle was fixed in law and observed in practice that this territory was subject to a single clerical leader. Although still designated by a variety of titles, this official was increasingly called rector (*rector*) or curate (*curatus*), both terms connoting the exercise of a specific authority. The rector was nominated by the patron, and appointed and installed by the bishop after the latter had ascertained the candidate's fitness. A constant stream of reforming legislation sought to define fitness in terms of age (at least twenty-five years), condition of birth (legitimate), celibacy, education (ability to read, knowledge of basic doctrine and liturgical usages), and moral qualities (sobriety, honesty, restraint in eating and dress), but the evidence suggests that these requirements were not strictly observed.

By 1300 the rector's responsibilities were clearly defined. Above all, he was responsible for the care of souls, centering on the celebration of Mass, the administration of sacraments, and the teaching of the faithful. The good pastor was expected to watch over his flock to see that each fulfilled his or her religious duties, and to report habitual sinners and heretics to the bishop for judgment and punishment. He carried out parish charitable works and administered the parish property in a way that would assure resources to carry on religious worship, to maintain church buildings, and to provide his own support. The typical rector also played an important social role in the parish as mediator of quarrels, chief scribe for drawing up wills and business documents for illiterate parishioners, reporter of crimes to civil authorities, and bearer of complaints to those who held power over the community. Taken together, these burdens were heavy. In most parishes the rector was assisted by priests, deacons, and lesser clergy, all of whom he chose and remunerated as he saw fit.

THE PARISH PATRIMONY

During the age of reform, popes and bishops made a concerted effort to provide adequate material support for parish churches and to develop a system of controls over these resources that would assure their use for religious purposes. As a result, a basic system of parish support became fairly clearly defined. Each parish had a patrimony that the bishop granted to the rector as a benefice. The rector was not permitted to dispose of any part of this patrimony or to use income from it for improper purposes; it was his duty to use the patrimony prudently and to increase it if possible. The patrimony was composed of several elements: the church building and its cemetery; the landed endowment, including the rector's living quarters, a garden, and fields with serfs attached; certain incomes due in kind or in money, including tithes, offerings made by the faithful, and contributions (increasingly fixed charges) made on the occasion of the administration of sacraments; and pious foundations established to provide for special religious services, especially masses for the dead. The bulk of the income went to support the parish clergy, to provide for religious ceremonies, to maintain the church building and its furnishings, and to assist the poor, sick, and aged. In addition, the rector was responsible for a variety of payments to the bishop and, increasingly, to the pope. Despite repeated prohibitions, patrons continued to exact a share of the income of the parish patrimony. There were so many variables in the constitution of the parish patrimony, in realizing its potential, and in dispensing its return that it is impossible to generalize, except perhaps to say that by the thirteenth and fourteenth centuries the support system was better defined and less subject to manipulation for nonreligious purposes than had been true earlier.

THE PARISHIONERS

There remained one more element of the medieval parish: its membership, as defined by residence within its boundaries. Each parishioner was required to fulfill all religious obligations within the parish; nonmembers were excluded from participation. Thus, the parish constituted a closed community whose members were bound together by virtue of following a common religious leader and sharing a common set of religious experiences focused in one spot, the parish church. In return for the spiritual gifts they received, the parishioners shared the responsibility for sustaining parish life by paying tithes, making offerings, and remembering the church in their wills. While ecclesiastical law generally presumed that the rector possessed complete authority over his flock, surviving evidence suggests that parishioners had some voice in parish affairs, particularly in urban parishes. They sometimes took part in selecting the rector, in the management of parish resources, in deciding on new church buildings, in determining charges for religious services, and in establishing the frequency and form of religious services. Thus, in a variety of ways the mature medieval parish, based on sustained involvement of a compact body of people in a common religious experience, represented a vital social organism providing stability in society.

While the medieval parish was assuming its internal structure, other developments served to incorporate the parish more tightly into the ecclesiastical hierarchy, especially the episcopal structure. This is not the place to describe the evolution of effective episcopal control over parish life or to discuss how it impacted on the parish. It is important to note, however, that this trend tended to standardize and universalize religious usages, which fostered a commonality between the members of a single parish and the members of thousands of others across the entire Roman Catholic world of the late Middle Ages.

LATE MEDIEVAL DEVELOPMENTS

By 1300 the parish had assumed its basic features over most of Europe: a clearly defined territory, a properly equipped church building, a rector, a patrimony, and a community of souls served by a well-defined set of religious practices. A body of law had evolved defining the parish structure, its internal workings, and its relationships to other agencies in the ecclesiastical and secular worlds. There were few fundamental changes in parish structure during the late Middle Ages—nor, in fact, long afterward.

To complete a picture of the medieval parish, however, it is necessary to note certain late medieval developments that led to adjustments and tensions in the system described above. Not surprisingly, the assault on the parish patrimony continued. Aside from the depredations of patrons, the most serious threat to parish properties in the late Middle Ages resulted from the large-scale appropriation of parish churches by monasteries and cathedral chapters, and the diversion of parish resources to the religious ends of these establishments—ends that often had little to do with the care of souls. New difficulties arose with respect to the designation of rectors, from the growing practice of separating the rector's office from the associated benefice. This meant that an individual could be granted the use of the parish patrimony without assuming the office of rector—as long as he found someone else, a vicar, to substitute for him in discharging the religious duties of the office. Those with rights to designate rectors—bishops, monasteries, cathedral chapters, lay patrons, popes—granted parish churches to those who were not equipped to serve, or who had no intention of serving, in the parish where the church was located. Enterprising clerics made a business of acquiring plural benefices, which increasingly left the care of souls in the hands of ill-trained, ill-paid vicars who were little respected by their parishioners. In this way, the resources of the parish were diverted to absentee titularies who derived a living from parish income but had nothing to do with parish life.

While parish leadership was being weakened by absenteeism and pluralism, other forces were also operating to undermine parish unity. Papal dispensations increasingly freed some parishioners, particularly those who could afford to pay, from parish religious observances and financial responsibilities. New organizational structures appeared within the parish boundaries to serve special needs of parishioners: confraternities to promote piety and charity; private chapels (chantries) served by specially designated priests who carried on religious activities for a donor's special benefit, especially masses for the dead; lay churchwardens who assumed responsibility for upkeep of the parish church and its furnishings, and took control of part of the parish resources for this purpose.

Particularly disruptive was the intrusion of the mendicant orders, which claimed a role in the care of souls. Zealously devoted to improving religious life among all the faithful and armed with papal sanction, the Franciscans and the Dominicans invaded parish after parish across Europe to preach, reconcile sinners, and intensify spiritual life. Because of their zeal and their superior preparation, they made a powerful impression on the parish populace. Their pride challenged and their income diverted to the intruders, the parish rectors and their bishops fought back. The result was an extended and unseemly quarrel that confused many concerning the locus of religious authority within the parish. Although many of these threats to parish unity represented new sources of spiritual vitality in the late Middle Ages, they still ran counter to the essential nature of the parish as it had been defined over a long period, and thus placed strains on that institution.

Finally, some evidence from the late Middle Ages suggests stress on the parish system resulting from what might be termed a missing ingredient in its structure or, perhaps better, an underdeveloped aspect of its mode of caring for souls. It is only from the thirteenth century on that records survive in sufficient fullness to permit the historian to get some feel for parish life. Even taking into account that these records—chiefly in the form of synodal legislation, episcopal visitation records, judicial proceedings, and moralists' tracts—are of a kind that emphasize shortcomings in Christian practice, one is still forced to conclude that parish religious life was far from ideal. The record portrays a badly trained, morally lax, materialistic clergy presiding over an ignorant, irreverent, and undisciplined flock. Everything points to the fact that the medieval parish always lacked the means to teach the meaning of Christianity in any depth or to sustain believers in disciplined observance of that religion. Perhaps this flaw in the medieval parish system explains why spiritual leaders throughout the Middle Ages advocated—to no avail—the need for parish schools directed by educated rectors.

Despite the travail that accompanied its definition and the problems that almost always beset its development, the medieval parish represented an effective means of aggregating people to serve what were perceived to be the fundamental ends of religious life. No less significant in terms of medieval society as a whole, the parish structure developed in such a way as to create discrete religious communities that usually coincided with the basic communities as defined by economic, social, and political structures. Thus, the medieval parish became one of the fundamental foci around which medieval life unfolded. An understanding of the structure and the function of the medieval parish provides a basic clue to understanding medieval civilization; its study warrants continued attention.

BIBLIOGRAPHY

Paul Adam, *La vie paroissiale en France au XIVe siècle* (1964); George W. O. Addleshaw, *The Development of the Parochial System from Charlemagne (768–814) to Urban II (1088–1099)* (1954, 2nd ed. 1970), *Rectors, Vicars, and Patrons in Twelfth and Early Thirteenth Century Canon Law* (1956), and *The Beginning of the Parochial System*, 3rd ed. (1970); Émile Amann and Auguste Dumas, *L'église au pouvoir des laïques (888–1057)* (1948), 265–290, 465–482; Henry G. J. Beck, *The Pastoral Care of Souls in South-east France During the Sixth Century* (1950); Catherine E. Boyd, *Tithes and Parishes in Medieval Italy: The Historical Roots of a Modern Problem* (1952); Olga Dobiache-Rojdestvensky, *La vie paroissiale en France au XIIIe siècle d'après les actes épiscopaux* (1911); Hans Feine, *Kirchliche Rechtsgeschichte*, I, 2nd ed. (1954), 35–42, 88–91, 114–121, 147–199, 227 240, 345–378; Giuseppe Forchielli, *La pieve rurale: Ricerche sulla storia costituzione della chiesa in Italia e particolarmente nel Veronese* (1938); Jean Gaudemet, *Le gouvernement de l'église à l'époque classique*, pt. 2, *Le gouvernement local* (1979), 217–320; John Godfrey, *The English Parish, 600–1300* (1969); Élie Griffe, *La Gaulle chrétienne à l'époque romaine*, new ed., rev. and enl., III (1964–1966), 260–298; Reginald A. R. Hartridge, *A History of Vicarages in the Middle Ages* (1930); Pierre Imbart de La Tour, *Les paroisses rurales du IVe au Xe siècle* (1900, repr. 1979); Dietrich Kurze, *Pfarrerwahlen im Mittelalter: Ein Beitrag zur Geschichte der Gemeinde und des Niederkirchenwesens* (1966); Gabriel Le Bras, *Institutions ecclésiastiques de la chrétienté médiévale*, 2 vols. (1959), esp. 203–230, 282–302, 363–441; Ferdinand Lot and Robert Fawtier, eds., *Histoire des institutions françaises au moyen âge*, III, Jean-François Lemarignier, Jean Gaudemet, and Guillaume Mollat, eds., *Institutions ecclésiastiques* (1962), 23–25, 98–114, 197–219, 380–406; John R. H. Moorman, *Church Life in England in the Thirteenth Century* (1945, repr. 1955), 1–241; Colin Platt, *The Parish Churches of Medieval England* (1981); Willibald M. Plöchl, *Geschichte des Kirchenrechts*, 2nd ed., I (1960), 47–61, 165–175, 342–359, 426–440, and II (1962), 141–176, 401–461; Ulrich Stutz, "The Proprietary Church as an Element of Mediaeval Germanic Ecclesiastical Law," in *Mediaeval Germany, 911–1250: Essays by German Historians*, Geoffrey Barraclough, trans., II (1938, repr. 1961), and *Geschichte des kirchlichen Benefizialwesens von seinen Anfängen bis auf die Zeit Alexanders III*, 3rd ed. (1972).

RICHARD E. SULLIVAN

[See also **Benefice, Ecclesiastical; Carolingians and the Carolingian Empire; Celibacy; Church, Latin: 1054–1305; Church, Latin: Organization; Clergy; Councils, Western (869–1179); Diocese, Ecclesiastical; Gregory VII, Pope; Penance and Penitentials; Religious Instruction; Simony; Tithes; Village Life.**]

PARLEMENT OF PARIS. The Parlement of Paris, the supreme tribunal of the French monarchy, evolved from the royal court and emerged as a distinct institution by the mid fourteenth century. French kings steadfastly maintained that they were the ultimate source of justice in their realm, and through the Parlement of Paris, they were able to make that claim a cornerstone of their authority.

For a very long time the kings' relatively small territorial possessions and lack of an effective bureaucracy made it impossible to enforce such claims. In the reign of Philip II Augustus (1180–1223), circumstances changed. As a result of fortuitous political events, the king gained control of important lands, including Normandy and Anjou, formerly under English authority. These acquisitions were naturally significant as a source of wealth for the French monarchy, but just as important was the fact that these lands required royal administration, necessitating the employment of officials to protect monarchical interests in the local areas and the development of a central bureaucracy to oversee those officers. Known as baillis in the north and seneschals in the south of France, the local representatives of the crown held vast jurisdictional and financial powers in their areas of governance. With zeal and great dedication to the extension of royal power, they asserted monarchical authority at every possible opportunity and enjoyed enormous success in so doing.

Simultaneously the French king's court began to develop as a necessary complement to the evolution of local administration. In the first half of the thirteenth century, however, the royal court was still a loosely organized body that assisted the king

PARLEMENT OF PARIS

in ruling but had no defined functions, specialized departments, nor stable membership. The court included the king's vassals, who participated when they were summoned, as when the monarch had a grievance against one of their peers. Other members of the court were the permanent advisers of the king, collectively known as the *hôtel dui roi,* who accompanied him everywhere he went. Among them were the experts in law (*iurisperiti*), who assisted in the judgment of suits involving the king and his vassals.

Under the guidance of Louis IX (1226–1270), there began within the royal court the development of a specific body concerned with matters of royal jurisdiction. While part of the court, the *grand conseil,* continued to accompany the king on his travels, other royal officials remained in Paris to look after the crown's financial and judicial interests. When those involved in matters of royal jurisdiction met, they constituted the group that became the Parlement of Paris. The word *parlement* had been used as early as 1239 to refer to discussions among the king and the members of his court, and in the early years of its development, Parlement not only served as a strictly judicial body but also provided an opportunity for the discussion of local interests and concerns between royal officials and subjects.

The 1259/1260 decision of Louis IX to abolish appeal by combat was very important in the early development of Parlement. That ancient practice had required a litigant who felt wronged by a verdict to challenge and fight the judge or his representative before a superior tribunal. In its place the king substituted the appeal procedure employed by the church, which required legal knowledge in the determination of every case. In this method the litigant appealed a verdict to a superior court, which would determine the legitimacy of his complaint, usually by examining evidence gathered by a commission of inquest. Thus an individual dissatisfied with the decision of a lower court, whether that of the king or of one of his vassals, might ultimately appeal the decision to Parlement, the highest jurisdictional body in the kingdom.

In the reigns of Louis IX and his successors, Parlement used still other jurisdictional claims to bring cases to its authority. According to one, somewhat related to appeal, any subject who believed he had been denied justice by the refusal or unreasonable delay of a lower court to hear his suit might bring that case to the attention of Parlement. In addition, the crown claimed that its court had immediate jurisdiction over all disputes involving the peace of the realm. As none of the Capetians ever precisely defined these so-called royal cases, they provided almost limitless opportunities for Parlement's assertion of the jurisdictional supremacy of the crown.

Through a complex of mechanisms, then, Parlement asserted its right to hear cases from virtually every part of France, either directly or on appeal. The system, as it developed, was anything but tidy, mixing original and appellate jurisdiction, and even civil and criminal cases. But Parlement was effective in asserting royal authority pretty much throughout the realm, and that is what the king wanted.

It is hardly surprising, however, that the Capetians' great vassals protested heartily as royal judicial claims began to weaken their authority in their domains. In the thirteenth and fourteenth centuries, the count of Flanders and the dukes of Aquitaine, Brittany, and Burgundy sought and worked out agreements with the crown to regulate the exercise of Parlement's jurisdiction in their areas. As Joseph Strayer has noted in his *The Reign of Philip the Fair:* "It was well to impress a great baron with the supremacy of royal justice, but it was folly to push these assertions of supremacy to a point where they might lead to revolt."

During the late thirteenth century the Parlement of Paris began to develop as a body with distinct characteristics. As early as 1254, official records of its sessions were being kept, although the earliest of them, the *Olim,* merely summarized some cases and ignored others. In the same period Parlement began to meet regularly, initially three times annually, a number gradually reduced in the following years as the terms lengthened. By the end of the thirteenth century, men who had been trained as jurists began to dominate the court. To be sure, the king's advisers, lay and ecclesiastical lords, and even local royal officials also acted as judges in Parlement from time to time. The specially trained *magistri,* however, had power because of their numbers and because of their tenure, which was coming to be virtually lifelong. These developments indicate that Parlement was becoming both more exclusively legal in its activities and increasingly stable as a body within the royal court.

Early on, Parlement organized itself into three main bodies. First and most important was the Grand'Chambre, which always rendered the final decision in a case. The Grand'Chambre was

PARLEMENT OF PARIS

assisted by the Chambre des Requêtes and the Chambre des Enquêtes. In general, Requêtes decided whether Parlement should take a case, and Enquêtes collected and summarized the evidence in cases that were taken. Over the centuries there were many variations in Parlement's structure, but these three bodies remained basic to its organization and procedure.

Criminal cases presented a problem for Parlement because many of its judges were churchmen, and the church did not want clerics deciding cases where the punishment involved the shedding of blood. A delegation of lay judges took to meeting separately to decide criminal cases; this body came to be called the Tournelle, from the small tower in the palace where it met. (The Grand'Chambre, however, did continue to judge many important criminal cases.)

Another stimulus to innovation was Roman law. During the thirteenth century, and especially in the aftermath of the Albigensian Crusade, the king's authority in the south of France increased dramatically. Legal traditions in the south were very different from those in the north; the south was far more dependent on Roman law, while the north relied more heavily on custom. The king's governors, or seneschals, generally knew little Roman law and had to take the advice of local men they named as judges. Philip III (1270–1285) tried to gain more control by sending a commission from Parlement to sit in Toulouse and judge all cases in the area according to written (that is, Roman) law. In 1291, the crown abolished this commission and reverted to the old system of local judges. All litigants from Languedoc, however, could appeal to the Parlement of Paris. These appeals increased the work load of Parlement and forced the judges there to acquire some knowledge of a legal tradition that had been relatively unimportant to them in the past.

As in other areas of monarchical authority, the reign of Philip IV (1285–1314) was a period of significant growth for Parlement. Indeed, that king was once thought to be its founder. While Louis IX now holds that title, it is nonetheless true that the brilliant and forceful expressions of royal legal authority by Philip IV and his advisers made Parlement more than ever before the embodiment of the crown's jurisdictional supremacy.

By the time of Philip's reign, Parlement's sessions were crowded spectacles. Some of the individuals present assisted the judges in the performance of their duties. These assistants included notaries to perform routine legal tasks, *huissiers* to maintain order, and *greffiers* to keep records. In addition to the numerous litigants and their families and friends, there were numerous proctors (*procureurs*) and advocates (*avocats*), who were roughly equivalent in functions to the modern English solicitors and barristers respectively.

As neither the king nor even his chancellor normally attended Parlement's sessions, the crown came to have its proctors and advocates, who were known collectively as the *gens du roi*. The most important of these, the *procureur-général*, was really a kind of medieval district attorney. Not only was he responsible for defending the king's rights, he was also charged with defending the king's peace, and he had the power to investigate and prosecute violations of the law even if there was no complaint from an injured party.

Most important, however, were the judges of the three chambers of Parlement. A royal ordinance issued around 1296 indicates that the bench had become crowded, with some forty-seven judges in the Grand'Chambre. Of those forty-seven, forty-one were jurists, an indication of the high degree of professionalism in Philip IV's Parlement.

It would be a mistake, however, to view the Parlement solely as a court of law at any time during its existence. In the modern American view of government, the division of judicial, legislative, and executive powers is basic; in medieval France it was not. The king was the source of law, and he relied on the Parlement to do much of his legal work for him. But neither king nor Parlement restricted its activities to sitting in judgment.

The Parlement exercised substantial police powers. It had the power, at least in theory, to enforce its judgments, and it had a more general police power that was the source of great authority in municipal administration. In 1499, for instance, when a bridge over the Seine collapsed into the river with its houses, Parlement immediately imprisoned the mayor and temporarily took over his duties. In general these powers of municipal administration extended wherever the royal power did, but it is perhaps understandable that Parlement was most concerned with Paris.

Parlement was also involved in overseeing—and protecting—the universities, particularly the ones in Paris and Orléans. Students were a boisterous lot in the Middle Ages, and town-gown conflicts were common. At Paris in 1404, a university procession met up with retainers of the king's chamberlain,

PARLEMENT OF PARIS

who were leading their horses to drink at the river's edge. The traffic jam developed into a riot in which a number of students were wounded. Parlement's punishment of the king's chamberlain was severe. Among other things he was required to tear down his house, of which he was particularly proud.

The Parlement was not just active in Paris; it was enmeshed in Paris. Situated in the old royal palace on the Île de la Cité, it was at the center of the city's hustle and bustle, and it was the best show in town. Parisians as well as visitors went there, even if they had no business, simply to watch the goings-on. The clerks who assisted in the court even took to putting on plays, which Parlement by turns approved and condemned. These clerks' farces were the only comic element in French theater before the Renaissance.

Parlement also exercised a form of legislative power. In a modern democracy such as the United States, legislative power derives from the people, who elect legislators to make laws for them. In medieval France the king was the source of law. When legislation was required, he could simply issue an ordinance. However, the king was expected to consult with his court before he made a law, and the practice arose of the king's sending his ordinances to Parlement to have them registered on its rolls. Occasionally, Parlement would find flaws in the proposed legislation and suggest changes. This procedure was eventually formalized and called a *remontrance.* The king could, of course, decline to make the changes. The Parlement could then decline to register the ordinance. The king could, however, by a mechanism known as a *lettre de jussion,* insist upon registration, and Parlement would comply. Sometimes, in such circumstances, the king would sit in Parlement, just to remind everyone who held ultimate power. This unusual procedure, in which time rolled backward, and the Parlement ceased for a moment to be a premodern governmental bureaucracy and became briefly the personal court of the king, was known as a *lit de justice.*

The king had various other mechanisms by which he circumscribed the powers of Parlement. One that Parlement found particularly galling was the creation of competing law courts. Perhaps the most upsetting was a late arrival, the Grand'Conseil, which acquired a distinct identity only in 1497, when it was separated from the king's council.

Other major challenges came from the various provincial Parlements that were created during the fifteenth century. These Parlements are best seen not as an innovation but simply as a new wrinkle in the long history of provincial judicial autonomy.

This process may perhaps be best seen in the Exchequer of Normandy. Originally set up by the dukes of Normandy, this court was taken over by Philip Augustus when he seized the duchy in 1202–1204. At that time there was no Parlement of Paris. The king sent men from his court to sit as judges in the Exchequer, and in later years Parlement began to hear appeals from the Exchequer. This provoked such opposition in Normandy, however, that in 1315 Louis X found it expedient to issue the *Charte aux Normands,* which, among other things, restored judicial sovereignty to the Exchequer—that is, the king abolished the mechanism of appeal from the Exchequer to the Parlement of Paris. However, Parlement continued to send judges to sit in the Exchequer, and the right of appeal to Parlement was reestablished after a few years.

In the fifteenth century the kings of France began to establish in various provinces Parlements that had the same final authority that the Parlement of Paris held in its (now diminishing) areas of jurisdiction. The first of these provincial Parlements was that of Toulouse, established in 1443. Others were established in Dauphiné, Bordeaux, and Burgundy. In 1499 the Norman Exchequer was reorganized on this new model; some years later it was renamed the Parlement of Rouen.

Even though the Parlement of Paris never succeeded in achieving a truly national jurisdiction, it did play a central role in the life of the French nation. It had a special relationship with the king of France that none of the provincial Parlements ever had, and it was a national institution in a way that they could never be. Its very uniqueness makes it a difficult institution for the modern mind to grasp. The eminent French historian Ferdinand Lot has called the Parlement of Paris the most original institution of medieval France; certainly he was correct when he said there was nothing like it anywhere else.

BIBLIOGRAPHY

Sources. Arthur Beugnot, *Les Olim,* 3 vols. in 4 (1839–1848); Edgard Boutaric, *Actes du Parlement de Paris, première série, de l 'an 1254 à l'an 1328,* 2 vols. (1863–1867); Henri Furgeot, *Actes du Parlement de Paris, deuxième série, de l'an 1328 à l'an 1350,* 3 vols. (1920–1975); Charles Victor Langlois, "Rouleaux d'ar-

PARLER FAMILY

rêts de la cour du roi au XIIIe siècle," in *Bibliothèque de l'École des chartes,* **48** (1887), and **50** (1889), and *Textes relatifs à l'histoire du Parlement depuis les origines jusqu'en 1314* (1888). See also Henri Stein, *Inventaire analytique des ordonnances enregistrées au Parlement de Paris* (1908).

Studies. In English, J. H. Shennan, *The Parlement of Paris* (1968), covers the medieval and later periods. Most of the principal studies are in French: Félix Aubert, *Le Parlement de Paris de Philippe le Bel à Charles VII (1314–1422)* (1886, repr. 1977), and *Histoire du Parlement de Paris de l'origine à Francois Ier (1250–1515),* 2 vols. (1894); Françoise Autrand, *Naissance d'un grand corps de l'état: Les gens du Parlement de Paris, 1345–1454* (1981); Thomas N. Bisson, "Consultative Functions in the King's Parlements (1250–1314)," in *Speculum,* **44** (1969); Gustave Ducoudray, *Les origines du Parlement de Paris,* 2 vols. (1902, repr. 1970); Marcel Fournier, *Essai sur l'histoire du droit d'appel* (1881); Paul Guilhiermoz, *Enquêtes et procès* (1892); Charles Victor Langlois, "Les origines du Parlement de Paris," in *Revue historique,* **42** (1890); Édouard Maugis, *Histoire du Parlement de Paris,* 3 vols. (1914–1916, repr. 1967); Ernest Perrot, *Les cas royaux* (1910); Carola M. Small, "Appeals from the Duchy of Burgundy to the Parlement of Paris in the Early Fourteenth Century," in *Mediaeval Studies,* **39** (1977).

JOSEPH A. KICKLIGHTER

[See also **Bailli; Beaumanoir, Philippe de; Châtelet; Coutumes de Beauvaisis; Custumals of Normandy; Établissements de St. Louis; France; Law, French; Livres de Jostice et de Plet, Li; Lo Codi; Louis IX of France; Nogaret, Guillaume de; Philip IV the Fair; Philip VI de Valois; Pierre de Fontaines; Seneschal.**]

PARLER FAMILY. *Parlier* carried the general meaning of "foreman" in the Middle Ages, and the dynasty of four generations of master masons, starting with Heinrich Parler the Elder, included one of the greatest architects of the late Gothic, Peter Parler.

Heinrich Parler the Elder worked as master at Schwäbisch Gmünd (Church of the Holy Cross) in the 1330's, and his name has been associated with the choir of the Frauenkirche in Nuremberg, Ulm Minster, and the choir of Augsburg Cathedral.

Peter Parler "von Gmünd" (1330–1399), eldest son of Heinrich, worked with his father at Schwäbish Gmünd. He is named in the inscription in the triforium of Prague Cathedral, where he replaced Mathieu d'Arras (*d.* 1352) as master in the 1350's. In addition to the completion of the choir of Prague

Net vaulting over choir of St. Vitus Cathedral, Prague, completed by Peter Parler, 1385. PHOTO: WERNER NEUMEISTER

Cathedral (St. Vitus), Peter is also associated with the Church of All Saints on the Hradčany, the choir of the church at Kolín on the Elbe (*ca.* 1360/1361), and the Charles Bridge over the Moldau (Vltava) River, Prague.

Heinrich had two other sons, Michael and Johannes. The former worked as mason at Goldenkron (1359) and with Peter Parler at Prague (1383). Johannes von Gmünd was named in a contract of 1359 as master of Freiburg Minster. After 1356 he was employed at Basel to repair the minster after the collapse of the upper choir. Johannes had two sons who both worked at Freiburg.

Peter Parler, twice married, had seven children. Of the children by his first wife, Nicholas was the eldest son; he studied at Prague University and entered holy orders. Wenzel (*fl.* 1390's) was master mason at Prague and Vienna. Johannes II (*d.* 1406) became *Dombaumeister* at Prague Cathedral from 1398 to 1406, where he worked on the south tower. He also worked at the Church of St. Barbara at Kuttenberg (Kutná Hora, *ca.* 1388). Both of

Peter's daughters married artisans in Prague, a leading goldsmith and Michael of Cologne, a mason. Peter's son Janco Parler, by his second wife, was born around 1383 and was also a mason.

A fourth generation of Parlers includes Johannes III, son of Johannes II, who is thought to have worked as a mason in Prague.

Associated with the Parler name are dazzling works of late Gothic vault construction, including types with multiple flying ribs and pendant keystones (Peter Parler's sacristy at Prague Cathedral). Some art historians have pointed to English precedents for the type of net vault used in the choir of Prague Cathedral, which tends to de-emphasize clear bay divisions.

BIBLIOGRAPHY

Paul Frankl, *Gothic Architecture* (1962), 161–170; Otto Kletzl, *Peter Parler der Dombaumeister von Prag* (1940); Anton Legner, *Die Parler und der schöne Stil, 1350–1400: Europäische Kunst unter der Luxemburgern*, 5 vols. (1978–1980), esp. vol. III; Josef Neuwirth, *Peter Parler von Gmünd, Dombaumeister in Prag, und seine Familie* (1891); Karl M. Swoboda, *Peter Parler, der Dombaumeister und Bildhauer* (1943).

STEPHEN MURRAY
FRANÇOIS BUCHER

[See also **Architect, Status of; Gothic Architecture; Gothic, International Style; Mathieu d'Arras; Prague; Vault.**]

PARLIAMENT was first of all a meeting where men spoke and parleyed, and then a process of governance. But before the Middle Ages ended, it had become a political institution with its own established procedures for conducting the king's and the kingdom's business. Yet parliament could not acquire an institutional character until it had passed the point of recognition, a time when these meetings received a name. The timing was imprecise, however, for men used several terms, like colloquium and council, on through the thirteenth century. The word itself—*parliamentum, parlement*, and *parliament* in the three languages of medieval English government—appeared on the plea rolls in 1237 and in the 1240's. In 1242 an assembly of magnates and prelates that met in London was called a parliament, and from 1244 to 1258 such an assembly met each year except 1250. In fact, three sessions met in April, June, and October 1258 at Westminster and at Oxford, and when King Henry III agreed to accept the Provisions of Oxford, which called this assembly a parliament, this formal document gave the word official recognition. By the 1290's, the author of *Fleta* tried to define the term when he wrote: "The king has his court in his council in his parliaments." Thus parliament was already a seat of authority. But whose authority? The king's or the kingdom's or the English people's? It was still the king's high court, or the king's parliament, for only his writ could call it into being. There the king exercised the authority of the crown and of the realm. But by 1484 Richard III's parliament made it clear that it, too, enjoyed England's authority and might recognize, and so authorize, a new king as it had done in 1461 and was to do again in 1485.

EARLY DEVELOPMENT: 1205–1307

A political purpose, to solve some immediate governmental problem, explains why the king summoned men of power to meet with him and his counselors. A series of councils, both small and large (a few were proto-parliaments), had met during the twelfth century, and they continued in King John's reign (1199–1216). His writs of summons to such a council in 1205 ordered archbishops, bishops, abbots, earls, and barons to come to London in order "to treat of our great and arduous affairs and the common profit of the realm." From these magnates King John also wished to obtain money and men with which to recover Normandy. Another such meeting at Oxford in 1207 granted the king, despite clerical and some baronial opposition, a tax of a thirteenth. The writ assessing this tax explained that it had been granted "by the common counsel and assent of our council at Oxford." To collect such nonfeudal aids and extraordinary revenues was easier when the prelates and magnates, as spokesmen for the kingdom, had given their consent. By 1213 political events were closing in on King John, and so he summoned a still larger council, one that included "four discreet knights" from each shire, to speak with the king about the affairs of his realm.

The men attending such a meeting were the king's earls and barons and his archbishops, bishops, and abbots (as king's tenants). All these appeared at meeting after meeting, and their experience afforded a core of continuity to transmit precedents and procedures that were to institutionalize the parliamentary process. At times there were present, in increasing numbers as the thirteenth century wore on, knights and burgesses chosen by the counties and boroughs to speak for their communities and for that community of communities, the kingdom. Only during the last decade of Edward I's reign (1272–1307) did diocesan clergy, knights of the shire, and burgesses appear with regularity. In 1305 ten priors, thirteen deans, and about fifty-seven archdeacons of England and Wales came to speak for the lower clergy. Also, twenty-three cathedral chapters sent proctors, and the clergy of twenty-one dioceses sent two from each. In all, this parliament included well over 600 men: 95 prelates, 145 members of the lower clergy, 103 earls and barons, 74 knights, and about 200 burgesses, all these in addition to the justices and members of the king's council. This was indeed a full parliament (*plenum parliamentum*), one larger than a great council, and it was an ample respresentation of the realm.

Representation, however, was not proportional—neither to the population or to the territory—for the south of England sent more burgesses than did the north. Yet members of the 1305 parliament did represent corporate entities: bishoprics, priories, and abbeys (four abbesses were summoned to an assembly in 1306), baronies and honors, and communities of counties, cities, and boroughs. So in a rather random fashion Edward I's larger parliaments contained spokesmen, if not proper representatives, for many kinds of freemen of England.

By 1307 parliament had acquired many features of a truly royal-national institution. Nevertheless, its institutional future remained potential, for the possibility still existed that the king's other courts and councils might usurp its functions. Writs of summons to a "general parliament" in 1275, Edward I's first, contain verbs that indicate what those summoned were expected to do: "to consider" and "to hear and to do" what would "be explained" to them by the king and his counselors. Also, those present at parliaments were "to talk" with the king, "to give" him counsel, "to settle" arduous business, "to treat, to ordain, to decide," and "to provide ways to meet the dangers" that then threatened the kingdom. Such activities afforded opportunities to discuss royal policies, foreign and domestic, to raise men and money for military ventures, and to reach decisions through the act of parleying. The ways that men did these things at parliaments, the procedures that they repeatedly followed, came to constitute the parliamentary process.

The first step occurred when the king and his advisers decided that the circumstances of the day required a parliament. Then the chancery clerks sent out writs of summons, individually, to earls and barons, to bishops and abbots. Later on and intermittently, writs ordered the sheriffs to have their counties choose and send two, at times three or four, knights for each shire and two or more burgesses from specified boroughs. Inclusion of these commoners came about gradually, and barely a dozen of the first seventy parliaments held after 1258 included popular representatives. A few such writs survive and date back to 1254 and 1242, yet in 1213 King John had ordered the sheriff of Oxfordshire to send "four discreet knights" to meet and "speak" with him "about the affairs" of the kingdom. But this meeting was not styled a parliament, and others with or without knights of the shire were called colloquiums and full councils. Writs went to sheriffs in 1226 to send four of the more lawful and discreet knights to Lincoln to present for the whole county any complaints against the sheriff over disputed interpretations of Magna Carta. The writ summoning two knights from each shire in 1254 stated the meeting's purpose: to grant Henry III an aid for his impending invasion of Gascony; and the "lawful and discreet knights" were to be empowered to answer "precisely" for their shires. When Edward I in 1283 raised forces to use against the Welsh, he instructed the sheriffs to send to Northampton freeholders armed for war who had land worth twenty pounds, and also "four knights from each of the aforesaid counties having full authority on behalf of the communities of the same counties."

The primal purpose of the parliamentary process was to win for the king his subjects' support. It also served to give the spokesmen for the kingdom a chance to speak out, for at a parliament they gave the king their counsel along with the kingdom's consent. The steady sequence of assemblies enabled the men coming from various parts of England to participate in the joint enterprise of governance. Originally an "occasion" when the king and his counselors performed "an act," as Maitland discerned, parliament was becoming the sum total of many procedures used to do the king's business. Maitland classified parliament's work under Edward I "under five heads, namely—(1) the discussion of affairs of state, more especially foreign affairs; (2) legislation; (3) taxation or supply; (4) the audience of petitions; and (5) judicial business, the determination of causes criminal and civil."

The kind of activity that predominated at a particular parliament varied according to the circumstances of the day. The records are too erratic and incomplete for any statistical appraisal. Foreign affairs included Edward I's troubles with Wales and Scotland, as well as with France and Gascony, and his military requirements meant a parliament or a full council in every year, except for 1303 and 1304, from 1290 through 1307. Legislation was another major function: witness the statutes of Westminster I and II and of Gloucester. The justices may have drafted the statutes; as Ralph Hengham, chief justice, remarked to a pleader: "Do not gloss the statute; we understand it better than you do, for we made it." Parliament, however, enacted them, and it also facilitated the transformation of feudal aids and services into a civic obligation in the form of grants. Such taxation was to supplement "the king's own," his income from his lands and properties, but in normal times he was expected "to live of his own." Petitions to remedy, by the king's grace, wrongs done to his subjects by royal officials were submitted to the king-in-council and sometimes decided in parliament. Then, too, a variety of judicial business, difficult cases referred from the common-law courts or others involving unprecedented points of law, eventually reached the king's council in his parliament.

Important persons might state their pleas before the king and his council at parliaments, and appeals from the common bench and the court *coram rege* (later called the King's Bench) were also heard. Sometimes cases of treason, like that of Nicholas Segrave in 1305, were tried at a parliament. Likewise, Almaric of St. Amand, governor of Oxford Castle, appeared at parliament and produced John of St. Amand because of a student riot in and about the castle. Then, too, charges were heard against cities, like Salisbury and Winchester, which had let a hostage from Bayonne escape. The royal justices might ask the king to approve in parliament their interpretations of ambiguous points of law; and a need to interpret statutes, or to provide new ones, required the justices' presence there. Certain acts were entered upon the Statute Rolls, in and after 1278, while others were entered on the Parliament Rolls as ordinances or memoranda.

The 1297 Parliament Roll contains the noun "taxation," and that of 1314–1315 the verb "to tax." Still, what modern men consider taxation, medieval men usually called grants or aids. These were gifts that the king's vassals and tenants gave to help their lord in times of extraordinary expenses, but by 1307 they had become an obligation: one that the parliamentary process had extended to the free members of England's communities of city, shire, and borough. Conversely, the subjects' grants of aids made at parliaments did much to enhance the kingdom's authority and to strengthen parliament's institutional character. Edward I's military ventures made him unable to "live of his own" and entailed expenses that required many contributions from his subjects. Time and again, the rents from the king's lands, the royal forest revenues, and established customs duties, like the wool prise, failed to suffice. So the spokesmen for England's men of property were called to a parliament to give their counsel and to consent to new levies. There agreement was reached as to the rate of assessment: a tenth, a fifteenth, or a twentieth of the value of "movables" (personal property). By 1300 the men attending a parliament, and those back home to whom they reported the terms agreed upon, had acknowledged that this was the lawful way for the king to procure additional revenues. The consent to taxes given at parliaments imbued the parliamentary process with the principle of contract.

This principle surfaced in 1297 with the agreements that the magnates made with Edward I concerning the raising of revenue. A baronial faction extracted from the king the first of his three Confirmations of the Charters—Magna Carta and the Charter of the Forest. They also got Edward I to declare in writing that the charters had been "made by common assent of all the realm" in Henry III's reign. The king had to go still further because "divers people" had feared that the aids paid "of their own grant and free will . . . might turn to a bondage to them and their heirs." So Edward I granted that "we shall never draw such aids, mises, nor prises into a custom"; and he even agreed not to take such aids "but by the common assent of all the realm and for the common profit thereof." The rule that the king could procure revenues beyond "his own" only with the kingdom's consent was formally fixed in 1297; and then in 1301 the Lords of parliament took the initiative and applied it successfully. These men of power, "on behalf of the whole community in the parliament of Lincoln," delivered to Edward I a bill. It requested the king's agreement to keep the charters, to annul any statutes to the contrary, and to settle procedural details about conducting the forest courts. Edward I answered the bill in writing, clause by clause, with the words "it expressly pleases"; and he also accepted the community's final stipulation, one contractual in nature: "on condition that the aforesaid matters are carried out, . . . the people of the kingdom granted him a fifteenth in place of the twentieth recently granted." The use of the parliamentary process to effect this agreement gave a lawful sanction to the contractual principle. Already Bracton and thirteenth-century common lawyers, as well as canonists and civilians, knew the maxim *Quod omnes tangit* (What touches all shall be approved by all). This rule gave a jurisprudential legitimacy to the doctrine of consent to new taxes and to new laws.

The right to make new laws was succinctly stated in 1291–1292 at an assembly styled a parliament. Those present laid down the rule that "the lord king, by reason of the preeminence of his royal dignity, can and should establish new law (*condere novam legem*) by the counsel of the nobles, prelates, great men, and magnates of his realm." Then, in 1301, when Edward I again confirmed the charters, he agreed "that if any statutes be contrary to the said charters . . . these may be emended or even annulled by the common counsel of our kingdom in due manner." Thus the fourteenth century opened with Edward I's full and conscious recognition that a valid way to amend old laws, to annul them, and to make new laws was through the parliamentary process.

Sessions of parliament often prepared the way for actions that dealt with affairs of state, and the recurrence of political crises best accounts for parliament's perpetuation. These exigencies, whether military, fiscal, or judicial, diplomatic, or dynastic, prompted the king to seek his subjects' support. Edward I's wars—French, Welsh, and Scottish—meant a sequence of demands for assistance. Thus the medieval parliament owed to Edward I, his wars, and his diplomacy, and to Edward II's troubles with his barons, much of its viability and its character as a national assembly. Parliament could also have been called the king's high court, for there the justices and the councillors did perform judicial functions. But not until the 1380's was it so styled; perhaps first in 1384, when the chancellor, Sir Michael de la Pole, spoke of "parliament which is the most high court of the realm." The sanest of the many contentious conclusions about the nature of medieval parliaments, however, seems to be that of the twentieth-century historian R. F. Treharne: "Despite the immensely important growth of the judicial and fiscal aspects of parliament, . . . it remained what it had been from the first, an essentially political assembly." For without political problems of royal-national import, the king with his justices and his councillors, in council or exchequer, might, and often did, dispose of fiscal and judicial matters. What the king had to have, besides his subjects' military and financial aid, was their moral support. And this he could best get from assemblies styled parliaments.

Those present at parliaments might make agreements, which Edward I swore to observe, but there remained the problem of how to make the king keep these contracts. Even England's Justinian (as Edward was called by later historians), asked his feudal lord, Pope Clement V, to release him from his various concessions. In a papal bull of 29 December 1305, Clement granted Edward's request, though he left the confirmed charters as a "part of the law of the land." By the end of his reign, however, parliament had become so much a part of the government that Edward I took along with him on his last campaign prelates, magnates, knights, burgesses, and diocesan clergy, who assembled 20 January 1307 at Carlisle to consider a proper settlement with the Scots. King Edward I was ill, but when he died on 7 July 1307, the earls and barons and the prelates carried on.

EDWARD II AND THE GROWTH OF PARLIAMENT

Edward's II's first parliament met at Northampton that October and granted him money for a trip to France to marry his twelve-year-old fiancée Isabella, daughter of the French king, and for his coronation on 25 February 1308. On that occasion Edward II swore a coronation oath that contained an additional promise: "to keep the rightful laws and customs which the community of your kingdom shall have chosen." To choose new laws, to hear pleas and petitions, and to vote the king revenues, parliament was to meet almost, but not quite, every year. Previous practices were maintained or modified, new procedures were begun, and men became conscious of the principles that were to control the parliamentary process. Most significant were representation, opposition, dissent, and, eventually, decision by majority instead of

PARLIAMENT, ENGLISH

unanimity. Edward II's quarrels with the magnates, the prelates, and the Commons set precedents that were to embed the parliamentary process in the structure of England's government. Three crises made his reign (1307–1327) a turning point in parliament's institutional growth. First came the Ordinances of 1311, then the 1322 Statute of York, which contained words recognizing the need for parliament's assent, and finally parliament's acceptance in 1327 of Edward II's "abdication."

Already barons at parliament in April 1308 had compelled Edward II to promise to banish his favorite, Peter (Piers) Gaveston; and then at the 1310 parliament the earls, some arriving armed, forced the king to appoint twenty-one Lords Ordainers with power to reform the realm. The Ordainers sought to maintain what they deemed to be traditions, and it took them over a year to produce the Ordinances of 1311, which Edward II agreed to accept and to publish throughout the land. Many of the Ordainers' proposals were too elaborate to be practicable, yet the Ordinances did serve to circulate certain political ideas that augmented the kingdom's authority and parliament's prestige. They attempted to establish as law controls over the appointment and dismissal of government personnel. They allowed Edward II to appoint the chancellor, the treasurer, the chief justices, and the household officers—but with the innovation that the king should do so "by the counsel and assent of his baronage, and this in parliament." Other royal actions also required the barons' approval, and the king was not to leave the country nor to undertake a war "without the common assent of his baronage, and this in parliament." Nor was the king to make changes in the coinage without the barons' advice, again in parliament, and men with complaints against the exchequer might seek recovery "by petitions in parliament." Likewise, pleas where the justices held differing opinions were to be concluded, "as law and reason" might require, in parliament. Perhaps their most utopian proposal was "that the king should hold parliament once a year, or two times if there be business, and this in a convenient place." The phrase "and this in parliament" implied the idea that the place for ultimate decisions, for making high policy, for legislation and taxation was at a parliament. The call for an annual parliament was a noble idea, but the king's needs and the kingdom's were what determined the frequency of parliaments.

Edward II and his baronial supporters were in control of the 1322 parliament, which enacted the Statute of York condemning the Ordinances of 1311. The Ordinances, they said, had restrained the royal power, had blemished the royal lordship, and were against the state of the crown. Since ordinances made by subjects in the past had led to "troubles and wars," the king, prelates, earls, barons, "and all the community of the realm at this parliament assembled" agreed that the Ordinances of 1311 should cease. Statutes made before 1311 were to remain in force; but any ordinance "made by the king's subjects" that impaired the royal power "should be null." Then came a redeeming clause for parliament's future:

> The things that should be established for the estate of our lord the king and his heirs, for the state of the realm and of the people, should be treated, agreed, established in parliaments by our lord the king, and by the assent of the prelates, earls, and barons, and the community of the kingdom just as has been accustomed to enact them.

This mention of the kingdom's assent implies that parliament contained representatives to speak for the corporate body of the realm. Already in the 1290's, the king's writs of summons had instructed the counties to bestow upon their knights "full authority on behalf of the community of the county," and burgesses, too, were empowered with "full and sufficient authority" to do what "common counsel" should ordain. Those present at a parliament were expected to answer before God for themselves and for the whole community of England. When these representatives did not agree unanimously, they sometimes reached decisions when the greater part agreed, thereby recognizing majority rule as an expedient way to conclude their arguments. Unanimity was obtained, however, in January 1327, when Edward II "was deposed from his pristine dignity" "by the unanimous consent of all the earls and barons, and of the archbishops and bishops, and of the whole clergy and people." Moreover, all "unanimously agreed" that Edward III should succeed his father.

The question has arisen as to whether this assembly at Westminster in January 1327 was indeed a proper parliament. Writs of summons in Edward II's name had been sent out in October 1326 for a parliament to meet 14 December. Then writs of supersedeas, dated 3 December, had postponed parliament until 7 January. When this assembly met at Westminster no king was present (according to the

PARLIAMENT, ENGLISH

modus the king's presence at parliament was required). For three days, 13, 14, and 15 January, bishops preached sermons explaining and justifying Edward II's removal with his own good will and "by common counsel and assent of . . . the whole community of the realm." Whether or not this assembly was a parliament is still argued. But before the fourteenth century ended, it was so construed, for some chronicles styled it a parliament; but the Lichfield Chronicle called it a "general council of all the clergy and people." Edward III's accession was proclaimed in London 24 January, his reign was dated from the twenty-fifth, and he was crowned 1 February. Two days later the assembly that had deposed his father and made him king reassembled as Edward III's first parliament.

CONFRONTATION AND COOPERATION: 1327–1399

Cooperation between king and parliament prevailed through most of Edward III's reign (1327–1377), although on occasion there were confrontations. Tradition, what was and had been, seemed good to many parliamentarians, and they confirmed past procedures more often than they innovated. Most of them were pragmatists and politicians, and their desires and demands were the forces that modified the character of parliament and made it distinct from the king's great councils. The great councils continued to compete as an alternative to parliament until well after 1485, however, although by then parliament had become an integral part—and in time of crisis an essential one—of England's government.

Forty-eight sessions of parliament met during Edward III's reign, and at most of them the barons and magnates rallied around their king and supported his wars. Cooperation between king, Lords, and Commons led to many exceptions to traditional rules, but often with a declaration that they were not to set precedents. Twice statutes declared that parliament should be held annually, but circumstances were what tended to confirm this goal. An act of 1330 stated that "a parliament shall be holden every year once, and more often if need be"; and again, in 1362, "for redress of divers mischiefs and grievances which daily happen, a parliament shall be holden every year, as another time was ordained by statute."

The use of commissions and committees fostered cooperation and made parliament men more active in the governmental process. Back in Edward I's reign, when petitions were presented at parliaments, they were often turned over to committees to answer. Receivers of petitions, and by 1315 auditors as well, were regularly appointed to deliver the replies. A committee to convert petitions into statutes in 1340 included bishops, barons, justices, and twelve knights and six burgesses chosen by the Commons. The Commons in 1379 and 1380 requested the appointment of committees to investigate the expense of the war and to examine the treasurer's accounts. Again in 1386 a commission of lords and prelates, appointed at the Commons' request, was to correct all the faults and defects of the crown and to do other things for its good. This commission was to last for only a year, and its members were to stay in London in order to have access to the "rolls and records" of the courts, the chancery, and the Exchequer. Such committees may suggest confrontation more than cooperation, but their repeated use afforded opportunities for the Lords and Commons to work together and for the king to yield to their requests.

Cooperation was even more apparent in the speeches and actions concerning Edward III's wars. When the question of peace with France arose in 1343, the lord chamberlain said in parliament: "As the war was begun by the common advice of the prelates, great men, and commons, the king could not treat of, or make, peace without the like assent." Lords and Commons, after separate discussions, advised the king to make an honorable peace. Should that fail, they agreed to aid him with all their power. But the war dragged on, and in 1348 the Commons cooperated by declaring themselves "so ignorant and simple that we cannot give you advice." So they begged to be excused and prayed the king to consult the magnates and sages of his council. Again, in 1354 the Commons' answer was that a treaty agreeable to the king and Lords would be the same to them. When asked again whether they could consent to a treaty of perpetual peace, they cried out with one voice, "Aye, Aye." When the Treaty of Bretigny brought peace in 1360, a parliament approved it formally. By working with his prelates, Lords, and Commons, the king confirmed the precedents of seeking their advice and assent.

Confrontation also contributed, in the long run, to parliament's institutional progress. Conflicts between the king and parliament, or some of its members, often ended in agreements that reinforced the principle of contract. During Edward III's reign

PARLIAMENT, ENGLISH

the Commons set more precedents that assured them of a major role in the governing process: taxation was not to be lawful without parliament's consent; both Lords and Commons must concur in legislation; and the Commons, through confrontations, acquired the right to inquire into and to redress abuses by other branches of the royal government. A statute of 1340 put into law the essence of the bargain the Commons had struck in 1339 that no common aid be made "if this is not by common assent of the prelates, earls, barons, and other magnates and commons of our said realm of England, and this in parliament." Edward III agreed that revenues arising from this aid and from wardships, marriages, customs duties, and escheats should be spent to safeguard his realm and to support his wars with Scotland and France. In 1348 the Commons also stipulated that the king should not levy any imposition, tallage, or charge "without the grant and assent of the commons in parliament." This agreement was to be entered on the roll "as a matter of record, whereby they may have remedy if anything should be attempted to the contrary in time to come." When Edward III promulgated the Ordinances of the Staple in 1353 at a great council that included a knight from every shire and some citizens and burgesses, the commoners present petitioned that the articles be read at the next parliament and be entered on the parliament roll. Their reason was that "ordinances and agreements made in council are not of record, as if they had been made in a general parliament." When parliament next met, the king and the magnates unanimously agreed that the articles be "held for a statute to endure forever."

By putting such conclusions to confrontations on the rolls as of record, parliamentarians built up a body of precedents. When Edward III quarreled with Archbishop John Stratford over administrative mismanagement in 1341, a committee of lords reported that peers had the right to be tried by their peers in parliament. The same parliament asked the king to ordain by their advice that important ministers and the chief justices be appointed in parliament and that they "be sworn before the peers in parliament to keep the laws." Edward III was reluctant to accept this control over his appointments, but he needed a subsidy. So he allowed the terms to be put into a statute after adding the phrase "with the advice of his council." Then, upon the dissolution of this parliament he issued a royal proclamation declaring the statute null and void. This confrontation also led to the first entry on the parliament rolls of a recorded dissent, one by the chancellor, treasurer, and justices. They declared that they could not enforce the act, as it was contrary to the laws and customs that they had sworn to keep.

Dissent, of course, was not new in 1341, but usually it was covered by the unanimous assent formally given to parliamentary decisions. Opposition as a principle, however, required an acceptance of majority rule in decision making and its corollary, the toleration of dissenting minorities. Not until 1826 was a parliamentary opposition institutionally recognized, and then only in jest as His Majesty's Opposition. Moreover, the viability of the practice of dissent and opposition depended upon the king's opponents finding a place for such actions in the existing structure of politics and government rather than on the battlefield. In this the peers and prelates were aided by the Commons, who held tight the strings to their purses and who struck many a bargain with a needy sovereign. Attempts to expel "evil counselors," to abolish "bad customs," to criticize unpopular administrative practices, and to reject, or to accept grudgingly, the king's request for money had an accumulative effect and kept alive criticism, opposition, and nonviolent dissent.

Two innovations under Edward III, the Commons' right to investigate the public accounts and to impeach the king's ministers, were reinforced by repetition in Richard II's reign (1377–1399). After John of Gaunt, a younger son of Edward III and the dominant power in politics during the years following 1376, left for Spain in 1386, his opponents persuaded the Commons to impeach the chancellor, Michael de la Pole, earl of Suffolk (*d.* 1389). When both Lords and Commons asked for his removal, Richard II arrogantly answered "that he would not for them, or at their instance, remove the meanest scullion from his kitchen." Parliament rejoined by refusing to do business until the king returned to Westminster and removed his minister. Richard carried this confrontation further by threatening to ask the king of France for advice, and this action provoked the 1386 parliament to mention Edward II's deposition, implying that they might do the same. In fact, the Knighton Chronicle (*ca.* 1395) gave as their words:

> We have an ancient statute . . . that if the king through any evil design . . . or by any other irregular courses,

> shall alienate himself from his people, and refuse to govern by the laws, statutes, and laudable ordinances of the realm, with the salutary counsel of the lords and great men of the realm, but will wantonly exercise his own singular arbitrary will—from that time it shall be lawful for his people, by their full and free assent and consent, to depose the king himself from his royal throne, and . . . to raise up some other of the royal race.

These words may be only a chronicler's invention, but they indicate the way some men were thinking as the fourteenth century closed.

Antagonism between Richard II and parliament continued in 1386, and parliament succeeded in impeaching Suffolk and having Thomas Arundel, bishop of Ely (1374, later archbishop of York, 1388, and of Canterbury, 1396; *d.* 1414), made chancellor. The next year the king put ten questions about his authority to the judges. Their answers favored the king's contentions, and several pertained to parliament. The king had the power to dissolve parliament at his pleasure. His consent was needed to impeach a minister, and Richard II might revoke Suffolk's impeachment. In response to these opinions, seven lords then appealed (that is, accused) several of Richard II's adherents of treason, and though the justices and the council declared the Appellants' case defective, they carried on the conflict. The Appellants asserted that matters concerning the peers of the realm should be determined according to the "law and course of the parliament." They went further and answered Richard II's contention that parliament was the king's, by claiming parliament's supremacy over any "lower courts or place in the realm." The judges who had answered Richard's questions were then impeached and banished, and parliament voted £20,000 to the Appellants for their services.

When Richard II reached twenty-two years of age in 1389, he repudiated the governance of the past twelve years and announced that hereafter he himself would direct the government. For over seven years there was apparent cooperation between the king and parliament, but discord arose anew in 1397 when the Commons petitioned the king for redress of their grievances. This time the Lords were with the king, and together they declared that anyone who moved the Commons to seek reform of anything pertaining to the royal person or to his rule and regality was guilty of treason. In January 1398 parliament annulled the proceedings of the 1386 and 1388 parliaments. Then parliament went still further and declared the judges' answers to Richard II's questions to be good law, and the Commons granted a tax on wool and hides for the duration of Richard II's life. Finally, this parliament empowered a committee of Lords and Commons to deal with any unanswered petitions after its dissolution "by authority and assent of the parliament."

Although this delegation of power was repealed in 1399, parliament had procured, through adversity, a recognition of its own authority. When Richard II renounced the throne that year, however, his abdication was accepted, not by parliament, but by "all the people." The "estates and communities" appointed deputies "to depose King Richard . . . in the place, name, and authority of all the . . . estates, as has been observed in similar cases by ancient custom of the said kingdom." These same estates "with all the people" were the ones who agreed that Henry IV should succeed to the kingship. However, a week later the same men who had given the people's and the estates' approval to the deposition and succession were converted, by new writs of Henry IV, into his first parliament. The idea of a parliamentary title to the throne was still an anachronism in 1399, but by 1484 and 1485 parliament's authority had become sufficient to sanction two new kings.

POLITICS, PERSONNEL, AND STRUCTURE: 1399–1485

Politics in and after 1399 was the animating force that determined the medieval parliament's destiny and its institutional structure. It became a forum for feuding factions and a court of last resort (short of force) for settling issues concerning the kingdom or the crown. When justices were confronted with cases politically too dangerous to decide, they passed them on to the king's high court of parliament. A series of decisions made in parliament prompted its advance toward its high position in England's governmental structure. When parliament bestowed the right to rule upon Richard, third duke of York (1411–1460), Edward IV (*r.* 1461–1470, 1471–1483), Richard III (*r.* 1483–1485), and Henry VII (*r.* 1485–1509), it did so with the kingdom's authority and its own. Thus parliament transcended the justices and men of law and even the kings, Henry VI (*r.* 1422–1461, 1470–1471) and Edward IV, and so became the kingdom's high court. There the estates of the realm were represented by the Lords Spiritual, the Lords

Parliament meeting at Westminster, 15th century. BY PERMISSION OF THE BRITISH LIBRARY, LONDON, MS HARLEY 1319, fol. 57

Temporal, and the Commons. Collectively, they spoke for the kingdom, formally with unanimity, though at times by majority rule. Paradoxically, parliament's authority was augmented through cooperation with these royal usurpers, each of whom acquired his right to rule with a parliament's approval.

Although the duke of York did not succeed to the throne, his agreement in 1460 to succeed Henry VI was a contract, "an accord . . . authorized by the authority of this present parliament." In fact, parliament's role went further, for the duke agreed that after Henry VI died, York's title to the crown would be one "entailed by authority of parliament," thus setting a precedent for Henry VIII's Succession Acts. Here was a crucial point of recognition that guaranteed for parliament and its authority a future. Before this accord had been reached, however, the Lords of parliament and the men of law had searched their souls and the records. First, the Lords called "the king's justices into the Parliament Chamber" and asked for "their advice and counsel." After a few days they reported to the Lords that they could give no decision regarding the rightful inheritor of the crown, for they were "the king's justices" and "this matter was so high and touched the king's high estate and regalie, which is above the law and passed their learning." The issue, they said, "pertained to the lords of the king's blood and the peerage of this his land." The Lords, irked, then called in the serjeants-at-law and the king's attorney, who waited two days and then replied that since the question "passed the learning of the justices, it must needs exceed their learning." So the Lords of parliament had to decide the question, and they had a debate with each lord free to speak "without any reporting or ill-will." In the end the agreement was "an act of accord by the king and the three estates, in this present parliament assembled."

This arrangement failed to work, however, because York died in battle 30 December 1460, and Henry VI survived. Then on 4 March 1461 several Yorkist lords and some London citizens acclaimed Edward IV king; but not until November were his title, his right to rule, and his authority to govern entered as "of record" on the rolls of parliament. Since Henry VI was still alive, York's agreement was inoperative, and so Edward IV, with "the advice and assent of the lords spiritual and temporal and of the commons," declared himself king "by God's law" of inheritance; and a Commons petition thanked God for his decision. The act of parliament declared the three Henrys kings *de facto* but not *de jure* because of Henry IV's "usurpation." Edward IV's right to rule was "by God's law, man's law, and the law of nature," and these sanctions were all confirmed "by the authority of parliament."

Once again in June 1483 England experienced a change of kings with no parliament in being. When Richard III supplanted his twelve-year-old nephew, Edward V, who had succeeded his father 9 April 1483, the uncle's lawyers and clerics devised an elaborate, but fictitious, scenario to explain his right to the throne. Richard III was a king whom "good law, reason, and the concord assent of the lords and commons of the realm have ordained to reign upon the people." Then at his coronation he was recognized as "inheritor by the laws of God and man to the crown and royal dignity of England . . . elect, chosen, and required by all three estates of the same land." Unfortunately, the three estates had met (fictitiously) out of parliament, and as King Richard's popularity began to wane, he deemed it wise to call a parliament to meet in January 1484. Perhaps no other medieval king did so much—on paper—to raise parliament's position and to exalt its authority in theory. Its rolls explain the extent of parliament's authority: "The court of parliament is of such authority, and the people of this land of such nature and disposition, . . . that manifestation and declaration of any truth or right, made by the three estates of this realm assembled in parliament, and by authority of the same, maketh, before all other things, most faith and certainty." Because the three estates were not "assembled in the form of parliament" in June 1483, doubts and ambiguities about Richard III's title had arisen. So the 1484 parliament declared and entered on its roll, as of record, that the petition asking him to be king was to "be of like effect, virtue, and force, as if all the same things had been so said . . . in a full parliament and by authority of the same accepted and approved." This enactment gave legality, if not legitimacy, to Richard III's "lawful election" by the three estates in June 1483 and conjoined the kingdom's authority with that of parliament.

Parliament also used its authority in 1485 to sanction the last medieval usurpation, that by Henry VII. With Richard III defeated and killed on Bosworth Field on 22 August, the wise new king sent out writs dated 15 September for a parliament to meet on 7 November. To prevent any ambiguities about Henry VII's right to rule, "the communities of the realm of England presented to the king in parliament" a bill in English. A single, long, straightforward sentence indicates the degree of authority that the medieval parliament had attained: "Be it ordained, established, and enacted, by authority of this present parliament, that the inheritance of the crown of the realms of England and of France . . . be, rest, remain, and abide in the most royal person of our now sovereign Lord King Harry the VIIth, and in the heirs of his body lawfully coming, perpetually." Henry's answer, in French, was that the king "wills it in all points." This contract was one based solely on an act of parliament and was a proper parliamentary title for the first Tudor.

Who were these men of power who spoke for the three estates with the kingdom's authority and parliament's? First, the Lords Spiritual were the archbishops and bishops, selected abbots who also enjoyed episcopal authority, and two priors. The Lords Temporal included dukes, earls, viscounts, and barons; while knights, esquires, and gentlemen from the counties and freemen from the cities and boroughs composed the Commons. Writs of summons indicate maximum numbers of lords who might have attended in the fifteenth century, and presence lists, kept by the clerks of parliament in and after 1449, probably earlier, give a few daily attendances by the lords. The two archbishops were both present at the 1461 parliament, as were sixteen of the nineteen bishops. Only twenty-two of the twenty-seven abbots and priors attended, and the one duke, Norfolk, summoned in 1461 died and left only a minor heir—although in 1453 five dukes had been summoned. Six of the twelve earls who received writs in 1461 attended, but the one viscount summoned in May had become an earl before parliament met on 4 November. Statistics on the barons are variable, but thirty-four of the thirty-nine who were summoned in 1461 appeared in November. The numbers summoned to Henry VII's first parliament declined to eighteen barons, but writs were sent to nine earls, two dukes, and two viscounts. The archbishops and abbots remained the same, two and twenty-seven, though the bishops dropped to sixteen. The total numbers of Lords Spiritual and Temporal summoned ranged from one hundred four in 1453 and ninety-three in 1461, with eighty, perhaps more, actually present, down to seventy-six in 1485. Attendance by a lord was obligatory; and those who failed to appear might be fined, as happened several times in the 1450's.

The number of commoners sent to parliament

also varied as some cities and boroughs were omitted and new ones added. A roll call was held on the first day of each parliament, and every knight, citizen, and burgess was to "answer by their names." Attendance varied, but was around 300, often less; and occasionally constituencies procured charters exempting them from sending members—as did Torrington, Malden, and Woodstock. Colchester was excused in 1404 but with the condition that the town would observe all statutes, ordinances, and charges that this parliament might grant. Before 1485, however, many towns had found it advantageous to have members of parliament look after their interests. In 1472 James Arblaster, the duchess of Norfolk's retainer, wrote to the bailiff of Malden urging him to choose Sir John Paston as a burgess, "my lady and you of the town could not have a meeter man to be for you in the parliament to have your needs sped at all seasons." The next year a letter to Sir John from his younger brother, John Paston, concluded with: "I pray God send you the Holy Ghost among you in the parliament house, and rather the Devil, we say, than you should grant any more taxes." How frequently these otherworldly members attended is not known. Yet bishops and parliamentary abbots familiar with canon law had held for long that the Holy Ghost was present at the church's general councils, to which they likened parliament, and inspired unanimous decisions.

The Commons made the rules governing the elections of their members, and they heard complaints against the sheriffs for having sent their friends or themselves to parliament. Cognizance of disputed elections was once a matter for the king and his council, but during and after Richard II's reign the Commons intervened. In 1404 the Commons petitioned the king and the Lords that parliament examine the sheriff of Rutland's return. The sheriff and the knight he had sent both appeared; parliament amended the return, and sent the sheriff to Fleet Prison until he had paid a fine. Later on, a statute of 1445 gave a defrauded candidate an action of debt against the sheriff in the court of common pleas.

Qualifications for both electors and elected were also prescribed by statute. An act of 1406 required that shire elections admit as electors not only freeholders, but all freemen present at the county court on election day. Then the 1430 parliament restricted the franchise to freeholders of land or tenement valued at forty shillings a year resident in the shire. Another act in 1445 required the knights of the shire to be notable knights, or notable esquires or gentlemen who could support the dignity of a knight, and not be yeomen. A motive for this may have been the Lords' desire to have a following in the lower house drawn from their retainers or household staffs. About a dozen retainers of Lord Hastings (*d.* 1483) were members of the Commons; and other lords, and the king and his henchmen, made sure that they had spokesmen for their interests among the Commons at politically critical parliaments.

The magnates and the king were not the only ones to use members of the Commons to promote their interests, however, for merchants and craftsmen did so too. A bill to protect the merchants of London against imports was put in as a Commons petition in 1461; and when it was sent to the Lords, it "was put in by the king's own hand and read." The Pewterers Company paid ten shillings and eight pence for legal advice in drafting a bill "to put into the parliament," and their archives also record "expense done on such as should put it up."

Structurally, parliament had attained its basic form, partition into two houses, an upper and a lower. When the Commons acquired a meeting place, a house of their own, their independence of the Lords was recognized. Their speaker asked the king in 1404 to order the Commons to meet daily at eight o'clock "at Westminster in their house assigned to them," and "the lords spiritual and temporal" were to meet in theirs. The term "house" still had a locative meaning in 1433 when the Commons took an oath "in their common house"; but by 1440 members were described as "of the Lower House," indicating an institutional connotation. When an act against Thomas Denyes passed "in the Higher House before the lords" in 1454, he "hoped to God" that it would not pass "in the Common House." Then in 1461 "there come up from the Lower House a notable number of the substance of the same House" to speak with the lords. The dual connotation of the Common House continued on through 1485, and its actual location was still the Chapter House of Westminster Abbey while the "Parliament Chamber," where the Lords sat, was the Painted Chamber in Westminster Palace.

This bicameral structure required refinements in the parliamentary process and its procedures. Communications between the two houses were made through the speaker accompanied by a few of the Commons. The speaker's office, begun about 1376, rapidly extended its functions, and in 1384 the chancellor's order to the Commons to choose a speaker was formally recorded. The speaker's first duty was to inform the Commons of the king's and the Lords' desires, and then to report back the Commons' reactions. This official intermediary was often after 1460 a member of the king's council and their nominee. While most speakers had been members of the lower house, a few had not served there previously. In one out of three parliaments the speaker had held the office before; and in eight parliaments (1432–1447) they were lawyers, many of whom had worked for the royal administration, and later on a few became justices. Experienced in politics and frequently attached to magnates and their retinues, speakers used their skills to maneuver government bills through the Commons. Just when the speaker came to preside over the lower house is not certain: perhaps in Richard II's reign, surely under the Lancastrians, for in 1453 the abbot of Wheathampstead wrote that the speaker had "the rule of the Lower House." As early as 1435 he received a royal monetary reward, and under Edward IV he was regularly paid a royal fee. This royal connection undoubtedly prompted the speaker to maintain control over what went on in the Common House, and in 1483 Bishop Russell, then chancellor, wrote that "all is directed" by the speaker, who acts as "president in their consultations" and who "maketh the questions." The speaker also kept a record of attendance, and he could authorize members to be absent or go home. So at the end of the Middle Ages, the speaker served to coordinate the parliamentary process and to facilitate cooperation between the two houses.

One procedural rule, important for the Commons' future, was their successful assertion that money bills should start in the lower house. In 1407 the Lords alone granted the king's request for a subsidy for national defense, and the Commons reacted. They responded that this was "much to the prejudice and derogation of their liberties," and Henry IV gave way. He agreed that each house, the king absent, might discuss the state of the realm and any needed remedies. But they were not to make grants until "by the commons granted, and the lords assented to." Nor was a grant to be sent to the king "before the lords and commons shall be of one assent and accord." Moreover, some of the Commons' grants were conditional, and this led to the practice of holding ministers to account. A large subsidy in 1404 required that it be spent on defense as prescribed in the grant itself. Two treasurers of war were then appointed and sworn in at that parliament, while at the next they were to account to the Commons.

When Henry V approved the Commons' right to petition in 1414, he agreed that nothing be enacted that was not in the original petition nor anything "contrary to their asking whereby they should be bound without their assent." Henry reserved, however, the "royal prerogative to grant and deny what him lust [pleases] of their petitions." Except for money bills, which were to begin in the lower house, and bills concerning the Lords, which were to start in the upper, either house might originate all other kinds of bills. The king still had the right to dispense with a penal law for a particular person, however, and in the Middle Ages he often used the dispensing power. The sovereignty of statute was still in the future.

By mid century, procedure in the upper house had become elaborate and bills sent up from the lower were amended. One article providing that franchises and liberties be granted by authority of parliament was rejected in 1461; and divers lords were to inform the Commons that the king would grant them, as his progenitors had done, of his liberality and in accordance with reason. Likewise, the Lords rejected a proposal to assign the justices' salaries by parliament's authority. Some bills were read three times, debate sometimes took place, and bills were committed to committees. By 1454 two and possibly three readings of a bill took place, and debate was probably on the second. When a bill, like one "against sheriffs" in 1461, was "read but not agreed," it might be amended; and amendments by the Lords as provisos or changes seem instigated by the government. Of twenty-six articles in one Commons bill, the Lords amended fourteen, rejected two, and passed ten as presented. When a Commons bill was altered, divers lords were "to declare unto the commons" their pleasure and the king's; and then the Commons were to ratify the amendments as happened in 1439, 1442, and 1445. Not all of the Lords' amendments required the Commons' ratification, however, and in 1455 the clerk of the *Rolls of Parliament* stated the rule: When the Lords altered a bill's intent or purpose, the Commons were to ratify the changes; but when the Lords merely modified details or added features inherent, like reducing a grant of money from four to two years, the bill need not be returned to the lower house.

An infrequency of parliaments under Edward IV—only seven in twenty-two years—and short sessions of only a few weeks enabled this king, his kinsmen, and his ministers to maintain an initiative in governance and a control over the parliamentary process. Edward IV was able to live much of the time from forfeited estates, feudal dues, and customs duties. Forced loans, called benevolences, also helped to reduce the king's dependence upon parliament. Parliament's importance may have waned under Edward IV, as some historians contend, but it soon enhanced its power and authority in 1484 and 1485, when the last two medieval parliaments sanctioned Richard III's and Henry VII's usurpations.

A parliamentary diary kept by the Colchester burgesses gives glimpses of what the 1485 parliament was like. It contains what the burgesses thought they should report to their constituents, "master baillies and all my masters," when they returned home and asked for their expenses. The first morning, 7 November, the Commons attended the king's grace at nine o'clock, and the king and the Lords "came down out of the Parliament Chamber into the church of Westminster, and there was said the mass of the Holy Ghost." During the mass, the lord steward declared in the king's name that the knights, citizens, and burgesses "should answer by their names." Then the king and the Lords returned to the Parliament Chamber, where the chancellor gave "a worshipful sermon." After that the king ordered the chancellor to instruct the Commons to assemble at nine o'clock in the morning to "choose" a speaker. This they did and chose Thomas Lovell, a gentleman of Lincoln's Inn, and the knights there present arose and set the speaker in his chair. The speaker thanked "the masters of the place," and the recorder of London explained that the custom was for the speaker and the Commons to command twenty-four knights and gentlemen to show the speaker to the chancellor and to learn when to present him to the king. At ten o'clock the next day all the Commons went into the Parliament Chamber and presented their speaker "before the king's grace and all his lords."

The Commons got down to business the following day and read a bill for a subsidy between the king and the merchants. They reached "no conclusion," but they passed the bill next day "as an act." The speaker then ordered four gentlemen to take the bill to the chancellor to have him "certify the king's good grace withal." Another bill that day was to restore to the former queen, Elizabeth, her castles and properties. Then came a Sunday and no sitting.

Day after day bills to restore properties to the many persons attainted by previous kings came in. One was to "restore blessed King Harry and Queen Margaret and Prince Edward," whom an "act of parliament" had attainted; and another was for Henry VII's mother, Margaret Beaufort, attainted by Richard III's parliament. The bills were read once, but there "were arguments and nothing passed." Three days later "there was a communing for the common weal of all the land" to seek a remedy for false money that had been deceiving "the king's liege people." The clerk of the crown came down, by order of the king and his lords, with a dozen bills that were read, and three days later the Commons received nine more. Finally, on 10 December, after the Commons had passed several bills, the king and his lords sent for the speaker and "all the House" to come to the Parliament Chamber. There they waited upon his grace, who commanded the lord chancellor "to prorogue His High Court of Parliament unto the 23 day of January." So ended England's medieval parliament, for January marked the advent of a new era, one when the king-in-parliament would assert, notably through Henry VIII's Reformation Parliament, his sovereign authority.

BIBLIOGRAPHY

For a full, critical bibliography of books and articles on the medieval parliament, see Edgar B. Graves, ed., *A Bibliography of English History to 1485* (1975), 503–524. See also R. G. Davies and J. H. Denton, eds., *The English Parliament in the Middle Ages* (1981); James Lydon, ed., *England and Ireland in the Later Middle Ages* (1981), 122–152; Nicholas Pronay and John Taylor, *Parliamentary Texts of the Later Middle Ages* (1980); Henry G. Richardson and George O. Sayles, *The English Parliament in the Middle Ages* (1981); John S. Roskell, *Parliament and Politics in Late Medieval England*, 3 vols. (1981); George O. Sayles, *The King's Parliament of England* (1974), and "The Deposition of Richard II: Three Lancastrian Narratives," in *The Bulletin of the Institute of Historical Research*, 54 (1981).

WILLIAM HUSE DUNHAM, JR.

[See also **Edward I; Edward II; Edward III; England: 1216–1485; Fleta; Henry III of England; Henry IV of England; Henry V of England; Law, English Common; Modus Tenendi Parliamentum; Provisions of Oxford; Richard II; Richard III.**]

PARLIAMENT, IRISH. The medieval Irish parliament was an institution established by English kings as lords of Ireland. Its history typified that of many governmental institutions in English Ireland, reflecting an attempt to extend the common-law system to a lordship that presented some rather different problems of government, while yet preserving substantial uniformity of form and function with the parent institution. Overall, this attempt was successful and laid the foundations of an Irish parliamentary tradition stretching down to the present. Yet parliament's development has provoked a still-unresolved controversy between nationalist historians who choose to emphasize parliament's role in fostering a sense of community consciousness and those who explore its changing role in royal government.

Nominally, parliament's jurisdiction extended over the whole island and its inhabitants. In practice, even at the lordship's height, around the year 1300, the Gaelic chiefs preserved their autonomy in at least two-thirds of the island; and "the community of Ireland" of parliament's proceedings meant the settlers of Anglo-Norman descent there. The first unambiguous reference to an Irish parliament dates from 1264, and it was probably established through Henry III's decision to implement in Ireland also the Provisions of Oxford, which had instituted regular parliaments in England. Administratively, parliament developed from the Irish counterpart of the king's council, the justiciar's council. Initially, the ministerial council comprised its nucleus, afforced by the magnates and some bishops and abbots; and though parliament was from the beginning a legislative body, its main function was then the administration of justice, especially matters referred by ministers. Between 1297 and the 1370's, however, a series of developments saw parliament achieve its classic late medieval form and functions, with the procedures as described in the Irish version of the *Modus Tenendi Parliamentum.*

Representatives of counties, franchises, and towns were first summoned to parliaments between 1297 and 1300, but for special purposes only: in 1300 taxation was for the first time discussed there. For many years, the Irish parliament did not, as in England, develop an upper chamber comprising magnates and prelates. Instead the earlier division between magnates and ministers survived, while elected representatives of the shires and towns attended only intermittently, in connection with the infrequent grants of taxation, occasional legislation, or petitions to the king. They were not yet seen as an essential part of parliament. Parliament's judicial functions were now less important—the newly developed justiciar's bench took over this work—and following the example of the English parliament, which by 1300 was receiving growing numbers of petitions from Irish litigants, it began to be approached chiefly by way of private petitions and bills. During the administration of William of Windsor (1369–1372, 1373–1376), however, parliament emerged from a period of obscurity as a tricameral institution. Since the assent of the Commons had long been necessary for a grant of taxation, the frequent demands for subsidies that characterized Windsor's governorship secured for them an established place in parliament. The assent of the proctors of the lower clergy was similarly necessary; in England this led to concurrent sittings of the clergy in convocation, but in Ireland the clerical proctors were accepted as a third house of parliament. Finally, the magnates and prelates sat with the ministerial council to form an upper house, although it was some years yet before there evolved the substantially modern concept of a limited peerage on English lines.

The character of disputes over Windsor's conduct in parliament also clarifies for us some of the Commons' powers at this time. They show that the principle of parliamentary consent to taxation was then accepted on all sides, that without the Commons' free consent a grant of subsidy was unlawful, and that the Commons' representatives had power of assent on behalf of their respective communities by virtue of a *plena potestas* (full power) clause in the writs of summons. Yet in 1375–1376, when the king summoned representatives of the Commons and clergy to England in an unprecedented bid to circumvent opposition to a subsidy, *plena potestas* was withheld by the communities.

In terms of the size and extent of representation, the Irish parliament was a good deal smaller than its English counterpart. The maximum number of counties and franchises represented was fourteen, and of towns twelve, but attendance in the commons usually fell well short of the potential fifty-two knights and burgesses which this indicates. Attendance was forty-two in 1420 and thirty-two and twenty-seven in 1499, but many mid-fifteenth-century parliaments probably had few representatives from areas outside the English Pale. About twenty bishops and a dozen abbots and priors were commonly summoned to the upper house in the late fourteenth century, while the number of temporal peers summoned was twenty or more. There was a similar tendency for numbers to decline in the fifteenth century, so that the maximum attendance of abbots and priors was eventually reduced to six, with around eleven bishops, and no more than fifteen temporal peers. Overall attendance in the Lords was eighteen in 1491, and twenty-nine and twenty-four in 1499. Periodically, the administration attempted to strengthen dwindling numbers by inflicting fines for absence from parliament, and in 1462 the creation of peerages on English lines began; but whereas attendance at parliaments had earlier been considered a burden, the dignity of a peer was by the mid fifteenth century highly prized. The numbers of clerical proctors elected by each diocese varied between four and one, but altogether twenty-seven proctors attended in 1420 and 1450; and of the maximum of eighteen dioceses, thirteen were represented in 1420 and eleven in 1499. The exact constitutional status of the house of clerical proctors is unclear; their assent was necessary to subsidy acts and probably other legislation affecting the church, but on other matters statutes might be validly enacted despite the proctors' disapproval. Eventually, in 1537, the proctors' opposition to the government's Reformation legislation prompted a statute denying their right to a place in parliament.

Thus the Irish parliament continued to develop along English lines, but with certain peculiarities to suit Irish conditions. One such characteristic was the frequency of local taxation, alongside general taxation, which stemmed from the stronger particularist traditions of the lordship's several communities. A unified system of taxation for the whole lordship really developed only in the 1370's, and then within the context of separate bargains with local communities in the manner of local subsidies. Indeed, local subsidies, frequently agreed with parliamentary authority, continued to yield substantial sums. The yields of general subsidies—rarely over £1,000 and commonly 700 marks (£467) or less in the fifteenth century—were never very considerable, but they provided a substantial proportion of the meager internal revenues available to the governor for the defense of the land. Thus taxation was at times a major raison d'être of the medieval parliament.

Throughout the Middle Ages legislation of the English parliament was periodically proclaimed and enforced in Ireland, but even in English parliaments legislation was of secondary importance between the reigns of Edward I and Henry VIII. And in Ireland legislation was limited to matters of purely local concern: apart from the Statutes of Kilkenny (1366) and Poynings' Law (1494), few medieval statutes were of major significance or lasting impact. Instead it was its administrative and quasi-judicial functions that provided the major continuing business of the Irish parliament. For these purposes, parliaments were convoked with an increasing frequency in the fifteenth century, so that between 1425 and 1494—at a time when English parliaments were meeting with a declining frequency—parliaments or great councils met almost every year. Starting with Edward IV's reign (1461–1470, 1471–1483), parliaments normally ran to several sessions; Dublin and Drogheda were the normal venues, as had been customary since Henry IV's reign, but sessions were occasionally held outside the Pale.

Many parliaments, apparently, drew up formal addresses to the king concerning the state of the land. Since Richard II was the only medieval king to visit the lordship (1394–1395) after King John in 1210, these addresses, and no doubt the consultations that lay behind them, were of particular importance in crown-community relations. Less frequently, we can detect behind them and parliament's other work the traces of friction between the king, royal officials, and subjects. Officials were anxious to control the channels of communication so as to protect themselves against charges of maladministration, while subjects sought redress of grievances at the highest level, and for his part the king sought full information but was also anxious not to undermine the authority of his ministers or to be pestered with the petty problems of a relatively unimportant part of his dominions.

For the rest, the fifteenth-century parliament rolls show that parliament now dealt with large numbers of petitions for matters of grace or of justice. These were predominantly from private individuals or particular interest groups, and many would earlier have been considered by the council outside parliament. By about 1450 a substantial portion of the petitions were directed to the Commons, which also sponsored proposals prepared by the council, magnates, and local authorities, so that the proportion of petitions actually prepared by the Commons must have been small. Manifestly, most petitions received perfunctory consideration: if a prima facie case were established, the Lords would remit the matter to an appropriate tribunal for determination. In this way the 1463–1464 parliament could pass 106 statutes in four sessions lasting twenty-three days. In practice, parliament was intervening in matters that would in England have been dealt with elsewhere. It was compensating for the weakness of royal government in Ireland by lending its authority, as the highest court in the land, to the work of inferior courts. And in the case of matters of equity that sprang from developments in the common law or the inability of the traditional courts to act effectively, it was establishing a new jurisdiction parallel to the development of chancery in England.

These developments were unwittingly curtailed by the enactment of Poynings' Law in 1494. This statute was part of a package of reform proposals devised by Henry VII. It provided that no parliament should be convoked except by license from the king, and that only such bills as had first been approved by him should be debated and either passed or rejected there without amendment. Its aim was conservative, but its effects were revolutionary. It attempted, rather awkwardly, to consolidate royal control over a key instrument of government that during the Wars of the Roses had been manipulated by successive governors against the king's interests. A notable instance was parliament's role in confirming Lambert Simnel's title as King Edward VI in 1487. Although successful in its aims, Poynings' Law effectively curtailed parliament's administrative and judicial functions, which devolved on the council, assisted by the development of chancery. Instead, parliament now met every five or ten years, primarily to approve a subsidy act; and until the Reformation (1536) and the need to endorse successive religious settlements, it was of comparatively minor importance. One further casualty of Poynings' Law was the representative great council, which had been peculiar to Ireland. None met after 1494, although for reasons that are now quite obscure they were in the fifteenth century sometimes summoned as an alternative to parliament. Provided they were of the same composition, Irish great councils could grant taxation and pass legislation (called ordinances, not statutes) just like parliaments. Otherwise, the only difference apparently concerned the period of summons, which might be less than the forty days required for parliament.

This account of the Irish parliament has concentrated on its role as an instrument of royal government. Given the particularism of the lordship's communities, their remoteness from court, and the relative weakness of the Dublin administration, parliament was vitally important and generally successful in the maintenance of consensus and cooperation between crown and community. Yet some friction was inevitable. Moreover, excepting the occasional magnate who was a peer of both parliaments, the lordship was unrepresented in the English parliament. Thus, at times the Irish parliament also became an instrument of the lordship's political community, helping to sustain and foster a separate sense of regional identity there. Most notably, with the encouragement of the lieutenant, Richard, duke of York, it even went so far as to declare in 1460 that the lordship was "corporate of itself" and not bound by English statutes. Yet such sentiments had little long-term impact before the mid sixteenth century. After 1541 parliament achieved a new status with the erection of the lordship into a kingdom comprising both English and Gaelic communities, and the admission to parliament of Gaelic representatives.

BIBLIOGRAPHY

F. W. A. Asplin, *Medieval Ireland c. 1170–1495: A Bibliography of Secondary Works* (1971), 53–55; Art Cosgrove and J. I. McGuire, eds., *Parliament and Community* (1983), 25–68; Steven G. Ellis, *Reform and Revival: English Government in Ireland, 1470–1534* (1986), chaps. 3 and 5; Brian Farrell, ed., *The Irish Parliamentary Tradition* (1973), 37–87; James F. Lydon, *England and Ireland in the Later Middle Ages* (1981), 122–152, "The Irish Church and Taxation in the Fourteenth Century," in *Irish Ecclesiastical Record,* 5th ser., **103** (1965), and "William of Windsor and the Irish Parliament," in *English Historical Review,* **80** (1965); Nicholas Pronay and John Taylor, *Parliamentary Texts of the Later Middle Ages* (1980), 117–152; David B. Quinn, "The Irish Parliamentary Subsidy in the Fifteenth and Sixteenth Centuries," in *Proceedings of the Royal Irish Academy,* **42** (1934–1935); Henry G. Richardson and George O. Sayles, *The Irish Parliament in the Middle Ages* (1952).

STEVEN G. ELLIS

[See also **Ireland; Modus Tenendi Parliamentum.**]

PARLIAMENT, SCOTTISH. The Scottish parliament is a subject comparatively understudied, its

PARLIAMENT, SCOTTISH

evolution ripe for reassessment. It is clear that it grew out of the Curia Regis of David I (*r.* 1124–1153), a court attended by prelates, tenants-in-chief, and members of the household. To what extent it owed anything to Celtic antecedents is totally unknown. As elsewhere one of the main functions of this body—the council—was to dispense justice, though it is doubtful if such was its sole concern. The first reference to a colloquium occurs in 1235. According to Duncan the term persisted even after the introduction of *parliamentum*, from the French *parlement,* because of the "small use of French in Scotland."

Parliament is first so recorded in 1293 with reference to the council sitting in its capacity as a supreme court of law. That the institution represented something more is indicated by a provision in the Treaty of Birgham (1290) safeguarding the inviolability of the Scottish parliament, disallowing summonses to non-Scottish courts, and forbidding deliberation of business concerning the kingdom or its inhabitants at any future parliament held outside Scotland. Parliament in some sense was already perceived to represent "the community in political action." The assemblies in 1290 and 1293 were both attended by bishops, abbots, priors, earls, and barons—the tenants-in-chief of the crown. While the pleas in 1293 reveal strong English influence, Scottish practice fairly quickly developed along its own lines.

In practice, parliament was a somewhat cumbersome body. Not only did attendance require a precept at forty days' notice but poor communications and extreme localism dictated a reluctance to participate. A treatise on the king's household that has been dated to the reign of John Balliol (1293) distinguishes between "full parliament" and "lesser council." One example of the latter was the privy or secret council, so called because its members were sworn to secrecy. Another, on record from the 1360's, was the council general, a lesser alternative to parliament, summoned by letter at short notice on the personal invitation of the king. Despite earlier claims the only apparent difference between the two bodies apart from the method of summons is that the presence of the king was essential to parliament whereas the council general could meet without him.

John Balliol appears to have been intent upon promoting parliament, to judge from frequent meetings in his short reign, and he possibly toyed with broadening the basis of representation. Novel participants were the burgesses who appended their seals to the Franco-Scottish treaty of 1295. They were also party to the Cambuskenneth indenture of 1326, which granted the tenth penny to Robert Bruce (Robert I of Scotland). Financial considerations may likewise have dictated their involvement in the Treaty of Edinburgh in 1328 and their attendance at the parliament of 1341, when the burghs were assessed for the "contribution." The evidence, however, does not indicate whether the burgesses were present on these occasions in an internal rather than an external capacity. By 1357 the documentation is explicit. The council general at Scone, which decided upon the means of paying David II's ransom, preserves the first mention of the three estates: *concordatum est et assensum per tres communitates ibidem existentes* (it was agreed and approved by the three estates present in the same place). The *tres communitates* were modeled upon French practice, and with their colleagues, the clergy and the magnates, the burgesses continued to sit in the unicameral chamber.

A clear measure of representation seems to be implied among those summoned to the parliament at Ayr in 1315, since among the ranks of the clergy the list included deans and archdeacons as well as "the rest of the prelates of the churches" together with earls, barons, knights, "and the rest of the community of the realm of Scotland, cleric and lay, gathered together to treat, discuss and ordain upon the state, defence and permanent security of the kingdom of Scotland." Since all were to meet in the parish church of Ayr, where presumably space was limited, it would appear that formality of summons conceals the reality of representation. David II's reign (1329–1371) produced the first attempt to lessen the burden of attendance when in 1367 "certain persons were chosen [by the estates] to hold the parliament and leave was given to the others to return home on account of the harvest." Such a rump was designated as a commission, whose findings had the force of law, as distinguished from a committee, which made findings and reported back to parliament. James I (*r.* 1406–1437) attempted to counter the potentially monopolistic or arbitrary tendencies of such commissions by demanding that representatives of the small barons and free tenants be elected as "commissioners of the shire." Fresh from a lengthy confinement in London that had afforded him ample opportunity to admire English practice, he also required that the commissioners elect "a wise and ane expert mann callit the common spekar of parliament" to act as spokesman for the "commonis." His demands were unheeded on both counts and shire representation was not adopted until the late sixteenth century.

James further attempted to overcome a native resistance to parliamentary attendance by relinquishing the blanket summons in favor of issuing precepts to individuals, among whom he distinguished "lords of parliament" drawn from the ranks of the small barons and soon to be known as "lairds." From the 1440's such lordships were regarded as hereditary. The question of whether James intended the creation of a parliamentary peerage remains open. Like his predecessors he continued to employ the device of the committee that drafted legislation for subsequent presentation to parliament, but it is not until 1467 that there occurs the first reference to a committee *ad formandum articulos.* From then on the committee of articles was regularly utilized, usually six or eight members being elected to it from each of the estates. By 1525 the spiritual lords elected the temporal lords and the temporal the spiritual to the committee. In other cases the estates would each elect their own representatives or the former would be elected by the estates as a whole. In James V's reign (1513–1542) the committee of articles was closely associated with the privy council and with the general council. Parliaments occasionally granted the privy council the powers of a commission and in 1535 the highly dangerous precedent was established of constituting the committee of articles as a commission. After the experiment was repeated in 1543 no other commission was appointed until the practice was revived during the following century.

Recent scholarly opinion has substantially revised the long-held view that the medieval Scottish parliament was merely a cipher or alternatively the hapless tool of the crown. It is difficult to know whether parliament played a part in the setting aside of John Balliol in 1296, though it is unlikely that it did not. Parliament in 1315 recognized Edward Bruce as *rex designatus.* There is more than a hint of the contractual theory of monarchy in the Declaration of Arbroath of 1320. Notwithstanding that the idea of mutual cooperation is a useful fiction in diplomatic transactions (a ploy manipulated with conspicuous success by both Robert I and David II), there is considerable evidence that parliament did not hesitate to oppose the king's wishes. This is most apparent in the presumed parliament of 1352, when David II's proposal to nominate a member of the English royal family as his successor was rejected, as it was again in 1364. Robert II's son was removed from the justiciary because he was "useless to the community." Confirmation of Nicholson's assertion that "the chief point of Scottish constitutional theory was that the king should live of his own" is found in parliamentary opposition to James I's insistence upon direct taxation, while kings and regents alike in the fifteenth century took care to secure parliament's consent to contentious legislation. The ideal of parliament, articulated in the Treaty of Birgham, as custodian of the rights and liberties of the kingdom and its subjects survived, however spasmodically, the Middle Ages.

The magnates always dominated the three estates, but the intensely regional nature of Scottish administration and the endurance of the kin based society ensured that the interests of the great ones were often identical to those of the humblest subject in the kingdom. The vast amount of legislation in the edited volumes of the *Acts of the Parliaments of Scotland* (now in need of revision) proves as much. The earliest surviving rolls date from the time of John Balliol and there are other fragments from the reigns of David II and Robert II. From 1466 the record is reasonably complete. The tighter bonds of Scottish society and less divisive stratification in a country where most people, however remotely, took pride in their aristocratic connections ensured a different development from the neighbor to the south. True demand for constitutional reform and parliamentary change awaited the collapse of the Scottish medieval order in the seventeenth century.

Existing studies of the Scottish parliament are bedeviled by absent or fragmentary evidence, by uncritical comparison with England's parliament, and by the circumstance that crucial innovations, particularly in the thirteenth century, took place during periods of English influence, thus obfuscating the record and distorting the uniqueness of the Scottish institution. The problem is further compounded because the major historian of parliament in Scotland, R. S. Rait, persisted in distinguishing it, throughout the Middle Ages, as the tool of the king.

BIBLIOGRAPHY

W. Croft Dickinson, Gordon Donaldson, and Isabel A. Milne, *A Source Book of Scottish History,* 3 vols., 2nd ed. (1958–1961); W. Croft Dickinson, *Scotland from the*

Earliest Times to 1603, 3rd ed., rev. by Archibald A. M. Duncan (1977); Gordon Donaldson, ed., *Scottish Historical Documents* (1970); Archibald A. M. Duncan, "The Early Parliaments of Scotland," in *Scottish Historical Review*, **45** (1966); Alexander Grant, *Independence and Nationhood: Scotland, 1306–1469* (1984); Ranald Nicholson, *Scotland: The Later Middle Ages* (1974); H. G. Richardson and George O. Sayles, "The Scottish Parliaments of Edward I," in *Scottish Historical Review*, **25** (1928); Thomas Thomson and Cosmo Innes, eds., *The Acts of the Parliaments of Scotland*, 12 vols. (1814–1875); Bruce Webster, *Scotland from the Eleventh Century to 1603 (Sources of History)* (1975).

EDWARD J. COWAN

[See also **David I of Scotland; David II of Scotland; Law, Scots; Robert I of Scotland; Robert II of Scotland; Scotland: History.**]

PARODY, LATIN. Parody consists in the manipulation of a well-known text or literary form for humorous (particularly bathetic) effect. It must be distinguished from imitation, such as the Ovidian epistles by Baudri of Bourgeuil (1046–1130) or the frequent use of Vergilian echoes in epic (as in the tenth-century *Waltharius*). The success of pure parody depends on the immediate recognition of the text that is being parodied and the awareness that it is being employed for absurd purposes. It requires a shared literary experience, which, in the Middle Ages, was provided principally by the classroom or by religion.

The basic Latin primer until the Renaissance was Donatus' *Ars minor* (fourth century), and its opening section, on the basic parts of speech, was a frequent source of parody: "What part of speech is Money? Preposition. Why? Because it is placed before everything else . . ." (Lehmann, No. 3); "Is there a comparative of "monk"? No. Why? Because it does not admit increase in virtue or decrease in vice . . ." (Lehmann, No. 4). The words "accusative," "genitive" and "dative" (accusing, engendering, giving) were naturally the source of many satirical puns. The *Doctrinale* (1199), an extremely popular grammar in verse by Alexander de Villa Dei, was parodied in a poem that opened with the same words, *Scribere clericulis:* "Now is the time to learn the compound shape of the feminine gender, the meaning of the inflexion of cases with Venus' maid-servants, the meaning of copulation and conjunction . . ." (Lehmann, No. 13).

In the early Middle Ages the works of Vergil were so well known that centos (utilizing individual lines and half-lines) were composed: Ausonius' *Cena nuptialis* (Marriage feast, fourth century) provided some startling effects in the consummation scene. A more serious *Cento Vergilianus* by Proba, wife of a consul, employed Vergilian lines to compose a life of Christ. Parody of style, however, is rare after late antiquity. Mock-heroic is common in the classical poets and continues in the *Appendix Vergiliana:* the *Moretum*, for example, a high-flown account of a peasant's breakfast, may be as late as the Carolingian period. Beast fable and beast epic, of course, always contain the materials of parody: the pomposity of many speeches is undercut simply by placing them in the mouths of animals. This is often seen in Nigel of Longchamp's *Speculum stultorum* (twelfth century), whose hero, Burnellus the Ass, makes many grandiloquent speeches.

The best-known texts in the Middle Ages (and thus the most common sources for parody) were the Bible and the liturgy. Composed sometime around 1200, one of the most popular satires against the papal curia was the *Evangelium secundum marcam argenti* (The Gospel according to [the Silver] Mark) (Lehmann, No. 1, in three versions), which is a tissue of reminiscences from the Gospels: "Blessed are the rich, for they shall be filled. Blessed are they that have, for they shall not go away empty. Blessed are they that have Money, for theirs is the Court of Rome." Or, "And the Cardinals said, 'Master, what shall we do to inherit money?' The Pope answered and said, 'What is written in the Law? How readest thou? Thou shalt love gold and silver with all thy heart and with all thy soul, and thy rich neighbour as thyself; this do, and thou shalt live. . . .'" The pattern of verse-response is parodied in a satire against monks, in which a Latin hexameter verse (for instance, "The monkish crowd, a noble host they are") is followed by a response from the Psalms ("Their sound is gone out throughout all the earth and their words to the end of the world"). The Divine Office was an obvious source of parody: "The Epistle: the reading of the Acts of the Potators to the Inebriates" (Lehmann, No. 17). Similarly, the Lord's Prayer: "Our Potation (*potus/pater*), which art in the wine-cup (*cypho/coelis*). . . . Lead us not into drunkenness (*ebrietatem/tentationem*) but deliver us from an empty cup (*cypho vacuo/malo*). A-bed! (*Stramen/Amen*)" (Lehmann, No. 19).

In another Gospel parody, the Ten Commandments are adapted: "Thou shalt not kill much, but thou shalt commit adultery; thou shalt not covet thy neighbour's property but his wife" (Lehmann, No. 20). The Archpoet of Cologne (twelfth century) asks for mercy not for "this sinner," but for "this drinker" (*potatori/peccatori*), but a later poet, Walter of Wimborne (thirteenth century), used drinking as a sign of divine ecstasy, and made the parody serious. A joke as old as Odysseus' deception of Polyphemus is revived in several elaborate Lives and Sermons on Saint No One—No One ascended to heaven, is happy in everything, is allowed to marry two wives, and alone (according to the Benedictine Rule) is permitted to speak after compline.

Hymns were a frequent inspiration. The hymn for prime, "Now the star of light has risen," continued "suppliants, we pray to God," but the parodist substituted "now is time to drink" (*Iam lucis orto sidere/Statim oportet bibere*). With the substitution of *vinum* for *verbum,* the famous Victorine hymn *Verbum bonum et suave* (Wholesome Word and sweet) was parodied many times. Two early hymns on the Cross, *Vexilla regis prodeunt* and *Pange lingua gloriosi* by Venantius Fortunatus (sixth century), were adapted to celebrate the death of Piers Gaveston, the hated favorite of Edward II: "Sing, tongue, the death of Peter. . . ." The Marian hymn *Ave Virgo gloriosa* reappears as: *Vinum dulce gloriosum/Pingue facit et carnosum/Atque pectus aperit* (How sweet and noble is the wine that makes the flesh grow fat and opens up the heart).

Some other literary forms were so well established as to be parodied. Several versions and copies exist of a letter from Satan to the Pope, thanking him for the good work the church is doing on Satan's behalf. Medical formulas are burlesqued in a poem against baldness (Lehmann, No. 22) and in the recipe given to Burnellus the Ass for growing a new tail. A love song in the Codex Buranus (No. 62: *Dum Diane vitrea*) is parodied in the drinking song *Dum domus lapidea* (No. 197), which keeps the elaborate rhyme scheme: both poems are unique, indicating a private joke.

BIBLIOGRAPHY

Paul Lehmann, *Die Parodie im Mittelalter,* 2nd ed. (1963).

A. G. RIGG

[See also **Archpoet; Goliards; Latin Literature; Nigel of Longchamp.**]

PAROIKOI, dependent peasants in the Byzantine Empire. The literal meaning is "dwelling near"; in the Code of Justinian a *paroikos* is described as one who has transferred his domicile to another region. The term is rarely encountered in the early period (fourth to sixth centuries). The texts differentiate it from a *colonus adscriptitius.* In this period a *paroikos* received land for cultivation, giving the landlord perhaps one-tenth of the produce; he seems to have been tied to the land. In the seventh to ninth centuries the few mentions of *paroikoi* concern ecclesiastical lands. Presumably the majority of the peasantry consisted of free farmers, not of *paroikoi.*

In the tenth century some monastic documents show the existence of various categories of *paroikoi.* The *demosiarioi* might possess land and were fiscally responsible to the state. The *ateleis* and *douloparoikoi* did not possess land and were fiscally responsible to the landlord. After having occupied land for thirty years, a *paroikos* could not be evicted but neither could he abandon voluntarily, according to the collection of legal writings known as the *peira.* According to Ostrogorskij, the *demosiarioi paroikoi* formed the bulk of the rural population, which thus consisted not of free peasants but of peasants tied to the land and paying their taxes to the state. This theory has not found wide acceptance.

In the eleventh century and later, the number of *paroikoi* increased, so that by the thirteenth century they were the vast majority of the rural population. The condition of a *paroikos* of this late period is better known, although the lack of uniformity still creates problems. A *paroikos* was not a slave; he was free in his person, and could own and alienate land. But the essence of his condition was that he, his taxes, and his services were granted to lay or monastic landlords by the state. He paid state taxes and rent to the landlord; he owed labor and other services, and was not supposed to leave the service of the landlord. The majority of monastic *paroikoi* of this period did not own arable land (as opposed to vineyards) but leased it from the landlords. The acute shortage of manpower in the late Byzantine period forced the landlords into fierce competition for *paroikoi.*

BIBLIOGRAPHY

Peter Charanis, "On the Social Structure and Economic Organization of the Byzantine Empire in the Thirteenth Century and Later," in *Byzantinoslavica,* 12 (1951); Angeliki E. Laiou-Thomadakis, *Peasant Society in the Late Byzantine Empire* (1977); Paul Lemerle, "Esquisse pour une histoire agraire de Byzance," in *Revue historique,* **219** and **220** (1958); Georgije Ostrogorskij, *Pour l'histoire de la féodalité byzantine,* Henri Grégoire, trans. (1954), and *Quelques problèmes d'histoire de la paysannerie byzantine* (1956); Germaine Rouillard, *La vie rurale dans l'empire byzantin* (1953).

ANGELIKI LAIOU

[See also **Byzantine Empire: Economic Life and Social Structure; Colonus; Taxation, Byzantine.**]

PAROUSIA (literally, "presence" or "arrival"), a term used to designate the Second Coming or the Last Judgment, generally derived from Matthew 25:31. The iconography of the image varies, but normally Christ/God is shown enthroned in glory above a group of the "saved," who are often placed inside walls representing Heavenly Jerusalem; below the elect is a group of damned souls in the fires of hell. Early images include miniatures in the *Sacra parallela* (Paris, Bibliothèque Nationale, MS grec 923) and the *Christian Topography* of Cosmas Indicopleustes (Rome, Biblioteca Apostolica Vaticana, MS greco 699), both from the ninth century.

BIBLIOGRAPHY

Yves Christe, *La vision de Matthieu* (1973), 68–72; André Grabar, *L'empereur dans l'art byzantin* (1936, repr. 1971), 252ff.

LESLIE BRUBAKER

[See also **Church, Early; Cosmas Indicopleustes; Early Christian Art; Pre-Romanesque Art.**]

PARRYS, JOHN. See **Pares, John.**

PARTALOPA SAGA. The tale of Partalopi is an anonymous *riddarasaga* (tale of chivalry) that derives from the French romance of adventure *Parténopeus de Blois.* The saga is preserved only in Icelandic manuscripts, but older scholarship assumed that it was translated into Norwegian in the thirteenth century along with other French romances. The major discrepancies between *Partalopa saga* and the extant continental versions of the tale suggest that *Partalopa saga* may have been translated from a version different from the one preserved today, or else may be a reworking of an originally faithful translation. That the romance of Parténopeus was popular in the Middle Ages is attested by the existence of Danish, English, Low and High German, Italian, Spanish, and Catalan versions of the tale.

Partalopa saga relates how Partalopi, son of King Hlöðvir of Frakkland (France), is transported under mysterious circumstances to Miklagarðr (Constantinople), where he becomes the lover of Marmoria, a maiden king and fairy mistress. The affair is unusual insofar as Marmoria remains invisible to Partalopi, and he remains invisible to her courtiers. Marmoria warns Partalopi not to attempt to see her, for that would also make him visible to her men and result in his death. But Partalopi succumbs to temptation: a magic stone renders Marmoria visible—with dire results. Only the intervention of Marmoria's sister saves the hero from death. After a succession of adventures, Partalopi is reconciled with Marmoria and marries her, and together they rule Miklagarðr, Grickland (Greece), and many other large countries.

As in many of the other *riddarasögur,* magical objects play a substantial role in the development of the narrative: a mysterious ship whisks Partalopi away from his native country and into Marmoria's realm; a wondrous bird rescues Partalopi from death at the hands of his enemies and drops him into the midst of his own men; a magic stone presented to Partalopi by the archbishop of Cologne enables him to see his fairy mistress.

Partalopa saga makes moderate use of the rhetorical and ornamental techniques associated with the courtly style of the *riddarasögur* translated in the thirteenth century. Synonymous collocations and alliterative clusters occur throughout the saga to emphasize significant dialogue and descriptive passages. Occasionally the author employs semantic or grammatical variation, or interweaves proverbs into the narrative, such as "Kavlld erv iafnan kvenna rad, þviat þav erv favitr ok brad" (Women's counsels are ever cruel, since they are foolish and rash). The saga is characterized by language both euphonious and rhythmical.

The sense for symmetry expressed stylistically through alliteration and synonymous collocations is apparent in the structure of the saga. The author balances narrative units against each other, as at the beginning of the work, where the two principals are introduced. The fifteen-year-old Marmoria is portrayed first: "er allra kvenna var vænst" (who was the most beautiful of all women), "ok svo godvr klerkvr at eingi fekzt henni jafngodvr i ǫllv Griklandi" (and such a well educated person that no one was her equal in all Greece). The portrait of Partalopi that follows presents in him a perfect match: "var þa .xv. vetra gamall enn gamall var hann at viti svoat eingi stodzt honvm j Franz, svo ok at allri atgerfi svo at vexti ok asynd eingi var ok betri klerkvr j Franz en hann. litillatvr var hann ok vinsæll" (he was then fifteen years old, but mature in understanding, so that no one equaled him in France, be that in all accomplishments, or in stature and appearance; there was no better educated person in France than he; he was gregarious and popular). Occasionally the author himself speaks, as when he modulates from one scene to the next: "Latvm hann nv leita P(artalopa) svo lengi sem honvm likar en rædvm nǫckvd vm Vrækiv" (Let us now permit him to search for Partalopi as long as he wishes, and let us relate something about Urækia).

Partalopa saga is transmitted in two fifteenth-century Icelandic vellums, in AM 533 4to (Arnamagnæan Institute, Copenhagen) and in Stockholm Perg. fol. 7 (Royal Library, Stockholm), in addition to a number of younger paper manuscripts.

BIBLIOGRAPHY

Sources. Lise Pexstgaard Andersen, ed., *Partalopa Saga* (1983), with English trans. by Foster W. Blaisdell; Oskar Klockhoff, ed., *Partalopa Saga för första gången utgifven* (1877); Bjarni Vilhjálmsson, ed., "Partalópa saga," in *Riddarasögur,* II (1949).

Studies. A. Trampe Bödtker, *Parténopeus de Blois: Étude comparative des versions islandaise et danoise* (1904); Eyvind Fjeld Halvorsen, "Partalopa saga," in *Kulturhistorisk leksikon for nordisk middelalder,* XIII (1968); Oskar Klockhoff, "Om Partalopa rímur," in *Små bidrag till nordiska literaturhistorien under medeltiden* (1880), 27–30; Eugen Kolbing, *Über die nordischen Gestaltungen der Partonopeus-Sage* (1873), and "Über die verschiedenen Gestaltungen der Partonopeus-Sage," in *Germanistische Studien,* II (1875); Henry Goddard Leach, "Is *Gibbonssaga* a Reflection of *Partonopeus?*" in *Medieval Studies in Memory of Gertrude Schoepperle Loomis* (1927).

MARIANNE E. KALINKE

[See also **Riddarasögur.**]

PARTHIANS, northeastern Iranian people whose empire, that of the Arsacids (founded by Aršak, Greek: Arsaces), freed Iran from Seleucid occupation. This dynasty existed longer than either of the other two great pre-Islamic Iranian dynasties, the Achaemenians and Sasanians, from 247 B.C. to A.D. 224/226. Aršak, leader of the nomadic Iranian tribe of the Parni, seized Parthia (Old Persian: Parthava; Greek: Parthyene), a former Achaemenian province, from its Seleucid satrap, Andragoras. Although the Seleucids managed to regain territory during the reign of Aršak's brother and successor, Tīrdat I (Greek: Tiridates; Armenian: Trdat), the Parthians, aided by local revolts among the Medes and other conquered Iranian peoples, pressed relentlessly across Iran, finally establishing themselves at Seleucia on the Tigris, where they built their western capital, Ctesiphon, in the reign of Mihrdāt I (Greek: Mithridates, *r. ca.* 171–138 B.C.). Despite invasions by the nomad Sakas in the east about 130 B.C. and the later challenge of the Kushan Empire, the Parthians established themselves as successors to the Achaemenians; Mihrdāt II (*ca.* 124–87 B.C.) styled himself king of kings and had a relief carved at Behistun (Bīsitūn) beneath that of Darius I.

From the first century B.C., Parthia faced the growing power of Rome along their common border on the Euphrates. The ill-fated invasion by the Roman general Marcus Licinius Crassus in 54 B.C. is described with dramatic detail by Plutarch. Armenia, which formed a buffer between the two superpowers, from the first century of the Christian era had a king of the Arsacid house appointed with Roman approval. Arsacid rule was tolerant—Jewish and Christian communities flourished—but notoriously decentralized and wracked by feuds among the noblity and within the royal house. Early in the third century the newly established Sasanian rulers of the semi-independent satrapy of Pārs (Greek: Pērsis), under Ardešir I, overthrew the last Arsacid king, Ardawān V (Greek: Artabanus V).

The Arsacids upheld Zoroastrianism. King Valaxš (Greek: Vologases) ordered the redaction of the Avesta, and fire temples were maintained (notably Ādur Burzen Mihr in Parthia; Isidore of Charax in his *Mansiones Parthicae* mentions also an ever-burning dynastic fire at Asaak). The *gōsāns* (minstrels) chanted the lays of the Kayanians, heroes of the epic age of the faith: one episode survives in a Sasanian redaction as the "Memorial of Zarer" (*Ayādgār ī Zarērān*). Legends transmitted by the Parthians, as well as Parthian kings and nobles, survive in Firdawsī's *Shāhnāma* (Book of kings). The Parthians were famed for the mounted soldiers the Romans called the *clibanarii,* and their "Parthian shot"—arrows fired while riding at full speed. They wore the distinctive felt helmet with earflaps, trousers, and soft boots of Central Asian horsemen, and they loved to adorn themselves with pearls. Their painting and architecture preserved Iranian traditions, and many of their administrative and social institutions were adopted by the Sasanians. Mani, the founder of Manichaeism, was a Parthian, and the Parthian language survived through the Sasanian period as the sacred tongue of the eastern Manichaeans, while the Persians called their own Zoroastrian literary language Pahlavi—Parthian. To this day a man of strength and nobility is called in Persian *pahlavān*—preserving the memory of that ancient great race, whose descendants, making their way to the sea from their homes in Parthia in the wake of the Arab conquest of Iran in the seventh century, fled to India, where they came to be known as Parsis—"Persians." They form today the majority of the adherents to Zoroastrianism.

BIBLIOGRAPHY

A. D. H. Bivar, "The Political History of Iran Under the Arsacids," in Ehsan Yarshater, ed., *Cambridge History of Iran,* III, pt. 1 (1983); Mary Boyce, "Manichaean Middle Persian Writings" and "Parthian Writings and Literature," *ibid.,* pt. 2 (1983); Malcolm A. R. Colledge, *Parthian Art* (1977); Nelson C. Debevoise, *A Political History of Parthia* (1938); Gennady A. Koshelenko, *Kul'tura Parfii* (1966); David Sellwood, *An Introduction to the Coinage of Parthia,* 2nd ed. (1980).

JAMES R. RUSSELL

[See also **Ardešīr I; Arsacids/Aršakuni, Armenian; Avesta; Ctesiphon; Manichaeans; Pahlavi Literature; Sasanians; Zoroastrianism.**]

PARTIMEN. The Old Provençal partimen, or *joc partit* (from *joc partir,* to choose, or to let someone choose, an alternative), is a lyric genre, created around 1170/1180, for two, or occasionally more, troubadours to debate the paradoxes of love and the problems of courtly life. The first poet introduced the alternatives of the dilemma, the second poet chose the better alternative, replying in the second strophe; in alternating strophes the poets then defended their own arguments, normally until there were six strophes. In the tornadas each poet appealed to a judge or summed up his argument. As the melody and strophe form of many partimens were borrowed from well-known lyrics, it has been suggested that improvisation may have occurred initially.

BIBLIOGRAPHY

Charles Camproux, "On the Subject of an Argument Between Elias and His Cousin," and Glynnis M. Cropp, "The *Partimen* Between Folquet de Marseille and Tostemps," in William T. H. Jackson, ed., *The Interpretation of Medieval Lyric Poetry* (1980); Erich Köhler, *Trobadorlyrik und höfischer Roman* (1962), 89–113, 153–192; Sebastian Neumeister, *Das Spiel mit der höfischen Liebe* (1969).

GLYNNIS M. CROPP

[See also **Provençal Literature; Tenso; Tornada; Troubadour, Trouvère, Trovador.**]

PASCHAL II, POPE (*ca.* 1058–1118), reigned during the investiture conflict. A north Italian, born Rainer at Bieda (near Ravenna), he became a monk in an unknown location in his early youth and rose to prominence when he was made a cardinal by Pope Gregory VII (*ca.* 1078). During the pontificate of Urban II (1088–1099), Cardinal Rainer was a leading member of the papal curia, traveling as legate to Spain in 1090. Apparently because of his long and loyal service as an aide to Gregory VII and Urban II he was regarded as the latter's obvious heir and was swiftly raised to the papal chair on Urban's death in 1099.

As events were soon to show, however, Paschal II lacked sufficient doctrinal sagacity and political acumen to be equal to the task of carrying on successfully the work of his predecessors. Paschal's greatest error was to transform the campaign for "freedom of the church" waged by Gregory VII and Urban II into a more narrowly defined controversy over investiture, and hence to abandon the goals his predecessors had held most dear. That is, whereas Gregory and Urban had been most intent on preventing the nomination of clerics by lay powers so that the church might be staffed by only the most reform-minded ministers, Paschal became so preoccupied with the issue of how clerics were to be installed into office that he lost sight of the truly central point of nomination. The result was that he tolerated compromise settlements of the investiture conflict in France and England that sacrificed the

PASCHAL II, POPE

most essential Gregorian principles and thereafter became embroiled in a humiliating confrontation with the emperor of Germany, in which he acted continually to his own disadvantage.

The first fatal step was taken in 1102, when Paschal promulgated a decree against lay investiture of clerics with the symbols of their tangible properties and governmental rights (known as their *temporalia*). Since Gregory VII and Urban II had already inveighed repeatedly against lay investiture of clerics with the symbols of their spiritual offices (*spiritualia*), Paschal no doubt thought that by forbidding lay powers to have any role at all in the ceremonics pertaining to clerical installation he was pursuing Gregorian principles to their most rigorous conclusion. But in fact once the pope drew attention to the question of what authority stood behind ecclesiastical holdings of *temporalia,* a matter of the most fundamental concern to all secular rulers, he made the entire issue of ceremonial investiture appear to be more important than it had ever seemed before and hence provoked a series of hostilities that led to ever-increasing difficulties. The compromise settlements of the investiture question in France and England (arrived at in 1106 and 1107, respectively) at least brought peace, but they can hardly be adduced to Paschal's credit. In both cases the kings of the respective countries agreed to cease investing bishops and abbots with the symbols of their *spiritualia* (ring and staff) and thereby lost some appearance of being theocratic monarchs. On the other hand, however, the crown in both countries retained its right of investing with the *temporalia* and, most important, retained its ability to control all higher ecclesiastical appointments. Whether Paschal realized it or not, by conceding this power of appointments he in effect abandoned the Gregorian campaign for "freedom of the church" in France and England.

Worse was to follow in Paschal's dealings with the German Empire. At the beginning of Paschal's pontificate Germany was still ruled by Gregory VII's original antagonist, Henry IV, but the old emperor had by now become worn down by decades of struggle with the papacy and in 1100 indicated a willingness to negotiate a reconciliation. Had Paschal seized on this initiative, he most likely could have resolved the long conflict between the empire and the papacy greatly to his own advantage. His conception of rigorous Gregorianism, however, led him to insist on holding out for an unconditional surrender. In 1104 it may have seemed as if the pope's intransigence was being rewarded, because Henry IV's son Henry rose up in that year against his father in the name of the papal cause. But civil war followed, and when Henry V came to rule without contest upon his father's death in 1106, he quickly made it clear that he had no intention at all of submitting to Paschal II on the investiture issue.

Matters came to a head early in the winter of 1110/1111, when Henry V advanced on Rome with a military force intending to intimidate Paschal into retracting his investiture rulings. Thus placed on the defensive, the pope responded in February 1111 with the amazing offer of surrendering all the *temporalia* held by all bishops and abbots from the empire in Germany and Italy since the days of Charlemagne. All such churchmen would henceforth be required to live solely from tithes and freely granted alms. Needless to say, Henry V was perfectly willing to appropriate the vast amount of lands and wealth that the pope was hereby offering to him, but since the bishops and abbots concerned had never been consulted they reacted with indignation when the agreement was read aloud in St. Peter's. Recognizing immediately that the pope's startling concession could never be implemented, Henry then took Paschal into protective custody and by April had wrung from him an entirely different but equally startling grant—a categorical and abject surrender on the issue of investiture. Thereupon the emperor returned to Germany in triumph, but Paschal, now faced with the likelihood of a revolt by his own clergy, repudiated his second concession in 1112. Since he was unwilling to go so far as to excommunicate Henry, however, he was unable to satisfy the extremists in his own camp, and when Henry advanced on Rome again, in 1117, the pope fled south to avoid having to repudiate his repudiation. A year later, with nothing settled, he died.

BIBLIOGRAPHY

Uta-Renate Blumenthal, *The Early Councils of Pope Paschal II, 1100–1110* (1978); Z. N. Brooke, "Gregory VII and the First Contest Between Empire and Papacy," in *Cambridge Medieval History,* V (1926), and "Lay Investiture and Its Relation to the Conflict of Empire and Papacy," in *Proceedings of the British Academy,* 25 (1939); Peter R. McKeon, "The Lateran Council of 1112, the 'Heresy' of Lay Investiture, and the Excommunication of Henry V," in *Medievalia et humanistica,* 17 (1966); Karl F. Morrison, *Tradition and Authority in the*

Western Church, 300–1140 (1969); Carlo Servatius, *Paschalis II, 1099–1118* (1979).

ROBERT E. LERNER

[See also **Councils, Western; Gregory VII, Pope; Henry IV of Germany; Investiture and Investiture Conflict; Papacy; Reform, Idea of; Urban II, Pope.**]

PASCHALE CHRONICON, a Byzantine chronicle covering the period from Adam to the twentieth year of Heraklios (629; the surviving text goes only to 628), composed by a cleric in Constantinople in the 630's. The latter part is important for contemporary history since it uses detailed eyewitness accounts. The significance of the earlier parts varies according to the sources used; many sections agree closely with the chronicle of Malalas. Even for the sixth century, the account is sketchy. The author has tried to enliven his material with anecdotal insertions from hagiographic and other sources, such as Cosmas Indicopleustes. The Greek is popular and the style unadorned.

BIBLIOGRAPHY

The text is in L. Dindorf, ed., *Historiae Byzantinae,* Corpus Scriptorum Historiae Byzantinae, X–XI (1832). See also Kyra Ericsson, "Revising a Date in the Chronicon Paschale," in *Jahrbuch der Österreichischen Byzantinistik,* **17** (1968); G. Mercati, "A Study of the Paschal Chronicle," in *Journal of Theological Studies,* 7 (1906); E. Schwartz, "Chronicon Paschale," in *Real-encyclopädie der classischen Altertumswissenschaft,* III (1899).

AVERIL CAMERON

[See also **Byzantine Literature; Cosmas Indicopleustes; Heraklios; Historiography, Byzantine; Malalas, John.**]

PASCHASIUS RADBERTUS OF CORBIE, ST. (*ca.* 790–*ca.* 860), Benedictine exegete and theologian who was born near Soissons and died in Corbie. Radbertus entered the famous abbey of Corbie before 820, where he served as teacher and, from 843 to about 851, as abbot. A disciplinary dispute led to his abdication and voluntary exile at the neighboring monastery of St. Riquier, but he returned to Corbie before his death. In 822 Radbertus assisted in the foundation of Corvey in Saxony.

Many of his writings were for the edification of the monks of Corbie and Corvey. These include a discussion of the feast of the Assumption (written under the name of St. Jerome), a life of the Virgin Mary, several homilies and saints' lives, and commentaries on the Gospel of Matthew, Psalm 44, and the Lamentations of Jeremiah. The treatise *De corpore et sanguine Domini,* the first theological treatise on the Eucharist, was originally written in 831 for the novices of Corvey. It was revised in 844 for the Frankish king Charles II the Bald, who had also commissioned a eucharistic treatise from another monk of Corbie, Ratramnus. The differing opinions of Radbertus and Ratramnus on the body of Christ in the Eucharist have been widely studied, and have been shown to be related to their different understandings of the Virgin Birth, expounded by Radbertus in *De partu Virginis.*

Although some modern scholars have portrayed Radbertus as a protoscholastic, he was better known to his contemporaries as a teacher and exegete than as a theologian.

BIBLIOGRAPHY

Sources. Works reprinted from earlier editions are in *Patrologia latina,* CXX (1852). Critical editions are *De corpore et sanguine Domini,* Bedae Paulus, ed., in *Corpus Christianorum, continuatio medievalis,* XVI (1969); *Expositio in Matheo libri XII,* B. Paulus, ed., in *Corpus Christianorum, continuatio medievalis,* LVI A–B (1984); *Cogitis me,* A. Ripberger, ed., *De partu Virginis,* E. A. Matter, ed., in *Corpus Christianorum, continuatio medievalis,* LVI C (1985).

Study. Henri Peltier, *Pascase Radbert* (1938).

E. ANN MATTER

[See also **Agius of Corvey; Benedictines; Biblical Interpretation; Carolingians; Exegesis, Latin; Philosophy and Theology, Western European.**]

PASSION CYCLE. The passion of Christ encompasses the events surrounding his suffering and death. Cycles in art were elaborated to illustrate the last week of Christ's life, beginning with his entry into Jerusalem and finishing with his entombment. Passion themes entered Christian art only in the third and fourth centuries, in a series of sculpted sarcophagi. Scenes such as the Seizure of Christ, the Kiss of Judas, Christ Before Pilate, and Pilate Washing His Hands are included, but initially the pictorial narrative did not extend to the crucifixion. Instead, a triumphal cross *(crux invicta)* or Christ holding a cross is represented to demonstrate his glory and victory over death.

The crucifixion appeared in the early fifth century on the wood doors of S. Sabina at Rome and an ivory plaque now in the British Museum. Nevertheless, the majority of surviving early Passion cycles, chief among them the mosaics of S. Apollinare Nuovo in Ravenna (early sixth century), the Gospels of St. Augustine (*ca.* 600), and the Rossano Gospels (sixth century), continued to omit the crucifixion.

From the ninth century on, the crucifixion became the focus of Passion imagery, and this veneration of the cross led to a monumentalization of the theme. The crucifixion was presented as the climax of Passion programs, as in the Naumburg Cathedral choir screen (1250–1260), or was raised to the level of an independent subject, as in the Wooden Gero Cross of Cologne Cathedral (acquired between 969 and 976, possibly completed by 965), or the so-called *Pestkreuz* (Plague Crucifix) of S. Maria im Kapitol, Cologne (1304). The process of excerpting the central figures from a broader narrative context for presentation as devotional images resulted in the appearance of such groups as Christ and St. John (extracted from the Last Supper) and the Pietà (an abbreviation of the Lamentation).

The large number of cycles that were created in the late Middle Ages indicates the growing interest in the Passion of Christ. In Italian painting, Giotto in frescoes for the Arena Chapel in Padua (1305–1312), and Pietro Lorenzetti in his Life of Christ cycle, in the lower church of S. Francesco in Assisi, depict elaborate Passion narratives. One of the fullest accounts was rendered by Duccio on the back of the *Maestà* (1308–1311); he presents twenty-six scenes, from the Entry into Jerusalem, the Last Supper, the Arrest, and the trials of Christ to the Crucifixion, Deposition, and Entombment. This expansion of the cyclical representation of the Passion, which culminated around 1500, has parallels in the rise of popular Passion plays, the widespread veneration of Passion relics, and the emergence of the sculptural stations of the cross.

BIBLIOGRAPHY

Louis Réau, *Iconographie de l'art chrétien*, II, pt. 2 (1957), 393–528; Gertrud Schiller, *Iconography of Christian Art*, II, *The Passion of Jesus Christ*, Janet Seligman, trans. (1972).

MICHAEL T. DAVIS

[See also **Arena Chapel; Assisi, San Francesco; Byzantine Art; Crucifixion; Deposition from the Cross; Duccio di Buoninsegna; Early Christian Art; Easter; Entry into Jerusalem; Fresco Painting; Giotto di Bondone; Gothic Art; Holy Week; Iconography; Lamentation; Last Supper; Lorenzetti, Pietro; Manuscript Illumination, European; Mosaic and Mosaic Making; Pietà; Pre-Romanesque Art; Romanesque Art; Stations of the Cross; Visigothic Art.**]

PASSION PLAYS, FRENCH. Plays depicting the Passion of Christ appeared in France at the beginning of the fourteenth century. More than simple dramatizations of the Passion story, these works often portrayed the whole of Christ's life. The playwrights took their material from many sources besides the Bible. Among the most important of these were the *Passion des jongleurs,* a verse narrative from the late twelfth or early thirteenth century, the apocryphal *Gospel of Nicodemus,* and the *Legenda aurea* of Jacobus de Varagine. Some of the plays also included events from the Old Testament, forming a historical cycle from Creation to Pentecost. The more elaborate plays were spectacular representations of the entire cosmos, including heaven and hell. Some involved 200 or more characters and mirrored many aspects of late medieval life.

The earliest surviving play in French is the *Passion du Palatinus* from the early fourteenth century; there, is however, evidence that earlier plays once existed. Also from the fourteenth century comes the *Passion Ste.-Geneviève* (named for the Paris library in which it is found). These two early plays dramatize only the events of Holy Week and are quite short (2,000 and 4,500 lines, respectively) compared to the later plays.

By the fifteenth century the custom of producing Passion plays covering all of Christ's life was well established in France. The plays of this period were generally much longer than the earlier plays, and their productions were far more elaborate. The *Passion de Semur* (9,500 lines), probably written in the early fifteenth century, introduces Old Testament events and comic characters. Even the traditional material is treated with originality in this play. The *Passion d'Arras* (25,000 lines) was written by Eustache Mercadé before 1440. Apparently the length of the play was considered unusual, since Mercadé apologizes for it. By mid century, however, when Arnoul Gréban wrote his *Mystère de la Passion* (34,000 lines), long plays were the norm.

Gréban's play was used as source and model for

many of the subsequent Passion plays. Jean Michel appropriated almost a third of it while writing his own *Mystère de la Passion* (30,000 lines); unlike Gréban, however, he concentrates almost exclusively on the events of Holy Week. The two sixteenth-century Passion plays from Valenciennes (more than 40,000 lines each) drew heavily on both Gréban and Michel.

Plays of such gigantic proportions were clearly not acted in one session. The practice was to divide them into *journées,* or days. Thus the plays of Gréban and Michel were produced in four days with morning and afternoon sessions each day. Sometimes the plays were staged in town squares; sometimes they were acted in specially built arena theaters. The great cost of mounting these enormous productions was first borne by municipal governments, but in the fifteenth century the practice of charging admission was introduced. By the sixteenth century wealthy merchants were investing in the productions for profit. Although the plays were usually put on for religious motives—to petition God for peace or to give thanks for the end of a plague—a town's decision to stage a Passion play was also influenced by the economic gains to be made from the influx of visitors.

As popular as the plays were, the religious and political tensions of the sixteenth century militated against them. In 1548 the Parlement of Paris banned all Passion plays in the capital. They gradually disappeared from the provinces as well, though in some remote areas they persisted into the eighteenth century.

BIBLIOGRAPHY

Maurice Accarie, *Le théâtre sacré de la fin du moyen âge: Étude sur le sens moral de la Passion de Jean Michel* (1979); Grace Frank, *The Medieval French Drama,* 2nd ed. (1960), 125–196. Louis Petit de Julleville, *Les mystères,* 2 vols. (1880); Émile Roy, *Le mystère de la passion en France du XIVe au XVIe siècle* (1903–1904, repr. 1974).

ALAN E. KNIGHT

[See also **Drama, French; French Literature: After 1200; Gréban, Arnoul; Mercadé, Eustache; Mystery Plays.**]

PASSIUN SEINT EDMUND, LA, an anonymous Anglo-Norman poem relating in four-line octosyllabic rhyming stanzas (1,696 lines) the martyrdom of St. Edmund, king of East Anglia, who was killed by invading Danes in 869. Written around 1200, the *Passiun* is based largely on the *Passio Sancti Eadmundi* by Abbo of Fleury, which dates from 985–987. The *Passiun* is not to be confused with the late-twelfth-century *Vie seint Edmund le Rei,* also Anglo-Norman, by Denis Piramus. In addition, there is an account of St. Edmund's death in Gaimar's *Estoire des Engleis* (vv. 2,867–2,920). A French continental prose life, written in the second half of the twelfth century, also exists.

BIBLIOGRAPHY

Judith Grant, ed., *La Passiun de seint Edmund* (1978).

BRIAN MERRILEES

[See also **Abbo of Fleury; Anglo-Norman Literature; Gaimar, Geffrei; Vie Seint Edmund le Roi, La.**]

PASTON LETTERS is the name generally given to a large number of documents mainly of the fifteenth century, all but a few in English, associated with the family of Paston, which was so called from the village of that name near the northeast coast of Norfolk. The family was living there when it first appears in the records, and continued in the county and in Norwich until the eighteenth century.

The collection is not precisely defined. Its core is about 780 letters written by and to members of the family, but some other letters and numerous related papers such as wills, indentures, and petitions have customarily been comprehended in the title since James Gairdner used it, with the addition of the dates "1422–1509 A.D.," for his first edition of the texts, which he began to publish in 1872.

These medieval documents are not the only surviving letters to come from the Paston family. Several hundred letters of the seventeenth century exist, but the earlier group forms a relatively independent record of the affairs of three generations of the family and there is a distinct break after it, so that its treatment as a separate entity is reasonable.

An important part of these papers was printed for the first time in 1787 by John Fenn, an antiquary of East Dereham in Norfolk, in two volumes containing 155 letters or extracts entitled *Original Letters, Written during the Reigns of Henry VI, Edward IV, and Richard III. By various Persons of Rank or Consequence.* The manuscripts of these and many others had been in the possession of William Paston, second earl of Yarmouth, with

PASTON LETTERS

whom the family line came to an end when he died in 1732. Some had evidently been sold by the earl in his lifetime, others remained as part of his estate. After several changes of ownership most of them came into the hands of a local dealer, from whom Fenn bought them.

The edition was received with great public interest; but some critics apparently doubted whether the letters were genuinely as ancient as they purported to be, and to allay such suspicions Fenn deposited the manuscripts on which these two volumes were based in the library of the Society of Antiquaries in London, so that scholars could examine them. At this stage King George III expressed a wish to see the manuscripts, and Fenn sent this part of his collection to the palace, intending that it should be added to the Royal Library. In recognition of this gift Fenn was knighted, but in fact the volumes were evidently never incorporated in the Library and they were lost to public view for a century. They reappeared in 1889 at the residence in Suffolk of a descendant of the secretary to William Pitt, who as prime minister had recommended that George III accept Fenn's dedication of his edition. While their whereabouts were unknown, these manuscripts could obviously not be consulted by scholars who might wish to verify Fenn's published text, and when Gairdner undertook his new edition in the 1870's he was obliged simply to reproduce Fenn's transcript of all the letters that had been included in these two volumes. Even after they came to light again, they remained in private hands, not available for study, until they were purchased by the British Museum in 1933.

In 1789, Fenn had continued his edition with two further volumes, containing 220 letters, and before his death in 1794 he had almost completed the preparation of a fifth, of 110 letters, which was published by his nephew William Frere in 1823. The manuscripts of those letters were also mislaid for a time, but they, together with many others which Fenn had owned but had not printed, were acquired by the British Museum in 1866 and later, so that the main body of Fenn's collection was eventually reunited there.

When Gairdner made his new edition he added to the letters that Fenn had collected a considerable number of documents variously related to the Paston family which had been preserved both in the British Museum and in other places such as the Probate Registry, the Bodleian Library and Magdalen College, Oxford, and Pembroke College, Cambridge. This edition came out in three volumes, the third in 1875, and a fourth, containing an important introduction and supplementary texts, was added in 1901. A large number of the documents he printed Gairdner himself transcribed, but of those that Fenn had printed he contented himself with partial checking, from which he decided that Fenn's text was in general correct enough. In fact there were considerable abridgments and rearrangements, and many minor inaccuracies which remained largely uncorrected even in the revised six-volume limited edition published in 1904. The additions made by Gairdner brought the number of published documents from the 485 in Fenn's five volumes to a total of more than 1,000. A small number of relevant texts, including a few letters, still remained separated from the main collections and unprinted. The first part of a new edition based directly on the manuscripts, edited by Norman Davis, appeared in 1971, a second part in 1976.

The author of the earliest letters in the collection was the founder of the family's prosperity, William Paston I, who was born in Norfolk of humble parentage in 1378 and lived until 1444. He became a successful lawyer in Norwich and London, and was made serjeant-at-law in 1421 and a judge of the court of common pleas in 1429. He was able to buy substantial lands, among them the manor of Oxnead near Aylsham, which remained in the family for 300 years. He married Agnes Berry, daughter of a Hertfordshire knight, who inherited additional lands. From this generation of the family not many records have been preserved: there are only seven drafts of letters and five other documents by William, the earliest of 1425, and by Agnes one letter to him probably of 1440 and a dozen to their two elder sons from 1445 onwards.

It was in the next generation that the bulk of the surviving papers were written. The eldest son of William and Agnes, John Paston I (1421–1466), was also a lawyer. He married Margaret, daughter and heiress of John Mautby of Mautby near Yarmouth, and left her in charge of his property in Norfolk during his frequent absences in London. Many of her letters to him survive, together with many from other correspondents. Though they do not now compose a regular file of letters and replies, it is likely that the preservation of these numerous papers is due primarily to John's careful habits and example—after his death Margaret wrote to their eldest son, "Your father . . . set more by his writings and evidence than he did by any of

PASTON LETTERS

his movable goods." The papers of which he was certainly or probably the author, which include various drafts of petitions and complaints as well as letters, number about forty-five, dating from the 1440's to 1465; there are sixty-nine letters from Margaret to him, extending from about 1441 to 1465, and thirty-five others by her mostly to their sons, continuing to 1478.

Other members of this generation are less well represented. The second son, Edmond, who died young, has left only one letter, perhaps of 1447; Elizabeth two, of 1459 and probably 1467; William II (1436–1496) about twenty, widely scattered from 1452 to 1480, as well as numerous memoranda; Clement seven, from 1461 to 1466.

Of the third generation about seventy letters remain from each of the eldest sons, both named John—John II (1442–1479), whose letters extend from 1461 to the year of his death, and John III (1444–1504), with letters from 1461 until after 1500—as well as miscellaneous memoranda; six from Edmond II between 1471 and about 1490; three from Walter, all from Oxford in 1479; nine from William III between about 1478 and 1492; and six from Margery, the wife of John III, from 1477 to 1489. Finally there is a single letter from the fourth William, son of John III, perhaps about 1495.

The great majority of these letters by members of the Paston family are to other members of it—those which are actual missives, not drafts or copies, necessarily so since otherwise they could not normally have been recovered. They are not at all evenly spread over the years during which they were written; for example, of Margaret's sixty-nine letters to John I, thirty-nine are of 1460 or later, sixteen of the one year 1465. Letters sent to members of the family from writers outside it are very various in origin and also uneven in distribution. Those addressed to William I number twelve, to Agnes three, but to John I no fewer than 262, to John II forty-seven, to John III sixty-nine—figures which confirm the predominance of John I in the affairs of the family during his lifetime. Many of his correspondents were estate servants, some were neighboring landowners; there are also more or less formal letters from magnates such as the duke of York, the duke of Norfolk, and the earl of Warwick.

A high proportion of the letters are concerned in one way or another with property, its acquisition, management, and defense. Some describe violent physical attacks on Paston residences. As early as 1448 the manor of Gresham, which John Paston I had inherited from his father, was seized by retainers of Lord Moleyns, who later forcibly ejected Margaret from her house. The greatest difficulties for the Pastons, as well as considerable gains in the long run, arose from John I's connection with Sir John Fastolf, of Caister near Yarmouth, a noted captain in the French wars who had amassed great wealth and estates. Margaret Paston was related to him through her mother, and John became one of his legal advisers and later an executor. (Some thirty letters from Fastolf to Paston survive.) When Fastolf died in 1459 his will, propounded by Paston, bequeathed his manors in Norfolk, Suffolk, and Norwich to Paston on condition that he should found a college of monks or priests and poor men to pray for the souls of Fastolf and his wife, father, and mother, and others that he was beholden to. The authenticity of this will was bitterly contested by other executors, who caused an inquiry to be held in the archbishop of Canterbury's court of audience.

The dispute was still unsettled when John I died in 1466, and the pursuit of it fell to John II, who had entered the service of King Edward IV in 1461 and had been knighted on coming of age in 1463. In 1465 a destructive assault was made by the duke of Suffolk's men on Hellesdon, one of Fastolf's manors of which Paston had taken possession, and in 1469 a still larger operation was mounted against Caister Castle, which had been Fastolf's principal residence, by the duke of Norfolk. John Paston III was in charge of it on behalf of his elder brother, but after a siege of five weeks he was forced to surrender and Norfolk occupied the castle.

In 1470, Edward IV was deposed and Henry VI restored for a time. In March 1471, Edward returned from exile. In April he successfully fought the battle of Barnet, in which the Paston brothers took part on the losing side and consequently had to sue for pardons. During 1470, John II had negotiated a compromise about the Fastolf estate with William Wainfleet, bishop of Winchester, the most influential of Fastolf's surviving executors. Wainfleet was to take over most of the disputed lands as part of the endowment of Magdalen College, Oxford, which he had recently founded, but Paston was to keep Caister and a few other manors; yet Norfolk refused to yield and it remained in his hands until he died in 1476. Paston then at last succeeded in making good his claim to it. He had meanwhile served in the English forces in Calais, and was later a member of parliament for Yarmouth.

PASTON LETTERS

After the death of John II in 1479 there was dissension between John III and his uncle William II about the inheritance of lands that had belonged to William I and Agnes, but no further external attacks are recorded. John III consolidated his standing in the county, becoming a member of parliament and sheriff. He was knighted at the battle of Stoke in 1487, and became a member of the earl of Oxford's council. When he died in 1504 he left an assured position to his son William IV, who in his turn became sheriff and was a knight by 1520, when he was present at the Field of the Cloth of Gold, when Henry VIII and Francis I of France met in an ostentatious "summit conference" not far from Calais.

In addition to the concern for family property some events of public importance are described by various writers, such as the murder of the duke of Suffolk in 1450, the recovery of Henry VI from insanity in 1454, and the outcome of the battle of Towton in 1461. Many more domestic matters also find a place in the letters. In 1469, Margery, the daughter of John Paston I and Margaret, gave great offense to her mother and brothers by insisting on marrying Richard Calle, head bailiff of the family estates. In 1477, John III married Margery Brews, after a suit whose prospects seemed at times unpromising because he hoped for a larger dowry than her father was willing to offer. She enlivened the courtship by two touching letters addressed to John as her "Valentine," the first known record of this custom. John II, besides being much interested in tournaments and known as "the best chooser of a gentlewoman," collected books of chivalry and romance. William II as a young man made some interesting notes on French grammar, and William III studied "versifying," among other things, at Eton. There is also much incidental information about daily life. Even the physical shape of the letters can be of interest—all the personal letters are on paper, in the early years often much cramped, evidently for economy, but the fair copies of legal documents are normally on parchment.

The most significant feature of all is the evidence the letters give about the currency and usage of the English language at a time of unique importance—unique because these documents were written during the period immediately preceding and contemporary with the introduction of printing by William Caxton. They richly exemplify the new status of English in the fifteenth century. Personal letters in England, so far as they have survived, were in earlier centuries nearly all written in French, legal and official documents in French or Latin. From early in the fifteenth century there was a major change toward the use of English in private papers and only slightly less in public documents.

It has often been remarked that the Paston papers show a competent command of English by an unexpectedly wide range of writers—not only clerics and gentry but minor estate officers and servants. This is certainly true, though caution is required in judging the documents because the person in whose name a letter appears need not have written it himself. Even the subscribed name of an author was sometimes not a signature, but written by the secretary who wrote the letter. It is generally apparent whether a letter is holograph or not, especially when a number in the same name survive.

Most of the men of the Paston family, and many of their correspondents, evidently wrote their own letters, but the women did not. Notably, from the fact that Margaret Paston's 104 extant letters are in more than twenty different hands, many of them identifiable as those of her servants or sons, it is reasonable to conclude that she could not write, or at any rate found it difficult. This makes it hard to analyze her language, for it can seldom be said with confidence whether a particular feature is her own or a secretary's. Ill-founded opinions have been reached by some scholars who have failed to take account of this problem.

For the study of linguistic history the letters attributable to known persons are of exceptional value because they provide precise evidence of usage at a particular place and date. The letters have too often been summarily characterized as "the Paston Letters, Norfolk"; the writers are of such varied experience that each must be considered individually. When an extended series of letters survives in the hand of a single author it may show, as the years pass, certain features characteristic of a limited area giving way to others in more general use, indicating that regional peculiarities were in the process of yielding to the tendency toward a more uniform written language. Good examples of this can be seen especially in the letters of John Paston III, who in the late 1460's altered some of his spelling habits and continued the new spellings in later writings. More generally, movements toward later "standard" forms can be seen in grammatical features such as the possessive and objective cases of the plural third personal pronoun, which in the earlier letters are normally *her* and *hem* but in later ones increasingly *ther* and *them.*

At a less technical level, the letters illustrate many aspects of familiar communication. Some writers use proverbs and common similes with colloquial freedom, yet the frequency with which formulas of address and conclusion recur, even in letters among family members, shows that the conventions of letter-writing were well taught. One detail which may seem unexpected to modern readers accustomed to the usage of other European languages is the all but universal use of the "polite" plural forms *ye* and *you,* not the singular *thou* and *thee,* in the family circle—by parents writing to children, husband to wife, one brother to another; the singular forms were used to express disapproval, but very rarely.

The range displayed in these letters, not only of technical "literacy" but of competence in putting a sentence together and constructing a coherent narrative, is remarkable. Some of the writers, too, show a real talent for conveying the effect of a vigorous or even quarrelsome dialogue—the first direct reports of colloquial speech in English, as distinct from the imagined conversations of poets or preachers. It is easy to see that current language of this kind could provide fertile ground to be cultivated by the writers of the sixteenth century, writers whose genius brought English prose to a new level of strength and eloquence.

BIBLIOGRAPHY

Sources. The modern edition is Norman Davis, ed., *Paston Letters and Papers of the Fifteenth Century,* I (1971), II (1976).

Several earlier editions are still useful. See John Fenn, ed., *Original Letters, Written During the Reigns of Henry VI, Edward IV, and Richard III. By Various Persons of Rank or Consequence,* 5 vols. (1787–1823). This edition contains an introduction on the manuscripts and illustrations of seals and watermarks. See also James Gairdner, ed., *The Paston Letters, 1422–1509 A.D.,* 3 vols. (1872–1875). This edition was reprinted in four volumes, with an introduction and supplement, in 1900–1901; and a library edition in six volumes came out in 1904. See also Curt F. Bühler, "Some New Paston Documents," in *The Review of English Studies,* **14** (1938).

For an edition in modern spelling, see Norman Davis, ed., *The Paston Letters: A Selection in Modern Spelling* (1963, rev. ed. 1983).

Studies. H. S. Bennett, *The Pastons and Their England* (1922); Norman Davis, "The Text of Margaret Paston's Letters," in *Medium aevum,* **18** (1949), "The Language of the Pastons," in *Proceedings of the British Academy,* **40** (1954), and "Style and Stereotype in Early English Letters," in *Leeds Studies in English,* n.s. **1** (1967); Asta Kihlbom, *A Contribution to the Study of Fifteenth Century English* (1926); G. A. Lester, *Sir John Paston's "Grete Boke"* (1984).

NORMAN DAVIS

[See also **Arches, Court of; Class Structure, Western (1300–1500); Common Pleas, Court of; England: 1216–1485; Estate Management; Family, Western European; Fortune; Henry VI of England; Inheritance, Western European; Law, English Common: After 1272; Middle English Language; Middle English Literature; Richard III; Tenure of Land, Western European; Wars of the Roses.**]

PASTOPHORY, a chamber attached to an early Christian or Byzantine church, normally designated as the prothesis or the diaconicon. By the end of the iconoclastic controversy, pastophories had been incorporated into the overall church design with standardized positions and functions. The naos was terminated by a tripartite sanctuary with apsed chambers flanking the bema. To the north, the prothesis was used for the preparation and storage of the species of the Eucharist. To the south, the diaconicon served as an archive, vestry, and library.

BIBLIOGRAPHY

Richard Krautheimer, *Early Christian and Byzantine Architecture,* 3rd ed. (1979).

ROBERT OUSTERHOUT

[See also **Apse; Bema; Diaconicon; Early Christian and Byzantine Architecture; Iconoclasm, Christian; Naos; Prothesis.**]

PASTOUREAUX. The word *pastoureaux,* meaning shepherds, has been applied to two popular uprisings (1251 and 1320) originating in northern France and, particularly in the case of the first, in Flanders as well.

Spurred on by the rumors of disaster on the crusade of Louis IX, which began in 1248, the first Pastoureaux left their flocks in 1251 ostensibly to aid the king of France in his struggle against the Muslims. On behalf of the crusade, the designated successor to the county of Flanders, Guillaume

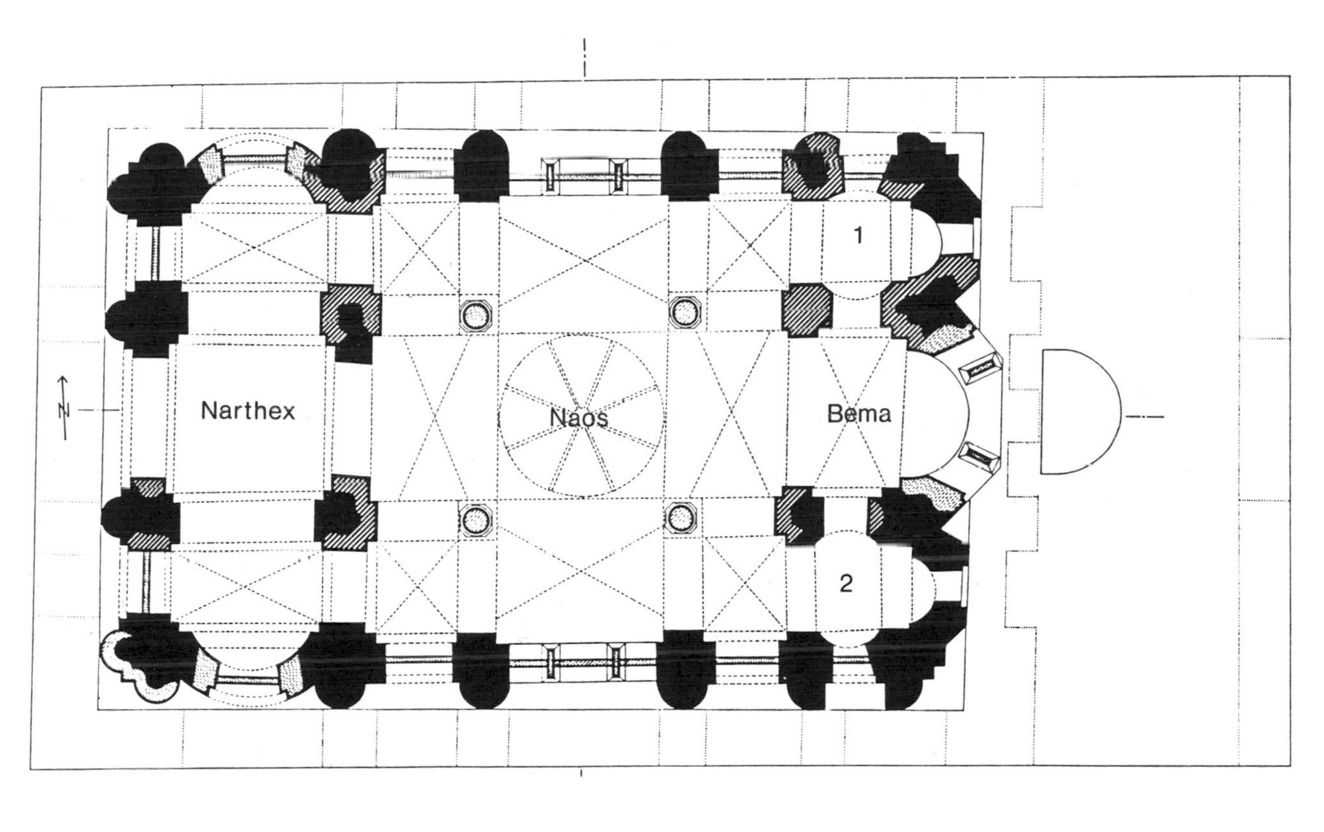

The Myrelaion church, Constantinople, *ca.* 920. Plan showing pastophories: prothesis (1) and diaconicon (2). Reproduced from Cecil L. Striker, *The Myrelaion (Bodrum Camii) in Istanbul.* © 1981 PRINCETON UNIVERSITY PRESS

Dampierre, who was a personal friend of Louis IX, had contributed an important contingent of troops. He and they suffered with the king in the early misfortunes of the war (1250). This may account for the sensitivity of people from Flanders, who had little loyalty to the French crown, or sympathy for the plight of a French king, in 1251.

The social composition of the Pastoureaux is difficult to determine. Certainly some were shepherds; but as the movement grew laborers of various sorts, including urban workers, joined their ranks. As the numbers increased (though never to the 100,000 given by one chronicler) conservative forces became uneasy, believing that the shepherds' real object was the overthrow of true religion and social hierarchy. Various chroniclers regarded the Pastoureaux as a mob of thieves, magicians, and prostitutes.

The leader of the Pastoureaux was called the Master of Hungary. He claimed the inspiration of the Virgin, and on his banner he displayed the Lamb of God Triumphant. Various rumors circulated about him. People conjectured that the Master was in some way responsible for the Children's Crusade of 1212; others thought he was in league with the Muslims, if not a demon of Muḥammad himself; still others regarded him as a necromancer.

In the late spring and early summer of 1251, the Pastoureaux became violent in the cities of Paris, Rouen, and Bourges. The primary objects of their outrage were prelates and Jews. Despite some initial interest in employing the Pastoureaux in King Louis' behalf, the regent Blanche of Castile ultimately committed royal forces to their suppression. No doubt many escaped—some may even have reached the Holy Land—but a number of them, including the Master of Hungary, were killed in the violence that followed.

Some seventy years after these events, in 1320, the king of France, Philip V, announced that he would lead a crusade to the East. Events conspired to render his promise empty. Nonetheless, the climate of opinion in 1320 could not have been better for the announcement. Years of scarcity and famine (1315–1317) had left people throughout the kingdom with a depressing feeling that France, the land of the new chosen people, had been stricken by the hand of God for sins only vaguely apprehended. A crusade would purify the land and reaffirm the bonds between the celestial kingdom of God and the terrestrial kingdom of the Franks.

Soon bands of shepherds gathered around self-proclaimed leaders of the crusade (themselves defrocked priests), and the second movement to be known as the Pastoureaux was launched. As in the earlier movement, the earnest desire to be soldiers for Christ justified otherwise unjustifiable violence. In Paris the Pastoureaux laid siege to the Châtelet, the seat of the governing authority (provost) of Paris. Popular support prevented the forces of suppression from overcoming the ever-increasing numbers of Pastoureaux. South and southwest of Paris the violence continued—often with popular support.

The Jews were a principal target of the violence. The 1306 order exiling Jews from France had been reversed in 1315. Consequently the south and southwest had significant Jewish settlements, and they became the preferred target of the shepherds—"from Toulouse to Narbonne."

The Pastoureaux were not content to focus on the Jews, however. The enemies of Christ, as they saw them, also included indifferent priests, prelates, and nobles, that is, the rich and the powerful in general. The Pastoureaux attempted to confront, humiliate, and, if the opposition is to be believed, annihilate these pillars of hierarchical society. The attempt provoked a terrible repression in which many of the Pastoureaux were killed, not in combat but by slow starvation as the forces of order effectively cut the supply of food to the disorganized rebels.

Remnants of the movement reached Aragon carrying with them intense hatred of the Jews and the unintegrated revolutionary program already being destroyed in France. For a while they were a menace in Spain, but ultimately they succumbed to the forces of the Aragonese crown.

BIBLIOGRAPHY

Malcolm Barber, "The Pastoureaux of 1320," in *Journal of Ecclesiastical History,* **32** (1981), and "The Crusade of the Shepherds in 1251," in Western Society for French History, *Proceedings of the Tenth Annual Meeting, 1982* (1984); Guy Fourquin, *The Anatomy of Popular Rebellion in the Middle Ages,* Anne Chesters, trans. (1978); Rodney Hilton, *Bond Men Made Free: Medieval Peasant Movements and the English Rising of 1381* (1973); William C. Jordan, *Louis IX and the Challenge of the Crusade* (1979); Michel Mollat and Philippe Wolff, *The Popular Revolutions of the Late Middle Ages,* A. Lytton-Sells, trans. (1973).

WILLIAM CHESTER JORDAN

[See also **Blanche of Castile; Châtelet; Class Structure, Western; Crusade, Children's; Crusades and Crusader States; Expulsion of Jews; Flanders and the Low Countries; France; Louis IX of France; Peasants' Rebellion.**]

PASTOURELLE, a short lyric dialogue in which a self-confident knight attempts to seduce a naive, greedy, or clever shepherdess. The outcome varies, but the knight is often outwitted. It uses three poetic structures—the amorous encounter, debate, and plaint—but depends heavily for its effect on the contrast in characterization.

BIBLIOGRAPHY

Pierre Bec, *La lyrique française au moyen âge,* I (1977), 119–136.

STEPHEN MANNING

[See also **French Literature: Lyric.**]

PASTURE, RIGHTS OF. Pasture was among the recognized rights of rural tenants throughout medieval Europe and was especially well developed in the cereal-growing region of the heavy-soiled north. But the right was circumscribed by lords' control over or claims to the commons and by village regulation. A good comparison is with rights of pannage in woods, but it is good only up to a point, for some of the most valuable pasture was on the harvested arable and roads, both areas where the presence of grazing animals could cause enormous problems. Rights of pasture were much less important where isolated farmsteads prevailed as the prime unit of agricultural organization.

Pasture on the village common was routinely afforded the animals of tenants of some substance in the high Middle Ages. Poorer tenants (such as cottagers) might be denied the right, and foreigners (people from other villages) might be suffered to pasture their animals only after the exercise of rights of pasture by natives. Such pasturing tended to take on the character of a collective enterprise. If, on the other hand, individuals were accorded separate rights of pasture, these were severely restricted.

The cycle of pasturing reflected the cycle of agricultural life. Fallow, for example, was not ordinarily subject to pasturing in the spring. Stubble often could not be pastured until it had been gleaned, and some of it had to be reserved for haulm (for thatching or other uses). Roads were not opened to grazing animals except in very restricted numbers and at very restricted times. Sheep could be pastured only under relatively close supervision because they inclined to extremely close cropping. Night pasturing was frowned upon because it was a cover for the invasion of the cultivated fields of others.

None of the restrictions or conditions mentioned above necessarily applied to every village. Studies of agrarian bylaws suggest that each village community, with or without the active urging of its lord, came up with an appropriate statement of the right of pasture. The historical problem concerns the evolution of rights of pasture during the Middle Ages, and on understanding this issue depends much of the agrarian history of premodern Europe.

Medieval village agriculture depended on cooperation. But cooperation was not merely expected; it was demanded—as the existence of village bylaws proves. It is very likely that the limited amount of pasturage was at the heart of this demand. The arable fields were held in strips and were plowed in long strips. The heavy soils of northern Europe required draft animals in abundance, and the draft animals required adequate pasturage. To assure that they would receive it, the village had to regulate access to the common, to the stubble, to the fallow, to roadways, and to the balks (the grassy swards occasionally found between cultivated strips). Any pressure on the balance between arable actually in cultivation and available pasturage for draft and food animals could be catastrophic.

Pressure came from many directions. Before the Black Death, one principal form of pressure was the burgeoning population. The competition for pasturage was not so much between peasants within the village (though this existed) as between lords and the villages in their seigniories. In the late thirteenth and early fourteenth centuries the tensions of this competition often took a nasty form as lords tried to protect their woods, for example, from encroachments by peasants while demanding the right to pasture their own herds on the village common.

A second consideration aggravated the pressure caused by population. This was the growth in the size of sheep herds in England and northern France as a consequence of the development of the cloth industry. Sheep were kept by ordinary peasants, but the large herds belonged to lay and monastic lords. The need for vast pasturages to supply these sheep put increasing pressure on the common, promoted frustration over the uncertainty of the status of the common, and led ultimately to the elaboration of a legal theory of seigniorial ownership of the common that was at variance with the manifest desires of villagers. The legal theory did not sweep all before it; village custom was too firmly entrenched for that. But the groundwork was laid for the tendentious legal struggle over tenants' rights of the late Middle Ages.

Connected with the developments thus far described was the increasing pace of enclosure in the late Middle Ages. The essence of medieval village agriculture had been (with major variations where geographical considerations made it inconvenient) the open-field system. Enclosure (with its usual concomitant, denial of traditional access to common or woods) threatened the very nature of agricultural life. In England the movement toward enclosure persisted over some centuries and was periodically fraught with social upheaval. The verdict on whether the enclosure movement materially benefited or impoverished the rural labor force is not yet in; but that there was a popular perception of enclosure as a threat to received notions of justice in rural life is absolutely certain. In France the social upheavals associated with enclosure manifested themselves less often and less intensively than in England, and have not given rise to acrimonious debate among historians about its impact.

BIBLIOGRAPHY

The bibliography on open-field agriculture, with which well-developed rights of pasture are most closely associated, is immense. Only a few of the more recent works are listed here. Warren O. Ault, "Open-Field Husbandry and the Village Community: A Study of Agrarian By-Laws in Medieval England," in *Transactions of the American Philosophical Society,* **55**, pt. 7 (1965), summarizes the findings of English scholars (including Howard L. Gray, Joan Thirsk, Charles and Christabel Orwin, and Eric Kerridge). He also publishes as an appendix a selection of agrarian bylaws, many of which deal with the regulation of pasturage. Herbert E. Hallam has attempted a general coverage of agricultural life—region by region—in England; rights of pasturage are described in context in his *Rural England (1066–1348)* (1981). French and other continental developments and their social consequences in the medieval and early modern period are surveyed in Georges Duby, ed., *Histoire de la France rurale,* I (1975), esp. 561–589; and Jerome Blum, *The End of the Old Order in Rural Europe* (1978), 120–125, 147–154. A judicious attempt to assess the impact of enclosure on England is Jerome Blum, "English Parliamentary Enclosure," in *Journal of Modern History,* **53** (1981). Though it deals with the parliamentary period of enclosure, its conclusions have relevance for the earlier period as well.

WILLIAM CHESTER JORDAN

[See also **Field Systems; Tenure of Land, Western European; Villages.**]

PATARINS. See **Bosnia.**

PATEN, a flat plate with a slightly raised rim or a shallow vessel used during the Mass to receive and serve the consecrated bread of communion. Mentioned in the *Liber pontificalis* as existing in the late second century, early examples were frequently made of glass with inset figural medallions, wood, or horn and sometimes adopted the form of a large, deep dish. In later centuries, the paten was made of precious materials such as gold and silver, encrusted with gems, and lavishly decorated with images in niello, enamel, or low relief; it generally assumed a circular form, although rectangular and hexagonal examples are known. With the introduction of small hosts in the West beginning in the ninth century, the paten's importance waned. In the eleventh century, it shrank dramatically in size, but gained further use as a chalice cover.

Alabaster paten with enameled medallion and silver gilt fitting. Constantinople, *ca.* 11th century. TESORO DI S. MARCO, VENICE, INV. 49

BIBLIOGRAPHY

Joseph Braun, *Das christliche Altargerät in seinem Sein und in seiner Entwicklung* (1932); Josef A. Jungmann, *The Mass of the Roman Rite,* Francis A. Brunner, trans., II (1955), 303–308; Henri Leclercq, "Patène," in *Dictionnaire d'archéologie chrétienne et de liturgie,* XIII, pt. 2 (1938).

MICHAEL T. DAVIS

[See also **Altar–Altar Apparatus; Mass.**]

PATERIKON. In Eastern Christianity, a *paterikon* is a history of a monastery or group of monasteries, taking the form of brief biographical sketches of its abbots and other monks particularly distinguished by their holy lives. In form and approach, *paterika* are modeled on the *Lausiac History (Historia lausiaca)* of Palladios, the *Spiritual Meadow* of John Moschos, and similar works of monastic antiquity. Later *paterika* may include additional historical material as well as devotional exhortations.

BIBLIOGRAPHY
Karl Krumbacher, *Geschichte der byzantinischen Litteratur: Von Justinian bis zum Ende des oströmischen Reiches (527–1453)*, I (1958), 179–182, 187–188.

JOHN H. ERICKSON

[See also **Monasticism, Origins.**]

PATMUTᶜIWN TARŌNOY (The history of [the province of] Tarōn) is one of the most curious works of medieval Armenian literature. Known under the single title since its first publication in 1719 at Constantinople, the numerous partial or complete manuscripts bear disparate titles given to each of its several parts. The *History* divides into two major sections, both of which finish with the colophon of one Yovhannēs (John) Mamikonean. In the colophon Yovhannēs provides some autobiographical information and explains the work's evolution: He is the thirty-fifth abbot of the monastery of St. John the Precursor in the province of Tarōn and, as the province was the hereditary property of the Mamikonean feudal house, he is also its bishop; he reveals an approximate date for his activities by stating that, at the request of the Armenian *katᶜołikos* Nersēs III the Builder (Šinoł, 641 661), he translated the work of the monastery's first abbot, the Syrian Zenob Glak, a contemporary and colleague of St. Gregory the Illuminator (*ca.* 240–*ca.* 332). This work by Zenob Glak, composed in Syriac, had been carried off by "several Persian soldiers" to Edessa, and for many years had been thought to be lost. Yovhannēs explains how he recovered Zenob's twenty-eight chapters, translated them and the additions of successor abbots, and then proceeded to write of events in and around the monastery through his own era. The entire work consists of thirty-eight chapters. Yovhannēs ends the colophon by asking future copyists to copy the work faithfully and not to find anything ridiculous in it. He also urges them to add the histories of their own times to it—something they evidently did not do.

The first part of the *History*—Zenob's section—is epistolary. It tells, inter alia, how the Arsacid kingdom of Greater Armenia was converted by St. Gregory the Illuminator and King Trdat III/IV the Great (*ca.* 280–*ca.* 330); how the relics of St. John the Precursor were brought from Caesarea of Cappadocia to Tarōn and housed in a monastery constructed on the ruins of a pagan Indian temple; and how Zenob was ordained as first bishop of the Mamikoneans and selected as first abbot of the Monastery of St. John. It ends with an extended account of King Trdat's war against "the king of the North."

Yovhannēs' section opens with a brief description of the interim period (in place of the writings of Zenob's successors?), including a reference to the expulsion of the Syrians and of their rites from the monastery. The account of his own era begins with a narration of miraculous events in the monastic enclave, which has evidently become a place of pilgrimage. Then he tells of the heroic acts of the Mamikoneans against the Persians in the decades from the reign of the emperor Maurice (*r.* 582–602) to that of Heraklios (*r.* 610–641). Battle after battle, deceit after deceit, and victory after victory (for the Armenians) are recounted. As with Zenob's section, prayers to St. John are recorded and the intercession of divine forces is related as having repeatedly occurred.

Until the end of the nineteenth century the *History*, as we have it, was accepted by scholars. This "orthodox" interpretation persists even among some scholars today. The "pseudorthodox" interpretation began with Victor Langlois's introduction to J.-R. Émine's French translation of the entire *History* in 1867. Langlois recognized that there were incredible elements in the extant manuscripts. He explained these, however, as textual corruptions, interpolations, and editorializing by the scribes. Ašot Abrahamyan's introduction to the 1941 Yerevan edition of the *History* remains the single best presentation of this position: The compiler was a man named Yovhannēs Mamikonean, albeit a later one than the present corrupted texts maintain. Moreover, most of the compiled materials are authentic.

The "iconoclastic" and most probable explanation is that the whole work is a later medieval forgery. Arguments for this position include the following points: (1) The date Yovhannēs provides for himself in the colophon is contradicted by the historically accepted dates of those individuals also mentioned in the work. (2) In antiquity and in the Middle Ages, stories of finding books were commonly used to introduce wholly new works. (3) Much of the material in the section purportedly by Zenob had been culled, with minor alterations of tenses and word forms, from works of the fifth century and later. (4) There is no way to distinguish thirty-eight chapters in the work. (5) The first mention of Zenob by another author occurs in Bishop Uχtanēs' *History,* which, at present, is dated in the tenth century. None of our *History*'s manuscripts predate that of Uχtanēs; thus, the tenth century is our *terminus ante quem.* (6) Stylistically, the first section contains few Syriacisms. (Many would be expected in a translation.) The entire work, in fact, is of the same style, and a late one at that. (7) Favorable treatment of Syrians can be explained more readily after the Council of Manazkert (726), at which communion between the Armenian and Syrian/Jacobite churches was restored.

What we have, then, is a work not about the Province of Tarōn but about one monastery in it. The emphasis on the Syrian element in the beginnings of Armenian Christianity may indicate a later trend to wrest the center of Armenian Christianity from the north, where Agatᶜangełos had taken it in the fifth century, back to the south of the country, in Tarōn, where another fifth-century source, Pᶜawstos Buzand, had located the "mother church" of Armenia. It is, moreover, an attempt to give not only legitimacy but also primacy to the Monastery of St. John the Precursor, and to authenticate its relics of St. John.

The work as a whole cannot be dated before the mid eighth century. Moreover, both internal and external evidence would be compatible with a date of 966–988 for the composition of the greater part of the work. The last two brief sections and Yovhannēs' colophon may have been added, with further editorial revisions, in a period of Mamikonid resurgence in Tarōn sometime before 1220, the date of the first complete manuscript.

BIBLIOGRAPHY

Sources. The *editio princeps* (1719), reprinted with new introduction (Calcutta, 1814), and by the Mekhitarists of S. Lazzaro (based on five manuscripts) (Venice, 1832); Ašot Abrahamyan, ed., *Yovhan Mamikonean: Patmutᶜiwn Tarōnoy* (based on twenty-three manuscripts) (1941). Translations include Jean-Raphael Émine's, in Victor Langlois, *Collection des historiens anciens et modernes de l'Arménie,* I (1867).

Studies. Levon Avdoyan, *Pseudo-Yovhannēs Mamikonean's History of Tarōn: Historical Investigation, Critical Translation, and Historical and Textual Commentaries* (diss., Columbia, 1985); Grigor Xalatᶜean, *Zenob Glak: Hamematakan Usumnasirutᶜiwn* [Zenob Glak: A Critical Study] (1893).

LEVON AVDOYAN

[See also **Armenian Literature.**]

PATRIARCH, from the Greek *patriarches,* literally the head of a *patria,* a family, group, or race. The term was introduced in the Greek translation of the Hebrew Bible (the Septuagint) to denote heads of families and tribes, more specifically Abraham, Isaac, Jacob, and Jacob's twelve sons, as in 1st Paralipomenon (1 Chronicles) 24:31, 27:22; 2nd Paralipomenon (2 Chronicles) 19:8, 23:20, 26:12; and 4 Maccabees 7:19, 16:25.

The early Christian church used the term patriarch in the same Old Testament sense (Acts 2:29, 7:8; Hebrews 7:4). Soon after the apostolic age and the church's transition from a congregational and unregulated organization to a more organized episcopal arrangement, the term patriarch was used for a bishop, the head of a spiritual family. More specifically it was employed for an elder or senior bishop and for church fathers in general (Gregory of Nazianzus, *Orations* 2.103 and 43.37; *Martyrium Theodoti,* Pio Franchi de' Cavalieri, ed., 1.15, 1.19).

The First Ecumenical Council (Nicaea, 325) singled out three bishops of leading civic and cultural centers for more jurisdictional power and honor. As bishops of large administrative divisions they were designated as exarchs, a title higher in honor and authority than that of metropolitan. During the fifth century, most probably after the Fourth Ecumenical Council, exarchs became known as patriarchs and the two terms were often used as synonyms. Canon 6 allowed the bishop of Alexandria to have authority over the churches of Egypt, Libya, and Pentapolis (the parts of Libya around Cyrene). The bishop of Rome had been given authority over the bishops of Italy, with the exception of northern Italy. The canon does not specify Antioch's jurisdiction, but we know from other sources that by the middle of the fourth century, Antioch exercised its jurisdiction over the bishops and metropolitans of the diocese of the Orient, which included Syria, Cilicia, and Mesopotamia.

Even though the canon mentions only these three bishops, there were others who received the dignity of patriarch. The fifth-century ecclesiastical historian Socrates Scholasticus relates that the First Council of Constantinople (381) appointed a patriarch over Constantinople and also speaks of the patriarchate of the Pontus diocese, divided between the bishops of Caesarea and Nyssa in Cappadocia and Melitene in Armenia. The Asian diocese (presumably another patriarchate) was divided between the bishops of Iconium and Antioch in Pisidia (Socrates, *Ecclesiastical History,* 5.8). The acts of the same council call other bishops patriarchs, an indication that by the end of the fourth century the title patriarch had come into accepted use in the church.

After the First Council of Constantinople the preeminence of five bishops was emphasized and their designation as patriarchs became established. The third canon of this council decreed that the bishop of Constantinople should enjoy primacy of honor after the bishop of Rome because he was the bishop of the new capital. Canon 28 of the Council of Chalcedon (451) decreed that the bishop of the new capital should enjoy equal honors with the bishop of Old Rome. Along with the bishops of Rome, Constantinople, Alexandria, and Antioch, Jerusalem's bishop was recognized as a patriarch.

During the reign of Justinian (527–565) the five patriarchs (pentarchy) achieved a definite rank of preeminence in the hierarchy of the church, with the patriarch of Old Rome as the *primus inter pares* (first among equals) among them. Church councils and imperial authority such as Justinian's legislation (*Novellae* 123.3) invested all five with a primacy over their respective areas, giving them the right to consecrate bishops and metropolitans under their jurisdiction.

With the decline of Rome as a center of political power and the rise of Constantinople in its place, the patriarch of Constantinople achieved preeminence and was elevated to equal seniority with the patriarch of Old Rome. The thirty-sixth canon of the *Quinisext* Synod (692), which completed the work of the Third Council of Constantinople (680), decreed that "the throne of Constantinople shall enjoy equal seniority (*presbeia*) with the throne of older Rome, and in ecclesiastical matters it shall be magnified like the latter and shall be second after it."

It was accommodation to the administrative divisions of the late Roman and early Byzantine empires as well as political and cultural considerations that contributed to the development of the pentarchy, including Rome's primacy of honor. The church of Rome, however, developed a different outlook and sought to transform its position of honor into a status of authority and supremacy, which contributed to friction between the Western and the Eastern patriarchs. From the Eastern point of view the pentarchy system was simply a matter of organization and not the result of any ecclesiological considerations. From a theological viewpoint all bishops are equal. The bishop of Rome had enjoyed the "first among equals" status because his see was in the old capital of the empire.

The four patriarchs of Eastern Christendom did not deny the patriarch, or pope, of Rome a primacy of honor, but they persistently refused to accept Rome's claims for supremacy in ecclesiological terms. Following the fall of Jerusalem, Antioch, and Alexandria to the Muslims (between 638 and 642) and the schism between the Western and the Eastern churches in the eleventh century, the patriarch of Constantinople became even more prominent and was acknowledged as the first among equals in the East in both Byzantine and post-Byzantine times. The system that prevailed was constitutional. The patriarch served as presiding officer rather than monarchical lawgiver. A patriarch presided over the synods of bishops in his province or jurisdiction, exercised juridical duties, and confirmed episcopal elections. But no patriarch could preside over every ecumenical council. Either directly or indirectly through representatives all five cooperated. The pentarchy authority survived until the eleventh century.

With the decline of the Byzantine state and the rise of national churches after the thirteenth century, the title of patriarch was sought by the heads of the Bulgarian, Serbian, and Russian churches. After years of controversy, the heads of these churches were named patriarchs.

In the early Christian centuries the election of a patriarch was similar to the election of a bishop—the choice of the clergy and the laity. In the eighth or ninth century only bishops in the rank of metropolitan participated in the election of a patriarch. But the system was never uniform, and the method of patriarchal election differed from church to church.

BIBLIOGRAPHY
Sources. Agapios Hieromonachus and Nikodemos Hagioreitēs, *Pedalion,* Denver Cummings, trans. (1957); Georgios Rhalles and Michael Potles, *Syntagma ton theion kai hieron kanonon,* 6 vols. (1852–1859); Panagiotes I. Zepos and Ioannes D. Zepos, eds., *Jus graecoromanum,* II (1931).
Studies. Louis Bréhier, *Le monde byzantin,* II (1949, 2nd ed. 1970); Claude D. Cobham, *The Patriarchs of Constantinople* (1911); Francis Dvornik, *The Idea of Apostolicity in Byzantium and the Legend of the Apostle Andrew* (1958), 3–105; George Every, *The Byzantine Patriarchate, 451–1204,* 2nd rev. ed. (1962); Pierre L'Huillier, "Patriarches," in *Thrēskeutikē kai ethike encyklopaideia,* X (1960); Maximos, Metropolitan of Sardis, *To oikoumenikon patriarcheion en te orthodoxo ekklesia* (1972); Steven Runciman, *The Eastern Schism* (1955), 1–27; Basileios T. Staurides (Istavrides), *Historia tou oikoumenikou patriarcheiou* (1967).

DEMETRIOS J. CONSTANTELOS

[See also **Autocephalos; Byzantine Church; Church, Latin; Clergy, Byzantine; Councils, Ecumenical; Ecumenical Patriarch; Katholikos; Papacy, Origins and Development; Pentarchy; Permanent Synod; Pope; Schisms, Eastern-Western Church.**]

PATRICIAN, ROMAN. In early Rome, members of the uppermost level of society were known as patricians, but in the Roman Empire the title fell into disuse. It was revived by the emperor Constantine I (*r.* 306–337) as a title of distinction reserved for the very highest officials. In the fifth century, the title also was applied to the most powerful general in the Western Roman Empire, and after the disintegration of the West, barbarian leaders such as Odoacar, Clovis, Theodoric, and Sigismund were granted the title by the Eastern Roman emperor; their acceptance of it has been taken to imply their recognition of Roman imperial sovereignty. In 754, Pope Stephen II named Pepin III the Short *patricius Romanorum* (patrician of the Romans), in a move apparently intended to place Pepin in the position of protector of the church of Rome. Charlemagne also received the title, but it was superseded in 800 when he became Holy Roman emperor. Modern historians also use the term "patricians" to refer to the upper crust of the medieval merchant or burgher class.

RALPH WHITNEY MATHISEN

[See also **Charlemagne; Class Structure, Western; Clovis; Constantine I, the Great; Holy Roman Empire; Odoacer; Pepin III and the Donation of Pepin; Roman Empire, Late; Stephen II, Pope; Theodoric the Ostrogoth.**]

PATRICIAN, URBAN. Historians have borrowed "patrician" from the Romans, rather anachronistically and with very little semantic precision, to designate a member of a presumably ruling elite in a medieval town. In the classic view, "patricians" led the struggle for town independence from feudal authority in the eleventh and twelfth centuries, thereby acquiring most of the positions of power in municipal institutions. This differentiation of political status, reinforced by their great wealth and by intermarriage, sometimes further bolstered by statutes that excluded artisans and other lesser persons from power, yielded a kind of urban aristocracy, the "patriciate," that dominated towns in the twelfth, thirteenth, and early fourteenth centuries. Forced in many towns to share power by guild or artisan revolts beginning in the later fourteenth century, an embattled patriciate nevertheless usually survived, perhaps with its own social institutions, well into the Renaissance-Reformation period, and some patrician families managed to secure recognition as part of the nobility.

There is no consensus on the origin or composition of the patriciate, and any historian's use of the term almost invariably reflects his or her assumptions about medieval urbanization and social stratification. For example, Henri Pirenne and his disciples, believing that trade was the driving force in town development, and thus commercial achievement was the factor most valued by townsmen, describe a patriciate of the richest merchants who successfully carved out a legal and political place for commerce in the agrarian (and therefore rather hostile) medieval world. The patricians came to grief only when they strayed too far from their roots, excluding new wealth or, as Fritz Rörig believed, becoming rentiers living on the income from their land, houses, and annuities, losing the urge for expansion and taking risks. Others—A. B. Hibbert, Jean Lestocquoy, and Karl Bosl—see towns as an integral part of a medieval society in which power and status were overwhelmingly ascriptive. Policies of bishops and princes brought the urban communities into existence, and the patricians emerged from the lesser nobility, free landowners, and ministerials. Descent and a knightly way of life gave them dominance that they parlayed into wealth; probably they dabbled in trade from the beginning, and as time passed, they expanded their commercial activities and absorbed successful great merchants through marriage. But in fact, no single factor explains all towns; both merchants and the landed, both achievement and ascription, were important in urban origins and later development.

The use and meaning of "patrician" varies enormously with the geographic area to which the historian applies it. A relatively self-conscious, self-perpetuating ruling elite in towns is probably most visible in northern Italy and Flanders, less clearly in Germany. There is little like the Italian or Flemish examples in France or Spain, and almost nothing in England. The basic variables were the state of the monarchy and the degree of urbanization; a ruling elite needs something to rule. In lands with weak central authority, as in the Holy Roman Empire, towns could achieve a measure of political independence, so that control of their governments meant a potential for power; in northern Italy, Flanders, and certain parts of Germany, towns generated the size and wealth to realize that potential.

Even there, however, a satisfactory patriciate remains hard to find. Italian humanists employed the word "patrician" mostly for cultural patrons. There is an isolated Flemish reference in 1306; the term appears occasionally in southern Germany in the later fifteenth century. But on the whole, the word was scarcely used in the Middle Ages; there was no medieval imperial patent for a patrician. Few towns legally defined their ruling families in the Middle Ages—notably Venice in 1297, but even in that classic case new men consistently found their way into a supposedly closed circle. The other famous "medieval" example, Nuremberg, in fact passed its legislation only in 1521.

As used by most historians, the term approximates an ideal type: a locus of power, wealth, and social status in families that monopolized political office and possessed great fortunes over generations, marrying only within their group. Actually, in most towns barely a handful of families ever fulfilled all of those criteria at any given time; officeholding, riches, and prestige usually spread significantly beyond those families, and new generations brought new families (or the return of other old ones). Patriciates invariably were marked as much by internal conflict as by working together to keep town rule to themselves; the uprisings "against" a patriciate usually prove to have been revolts against high taxes and poor government that some artisans, some merchants, and some patricians supported; a number of ostensibly patrician associations, supposedly indicating some degree of class consciousness, dissolve, on investigation, into groups that drew from more than one socioeconomic level. Above all, every town's patriciate seems to have been different in its control of political power, level of wealth, and extent of closure and intermarriage.

A term used for such dissimilar phenomena ought to be applied with more caution than is usually the case. "Patrician family," indicating a strong urban lineage, works reasonably well in describing medieval reality. "Patriciate," with its implications of class and class awareness, which for most towns are extremely elusive, is much less successful. To make "patrician" cover even most of the cases in which historians have used it, at best it can be a shorthand for saying that medieval towns generated their own leaders, and that the leaders of important towns had an impact on medieval history. Those leaders, whose dealings brought them into contact with nobles, princes, and kings, sometimes fancied themselves as being above other townsfolk. Among them, power, wealth, and family and lineage were all-important; the powerful were often wealthy and the wealthy often powerful, and those who inherited wealth or power or both had a head start. None of this is terribly surprising, but perhaps we do need a word for it.

BIBLIOGRAPHY

Ingrid Bátori, "Das Patriziat der deutschen Stadt," in *Zeitschrift für Stadtgeschichte, Stadtsoziologie und Denkmalpflege,* 2 (1975); Karl Bösl, *Die Gesellschaft in der Geschichte des Mittelalters* (1969); Stanley Chojnacki, "In Search of the Venetian Patriciate: Families and Factions in the Fourteenth Century," in John R. Hale, ed., *Renaissance Venice* (1973); A. B. Hibbert, "The Origins of the Medieval Town Patriciate," in *Past and Present,* no. 3 (1953); Jean Lestocquoy, *Les villes de Flandre et d'Italie sous le gouvernement des patriciens (XIe–XVe siècles)* (1952); Henri Pirenne, *Medieval Cities* (1956); Fritz Rörig, *Wirtschaftskräfte im Mittelalter* (1971).

RHIMAN A. ROTZ

[See Also **Bruges; Class Structure, Western; Cologne; Échevin; German Towns; Ghent; Italy, Rise of Towns in; Urbanism, Western European; Venice.**]

PATRICK, ST.

PATRICK, ST. (*ca.* 389–*ca.* 461). Although St. Patrick has long since been enshrined in the popular mind as the saint who threw the snakes out of Ireland, he remains the most enigmatic and controversial figure in early Christian Irish history. His legend has obscured his life for centuries. Paradoxically, we know some of the most intimate details of his life and career, for he is the primary source of information about himself. St. Patrick left two short works, both written for a specific occasion. Hence, though they allow an intimate view of the author's personality and character, they raise many questions about St. Patrick's mission and its historical context.

From internal evidence it is clear that the *Confession* was written late in Patrick's life, ostensibly to counter charges brought against him by his superiors. These charges are not specified, but judging from Patrick's response they must have impugned his qualifications to be a bishop and/or leader of a Christian mission in Ireland. Patrick begins with a lengthy exposition of the Creed. Perhaps his orthodoxy was in question, but it may be part of the broader question of his general level of education. Patrick readily admits that he is lacking in formal education in his *Confession.* He counters this failing by describing the origin and development of his spiritual commitment to the mission he has undertaken in Ireland. There is no doubt in Patrick's mind that he has been chosen by God for the task, whatever his personal shortcomings.

Most of the information Patrick supplies about his background comes from the *Confession.* Patrick was a Briton, the son of Calpurnius, a deacon and decurion, son of Potitus the presbyter. His father had a villa near a village called Bannavem Taburniae, where Patrick was captured in a raid when he was about sixteen. He spent the next six years in Ireland as a slave working as a herdsman. During this time the nominal faith of his childhood turned to deep conviction. Encouraged by divine voices, Patrick escaped and made his way to a port, where he took ship for home. After weathering a severe storm the ship came ashore in desolate country through which Patrick and the crew wandered for nearly a month before making human contact. Eventually, Patrick was reunited with his family in Britain, but the voices and visions that prompted his escape continued to trouble his mind. Sometimes they seemed to be part of his own spiritual awakening, at another time they urged him in a particularly vivid experience to return to Ireland, to the forest of Foclut.

In his writings Patrick gives no indication of when he returned as a missionary to Ireland, or what authority backed the enterprise. He speaks instead of the crisis that, apparently, prompted the *Confession.* Some youthful sin confessed to a friend in confidence was revealed by his friend to Patrick's superiors and raised doubts among them as to Patrick's fitness. Hurt as he was by the personal betrayal of his friend, Patrick was equally distressed that all God had accomplished through him in Ireland should be discounted by his youthful transgression. He makes vague allusions to the dangers he faced and the plots against him. He traveled to the hinterlands to preach and baptize. There, he witnessed the growth of the Christian community against great odds, refused the offerings of the faithful for his services, and spent only what was necessary to further his work. Patrick mentions in particular the plight of the women converts who faced the opposition of their families or masters. In closing, Patrick reiterates his conviction that God chose him for the task to which he has joyfully dedicated his life.

The second authentic piece by St. Patrick is an entirely different sort of composition. It is an open letter sent in his official capacity as the bishop of the Irish to the soldiers of the British chieftain Coroticus and the Christian communities of Ireland and Britain. Though nominally Christian themselves, these soldiers had captured and enslaved a number of recently baptized Irish converts in a raid. In his letter Patrick demands that the raiders return their prisoners and other plunder, and do penance. He admonishes other Christians to treat the soldiers as excommunicates until they comply with these demands. There is no surviving evidence as to the efficacy of Patrick's letter or its date.

Beyond the primary material, the medieval evidence for Patrick and his mission consists of some brief statements called the *dicta,* two early hymns, some canons, entries in the various Irish annals, and a number of *vitae,* or lives, of St. Patrick in Latin and Irish. Though this later evidence is copious, it is also conflicting, sometimes dubious, and frequently fabulous. Numerous scholars have attempted to sift it, winnowing history from legend; inevitably, controversy has resulted.

In 1905 John B. Bury published a reconstruction of Patrick's life that depended largely on the *Confession* and the *Letter to Coroticus,* the two late seventh-century lives of Patrick by Muirchú and Tiréchán and the Irish annals. He believed that Patrick was born about 389. After his sojourn in Ireland as a slave and his return to Britain, he went to the Continent, where he studied at Lerins and Auxerre. In 431 Pope Celestine I sent a mission to Ireland under Palladius of Auxerre, who died a short time later. Patrick was hastily ordained bishop by St. Germanus of Auxerre and sent to Ireland as the successor to Palladius. Patrick arrived in Ireland in 432, converted the king of Tara, Lóegaire m Néill, after a dramatic confrontation with the druids of Lóegaire's court, and established a headquarters for himself at Armagh. After a successful career of more than thirty years spent traveling throughout Ireland to preach, convert, and baptize, Patrick died in 461 and was buried at Saul.

Bury's magisterial summation was the standard work on Patrick for some forty years, until 1942, when Thomas F. O'Rahilly revived an older theory of two historical Patricks. In O'Rahilly's view the Patrick of the medieval hagiographers was a composite of the lives and careers of Palladius and Patrick the Briton. He posited that Palladius had worked in Ireland from 431 to 461 and was succeeded by Patrick, who labored from 461/462 to about 492. The Patrician debate began again.

Much of the debate has centered on the chronology of Patrick's mission, and, if the legendary Patrick is indeed a composite, whether he was the predecessor, contemporary, or successor of the one or more individuals whose lives have become so inextricably mingled with his own. Both schools of thought, those who favor the single Patrick and those who argue for the composite Patrick, have offered modifications and alternative theories to those put forward by Bury and O'Rahilly. Hardly any detail of Patrick's life and career not confirmed by his own words is uncontested, and even his curious Latin allows differing interpretation. These points of controversy span the entire fifth century, spilling over at either end.

The date of Patrick's birth usually has been reckoned retroactively from the time of his arrival as a missionary in Ireland, a calculated guess in itself. The various Irish annals offer several different dates, from 313 to 353, for his birth, but most modern scholars are loath to accept the testimony of the annals without supporting evidence. The earliest birthdate was suggested by Mario Esposito, who believed Patrick came to Ireland as a missionary in 395, pushing the birthdate well back into the fourth century. The latest birthdate, 418, has been argued by James Carney, who believes Patrick's mission began in 456. Between these extremes, a number of scholars still prefer dates near the 389 birthdate proposed by Bury. R. P. Hanson advanced an argument based on the statement by Patrick that his father was a deacon and a decurion. He investigated the periods in which the combination of sacred and secular offices would have been easiest, entirely avoiding any reference to Irish sources, to arrive at the conclusion that Patrick was born about 390.

The place of Patrick's birth has also been a disputed question. Though Patrick's family was obviously part of the romanized British aristocracy and he mentions the name of a town near his father's villa, the location is unknown. Muirchú, one of Patrick's earliest medieval biographers, located his home in the Strathclyde area. This is still the favored site for many scholars; others prefer sites near the Severn estuary, southern Cornwall, or the Glastonbury area as regions more subject to Roman influences than Strathclyde.

The part of Ireland in which Patrick spent his captivity has never been established either. Both Tiréchán and Muirchú claimed it was in Slemish in Antrim. This is entirely possible, especially if Patrick's home was in Strathclyde, but several points in the *Confession* raise serious objections to it. The famous passage in the *Confession* about the vision of the letter from Ireland and the voices of the people in the forest of Foclut could not have so strongly affected Patrick if he had never been to the region and knew no one there. The forest of Foclut, however, is in Sligo on the west coast of Ireland. Furthermore, the difficulties Patrick encountered in escaping and returning to Britain are extraordinary if he was in fact in Slemish, just across the narrows of the Irish Sea from Britain.

These questions of geographical identification seem mere quibbles indeed, compared to those surrounding Patrick's education and the circumstances of his return to Ireland. The medieval biographies of Patrick all provide him with a lengthy period of study in Gaul and Italy. The only support provided for such claims in the *Confession* is a quite brief allusion made by Patrick to his wish to visit Gaul, which some scholars have read as a reference to friends whom Patrick wished to see again. Stronger evidence comes from the so-called *dicta*, the sayings attributed to Patrick first recorded in the Book of Armagh (ninth century). One of them is a remark about Patrick's travels through Gaul, Italy, and the Tyrrhenian Sea islands. These frail supports alone hardly suffice for claims of thirty or forty years of study, but the tradition of Patrick's sojourn on the Continent is very strong in the early lives.

As a strong counter to this tradition, the candid admissions Patrick makes in the *Confession* about his lack of education and formal training—borne out by his obvious difficulties in writing Latin—hardly befit a man educated at Lerins, Auxerre, or Tours. Patrick was thoroughly versed in Scripture and the Bible, apparently Jerome's Vulgate was known to him, but as yet no textual investigation has been able to prove that Patrick was familiar with the works of the church fathers and his own contemporaries. After careful study of Patrick's Latin, Christine Mohrmann concluded that it could reflect continental popular Latin usage. Subsequently, both Kenneth Jackson and Daniel Binchy have pointed out that so little is known of fifth-century British Latin that it is impossible to determine how it differed from contemporary continental usage. Indeed, some of Patrick's odder constructions seem closer to Irish syntax than Latin.

This paradox is explained by the scholars who favor the composite Patrick theory as the result of the incorporation of the life of the continental missionary Palladius into the life of the British missionary Patrick. The mission of Palladius to Ireland is attested by the sound authority of a contemporary, the continental chronicler Prosper. According to him, in the year 431 Pope Celestine sent Palladius, a deacon at Auxerre, as a bishop to the Irish Christian community.

Unfortunately, Prosper provides no further details about Palladius and his mission. The Irish sources unanimously declare that Palladius died or was martyred almost immediately and that Patrick was his successor, arriving in Ireland in 432. There is a surviving, though faint, tradition that the Palladian mission did manage to establish three churches in southern Ireland in the Wicklow area before it collapsed: Cell-Fine, Tech-na-Roman, and Domnach-Airte. The fullest account is found in the *Tripartite Life* (late ninth to tenth century), but there are serious chronology problems in its version of the Palladian mission's fate. These hints, however faint, have led some scholars to doubt the Irish reports and to credit the Palladian mission with at least some success. The early work of this mission was either annexed to the subsequent mission of St. Patrick or simply overshadowed by it in their view.

There is no clearly identified authority for the Patrician mission. Patrick does not say who consecrated him "bishop to the Irish," though he uses that title. He may have begun without official sanction at all, winning belated recognition by the success of his efforts. The seniors he refers to in the *Confession* could be in Britain or Gaul or both. The Irish tradition that he was consecrated and sent by Pope Celestine is probably a native attempt to give Patrick the kind of credentials held by his rival Palladius, but it is not utterly impossible.

If there were two separate missions to Ireland, it does not necessarily follow that Patrick was able to take advantage of whatever headway the mission of Palladius made. If Mario Esposito is correct, the Patrician mission preceded that of Palladius. If Patrick succeeded him, the fact remains that Patrick was active in the north, while Palladius was active in the south. It was only much later as Patrick's cult spread that he became the national apostle of legend.

Patrick's original northern focus is most evident in the earliest material, which associates him with the principal sites of Down, Armagh, and Tara. Down was probably the original site of Patrick's mission, but Armagh became the center of his cult. Traditionally, Patrick is portrayed as the apostle to the powerful Uí Néill dynasty at Tara in the Boyne valley. Daniel Binchy observed in 1962 that if the historical St. Patrick had been allied with the Uí Néill, it is most unlikely that he would have established himself at Armagh, which was very close to Emain Macha, the royal site of the Ulster kings who opposed the Uí Néill.

More recently, however, Richard Sharpe has argued that Patrick was not the founder of Armagh. He cites archaeological evidence to show that Emain Macha was deserted before Patrick's time, while Armagh was occupied from the third century on into the Christian period. More evidence against Patrick's legendary patronage of the Uí Néill is found in the Book of Armagh, which gives a geographic description of an area called the *termon* of Armagh. Eoin MacNeil considered the area described to be the original Patrician see. This area lies entirely within the territory of the Ulster and eastern Airgialla kingdoms, well to the north of the Tara Uí Néill. There are references in Patrick's writings to his travels, but his own accounts of the dangers he encountered attest to the difficulties of travel in Patrick's time. The extensive circuits of Ireland found in Tiréchán's account, therefore, are suspect.

Whatever the extent of Patrick's mission, it would obviously help to establish the date of that mission if the ruler Coroticus addressed in Patrick's letter could be identified. It is not clear at what point in his career Patrick wrote it, but certainly he had been in Ireland a number of years before the incident. Unfortunately, there are two fifth-century British chieftains of that name. The earlier one is Coroticus, or Ceretic, of Dumbarton in Strathclyde (*fl.* 410–440). The other possible target of the letter is Ceretic, son of Cunedda, prince of North Wales, who reigned during the second half of the fifth century. Those scholars who favor an early date for the mission of St. Patrick argue for Ceretic of Dumbarton, and those who prefer a later date argue for Ceretic of Wales.

It is most unfortunate that Coroticus is the only contemporary that Patrick cites by name in his writing. He alludes to his converts and companions, but they cannot be identified. The biographers provide Patrick with a number of assistants and contemporaries, as do the Irish annals. The most prominent of his immediate associates are Secundinus (Irish: Sechnall), Iserninus, and Ausaille (Irish: Usaille). The annals disagree as to the death dates of these three, but even the latest obituary, one for Iserninus in 468/469, is compatible with a 461 date for Patrick himself. This is not true for the obituaries of all Patrick's supposed contemporaries recorded in the annals. Some of the dates are as late as the mid sixth century. Though the annals' entries for the fifth and sixth centuries are not contemporary with the events recorded, the net implication of these later obituary entries can be cited as an argument for the later obituary date for Patrick of 490 or later.

The problem of determining who Patrick's contemporaries were, however, is a tautology in and of itself. The death dates for Patrick given in the annals range from 457 to 496. Obituaries stating that someone was Patrick's disciple or colleague do not provide a means of objective verification for their claims. The date of 461 for Patrick's death is still favored by some scholars, but the majority of the annal entries for his death put it much later, toward the end of the fifth century. If Patrick arrived in Ireland in 432 and lived until the early 490's, he could not have been much past his mid-twenties when he came. Scholars who believe that Patrick spent a number of years in Gaul and Italy before his return to Ireland have traditionally sided with Bury and the early date, while those preferring a composite Patrick legend have argued for the later one(s).

The confusion in the annals over the obituary of St. Patrick arises from the apparent existence of two Patricks. The earlier date of 461 is cited in the *Annals of Ulster* and the *Annals of Ireland (Annals of the Four Masters)* as the obit of the "Old Patrick" as distinct from the 492/493 obit for Patrick the "archbishop." Scholars arguing the existence of a single historical Patrick believe this to be a textual confusion in the later sources, but others accept the possibility of two distinct historical personages. These scholars, however, do not agree on the identity of the two (or more) Patricks. If Patrick the Briton was the successor to Palladius, O'Rahilly argued, then Palladius would be "Old Patrick." This argument is completely reversed by Esposito, who believes that Patrick the Briton preceded Palladius. The earliest mention of the two Patricks comes in the appended material to Tiréchán preserved in the *Book of Armagh*. Consequently, if it is to be dismissed as a textual problem in the written sources, it must have arisen very early to have established itself by the ninth century, and perhaps as early as Tiréchán's time, about 700. In the *Book of Armagh* reference, the "Old Patrick" designation is given to Palladius. The theory of a youthful successor to Patrick the Briton, omitting Palladius from consideration entirely, has the advantage of reconciling the apparent confusion of the annals' version of the post-Palladian mission of St. Patrick and his extreme longevity. To date no scholar has been able to provide a completely satisfactory explanation to the "Old Patrick" puzzle.

To match the confusion over the date of Patrick's death, there is also great uncertainty over his burial. All the early sources agree that he died at Saul in the territory of the remains of the old Ulster kingdoms. The Airgialla peoples around Armagh, according to legend, attempted to ambush the funeral party but were outwitted by the miraculous appearance of a second burial cortege. The "triumphant" Airgialla led this second cortege back to Armagh, where it abruptly vanished. Patrick's relics subsequently were said to have been translated to Downpatrick. Saul, Armagh, and Downpatrick have all claimed to be the true burial sites, but the exact location of Patrick's grave remains unknown.

Contemporary scholars of the period readily admit that too much vital evidence is lacking to permit solutions to the many problems surrounding St. Patrick. The final irony is that the force of the personality revealed in the *Confession* and the *Letter to Coroticus* continues to attract their interest and invite investigation.

BIBLIOGRAPHY

Sources and editions include A. B. E. Hood, *St. Patrick: His Writings and Muirchu's Life* (1978), a popular rather than scholarly presentation, containing the Latin text with facing English translation; and Whitley Stokes, ed., *Tripartite Life of Patrick*, 2 vols. (1887, repr. 1965), containing Irish and Latin texts with English translation.

Studies include John B. Bury, *The Life of St. Patrick* (1905), the standard biography; and Thomas F. O'Rahilly, *The Two Patricks* (1942), which equates the old(er) Patrick with Palladius. Other studies include Daniel Binchy, "Patrick and His Biographers: Ancient and Modern," in *Studia hibernica,* **2** (1962); Brian De Breffny, *In the Steps of St. Patrick* (1982); Mario Esposito, "The Patrician Problem and a Possible Solution," in *Irish Historical Studies,* **10** (1956); Richard P. C. Hanson, *Saint Patrick: His Origins and Career* (1968); Richard Sharpe, "St. Patrick and the See of Armagh," in *Cambridge Medieval Celtic Studies,* **4** (1982); Francis Shaw, "The Myth of the Second Patrick," in *Studies,* **50** (1961), which answers O'Rahilly's theory with arguments that textual confusions created the second Patrick theory.

DOROTHY AFRICA

[See also **Celtic Church; Germanus of Auxerre; Ireland, Early History; Missions and Missionaries.**]

PATRISTIC LITERATURE. See **Church Fathers.**

PATRONQMOBA (Georgian: *patroni,* lord; *qmoba,* slavery, serfdom), the system of personal dependence or vassalage in ancient and medieval Georgia. The Georgian "feudal" system arose from a tribal-dynastic organization of society upon which was imposed, by royal authority, an official hierarchy of regional governors, local officials, and subordinates. Established as early as the fourth century B.C., the Georgian sociopolitical system fluctuated between periods of dynastic assertion by local princes and reimpositions of royal "feudalism."

In the medieval period Georgian "feudalism," or *patronqmoba,* went through three distinct phases. From the eighth to the eleventh centuries, Georgian society was organized on a network of personal ties or contracts linking the king and the princes, the princes and the nobles. Already in the eighth and ninth centuries, a system of receiving homage in exchange for benefices developed. Beginning in the eleventh century, ties based on service became more important, and land gradually became hereditary. After a brief feudal revival in the fourteenth century, vassal-lord relations disintegrated, and Georgian *patronqmoba* metamorphosed into *tavadoba,* rule by the princes.

BIBLIOGRAPHY

William E. D. Allen, *A History of the Georgian People,* 2nd ed. (1971); Nikolai Aleksandrovich Berdzenishvili, *Ocherk iz istorii razvitiia feodal'nykh otnozhenii v Gruzii* (1938); Georges Charachidzé, *Introduction à l'étude de la féodalité géorgienne* (1971); Cyril Toumanoff, *Studies in Christian Caucasian History* (1963).

RONALD GRIGOR SUNY

[See also **Feudalism; Georgia: Political History; Georgians (Iberians).**]

PATZINAKS. See **Russia, Nomadic Invasions of.**

PAUCAPALEA (*fl.* mid twelfth century) was "present at the creation" in Bologna of the *Concordia discordantium canonum,* the only identified name among those who revised and completed the work traditionally ascribed to Gratian. Paucapalea inserted a number of canons, brought order into the distinctions of part 1 and part 3, and probably contributed the climactic dictum on marriage, case 27, question 2, dictum post chapter 50. His own commentary on the *Concordia,* the earliest known, has not been definitively identified. In 1890 Johann Schulte published *Quoniam in omnibus,* describing it as Paucapalea's summa, but it is more likely that this truncated work is dependent on *Sicut uetus testamentum,* a major commentary, a passage from which Rolandus ascribes to Paucapalea. *Sicut uetus* *testamentum* strikes a balance between biblical material and Roman law characteristic of the *Concordia* itself and is rich in canonical analysis. It was composed after midsummer 1146 and probably before 1150. The author of *Sicut uetus testamentum* is learned in law, interested in classical allusions, sensitive to biblical poetry, and intrigued by Greek etymologies. His humane culture, and a set of anti-Genoese cases, suggest a Pisan.

Two Paucapaleas appear in records of this period: one witnesses documents at S. Vittore, Bologna, in 1165; another, probably Pisan, is bishop of S. Giusta, Sardinia, in 1146 or 1147. Neither has been proved to be identical with the canonist, who is known only by references in Bolognese commentators.

BIBLIOGRAPHY

Antonio Mocci, "Documenti inediti sul canonista Paucapalea," in *Atti della Reale accademia delle scienze di Torino,* 40 (1905); John T. Noonan, Jr., "The True Paucapalea?" in Wendy D. O'Flaherty, ed., *The Critical Study of Sacred Texts* (1979); Paucapalea, *Die Summa des Paucapalea über das Decretum Gratiani,* Johann Schulte, ed. (1890, repr. 1965).

JOHN T. NOONAN, JR.

[See also **Bologna, University of; Corpus Iuris Civilis; Decretists; Decretum; Gratian; Law, Canon; Rolandus.**]

PAUL THE DEACON (*ca.* 720–*ca.* 799), historian, teacher, poet, and monk of Monte Cassino, is best known for his *History of the Lombards,* which tells the story of his people from their legendary origins to the death of King Liutprand in 744.

Son of a noble Lombard couple named Warnefrid and Theodolinda, Paul was sent for his education to the court of King Rachis at Pavia. There his tutor, Flavianus, taught him some Greek and Hebrew along with the regular course of studies in Latin authors, though in later years Paul was inclined to dismiss his Greek learning. About 770 he came to know King Desiderius and his reputedly beautiful daughter Adelperga, who in time persuaded Paul to come to Benevento, where she and her husband Arichis ruled. Paul probably entered Monte Cassino in 773 or 774, when Charlemagne broke Lombard power in Italy. There is no evidence that he had been a monk at St. Peter's in Civate or that he composed a commentary on the Rule of Benedict there, as earlier scholars thought.

In 782/783 Paul journeyed to Aachen to intervene with Charlemagne on his brother's behalf. Seven years earlier his brother, Arichis, had been involved in the revolt of Duke Hrodgaud of Friuli against Charlemagne, had lost all his property, and had been imprisoned. The best evidence is that this meeting had been arranged by Paul's friend and countryman Peter of Pisa, and that Paul's brother was released the same year. The contact with the court at Aachen apparently was decisive for Paul. He remained for perhaps two or three years as an honored guest of Charlemagne, and when he returned to Monte Cassino, he seems to have done so with a deeper commitment to the spiritual life than he had displayed before. The last decade of his life was his best and most productive. Most scholars think he lived nearly to the end of the century, but at least one has suggested that he was dead before 790.

The earliest (*ca.* 770) work of Paul's to survive is an acrostic poem of thirty-six lines written while he was at the court of Desiderius and spelling out the name of Princess Adelperga in the initial letters of each stanza. The poem outlines the chronology of sacred history, giving the traditionally accepted number of years from the Creation to the time of Abraham, to Moses, and so on, down to Paul's own day. Like much of Paul's verse, this does not suggest great poetry, but it does reveal something about the care he took in educating his prince's daughter. Better known are his moving lines to Charlemagne on behalf of his brother, in which he describes the plight of his sister-in-law and her children, left to "beg their bread in the streets with trembling lip." Also remembered is his poem in praise of Lake Como, which would have surpassed even the Sea of Galilee, as it surpassed all other lakes, had Jesus walked on its waters. Inscriptions, epitaphs, and dedicatory poems make up the balance of Paul's poetry, and though their subjects seem unpromising, they frequently repay careful study.

Very influential was Paul's homiliary, a collection of patristic homilies that was textually sound and covered the whole ecclesiastical year. Charlemagne's *Epistola generalis* recommended its use throughout his empire.

Evidence of Paul's scholarly and pedagogic interests are his *Grammar* and his epitome of Festus' *De verborum significatu,* but deservedly best known are his historical works. Among these may be counted his *Life* of Gregory the Great, though more hagiography than history, as well as the *History of the Bishops of Metz* and his masterpiece, the *History of the Lombards.* Based on the now-lost, anonymous *Origo gentis Langobardorum* and the chronicle of Secundus, Paul's *History* is a simple and compelling narrative of his nation's past, chronologically vague but generally quite accurate. Either because he died or because he was unwilling to chronicle the story of the Lombards' defeat by the forces of Charlemagne, Paul stopped his narrative just short of the half-century of history after 744 that he had personally witnessed.

BIBLIOGRAPHY

Only the *Historia Langobardorum* has been translated into English: Paul the Deacon, *History of the Lombards,* William D. Foulke, trans. (1907, repr. 1974). It is edited in *Monumenta Germaniae historica: Scriptores rerum Langobardicarum et Italicarum Saec.* VI–IX (1878), 45–187. The best edition of the poetry is Karl Neff, *Die Gedichte des Paulus Diaconus* (1908), also available in *Monumenta Germaniae historica: Poetae latini aevi carolini,* I (1880), 35–86.

Commentary in English is to some extent dated: Max L. W. Laistner, *Thought and Letters in Western Europe: A.D. 500 to 900* (1931, rev. ed. 1957); Frederic J. E. Raby, *A History of Christian-Latin Poetry from the Beginnings to the Close of the Middle Ages* (1927, 2nd ed. 1953). More up to date are Franz Brunhölzl, *Geschichte der lateinischen Literatur des Mittelalters,* I (1975), 257–268; Josef Szövérffy, *Weltliche Dichtungen des lateinischen Mittelalters* (1970).

COLIN CHASE

[See also **Carolingian Latin Poetry; Lombards, Kingdom of; Peter of Pisa.**]

PAULICIANS, a sect, named after a Paul whose identity is disputed, which seriously disturbed the eastern provinces of the Byzantine Empire in the ninth century. When the Paulicians, driven from the capital by the persecution of the empress Theodora II in 842, established themselves on the Upper Euphrates, they created a state whose capital was Tephrikē (modern Divrigi). According to the historians of the Macedonian dynasty, Genesios, George the Monk, and Theophanes Continuatus, the Paulicians—considered heretics—collaborated with the Muslim emir of Melitene and threatened the eastern frontier of the empire until Basil I in a major campaign seized Tephrikē in 872 and destroyed the Paulician state. Thereafter, the Paulicians fled to Islamic lands, where the crusaders met them around Antioch in the late eleventh century. Others probably fled to Armenia. A number of them served in the Byzantine armies in southern Italy during the wars against the Normans in the mid eleventh century. Finally, still other Paulicians settled in the Balkans around Philippopolis (modern Plovdiv) in Komnenian times. They were met there by the Third Crusade, and some of them survived to modern times, although they converted to Roman Catholicism in the eighteenth century.

ORIGINS AND DOCTRINES OF THE SECT

The history and particularly the doctrine of the Paulicians are still the subject of active scholarly controversy. There seems to be no doubt that the sectarians rejected the sacraments of the Orthodox churches, which they considered tainted, and the authority of the ecclesiastical hierarchy, preferring to follow only their own leaders. They were intransigent iconoclasts rejecting reverence not only of holy images but of the cross itself, which they viewed as the "accursed instrument" of Christ's crucifixion. Beyond these points, however, disagreement in the sources have led to two main theses among scholars.

Greek theories. On the basis of Greek polemical sources, and especially of the *History of the Manichaeans Called Paulicians* by one Peter of Sicily, whose dates and authenticity have been questioned, the Paulicians have been identified as descendants of the earlier Manichaeans and thus as dualists recognizing two principles—one good, the other evil—personified by the Heavenly Father, the Lord of Eternity whose power lay outside the visible world, and the Creator of the World, who holds power in the finite material world. Since matter pertained to the realm of evil, the incarnation of Christ must therefore have been illusory or Docetic, and the true Mother of God was to be identified with the Heavenly Jerusalem.

According to these Greek sources, the sect, taking its name from a certain Paul of Samosata, the son of a Manichaean woman named Kallinike, first appeared in the eastern theme of Armeniakon. Its true founder, however, was an Armenian named Constantine, who learned the heretical doctrine from a Syrian deacon in the mid seventh century, and who took the pastoral name of Silvanos in honor of the disciple of St. Paul. Though Constantine-Silvanos was soon put to death by the Byzantine authorities and persecutions continued, the sect survived in Asia Minor under the guidance of a number of successive leaders: Symeon-Titos; Paul; Genesios-Timothy; Zacharias; Joseph-Epaphroditos; the most distinguished of all, Sergios-Tychikos, in the first half of the ninth century; Baanes; and finally the leaders known to the historical sources, the imperial officers Karbeas and his nephew Chrysocheir, who ruled at Tephrikē. Most of the heresiarchs took Pauline pastoral names, and they founded a number of churches in Asia Minor whose names were also associated with St. Paul (Macedonia, Achaia, Philippi, Laodikeia, Ephesos, and Kolosses), as well as the political centers of Argaous, Amara, and Tephrikē on the Euphrates. According to this interpretation, the Paulicians are seen as part of a continuing dualist tradition reaching back to the third-century Manichaeans and in turn influencing the Bogomils in the Balkans and ultimately the Albigensians of southern France.

Armenian theories. Both the name of the Paulicians, which contains the pejorative Armenian suffix *-ik,* meaning small or wretched, and the traditional background of the first heresiarch, Constantine-Silvanos, point to Armenia rather than Byzantium as the original home of the sect. Consequently, the numerous Armenian sources relating to the Paulicians are of obvious interest in their study, but they create the basic problem in the interpretation of Paulicianism through their disagreement with the Greek evidence. Even if the *mcłnēutᶜiwn* (filth) condemned at the Council of Šahapiwan in 444 and the nameless heretics mentioned in the historian Łazar Pᶜarpecᶜi's *Letter to Lord Vahan Mamikonean* later in the same century are not to be identified with Paulicians, as has been suggested by some scholars, these heretics are condemned by name in the *Call to Repentance* of the *katᶜołikos* John Mandakuni (478–490), long before the appearance of Constantine-Silvanos, and in the "Oath of Union" of the Council of Dwin in 555, where they are identified with Nestorians. In the seventh and eighth centuries the sectarians are explicitly mentioned in the "Canons and Constitutions" of the Council of Albania, at the Council of Dwin in 719/720, and in a separate treatise *Against the Paulicians* of the *katᶜołikos* John of Ōjun (717–728), as well as in later lists of heresies. The Paulicians are probably also to be identified with the iconoclasts condemned by the theologian Vrtᶜanēs Kᶜertᶜoł at the beginning of the seventh century in his *Treatise Against the Iconoclasts,* and with the "sons of sinfulness" known to the historian Łewond the Priest in the eighth century. Finally, they are usually taken to be the predecessors of the Tᶜondrakecᶜi, who flourished in Armenia from the ninth century on.

Even if one does not accept the presumed manual of the heretics known as *The Key of Truth,* whose authenticity has been questioned, the doctrine of the sect that emerges from the Armenian sources differs radically from the one set forth by the Greek polemicists. In Armenia, the heretics were said to be descended from Paul of Samosata, bishop of Antioch late in the third century, and they were identified with Nestorians and iconoclasts. Their doctrine was given not as dualism but rather as the condemned adoptionist Christology of Paul of Samosata wherein Jesus, born an ordinary man, was adopted for his sinlessness as Son of God, an apotheosis achievable to all those who equaled his virtues, and particularly by the Paulician leaders. On the basis of this evidence, it has been argued that the Armenian Paulicians dated back to a much earlier period than those in the Byzantine Empire; that they were not linked to Gnostic traditions but were in effect Old Believers holding to the original Syrian form of Armenian Christianity, adoptionist and iconoclastic in character, which had been brought from Antioch and Samosata to southern Armenia and subsequently been rejected by the Hellenization of the northern Armenian church beginning in the late fourth century. This original form of Paulicianism survived in Armenia, where it was taken over by the Tᶜondrakecᶜi, and it also manifested itself among the later Paulicians in southern Italy. Another group fled to the Byzantine Empire, where they were welcomed in the period of the iconoclastic emperors Leo III and Constantine V. There, under the influence of extreme iconoclastic groups, accused of Manichaean dualism and Docetism by their opponents, such as St. John of Damascus, and perhaps in the time of the great heresiarch Sergios-Tychikos, who is accused of major innovations, the Byzantine Paulicians gradually accepted a docetic Christology rejecting matter as evil and ultimately became dualists. This neo-Paulicianism was the one described by the Greek sources and may have influenced the Bogomils, but it marked a radical departure from the original Armenian doctrine.

CONCLUSIONS

There seems to be little doubt that Paulicianism was a major political and religious movement in

Armenia and the Byzantine Empire. Its recently suggested social thrust is less probable since its last leaders, at least, were army officers of considerable social standing. The historical and theological problems associated with the sect, however, still present considerable difficulties. For their solution all the relevant sources, Armenian as well as the more familiar Greek ones, will require equal attention.

BIBLIOGRAPHY
Karapet Ter-Měkěrttschian, *Die Paulikianer im byzantinischen Kaiserreiche und verwandte ketzerische Erscheinungen in Armenien* (1893); Frederick Cornwallis Conybeare, *The Key of Truth: A Manual of the Paulician Church in Armenia* (1898); Steven Runciman, *The Medieval Manichee: A Study of the Christian Dualist Heresy* (1948); Paul Lemerle, "Les sources grecques pour l'histoire des Pauliciens d'Asie Mineure," in *Travaux et mémoires,* **4** (1970), and "L'histoire des Pauliciens d'Asie Mineure d'après les sources grecques," *ibid.,* **5** (1973); Milan Loos, *Dualist Heresy in the Middle Ages* (1974); Nina G. Garsoïan, *The Paulician Heresy* (1967), "Byzantine Heresy: A Reinterpretation," in *Dumbarton Oaks Papers,* **25** (1975), and "L'abjuration du Moine Nil de Calabre," in *Byzantinoslavica,* **25** (1974); Erwand Ter-Minassiantz, *Die armenische Kirche in ihren Beziehungen zu den syrischen Kirchen bis zum Ende des 13. Jahrhunderts* (1904). See also the numerous Russian and Armenian articles, some translated in the *Revue des études arméniennes,* n.s. **1** (1964), **9** (1972), **10** (1973–1974), by Karen N. Yuzbashyan and Hratch M. Bartikyan.

NINA G. GARSOÏAN

[See also **Adoptionism; Albigensians; Armeniakon, Theme of; Bogomilism; Docetism; Dualism; Genesios, Joseph; George the Monk; Heresies; Iconoclasm; Łazar P^{c}arpec^{c}i; Manichaeans; Theophanes Continuatus.**]

PAULINUS OF AQUILEIA, ST. (before 750–802). Born in Friuli in northern Italy, Paulinus became a grammarian and found favor under Charlemagne, who granted him land and summoned him to his court school in 776. In 787 he was made patriarch of Aquileia by Charlemagne, whom he represented at several subsequent church councils. He was particularly involved in the suppression of the Spanish heresy of adoptionism, and in 794 at the Council of Frankfurt, at the order of Charlemagne, he drafted the *Holy Syllabus Against Elipandus,* the bishop of Toledo. Also at the order of Charlemagne, conveyed by Alcuin, he wrote *On the Divinity of the Son Against Felix of Urgel* (796–800). In conjunction with this work he seems also to have composed his metrical *Rule of Faith,* which, according to one commentator, "neglected the Rule of Metrics." In his quest for orthodoxy, Paulinus also supported the Nicene-Constantinopolitan Creed. In 801, at the Council of Aachen, he obtained a guarantee of free episcopal elections. His epitaph was composed by Alcuin, who called him "lux Ausoniae patriae" (the light of his [Italian] homeland).

Paulinus was remembered for his missionary activities on behalf of the Carinthians, the Styrians, and the Huns, although he opposed the mass baptisms of uncatechized barbarians. He is considered primarily a theologian, but his extant works also include poems ("On Lazarus," "On the Resurrection of the Lord," "On the Sorrow of Repentence," and "On the Destruction of Aquileia," among others), letters, and hymns. His literary circle included Alcuin, from whom he received poems and letters, and the duke Hericus of Friuli, for whom he wrote a *Book of Exhortation,* as well as *Verses on the Death of the Duke Hericus* after the latter's death in 799.

BIBLIOGRAPHY
Sources. Analecta hymnica medii aevi, L (1906), 127–151; *Monumenta Germaniae historica: Epistolae,* IV (1895), 516–527; *Monumenta Germaniae historica: Poetae latini medii aevi,* I (1881), 122–148, IV, pt. 2 (1923), 911–914, VI, pt. 1 (1951), 208–225; *Patrologia latina,* XCIX (1851), 1–684.
Studies. Giuseppe Ellero, *San Paolino d'Aquileia* (1901); Karl Giannoni, *Paulinus II, Patriarch von Aquileia* (1896); *Miscellanea di studi storici e ricerche critiche, ricorrendo il XI centenario della morte di Paolino* (1905); Pio Paschina, *San Paolino patriarca e la chiesa aquileise alla fine del secolo VIII* (1906, repr. 1977).

RALPH W. MATHISEN

[See also **Adoptionism; Alcuin of York; Carolingian Latin Poetry; Carolingians; Charlemagne.**]

PAULINUS OF BÉZIERS (*fl.* early fifth century), bishop of Béziers, usually thought to have been the "St. Paulinus" who wrote the *Epigram* in 110 hexameters. This poem, in the form of a dialogue between the monks Salmon and Thesbon, was probably written about 407 and tells of the devastation and misery in Gaul caused by the barbarian invasions. It blames these troubles on contemporary immorality and the unwillingness of people to reform; in this it foreshadows the works of Salvian of Marseilles (*d.* after 470) and others. Some believe that this is the Paulinus who wrote the *Passion of Saint Genesius of Arles,* one of the earliest hagiographical texts.

BIBLIOGRAPHY

Sources. Corpus scriptorum ecclesiasticorum latinorum, XVI (1888), 499–510, XXIX (1894), 425–428; J. N. Hillgarth, *The Conversion of Western Europe* (1969), 68–69; *Patrologia latina,* LXI (1847), 418–420.

Studies. Eleanor S. Duckett, *Latin Writers of the Fifth Century* (1930); E. Griffe, "L'*Epigramma Paulini,* poème gallo-romain du Ve siècle," in *Revue des études augustiniennes,* 2 (1956); John Martindale, ed., *Prosopography of the Later Roman Empire,* II, *A.D. 395–527* (1980), 845–846; Martin von Schanz *et al., Geschichte der römischen Litteratur bis zum Gesetzgebungswerk des Kaisers Justinian,* IV, pt. 2 (1920), 361–363.

RALPH W. MATHISEN

[See also **Hagiography, Western European; Salvian of Marseilles.**]

PAULINUS OF NOLA, ST. (353/354—431), bishop of Nola and writer. Born of a senatorial family of Bordeaux, he was named Meropius Pontius Paulinus. After being educated by the Gallic poet Ausonius (*d. ca.* 393), Paulinus rose to become suffect consul around 378 and governor of Campania in 381. Around 389 he suffered a series of personal misfortunes, and he and his Spanish wife, Therasia, adopted a very ascetic religious life. For this he was much criticized by some members of the senatorial order, although other aristocratic Christians, such as St. Melania the Younger (383–439), adopted a similar way of life at this time. On 25 December 394 he was forcibly ordained a priest at Barcelona, and in the following year he and his wife retired to a family estate at Nola, where he established a monastery and in 409 became bishop. He died on 22 June 431, and the priest Uranius wrote the extant *On the Death of St. Paulinus.*

Paulinus was a prolific writer; extant works include fifty letters to such men as Sulpicius Severus, Augustine, Jerome, and Eucherius of Lyons, and thirty-three poems on religious topics, including fourteen homilies on his patron saint, Felix of Nola. He also wrote a lost panegyric on the emperor Theodosius I and an influential sacramentary, also lost. His elegant style has led to his being called "the Christian Cicero."

BIBLIOGRAPHY

Sources. Acta sanctorum: June, V (1867), 170–172; *Corpus scriptorum ecclesiasticorum latinorum,* XXIX and XXX (1894); *Patrologia latina,* LIII (1847), 858–866 and LXI (1847), 153–438; P. G. Walsh, *Letters of St. Paulinus of Nola,* 2 vols. (1966–1968), and *The Poems of St. Paulinus of Nola* (1975).

Studies. Nora K. Chadwick, *Poetry and Letters in Early Christian Gaul* (1955); W. C. Frend, "Paulinus of Nola and the Last Century of the Western Empire," in *Journal of Roman Studies,* 59 (1969); R. C. Goldschmidt, ed., *Paulinus' Church at Nola* (1940); A. H. M. Jones *et al.,* eds., *Prosopography of the Later Roman Empire,* I, *A.D. 260–395* (1971); Martin von Schanz *et al., Geschichte der römischen Litteratur,* IV, pt. 1 (1920).

RALPH W. MATHISEN

[See also **Bells; Beneventan Rite; Cassian, John; Latin Literature; Sacramentary.**]

PAULINUS OF PELLA (376–*ca.* 459). Born at Pella in Macedonia, where his father was in imperial office, Paulinus was the grandson of the Gallic poet Ausonius, and he demonstrated his own literary inclinations by composing, in 459 at the age of eighty-three, an autobiographical poem, the *Thanksgiving to God in an Account of My Life* (*Eucharisticos*). The poem, in 616 hexameter verses of mediocre quality, describes the indulgences of his youth and the subsequent misfortunes he suffered as a result of the barbarian invasions beginning in 406. In 414/415 he was appointed count of the treasury by the usurper Attalus, and in 421 he experienced a religious conversion but failed in an attempt to become a monk. His declining years were spent in poverty, first in Marseilles and finally in Bordeaux.

Despite its emphasis on Paulinus' miseries and afflictions, his poem was written as a thanksgiving to God for his guidance and mercy. It is primarily useful for its descriptions of Gallic life during the first half-century of the barbarian occupation. Paulinus is also thought to have been the author of an extant *Oratio* (*Prayer*) in nineteen hexameter verses.

BIBLIOGRAPHY

Sources. Corpus scriptorum ecclesiasticorum latinorum, XVI (1888), 263–314; Claude Moussy, *Poème d'action de grâces et prière: Paulin de Pella* (1974); Hugh G. Evelyn White, trans., *Ausonius,* II (1921), 295–351.

Studies. Nora K. Chadwick, *Poetry and Letters in Early Christian Gaul* (1955); Eleanor S. Duckett, *Latin Writers of the Fifth Century* (1930); A. H. M. Jones *et al.*, eds., *Prosopography of the Later Roman Empire,* I, *A.D. 260–395* (1971), 677–678; Martin von Schanz *et al.*, *Geschichte der römischen Litteratur,* IV, pt. 2 (1920), 374–376.

RALPH W. MATHISEN

PAULINUS OF PÉRIGUEUX (*fl.* 459–472), poet, native of Gaul. Paulinus was born in the early fifth century and converted to Christianity late in life. Around 470 he dedicated to Bishop Perpetuus of Tours (461–491) a poem *On the Life of St. Martin* in six books and 3,622 hexameter verses. The first five books were based on the works of the Gallic Christian Sulpicius Severus (*ca.* 360–*ca.* 430), and the last recounted miracles that had occurred after the saint's death. His other extant works include a twenty-five-line hexameter poem for the wall of Perpetuus' new church of St. Martin, an eighty-line poem on his grandchild, and a dedicatory letter to Perpetuus. He probably is to be identified with the rhetor Paulinus of Périgueux mentioned by Sidonius Apollinaris.

BIBLIOGRAPHY

Sources. Corpus scriptorum ecclesiasticorum latinorum, XVI (1888), 17–165; *Patrologia latina,* LXI (1847), 1007–1076, and LXXIV (1850), 673.

Studies. Alston H. Chase, "The Metrical Lives of St. Martin of Tours by Paulinus and Fortunatus and the Prose Life by Sulpicius Severus," in *Harvard Studies in Classical Philology,* **43** (1932); Martin von Schanz *et al.*, *Geschichte der römischen Litteratur,* IV, pt. 2 (1920), 376–378.

RALPH W. MATHISEN

[See also **Sidonius Apollinaris.**]

PAULUS DIACONUS. See **Paul the Deacon.**

P^cAWSTOS BUZAND is the name given to a putative Armenian medieval historian also known as Faustus of Byzantium or Faustos of Buzanta. The *History of Armenia* attributed to him covers the period of the later Arsacid dynasty from Xosrov II/III (*ca.* 330–338) to Aršak III/IV (378–386/390), or roughly to the partition of Armenia about 387. This *History* consists of four "books" or rather "registers," *dprut^ciwnk^c*, numbered III to VI, of which the last is much shorter than the others and does not give a chronological account of events but rather a series of brief ecclesiastical biographies.

The study of this text has provoked a number of scholarly controversies centering on the identification of the author, the number of books contained in the original, the language (Greek, Syriac, or Armenian) of its composition, and its date. Despite some lingering hesitations, the accepted thesis at present is that the so-called *History of Armenia* is an original work composed in Armenian and not a translation from Greek, and that it dates from the later fifth century (460's or 470's), although its subject is the fourth century. The work was known to the historian Łazar P^carpec^ci, who wrote at the end of the fifth century, and it seems to have had common sources with the contemporary compilation now known as the "Agat^cangełos cycle." As such, it is one of the earliest monuments of Armenian historiography. Despite the confusion created by the identification of "the beginning" as Lesson [book] III, this "Lesson" is now taken as having been the first one, with no initial books lost, so that the entire text is still extant. Finally, twentieth-century scholarship has confirmed that both the title of the work and the name of its author are incorrect. An analysis of the title of the work as given in the text, *Buzandaran patmut^ciwnk^c*, as opposed to the customary one, which is a later addition, has shown that the first term is not a toponym (Byzantium or Buzanta/Podandos in Cilicia) but a derivation from Parthian **bōzand,* Old Persian **bavant-zanda-* or **bava-zanta/i,* "a reciter of epic poems, a bard." Taken in conjunction with the second term, *patmut^ciwnk^c*, "histories" (in the plural), the correct title which is entirely suited to the nature of the work is now clearly set forth. It is an anonymous compilation of epic tales or histories that were subsequently attributed to a bishop P^cawstos or Faustos mentioned in the text and known to other contemporary sources.

The *Epic Histories* attributed to P^cawstos have never achieved the status granted to the other

 PEACE OF GOD, TRUCE OF GOD

medieval histories that form the Armenian "received tradition." Their chronology is demonstrably weak, a number of anachronisms have been noted (the Roman emperors Constantius II and Valens are confused), and a number of episodes from the life of St. Basil of Caesarea have been attributed to the Armenian patriarch St. Nersēs I (*ca.* 310–373). The unbounded admiration expressed for the Mamikonean house and the antagonism toward the Arsacid kings also give an unquestionable bias to the text. Nevertheless, it is a document of major importance, not only because of its early date, but because of its popular, uncontrived character, which serves to balance the more scholarly historians of the "received tradition." It is also the most extensive source for the characteristic *naxarar* social structure of early medieval Armenia. Finally, its reliance on epic tales makes it the main repository for the extensive and otherwise almost completely lost oral literature of the period.

BIBLIOGRAPHY

Manuk Abełean (Abeghian), *Istoriia Drevnearmianskoĭ Literatury [Hayocʿ hin grakanowtʿian patmutʿyun]* (1975); Nikolay Adontz (Adonts), "Faust Vizantiĭskiĭ kak istorik," in *Khristianskiĭ Vostok,* VI (1917–1920); Norman H. Baynes, "Rome and Armenia in the Fourth Century," in *English Historical Review,* **25** (1910), repr. in *Byzantine Studies and Other Essays* (1955); Fréderic Feydit, "L'histoire de Fauste de Byzance comprenait-elle deux livres aujourd'hui perdus?" in *Pazmaveb,* **116** (1958); Nina G. Garsoïan, *Armenia Between Byzantium and the Sasanians* (1985); Karapet Melikʿ-Ōhanǰanyan, "Tiran-Trdati vēpə əst Pʿawstos Buzandi," in *Tełekagir* (1947); Paul Peeters, "Le début de la persécution de Sapor d'après Fauste de Byzance, in *Revue des études arméniennes,* **1** (1920); Anahit Perikhanian, "Sur arm. *Buzand,*" in *Mélanges Haig Bérbérian*; Ernest Stein, "Fauste de Buzanta a-t-il écrit en Grec?" in *Histoire du Bas-Empire,* II (1949, repr. 1968), 835–836.

An edition of the "History of Armenia" in Armenian is Pʿawstos Buzand, *Hayocʿ Patmutʿyun,* Stepʿannos Malxasyancʿ (Stepan Malkhasiants), ed. and trans. (1947, repr. 1968). The English edition is Nina G. Garsoïan, *Epic Histories* (1987).

NINA G. GARSOÏAN

[See also **Agatʿangełos; Armenia: History of; Armenian Literature; Historiography, Armenian.**]

PEACE OF GOD, TRUCE OF GOD. The movement known as the Peace of God arose in the tenth century as a reaction against the ravages of warfare in southern and central France. In a series of councils, of which those at Le Puy in 975 and again about 990–993, at Charroux in 989, and at Narbonne in 990 are the earliest recorded, the bishops of Aquitaine and Septimania imposed on their diocesan populations a statute of protection for churches, unarmed clergymen, peasants, and the poor. Violators were to be excommunicated, according to the articles of Charroux; and although the precise terms varied from the start, it is clear that the bishops took the initiative in these councils and in others that followed, such as those at Limoges (994) and at Poitiers (*ca.* 1011–1014). The impulse spread to Burgundy in the early eleventh century and was renewed in Aquitaine after 1027.

In this early instituted form, the Peace was not altogether new. Episcopal sanctions against violators of churches existed in Frankland as early as the sixth century, and the protection of clergy, widows, orphans, and the poor was a function of Carolingian kingship long since promoted by the bishops. The early fathers of the Peace clearly were seeking to uphold the lawful regalian order of the counties. In 975 the bishop of Le Puy called on neighboring counts to enforce his demands, and about 1014 the statutes of Poitiers provided for spiritual sanctions against violators only in case of the failure of princely justice.

But the statutes tell only part of the story. The councils in which they were issued were occasions for popular manifestations of penitential enthusiasm that transformed the old program of ecclesiastical and regalian sanctions. Raoul Glaber, a monk of Cluny, saw the "renewal of peace" as part of a wider movement of religious revival in which abbots and monks joined the bishops, convoking the masses of lay people to ceremonies centered upon the display and veneration of saints' relics. There were miraculous cures; there were moving sermons that did not fail to evoke St. Paul's identification of peace with Christ; cries of "Peace, peace, peace!" rose in token of a common pact with God. Moreover, the prelates began to impose oaths to uphold the Peace on the laymen who attended such assemblies or, more exactly, upon those—the knights—whose ravages were particularly feared.

What was new, in short, was the movement of pacification that grew out of the tenth-century councils. The early chronology of this movement is very obscure. There is some evidence for the imposition of oaths and for reliquary veneration associ-

PEACE OF GOD, TRUCE OF GOD

ated with the Peace already before the year 1000; and the assimilation of physical violence to simony and clerical incontinence may likewise be traced back to the first assemblies. But it is only the records of the Aquitanian councils after 1020 that reveal an enlarged conception of disorder giving rise to a correspondingly enlarged and contagious ideal of peace. Pacification came to mean purification, that is, a more radical critique of existing behavior in the light of God's dispensation than was represented by the statutes. And it was this critique that produced the most original innovation of the medieval peace movement: the Truce of God.

Whereas the Peace sought to protect certain classes of persons and their property at all times, the Truce was an attempt to prohibit all fighting at certain times. The notion is first perceptible in a north French oath of 1023–1025 in which knights are to be given the protection of the unarmed if they lay down their weapons during Lent. In 1027 a council at Toulouges (in the county of Roussillon) imposed a general truce from Saturday evening to Monday morning. The importance of these early prohibitions should not be exaggerated: neither one was absolutely new in its context, neither immediately influential. But they show that people were beginning to think that war itself might be brought under religious constraints. Comprehensive legislation to that effect was first produced in a synod at Arles (*ca.* 1041–1043); it extended the Truce from Thursday to Monday morning (these being the days commemorative of Christ's Passion), and added the greater saints' days and the seasons of Advent and Lent to the prohibition. It appears that an ascetic ethic was being proposed for the military class of society, and it is perhaps no accident that Abbot Odilo of Cluny was among the prelates acting at Arles. It was merely a logical step to move from a truce so defined to an absolute prohibition of internal warfare—and this step was soon taken. In a council at Narbonne in 1054, it was laid down that "no Christian should kill another Christian, for whoever kills a Christian undoubtedly sheds the blood of Christ."

By the middle of the eleventh century, the medieval peace movement had reached the end of its early evolution. The prelates at Arles not only referred to the Peace of God and the Truce of God as such for the first time, but also represented their statutes as if generally accepted throughout France. In reality, the movement could make headway only where lay powers were willing to recognize it and enforce it. This had been a major difficulty from the outset. In fact, Bishop Gerard of Cambrai had resisted the imposition of peace oaths in his diocese on the grounds that it was a usurpation of the king's right.

It is understandable that the Peace began in and spread from those dioceses where the king had failed to keep order. The movement was thus related to two other aspects of institutional change: the breakdown of public order at the level of the county and the rise of the knights as a military class. In the second half of the tenth century the regalian powers reserved to counts and viscounts were passing to castellans and lesser lords, whose multiplying clienteles of vassals could escape subjection only by subordinating and exploiting peasants. As new lordships proliferated, the competition for wealth and incomes intensified; a gulf was opened up between knights and peasants.

That the knights rightfully bore arms was not questioned in the early peace councils and oaths. But as the movement evolved, the principle of private war itself came into question, and as the idea of the Truce gained adherents among clerical reformers, knights must have been encouraged to think of fighting as a religious duty properly engaged in only against infidel enemies beyond the borders of Christendom. That the papacy drew such a conclusion is clear from the Council of Clermont (1095), where, together with Pope Urban II's exhortation to undertake the First Crusade, the Peace and Truce of God were imposed anew on the kingdom of France.

This step carried the instituted Peace to an ideal extreme. Diocesan legislation was still poorly coordinated even for routine matters of discipline, and there was nothing routine about the enforcement of peace and justice around 1100. Although the Peace and Truce found a place in Lateran conciliar legislation, the popes of the twelfth century shrewdly left their administration to local authorities.

In the later history of the Peace, three tendencies are evident. First, the ideological enthusiasm of the early councils was seldom rekindled after the 1030's. Only where local violence persisted in the absence of effective lay justice, as in Gévaudan and Auvergne, were there religious promotions for the Peace in the twelfth century. Second, the instituted or statutory Peace was progressively appropriated by secular authorities in territorial legislation: this happened in Normandy, Flanders, and Catalonia in the eleventh century, and in some parts of Germany, and the Peace was imposed on the kingdom of France by Louis VII in 1155 (if not by his father half a century earlier). This evolution was a natural consequence of the revival of secular justice, which in northern principalities soon lost all traces of the early diocesan inspiration.

Third, in much of the south—from Aragon to Provence—the instituted Peace and Truce were revived toward the middle of the twelfth century. It was not so much that lay powers were weaker here than in the north—that was clearly true only of Occitania—but that conceptions of public territorial order under the old condominium of greater princes and prelates had persisted more completely. The law of the Peace was made to play the role of the law of fiefs in the north, but to accomplish this the diocesan statutes had to be given teeth. So for the first time provision was regularly made not only for diocesan jurisdiction and episcopal sanctions but also for diocesan armies to be deployed against recalcitrant marauders, for taxes to support such armies or to compensate the victims of violence, and for officers to police the peace. Oaths were reinstituted with a newly extended meaning; no longer purely negative, they included positive commitments to serve in the peace force and to pay the peace tax. Moreover, the legislators of the twelfth century widened the scope of the Peace, creating a new protection of plow animals (the "peace of beasts") in Catalonia and the province of Narbonne, and from the time of the Third Lateran Council (1179) the popes, in promoting the "business of the peace and faith," encouraged the faithful to think of heretics as violators of the Peace.

Thus reorganized and expanded, the instituted Peace survived the Albigensian crusades to become the basis of the royal administration imposed on Languedoc by the Capetians. In Catalonia, where the statutes of Peace and Truce remained the nucleus of territorial legislation promulgated in the *Corts* of the thirteenth century, the peace tax was transformed into a general subsidy—often for war or crusade—that was to have a long history. The institutional influence of the Peace of God was less pronounced in the north, but the adaptability of the old legislation may perhaps be discerned in communal charters "of peace" for Laon and other Capetian towns in the twelfth century.

How well the Peace and Truce answered to the need for which they arose is hard to say. The more emotional reliquary demonstrations may well have had some temporary effect in reducing the damage of local feuds and reprisals; but it is hardly proof of efficacy to note that the Peace persisted or was revived chiefly in regions known to have been most disturbed. The Truce may never have been taken seriously by the great men, although it continued to be enforced against petty marauders in the south. But both institutions were assuredly influential in the molding of opinion: the Peace, because it placed violators against the defenseless absolutely in the wrong at a time when spiritual sanctions were taken seriously, and because it lent dignity as well as statutory form to the Carolingian idea of judicial responsibility; the Truce, because it helped define Christian ideals of knighthood and warfare that were widely recognized in the age of the crusades.

BIBLIOGRAPHY

The sources for the Peace and Truce of God have not been well collected or edited; most, however, are gathered in Ludwig Huberti, *Studien zur Rechtsgeschichte der Gottesfrieden und Landesfrieden* (1892). The major recent study is Hartmut Hoffmann, *Gottesfriede und Treuga Dei* (1964).

For valuable interpretations of several aspects of the peace movement, see Roger Bonnaud-Delamare, "Fondement des institutions de paix au XIe siècle," in *Mélanges d'histoire du moyen âge dédiés à la mémoire de Louis Halphen* (1951); Georges Duby, "Laity and the Peace of God," in his book *The Chivalrous Society,* Cynthia Postan, trans. (1977); Bernhard Töpfer, *Volk und Kirche zur Zeit der beginnenden Gottesfriedensbewegung in Frankreich* (1957). H. E. J. Cowdrey, "The Peace and the Truce of God in the Eleventh Century," in *Past & Present,* no. 46 (1970), reviews and supplements recent work.

On the beginnings of the Truce, see Pierre Bonnassie, *La Catalogne du milieu du Xe à la fin du XIe siècle,* II (1976), 656–662; Jean-Pierre Poly, *La Provence et la société féodale, 879–1166* (1976), 191–204.

For the later history, see Thomas N. Bisson, "The Organized Peace in Southern France and Catalonia, *ca.* 1140–*ca.* 1233," in *American Historical Review,* 82 (1977); Aryeh Graboïs, "De la trêve de Dieu à la paix du roi," in Pierre Gallais and Yves-Jean Riou, eds., *Mélanges offerts à René Crozet,* I (1966).

THOMAS N. BISSON

[See also **Aquitaine; Catalonia; Church, Latin: To 1054; Clermont, Council of; Cluny, Order of; Cortes; Excommunication, Feudalism; France: 987–1223; Interdict; Knights and Knight Service; Languedoc; Law, Canon; Law, French: In South, Odilo of Cluny, St.; Raoul Glaber; Reform, Idea of; Taxation, Church; Taxation, French; Urban II, Pope.**]

PEARL, an elegy in the form of a symbolic dream vision, appears in a unique manuscript (British Library, MS Cotton Nero A.x)—a small quarto volume that also contains the chivalric romance *Sir Gawain and the Green Knight* and two biblical homilies employing exempla, *Purity* (or *Cleanness*) and *Patience.* Composed in the latter part of the fourteenth century and preserved in an early-fifteenth-century scribal hand, the Cotton Nero poems are customarily attributed to a single anonymous author, possibly a member of an aristocrat's household in the northwest Midlands.

Although the Cotton Nero poems present varying degrees of complexity in structure, theme, and imagery, *Pearl* is invested with a particularly intricate design and symbolic meaning. In the opening section of the poem, a jeweler-narrator laments the loss of a valuable pearl in a garden. While the narrator employs courtly-love phraseology to express his longing for the gem, such terms also suggest his love for a woman or a girl. After he enters a spice garden, the jeweler's sorrow and the fragrance exuding from the spice flowers gradually release him from consciousness. His body in a trance, his spirit soars to a radiant landscape containing shimmering jewels, lustrous groves, and multicolored birds. His sorrow somewhat dispelled, the jeweler wanders along the banks of a river separating the jeweled land from a region of consummate loveliness. Suddenly he perceives a resplendent maiden, a child garbed in gleaming white robes ornamented with numerous pearls. A pearl-studded crown rests on her head, and one flawless pearl adorns her breast. Gradually realizing that he "knew her well," for she was "nearer to me than aunt or niece," he identifies the maiden with the lost pearl.

At this point a debate between the dreamer and the maiden begins. Since he clings to earthly values, the pearl-maiden rebukes him for numerous false assumptions and misapprehensions. Attempting to deflect the dreamer's objections to her heavenly rank, she then describes her union with Christ and alludes to the principle of charity, which links all Christians with the Mystical Body of Christ. Inasmuch as the dreamer is still skeptical about the justice of the maiden's heavenly reward, she recounts the New Testament parable of the vineyard (Matt. 20:1–16).

In the ensuing discussion of divine grace and heavenly rewards, particularly the distinction between salvation for the righteous and salvation for the baptized innocent child, the maiden cites the parable of the pearl of great price (Matt. 13:45–46), wherein a merchant sells all his goods in order to buy that pearl. She also associates the single wondrous pearl adorning her breast with the pearl of Matthew's parable and urges the dreamer, like the merchant, to forsake the world in order to obtain the immaculate pearl (eternal life in heaven). Later she informs him that she is one of the 144,000 virgins in the New Jerusalem—brides of the Lamb whom St. John the Evangelist describes in Revelation (14:1–4). The maiden then directs the dreamer to a hilltop, where he gazes at the heavenly city.

Rooted in the apocalyptic portrait of the New Jerusalem presented in Revelation 21:10–21, the dreamer's vision focuses upon the twelve foundation stones, each of which is fashioned from a single gem; the streets of gold; the twelve pearly gates; and the city's supernal radiance. Suddenly aware of a procession of virgins before the Lamb's throne, he notes that each virgin, like the pearl-maiden, is arrayed in white robes and pearls and wears the pearl of great price. Beholding his pearl-maiden in the group, he attempts to cross the river. The vision ends abruptly, for the dreamer finds himself once again in the original earthly garden. At the end of *Pearl,* however, the narrator accepts God's will and perceives the true role of his creatures—to act as humble servants and precious pearls pleasing to God.

The complex plot of *Pearl* is reinforced by an elaborate design and symbolic meaning. Although the poet employs the native provincial tradition (alliterative verse) of the Midlands, the metrical form of *Pearl* is highly stylized. Composed of 101 twelve-line stanzas, each line of which has four stresses, the poem contains a difficult rhyme scheme (*a b a b a b a b b c b c*). Furthermore, *Pearl* is divided into twenty sections, each of which, with the exception of section XV, has five stanzas. Individual stanzas within a section are interlocked through the employment of a key word, often in the form of a refrain, in the last line of each stanza and in the first line of the following stanza. Even the major sections are linked through concatenation, for the key word of one section appears in the first line of the following section. Finally, the key words ("Prynceȝ paye") of the concluding section echo the first line of the poem, thereby creating a pearl-like circularity and completeness. Although line 1 of *Pearl* designates an earthly monarch, the last line points to Christ, the prince of heaven.

Pearl's intricate metrical structure is mirrored in number symbolism, an aspect of symmetrical design. In a symbolic fusion of 100, the emblem of perfection, and 12, a representation of eternity, the poet composes 1,212 lines. Furthermore, in the dreamer's vision of the New Jerusalem—the vision in which time comes to an end and eternity reigns—the poet highlights the significance of twelve: the twelve gates, foundation stones, fruits of life, and furlongs in height, width, and length of each square side (12,000 furlongs in Revelation 21:16). The number of virgins in the celestial city is 144,000, a multiple of twelve.

Equally complex is the shifting symbolism of the pearl. Although it initially signifies an earthly jewel as well as a dead child, this precious gem is gradually disclosed as an emblem of the immaculate nature of the beatified maiden, innocence, purity, the pearl of great price, heaven, everlasting life, perfection, redeemed souls, and eternity. Through the dramatic transformation of such pearl symbolism, the poet slowly reveals his theme —the jeweler-narrator's need to abandon earthly values and to humbly embrace and seek consolation in Christ, the true wellspring of spiritual joy.

BIBLIOGRAPHY

The standard edition is Eric V. Gordon, ed., *Pearl* (1953). The most sensitive translation is Marie Borroff, trans., *Pearl: A New Verse Translation* (1977).

Anthologies of criticism are Robert J. Blanch, ed., *Sir Gawain and Pearl: Critical Essays* (1966); John Conley, ed., *The Middle English Pearl: Critical Essays* (1970). A review of scholarship is Laurence Eldredge, "The State of 'Pearl' Studies Since 1933," in *Viator,* 6 (1975). Bibliographies are Malcolm Andrew, *The Gawain-Poet: An Annotated Bibliography, 1839–1977* (1979); Marie P. Hamilton, "The *Pearl* Poet," in J. Burke Severs, gen. ed., *A Manual of the Writings in Middle English: 1050–1500,* II (1970).

On number symbolism, see Russell A. Peck, "Number as Cosmic Language," in Caroline D. Eckhardt, ed., *Essays in the Numerical Criticism of Medieval Literature* (1980); Maren-Sofie Røstvig, "Numerical Composition in *Pearl*: A Theory," in *English Studies,* 48 (1967).

Full-length studies of *Pearl* include Ian Bishop, *Pearl in Its Setting: A Critical Study of the Structure and Meaning of the Middle English Poem* (1968); Theodore Bogdanos, *Pearl, Image of the Ineffable: A Study in Medieval Poetic Symbolism* (1983); Patricia M. Kean, *The Pearl: An Interpretation* (1967). General studies include John A. Burrow, *Ricardian Poetry: Chaucer, Gower, Langland, and the Gawain Poet* (1971); William A. Davenport, *The Art of the Gawain-Poet* (1978); Lynn Staley Johnson, *The Voice of the Gawain-Poet* (1984); Charles Muscatine, "The *Pearl* Poet: Style as Defense," in his *Poetry and Crisis in the Age of Chaucer* (1972); A. C. Spearing, *The Gawain-Poet: A Critical Study* (1970); Edward Wilson, *The Gawain-Poet* (1976).

ROBERT J. BLANCH

[See also **Allegory; Gawain and the Green Knight, Sir; Middle English Literature.**]

PEASANTS' REBELLION. Although its forms and scope varied, peasant revolt was endemic in the Middle Ages. The demands of the landlords and of the lord king vastly increased the burden carried by peasants trying to maintain a livelihood with resources severely limited by a primitive technology. Nightmares like that of Henry I of England, in which overburdened villagers assaulted him with forks and scythes, must have troubled the sleep of many lords.

But the fear of concerted risings became reality only in the late Middle Ages. Almost all aspects of the social and economic history of the period linked with peasant revolt can be debated, but the effect of demographic change on the supply of labor and the level of pay is one factor. Closely related is the economic depression, which most historians consider a feature of late medieval Europe. A third important force, too often overlooked, is the more "political" factor of the demands of the crown, particularly as a result of the expanded warfare waged by the states from the 1290's on. The two major Western European revolts of the period, the Jacquerie in France (1358) and the Great Rising of 1381 in England, illustrate the workings of these forces.

THE JACQUERIE

In historical writing the French revolt of 1358 has become a classic type or model of rural rising; "Jacquerie" has thus become a generic term. The name is drawn from Jacques Bonhomme, the representative term for any peasant (whose traditional garb was a short garment similar to the present-day jacket). The original Jacquerie was characterized by suddenness, great violence, and a widespread attack on all nobles in the area affected. The rebels seemed to act without clear warning and lashed out against all the privileged—men, women, and children—in an awesome, if temporary, surge of killing and destruction. The shocking incidents recounted in contemporary chronicles such as Froissart may not exaggerate the fierce and brutal nature of the rising. The noble reaction that crushed the Jacquerie was, in turn, severe and bloody.

The rising began with a clash between men-at-arms and villagers on 28 May 1358 at St. Leu d'Esserent, about twenty-five miles to the north of Paris. With great speed the rising spread from village to village; eventually, it covered an area around Pàris reaching Orléans in the south, Amiens in the north, and Laon in the east; at least fourteen departments of modern France were affected. Rebel ranks may have been filled with rural artisans rather than simple peasants. In fact, the "Jacques" included wealthy villagers, clerics, and minor royal functionaries. Leadership fell to an obscure man called Guillaume Cale, who had some military knowledge.

In early June many Jacques were cut down in an unsuccessful attack on the fortified market area in the town of Meaux (in which a number of noble ladies, including the dauphin's wife, had taken refuge). At the same time the nobles of Picardy, led by Charles II the Bad, king of Navarre, crushed a large force of Jacques between Mello and Claremont, after luring Cale into a trap and seizing him. The movement was now a lost cause and brutal repression fell on the peasantry, sometimes without discrimination between rebels and nonrebels.

Historians have long sought to understand the Jacquerie and their explanations have ranged widely. At present, the tendency is to emphasize a political and military crisis emerging from the disasters of the Hundred Years War and working in a context of long-range social and economic problems. Among the latter, the changed balance between supply and demand for rural labor brought by the terrible mortality of the Black Death seems especially important. The Jacquerie broke out in the crisis that shook the kingdom after the ignominious defeat of French arms and the capture of the French king at Poitiers in 1356. Three parties contended for control, or at least for advantage, in this period of turmoil: the king's eldest son, Charles, duke of Normandy (1337–1380, the future Charles V), who was acting as regent; Étienne Marcel (*d.* 1358), provost of the merchants of Paris and head of a leading bourgeois clan in the capital; and Charles II the Bad, count of Évreux and king of Navarre (*r.* 1349–1387), a cousin and brother-in-law of the regent, who had territorial ambitions and probably designs on the throne.

This triangular struggle was complicated by the presence of roving bands of soldiers, English and others, who were eager for employment and were a constant scourge on the villagers of the region. At the top of French society this situation produced a series of meetings of assemblies in which reform was much discussed, and finally a state of virtual civil war. In the countryside the consequences of the crisis contributed significantly to the Jacquerie. Animating all of the struggles in town and countryside, as Raymond Cazelles insists, was a deep, mutual hatred between noble and non-noble (both burgher and peasant). The villagers' hatred can well be imagined: the nobles had failed to prevent the invasion of their region, and peasant lands and homes were being overrun by brigands; the nobles who failed to check the brigands were thought to be treating with them and, in some cases, even joining them. Noble, chivalric glory had been diminished on the field at Crécy and all but extinguished at Poitiers. The villagers might simultaneously be paying war taxes, seigneurial dues, ransoms for lords captured at Poitiers, and protection money to ward off soldiers carrying one banner or another, or no banner at all. They lived in a region crackling with rumors of disaster and plot, which seem to have been more potent than the hope of reform at work in some minds. The Jacquerie has traditionally been described as incoherent, but Raymond Cazelles has argued that the attacks reveal a political program. The castles assaulted were those helpful to the dauphin and his allies among the nobles as they tried to blockade rebellious Paris and to intimidate other towns. This interpretation stresses the involvement of townsmen and the importance of the political crisis in France in 1358.

THE ENGLISH PEASANTS' REVOLT

Fears of revolt had been expressed in England across the fourteenth century and were repeated with more point after 1358. Such fears came true in late May or early June of 1381. Trouble began when the men of several villages in southwest Essex assaulted government officials investigating widespread tax evasion. Resistance soon became a major revolt that spread to include most of the counties of Essex, Kent, Norfolk, Suffolk, Hertfordshire, Cambridgeshire, and parts of Sussex, Surrey, and Middlesex.

By early June the Kent rebels were led by Wat

Tyler, an able leader whose career before the rising is totally unknown. He took the rebels into Canterbury, seized the sheriff of Kent, and destroyed country muniments. Some coordination between the Kent and Essex rebels seems likely; as Tyler overwhelmed county authority in Kent, the Essex men did the same in their locale. Though the sheriff of Essex, John Sewall, escaped when they plundered his home, the rebels killed the escheator, John Ewell; they also destroyed a manor associated with Robert Hales, the royal treasurer. Then both main groups swiftly marched along either side of the Thames to London, where they planned to see the king and save king and kingdom from "traitors." On their march to London, Wat Tyler's men apparently liberated John Ball (*d.* 1381) from the archbishop's prison in Maidstone, Kent. Though he had been a priest himself, Ball had spent the last two decades denouncing the evils of clerical power and wealth to all who would listen. Ball's sermons may have inspired Tyler's rebels. His ideas certainly sent a shiver of horror through monastic writers of the age. But his influence and the supposed connection between rebellion and Wycliffite heresy have both been exaggerated.

Richard II was then only a boy of fourteen. On 12 June he was rowed down the Thames in the royal barge and met the Kentish rebels near Greenwich, but he was dissuaded from landing by courtiers who feared they might be on the rebels' list of traitors deserving death. The rebels could easily have loosed a deadly flight of arrows on the royal barge, but they showed a reverence for the person of the king that was to mark all of their actions. Negotiation with the king seemed, in fact, the main hope for rebel success. But another form of success would be to enter London. According to the chronicler Froissart they were desperately in need of the food supplies they could find in the city. In fact, a change in London city government in 1376 (following the "Good Parliament" of that year) had made politics in the city more radical and more turbulent. With some conservatives ousted from influence, radicals revised the city's ordinances and established the annual election of aldermen. In the years before the Peasants' Revolt, powerful patrons clashed and mob violence produced an urban form of the "bastard feudalism" characteristic of later medieval England. Under these conditions the rebels easily entered London. With willing help from ordinary Londoners, the rebels swiftly and thoroughly destroyed the Savoy palace, home of the king's uncle, John of Gaunt, duke of Lancaster, whose name stood at the head of the rebels' proscription list and who was the bête noire of many Londoners. Richard and his entourage could see the flames from their vantage point on the walls of the Tower of London, in which they were virtually besieged. Richard agreed to discussion with the rebels, who always professed the greatest reverence for the crown, and left the Tower on 14 June to go to the camp of the men from Essex at Mile End, beyond the east line of city walls. The details of this meeting are uncertain; we are even in doubt if Wat Tyler was present. But the king agreed to pardons for the rebels and promised an end to serfdom in Essex and Hertfordshire. Perhaps the royal aim was achieved when many of the rebels went home, carrying charters that were later revoked. Yet, he had also given royal approval for the rebels to seize traitors and bring them to him. Some sources connect this grant and the entry of the rebels on that same day into the Tower to seize the chancellor, Simon Sudbury (archbishop of Canterbury), the treasurer, Robert Hales, and the physician to John of Gaunt. These three men were speedily executed on Tower Hill.

By 15 June the number of rebels and their capacity were diminishing and royal and city authorities were apparently cooperating and recovering initiative. Richard met the remaining rebels (mainly men from Kent) in the open market at Smithfield, just beyond the northwest corner of the city walls. Again, an exact reconstruction of the meeting is impossible, but it seems that Wat Tyler (possibly struggling to maintain momentum) behaved in a deliberately provocative manner to the king and presented demands designed to cause a crisis that would end Richard's successful temporizing: in addition to the abolition of serfdom, he wanted no law save (apparently) the 1285 Statute of Winchester, no lordship save that of the king, no bishop except one, and the distribution of church property to parishioners. In a confused scuffle Tyler was cut down and rebel longbows were drawn. But Richard II bravely called out to the rebels that he would be their leader and, in a remarkable scene, led the peasants away from the city. Surrounded by the professional soldiers brought by the mayor, the rebels were sent home. The major thrust of the rising was over, though related risings would continue to occur in other parts of England.

As in France, the English rebels were recruited not mainly from the lowest ranks of society, but from landowners and artisans, often those who played a prominent role in local government, whether a manor, village, or hundred. But the English rising differs sharply from the Jacquerie in its relatively low level of violence. As peasant rebellions go, the English rising was almost restrained. Very few lords (and no women and children) were put to death. Suppression of the rising generally followed established legal forms and resulted in fewer than 200 executions.

As even a brief narrative indicates, a combination of socioeconomic and political grievances stands behind the rising. Peasants bitterly resented the attempt to hold their wages to the low levels that obtained before the Black Death reduced the supply of labor and loosened the hold of lords over servile tenants. In fact, the labor legislation (the Ordinance of Laborers of 1349 and the Statute of Laborers of 1351) was most zealously enforced in just those areas where rebellion would be most intense. Although many historians no longer support the idea of a rigorous "seigniorial reaction" after the Black Death in which lords increased labor services, lordly control does appear to have frustrated the rising expectations of the peasants. In their hour of revolt the peasants, whenever possible, burned manorial records of hated obligations and repeatedly demanded royal abolition of serfdom.

But as E. B. Fryde suggests, "Seigniorial demands were universally disliked but accepted as inevitable, like spells of bad weather. It was royal demands, like the poll tax, which were most likely to spark off an armed rising." In 1381 the burden of heavy war taxation was being shifted to the poor; the poll tax of 1380 was the third such tax since 1377 and the heaviest. Though the crown announced that in each locality the rich would bear a larger proportion of the assessment, this policy was in no way enforced. The effects of royal action, moreover, extended beyond taxation. The high claims of the English crown in the areas of justice and public order contrasted sharply with popular perceptions of misgovernment, corruption, and gross injustice. Unlike the Jacques, the English rebels did not attack lords indiscriminately; their anger was regularly directed at those landlords who were also local government officials and against agents—for example, justices of the peace and lawyers—of the judicial apparatus at all levels. This was as true in London as in smaller towns and the countryside. The "new legal professionalism threatened both manorial and civic custom" and so sparked the wrath of rebels everywhere. Though these targets might be termed "political" rather than "social," the very distinction may be unnecessary. The well-developed power of the English government made the crown a potent force not only in "political" issues such as defense, taxation, and justice, but also in the "social" issues of regulating the supply and pay of laborers. The rebels' decision to march on London and demand to see the king thus is understandable, even if their faith in his speedy concessions seems naive.

Royal promises were, of course, revoked, and the rising did not in itself end serfdom in England, nor break lordly control. But over the next several generations fear of another rising probably contributed to the decline of serfdom, which economic change was affecting. The rising also, and more immediately, ended poll taxes and the high level of war expenditure.

BIBLIOGRAPHY

Margaret E. Ashton, "Lollardy and Sedition, 1381–1431," in *Past and Present,* **17** (1960); Richard B. Dobson, *The Peasants' Revolt of 1381* (1979); The Past and Present Society, *The English Rising of 1381* (1981), includes a paper on the Jacquerie by Raymond Cazelles; Jean Froissart, *Chronicles,* Geoffrey Brereton, trans. (1968); Edmund B. Fryde, *The Great Revolt of 1381* (1981); Guy Fourquin, *Les soulèvements populaires au moyen âge* (1972); Vivian H. Galbraith, *The Anonimalle Chronicle, 1333–1381* (1927); Rodney H. Hilton, *Bond Men Made Free: Medieval Peasant Movements and the English Rising of 1381* (1973); Simeon Luce, *Historie de la Jacquerie,* 2nd rev. ed. (1984); John R. Maddicott, *The English Peasantry and the Demands of the Crown, 1294–1341* (1975), and *Law and Lordship: Royal Justices as Retainers in Thirteenth- and Fourteenth-century England* (1978); Michel Mollat and Philippe Wolff, *The Popular Revolutions of the Late Middle Ages,* A. L. Lytton-Sells, trans. (1973); Richard A. Newhall, ed., and Jean Birdsall, trans., *The Chronicle of Jean de Venette* (1953); Charles W. Oman, *The Great Revolt of 1381,* E. B. Fryde, ed. (1969); A. Reville, *Le soulèvement des travailleurs d'Angleterre en 1381* (1898); Jules Viard and Eugène Déprez, eds., *Chronique de Jean le Bel,* 2 vols. (1904–1905); Bertie Wilkinson, "The Peasants' Revolt of 1381," in *Speculum,* **15** (1940).

RICHARD W. KAEUPER

[See also **Class Structure, Western; England: 1216–1485; France: 1314–1494; Jacquerie; Richard II; Serf; Serfdom: Western European.**]

PEASANTS' WEDDING. See **Bauernhochzeit, Die.**

PECHAM, JOHN. See **Peckham, John.**

PECHENEGS. See **Russia, Nomadic Invasions of.**

PECHERSKAYA LAVRA (Pechersky Monastery, literally "monastery of the caves") in Kiev was the oldest (founded by the monk Antoni in 1060) and most important monastery in Russia. Beginning as a cave abbey in which the monks lived, the establishment gradually grew into a cluster of structures built and rebuilt through the centuries. The first church was founded in 1073. Pecherskaya Lavra was a center for religious writings and art, as well as for religious devotion.

BIBLIOGRAPHY

John Beckwith, *Early Christian and Byzantine Art,* 2nd ed. (1979), 236, 254–256; Hubert Faensen and Vladimir Ivanov, *Early Russian Architecture* (1975), 335–336, 367, pl. 38; George H. Hamilton, *The Art and Architecture of Russia* (1954); Victor N. Lazarev, *Old Russian Murals and Mosaics* (1966), 67; M. J. Rouët de Journel, *Monarchisme et monastères russe* (1952).

ANN E. FARKAS

[See also **Alimpi; Athos, Mount; Kievan Rus; Monasticism, Byzantine; Russian and Slavic Art; Theodosius of the Caves, St.**]

PECIA (Medieval Latin: "part," "piece"). Early medieval culture was characterized by very limited literate audiences and needs. Under these circumstances, the multiplication of copies of a given text did not generally require particular speed or efficiency. New manuscript books were often obtained by copying a needed work from beginning to end in a continuous operation. Each new copy could serve as a model for further copies. This approach presented a dual disadvantage. On one hand, the model or its constituent elements (quires) were immobilized during the copying, so that one model might produce only one copy at a time. On the other, the use of derivative copies as models for further copies increased and compounded the copyists' mistakes, which inevitably attended each new transcription. Thus texts were often produced slowly and tended to display a progressive deterioration in quality.

The new needs of the medieval universities resulted in the development of a different technique, which prevailed from the thirteenth through the fourteenth and fifteenth centuries. A copy of the required text was obtained and corrected, probably by a stationer. This "exemplar" was copied into segments or *peciae,* which varied in length according to local usage. The individual *peciae* were rented out one by one, often for one week, and copied at the student's expense. An individual *pecia* might consist of four to twelve good-sized folios or leaves, each bearing two columns of text per side. Surviving examples are characterized by signs of wear and tear and repairs; they often have the *pecia* number in the upper margin of the first page of each segment; *corrigitur* ("it is corrected") is often written in the lower margin of the first or last page. After the copy was finished, the *pecia* was returned to the stationer and again put into circulation. Copies made from *peciae* are identifiable by numbers, often accompanied by an abbreviation for the word *pecia* in the side margin and corresponding to a break in the transcription of the text. In this way, all copies of a text theoretically descended from the same exemplar and thereby avoided the introduction of new, compound mistakes. Moreover, the systematic distribution of long texts in small pieces prevented the immobilization of extensive segments of the text in one copyist's hands. In other words, the new system allowed faster and more correct multiplication of copies of a given text. Unfortunately, comparison of exemplars and surviving author's autographs shows that the spread of this system was not accompanied by efforts of stationers to obtain particularly correct texts for use as exemplars.

BIBLIOGRAPHY

Jean Destrez, *La pecia dans les manuscrits universitaires du XIIIe et du XIVe siècle* (1935), is the fundamental study; a recent overview can be found in Graham Pollard, "The *Pecia* System in the Medieval Universities," in *Medieval Scribes, Manuscripts, and Libraries: Essays Presented to N. R. Ker,* Malcolm B. Parkes and Andrew G. Watson, eds. (1978).

MICHAEL MCCORMICK

[See also **Manuscript Books, Production of; Quire.**]

PECK, a measure of capacity for dry products in Scotland and England. The Scots peck contained 4 lippies equal to 0.25 firlot or 0.0625 boll: 549.333 cubic inches (9.004 liters) or 5.3125 Scots pints equal to 0.2554 Winchester bushel for wheat, peas, beans, rye, and white salt, and 801.381 cubic inches (13.125 liters) or 7.75 Scots pints equal to 0.3727 Winchester bushel for oats, barley, and malt. During the Middle Ages the English peck contained 537.6 cubic inches (8.810 liters) or 2 gallons equal to 0.25 Winchester bushel. Regionally, however, there were numerous variations for these and other products. One of the most common of capacity measures, the name appears in medieval manuscripts under such variants as pec, peccum, pek, pekke, peke, pecke, peccus, and pect.

RONALD EDWARD ZUPKO

[See also **Boll; Bushel; Weights and Measures, Western European.**]

PECKHAM, JOHN (Pecham) (*ca.* 1230–1292), archbishop of Canterbury, physicist, mathematician, probably grew up near Lewes and received his early schooling there. He went on to Oxford, where he studied arts and became a Franciscan. In the late 1250's he studied theology at the University of Paris, receiving his doctorate in 1269 and remaining there as regent master in theology. Peckham then lectured at the Franciscan school at Oxford. In 1275 he was elected provincial of the English Franciscans. In 1277 he went to Italy as lecturer at the papal university in Viterbo. While there Peckham was nominated archbishop of Canterbury. He was consecrated in 1279 and served as archbishop until his death in 1292.

Peckham was an active participant in the intellectual life of his time, as well as an energetic, reforming archbishop whose zeal more than once brought him into conflict with abbot, bishop, or king. He produced important scientific treatises, was a proponent of the conservative, Augustinian position in the debates at Paris and Oxford over the unity of form, wrote in defense of the mendicants in their controversy with the seculars, and composed poetry. While Peckham was not an original mind or a great writer, both his treatise on perspective and his synodal legislation had enduring significance.

BIBLIOGRAPHY

Sources. Peckham's register has been edited by Charles Trice Martin, *Registrum epistolarum fratris Johannis Peckham archiepiscopi Cantuariensis,* 3 vols. (1882–1885), and by F. N. Davis (vol. I) and Decima L. Douie (vol. II), *The Register of John Pecham, Archbishop of Canterbury, 1279–1292* (1968–1969). Peckham's *Perspectiva communis* has been edited and translated by David C. Lindberg in his *John Pecham and the Science of Optics* (1970). The *Tractatus de sphera* has been edited by B. R. Maclaren (diss., Univ. of Wisconsin, 1978). For the poetry, see *Philomena, a Poem by John Peckham,* William Dobell, trans. (1924), and J. L. Baird and John R. Kane, *Rossignol* (1978).

Studies. The standard biography is Decima L. Douie, *Archbishop Pecham* (1952). See also Lindberg (above) for a good brief biography. Other studies are A. G. Little, "The Franciscan School at Oxford in the Thirteenth Century," in *Archivum franciscanum historicum,* **19** (1926); P. G. Melani, "La predicazione di Giovanni Pecham," in *Studi francescani,* **38** (1941); D. E. Sharp, *Franciscan Philosophy at Oxford in the Thirteenth Century* (1930); Hieronymus Spettman, "Die Psychologie des Johannes Pecham," in *Beiträge zur Geschichte der Philosophie des Mittelalters,* **20** (1922), and "Der Ethikkommentar des Johannes Pecham," *ibid.,* supp. 2 (1923).

KATHLEEN GREENFIELD

[See also **Anglo-Latin Poetry; Anglo-Norman Literature; Bacon, Roger; Franciscans; Optics, Western European.**]

PECOCK, REGINALD (*ca.* 1395–*ca.* 1460), English bishop and theologian who was tried for, and convicted of, heresy. Born in Wales, he earned his bachelor's, master's, and divinity degrees at Oxford before 1424. He was ordained a priest in 1421. From 1425 to 1431 he was rector at St. Michael's, Gloucester. In 1431 he moved to London, where he became master of Whittington College and rector of St. Michael Paternoster Royal. Here, as a Catholic educator seeking to allay the religious discontent sweeping through the working classes, Pecock found his lifework. At Whittington he began to write religious treatises in English for the laity. In 1444 he became bishop of St. Asaph, on which occasion he also received his doctor of divinity degree. In 1450 he was raised to bishop of Chichester, his last important ecclesiastical post. Pecock does not seem to have resided in either bishopric, preferring to stay in London to continue writing and preaching in defense of the church against the Lollard heresy. In 1447, for example, at St. Paul's Cross he preached a controversial sermon defending the nonpreaching and nonresidence of bishops, a sermon that roused the ire of both the laity and his fellow bishops.

Pecock's work was in three major areas: defending the faith, writing religious treatises in English, and reorganizing the faith. In defending the faith he noted that the Lollards did not accept the authority of the church, and that therefore the argument "This is right because I say it is right" was not likely to convince or convert them. He decided to argue rationally the correctness of the church's teachings. Pecock elevated reason over authority. In order to communicate his arguments to the laity, he developed a prose style based on the syllogism. And since he was trying to teach the rudiments of the faith, he reorganized that faith into what he considered a more coherent, more easily taught pattern that he called the "seven matters of knowledge." Pecock was especially interested in the fourth matter: God's law, which he organized into four tables to replace the various works, gifts, creeds, and virtues then in vogue.

The major event in Pecock's life was his trial for heresy in 1457. His reliance on reason and logic created problems for him with his more authority-oriented superiors. At his trial he was asked to choose one of two lines of action: either he could stand by his real views, which the court had not considered, and thus set himself against the church as it was represented in his judges; or he could recant a position he never held, and thus destroy the effectiveness of his lifework by apparently admitting it to be heretical. Pecock chose to murder his lifework and reputation rather than cut himself off from the church he had labored so long to defend. On Sunday, 4 December 1457, he made a public abjuration at St. Paul's Cross and his books were burned. Of the more than fifty he wrote, a mere half dozen are extant. The next year he was immured at Thorney Abbey, forbidden the company of books, and given nothing to write with or upon. This prolific defender of the faith died at Thorney Abbey, perhaps as early as 1460.

BIBLIOGRAPHY

Sources. The Repressor of Over Much Blaming of the Clergy, Churchill Babington, ed., 2 vols. (1860); *The Book of Faith,* J. L. Morison, ed. (1909); *The Donet,* Elsie Vaughan Hitchcock, ed. (1921); *The Folewer to the Donet,* Elsie Vaughan Hitchcock, ed. (1924); *The Reule of Crysten Religioun,* William Cabell Greet, ed. (1927).

Studies. "Bishop Pecock, His Character and Fortunes," in *Dublin Review,* **24** (1875); E. M. Blackie, "Reginald Pecock," in *English Historical Review,* **26** (1911); Everett H. Emerson, "Reginald Pecock: Christian Rationalist," in *Speculum,* **31** (1956); V. H. H. Green, *Bishop Reginald Pecock* (1945); Ernest F. Jacob, "Reynold Pecock, Bishop of Chichester," in *Proceedings of the British Academy,* 37 (1951); John Lewis, *The Life of Reynold Pecock* (1820); Joseph F. Patrouch, *Reginald Pecock* (1970).

JOSEPH F. PATROUCH, JR.

[See also **England (1216–1485); Lollards.**]

PEDILAVIUM. See **Feet, Washing of.**

PEDRO DE CÓRDOBA (*fl.* second half of the fifteenth century), a painter of Córdoba. He is chiefly known from a signed altarpiece of 1475 in the Cathedral of Córdoba, a large and exceptionally detailed *Annunciation,* in which firm knowledge of Flemish painting is revealed. He is sometimes postulated to be the master of Bartolomé Bermejo (*fl.* 1470–1498).

BIBLIOGRAPHY

David G. Carter, "Primitive of the Mass of St. Gregory," in *John Herron Institute Bulletin,* **45** (1958); Chandler R. Post, *A History of Spanish Painting,* V (1934), 60–72.

JOHN WILLIAMS

[See also **Bermejo, Bartolomé; Flemish Painting; Gothic Art: Painting;** and illustration overleaf.]

PEDRO EL CEREMONIOSO. See **Peter IV the Ceremonious.**

PEDRO SERRA. See **Serra, Pedro and Jaime.**

PEIRE CARDENAL (**Pierre Cardinal**) (1180 *ca.* 1278), Provençal poet, son of a knight, scarcely fits the accepted notion of the troubadour as writer of

The Annunciation, with Sts. Barbara, Ivo, James, John the Baptist, Lawrence, and Pius I. Panel painting by Pedro de Córdoba, 1475. CÓRDOBA CATHEDRAL. FOTO MAS, BARCELONA

courtly love lyrics. He captured the attention of his contemporaries by his virulent satiric portraits of clerical decadence and by his almost biblical longevity—he lived for nearly a century at a time when old age began at forty.

Peire's fame in his own era may be judged from the fact that shortly after his death, Michel de la Tour (Miquel de la Tor) of Nîmes wrote a biography *(vida)* of him, short by modern standards (twenty prose lines) but long for the time.

Michel de la Tour reports that King James I the Conqueror of Aragon (*r.* 1213–1276) "honored and protected" Peire for his vigorous satiric ballads *(sirventes)* chastising the follies of the world, particularly of venal clerics and prelates. Michel states that Peire frequented "the courts of kings and noble lords," by which we may judge the extent of the reformist religious sentiments during the period.

Such lines as the following give us the measure of Peire's reformist zeal: "Neither buzzard nor vulture smells the stench of carrion faster than a prelate scents a rich patron." "Year-round the clergy's greedily occupied with dressing well in costly garb; the princes of the church finance courtly splendor by raising rents and holding for ransom other people's rightful fiefs."

In keeping with the simple piety he extolled, Peire developed a kind of poem called the "sermon," not unlike a homily, to complement the satiric verse. Thus, he wrote exhortations to attain nobility by deed rather than birth; or to link honesty, piety, and charity: "Speak the truth, manifest faith by supporting and sheltering the poor, for the rich should help the poor."

Peire's poems also innovate by invoking God in ways that earlier troubadours used to address their *domna,* the lady who was "lord" over their affections. The religious tone of such poems, coupled with the strongly reformist slant of the satiric verse, anticipates the Italian *dolce stil nuovo* (sweet new style) and identifies Peire as a direct precursor of Dante, who made no secret of his admiration for Provençal poetry.

Peire belongs to the last strong generation of troubadours. When he writes with feeling of the virtues of Toulouse, his verse may be taken as an elegy for the end of a poetic tradition, the eclipse of a culture: "Toulouse! when I contemplate your brave ways and beautiful language, I come to detest other cities who cannot match your peerless art and learning." Peire wrote ninety-six poems, three of which contain musical notations; eight other poems of doubtful origin have been attributed to him. The poems survive in twenty-one manuscripts.

BIBLIOGRAPHY

Sources. Poésies complètes du troubadour Peire Cardenal . . . , René Lavaud, ed. (1957). Commentary and corrections of this edition have been published by Kurt Lewin in *Neuphilologische Mitteilungen,* **62** (1961). A further source is Frédéric Fabre, "Deux pièces du troubadour Peire Cardenal," in *Lettres romanes,* **13** (1959).

Studies. Charles Camproux, "Présence de Peire Cardenal," in Pierre Bec, ed., *Présence des troubadours* (1970), and "Cardenal et Rutebeuf, poètes satiriques," in *Revue des langues romanes,* **79** (1971); Frederick Goldin, "The Law's Homage to Grace: Peire Cardenal's *Vera vergena, Maria,*" in *Romance Philology,* **20** (1967); Roger Lassalle, "Proverbe et paradoxe chez Peire Cardenal, auteur de *sirventès,*" in *Romanistique* (Nice), **14** (1971), and "Peire Cardinal, Juvénal d'Occitanie?" in *Bulletin de l'association Guillaume Budé,* 4th ser., **1** (1973).

STEPHEN G. NICHOLS, JR.

[See also **Aragon, Crown of (1137–1479); Provençal Literature: After 1200; Troubadour, Trouvère, Trovador.**]

PEIRE D'ALVERNHA (*fl.* 1150–1170), one of the early Provençal troubadours of Auvergne. In twenty-four extant poems of elaborate technique and austere, difficult style, he insisted on the need for poetry to be new and original. Ironically, his best-known poem is the burlesque "troubadour gallery," in which he pokes sharp-witted fun at twelve of his fellow poets.

BIBLIOGRAPHY

Rita Lejeune, "La 'Galerie littéraire' du troubadour Peire d'Alvernhe," in *Actes et mémoires du 3ème Congrès international des langue et littérature d'Oc et d'études franco-provençales, Bordeaux 1961* (1965), 35–54; Alberto del Monte, ed., *Peire d'Alvernha: Liriche, testo, traduzione e note* (1955).

ROBERT TAYLOR

[See also **Provençal Literature; Troubadour, Trouvère, Trovador.**]

PEIRE VIDAL (*fl. ca.* 1175–*ca.* 1210), troubadour poet and perhaps composer. He was employed at the courts of Toulouse, Marseilles, Aragon, Castile, and Montferrat, and lived as well in Genoa, Pisa, Cyprus, and Hungary. Some of his poems are political in content, and he was known as a supporter of Richard I the Lionhearted of England.

Scholarly opinion attributes about fifty poems to Peire, of which twelve survive with music. His verse was known in his time for irony, wit, and boasting; his music is remarkable for its wide spans of vocal range. One of his songs has two extant melodies, and two others show major structural variants among known versions.

BIBLIOGRAPHY

Les poésies de Peire Vidal, Joseph Anglade, ed. (1913, 2nd rev. ed. 1923, repr. 1966); Ugo Sesini, *Le melodie trobadoriche nel Canzoniere provenzale della Biblioteca Ambrosiana* (1942); Nicola Zingarelli, "Pietro Vidal e le cose d'Italia," in *Studi medievali,* **1** (1928).

MARCIA J. EPSTEIN

[See also **Provençal Literature: After 1200; Troubadour, Trouvère, Trovador.**]

PELAGIUS (*ca.* 360–*ca.* 418), Romano-British theologian. Born in Britain or Ireland, he went to Rome about 384 and remained there until 409. During this period he composed his most substantial works, especially his monumental commentary on the Epistles of St. Paul. In these writings Pelagius displays evidence of his wide reading in classical Latin and in the Greek and Latin fathers, together with his exhaustive knowledge of Scripture. Although not ordained a priest, he was renowned for his asceticism. Augustine, who speaks of him with respect and affection, calls him "a holy man" and "a distinguished Christian."

With Rome under threat from the Visigoths led by Alaric, Pelagius fled with Celestius (Caelestius), his close friend and supporter, first to Sicily (409) and then to Hippo and Carthage (410). He soon proceeded to Palestine, his home until he disappeared from the historical record in 418.

The doctrine of Pelagius is based on the belief in the complete freedom of the human will to do either good or evil: this free will cannot be prejudiced by the sin of a forebear or the grace of God. For Pelagius, people can fulfill all divine commands without the assistance of divine grace. The heresy to which Pelagius gave his name consisted of the theological implications of this basic tenet: there is no such thing as original sin, since sin is always a matter of individual will and not of human nature transmitted from Adam to posterity; the human race did not incur spiritual death with the sin of Adam, nor was it redeemed by the death and resurrection of Christ; there were sinless people before the coming of Christ; infant baptism is unnecessary, since all children are born without sin; infants who die without baptism go straight to heaven; prayer for the conversion of sinners is futile, since only free will makes one good, and grace is always given in proportion to one's merits.

Celestius, who propagated these views much more vigorously than his master, was excommunicated by a council at Carthage in 411 and went to Ephesus. In 415 Pelagius cleared himself at Diospolis of the charge that he had denied the necessity of grace. At this point Augustine began to write and preach against Pelagianism, emphasizing the weakness of the human will as a result of the sin of Adam and insisting on the necessity of the gratuitous gift of divine grace for salvation.

In early 417, largely due to the influence of Augustine, Pope Innocent I (*d.* 417) confirmed the findings of the councils of Carthage and Milevis (416), and excommunicated both Pelagius and Celestius. In the face of appeals by the latter, the Sixteenth Council of Carthage (418) issued nine canons condemning specific errors of Pelagius: on original sin and its transmission, the nature and necessity of grace, and the universality of sin. As a result, Pope Zosimus (417–418) reaffirmed his predecessor's excommunications. Henceforth, the new champion of Pelagianism was Julian, bishop of Eclanum in Italy, who argued against Augustine that his doctrine of original sin was a revival of Manichaeism.

A movement later referred to as Semi-Pelagianism, led by the monk John Cassian (*ca.* 360–*ca.*432/435), repudiated Pelagianism but rejected Augustine's extreme form of predestination. Since the formal condemnation of Pelagianism and Semi-Pelagianism by the Second Council of Orange in 529, the Augustinian concept of grace as a gratuitous and undeserved gift of God has been generally accepted in orthodox Western theology.

The philosophical significance of Pelagianism lies in its insistence on the independence of ethics from religious dogma: People are free to choose either good or evil. Pelagius' chief concern was to emphasize the necessity of human moral effort, in contrast to the widespread moral indifference of the times.

BIBLIOGRAPHY

Sources. Because of Pelagius' condemnation, few of his extensive writings have survived. Two sources are Alexander Souter, ed., *Pelagius' Expositions of Thirteen Epistles of St. Paul,* 3 vols. (1922–1931); and St. Augustine's quotations from Pelagius' *On Nature,* found in Augustine's "On Nature and Grace," in *A Select Library of the Nicene and Post-Nicene Fathers of the Christian Church,* 1st ser., V, Philip Schaff, ed., with an introductory essay by B. B. Warfield (1893, repr. 1971).

Studies. Gerald Bonner, "Rufinus of Syria and African Pelagianism," in *Augustinian Studies* (1970), and *Augustine and Modern Research on Pelagianism* (1972); Peter R. L. Brown, "Pelagius and His Supporters: Aims and Environment," in *Journal of Theological Studies*, n.s. **19** (1968), and, for the controversy between Pelagius and Augustine, *Religion and Society in the Age of Saint Augustine* (1972); Robert F. Evans, *Four Letters of Pelagius* (1968), and *Pelagius: Inquiries and Reappraisals* (1968); John Ferguson, *Pelagius: A Historical and Theological Study* (1956), containing an excellent bibliography; Alexander Souter, *The Earliest Latin Commentaries on the Epistles of St. Paul* (1927), 205–230. Other works containing references to the Pelagius–Augustine controversy include Gerald Bonner, *St. Augustine of Hippo* (1963), 312–393; James Bowling Mozley, *A Treatise on the Augustinian Doctrine of Predestination* (1855, 3rd ed. 1883).

BERNARD CULLEN

[See also **Augustine of Hippo, Saint; Cassian, John; Church, Early; Julian of Eclanum; Philosophy and Theology, Western European.**]

PELAGONIA, in western Macedonia, was the site of a battle (1259) in which the Byzantine emperor of Nicaea, Michael VIII Palaiologos, decisively defeated the coalition of William of Achaia (Guillaume de Villehardouin), Manfred, king of Sicily, and Michael II of Epiros. This victory marked the beginning of the decline of Latin supremacy in medieval Greece; brought Epiros, Nicaea's archrival for hegemony over the Byzantines, to the brink of ruin; and, most important, paved the way for the Nicene restoration of the Byzantine Empire by removing the threat of a Latin attack from the West. As a result, Michael VIII Palaiologos of Nicaea was able to advance on (and then to capture) Latin-held Constantinople in 1261.

BIBLIOGRAPHY

Deno J. Geanakoplos, "The Battle of Pelagonia," in his *Emperor Michael Palaeologus and the West* (1959, repr. 1973), 47–74.

DENO J. GEANAKOPLOS

[See also **Byzantine History (1204–1453); Epiros, Despotate of; Latin Principalities and Frankish States in Greece; Michael II of Epiros; Michael VIII Palaiologos; Nicaea, Empire of.**]

PELENA (plural: *peleny;* literally, "shroud"), a richly decorated square or rectangular cloth used as an altar covering in Slavic Orthodox churches or hung below or around icons. *Peleny* are of two types: one is normally made of silk or velvet and heavily embroidered, often with gold or silver thread, and sometimes has precious or semiprecious stones incorporated into the decorations; the other type is of linen and is embroidered with folk motifs, most often in red thread.

BIBLIOGRAPHY

Natalia Andreevna Maiasova, *Drevnerusskoe shit'e* (1971), with French summary; I. I. Pleshanova and L. D. Likhacheva, *Drevnerusskoe dekorativno-prikladnoe iskusstvo v sobranii Gosudarstvennogo Russkogo Muzeia* (1985), with English summary.

GEORGE P. MAJESKA

[See also **Russian and Slavic Art.**]

PENANCE AND PENITENTIALS. In medieval ecclesiastical literature the word "penance" is used to connote different but interrelated practices: (1) a public liturgical rite; (2) a private liturgical rite; (3) expiatory acts, particularly fasting, imposed on sinners who had acknowledged their sins; (4) interior dispositions of repentance, sorrow, conversion. It is usually clear from the context of the discussion which of these meanings is intended.

FORMS OF PENANCE

The early Christian church understood itself to be the vehicle through which sinners could receive God's forgiveness. However, the particular ways and institutions through which this understanding was realized in practice underwent a long evolution and development from the patristic period to the speculative theologians of the thirteenth century. By the fifth century certain lines of development are clear and are generally acknowledged by historians of penance: forgiveness for all sins after baptism was available to all Christians; forgiveness for the major or capital sins (such as adultery, murder, idolatry) was obtained through the rite of public penance that began on Ash Wednesday with the excommunication of the penitents from the church and the Eucharist, prayers for their forgiveness, and the enjoining of penance. The penance ended on Holy Thursday with reconciliation and readmission to the Eucharist.

The discipline of public penance was the one

PENANCE AND PENITENTIALS

chance open to ordinary Christians to obtain remission of their sins. However, it was a severe practice that could be undertaken only once in a lifetime and that carried heavy disabilities. Those who underwent public penance could not marry if they were single, could not engage in sexual relations during and after public penance if they were already married, could not enter military service, and were barred from becoming clerics in the future. To undergo public penance was a serious decision not to be made lightly, particularly by young people and by those newly married. The sermons of Caesarius of Arles suggest that the practice of deferring penance until the end of one's life may have been prevalent by the beginning of the sixth century.

There is some dispute about whether the practice of private penance existed in the West prior to the sixth century, but it is not always clear what the parties to the dispute mean by "private penance." The church certainly did not believe that the rite of public penance was the only way to extend forgiveness to various sinners, that is, it did not believe that its power to forgive was restricted to the public rite. Clerics, who were barred from undertaking public penance, were deposed from office for a serious offense, and then could be forgiven and reconciled. Likewise, those who were in danger of death and converts from heresy could receive forgiveness and reconciliation.

Although these extraordinary situations show that the church understood its power to extend beyond the strict rite of public penance, they do not prove that private penance, in the sense of penitents confessing their sins to a priest and receiving forgiveness as often as they wished, existed prior to the sixth century. Furthermore, the existence of private penance in that sense would be difficult to reconcile with the caution expressed to young people about undertaking public penance and with the practice of deferring penance. Neither concern would be intelligible if there had been private penance. Perhaps the clearest indication that this form of reconciliation was not common is seen in the reaction of the Third Council of Toledo (589) to the practice, which apparently was beginning to be evident in Spain at that time. The council censured the practice, which it considered a presumptuous departure from tradition, of seeking forgiveness from a priest as often as one sinned and commanded that "penance be given according to the canonical form of the ancients." It outlines what it means: the penitent is to be excluded from Communion and to take his place among the penitents; after the time of penance has passed, he is to be restored to Communion at the priest's discretion.

Whatever the circumstances that occasioned the reaction of the Toledo council, by the end of the sixth century there are signs of private penance in Ireland, where there seems to have been no tradition of public penance. A century later Theodore of Canterbury (Tarsus) is reported to have said the same of Anglo-Saxon England: "Reconciliation is not publicly established in this province, for the reason that there is no public penance either." On the other hand, the canons of the First Synod of St. Patrick (457) use excommunication as the most frequent form of punishment, indicating a relation to the rite of public penance. It has been suggested that this document marks the transition to the characteristic form of Irish private penance. The reasons for this development in Ireland probably lie in the tradition of a soul-friend (*anmchara*) or personal spiritual director, a monastic tradition that encouraged the confession of faults to a superior who imposed appropriate penances, and the scattered rural structure of the society whose principal ecclesiastical leaders were abbots rather than bishops. The practice of private penance is also evident earlier in the sixth century in some Welsh documents—*Preface of Gildas on Penance,* Synod of North Britain (Brevi), Synod of the Grove of Victory, *Excerpts from a Book of David (of Menevia)*—and is best exemplified by the penitentials that were taken by Irish missionaries to the Continent, where they spread rapidly and eventually found their way to England.

Private penance never replaced public penance, and throughout the Middle Ages the two developed side by side. In times of ecclesiastical reform, such as in the early ninth century and in the late eleventh century, laments over the demise of the ancient tradition of public penance and calls for its restoration are frequently encountered. However, the different types of penance were grounded on a principle that is formulated in the Rheims Penitential of the eighth century: secret (private) penance for secret sins, public penance for public sins. In fact, by the beginning of the thirteenth century, three forms of penance had developed which are described by Robert of Flamborough: solemn, public, and private. Solemn penance was, in effect, similar to the ancient public penance and carried with it the harsh disabilities of the latter. Public

PENANCE AND PENITENTIALS

penance (nonsolemn) referred to the openness of the penance, such as going on pilgrimage, and could be imposed by an ordinary priest at any time. Private penance was the penance that took place in private before the priest—what in more recent times is generally called confession.

PENITENTIALS

The significant medieval development in the history of penance was the general acceptance of private, repeatable confession of sins to a priest, a practice whose origins are found in Ireland. Penitentials were handbooks devised to aid the priest-confessor in the administration of private penance. These manuals took many forms, but central to all of them is a list of canons, each canon comprising two parts: the specification of an offense and the determination of an appropriate penance for that offense. Many penitentials have prefatory material counseling the priest on how to deal with penitents and reminding him of his curative role. Penance was not seen primarily as punitive but as curative, the medicine for sins administered by the physician of souls.

Penitentials usually bear no titles and are named after their reputed authors (such as Vinnian, Cummean, Theodore, Bede, Egbert [of York]), or after the manuscripts in which they are found (such as Bobbio, Burgundian, Vallicellian, Monte Cassino), or even after their early editor (Martenianum). The earliest Irish manual is the Penitential of Finnian, thought to be the work of Finnian of Clonard (*d.* 549) or Finnian of Moville (or Magh Bile; *d.* 579). It would have to have been written perhaps before 591, the year Columbanus went to the Continent, where he wrote a penitential that incorporates material from the work of Finnian. The Latin Irish penitentials are those of Finnian, Columbanus, and Cummean. The Bigotian Penitential in its present form shows signs of continental and Anglo-Saxon influence. The Old-Irish Penitential is a manual written in the vernacular that is dated not later than the end of the eighth century by its recent editor (D. A. Binchy).

Aside from being the first manual of its kind on the Continent, the Penitential of Columbanus had considerable influence on a group of handbooks of the eighth and ninth centuries, collectively referred to as Frankish penitentials (such as Bobbio, Burgundian, Paris, Fleury, Merseberg *a,* St. Gall, Vienna). By far the most influential of the Irish penitentials is that ascribed to Cummean, probably Cumineus Longus, bishop of Clonfort (*d.* 662). This comprehensive penitential had wide circulation on the Continent in the eighth century and exerted considerable influence on the early Anglo-Saxon tradition that began with penitential materials associated with Theodore of Canterbury. Aside from several relatively unstructured works (*Canones Gregorii, Canones Cottoniani, Capitula Dacheriana, Canones Basilienses*) there is a penitential ascribed to Theodore, divided into books and chapters, probably completed by 741. Other penitentials associated with the early English church are the individual works ascribed to Bede and to Egbert of York. The combined form incorporating most of the material from Bede and Egbert, in addition to other sources, is certainly a work of Frankish origin, probably from the second half of the ninth century.

Several penitentials of the eighth and ninth centuries have a tripartite structure, drawing most of their canons from (1) Frankish sources, (2) Cummean, and (3) Theodore. The best-known of these works are *Excarpsus* of Cummean, Rheims Penitential, *Capitula iudiciorum,* Tripartite of St. Gall, Merseberg *a,* and Vallicellian I, which was dependent on Merseberg *a.*

The penitentials seem to have been welcomed on the Continent after Columbanus, and it would probably be correct to read the eighth canon of the Council of Chalon (647–653) as sanctioning the form of private penance that these manuals were meant to serve. Jonas of Bobbio in his Life of Columbanus speaks of people flocking to the saint for the medicine of penance. On reflection, this lack of opposition is curious and might suggest an already existing continental tradition of private penance that could accommodate the Irish system. However, there is no evidence for an ordinary system of private penance prior to the missionary activity of Columbanus.

The wide diffusion of penitentials in the seventh and eighth centuries bears witness to their popularity, and by the beginning of the Carolingian reform in the early years of the ninth century, one encounters rules directing that a penitential be one of the books in the priest's possession. However, about the same time a reaction to the penitentials seems to have begun to lead to their outright condemnation by the Council of Chalon (813) and the Council of Paris (829). The reasons given for the censures were that the penitentials did not reflect the authentic tradition and that the penances they imposed were not consistent with the gravity of the sins. However, the demands of the pastoral ministry guaranteed the continued existence of penitentials, seen in the manuscript evidence of ninth- and tenth-century copies of older penitentials and in the composition of new ones in the traditional style (for instance, St. Hubert, Monte Cassino, Pseudo-Gregory, Pseudo-Theodore, Double Penitential of Bede/Egbert).

Nonetheless, the condemnations did have some effect, since it is not until the beginning of the tenth century that recommendations to own a penitential are again encountered. Little evidence of material from the penitentials is found in the statutes drawn up after 813 by bishops for their dioceses; collections of church law such as the *Dacheriana* (*ca.* 800) do not use canons from these manuals; and there is little trace of them in the councils of the period.

Some effort was made to create penitentials that met the criticisms of the conciliar censures, two of which are worthy of note. Halitgar of Cambrai, perhaps about 830, composed a work in six books that was a balanced and judicious compromise between ancient authority and the penitentials. The first two books deal with the virtues and vices, drawing on Gregory the Great and Julianus Pomerius (cited as Prosper of Aquitaine). Books III, IV, and V deal with penance, the sins of the laity, and the sins of the clergy, respectively, drawing on traditional sources of ecclesiastical councils and the letters of popes. The sixth book is a traditional manual using older penitential sources that Halitgar claims was drawn from a Roman document; hence its traditional name, the Roman Penitential (called by some scholars the Pseudo-Roman Penitential). In fact, it has been shown that Halitgar drew his materials from traditional tripartite sources: Irish materials, Theodore, and Frankish canons.

Later in the century Hrabanus Maurus composed two penitentials that are radical departures from the older style of manual, being closer to miniature collections of traditional ecclesiastical law. The Penitential Addressed to Otgar (842) has no older penitential materials, and the Penitential Addressed to Heribald (856) incorporates only a few penitential canons.

By the end of the ninth century the creative period of traditional-type penitentials was completed. In the tenth century the penitentials took on a new role marked by their incorporation into collections of church law. Regino of Prüm's *Libri duo de synodalibus causis et disciplinis ecclesiasticis* (906) drew on the Double Penitential of Bede/Egbert; the ninth book of the unedited Collection in Nine Books virtually reproduces the *Capitula iudiciorum* and Pseudo-Gregory Penitential. A new impetus to the penitentials came from the work of Burchard of Worms at the beginning of the eleventh century. He used several penitential sources for his *Decretum* and began a new tradition with its nineteenth book, called "Corrector et medicus." This book had a profound influence on subsequent collections and even circulated separately as an independent penitential manual. This phase of the history of the penitentials continued well into the twelfth century, but after Gratian there began a new tradition of confessional manuals that gradually replaced the older works with what have come to be called "summas for confessors" (*summae confessorum*).

It is sometimes supposed that from the middle of the eleventh century a reaction set in against the penitentials similar to the one at the beginning of the ninth century. The fierce attack on the penitentials by Peter Damian in his *Book of Gomorrah* is often cited in support of this claim. However, aside from Peter Damian there are no indications of opposition to these manuals from the period of the Gregorian reform up to Gratian. They tended not to be used as frequently in collections of church law as they had been used by Burchard, but this is probably because of the growing sophistication of the law and of the availability of more authoritative texts. It should be noted that a text attributed to Augustine by Burchard that recommends the possession of a penitential is found later in Ivo of Chartres and in the *Decretum* of Gratian.

One of the salient features of the penitentials is their often harsh and frequently lengthy penances. Whether these penances were carried out is not known, but it is clear that for many combinations of serious sins a person would be condemned to doing penance for his or her whole life, and perhaps would need several lifetimes if the penances were implemented. Such a system would be intolerable for the general population. In fact, a system of commutations and redemptions was introduced very early that allowed penitents to satisfy years of penitential fasting with psalms, almsgiving, monetary payments, and even, in some cases, having someone else do the penance. From the middle of the eighth century, many of the more complete penitentials incorporated detailed instructions for commutations. Needless to say, such practices could lead to abuses, particularly to a mechanistic view of penance that derogated the core of confession, which was personal sorrow and satisfaction for one's offenses.

Another feature that distinguishes continental penitentials from their Irish and Anglo-Saxon forebears is the liturgical context in which some of the former are found. From the beginning of the Middle Ages the administration of penance, whether public or private, was the preserve of the church. The initiation into public penance was associated with Ash Wednesday, and its conclusion through reconciliation and readmission to the Eucharist took place on Holy Thursday. Rituals and prayers developed to accompany the rites of public penance, and were incorporated into the earliest sacramentaries, frequently under the rubric "Order for Giving Penance at the Beginning of the Fast."

A similar rite grew up around private penance, often borrowing prayers from the older public rites. Several penitentials that have come down to us are found only in a liturgical setting: the Bobbio Penitential in the Bobbio Missal, the Fleury Penitential in a liturgical ordo of penance, and the Paris Penitential in a Paris manuscript (Cod. Paris 7193) that seems to have been originally attached to a well-known manuscript of the Vatican Library (Codex Vat. Regin. 316) containing the Gelasian Sacramentary. The elaborate ordo for private penance in the tenth-century Romano-German Pontifical contains an interrogatory to be used by the priest in questioning the penitent that closely resembles the interrogatory at the beginning of the Double Penitential of Bede/Egbert. A liturgical order in various forms accompanies many of the continental penitentials (such as Merseberg *a*, Vallicellian I, Tripartite of St. Gall, and Halitgar), and although they are of varying length, it is difficult to imagine how any ordo for private penance containing more than a few short prayers could be used in practice.

Little is known of the day-to-day administration of private penance, but it is evident that if the general Christian population did private penance even a few times in a year, there would be no time to use the elaborate ritual for private penance found in the Romano-German Pontifical, for instance. Perhaps private penance was actually a combination of public prayers, admonition, general interrogatories that served as reminders, and formalized confession of sins before a general congregation, followed by the private confession of personal sins to the priest and the fulfillment of the individual penances in private.

DOCTRINAL DEVELOPMENT

Throughout the early Middle Ages penance as an institution developed primarily within the context of practice and a relatively unreflective intellectual atmosphere. Even the lengthy section on penance in collections of church law are no more than anthologies of papal letters, conciliar statements, and excerpts from the Fathers and other ecclesiastical sources on the subject of penance. The eleventh century, however, marks the beginning of the introduction of a reflective, questioning, didactic approach to penance that can be detected in Bonizo of Sutri's work on the Christian life. At this time there appeared a work entitled *De vera et falsa poenitentia* (Concerning true and false penance), of which nothing is known except that it was attributed to St. Augustine but probably was composed about the middle of the eleventh century. This is the first serious intellectual treatment of penance in the medieval period, and its influence was lasting, no doubt because of its reputed author and because it was used by Gratian in his treatise on penance and, through him, entered the *Books of Sentences* of Peter Lombard.

The medieval doctrinal history of penance received its impetus from Peter Lombard and developed in the context of commentaries on the *Books of Sentences* and in independent theological works such as Thomas Aquinas' *Summa theologiae*. Some of the central questions touched on the sacramental nature of penance, the power of the priest, the effect of absolution, the role of the internal dispositions of the penitent, and the revival of sins already forgiven. Perhaps the most significant impetus both to the development of the practice of private penance and to its doctrinal treatment by church law and theology was the decree *Omnis utriusque sexus* of the Fourth Lateran Council (1215), which formulated the requirement of annual confession for all Christians.

BIBLIOGRAPHY

Sources. Collections include Franz B. Asbach, ed., *Das Poenitentiale Remense und der sogen. Excarpsus Cummeani* (1975): the *Canones Basilienses* (App., 79–89) and *Rheims Penitential* (App., 2–77, esp. 30 [Rheims 4.50 and 4.51, distinction between public and private penance]); Ludwig Bieler, ed., *The Irish Penitentials* (1963, repr. 1975), edition and English trans. of Welsh

PENANCE AND PENITENTIALS

penitential materials, Irish penitentials with related material, and English trans. of Bigotian Penitential and Old-Irish Penitential: First Synod of St. Patrick (54–59), Welsh documents relating to penance (60–73); Carlo de Clercq, ed., *Concilia Galliae A.511–A.695* (1963): Council of Chalon canon 8 (304), and Council of Orléans canon 27/24 (124); Severino González-Rivas, *La penitencia en la primitiva iglesia española* (1949); John T. McNeill and Helena M. Gamer, trans., *Medieval Handbooks of Penance* (1938, repr. 1965), translations of the principal *libri poenitentiales* and selections from related documents: Theodore of Canterbury's Penitential 1.13.4 (195), rules stipulating the possession of a penitential (390–391), Council of Chalon canon 38 (401–402), Council of Paris canon 32 (402–403), Fourth Lateran Council canon 21 (413–414); Leo C. Mohlberg, Leo Eizenhöfer, and Petrus Siffrin, eds., *Liber sacramentorum Romanae aecclesiae ordinis anni circuli (Cod. Vat. Reg. 316/Paris Bibl. Nat. 7193, 41/56)* (1960): Paris Penitential (254–259); C. Munier, ed., *Concilia Galliae A.511–A.695* (1963): Council of Agde canon 15 (201); *Patrologia latina:* Burchard of Worms's *Decretum XIX* (CXL, 949–1014), text attributed to Augustine that recommends possession of a penitential (CXL, 625), Third Council of Toledo canon 11 (LXXXIV, 353), *De vera et falsa poenitentia* (XL, 1113–1130), Halitgar of Cambrai's *De vitiis et virtutibus et de ordine poenitentium* (CV, 651–700), Hrabanus Maurus' *Poenitentium liber* [to Otgar] (CXII, 1397–1424) and *Paenitentiale ad Heribaldum* (CX, 467–494), Ivo of Chartres's *Decretum* 6.22, recommending possession of a penitential (CLXI, 450D), Peter Damian's *Liber Gomorrhianus* 10–12 (CXLV, 169–172), trans. by Pierre J. Payer as *Book of Gomorrah* (1982); Hermann Josef Schmitz, *Die Bussbücher und die Bussdisciplin der Kirche*, 2 vols. (1958, repr. of 1883 ed.), and *Die Bussbücher und das kanonische Bussverfahren* (1898, repr. 1958), which includes Halitgar's *De vitiis et virtutibus* bks. 3–6 (275–300); Cyrille Vogel, *Les 'libri paenitentiales'* (1978), which includes a survey of individual penitentials with information on extant editions and secondary literature and bibliography (updated in A. J. Frantzen, *Mise à jour* [1985]); Hermann Wasserschleben, ed., *Die Bussordnungen der abendländischen Kirche* (1851, repr. 1958).

Individual works include Bonizo of Sutri, *Liber de vita christiana,* E. Perels, ed. (1930), books 9–10; Caesarius of Arles, *Sermons,* Sister Mary Magdeleine Mueller, O.S.F., trans. (1956), 295–311; Collection in Nine Books, Vatican Library, MS Vat. lat. 1349; Gratian, *Decretum,* Emil Friedberg, ed. (1879, repr. 1959), D. 38, c. 5 (col. 141); J. Madoz, "Una neuva recensión del penitencial 'Vallicellanum I,'" in *Andlecta Sacra Tarraconensia,* 18 (1945); Peter Lombard, *Libri IV sententiarum,* 3rd ed. (1981), bk. 4, dists. 14–22; Regino of Prüm, *Libri duo de synodalibus causis et disciplinis ecclesiasticis,* F. G. [W.] H. Wasserschleben, ed. (1840); Robert of Flamborough, *Liber poenitentialis: A Critical Edition with Introduction and Notes,* J. J. Francis Firth, ed. (1971), 205–208; Thomas Aquinas, *Summa theologiae,* pt. III, ques. 84–90, and supp., ques. 1–28; Cyrille Vogel and Reinhard Elze, eds., *Le pontifical romano-germanique du dixième siècle,* 3 vols. (1963–1972), on developed rite of public penance, II, 14–21, 59–67, and on private penance, II, 234–245.

Studies. On penance, see Karl Adam, *Die geheime Kirchenbusse nach dem heiligen Augustin* (1921); Émile Amann, "Peñitence," in *Dictionnaire de théologie catholique,* XII (1933), the most comprehensive introduction to the subject; Paul Anciaux, *La théologie du sacrement de pénitence au XIIe siècle* (1949); Paul Galtier, *L'église et la rémission des péchés aux premiers siècles* (1932), the clearest presentation of the case for the early existence of private penance, and *De paenitentia* (1923, new ed. 1950), esp. 221–261; Josef Andreas Jungmann, *Die lateinischen Bussriten in ihrer geschichtlichen Entwicklung* (1932), an excellent introduction to the liturgical rites of penance with ample references to primary and secondary sources; Henry C. Lea, *A History of Auricular Confession . . . ,* 3 vols. (1896, repr. 1968), still useful for documentation; A. Michel, "Pénitence du IVe concile du Latran à la réforme," in *Dictionnaire de théologie catholique,* XII (1933); Jean Morin, *Commentarius historicus de disciplina in administratione sacramenti poenitentiae* (1651, 2nd ed. 1682, 1702); Robert Cecil Mortimer, *The Origins of Private Penance in the Western Church* (1939), a convincing position against Galtier's thesis on the subject of private penance; Bernhard Poschmann, *Die abendländische Kirchenbusse im frühen Mittelalter* (1930), *S. Aurelii Augustini episcopi Hipponensis, textus selecti de paenitentia* (1934), a useful collection of texts on penance by Augustine, and *Penance and the Anointing of the Sick,* Francis Courtney, trans. and rev.(1964), an excellent English summary of Poschmann's major works on penance, with ample bibliographies; Karl Rahner, "Bussdiziplin, altkirchliche," in *Lexikon für Theologie und Kirche,* 2nd ed., II (1958); Amédée Teetaert, *La confession aux laïques dans l'église latine dupuis le VIIIe jusqu'au XIVe siècle* (1926); Cyrille Vogel, *La discipline pénitentielle en Gaule dès origines à la fin du VIIe siècle* (1952), "Le péché et la pénitence," in *Pastorale du péché* (1961), "Le pontifical romano-germanique du Xe siècle: Nature, date, et importance du document," in *Cahiers de civilisation médiévale,* 6 (1963), and "Les rites de la pénitence publique au Xe et XIe siècles," in Pierre Gallais and Yves-Jean Riou, eds., *Mélanges offerts à René Crozet,* I (1966); Oscar D. Watkins, *A History of Penance,* 2 vols. (1920, repr. 1961), particularly useful for the reproduction of primary texts, many of which are translated in the course of the author's discussion.

On penitentials, see H. P. Forshaw, "The Pastoral Ministry of the Priest-Confessor in the Early Middle Ages, 600–1100" (diss., Univ. of London, 1975), on the origin and development of the role of the priest-confessor in the administration of private penance in the West; Paul Fournier, "Études sur les pénitentiels," in *Revue d'histoire et de littérature religieuses,* 6–9 (1901–1904), showing the insular and Frankish origins of the later penitentials (against Schmitz, who argued for a Roman origin); Allen J. Frantzen, "The Significance of the Frankish Penitentials," in *Journal of Ecclesiastical History,* 30 (1979), and *The Literature of Penance in Anglo-Saxon England* (1983); Raymund Kottje, *Die Bussbücher Halitgars von Cambrai und des Hrabanus Maurus* (1980); Gabriel Le Bras, "Pénitentiels," in *Dictionnaire de théologie catholique,* XII (1933), a classic introduction to penitentials; Pierre Michaud-Quantin, "Un manuel de confession archaïque dans le manuscrit Avranches 136," in *Sacris erudiri,* 17 (1966), an example of the continuing influence of the penitential literature into the twelfth century; Pierre J. Payer, "The Humanism of the Penitentials and the Continuity of the Penitential Tradition" in *Mediaeval Studies,* 46 (1984), and *Sex and the Penitentials* (1984); Rosamund Pierce, "The 'Frankish' Penitentials," in Derek Baker, ed., *Studies in Church History,* 11 (1975); Thomas P. Oakley, "The Penitentials as Sources for Mediaeval History," in *Speculum,* 15 (1940); Cyrille Vogel, "Composition légale et commutations dans le système de la pénitence tarifée," in *Revue de droit canonique,* 8 (1958) and 9 (1959), the only thorough study of the complex commutations or redemptions introduced to alleviate the strict penances found in the penitentials.

PIERRE J. PAYER

[See also **Aquinas, St. Thomas; Baptism; Bede; Burchard of Worms; Celtic Church; Columbanus, St.; Confession; Excommunication; Gildas, St.; Hrabanus Maurus; Indulgences; Law, Canon; Lent; Peter Damian, St.; Peter Lombard; Regino of Prüm; Seven Deadly Sins; Theodore of Canterbury, St.**]

PENDANT VAULT. See **Vault.**

PENDENTIVE, an architectural term describing the concave triangle (point down) that bridges the gap between the corners of a square or rectangular room and its domed ceiling. The four pendentives thus formed are rarely weight bearing; instead, they function visually to unify the square ground plan with the circular roof. Early examples appear at Hagia Sophia in Constantinople (532–537).

LESLIE BRUBAKER

[See also **Dome; Hagia Sophia (Constantinople); Vault;** and illustration overleaf.]

PENETES. This term is used in Byzantine texts to designate the "poor" as a social category derived from an economic condition. *Penes* is to be distinguished from *ptochos,* which signifies indigence. The two terms were often used interchangeably, however.

An economic definition of *penes* is found in legislative texts and remains unchanged from the time of Justinian I (527–565) through the legislation of the Macedonians (tenth century) and into the fourteenth-century *Hexabiblos.* According to these texts, a *penes* is a person who owns property with a value of less than fifty nomismata (solidi). The condition carried a legal disability: the *penetes* were not allowed to appear in court as witnesses.

The *penetes,* like the *ptochoi,* were the object of philanthropy in the Byzantine Empire, a fact explicable by their economic position as well as by social necessity expressed as religious (or, in the fourteenth century, as civic) duty. But the *penetes* were not indigent, for the term was used to describe productive members of society. In the sixth century it encompassed the various laborers; in the fourteenth-century *Dialogue Between the Rich and the Poor,* the *penetes* are those who work the land, the masons, the sailors, and the artisans. These people were considered unable, by nature and by position, to govern (see the "Homilies" of Isidore of Thessaloniki).

The term *penetes* was generally used in a social context, as the opposite of the rich. In the *Eclogue* (*Ekloga*), the Isaurian law code, a differentiation was made between the wealthy, the less wealthy, and those who were "entirely poor." In the legislation of the Macedonians, the emperors posited two social groups, the powerful (*dunatoi*) and the *penetes* (occasionally also called *ptochoi*), who comprised the majority of the rural population; they were the smallholders who paid taxes and served as soldiers and whom the state tried, unsuccessfully, to protect.

Hagia Sophia, İstanbul, showing two of the four pendentives formed beneath the main dome. FROM GASPARD FOSSATI, *AYA SOFIA, CONSTANTINOPLE* (1852). Art, Prints & Photographs Division, New York Public Library

BIBLIOGRAPHY
Phaidon Koukoules, *Byzantinon bios kai politismos,* II.1 (1948), 156–168; Evelyne Patlagean, *Pauvreté économique et pauvreté sociale à Byzance, 4e–7e siècles* (1977); I Ševčenko, "Alexios Makrembolites and His 'Dialogue Between the Rich and the Poor,'" in *Zbornik radova vizantoloshkog instituta,* 6 (1960).

ANGELIKI LAIOU

[See also **Byzantine Empire: Economic Life and Social Structure; Dunatoi; Eclogue; Hospitals and Poor Relief, Byzantine.**]

PENITENTIALS. See **Penance and Penitentials.**

PENNY. At the end of the eighth century Charlemagne undertook a currency reform. Retaining Roman terminology, he issued as his principal coin a silver *denarius* of about 24 troy grains (or about 1.5 grams) of pure silver. This monetary reform soon spread to other parts of Europe, and until the second half of the thirteenth century the *denarius* was the dominant Western European circulating coin in domestic and international transactions. In French the *denarius* was called a *denier;* in English it was called a penny.

For small transactions, pennies were sometimes cut into halves, quarters, and even smaller fragments. For ease of bookkeeping, there were also units of account larger than the penny. A solidus, or shilling, was equal to 12 pennies, and 20 shillings were reckoned to be a *libra,* or pound. The Latin terms once again derive from the Roman monetary system.

The shilling and the pound were not circulating currencies in Western Europe. Denominations larger than the penny were not regularly struck in the West until the thirteenth century, when the gold florin and ducat began to replace the penny in international commerce. The gold Byzantine solidus (also called nomisma or bezant) and the gold Muslim dinar were both minted regularly and used in international trade.

In England standardized coinages began in Kent and Mercia during the later eighth century and were influenced by the Frankish reforms. During the next century minting of pennies spread to other Anglo-Saxon kingdoms, all of them reckoning pennies at 240 to the pound. By the tenth century there were approximately sixty to seventy mints receiving dies from a number of die-cutting centers, but all were supervised by the royal court. The actual pennies, however, were minted crudely, which made clipping and counterfeiting easy. On most of Offa's (*r.* 757–796) coins the king's name appears on the obverse and the moneyer's on the reverse. Under Athelstan (*r.* 924–940) the custom began of placing both the moneyer's and the mint's name on the reverse. With Edgar (*r.* 959–975) the royal head was standardized and faced to the left until the Norman conquest.

Early in the twelfth century the penny began to be called a "sterling," a word of uncertain origin although at times it was thought to derive from *steorra,* a star on some of the older issues; from *staer,* a starling, since some of Edward the Confessor's (*r.* 1042–1066) pennies had four birds stamped on them; or from coins circulated by the Easterling moneyers, a name that in Norman times was applied at English ports to traders from the North and Baltic seas who used good silver money.

The weight of the English silver penny was reckoned generally at 24 troy grains before the Norman conquest. Thereafter it was reduced gradually, in large part because of increasing shortages of silver and because of expanded coinage needs, to 22.5 (1066), 22 (1300), 20.25 (1344), 20 (1346), 18 (1351), 15 (1412), 12 (1464), 10.5 (1527), 10 (1543), 8 (1552), 7.5 (1601).

The Middle English word *penny* or *peny* derived from the Old English *penig* or *penning,* forms akin to the Old High German *pfenning* or *pfenting* (a coin, penny) and the Old Norse *penningr.* The first written reference to it in England occurs in Ine's laws, where the form *pæning* or *pæninga* is used. For centuries it was believed erroneously that it was derived from "pending" (money of Penda) or from "oiffing," an Irish term for "penny" presumably meaning "money of Offa," or as a loanword from the Latin *pecunia* (money) or *pendere* (to weigh).

The English Tower pennyweight was originally simply the weight of a silver penny. It was later reckoned at 32 wheat grains or 22.5 troy grains (1.458 grams), equal to 1/20 Tower ounce of 450 grains (29.160 grams) or 1/240 Tower pound of 5,400 grains. Named after the currency pound at the mint in the Tower of London, this weight system was replaced eventually by the troy, whose pennyweight contained 24 grains of barleycorns (1.555 grams), equal to 1/20 troy ounce of 480 grains (31.103 grams) or 1/240 troy pound of 5,760 grains.

Since after the middle of the thirteenth century European states began minting larger silver denominations and new gold coins, the reign of the penny came to an end.

BIBLIOGRAPHY

Howard W. Bradley, *Handbook of Coins of the British Isles* (1978); George Brooke, *English Coins* (1932, 3rd rev. ed. 1950); Carol Humphrey Vivian Sutherland, *English Coinage, 600–1900* (1973).

RONALD EDWARD ZUPKO

[See also **Dinar; Dirham; Ducat; Florin; Mints and Money, Western European; Nomisma; Pound (Money); Shilling.**]

PENTARCHY, an early medieval concept according to which, within the theoretically universal Christian world, ecclesiastical power was divided among the patriarchs of Rome, Constantinople, Alexandria, Antioch, and Jerusalem. The concept of pentarchy emerged in the fifth century, when de facto the archbishops of these five cities exerted influence within the church. Emperor Justinian I (*r.* 527–565) gave the system legal sanction in his *Novellae* (6, 109, 123). In 692 the idea was accepted in Byzantine canon law at the Synod in Trullo: "We define that the throne of Constantinople should enjoy equal privileges with the throne of Old Rome . . . , after it should be numbered the throne of the great city of the Alexandrians, then the throne of Antioch and, after it, the throne of the city of Jerusalem."

Precisely at the time the pentarchic theory received this legal and canonical recognition, however, it lost much of its real substance: during the reign of Justinian, the vast majority of Christians in Egypt and at least half of the population of Syria joined the Monophysite schism, and thus the Orthodox patriarchs of Alexandria and Antioch inevitably lost much of their prestige within the empire. In the seventh century the Arab conquest isolated them entirely (together with their colleague at Jerusalem) from Constantinople and Rome. The incumbents of the latter two patriarchal sees faced each other as the real heads of Christendom until the schism of the eleventh century separated them.

On the other hand, within the Byzantine Orthodox world the number of patriarchs was never formally restricted to the orginal five. The katholikos of Georgia, the Bulgarian archbishops of Preslav, Ochrid, and Trnovo, and the archbishop of Serbia also adopted the title of patriarch whenever historical circumstances allowed them to do so. Nevertheless, the pentarchy, as an ideal model, continued to be mentioned in canonical texts and to be used in Byzantine polemics against the papacy.

BIBLIOGRAPHY

See John Meyendorff *et al.*, *The Primacy of Peter* (1963); "Patriarche," in *Dictionnaire de droit canonique* and *Dictionnaire de théologie catholique.* See also Joan M. Hussey, *The Orthodox Church in the Byzantine Empire* (1986), 297–312.

JOHN MEYENDORFF

[See also **Autocephalos; Byzantine Church; Heresies, Byzantine; Islam, Conquests of; Monophysitism; Patriarch; Schisms, Eastern-Western Church.**]

PENTATEUCH, the first five books of the Old Testament (Genesis, Exodus, Leviticus, Numbers, Deuteronomy), also known as the five Books of Moses. In the early medieval period, size, practicality, and expense conditioned patrons to commission single books (such as Genesis) or small units of the Bible when they desired an illustrated manuscript; the Pentateuch was one of the textual units deemed suitable for this purpose, especially in the Latin West. The oldest illustrated copy is the enigmatic Ashburnham Pentateuch (Paris, Bibliothèque Nationale, MS nouv. acq. lat. 2334), a Latin book of uncertain origin; it is known to have been in Tours by the ninth century and is therefore generally attributed to the seventh or, less likely, eighth century. The Ashburnham manuscript contains full-page miniatures, most of which illustrate several verses of text. This has led several scholars to speculate that earlier illustrated pentateuchs existed with smaller pictures inserted in the writing columns at appropriate intervals. Because some details in the Ashburnham Pentateuch's miniatures derive from Jewish texts, it has been argued that pentateuchs were first illustrated for Jewish use and that these provided models for later Christian adaptation.

BIBLIOGRAPHY

Oscar von Gebhardt, ed., *The Miniatures of the Ashburnham Pentateuch* (facsimile) (1883); Joseph Gutmann, "The Jewish Origin of the Ashburnham Pentateuch Miniatures," in *Jewish Quarterly Review,* **44** (1953); Bezalel Narkiss, "Towards a Further Study of the Ashburnham Pentateuch (Pentateuque de Tours)," in *Cahiers archéologiques,* **19** (1969), and "Reconstruction of Some of the Original Quires of the Ashburnham Pentateuch," in *Cahiers archéologiques,* **22** (1972); Kurt Weitzmann, *Late Antique and Early Christian Book Illumination* (1977), 17, 118–125.

LESLIE BRUBAKER

[See also **Jewish Art; Manuscript Illumination: European; Manuscript Illumination: Hebrew; Pre-Romanesque Art.**]

PENTECOST (from the Greek *pentēchostos,* fiftieth), the Christian feast day commemorating the descent of the Holy Ghost to the apostles and to the Virgin Mary. Celebrated on the seventh Sunday or the fiftieth day after Easter, this movable feast is also called Whitsunday. Acts 2:1–41 recounts the appearance of the Holy Ghost to a number of Christ's followers.

In Christian iconography, the Byzantine tradition typically depicts the Virgin and the apostles seated in a space covered by a rounded arch. Within the arch are figures representing the world that the apostles are to evangelize or the tongues of flame, symbolizing the Holy Ghost, that descend on the group.

In Judaism the equivalent of Pentecost is Shavuot, the Festival of Weeks, on the sixth day of Sivan, the ninth Jewish month. Shavuot originally was the festival that ended the grain harvest. The Pentateuch states that the festival is to commence fifty days after the offering of the first Omer (the first-cut sheaf of barley; see Lev. 23: 15–16). Pentecost acquired a second purpose: commemoration of the pact between God and mankind, in which God promised Noah no further general flood.

BIBLIOGRAPHY

Ormonde M. Dalton, *Byzantine Art and Archaeology* (1911, repr. 1961); Hayyim Schauss, *The Jewish Festivals: From Their Beginnings to Our Own Day*, Samuel Jaffe, trans. (1938).

JENNIFER E. JONES

[See also **Feasts and Festivals, European; Twelve Great Feasts.**]

Pentecost. Miniature from the Rabula Gospels of 586 (the earliest known signed and dated Christian codex with miniatures). FLORENCE, BIBLIOTECA MEDICEA LAURENZIANA, COD. PLUT. I, 56, fol. 14v

PEOPLE OF THE BOOK. By this term, a translation of the Arabic expression *ahl al-kitāb,* Muslims refer to those people whose religion is based on a divinely revealed scripture. Initially, at the time of Muḥammad, the prophet of Islam, the principal "people of the book" were Jews and Christians. They are mentioned frequently in the Koran, which records Muḥammad's divinely inspired religious message. In fact, Muḥammad preached that his own book represented the latest stage in a long process of progressive revelation of true belief in one God.

There is little doubt that Muḥammad was influenced by both Judaism and Christianity in the formulation of his own brand of revealed monotheism. It is less clear, however, how he became acquainted with the "books" of the people of the book and how much of their specific content he actually knew. He speaks of the *Tawrāt*, which means the Torah, of the *Zabūr*, identical with the Psalms of David, and of the *Injīl,* the Evangelion or Gospel. Muḥammad may have met and conversed with Jewish and Christian merchants traversing the Arabian Peninsula, or he may have absorbed some knowledge of Christianity from Christian Arab tribes and of Judaism from Jews settled in northern Arabia. Possibly he heard the sermons of Christian monks and learned about Christian scripture in this way. At any rate, Jewish and Christian ideas were "in the air" in Muḥammad's Arabia, and they certainly helped pave the way for acceptance by the pagan Arabs of his monotheistic message.

At the outset, Muḥammad probably expected the people of the book to acknowledge him as Prophet and as bearer of the newest, and hence most authentic, version of the divine word, especially since, to him at least, the essentials of his faith were shared by Jews and Christians. In hopes of attracting Jewish converts, he even adopted some Jewish rituals, like the fast known as *ᶜAshūrāᵓ*, modeled on the Day of Atonement, and the custom of facing Jerusalem during prayer. Similarly, he retold, albeit in a somewhat confused fashion, many stories from Christian and Jewish scriptures, the latter often infused with details deriving from Jewish legendary Midrash. He also revered as prophets, that is, as recipients of divine revelation, biblical personages such as Abraham, Moses, David, and Jesus.

However, the people of the book, especially the

Jews of Medina, with whom Muḥammad was in close contact during the final, crucial years of his mission, rejected his overtures and even greeted his preaching with outright hostility and mockery. As a result the Prophet cast off or transformed the Jewish observances he had initially adopted and came to view the people of the book as obstinate and rebellious and as people to be shunned. Biblical Abraham, the ancestor of the Arabs through his son Ishmael, became for Muḥammad the first true Muslim, a staunch monotheist whose faith was distorted by later generations in their scriptures.

In later Islamic polemics against the people of the book, the status and content of Jewish and Christian scriptures played a significant role. The idea that the Torah contained a distorted version of pristine Abrahamic monotheism was elaborated in the accusation of "falsification" (*taḥrīf*). Current Jewish scripture was portrayed as a concoction of Ezra during the Babylonian exile. It replaced the original and true revelation given Moses, which had been largely forgotten as a result of the many tribulations experienced by the Israelites. The doctrine of abrogation (*naskh*) of previous revelations, used in the first instance to rationalize contradictory verses in the Koran, was applied to the scriptures of the people of the book and took the place of Muḥammad's original teaching about the community of belief between Jew, Christian, and Muslim. Similarly, the anthropomorphic descriptions of God in the Jewish Bible came under heavy attack as a perversion of proper monotheistic belief.

Against the Christians, the charge of "falsification" found expression, for instance, in the claim that Paul had altered the teachings of Jesus. Central Christian theological doctrines like the Trinity and the Incarnation came under fire for their incompatibility with the absolute monotheism of Abraham.

In general, the later Islamic polemic against the people of the book is both quantitatively and qualitatively weighted toward the refutation of Christianity. This is understandable. Christians comprised a much larger segment of the people of the book than did Jews, and Christians were more visible than Jews in government posts. The greater incidence of Muslim-Christian encounter, coupled with the fact that the Christians were coreligionists of powerful Christian states on the borders of the Islamic domain, made the Christians more important targets of Muslim religious polemic than the powerless Jews.

Despite the consistent hostility toward the people of the book in Muslim polemical and other writings, Muḥammad's own original admiration for them was translated into a relatively tolerant legal status. They became known as "people of protection" (*ahl al-dhimma;* also *dhimmīs*) and were not required, as were the pagan Arabs, to accept Islam as the price of being allowed to live. Rather, they paid tribute to the Islamic state and were made to endure discriminatory disabilities, ultimately codified in the so-called Pact of ᶜUmar, in return for security and freedom to practice their religion, however imperfect.

Eventually, as Islam expanded by conquest, other religious communities not specifically identified as people of the book in the Koran were assimilated to this protected status, it being unwise and impractical to extirpate such significant populations. These included the dualist Zoroastrians and some groups of Manichaeans, the gnostic baptizing sect of the Sabians (Mandeans) of Iraq (mentioned in the Koran), and the polytheistic Hindus of India.

BIBLIOGRAPHY

The article "Ahl al-Kitāb" in the *Encyclopaedia of Islam,* new ed., I (1960); Erdmann Fritsch, *Islam und Christentum in Mittelalter* (1930); Moshe Perlmann, "The Medieval Polemics Between Islam and Judaism," in Solomon D. Goitein, ed., *Religion in a Religious Age* (1974); Moritz Steinschneider, *Polemische und apologetische Literatur in arabischer Sprache, zwischen Muslimen, Christen, und Juden* (1877, repr. 1966); Arthur S. Tritton, *The Caliphs and Their Non-Muslim Subjects: A Critical Study of the Covenant of ᶜUmar* (1930, repr. 1970).

MARK R. COHEN

[See also **Abode of Islam—Abode of War; Arabia, Islamic; Costume, Islamic; Costume, Jewish; Diplomacy, Islamic; Islam, Religion; Jews in the Middle East; Jews in Muslim Spain; Jews in North Africa; Koran; Muḥammad; Palestine; Polemics, Islamic-Jewish; Taxation, Islamic.**]

PEPIN I (of Landen) (*d.* 640), also known as Pepin the Elder, mayor of the palace (628–639). He is most famous (with Bishop Arnulf of Metz) as one of the two founding ancestors of the Carolingian dynasty, but this conception is anachronistic because no one in the mid seventh century could have known that his great-great-grandson Pepin III would become king in 751. Pepin's career is in reality most revealing of the aristocratic politics in the Frankish world.

Pepin was one of the greatest landholders in Austrasia (East Francia), with vast estates in what is now eastern Belgium, near a site called Landen, whence his name. His landholdings were augmented in the region around Trier by his marriage (date unknown) to Itta, a noble heiress and sister of Bishop Modoald of Trier (*d.* before 647). Pepin supported the efforts of King Chothar II of Neustria (*r.* 584–628) to unite the Merovingian kingdoms in 613 and was rewarded with the office of mayor of the palace (*maior domus*) in Austrasia, basically an administrative and judicial position. Chothar's other major supporter was Arnulf, a great nobleman and landowner, who was rewarded with the bishopric of Metz (614). Pepin and Arnulf cemented an alliance between their families by arranging in 629 or 630 a marriage, carried out between 630 and 640, between Pepin's daughter Begga (*d.* 693) and Arnulf's son Ansegisel (*d.* before 679). Pepin II, the principal heir of this marriage, became through his double inheritance the greatest landowner after the king in Austrasia, perhaps in the whole Frankish world.

Pepin I used his mayoral office, his wealth, his monastic foundations and promotion of Columbanian monasticism, his growing control of bishoprics, and—according to some sources—his powerful personality to achieve a position of unprecedented power in the Frankish world. Although he endured a temporary eclipse in the 630's engineered by King Dagobert I (*r.* 629–639) and the powerful Adalgisel-Grimo clan, he overcame most rivals, recovered his mayoral office, and handed the office on to his son Grimoald (*d.* 661/662). More than anyone else Pepin transformed the mayoral office from a simple court dignity to a post equal to and eventually greater than the monarchy.

Pepin the Elder, of Landen, should not be confused either with Pepin I, king of Italy (781–810), a son of Charlemagne, or with King Pepin I of Aquitaine (*r.* 817–838), a son of Louis the Pious. Note too that in the Anglophone world Pepin is considered an ancestor of the Carolingians, who actually take their name from Charlemagne (Carolus Magnus), but Europeans often refer to his family as Arnulfings (more rarely Arnulfians) or as Pippinids (from the German spelling, Pippin).

BIBLIOGRAPHY

Pepin's life is sketched in Rosamond McKitterick, *The Frankish Kingdoms Under the Carolingians, 751–987* (1983), 16–27, and Pierre Riché, *Les carolingiens: Une famille qui fit l'Europe* (1983), 23–29. The genealogy of the family is treated in Eduard Hlawitschka, "Die Vorfahren Karls des Grossen," in Wolfgang Braunfels, ed., *Karl der Grosse,* I: Helmut Beumann, ed., *Persönlichkeit und Geschichte* (1965), 51–82. Pepin's historical environment is superbly reconstructed in Matthias Werner, *Der lütticher Raum in frühkarolingischer Zeit: Untersuchungen zur Geschichte einer karolingischen Stammlandschaft* (1980), 341–404.

THOMAS F. X. NOBLE

[See also **Carolingians and the Carolingian Empire; Mayor of the Palace; Merovingians.**]

PEPIN II (of Herstal) (635/655–714), grandson of Pepin I of Landen and duke of Austrasia (East Francia), inherited from his parents, Ansegisel and Begga, immense landholdings—concentrated in the Trier-Metz region and in the neighborhood of Liège—plus a tradition of officeholding and social prominence.

As Pepin came to adulthood, his position was extremely precarious. His uncle Grimoald had succeeded his grandfather Pepin I as mayor of the palace in Austrasia and totally dominated the ineffective Merovingian king Sigibert III (*r.* 639–656). Grimoald went so far as to prevail upon Sigibert to adopt as his son and successor his own son Childebert. Sigibert seems to have been childless when this bargain was struck, though he later had a son, Dagobert, who was exiled to Ireland. Childebert did reign for a time, perhaps from 656 to 662 but certainly after 660. Grimoald's pretensions angered many in the Frankish kingdoms, and in about 662 Grimoald and his son were murdered.

It seemed as though the political fortunes of Pepin's family had been checked, although they were not ruined entirely: Pepin became duke of Austrasia, an office whose precise significance is difficult to gauge. A powerful rival to Pepin's family, Wulfoald, was installed as mayor of the palace in Austrasia, however, and the new king of Austrasia, Childeric II (*d.* 673), became a pawn in the hands of the Neustrian nobility, which was itself dominated by its mayor, Ebroin (*d.* 681), until 680. Pepin, meanwhile, used his position as duke, his vast wealth, and Austrasian distaste for Neustrian domination to begin rebuilding his family's political fortunes. Twice Pepin II led the Austrasians in battle against the Neustrians. At Tertry in 687 he won a decisive victory, seized control of King Theuderich III (*d.* 690/691) and his treasure, and became mayor of all the Merovingian kingdoms. Historians are frustrated that a lack of sources prevents a careful documentation and understanding of Pepin's remarkable achievements between 662 and 687.

After 687 Pepin II of Herstal resided in Austrasia and continued building strong ties with the local nobility, enhancing them by his marriage to Plectrude, whose family connections can no longer be considered as certainly established, but whose nobility and importance to Pepin are beyond doubt. Pepin II controlled Neustria through its kings—four undistinguished ones in succession—and, after 700, through his son Grimoald as mayor. Burgundy was controlled for a time by his son Drogo. Throughout the Frankish realms Pepin II kept close control of key bishoprics, such as those of Rheims in Neustria and Lyons in Burgundy. He also continued the family tradition of founding and promoting monasteries, and he supported missionaries, especially in Frisia. These actions brought him wealth, prestige, and talent. Once he had settled internal Frankish affairs Pepin turned to an aggressive military policy that involved campaigns against the Saxons, Frisians, Alemans, Bavarians, Aquitainians, Gascons, and Bretons. With virtually all of these peoples Pepin established relations on terms advantageous to the Franks.

Pepin's sons by Plectrude, Grimoald and Drogo, predeceased him in 708 and 714 respectively. He also had two sons by a concubine, Chalpaida, Charles (later known as Martel, the "hammer") and Childebrand. In 714 Plectrude prevailed upon Pepin to name as his successor Theudoald, an illegitimate son of Grimoald, so that she could retain control and exclude the sons of her rival. By 721, however, Charles had taken up his father's succession.

Pepin II of Herstal should not be confused with the Pepin II (*d.* 864) who was a grandson of Louis the Pious and for a time a rival of his uncle Charles II the Bald (king of France 840–877) in Aquitaine.

BIBLIOGRAPHY

Two accounts of Pepin's life and career are Rosamond McKitterick, *The Frankish Kingdoms Under the Carolingians, 751–987* (1983), 27–30, and Pierre Riché, *Les carolingiens: Une famille qui fit l'Europe* (1983), 29–43. Fundamental in its treatment of the Carolingian ruling family and its environment are Matthias Werner, *Der lütticher Raum in frühkarolingischer Zeit: Untersuchungen zur Geschichte einer karolingischen Stammlandschaft* (1980), 159–174, 275–280, 396–409, and *Adelsfamilien im Umkreis der frühen Karolinger: Die Verwandschaft Irminas von Oeren und Adelas von Pfalzel* (1982). The genealogy of the family is treated in Eduard Hlawitschka, "Die Vorfahren Karls des Grossen," in Wolfgang Braunfels, ed., *Karl der Grosse,* I: Helmut Beumann, ed., *Persönlichkeit und Geschichte* (1965), 51–82.

THOMAS F. X. NOBLE

[See also **Carolingians and the Carolingian Empire; Mayor of the Palace; Merovingians.**]

PEPIN III AND THE DONATION OF PEPIN

LIFE

Pepin the Short (714–768) was born to Charles Martel and his first wife, Chrotrudis. He was baptized by the Anglo-Saxon missionary Willibrord, and his godfather was Raginfred, later archbishop of Rouen. Pepin had a brother, Carloman, who was at least fifteen in 722, a sister, Hiltrud, and a half-brother, Grifo, by his father's second marriage to the Bavarian Swanahild. He also had three illegitimate half-brothers, Bernhard, Hieronymus, and Remedius.

Of Pepin's youth little is known, except that he was educated at St. Denis and sent, about 735, to the Lombard king Liutprand (*r.* 712–744) to have his hair cut, which was a symbolic rite of passage to manhood that created a fictive kinship between Pepin and Liutprand and consolidated the alliance between the Franks and Lombards concluded some years earlier. In 749 Pepin married a distant relative, Bertrada, who was a daughter of Count Charibert of Laon and a granddaughter of that Bertrada who founded the great monastery of Prüm. This marriage brought Pepin extensive landholdings in the Moselle region. Pepin had two sons, Charles (the future Charlemagne), born in 747, and Carloman, born around 751. He also had a daughter, Gisela, who died as abbess of Chelles in 810. Shortly before his death, following the Frankish tradition, Pepin divided his kingdom between his two sons. He died 24 September 768 and was buried at St. Denis.

In 741 Pepin and Carloman succeeded their father, Charles, as mayors of the palace even though the Merovingian throne had been vacant since 737. Pepin received Burgundy, Neustria, and Provence, whereas Carloman got Austrasia, Alemannia, and Thuringia. Together the brothers summoned synods, the first that had met in eighty years, and issued capitularies, the first since 614. They also issued diplomas in their own names, styling themselves "dukes and princes of the Franks." Rebellions in Aquitaine, Bavaria, Saxony, and Swabia, due in part to a reluctance by these peoples to submit to the mayors in the absence of a king and in part to the machinations of Grifo, led the brothers to put the Merovingian Childeric III on the throne in 743. In 747 Carloman retired to Monte Cassino; he entrusted his two sons, one of them called Drago, to Pepin, but Pepin did not share power with them and became the sole mayor for the entire Frankish kingdom.

By late 749 or early 750 Pepin had decided to make himself king. He sent Abbot Fulrad of St. Denis and Bishop Burchard of Würzburg to Pope Zacharias I (*r.* 741–752) to ask "concerning the kings in Francia who had no royal power, and whether this was fitting or not." Zacharias responded that such a situation offended the divine order and urged that Pepin be made king. In November 751, before the assembled Franks at Soissons, Pepin the Short was acclaimed king by the Franks and anointed by the Anglo-Saxon Benedictine Boniface, as papal legate, and the Frankish bishops present, after Childeric had been sent into a monastery. This was the first anointing of a Frankish king.

As virtually all sources are later and written from a Carolingian point of view, it is difficult to reconstruct the situation, but Pepin undoubtedly faced strong opposition. This opposition probably had little to do with sentiments in favor of Merovingian legitimacy and much to do with support for Grifo, Carloman, and Carloman's sons. Powerful Frankish nobles might have also balked at seeing one of their number rise so high. Papal approval and episcopal anointing were probably employed to appease critics. When Pope Stephen II (*r.* 752–757) visited Francia in 754 he crowned and anointed Pepin, his wife, and his two sons, and, according to a source whose authenticity is at least questionable, he forbade the Franks ever to choose a king from another family. At that time, opposition from Pepin's own family must have been insignificant because Grifo had been assassinated in 753, Carloman was incarcerated at Vienne, and the latter's sons were tonsured.

As king, Pepin continued the work begun by him and Carloman while they had been mayors. Two broad programs are evident. The first consisted of a reform of the Frankish church, initiated under the inspiration of Boniface. Efforts were made to regularize the ecclesiastical hierarchy, impose canon law, regularize the lives of the cathedral clergy (canons), bring about semiannual synods, compensate churches for properties seized by, and granted to, laymen, and in general improve the moral and spiritual discipline of all the clergy. The success of Pepin's work should not be exaggerated, but it was a good beginning. He was a cunning and resourceful ruler who simultaneously exploited and benefited the church.

The second program was designed to consolidate the kingdom. Pepin campaigned with limited success in Brittany and Saxony but submitted Alemannia and Aquitaine to Frankish rule by defeating, respectively, dukes Theodebald and Waifar. Pepin forced the submission of Duke Odilo of Bavaria and then exercised a protectorate over Odilo's son Tassilo III until the latter became his vassal in 757. In 763 Tassilo broke free and remained virtually independent for more than two decades. Pepin's military successes were considerable, but much work was left for his successors.

THE DONATION OF PEPIN

The "Donation of Pepin" refers to Pepin's grant to Pope Stephen II of a strip of land in Italy that would become the papal states. When the Lombard king Aistulf (*r.* 749–756) conquered the exarchate of Ravenna in 751 and announced his intention of subjecting Rome to his authority, Stephen appealed to Pepin. Pepin's family had long been allied to the Lombards, and a decision to intervene in Italy cannot have been easy for Pepin to make, especially in view of latent resentment after his usurpation of royal power. Stephen was theoretically a Byzantine subject, and the lands seized by Aistulf belonged to the emperor. But Emperor Constantine V was considered a heretic in the West because of his iconoclasm, and he was in no position to aid the pope in Italy. Although Constantine commanded Stephen to negotiate with the Lombards on behalf of the empire, which Stephen did with little discernible enthusiasm, in reality the pope had no choice but to turn to the Franks. On 6 January 754 Stephen arrived at Ponthion, where Pepin accorded him high honors and promised on oath to protect the Roman church. Stephen wintered at the monastery of St. Denis while Pepin negotiated fruitlessly with the Lombards and more successfully with the Franks. At Quierzy (a Frankish royal residence near Soissons) in April Pepin promised to restore to the pope certain specified lands in Italy, and Stephen anointed him and named him *patricius romanorum* to give some public expression to Pepin's new role as defender of the Roman church. In 755 Pepin defeated Aistulf and in the First Peace of Pavia, concluded among "Franks, Lombards, and Romans," Aistulf agreed to make restitutions. No sooner had Pepin returned to Francia than Aistulf refused to give up "one hand's width of land" and laid siege to Rome. Pepin, on the urgent appeal of Stephen, returned in 756, defeated Aistulf again, and, in the Second Peace of Pavia, took hostages for surety, imposed a heavy tribute, and demanded restitutions. This time Fulrad, abbot of St. Denis, was left in Italy to travel from city to city receiving their keys and hostages as tokens of submission to the pope. His work completed, Fulrad deposited at the Confession of St. Peter a document detailing the cities and territories given to the pope. Thus, the term "Donation of Pepin" should be used to refer to the latter document of 756 and not to the Promise of Quierzy or to the written instrument, if one existed, of the First Peace of Pavia.

In fact donation is the wrong term altogether, for the lands in question were never Pepin's to donate. Restoration is also misleading because, by strict legal title, the lands belonged to the emperor and not to the pope, to whom they were "restored." Pepin had simply acted to repay the papacy for its efforts on his behalf, and when a Byzantine representative protested about Pepin's conduct, the king replied that he had acted for the salvation of his own soul and for love of St. Peter.

BIBLIOGRAPHY

For general accounts of Pepin's life and reign older works remain indispensable: Heinrich Hahn, *Jahrbücher des fränkischen Reiches, 741–752* (1863); Ludwig Oelsner, *Jahrbücher des fränkischen Reiches unter König Pippin* (1871); Englebert Mühlbacher, *Deutsche Geschichte unter den Karolingern* (1896), 23–83; Louis Halphen, *Charlemagne et l'empire carolingienne* (1947) 17–55. Genealogical matters are best treated by Eduard Hlawitschka, "Die Vorfahren Karls des Grossen," in Wolfgang Braunfels, ed., *Karl der Grosse,* I (1966–1967), 51–82.

Inner tensions in Pepin's kingdom are treated by Leo Mikoletzky, "Karl Martell und Grifo," in *Festschrift für Edmund Stengel* (1952); Walter Mohr, *Studien zur Charakteristik des karolingischen Königtums im 8 Jahrhundert* (1955).

Religious affairs in Pepin's time may be studied from many perspectives. See *The Church in the Age of Feudalism, Handbook of Church History,* III, Hubert Jedin and John Dolan, eds., Anselm Biggs, trans. (1969), 7–25; Giles Constable, "Nona et Decima: An Aspect of Carolingian Economy," in *Speculum,* **35** (1960); Carlo De Clercq, *La législation réligieuse franque de Clovis à Charlemagne* (1936), 115–136; Theodor Schieffer, *Winfrid-Bonifatius und die christliche Grundlegung Europas* (1954).

The relations between Pepin and the Roman church, including Pepin's kingship, have elicited a voluminous literature. Works of enduring value include Ottorino Bertolini, "Le origini del potere temporale e del dominio temporale dei papi," in *Settimane di studio del Centro Italiano di Studi sull'alto Medioevo,* **20** (1973), and "Il problema delle origini del potere temporale dei papi nei suoi presuppositi teoretici iniziali: Il concetto di 'restitutio' nelle prime cessioni territoriali alla Chiesa di Roma," in Ottavio Banti, ed., *Scritti Scelti di Storia Medioevale,* II (1968), 485–547; Heinrich Buttner, "Aus den Anfängen des abendländischen Staatsgedankens," in Theodor Mayer, ed., *Das Königtum,* (1956), 155–167; Erich Caspar, *Pippin und die römische Kirche* (1914); Anna M. Drabek, *Die Verträge der fränkischen und deutschen Herrscher mit dem Papsttum* (1976); Louis M. O. Duchesne, *The Beginnings of the Temporal Sovereignty of the Popes, A.D. 754–1073,* Arnold H. Matthew, trans. (1908 repr. 1972), 21–48; Eugen Ewig, "Zum christlichen Königsgedanken in Frühmittelalter," in *Das Königtum,* 7–73; Wolfgang Fritze, *Papst und Frankenkönig* (1973); Johannes Haller, "Die Karolinger und das Papsttum," in *Historische Zeitschrift,* **108** (1912); Jörg Jarnut, "Quierzy und Rom: Bemerkungen zu den 'Promissiones donationis' Pippins und Karls," in *Historische Zeitschrift,* **220** (1975); Leon Levillain, "L'avènement de la dynastie carolingienne et les origines de l'état pontifical," in *Bibliothèque de l'école des chartes,* **94** (1933); David Harry Miller, "The Motivation of Pepin's Italian Policy, 754–768," in *Studies in Medieval Culture,* **4.1** (1973), 44–54, and "The Roman Revolution of the Eighth Century: A Study of the Ideological Background of the Papal Separation from Byzantium and Alliance with the Franks," in *Mediaeval Studies,* **36** (1974); Walter Mohr, *Die karolingische Reichsidee* (1962), 1–38; Ernst Perels, "Pippins Erhebung zum König," in *Zeitschrift für Kirchengeschichte,* **53** (1934); Percy Ernst Schramm, "Das Versprechen Pippins und Karls des Grossen für die römische Kirche," in *Zeitschrift der Savigny-Stiftung für Rechtsgeschichte, Kanonistische Abteilung,* **27** (1938);

Walter Ullmann, *The Growth of Papal Government in the Middle Ages,* 3rd ed. (1970), 44–86.

THOMAS F. X. NOBLE

[See also **Carolingians; Charlemagne; Charles Martel; Constantine V; Deposition of Rulers; Merovingians; Papal States; Stephen II, Pope.**]

PERA-GALATA, the Genoese colony on the north shore of the Golden Horn opposite Constantinople (Pera in Genoese sources, Galata in Byzantine, earlier Sykai, modern Beyoğlu), was established in 1267 or 1268 after Michael VIII Palaiologos had expelled his erstwhile Genoese allies from the their old commercial quarter in the city (1264). The new location, intended to remove the colonists from anti-Latin mobs, was convenient for their trade and enhanced their independence, though Michael retained effective authority. Prosperity was assured by the Genoese ascendancy in the Black Sea. The podesta of Pera took precedence of all other Latins at the Byzantine court, and the Genoese enjoyed special juridical status.

Destroyed by the Venetians in 1296, Pera was soon rebuilt on a larger scale, and by 1308 the empire's customs receipts were suffering from the exemptions granted the colonists. Wooden houses were replaced with stone, and although Pera was slow to take on a substantial appearance it came to be known as a cosmopolitan place, hospitable and tolerant. After 1328 a city wall rose over the emperors' objections, and the Ghibelline population showed no greater deference to Genoa when in 1324 they repulsed a fleet sent out to subdue them by the dominant Guelphs. The clergy and churches of Pera depended directly on the archbishop of Genoa, and the Dominican and Franciscan convents served as headquarters for missions into Asia and as shelter for learned Latin Christians who sought to convert the Greeks and whose intellectual exchanges with them were important for the Italian Renaissance.

By 1346 Pera's customs receipts were seven times Constantinople's. In 1348 the colonists destroyed a Byzantine fleet built to reassert authority over them and went on to enlarge their settlement. John VI Kantakouzenos had to ratify their virtual autonomy (1352). From this time even the Venetians had to conduct their business at Pera. The link to Genoa was the podesta, appointed annually from home, who served as continuing diplomatic representative to the Byzantine court. Two assemblies, each reserving one-sixth of their seats for non-Genoese, came to be divided equally between nobles and people, and after 1306 a civil official, the *abate del popolo,* functioned like a Roman tribune. A compilation of Genoese customary law, augmented by statutes, served as the colony's organic code.

Changing trade patterns caused by the collapse of the Mongol states led to economic decline which, though it could be mitigated by slave-trading profits, still left Pera's receipts by 1423 at only one-seventh of the level of 1334. The colony was now a place of about 2,000 inhabitants, thickly built up within its well-maintained defenses, but long habituated to subservient cooperation with the Turks. In 1453 it fell to Mehmed II without a struggle. At his order all its fortifications were demolished and all its independence given up except for limited freedom of worship and commercial jurisdiction, though as a base for Christian merchants and missionaries Pera long retained a distinct Latin character.

BIBLIOGRAPHY

Wilhelm Heyd, *Histoire du commerce du Levant au moyen-âge,* rev. ed., Furey Raynaud, trans., 2 vols. (1885–1886, repr. 1959, 1967), remains the most informative work. Kenneth M. Setton, *The Papacy and the Levant, 1204–1571,* I and II (1976, 1978), discusses many aspects of Byzantine-Latin relations that involve Pera. Raymond J. Loenertz, *La société des frères pérégrinantes: Étude sur l'orient dominicain* (1937), and Thomas Kaeppeli, "Deux nouveaux ouvrages de Frère Philippe Incontri de Péra," in *Archivum Fratrum Praedicatorum,* 23 (1953), treat the ecclesiastical and intellectual life of the colony. Works on the topography of Constantinople normally include Pera: Jean Sauvaget, "Notes sur la colonie génoise de Péra," in *Syria,* 15 (1934), is reliable. See bibliography under **Caffa** for Genoese colonization in the Black Sea region, including Pera.

AVERY ANDREWS

[See also **Byzantine Empire: History (1204–1453); Caffa; Constantinople; Genoa; Golden Horn; Trade, Byzantine; Trade, European.**]

PERCEVAL. See **Arthurian Literature; Grail, Legend of; French Literature; Matter of Britain.**

PERCEVALS SAGA. See **Parcevals Saga.**

PERCH, a measure of length for land in the British Isles. It generally contained 16.5 feet or 5.5 yards (5.029 meters), but perches of 9, 9.33, 10, 11, 11.5, 12, 15, 16, 18, 18.25, 18.75, 19.5, 20, 21, 22, 22.5, 24, 25, and 26 feet (2.743 to 7.925 meters) were also used. Perches of 16.5 feet and smaller were usually agricultural land measures, while those larger than 16.5 were feet used in forest regions and in urban draining, fencing, hedging, and walling operations. Etymologically the word was ultimately derived from the Latin *pertica* (a pole, long staff, or measuring rod), and it was used interchangeably with other linear measuring units such as the gad, lug, pole, and rod.

RONALD EDWARD ZUPKO

[See also **Weights and Measures, Western European.**]

PEREDUR. See **Mabinogi.**

PEREGRINATIO AETHERIAE. See **Itinerarium Egeriae.**

PÈRES, LA VIE DES ANCIENS. See **Vie des Anciens Pères, La.**

PÉREZ DE GUZMÁN, FERNA. See **Spanish Literature: Biography.**

PERFECTIO, a term used in mensural notational theory from the late thirteenth century to describe (1) the manner of writing a ligature and (2) the threefold grouping of values in a mensural series.

A ligature *cum perfectione,* regardless of the number of notes ligated, ends with the rhythmic value of a *longa.* A ligature *sine perfectione* ends with the rhythmic value of a *brevis.* The lack of perfection (*sine perfectione*), or "incompleteness," of the ligature refers to the alteration of the normal written form for any given ligature. The earliest use of *perfectio* denoting a form of ligature is found in John of Garland's *De mensurabili musica* (*ca.* 1240).

Perfectio as a threefold grouping was first applied to combinations of *longae* and *breves;* three *tempora* (one *tempus* is the value of one *brevis*) formed a "perfection." Similarly, one *longa* of three *tempora* or a combination of a *brevis* (one *tempus*) and a *longa imperfecta* (two *tempora*) formed a "perfection." The earliest use of *perfectio* to describe such groups of three *tempora* is found in Magister Lambertus' *Tractatus de musica* (*ca.* 1279) and Franco of Cologne's *Ars cantus mensurabilis* (*ca.* 1280). The concept of *perfectio* from mensural theory replaced the concepts of *longa recta* (two *tempora*) and *longa ultra mensuram* (three *tempora*) from the modal rhythmic theory of the early thirteenth century. In the fourteenth century, in the treatises of Jehan des Murs, *Compendium musicae practicae* (*ca.* 1322) and *Libellus cantus mensurabilis* (*ca.* 1340), the concept of *perfectio* was extended beyond the *longa,* and threefold divisions of the *brevis* (three *semibreves*) and *semibrevis* (three *minimae*) came to be called "perfect."

BIBLIOGRAPHY

Wolf Frobenius, "Perfectio," in *Handwörterbuch der musikalischen Terminologie* (1973); Fritz Reckow, "Proprietas und Perfectio: Geschichte der Rhythmus, seiner Aufzeichnung und Terminologie im 13. Jahrhunderts," in *Acta musicologica,* 39 (1967); William G. Waite, *The Rhythm of Twelfth-century Polyphony* (1954).

CALVIN M. BOWER

[See also **Ars Antiqua; Ars Nova; Jehan des Murs; John of Garland; Musical Notation, Western.**]

PERICOPE (Greek: *perikopē,* cutting or section), a passage from the Bible read as part of the Christian liturgy. Although "pericope" was used by the Fathers of the church to mean any section of Scripture, the term came to refer to the Mass readings in particular. The standardization of pericopes, a liturgical development of the fourth or fifth century in both East and West, required their collection in separate lectionaries (epistolaries and evangeliaries) until the adoption of a complete missal in the tenth century.

BIBLIOGRAPHY
Gerhard Kunze, *Die gottesdienstliche Schriftlesung,* I, *Stand und Aufgabe der Perikopenforschung* (1947); A. Allan McArthur, *The Christian Year and Lectionary Reform* (1958).

WILLIAM J. DIEBOLD

[See also **Breviary; Divine Office; Evangeliary; Gospelbook; Lectionary; Liturgy, Treatises on; Mass, Liturgy of; Missal.**]

PERLESVAUS is an early-thirteenth-century Arthurian romance written in Old French prose by an unknown author. Its subtitle, *Le haut livre du graal,* indicates the story's principal subject, the Grail quest of Perceval, here called Perlesvaus. The romance is full of Christian allegories placed within the larger thematic context of the battle between the forces of good (New Law) and evil (Old Law). Perceval's Grail quest is related as a series of conquests of the enemies of the New Law. Many questions remain unanswered as to the work's exact place in the development of the Grail legend and its relationship to other Grail romances. Of particular interest is the treatment of Lancelot's sinful love for Arthur's queen, Guinevere, who remains the knight's inspiring influence even after her death—a twist peculiar to *Perlesvaus.*

BIBLIOGRAPHY
Sources. The text is available in William A. Nitze and T. Atkinson Jenkins, eds., *Le haut livre du graal: Perlesvaus,* 2 vols. (1932–1937, repr. 1972). A translation is also available: Nigel Bryant, trans., *The High Book of the Grail* (1978).
Studies. Keith Busby, " 'Li buens chevaliers' ou 'uns buens chevaliers'? Perlesvaus et Gauvain dans le *Perlesvaus,*" in Jacques de Caluwé, ed., *Lancelot, Yvain, Gauvain* (1981); Thomas E. Kelly, *Le haut livre du graal: Perlesvaus—A Structural Study* (1974)

THOMAS E. KELLY

[See also **Arthurian Literature; French Literature; Grail, Legend of; Parcevals Saga; Perceval, Roman de.**]

PERMANENT SYNOD, one of the most important institutions of the Byzantine church, reflecting episcopal collegiality in the government of the "ecumenical patriarchate." Partly as a reflection of the Roman practice of the pope's taking some important decisions together with the council of neighboring bishops (*suburbicarii*), the archbishop of Constantinople—the "New Rome"—who had received the second place of honor after the pope in 381 (First Council of Constantinople, canon 3), gathered around himself, on a regular basis, an assembly of metropolitans to solve pending issues. The assembly was soon referred to as a "permanent synod" (*synodos endēmousa*). Neither the frequency of meetings nor the membership was ever strictly defined. The metropolitans of neighboring cities—Heraclea and Chalcedon, for instance—were regularly present, and bishops from more remote provinces, as well as the patriarchs of Alexandria, Antioch, and Jerusalem, if they were visiting the capital, could be invited to participate in decisions. The existence of the permanent synod was supposed to assure that the patriarch of Constantinople, who in virtue of his position as bishop of the imperial capital was invested with extraordinary powers, would not use those powers without some control by his brother bishops.

The synod played a central role in the patriarchal elections. When the patriarchal throne became vacant, it was called to nominate three candidates, from whom the emperor would choose one. Only in exceptional cases was this normal procedure replaced by a direct choice of the new incumbent by the emperor. The deposition of the patriarch—even when it was imposed by the emperor—required the sanction of the synod. The synod also functioned as the highest ecclesiastical tribunal for doctrinal or disciplinary matters.

When matters of extraordinary importance arose, the membership of the synod was enlarged to include as many as twenty, thirty, or even forty bishops. Some important sessions were attended by senators and presided over by the emperor (such as the synods of 1166 and 1170, presided over by Manuel I Komnenos, and the synod of 1341, presided over by Andronikos III Palaiologos).

The sack of Constantinople by the crusaders in 1204 and by the Turks in 1453 caused the disappearance of Byzantine patriarchal archives, except for a few isolated documents and a continuous, though incomplete, collection of synodal acts for the period 1315–1402. These documents constitute a major source of Byzantine institutional history.

BIBLIOGRAPHY
Jean Darrouzès, *Le registre synodal du patriarcat byzantin au XIVe siècle: Étude paléographique et diplomatique* (1971); Vanance Grumel, *Les régestes des actes du patriarcat de Constantinople,* I, *Les actes des patriarches,* 6 fasc. (1932–1979); Joseph Hajjar, *Le synode permanent dans l'église byzantine dès origines au XIe siècle* (1962).

JOHN MEYENDORFF

[See also **Byzantine Church; Caesaropapism; Clergy, Byzantine; Councils, Byzantine; Ecumenical Patriarch; Law, Canon: Byzantine; Patriarch.**]

PERO DE TAFUR. See **Tafur, Pero de.**

PEROTINUS (Pérotin) (*ca.* 1165–*ca.* 1225). An English writer on music, generally referred to as Anonymous IV (he is the fourth of a number of anonymous authors in Edmond de Coussemaker's edition of medieval writers on music), in his treatise (*ca.* 1275–1280) briefly mentions a certain Leoninus, "generally known as the best composer of organa [*optimus organista*], who produced [*fecit*] the great book of organum for Mass and Office [*Magnus liber organi de gradali et antifonario*] for the enhancement of the divine service." After this tantalizingly minimal reference to Leoninus and his epochal volume, Anonymous IV continues with a more detailed report about later developments:

> This book was in use until the time of Perotinus Magnus, who shortened it and composed a great many better clausulae or [*puncta*] [short pieces of discant polyphony], because he was the best composer of discant [*optimus discantor*] and better than Leoninus. . . . Moreover, this same Magister Perotinus wrote excellent compositions for four voices [quadrupla], such as "Viderunt" and "Sederunt," replete with artful musical turns and figures, as well as a considerable number of very famous *tripla,* such as "Alleluia Posui adiutorium," "[Alleluia] Nativitas," etc. Besides, he also composed conducti for three voices, e.g., "Salvatoris hodie"; and two-part conducti, such as "Dum sigillum summi patris," and monophonic conducti, e.g., "Beata viscera," and many more. The book, or rather the books, of Magister Perotinus [have been] in use . . . in the choir of the Cathedral of Our Blessed Virgin in Paris . . . until the present day. . . .

Perotinus is also mentioned in the treatise by the musical commentator John of Garland (*fl. ca.* 1240). Though the relevant musical sources carry no ascriptions, each of the few compositions cited by Anonymous IV is preserved in them.

Of the two views of the chronology of Perotinus' oeuvre, the one that his works for four voices were his crowning achievement, written late in his life, must be judged incompatible with the stylistic and evolutional evidence. Anonymous IV's designation of Leoninus as *optimus organista* is borne out by the fact that in the manuscript preserving the oldest available version of the *Magnus liber* (though certainly not the original) organal portions preponderate, often with astonishingly long melismas in the upper part (*duplum*) decorating single sustained notes of the cantus firmus in the lower voice (tenor). Perotinus' *quadrupla* (organa for four voices) and most of his *tripla* (organa for three voices) are stylistically more conservative than the clausulae. The former, especially the *quadrupla,* are compositions of monumental length favoring organal style (that is, the long notes of the tenor sustain extensive melismas in the upper voices, which always exhibit precise rhythm). Second-mode rhythms are rare in the *tripla* and do not appear at all in the *quadrupla.* The tenors of the latter are still unpatterned in the discant sections, while only the three earliest tenor patterns occur in any of the *tripla.* The inevitable conclusion is that the *quadrupla* and a good many of the *tripla* must have preceded the clausulae, which are more progressive both in style and as a genre. If it is assumed that Leoninus "made" the *Magnus liber* around 1180—the choir of the new cathedral was finished in 1177 (except for the roofing) and the high altar was consecrated in 1182—the traditional view, based on persuasive circumstantial evidence, that the two *quadrupla* were written in the late 1190's makes the intervening time interval entirely convincing. Thus, the composition of most of the clausulae after that of the *quadrupla,* as well as the appearance of the second rhythmic mode late in the first decade of the thirteenth century, makes it impossible to fix Perotinus' date of death as early as 1200/1205.

Nearly all polyphonic music written prior to Perotinus' *tripla* consists of only two voices. (The relatively primitive exceptions are one of the compositions in Cambridge University Library MS Ff.1.17, one of the organums in the manuscript containing the Milan organum treatise, and, perhaps, one of the compositions in the Codex Calixtinus at Santiago de Compostela.) Thus, Perotinus' development of a regular three-part idiom is a major technical advance and the four-part compositions represent an absolutely stunning feat.

Yet, with all their full sonority, variety, and organal monumentality, the *quadrupla* remained isolated accomplishments. Even three-part writing declined temporarily as Perotinus (and presumably others), turning to the further development of melismatic discant style, began to cultivate a less imposing genre, the clausula, which soon started to serve as the conceptual and notational melismatic model for the motet. (Syllabic music, monophonic as well as polyphonic, had no set of single-note symbols denoting fixed rhythmic values and relationships.)

It seems that the notion of the polyphonic clausula, mostly for two voices (tenor and *duplum*), arose from the shortening of the *Magnus liber* referred to by Anonymous IV. Fortunately there is concrete evidence of what seems to have been a process of modernization and tightening. One of the "Notre Dame manuscripts" contains 156 concise snippets of discant polyphony, most of which were intended to serve as replacements for long organal passages in the *Magnus liber*. Both the grouping of the notes of the tenor and the particularly meticulous shaping of the few phrases of the *duplum* reveal that about half a dozen of these substitutes are not merely brief, amorphous passages whose sole raison d'être is to be inserted somewhere in place of old-fashioned passages, but real miniature pieces of music with a life of their own. This is, in all probability, the birth of the species of composition that Anonymous IV called clausula. Hundreds of these have been preserved, constituting the first repertory of self-contained and independently shaped pieces of polyphonic music (discant) whose cantus firmi are Gregorian melismas excised from certain chants. In several of the clausulae the notes of the tenor are still treated as they were in Leoninian discant sections, that is, isochronously, with or without regular grouping. But it seems almost inevitable that the tendency to write *dupla* with balanced phrase designs, which had caused the increasing practice of regular grouping in the tenor, would lead to the shaping of more clearly defined reiterated groups, that is, rhythmic patterns. Unfortunately, it is impossible to hazard any guess as to how many of the preserved clausulae and early Latin motets were composed by Perotinus, though the combination of stylistic features, dissemination, and placement in manuscripts allows the positing of a few plausible hypotheses.

The accomplishments of Perotinus reveal a creative mind of staggering brilliance. It was he who for the first time wrote polyphony not just for two voices but "tripla plurima nobilissima" and even compositions for four voices; he modernized Leoninus' *Magnus liber;* and he gave greater strength and precision to the rhythmic component of music. The "music of the future" (the motet of the thirteenth and fourteenth centuries) evolved from his radical notion of carving a suitable melismatic segment out of a chant in order to produce a clausula, a precisely measured polyphonic composition based on a rhythmically patterned tenor that functions as the yardstick for the numerically interrelated parts (rhythms and phrases) of the piece. It was doubtless his concept to present a chant melisma two or more times in the tenor of one clausula (or motet) in order to produce a well-proportioned piece of music; and we need not shrink from crediting Perotinus with the introduction of new rhythms, with the codification of the (rhythmic) modal system, and with many features of its ingenious notation. In addition, both his melodic style and his counterpoint exhibit great suppleness, élan, and energy. And, finally, certain aspects of his style indicate resourceful assimilation of English musical traits.

The greatness of Perotinus Magnus, as he was called, rests essentially on qualities he shares with the other outstanding "classical" masters among European composers. Like them he focused diverse "national" influences, created well-organized masterpieces that stylistically and formally are the consummate high points of the period, and bequeathed an important artistic heritage with diverse potentialities. Small wonder that throughout the thirteenth century and still in the early fourteenth, manuscripts written in France, England, Spain, Italy, and Germany continued to transmit music by Perotinus and his immediate successors. His activity in Paris coincided with the erection of Notre Dame. Both the cathedral and the oeuvre of Perotinus are climactic monuments of the classic Gothic.

BIBLIOGRAPHY

Ian D. Bent, "Pérotin," in *The New Grove Dictionary of Music and Musicians*, XIV (1980); Frederick W. Sternfeld, ed., *Music from the Middle Ages to the Renaissance* (1973); Craig Wright, "Leoninus, Poet and Musician," in *Journal of the American Musicological Society,* 39 (1986)

ERNEST H. SANDERS

[See also **Anonymous IV; Art Antiqua; Clausula; Conductus; Duplum; Hocket; John of Garland; Leoninus; Magnus Liber Organi; Melisma; Motet; Music; Musical Notation, Modal; Musical Treatises; Notre Dame School; Organum.**]

PERSIA. See **Iran; Sasanians.**

PETER DAMIAN, ST. (Petrus Damiani) (1007–1072), a leading clerical reformer. Little is known of Peter Damian's early life except that he was born at Ravenna, took the name "Damiani" from an elder brother who looked after him and sent him to school, and later studied the liberal arts at Faenza and Parma. His studies completed, he was teaching at Ravenna when he became attracted by the ascetic life led by groups of hermits in the area, a way of life that owed much to the influence of Romuald of Ravenna, whose biographer Peter was to become. About 1035 (or 1038) Peter joined a group of such hermits at Fonte Avellana, a hermitage in the Apennines whose origins are obscure but where memories of Romuald were apparently vivid. Though Peter frequently spent long periods away from Fonte Avellana, it was to remain his base of operations for the rest of his life.

It is in connection with Damian's teaching and his early years at Fonte Avellana that we first learn, from his disciple and biographer, John of Lodi, of that eloquence which made his writings so popular during the rest of the Middle Ages and which doubtless does much to explain his success as a reformer. John states that his sermons were capable of holding audiences for six hours at a time, and almost immediately after entering Fonte Avellana he was borrowed, for purposes of instruction, by similarly minded monasteries (Pomposa, near Ravenna, and S. Vincenzo, near Fossombrone).

It was in 1042, probably near the end of his stay at S. Vincenzo, that Peter wrote his biography of Romuald, and in doing so traced for himself, as it were, a model for his own actions and intent—as he said of Romuald, "to turn the whole world into a hermitage." Neither Romuald nor Peter came close to this goal, and Peter's phrase itself is an overstatement, since it is clear that neither of the two men aimed in practice at more than a wide diffusion of the ideals, and of some of the practices, of the hermits. In the early years after his biography of Romuald, however, Peter founded new hermitages and monasteries, or had existing ones entrusted to his care. These formed the nucleus of what later became a "congregation" of monasteries and hermitages, held together (as the congregations of Vallombrosa and Cîteaux were later held together) by a quasi-juridical "bond of charity" and centered at Fonte Avellana.

It was probably in the mid 1040's that Peter began to come to grips with an issue that plagued him—as it did his world—for some years to come: the validity of the sacraments performed by simoniacs. Simony was a problem that troubled the church throughout the Middle Ages, but at no time, perhaps, was the agitation against it so intense as in the second half of the eleventh century. In Italy the struggle seems to go back very largely to Romuald, with his most active Italian successors in this respect probably being Peter Damian and Giovanni Gualberti. The former took a "moderate" position that, while condemning simoniacs, held they could perform valid sacraments. Gualberti's position was that a simoniac could not perform a valid sacrament, which meant that bishops and priests consecrated—even gratis—by a simoniac had received invalid consecrations and therefore could not perform valid sacraments themselves. (Peter had been ordained gratis by a simoniac.) This position was later to become the basis for what have been called "liturgical strikes" in Tuscany and Lombardy, in which the laity were urged to boycott the services of allegedly simoniac priests.

Peter Damian naturally seconded the efforts in the late 1040's to use the papacy to reform the church at large, and he was not slow to remind popes of their duties in that regard. His first extant letter to a pope, that of 1045 to Gregory VI, warns that if energetic measures were not taken, the people's "entire hope for the renewal of the world" would be disappointed. Collaborating with Emperor Henry III in the latter's reform of the papacy, Peter attended at least some of the councils of Pope Leo IX, one of which occasioned the most extended discussion he has left of the question of simoniac sacraments, the *Liber gratissimus* of 1052. Appointed cardinal-bishop of Ostia in 1057 by Stephen IX, Peter was thenceforth (despite a number of threats to resign) a leading figure in the college of cardinals and was at least partly responsible for the drawing up of the papal election decree of 1059, in which Nicholas II defended his rather irregular election, took the first step toward concentrating papal elections in the hands of the cardinals, and spoke of imperial rights in papal elections in terms that remain controversial.

The question of simoniac sacraments was debated during the 1060's at a number of councils where Peter presumably found himself at odds with Cardinal Bishop Humbert of Silva Candida; Peter's references to Humbert, however, are always cordial and respectful. The simony problem also occasioned legations by Peter to Milan (1059–1060) and to Florence (1066), the first of which was notable for his successful assertion of the prerogatives of the see of St. Peter, the second for emotional altercations with Gualberti's adherents. Gualberti's views eventually won out in Florence, and it is possible that Damian modified some of his own views in the direction of Gualberti's.

Peter Damian stood in the intellectual tradition that led back through Gregory the Great to St. Augustine. He has acquired the reputation of an anti-intellectual largely because of the ideas expressed in his *De divina omnipotentia,* which culminates in a very close approach to the assertion that God can undo the done. On the one hand, Peter expresses, in many of his writings, a strong sense of God's omnipotence and of man's severe limitations; on the other, he was probably as learned as any man of his time, made ample use of the rhetoric he had been taught, and urged the schooling of clerics as one way to their reform. Like Romuald and Gualberti, Peter energetically advocated the adoption of the Augustinian ideal of a semimonastic life for the clergy, and it is sometimes held that he was one of the first to voice the ideal of apostolic poverty that spread in the following century and culminated in the mendicant orders.

BIBLIOGRAPHY

Sources. The most commonly used edition of Damian's works is that in *Patrologia latina,* CXLIV (1853) and CXLV (1853). Unfortunately, in an attempt to mark nineteen sermons commonly ascribed to Damian but really by Nicholas of Clairvaux, the editors of the *Patrologia latina* often marked the wrong sermons, a mistake that has occasioned a good deal of misinterpretation of Peter Damian's thought. The sermons that should have been marked as belonging to Nicholas are: 9, 11, 23, 26, 27, 29, 40, 43, 44, 47, 52, 55, 56, 58, 59, 60, the "anonymous" sermon after 61, 62, and 69. Also generally considered spurious are sermons 1, 7, 12, 70, and 71, and *opusculum* 28. Works by Peter Damian published since the *Patrologia* are in Giovanni Lucchesi, "Clavis S. Petri Damiani," in *Studi su s. Pier Damiano in onore del cardinale Amleto Giovanni Cicognani,* 2nd ed. (1970). Peter Damian's writings may also be found in *De divina omnipotentia: Lettre sur la toute-puissance divine,* André Cantin, ed. (1972). A critical edition of the *Liber gratissimus,* L. von Heinemann, ed., is in *Monumenta Germaniae historica: Libelli de lite,* I (1891), 15–75. See also *Discepta synodalis, ibid.,* 76–94. A number of Damian's works are translated into English in *St. Peter Damian: Selected Writings on the Spiritual Life,* Patricia McNulty, trans. (1959).

Studies. The pioneering work on the thorny problem of the chronology of Damian's works is J. B. Mittarelli and Anselmo Costadoni, *Annales Camaldulenses,* II (1756), revised in Franz Neukirch, *Das Leben des Petrus Damiani* (1875). Further revisions are Kennerly M. Woody, "Damiani and the Radicals" (diss., Columbia, 1966); and Giovanni Lucchesi, "Per una vita di San Pier Damiani," in *San Pier Damiano: Nel IX centenario della morte,* 2 vols. (1972), I: 13–179, II: 13–160. Studies in English are Owen Blum, *St. Peter Damian: His Teaching on the Spiritual Life* (1947); and John Joseph Ryan, *St. Peter Damiani and His Canonical Sources* (1956).

Two useful biographies are Fridolin Dressler, *Petrus Damiani: Leben und Werk* (1954); and Jean Leclercq, *St. Pierre Damian: Ermite et homme d'église* (1960). The Dressler biography contains an extensive bibliography, brought up to date in Kurt Reindel, "Neue Literatur zu Petrus Damiani," in *Deutsches Archiv für Erforschung des Mittelalters,* **32** (1976).

KENNERLY M. WOODY

[See also **Blessed Virgin Mary, Little Office of; Camaldolese, Order of; Church, Latin; Excommunication; Hermits, Eremitism; Humbert of Silva Candida; Reform, Idea of; Romuald of Ravenna, St.; Simony.**]

PETER AND ASEN, twelfth-century rulers of Bulgaria. With his brother Peter (*d.* 1197), Asen (*d.* 1196) led a Vlach-Bulgarian uprising in 1186 against Byzantium, liberating Bulgaria after 168 years of Byzantine rule. Then, with Cuman (Polovtsy) aid, they defended Bulgaria's newly won independence against a series of Byzantine attacks over the next decade and won recognition of Bulgaria's liberation in a treaty with Byzantium in 1188. Thus was established the Second Bulgarian Empire and the Asenović dynasty, which ruled

Bulgaria until 1257. Asen made Trnovo his capital; it remained the capital until the state fell to the Ottomans in 1393. The sources are confused about the relations between the two brothers in the years immediately following the initial uprising; but by 1188 Asen emerged as the dominant figure, having been crowned in that year by the newly created archbishop of Trnovo. Asen governed in Trnovo while Peter held Preslav. Asen was murdered in 1196 by a nobleman named Ivanko, who then was forced to flee to Byzantium when Trnovo was attacked by Peter. Peter ruled for only a year; he died in 1197 and was succeeded by their able younger brother Kalojan.

BIBLIOGRAPHY

John V. A. Fine, Jr., *The Early Medieval Balkans* (1982).

JOHN V. A. FINE, JR.

[See also **Bulgaria; Kalojan.**]

PETER OF BULGARIA (*d.* 969) acquired the Bulgarian throne upon his father, Symeon's, death in 927; initially his maternal uncle George Sursuvul was regent. They continued the ongoing war with Byzantium until they obtained an advantageous treaty in late 927. Byzantium recognized Peter's title "emperor of Bulgaria" and the autocephaly of the Bulgarian church under a patriarch; Peter also married Maria Lekapena, granddaughter of Emperor Romanos Lekapenos. Between 928 and 930 Peter suppressed two revolts by his brothers Ivan and Michael. Thereafter he kept Bulgaria at peace, enabling it to enjoy commerical prosperity until war broke out with Byzantium in 965. After the Russians, as Byzantine allies, invaded Bulgaria and defeated its army in 967, Peter suffered a stroke. He abdicated, to be succeeded by his son Boris II, and died two years later in a monastery. A religious man, Peter built many churches and was canonized by the Bulgarian church. During his reign the Bogomil heresy arose.

BIBLIOGRAPHY

John V. A. Fine, Jr., "A Fresh Look at Bulgaria Under Tsar Peter I (927–69)," in *Byzantine Studies,* 5 (1978), and *The Early Medieval Balkans* (1983).

JOHN V. A. FINE, JR.

[See also **Bogomilism; Bulgaria; Maria Lekapena.**]

PETER IV THE CEREMONIOUS (Pedro IV of Aragon, Pere III of Catalonia) (1319–1387), born at Balaguer, succeeded his father, Alfonso IV of Aragon (Alfons III of Catalonia), as king on 25 January 1336. He died at Barcelona. His fifty-year reign, though filled with wars, constituted the cultural climax of the Crown of Aragon, especially as regards law, science, and history. Peter's role as patron closely resembled that of Alfonso X of Castile. Like Alfonso, he was interested in law, astrology, poetry, and history, in Islamic and Jewish as well as Christian learning. Also like Alfonso, he used Jewish artists and scientists (in Peter's case from Majorca, Perpignan, Catalonia, and Andalusia) to write scientific treatises and devise scientific instruments. Peter also encouraged educated Christian administrators, who created a new prose style that was imitated by nonofficial writers and raised the standards of composition, particularly in Catalan.

As in Alfonso's court, the main influences on Peter's court were Eastern (astrology and medicine) and French (religious literature, poetry, and the novel in particular). Classical ideas appeared late in his reign, in Peter's famous eulogy of the Acropolis and in the document, inspired by Sallust, in which he declared his wish to be commemorated by a historian comparable with those of ancient Athens. Both documents are of 1380.

In 1346 Peter formally reorganized the royal archive. He collected an important library, part of which he left to the Cistercian monastery of Poblet, as an accompaniment to the visual presentation of his dynasty's history in the royal tombs he built there, the most unified dynastic mausoleum of medieval Spain. Peter's extreme attention to detail also appears in his supervision of work on other buildings, from palaces to dockyards. He attempted to create two new universities (Perpignan in 1350, Huesca in 1354) and to endow Lérida University with a theological faculty. He supported students of law and theology in foreign universities and encouraged original thinkers, notably the leading theologian Francesc Eiximenis.

The many translations promoted by Peter included one of the Koran (from Latin), legal texts of Maimonides (from Hebrew), and Arabic works on medicine and agriculture translated by Jewish scholars. Peter ordered a translation of Julius Frontinus' *Strategemata*; Catalan versions of Guido delle Colonne's *Historia destructionis Troiae* and Palladius' *De re rustica,* made by royal officials,

PETER IV THE CEREMONIOUS

survive. Mateu Adrià, a royal protonotary, translated Alfonso X's *Siete partidas* and James (Jaime) III of Majorca's *Leges palatinae.*

The *Siete partidas* provided a vernacular model for the systematic application of Roman law. Peter's *Tractat de cavalleria de Sant Jordi* is a Catalan version of portions of *Siete partidas* II; its preface contains theological considerations that recur in the prologue to Peter's own *Chronicle.* The Catalan *Ordinances* for the royal household and chancery (1344) expand James III's *Leges.* Later ordinances dealt with naval and financial questions. The final version of the Catalan maritime legal code, the *Libre del Consolat del mar,* was issued after Peter had made additions to it.

In 1360–1366 Peter's Christian and Jewish astronomers (Pere Gilbert, Dalmau Ses Planes, and Jacob Corsino) made new observations and drew up new tables calculated on the meridian of Barcelona, in Hebrew, Latin, and Catalan, which constituted a major advance on Alfonso X's *Tablas alfonsíes.* Peter's prologue shows that the inspiration for this work was pragmatic, the ability to use the movements of stars and planets as a guide to actions in this world. Royal letters show that this was how they were used. Peter said he believed that astrology could help him "to be fortunate and escape celestial misfortune."

The same pragmatic, patriotic inspiration appears in the few short poems by Peter that are known. Peter encouraged poets attached to his court and promoted the first Catalan poetic consistory (1338), in imitation of the existing consistory of Toulouse. His own ideas appear more clearly in his remarkable speeches to the Corts, in his personal letters—of which only a selection has been published—and in his *Chronicle.*

History was perhaps the predominant interest of Peter's life. He was deeply interested in the historical works commissioned by his subject Juan Fernández de Heredia, grand master of the Hospitalers from 1377 to 1396. Peter collected chronicles from other countries, especially France and Castile; he had Alfonso X's historical works partially translated. The Catalan adaptation of Vincent of Beauvais's *Speculum historiale* was entrusted to two Dominicans, Jaume Domènech and Antoni de Ginebreda. The *Chronicle of the Kings of Aragon and Counts of Barcelona* (*Cròniques dels reys d'Aragó e comtes de Barchinona,* or the *Crónica de San Juan de la Peña*), written at Pedro's command, was intended to match the official French and Castilian chronicles and to provide an introduction to the history of Peter's own reign. Written in the three official languages of the Crown of Aragon—Latin, Catalan, and Aragonese—it originally ended in 1336.

Peter's own chronicle is the fourth (the last to survive) of the great Catalan chronicles of the thirteenth and fourteenth centuries. It covers, unevenly, the period from 1319 to 1369. An appendix, probably partly due to Peter, continues to 1385. Over half of the *Crònica* was completed by 1375. The first redaction was probably finished by 1383, the second shortly thereafter. Peter's letters show that the work was drawn up by a number of royal officials, notably Bernat Descoll and Arnau de Torrelles, and closely revised by Peter, who, according to Abadal, "controlled the text, both in what was included and what was possibly excluded." Peter's intervention was responsible for many omissions and distortions but also for much of the work's interest. The *Chronicle* is dynastic history, intended to present the providential role of the house of Aragon in a popular style calculated to appeal to Peter's subjects as well as to instruct his successors. As the work of a major historical figure it differs greatly from other contemporary chronicles. It sheds light on Peter's complex character, his cunning and his caution, his legalism and his combativeness.

During the reigns of Peter's successors there was an increased influence of Italian humanism in the Crown of Aragon and more original achievements in poetry and the novel—achievements for which Peter's activities as cultural patron had laid the foundation.

BIBLIOGRAPHY

Sources. Crònica: Chronique catalane de Pierre IV d'Aragon III de Catalogne, dit le cérémonieux ou "del Punyalet," Amédée Pagès, ed. (1941). The English translation is *Pere III of Catalonia (Pedro IV of Aragon): Chronicle,* Mary Hillgarth, trans., J. N. Hillgarth, introduction and notes, 2 vols. (1980). The Catalan text is *Crònica general de Pere III,* A. J. Soberanas Lleó, ed. (1961). The Latin text is *Crónica de San Juan de la Peña,* A. Ubieto, ed. (1961). The Aragonese text, with the Latin, is *Historia de la corona de Aragón,* T. Ximénez de Embrun, ed. (1876). Also *Làs tàblàs astronómicas del rey Don Pedro el Ceremonioso,* J. Mª. Millás Vallicrosa, ed. (1962).

Other writings are in *Tractats de Cavalleria,* P. Bohigas, ed. (1947), 97–154; Ricard Albert and Joan Gassiot, eds., *Parlaments a les Corts Catalanes* (1928),

24–56; *Epistolari de Pere III,* Ramon Gubern, ed. (1955).

Documents may be found in Antoni Rubió i Lluch, *Documents per l'història de la cultura catalana mig-eval,* 2 vols. (1908–1921).

Studies. Jorge Rubió i Balaguer, "Literatura catalana," in *Historia general de las literaturas hispánicas,* Guillermo Díaz-Plaja, ed., I (1949), 708–718.

Specific studies include Ramón d'Abadal i de Vinyals, "Pedro el Ceremonioso y los comienzos de la decadencia política de Cataluña," in *Historia de España,* Ramón Menéndez Pidal, ed., XIV, 2nd ed. (1976); Mª. del C. Gómez Mutané, *La música en la casa real catalano-aragonesa durante los años 1336–1442,* I (1979); Josep Maria Madurell y Marimon, "Pere el Ceremoniós i les obres públiques," in *Analecta sacra Tarraconensia,* **11** (1935), 371–393, and "El palau reial major de Barcelona," in *Analecta sacra Tarraconensia,* **12** (1936), **13** (1937–1940), **14** (1941); Jordi Rubió i Balaguer, "Sobre els orígens de l'humanisme a Catalunya," in *Bulletin of Spanish Studies,* **24** (1947); Antoni Rubió i Lluch, "Estudi sobre la elaboració de la Crònica de Pere I Ceremoniós," in *Anuari de l'institut d'estudis Catalans,* **3** (1909–1910), and "La cultura catalana en el regnat de Pere III," in *Estudis universitaris Catalans,* **8** (1914); Francisco Sevillano Colom, "Apuntes para el estudio de la Cancillería de Pedro IV el Ceremonioso," in *Anuario de historia del derecho español,* **20** (1950).

J. N. HILLGARTH

[See also **Aragon, Crown of; Catalan Literature; Eiximenis, Francesc.**]

PETER (*d.* 1326), metropolitan of Kiev and all Russia (1308–1326), who by transferring the metropolitan's permanent residence from Kiev to northern Russia contributed greatly to the political rise of Moscow. Formerly the head of a monastery in Galicia, he was presented to the patriarchate of Constantinople as candidate for the metropolitanate by the Galician prince Yurii I (*r.* 1324/1325–1340), who opposed the nomination of a "northern" candidate. The Galician origin of Peter did not prevent him from becoming a staunch supporter of northern claims of supremacy among Russian principalities. A close friend of the Muscovite prince, Ivan I Kalita (*r.* 1325–1341), he presided over the building of the first stone church in the Moscow Kremlin—the original church of the Dormition—and was buried in it in 1326.

BIBLIOGRAPHY

The two contemporary lives of Peter are published in B. S. Angelov, *Iz starata Bulgarska, Russka i Serbska literatura* (1958), and in Makary, *Istoriya Russkoy Tserkvi,* IV, 1 (1866). General information and bibliography are in John Meyendorff, *Byzantium and the Rise of Moscow* (1981), 93–94, 148–154.

JOHN MEYENDORFF

[See also **Muscovy, Rise of.**]

PETER, MASTER (*fl.* early twelfth century), a Russian architect named in a late local chronicle as builder of the Yur'ev (St. George) monastery church near Novgorod (begun 1119). Peter is particularly known for integrating asymmetrical stair towers into the main body of the church building and for his interesting use of proportions inside and out. His Yur'ev monastery church is particularly noteworthy for its clear articulation of the facades: horizontally by two levels of niches and windows,

Yur'ev (St. George) monastery church, Novgorod, showing the square stair tower projecting from the sanctuary. Designed by Master Peter, 1119–1130. PHOTO: WILLIAM BRUMFIELD

and vertically by engaged arches and pilasters reflecting the internal divisions of the building. Peter is sometimes thought also to have designed the St. Nicholas Church in the Market and the Nativity of the Virgin Church of the Anton'ev (St. Anthony) monastery. Both churches are in Novgorod and almost contemporary with the Yur'ev monastery church.

BIBLIOGRAPHY

Hubert Faensen and Vladimir Ivanov, *Early Russian Architecture* (1975), 367–370; Igor Grabar, ed., *Istoria russkogo isskusstva,* I (1911), 171–180; Igor Grabar *et al.*, eds., *Istoria russkogo iskusstva,* II (1954), 24–30; Mikhail K. Karger, *Novgorod the Great* (1973), 147–152, 210–212, 219–225.

GEORGE P. MAJESKA

[See also **Novgorod; Russian Architecture.**]

PETER AUREOLI (*ca.* 1280–1322) was a French Franciscan who from his earliest days in the order seems to have been a good friend of Pope John XXII. Peter testifies to this relationship in the dedicatory note to his chief work, *Scriptum super primum Sententiarum;* their common origin in the county of Quercy in southern France, coupled with the pope's consecration of Peter as archbishop of Aix-en-Provence in 1321, provides further evidence of their friendship.

In his relatively short life, Peter established himself as a prominent Scholastic. William of Ockham, for example, quotes Peter rather extensively (in order to criticize him) in his own *Scriptum* on the *Sentences,* in the very important question dealing with intuitive cognition. In fact, in this passage Ockham laments having had so little opportunity to study Peter's work. After lecturing at Bologna (*ca.* 1312), Peter probably lectured at Toulouse (*ca.* 1314), and from 1316 to 1318 he taught at Paris. The appointment to the prestigious chair at Paris by his powerful opponent, the new Franciscan minister general, Michael of Cesena, has puzzled some modern scholars. It is possible that his friend John XXII had a hand in this advancement, for in 1318 the pope wrote a letter to the chancellor of the University of Paris, asking that Peter be promoted to master of theology. It would, however, be a mistake to imagine that Peter owed his success only to fortunate connections. He was a competent theologician and philosopher, often critical of predecessors like Thomas Aquinas and Duns Scotus, and on occasion innovative.

It is sometimes suggested that Peter came under the influence of Duns Scotus while a student at Paris in the early fourteenth century. His defense of the doctrine of the Immaculate Conception has tempted some to draw this connection with the Subtle Doctor, Scotus, who is celebrated for his support of that doctrine. The available evidence, however, shows little likelihood that Peter could have been a student of Scotus'.

BIBLIOGRAPHY

The edition of Peter's chief work is *Scriptum super primum Sententiarum,* Eligius M. Buytaert, ed. (1952). See also Stephen Brown, "Avicenna and the Unity of the Concept of Being: The Interpretations of Henry of Ghent, Duns Scotus, Gerard of Bologna, and Peter Aureoli," in *Franciscan Studies,* n.s. **25** (1965); Francis Kelley, "Walter Chatton vs. Aureoli and Ockham Regarding the Universal Concept," *ibid.,* n.s. **41** (1981).

FRANCIS KELLEY

[See also **Duns Scotus, John; John XXII, Pope; Ockham, William of; Philosophy and Theology, Western European.**]

PETER COMESTOR (Peter Manducator) (*ca.* 1100–1178), theologian, was born in Troyes and became dean of its cathedral church (St. Peter's) in 1147. He was also a canon at the abbey of St. Loup near Troyes. It seems that he had heard Peter Abelard and had been a student of John of Tours before going to Paris. Well before 1159 he had settled in that city, where he studied under Peter Lombard and then taught theology. Sometime between 1164 and 1168 Peter resigned his chair of theology and became chancellor of the Paris cathedral school; he retained that position until his death. He was buried at the abbey of St. Victor, probably because of his close ties with the Victorines and his association with the affiliated abbey of canons regular at St. Loup.

Peter's most important contribution to theology is the *Historia scholastica* (dedicated 1169). It enjoyed a tremendous popularity throughout the Middle Ages and was a "set book" in the theological curriculum. Originally written in Latin, it was translated into most of the European vernaculars.

Very quickly Peter became known as the "Master of the *Histories.*"

In the *Historia,* Peter provided a foundation for the study of the Bible and of theology as outlined in Hugh of St. Victor's *Didascalicon.* He presents a careful chronological reckoning of the history of the Bible from Genesis through the Gospels. (Peter of Poitiers extended it through Acts.) Apart from the usual patristic authors, one of his principal sources for the Octateuch was the work of a contemporary, Andrew of St. Victor. Peter also made extensive use of the *Jewish Antiquities* of Josephus. Through his work much Hebrew lore and learning became known in the Latin West.

In addition to the *Histories,* Peter left some 150 sermons that frequently employ theme texts from the Hebrew Scriptures. Most often he gives these texts a moral interpretation—for example, exhorting his hearers to a holier way of life. The sermons complement the *Histories* and were used as models for preaching.

Of Peter's other works, only the *Sententiae de sacramentis* and a few theological *quaestiones* have been printed. The *Sententiae* (1165–1170) are largely an abridgment of Peter Lombard's discussion of the first four sacraments. The introduction to this work influenced many subsequent works of the same genre. In the *Sententiae* Peter seems to have been the first to use the Latin equivalent of "transubstantiation" in relation to the normative Roman Catholic doctrine of the Eucharist. The tract on penance occupies nearly half of the *Sententiae.* Finally, Peter's *quaestiones* are a valuable witness to the oral teaching of Peter Lombard.

Peter also wrote commentaries on the Gospels, a gloss on the twelfth-century *Glossa ordinaria* on the Bible, a gloss on the *Magna glossatura* of Lombard, and perhaps also a gloss on Lombard's *Sentences.*

In his *Divine Comedy,* Dante puts Peter Comestor next to Hugh of St. Victor in the outer circle of lights in the fourth heaven of Paradise (*Paradiso,* canto XII).

BIBLIOGRAPHY

Sources. Historia scholastica and the *Sermons* are in *Patrologica latina,* CXCVIII (1855), 1045–1844; for *Sententiae de sacramentis,* Raymond M. Martin, appendix to *Maître Simon et son groupe: De sacramentis,* Heinrich Weisweiler, ed. (1937); for *quaestiones,* Jean B. Pitra, ed., *Analecta novissima spicilegii solesmensis: Altera continuatio,* II (1888), 98–187.

Studies. Ignatius Brady, "Peter Manducator and the Oral Teachings of Peter Lombard," in *Antonianum,* **41** (1966); "Pierre Comestor," in *Dictionnaire du theólogie catholique;* Johannes S. Schneyer, "Repertorium der lateinischen Sermones des Mittelaters für die Zeit von 1150–1350," in *Beiträge zur Geschichte der Philosophie und Theologie des Mittelalters: Texte und Untersuchungen,* **43,** Heft 4 (1972); Beryl Smalley, *The Study of the Bible in the Middle Ages,* 3rd ed. (1982); Friedrich Stegmüller, *Repertorium biblicum medii aevi,* IV (1954) and IX (1977).

MARK A. ZIER

[See also **Andrew of St. Victor; Bible; Exegesis, Latin; Hugh of St. Victor; Peter Lombard.**]

PETER GETADARZ. See **Petros Getadarj.**

PETER JOHN OLIVI (1247/1248–1298), philosopher and theologian. Born in Serignan, near Béziers in southern France, he entered the Franciscan order at the age of twelve, serving his novitiate at Béziers. After a period of study in Paris, he began his teaching career in the 1270's as lector in the Franciscan houses of southern France, probably at Montpellier and Narbonne, perhaps elsewhere as well. By the early 1280's he was a prolific and respected scholar. For example, in 1279 his aid was solicited in connection with the writing of the papal bull *Exiit qui seminat,* issued by Nicholas III.

Nevertheless, during these same years a succession of quarrels and accusations kept Peter from becoming a master and eventually resulted in his censure. In 1283 the minister general, Bonagratia S. Giovanni in Persiceto, selected a committee of seven Parisian scholars who examined Olivi's works and censured a series of propositions. These included theological views, such as Olivi's suggestion that marriage was not a sacrament in the full sense of the word; philosophical views, including his refusal to identify the intellective soul as the form of the human body; and views on Franciscan poverty, especially his insistence that the Franciscan vow bound its adherents not only to lack of ownership, but also to restricted use of whatever goods were placed at their disposal. This last issue may have been the most important one. Olivi's argument for restricted use (*usus pauper*) and his insistence that Franciscans could never be dispensed from it made

PETER JOHN OLIVI

him chief spokesman for a reforming faction later known as the Spirituals. Opponents of his position argued that it put undue strain on Franciscan consciences and hindered friars from performing duties assigned them by the church.

That fall Olivi was summoned to Avignon and forced to accept the so-called *Letter of the Seven Seals,* in which the commission set forth their own views on these subjects. Olivi's works were banned, and he was denied permission to confront his censors; yet in 1285 he finally managed to gain the documents necessary for a reasoned defense and addressed an apologia to the committee. There is no record of a reply, but his effort may not have been wasted. Arlotto of Prato, a former member of the examining committee who had been elected minister general in 1285, summoned Olivi to Paris so that he could defend himself personally. There is no reliable evidence on the immediate outcome of this interview, but in 1287, at the general chapter held at Montpellier, Olivi was allowed to clarify his views on poverty; he was then appointed lector at the convent of S. Croce in Florence. He stayed there until 1289, when he was chosen to perform the same function at Montpellier. The last decade of his life seems to have been spent teaching in southern France.

When he died at Narbonne, Peter John Olivi was venerated by many, and his tomb became the goal of pilgrimages. This unofficial cult might have led to canonization in time if other factors had not tipped the balance in favor of condemnation.

By 1298 the order was increasingly polarized, and the Spirituals were losing ground. In 1299 the minister general, John of Murrovalle, launched a persecution of the Spirituals which continued until 1309. Olivi's works were again banned. Although his views on poverty were central in this renewed attack, opponents of the Spirituals tried to discredit Olivi as thoroughly as possible by reviving the theological and philosophical charges of the 1280's. By 1309, when Pope Clement V intervened and attempted to repair the rift within the order, Olivi's orthodoxy had become such a bone of contention that it was one of the four main issues Clement wanted settled. In 1312, at the Council of Vienne, Clement tried to end all dispute with two bulls. One, *Exivi de paradiso,* addressed the poverty question. It demanded reform and attempted to describe the relationship between restricted use and the vow in terms which would have made little sense to Olivi or his opponents. The other bull, *Fidei catholocae fundamento,* announced that the lance pierced Christ's side after his death on the cross; that baptism confers informing grace and the virtues; and that the intellective soul is the form of the human body. Olivi's name was not mentioned in the bull; yet all three assertions implicitly refuted views which had been ascribed to him by his enemies, and which, in at least the first two cases, he probably held.

Neither the poverty question nor that of Olivi's orthodoxy was really settled. Between 1318 and 1326 Pope John XXII conducted an investigation leading to the condemnation of Olivi's Apocalypse commentary and perhaps of other works as well. This action was closely related to John's support of the Franciscan minister general, Michael of Cesena, who was attempting to suppress the Spirituals. In the Apocalypse commentary, Olivi had argued that Francis and his rule inaugurated the third age (*statūs*) of the Holy Spirit predicted by Joachim of Fiore (*d.* 1202). Olivi had pictured his own time as one of escalating conflict between "spiritual men" and carnal opponents of the new era. Moreover, he had suggested that the mystical antichrist would soon gain control over the church and persecute the godly. Once pressed by John and the order, the embattled Spirituals saw Olivi's scenario as a prophecy of their own situation. Thus, they converted vague speculation into an apologia for rebellion.

Olivi received little scholarly attention before the end of the nineteenth century. Since then, historians have invested him with increasingly greater significance in a wide variety of areas. He has been described as the most acute economic thinker of the Middle Ages, as a precursor of nominalism, and as the author of the first serious attempt to formulate a doctrine of papal infallibility. His views on Franciscan poverty are now seen as essentially moderate, an attempt to preserve original Franciscan ideals while accepting the new functions assumed by the order in the course of the thirteenth century. Nevertheless, since less than half of Olivi's extensive writings have been published, a definitive appraisal of his contribution cannot be expected until substantially more editorial work has been done.

BIBLIOGRAPHY

David Burr, "The Persecution of Peter Olivi," in *Transactions of the American Philosophical Society,* 66 (1976), which is an introduction to Olivi's life and thought. See also David Burr and David Flood, "Peter Olivi: On Poverty and Revenue," in *Franciscan Studies,* **40** (1980), David Burr, "The Correctorium Controversy and the Origins of the *usus pauper* Controversy," in *Speculum,* **60** (1985), and "Olivi, Apocalyptic Expectation, and Visionary Experience," in *Traditio,* **41** (1985); David Flood, ed., *Peter Olivi's Rule Commentary* (1972); Servus Gieben, "Bibliographia Oliviana (1885–1967)," in *Collectanea franciscana,* **38** (1968); Julius Kirshner and Kimberly Lo Prete, "Peter John Olivi's Treatises on Contracts of Sale, Usury, and Restitution: Minorite Economics or Minor Works?" in *Quaderni fiorentini,* **13** (1984); Brian Tierney, *Origins of Papal Infallibility,* 1150–1350 (1972).

DAVID BURR

[See also **Beguins; Clement V, Pope; Councils, Western (1311–1449); Franciscans; Heresies, Western European; Joachim of Fiore; John XXII, Pope.**]

PETER LANGTOFT (*fl.* 1271–1307), canon of the Augustinian priory of Bridlington in Yorkshire. He served as attorney (procurator) there from 1271 to 1286 and was the author of an Anglo-Norman French *Chronicle* of the history of England beginning with Brutus. Composed in alexandrine laisses, the *Chronicle* is patriotic and virulently anti-Scottish in outlook. Its first two parts are unoriginal, but the third section, on Edward I (1272–1307), is a valuable firsthand account. Robert Mannyng of Brunne translated the latter two parts into English in 1338.

BIBLIOGRAPHY

Sources. Jean-Claude Thiolier, ed., "Édition critique et commentée du 'Règne d'Édouard Ier' de Pierre de Langtoft" (thèse d'état, Univ. de Paris-IV, 1978); Thomas Wright, ed., *The Chronicle of Pierre de Langtoft, in French Verse from the Earliest Period to the Death of Edward I,* 2 vols. (1866–1868).

Study. Robert P. Stepsis, "Pierre de Langtoft's Chronicle: An Essay in Medieval Historiography," in *Medievalia et humanistica,* n.s., 3 (1972).

ELLEN T. WEHNER

[See also **Anglo-Norman Literature; Edward I of England.**]

PETER LOMBARD (*ca.* 1095–1160), theologian. Born in the town of Lumellogno near Novara in Lombardy, Peter received his early education in Italy. In 1133 Bishop Humbert of Lucca commended him to Bernard of Clairvaux in order that he might continue his studies in France. Peter studied theology first at Rheims, and he then went to Paris, initially to the abbey of St. Victor. He achieved a reputation as a "celebrated theologian" by 1144 and became a canon at the cathedral church about 1143–1145. By 1147 he had become a subdeacon, and in 1148 he took part in the Rheims consistory of Pope Eugene III, which dealt with the controversial teachings of Gilbert of Poitiers. Late in 1154 he traveled to Rome, where he encountered John Damascene's work *De fide orthodoxa* in the recent Latin translation of Burgundio of Pisa. By 1157 he was priest and archdeacon, and following the death of Bishop Theobald he was elected bishop of Paris in 1159. He died in office the next year.

Peter's authentic works include a *Glossa in Psalmos,* a *Glossa in Epistolas beati Pauli* (which together were known as the *Magna glossatura*), more than thirty sermons (undated), and the *Sententiae in IV libris distinctae,* the work that earned him the title "Master of the *Sentences.*"

According to Herbert of Bosham, a student of Lombard and later secretary to Thomas Becket, Lombard began to compose his *Glossa in Psalmos* shortly after arriving in France as a private composition of spiritual edification, and not for teaching. A work of moral and spiritual exegesis, this *Glossa* shows little interest in theological doctrine per se and depends almost entirely on Anselm of Laon's *Glossa in Psalmos* and the *Media glossatura* of Gilbert of Poitiers. According to Herbert, only a short time before his elevation to the episcopacy did Peter in fact begin to read this work publicly in the schools, at which time he also started to correct it. Thus, although Peter began to compose this work shortly after his arrival in France (*ca.* 1135–1136), it was only published some twenty years later.

Lombard's next major work was the *Glossa in Epistolas,* sometimes called the *Collectanea.* This work exhibits much more mature theological reflection than his first *Glossa.* In addition to the glosses on Paul by Anselm and Gilbert, Lombard also used that of Florus of Lyons (a major source of Lombard's citations of Augustine), the anonymous *Summa sententiarum,* and various other theological opuscula.

Great confusion has surrounded the dating of this work. It now seems that the apparent witness of

Gerhoch of Reichersberg (used to date the work ante 1142) can be discounted. Moreover, certain theological questions appear in the earlier—but not the later—recension of it that seem to be inspired by the debates over Gilbert's teaching, from about 1147 to 1148. Thus it seems that the earlier redaction of this *Glossa* was composed after the consistory of 1148. It did not reach its final form until after 1154, when the text was corrected against Burgundio's translation of *De fide orthodoxa,* and the questions of the earlier redaction were transferred to the *Sententiae.* Indeed, Peter may have continued to revise this *Glossa* until his episcopal election in 1159.

Lombard's most celebrated work is the *Sententia.* Here he sets out the whole of Christian doctrine: Book I treats of the Trinity and the divine essence; Book II, Creation and the Fall; Book III, the Incarnation, the Redemption, the virtues of Christ and Christian virtues in general; Book IV, the sacraments and eschatology. Inspired by Peter Abelard's *Sic et non,* and following a method similar to that of Gratian, Lombard proceeds by seeking to reconcile apparently conflicting authorities by a thoughtful application of dialectics.

Peter's sources for the *Sententiae* demonstrate the comprehensive nature of the work: the Bible, Hilary, Augustine, Julian of Toledo, Ivo of Chartres, the *Glossa ordinaria* on the Bible, Abelard, Hugh of St. Victor, the *Summa Sententiarum,* Gratian, John Damascene, as well as his own glosses.

It now seems that the *Sententiae* were composed during the period from 1155 to 1158. Their terminus a quo is fixed by Lombard's use of Damascene (post 1154). He composed the work and read it to his students during the years 1155–1157 at the end of which period it was published. Peter read the *Sententiae* a second time in 1157–1158, emending and adding to the text as he went along, though without issuing a second edition. The works of his students, John of Cornwall and Peter Comestor, attest to this second reading. The terminus ad quem is fixed by a note at the end of the text in a manuscript of the second half of the twelfth century (Troyes, Bibliothèque Municipale MS 900 folio 225vb) that reads: "This book was composed [*conscriptus est*] in 1158."

The genius of this work lies in its organization and in its brevity. It was ideally suited to the teaching of theology and was a standard text in the theological curriculum into the seventeenth century. As part of his teaching responsibility, every master of theology commented in depth on at least part of the *Sententiae.* Among such theologians are to be numbered Thomas Aquinas, Bonaventure, Albertus Magnus, John Duns Scotus, William of Ockham, John Gerson, and Martin Luther.

A number of Lombard's opinions gave rise to considerable debate. In his own lifetime he was implicated in the error of christological nihilism, namely that Christ, insofar as he is *human,* has no substantial reality. With regard to the trinitarian processions, he was accused by some at the end of the twelfth century of holding that the divine persons were something other than the divine essence, but his teaching was approved by the Fourth Lateran Council (1215). His teaching on the indwelling of the Holy Spirit, whereby the love of God that dwells in a person is not some created reality but rather the very person of the Holy Spirit, was not widely accepted in the Middle Ages, though it was taken up again by the Protestant reformers.

In his *Divine Comedy,* Dante puts Lombard next to Gratian in the inner circle of lights in the fourth heaven of Paradise (*Paradiso,* canto X).

BIBLIOGRAPHY

Sources. Petrus Lombardus, *Sententiae in IV libris distinctae,* 3rd ed., 2 vols in 3 (1971–1981); Johann B. Schneyer, "Repertorium der lateinischen Sermones des Mittelalters, für die Zeit von 1150–1350," in *Beiträge zur Geschichte des Philosophie und Theologie des Mittelalters,* **43.4** (1972), 700–704; Friedrich Stegmüller, *Repertorium biblicum medii aevi,* IV (1954), nos. 6625–6669.2, IX (1977), nos. 6625–6668, and *Repertorium commentariorum in Sententias Petri Lombardi,* 2 vols. (1947) (full texts of commentaries on Lombard), supplemented by Victorin Doucet, *Commentaires sur les Sentences: Supplément au répertoire de M. Frédéric Stegmüller* (1954).

Studies. I. Brady, O.F.M., "Peter Lombard, Canon of Notre Dame," in *Recherches de théologie ancienne et médiévale,* 32 (1965); Joseph de Ghellinck, *Le mouvement théologique du XIIe siècle,* 2nd ed. (1948); Elizabeth F. Rogers, *Peter Lombard and the Sacramental System* (1917); Beryl Smalley and George Lacombe, "The Lombard's Commentary on Isaias and Other Fragments," in *New Scholasticism,* 5 (1931).

MARK A. ZIER

[See also **Aquinas, St. Thomas; Bible; Bonaventure, St.; Exegesis, Latin; Gilbert of Poitiers; Peter Comestor; Philosophy and Theology, Western European.**]

PETER OF BLOIS (*ca.* 1135–1211). Almost all our knowledge of Peter of Blois is gleaned from his letters. He received the best education then available: grammar and literature at Tours and Paris (perhaps with John of Salisbury), law at Bologna, and theology, again at Paris, where Peter Lombard lectured. But Peter of Blois put rhetoric before theology and law, and began a career as a tutor and secretary. In 1166, with a party of Frenchmen, he went to Sicily as tutor to William II, the young Sicilian king; about a year later illness saved him from the massacre of the French by local opposition. Not finding a subsequent satisfactory situation in France, Peter finally chose "exile" in England about 1174. For various employers he traveled on diplomatic missions to France and Italy; he wrote letters for, among others, the archbishops of Rouen, Sens, and York, Henry II, Queen Eleanor, and even Pope Alexander III; he was an important member of the households of Richard, Baldwin, and Hubert, archbishops of Canterbury. He accumulated minor benefices at Chartres, Rouen, Bayeux, Salisbury, Ripon, and Wolverhampton, but rose no higher than archdeacon of Bath (1182) and of London (*ca.* 1200).

Peter mentions little but tribulation in connection with his ecclesiastical positions. Although failing to attain wealth or high position, as a ready writer Peter was confident of immortality through his pen. He composed treatises on moral and religious topics, a manual on letter writing entitled *Libellus de arte dictandi rhetorice* (Cambridge University Library, MS Dd. ix. 381 fols. 115–121), and some highly accomplished lyrics preserved in the *Carmina Burana.*

The most absorbing and successful, however, were his letters. It was a novelty for someone to publish his own letters during his lifetime, but Peter published his own collection in 1184, and continued to rework and circulate it for about twenty years. More than 250 manuscripts survive, and they were reproduced up to the seventh century. They provided models for every type of letter, with eloquent language and sound moral views required for students to learn by heart, and earnest advice for most situations a literate cleric would encounter. Surprisingly most letters, even the *comminatoriae* (denunciations), are addressed to identifiable persons, mainly churchmen in England and France. Many touch on notable issues of the day: the murder of Becket, Henry II and his conflict with his sons, the Third Crusade and Richard I's captivity, the growth of the Cathar hersey, and the interdict against King John. Peter's notorious tendency to use other men's words enabled him to transmit his own wide reading, both traditional and contemporary: countless quotations and examples from the classics and even more from the Bible, as well as pronouncements of civil and canon law, fragments of Aristotle, passages from a Salernitan medical treatise, and Arab astronomy from Toledo. Later Peter attempted Scholastic disputation, but was out of sympathy with that approach. He excels his contemporaries, however, when he can use his genuine literary and historical sensitivity, discussing such problems as the institution and abolition of the old law, the development of heresy, or the text of the Mass. In his late letters and the unpublished *De fide* (a collection of arguments used against heresies [Oxford, Jesus College, MS 38, fols. 84–103]) Peter shows an emotional fervor akin to that of the Cistercians, and an honest facing of his own doubts.

BIBLIOGRAPHY

Sources. Petri Blesensis Bathoniensis archidiaconi opera, John A. Giles, ed., 4 vols. (1847–1848), repr. in *Patrologia latina,* CCVII (1904). Unprinted letters are in Erfurt, Wissenschaftliche Allgemeinbibliothek, MS Amplonianus F. 71, fols. 186–197, 200–224; Bamberg Staatsbibliothek, MS B. iv. 38, fols. 86–110. See *The Late Letters of Peter of Blois,* Elizabeth Revell, ed.

Studies. Martin Camargo, "The *Libellus de arte dictandi rhetorice* attributed to Peter of Blois," in *Speculum,* 59 (1984); Peter Dronke, "Peter of Blois and Poetry at the Court of Henry II," in *Mediaeval Studies,* 38 (1976); Joseph Gildea, "Extant Manuscripts of *Compendium in Job* by Peter of Blois," in *Scriptorium,* 30 (1976); Ethel C. Higonnet, "Spiritual Ideas in the Letters of Peter of Blois," in *Speculum,* 50 (1975); Joseph Armitage Robinson, *Somerset Historical Essays* (1921), 100–140; Richard W. Southern, *The Making of the Middle Ages* (1953), 210–215, and *Mediaeval Humanism and Other Studies* (1970), 105–132.

ELIZABETH REVELL

[See also **Dictamen; Rhetoric, Western European.**]

PETER OF CANDIA. See **Alexander V.**

PETER OF MARICOURT. See **Peter Peregrinus of Maricourt.**

PETER OF PISA (*fl.* eighth century) was one of the first scholars drawn to the court of Charlemagne as a participant in the intellectual and religious revival known as the Carolingian renaissance. He probably served in the court of the Lombard kings of northern Italy before joining Charlemagne after Lombardy had been conquered by the Franks. Peter, who instructed the king in Latin and answered his questions on the biblical Book of Daniel, enjoyed a close personal relationship with Charlemagne. He was also the court grammarian and he prepared a grammar book, wrote poems, and compiled a small treatise on Daniel. A debate he had in 767, while still in Italy, with the Jew Lullus, does not survive. Peter died before 799.

BIBLIOGRAPHY

Franz Brunhölzl, *Geschichte der lateinischen Literatur des Mittelalters,* I (1975), 249–250; Michael Lapidge, "The Authorship of the Adonic Verses 'ad Fidolium' Attributed to Columbanus," in *Studi medievali,* n.s. **18** (1977); Wilhelm Levison and Heinz Löwe, eds., *Wattenbach-Levison: Deutschlands Geschichtsquellen in Mittelalter,* II. Heft (1953); Max Manitius, *Geschichte der lateinischen Literatur des Mittelalters,* I (1911, repr. 1974), 452–456.

JOHN J. CONTRENI

[See also **Carolingian Latin Poetry; Classical Literary Studies.**]

PETER OF SPAIN (Petrus Hispanus). In his *Speculum iudiciale* (*ca.* 1271–1276), Guillaume Durand lists twenty-three writers who achieved special eminence in glossing the *Decretum* of Gratian. On this list is "Petrus Hispanus," and manuscripts with his decretist glosses of the 1170's are numerous. In the 1190's, when the attention of canon-law writers began to be directed to the papal decretals, Peter became a decretalist as well as a decretist. After Bernard of Pavia published (*ca.* 1188–1192) his *Compilatio prima,* the earliest of the *Quinque compilationes antiquae,* Peter wrote, between 1193 and 1198, an entire apparatus of glosses to Bernard's *Compilatio.* Although no complete manuscript of this apparatus has survived, there are many decretalist commentaries that make heavy use of it. According to Alphons Stickler, Peter's glosses consist largely of elucidations of the decretals in light of Roman law; Peter had been a student of the preeminent Roman law glossator Azo. The elder Peter of Spain is also sometimes called Petrus Hispanus Bononiensis (of Bologna) to distinguish him from his younger namesake.

During the 1220's two documents attest the presence of "Petrus Hispanus" as a professor of canon law at Bologna and Padua. This Lisbon-born Peter of Spain the Younger, sometimes called Petrus Hispanus Portugalensis, wrote *Notabilia ad Compilationem quartam* (after 1215). He also may have written two small treatises, *De ordine iudiciorum,* expositions of Roman-law procedure. This was a genre of civil-law commentary largely developed by canonists. Peter's particular contributions were later conflated with similar works of other authorities, such as Bartolus (Bartolo da Sassoferrato).

Outside the realm of canon law the most eminent Peter of Spain was undoubtedly Pedro Juliano Rebolo or Rebello (Petrus Hispanus Portugalensis), *ca.* 1205–1277, who was renowned both as a philosopher and as a physician. The popular medieval medical handbook *Thesaurus pauperum* has traditionally been regarded as his work, although modern editors have recently questioned his authorship. The most famous of his many writings was his enduringly popular textbook of logic, *Tractatus,* better known as *Summule logicales.* On 13 September 1276 he was elected pope as a compromise candidate acceptable to both the French and Italian curial parties. His brief reign as Pope John XXI ended with his death on 20 May 1277.

BIBLIOGRAPHY

There is no printed edition of any work written by the first two Peters of Spain discussed in the article. Many of the elder Peter's glosses are printed either in the commentaries of other canonists or in modern scholarly works.

On the elder Peter, see Franz Gillman, "Des Petrus Hispanus Glosse zur Compilatio prima auf der Würzburger Universitätsbibliothek," in *Archiv fur katholischen Kirchenrecht,* **102** (1922); Stephan Kuttner, *Repertorium der Kanonistik (1140–1234)* (1937), *passim;* Alphons M. Stickler, "Decretisti bolognesi dimenticati," in *Studia gratiana,* **3** (1955).

On Peter of Spain the Younger, see Helmut Coing, *Handbuch der Quellen und Literatur der neueren europäischen Privatrechtsgeschichte,* I (1973).

The most recent edition of Peter of Spain's (John XXI's) logical treatise is *Tractatus, Called Afterwards Summule logicales,* L. M. de Rijk, ed. (1972), which includes useful biographical and bibliographical sections. For a Latin/English edition, see Joseph P. Mullally, ed.and trans., *The "Summulae logicales" of Peter of Spain* (1945).

ELAINE GOLDEN ROBISON

[See also **Azo; Decretals; Decretist; Decretum; Dialectic; Durand, Guillaume; Gratian; Law, Canon: After Gratian.**]

PETER OLIVI. See **Peter John Olivi.**

PETER PECKHAM (Peter Fetcham, Pierre d'Abernun) (*fl.* thirteenth century). An English cleric, probably of Norman descent, he was author of three works in Anglo-Norman French verse: the *Lumiere as Lais* (1267), a compendium of theology for the laity modeled on the *Elucidarium* of Honorius Augustodunensis; the *Vie de saint Richard* (1270–1271), a translation of Ralph Bocking's Latin *Life and Miracles* of St. Richard Wyche, bishop of Chichester; and the *Secret des secrets* (after 1267), a book of advice on ruling and hygiene translated from Pseudo-Aristotle's *Secretum secretorum* and completed with material from the *Liber almansoris,* the Latin version of the *Kitāb al-ṭibb al-Manṣūrī* by al-Rāzī.

BIBLIOGRAPHY

Sources. "Vie de saint Richard, évêque de Chichester," Alfred T. Baker, ed., in *Revue des langues romanes,* **53** (1910), a partial edition; Charles-Victor Langlois, "La lumiere as Lais," in his *Vie en France au moyen âge,* IV (1928), a summary of the *Lumiere; Le secré de secrez, by Pierre d'Abernun of Fetcham,* Oliver A. Beckerlegge, ed. (1944).

Studies. Mary Dominica Legge, "Pierre de Peckham and His '*Lumiere as Lais,*'" in *Modern Language Review,* **24** (1929); Jean Monfrin, "La place du 'Secret des secrets' dans la littérature française médiévale," in W. F. Ryan and Charles B. Schmitt, eds., *Pseudo-Aristotle, the "Secret of Secrets": Sources and Influences* (1982).

ELLEN T. WEHNER

[See also **Anglo-Norman Literature; Honorius Augustodunensis; Rāzī, Abū Bakr Muḥammad ibn Zakarīya al-.**]

PETER PEREGRINUS OF MARICOURT (*fl.* 1260's) wrote the earliest extant scientific treatise specifically concerned with magnetism, *Epistola Petri Peregrini de Maricourt and Sygerium de Foucaucourt, militem, De magnete,* dated 8 August 1269. Apart from his substantive contributions to the knowledge of magnetism, Peter emerges as an enthusiastic and convincing advocate of experimentation. Many things that can be deduced by the operation of reason, he says, cannot be proved without manual skill, such as experimental technique. Repeatedly he advises his dear friend Sygerius to demonstrate the truth of his assertions by performing the experiments he describes.

After some introductory material, Peter lays down the rules for determining magnetic polarity. Take a lodestone (natural magnet); polish it into a sphere. Now lay a needle on its surface at many different points. Each time the needle comes to rest, mark the sphere along the needle's orientation with a line that divides the sphere in half. All these lines, or meridians, will converge at two points: the poles. Now determine which pole is north and which is south. Place the magnet in a wooden cup and place the cup in a large basin of water. If you do this a thousand times, the same pole will point north a thousand times. There follow some experiments concerning the magnetization of iron, and some theorizing on magnetic attraction and repulsion. Peter believed that the source of magnetic attraction was the poles of the celestial sphere inside which the earth was located; he was unaware that the earth had its own magnetic poles.

From experiments dealing with the nature of magnetism, Peter moves on to describe several instruments that can be made with magnets. One of these is a perpetual-motion machine, and two are improved compasses that represent real advances in construction.

Peter of Maricourt's *De magnete* was highly esteemed during the Middle Ages (thirty-one manuscripts survive), and William Gilbert cited it by name in his own treatise *De magnete,* which he wrote in 1600.

BIBLIOGRAPHY

Sources. The edition is P. Radelet–de Grave and D. Speiser, eds., "Le *De magnete* de Pierre de Maricourt: Traduction et commentaire," in *Revue d'histoire des sciences,* **28** (1975). Peter is generally credited with a treatise on the construction of an astrolabe, only excerpts of which have been published; see Giuseppe Boffito and Camillo Melzi d'Eril, *Il trattato dell'astrolabio di Pietro Peregrino di Maricourt* (1927).

Studies. Eduard J. Dijksterhuis, *The Mechanization of*

the World Picture, C. Dikshoorn, trans. (1961), 152–153; Silvanus P. Thompson, "Petrus Peregrinus de Maricourt and His *Epistola de Magnete,*" in *Proceedings of the British Academy,* 2 (1905–1906).

ELAINE GOLDEN ROBISON

[See also **Astrolabe; Compass, Magnetic.**]

PETER RIGA (*ca.* 1140–1209), Latin religious poet, was born at Rheims—he has no connection with the city on the Baltic—and studied at Paris in the 1160's. He dedicated the *Floridus aspectus,* a collection of miscellaneous short poems, to Samson, archbishop of Rheims; the poems—secular, moral, and religious—became inextricably mixed in the anthologies with the short poems of Marbod, Hildebert, and the *Anthologia latina.* He wrote short poems on biblical themes, such as the very popular *Susanna,* which dramatizes the story by beginning with the accusations of the judges, who are refuted by Daniel. Peter's major work is the *Aurora,* a versification of the principal books of the Bible, with verse moral interpretations; according to Paul Beichner, Peter produced three editions, adding new works and his earlier separate poems. The *Aurora* was further "edited" by Peter's younger contemporary Egidius (Giles) of Paris, who added verses of his own. Drawing on standard authorities, such as Peter Comestor's *Historia scholastica,* the *Aurora* was widely quoted by medieval writers (including Chaucer). Most of the poems are in unrhymed elegiac couplets, but the third edition has hexameters with final rhyme (*caudati*).

BIBLIOGRAPHY

Peter's works are in *Patrologia latina,* CLXXI (1854), 1381–1442, and in *Aurora: Petri Rigae Biblia versificata,* Paul E. Beichner, ed., 2 vols. (1965). See also André Boutemy, "Recherches sur le *Floridus aspectus* de Pierre la Rigge," in *Moyen âge,* 54 (1948), continued in *Latomus,* 8 (1949).

A. G. RIGG

[See also **Latin Literature.**]

PETER THE CHANTER (*d.* 1197), a prominent theologian, churchman, and reformer, flourished at Paris in the last quarter of the twelfth century. Originating from a family of minor knights at Hodenc-en-Bray near Beauvais, he went to school at Rheims, where his teacher was probably Robert de Camera, who later became bishop of Amiens (1166–1169). By 1173 Peter was at Paris as a master, and he taught theology until the end of his career. His most influential students were Robert of Courson, later papal legate for France (1212–1219); Stephen Langton, archbishop of Canterbury (1206–1228); and very likely the future Pope Innocent III (1198–1216). In 1183 Peter was chosen chanter of Notre Dame (whence his name); this function was exercised concurrently with his teaching. Active in ecclesiastical affairs, he was appointed by the popes as judge delegate in at least fifteen cases, including the divorce trial of King Philip II Augustus in 1196. An outspoken churchman, he was reported to have advised a leading merchant of Paris, Thibaut the Rich, on making restitution of ill-gotten gains and to have upbraided King Philip on the quality of contemporary bishops. Promotion to high office for himself, however, came with difficulty. The chapter of Tournai elected him bishop in 1190, but William, archbishop of Rheims and regent during the king's absence on crusade, annulled the election because of a procedural irregularity. It was later rumored that Peter was considered for the bishopric of Paris, but nothing came of the matter. Finally, in 1196 the chapter of Rheims elected him dean, but before he could occupy the new position, he fell seriously ill. Journeying to the Cistercian abbey of Longpont, near Soissons, he took the habit of a monk and died there on 25 September 1197.

In a celebrated passage, Peter likened the study of theology to a building. Lecturing represented the foundations, disputation the walls, and preaching the roof. Composed with the collaboration of his students, Peter's own writings reflect this threefold division. His lectures on the Bible were transcribed in the form of commentaries. While earlier theologians had concentrated on the Psalms and the Epistles of Paul, Peter was the first to encompass the entire corpus of Scripture. (In addition, he wrote other aids to scriptural study.) Peter set aside special times for disputing difficult problems arising from his lectures, which were formulated as *questiones* and collected under the title *Summa de sacramentis.* The *Summa* of his student Robert of Courson constituted a final reworking of this collection. Although Peter was reputed to be a celebrated preacher, virtually no sermons have survived. But he did compose a widely copied treatise, the

Verbum abbreviatum (1191–1192), that publicized his moral theories for a larger audience.

What distinguished Peter the Chanter from contemporary theologians was his intensely practical orientation. Focusing on the doctrine of penance, he formulated a casuistic approach to moral questions through individual cases. By debating the ethical issues involved in these specific cases, Peter laid the groundwork for the guides to confessors that were composed for priests administering penance in the following century. He was sensitive to problems around him. For example, as a dignitary of Notre Dame during its reconstruction in the new and imposing Gothic style, Peter objected, on moral grounds, to the great expenditure of money. Responsible for the services in the choir, he was critical of the frivolity of the subdeacons during the Feast of Fools (1 January). As teacher he examined masters' claims for demanding fees from their students. But Peter's interests extended beyond his personal experience to the whole range of human conduct, and he probed the moral conditions of occupations as diverse as chancery clerics, lawyers, mercenary soldiers, merchants, prostitutes, and jongleurs. In the process he examined such important contemporary issues as the just war, forest laws, tallages on towns, the just price, mortgage credit, and commercial partnerships. Few facets of everyday life escaped scrutiny in his classroom.

As a biblical scholar, Peter believed that true reform consisted in cutting away the accretions of tradition to uncover the simple word of God. Following this course, his scriptural studies inspired him to attack certain established social institutions. For example, he believed that ordeals, the so-called judgments of God, customarily employed for centuries in the law courts, were immoral because they violated the biblical commandment "Thou shalt not tempt God." (Besides, Peter argued, they did not work.) Moreover, he felt that the application of capital punishment to petty thievery, poaching deer in the royal forests, and heresy had no scriptural justification. In the realm of marriage he contended that the system of impediments designed to forbid marriage within seven degrees of consanguinity far exceeded the biblical limitations against incest and encouraged divorce. (Since most people in an age of restricted mobility were related within the prohibited degrees, they were eligible to dissolve their marriages.) For the secular clergy he asserted that since the primitive church allowed marriage for deacons and subdeacons, only priests and bishops were bound by celibacy.

The impact of Peter's reform proposals met with mixed results. Although the Forest Charter of 1217 abolished capital punishment for crimes against the king's venison in England, elsewhere the penalty remained in effect, as it did for punishing thieves and heretics. And in 1207 the papacy constituted subdeacons and above as sacred orders, thus expanding the range of clerical celibacy. But two of Peter's important reforms did take root. At the Fourth Lateran Council (1215) Pope Innocent III, citing Peter's arguments, reduced the impediments of consanguinity from seven to four degrees, thereby limiting the scope for divorce. Equally important, the council solemnly prohibited the clergy from participating in ordeals, thus laying an axe to the root of this legal barbarity. Because of the success of such proposals as these, Peter must be seen not merely as a local churchman and scholar but as an influential reformer as well.

BIBLIOGRAPHY

Sources. The short version of the *Verbum abbreviatum* was edited by Georges Galopin (1639) and reprinted in *Patrologia latina,* CCV (1855), 1–554. The *Summa de sacramentis et animae consiliis* has been edited by Jean-Albert Dugauquier, 3 vols. in 5 (1954–1967). Peter's biblical commentaries remain unedited, but their MSS are inventoried in Friedrich Stegmüller, *Repertorium biblicum medii aevi,* 7 vols. (1950–1961).

Studies. The most recent study, which forms the basis of this article, is John W. Baldwin, *Masters, Princes, and Merchants: The Social Views of Peter the Chanter and His Circle,* 2 vols. (1970). It supersedes Franz S. Gutjahr, *Petrus Cantor Parisiensis: Sein Leben und seine Schriften* (1899). Peter's biblical scholarship is studied in Beryl Smalley, *The Study of the Bible in the Middle Ages* (1952), 196–263.

JOHN W. BALDWIN

[See also **Courson (Courçon), Robert of; Innocent III, Pope; Langton, Stephen; Paris, University of; Philip II Augustus.**]

PETER THE DEACON OF MONTE CASSINO (*ca.* 1107–after 1153). The librarian (*bibliothecarius*) of the abbey of Monte Cassino from 1130, Peter oversaw the compilation of the abbey's cartulary—the *Registrum Petri Diaconi,* which played a role in the struggle between pope and emperor—and other historical works. A man of demonstrated literary skill, Peter has been exposed as a notorious forger.

BIBLIOGRAPHY

The bulk of Peter the Deacon's work is contained in Migne, *Patrologia latina,* CLXXIII (1854). "Peter the Deacon of Monte Cassino," in *New Catholic Encyclopedia,* XI (1967), 215–216, has a good bibliography. An edition is Robert H. Rogers, *Petri Diaconi: Ortus et vita iustorum cenobii Casinensis* (1972).

MARK A. ZIER

[See also **Constantine the African; Forgery; Monte Cassino.**]

PETER THE HERMIT (*fl.* eleventh century), perhaps a native of Picardy, has received credit for persuading Pope Urban II (*r.* 1088–1099) to launch the First Crusade. The chroniclers Albert of Aix (Albertus Aquensis, whose great history was written between 1119 and 1150) and William of Tyre (*d. ca.* 1185) gave rise to this legend, which was accepted for centuries. Albertus' history, the main source of information on Peter the Hermit, is not an eyewitness account, but depends upon the stories of pilgrims. Stories circulated that Peter had a letter from heaven prophesying that Christians would recover the Holy Sepulcher. Rumors spread that he had tried to visit Jerusalem, only to receive bad treatment at the hands of the Turks. He supposedly used accounts of Turkish atrocities to inflame audiences of concerned Christians.

The nineteenth-century historian Heinrich Hagenmeyer has shown that Peter had no influence on Pope Urban's decision. Once the crusade was proclaimed, however, Peter's rabble-rousing techniques caused large crowds of ignorant and poor people to follow him in taking the cross. The pope, no doubt, preferred an orderly crusade led by great lords, but Peter and other preachers stirred up a peasants' crusade with no leaders of any standing. Following the council at Clermont (1095), Peter enlisted the services of Walter the Penniless (sans Avoir) at Poissy and Geoffrey Burel at Étampes. Later in Germany he gathered an army of Germans, Lorrainers, Swabians, and Bavarians.

Peter's march through Hungary was orderly until unruly elements captured Semlin (present-day Zemun, in northeastern Yugoslavia). He then crossed into Bulgaria and by 2 or 3 July 1096 reached Nish (then military headquarters of Bulgaria, present-day Niš in eastern Yugoslavia). Following skirmishes with forces of the Byzantine governor, Niketas, Peter arrived at Constantinople on 30 July 1096. Emperor Alexios I Komnenos interviewed Peter, gave him presents, and advised him to await the main army of the crusaders.

Unfortunately, the unruly elements in the peasant army caused the emperor to send the forces of Peter and Walter across the straits on 6 August. In the ensuing weeks Peter lost control of his forces. Reginald (Rainaldus), an Italian nobleman, led an ill-fated expedition to a Turkish fortress, Xerigordon, which resulted in the massacre of his forces. In the beginning of October Peter returned to Constantinople to enlist Byzantine aid. In the meantime, the forces of Walter the Penniless and Geoffrey Burel were ambushed near Dracon, and the peasants' crusade came to a tragic end.

The activities of Peter following the loss of his forces are sketchy. During the siege of Antioch, in the days of famine and cold, Peter fled on 20 January 1098 only to be apprehended by the Norman Tancred (*d.* 1112) and returned to the siege. Later, Peter and an obscure Frank, Herluin, met with Kerbogha, atabeg of Mosul. Their efforts to persuade Kerbogha to lift the siege of Antioch failed, but Peter's efforts erased the shame of his flight.

Later, during the siege of Jerusalem on 8 July 1099, the crusaders formed a procession around the city and listened to Peter and Arnulf of Chocques, chaplain of Robert of Normandy (*d.* 1134), as they spoke on the Mount of Olives. Apparently, Peter continued to sway the masses. On 11 August 1099, when the crusaders marched against the forces of al-Afdal, Peter held services of intercession for Latin newcomers and natives. He also advised Greeks and Latins to form processions, offer prayers, and give alms so that God would bestow victory upon his people. The activities of Peter following the First Crusade are poorly recorded. He probably returned to Europe in 1101 and supposedly died in 1115. In an age of superstition and mass hysteria Peter remains a legendary preacher who stirred the lowly to take the cross and give their lives in a futile effort to recover the Holy Sepulcher.

BIBLIOGRAPHY

Albertus Aquensis, *Historia Hierosolymitana,* in *Recueil des historiens croisades— historiens occidentaux,*

IV (1879), Albert was not present but gave the best account of the Peasants' Crusade; Louis Bréhier, ed. and trans., *Histoire anonyme de la première croisade* (1924); Frederic Duncalf, "The Peasants' Crusade," in *American Historical Review,* **26** (1921); Heinrich Hagenmeyer, *Peter der Eremite* (1879); John H. Hill and Laurita L. Hill, trans., "*Peter Tudebode: Historia de Hiersolymitano Itinere,*" in *Memoirs of the American Philosophical Society,* **101** (1974); Rosiland Hill, ed. and trans., *Gesta Francorum et aliorum Hierosolymitanorum: The Deeds of the Franks and Other Pilgrims to Jerusalem* (1962).

JOHN H. HILL

[See also **Alexios I Komnenos; Clermont, Council of; Crusades and Crusader States: To 1192; Tancred (Crusader); Urban II, Pope; William of Tyre.**]

PETER THE VENERABLE (*ca.* 1092–1156), ninth abbot of Cluny and foremost spokesman for traditional Benedictine observance during the twelfth-century monastic revival, was born in Auvergne of the noble Montboissier family. He received his education as an oblate at the Cluniac house of Sauxillanges, governed as prior first at Vézelay and then at Domène (near Grenoble), and was elected by acclamation as abbot of Cluny in 1122.

The thirty-year-old abbot began his thirty-four years of administration amid the shambles left by the deplorable Pons de Melgeuil (1109–1122) and Pons's immediate successor of four months, Hugh II. Under Peter's humane but firm direction, discipline was soon restored and consolidated; and the Cluniac empire (some 300 to 400 monks at Cluny, along with some 2,000 houses subject to Cluny in varying degrees) attained its zenith of prosperity and influence in church and state. Popularly known chiefly because of his attractive personality, his championship of traditional Benedictine observance in the controversy between the Cistercians and the Cluniacs, and his warm-hearted generosity to Peter Abelard after the latter's condemnation at Sens in 1140, the last and perhaps greatest of the "holy abbots of Cluny" left a considerable body of letters, theological and polemical treatises, sermons, and hymns and other liturgical texts. Though physically frail, Peter traveled extensively in the interests of monastic discipline and ecclesiastical affairs: to England in 1130 and 1155; to Spain in 1142 (and perhaps also in 1124 and 1127)—it was there that he commissioned the Latin translation of five Arabic works, including the Koran; six journeys to Rome; and an almost uninterrupted trajectory of occasional trips throughout France and the Rhineland.

Peter's numerous writings attest to the wide range of his interests, to his balanced judgment, and to his general competence and reasonableness in an age given to extremes in matters of controversy. The collection of his letters assembled by his secretary, Peter of Poitiers, ranks high among the most valuable letter collections of the Middle Ages and includes everything from letters of counsel to full-length theological treatises. The *Contra Petrobrusianos* is the most objective source of information about the tenets of the followers of Pierre de Bruys; the tract *Adversus Judaeorum inveteratum duritiem* excludes apologetic recourse to New Testament texts, takes into account the Hebrew version of biblical passages cited, eliminates allegorical interpretations, and carefully avoids questions of secondary importance. In his two apologetic writings against Islam, written only after he had failed to persuade his friend Bernard of Clairvaux to take the initiative, Peter reveals a knowledge of Islamic doctrine remarkable for his century and milieu. His conviction that Muslims are to be approached "not by force, but by reason; not in hatred, but in love," expresses a general attitude that makes Peter, even in the midst of controversy, an extremely attractive figure. Of less interest to the theologian, but no less characteristic of Peter's interests, are his works of edification: the *De miraculis,* four sermons, an Office of the Transfiguration, and various hymns and other liturgical compositions.

But Peter's chief importance lies not so much in his writings as in his person, "a fruit of Cluny, and the symbol of monastic holiness fed at the sources of Benedictine tradition," as Jean Leclercq put it. The only medieval life of Peter is by his constant companion and disciple, Radulphus; another important source is provided by the Chronicle of Cluny. But these works have to be fleshed out and controlled by the data provided by Peter's own extensive correspondence. Though Peter was never formally canonized, his popular cult at Clermont received papal approbation in 1862, and his memorial is now inscribed in the monastic calendar along with the other holy abbots of Cluny on May 11.

BIBLIOGRAPHY

Sources. Most of Peter's works are in *Patrologia latina,* CLXXXIX (1854), 61–1054. Giles Constable has edited three collections of Peter's writings: "Petri Venerabilis sermones tres," in *Revue bénédictine,* **64** (1954), *The Letters of Peter the Venerable,* 2 vols. (1967), and *Statuta Petri Venerabilis,* in *Corpus consuetudinum monasticarum,* VI (1975). For the apologetic treatises against the Petrobrusians and the Saracens, see *Petri Venerabilis: Contra Petrobrusianos hereticos,* James Fearns, ed. (1968).

Studies. The best study of Peter's life and work is Jean Leclercq, *Pierre le Vénérable* (1946). Valuable essays are in Giles Constable and James Kritzeck, ed., *Petrus Venerabilis 1156–1956* (1956). See also James Kritzeck, *Peter the Venerable and Islam* (1964).

CHRYSOGONUS WADDELL

[See also **Abelard, Peter; Bernard of Clairvaux, St.; Cluny, Order of; Polemics, Christian-Jewish.**]

PETER URSEOLUS, ST. (928–997). After serving as ambassador of the Republic of Venice to the court of Otto I, Peter Urseolus was acclaimed doge on 12 August 976. During his two-year reign he subsidized much of the restoration of S. Marco. In 978 Urseolus abdicated and, in the company of Guarin and St. Romuald, retreated to the Benedictine abbey of St. Michel at Cuxa, where he spent the remainder of his life as a monk. He is represented in a fourteenth-century mosaic in the baptistery of S. Marco. In 1731 Peter Urseolus was canonized.

BIBLIOGRAPHY

"Pietro Orseolo," in *Bibliotheca sanctorum,* X (1968); "Petrus Urseolus," in *Lexikon der christlichen Ikonographie,* VIII (1976); Louis Réau, *Iconographie de l'art chrétien,* III, pt. 3 (1959), 1,101.

MICHAEL T. DAVIS

[See also **Romuald of Ravenna, St.; S. Marco; Venice.**]

PETER VON PRACHTATITZ (**Prachatitz**) (*fl.* first half of the fifteenth century) directed the atelier at St. Stephen's, Vienna, between 1404 and 1429. While he advanced the construction of the nave, the major focus of his activity was the great south tower of the transept above the second story. Working in what has been termed a post-Parler style, Peter created an elegant yet dramatic composition that achieves an astonishing degree of unity through the repetition of gables and overlapping

St. Stephen's Cathedral, Vienna, showing the south tower of Peter von Prachtatitz. Pen and ink drawing by Salomon Kleiner, 1721. VIENNA, ÖSTERREICHISCHE NATIONALBIBLIOTHEK, COD. MIN. 9, Bl. 58

and diagonally interpenetrating forms. Peter may have been related to the Parler family, but his work displays little resemblance to the contemporaneous Prague Cathedral. He was succeeded at Vienna by Hans Prachtatitz, presumably his son.

BIBLIOGRAPHY

Walter Buchowiecki, *Die gotischen Kirchen Österreichs* (1952), 170–173; Rupert Feuchtmüller, *Der Wiener Stephansdom* (1978), 141–144, 169–174, 377–379; Paul Frankl, *Gothic Architecture* (1962), 165–168; Richard Perger, "Die Baumeister des Wiener Stephansdomes im Spätmittelalter," in *Wiener Jahrbuch für Kunstgeschichte,* 23 (1970); Hans Tietze, *Geschichte und Beschreibung des St. Stephansdomes in Wien* (1931), 13–14, 17–25; Josef Zykan, "Der Stephansturm: Zu den Problemen der Instandsetzung und zur Frage der Baugeschichte," in *Österreichische Zeitschrift für Kunst und Denkmalpflege,* 9 (1955); Marlene Zykan, "Zur Baugeschichte des Hochturmes von St. Stephan," in

Wiener Jahrbuch für Kunstgeschichte, **23** (1970), and *Der Stephansdom* (1981), 84–98.

MICHAEL T. DAVIS

[See also **Gothic Architecture; Masons and Builders; Parler Family.**]

PETER WALDO. See **Waldes.**

PETER'S PENCE originated during the Anglo-Saxon period as a freewill offering on the part of one of the Anglo-Saxon kings to the Roman pontiffs. The traditions regarding its origin date from the subsequent Norman period. It has been attributed to King Ine of Wessex, who abdicated in 727, but this report is not confirmed by Bede. Henry of Huntington traces it to King Offa of Mercia, and there is some confirmation of this in a letter from Pope Leo III to Offa's successor, Cenulf, in 797 or 798. William of Malmesbury relates that Aethelwulf of Wessex originated the payment during the pontificate of Leo IV. It is highly probable that it was extended by King Alfred to all the territories he conquered from the Danes in the ninth century, and it is certain that it was being sent to Rome regularly under his successors.

Peter's Pence appeared under various names in Anglo-Saxon sources. It was called "Romefeoh" or "Romescot," and "hearthpenny," though the latter term was used of other payments as well. The Anglo-Saxon Chronicle referred to it as "the alms of the West Saxons and of King Alfred." The earliest mention in an English law dates from the early tenth century. There can be no real doubt about its royal origin. Under Edward the Confessor it was enforced in the royal courts. Although normally collected by the bishops, it was transmitted to Rome in the name of the king. It provides interesting testimony of the close ties between England and Rome in the Anglo-Saxon period.

The beginnings of the reform movement in Rome in the mid eleventh century marked a significant change in the attitude of the papacy toward Peter's Pence. Prior to this period there is no evidence that any pope wrote an English king to demand its payment, though the letter of Leo III was in the nature of a request that Cenulf fulfill the commitment made by Offa. Now, however, and especially after the conquest of England by William of Normandy in 1066, the papacy increasingly attempted to ensure the prompt payment of Peter's Pence, treating it more as a tax than as a freewill offering. In twelfth-century sources it is quite commonly referred to as *census sancti Petri,* a term that makes clear this process of transformation from freewill offering to proprietary right. In this way it came to be listed in the *Liber censuum romanae ecclesiae,* prepared by Cardinal Cencius in the late twelfth century. At that time the amount of the payment was fixed at 299 marks. Although there were efforts under Celestine III and Innocent III to have the payment increased so that it would more closely reflect the increment in the actual collections, the crown and the bishops resisted. In 1273 the same amount was being recorded as in the *Liber censuum.* However, the papacy was more successful in gaining recognition of its right to the payment. This was acknowledged by King John in 1213, in connection with the settlement of his conflict with the papacy and the raising of his excommunication and the interdict.

Payment of Peter's Pence was often subject to political conditions. During the early twelfth century the investiture controversy led to its suspension, as did the later Becket conflict. In the early fourteenth century there was increased royal opposition, but it remained on the books until it was suppressed by King Henry VIII in 1534.

The introduction of Peter's Pence into other kingdoms seems to have been influenced in part by the English precedent. Nicholas Breakspear, cardinal legate of Pope Eugene III and later the first English pope, was responsible for its introduction into Norway (1152) and Sweden (1153). Undoubtedly it spread from these kingdoms to Iceland. Less clear are the cases of Hungary, Dalmatia, Istria, and Poland, which may also have made offerings of this type distinct from feudal dues.

The modern Peter's Pence originated in 1860 at Vienna as a freewill offering and was taken up by the papacy to help make up for the loss of papal revenues following the expropriation of the papal states and Rome. Pope Pius IX extended the practice to the entire church by the encyclical *Saepe venerabiles fratres* (1871). It thus has no relationship to the medieval offering.

BIBLIOGRAPHY

Camille Daux, *Le denier de saint Pierre* (1907); Karl Jordan, "Zur päpstlichen Finanzgeschichte im 11. und

12. Jahrhundert," in *Quellen und Forschungen aus italienischen Archiven und Bibliotheken,* **25** (1933–1934); William E. Lunt, *Financial Relations of the Papacy with England,* 2 vols. (1939): I, 3–84, II, 1–53.

JAMES M. POWELL

[See also **Church, Latin: Organization; Innocent III, Pope; Taxation, Church.**]

PETITE PHILOSOPHIE, LA, is an anonymous Anglo-Norman poem, written about 1230, which deals with the nature of the universe. Based mostly on book I of the Latin treatise *De imagine mundi libri tres,* with some influence from the *Elucidarium* of Honorius Augustodunensis, the poem explains, with suitable references to etymologies and allegorical significance, the elements, the planets, other heavenly bodies, various natural phenomena, and the signs of the zodiac. It concludes with a sermon on the torments of hell and the joys of heaven.

BIBLIOGRAPHY

The edition is William Hilliard Trethewey, ed., *La petite philosophie: An Anglo-Norman Poem of the Thirteenth Century* (1939).

BRIAN MERRILEES

[See also **Anglo-Norman Literature; Astrology/Astronomy; Elucidarium and Spanish Lucidario; Encyclopedias and Dictionaries, Western European; Honorius Augustodunensis.**]

PETRARCH (Francesco Petrarca) (1304–1374) continues to be considered Italy's greatest lyric stylist and poet with an unparalleled international influence, the literary arbiter of his time, the "father" of the humanistic movement in his recovery of classical texts, and "the first modern man of letters" in his attempt to integrate Christian and classical thought. Nevertheless, he is one of the most difficult literary figures to assess.

On the one hand, the American scholar Ernest H. Wilkins states that "Petrarch was the most remarkable man of his time; and he is one of the most remarkable men of all time . . . for we know far more about his experiences in life than about the experiences of any human being who had lived before his time." On the other hand, Antonio Quaglio speaks of Petrarch's constant attempt to manipulate all biographical elements in his works "for the purpose of composing an ideal profile of himself, of enclosing his earthly experiences, shorn of all realistic particulars . . . in a dimension at once human and historical, having a particular literary significance as a model for posterity of a life based on the illustrious models of classical culture."

The distance between the two statements marks the distance between Petrarch the man and the scholar, and the Petrarch who found it impossible to lead a life that did not partake of and exude the fullness and beauty of poetry. The three ingredients that most contributed to this complexity were his rediscovery of the spirit of the great classical authors, his desire to restore some measure of that spirit to the literature and society of Christian Europe, and his poetic sensitivity that enabled him to convey the essence of life both in an impeccable vernacular and in a Latin verse and prose reflecting clear classical echoes.

The times in which Petrarch lived doubtless deeply influenced his character. It was a period in which the societal structures of the Middle Ages were slowly weakening. Communal governments were yielding to various forms of seigniories; faith in the Avignon papacy and the Holy Roman Empire was badly shaken; Italy was being torn by internecine struggles and France by the Hundred Years War; and the pursuit of learning and culture seemed to have reached new lows. Petrarch emitted two outcries that can serve as a framework to his biography.

The first is in his *Rerum memorandarum libri* (I.19), where he decries the manner in which the generations after Pliny had allowed so many great works to disappear, and concludes that it is his painful experience to feel "as though on the confines of two civilizations, capable of looking simultaneously backward and forward, wanting to convey this complaint to posterity, since my elders do not feel as I do." The second appears in the *Letter to Posterity,* his unfinished autobiography that paints in broad strokes his life to 1351: "Among my many activities, I applied myself particularly to the knowledge of the ancient world, inasmuch as this present age has always displeased me to the point that, were it not for my affection for my dear ones, I should always have preferred to have been born in any other age. . . . "

This self-portrait reveals the extent to which Petrarch was to try to be a classical model for his own decadent times. Addressing posterity, he asserts: "I was one of your species, an insignificant mortal, from roots neither elevated nor lowly, but of ancient stock, *as Caesar Augustus says of himself*" (italics added). There follows an observation revealing his sensitive humanity: "Adolescence deluded me, youth misled me, but old age has set me right and through experience has convinced me of the truth of what I had read long before: that the pleasures of adolescence are vain." The universal resonances in these statements permeate not only Petrarch's "actual" life and works but also his life as artist, and as literary and cultural arbiter of his day and of the humanistic and Renaissance eras.

By examining first the highlights of Petrarch's life, then the nature of his Latin works, and finally the two Italian works on which his fame primarily rests, the *Canzoniere* and the *Trionfi,* one can discern to some degree why Petrarch was a truly remarkable man of letters and citizen of the world.

LIFE

Petrarch was born in Arezzo on 20 July 1304; his parents were Eletta Canigiani and ser Pietro di ser Parenzo, commonly called Petracco, a friend of Dante and, like him, banished from Florence on political grounds. Soon after Petrarch's birth he was, in 1305, taken by his mother to the family home at Incisa, where his brother Gherardo was born in 1307. They moved in 1311 to Pisa, and shortly thereafter Petracco decided to seek his fortune at the court of Pope Clement V (*r.* 1305–1314), which had moved to Avignon in 1309. The city's crowded conditions forced the family to settle in nearby Carpentras, where the young Petrarch began his studies under Convenevole da Prato.

Following his mother's death in 1318/1319, Petrarch composed his first poem in Latin (*Epistola metrica* I.7) in her memory. Containing thirty-eight verses, one for each year of her life, the piece already shows his concern for form. After completing law studies at Montpellier, Petrarch and his brother were sent to Bologna in 1320 to continue the study of law. Their father's death in 1326 compelled them to return to Avignon.

The brothers spent some carefree years in Avignon, years that Petrarch later recalled with nostalgia. It was during this period, on 6 April 1327, that he presumably first saw his beloved Laura in church on Good Friday. Although scholars have failed to establish her identity with absolute certainty, her existence was very real to the poet, who traces the "mythic story" of his unrequited love in his Italian and Latin works. The announcement of her death on the first guard leaf of his precious Vergil lends special credence to her existence.

Having squandered, with his brother, the family patrimony, Petrarch embarked upon an ecclesiastical career by embracing minor orders with the hope of gaining some financial security. His acquaintance with Giacomo Colonna, member of the powerful Roman family, led to the position of chaplain to Cardinal Giovanni Colonna, with whom he was long associated. His presence in the Colonna household from 1330 to 1337 led to friendships that Petrarch was to cultivate throughout his life and that, together with his restless curiosity and insatiable thirst for knowledge, were the causes for his countless trips throughout Europe. He visited Paris, Ghent, Liège (where he discovered two of Cicero's lost orations), Cologne, and Lyons. In either Paris or Avignon, Petrarch came to know Dionigi di Borgo San Sepolcro, an Augustian friar and later bishop, who first attracted him to St. Augustine, and eventually to the study of sacred letters, through a gift of the *Confessions.*

Early in 1335 Petrarch received a canonry in Lombez from Benedict XII (*r.* 1334–1342), but he remained in Avignon. He successfully argued before the pope in behalf of the powerful Mastino della Scala, who sought to remain lord of Parma. His participation in the polemic concerning the location of the papal court resulted in metrical letters (I.2, I. 5) to Benedict urging him to return the papal see to Rome. In 1337 he visited Rome for the first time, as guest of the Colonnas. Upon his return to Avignon, Petrarch retired to the seclusion of his new home in nearby Vaucluse (to become his "dearest spot on earth"), where he prepared the first "collected edition" of his poems in Italian. The same year his first illegitimate child, Giovanni, was born.

At the end of 1338 Petrarch started his serious works: the *De viris illustribus,* the *Africa* (on Scipio), perhaps the *Trionfi,* and numerous lyrics in the vernacular. As word of his classical epic on Scipio spread through learned circles, his reputation in both France and Italy became such that on 1 September 1340 he received invitations from the University of Paris and the Roman Senate to accept the laurel crown for poetry. Petrarch chose Rome, but first went to Naples to be "examined" on the purpose and function of poetry by the enlightened King Robert. On Easter Sunday, 8 April 1341, on the Capitoline before the public and Senate of Rome, he was crowned "magnus poeta et historicus." After delivering a learned oration on the nature of poetry, Petrarch led a solemn procession to St. Peter's, where he placed his laurel crown on the high altar.

After a stay in Parma as guest of Azzo da Correggio, whose ascent to power he had supported, Petrarch returned to Avignon in 1342, then joined a delegation of Roman nobles in petitioning Clement VI (*r.* 1342–1352) to return the Holy See to Rome. While the French pontiff agreed to proclaim 1350 a jubilee year, he was not convinced that it was yet time for the return of the papacy. The visit of Cola di Rienzo (who opposed the aristocratic government of Rome) to Avignon in 1343 prompted yet another appeal from Petrarch for the return of the papacy to Rome. In the same year his brother Gherardo became a Carthusian; another illegitimate child, Francesca, was born; and King Robert of Naples died. These events led him to begin the confessional *Secretum* and the scholarly *Rerum memorandarum libri.* As special emissary of the pope and of Cardinal Colonna, Petrarch again went to Naples to plead a case before the governing body. Having cultivated new friendships there (Giovanni Barrili and Barbato da Sulmona), he then visited Parma as guest of the Correggi, but internecine warfare forced him to flee in February 1345. He stopped for several months in Verona, where he met Dante's son, Pietro, and discovered the first sixteen books of Cicero's letters to Atticus and his letters to Quintus and to Brutus, which he personally transcribed in order to incorporate them into his already sizable library.

From 1345 to 1347 Petrarch spent a prolific period at Vaucluse, where he started still other works (*De vita solitaria, Bucolicum carmen, De otio religioso*), and where, in 1347, his enthusiasm for the rebirth of Rome was again aroused upon hearing that Cola di Rienzo had been declared tribune of the people. The event prompted him to direct to Cola a Latin eclogue (V) and three letters (*Variae* 38, 42, 48) exhorting him to restore the ancient glory of Rome. Cola's coup was short-lived, for he alarmed the pope by his arrogation of all temporal authority to Rome and the Roman people, by his dismissal of the papal vicar, and by his humiliation of the Roman nobility. Even as Petrarch was leaving Provence to join him in Rome, he learned of Cola's failure and thereupon changed his itinerary.

A severe earthquake in Verona and a canonry at the cathedral of Parma caused Petrarch to settle for some time in the latter city, where in 1348 he was appointed archdeacon. It was here that he learned of the terrible toll of friends, including Laura, taken by the Black Death. The writings of this sojourn, including perhaps his *Psalmi poenitentiales,* reflect the depression and desolation that overcame him as a result of these losses. Worsening relations with the bishop of Parma caused Petrarch to accept the invitation of Iacopo da Carrara, lord of Padua, who assigned him a canonry in his city. Following a brief return to Parma and further losses of friends, Petrarch continued to search for a permanent abode: in 1349 at Carpi, shortly thereafter in Ferrara, then in Padua, where he began his collection of personal letters, the *Familiares.*

After having spent much of 1350 in Mantua and Parma, Petrarch visited Rome in the fall for the jubilee year. At Boccaccio's insistence he stopped en route in Florence, where he made a number of lifelong friends. A short stay in Rome was followed by a return to Parma via Arezzo and Florence, where he was given Quintilian's *Institutiones oratoriae* (with which he was unacquainted). Early in 1351, Petrarch was called to Padua by Francesco da Carrara after the assassination of his father, Iacopo. Complex political events in Rome and Naples, as well as the war between Genoa and Venice, caused him to direct letters to Emperor Charles IV and to the doges of Genoa and Venice appealing for the reestablishment of peace.

Meantime, Avignon and Florence began to vie for Petrarch's presence, the former at the pope's request, the latter at Boccaccio's instigation (with the offer of a university professorship and of the restitution of his family's property). He opted for Avignon, traveling there by way of Vicenza, Lonigo, Mantua, Parma, Piacenza, and Verona. In the autumn of 1351, after a lengthy stay with friends in Avignon, he went to Vaucluse, turning down the pope's offer of a papal secretaryship and a bishopric. Petrarch devoted himself instead to his uncompleted works and discovered the extent to which he now viewed Avignon as a new Babylon. The clerical hostility he had encountered in Avignon haunted him in Vaucluse as well, instilling in him the desire to leave Provence, but the difficulty of deciding where to settle in Italy detained him.

Even at his departure in 1353, Petrarch was still uncertain of his destination. By coincidence he stopped in Milan as guest of Giovanni Visconti, archbishop and lord of the city, who was mistrusted by the Italian communes. Petrarch remained in Milan for eight years despite the criticism of his closest friends that he had forsaken his liberty. While performing small favors (brief periods as orator and ambassador) for the Visconti family, he enjoyed the tranquillity necessary to work with great zest on his literary projects. He survived a series of political misfortunes that culminated in the long-awaited descent of Charles IV of Luxembourg (*d.* 1378). In late 1354 Petrarch welcomed Charles in Mantua, where he had been summoned, and accompanied him to Milan to be crowned king of the Italians and to Rome to be crowned emperor (1355). The descent, however, only served to fan political fires. Charles hastily retreated, much to Petrarch's chagrin.

Despite such setbacks, in 1358 Petrarch accepted a mission as emissary for the Visconti to gain the emperor's mediation for peace between Milan and the Venetian League. He traveled to Basel and Prague, where the emperor bestowed upon him the titles of palatine count and counselor. The journey was primarily a social success for Petrarch, who made numerous friends, including the empress.

Once again in Milan, Petrarch returned to work with renewed fervor on unfinished works (the *Canzoniere* and the *De viris*) and started new ones (the *De remediis*). In 1359–1360 he welcomed Boccaccio to his home and enjoyed brief trips to Bergamo, Padua, and Venice. As the Milanese political situation improved, Petrarch was called upon for ceremonial occasions and political advice. In early 1361, at Galeazzo's invitation, he journeyed to Paris to deliver an oration celebrating the return of King John II (*d.* 1364) to the throne. Even more demanding was the request of Emperor Charles IV of Luxembourg that he judge the validity of two ancient documents that the Austrian ruler, Duke Rudolf IV (*d.* 1365), considered special privileges, deriving from Caesar and Nero, dispensing Austria from submission to the empire. Petrarch disproved their authenticity, and once again asked Charles to make Rome the capital of the empire.

The plague of 1361 caused more losses of friends and family (his son), and prompted Petrarch's temporary residency in Padua, where he finished his impressive *Familiares* and began a second collection of personal letters, the *Seniles*. His decision to return to Avignon at the pope's behest had to be canceled because of widespread wars in Lombardy. Even an invitation from the emperor to join his staff did not tempt Petrarch. He instead approached the chancellor of Venice with a request for hospitality in exchange for his personal library, which would become the city's public library at his death. The Venetian Republic offered him a house in which Petrarch did considerable work and entertained a number of friends; he also traveled extensively. For a time his residence in Venice appeared permanent, and he continued to participate in important world events. His delight at the election of Urban V (*r.* 1362–1370) as pope resulted in a persuasive letter (*Sen.* VII.1) inciting the pope not only to move to Rome but also to withstand the many pressures that would urge his return to Avignon. Unfortunately, upon returning to the Holy City, Urban found the chaotic situation of its government unbearable and was obliged to return to Avignon.

By 1367 Venice became intolerable as a result of its government's indifference to vicious attacks by four "Aristotelians" upon Petrarch and his works, attacks that he countered with a violent invective, *De sui ipsius et multorum ignorantia*. By 1369 he was again spending much of his time in Padua at the insistence of the lord, Francesco da Carrara, through whose generosity he received some land in Arquà, among the Euganean Hills, not too distant from Padua. There, with the assistance of friends, he built a comfortable house (which still stands), and there he transferred himself and all his belongings in 1370. His fame had by this time become such that Petrarch continued receiving (and refusing) invitations to change his domicile from the most powerful men of the time, including Urban's successor, Gregory XI (*r.* 1370–1378). Even in isolated Arquà there was no diminution in Petrarch's activities as writer and emissary. In addition to conveying the surrender of the Carrara family to the victorious Venetians, he gave his *Canzoniere* its final ordering, added the last two chapters to the *Trionfi,* rearranged his letters for their final edition, found time to write some of his best and longest letters and to translate Boccaccio's tale "Griselda" into Latin, and, perhaps most important, was able to live with tranquillity and joy once his daughter and her family agreed to join him in his final hermitage.

Petrarch died on the eve of his seventieth birthday shortly after midnight on 18/19 July 1374, while reading his Vergil. He was buried in the

PETRARCH

parish church of Arquà according to the instructions contained in his will, but was soon transferred by his son-in-law to the marble tomb that still stands beside the church in the village square.

As extraordinary as this life may appear in its barest outlines, the records through which it is distilled down to the present, especially those left by Petrarch himself, reflect a prophetic figure without whom the history of Western civilization would not have been exactly the same. The "transalpine Helicon," as he referred to his hermitage at Vaucluse, became the headquarters for activities that eventually led to his becoming not only a literary and cultural czar for all of Europe but also a consultant to emperors, popes, and kings. As Pier Giorgio Ricci has observed: "He was a prophet: and it was from him that Humanism took its basic form and shading, and from him that many fundamental threads of Renaissance civilization assumed particular characteristics." The reference is to Petrarch's sense of isolation in his conviction that what antiquity had to offer mankind was precisely what the society of his day seemed to lack, that is, not only the four cardinal virtues but also the awareness that men must interact with fellow men as well as with God. For him true virtue consisted of the Stoic definition "recte sentire de Deo et recte inter homines agere" (to feel rightly about God and to act rightly among men; *Fam.* XI.3).

THE SCHOLARLY PETRARCH

Petrarch the scholar and man of letters is reflected primarily in his Latin works (the later dates are of either the latest or the final revision).

Poetry. Africa (1338–1345); *Psalmi poenitentiales* (1342–1348); *Bucolicum carmen* (1347–1364); *Epistolae metricae* (composed 1331–1355, collected 1350–1358); miscellaneous pieces.

Prose. De viris illustribus (1338/1339, 1353); *Secretum* (1342/1343–1358); *Rerum memorandarum libri* (1343–1345); *Familiarium rerum libri XXIV* (1345–1366); *De vita solitaria* (1346–1371); *De otio religioso* (1347–1357); *Invective contra medicum* (1352–1353); *De remediis utriusque fortune* (1354–1366); *Invectiva contra quendam magni status hominem sed nullius scientie aut virtutis* (1355); *Itinerarium syriacum* (1358); *Senilium rerum libri XVII* (1361–1374); *De sui ipsius et multorum ignorantia* (1367); *Posteritati* (1367–1371); *Invectiva contra eum qui maledixit Italie* (1373); *Variae;* miscellaneous pieces including six orations and a personal will.

Servius reveals the poet Vergil to soldier, vinedresser, and shepherd, representing the *Aeneid*, the *Georgics*, and the *Eclogues*. Frontispiece by Simone Martini, commissioned by Petrarch for his personal copy of Vergil (the *Ambrosian Vergil*), before 1344. MILAN, BIBLIOTECA AMBROSIANA, CONS. I.VIII.74, fol. 1v

The epistolaries. Ernest Wilkins characterizes Petrarch's letter-writing as follows:

> Petrarch wrote an immense number of letters—more, perhaps, than anyone had ever written before him. The earliest appear to date from his university days; the latest of all, written a month before his death, ends with the words *Valete amici, valete epistole.* The number of his addressees is great beyond any precedent: a hundred and fifty are known to us by name. They include the Emperor Charles IV and his Empress, King Robert, Charles of Valois, members of the Visconti and of several other ruling families, doges of Genoa and of Venice, the people of Florence and the people of Rome, Rienzi, several chancellors, two popes, several cardinals, many bishops and archbishops.

There are many other addressees from all walks of life.

In describing the contents of the letters, Wilkins writes:

> They include . . . reminiscences; letters of invitation, thanks, excuse, congratulation, consolation; exhortation, reproof, and recommendation; praises of Italy and of certain Italian cities; characterizations; discussions of antiquity, poetry, authorship, style, scholarship, and the collecting of books; discussions of abstract subjects, such as fame, fortune, friendship, humility, and solitude.

A seemingly endless number of specific subjects are covered as well.

While Petrarch's two principal collections of letters, the *Rerum familiarium libri XXIV* (Letters on familiar matters) and the *Rerum senilium libri XVII* (Letters of later years), provide insights into his extensive involvements with events and individuals of his day, they also reflect his concern for form and classical norms, including countless citations from classical *auctores* and the recurring use of exempla from antiquity. In addition they project the image of a man of letters aware of the coalescence of time in each dimension of his work. Thus, while the *Familiares* ends with letters directed to such ancients as Vergil, Livy, Cicero, and Seneca, the *Seniles* concludes with a letter addressed to posterity. But most of all there are the innumerable indications of Petrarch's care in revising, rewriting, subdividing, eliminating, and even inventing letters to achieve desired artistic effects intended to reproduce the spirit of Cicero's epistolaries, especially his *Epistolae ad Atticum*. The names invented for the two friends to whom the collections are dedicated, "Socrates" and "Simonides," are suggestive of the same intent.

It was his discovery of Cicero's letters in 1345 that prompted Petrarch to begin collecting a corpus of his own missives, and by 1366 the *Familiares* included the present 350 letters. Some fifty-seven letters not qualifying for insertion were collected under the title *Variae,* and nineteen strong letters against the Avignon papacy were gathered into a separate group, entitled *Sine nomine*.

In 1361 Petrarch initiated a second major corpus containing letters of his later years. The *Seniles* were divided into seventeen books and contained 125 letters, but never underwent the polishing of the *Familiares*.

While the epistolaries suggest a need to communicate with kindred souls, the general contents and tone are far different from those of Dante and Boccaccio. Rather than practical or mundane information, they convey the inner movements of the writer's mind as it contemplates a problem or question or opinion. They provide a means for cultivating "the art of friendship" by having friends participate in the writer's literary conquests or moral stance on contemporary events. No letter, however, overlooks the exigencies of the epistle as a classical genre, with its style reflecting classical Latin or the Latin of the church fathers. The resulting portrait is of a cultured man of letters who may begin with a response to a correspondent but who makes that the vehicle for expressing his views and recollections. This explains why the addressee's name often fails to appear and why many letters either are fictitious or were never sent. Thus, the exigencies of the genre make the letter primarily a rhetorical exercise or a treatise.

Though Petrarch contends that his model is Cicero rather than Seneca, the themes reflect the Senecan tendency toward the moral and learned treatise, while the external format does remain Ciceronian. At times the classical superstructures and repetitive "sentences" are excessive, but at others the writer's involvement results in an intimacy and an eloquence reminiscent of his masterpieces. In the *Familiares* this is especially true when he treats such themes as the brevity of life and the flight of time (I.3; XXIV.1), the vanity of the desire for glory (I.2), the sense of an unhappy fate and the fragility of existence (V.8; VII.8; VIII.8; XIV.1), the introspective delight in analyzing his own passions and restlessness (XIX.16, 17), or life as a perilous journey. His letters to Giacomo Colonna (II.9), to Dionigi on the scaling of Mont Ventoux (IV.1), and to his brother (X.3) may serve to introduce his great exemplary epistles.

A large number are dedicated to Petrarch's tender relationships with friends, whether it be reconciling differences (XX.13–15), offering consolation in the midst of crises (II.1–4; VII.13), or mourning their deaths (IV.10–13; V.1). On occasion the letters reflect the portrait of a sage, but also the ideals and life of the writer satisfied with his lot (XVI.3), seeking only to enjoy the pleasures of learning (XXI.12). On the other hand, Petrarch does not hesitate to attack frauds, whether they be false poets, false philosophers, or false scientists (XIII.6–7; V.19; XV.6). Some reveal the curiosity of the ordinary traveler (II.12–14; I.5), at times with realistic narratives (V.5; XI.7) or with fanciful ones (I.4); some sketch such types as the miser (I.10), the lecher (V.9), the parasite (I.11), the lover (V.8); others are apologues or fables (IX.7; XVI.12). Numerous letters touch upon political or religious problems: from the description of the ideal government, monarchy (III.7), to the ideal prince (VII.15; XII.2), from excitement over Cola's coup (VII.5, 7; XIII.6) to appeals for the descent of Charles IV into Italy (X.1; XII.1; XVIII.1). Ultimately, the dominant spirit of his political and religious letters is the dream of a reborn Rome uniting, as it once did, popes and caesars.

The thematics become less strident in the later *Seniles*. Interested less in the world and more in his internal state, Petrarch writes to his closest friends with new maturity. The vision of death is countered with readings of pagan and Christian works. The comfort of art and the awareness of his dignity as a man of letters remain with him, giving him the strength to defend himself against unjust critics, to reaffirm the freedom of the writer (II.1) and the nobility of the pursuit of poetry (XVII.2). There continue to be observations on social and/or historical matters: the duties of a good prince (XIV.1), Dido in history and legend (IV.5), and the disproving of the caesarean diplomas claimed by the Hapsburgs (XVI.5). Polemical letters against groups such as doctors and Averroists abate, although literary interests still hold his attention (for instance, the acquisition of the Homeric poems in Latin), but the most sincere letters reflect a weariness and sadness not present in the *Familiares*. Petrarch lingers over memories of a life that is forever gone, yet with the wise serenity of a person expert at restraining his melancholy and nostalgia (X.2).

The unfinished *Letter to Posterity* that was to complete the *Seniles* as book XVIII reproduces a stereotyped portrait of the poet based primarily on the biography that Boccaccio had written. In it, however, Petrarch, aware of his cultural mission, centers his message for renewal on the *Africa*, which, though unfinished, was to contain the essential ingredients of humanism's dream: a classical epic with Christian overtones.

Polemical works. Petrarch wrote four invectives in Latin, all of them in response to attacks against his ideologies or convictions. All reflect his commitment to deeply felt values and his readiness to oppose any position that might jeopardize the human values relating to life and death, man's happiness on earth, and his aspirations after death. His main targets were Averroistic Aristotelianism, reactionary Scholasticism, and philosophical movements based on dialectic alone. In attacking the Averroists' doctrine of double truth, he employed texts and arguments from patristic and pagan sources. Yet, unlike Dante's invectives, Petrarch's tend to demolish systematically both the accusations and the attackers.

The *Invective contra medicum*, in four books, is directed against physicans in general. The pope's doctor became angry at Petrarch's letter to his patient (*Fam.* V.19) warning him against doctors' pretensions, and counterattacked by ridiculing Petrarch's dedication to letters. In books 2 and 3 the poet mocks the doctor's rhetoric, and in book 3 defends poetry as superior to the practical arts. This book became a fundamental text for the humanists, together with the defense in the fourth book of the life of solitude and the pursuit of virtue.

The *Invectiva contra quendam . . . hominem . . .* is against a French cardinal who attacked Petrarch for his servility to the Visconti and for plagiarizing the ancients. Petrarch's irony views the cardinal as an adventurer fated to fall from his high position, thus demolishing the saintly figure of his opponent. His scorn for ecclesiastical corruption, curial intrigues, and hypocritical culture (contrasted with the virtues and dedication to letters of both the Visconti and himself) contributes to the portrait of the poet accomplishing far more good than the cardinal.

De sui ipsius et multorum ignorantia is considered Petrarch's most original and powerful invective. Some Venetian "Aristotelians" who had said Petrarch was well-meaning but ignorant provoked the poet's acerbic attack against formal logic, the worship of the syllogism, and the submission to Aristotle as dehumanizing and dangerous to the Christian. To such "useless" knowledge Petrarch opposes the Augustinian ideal of a *sapientia* that is also *pietas*, and proclaims his dedication to virtue and truth. Aristotle is made Christianity's enemy in his pretense to explain God, while Cicero, Seneca, and Plato appear as precursors of the son of God. Thus his own knowledge fuses pagan and patristic culture, Cicero and Augustine, a far cry from his alleged ignorance.

The *Invectiva contra eum qui maledixit Italie* stemmed from Petrarch's continual campaign to return the papacy to Rome. It is directed against a professor at the University of Paris, champion of the French position that Avignon was the rightful see. One of Petrarch's most vitriolic invectives, it overwhelms the Frenchman with exempla that define the Christian religion in the spirit of charity to which French corruption could never aspire. It was Rome that had prepared the way of the Lord through its famous *pax*. The apology of the classical world is slowly transformed into the affirmation of the value of letters that transmit the lasting values of the past—a process in which Rome always led the way.

The spirit of Petrarch's polemical writings taught future humanists to intervene whenever their ideals were threatened by critics whose sole credentials are vanity and useless erudition.

Works in Latin verse. Petrarch attempted two other classical forms, the eclogue and the metrical letter. The *Bucolicum carmen* contains twelve eclogues of Vergilian stamp, started between 1346 and 1348, completed in 1352, but revised until 1364. The varied themes are usually hidden, if not crushed, by a thick allegory that often requires the author's explanation or the reader's deciphering. Such are the two on the corruption of the papal court (VI, VII) and the one on the Hundred Years War (XII). Of greater interest are those dealing with personal themes, such as the lament over the death of King Robert (II), the discussion between Petrarch and his brother on the relative merits of the classical epic and the poetry of David (I), a touching description of his move from Provence and his separation from Cardinal Colonna following Cola's coup in Rome (VIII), and Laura's death (X). While greatly admired, the eclogues often suffer from the rigid personifications.

Petrarch wrote over a hundred relatively short Latin poems, nearly all in unrhymed hexameters, entitled *Epistole metrice.* Originally youthful love poems, their scope was enlarged to contain verse letters on subjects similar to the other epistolaries. His formal criteria, at the beginning chronological, were abandoned as the collection grew to sixty-six letters divided into three books. Among these writings also, the most effective are those reflecting the poet's interests: descriptions of Vaucluse and of his life there, exhortations to successive popes to return to Rome, an account of his coronation, his love for Laura, the importance of preserving Roman ruins, his house in Parma, the prerogatives of Italy, and an extensive comment on the *Roman de la Rose* (III.30). Of particular merit are I.8, an extended though morbid autobiography, and III.10, on the precariousness of daily life, the flight of time, and the approach of death. These all are recapitulated in I.14, which is a disturbed but lucid meditation on his personal life at the approach of death. The best poems of the collection, according to Wilkins, "are worthy companions to the best of the Italian lyrics."

Historical works. The three works constituting Petrarch's highest aspirations, and primarily responsible for his reputation in his own time, were the *Africa,* the *De viris illustribus,* and the *Rerum memorandarum libri,* all dealing with the personalities and qualities that made antiquity the mother of civilization. For the first two he received the laurel crown in 1341 as poet and historian, since the *Africa* was an attempt at Vergilian epic and the *De viris* was to consist of biographies of the greatest individuals of all time. Unquestionably these two were the basis of Petrarch's hope for enduring fame.

Although incomplete, the *Africa* is the Latin work to which Petrarch devoted more time and energy than to any other. Like the *Aeneid,* it was to consist of twelve books, to use the same meter, and to exude the same spirit. It was this last objective that was most difficult to achieve, and perhaps explains why the poet never went beyond book IX and why scholars have failed to see why it was one of the most ambitious attempts at formal Latin epic undertaken since the *Aeneid.*

Petrarch suggests this in his *Letter to Posterity:* "One Holy Friday . . . I was overtaken by a desire to write an epic poem on that first Scipio Africanus, whose extraordinary fame, strange as it may seem, had appealed to me since my early years. The nature of the subject prompted me to entitle it *Africa.* . . . " Petrarch was thus inspired to begin the epic on the same holy day he had met his beloved, Laura; that is, not only a Good Friday but the actual Good Friday in liturgical time that Carlo Calcaterra has shown to be 6 April. Petrarch's Vergilian epic was to reflect the highest moment in the history of Roman valor as seen in the exploits of one of the most perfect leaders, morally and militarily, that Rome had ever boasted. The first section was inspired by Cicero's *Somnium Scipionis,* which had existed as an extract with many commentaries since early Christian times. Macrobius' commentary had made the dream a compendium of knowledge and philosophy. When one adds to this Livy's account of Scipio's feats and of his character, as well as the significance to Rome and to Western civilization of the defeat of Hannibal's invasion of Italy, the starting date of 6 April becomes as appropriate for such an epic as it had been for his meeting with Laura. As I have shown in my book on the *Africa*, in Petrarch's view,

> Here was a man who, as a living paragon of virtue, valor, and glory, had not only saved Rome, the capital of antiquity and of Christianity, in its darkest hour, but had been able to reach into the future and incite his adopted grandson to the final destruction of Carthage and the establishment of Rome as a truly eternal city. . . . (*Petrarch, Scipio, and the "Africa"*)

Petrarch read a good portion of the poem to King Robert prior to the coronation ceremony, which had probably spurred him to add the portion inspired by Livy. It is this portion that contains sections celebrated for their poetic appeal: the Sophonisba-Massinissa episode (V–VI), the death of Mago (VI), the Battle of Zama (VII). Book IX, although awkward, is important for Petrarch's ideas on poetry and on the poet's role in society. In the description of Scipio's triumph, the poet Ennius stands at his right, thus showing Scipio's high regard for poetry and the arts. Thomas Bergin defines the value of the *Africa* as an essential document in the history of culture:

> Petrarch set for himself the goal of integrating Livy's history, Cicero's philosophy, and Virgil's poetry: the *Africa* is his great heroic statement on history and poetry and all the *studia humanitatis*. . . . And we believe it serves to deepen our understanding of a great poet and a remarkably sensitive human being.

Petrarch considered himself a historian as well as a poet, but his interest in the past lay in men rather than in events. He was thus closer to a biographer than to a general historian. The *De viris* was originally to be a series of biographies starting with Romulus and ending with Titus. He completed twenty-four, the biography of Julius Caesar being the last and longest. The work was enlarged at the beginning and end by prefixing the lives of twelve biblical and mythological figures, from Adam to Hercules, and by adding lives, never actually written, of twelve more Romans, from Flaminius to Trajan. His primary source was Livy, but many others (such as Suetonius and Florus) were used with discrimination.

The collection was clearly intended to inspire in the reader the *animi vis et acrimonia* (strength and keenness of mind) of the great men. The writer follows their vicissitudes, commenting on both kinds of fortune in order to give a sense of deeds and lives as real and lived. Although Petrarch always seems to seek the exemplary moralistic value of his heroes, the work does depart from the ordinary medieval chronicle in that his interpretations are free of providential colorations or preordained conceptions.

Like the *De viris illustribus*, the *Rerum memorandarum libri* was to be a supplement to, or exegesis of, the *Africa*, but in a different manner. The work was planned as a voluminous treatise on the cardinal virtues and was structured as a temple of virtues. Its opening book is called the "vestibule," or the necessary "preludes" to virtue (leisure, solitude, enthusiasm, and learning), with Scipio presiding as the paragon of all virtues. Biography is here fused with anecdotes to provide exempla for which Greek, Roman, and modern figures are given in order to compare ancient virtues with later ones.

As with the *Invectives*, Petrarch's attitude is critical of the present and expresses his conviction that were the glorious history of the past reexperienced through the testimony of the past, it would be possible to direct man toward the exercise of the moral virtues. Petrarch never went beyond the introductory book and three books on Prudence, despite the novelty and originality of design and a philological methodology based on reliable sources.

These three historical works were destined to remain unfinished for a variety of reasons, but their message was clear. Greece and Rome had much to offer man that sooner or later had to be recognized and accepted. Increasingly, Petrarch realized that discovering and restructuring authentic documents of ancient culture was as important as trying to contrast past and present. He assumed the task with a zeal that was to inspire future humanists.

Though written for a friend as a geographical guide to the Holy Land, the *Itinerarium syriacum* is really an archaeological guide woven with literary allusions. The information useful for the pilgrimage includes much historical and anecdotal data concerning the route, enhanced by moralistic observations. The descriptions of the Italian coast from Genoa to Naples, and of Naples itself, are based on personal experience. Typical of the commentary is the following: "You must not fail to visit the Royal Chapel where my fellow-townsman [Giotto] . . . has left great monuments of his genius and his skill." Together with Boccaccio's *De montibus* this work marks a revival of geography based on factual sources, a genre forgotten since antiquity.

The personal treatises. With the passage of time the Latin works begin applying the lessons learned from classical *auctores* to Petrarch's own life and

Christian viewpoint. In the mid 1340's he discovered two concepts that acted as practical links between classical wisdom and Christian spirituality: the ideals of *otium litteratum* and *vita solitaria,* both of which applied to the lives of the ancient greats and of the Christian Fathers.

De vita solitaria is divided into two books, the first containing a dedication and eight chapters, the second fifteen chapters. The dedication affirms that the treatise is based on the writer's conviction that to understand oneself and to rediscover the word of God in order to achieve salvation, one must seek a refuge away from the city. He thus contrasts the harried life of the city dweller with that of the country dweller, close to nature and to God (I.2). The portrait reveals an aristocratic isolation that allows the learned man to become a repository of the wisdom of the past without any sense of contradiction with the Christian precept of charity. This ideal is not to be imposed on society as a whole, but is, rather, an invitation to a select minority, those who know how to interact with books and knowledge, to reject hypocrisy and temptation.

Despite the many exempla from many ages and many places, the final profession of faith is the value of a life spent amid books and friends with the background of a nature silent and apart, whose presence encourages the remembrance of things past, the common interests and tastes that provide deeper insights into one's very being. The message is addressed to his restricted circle of friends who may have a vocation for the religious or the literary life. While the work does end in the name of Christ, its main thrust is literary and its principal exempla are drawn from the great spirits of the classical past.

De otio religioso reflects the same themes as *De vita solitaria,* but the perspective and intent are different. Though the original title was *De otio religiosorum,* it is considered incorrect. The treatise is divided into two books composed in 1347 and revised extensively over the next ten years. It resulted from Petrarch's visit to his brother's Carthusian monastery, and is dedicated to Gherardo. Addressed to the French Carthusians as a celebration of the monastic life and the cloistered leisure (*otium*) it offers for contemplating the divine, it follows roughly Augustine's *De vera religione.*

The work is structured and proceeds in a manner much inferior to the *De vita solitaria.* The theme of celebrating the monastic ideal is interrupted by digressions on the dangers and obstacles threatening such a life. The learned citations fail to breathe life into the pages, and the theme lacks organic development because of the writer's lack of conviction for the ascetic life, despite his admiration for it.

The same religious echoes, intensified by the many deaths from the plague of 1348, inspired the seven *Psalmi poenitentiales* that are prayers and/or confessions in short prosaic verses. Using material from the Psalms and other portions of the Old Testament, Petrarch creates a distinctly Augustinian tone. While he maintains that the *Psalmi* were composed without literary concern, they are effective in their lack of direct translation from the various sources and for their reflection of a lyric intonation of the highest order.

The vast and uneven contents of *De remediis utriusque fortune* represent Petrarch's most important and committed work from the philosophical point of view, as well as the work most pertinent to man's daily life. As a result it was the most popular of his treatises down to the eighteenth century. The full story of its evolution has yet to be written, but the first draft falls in 1356–1357, although it was not published until 1366. Dedicated to Azzo da Correggio, who, of all Petrarch's friends, had felt most painfully the wheel of fortune, the final version is divided into two parts, with book I, containing 122 dialogues involving Reason, Joy, and Hope, giving remedies for the dangers inherent in more than 100 kinds of good fortune, and with book II giving remedies for more than 100 kinds of adverse fortune in 131 dialogues.

It is perhaps the most attractive of Petrarch's treatises because of the variety of human interests involved. Its theme is the mutability of fortune; the mood is essentially Stoic; its primary purpose is to assist man in attaining moral dignity. Thus readers found in the detailed expositions divided into brief dialogues a reference book for coping with the vicissitudes of fortune and the problem of good and evil. For Petrarch, human nature is fundamentally miserable, whether fortune smiles upon it or not. Yet there is an almost heroic belief that misery can be mitigated and fleeting joys controlled through the use of the wisdom of the great writers. Faith in the human ability to act or to react never falters throughout the book. In I.2.93, the humanistic message becomes wedded to the Christian one inherited from the Fathers, one that opens the doors of heaven without closing the garden and desert of earth as Reason cries out: "Tell me, I beg you, what could man ever, I do not say hope to have, but desire or consider of greater account, than the fact that man may become God?"

Despite the clear echoes of Boethius, Cicero, and Seneca, this treatise exudes a freshness and originality not found in the *summae* of the time.

THE INTROSPECTIVE AND LYRICAL PETRARCH

All the works treated thus far were projects aimed at learned readers and intended to produce an image of the writer who hoped to restore to European culture the grandeur and values of the fading classical past.

The unique coronation ceremony, however, had left Petrarch with an uneasy conscience. The result was a spiritual and psychological crisis caused not only by his scruples about deserving the laurel crown but also by a series of other events. The birth of his illegitimate daughter offered him living proof of his carnal weakness, while his brother's decision to enter a monastery and the death of Robert of Sicily resulted in what Bergin calls "the sense of unease and even despair . . . which led to a thorough soul-searching, of which the *Secretum* is the record."

The Secretum. Though written in Latin prose, the *Secretum,* together with the *Canzoniere* and the *Trionfi,* is the most intimate of Petrarch's works, and is thus included in this section. In many ways it serves as a watershed from which all his works and activities seem to flow, the "tranquil waters" of moral justification that even a kindred soul such as St. Augustine cannot fully accept. Its searching self-analysis, while seemingly unresolved at the end, does appear to provide Petrarch with a distinct conviction that his works and activities may not necessarily lead to damnation.

While *Secretum meum* is the title given within the text, the title *De secreto conflictu curarum mearum* appearing on a number of manuscripts is preferred by many critics. The work was never published, since it was presumably intended for the author alone. It is divided into three books representing three days of discussion between St. Augustine and Francesco, in the presence of the silent allegorical figure of Truth. The fictitious framework is quite simple: Petrarch imagines that in a kind of waking dream there appear to him Lady Truth and Augustine, who at her request tries to free the writer from the dangerous spiritual illness from which he has long suffered and to direct him toward the path of a Christian life. The two interlocutors stand for Petrarch's divided personality, with Augustine representing the religious ideal and Francesco the secular. The choice of Augustine is natural because the *Secretum* is modeled on his *Confessions,* but there are also Stoic echoes of Boethius, Cicero, and Seneca.

The opening borrows from the "vision" genre with which Petrarch had experimented in the *Africa.* Lady Truth introduces herself in the dream as "the one whom in your *Africa* you depicted with loving elegance," implying that she has come to help one who had once been able to see her clearly but now needs assistance. Francesco tries to contemplate her, but his sight cannot tolerate her brightness. She thus has him turn to Augustine, who has mysteriously appeared. As in the opening of the *Divine Comedy,* the Lady urges the ancient seer to save Francesco from his dangerous illness. Despite condemnations of himself and of all mankind throughout the three-day conversation, the poet admits finding it so helpful that he decided to record it for himself alone.

Augustine sets the theme of book I by stressing the realization that earthly life will cease and the necessity of preparation for eternal life. As long as man does not train his will to turn away from earthly delights, such happiness is impossible. Rather than the laurel (Latin poetry) or the myrtle (vernacular poetry), Francesco should recall Augustine's fig tree. Earthly matters can only lead to "fantasma," the greatest of all impediments because they reflect false images of reality that keep the mind from ascending to "the one and greatest light."

In the second book, Augustine examines Francesco with respect to the Seven Deadly Sins. Accused of pride of talent, of the superficial beauty of his works, of his sense of personal attractiveness, and of aspiring to earthly glory, Francesco responds with equivocation. He admits serious failure only in the case of the seventh deadly sin, *accidia* (slothful melancholy): ". . . this plague seizes me at times with such tenacity that for whole days and nights it holds me in its grasp and tortures me; and my life then has the semblance not of light and of true life, but of Tartarean night and bitter death."

Book III explores what prevents Francesco's proper meditation on life and death. Augustine accuses him of being bound by two adamantine chains: his love for Laura and his desire for glory. Francesco, greatly shocked, had considered them his brightest ideals and the least harmful to his soul. For him, love can be noble or abject, but this depends on the beloved; and his had been a rare model of virtue and beauty. For Augustine, Laura is still a mortal woman who has wasted too much of

PETRARCH

Francesco's life, causing him to overlook the Creator because of a creature. Her very name had made him fall into a "splendid abyss" and stray from the straight path to take the byway to earthly glory. Of all the bad effects singled out by Augustine, the worst was the poet's worship of the laurel. The danger in such madness is the neglect of self and of God, which would lead to perdition.

While the poet nearly concedes that perhaps Augustine is right in his indictment of Laura, he withstands Augustine's warnings against the desire for earthly glory. He believes that there is a legitimate earthly glory that does not interfere with salvation. He is, in fact, in the midst of writing "an illustrious work, rare and outstanding." Thereupon Augustine argues that such time-consuming works may lead to damnation because they distract him from the path to salvation. But Francesco rebuts this:

> You must come forth with something more persuasive than that if you can, for I find that [argument] expedient rather than effective. I am not contemplating becoming a god. . . . Human glory is sufficient for me; only this do I long for, and, mortal that I am, I desire only mortal things.

Francesco listens politely to the remainder of Augustine's arguments, but he makes it clear that, while he hopes someday to follow the saint's advice, he cannot yet abandon his pursuits, above all the *De viris illustribus* and the *Africa,* the objects of Augustine's attack. The *Secretum* thus ends in a staunch defense not only of classical studies but also of those works of Petrarch intended to exalt the greatest heroes of antiquity. For Petrarch, Augustine's "chains" and "phantasms" can also serve as goads.

Better known as the *Canzoniere,* the *Rerum vulgarium fragmenta* is unique for a number of reasons: Petrarch considers his poems "trifles"; he worked diligently both on the poems and on their ordering for at least thirty years; we still possess a large number of the worksheets (Vat. Lat. 3196) on which he entered and revised particular poems; we still possess the final manuscript of the collection (Vat. lat. 3195), which is partially autograph and reveals the poet's dissatisfaction to the very end with his ordering (the autograph marginalia give yet another ordering of the last thirty poems); unlike any previous collection of vernacular love lyrics, it reflects all of Petrarch's aspirations, desires, fears, conflicts, and learning instead of only his love for a woman. In fact, its central inspiration is as humanistic as it is courtly or stilnovistic; Laura, whose name recalls the laurel crown of Roman greatness, substitutes for his favorite Roman hero, Scipio, just as Beatrice replaces Vergil in Dante's *Comedy.*

Ernest H. Wilkins proved with sound methodology that the *Canzoniere* went through at least nine versions before transcription into the manuscript Vat. lat. 3195. The definitive collection consists of 366 poems in five different metrical forms: 317 sonnets, 29 *canzoni,* 9 *sestine,* 7 ballates, and 4 madrigals. (Excluded poems still extant are known as *Rime disperse.*) The collection is divided into two parts: "In vita" (1–263) and "In morte di Madonna Laura" (264–366). Most of the poems relate the poet's love for Laura, a woman of beauty and excellence. Some thirty-seven poems deal with various other subjects: religious, moral, political, or matters pertaining to friends. Increasingly, scholars are seeing new dimensions in the collection that make it a "breviary" of a sensitive man of letters attempting to fuse classical and Christian values.

Though the first poem seems to recant his love poems and the last poem seems to be a hymn of thanksgiving to the Virgin Mary, the last poem of part I (263) and the first poem of part II (264) identify the central conflict in terms reminiscent of the *Secretum.* Poem 263, the last to the "live" Laura and the last to be entered, is perhaps the key poem, since it seems to provide her with a complex definition through recapitulating various images. She is first addressed as the "Victorious triumphal tree, honor of emperor and of poets," then as "True Lady, concerned for naught but honor," and finally as the one who despises what is "prized among us," including her "high beauty, which has no equal in the world, . . . except insofar as it seems to adorn and set off your lovely treasure of chastity." Throughout her life, then, Laura was an inspiration not unlike that which Apollo found in Daphne, whom he transformed into a laurel tree precisely for the qualities exemplified by Laura: beauty and purity.

Poem 264 declares it impossible to fulfill the recantation of poem 1 because the poet now feels both the dangers and the appeal of Laura's image as defined in poem 263; Augustine's two adamantine chains have become two knots. Indeed, the poet even tries to recall the "crossroads" mentioned in the *Secretum* where he abandoned "the journey to the right," but to no avail; the poem ends with the famous cry, "And I see what is best, but cling to the worst."

The abiding theme of the *Canzoniere* is love, but its scope widens from the love of a beautiful lady to the love of an indefinable beauty reflected by Laura and partaking of the human and the divine, the classical and the Christian; to a beauty that can attract an Apollo or lead a Christian sinner to Mary and her Son; to the love of Italy and the church of Christ; to the love of one's fellow man; to the love of learning and antiquity; to the love of nature and solitude, to the love of goodness, truth, virtue, and glory. At times, some or all of these loves are implicitly or explicitly sung in a poem to Laura.

Everywhere there are echoes of Horace, Vergil, Ovid, Seneca, Livy, Lucan, Cicero, and Catullus, as well as Arnaut Daniel, Bernart de Ventadorn, Calvacanti, Sennuccio del Bene, and particularly Cino da Pistoia and Dante. Obviously, then, unlike Dante's poetry, Petrarch's is addressed to the learned reader. There are also borrowings from religious models, from Augustine to Boethius, the Scriptures, and the Psalms. And yet this fusion of life and literature, so typical of Petrarch, does achieve an unparalleled lyricism. The springboard is his profound need to resolve his inner conflicts—which never actually happens except, perhaps, through its verbalization. His elegiac tone results not only from unhappiness over the transience of all that is human but also from disappointment in a divinity that fails to placate a believer desirous of both the earthly and the divine. Whence the sense that the real theme goes beyond love as a passion, and becomes a soliloquy or dialogue with himself or the reader, with nature, or with Laura, dialogues that the poet's sensitivity subjects to a psychological analysis in the light of spiritual uncertainties.

This may be observed in the formal structure given to the collection. In the first form (fourteen poems), nine revolve around a classical theme, especially the Apollo-Daphne myth, in which Laura becomes Daphne and the poet, Apollo. With the second form, however, Petrarch clearly decided to open with poems providing a Christian framework. Aside from the recantation theme (1), the next poems (2–4) describe the beginnings of his love as having occurred on a Good Friday, which he elsewhere dates as 6 April 1327. Scholarship has proven that this date was not a Good Friday, but the actual date of Christ's Passion. Eventually it seemed to encompass Petrarch's entire life: on 6 April he began the *Africa* and the *Trionfi*, he arrived in Rome for his coronation, and Laura died on a 6 April (1348), which was an Easter Sunday. She thus, according to Carlo Calcaterra, captured him on the day of Christ's Passion and freed him on the day of the Resurrection. Even the twenty-one years that had intervened found meaning in medieval numerology with the numbers 7 and 3.

More recently, Thomas Roche, Jr., went even further than Calcaterra in analyzing Petrarch's use of a Christian calendrical structure in order to explain the placement of the nonsonnet forms within the collection. Accepting the centrality of the date 6 April and of the year 1327 in Petrarch's life, he assigns that date to the first poem. By so doing and by following the calendrical sequence for each subsequent poem, he shows how no. 264, which opens the second part, would fall on Christmas and the last poem, to the Virgin, would fall on Palm Sunday. Furthermore, the beginning of his love on the day of Christ's death counterpoints the Augustinian distinction between *caritas* and *cupiditas* by proclaiming his love to be essentially selfish. By beginning part II on the day of Christ's birth, the poem proclaims "the possibility of rejuvenation and of truer understanding of both earthly and heavenly love."

While this theory of the *Canzoniere* being structured around the liturgical year may be valid, another interpretation may be just as valid, especially in explaining the *Trionfi*, which may be viewed as complementing the *Canzoniere*. This interpretation centers on the arguments against earthly glory made by Augustine in the *Secretum* and Petrarch's lifelong desire to be an intermediary between classical and Christian learning.

Like his view of ancient myths, Petrarch's lyrics contain images of a perennially grieving and restless humanity finding redemption in the very contemplation of the forbidden fruit. Only through a sound knowledge of his Latin works may one see what might be called the humanistic dimension of his Italian lyrics. By identifying his passion for Laura with the myth of Daphne, symbolic not only of a selfish and fleeting love but also of the eternal beauty sought by the god of light, moral purity, music, and poetry, Petrarch endows his "book of songs" with a highly personal sense of love possessing new artistic dimensions.

In his Latin works Petrarch reveals a noble view of mankind deriving from a literary-historical study of its pagan and Christian past. While extolling the achievements of ancient heroes and writers, he seals them with the same imprint of a grieving and transient humanity searching for a timeless happiness. When viewed within the Christian framework, however, all past achievements and knowledge reflect man's greatness and his limitations; yet with proper understanding through the light of God, all past knowledge can become true wisdom.

For this reason, then, Petrarch's Italian lyrics seem to reflect both a pagan Parnassus and a Christian Calvary. By superimposing a Christian awareness on a pagan myth, the love poems mirror the kind of redemption that Petrarch feels is needed by suffering humanity. Laura as Beauty, Poetry, and Earthly Love may deserve veneration, but not at the expense of Christian salvation. The Christian superstructure of part II begins to counterbalance the Apollo-Daphne motif of part I, meshing the two themes, first by orchestrating the hidden meanings of the Apollo-Daphne myth, and then by immersing Laura's image within the framework of the Passion and Redemption. With *canzoni* 359, 360, and 366, the poet's new dilemma is defined: whether one must reject earthly endeavors in order to gain Christian salvation. The final hymn to the Virgin seems a positive response, but most of the Virgin's attributes are Laura's, while her primary attribute, her virginity, is celebrated twenty-one times in the word "Virgin," recalling the length of the poet's love drama.

The poetry can thus be said to express throughout not only the enchantment felt by a Christian Apollo for a Christian Daphne, but also a sense of the contradictory nature of the two terms. As a result, the poet's endless attempts to reconcile the two dimensions of the myth in the figure of Laura endow his "trifles" with a poetic power that far surpasses any and all traditions from which they derived.

These overall interpretations are in no way meant to deprive individual poems of their gemlike beauty and perfection. The manner in which Petrarch gave a kind of final set to the sonnet, the *canzone,* and the *sestina* has been the subject of innumerable studies. Indeed, it was this type of accomplishment, especially in the dazzling development of some of the sonnets, that was to attract future generations of Petrarchists and was to divide scholars over what constituted the truly aesthetic dimension of the *Canzoniere.* In recent years it has been shown that perhaps Petrarch's collection may well satisfy the criteria of both modern and medieval-Augustinian theories of aesthetics.

Simultaneously with his lifelong work on the *Canzoniere,* Petrarch was also trying to fulfill another ambition—the composition of a work in Italian that would both portray his humanistic Laura and vie with Dante's masterpiece. Even a surface perusal of his six *Trionfi,* all with Latin titles, reveals the extent of Dante's influence: the *terza rima,* the poet's journey beyond this world and beyond time with the aid of a guide, a vision of humanity victim of its own foibles and greatness, a concluding vision that leads beyond death and time with the poet's beloved playing the central role, and similar rhetorical devices and phraseology. The challenge also recalls Petrarch's correspondence with Boccaccio on his judgment of Dante (*Fam.* XXI.15; *Sen.* V.2), as well as his letter to his brother on the value and function of secular (as contrasted with religious) literature (*Fam.* X.4). The poetry he sought not only teaches the virtues in the manner of the great ancients, but it does so without overlooking Christian charity.

Since Petrarch never gave the *Trionfi* a final set, it is impossible to give the exact dates of composition (somewhere between 1338 and 1374), or the sequence of subsections desired by the poet. The basic structure and theme, however, provide sufficient evidence of the author's purpose. There are six triumphs, each divided into *capitoli,* each portraying the best of humanity in its struggle against mysterious forces in order to achieve an eternity of fulfillment. These forces are Love, Chastity, Death, Fame, Time, and Eternity, and each is depicted as triumphing in some form over the preceding one. The significance of the number 6 for Petrarch has already been broached, but it may be well to recall that, in Christian tradition, God created man on the sixth day, man fell on the sixth day, and on the sixth day Christ's death redeemed that fall. Also significant is the opening scene of the first triumph, 6 April.

We note also the centrality of the ancient Roman triumph for victorious figures, "Such as triumphal chariots used to bear / To glorious honor on the Capitol" ("Tr. of Love," vv. 14–15). Each triumph presents a large number of persons moving processionally under the dominance of a single figure. Of the six triumphant figures, all are medieval allegories except the first, the classical figure of Cupid, whose dominance as *cupiditas* contrasts the classical motif with Augustinian *caritas.*

On 6 April, then, while walking through the woods near Vaucluse, the poet dreams of the triumph of Cupid sitting atop a chariot, herding countless prisoners whom Petrarch does not recognize. A shade appears, at first unknown to him but then recognized by him (he remains unnamed, unlike Dante's Vergil), with whom the poet views the spectacle. The shade expresses surprise that the poet is not in the procession, but Petrarch insists that "the toils of love dismayed me" (vv. 55–56), thus giving a different account of his pre-Laura loves than in the *Canzoniere*. To the poet's shock, few are the past greats not included among Cupid's victims, from the two Caesars and Nero to Aeneas and a host of Greek and mythological figures; from Phaedra to Phyllis, who was changed into a tree that blossomed through her lover's tears. This reminiscence of the Laura-Daphne motif leads at the end of the *capitolo* to a view of Apollo standing haughtily alone without a mate, obviously meant to reflect the once victimized lover who is now an uninvolved observer. The presence of Apollo and Phyllis is essential to an understanding of Laura as the central poetic image in the *Trionfi*.

The second *capitolo* of the first triumph continues to reinforce Petrarch's concept of love as more than passion, based somehow on the ancient cardinal virtues. The episode of Massinissa and Sophonisba, echoing Paolo and Francesca as well as Aeneas and Dido, with its resolution through the "holy words" of Scipio Africanus, once more reflects Scipio's moral and military heroism. In the third *capitolo* the throng of Cupid's victims, "all stained with the same pitch" (v. 99), enlarges to include examples from Greek, scriptural, Hebraic-Christian, and courtly times. Suddenly, a maid "took me captive: I . . . was bound by her words and by her ways" (vv. 91–93). The guide thereupon laughs and welcomes him among the victims. Interestingly, Laura stands outside the procession and the poet notes that Cupid himself seems to fear "the fair beast," since it seems that "no one can bind her with the bonds of love . . ." (vv. 130ff).

In *capitolo* IV the dreaming lover realizes that he was swiftly tamed. He thus joins other poet-victims who include Orpheus, Vergil, Ovid, Dante, Arnaut, and some friends with whom he had sought perhaps a premature glory: "With them I plucked the glorious laurel branch / Wherewith—perhaps too soon—I decked my brow" (vv. 79ff). He also recalls having failed to do Laura's bidding as expressed in one of the last poems of the *Canzoniere:* "Yet from her, . . . / Ne'er have I gathered either branch or leaf, / So hard and unyielding were her roots" (vv. 82–84). Finally, the poet describes Cupid taking his triumph from Vaucluse to Cyprus, the abode of Venus, where he encloses all in a cage and where his allegorical "troops," mostly phantasms, subject the imprisoned victims to the sufferings of love.

In the second triumph, of Chastity, Cupid does battle with Laura and loses, thus becoming "captive and reft of his wings" (v. 18). In contrast with Cupid's troops, Laura's are more civilized, with Beauty and Chastity leading all others. And her victory is compared with those of Scipio, Goliath, and Cyrus. The remainder of the triumph contains the moment that is the core of Petrarch's concept of Laura. In leading what had been Cupid's triumph to Rome, she has Scipio join her band. Then she leads her triumph first to the Roman temple of Venus Verticordia, the "good" Venus who freed hearts from mad passions, and then to the temple of patrician chastity, where she deposits Cupid's spoils and the "laurel crown of victory" (v. 186), recalling Petrarch's symbolic gesture at his coronation. The implications of Laura's triumph over Cupid are most complex, for the Chastity she represents is not the simple guarding of her virginity, but the conquest of those passions that dehumanize man, making him a caged animal. She is thus the force that can free humanity from such a condition; and when she makes Scipio her lieutenant, we feel the extent to which chaste forces can contribute to the concept of the hero.

Some of these meanings emerge in the following "Triumph of Death." The opening verses describe Laura as "Glad for her victory over the great foe / Who with his fraudulence afflicts the world" (vv. 5–6), recalling Dante's definition of Satan. Just as it was impossible for Laura to eliminate Cupid except perhaps in the lover's heart, so it is with Laura's death, which symbolizes the destruction not of Chastity but of the chastity affecting the poet most directly. Furthermore, just as Cupid was subdued in Venus' abode, Laura as Chastity is subdued in the poet's Helicon. The description of Laura's death is actually a triumph over death, a triumph that suggests Christ's in certain details and in the concluding verse: "And even death seemed beautiful in her beautiful face."

The following *capitolo* provides a vision, within the dream, of the poet in intimate conversation with Laura under a laurel tree. Like Augustine, she defines his problem as one involving the reason and the will. Indeed, his reaction to her death still shows his excessive attraction to her physical beauty.

In the fourth triumph, of Fame, we again behold a triumph of "Laura," although most critics deny the clear resemblances between Lady Fame and Laura. Yet Lady Fame can only reflect, if not Laura herself, then at least the kind of fame that Petrarch saw in Laura. In fact, in an unfinished *capitolo* among the appendices of the *Trionfi,* he includes himself with Scipio and Laura among those who did triumph over *cupiditas,* a triumph worthy of the Capitoline crown. In addition, the greats led by Lady Fame include many of those freed by Laura in the "Triumph of Chastity." When the poet observes that the Latins had acquired fame because of a selfless concern for the people, the reader senses that true glory involves a love that could only be called chaste. The following *capitolo* depicts the fame earned by the great non-Roman peoples. Once again it resulted from *ben far* (good works) that Laura repeatedly effects in the poet throughout the *Canzoniere;* indeed in a discarded appendix (Appendix 1) to the "Triumph of Chastity" he calls her the one "for whom I first found pleasure in doing good works."

The last *capitolo* of the "Triumph of Fame" deals with those who had gained fame for reasons other than military prowess. In the guide's words, "Tis not in arms alone that fame is won" (v. 3). Here are the great philosophers, thinkers, and poets whose lofty goals include both the pleasures of beauty and the beauty of virtue. Once again the recurring image of Laura comes to mind.

In the "Triumph of Time" the sun (Apollo?) cannot conceive of human fame lasting ad infinitum, and thus accelerates to allow Time to take its toll of human glory, a theme appearing in both the *Secretum* and the *Canzoniere.* By comparing Augustine's "splendid abysses" to the words of the angry sun in this triumph ("What dark abyss of blind oblivion / Awaits these slight and tender human flowers!": vv. 101–102), the reader feels that the poet is preparing for the return of Laura as a new sun. And this is indeed what happens in the "Triumph of Eternity."

At the opening, the dreaming poet seems near despair because there is nothing stable under the heavens. His heart warns him that he must turn to the Creator, in whom he can trust, but the poet also utters the hope that divine mercy will still work within him "lofty and rare effects." These words might be taken as an abiding hope that the poet will be allowed to salvage certain secular and praiseworthy values, even while going beyond earthly aspirations. He then asks, "If all things / That are beneath the heavens are to fail, / How, after many circlings, will they end?" (vv. 16–18). While pondering such things, he beholds the world as he knew it unmade, and then remade "more beauteous and joyous than before" (v. 24). The basic characteristic of this new world is timelessness. Mortal fame will no longer be controlled by the years; instead "the glorious / Will glorious be to all eternity" (vv. 90–91).

Thus does Petrarch try to resolve the problem of the frailty of human endeavor and glory. Mortal fame will endure provided it was truly meritorious and partook of qualities that the poet once again associates with his beloved. In this new world Laura will stand out among those who are "rare and beauteous," and her "angelic modes" and "chaste thoughts" will be perfectly visible. When this will be, the poet cannot say any more than could Christ's disciples (vv. 100–102). But true merit will be identifiable at the right moment, for without time all such mysteries will become as transparent as a spiderweb. Those who "merited illustrious fame" will, in the flower of their new youth, possess "immortal beauty and eternal glory" (vv. 133–134). And leading them all will be his Laura, who has assumed her glorified beauty.

Once again Laura leads a triumph and seems to stand in the place of the figure of Eternity, leading a group that doubtless must include the followers of Lady Fame. The ending of the *Trionfi* recalls the ending of the *Africa,* where Scipio stood with Ennius at his side. Laura heads a host of past greats, including Scipio and Caesar, because they had all been inspired by the beauty inherent in the laurel crown. It resembles a movement from the laurel back to Daphne, a new world in which a Christian Apollo is now able to convert the laurel back to its human form. Laura and her selected retinue are destined to partake of the eternal verdure of the classical laurel because their deeds and accomplishments are marked by beauty and goodness.

Thus does Petrarch resolve the dilemma of his twofold vocation, the learned man of letters with an unrivaled knowledge of antiquity, and the deeply sensitive Christian poet in the vernacular who is aware of Dante's great accomplishment and desirous of outdoing him. By reflecting the learning of his Latin works in his Italian poetry in a manner almost contrary to Dante's, he managed to achieve something that for centuries made his poetry the norm for love poetry. But there is little doubt that Petrarch would have denied any value to the movement that became known as Petrarchism. What he wished to express in his vernacular poetry was a message different from, but just as important as,

Dante's. This message he had conveyed to Boccaccio in *Seniles* I.5, in which he declares that, while the journey to salvation may be a blessed experience for all, "that journey is more glorious that achieves the summit accompanied by the loveliest light; whence the piety of an ignorant but pious man is inferior to the piety of the man of letters." The incredible procession led by Laura in the "Triumph of Eternity" reveals a vision far more daring than Dante's, for it seems to be saying that only when the ancient republic of letters, knowledge, selfless achievement, and beauty is seen as consonant with Christian doctrine can mankind be said to have grasped the essential meaning of salvation.

BIBLIOGRAPHY

Editions. There is no modern edition of Petrarch's complete works. The most complete edition of all his works was printed at Basel in 1554 and 1581, as *Francisci Petrarchae . . . opera quae extant omnia* (repr. 1965); a complete edition of only his Latin works appeared at Basel in 1496 and at Venice in 1501 and 1503 as *Librorum Francisci Petrarche impressorum annotatio.* A national edition was undertaken in 1926, but the only volumes to have appeared by the 1980's are *Africa,* N. Festa, ed. (1936); *Le familiari,* 4 vols.: I–III, Vittorio Rossi, ed., IV, Umberto Bosco, ed. (1926–1942); *Rerum memorandarum libri,* Giuseppe Billanovich, ed. (1943); *De viris illustribus,* Guido Martellotti, ed. (1964). Ample selections from Petrarch's works are in two volumes with facing translations for all Latin works: *Rime, Trionfi e poesie latine,* Ferdinando Neri, Guido Martellotti, Enrico Bianchi, and Natalino Sapegno, eds. (1951); *Prose,* Guido Martellotti, Pier Giorgio Ricci, Enrico Carrara, and Enrico Bianchi, eds. (1955).

Bibliographies. The best single, though limited, bibliography is the Cornell University Library *Catalogue of the Petrarch Collection Bequeathed by W. Fiske,* Mary Fowler, comp. and ed. (1916, repr. 1971), expanded as *Catalogue of the Petrarch Collection in Cornell University Library* (1974). Other bibliographies are in "Literature of the Renaissance: Italian," in *Studies in Philology,* and *MLA International Bibliography* (1957–); and Antonio E. Quaglio, *Francesco Petrarca* (1967), 197–237. Joseph C. Fucilla has compiled what he terms a "virtually complete bibliography" in his *Oltre un cinquantiennio di scritti sul Petrarca (1916–1973)* (1982).

Concordances. A. Duro, ed., *Concordanze del "Canzoniere" di Francesco Petrarca,* 2 vols. (1971). On microfiche is Aldo S. Bernardo, ed., *A Concordance to Francesco Petrarca's Rerum familiarium libri* (1977).

Biographies. Thomas G. Bergin, *Petrarch* (1970); Giovanni Boccaccio, *De vita et moribus Domini Francisci Petracchi de Florentia,* in his *Opere latine minori,* Aldo F. Massera, ed. (1928); Giovanni A. Cesareo, *F. Petrarca: La vita* (1920); A. M. Cuomo, *Appunti per la biografia di Francesco Petrarca* (1926); L. di Benedetto, *Aspetti del Petrarca uomo* (1951); Arnoldo Foresti, *Aneddoti della vita di Francesco Petrarca* (1977); Giuseppe Frasso, *Itinerari con Francesco Petrarca* (1974); Henry Hollway-Calthrop, *Petrarch: His Life and Times* (1907); James Robinson and Henry W. Rolfe, *Petrarch, the First Modern Scholar and Man of Letters* (1898, 2nd ed., rev. and enl., 1914); Angelo Solerti, *Le vite di Dante, Petrarca, e Boccaccio scritte fino al secolo decimosesto* (1904); E. H. R. Tatham, *Francesco Petrarca, the First Modern Man of Letters,* 2 vols. (1925–1926); L. Tonelli, *Petrarca* (1930); Luigi Ugolino, *Il romanzo di Messer Francesco Petrarca* (1946); Ernest H. Wilkins, *Petrarch's Eight Years in Milan* (1958), *Petrarch's Later Years* (1959), and *Life of Petrarch* (1961).

Studies. Aldo S. Bernardo, "Petrarch's Attitude Toward Dante," in *PMLA,* **20** (1955), "Dante, Petrarch, and Boccaccio," in Beatrice Corrigan, ed., *Italian Poets and English Critics, 1755–1859* (1969), "Petrarch and the Art of Literature," in Julius A. Molinari, ed., *Petrarch to Pirandello* (1973), 19–43, "Laura as *nova figura,*" in *idem,* ed., *Francesco Petrarca, Citizen of the World* (1980), and "Petrarch's Autobiography: Circularity Revisited," in *Annali d'italianistica* (1986); Giuseppe Billanovich, *Petrarca letterato,* I: *Lo scrittoio del Petrarca* (1947), and "Dalle prime alle ultime letture del Petrarca," in Giuseppe Billanovich and Giuseppe Frasso, eds., *Il Petrarca ad Arquà* (1975); M. Boni, *Francesco Petrarca nel sesto centenario della morte* (1976); Umberto Bosco, *Francesco Petrarca* (1946, 2nd ed. 1961); Carlo Calcaterra, *Nella selva del Petrarca* (1942); Enrico Carrara, *Studi petrarcheschi ed altri scritti* (1959); Gianfranco Contini, "Petrarca e le arti figurative," in Bernardo, ed., *Petrarca, Citizen;* Pierre de Nolhac, *Pétrarque et l'humanisme,* 2 vols. (1907); F. de Sanctis, *Saggio critico sul Petrarca* (1978); Kevelin Foster, *Petrarch: Poet and Humanist* (1984); Pier Paolo Gerosa, *Umanesimo cristiano del Petrarca* (1966); U. Mariani, *Il Petrarca e gli agostiniani* (1946); Guido Martellotti, "L'umanesimo del Petrarca," in *Il veltro,* **24** (1980); Antonio E. Quaglio, *Francesco Petrarca* (1967), which is a most comprehensive overview, with bibliography; Charles Trinkaus, *The Poet as Philosopher: Petrarch and the Formation of Renaissance Consciousness* (1979); Ernest H. Wilkins, *The Making of the "Canzoniere" and Other Petrarchan Studies* (1951), and *Studies in the Life and Works of Petrarch* (1955).

ALDO S. BERNARDO

[See also **Babylonian Captivity; Biography, Secular; Boccaccio, Giovanni; Classical Literary Studies; Cola di Rienzo; Dante Alighieri; Florence; Italian Literature: Lyric Poetry; Italy, Fourteenth and Fifteenth Centuries; Middle Ages; Philosophy and Theology, Western European: Late Medieval.**]

PETRI EXCEPTIONES. Among the medieval lawbooks that abbreviated and excerpted the sources and literature of Roman law, one of the most important was the *Exceptiones legum Romanarum* of a jurist named Petrus, produced in southern France in the mid twelfth century. The work was compiled from two earlier collections known as the Tübingen and Ashburnham lawbooks, but was completely rearranged into four books treating persons, contracts, delicts, and actions, respectively. The rubric and prologue to the work are the only source of information about the author and his purpose. It names Petrus as the author, a *vir disertissimus* (very eloquent man), and reports that he dedicated the work to Odilo, the vicar of Valence. His purpose was to write a handbook for judges that would introduce them to the basic principles of Roman law and help them perform their judicial duties.

BIBLIOGRAPHY

Sources. Carlo Guido Mor, ed., *Scritti giuridici preirneriani,* II, *Exceptiones legum Romanarum* (1938, repr. 1980).

Studies. Max Conrat, *Geschichte der Quellen und Literatur des römischen Rechts im frühen Mittelalter* (1891, repr. 1963), 420–549; Hermann Kantorowicz, "Les origines françaises des 'Exceptiones Petri,' " in his *Rechtshistorische Schriften,* Helmut Coing and Gerhard Immel, eds. (1970); Giovanni Santini, *Ricerche sulle "Exceptiones legum Romanarum"* (1969); Paul Vinogradoff, *Roman Law in Mediaeval Europe* (1909, 2nd ed. 1929, repr. 1968), 44–48; P. Weimar, "Zur Entstehung des sogenannten Tübinger Rechtsbuchs und der Exceptiones legum Romanarum des Petrus," in Walter Wilhelm, ed., *Studien zur europäischen Rechtsgeschichte* (1972).

KENNETH PENNINGTON

[See also **Corpus Iuris Civilis; Law, Civil—Corpus Iuris, Revival and Spread; Law, French: In South.**]

PETROS GETADARJ (*d.* 1058), *Katᶜołikos* of Armenia from 1019 to 1058, is known for his role in the annexation of the Bagratid kingdom of Ani to the Byzantine Empire. Educated in a Byzantine monastery in Trebizond, Petros was well versed in classical literature. At the end of 1022 he met the Byzantine emperor Basil II (976–1025) at Trebizond and presented him with a document whereby the Bagratid king Yovhannēs-Smbat III (*d.* 1040) willed his kingdom to the empire. Petros had a very turbulent pontificate and was forced to spend most of it away from his see. In 1037 he was deposed from his throne and incarcerated in the fortress of Bǰni under the control of Grigor Magistros Pahlawuni (*ca.* 990–*ca.* 1058), with whom he became friends. He was restored to his former honor in 1039. After the fall of the Bagratid kingdom in 1045, the Byzantines treated him with respect, but in 1046 he was exiled first to Arcn and Xałtoyaṙiǰ, and then to Constantinople, where he was forced to stay for four years. He was permitted to spend his last years in Sebaste, in the monastery of S. Nšan.

Petros is known as a hymnographer; the medieval tradition attributes to him several *Patrum* hymns that are dedicated to the deceased and *Pueri* hymns commemorating Sts. Sargis, George, and Minas. His letters to Grigor Magistros have not survived.

BIBLIOGRAPHY

Karapet Kostanian, *Tēr Petros I Getadarj* (1897); Henri F. Tournebize, *Histoire politique et religieuse de l'Arménie* (1910).

KRIKOR H. MAKSOUDIAN

[See also **Ani in Širak; Armenia, History of; Bagratids; Grigor Magistros.**]

PETRUS (*fl.* early twelfth century), the illuminator who in 1109 illustrated the copy of the Beatus *Commentary on the Apocalypse,* written in 1091 in the Castilian monastery of Santo Domingo de Silos (London, British Library, Add. MS 11695). It is one of the last *Commentaries* to perpetuate the Mozarabic tradition. Still, Romanesque elements from beyond the Pyrenees appear in both the style and the iconography.

BIBLIOGRAPHY

Meyer Schapiro, "From Mozarabic to Romanesque at Silos," in *Art Bulletin,* **21** (1939); John Williams, *Early Spanish Manuscript Illumination* (1977), 110–119.

JOHN WILLIAMS

[See also **Apocalypse, Illustration of; Beatus Manuscripts; Manuscript Illumination: European; Mozarabic Art.**]

PETRUS. See **Petri Exceptiones.**

PETRUS. See also **Peire; Peter; Piero; Pierre; Pietro.**

PETRUS DE CRUCE (Pierre de la Croix) (*fl. ca.* 1290's), motet composer and theorist from Amiens. He is credited by fourteenth-century theorists with being the first composer to subdivide the breve into more parts than had been allowed by Franco of Cologne.

Little is known about Petrus' life. Documents of the French royal treasury from 1298 concerning the Office of St. Louis record money paid to a Magister Petrus de Cruce of Amiens for his part in compiling the *historia,* that is, the rhymed antiphons, responsories, and other elements that make up that Office. Further reference to a Petrus de Cruce of Amiens is found at the end of a *Tractatus de tonis* (tonary).

The most complete information about his musical accomplishments is in book VII of the treatise *Speculum musicae* (*ca.* 1324) by Jacques de Liège: "For that worthy *cantor,* Petrus de Cruce, who composed so many beautiful and good measured songs and followed the techniques of Franco, sometimes placed more than three semibreves for a perfect breve." Franco had allowed only two semibreves (read as short-long) or three equal semibreves (all short) for each breve. In Petrus' system, anywhere from two to seven semibreves could be fitted into the space of a breve, marking a definitive break with the predictable pattern of modal rhythm. These groups of semibreves were separated from one another by a dot (*punctus*). Both French and English theorists singled out the separation of series of semibreves by *puncti* as the innovative aspect of Petrus' music, and works exhibiting this manner of notation are often termed "Petronian" by modern writers. (The dot as a sign of separation of notes was to become a notational device of great importance in both English and Italian notational systems in the fourteenth century.) In the *Speculum musicae,* Jacques de Liège cites passages from two motets as examples of this notational system, and attributes them specifically to Petrus de Cruce. Thus, Petrus de Cruce is one of the very few composers who can be associated with specific thirteenth-century motets. Their distinctive style has led music historians tentatively to identify other motets with similar traits as possible works by him.

Petrus' style can be identified by the *triplum,* or upper voice. The fast movement in the *triplum* contrasts with the slow-moving *duplum* and tenor (to accommodate the fast semibreves, a slower beat is required than for earlier motets, which move primarily in longs and breves). Syllables are set to the fast semibreves, and passages of very rapid declamation alternate capriciously with passages of slow declamation. The word accents are not reinforced by the music. Petrus' motets also lack hocket passages and have unpatterned tenors.

One of the main problems associated with works in "Petronian" notation is the rhythmic interpretation of the semibreves, which all have the same shape in the manuscripts. In modern editions, the semibreves are usually transcribed as groups of notes of equal value. It is possible, however, that specific rhythmic patterns were realized in the performance of the groups of semibreves, and that the addition in the first quarter of the fourteenth century of a new note shape, the minim (like the semibreve, but with an ascending stem), may have served at first to clarify rhythmic patterns that were already present in the old notation, while at the same time allowing the possibility of introducing new rhythmic patterns unavailable before.

BIBLIOGRAPHY

The *Tractatus de tonis* of Petrus de Cruce is edited by Denis Harbinson as vol. 29 of the *Corpus scriptorum de musica* (1976). Concerning this treatise, and the Office of St. Louis, see Michel Huglo, *Les tonaires: Inventaire, analyse, comparaison* (1971), 336, 429. Further references to the Office of St. Louis are given in Heinrich Besseler, "Studien zur Musik des Mittelalters: I. Neue Quellen des 14. und beginnenden 15. Jahrhunderts," in *Archiv für Musikwissenschaft,* 7 (1925), 210 n. See also "Petrus de Cruce" in *New Grove Dictionary of Music and Musicians,* XIV (1980).

One of the two motets attributed to Petrus by Jacques de Liège is in Archibald T. Davison and Willi Apel, eds., *Historical Anthology of Music,* rev. ed. (1949), p. 36 (item 34; item 35 shares many Petronian characteristics).

LAWRENCE M. EARP

[See also **Ars Antiqua; Ars Nova; Franco of Cologne; Jacques de Liège; Motet; Music, Western European; Musical Notation, Western.**]

PETRUS HISPANUS. See **Peter of Spain.**

PETRUSLIED. A manuscript from Freising, now in Munich, contains three two-line strophes of Old High German rhyming verse, each followed by "Kyrie eleison, Christe eleison." The first tells of Peter's power to save, the second of his having charge of the gates of Heaven, and the third exhorts us to pray to him for mercy. The text is provided with neumes and was probably meant to be sung in procession. The dialect is Bavarian with traces of Frankish. Some scholars believe that the poem testifies to a tradition of rhyming verse antedating Otfrid's *Evangelienbuch,* with which it has one line in common.

BIBLIOGRAPHY

J. Knight Bostock, *A Handbook on Old High German Literature,* 2nd ed. (1976), 213–214; J. Sidney Groseclose and Brian O. Murdoch, *Die althochdeutschen poetischen Denkmäler* (1976), 77–81.

DAVID R. MCLINTOCK

[See also **Old High German Literature; Otfrid von Weissenburg.**]

PETTY ASSIZES, ENGLISH. Medieval Englishmen were forever quarreling about real property. In the twelfth century, down to the 1160's, the means of pressing and defending claims were ill-defined. Some disputes could be settled by a regular action of right, which led to a solemn, definitive judgment, but far less formal methods were usually employed. In unpatterned whirls of moves and countermoves the parties might negotiate; seize the property by turns; invoke the help of friends, sheriff, or lord; and petition the king to intervene. Authorities would investigate in ways they thought best (often by taking verdicts from juries) and would seize and deliver property and issue orders as seemed appropriate.

King Henry II was a systematizer. In the 1160's and 1170's he sought to substitute ordered system for these unstructured ways. To this end he introduced the four standard procedures that were later called the petty assizes.

The first of these was the assize *utrum,* which appeared in 1164 in the Constitutions of Clarendon and which provided:

> If a dispute arises between a cleric and a layman, or between a layman and a cleric, about a tenement which the cleric contends is held in alms and the layman as lay fee, it shall be settled by judgment of the king's chief justiciar upon the verdict of twelve lawful men . . . whether the tenement belongs to alms or lay fee. . . .

"Tenement" was the common-law term for real property. "Alms" were tenements held by churches and subject to church courts alone, while "lay fee" meant all other tenements, subject to secular jurisdiction, whether held by churches or private persons. As the Constitutions here provided, a case was to go to the church court if the property was found to be alms, to the appropriate lay court if it was lay fee.

The second assize Henry II introduced was the assize of novel disseisin, which seems to have been enacted in 1165 or 1166. It provided that any holder of free tenements who was illegally disseised (dispossessed) might if he acted without delay obtain a royal writ ordering the sheriff to empanel jurors, who would investigate and appear before the king's justices to state their findings. If they said that the plaintiff had indeed been disseised of a free tenement, wrongfully and without judgment, the court would restore him the property. An associated "assize of nuisance" made the same procedure available to owners who had suffered mere interference with their property, such as obstruction of a right-of-way.

The third assize was that of mort d'ancestor. Instituted in 1176, this was for the benefit of the heir who was kept out of his heritage. In the commonest case, such a person would be claiming as heir of a close relative who had recently "died seised as of fee," that is, died in actual possession of heritable property. The assize of mort d'ancestor allowed the claimant in such a case to have a royal writ sent to the sheriff, directing him to empanel jurors who would inquire and return a verdict before the king's justices. If the jury confirmed that the claimant was the immediate heir of an "ancestor" who had not long since died seised as of fee, the justices would award him seisin (possession) of the property. The claimant could not in this way take the property away from any near kinsman of his who already had taken it, by pretending to be the rightful heir of the same ancestor, for the assize of mort d'ancestor was not meant to resolve fine points of the rules of inheritance. Nevertheless, except in such cases, the assize would serve the heir.

The fourth assize is that of darrein (last) presentment, designed apparently in 1179 or 1180. When an ecclesiastical position such as a parish church fell vacant on the death or removal of the incumbent clergyman, it belonged to the patron, who held the advowson of the church, to select a successor and present him to the bishop. On such occasions it often happened that two rival patrons made competing presentments. The bishop might not judge between them. The issue in such a case was about the ownership of the advowson, to which of them it belonged; and in England claims to advowsons were for the king's court to judge. The assize of darrein presentment allowed either of the rivals to have the sheriff send a jury into the king's court to tell which of them it was, or whose ancestor it was, who had successfully presented to that church the last time it had been vacant. The king's court would then direct the bishop to accept the presentment of the party in whose favor the jury found.

Nothing in the petty assizes went to replace the action of right, which on the score of regularity of procedure needed no reform. For the kinds of cases that it could serve (it could enforce only claims to inherited property), the action of right was still the source of final, definitive judgments. Trial in an action of right was by battle or the grand assize, the latter distinguished from the petty assizes by its use in such a procedure that determined the right to a tenement and not merely a right to possession subject to further determinations. A party who wanted to obtain such a definitive resolution would have to resort to an action of right after all negotiations, maneuverings, and petty assizes had been utilized. But as standardized procedures that offered to take the place of other informal maneuverings, the petty assizes were a brilliant success. *Utrum* was fairly imposed by decree as the required solution for the jurisdictional question with which it dealt. The other three were merely made available to men and women who found themselves in some of the commonest circumstances of parties to disputes—disseised, kept out of an inheritance of which an ancestor had died seised, or faced with a competing presentment to a church. They might use them if they liked, as alternatives to other means of seeking their own. Increasingly, parties chose the petty assizes; the number of assizes brought and prosecuted grew in the late twelfth century and became very large in the thirteenth.

Novel disseisin and mort d'ancestor, the most broadly applicable of the assizes and the most frequently used, may have been designed especially to serve parties who could not rely on their lords for informal justice because the lords were taking the side of their opponents or were themselves the opponents. The legislation at Northampton in 1176 that founded mort d'ancestor did so by saying that the procedure of the assize should be available "if the lord of the fee denies to the heirs of the decedent, when they ask for it, the seisin which the decedent had," which is as much as to say that the assize was directed against lords who did wrong in this matter. The association of the assize of nuisance with novel disseisin tends to the same conclusion: the lord was by far most likely to interfere with a tenant's free enjoyment of his holding, as by blocking a right-of-way.

But whether this was the special purpose of these two assizes or not, it is certain that after they were founded, holders of tenements often used them against their lords. Through the late twelfth and early thirteenth centuries the two assizes exerted a gradual but massive chilling effect on what had before this time been firmly established traditions of the powers and responsibilities of lords. The lords now hesitated to enforce their own rights by seizing tenements, even from tenants who defaulted outrageously in their obligations, for fear that the tenants would bring novel disseisin. They hesitated to intervene in disputes about tenements held of them. The party who was in the right in the dispute stood in less need of the lord's help than in former times, for he could now invoke novel disseisin or mort d'ancestor, while if the lord did lend his help to either party he was likely to find himself a defendant in an assize brought by the other. The consequent fading of the disciplinary and protective powers of the lord was the beginning of the end of English feudalism. Henry II may have planned it that way, if uncanny foresight was among his undoubtedly remarkable talents.

The four petty assizes developed in diverse and unexpected ways. *Utrum* did not function for long in the manner prescribed in 1164. In the 1170's appeals began to be allowed from English ecclesiastical courts to Rome, and it may be that the king was then no longer willing to allow the church courts the jurisdiction over land held in alms which *utrum* was designed to protect. Around 1200 the assize served not to award jurisdiction to the ecclesiastical or lay court but to award seisin of the property by judgment of the king's court in which the assize was held, where the dispute was between a church that claimed to hold in alms and an adversary who claimed to hold by a lay tenure. Later on, the conclusion was somehow reached that

PETTY ASSIZES, ENGLISH

it was inappropriate for laymen to use this assize or for any churchmen to use it except parsons who had to sue to recover lands held in alms by their parish churches. For parsons who were so circumstanced that they had no other legal remedy, the assize resulted in definitive judgment, like an action of right. With this strange metamorphosis, which was complete by about 1235, *utrum* entered upon a long, modest career as "the parson's writ of right."

In or about the year 1200, darrein presentment was supplemented by an additional procedure called *quare impedit* (literally, why he impedes). This allowed a claimant to an advowson, when faced with a competing presentment, to hale his rival into the king's court on a general challenge "to permit him to present . . . in this case in which he complains that the defendant is wrongfully impeding him." *Quare impedit* was probably meant to serve men who had demonstrably good claims to advowsons but for some reason could not show, as darrein presentment required, that they or their ancestors had made the last presentment. One who had purchased the advowson since the last presentment would, for example, be in this situation. But by around 1300 *quare impedit* was recognized as an alternative available even to those whose cases darrein presentment could accommodate. Once able to choose, litigants more and more chose *quare impedit*. By the late 1300's darrein presentment had dropped out of use, never to be revived.

Meanwhile, novel disseisin became more broadly serviceable than ever. Of the devices which the law adopted to bring this about, one in particular proved of enormous effect. An owner who was out of seisin of his property often had a right to go and take seisin of it. For example, if the owner had granted a life interest, he could reassume seisin when the life tenant died. Where it existed, the right to take seisin was good even in the face of an adversary who was in wrongful occupation. From the 1270's on, the courts held that when an owner exercised this right, any show of taking seisin would put him in seisin in the eyes of the law even if he did not gain actual control. It followed then that any adversary who continued from that time to hold against him, technically had disseised him, and he could recover by novel disseisin. With that much established, the courts proceeded during the course of the following century to concede this right of taking nominal seisin more and more generously to owners whose lands were for one reason or another being held against them. By about 1390 nearly all owners had it. Therefore, nearly all could vindicate their claims by novel disseisin, which thus became a general-purpose action for real property. Mort d'ancestor was rendered obsolete. The heir who found himself shut out of his inheritance could make a show of taking seisin and then sue by novel disseisin.

Novel disseisin might have served for centuries in this way. But by 1400 it was recognized that if a show of taking seisin would entitle an owner to say that he had been disseised, it would equally entitle him to say that the adversary who was holding the property against him had trespassed. As an alternative to novel disseisin, he could sue for trespass. For several reasons claimants to property more and more chose the suit for trespass, and novel disseisin came to be used less and less. It was still a familiar proceeding at the end of the Middle Ages, but its decline continued until it became obsolete around 1600.

BIBLIOGRAPHY

The twelfth-century origins of the petty assizes are carefully studied by R. C. van Caenegem, *Royal Writs in England from the Conquest to Glanvill: Studies in the Early History of the Common Law* (1959), esp. chap. 3, 261–335. For a shorter account see the same author's *Birth of the English Common Law* (1973). Some of his views are disputed by Doris M. Stenton, *English Justice Between the Norman Conquest and the Great Charter, 1066–1215* (1964), esp. chaps. 2 and 3. Stroud F. C. Milsom advanced the thesis that novel disseisin and mort d'ancestor were intended specifically for use against feudal lords in his introduction to the reissue of Frederick Pollock and Frederic W. Maitland, *The History of English Law, Before the Time of Edward I,* 2nd ed., I (1968), xxvii–xlix. He develops the view fully in *The Legal Framework of English Feudalism* (1976).

On the assize *utrum* see Elizabeth G. Kimball, "The Judicial Aspects of Frank Almoign Tenure," in *English Historical Review,* 47 (1932); S. E. Thorne, "The Assize Utrum and Canon Law," in *Columbia Law Review,* 33 (1933); Alexandra Nicol, ed., "Changes in the Assize Utrum Between the Constitutions of Clarendon and Bracton," in R. F. Hunnisett and J. B. Post, eds., *Medieval Legal Records: Edited in Memory of C. A. F. Meekings* (1978), 18–24. The award of seisin in this action, around 1200, is illustrated in several early records, for example in Doris M. Stenton, ed., *Pleas Before the King or His Justices, 1198–1212,* IV (1967).

The development of novel disseisin from its beginnings to its obsolescence around 1600 is traced by Donald W. Sutherland, *The Assize of Novel Disseisin* (1973). There are no similar studies of the other petty assizes; but for the growth of *quare impedit* at the expense of darrein presentment, see Stroud F. C. Milsom's legal introduction to Elsie Shanks and Stroud F. C. Milsom, eds., *Novae narrationes* (1963), xli–xlvi. In 1271 business was about equally divided between darrein presentment and *quare impedit:* Frederick Pollock and Frederic W. Maitland, *History of English Law* (1968).

By 1378–1379 darrein presentment was no longer being used, as appears from Morris S. Arnold, ed., *Year Books of Richard II: 2 Richard II, 1378–1379* (1975), xii–xv. The gradual shift of business to *quare impedit* in the intervening century can be traced, in part and very roughly, in the several volumes of *Year Books of Edward II* published by the Selden Society for the years 1307–1319.

DONALD W. SUTHERLAND

[See also **Assize, English; Clarendon, Assize of; Clarendon, Constitutions of; Henry II of England; Inheritance; Law, English Common; Seisin, Disseisin; Tenure of Land.**]

PFAFFE AMIS. See **Stricker, Der.**

PFAFFE KONRAD. See **Rolandslied.**

PFAFFE LAMPRECHT. See **Lamprecht.**

PHARMACOPEIA. As a headache sufferer today swallows for relief the cure-all aspirin, so the medieval citizen reached for the panacea called theriac. That pill (*pilula,* little ball) plus a drink of dill wine was considered a dependable alleviator of aches and illnesses of the head. Headache treatments exemplify methods of medieval pharmacotherapeutics. The same potherb cultivated in kitchen gardens to adorn salads and stuff sausages also could be a drug, a chemical agent affecting the living organism. Dill, the fragrant plant that flavors the modern dilled pickle, typifies the multiple uses of medieval vegetable, animal, and mineral substances in medicine.

Medieval physicians and pharmacists distinguished between two classes of drugs. First were

A pharmacist dispenses theriac. Lombard miniature from the *Tacuinum sanitatis in medicina, ca.* 1390. VIENNA, ÖSTERREICHISCHE NATIONAL BIBLIOTHEK, CODEX SER. NOV. 2644, fol. 53v

natural substances potent in their natural state, prescribed and taken "as is," without essential change, preparation, or admixture with other drugs. Called "simples," these drugs were the subject of pharmacognosy, meaning knowledge of natural substances in natural forms. Dill was a "simple" when prescribed for headache as the raw or dried herb tossed with salad or as baked with flour, butter, and sugar into "headache cakes."

As a component of theriac, however, dill also was a material for pharmacy: the preparing, compounding, and dispensing of medicine, changing the natural substance to make it more potent, or joining it with other drugs to enhance its effect for healing. Such combinations were called compound drugs; theriac's sixty-one ingredients (or sixty-three, according to the best medical opinions in fifteenth-century Bologna) included viper flesh, cardamom, and dill.

Actions of particular drugs within the living body were thought pharmacodynamic (in modern parlance), having an effect upon the total body, which, thus empowered, changed the course of the illness or disease. A drug increasing or decreasing one of the four humors—blood, phlegm, choler, and black bile—thus changed balances among them and indirectly affected the disease process. This changing of the intrinsic environment to effectively combat extrinsic disease prefigures modern understanding of the immune system. Medieval physicians also utilized drugs to favorably influence the patient's mood and psychological affect. Conversely, other medieval drugs were considered chemotherapeutic (in Paul Ehrlich's phrase), changing not the host but the agent causing the illness, such as treatments for lice, worms, and other invading, indwelling organisms.

Pharmacists prepared remedies according to physicians' prescription. Physicians themselves also utilized time-honored pharmacological methods for preparing drugs which, attributed to the second-century Greek physician Galen, were therefore called galenicals. Dillweed leaves steeped in boiling water made a tea or decoction, drunk warm or cool. Or dill leaves, stem, and seeds were served in a temperate water infusion. A tincture of dill was an alcoholic or hydroalcoholic solution, easily purchasable from a market pharmacy. Dill also was prepared in fluidextract, a concentrated liquid preparation with alcohol as solvent and preservative. And a thick, concentrated, semisolid extract could be diluted as dill broth or added to wine, ale, beer, fruit juice, or mixed into fruit sauces or cakes.

Dill sometimes was an ingredient in collyria, highly concentrated compound drugs usually diluted with egg white, applied externally for treating diseases of the eye and head. In all these forms dill was thought to alleviate headache, relieve nervous tension, and relax the muscles. Likewise, dill was important for easing headaches of insomnia and overcoming symptoms concomitant with headaches; it helped digestion, settled colic, checked bowels, relieved upset stomach, and reduced fevers. Heated in a fluid and then inhaled, dill seeds stopped uncontrollable sobbing and its attendant headache. As an aid to physicians and cooks, dill was so popular a stimulus for headache-free physical fitness that medieval medical texts enthusiastically refer to Greek Masters of Games who would not permit their athletes to eat any food without dill.

Since medieval physicians and surgeons understood that not all similar pains had the same etiology nor the same qualities, headache treatments, for example, had various purposes: to reduce pain, to diminish frequency, to eliminate headaches by curing the body of their stimuli, or to prevent them prophylactically by avoiding foods or activities causing headaches. Medico-pharmacological manuscripts refer to a number of specific headache types, each with a recommended remedy: "stinging head pain," "half-head headache" (migraine), "searing pain circumnavigating the skull," nervous-tension head pain, headache associated with trauma, paralysis, epilepsy, or brain tumor. In addition to the panaceas theriac and potable gold (Chaucer's Physician prescribes "gold in cordial," a liquid preparation of gold salts), the pharmacopeia for headache basically included variations upon the active ingredients of dill, marjoram, mandrake, and almonds.

Sweet marjoram was added to foods as a condiment or taken as a galenical. Not only good against headaches, marjoram was also thought useful for the brain because it helped "remove occlusions of the brain." Like dill, marjoram was effective for upset stomach and irritated intestines.

The powerful botanical mandrake (mandragora) alleviated both pain in the head and insomnia. Mandrake dulled the senses and induced sleepiness, thereby acting as analgesic and soporific. Along with opium poppy, hyoscyamus, and poison hemlock, mandrake was an important surgical anesthetic as well as an ameliorator of postsurgical pain.

Almonds served in the pharmacopeia to relieve headache and to overcome anxiety. Raw, roasted, or toasted, they were added whole, cut, slivered, ground, or pulverized to omelettes, fruit sauces, gravies, stuffings, stews, salads, cakes, breads, and pastries. As mood food, almonds were thought a defense against melancholy, particularly when used in marzipan—a sweet dense almond paste used to make festive food sculptures, from simple, brightly colored fruits and flowers to startling, delectable "subtletie" illusion foods. Almond milk was a base for hygienic soups and sauces as well as a disguise for ill-tasting medications. To prevent drunkenness, whole almonds were prescribed to precede alcoholic beverages. (Modern cocktail favors have a long utilitarian heritage.)

Foods and flowers thought to cause headache included roses. Medical manuals accuse roses of causing severe headache consequent upon blockage of nasal passages and sensations of heaviness and constriction in the nose, sinuses, and forehead. Nevertheless, gardeners copiously bred roses for aesthetics, symbolism, and cookery. In art and literature the rose represented perfect beauty: witness the secular, erotic *Romance of the Rose* and the ecclesiastically encouraged gardens of love with the madonna in the rose garden; the Virgin Mary was called "Rose Without Thorns" (*flos sine spinata*) and "Rose of Sharon" (*flos campi*). Moreover, rose petals were common in cookery, as in exquisite rose-petal bread, and rose water was a flavoring liquid in baking and an astringent and enfragrancer in cosmetics. Pharmacology caused rose gardens in art and reality to include crocuses, and recipes for rose foods to add saffron, made from flowering crocus. Symbolic values of the flowers notwithstanding, crocus neutralized the power of roses to cause headaches and nasal constrictions, and thus was a necessary companion in cookery and imagery. Rose-adorers who were olfactorily sensitive required crocus, camphor, or rose-abstinence.

For almost every pharmacopeic negative there was a positive, and the texts specify balancing agents for each. Celery's tendency to stimulate head pain could be neutralized by lettuce. Likewise, the plant elecampane's headache-effect could be countered with coriander seed. Garden nasturtium caused migraine headache. Cultivated for its ornamental cruciferous appearance and tangy, pungent taste, nasturtium also was a potent aphrodisiac. Recipes for "potent salad" suggest tossing watercress and nasturtium with vinegar plus chopped escarole (endive) to accentuate the positive effect while counteracting the attendant headache. Neutralizers were listed for other sexual energizers that stimulated head pain, such as roasted chestnuts, onion, garlic, and eggs.

Included in medical manuals was an unexpected though common cause of headache: anger, *ira*, unbridled fury or ire. Its positive medical purposes were relieving toothache and mouth "torments" (anger's distraction might preclude extraction) and benefiting patients with paralysis; anger might stimulate those with physiological paresis to exercise with vestigial muscle power and forcibly shock hysterical paralytics out of immobility. Fury-caused headache, however, could be alleviated by dill, marjoram, mandrake, or almonds, plus, as the *Tacuinum sanitatis* advises, a dose of the dictates of reason and philosophy!

The most acute test of the pharmacopeia was in the field of toxicology, the study of poisons, where considerable ingenuity was devoted to developing techniques for identifying toxins as well as lists of their antidotes. Most writers on poison agreed that prevention was the only infallible antidote. To avoid accidental or politically motivated poisoning, a noble or clerical court customarily employed credence testers. These highly paid servants tested all suspicious food and drink by tasting; they were required to be trustworthy and were replaced frequently. Credence stones were believed to change color in the presence of particular poisons; the bezoar stone, a calcareous concretion from the alimentary canal of a ruminant, does indeed change color when dipped in solution of arsenic. Credence cups made of minerals, metals, jewels, or animal horns thought to be identifiers of poison varied in their efficacy according to the powers of chemistry and luck. Shining silver that tarnished to black when touched by a poison sulfide performed less well for other chemicals.

Under duress, however, the medieval physician could consult various poison texts, which often took both the name and form of a list of antidotes, *Antidotarium*, enumerating on one side of a page the toxic substance, be it animal, vegetable, or mineral, with a parallel column of neutralizers. Others, like Francis of Siena's late-fourteenth-century book of eighty chapters, dedicated to Philip of Alençon, patriarch of Jerusalem, includes with lists of poisons more discursive preventive, diagnostic, and prognostic advice. His *notificatio* section offers poison identifiers; *complexio* suggests their injurious effects; *prognosticatio* illuminates prospects for cure or death; and *curatio* recommends antidotes and ancillary methods for cure. Like their contemporary Francis of Siena, other writers on poisons such as William of Marra, Peter of Abano, Gentile da Foligno, Christopher de Honestis, John Martin of Ferrara, and Ferdinando Ponzetti quoted Galen and Greek sources as well as Avicenna and Arabic antecedents, offering advice on prevention and practical succor from the pharmacopeia.

A century earlier, the thirteenth-century physician Peter Juliani established a set of six questions for testing true medical effect of an administered drug. In his commentaries on the nutrition and drug treatises of the Jewish physician Isaac Judaeus (Isaac Israeli), Peter demonstrated the protoscientific method of medieval pharmacology: (1) The tested drug must be unadulterated so its active agent will be demonstrable. (2) The diagnosis of the patient's illness must be unequivocal, and the one the drug is expected to treat. (3) The drug must be given exclusively, not accompanied by any other. (4) The drug's qualities of heat, cold, moisture, and dryness must be opposite to the qualities of the ailment. The humoral demands of a "warm and dry" illness were a "cold and moist" drug. (5) Experiments on cause and effect must be repeated and replicable. (6) Patients must be human, not animal.

The pharmacopeia was characterized by a balancing of negatives and positives, poisons and antidotes, and diseases and their galenicals.

BIBLIOGRAPHY

Sources. Richard Banckes [Banks], *Banckes's Herbal,* Sanford Larkey and Thomas Pyles, eds. (1941); Andrew Boorde, *A Dyetary of Helth,* Frederick J. Furnivall, ed. (1870); Carolous Clusius [Ch. de l'Écluse], *Rariorum plantarum historia* (1601); Petrus Crescentius, *In commodu ruralium* [or] *Opus ruralium commodorum* (1490); Dioscorides, *The Greek Herbal* (512), R. T. Gunther, ed. (1959); *Garten der Gesundheit* [or] *Hortus sanitatis* (1485); John Gerard, *The Herbal or General History of Plants* (1597, 1633, repr. 1975); M. Levey, ed. and trans., *The Medical Formulary or Aqrabadhin of Al-Kindi* (1966); Maimonides, *Treatise on Asthma* [or] *Sefer Hakazerith* (1199), Suessman Muntner, ed. and trans. (1963); *Le menagier de Paris* (1393) [*The Goodman of Paris,* Eileen Power, trans. (1928)]; Bartolomeo Platina, *De honesta voluptate* (1475) [*On Honest Indulgence and Good Health,* E. B. Andrews, trans. (1967)]; *Tacuinum sanitatis* (*ca.* 1475, New York Public Library, Spencer Coll., MS 65).

Studies. F. J. Anderson, *An Illustrated History of the Herbals* (1977); Luisa Cogliati Arano, *The Medieval Health Handbook: Tacuinum sanitatis,* Oscar Ratti and Adele Westbrook, trans. (1976, repr. 1981); W. Blunt and S. Raphael, *The Illustrated Herbal* (1979); Madeleine Pelner Cosman, *Fabulous Feasts: Medieval Cookery and Ceremony* (1976, repr. 1979), "Machaut's Medical Musical World," in *Machaut's World: Science and Art in the 14th Century* (1978), and "A Feast for Aesculapius: Historical Diets for Asthma and Sexual Pleasure," in *Annual Review of Nutrition* (1983); Margaret B. Freeman, *Herbs for the Mediaeval Household, for Cooking, Healing, and Divers Uses* (1943); Muriel Joy Hughes, *Women Healers in Medieval Life and Literature* (1943, repr. 1968), 22–29, 34–36, 148–154; Linda Voigts, "Anglo-Saxon Plant Remedies and the Anglo-Saxons," in *Isis,* 70 (1979).

MADELEINE PELNER COSMAN

[See also **Biology; Herbals; Herbs; Medicine, History of.**]

PHILARETOS VAKHRAMIOS. See **P^cilartos Varažnuni.**

PHILIP II AUGUSTUS (1165–1223), king of France from 1179 until his death, was responsible for laying the foundations for the ascendancy of the French monarchy in the thirteenth century. His birth at Paris on 21 August 1165 was the occasion for unusual rejoicing. The marriages of his father, Louis VII, to three successive wives over a span of thirty years had resulted only in daughters ineligible to inherit the throne. When the third queen, Adela of Champagne, gave birth to a son, the royal city erupted in jubilation and undoubted relief. The king's advanced age, however, and the prince's youth still rendered the dynasty's future precarious. Immobilized by a stroke, Louis decided to have his son crowned in August 1179, according to a long-established Capetian tradition of associating heirs during the king's lifetime. Shortly before the ceremony, however, the young prince fell gravely ill from a hunting accident. In desperation Louis roused himself from his sickbed and journeyed to Canterbury to pray at the tomb of Thomas Becket, his old friend and now martyred saint. Apparently the saint's intercessions were efficacious, because Philip recovered and was crowned at Rheims on 1 November 1179. With the old king again confined to bed, the ceremonies provided a stage for the great lords of Flanders, Champagne, and England to dramatize their power over the fourteen-year-old king, as they, in fact, competed for dominion over the kingdom. The count of Flanders demonstrated his influence at court by marrying his niece, Isabella of Hainaut, to the king on 28 April 1180.

These rivalries were interrupted by the staggering news of the fall of Jerusalem to the Muslims in October 1187 and the resulting papal appeals for a new crusade to rescue the Holy Land. King Richard I the Lionhearted of England, the successor to the Angevin continental lands, had taken the cross immediately, but Philip II Augustus delayed this step because Queen Isabella had in 1187 given birth to a son, Louis, and the king wished to be assured of the survival of his heir. Philip finally consented to papal entreaties, and the two kings departed in July 1190 on an expedition that included winter quarters in Sicily, the siege of Acre, the key seaport in Palestine, and its capture in July 1191. While the departure of the two kings afforded respite to their lands, they continued their mutual competition on the crusade. The venture was particularly frustrating for Philip because at every stage he arrived first, and initiated careful plans, only to be followed by Richard, whose

PHILIP II AUGUSTUS

greater wealth and flamboyant manner upstaged the French king. After the fall of Acre, Philip precipitously left the Holy Land and returned to France in December 1191.

Other considerations prompted Philip's departure, among them a change in dynastic plans. Queen Isabella had died in March 1190 and Prince Louis had barely survived a serious illness during the king's absence. Philip was therefore intent on seeking another wife to strengthen his lineage. While this ultimate goal was clear, his means to obtain it remain a mystery. No satisfactory explanation has emerged to explain his choice of Ingeborg (Ingeburge), the sister of Cnut VI of Denmark. The nuptial ceremonies were barely concluded on 14 August 1193 when the king exhibited an aversion to his bride. Determined to divorce her, he was granted his wish in November 1193 from a council of obliging bishops. He then married Agnes of Meran, from the Bavarian nobility. Refusing to recognize the divorce and remarriage, the pope intervened in response to Ingeborg's pleas. When Philip stubbornly resisted, Innocent III levied an interdict on the royal lands in January 1200. Coming at an inopportune moment, this awesome measure induced Philip to take Ingeborg back as queen but did not succeed in restoring her marital rights. Agnes, however, released Philip from this bigamous predicament by dying in July 1201, after having given birth to two children, Marie and Philip. Through political inducements the king persuaded the pope to legitimize them in November 1201, thus granting Philip his ultimate objective of another male heir. Despite continued and persistent efforts, however, he was never able to separate himself legally from Ingeborg.

More important, the Third Crusade also coincided with the pivotal developments that give significance to Philip II Augustus' reign. His departure in 1190 provided opportunity to publish an ordinance in which he expanded the judiciary by appointing baillis and reorganized the finances by creating a central accounting bureau. Henceforth, these governmental functions were no longer performed in an itinerant royal court but were centered in Paris. Later, in July 1194, an unfortunate loss of his baggage train persuaded Philip to store his documents permanently at Paris and to improve the keeping of records. The death of the great baronial counselors in the Holy Land enabled him to appoint new, young men of lesser rank, who were more amenable to his wishes. The death of the count of Flanders, in particular, permitted the king to set in motion long-laid plans to acquire the rich provinces of Artois, Vermandois, and Valois through inheritance. Finally, Richard's capture and imprisonment by the German emperor on his return from Palestine in December 1192 presented Philip the opportunity to attack his rival's lands.

Although he realized no permanent gains during Richard's lifetime, in 1204 he was able to wrest Normandy from Richard's successor, John, and to drive the English south of the Loire Valley by 1206. These territorial acquisitions were confirmed at the great Battle of Bouvines on 27 July 1214 when Philip defeated a coalition of English, Flemish, and German armies. He thereby increased the royal domain significantly beyond its former size and securely incorporated these lands into royal administration. When the king died on 14 July 1223, he was buried in regal splendor at the royal abbey of St. Denis in the first amply reported funeral ceremony of the Capetian dynasty. His son Louis VIII's coronation took place on 6 August. For the first time, a Capetian was crowned after the death of the king, a token of the permanence of Philip Augustus' achievements and of the royal dynasty's confidence in its future.

BIBLIOGRAPHY

Sources. John W. Baldwin, Françoise Gasparri, Michel Nortier, and Elisabeth Lalou, eds., *Les registres de Philippe Auguste* (1987); Henri-François Delaborde, ed., *Oeuvres de Rigord et de Guillaume le Breton,* 2 vols. (1882), which gives the chief royal chroniclers of the reign, and, with Charles Petit-Dutaillis, Jacques Boussard, and Michel Nortier, eds., *Recueil des actes de Philippe Auguste,* 4 vols. (1916–1979), containing the royal charters of Philip II Augustus as cataloged by Léopold V. Delisle in 1856; Léopold V. Delisle, ed., *Recueil des jugements de l'échiquier de Normandie* (1864), which prints the one surviving judicial roll from Philip's reign, and "Scripta de feodis," in *Recueil des historiens des Gaules et de la France,* XXIII (1876), which inventories the fiefs. Ferdinand Lot and Robert Fawtier, eds., *Le premier budget de la monarchie française: Le compte général de 1202–1203* (1932); and Michel Nortier and John W. Baldwin, "Contributions à l'étude des finances de Philippe Auguste," in *Bibliothèque de l'École des Chartes,* 138 (1980), print the surviving financial documents. The royal archives are collected in Alexandre Teulet, ed., *Layettes du trésor des Chartes,* I (1863).

Studies. John W. Baldwin, *The Government of Philip Augustus: Foundations of French Royal Power in the Middle Ages* (1986), approaches the reign from the viewpoint of governmental documentation; Robert-

PHILIP IV THE FAIR

Henri Bautier, ed., *La France de Philippe Auguste: Le temps des mutations* (1982), offers the most comprehensive collection of studies of Philip's time; Alexander Cartellieri, *Philipp II. August, König von Frankreich*, 5 vols. in 4 (1899–1922), remains the fullest study of Philip II Augustus based on chronicle materials; Robert Davidsohn, *Philipp II. August von Frankreich und Ingeborg* (1888), is the best account of Philip's marital problems.

For an interpretation of his reign, see C. Warren Hollister and John W. Baldwin, "The Rise of Administrative Kingship: Henry I and Philip Augustus," in *The American Historical Review*, 83 (1978).

JOHN W. BALDWIN

[See also **Crusades and Crusader States: To 1192; France; John, King of England; Richard I the Lionhearted.**]

PHILIP IV THE FAIR (1267/1268–1314), king of France. He was the son of Philip III (*r.* 1270–1285), and became heir to the French throne in 1276, when his elder brother, Louis, died. (His mother, Isabella of Aragon, had died in 1270.) Philip in 1284 married Jeanne of Champagne, heiress of the wealthy county of Champagne and of the kingdom of Navarre. He became king of France in 1285 when Philip III died on a futile crusade against Aragon.

Philip may have been embittered by his father's death. He showed no interest in crusades and had little respect for papal admonitions. He filled many French bishoprics with his supporters and taxed the French clergy—with the pope's consent, when he could get it, and through ostensibly free gifts from local councils of the clergy when the pope refused to act.

Philip also taxed his subjects—heavily at times—and was the first French king to impose general taxes. These taxes brought in large sums of money (about 735,000 livres tournois in 1304, the peak year) and caused such bitter complaints that they could not be continued. After 1304, there were only three general taxes. Two were based on old precedents (an aid for marrying his eldest daughter, and an aid for knighting his eldest son). The third, to support a war with Flanders (1314), was never fully collected because peace was made.

Philip's need for taxes was caused by his efforts to keep his two most powerful vassals, the count of Flanders and the king of England (as duke of Aquitaine), from becoming practically independent rulers of their fiefs. He certainly checked these tendencies and in the process gained some useful border territories, but he did not end the threat. His successors had to renew the struggles.

Philip also continued the process of increasing the size and expanding the powers of the French bureaucracy. The Parlement of Paris, the highest court of the kingdom, perfected its organization and expanded its jurisdiction, especially in hearing appeals from the courts of the count of Flanders and those of the king of England in the English-held duchy of Aquitaine. The Chambre des Comptes (treasury department) also became better organized and more efficient in collecting royal income. The king's council, where final decisions on policy were made, was not yet formally organized, but the king was free to determine its composition for each term. Its agenda expanded, and the frequency of its meetings increased. At the local level, there were more officials to aid the baillis in the north and the seneschals in the south in their work of collecting revenues and administering justice.

Philip's policies led, almost inevitably, to a quarrel with the church. He was obviously taxing the clergy (the so-called free grants by local councils were anything but free), and he was trying to limit the jurisdiction of ecclesiastical courts, as were most contemporary rulers. In return, he protected the rights of the clergy against feudal lords and urban governments more rapidly and efficaciously than could the pope. Nevertheless, it was clear that the church in France was being treated as if it were an arm of the French government, and that French bishops were either not willing or not able to preserve their independence. Thus, when Philip, in 1303, arrested Bernard Saisset, bishop of Pamiers (a southern diocese), on a flimsy charge of treason, the pope (Boniface VIII) felt that he had to act. His exact plans are uncertain, but he called the prelates of France to come to a council which could have excommunicated the king and thus have released his subjects from their allegiance.

Philip could not risk such a council. He had his own list of accusations against Boniface VIII, who had been elected only after his predecessor had resigned (an almost unprecedented action) and who certainly had been guilty of intemperate language. He sent Guillaume de Nogaret to arrest the pope and bring him to France to be tried by a church council. It is unlikely that this plan could have succeeded, but Nogaret at least accomplished the first part of it by seizing the pope at the papal palace of Anagni (September 1303). Boniface, who was an elderly man, was soon released by an uprising of the people of Anagni, but died a few days later, probably of shock. His immediate successor, Benedict XI, did nothing to avenge him and reigned for only a year. The cardinals then completely capitulated by electing a French archbishop, who took the name Clement V (1305–1314). Clement talked of leaving France for the old papal capital of Rome, but somehow never found a good time to do so. Admittedly, Rome and the nearby papal lands were in such a state of turmoil that they were not very attractive places from which to administer a European-wide church. Clement's successors also found it unwise to return to their old capital. Not until 1378 did a pope return (reluctantly) to Rome, and by that time papal prestige and authority had greatly diminished. Philip had certainly not foreseen these results of his actions, but they would not have displeased him.

Philip died in 1314. During the brief reigns of his sons, Louis X (1314–1316), Philip V (1316–1322), and Charles IV (1322–1328), his basic policies were confirmed. When they died without leaving sons who could succeed them, the nearest male relative was their nephew, Edward III, king of England (*r.* 1327–1377). Edward's mother was a daughter of Philip the Fair, but for obvious reasons, neither the bureaucrats nor the nobility wanted to be ruled by an English king, and so they invented a rule (the so-called Salic Law) that barred women and their heirs from the throne. This was bad law but good politics. It would have been almost impossible for a fourteenth-century king to have governed two such different countries. Edward I of England had found it impossible to govern both England and Scotland. A combination of England and France would have been even worse. Unfortunately, the English claim was good enough to be one of the excuses for starting the Hundred Years War. Thus, one of Philip's most statesmanlike acts—securing peace with England through a marriage alliance—came back to trouble his successors. On the other hand, involving the Salic Law ensured that the French government could continue to develop along the lines devised by Philip IV the Fair.

BIBLIOGRAPHY

Joseph R. Strayer, *The Reign of Philip the Fair* (1980), with detailed bibliography.

JOSEPH R. STRAYER

[See also **Boniface VIII, Pope; Bruges; Burgundy; Champagne; Chivalry, Orders of; Councils, Western; Disputatio Inter Clericum et Militem; Ecclesiology; Flanders and the Low Countries; France; Ghent; Kingship, Theories of; Lyons; Marigny, Enguerran de; Nogaret, Guillaume de; Parlement of Paris; Political Theory, Western European; Representative Assemblies, French.**]

PHILIP VI OF VALOIS (1293–1350), king of France from 1328 to 1350, was the first monarch of the Valois dynasty. His father, Charles, count of Valois, Anjou, and Maine, was a younger brother of Philip IV and a grandson of St. Louis. When Philip IV died in 1314, he left three sons, the oldest of whom (Louis X) had a posthumous son. The early deaths of these four princes in rapid succession (1316–1328) ultimately brought Philip of Valois to the throne, but not without a political crisis that established new rules for the French succession: henceforth, a woman could neither inherit the throne nor transmit a claim to it.

Although Philip was a first cousin of his predecessor, Charles IV, and was on congenial terms with him both personally and politically, the succession was complicated by the strong French tradition of legitimacy. It was impossible to banish all doubts about the validity of Philip's claim, and malcontents could always have recourse to the alternative of the opposing claimant, Edward III of England. Philip had to find places for his own followers as well as those who had served Charles IV. He had to honor a promise to help the count of Flanders put down a rebellion, and he had to banish his longtime friend, Robert of Artois, in 1332 when the latter's interests conflicted with those of the count of Flanders and duke of Burgundy, whom Philip could not afford to alienate. After 1332, Philip drew heavily on advisers from Burgundy and Auvergne. Powerful interests in the north and west felt slighted, and their resentments weakened Philip's position when the Hundred Years War with England broke out in 1337.

The first French king in many generations to suffer military defeat at the hands of England, Philip is best known for the disaster at Crécy, soon to be dwarfed by the greater misfortunes of his son. Historians have recently begun to appreciate Philip's deft political maneuvering in the face of intense pressures. Although the reign began with a victory over Flemish rebels at Cassel, Philip's military position was hampered by a perpetual shortage of revenue, especially during times of truce. His subjects objected to paying taxes unless they felt a sense of acute danger from a foreign enemy.

For nearly a decade after the mid 1330's, financial officers dominated the government but failed to find a financial solution. The English gained command of the sea at Sluys (1340), intervened in Brittany (1341), made substantial conquests in Guienne (1345), defeated Philip at Crécy (1346), and took Calais (1347). These last defeats led to several reshufflings of the government and persuaded the Estates General that a military recovery required substantial taxes. Assemblies granted very large sums during the winter of 1347–1348, but collection had barely begun when the Black Death reached France, bringing administrative chaos as well as demographic disaster. This final setback ended hopes for a speedy French recovery, and when Philip died in August 1350, his son, John II, inherited serious unresolved problems of a financial and political nature.

BIBLIOGRAPHY

The indispensable source for the reign is Raymond Cazelles, *La société politique et la crise de la royauté sous Philippe de Valois* (1958). A more recent book that concentrates on fiscal politics is John Bell Henneman, *Royal Taxation in Fourteenth-century France: The Development of War Financing, 1322–1356* (1971). The extensive, if somewhat overlapping, bibliographies of these two works list most other major works, including the many articles of Jules Viard, the principal historian of Philip VI before Cazelles.

JOHN BELL HENNEMAN

[See also **Black Death; Edward III of England; France; Hundred Years War; Taxation, French; Valois Dynasty.**]

PHILIP OF HARVENGT (*ca.* 1100–1183), theologian and hagiographer. Born to a humble family, Philip became a Premonstratensian canon and served as prior and then abbot of the abbey of Bonne Espérance (1156/1157–1182). He was a prominent monastic theologian who engaged in controversy with Bernard of Clairvaux.

Philip's works show that he was an excellent Latinist who delighted in the massive use of rhyming prose. He has left several treatises on the spirituality and conduct of clerics and on scriptural questions as well as a *Commentary on the Song of Songs*. Philip wrote updated versions of several biographies of saints from northern France and southern Belgium; he also composed a *Life of St. Augustine* and an interesting biography of his contemporary Oda of Rivreulle. The poems formerly ascribed to him are no longer considered authentic.

BIBLIOGRAPHY

Philip's works are in *Patrologia latina,* CCIII (1855). For further details and bibliography, see Michael McCormick, *Index scriptorum operumque latino-belgicorum medii aevi: Nouveau répertoire des oeuvres médiolatines belges,* pt. 3, II (1979), 183–194. For Philip's hagiographical production, see Michael McCormick and Paul Fransen, *Index scriptorum operumque latino-belgiocorum medii aevi: Nouveau répertoire des oeuvres médiolatines belges,* pt. 3, I (1977), 37–38, 69–70, 75–76, 98–99, 133, and 142.

MICHAEL MCCORMICK

[See also **Bernard of Clairvaux, St.; Hagiography, Western; Premonstratensians.**]

PHILIP THE CHANCELLOR (*ca.* 1160/1185—1236/1237), theologian, philosopher, administrator, and poet. From the sixteenth to the present century, he was often confused with Philippe de Grève, although contemporary documents clearly distinguish them. He was born in Paris, the son of Archdeacon Philippe of Paris. There is no extant information on his early life, although he most likely studied theology, and perhaps also canon law, in Paris. He is first mentioned in a charter of 1211 as deacon of Noyon.

In 1217, Pope Honorius III granted him permission to transfer to the Parisian diocese, where he became chancellor of Notre Dame (by 1218). In the early years of his tenure, he came into conflict with the University of Paris (over which he, as chancellor, had limited jurisdiction), then struggling for some measure of autonomy. In 1219 he excommunicated the masters and imprisoned the students, but his excommunication order was rescinded by Honorius III. By the time of the great university strike of 1229–1231, however, he had become more tolerant of university concerns and sided with the pope and university against the bishop and regent. Thus he readily submitted to the bull of Gregory IX (*Deus parens scientiarum,* 1231), which established regulations for the governance of the university and ended the strike. During his tenure the Dominicans and Franciscans received their first chairs of theology at the university. While he later earned the enmity of the Dominicans through his defense of benefice cumulation at the assembly of 1235, he remained friendly with the Franciscans and at his death was buried in their church.

Philip's wide-ranging literary production includes philosophical treatises, commentaries, sermons, and poetry. His major philosophical work, the *Summa quaestionum theologicarum (Summa de bono)*, written about 1230–1236, was probably incomplete at his death. It is the first systematic presentation of theology dealing with the metaphysical concept of the good and its relation to truth and being, the various species of good, and the transcendental properties of being and free will. The problems themselves derive from the Augustinian tradition and demonstrate the profound influence of Christian Neoplatonism, while the solutions proposed show Philip to be among the pioneers of the newly emerging Aristotelian philosophical method (and one of the first to refer to a Latin Averroës). While portions of the *Summa* depend directly on the *Glossa* of Alexander of Hales, the philosophical foundations of the work are original. The *Summa* exercised great influence on pre-Thomist philosophy, especially on early Franciscan thought and Albertus Magnus, and the work established Philip as a major forerunner of Scholasticism.

The controversial work *Summa duacensis* has been variously viewed either as one of the sources of Philip's *Summa* or as his own early outline of the larger work. His *Distinctiones super Psalterium* is a collection of practical commentaries on the Psalms (for use in sermons), giving a verse-by-verse explication of their fourfold sense. He also wrote twenty theological *Quaestiones* and was a prolific and renowned preacher (more than 700 sermons).

Philip's reputation as a poet, in both Old French and Latin, was wide and, judging from the extensive corpus of Latin works (only one, disputed, vernacular poem survives), well deserved. His highest poetic achievement was in nonliturgical, religious verse (hymns, motets, conducti), but he also composed moralizing and satirical poems, especially on ecclesiastical abuses. The poems are intellectually challenging and exhibit a rare command of the characteristically medieval rhythmic, rhyming mode, often with the added embellishment of a refrain.

BIBLIOGRAPHY

A list of Philip's edited poetic works appears in *Analecta hymnica medii aevi,* 50 (1907, repr. 1961), 529–531; a list of manuscripts of philosophical works is in Artur M. Landgraf, *Einführung in die Geschichte der theologischen Literatur der Frühscholastik* (1948), 132–133.

See also E. Bettoni, "Filippo il Cancelliere," in *Pier Lombardo,* 4 (1960); Odon Lottin, *Psychologie et morale aux xiie et xiiie siècles,* VI (1960); Henry Meylan, "Les 'Questions' de Philippe le Chancelier" (thesis, École Nationale des Chartes, 1927); Walter H. Principe, *The Theology of the Hypostatic Union in the Early Thirteenth Century,* IV, *Philip the Chancellor's Theology of Hypostatic Union* (1975); Frederic J. E. Raby, *A History of Secular Latin Poetry in the Middle Ages,* 2nd ed., II (1957), and *A History of Christian Latin Poetry from the Beginnings to the Close of the Middle Ages,* 2nd ed. (1953); Johann B. Schneyer, *Die Sittenkritik in den Predigten Philipp des Kanzlers,* Beiträge zur Geschichte der Philologie und Theologie des Mittelalters, XXXIX.4 (1963); Jean-Pierre Torrell, *Théorie de la prophétie et philosophie de la connaissance* (1977); Maurice de Wulf, *History of Mediaeval Philosophy,* Ernest C. Messenger, trans., II (1938).

JEROLD C. FRAKES

[See also **Aristotle in the Middle Ages; Conductus; Notre Dame School; Paris, University of; Poetry, Liturgical; Scholasticism, Scholastic Method.**]

PHILIPPE DE BEAUMANOIR. See **Beaumanoir, Philippe de.**

PHILIPPE DE GRÈVE (*d. ca.* 1220), from 1181 a canon of Notre Dame and later dean of the cathedral chapter of Sens. Due to an incorrect attribution in the 1523 edition of *Summa in Psalterium* by Josse Bade, he was for centuries identified with his contemporary, Philip the Chancellor. Henry Meylan in 1927 clearly showed, by comparing manuscripts and obituaries, that all the extant writings hitherto ascribed to Philippe de Grève were in fact authored by Philip the Chancellor.

[See also **Philip the Chancellor.**]

PHILIPPE DE NOVARE, also known as Philippe de Navara or Navarre (*ca.* 1195–*ca.* 1265), jurist, was born in Novara, Lombardy, but spent almost his entire life in the Latin Orient, where he pursued a successful career as knight, diplomat, and man of letters. It was his legal expertise, however, that brought him the greatest renown during his lifetime.

Shortly after the siege of Damietta in 1218, Philippe entered the service of Jean I d'Ibelin, lord of Beirut. Between *ca.* 1221 and 1226 he married and settled on Cyprus. During the extended war (1229–1243) between the Ibelins and the supporters of Emperor Frederick II, Philippe played a leading role. His accomplishments as soldier and diplomat were instrumental in the first phase of the war, which ended with the definitive reconquest of Cyprus by the Ibelin party in 1233. Three years later Philippe took part in the last rites administered to Jean I d'Ibelin and then passed into the service of his son and successor, Balian III d'Ibelin. The latter presided over the second and final phase of the war, during which the imperial forces were driven out of their last stronghold on the Lebanese mainland in 1243. Philippe's contribution to this victory was invaluable, for it was his juridical and polemical skill that resulted in the establishment of Alice of Champagne as ruler of the kingdom of Jerusalem. For the rest of his life, Philippe was an important figure in the political and legal affairs of both Cyprus and Syria. He was one of the principal advisers of King Henry I of Cyprus and an executor of his will. The last documented reference to Philippe dates from 1264, when (during a legal dispute at Acre) mention was made of his reputation as the "best pleader (*pledeour*) on this side of the sea."

Philippe is the author of three works. The first is a prose history of the imperial-Ibelin wars, with intercalated occasional poems on the same subject, which frequently treat historical events in terms of the animal characters from the *Roman de Renart.* These *Mémoires* were apparently part of a composite larger work (now lost) that included an autobiographical account of Philippe's early life as well as his love and religious poetry. Philippe's history was written shortly after the close of the war (*ca.* 1243–1247) and was later revised by him (*ca.* 1254–1258). The work's polemical aim has been identified by Alfred Foulet: to justify and valorize the house of Ibelin. Philippe composed his *Livre de forme de plait* (also called *Livre à un sien ami*) between 1252 and 1257. The work is a "practical" manual for lawyers, providing detailed instruction on how to plead most effectively in the courts of Outremer. The *Livre* became an important component of the Assizes of Jerusalem. The moral-didactic treatise *Les quatre âges de l'homme* (*ca.* 1265) is the product of Philippe's old age. It treats in sequence the activities most appropriate to each of the four stages of a human life and ends by stressing the religious dimension of the final stage, considered a preparation for the life to come.

BIBLIOGRAPHY

Sources. Les quatre âges de l'homme, Marcel de Fréville, ed. (1888); *Livre de Philippe de Navarre (Livre de forme de plait),* in *Les assises de Jérusalem,* Arthur A. Beugnot, ed., I (1841), 469–571; *Mémoires, 1218–1243,* Charles Kohler, ed. (1913); *The Wars of Frederick II Against the Ibelins in Syria and Cyprus,* John L. La Monte and Merton J. Hubert, trans. (1936).

Studies. Alfred L. Foulet, "Les mémoires de Philippe de Novare sont-ils un plaidoyer?" in *Romania,* **56** (1930); Charles V. Langlois, *La vie en France au moyen âge, de la fin du XIIe au milieu du XIVe siècle* (1925), 205–240; Gaston Paris, "Philippe de Novare," in *Romania,* **19** (1890), which establishes Philippe's correct name and birthplace as Novare (Italian Novara, in Lombardy) rather than Navarre, as had previously been thought, and "Les *Mémoires* de Philippe de Novare," in his *Mélanges de littérature française du moyen âge* (1912), 427–470; Aldo Bart Rossebastiano, "La 'chanson d'aube' di Filippo de Novara," in Naples, Istituto universitario orientale sezione romanza, *Annali,* **21** (1979).

KEVIN BROWNLEE

[See also **Assizes of Jerusalem; Crusades and Crusader States: 1212–1272; Cyprus, Kingdom of; Frederick II; Ibelin, Jean d' (of Beirut); Ibelin, Jean d' (of Jaffa).**]

PHILIPPE DE THAON (*fl.* 1113–1139), probably a cleric of Norman descent associated with the English royal court, was the author of some of the earliest works in Anglo-Norman French, most in hexasyllabic rhymed couplets. His writings include a *Cumpoz* (1113) or *computus* for calculating the movable feasts of the church; a *Bestiaire* (1121–1139, but probably before 1135), which describes the characteristics and allegorical significance of various animals, birds, and stones, based primarily on the *Physiologus* tradition; and the *Livre de Sibile* (1139 or shortly thereafter), a faithful translation of the book of prophecy *Sibylla*

Tiburtina, with additional material from the *Libellus de Antichristo* by Adso of Montier-en-Der. Less certainly attributed to Philippe are an "Alphabetical Lapidary," recounting the physical, magical, and medicinal properties of stones, and an "Apocalyptic Lapidary" on the twelve foundation stones of the heavenly Jerusalem (Rev. 21:14). Philippe perhaps also wrote a *Débat de l'âme et du corps* (Debate of the body and the soul).

BIBLIOGRAPHY

Sources. Eduard Mall, ed., *Li Cumpoz Philipe de Thaün: Der Computus des Philipp von Thaün, mit einer Einleitung* (1873); Paul Meyer, ed., "Les plus anciens lapidaires français," in *Romania,* **38** (1909); Hugh Shields, ed., *Le livre de Sibile by Philippe de Thaon* (1979); Paul Studer and Joan Evans, eds., "The Alphabetical Lapidary" and "The Apocalyptic Lapidary," in their *Anglo-Norman Lapidaries* (1924); Hermann Varnhagen, ed., "Das altfranzösische Gedicht 'Un samedi par nuit,'" in *Erlanger Beiträge zur englischen Philologie,* I, 1 (1889); Emmanuel Walberg, ed., *Le bestiaire de Philippe de Thaün* (1900).

Study. Rupert T. Pickens, "The Literary Activity of Philippe de Thaün," in *Romance Notes,* **12** (1970).

ELLEN T. WEHNER

[See also **Anglo-Norman Literature; Bestiary; Lapidarium.**]

PHILIPPE DE VITRY. See **Vitry, Philippe de.**

PHILIPPE MOUSKET (*d. ca.* 1243), French chronicler—who called himself Mouskés in the first line of his work—belonged to the upper bourgeoisie of Tournai (Belgian Hainaut). He composed *Chronique rimée* (31,286 octosyllabic couplets) just before his death. This is a partisan account of the French monarchy from the Trojan War until the author's own time. He claims to have translated a Latin book found in the Abbey of St. Denis. More probably, he relied chiefly on French sources, including the chansons de geste, as well as on such popularly slanted histories as the *Chronique française des rois de France* by the Anonymous of Béthune and a French version of the Pseudo-Turpin. *Chronique rimée* testifies to the ever-growing fascination of the lay public with the history of France.

BIBLIOGRAPHY

Frédéric-Auguste Reiffenberg, ed., *Chronique rimée de Philippe Mouskés,* 2 vols. (1836–1838), and *Supplément* (1845); Robert C. Bates, "Philippe Mouskés Seven Centuries Ago," in Henri M. Peyre, ed., *Essays in Honor of Albert Feuillerat* (1943); Ronald N. Walpole, "Philippe Mouskés and the Pseudo-Turpin Chronicle," in *University of California Publications in Modern Philology,* **26** (1947), a thorough study of Mousket's sources, which Walpole believes to be chiefly French.

PETER F. DEMBOWSKI

[See also **Chansons de Geste; French Literature; Pseudo-Turpin.**]

PHILIPPOPOLIS. Situated on the Marica River in Thrace, Philippopolis (modern Plovdiv, Bulgaria) was an important town involved in the Byzantine-Bulgar wars of the ninth century. In 831 it was occupied by the Bulgars but was retaken by the Byzantines. At the end of the tenth century, Emperor Basil II fortified it heavily and placed a permanent governor there. It was subsequently taken by Frederick Barbarossa during the Third Crusade in 1189, was retaken by the Byzantines in 1263, fell to the Bulgars in the early 1340's, and finally fell to the Turks in 1363. Philippopolis was an important stronghold of the Paulician sect and also had an Armenian and a Hungarian trading community.

BIBLIOGRAPHY

George Ostrogorsky, *History of the Byzantine State,* Joan Hussey, trans. (1956, rev. ed. 1969).

LINDA C. ROSE

[See also **Bulgaria; Paulicians.**]

PHILOBIBLON. See **Richard de Bury.**

PHILOSOPHY AND THEOLOGY. The development of medieval philosophy and theology is treated below in the following nine articles: **Byzantine; Islamic; Jewish (in the Islamic World); Jewish (in Northern Europe); Western European (Origins to Mid Twelfth Century; Twelfth Century; Thirteenth-century Crisis; Late Medieval; Terminology).**

PHILOSOPHY AND THEOLOGY, BYZANTINE

THEOLOGY

The theology of the Eastern church is first and foremost a theology of definition. Its key word is orthodoxy, the "right doctrine," which, with its claim of absolute accuracy, allows no "turning aside to the right hand or to the left." Historically it stems from the concern for Christian unity, apparent from the earliest days of the church ("one Lord, one faith, one baptism"), that after the Christianization of the Roman Empire became a political necessity as much as a spiritual ideal. The formulas that defined the one faith were decreed by the seven ecumenical councils and guaranteed by their authority.

A second major factor in patristic and Byzantine theology is the merging of a Jewish with a Hellenistic heritage; the result is a speculative theology, sometimes more closely, sometimes only loosely, connected with the controversies of conciliar orthodoxy, and characterized by a marked influence of Greek philosophical thought and terminology. The interpretation of Scripture plays a part in both, but in its independent, systematic form it is important enough to be dealt with separately as a third aspect of theology.

Orthodoxy. The question in what sense Jesus was the Son of God, the first that the early church faced in its confrontation with Judaic monotheism, was the cardinal issue of Pauline and Johannine theology; and it loomed large in the philosophical reflection of the third century as well. It is therefore not surprising that when the universal church began meeting to define its position on essential points, this, rather than matters of morals, discipline, and organization, should have become the subject of discussions that unfailingly ended in bitter, often violent, controversy. Whatever the role played in these doctrinal disputes by personal ambition (Cyril of Alexandria, Dioscoros of Alexandria), ethnic identity (the Arianism of the Germans; the Monophysitism of Syria, Egypt, and Armenia), and political expediency, the faith as established by the ecumenical councils became the basis of orthodoxy. Of these councils the first two, which centered on the interpretation of the text "In the beginning was the Word," are traditionally described as theological, and the following four, which dealt with the sequel, "And the Word became flesh," as christological.

Originally there were three predominant formulas to define the relation among the Father, the Son, and the Holy Spirit: modalism or modalistic monarchianism (the three are "modes" or manifestations of the one God), subordinationism (the Father is the supreme God, and the Son and Holy Spirit are subordinate to him), and Trinitarianism. The first, generally known as Sabellianism, was condemned as early as the third century and had only minor significance in the subsequent period. The decisive dispute of the nascent Christian world was between the Trinitarianism of Athanasius of Alexandria (*ca.* 295–373) and subordinationism, held in the third century by such prominent thinkers as Origen (*d. ca.* 254) and Lucian of Antioch (*d.* 312), and renewed by the Alexandrian presbyter Arius (*d.* 336), with Eusebius of Nicomedia (*d. ca.* 342) as its most influential champion at court. The First Council of Nicaea, convoked in 325 by Constantine I, adopted the Athanasian formula "consubstantial with the Father" in the face of strong opposition, not only from the Arians but also from conservative Trinitarians, who objected to the use of a nonbiblical term. The victory was by no means final, for during the following half-century the political powers tended to favor Arianism.

The same period, however, was also the golden age of orthodox theology, that of the Cappadocian fathers: Gregory of Nazianzus (the Theologian, *d.* 389/390), Basil the Great (*d.* 379), and his younger brother Gregory of Nyssa (*d. ca.* 394). They defended and expanded the Athanasian theology, which with the accession of Theodosius I in 379 definitively defeated Arianism, at least within the confines of the empire—it survived for several centuries among most of the Germanic tribes (Goths, Vandals, and Lombards). The First Council of Constantinople (381) proclaimed the Holy Spirit equal to the Father and the Son against the alleged objections of Macedonius, bishop of Constantinople (bishop 341–348, 350–360; by 381 already deceased). Reaffirming the Nicene Creed, which in its original form ended with the words "and in the Holy Spirit," it adopted what is now known as the Nicaeno-Constantinopolitanum, or more commonly as the Nicene Creed, an already existing formula, which continues: "the Lord and Giver of Life, who proceeds from the Father and the Son; who together with the Father and the Son is worshiped and glorified, who has spoken through the prophets. . . ." The restraint used in not explicitly declaring the Holy Spirit consubstantial with the

Father reflects Basil's cautious attitude in this matter.

The conflict that dominated the fifth century concerned the relationship between the Divine Word and Jesus the man. It was as much a clash between rival sees as between doctrines, the protagonists being, on the one side, Cyril, archbishop of Alexandria (*d.* 444), and, on the other, Nestorius, archbishop of Constantinople (428–431; *d. ca.* 451), who refused to grant the Virgin Mary the predicate "mother of God" (*Theotokos*) rather than "mother of the man Jesus," because he held Christ's divinity and humanity to be distinct. Cyril's formula "one nature incarnate of (God) the Word incarnate" was accepted by the Council of Ephesus (431) but failed to win general approval until he had made the concession of declaring it equivalent to the Antiochene formula "union, without confusion, of two natures." The brutal tactics used by Cyril's successor Dioscoros I at the Second Council of Ephesus (449, called the Robber Synod) to obtain the reinstatement of the professed Monophysite Eutyches resulted in a countermovement led by Leo I of Rome (*r.* 440–461). The Council of Chalcedon (451) deposed Dioscoros and, while declaring Cyril's theology orthodox, adopted as its own definition "two indivisible and unconfused natures in one person and one hypostasis." This decision had far-reaching consequences: not only did the Alexandrian see lose its dominant position but Egypt, Syria, and Armenia were severed for good from the universal church.

In the following two centuries the ecclesiastical policy of the empire was aimed at healing the schism, and official theology consisted mainly in footnotes to the definitions of Ephesus and Chalcedon. Emperor Zeno's *Edict of Union* (482), Justinian's condemnation of some writings by leading Antiochene theologians through the Second Council of Constantinople (553), and Heraklios' edict *Exposition* (*Ekthesis,* 638, written by the patriarch Sergios), which propounded the doctrine of a single will and a single operation common to the two natures in the one person of Christ, represent three abortive attempts to arrive at an understanding with the Monophysites. The last of these compromise solutions (Monothelitism) was defeated at the Third Council of Constantinople (680–681), chiefly through the activity of St. Maximus the Confessor (*d.* 662), the outstanding theologian of medieval Byzantium. The decisive factor, however, in the restoration of religious unity within the empire was not Maximus' theology but the Arabic conquest of the Monophysite provinces, Syria and Egypt (634–642). It is significant that further endeavors to convince and convert Monophysites were almost without exception aimed not at the dissenting churches of these lost provinces but at Armenia, which politically maintained a precarious balance between Byzantium and Islam.

The next controversy that divided the Eastern church, iconoclasm versus image worship, while in the first place a matter of cult practice, contributed to orthodox theology a theory of the significance of the image. The circumstances that gave rise to the iconoclast movement remain obscure; but whatever the possible explanations, it would be easier to understand it in the setting of the third or the fourth century than in that of the eighth. The driving force behind iconoclasm was, in any case, the personal conviction of Leo III the Isaurian (*r.* 717–741) and the son (Constantine V, *r.* 741–775) and grandson (Leo IV, *r.* 775–780) who succeeded him, while the resistance or indifference of the majority of their subjects brought about its ultimate failure. In 787 the Second Council of Nicaea, the seventh and last ecumenical council recognized as such by both the Western and the Eastern churches, solemnly proclaimed the restoration of image worship.

Nevertheless, the revival of iconoclasm a quarter of a century later under the emperors Leo V (*r.* 813–820), Michael II (820–829), and Theophilos I (829–842) proves that there was still considerable support for it, at least among some sections of the population. But by the end of this period its force was apparently spent; its total disappearance was only a matter of a few decades. (The Sunday of Orthodoxy, the first Sunday of Lent, commemorates the end of iconoclasm in 843.) In Constantinople the principal theoreticians of image worship were the patriarchs Germanos I (deposed 730), Tarasios (784–806), and Nikephoros I (deposed 815). A more important contribution and more effective support came from Muslim territory, in the writings of St. John of Damascus (Damascene), the great eighth-century systematizer of orthodox theology.

The iconoclast schism was followed almost immediately by the Photian schism (ninth century), which caused a division within the Constantinopolitan church (Photians against Ignatians) as well as between Constantinople and Rome. Neither the real issue in the conflict between the two sees (jurisdiction over certain dioceses in Italy, Sicily, and the Balkan Peninsula, in particular over the recently converted Bulgarians) nor the position taken by Rome (canonical invalidity of Photios' election to the patriarchate in 858) is relevant to the present subject. It was Photios (*ca.* 810–*ca.* 893) who, in addition to some points of ritual and discipline, raised the dogmatic question of the procession of the Holy Spirit from the Father and Son (*a Patre Filioque*), maintaining that the Holy Spirit proceeds from the Father alone. This controversy eventually separated the churches for good. Photios first discussed the question at length in an encyclical to the Eastern patriarchs, then made it the principal charge in his anathematization of Pope Nicholas I in 867.

While the doctrine of procession from the Son as well as from the Father had by that time found general acceptance in the Frankish West, no addition to the creed had been authorized by Rome, so that at the Council of Reconciliation (879–880) the Constantinopolitan clergy and the Roman legates could subscribe jointly to the Nicene-Constantinopolitan creed in its original form, regardless of the interpretation each party chose to put on it. Even after the reconciliation, Photios returned to the question at least twice: in a letter to the archbishop of Aquileia and in his *Mystagogia* (*Mystagogy of the Holy Spirit*), after which the matter rested for nearly two centuries.

In the confrontation of 1054 between legates of Pope Leo IX and Patriarch Michael Keroullarios, which resulted in the irreparable schism, the *filioque* controversy was not the most prominent factor, though by that time the doctrine that the Holy Spirit proceeds from both Father and Son had officially become a part of the Latin creed. Among the Greeks there were no new theological developments until increasingly close contacts with the Western world, especially after the Latin conquest of Constantinople in 1204, induced them to reconsider the problem—as seen in the arguments of Nikephoros Blemmydes (*ca.* 1197–*ca.* 1272), the most significant theologian of the Empire of Nicaea. When, after the recapture of the capital, the precarious military and political situation made papal support indispensable, Emperor Michael VIII Palaiologos consented to accept the Roman creed (Council of Lyons, 1274). Patriarch John XI Bekkos, an able and erudite theologian, became the defender of this short-lived union. The continued literary debate for and against (of which the translations of Latin theological works, chiefly by Maximus Planudes [*d. ca.* 1330] and Demetrios Kydones [*d. ca.* 1398], were an important byproduct), together with renewed attempts at a settlement, culminated in the equally unsuccessful Council of Ferrara-Florence (1438–1439), where the metropolitan of Nicaea, the future Cardinal Bessarion (*d.* 1472), acted as the chief Byzantine unionist against the unyielding opposition of Mark Eugenikos of Ephesus.

Throughout this period, from the ninth century to the fall of Constantinople (1453), there was a constantly increasing stream of dogmatic literature (a great deal of it still unpublished in the twentieth century), but there were no significant developments in doctrine. The content is mostly polemical or apologetical. Next in quantity to writings against the Latins is a very considerable body of literature directed aginst Islam, which served various purposes: Some of it, perhaps most of it, is purely academic; another part is linked to Byzantine diplomacy, trying to justify the Christian position in exchanges with Muslim rulers; finally, if there was any real attempt to persuade or convince, it must have been aimed at potential renegade Christians in occuped territory or at Muslim settlers in the empire, mainly in the capital. Third in importance is the debate against the Armenian Monophysites, whose relation to Byzantium was much the same as Byzantium's relation to the Western countries in the time of its decline: a need for military support, on the one hand, and unwillingness to sacrifice traditional beliefs, on the other. A part of this kind of polemical material appears, in combination with accounts of long-extinct heresies, in the comprehensive heresiological compilations of the monk Euthymios Zigabenos (*Panoplia dogmatica,* early twelfth century) and of the statesman Niketas Choniates (thirteenth century). There was also a great deal of internal conflict, but almost entirely over personal, disciplinary, or canonical issues.

The only dispute within the Orthodox church after iconoclasm that affected dogmatic thinking at all was the hesychast controversy in the fourteenth century. It originated in the contemplative practices of some Mt. Athos visionaries, who claimed the light that revealed itself to them in their state of trance was the same divine, uncreated light that shone upon Christ on the mountain of the Transfiguration (Mt. Tabor). To defend this claim against the objections of the Calabrian monk Barlaam (*ca.* 1290–*ca.* 1348, until 1341 still considered orthodox), who attacked it with the tools of Western Scholasticism, Gregory Palamas (1296–1359), at one time an Athos monk, worked out a theory distinguishing between God's absolutely unknowable essence and his knowable, sometimes visible, operations. Despite strong opposition from Gregory Akindynos (*d. ca.* 1349) and Nikephoros Gregoras, Palamas' doctrine was approved by the synod of 1351, and he became a saint of the Orthodox church as early as 1368.

Speculative and mystical theology. Besides conciliar theology, which of course can also be described as speculative, there is an important theological literature originating in reflection rather than in controversy. Its main source of inspiration was the need to adapt the Jewish tradition of Scripture to Hellenistic thought. Throughout the patristic period, but more conspicuously from Origen on, there was a constant influx of Platonism, successively in its Middle Platonic, Plotinian, and post-Plotinian forms. What made it acceptable, notwithstanding the antagonistic attitude toward Christianity of many of its chief representatives (Porphyry, Julian the Apostate, the Athenian school), was its moderate dualism. Stoicism, which was no less profoundly religious, had a certain influence on Christian ethics and asceticism, but its materialistic monism made it unfit for assimilation.

The Cappadocian fathers were Platonists in various degrees. Gregory of Nazianzus explicitly recognized Platonic philosophy as most closely related to Christianity. Words and concepts are freely adapted: the Trinity is defined in the "Neopythagorean" terms of monad-dyad-triad, and God's action in the world described in terms of remaining-proceeding-reverting, current since Plotinus. Gregory of Nyssa's account of the creation, fall, and ascent of the soul is a remarkable synthesis of Plotinian and scriptural elements, the latter to a great extent transformed by allegorical interpretation.

Just when, toward the end of the fifth century, Christian philosophy had begun to move away from the emphatically pagan Platonism of the Athenian school, the Platonizing trend reached its climax thanks to one of the most remarkable mystifications of world literature: the *Corpus areopagiticum*, a small collection of treatises and letters produced between about 475 and 528, and purporting to be the work of Paul's convert Dionysius the Areopagite. An amalgam of the Platonism of the Cappadocians with Athenian Neoplatonism, but bearing most visibly the imprint of Proclus' system, terminology, and stylistic mannerisms, it perpetuated the latter's ideas in the East principally through St. Maximus the Confessor (*d.* 662). In the ninth century, through John Scottus Eriugena (*d. ca.* 877/879), it became the principal, and for a long time the only, channel by which later Neoplatonism reached the West.

Aside from this exceptional phenomenon, however, the sixth century was the beginning of a long and almost complete break in the Platonic tradition. Henceforth, the mainstream of Byzantine mystical theology had a different origin and took a different course: its context was monastic spirituality, and the reading public it addressed consisted of ascetics of widely varying degrees of spiritual perfection and secular education. Basil's disciplinary rules and Theodore of Studios' (759–826) guidance for practical conduct, for example, belong to this literature to the extent that their goal is salvation. In the fourth century Evagrius of Pontus distinguished this first step in the ascent to perfection from a higher and a highest: first practice, next natural contemplation, finally knowledge of God. The idea of step-by-step progress is the main theme in the seventh-century hermit John Klimakos' (*ca.* 570–*ca.* 649) *Ladder of Paradise* (*Klimax,* whence his name), one of the most widely read books of its kind. The greatest names in Byzantine mystical theology are St. Maximus the Confessor and Symeon the New Theologian (949–1022). Unique in many ways is a work of the fourteenth century, by Nikolaos Kavasilas, who addresses himself to all Christians without exception and gives the sacraments—that is, God's action rather than the ascetic's efforts—the central place in the "life in Christ."

Exegesis. The creative period of scriptural interpretation is characterized by two concurrent, sometimes rival, methods: literal explanation and allegory. The latter, of Stoic origin, was applied, under that name, in Galatians 4:21–31, about the time the Jewish philosopher Philo Judaeus (Philo of Alexandria, *d. ca.* A.D. 50) was practicing it systematically with a view to a Platonic interpretation of the Septuagint. Philo's example was followed, for a similar purpose, by the Christian Alexandrians (Origen, later Cyril), but no less by others (Gregory of Nyssa, for instance). The methods were not considered mutually exclusive: a literal interpretation can be offered conjointly with a moral and a spiritual one.

The clash occurred only when the Antiochene

school, in deliberate opposition to allegory, insisted on a purely historical and pragmatic approach. Its chief exponents were Diodorus of Tarsus (fourth century), his pupil Theodore of Mopsuestia (*d.* 428), and, half a century later, Theodoret, bishop of Cyrrhus (Theodoret of Cyr); the most famous and successful was without any doubt St. John Chrysostom (348–407). Diodorus and Theodore were later considered the "fathers" of Nestorianism, to which their exegesis, with its emphasis on historical and human factors, was felt to be the natural complement; Theodoret of Cyr was condemned by the Second Council of Constantinople (553) for his opposition to Cyril. Nevertheless, although Theodore of Mopsuestia's writings were also condemned at the 553 council, his commentary on the twelve minor prophets and most of his other works have survived. Photios' partiality for their exegetical method may have had a share in this; also, until well into the Middle Ages there was a lingering feeling of dissatisfaction with the condemnation of Theodoret.

By the sixth century the view began to prevail that in the matter of exegesis, as in many others, everything worth saying had already been said, a view that led to the compiling of the so-called catenae, variorum editions of single Bible books or groups of books. Some known compilers are Procopius of Gaza (*d. ca.* 528), Olympiodorus of Alexandria (sixth century), Theophylact, archbishop of Bulgaria (*ca.* 1090–1109), and Niketas of Heraclea (eleventh century), but most of these often huge compilations are anonymous. If a name is attached to them, it may be that of a reviser, since in this type of literature there was usually a continuous process of adding and abridging. Even the original editor may no longer have a valid claim to authorship. In these collections Alexandrian and Antiochene, orthodox and heterodox materials are gathered together indiscriminately. It is precisely this uncritical assemblage that makes them valuable from a present-day point of view.

Next in popularity to the catena ranks another genre: miscellaneous essays on isolated passages in the form of questions and answers (*eratopokriseis*). An early author is Theodoret, who, however, follows the order of the text. Truly miscellaneous are a large collection attributed to St. Anastasios Sinaita, St. Maximus the Confessor's *Questions to Thalassius,* Photios' *Amphilochia,* and similar works by Michael Psellos and Michael Glycas. In comparison, new running commentaries become rare. A special case is the Apocalypse, which after early recognition was almost entirely ignored during the patristic period and only slowly regained some ground in the Middle Ages. The oldest extant commentaries on it were written in the sixth century by Oecumenios and by Andrew of Caesarea; Arethas of Patras' commentary (beginning of the tenth century) is a revised version of Andrew's.

Literal and allegorical exegesis remained equally acceptable to the church, provided the results conformed to orthodox doctrine. Yet from time to time strong sympathies or antipathies are expressed. St. Maximus the Confessor declared the literalistic method to be Jewish, and therefore irreconcilable with a Christian conception of Scripture. Photios, reviewing Maximus' *Questions to Thalassius,* disapproved of his exegesis as arbitrary and too far remote from the text; in his own *Questions to Amphilochios* (the *Amphilachia*) Photios tried to visualize the situation as strictly historical and to determine why the persons involved (human or divine) acted as they did. About two centuries later, Michael Psellos began a treatise with the statement "Trees of Life or of Knowledge have never been seen on the earth before, nor are they likely to appear in the future."

PHILOSOPHY

The only possible definition of Byzantine philosophy, unless one chooses to apply the term loosely to Byzantine speculative thought in general, is "involvement with the wide variety of subjects that in classical antiquity, down to the sixth century, passed under the common name of 'philosophy.'" This is what the Byzantines themselves—in spite of frequent but halfhearted claims that Christian dogma was the only true theoretical philosophy and the monastic life the only true practical philosophy—usually understood by the word.

After the sixth century there were no schools representing and developing a specific philosophical system; whatever philosophical instruction there was, was occasional and intermittent. Accordingly, there were no philosophers, unless the term is extended to include theologians, as it was in the case of St. Maximus. There were certainly authors who wrote on philosophical subjects, but with rare exceptions (partly due to the chance nature of manuscript tradition) these writings are outweighed by their production in other fields.

Those elements of the ancient tradition that survived the Christianization of the existing society served several divergent purposes. In the first place, philosophy, though often in a simplified and elementary form, continued to function as a part of a general education. Further, there was a good deal of interaction with theology, which either underwent the influence of philosophical systems or adapted them to its own purposes. Finally, along with other components of the pagan heritage, such as the fantasies of ancient myth, the erotic poetry of the Greek Anthology, and the impertinent jokes of Lucian, it provided an escape from the exacting ideology that monopolized Byzantine life.

Education. Throughout antiquity, from the fourth century B.C. on, philosophy had fought a losing battle against rhetoric in the education of the young, and Christianity did not do much to tip the balance in its favor. Most of the Fathers studied with rhetoricians, and whatever philosophical knowledge they possessed, they acquired by reading. Of the leading philosophical schools, Stoicism and Epicureanism had succumbed by the fourth century; the Platonic tradition, as far as oral teaching is concerned, ended toward the middle of the sixth century at Athens, and not much later at Alexandria, mainly owing to its polytheistic theology, which identified transcendent realities with the gods of the old cults and myths. The (Platonizing) Aristotelianism of Alexandria did not survive much longer.

This amounts to saying that the takeover of philosophical instruction by Christians was a failure. No attempt was made, after Origen, to found institutions for the development of a Christian, or christianized, philosophy. The school of Gaza was a school of rhetoric, though some of its members (Procopius, Aeneas, Zacharias of Mytilene, also called Scholasticus [*d.* 553]) engaged in polemics against certain Neoplatonic doctrines, such as reincarnation and the eternity of the world. Athens, in spite of its religious bias, did attract some Christian students, but none of them, as far as we know, ever made a contribution to philosophy (unless, of course, the Pseudo-Dionysius was among them).

At Alexandria, however, things took a somewhat different turn. Ammonius, the son of Hermias, in the course of his long professorate (*ca.* 470–*ca.* 520) was forced by financial pressure to compromise with the local patriarch; the terms of the agreement are not known, but it must somehow have limited his freedom of speech. Meanwhile a Christian student, John Philoponus (*fl. ca.* 500–*ca.* 550), edited Ammonius' lectures, providing them with critical observations; he was not, however, accepted as a legitimate member of the school and was not appointed to the chair. There seem to have been at least two pagan successors before the leadership finally passed into Christian hands (after 565). Those in charge, however, were faced with the fundamental problem that teaching could only be teaching of the truth. In consequence, major issues were avoided, and in the next half-century or so philosophical instruction was reduced to an elementary general introduction and an equally elementary course in logic, which did not differ significantly from the courses as Ammonius had taught them, except in inaccuracy and wordiness. Curiously, in this impoverished form the Greek philosophical heritage had a geographical expansion as never before: Through Boethius it spread over most of Western Europe; in the East, it reached Armenia and Syria, and, via Syria, eventually the entire Muslim world.

The eleventh century saw a return to the formal teaching of Aristotelian philosophy, documented by Psellos' commentaries on the *De interpretatione* and *Physics.* This activity was continued in the next century by Michael of Ephesus, Eustratius, Stephanus, and others; apart from the *Organon,* they devoted most of their efforts to works for which no Alexandrian commentaries were available (physiological and biological writings, *Ethics, Politics, Rhetoric*). Their choice may also have been determined by the wish to steer clear of subjects that were theologically sensitive. Further commentaries on Aristotle continued to be produced up to the late Middle Ages and beyond (Magentinus, George Pachymeres [*d. ca.* 1310]).

Throughout the Byzantine period, short surveys derived from the traditional course in logic (including the introduction) continued to be produced. A favorite source of popularized information in the field of philosophy was the doxographical manual *Placita philosophorum* (*Peri tōn areskonton philosophois physikon dogmatōn*) ascribed to Plutarch; its pattern was followed in compilations by Symeon Seth (eleventh century) and Michael Psellos that enjoyed a wide circulation. Equally successful, but better organized and of a generally higher quality, were Nikephoros Blemmydes' two epitomes of Aristotelian logic and physics.

Terminology. The part played by (later) ancient philosophy in the shaping of Christian theological speculation has already been dealt with in the context of theology. In addition, philosophy became increasingly important to conciliar dogmatics in its role of "handmaiden of theology," by providing the necessary distinctive terminology. Once the first, much-disputed step of accepting the word "consubstantial" in the Nicene Creed had been taken (against the Arians, themselves accused of adulterating the faith with profane terminology and argument), further steps were easy: in the Christological debates of the fifth century, "nature," "hypostasis," and "union" were the key terms. Not much later, during the first stage of the Christianization of the Alexandrian school, logical terminology was deliberately adapted and expanded to serve this purpose. John Philoponus' "tritheism" was the direct result of the application to theology of Aristotelian modes of thought. In the anthology known as *Doctrina patrum de incarnatione Verbi* (compiled about the middle of the seventh century), extracts from the Alexandrian professor Elias figure among quotations from the Fathers. About the same time there was a spate of small manuals of logic written specifically for use in theology, in both Greek and Syriac; in some cases secular and theological definitions of the same terms were set side by side. The genre culminates in St. John of Damascus' *Dialectics,* in which the "handmaiden" metaphor appears for the first time in Greek.

Philosophy seen as a danger. Classical culture, literary as well as philosophical, though accepted as useful and even indispensable for a liberal education (not least owing to the weight of Basil's authority), nevertheless continued to be looked upon with a certain suspicion as a potential danger to the faith and to morality. This ambivalent attitude is nowhere more manifest than in the case of Neoplatonic writings. As "ancient" literature (by the ninth century) they were tolerated, with the sole exception of deliberately anti-Christian books; because of their strange, esoteric character, they were suspect to some while exercising an insidious attraction on others who, for various reasons, might experience the rigid orthodoxy of the community as oppressive. Because it could not be expressed in writing, this last trend remains to a great extent elusive; it becomes tangible, however, in the manuscript tradition.

Thanks to the long survival of the Alexandrian school, a great part of its library holdings were available to Constantinopolitan scholars in the ninth century, the critically important period when most of the extant classical literature was transliterated from uncial into minuscule script, among it a disproportionate quantity of Neoplatonic works. Excluding Platonizing interpretations of Aristotle, what we still have at present of strictly Neoplatonic literature (Plotinus, Porphyry, Iamblichus, Hermias, Proclus, and Damascius) amounts to roughly 2.5 million words, about four times the complete Plato; this figure does not allow for losses between the ninth and sixteenth centuries. Those losses must have been considerable, and are in several cases demonstrable. We still possess some of the finest copies from the library of an unknown scholar of the end of the ninth century (Leo Choirosphaktes?) who read, corrected, and annotated a number of them himself. The rest has been preserved in later transcripts. The effort and expenditure bestowed on these volumes are in strange contrast with the almost complete silence on Neoplatonism in contemporary authors: over a period of about two centuries there is no evidence whatever of familiarity with Neoplatonic thought and terminology, and its very existence is barely mentioned. The likeliest explanation is that the material was regarded as dangerous.

Some incidents of the same time confirm this: Leo the Mathematician (also known as Leo the Philosopher, surnamed the Hellene, that is, the Pagan [*d.* after 869]) was posthumously attacked as an apostate in a satirical poem by a former pupil; the scholar and diplomat Leo Choirosphaktes became the target of an equally crude prose satire by Arethas of Patras, archbishop of Caesarea (*fl.* 895–932), who accused him of friendship with the enemies of the faith, Porphyry and Julian the Apostate. Arethas himself, while still a deacon, had been formally charged with impiety in a patriarchal court, probably on similar grounds.

Neoplatonism surfaced at last in the eleventh century owing to the interest of Michael Psellos, who quoted freely from all the leading Neoplatonists; the Chaldean Oracles, in their Neoplatonic interpretation, had a special fascination for him. He was careful, however, to make it clear at every turn that his use of these texts was selective and critical, and that it had not led him into any conflict with revealed truth. Nevertheless, at a certain point in his career, he was obliged to produce a written profession of faith. While Psellos himself escaped scot-free, his student and successor John Italos (*ca.* 1025–after 1082), who was less cautious, or less fortunate, was indicted before a synod and forced to recant a number of specific Platonic and Origenistic tenets in 1082, at the beginning of the reign of Alexios I Komnenos (*r.* 1081–1118). The reaction to this was, on the one hand, a preference for Aristotelian studies, and on the other, a more circumspect attitude toward Platonism. Isaac the Sebastokrator, a prince of the Komnenan house (probably a younger son of Alexios), rewrote Proclus' three treatises on providence and evil, eliminating everything that could be considered at variance with Christian dogma or even remind a reader of the pagan origin of the essays; Nikolaos, bishop of Methone, wrote a refutation of Proclus' *Elements of Theology,* also in the twelfth century.

The thirteenth and fourteenth centuries witnessed a new proliferation of manuscripts: For many of the major works (Iamblichus on Pythagorean doctrine, Proclus' *Platonic Theology* and his commentaries on the *Alcibiades* and *Parmenides,* Hermias on the *Phaedrus*), our oldest copies belong to this period, often written by scholars who produced their own transcripts. At this time, involvement in Platonic doctrine seems no longer to be a problem: both Plato and Aristotle were freely discussed by such leading writers as Nikephoros Choumnos (*ca.* 1250–1327), Theodore Metochites, Nikephoros Gregoras, and Demetrios Kydones (*ca.* 1324–1398). Protests from conservative theologians were not lacking, but they were no longer heeded. Their concern was not wholly unjustified, for in this era of political disintegration, when Orthodox, Catholics, and Muslims were mixing everywhere, changing one's persuasion had become relatively easy. In the early fourteenth century the astronomer and physician Gregory Chioniades (later archbishop of Tabriz) had to defend himself against allegations of fatalism and Islamic beliefs. A century later the worst fears came true, when in the person of Georgios Gemistos Plethon (*ca.* 1355–1452) Platonism once more became a menace and a rival to Christianity.

BIBLIOGRAPHY

Bibliographical publications include Maurice Geerard, *Clavis patrum graecorum,* II–IV (1974–1980); Thomas P. Halton and Robert D. Sider, "A Decade of Patristic Scholarship, 1970–1979," in *The Classical World,* 76 (1982–1983); Wilhelm Schneemelcher, ed., *Bibliographia patristica,* I (1956); C. N. Tsirpanlis, "A Bibliography of Orthodox Theology (1970–1979)," in *The Patristic and Byzantine Review,* 1 (1982).

Two earlier publications dealing specifically with the church councils are Giovanni Domenico Mansi, *Sacrorum conciliorum nova, et amplissima collectio,* II–XXXI (1901); Eduard Schwartz and Johannes A. Straub, eds., *Acta conciliorum oecumenicorum,* 4 vols. (1914).

Studies include Berthold Altaner, *Patrology* (1960); Arthur H. Armstrong, ed., *The Cambridge History of Later Greek and Early Medieval Philosophy* (1967); Hans Georg Beck, *Kirche und theologische Literatur im byzantinischen Reich* (1959); Francis Dvornik, *The Photian Schism* (1948), and *The Ecumenical Councils* (1961); Adolf von Harnack, *History of Dogma,* Neil Buchanan, trans., 7 vols. in 4 (1961, repr. 1976); Herbert Hunger, *Reich der neuen Mitte: Der christliche Geist der byzantinischen Kulture* (1965), and *Die hochsprachliche profane Literatur der Byzantiner,* I (1978); J. M. Hussey, *Church and Learning in the Byzantine Empire* (1937); Hubert Jedin and John Dolan, *Handbook of Church History,* II–IV (1968–1980); M. J. Le Guillou, *The Spirit of Eastern Orthodoxy,* David Attwater, trans. (1962); Vladimir Lossky, *The Mystical Theology of the Eastern Church,* 2nd ed. (1975); John Meyendorff, *Byzantine Theology: Historical Trends and Doctrinal Themes,* 2nd ed. (1974); Jaroslav Pelikan, *The Christian Tradition: A History of the Development of Doctrine,* I: *The Emergence of the Catholic Tradition* (1971), II: *The Spirit of Eastern Christendom* (1974); Gerhard Podskalsky, *Theologie und Philosophie in Byzanz* (1977); Johannes Quasten, *Patrology,* III (1960); Basile Tatakis, *La philosophie byzantine* (1949); Friedrich Ueberweg, *Grundriss der Geschichte der Philosophie,* I: *Die Philosophie des Altertums,* Karl Praechter, ed. (1926), and II: *Die patristische und scholastische Philosophie,* Bernhard Geyer, ed. (1928); Harry A. Wolfson, *The Philosophy of the Church Fathers,* I (1956).

L. G. WESTERINK

[See also **Arianism; Aristotle in the Middle Ages; Athos, Mount; Byzantine Church; Christology; Church, Early; Councils, Byzantine; Councils, Ecumenical; Doctors of the Church; Filioque; Heresies, Byzantine; Hesychasm; Icon, Theology of; Iconoclasm; Liturgy, Byzantine Church; Monothelitism; Mysticism, Christian: Byzantine; Neoplatonism; Nestorianism; Plato in the Middle Ages; Schism, Eastern-Western Church; Schism, Photian; Trinitarian Doctrine; Theotokos;** and individual personalities.]

PHILOSOPHY AND THEOLOGY, ISLAMIC. In the early centuries of Islam, theology and philosophy were regarded as two distinct disciplines, following their own assumptions and intellectual traditions. "The science of dialectic" (*ᶜilm al-kalam*) meant Islamic theology, derived only from the revealed Koran and the traditions of the prophet Muḥammad. Philosophy (*al-falsafa*) was a "foreign" science based on natural knowledge and largely inspired by ancient Greek philosophy. As time passed theology and philosophy interacted increasingly, with varying relations in different parts of the Muslim world. But we must begin by describing them as separate, as they generally were until about the eleventh century.

THEOLOGY

Almost all teaching, discussion, and writing on this subject were conducted in Arabic, the language of the Koran and of other Islamic subjects such as exegesis and jurisprudence. The principal centers of theology were in Iraq and Iran.

After early discussions on conditions for salvation and the moral qualifications of caliphs, the first systematic school, the Muʿtazilites, arose in Iraq in the eighth century, about a century after Muḥammad's death in 632. Their self-description as "the party of unity and justice" announced their central doctrines.

The unity of God (Allah) was understood very strictly by them, reflecting the emphasis of the Koran. Polytheism and the Christian Trinity were rejected as a matter of course. The Koran could not be eternal beside God but must have been created by the one eternal being. Even the attributes of God, such as his power and wisdom, would raise problems if they were thought of as separate eternal entities; they had to be somehow united with an essence of God which was purely simple, since "unity" included simplicity.

Muʿtazilite ethical theology insisted that God was just in an objective sense as understood by man. Therefore he would treat man with this intelligible justice in distributing rewards and punishments on the Day of Judgment. Thus men would be punished only for sins which they had had the power to avoid. This implied that men had power to choose their own conduct, free from predestination. God has delegated to man this power to decide and even (according to the later Muʿtazilites) to "create" his own acts.

These doctrines of God's unity and justice were worked out with much refinement and far-reaching related theories over a period of three centuries by theologians of two schools, those of Basra and Baghdad, with constant controversy among themselves and with opponents. They seldom enjoyed government support and were increasingly denounced. The Basran tradition culminated in the work of ʿAbd al-Jabbār (*ca.* 935–1025), a Persian who wrote a long summa presenting the latest positions in dialectical form. After him there were few Muʿtazilites, and most of their books were destroyed by opponents or neglected in libraries.

Their method was rationalist in the sense that they started from a few principles stated or implicit in the Koran, then deduced their logical consequences, without too much regard to problems of consistency presented by other assertions of the Koran. Their theory of knowledge supported confidently the powers of human intellect (*al-ʿaql*).

The Muʿtazilites met with opposition from the beginning from a variety of viewpoints. Ibn Ḥanbal (780–855), a famous jurist of Baghdad, disapproved of all theology on the ground that it was bound to go beyond the Koran by interpreting it according to human ideas, thus distorting its messages, which were perfectly expressed in the Book of God. Theology was idle speculation that had not been practiced by Muhammad and his Arab companions, the models for later Muslims to follow; it could only raise needless doubts about Islam. Nonetheless, there were later Hanbalite theologians, even if their intent was negative. Ibn Taymīya of Damascus (1263–1328) was the most influential. He made a rare attempt to refute Aristotelian logic. The Hanbalite school persists today in Saudi Arabia as one of the four orthodox schools of jurisprudence.

Some early Shiite theologians of the Imamite sect (also called Twelvers, now the majority in Iran), such as Hishām ibn al-Ḥakam (*d.* 795/796), disagreed with the Muʿtazilites in a different way. They accepted theology but opposed the transcendental Muʿtazilite doctrine of God, and interpreted the Koran more literally. God moves in space. His knowledge changes with the changes in its objects. But later Imamite theologians absorbed many of the Muʿtazilite doctrines, such as the objective justice of God and the freedom of man.

A more formidable opposition to Muʿtazilism emerged around the ninth century from Sunnite theologians who may be called traditionalist, in the sense that they tried hard to follow closely the precise meaning of the Koran. If this effort created apparent problems of consistency, Sunnite theologians would interpret the text cautiously with the help of the traditions and a careful study of the Arabic language and grammar at the time of the Prophet. Thus they were known as "the party of tradition" (*ahl as-sunna*), who followed the guidance of transmitted sources (*an-naql*) rather than independent human intellect. In fact, however, they were unable to follow this program with complete consistency since they, like the Muᶜtazilites, emphasized one principle found in the Koran rather than others, as will be shown.

The moderate literalism of the traditionalist school is seen in their doctrine of God's attributes. These could not be assimilated to a single essence of God, as the Muᶜtazilites proposed, because the Koran mentions many attributes, often by an abstract name; for example, God is not merely "knowing"; he also has "knowledge." Thus his attributes are real and distinguishable, without impairing his unity; for a single existent can have many attributes, as is commonly believed. So, too, they insisted that the Koran is the eternal, uncreated Word of God, being his very thought.

The principle which the traditionalists singled out as supreme was that of God's omnipotence. This is indeed stressed greatly in the Koran. Some of this school even denied natural causation in the world, because it would imply power in things other than God. In its place they constructed an "atomic" theory of causes, by which God is the sole cause of the successive states of the world, in themselves causally unconnected with each other.

Again, respecting omnipotence they found fault with the Muᶜtazilite view that there are objective standards of good and evil which God follows. Even though the Muᶜtazilites had been careful to state that God follows these standards freely, their very existence was now rejected because they would be independent and prior to his thought and will. The only standard of value for God and man was the will of God; whatever he wills is good by definition. This is ethical voluntarism, which, after the jurist al-Shāfiᶜī (*d.* 820), became the first principle of Islamic law in most schools. By adopting it traditionalist theologians could claim that God's will suffers no ethical limits. Thus, even if he punishes sinners whose acts he has predestined, he cannot be called "unjust," for justice means nothing but obedience to divine laws, and God is not subject to any laws.

Such a position, however neat as a theory, could hardly satisfy believers in an intelligible divine justice. The Sunnite theologian al-Ashᶜarī of Basra (873–935) then elaborated a subtler theory of justice, which might leave man responsible for his acts and so rightly culpable for his sins. This was the theory of "acquisition" (*al-iktisāb*), suggested by the Koran and already proposed by earlier traditionalists. While God creates every act of man and enables him to do it, the act is still that of the human agent, making him responsible for its consequences to himself. Ultimately, however, God predestines what act a man chooses; thus the problem is dismissed but not solved.

A solution closer to the Muᶜtazilite one was worked out by al-Māturīdī of Samarkand (*d.* 944). A man really chooses how to act, then God creates for him the act that he has chosen. Man "acquires" his act, while God "creates" it. Thus freedom and justice are preserved, but "creation" remains God's privilege, contrary to the later Muᶜtazilite vocabulary.

The schools of al-Ashᶜarī and al-Māturīdī became predominant in Sunnite Islam: the Ashʿarites in all the Arab countries and for a while in Iran, the Maturidites in Transoxania (now Uzbekistan), Turkey, and India.

PHILOSOPHY

Al-falsafa began to be studied in the ninth century, after Syriac Christian scholars at Baghdad had made accurate Arabic translations of most of Aristotle and some later Greek commentaries on him. Plato's dialogues became known through translated summaries. Parts of the *Enneads* of Plotinus were translated and became very influential, but they were generally ascribed to Aristotle—a cause of much confusion. Major works of Greek science were also translated, such as Galen's medicine, Ptolemy's astronomy and geography, and Euclid's geometry. These were regarded as the most advanced scientific books in the world, and since philosophy was not distinguished from science it shared in their prestige and came to be viewed by educated people as giving equally certain knowledge. All the philosophers were learned in one or more of the other sciences. Most of them were Muslims, but philosophy was not consciously Islamic until a later period.

The first Muslim philosopher, al-Kindī (*d. ca.* 870), an Arab of Basra, was a pioneer in Arabic philosophical writing. He showed some independence from the Greeks in holding that the world is not everlasting but was created in time, as the Koran declares.

Al-Farabī (873–950) was a Turk of Transoxania who studied and wrote in Baghdad and Aleppo. He gained a high reputation as an Arabic commentator on Aristotle, but his own philosophy was more Neoplatonic. Thus he propounded the emanation of the world in successive stages from God and the higher intellectual beings. Man must strive for happiness by climbing through intellectual discipline toward a conjunction of his soul with the world's active intellect. The ideal community requires a political organization such as the caliphate, in which a code of divine law (*sharīʿa*) has been provided by a philosophic prophet. Prophets are distinguished by imaginative powers which enable them to teach the law to the people in a convincing style.

Ibn Sīnā (Latin: Avicenna, 980–1037) was a Persian of Bukhara who was chief physician and minister to several princes in Iran. Besides his major medical and philosophical works in Arabic he also wrote a few in Persian, being the first to do so since the inception of Islam. His philosophy resembles that of al-Fārābī in being a synthesis of Aristotelian, later Greek, and original views. He accepted the emanation of the world, the Aristotelian psychology of active and passive intellects, and the ascent of the soul. But he was not strictly a Neoplatonist, in view of a number of differences. His cosmological argument for the existence of a first cause is widely known. Every ordinary essence is in itself contingent, so that its existence requires an external cause. But the chain of such causes cannot be infinite. Therefore there must be one noncontingent essence that exists without a prior cause and gives existence to everything else.

The world is everlasting; "creation" means continual emanation. The human mind is completely determined by causes, like the rest of the world. Ibn Sīnā describes a mystical path in an allegorical fable but was not himself known as a practicing Sufi. His philosophy is a wide-ranging and self-consistent synthesis which is central in Islamic philosophy, drawing upon his predecessors and providing the classical base for all his successors in the Eastern countries. He himself thought it harmonious with Islam, but it was soon to be criticized as contrary to Islam in certain respects.

THE INTERACTION OF THEOLOGY AND PHILOSOPHY

The Ismaili sect of Shiism had in the tenth century already incorporated into its esoteric theology a Neoplatonic cosmology of emanation. By contrast, Sunnite theologians generally ignored philosophy until well into the eleventh century. But now two brilliant theologians educated themselves in the philosophic tradition and reacted to it.

One was Ibn Ḥazm of Córdoba (994–1064), a literary author who joined the Zahirite school of law, which derived all Islamic law from a literal construction of the Koran and traditions. An imaginative writer and a learned critic of all religions other than Islam, Ibn Ḥazm applied literalism to theology in a logical and sweeping fashion that allowed no other source of religious truth than revelation. Greek logic and even metaphysical concepts could be used to explain and defend this truth but never as independent sources of religious knowledge.

The Persian al-Ghazālī (Latin: Algazel, 1058–1111) held a somewhat similar view of philosophy, although from a more traditionalist standpoint. After studying Shafiʿite law and Ashʿarite theology under the eminent al-Juwaynī (*d.* 1085) at the college of law (madrasa) at Nishapur, he became professor in an important madrasa at Baghdad. There he made a deep study of the philosophies of al-Fārābī and Ibn Sīnā, then wrote a devastating attack on them, showing many inconsistencies and unproved conclusions. He also condemned many of their views as contrary to Islam, especially their denial of three central doctrines: creation of the world in time, God's knowledge of particulars, and man's corporeal resurrection. But he appreciated Greek logic as a neutral instrument which could be used in support of Islam.

Resigning from his chair in 1095, he brought a new tone to these controversies by his personal conversion to Sufism. This Islamic mysticism had already been practiced by a long line of spiritual leaders, not adhering to any one school of theology or philosophy. Al-Ghazālī emphasized the inward and practical sides of Islam, while drawing cautiously upon Aristotelian ethics and Neoplatonic mysticism where they seemed in harmony with his religious purposes. The Koran as revelation always remained for him the ultimate source of truth in religion. All these directions of Islamic thought were fused together in his greatest work, *The Revival of the Religious Sciences.* Its impact has remained profound among Muslims owing to the sincerity of his thought and the force of his Arabic writing style.

ANDALUSIAN PHILOSOPHY

Philosophy was studied at Córdoba from the tenth century on. The most important work was done in the twelfth century. Ibn Bājja (Latin:

Avempace, *d.* 1139) of Saragossa wrote in the Neoplatonic tradition of intellectual mysticism, with some political interest as well. Ibn Ṭufayl (*d.* 1185) is chiefly known for his philosophical romance, *Ḥayy ibn Yaqẓān,* showing the possibility of attaining scientific, philosophical, and religious knowledge by untutored natural reason.

The foremost Andalusian philosopher was Ibn Rushd (Latin: Averroës, 1126–1198). Being broadly educated in Islamic law, the secular sciences, and philosophy, he was commissioned as a young man by the Almohad ruler of Morocco and al-Andalus to write Arabic commentaries on all the translated works of Aristotle. This huge task occupied him for the last thirty or—according to some scholars—forty years of his life. The commentaries are in three forms: summaries, middle commentaries, and long commentaries—the last two kinds annotating the texts sentence by sentence. Complete sets of three have mostly not survived in Arabic, but many of the missing ones are available in medieval Latin and Hebrew translations. There is also, in Hebrew translation only, a lengthy summary and commentary of Plato's *Republic,* meant to take the place of Aristotle's *Politics,* which had never been translated into Arabic.

While the Aristotelian commentaries are faithful to the thought of the master, they contain a great deal of Ibn Rushd's own philosophy. Moreover, he wrote several independent works, having as their main purpose the defense of philosophy, especially that of Aristotle, against the attacks of al-Ghazālī and others. He did this with a variety of arguments of general scope such as the following: that Islam allows latitude to qualified scholars to interpret the Koran, and that philosophers are the best qualified to do so by their understanding of the truths of science, including philosophy. Revelation and science must agree, for truth is single—contrary to the medieval Christian attribution to Averroës of a theory of "double truth." But science and philosophy may contradict theology (*al-kalām*), which did not have the same authority in Islam as Catholic doctrine in the Christian West.

Ibn Rushd's philosophy is a revived Aristotelianism, purified of most of the accretions of later Greek and earlier Islamic philosophy. In ethics he upheld the objectivity of value against the Greek sophists and the Ash'arite theologians. He had no sympathy for Sufism. His attacks on theologians brought on him a trial for heresy in Córdoba (1195) and resulting condemnation and exile.

This event was part of a growing disapproval of philosophy in the Arab countries. But it did not fade altogether. The Aristotelian-Rushdian tradition may still be seen in Ibn Khaldūn of Tunis (1332–1406). His study of historical method led him to create a new "science of culture" or social science, whose laws would guide the historian in judging the possibility or probability of recorded events. These ideas were set forth in his wide-ranging and penetrating *Introduction* (*al-Muqaddima*) to the study of history.

THE LATIN AND HEBREW TRANSLATIONS

When the Christian Spanish Reconquista took Toledo (1085) and Saragossa (1118) from the Muslims, Christian scholars gained easy access to books of Islamic science and philosophy, which they found more advanced than their own. From 1130 on, Latin translations of parts of Avicenna's *al-Shifā*ᵓ (Latin: *Sufficientia*) were being made. Toledo from 1160 to 1187 was a busy center of translation, led by Gerard of Cremona (1114–1187). The Aristotelian commentaries of Averroës became available in Latin in the early decades of the thirteenth century. Some texts of Aristotle were also translated from their Arabic versions. In the same period many philosophical works were also being translated directly from ancient Greek. Thus the Latin philosophers from Albertus Magnus (*ca.* 1200–1280) on had at their disposal a far richer philosophical library than their predecessors.

A parallel activity occurred as part of the Hebrew revival in Spain and southern France, including Hebrew translations of many of Averroës' commentaries. In addition, works of Jewish philosophers who had written in Arabic, such as the *Guide of the Perplexed* of Moses ben Maimon (Maimonides, 1135–1204), were now put into Hebrew.

LATER EASTERN PHILOSOPHY

Al-Ghazalı had started a trend toward the coalescence of theology, philosophy, and Sufism. The use of philosophical concepts and terms in elaborating an Islamic theology became bolder and more open in the works of Fakhr al-Dīn al-Rāzī (1149–1209), a learned and prolific commentator on both the Koran and Ibn Sīnā. Another commentator on Ibn Sına, Naṣīr al-Dīn al-Ṭūsī (1201–1274), is important as an encyclopedist, expounding Greek and Islamic philosophy and science, at times in Persian. His *Nasirean Ethics*, in the Aristotelian mode (happiness and the virtues), is wider in scope than the earlier Arabic *Ethics* of Miskawayh (*d.* 1030), since it continues with a treatment of domestic economy and politics.

Sufism pervaded the illuminationism of Suhrawardī al-Maqtūl (1155–1191), a philosophy, or rather Wisdom, which has Zoroastrian, Hermetic, and Platonic roots. Reality consists of degrees of light, from the pure light of God to the most negative darkness. Unfortunately he also stated that existence was only a logical notion, prolonging a widespread misunderstanding of Ibn Sīnā, who had sometimes referred to existence as an "accident." (Ibn Sīnā had only meant by this that the existence of any essence is contingent, not necessary.)

Ibn al-ᶜArabī of Murcia (1165–1240) lived in many cities of western and eastern Islam, latterly in Malatya (east-central Turkey) and Damascus. His comprehensive but unsystematic mystical philosophy attempted to unify all aspects of the world by relating it closely to God. The world is the manifestation of God, who perceives himself reflected in it. Man is an image of the divine and in turn perceives God in the beauty of the world around him. In line with a common Sufi outlook, Ibn al-ᶜArabī finds the same truths expressed in all religions in their different ways. His vast writings in prose and verse are full of symbolism, making his philosophy difficult to describe but rich in poetic and religious imagination. As a Sufi with personal mystical experience as well as intellectual power, he became a major influence on all later Sufi philosophy.

The line of mystical poets was continued in Islam most strongly in Iran. The greatest of this genre was Jalāl al-Dīn Rūmī (1207–1273), who wove theological and philosophical ideas in endless profusion into his long Persian poem *Couplets (Masnavī)*.

The later Persian philosophers, still writing mostly in Arabic, developed the concept of philosophy as Wisdom (*al-ḥikma*) or theosophy, in an unbroken chain of thought from Ibn Sīnā through Suhrawardī to the present time.

BIBLIOGRAPHY

General Works. See the second edition of the *Encyclopedia of Islam* for articles on "Falsafa," "ᶜIlm al-kalām," and individual philosophers and schools. See also Majid Fakhry, *A History of Islamic Philosophy* (1970); Louis Gardet and M.-M. Anawati, *Introduction à la théologie musulmane: Essai de théologie comparée* (1948); Mian Mohammad Sharif, ed., *A History of Muslim Philosophy,* 2 vols. (1963–1966); Harry A. Wolfson, *The Philosophy of the Kalam* (1976).

Monographs. Miguel Cruz Hernández, *Filosofía hispano-musulmana,* 2 vols. (1957); Richard Frank, *Beings and Their Attributes: The Teaching of the Basrian School of the Muᶜtazila in the Classical Period* (1978); Louis Gardet, *La pensée religieuse d'Avicenne (Ibn Sīnā)* (1951); George F. Hourani, *Islamic Rationalism: The Ethics of ᶜAbd al-Jabbār* (1971); Muhsin Mahdi, *Ibn Khaldūn's Philosophy of History* (1957); Nicholas Rescher, *The Development of Arabic Logic* (1964).

Translations. Ibn al-ᶜArabī, *The Wisdom of the Prophets (Fuṣūṣ al-ḥikam),* Titus Burckhardt and Angela Culme-Seymour, trans. (1975); al-Ashᶜarī, *The Theology of al-Ashᶜarī,* Richard J. McCarthy, ed. and trans. (1953); al-Fārābī, *Philosophy of Plato and Aristotle,* Muhsin Mahdi, trans. (1962); al-Ghazālī, *al-Munqidh min al ḍalāl and Other Relevant Works,* Richard J. McCarthy, trans. (1980); Ibn Khaldūn, *The Muqaddima,* Franz Rosenthal, trans., 3 vols. (1958); Ibn Rushd, *Averroës on the Harmony of Religion and Philosophy,* George F. Hourani, trans. (1961), and *Averroës' Tahāfut al-tahāfut (The Incoherence of the Incoherence),* Simon Van den Bergh, trans., 2 vols. (1954); Ibn Sīnā, *The Metaphysics of Avicenna (Ibn Sīnā),* Parviz Morewedge, trans. (1973); Ṭūsī, *The Nasirean Ethics, by Naṣīr ad-Dīn Ṭūsī,* G. M. Wickens, trans. (1964).

GEORGE F. HOURANI

[See also **Allah; Aristotle, in the Middle Ages; Islam, Religion; Law, Islamic; Mysticism, Islamic; Muᶜtazila; Neoplatonism; Plato in the Middle Ages; Shīᶜa; Sunna; Translation and Translators, Islamic;** and individual personalities.]

PHILOSOPHY AND THEOLOGY, JEWISH: ISLAMIC WORLD

PHILOSOPHY VERSUS THEOLOGY

Jewish philosophy came of age in the Islamic world during the late ninth and tenth centuries. By then the works of classical and Hellenistic philosophy read in late antiquity had been translated into Arabic; and Jews, together with other Arabic-speaking peoples living in the orbit of Islam, were able to satisfy their curiosity concerning this "foreign" and "secular" science. To some Jews it became apparent, as it had to some Muslims, that philosophy per se is not necessarily foreign or inimical to traditional faith and that it should be regarded, rather, as a necessary component of faith, particularly for the intelligent and educated person.

The relationship of faith and reason—of traditional beliefs rooted in the Bible and rabbinic commandment-oriented literature, on the one hand, and of logically constructed theories and arguments deriving from Greek and Muslim authors, on the other—became a frequently discussed issue in the philosophical literature. The type of faith that emerged from this discussion was conceived along mostly theoretical and rational lines, though a significant part of Jewish philosophy (as of medieval philosophy in general) remained intuitive in its assumptions, "practical" in its applications, and mystical in its conclusions.

Asserting and defending the apposite religiosity of philosophical texts, or the philosophical interpretation of religious texts—commonly using allegory for the latter—was not the sole concern of those Jews who became philosophers, though it did leave many stylistic marks upon their work, and often gave it an apologetic and political appearance. Of at least equal concern to the philosophers was the particular doctrine they espoused, which was located in Scripture but was not dependent upon Scripture for its truth value. Jewish philosophy thus took its place alongside Islamic philosophy in being intrinsically concerned with the entire range of philosophical investigation, as maintained and transmitted through late antiquity: the logic of the *Organon;* the "practical" sciences of politics, economics, and ethics; and the "theoretical" ones of mathematics, physics, and metaphysics.

Like their Muslim counterparts, Jewish philosophers eventually came to know more Aristotle than Plato, though Neoplatonic views infiltrated through such pseudo-Aristotelian works as the *Theology of Aristotle* (an abridgment of Plotinus' *Enneads*) and the *Book of the Pure Good* (the Arabic version of the *Liber de causis,* an abridgment of Proclus' *Elements of Theology*).

The two main schools of medieval philosophical investigation are usually characterized as Neoplatonic and Aristotelian, though for the Jews even more, perhaps, than for others this is a rough and inadequate distinction. For instance, Saadiah Gaon in the tenth century is closer to the Muʿtazilite theologians (the *mutakallimun*) of Islam than to any of the *falāsifa;* and Baḥya ben Joseph ibn Paquda (eleventh century) is more inspired by the Sufi mystics of Islam than by its rationalists. These men and others developed views of Judaism closer, respectively, to theology and pietism than to what is considered technically as philosophy, though they were familiar with and partially incorporated into their work the philosophical tradition that began in Athens and was transmitted through Baghdad.

Jewish philosophy in the Islamic world is thus a multifaceted creation encompassing theology, mysticism, apologetics, and polemics as well as "straight" philosophy. Its practitioners were men of diverse sorts and many parts: rabbis, statesmen, doctors, poets, and mystics as well as logicians and rationalists. They reflected a high degree of acculturation and achievement in the Islamic world and at the same time introduced a new cultural dimension into Judaism.

Part of this achievement, it should be recognized, was the first systematic articulation of a Jewish theology, a feat that biblical literature had not imagined and that the sages of the Talmud had not attempted. The beliefs and values of these earlier periods were assembled and rationalized by medieval philosophers, often with the aid of metaphysical concepts hitherto absent, and now "discovered" in the Bible. The Jews of the Middle Ages, however—as well as of later periods—never adopted one particular theology, and no separate class of theologians comparable with the *mutakallimun* (known in the medieval West as *loquentes*) emerged in Judaism. Similarly, few Jewish thinkers outside Karaite circles adopted a kalam-style separate theology. Within Judaism, therefore—in contrast with Islam and Christianity—the line between theologian and philosopher was blurred, and the representative of each was distinct from the classical and continuing role of rabbi.

It must be noted that many, if not most, rabbis and Jews, even in the "golden age" of Islam, viewed the new philosophical/theological literature suspiciously, as an essentially alien enterprise. Rabbinic literature continued through the Middle Ages to maintain its distinctive identity, concerned primarily with biblical exegesis and Talmudic hermeneutics, defying facile categorization and philosophical investigation. Even Maimonides' attempt in the *Mishneh Torah* to systematize and explain Jewish law (the halakhah), however rational in approach, was consciously divorced from explicit philosophical analysis. The process of halakhic codification and organization inaugurated by Sephardic Jews thus developed along lines separate from those of Jewish philosophy and theology.

Organized political opposition to philosophy was, however, never attempted within the world of Islam; indeed, the most vocal opponent of philosophy in that world, Judah Halevi (*ca.* 1075–1141), may be described in part as a practitioner of the art. The opponents of philosophy could not accept the apparent primacy of reason and autonomy of nature that philosophy allegedly affirmed, despite the attempts of the philosophers to accommodate such concepts to beliefs in the supremacy of God's will and the ultimate dependence of nature upon that will. Philosophy was widely regarded as deficient also in its ability to address the specific laws, needs, and nature of the Jewish people and of the individual Jew; the universal and ostensibly impersonal theories of which philosophy speaks were seen as insufficient assistance in the struggle for national survival and individual immortality.

The suspicion of philosophy as a tool of assimilation for the educated was already present in the Islamic world, though it was not to be targeted as such publicly. Official rabbinic opposition to philosophy in general, and to Maimonides' philosophical writing in particular, first surfaced in Christian France in the thirteenth century, and from there influenced Jews living in the Muslim world. The concurrent demise of Jewish philosophy in the orbit of Islam was, however, due to the general decline and disappearance of the secular sciences there, part of the particular orthodox and mystical direction that Islam took from the twelfth century on.

MAJOR PHILOSOPHERS AND THEIR IDEAS

For some three centuries, however, from about 900 to 1200, Jewish philosophy flourished in the Muslim world; its literature was transmitted via Hebrew translations to Jews living in Christian Europe, who maintained the tradition through the Middle Ages and into the Renaissance. European Jews (of Sephardic extraction) were also responsible for much of the translation of philosophical works from Arabic and Hebrew into Latin, and thus for bringing the fruits of Muslim and Greek, as well as Jewish, philosophy to Western Europe. Of course, the study of Jewish philosophy did not cease among Jews in the Islamic world in the thirteenth century; Judah ben Nissim ibn Malkah was responsible for its continuation (mingled with concepts taken from Jewish mysticism) in the Maghrib during the fourteenth century. The major figures of Jewish philosophy in the Islamic world, however, were Isaac Israeli (*ca.* 855–*ca.* 955), Saadiah Gaon (882–942), Solomon ibn Gabirol (1020–*ca.* 1058/1070), Baḥya ben Joseph ibn Paquda (late eleventh century), Judah Halevi (*ca.* 1075–1141), Abraham ibn Daud (*ca.* 1110–1180), and Moses Maimonides (*ca.* 1135–1204).

The provenance of these figures ranges from Baghdad in the East, through the Maghrib states of North Africa to Moorish Spain in the West. The first philosopher of record in this group, Isaac Israeli, is only incidentally a resident of the Maghrib, for his philosophy is heavily influenced by writings that originated in the East, both late Neoplatonic works transmitted from the Greek and those written by the first Muslim philosopher, the Baghdad-based Abū Yūsuf Yaᶜqūb ibn Isḥāq al-Kindī (*ca.* 800–*ca.* 870). Similarly, the Toledan Judah Halevi responded to the philosophy and theology of the Persians Ibn Sīnā and al-Ghazālī; and the Egypt-based Maimonides reacted to the Turkish al-Fārābī.

Jewish philosophy in this period was thus broad in scope and origins, limited solely by the boundaries of the Islamic world (*Dār al-Islām*). Jews living outside this world, in Provence, in southern Italy, or in the areas claimed by the Christian reconquest of Spain, were nevertheless part of it intellectually, though politically, geographically, and linguistically separate. Jewish philosophy in the Christian world was essentially a continuation of that of Jews under Islamic rule, and the influence of Scholastic thought was far less than that of the *falāsifa* of Islam, particularly Ibn Rushd and Ibn Sīnā and their Jewish disciples. Jewish philosophers of the fourteenth and fifteenth centuries, such as Levi ben Gershom (Gersonides) and Ḥasdai Crescas, in many ways represent a culmination of the philosophy studied and taught in the Islamic world. Yet, as this culmination was also a response to that philosophy, a response molded to some degree by the new circumstances and intellectual currents of Christian Europe, this later period in medieval Jewish philosophy may be treated separately.

The first two representatives of Jewish philosophy in the Islamic world are Isaac Israeli and Saadiah Gaon, and in their work most, if not all, the main concerns and tensions of the new discipline are outlined. Both men considered the world spread before their eyes to be the basic datum that must be accounted for; the explanation must conform to the reality commonly experienced. Explanations that invoked spiritual entities such as pure forms, separate intelligences, and God were ultimately to be controlled by what is discernible to the senses and basic intelligence. This did not, to be sure, lead these men and those who followed into actual experimentation with the real world, into science as we know it, for the *scientia* of the Middle Ages was a theoretical activity that followed prescribed lines of inquiry and recognized authorities. That a textbook by Aristotle or Ptolemy served as the world for medieval scholars and would-be scientists does not alter the fact that the text for this book was the world itself, and that the philosophers were interested primarily in understanding the reality behind the text. Medieval Jewish philosophy is thus both typically Jewish and typically medieval in approaching reality through authoritative texts, while being typically philosophical in striving for explanations of this reality that do justice to normative (as well as extraordinary) experience.

It was primarily for this reason that Saadiah rejected the extreme approach of the kalam theologians of Islam, who essentially repudiated the testimony of their senses and insisted that nothing has a nature of its own, that everything is created anew each moment by God. This type of occasionalism did not appeal to Jewish philosophers even though it places as strong an emphasis upon God's power and uniqueness as could be desired. Though Saadiah was obviously attracted to various other kalam themes and arguments, he was not at all tempted by the anticausal position of occasionalism and the atomistic physics that underlies it. For this Islamic variety of atomism posits a world of objects that have no essential identity or duration, a world radically contingent upon the ever-present will of God, a will that can endow an atom with any "accident" it wishes. The deity in this scheme overwhelms and undermines the world, the philosophers felt, for he creates a situation in which practically anything is possible, and therefore nothing is true in general and nothing universal can be known with certainty.

It was against such a world view, common in the Islamic world, that Jewish (and Muslim) philosophers did battle, asserting the innate reality of the sensible world and seeking explanations of it. This was not a mere bias of the philosophers, but a conviction that such a view is a necessary condition of all discourse. Such a world does not exclude such nonsensible objects as souls and intelligences (traditionally called angels)—indeed, they were a main attraction for most medieval philosophers; but such immaterial entities, and even God, are comprehensible philosophically only to the degree they relate to and help to explicate corporeal reality.

Isaac Israeli conformed to this standard, though as a "Neoplatonist" he could well be misunderstood in this respect. He posited an entire incorporeal structure of universal substances that is prior to the physical world and separate from it. This structure, however, like the emanative process that explains its dynamics, is best conceivable as an attempt to make sense of the reality in which man finds himself, a reality of formal as well as material dimensions. If he appears overwhelmed by the cosmic substances that precede and loom above him, man may yet be reassured that they exist—if not for him, then with him, complementing on a global scale and in a paradigmatic manner the diverse aspects of existence we all experience. The world of the philosophers is thus one, finite world, with all being, excluding only God—and that exclusion being only a partial one—contained within it.

For this reason popular distinctions between "the world above the moon" and that "below" it, between "metaphysics" and "physics," are generally misleading in their emphasis upon the two different realities of each sphere. It is true that the translunar world is conceived of as essentially unchanging and permanent in its existence, and the sublunar world as characterized by generation and corruption; the matter of the upper sphere, as a fifth element different from the four believed to be found in all sublunar bodies. Yet it is also true that both spheres are conceived of as having a material base, and that the matter in each has the same function: to provide a physical anchor for form. This is true, paradoxically, even for those forms regarded as pure or "separate." For these substances, be they the intelligences of the spheres of Abraham ibn Daud or Maimonides, the Universal Intellect and World Soul of Isaac Israeli or the Universal Form and Matter of Ibn Gabirol, are "separate" vis-à-vis the matter or body to which they are inevitably related, as its noncorporeal, formal principle. Form and matter, whether singly or in combination, are thus conceived of as universal and ubiquitous entities, principles as well as explanations of being.

The concepts of form and matter alone are not, however, sufficient to explain the actual nature of all substances; and most Jewish philosophers, like the majority of other medieval philosophers, accepted the Aristotelian categories as ontologically valid qualifications of substance found in states of being formed by a concatenation of factors known as the four causes. While "cause" is commonly thought to be a force external to the object,

Aristotle's "material" cause in particular, and the formal and often the efficient cause as well, are to be located within the object in question, providing its definition and identity. The nature of something is therefore best explained by a description of the causes consiting that nature; and these causes, as causes, are also universal. In the widely accepted notion of a final cause, moreover, the inner-directed explanation of substance is turned outward, and the parameters of an object are expanded toward goals beyond its immediately present reality. The principle of causation thus serves, with the categories and the notion of four elementary substances, to explain the substances that comprise the world both in their dynamic interaction and change, and in their discrete identifications and states of being.

The notion of potential being is subsumed within the concept of final cause, and the concept of potentiality was a mainstay of medieval philosophy, particularly of those who shared an Aristotelian world view. For it is in accepting this concept that Aristotle's arguments for an eternal universe were judged credible, if not compelling. These arguments were nourished by the conviction that the concept of creation from nothing taken literally was indefensible, it being impossible for that which is absolutely nothing to be a source for being. For those who accepted the Aristotelian alternative of an eternal universe, the infinite extension of time and the eternity of the world's motion, which time measured, entailed belief in the reality of potential being. This, because the causal series and time spans that in the aggregate constitute an infinite number are each also discrete and capable of being measured, and as such are finite. An actual infinity is for this reason infinite theoretically, something that has the (real) potentiality to be infinite, though in actual experience it is finite.

In this view, potential being conforms to what is actual, and future possibilities are delimited by actual experience—another example of the predictable and knowable world of medieval philosophy. Yet this closed and self-contained feature of an eternal universe, for all its open-ended horizons, struck many medieval Jewish philosophers as unacceptably restrictive upon the freedom and nature of God, and consequently upon the freedom and nature of man and the world. The philosophical mechanisms for explaining the world clashed here with prior and passionately held theological convictions. At stake were traditional beliefs in the createdness of the world, and in God as creator. It was generally felt, moreover, that only belief in a voluntaristic *creatio ex nihilo* could justify the notion of subsequent divine intervention in the world. Belief in revelation and miracles, and the image of a concerned and loving deity, were thus tied to acceptance of the concept of creation. While few were prepared, like Isaac Israeli, to argue unequivocally as philosophers for the notion of *creatio ex nihilo,* most Jewish philosophers in the Islamic world felt the alternative concept of an eternal universe was at least as vulnerable to philosophical analysis, regarding its premise of potential infinity as mere speculative theory.

We find, then, that much of the medieval philosophical literature of the Islamic world (and later in Europe as well) is concerned with concepts of physics, and that the theology that emerges is one rooted in the science of the day. Yet, creation aside, most Jewish philosophers accepted the Aristotelian physics outlined above, once it became well known, even though in the celestial realm various Neoplatonic variations were adopted, particularly as regards the separate existence of pure universal formal substances. Most of the physical arguments were considered logically demonstrable, nature seen as perfectly definable and thus predictable. This view was reconciled with the belief in God's presence in history and his ability to effect miracles through the rationalization, in various ways, of that presence, incorporating it, in effect, within a "natural" world view.

Thus the will of God and his wisdom were seen by Ibn Gabirol as responsible for universal form and matter, infusing the universe at all levels with God's presence, while for Saadiah and Halevi a permanent though unique "created glory" and "divine presence," respectively, were instruments of the divine will. That this will affected the Children of Israel particularly was seen as a natural fact by most Jewish philosophers, though hardly anyone emulated Halevi in fashioning a physics centered upon the people and land of Israel. Most, rather, presented the Jewish experience as an example (albeit the prime one) of universal truth, and not its arbiter; the Torah taken as the repository of wisdom rather than as its author (though these two aspects were seen as ultimately united in God).

The commandments of the Bible were, accordingly, explained in conformity with universal standards of ethics that Maimonides, for example, was not distressed to find illustrated in prior Greek and Islamic philosophical texts. Even the most arcane ritual laws were assumed to have a place within a divine plan that was believed to be rational to the core. The Torah was seen as a blueprint for individual salvation and for a perfect society, an ideal state; the influence of Plato's *Republic,* as filtered through al-Fārābī's political writings, was evident in Maimonides' *Guide of the Perplexed.*

MAIMONIDES' *GUIDE*

The *Guide* is clearly the masterpiece of medieval Jewish philosophy, as celebrated for its ambiguities as for the attempt to resolve them. It is concerned with all the philosophical themes adumbrated above, and others as well. The book is at once a work of biblical exegesis and philosophical polemic, of political and ethical philosophy, of physics and metaphysics. It seeks an exact identification of God's being and, like its predecessors, settles for indirect information (deduced from phenomena inferred to be the effects of divine actions) and negative predication, knowledge of what God is not. Convinced that man's nature and salvation lay in knowing the truth, Maimonides was nevertheless practically silent here as to the consequences of that salvation. The immortality of man's soul, and the personal or impersonal nature of such immortality, are subjects conspicuously absent from this work, though they are major subjects of concern in the philosophical literature of the period. Presumably Maimonides agreed with his predecessors that through his intellectual attainments man achieves some sort of immortality, though it is unlikely that Maimonides literally accepted the popular notions of an enduring individual soul and a resurrected body that he affirms elsewhere.

Following his Islamic mentors and Jewish predecessors, Maimonides superimposed the figure of the prophet upon Plato's philosopher-king, finding the prophets in general and Moses in particular to have a cognitive faculty for transmitting intellectual propositions in imaginative form. The Bible is thus revealed as a philosophical document when properly decoded. The philosopher is then the equal of the prophet in comprehending universal truth, though the prophet is uniquely gifted to communicate it in popular form. This makes it possible for any moral and properly educated man to reach the same cognitive level as the prophet and to know what the prophet knew, which is to approach God through conjunction with the world of eternal truth and being. This is the ultimate goal of medieval Jewish philosophy, though its adherents took exception to the belief that anyone could attain the knowledge of Moses and know God as intimately as he did, however qualified that knowledge was. The Torah thus remained knowable and unknowable even for philosophers as they strove to attain the perfection of Moses.

Though identified with pure intelligent being, Maimonides' God is more than Aristotle's thought thinking itself, for he is the creator, sustainer, and redeemer of the world, a redeemer whose will is an expression of his wisdom and is equal to it. This divine will knows all of being, though Maimonides is equivocal as to the manner in which particular knowledge is known by God. Also ambiguous are his expressions of God's love and personal concern, which run the risk for Maimonides—as for his predecessors—of introducing notions of corporeality and multiplicity into the concept of the one God. Maimonides thus brought to a classic formulation the medieval doctrine of negative attributes, in which ostensibly nothing is known about God's essence other than that he is purely one, a source of being and truth whose existence is necessary and "part of" (equal to) its essence. That the world needs such a being—and only one such—was demonstrable to Maimonides by physical and logical arguments, though they did not adequately support the image of a personal God, much less a historical one, which Maimonides also wished to proclaim.

It is this personal God of Israel's history whom Halevi celebrated, even as it is the personal God sensed in one's heart to whom Baḥya ibn Paquda and Maimonides' son Abraham bore witness. Responding to the inner-directed focus of Sufi thought, Baḥya nevertheless showed familiarity with philosophical concepts and modes of thought. Jewish mysticism of this period and later was thus intellectually oriented, although scientific technique was dissociated from its original subject matter to follow a spiritual geography of its own. However, medieval Jewish mystics shared with the philosophers a theology that generally emphasized the unique and strictly unitary nature of the divine being, a transcendent nature that yet somehow related to the world as its creator and lawgiver. Also similar was the view of man as a free agent capable to some degree of participating in the divine world of eternal being. Observance of the law was a minimal requirement for both groups, a necessary ethical as well as political condition for the solitary ascent of the soul into the divine presence.

BIBLIOGRAPHY

Sources. English translations of the main works discussed in the article are Abraham Ibn Daud, *Sefer Ha-Qabbalah: The Book of Tradition,* Gerson G. Cohen, trans. (1967); Baḥya ben Joseph, *The Book of Directions to the Duties of the Heart,* Menahem Mansoor, trans. (1973); Isaac Israeli, *Isaac Israeli: A Neoplatonic Philosopher of the Early Tenth Century,* Alexander Altmann and Samuel M. Stern, trans. (1958, repr. 1979); Judah Halevi, *Kitab al Khazari,* Hartwig Hirschfield, trans. (1905 and later eds.); Moses Maimonides, *Guide of the Perplexed,* Shlomo Pines, trans. (1963); Saadiah Gaon, *The Book of Doctrines and Opinions,* Samuel Rosenblatt, trans. (1948); Solomon ben Judah Ibn Gabirol, *The Fountain of Life, Fons Vitae,* Harry E. Wedeck, trans. (1962).

Studies and bibliographies. A lengthy discussion of medieval Jewish philosophy in the Islamic world is in Julius Guttmann, *Philosophies of Judaism,* David Silverman, trans. (1964), 47–182. See also Georges Vajda, *Introduction à la pensée juive du moyen âge* (1947), 19–146, and "Les études de philosophie juive du moyen âge depuis la synthèse du Julius Guttmann," in *Hebrew Union College Annual,* **43** (1972) and **45** (1974). A less detailed bibliographical study is Lawrence Berman, "Medieval Jewish Religious Philosophy," in *Bibliographical Essays in Medieval Jewish Studies,* II (1976). See also Colette Sirat, *A History of Jewish Philosophy in the Middle Ages* (1985), 15–211. Secondary literature is listed in the "History of Jewish Philosophy," in the annual *Index of Articles on Jewish Studies* (1966–).

ALFRED L. IVRY

[See also **Abraham ibn Daud; Aristotle in the Middle Ages; Baḥya ben Joseph ibn Paquda; Exegesis, Jewish; Israeli, Isaac; Judah Halevi; Judaism; Maimonides, Moses; Neoplatonism; Plato in the Middle Ages; Saadiah Gaon; Solomon ben Judah ibn Gabirol.**]

PHILOSOPHY AND THEOLOGY, JEWISH: IN NORTHERN EUROPE. Of the three major Jewish theological movements of the Middle Ages—Jewish rationalistic philosophy, cabalistic mysticism, and Ashkenazi Hasidism (*Ḥasidei Ashkenaz*)—only the third originated in central or northern Europe. It was dominant for several generations, and the other two were incorporated within it at least until the end of the thirteenth century. It is necessary, therefore, to describe Ashkenazi Hasidism first, and then to analyze briefly the impact of the other systems on later Jewish generations.

ASHKENAZI HASIDISM

Ashkenazi Hasidism (Jewish-German pietism) flourished in the twelfth and thirteenth centuries, and produced both a school of ethical thought and an esoteric theology that is sometimes described as mystical. The earliest writer of this school known to us by name is Rabbi Samuel ben Kalonymus, who lived in the mid twelfth century. Ashkenazi Hasidic traditions insist, however, that Rabbi Samuel was the recipient of old material, transmitted orally from father to son and rabbi to disciple for many generations. Some of these traditions connect the beginnings of Ashkenazi Hasidic esoteric doctrines with the appearance in the mid ninth century of a sage from Babylonia, Aaron Ben Samuel of Baghdad, in the Jewish communities of southern Italy, where he taught his secrets to the sages of the Kalonymus family. When members of this family settled later in the Rhine cities, especially Mainz, they brought with them these traditions and laid the foundations for the esoteric school of Ashkenazi Hasidic mystics. It is doubtful that these legends can be regarded as historical, though it is quite possible that some elements of Ashkenazi Hasidic doctrines were transmitted by a migrant sage, especially their unusual system of prayer exegesis.

The central figure in the history of Ashkenazi Hasidism was Rabbi Judah ben Samuel he-Hasid (the Pietist, *ca.* 1149–1217), the son of Rabbi Samuel. Rabbi Judah lived in Speyer and in Regensburg. He was the central author of the magnum opus of the Ashkenazi Hasidic ethical lore, *Sefer Ḥasidim* (The book of the pietist), as well as of many works in esoteric theology. It is very difficult to identify Rabbi Judah's works because he insisted on anonymity, explaining that when an author mentions his name within his work, he causes his descendants to commit the worst sin in Ashkenazi Hasidic ethics: the sin of pride. It seems that he was alone in this demand, for other Ashkenazi Hasidic authors included their names in full in the titles of their works. Rabbi Judah wrote a theological work that is now lost, *Sefer ha-Kavod* (The book of divine glory), and it is quite possible that he produced a series of theological works now at Oxford (Bodleian Library, MSS 1566–1567 [MS Oppenheim 540]). Tradition attributes to him the most famous Jewish-German theological poem, *Shir ha-Yiḥud* (Hymn of divine unity), which became a part of the Jewish prayer book.

The most prolific writer of this movement was Rabbi Judah's relative and disciple, Rabbi Eleazar ben Judah of Worms (*ca.* 1165–*ca.* 1230). Rabbi

Eleazar wrote an extensive commentary on the prayers (probably in two or three different versions), a major book of Jewish customary law (*Sefer ha-Roqeaḥ* [Book of the perfumer]), and several treatises in esoteric doctrines, the most important of which is *Sode Razayya* (The most secret secrets), which included five separate books: (1) an interpretation of the alphabet and the secrets of creation; (2) the secret of the Holy Chariot; (3) the secret of the Holy Name; (4) the secret of the soul; (5) a commentary on the *Sefer Yeẓirah* (The book of creation, an ancient text probably from the late Talmudic period) [fourth to sixth centuries]). Beside these there are many shorter works and commentaries by him.

OTHER ESOTERIC WRITERS AND WORKS

Rabbi Samuel, Rabbi Judah, and Rabbi Eleazar were regarded by later generations as the representatives of Ashkenazi Hasidism. But in the second half of the twelfth century and the beginning of the thirteenth, there were several other groups of mystics and esoteric writers who helped to create the cultural and theological environment of the Jewish communities, and whose ideas became incorporated into the larger body referred to as "Ashkenazi Hasidic." Among them is the anonymous author of the *Sefer ha-Ḥayyim* (Book of life), a relatively systematic theological work dealing with the nature of the divine worlds, the cosmos, and especially man and his soul. Another is the anonymous author of the *Sefer ha-Navon* (The book of the wise), a theological commentary on the verse "Shema Ysrael" (Deut. 6:4). Ashkenazi Hasidism had a fierce opponent in Rabbi Moses Taku, who wrote a bitter treatise against Ashkenazi Hasidic theology (probably *ca.* 1220) entitled *Ketav Tammim* (The book of perfection), in which he attacked the Hasidim and their various sources.

The most important group of creative theological writers outside the school of Rabbi Judah the Pious was a circle of mystically inclined writers who attributed their works to traditions initiated by the prophet Jeremiah, his son Ben Sira (pseudo-Ecclesiasticus), and his great-grandson Joseph ben Uzziel. This line of tradition is found in a ninth-century collection of stories attributed to Ben Sira (*Alphabet of Ben Sira*), and the writers in medieval Germany adopted it for their own uses. The main figure in this circle was Rabbi Avigdor ha-Zarefati (the Frenchman), who lived probably in the second half of the twelfth century. Their works deal mainly with the secret of creation, commentaries on the *Sefer Yeẓirah*, and theological poetry incorporating their ideas.

SOURCES OF ASHKENAZI HASIDISM

The main sources used by all Ashkenazi Hasidic writers belong to two distinct groups. The first is the ancient Jewish mystical traditions, usually called the *Heikhalot* and *Merkabah* literature (*Heikhalot:* Holy Palaces, the various parts of the divine realm; *Merkabah:* the Divine Chariot seen by Ezekiel). This vast literature, which flourished between the third and the ninth centuries, has been preserved by the Ashkenazi Hasidim, who even today are our main source of knowledge of this literary corpus. Some works have been lost; others survived only because of their editions and commentaries. It seems that this literature was very much alive among the Ashkenazi Hasidim, and it is even possible that some mystics in medieval Germany followed the ancient traditions and tried to gain visionary and mystical entrance into the realm of the Palaces and the Chariot.

The second main source was the works of Jewish philosophers from the tenth to the twelfth centuries, the most important among them being Rabbi Saadiah Gaon (Babylonia, tenth century) and Rabbis Abraham bar Hiyya and Abraham ben Meïr ibn Ezra (Spain, twelfth century). The latter two wrote their works in Hebrew; Saadiah's Arabic works were translated into Hebrew probably in the eleventh century in a poetic, nonphilosophical paraphrase. The Ashkenazi Hasidim derived from these writers many Neoplatonic ideas, but they did not become acquainted with philosophical methods, for the Hebrew works were written as biblical commentaries or homiletical works that did not convey philosophical systematic reasoning. The Ashkenazi Hasidim remained opposed to medieval philosophy and dialectic. They regarded Saadiah and Ibn Ezra as mystics and guardians of esoteric secrets, not as creative philosophical thinkers.

The third major source was the impact of the surrounding culture in medieval Germany. The Hasidim did not take part in the literary culture of their period, and as far as we can tell today, most of them did not know Latin. They regarded Latin as the language of the church, and their insistence upon creating as many barriers as possible between the Jewish community and Christian influences made them withdraw from any facet of the official culture. This, however, did not apply to the popular culture of the people among whom they lived. Thus we find an enormous impact of popular beliefs, stories, and demonology derived from vernacular-speaking neighbors, while Latin theology had hardly any influence upon their works.

THEOLOGY AND ETHICS OF ASHKENAZI HASIDISM

The basic theological problem that the Ashkenazi Hasidim tried to solve—and the solution accepted by them influenced all other parts of their thought—was that of divine transcendence and divine immanence. The Hasidim inherited from ancient times the biblical and talmudic picture of a personal God, described in detailed anthropomorphic terms, who is revealed in the process of creation and guides history and human affairs. This concept was in sharp conflict with the medieval tendency—universal to all schools of Jewish thought and reflecting the impact of Greek philosophy transmitted by the Arabs—to describe God as completely transcendent, unchangeable, and therefore removed from any possibility of revelation.

The Ashkenazi Hasidim approached this problem with the help of Saadiah's explanation that revelation to the prophets and the subject of biblical anthropomorphic descriptions is not God himself but a created angel, the *kavod* (or *Shekinah,* divine glory). Saadiah made a clear distinction between the Creator, God himself, and the revealed power, which is a creature like all other creatures, though more magnificent than—and supreme over—all other beings. The Ashkenazi Hasidim accepted Saadiah's solution in principle, but could not follow his attitude toward the *kavod.* If this divine glory was seen by Moses, and if one has to turn to the same being when one prays to God, and if the biblical names for God, including YHWH, refer to the *kavod,* then it cannot be just one more created angel. They therefore adopted an approach found in Abraham ibn Ezra's commentary to the book of Exodus (chap. 33), according to which the *kavod* is an emanated being; its upper realms are purely divine, and therefore no revelation of this "supreme face" of the divine glory is possible. Its "lower face," however, is turned toward the created world, and this face has been revealed to the prophets and serves as an object of human prayers. The Ashkenazi Hasidim perceived the divine world as a complex series of emanations, but they did not create a detailed system of such powers. Divine transcendence was preserved, and secondary divine powers were regarded as revealed in the created world.

The immanence of God was regarded as twofold: a selective immanence of the divine glory, which is revealed when, where, and to whom divine providence decides; and the immanence of the supreme Godhead, which is present everywhere and at all times, but is not perceived by human beings and does not take part in guidance of history. To the problem of the divine presence in dirty, ugly, and sinful places the Hasidim answered that the *kavod* really cannot be present in such places, but the Godhead can be. It is not affected by the character of the place in the same manner that the sun is not affected by dirt when it shines on it. Their paradoxical formulation holds, therefore, that revelation in sinful places is of a higher divine order than revelation in holy places, where the *kavod* chooses to shine.

This view can be understood if the Ashkenazi Hasidim's attitude toward miracles is taken into account. This chapter in their theology sets them apart from all other Jewish schools of thought, and it may reflect the specific historical experience of German Jewry during the Middle Ages. According to the Hasidim, God's attributes cannot be learned from a study of natural, social, and historical laws. When God created the world and laid the foundations for human history, he did not reveal his divine characteristics. These are manifest only in the miracles shown in the world; not in the natural way of things, but in the exceptional and the unique. The sole purpose of this world is to bring forth the *zaddikim,* the Righteous Ones, who are very few. The *zaddikim* are characterized by their ability to overcome enormous difficulties, even impossible ones, and by their success they enable the world to exist. In order that such *zaddikim* will be able to reveal their abilities, the world should be as wicked as possible; the more evil the circumstances, the greater the spiritual powers revealed when one of the Righteous overcomes them. In the beginning, according to Rabbi Eleazar of Worms, God wanted to create a world ruled by evil powers alone. After a succession of such creations, which failed to produce *zaddikim* and therefore were destroyed, God created this world as a compromise, adding some good element to it so that righteousness will be possible.

When one observes the created world, therefore, one does not meet God's goodness, but the obstacles he created in order that the *zaddikim* will overcome them. Only when observing miracles one can comprehend divine providence. History as a whole is just one of the trials that God put forth in order to try the *zaddikim*. It is possible that the Ashkenazi Hasidim regarded the powers of the stars, in which they believed, as another divine law that the righteous have to overcome to prove their adherence to the real divine wishes, by overcoming the difficulties God put in their way.

Ashkenazi Hasidic ethics, presented mainly in the *Sefer Ḥasidim*, are to be understood as a practical system for educating believers so they will be able to overcome the world's trials and become righteous. The laws of the Torah, according to them, are not intended to facilitate and regulate human social and religious life. Their purpose is constantly to test man's devotion to God against the physical attractions of this world. Sin, therefore, always gives pleasure, while the service of God and compliance with his commandments always mean negation of human desires.

Ashkenazi Hasidic ethics are, therefore, a constant attempt to maximize the demands of Jewish religious law, to develop more and more restrictions and demands that will make compliance ever more difficult and rare. The ultimate achievement is the *kiddush ha-shem* (sanctification of the holy name), which means giving one's life for God's name. The victims of the massacres during the crusades—Jews who died because they refused to convert to Christianity—were regarded as the standard to be adopted and the ideal according to which everybody should educate himself. *Kiddush ha-shem* means the complete denial of the physical world and ultimate submission to the divine will, and every religious act should be carried out as a *kiddush ha-shem* in miniature. Seldom does one find such a close relationship between the theology and ethics of a religious movement and the specific historical situation in which it was created. Ashkenazi Hasidism did not initiate Jewish martyrdom during the early crusades; rather, it explained God's purpose in creating these historical circumstances and fashioned a system of ethics that preserved the spirit of the martyrs of 1096 and made them a symbol for later generations to follow.

The Ashkenazi Hasidim also developed a body of repentance literature that emphasized the same motifs. If sin brings pleasure, repentance (*teshuvah*) should include pain and suffering in the same amount. They made extensive lists of sufferings to be undergone for every specific sin, usually prescribing many days of fasting. Sometimes, especially for sexual sins, they demanded more picturesque tortures, such as sitting naked among insects in the summer or immersing in an icy river in the winter. It should be noted, however, that the Hasidim demanded such self-inflicted tortures only within the framework of *teshuvah*, never as a way of life.

A more mystical aspect of Ashkenazi Hasidic theology is the attitude toward prayer, as reflected in the many works dealing with interpretation of the Jewish prayer book. According to them, there is a mystical harmony among the structure of the prayers, the letters used in them and the numerical value of these letters, and other parts of sacred literature, especially the Bible and the Midrash. Even though the prayers were composed by men, the sages of the Second Temple period, divine secrets are hidden in esoteric numerical structures within them. Both Rabbi Judah the Pious and Rabbi Eleazar of Worms wrote their major books on this subject, and they insisted that these secrets reached them through a long oral tradition from antiquity. The name of Rabbi Aaron ben Samuel of Baghdad appears as the transmitter of these secrets from Babylonia to the Kalonymus family in Italy, and there may be some basis to this claim. It is unclear, however, whether these commentaries on the prayer book actually influenced everyday practice during prayer, or were written in a speculative way, without practical consequences. It is very difficult, therefore, to decide whether the Ashkenazi Hasidim adopted mystical practices, or whether some mystical aspects in their theology sum up their connection with mysticism.

THE CABALA

During the second half of the thirteenth century and the beginning of the fourteenth, Jewish theology in Germany came under the influence of the cabala, the mystical system developed in Spain and the Provence in the late twelfth century. The theological ideas of the Ashkenazi Hasidim were absorbed to a very large extent by the cabala, though they remained marginal in the new system. Some of the Jewish theologians of the late thirteenth and early fourteenth centuries interpreted Ashkenazi Hasidic ideas, texts, and terminology in a cabalistic manner. Rabbi Menahem Ziyyoni, the author of a major commentary on the Torah and other works (probably late in the fourteenth century), can be regarded as the perfect example of this absorption of Ashkenazi Hasidic theology within the cabalistic system.

Ashkenazi Hasidic ethics, however, remained an independent system in Jewish thought in Northern Europe throughout the Middle Ages, and in early modern times many of its ideas and precepts were adopted by other Jewish schools. In the works of many later cabalists, in Europe and the Near East, it was dominant for many centuries, and it comprises one of the most important contributions of the Middle Ages to Jewish thought in early modern times.

BIBLIOGRAPHY

In Hebrew. Itzak F. Baer, "The Religious-Social Tendency of Sepher Hassidim," in *Zion,* 3 (1937/1938), and "The 1096 Massacres," in *Sefer Assaf* (1953); Abraham Berliner, *Selected Works* (1945), 142–170; Joseph Dan, *The Esoteric Theology of the Ashkenazi Hasidism* (1968), "Rabbi Eleazar's Shaarey ha-Sod, ha-Yihud veha-Emunah," in Israel Weinstock, ed., *Temirin: Texts and Studies in Kabbala and Hasidim* (1972), I, *Studies in Ashkenazi Hasidic Literature* (1975), and *Hebrew Ethical and Homiletic Literature* (1975), 121–145, with detailed bibliography on 289–293; Efraim Elimenech Urbach, ed., *'Arugat ha-bosem,* 4 vols. (1939–1963), and *The Tosafists: Their History, Writings, and Methods* (1955).

In other languages. Alexander Altmann, "Eleazar of Worms' Ḥokhmat ha-ʾEgoz," in *Journal of Jewish Studies,* **11** (1960); Haim Hillel Ben-Sasson, "The Middle Ages," in *idem,* ed., *A History of the Jewish People* (1976), 545–560; Abraham Cronbach, "Social Thinking in the *Sefer Ḥasidim,*" in *Hebrew Union College Annual,* **22** (1949); Joseph Dan, "The Beginnings of Jewish Mysticism in Europe," in *The World History of the Jewish People,* 2nd ser., II, *The Dark Ages* (1966), and "Ḥokhmath ha-ʾEgoz: Its Origin and Development," in *Journal of Jewish Studies,* **17** (1966); Monford Harris, "The Concept of Love in Sepher Hassidim," in *Jewish Quarterly Review,* **50** (1959); Gershom G. Scholem, *Major Trends in Jewish Mysticism* (1954), and *Ursprung und Anfange der Kabbala* (1962); Haym Soloveitchik, "Three Themes in the *Sefer Ḥasidim,*" in *Association for Jewish Studies Review,* **1** (1976).

JOSEPH DAN

[See also **Abraham Bar Ḥiyya; Abraham ben Meïr Ibn Ezra; Cabala; Eleazar ben Judah of Worms; Ḥasidei Ashkenaz; Judah ben Samuel he-Hasid; Kalonymus Family; Saadiah Gaon.**]

PHILOSOPHY AND THEOLOGY, WESTERN EUROPEAN: TO MID TWELFTH CENTURY. The encounter between pagan philosophies based on reason and Christian doctrines based on faith in the Gospel kerygma occurred as soon as Christianity penetrated Hellenic culture. But the concept of Christian theology defined in the modern sense, juxtaposing an autonomous philosophy to a systematically ordered, speculative discipline about the God of Hebrew-Christian revelation, took at least eleven centuries to emerge from that encounter. In the Latin West, the emergence of the high medieval conceptions of theology that bear significantly on the various historical conceptions of the relationship between philosophy and theology can be primarily traced, prior to the thirteenth century, in the writings of Tertullian, Augustine, Boethius, Eriugena, Anselm of Canterbury, and Abelard.

"Theology," a word not found in the Bible, first appeared with a technical sense in the Greek philosophers. But its usage among them is ambivalent. Plato and Aristotle derogated poetry and myths as "theology." Yet, "theology" also designated, for Plato, a rationally or philosophically correct discourse about God (*Republic,* Book II, 377–383), and, for Aristotle, it was "first philosophy" or the highest philosophical science of "being qua being" (*Metaphysics,* 1026a; 1064b).

The Greek fathers of the second and third centuries retained this ambivalence in the meaning of the term. "Theology," for the apologists, usually connoted the pagan myths. Subsequently, Clement of Alexandria (*ca.* 150–*ca.* 215) and Origen (*ca.* 185–*ca.* 254) distinguished pagan or mythic theology from the theology of Christian revelation. By the fourth century, in the writings of Eusebius of Caesarea (*ca.* 263–*ca.* 340), there is evidence that "theology" had attained its normative Christian usage: the true, ecclesiastical knowledge of the God of revelation.

Characteristically, the Greek fathers distinguished *theologia* and *oikonomia;* the former term refers to knowledge of the Trinity, the latter to knowledge of the divine redemptive activity in history and the church. The Latin Middle Ages admitted a variety of synonyms for "theology": *sacra pagina, divina pagina,* and *sacra doctrina.* All the terms tie theology to biblical exegesis.

Likewise, the term "philosophy" has a complex history. Among third- and fourth-century authors such as Cyprian (*ca.* 200–258) and Ambrose (*ca.* 340–397), it often connoted the practical exercise of the Christian virtues. In the Carolingian period, "philosophy" designated the ensemble of all the sciences. In the eleventh century, under Abelard's influence, there first appeared the antithesis between an autonomous rationality (philosophy) and a theology dependent on biblical exegesis and ecclesiastical authorities.

TERTULLIAN

Compared with their Greek counterparts, the Latin fathers were less speculative and more concerned with the practical business of living a Christian life in a pagan milieu. Tertullian (*ca.* 155–*ca.* 220) set the pattern. Although erudite, he was not attracted to Christianity by a theoretical appreciation of its philosophical merits, but by the moral heroism of persecuted Christians. Posterity reiterates the judgment of his contemporaries. Embodying a strenuous moralism of their own, Tertullian's writings display a lawyer's impassioned rhetoric and advocacy. But, for Tertullian, this vehemence exemplifies rather than detracts from the intrinsic truth of the Christian religion. Here the great African Father parted company with the Greek fathers.

Tertullian, unlike Clement of Alexandria, repudiated any similarity between the Christian and the philosopher. He castigated Socrates, a "corrupter of youth" (*Apologeticum,* 46), and Aristotle, a "miserable" man responsible for inventing the vanities of dialectic (*De praescriptione haereticorum,* 7). Nonetheless, Tertullian did acknowledge a certain concordance between philosophy and Christianity. Sometimes philosophers happen to agree with church doctrine. The concordance, however, is deceptive. They have stolen these ideas from the Old Testament. Philosophical thievery is always selective and subordinate to the misguided pursuit of originality.

Tertullian, accordingly, rejected the method of his predecessor, Justin Martyr (*d. ca.* 165), and his contemporary, Minucius Felix (*d. ca.* 250), both of whom assiduously culled the philosophers for evidence in support of Christian faith. Tertullian knew these philosophical parallels to Christianity but disavowed them, believing that revelation alone guarantees the truth of Christian faith. Philosophy distorts the truth and academic philosophers, time and again, prove to be the "patriarchs of heretics" (*De anima,* 3).

Nonetheless, Tertullian's opposition to philosophy should not be construed as a formal opposition between faith and reason but as a critical juxtaposition of the Gospel and pagan philosophy. Tertullian voiced, if not the exact phrase, views comparable to the famous "credo, quia absurdum" (I believe because it is absurd) usually attributed to him. But, precisely against the philosophers, he asserted that natural reason, if kept uncontaminated from sophistry, could attain a knowledge of God. To the pure of mind, that God exists and that men should fear his judgment are self-evident truths. Tertullian opposed, then, not reason but a self-contained rationalism that would place philosophy above the Gospel.

In fact, Tertullian's writings incorporate many philosophical elements. His treatment of the proof of God's existence from universal consent, the corporeal nature of God, the function of the Logos in the creation of the world, the unity of the soul, the character of the moral virtues, and his criticism of the Platonist theory of metempsychosis are heavily imbued with Stoicism. But, for all their influence, Tertullian remained independent of the Stoics.

Tertullian never pursued philosophical argumentation for its own sake; his use of philosophy is exclusively apologetic, and the philosophical elements in his thought are neither original nor integrated. Accordingly, Tertullian did not attempt to harmonize faith and reason or to correlate theology and philosophy.

AUGUSTINE

Properly speaking, this latter duality does not structure even the thought of Augustine (354–430). His debate with the philosophers signaled the victory of a personal faith over a personal despair. Philosophy did not provide the certitude which Augustine had sought but did not find until his religious conversion in 386. He was looking for an answer to life's most important question: what will make men abidingly happy? There are numerous philosophical answers to this question. Augustine decided, therefore, that the question should be rescued from the philosophers, who are incapable of understanding the actual conditions in which they philosophize. Their achievements, consequently, cannot possibly match their aspirations.

Philosophers attempt to reach the truth by reason alone. But they, like all men, suffer from deranged appetites that darken their intellects. As Augustine discovered after a long odyssey, Scripture, and not philosophy, correctly diagnoses reason's peculiar malady and provides the effective cure. Since sin has disordered man's will and weakened his intellect, only divine grace can restore order and enlightenment. True knowledge begins, then, in humility and repentance.

Augustine, however, could not and did not divorce faith from understanding. He himself had first read Plotinus and then Scripture. The experience taught him that philosophy, especially that of the Platonists, can be used to understand what is believed. Thus Aristotle's famous formulas encapsulated his personal experience and what he regarded as the universally correct procedure: "Believe that you may understand," and "Understand that you may believe" (*Sermon,* 43). These formulas, simple as they sound, need careful interpretation.

The Augustinian unity of faith and understanding cannot be resolved into the modern distinction between theology and philosophy. Augustine did not recognize and certainly did not practice, however strong his allegiance to the Platonists, a methodologically or existentially autonomous philosophical science. He accepted, from the time of his conversion, that Christianity is the true philosophy and the necessary corrective for all pagan philosophies.

Yet, Augustine did not conflate theological arguments that take as a premise some indemonstrable article of faith, from which further conclusions can be deduced, and philosophical arguments that attempt a rational demonstration of some truth of faith. Within the existential ambience of faith seeking understanding, there exists a philosophy that is both fully Christian and fully rational. For such a philosophy, faith indeed determines the range of objects that reason attempts to contemplate, but faith in no way renders strictly rational argumentation superfluous or nugatory.

Augustinian wisdom, in the light of posterity's sharp methodological distinction between philosophy and theology, appears to be entirely or merely theological. Augustine himself admitted that faith adverts to the concrete, contingent events of a sacred history. This historical orientation permeates Christian philosophy and distinguishes it from the avowedly timeless pursuits of pagan philosophy. But the late medieval disjunction of theology and philosophy obscures or misconstrues the role that reason plays for Augustine. Augustine's Christian philosophy is not the scholastic handmaiden eager to serve theology; rather, it is the integrally rational dimension of an understanding whose horizon is set by the Christian faith. Augustinian wisdom has its own axis; it turns not upon a distinction between separate disciplines, theology and philosophy, but upon a distinction between separable moments, faith and understanding, in the one Christian consciousness.

BOETHIUS

A different tendency, toward the standardization of philosophical vocabulary, the method of logical division and definition, and the systematization of scholastic theology, originated with Boethius (*ca.* 480–524/525). Boethius, who has been described as both the last Greek philosopher and the first Schoolman, wanted to translate into Latin, in imitation of Cicero, all the works of Plato and Aristotle and to show the compatibility of their philosophical doctrines. Although Boethius did not complete this ambitious project, and presented an Aristotle dubiously colored by Plato, he did, in fact, provide the basic translations and commentaries on the Greek philosophers upon which subsequent theology focused.

One of his translations, Porphyry's Introduction (*Isagoge*) to Aristotle's *Categories,* was widely read in the ninth and tenth centuries. But during the same period, Boethius' own commentary on the *Categories* and his two commentaries on the *Isagoge* went unused. For the early Middle Ages, the pseudo-Augustinian treatise the *Categoriae decem,* the *Liber de generatione divini verbi* and *Adversus Arium* of Marius Victorinus, and, especially, Augustine's *De Trinitate* were more prominent sources of logical doctrine. In the twelfth century, which can be appropriately called the "Age of Boethius," a passage from his commentary on the *Isagoge,* wherein Boethius personally avoided choosing between Plato and Aristotle, focused the debate between the realists and the nominalists on the status of universals.

Boethius schematized philosophy into the practical and speculative, both of which are tripartite. Practical philosophy deals with the acquisition of the virtues, the role of the virtues in the administration of the state, and the administration of the household. Speculative philosophy, since there are three kinds of beings, consists of a theology of immaterial beings (*intellectibilia*), a psychology of embodied souls (*intelligibilia*), and a physiology of material natures (*naturalia*). The latter science constitues, to use Boethius' new label, a quadrivium of disciplines: geometry, astronomy, music, and arithmetic. The conjunction of Boethius' quadrivium with the traditional trivium (grammar, rhetoric, and logic) formed the core of medieval education.

Written while he was in detention, under sentence of death for allegedly plotting with Constantinople against the Ostrogothic emperor Theodoric, Boethius' most famous work, the *De consolatione Philosophiae* (The consolation of Philosophy), studiously avoids mentioning ecclesiastical or biblical authors but adopts, instead, a Neoplatonic view of divine providence and human freedom. On a benign reading, Boethius' philosophical opinions do not contradict Christian dogma but stand, as a humanistic rationalism, outside the proper ambience of religious faith. Whatever be the explanation of this fact, it is implausible to infer that Boethius formally abandoned Christianity at the end of his life. Other explanations must, therefore, be advanced. Perhaps Boethius, out of love of the classical tradition, conflated philosophy and Christianity; perhaps in the hope of a reprieve, he chose to remain prudently silent about those theological doctrines that had provoked his political calamity; or perhaps he intended to provide, what subsequent readers have claimed to find, a philosophical propaedeutic to Christianity. In any case, despite its ambivalent character, the *De consolatione Philosophiae* attained great popularity, and it merits, for its literary and philosophical importance, comparison with Augustine's *Confessions*.

AFTER BOETHIUS

The period after Boethius was barren of original philosophical speculation. The *Institutiones* of Cassiodorus (*ca.* 490–*ca.* 583) contains a summary of the liberal arts and fragmentary information about dialectic, logic, and the history of philosophy. The *Etymologiae* of Isidore of Seville (*ca.* 560–636), a major source for five hundred years, is an often fanciful work of a grammarian. In it, Isidore recapitulated all the ancient knowledge that he thought useful for the educational program of the church, including outlines of the history and divisions of philosophy. During the seventh and eighth centuries, the Irish monastic scholars produced exegesis which, luxuriant in allegories, was singularly impoverished of metaphysics. In England, Bede (672/673–735) redacted patristic exegesis but specifically omitted passages that contained metaphysical speculation.

By 800, in the school of Alcuin (730–804), early medieval theology began to incorporate the "old logic," that is, Aristotle's *Categories.* The *Categories* existed in three Latin versions: a generally accurate but unread (until the eleventh century) translation of Boethius, a composite of Boethius' commentary on the *Categories,* and a loose paraphrase (*Categoriae decem*) attributed to Augustine. The latter, used extensively in the ninth and tenth centuries, was the primary source for logical doctrine, despite its considerable deviations from Aristotle, until finally supplanted by Boethius' translation of the *Categories* in the twelfth century.

The *Categoriae decem* disseminated from Alcuin's circle. Alcuin, a British monk and the leading scholar to whom Charlemagne entrusted the restoration of the humanities, wrote a compendium of logic (*De dialectica*) and a commentary on Genesis (*Dicta Albani*) that changed somewhat the psychological analogies of Augustine's *De Trinitate.* Alcuin's star pupil, a German monk named Bruun, also known as Candidus of Fulda, continued (in the *Dicta Candidi*) his teacher's discussion of the Trinity, the categories, and the syllogism, and presented a proof for the existence of God based on the imperfection of man. Another pupil, Fridugisus (*d.* 834), who succeeded Alcuin as abbot of St. Martin of Tours, wrote an important letter (*De nihilo et tenebris, ca.* 800) in which he claimed that darkness and nothingness signify a common matter from which God created the cosmos. About 830, Agobard of Lyons (769–840) controverted Fridugisus on the interpretation of Scripture, the relationship of truth to God, and the preexistence of the soul. The latter doctrine exposed, in Agobard's view, Fridugisus' false allegiance to pagan philosophy.

A similar repudiation of purportedly pagan conceptions, now in the context of a theological apology for the Frankish political order, marks the *Libri Carolini.* The anonymous authors (the chief of whom was probably Theodulf of Orléans) contravened the restoration and defense of icons propounded by the Council of Nicaea (787). In sanctioning the cult of icons, the council uncritically incorporated, according to Charlemagne's apologists, the pagan practice of worshiping the images of the absent emperor. Underlying the cult of icons is a Neoplatonic philosophy that confuses time and eternity. At issue is the Neoplatonic justification for Byzantine political theory. The Frankish theologians rejected the Byzantine claim that God and the emperor were simultaneously corulers of the empire.

Neoplatonic doctrines also disturbed Ratramnus (*d. ca.* 868), a monk at Corbie, who devoted two treatises to problems about the nature of the soul. The first treatise (written *ca.* 850, about the time of King Charles the Bald's official inquiry on the soul's immateriality and relation to space) collects patristic opinions. The second treatise (*Liber de anima ad Odonem, ca.* 860), a reply to Ratramnus' bishop, Odo, attacks the heretical notion of a world soul propounded by a pupil of the Irishman Macarius.

Macarius' pupil, an unknown monk of St. Germer de Fly, imposed a Neoplatonic interpretation on an ambiguous text of Augustine's *De quantitate animae.* In reference to the unity and multiplicity of souls, Augustine envisaged three alternatives: (1) all souls are somehow one, (2) each is unique and separate, and (3) all souls are both one and many. Augustine regarded the third option as unintelligible but appeared not to choose between alternatives one and two. Marcarius, for his part, decided that the third option was the only correct possibility and explained what Augustine, purportedly out of respect for the intellectual limitations of his readers, had left unsaid. The world soul is an existent species from which individual souls derive. Ratramnus rejected Macarius' interpretation: only individuals exist in reality; universals are merely concepts existing in the mind.

ERIUGENA

Neoplatonism, however, gained impetus from a gift of Emperor Michael II Balbus (the Stammerer). In 827, the emperor presented Louis I (the Pious or the Debonair) with a Greek codex of Pseudo-Dionysius (whose fifth-century origins remain obscure), which Charles the Bald around 860 requested John Scottus Eriugena (*ca.* 820–*ca.* 877/879) to translate anew. Subsequently, Eriugena also translated the *Ambigua* of Maximus the Confessor (580–662) and the *De hominis opificio* of Gregory of Nyssa.

Eriugena, in his own *Periphyseon,* employed the Neoplatonic scheme of *divisio* (*prodos*) and *reversio* (*epistrophē*), versions of which are found in Maximus and Pseudo-Dionysius, to explain the emanation of creation and its unity in God. The treatise applies to universal nature (*physis*), the cosmological doctrine of the syzygies, the theory that one element can pass into another by means of a common property.

Eriugena divided nature into (1) that which creates and is not created (God as principle of all things); (2) that which is created and creates (the archetypal divine ideas); (3) that which is created and does not create (things); and (4) that which is not created and does not create (God as the end of all things). But these divisions, since they can be reduced to two (Creator and creation), are less important than the total parallelism that Eriugena posited between human and divine dialectics.

Human dialectic, which resolves genera into species and species into individuals and then reverts, in search of an intelligible unity, from the many back to the one, imitates the hypostasizations of the divine dialectic of procession and return. Emanation from the divine reaches its limit with matter and, at that point, begins to revert by means of the motion of the world soul (identified as the *vita communis*) that emerges from matter. Man's function, in relation to the sensible world, is analogous to God's ultimate function in relation to the whole process of emanation. Man is the proximate final cause that draws the sensible world into the realm of intelligibility, draws intelligibility into a unified concept within himself, and draws himself (and thus the sensible world) into God.

Eriugena's metaphysics has pantheistic overtones: God himself is *divisio* and *collectio,* genus and species, whole and part. But Eriugena, borrowing an image from Maximus, maintained that as light is not destroyed by uniting with air, so nature, though deified in the process of return, is not destroyed or collapsed into the divine. The same point can be expressed philosophically: the categories cannot be applied to God. Even in the beatific vision, contemplation reaches only to the theophanies and not to the divine nature itself. God, although he is the being of all creatures, is himself beyond being and, therefore, imparticipable.

Eriugena's cosmology, especially his gloss on a text of Martianus Capella describing the soul's journey to and from the celestial spheres, provoked the criticism of a sometime colleague, Prudentius, after the latter became (in 843) bishop of Troyes. Eriugena's gloss refers to the Neoplatonic doctrine that there is no extracosmic place of punishment for the soul, and to Varro's identification of God with the *anima mundi* (world soul) and the individual gods with the zones of the cosmos. Prudentius objected that Eriugena's references, whose direct source is *De civitate Dei,* do not convey Augustine's polemic against these pagan doctrines, which contradict the Christian belief in an extracosmic destiny.

Hincmar, archbishop of Rheims, commissioned (*ca.* 850) Eriugena to combat the theory of double predestination formulated by a rebellious monk, Gottschalk. This time, Eriugena transformed Augustine, much to Hincmar's chagrin, into an almost Pelagian champion of human freedom. To eliminate the idea that God has prepared a specific place of eternal damnation, Eriugena appealed to Augustine's early anti-Manichaean writings and to Origen's *De principiis.* Both good and evil souls, although their experiences ultimately differ, migrate to the same cosmic stratum. In that place, however, the evil soul experiences a self-inflicted misery.

On Eriugena's reading, Gottschalk's theory of double predestination fails to comprehend that punishment is a consequence of the human misuse of freedom. Evil and punishment for sin are but corruptions of good. They are, strictly speaking, nothings. Since God knows only being or what can participate in being, he has no proper foreknowledge of evil and does not predestinate man to punishment. Eriugena's theory, however, was condemned by the Council of Valence (855) and the Council of Langres (859).

The work of Eriugena attracted the attention of his contemporaries. The decline of the Carolingian dynasty, following the death of Charles the Bald (877), initiated a period of cultural and political disorder. Fifty years after Eriugena's death, scholars were mainly involved in glossing the standard texts, the *Categoriae decem* and Boethius' *Opuscula sacra.* By the tenth century, glosses on these texts indicate more interest in Aristotle than Eriugena.

TENTH TO EARLY ELEVENTH CENTURIES

In the tenth century, intellectual life survived in the Benedictine monasteries. Dialectic, as preparation for writing letters and official documents in Latin, remained part of the curriculum of the monastic schools. Prominent among tenth-century logicians was Gerbert of Aurillac (945–1003), who became (999) Pope Sylvester II. Gerbert is the first person known to have taught, while at Rheims (972–991), a full course, such as it could be derived from Boethius, of the (old) logic of Aristotle.

The early-eleventh-century debates between dialecticians and antidialecticians were theological debates about the proper application of dialectics to Christian dogma. The debate between Berengar of Tours (*ca.* 1000–1088) and Lanfranc of Bec (1005–1089), about the nature of the Eucharist, is typical. Berengar argued that, after the consecration, the substance of the bread remains since it is logically impossible for accidents of bread to exist apart from their proper substance. Thus logic would render invalid the doctrine of transubstantiation. Lanfranc, while not repudiating dialectic, demanded that it be subordinated to faith, in this case, to the belief that the substance of the consecrated bread (despite the preservation of its accidents) is substantially changed.

These theological debates had ramifications for political and monastic life. To Manegold of Lautenbach (writing *ca.* 1080), Neoplatonic cosmology not only blatantly contradicted the Bible but also inculcated a spirit of intellectual arrogance that found expression in antipapal politics. But Manegold's negative evaluation of philosophy did not prevent him from using all the resources of dialectic to defend the prerogatives of Pope Gregory VII (1073–1085) against Emperor Henry IV (1056–1106). Otloh of St. Emmeram (1010–1070) lamented the fact that certain monks preferred Boethius to Scripture. Peter Damian (1007–1072), who had taught grammar and dialectic before his conversion (*ca.* 1035) to the eremetical life, became a radical antidialectician. Monks should not study philosophy and dialecticians should not presume to judge faith. Logic governs man's temporal understanding of natural phenomena. Man, for example, cannot understand the past to be possibly different than it actually was. But, for God, all time is a simultaneous present; in the divine eternity, it is possible for the past not to have been or to have been differently than it was. For God simply transcends human logic.

ANSELM OF CANTERBURY

Anselm of Canterbury (1033–1109) was both a devout monk and an original philosopher. But philosophy for Anselm was dialectic, a circumstance that uniquely determined the Anselmian synthesis of faith and reason. Anselm knew well and followed the doctrine of Augustine: Faith must precede reason but reason, once given its object of investigation by faith, can understand. Reason attempts to understand, not so that it can construct an apologetic designed to convince the nonbeliever, but so that the believer may take delight in the rational demonstration of a truth first held only on faith. Such demonstrations, although they can be validly and certainly derived from reason, are, in a certain sense, hypothetical, since, for the obedient Christian, they remain open to correction from ecclesiastical authority.

Anselm's *Monologium,* written about 1076 for the monks at the Abbey of Bec, elaborates, on the basis of an Augustinian-Platonic metaphysics, three proofs for the existence of God. The proofs attempt to find the ultimate source of an observed property or quality in finite things: their goodness, their being, and their degree of perfection. By appealing to the theory of participation, that every relative instantiation of a property shares in or derives from a single, absolute instantiation of that property, the proofs attain a supreme Goodness, Being, and Perfection, which the believer can identify as the God of faith.

The famous ontological proof of the *Proslogion,* written because Anselm was not satisfied with the complex arguments of the *Monologium,* has an almost unparalleled importance in the history of philosophy. Subsequent discussion has refined but hardly moved beyond the parameters of Gaunilo's objection to the proof and Anselm's defense of it. The concept of a perfect being (the Being greater than which one cannot think), and only this concept, necessitates passage from thought to actual existence.

Anselm's dialectical proofs for Christian dogma exceed Augustine's analogical use of philosophical concepts to exegete theological doctrine. Anselm, for example, did not hesitate to offer the necessary reasons for the Trinity and the Incarnation. Anselm's Christian philosophy, however, is not a rationalism; the rational comprehension it attains always presupposes an article of faith to be comprehended. For this reason, Anselm did not draw, as the thirteenth-century Scholastics would, a clear distinction between an autonomous philosophy and a rationally schematized theology. Nonetheless, Anselm's philosophical demonstrations of the basic tenets of Augustinian theology foreshadowed the efforts of the thirteenth-century Scholastics to construct scientific theologies. In this sense, Anselm is the "father of Scholasticism."

TWELFTH-CENTURY PLATONISM

In the twelfth century, a Platonist movement developed, despite the paucity of primary sources, around the cathedral at Chartres. One of this school's first masters, the humanist Bernard of Chartres (*d. ca.* 1130), whose philosophical interest in grammar anticipated the speculative grammars of the thirteenth century, explained the relationship of terms and their grammatical derivatives by means of the theory of participation. Bernard's student, Gilbert of Poitiers (*ca.* 1075–1154), gave a metaphysical interpretation of Aristotle's *Categories* and wrote influential commentaries on Boethius. Gilbert introduced into theological speculation an emphasis on the reality of essences, an emphasis that culminated in the theology of Duns Scotus (*ca.* 1266–1308). For Gilbert, the divine essence, which is being pure and simple, is the source of all created entities, which are compounds of a generic essence concretized by the addition of other essential forms.

Thierry of Chartres (*d.* after 1151), brother of Bernard and Gilbert's successor as chancellor of Chartres (1141), was called "the greatest philosopher of all Europe." Thierry's *Heptateuchon,* which covers both the trivium and the quadrivium, shows a deep commitment to classical culture. His *De septem diebus* applies the subject matters of the quadrivium, in particular the physics of Calcidius' commentary on the *Timaeus,* to the exegesis of Genesis. Thierry identified the biblical heaven and earth with the four elements. The elements have interchangeable particles which, moving mechanistically, constitute nature. Because nature is multiple, it can be interpreted mathematically; God, however, is One, superior to being and number. Thierry's theology, then, although not itself pantheistic, slanted toward Neoplatonism, and thus encouraged the important role afforded, in the fourteenth century, to Proclus.

In the school of Chartres, the Platonism of Boethius and Calcidius dominated such figures as William of Conches (*ca.* 1080–*ca.* 1154) and Clarenbaud of Arras (*d.* 1170). But for the preeminent humanist of Chartres, John of Salisbury (*ca.* 1125–1180), not Plato but Cicero and Quintilian were the exemplars of an enlightened, because modest, philosophical stance.

John allowed that the senses, reason, and faith are sources of truth, but severely restricted the number of philosophical certitudes that could be thereby attained. The ultimate metaphysical status of universals, to take a central question, is an unsolvable problem, even if one grants that Aristotle has provided the correct account of their psychological genesis. Philosophy, as the classical academicians realized, is the erudite discussion of probable explanations for unsolvable problems. Such probable explanations have great value; they free the mind of the philosopher from false dogmatism and enable him to love and follow the divine wisdom.

PETER ABELARD

No such philosophical modesty restrained Peter Abelard (*ca.* 1079–*ca.* 1142), whose dialectic was as expansive as his life was restless. Abelard, whom John of Salisbury called after his birthplace the "Peripatetic of Pallet," wandered from monastery to monastery capturing the attention and the admiration of his contemporaries (with the notable exception of Bernard of Clairvaux). Praised for the clarity of his teaching, Abelard relentlessly exposed the inadequacies of his own teachers, Roscelinus (*ca.* 1050–1125) and William of Champeaux (*ca.* 1070–1122). In fact, Abelard's explanation of universals resembles the doctrine of Roscelinus: universals, or the meanings of words, exist in the intellect but they designate, since there are no essences in things, only individuals.

Abelard's brilliance, which shaped the development of logic in the twelfth century, also inspired a school of theology, but it did not save Abelard himself from condemnation for heterodoxy at the Councils of Soissons (1121) and Sens (1140), after which many of his theological works were destroyed. One that survives, the *Sic et non,* is a collection of juxtaposed biblical, patristic, and conciliar texts in which various authorities argue, contradictorily, for and against 158 different theological doctrines. This format, which did not occasion offense, had already been used in compilations of canon laws; it did not represent, therefore, a rationalist attack on tradition but was, rather, a methodological step toward the scientific theologies of the thirteenth century. For his part, Abelard confidently assumed that where traditional texts were at variance, dialectic could and should settle the meaning of the basic terms and thus resolve at least some of the contradictions. While his approach was somewhat facile, lacking any mystagogical sense, no theologian, after Abelard, could doubt that sound theology must fulfill the requirements of logic.

Abelard's fascination with logic colored and, to his critics, distorted his Trinitarian and christological speculation. He was condemned because his theology seemed to obscure the distinctions in the Godhead and the unity of Christ's humanity and divinity. In ethics, Abelard courted controversy; he challenged traditional teaching by claiming that the intention of the agent and not the content of the act determines morality. Still, on these and other issues, Abelard did not regard his own terminology or ideas as fixed. He wrote and rewrote and, in the process, became increasingly orthodox in his opinions.

To what may we attribute the humane character of his thoughts? Perhaps Abelard, not unlike but with fewer scruples than Anselm of Canterbury, simply took for granted that faith, although rooted in the authority of Christ and the church, is inwardly rational. Read in this light, the ancient philosophers show a remarkable harmony with, if not an actual anticipation of, the Christian Gospel. This, in any case, was Abelard's perspective: that Christian wisdom completes rather than transcends philosophical insight.

Yet, Abelard remained suspect, as much for the spirit behind his opinions as for their specific content. The ambiguity lay in his failure to distinguish sharply faith and reason, philosophy and theology. Without such a distinction, his thinking always seemed a danger to religious authority and to faith in revealed truth.

THE INFLUENCE OF ARISTOTLE AND AUGUSTINE

By the middle of the twelfth century, Boethius' Latin translations of Aristotle's *Prior* and *Posterior Analytics, Sophistical Refutations,* and *Topics* became established as the "new logic." The old and the new logics, introduced by stages, played an essential role in the development of a theology that could claim, by the thirteenth century, to be in conformity with the Aristotelian model of science. Boethius' theological treatises, which utilized the logical terminology of Aristotle, had set the precedent. Seven hundred years later, the precedent was the norm. Thenceforth, logic was accepted as the necessary instrument by which the theologian could define terms, deduce remote conclusions from immediately revealed truths, and fashion theological discourse into a rationally ordered science.

The introduction of Aristotle into Western theology occurred in three major stages. (1) During the ninth, tenth, and eleventh centuries the assimilation of the old logic (Boethius' logical treatises, and his translations and commentaries on Aristotle's *Categories* and *De interpretatione,* Porphyry's *Isagoge,* and Cicero's *Topics*) enabled theologians to classify terms and to analyze propositions found in the Bible and the Fathers. (2) In the twelfth century, the new logic prompted theories of knowledge and of demonstrative reasoning that allowed, in the urban schools of theology, the development of standardized problems and questions. (3) In the late twelfth and early thirteenth centuries, the appearance of Latin translations of Aristotle's *Metaphysics, Nicomachean Ethics,* and *De anima* transformed, in the great theological summae, the subject matter, principles, and method of theological speculation.

During the sixth to the twelfth centuries, however, Aristotle was only one influence, certainly not the most powerful, among others. By comparison, the influence of Augustine can hardly be overemphasized. In the *De doctrina christiana,* Augustine had enjoined that dialectic should serve as a propaedeutic, and the liberal arts should function as an auxiliary to scriptural exegesis and theology. In turn, Augustine's own works served as the preeminent authority and model for the elaboration of theological themes and dogmatic controversies and the exploration and criticism of philosophical arguments and theories of knowledge.

Augustine's Plotinian philosophy focused and controlled the diverse, syncretic Neoplatonisms that pervaded Latin theology until the end of the twelfth century. On the two major issues, whose continual resurfacing betrayed the innate, heterodox tendencies in Neoplatonism, Augustine had clearly adhered to biblical orthodoxy: God creates immediately, as the soul relates to God immediately, without need of a hierarchy of beings; and only God—and not matter or separate ideas—is eternal. Augustinism provided a legacy of common philosophical themes: in metaphysics—the ordered character of the universe, the negative ontological status of evil, and the depreciation of the world of becoming; in noetic theory—the distinction between the sensible and the intelligible worlds and the primacy of the latter; in anthropology—the duality of body and soul, the immortality and substantiality of soul, and the interiority and subjectivity of mind. The variety of Neoplatonisms did not disappear in the thirteenth century. But the introduction of Aristotle put their interpretation, as well as that of Augustine himself, in a radically new context.

BIBLIOGRAPHY

Berthold Altaner, *Patrology,* Hilda C. Graef, trans. (1960); *The Cambridge History of Later Greek and Early Medieval Philosophy,* A. H. Armstrong, ed. (1967); Marie-Dominique Chenu, O.P., *La théologie au douzième siècle* (1957), partial translation in his *Nature, Man, and Society in the Twelfth Century,* Jerome Taylor and Lester K. Little, trans. and eds. (1968); Yves Congar, O.P., *A History of Theology,* Hunter Guthrie, S. J., trans. and ed. (1968); Hubert Cunliffe-Jones, *A History of Christian Doctrine* (1978); Jean Daniélou, *The Origins of Latin Christianity,* John Austin Baker, ed., David Smith and John Austin Baker, trans. (1977); G. R. Evans, *Old Arts and New Theology: The Beginnings of Theology as an Academic Discipline* (1980); Joseph de Ghellnick, S. J., *Le mouvement théologique du xiie siècle,* 2nd ed. (1969); Étienne Gilson, *History of Christian Philosophy in the Middle Ages* (1955), containing a superb bibliography, and *The Spirit of Mediaeval Philosophy,* A. H. C. Downes, trans. (1940); Werner Jaeger, *The Theology of the Early Greek Philosophers* (1947); David Knowles, *The Evolution of Medieval Thought* (1964); John Marenbon, *From the Circle of Alcuin to the School of Auxerre: Logic, Theology, and Philosophy in the Early Middle Ages* (1981); Franz Overbeck, *Vorgeschichte und Jugend der mittelalterlichen Scholastik* (1971); William G. Rusch, *The Later Latin Fathers* (1977); Harry Austryn Wolfson, *The Philosophy of the Church Fathers,* I, *Faith, Trinity, Incarnation,* 3rd ed. (1970).

DENIS J. M. BRADLEY

[See also **Aristotle in the Middle Ages; Augustinism; Carolingians and the Carolingian Empire; Church Fathers; Councils; Dialectic; Manichaeans; Neoplatonism; Nominalism; Plato in the Middle Ages; Quadrivium; Realism; Scholasticism; Scholastic Method; Trivium; Universals;** and individual philosophers and theologians.]

PHILOSOPHY AND THEOLOGY, WESTERN EUROPEAN: TWELFTH CENTURY TO AQUINAS

ABELARD

Peter Abelard introduced into philosophy and theology standards of technical exactness that influenced subsequent school practice even while his methods, personal style, and particular teachings aroused opposition from monastic authors such as Bernard of Clairvaux and William of St. Thierry. More thoroughly than his predecessors, Abelard used reasoning to examine the meaning of propositions in philosophy and faith and used dialectics in disputation. This attention to propositional meaning may have come from Abelard's moderate nominalism. For him universals are not, as for Roscelinus, simply words, but words with meaning. Abelard denies that individuals share an essence or substance. If they belong to the same genus or species, they have the same *status,* but this is not an essence.

In theology one of Abelard's major contributions was his *Sic et non,* especially its prologue containing principles for interpreting the many discordant authoritative texts given in the work. In this prologue he states that doubt leads to inquiry and inquiry to truth; hence he both advocated and practiced use of the question method. Abelard was the first in the West to use the term "theology" for a discipline studying God (*sacra doctrina* and *sacra pagina* were the usual terms). He produced several theological systematizations, calling each a summa. He and his considerable "school" studied "the sum (summa) of human salvation" under the three headings of faith, charity, and sacrament. In this plan faith included hope; charity, in accord with his emphasis on interior intention and his stress on the primacy of love in Christian activity, included moral questions; sacrament included the Incarnation.

Abelard taught that non-Christians could find salvation either through direct revelation or by acting with good faith and right intention. Suspicion about his teachings on the Trinity, grace, the Incarnation, and Christ's saving work led to condemnations at the local Council of Sens (1140). Since at least some of the condemned propositions reflected tendentious views about his teaching, he wrote to correct these misinterpretations and to defend his sincere faith and orthodoxy.

THE SCHOOL OF CHARTRES

This cathedral school was an important center of philosophy and theology, its most outstanding scholars being Bernard Silvester, Thierry of Chartres, William of Conches, and Gilbert of Poitiers. Gilbert wrote a frequently used commentary on the Psalms and Pauline Epistles called the *Media glosatura* to distinguish it from the *Glossa ordinaria* and the *Glossa interlinearis,* biblical commentaries produced mainly by the school of Anselm and Radulphus of Laon.

Gilbert's *Expositiones* on four opuscula of Boethius influenced the metaphysical outlook and theology of scholars well into the thirteenth century. His philosophy, a logical realism, paid constant attention to the rules of grammar, logic, dialectics, and rhetoric, especially to application of them in the distinct discipline (*facultas*) of theology.

For Gilbert, in all created reality there is a distinction between the *id quo,* the concrete entity, and the substantial form and the many accidental forms (each a *quo est*) by which the concrete entity is what it is substantially and accidentally. In grammar, the *quod est* is the subject of statements, whereas each *quo est,* signifying a universal form, must refer to the predicate. For example, Plato (*id quod*) is man by humanity (*quo est*). These forms are universal, whereas an *id quod* or subject like Plato is individuated by the "collected property of Plato," which is "collected from all the things belonging to him," that is, from the many forms in him. Because this "total form of Plato" (called *Platonitas*) lacks conformity with any other, Plato is a unique individual. Although Gilbert rejected Boethius' teaching that a unique variety of accidents produce individuation, some of his followers (the anonymous author of the *Sententiae divinitatis,* Alan of Lille, Simon of Tournai) included accidents among the forms or properties whose coalescence produces individuation.

Thierry of Chartres, to develop his interest in cosmogony, combined Neoplatonism with a commentary on Genesis. Although Thierry knew and used Plato's *Timaeus,* he and his pupil Clarembald (Clarenbaldus) proposed a philosophical view of God not as the orderer of existing chaotic matter but as the Creator of everything, including matter. Thus God is the "form of being" (*forma essendi*), not as an intrinsic form but as one participated by all beings. God creates the universe through Ideas conceived in his mind. William of Conches speaks in the same way of divine Ideas. He identifies efficient causality with the Father, formal causality with the Son, and final causality with the Holy Spirit. In his earlier writings William identified the world-soul with the Holy Spirit, but later, viewing the world-soul as created, he rejected its identification with a divine person. For some the world-soul was thought to be a power introduced by God into sensible reality or, as in Alan of Lille, something identical with nature, positions that may reflect Stoic influence. Bernard of Chartres differs from the others by saying that the divine Ideas are not coeternal with God.

Important for medieval philosophy and theology was this school's focus on natures intrinsic to things, by which things have their proper activity. This theme was to be strengthened by the subsequent entry of the "new" Aristotle and his commentators. Alan of Lille, who was influenced by Boethius, Gilbert, and the *Liber de causis,* attempted to construct in his *Distinctiones* and his *Theologicae regulae* an organized deductive theology with its own initial axioms or principles analogous to those of other disciplines. The Pseudo-Dionysius influenced him, more than his mentors, to emphasize negative theology.

Alan of Lille also wrote an important work of apologetics against the Cathars, Waldensians, Jews, and Muslims, a work that recalls the importance of these religions and their theology in the medieval context. Increased contact with Jewish scholars, for example, influenced scriptural exegesis, theology concerning the Divinity, discussions of salvation history, and the relations of church and synagogue, especially as Talmudic commentaries became better known to Christian scholars and challenged their assumptions about the meaning of the biblical texts.

MONASTIC AUTHORS

While scholastic philosophy and theology were developing in the cathedral schools and later in the universities, the more traditional theology continued in the monasteries, taking on new vigor in such important figures as the Benedictines Rupert of Deutz, Peter the Venerable, and William of St. Thierry (later a Cistercian), the Carthusians Guigo I and Guigo II, and the Cistercians Bernard of Clairvaux, Aelred (Ethelred) of Rievaulx, and Isaac of Stella. In general this so-called "monastic theology" practices Augustine's ideal of *intellectus fidei* or Anselm of Canterbury's *fides quaerens intellectum* by seeking a type of understanding achieved by penetration of the mysteries of faith, under the Holy Spirit's guidance, through contemplative prayer culminating in mystical experience of God.

The interest of monastic authors in spiritual growth led them to important discussions of anthropology, human psychology, and grace, as well as to the phenomenology of spiritual advance, which was seen as developing from *lectio divina* through meditation to prayer (*oratio*) and finally to contemplation. A work of anthropology and psychology, greatly influential until the mid thirteenth century because it was attributed to Augustine, was the *De spiritu et anima* of Alcher of Clairvaux. His compilation drew on various Latin sources for numerous definitions of the soul and classifications of its faculties. Although these are listed with little concern for consistency or harmonization, the wide use of this encyclopedic work reveals the increased interest in such matters among monastic spiritual authors; indeed, the work's influence extended beyond the monasteries to many scholars.

Bernard of Clairvaux combined Augustinian doctrine with important ideas from Eastern authors. The Christian, made in God's image according to *liberum arbitrium* (the faculty of free choice), is called to become, by the divine gift of grace, the likeness of God, which is the freedom to know, choose, possess, and enjoy the good. Sin destroys this likeness and leads a person into dissimilitude; the divine likeness can be recovered by three degrees of humility, by faith and hope, and above all by progress in four degrees of love, that is, from love of self for one's own sake to love of God for one's own sake, then to love of God for God's sake, and finally to love even of oneself for God's sake. Christ's humanity, including the mysteries of his life, attracts the Christian in the human bodily condition and draws the person to the Word, who is the perfect Image of God and who in spiritual espousal becomes the Bridegroom of the individual Christian as well as of the whole church.

Bernard speaks of contemplation by the intellect and by the heart. William of St. Thierry, while elaborating many details of spiritual growth, develops a theory of mystical contemplation summarized in his phrase, derived from Gregory the Great, "Love itself is understanding," that is, loving union with God begets an experiential knowledge beyond imagining or reasoning. In the next century Thomas Aquinas developed a similar theory of knowledge by "connaturality," achieved through love and the Holy Spirit's gifts of wisdom and understanding. Among the many Cistercian authors Aelred of Rievaulx is best known for his remarkable treatise on friendship, modeled on Cicero's *De amicitia* but giving it a profound Christian spiritual application.

THE SCHOOL OF ST. VICTOR

The canons regular of St. Victor, whose school at Paris was founded by William of Champeaux, occupied a position between Abelard's dialectical rigor and the spiritual interests of monastic theologians. Abelard had said that it sufficed to use the tools of philosophy to grasp the meaning of Scripture; Hugh replied that uniquely in the Scriptures "not only the words but things as well have meaning." Philosophers can grasp only the meaning of words, whereas the meaning of things is spoken to us by God, and their meaning is established by "use." Hugh, however, is far from disdaining human reason: in his *Didascalicon* he urges use of the liberal arts and describes twenty-one disciplines that can serve the religious penetration of revelation.

Hugh's influential *De sacramentis* was "a kind of brief summation (*summa*) of all things in an ordered sequence," a systematic exposition of all mysteries (*sacramenta*) of faith designed to help anyone reading the Scriptures. Whereas the logical systems of Abelard's summae neglected history, Hugh's work orders its topics historically, beginning with creation, moving through the sin of Adam and Eve to Christ and his saving work, then to the church and the sacraments, lastly examining the Christian life and the final end of all. Hugh calls this entire ordered structure "the whole of divinity" (*tota divinitas*).

Within Christology, Hugh develops his view that a person is, properly, the rational spirit or soul, for even when separated from the body the soul exists through itself (per se) and so remains a person; united to the body, the soul is one person with the body. Thus for Hugh the soul by itself fulfills Boethius' definition of "person" as "an individual substance of a rational nature."

Spirituality was vitally important to Hugh and to the whole Victorine school. Hugh's commentary on Pseudo-Dionysius the Areopagite's *Celestial Hierarchy* made him among the first in the twelfth century to introduce this author's works, which were to become very influential in theology, including spirituality. In spiritual teaching Richard of St. Victor was outstanding; Cayré speaks of him as "le plus grand théoricien de la mystique au moyen âge" (II, 388). For Richard, as for Bernard of Clairvaux and others, the *Song of Songs* provided the occasion for a commentary related to the spiritual life. In addition, Richard's *Benjamin minor* or *Preparation of the Soul for Contemplation* and his *Benjamin maior* or *The Grace of Contemplation* give a theology of mysticism that was to influence all later periods of the Middle Ages.

The Victorine school also included Andrew of St. Victor, important for his insistence on the literal sense in biblical exegesis; the theologian Achard of St. Victor; Walter of St. Victor, an acid-tongued critic of dialectics in theology and a virulent attacker of Abelard, Gilbert, Lombard, and Peter of Poitiers; and the liturgical poet Adam of St. Victor. Important for philosophy was Godfrey of St. Victor, author of the *Fons philosophiae,* a philosophical poem, and the *Microcosmus,* an allegorical application of the hexaemeron in Genesis to the "microcosm," that is, the human person. This work, which includes elements of physica, psychology, ethics, and theology, is an optimistic product of Christian humanism because it sees in the call of human beings to supernatural life no depreciation of human nature.

PETER LOMBARD

The commentaries on the Psalms and the Pauline Epistles by Lombard and his pupil and posthumous editor, Herbert of Bosham, were known as the *Magna glosatura;* later citations of the *Glossa* often refer to it rather than to the *Glossa ordinaria* and *Glossa interlinearis* or to the *Media glosatura.* Lombard's commentaries contain many topics not treated in his more famous *Sentences,* for example, discussions of the Mystical Body of Christ that were to influence growth of this topic among medieval theologians.

Lombard's *Sentences* combined quotations of patristic sources with a judicious use of dialectics in a way well adapted to the needs of the schools. For his patristic texts he often employs Abelard's works, Otto of Lucca's *Summa sententiarum,* Hugh of St. Victor's *De sacramentis,* and the canonical collections of Ivo of Chartres and Gratian. *Sententiae* in the title refers mainly to its ordered collections of patristic opinions on particular topics, but it also refers to the personal opinions of judgments that Lombard occasionally inserts. Although it was useful for its clear plan, relative brevity, and organic unity, its sparse use of philosophy fostered imprecise terminology that afterward led to fruitless discussions. Nor did the work help to reconcile conflicting authorities.

Lombard's first book deals at length with the Trinity before examining the essential attributes of God. The second book gives texts and discussions concerning creation, grace, sin, and the vices. The third book deals with Christology and then, starting from Christ's virtues, examines Christian virtues. Lombard's presentation of three school opinions on the Incarnation helped focus subsequent discussion of this topic. Christ's saving work is presented in traditional patristic, and especially Augustinian, terms rather than by Anselm's satisfaction theory, which in fact only gradually found entry into some twelfth-century theological traditions. Lombard's fourth book views the sacraments as extensions of Christ's saving work and concludes with eschatology.

The *Sentences* soon began to be glossed, then commented on in greater detail. In the early thirteenth century Alexander of Hales introduced it as a textbook, and soon, despite the protests of Roger Bacon that it was supplanting the Bible, it became the required text for commentary by bachelors in theology aspiring to the mastership.

ETHICS

In addition to the moral and spiritual doctrine of the theologians of the twelfth century, ethics was studied within commentaries on grammatical and rhetorical works in courses on the liberal arts, and some of this teaching was used as well by theologians, who distinguished between the useful but limited ethics of the pagan moralists and theological moral doctrine often influenced by Gregory the Great. Added to such continuous commentary were collections of florilegia giving moral maxims and texts from classical pagan moralists, for example, the *Florilegium Gallicum,* or the *Moralium dogma* attributed to William of Conches, which is a series of quotations from Cicero's *De officiis,* and from Seneca. A certain amount of ancient ethics was also transmitted through Fathers such as Jerome and Augustine. Whether through such indirect avenues or by direct reading of the texts, the Stoic doctrines of Seneca and Cicero attracted and influenced many Christian moralists and theologians, as well as writers on spirituality such as William of St. Thierry.

There were, however, others who dealt directly with ethics. Abelard, for example, applied his nominalist principles to ethical matters. He stressed the individual as the moral agent and insisted on the primacy of personal intention in moral activity rather than on finding goodness or evil in a supposed common nature or in the finality of an act. For him the criterion of good intention is conformity to God's revealed will. Abelard's views that virtue is universally human and that moral life is a coherent unity are in accord with typically Stoic doctrines, which he knew from the works of Seneca. John of Salisbury set forth a fundamental theory of morality based on the ideas of the good, of virtue, and of particular human duties.

This more direct ethical study generally concentrated on human subjects rather than on God or Christ and his New Law; sin as disobedience to God or loss of friendship with God was less emphasized than in theological works. The virtues were examined without reference to Gospel virtues, gifts of the Holy Spirit, or the beatitudes; at the same time, the list of virtues given by Cicero and Macrobius often entered theological summae; this was a normal area where natural ethics and theological moral doctrine would meet. Alan of Lille, who first used the term *theologia moralis* in his *De virtutibus et vitiis,* saw the distinction between virtues as discussed in ethics and virtues of the graced Christian; he also studied the collaboration between nature and grace in moral and spiritual action. His poetical works, the *De planctu naturae* and the *Anticlaudianus,* portray the interplay of the virtues as well as the relations between reason, faith, and theology.

In the late twelfth and thirteenth centuries, the development of universities and the growing maturity of scholastic philosophers and theologians gave rise to two distinct types of debated questions, the more formally organized "disputed question," controlled by the master, and the more spontaneous, unstructured "quodlibetal question," in which the master accepted and answered arguments on any topic whatsoever. Theological summae became more complex and better ordered, and the former glosses of Lombard grew into full commentaries that soon went beyond the limits of Lombard's text to examine many topics only partially linked with his data. Commentaries on Scripture, products of one essential duty of a master in the faculty of theology, increased in volume and profundity, at times incorporating questions within their structure.

In philosophy the newly acquired ethics, psychology, physics, and metaphysics of Aristotle became objects of commentary and debate, to which the works and commentaries of Ibn Sīnā (Avicenna) and, in the 1230's, those of Ibn Rushd (Averroës) brought insights while raising new problems. The works of al-Fārābī and al-Ghazālī, of the Jewish thinkers Solomon ben Judah ibn Gabirol and Moses Maimonides, as well as such Neoplatonic writings as the *Liber de causis,* also became available through translations.

Whereas the logical works of Aristotle had provided the twelfth century with a theory of knowledge and demonstration and had reinforced the largely dialectical or rhetorical theology of that period, the entry of his newly translated works, together with other philosophical writings, gave scholars new concepts and doctrines to be examined within their formal methodology. These included ideas concerning the physical universe, the human person, the soul, human activities and virtues, as well as the concepts of matter and form, potency and act, of being and the transcendental modes of being.

These themes were discussed by professors in the faculty of arts when, after initial ecclesiastical reserve at Paris, the new works were accepted for teaching and comment. At Oxford, where there was more freedom, Alfred of Sareshel commented on Aristotle's *Physics,* John Blund produced a treatise on the soul influenced by Ibn Sīnā through Gundissalinus, and Adam of Buckfield worked extensively on Ibn Rushd. Scholars in the faculties of arts of the developing universities produced commentaries on the metaphysics of Aristotle, and the independent ethical studies of some twelfth-century authors were continued by similar commentaries on Aristotle's ethical works. Knowledge of this independent and mostly unedited work is only gradually coming to light.

Masters of theology also began to use these new works, some with hesitation but others, such as Albertus Magnus and Thomas Aquinas, enthusiastically and yet critically. In England, Robert Grosseteste used a certain amount of Aristotelian science and cosmology but developed it within a Neoplatonic hierarchical view of reality that reinforced his strongly authoritarian notion of the papacy and of his own episcopacy. Richard Fishacre, the first Oxford theologian to comment on Lombard's *Sentences,* applied Aristotelian and Averroist notions in theology. For example, he found their teaching on motion useful to show the existence of a human soul in Christ and for discussing certain aspects of eschatology.

The understanding of the natures of things, giving things their inner consistency and finalities, transformed many discussions and led to a clearer distinction between the natural and the supernatural. Understanding the difference between the soul and its powers led Philip the Chancellor and others after him to distinguish clearly between sanctifying grace in the essence of the soul and virtues such as faith, hope, and charity in the powers. Human activity, its objects or ends, and the virtues aiding it were analyzed more carefully.

Aristotle's teaching on unity and forms of union were applied within Christology; a deeper notion of relation was applied to the Trinity and to creatures with respect to God. Efficient, final, material, and formal causes constantly entered philosophical and theological discussions. Instrumental causality became an important concept, especially for Aquinas, in dealing with many theological areas where the joint actions of God and human persons were involved.

METHOD IN THEOLOGY

The influence of Aristotle's *Posterior Analytics* led to debates on whether theology is a science. Because of the certitude of the truths of faith, William of Auxerre compared them to the evident first principles of other sciences. Others extended this by saying that these truths of faith are the starting points from which theology may reason to conclusions, thereby showing itself to be a science in some sense.

Although all school theologians began practicing theology in this deductive manner and using the new concepts, differences in emphasis appeared. The so-called Augustinian theologians, who can be seen as continuing the Victorine approach and who included the Franciscans and earlier Dominicans, tended to view theology as a practical discipline or science whose function was to lead to an inflaming of the mind through love. Thus Bonaventure stated that the end of theology is "that we may become good." For this group reason and philosophy were useful for considering earthly things but fell short of the higher wisdom concerned with spiritual and eternal things. Hence they were more cautious in use of the new thought. For Bonaventure all the arts are to be "led back to theology" by being organically connected under and with it.

Robert Grosseteste, although a translator of Aristotle's *Ethics,* an enthusiast for mathematics, and developer of a metaphysics of light, insisted, with the Franciscan Roger Bacon, that scriptural commentary should have pride of place in theology; questions should be raised only within such commentary. Each opposed using Lombard's *Sentences* as a textbook, fearing this would lead to the demeaning of Scripture. Natural knowledge should be cultivated in theology to help understand the Scriptures. Yet Grosseteste himself raised theological questions such as whether the Son of God would have become incarnate had there been no sin.

Bacon severely criticized Alexander of Hales and Albertus Magnus for their manner of theologizing. But, when not dealing with theology, Bacon strongly supported experience and experimental science; their role for him is to confirm the conclusions of reason. Moreover, Bacon greatly admired the ethical thought of Aristotle and Seneca. Seeking to unite the ethics of the philosophers and his Christian faith, he frequently quotes each of them in his *Moralis philosophia.*

Others in the Augustinian tradition were less conservative but tended to equate "sacred doctrine" with wisdom and, to some extent, revelation. They viewed it as a science only broadly, that is, as certain knowledge; it cannot be strictly scientific because it deals with God's free contingent acts and not only with universals; also, its principles are not self-evident.

Aquinas replied to such views by applying Aristotle's teaching on subordinated sciences. He held that theology, like a subordinated science, receives its certain first principles, through faith, from the higher and self-evident knowledge or science possessed by God and the blessed in heaven who see God. If not self-evident, these principles given through revelation and received through faith are nevertheless certain, and from them one can argue to conclusions in a truly scientific way. By using the Neoplatonic theme of the procession of all creation from God and its return to God as its end, Aquinas includes contingent salvation history within this science and, by examining the fittingness (*convenientia*) of historical acts, links them with the universal truths of sacred doctrine.

Albertus Magnus and Aquinas adopted Aristotelian philosophy programmatically within their theology but always subordinated its use to their faith, which was deeply nourished by their continual commentaries on the Bible. Each (Albert even more than Aquinas) also preserved many elements of Augustinian and Neoplatonic thought, including that of the Pseudo-Dionysius. In addition, they made considerable use of John of Damascus' *De fide orthodoxa.* Moreover, although Aquinas used Aristotelian concepts and teachings, his own doctrine of *esse,* or the act of existing, went far beyond Aristotle's substantial formalism.

Viewing natures in themselves, with a finality inscribed in their very being, Aquinas sometimes disagreed with the Augustinian theologians, including Bonaventure. Where these, Albert included, held that in all human knowing the mind needs a special illumination from God to attain certitude, Aquinas insisted that God's very creating of human intellects provides sufficient light for natural knowledge and that only regarding supernatural mysteries of faith is added light needed from God.

THE NEW PHILOSOPHIES

Ibn Sīnā's philosophy gave many insights to Western thinkers, for example, his proofs of the existence of God by causality and by comparison of possibility and necessity, as well as the distinction between essence and existence in creatures that he learned from al-Fārābī. In varying degrees many Christian authors, above all Gundissalinus, incorporated elements of Ibn-Sīnā's philosophy into their generally Augustianian outlook. On other points, however, his positions met opposition from Christian thinkers such as William of Auvergne. Ibn Sīnā held that the First Cause can and does create only one immediate effect, the First Intelligence, and that other Intelligences, human souls, and matter are produced by a descending order of causes. Against this, William and others insisted that God is the omnipotent and free creator of all things, including matter. Ibn Sīnā denied creation by God and God's knowledge of individuals; these tenets were rejected as opposed to God's providence. To his doctrine that we have only a possible intellect which receives knowledge from a separate Agent Intellect, Christian thinkers opposed either God's active role in illumination or the sufficiency of an individual Agent Intellect in each person actuating the possible intellect.

Another problem raised by the new thought was Aristotle's and Ibn Rushd's teaching that the universe is eternal, and Ibn Sīnā's doctrine that God created the world eternally. Basing their views on scriptural revelation, Christian thinkers denied that the universe was created eternally, a denial confirmed in 1215 by the Fourth Lateran Council's statement that God created all "from the beginning of time." Most held, on philosophical grounds, that an eternal creation was impossible; Aquinas, however, maintained that although God did not eternally create the world, he could have done so.

PHILOSOPHY OF INDIVIDUATION AND BEING

Whereas Aquinas and others who followed Aristotle more closely looked to matter as the principle of individuation among members of the same species, most maintained some type of Boethian-Gilbertian individuation by forms. A widespread essentialist philosophy of being saw the metaphysical perfection of a thing in terms of its form, essence, or *quo est;* in a creature the various forms coalesce to constitute the concrete subject or *quod est,* so that the metaphysical structure of a being corresponds in such a view to the logical pattern of genus, specific difference, properties, and accidents. The object of metaphysics is thus essential being, whereas existence, even when held to be distinct from essence (as in William of Auvergne), is considered merely a fact on the level of nature together with matter and physical form. For Aquinas, by contrast, the most profound metaphysical perfection of a creature participating in the self-subsisting existing of God, who is Pure Act, is its created act of existing giving actuality to every other perfection in it, including its form and individuating matter. For Aquinas, since angels as pure spiritual beings lack matter of any kind, each angel constitutes a distinct species. Essentialist theologians denied this and thought angelic individuation to be constituted, as in other creatures, through coalescence of formal properties, or, Bonaventure held, through "spiritual" matter.

According to this logical realism the human person is constituted through a threefold distinction achieved by its formal perfections: the distinctions of singularity, of incommunicability, and of dignity. The person is singular and not universal by reason of its unique collection of properties and accidents; it is incommunicable because it enters nothing else as a part; the third distinction, dignity, is in the person because its individual nature is not mixed with or assumed by a nobler form or being. This doctrine was worked out especially within Christology. Since this approach played down personality as a positive perfection, seeing it as merely the fact of not being assumed by another person, theologians such as Philip the Chancellor and Albertus Magnus tried to go beyond it. Aquinas' doctrine of *esse,* distinct from essence, made personality a positive perfection since for him the act of existing, "the most formall of all" and "the most perfect of all," as "it is the actuality of all things, even of forms," actuates the individual so as to make it "a complete substance subsisting through itself separately from others."

Within the human person, the mind, spirit, or soul was for most Augustinians the essential element using the body as an instrument, a doctrine that weakened the substantial unity of human persons. For them, the human composite is constituted by many distinct substantial and accidental forms; on this point Albert joined the Augustinians by accepting a plurality of substantial forms. For Aquinas the human soul is the unique substantial form of the body, needing the body as an instrument for its highest operations of intellectual knowing and loving. The unity of the human person is guaranteed by its one act of existing making the soul to be; in turn the soul communicates existence to the body, thus achieving an integral unity. The doctrine of substantial forms had consequences for Christology. Because Thomas' doctrine of one human substantial form seemed to threaten the continuity between Christ's living and dead body, it met opposition and in 1277, after his death, was condemned by the Dominican archbishop of Canterbury, Robert Kilwardby.

AVERROISM

Although the commentaries of Ibn Rushd (Averroës) on Aristotle greatly helped understanding difficult passages, some of his interpretations and his own personal doctrines raised problems for Christian thinkers. Starting from the experience of motion, he developed a proof for God's existence as Prime Mover that was used in modified form by Aquinas, but his teaching on the eternity of the world and on divine causality as a final but not efficient causality clashed with the Christian doctrine of creation. By asserting that the soul is not spiritual and that there is only one Agent Intellect and one Possible Intellect, he gave human beings the status of a higher animal without personal intellectual knowledge. The individual knows because of the union (*continuatio*) of the separate intellect with the sense powers of the individual. These doctrines of Averroës also compromised human free choice and human immortality.

Siger of Brabant, Boethius of Dacia, and others in the faculty of arts at Paris were strongly influenced by these teachings, which appeared to them to be rationally certain. These tenets were sharply criticized by Albert, Bonaventure, and Thomas Aquinas, and in 1270 Bishop Étienne Tempier of Paris condemned thirteen propositions reflecting this Averroist background as well as some Avicennian roots or, in the question of freedom, Stoic determinism and fatalism. Although Tempier's condemnation seems to suggest that these professors taught the possibility of a double truth, there is no evidence to show they did. They held that if reason conflicted with faith, the higher light of faith must prevail. Boethius of Dacia protested, however, that philosophers have the right to teach positions contrary to faith because these conclusions of reason, which Siger sometimes called "probable," come from a limited faculty of knowing. Boethius held that because the higher light of faith makes one aware of the divine omnipotence and so of the possibility of truths unknowable to the philosopher such as the beginning of the world in time, or the resurrection of the dead, faith must prevail when it disagrees with reason. For his part, Siger always upheld human free will, and in his later works he accepted some of Aquinas' criticisms and abandoned Averroës' notion of intellect.

GOD

The Anselmian approach to the existence of God was accepted by Richard of St. Victor and, with some modifications, by the Franciscan school's *Summa Fratris Alexandri* and by Bonaventure, for whom the essentiality of God dominates the question. Bonaventure argues that God cannot be thought not to be. Once he takes this position, a further proof of God's existence is hardly necessary. Aquinas' existentialism rejects this type of proof as an unwarranted move from thought to real existence. He begins from the experience of motion, causation, contingency, degrees of existing perfections, and order in the universe, and reasons to the need to posit a First Mover, First Cause, Necessary Being, Perfect Being, and Universal Orderer, whom all call or name "God"; these "ways" lead to God as Self-Subsisting Existing Itself, imperfectly but truly and properly known by analogy from creatures who are remotely like their Cause.

Concerning knowledge of God, Augustine's divine exemplarism inspired all theologians of this period, especially Bonaventure, but also Albert and Aquinas. The influential negative theology of the Pseudo-Dionysius helped maintain the sense of God's mysterious transcendence and set limits to any exaggerated use of reason; it also entered the teaching on mystical contemplation of Albert, Bonaventure, and Aquinas. Albert's use of this author was taken up by his disciple, Ulrich of Strasbourg, and their joint teachings strongly influenced German spirituality, especially the later Rhineland mystics.

THE TRINITY

Abelard was accused of holding that only the Father has the fullness of power, and that the Holy Spirit was the soul of the world (a doctrine to be found in William of Conches); Abelard defended his orthodoxy against such interpretations. When Gilbert of Poitiers applied his rules of speculative grammar and metaphysics to the theology of the Trinity (and the Incarnation), he met opposition. According to his rules, one must say, "God is God by divinity" rather than "God is divinity." Further, according to Gilbert, each divine person is distinct from the others by a unique personal property "affixed" to the person, a property not to be identified with the person, at least in predication. To Bernard and other critics this amounted to positing a fourth person and so a quaternity in God.

Since for Gilbert humanity is a form, he judged it incorrect to say that Christ as man is an *id quod* or *aliquid,* for this would imply that Christ as man is a human subject and person; his teaching stood behind the *non est aliquid* doctrine later condemned by Pope Alexander III. Yet Gilbert's philosophy of the subject subsisting under many forms was adopted by many theologians; in Christology, for example, it led to the subsistence theory, the second opinion described in Lombard's *Sentences,* which later became the common opinion.

In his *De sacramentis,* Hugh of St. Victor, like many theologians of this time, followed Augustine in discerning vestiges of the Trinity in all creation and a special image in the human soul by reason of its memory, intellect, and will. The power, wisdom, and goodness of God were appropriated respectively to the Father, Son, and Holy Spirit although each person was held to possess all these divine attributes.

Peter Lombard's *Sentences* belie the frequent cliché that Western theology begins with the divine essence before coming to the divine persons. The first book of his work discusses the Trinity at great length before coming to the divine essential attributes. His statement, taken from Augustine, that "the Father, Son, and Holy Spirit are, as it were, one supreme reality" (*una quaedam summa res*) led Joachim of Fiore to accuse him of accepting four persons in God. Yet his statement was approved by the Fourth Lateran Council, which said: "We believe and confess" this doctrine "together with Master Peter Lombard." The council also denied that the phrase involved a quaternity of persons. This was a remarkable conciliar approbation of an individual theologian whose work, despite earlier opposition from Walter of St. Victor and others, by then had been widely accepted and used by theologians; indeed, even canonists found the work a useful source for canonical texts. Lombard's theology of the Holy Spirit included his personal opinion that the individual Christian's charity is the very person of the Holy Spirit and not some created reality, an opinion that met unanimous rejection from other theologians.

The dictum, drawn from the Pseudo-Dionysius, that goodness is self-diffusive strongly influenced Richard of St. Victor, who used it in an Anselmian attempt to find "necessary reasons" for the trinity of persons in God. After a more traditional study of the divine properties in the first two books of his *De Trinitate,* Richard seeks an argument for the trinity of persons from an analogy mentioned but set aside by Augustine, that of interpersonal love. God's love overflows into another person worthy of his love, who to be worthy must also be divine; these two seek a "consort of love," a "commonly loved" third person so as to have someone to share their generous joyful love.

In trinitarian (and christological) discussions of the period, Boethius' definition of person as "an individual substance of a rational nature" raised difficulties. Richard gave a new definition of person that was to become part of the school tradition. In his view a person "exists through itself alone according to a certain singular mode of rational existence." In this definition *exsistere* signifies not simply the fact or act of existing but also being through oneself (*per se*) and being from another (*ex-sistere*). Two of Richard's trinitarian dicta, however, found less favor: "The substance begot a substance" (understanding "substance" as divine substance), and "The person of the Son is a begotten substance (*substantia genita*)." These statements, taken up by Joachim of Fiore, were condemned by the Fourth Lateran Council.

In studying the Trinity, theologians frequently used the couplet of the Son's generation by nature and the Holy Spirit's procession by love in the will. Albert once suggested and Aquinas in his later works chose the replacement of this nature-will couplet with the intellect-will couplet, making the intellectual conception of the Word prior in thought to, but identical with, the generation of the Son. Augustine had left only partially solved the question why the Holy Spirit is not born as the Son within the Trinity even though this third person proceeds within the identically one nature of the Father and so is, like the Son and any son, the same in nature as the Father. Both Albert and Thomas Aquinas solved this problem by teaching that in the Trinity God's act of willing and loving does not, by reason of the kind of procession it entails, produce a likeness, as does the intellectual generation of the Word-Son. The Holy Spirit is the same in nature as the Father (and Son) not because of the procession by will or love but because this procession terminates within rather than outside the divine nature. In applying Boethius' definition of "person" to the Trinity, Aquinas stressed the element of distinctness in persons and thus viewed the Father, Son, and Holy Spirit as distinct relations sharing the one divine subsistence.

The theology of the missions and indwelling of the persons of the Trinity advanced in the thirteenth century. For Albert and Bonaventure the indwelling is achieved when the graced human person images the exemplarity of divine immanent processions through knowledge and love. The early Aquinas emphasized this aspect but already added what would later be his main view, that the persons dwell in intellectual creatures by becoming intentional objects of their experiential knowledge and love exercised through faith, charity, and the gifts of the Holy Spirit.

The analogy of the Holy Spirit as proceeding in the mutual love between the Father and Son helped Western theologians express the doctrine, reaffirmed by the Fourth Lateran Council, that the Spirit proceeds from the Son as well as from the Father (the doctrine of the *Filioque*). However, since this analogy was not used in the Eastern tradition, their basic reply to the Orthodox rejection of the *Filioque* was Anselm's argument that the Holy Spirit, unless proceeding from the Son, would not be distinct from the Son. A Western attempt to reconcile the two views suggested that, as bond of love, the third person proceeds from the Father alone but, as Spirit, proceeds from both Father and Son. This attempted reconciliation, however, was rejected, together with several other propositions, by the masters of Paris in the 1240's, an action showing the magisterial authority of the corpus of university theologians at this period.

CREATION

Heretical sects of the early thirteenth century viewed matter as evil; some dualists held that matter was created by an evil god. Against them the Fourth Lateran Council affirmed that God is "the Creator of all things visible and invisible, spiritual and corporal," including angels, the material universe, and man. "The devil and other demons," it said, "were created by God good in nature but made themselves evil through themselves." This teaching and the need to resist heresies led to the writing of treatises on the good (*De bono*), as well as to elaboration of the transcendental properties of being (*res, aliquid,* one, true, good), for example, by Philip the Chancellor, Albertus Magnus, and Aquinas.

Theologians taught that God created all things, keeps them in existence by his conserving power, and guides them by a loving providence. Augustinians tended to view this conservation and guidance as staying the innate tendency toward nonbeing of all created being. Aquinas, however, held that spiritual beings and matter, once created and continually conserved by God, will always exist; God could withdraw his conservation, but for Aquinas this is unthinkable of God, nor is there any metaphysical deficiency in the structure of created being to suggest it. Further, for Aquinas, the creature's attainment of its perfection, especially by the free activity of intellectual beings, is part of God's intention in creating and itself glorifies God.

HUMAN DESTINY

In this period, it was commonly held with respect to human destiny that, as Augustine taught, all are *capax Dei* and so are called to a life of blessedness with God, which is the only end that will fulfill them. Although Aquinas discerns finalities inscribed in created natures and speaks of particular natural ends for the human subject, he likewise holds that this subject is *capax Dei,* that is, positively oriented toward God by more than an obediential potency, and insists that the absolutely final, beatifying end of intellectual creatures can only be the vision of God. His doctrine of grace emphasized, in Pauline and Augustinian terms, the primary graciousness of God resulting in a real ontological change in the graced creature, a supernatural qualitative intensification of creaturely existence giving a share in divine life. Aquinas and other theologians of the thirteenth century located the possibility of human merit only within this primary graciousness of God and only in subordinate relationship to the merits won by Christ through his passion and death. Aquinas saw this subordinate human meriting as adding to rather than taking from God's glory since it reveals God as generously allowing creatures a positive if secondary instrumental role in achieving their destiny.

Difficult questions remained, however, owing to Augustine's teachings on predestination. In this period the theory of limbo was developed to soften Augustine's view that unbaptized children suffer some light penalties in hell. The milder position was that although they cannot enter heaven, they exist in a state of natural happiness.

ORIGINAL JUSTICE AND ORIGINAL SIN

Numerous questions were raised about the original state of the first couple, among others whether they were created in grace or whether this and the preternatural gifts (immortality and freedom from ignorance, suffering, and concupiscence) were added to nature after creation. Debates about the nature of original sin turned on the predominant twelfth-century view, derived from Augustine, that it consists in disordered concupiscence, not as an act but as an innate tendency affecting the sensitive powers. Answering arguments that this disorder is not effaced by Baptism, William of Auxerre in the next century concluded that original sin is not precisely the disorder but rather sinful concupiscence, and it is this that is removed by Baptism.

By contrast with the prevailing Augustinian view, Anselm of Canterbury had distinguished original sin from concupiscence by viewing original sin as essentially the privation of that original justice or rectitude of will first enjoyed by Adam and Eve but lost for their descendants by their transgression; from this loss followed the disorder in human nature. Abelard for his part denied that Adam's guilt was transmitted to all his descendants, but this tenet was condemned by the Council of Sens in 1140. Albert, Bonaventure, and Aquinas refined Anselm's position. They distinguished the formal element as loss of original justice and so loss of the mind's and will's order to God and the material element as disordered concupiscence following upon this previous disorder. It is transmitted, Aquinas said, because all Adam's descendants share his primary sin as members of a vast organic whole somewhat as they share Christ's merits as members of his Mystical Body.

MORAL DOCTRINE AND SPIRITUALITY

If Augustine's views on original sin did not prevail, they do seem to have led theologians to adopt a rigorist position on sins of ignorance and on indeliberate movements of the sensitive appetite. These were but two of many debated topics in the field of moral doctrine, which developed greatly in this period, especially as the thirteenth century saw the influx of new psychological and ethical ideas. Also discussed were the relation of intention, synderesis, and conscience to morality; questions of natural and positive law; and the interrelation of practical judgment and the will in human activity. Among these, the introduction of such notions as synderesis, conscience, and natural law was the result of Stoic influence. They were developed in the thirteenth century in combination with Aristotle's teaching on practical reason.

Natural law was generally seen to coincide with reason and to be the supreme law that is the basic norm of moral conduct for all nations. It was held to be immutable in its fundamental principles, allied with an inborn inclination in every human being, present and knowable by an intuition in all, and foundational for every moral or legal prescription.

The way moral doctrine was organized in various summae reveals fundamental choices. William of Auxerre's *Summa aurea,* linking human sin and vices with those of Adam, treats them at great length before the virtues. Philip the Chancellor, however, is much more positive. His *Summa de bono,* after studying the good of nature and the good in general, presents the good of grace, including the theological virtues (faith, hope, and charity) and the cardinal virtues (prudence, fortitude, temperance, and justice); evil and sin are seen as opposed to these goods (an idea first introduced by Hugh of St. Cher). In the influential *Summa Fratris Alexandri* of the Franciscan school, however, laws, negative commands, and precepts dominate the order and discussion of morality. On the other hand, Bonaventure's *Breviloquium* presents Christ's saving work as issuing first of all in the positive gifts of the Holy Spirit (grace, virtues, gifts, and beatitudes); only after this does he discuss the obligations of faith, love, action, precepts, and counsels.

Within Aquinas' unified theology his moral-spiritual doctrine is a most original contribution. For him the human subject images the freedom and self-determination of God by exercising the virtue of prudence and the other acquired and infused virtues, especially faith, hope, and charity, all this under the guidance of the Holy Spirit's gifts. These gifts are needed in addition to the virtues so that the person, directly related to God by the theological virtues, may be helped to live on this lofty supernatural plane. Thus for Aquinas the New Law is the very grace and interior presence of the Holy Spirit. Laws, commands, and even the letter of Scripture are secondary to this, their role being to educate and nurture the person's moral life toward mature Christian self-direction. In the second part of his *Summa theologiae,* God as sole beatitude comes first, then the virtues and gifts of the Spirit by which God is reached through graced activity. Vices and sin are treated as defects in or failures of these virtues. Lastly, the commandments are related to the corresponding virtues and vices but are not given prominence or central organizing force. Aquinas explicitly rejects the Stoic moral depreciation of the passions or emotions. For him these, in so far as they are in accord with reason and will, contain moral good and in fact increase it; conversely, their disaccord with reason and will entails and increases moral evil. Aquinas deals with the moral-spiritual life before his Christology; nevertheless, because he holds Christ to be the unique way of salvation in actual human history, his moral-spiritual doctrine for present human existence has a Christic context.

All this shows that the moral doctrine of these theologians is not something distinct from their spirituality, that is, their teaching about the spiritual life; for them true moral life means seeking union with God in and through Christ and his church. This is clear from their systematic works and even more from their regularly taught scriptural commentaries. Albert, Bonaventure, and Aquinas also wrote special treatises, theologically based, to guide spiritual progress.

THE CHURCH

The Christology of this period had important consequences for the theology of the church and the sacraments. Hugh of St. Victor's *De sacramentis* has a well-organized section on the church immediately following his study of Christ. The church is both Body of Christ unified by the Holy Spirit and an ordered hierarchical structure resembling the heavenly hierarchy that Hugh knew from the Pseudo-Dionysius. Because Hugh asserts that things spiritual are of greater value than things temporal, he concludes that the ecclesiastical order has power over the secular order; he passes on to theologians many canonists' views concerning the papacy and episcopacy in relation to secular rulers. His doctrine on the sacrament of Order and degrees within this sacrament was significant for the entire period examined here.

In the later twelfth century disputed questions began to examine the church as the Mystical Body of Christ, the church's unity, Christ's grace of headship, and membership in the church. Commentaries on Lombard's *Sentences* soon inserted discussions of these topics in the places where Lombard dealt with Christ's grace and knowledge. Summae of the thirteenth century likewise included these topics in their Christological sections. Most theologians taught that Christ's headship makes him the exemplar of all virtues as well as teacher and moral influence for his members. To these considerations Aquinas added the idea that Christ's graced humanity is the instrumental efficient cause of all saving effects in those united to him by faith, charity, and what Aquinas frequently refers to as "the sacraments of faith."

Except for these later discussions, for Hugh of St. Victor's earlier section on the church, and for apologetic works by authors such as Hugh of Rouen, Alan of Lille, Durandus of Huesca, and Moneta of Cremona, there was no distinct treatment of the church by theologians during this whole period. Many elements of ecclesiology were left to canonists, although in the thirteenth century Alexander of Hales, Richard Fishacre, and Albertus Magnus led the way in introducing canonical materials into theology, especially in sacramental theology. In this area many aspects of the theology of the church were treated, for example, in sections on Baptism, the Eucharist, Penance (including the power of the keys and indulgences, where the theology of the papacy's universal power and teaching office was developed, especially by Franciscans and Dominicans). Medieval theologians often used the hierarchical views of Pseudo-Dionysius in ecclesiology. In the thirteenth century, for example, some followed Guido of Orchelles' lead by linking the various grades of Order with the nine grades of the angelic hierarchy, adding the episcopacy and the papacy to the usual seven grades. Others maintained the seven degrees because they saw as fundamental to Order the power to consecrate the Eucharist, possessed by priests equally with bishops and the pope, who were considered superior in dignity but not in Order.

THE SACRAMENTS IN GENERAL

The twelfth and thirteenth centuries saw intense study and thorough systematizing of the theology of the sacraments. Abelard and his school used variations of Augustine's definition of sacrament as "a visible sign of invisible grace." Hugh of St. Victor narrowed this somewhat by stressing the likeness between a sacrament and its effect as well as Christ's institution of sacramental signification (*ex institutione significans*). Lombard used the metaphor of Christ, the Good Samaritan, healing the wounds of sinful humanity by applying the balm of the sacraments; this metaphor and view influenced theologians to see the sacraments primarily as remedies for sin.

Before Lombard and Hugh, the *Summa sententiarum* had distinguished "major" from "minor" sacraments; the former were efficacious signs conferring what they signify. Applying this principle, Lombard defined a sacrament as "a sign of God's grace and a form of invisible grace such that it images this grace and causes it." By introducing causality into the definition of sacrament, Lombard influenced all subsequent sacramental theology, which increasingly asked how the sacraments cause grace. Using this definition, Lombard listed seven sacraments: Baptism, Confirmation, the Eucharist, Penance, Extreme Unction, Order, and Matrimony. These he distinguished from simple sacred signs such as holy water, the sign of the cross, blessings, and blessed objects, which he called "sacramentals."

To solve problems concerning the nonrepetition of Baptism, Confirmation, and Order, and the real presence of Christ in the Eucharist, closer attention was paid to the relation of sign and of reality signified, and a third element was distinguished, called "the sign and reality" (*sacramentum et res*). The visible sign, for example, washing with water together with the words of Baptism, or the consecration of bread and wine, was called "the sign alone" (*sacramentum tantum*), while the final reality signified, for example, the interior cleansing from sin in Baptism or the spiritual nourishment of the soul in the Eucharist, was called "the reality alone" (*res tantum*). In the three nonrepeatable sacraments the intermediate "sign and reality" came to be called the "character" of each sacrament.

Thirteenth-century theologians sought to find the correct Aristotelian category for this sacramental character and usually assigned it to one of the subspecies of quality. For some, like William of Auxerre, the character was a "disposition" for grace; in the *Summa Fratris Alexandri* it was called a "figure," that is, a configuration of the Christian to Christ, the Redeemer, and thereby to the whole Trinity. For Aquinas (in a direction begun by Philip the Chancellor) the character is of the order of worship and gives the Christian a sharing in Christ's priestly worship. Understood within the category of quality, it is a power. The character of Baptism gives a passive power to receive the other sacraments; the characters of Confirmation and Order give different degrees of active power with respect to the sacraments and worship. In the Eucharist the intermediate "sign and reality" was seen to be the Body and Blood of Christ, reception of which effected the "reality alone" of spiritual nourishment and communion with Christ and the members of his Mystical Body.

Theologians tried but found it more difficult to apply the threefold distinction to the other sacraments. Another way to include all the sacraments within one theological system was to use the concept of matter for the sensible gestures or objects and form for the deeper meaning signified in most cases by words. Hugh of St. Cher, the first to write a full commentary on Lombard's *Sentences,* was also the first to discern in all the sacraments a matter and a form, these being understood in the Aristotelian sense of determinable and determining elements.

Although in the twelfth century some theologians held that only certain sacraments caused grace, in the thirteenth century all seven sacraments were viewed as causing grace, although the way they did so was debated. Some judged this causality to be dispositive, while others viewed it as occasional. Aquinas taught that the sacraments were "separated instruments" of God's efficient causality operating through the "conjoined instrument" of the humanity of Christ. He also balanced the causality aspect of the sacraments by insisting on their sign value; in fact, for him the sacraments cause by signifying. However, they are more than causes because they are worshipful acts of God even while signifying and causing the gifts of God in the recipient. One of Aquinas' most important contributions, especially in his later works, was his view that the remedial role of the sacraments, though still important, is secondary to their more positive and primary role as powerful aids to spiritual growth at key moments of individual and social life.

THE EUCHARIST

The intermediate "sign and reality" in the Eucharist was seen to be the Body and Blood of Christ resulting from what, beginning with Rolando Bandinelli in the twelfth century, was called "transubstantiation," that is, the change of the substance (but not of the outward forms or appearances, sometimes called "accidents") of the bread and wine into the Body and Blood of Christ. This eucharistic doctrine, distinguishing outward appearances from the new substance and from the spiritual effects of union, was developed to solve the problems raised by Berengar of Tours in the eleventh century. It was officially accepted by the Fourth Lateran Council in 1215, which said that in the church Jesus Christ is both priest and sacrifice and that "his body and blood are truly contained in the sacrament of the altar under the appearances of bread and wine, the bread having by divine power been transubstantiated (*transsubstantiatis*) into the Body and the wine into the Blood, so that, to complete the mystery of unity, we receive from what is his and he receives from what is ours." It should be noted that the council uses "appearances" (*speciebus*) rather than the more philosophical term "accidents." The "mystery of unity" mentioned in the text is what theologians called the *res tantum* or "the reality alone." Aquinas later described this reality as the unity of the Mystical Body of Christ.

Theologians discussed many other aspects of the Eucharist: its necessity for salvation; the use of leavened or unleavened bread (a sore point between Eastern and Western Christians); what happens when the eucharistic elements are moved locally or divided; how the appearances or accidents continue without their usual substantial subject (Aquinas held that the accident of quantity, sustained by God, supported other accidents such as as the qualities or place of the consecrated species); and the effects of sacramental and spiritual reception of the sacrament (a question debated strongly in the twelfth century). The significance of eucharistic rites was studied in individual works by Hugh of St. Cher and Albertus Magnus and by Aquinas in his *Summa theologiae.* Thomas also composed, in whole or in great part, the Office of Corpus Christi, a feast established universally in the West at this time as a result of the flowering of devotion to Christ "truly present" in this sacrament.

PENANCE

Hugh of St. Cher was the first to achieve a complete assimilation of the sacrament of Penance to the other sacraments through use of the concepts of matter and form. Before him, in the twelfth century, many theologians had distinguished between confession and satisfaction as the external sacrament and interior sorrow or penance as the internal sacrament. For Abelard, interior penance was essential while confession was only relatively necessary. Lombard agreed and also taught that the priest's absolution was a sign showing the reconciliation that had already been achieved by the penitent's loving sorrow, or indicating that some of the punishment due to sin had been remitted.

The Victorines insisted that priestly absolution was strictly necessary for mortal sins. William of Auvergne and Thomas Aquinas later followed this view. For William the priest's absolution perfects the penitent's imperfect sorrow, while Aquinas, in a manner somewhat like Hugh's, held that the confession and expression of sorrow are the quasi matter of the sacrament whereas the absolution is the formal element integrating the confession of sins, the penitent's sorrow, and the priest's absolution into one composite whole.

MATRIMONY

Theologians found some difficulty in accepting Matrimony as a true sacrament: financial arrangements surrounding it suggested the danger of buying and selling grace; it existed before Christ, the founder of sacraments; it involved sexual intercourse, which theologians thought always involved at least a slight sin (Augustine had taught that this ever-present sinfulness was the cause of original sin being transmitted to children in their conception). Lombard, however, listed it among the sacraments even if he said it did not confer grace but was only a "remedy for sin." Reaction against Albigensian and other unorthodox views condemning all marriage and intercourse, as well as further thought about the notion of a sacrament as such, led to a more positive view. Yet it was only in the thirteenth century, and with some hesitation, that theologians came to admit that matrimony conferred grace and even then only through the blessing of the priest. Albert and Aquinas were the most positive; from Aristotle they learned that the pleasure of intercourse, being of nature, must be good. They viewed the sacramental grace of Matrimony as helping to a holy married life, aiding fidelity, and making the union of married persons an image or sign of the faithful union of Christ with his church; this last was the reason they and many others gave for the indissolubility of marriage.

ESCHATOLOGY

A whole range of problems presented themselves to theologians regarding eschatology: the nature of the beatific vision; the question whether knowledge or love constitutes the essence of beatitude; the place and state of heaven, hell, purgatory, and limbo; the individual and the universal judgment, including the circumstances of Christ's final coming and his judgment of all; the circumstances and qualities of the resurrection and glorification of the bodies of the just. This last topic provided a locus for reflections on matters of biology; theologians believed that all that is truly of human nature would share the resurrection and so were led to ask biological questions about what is truly a part of human nature.

Joachim of Fiore's theology of history involved his prediction of a new age of the Holy Spirit to come in the thirteenth century, which would replace the reign of Christ. This aspect of the highly respected abbot's doctrine was opposed by the great theologians of the thirteenth century even though it attracted some groups of Franciscans. Medieval eschatology has sometimes been criticized as overly individualistic, but these debates about Joachim show that this was not necessarily the case, for Joachim's doctrine and the responses it elicited focused attention on the ecclesial or corporate aspects of "the last things." Moreover, it should be recalled that all Scripture was read not only in a literal historical sense but also, in addition to the allegorical and tropological senses, according to the anagogical sense. This sense of Scripture led the biblical interpreter to see the ultimate fulfilment of texts concerning the People of God or the church in Christ's final coming as Savior and Judge not only of individuals but of the whole visible church and indeed of all peoples.

BIBLIOGRAPHY

General works. Philotheus Boehner, *Medieval Logic* (1952); *The Cambridge History of Later Medieval Philosophy,* Norman Kretzmann, Anthony Kenny, and Jan Pinborg, eds. (1982); *The Cambridge History of the Bible,* G. W. H. Lampe, ed., II (1969); Fulbert Cayré, *Patrologie et histoire de la théologie,* II, rev. ed. (1955);

Marie-Dominique Chenu, *La théologie au douzième siècle* (1957), *Nature, Man, and Society in the Twelfth Century*, Jerome Taylor and Lester Little, trans. (1968), and *La théologie comme science au XIIIe siècle*, 3rd ed., rev. (1969); Henri Cloes, "La systématisation théologique pendant la première moitié du XIIe siècle," in *Ephemerides theologicae Lovanienses*, **34** (1958); Yves Congar, *A History of Theology*, Hunter Guthrie, trans. and ed. (1968), 69–127; Frederick Copleston, *A History of Philosophy*, II; *Mediaeval Philosophy* (1950, repr. 1962); Joseph De Ghellinck, *Le mouvement théologique du XIIe siècle*, 2nd ed. (1948); Philippe Delhaye, *Medieval Christian Philosophy*, S. J. Tester, trans. (1960); Pierre Duhem, *Le système du monde: Histoire des doctrines cosmologiques de Platon à Copernic*, IV (1916), 309–575, V (1917), VI (1954); Aimé Forest, Fernand Van Steenberghen, and Maurice de Gandillac, *Le mouvement doctrinal du XIe au XIVe siècle* (1951); Bernhard Geyer, ed., *Die patristische und scholastische Philosophie*, 11th ed. (1928).

Étienne Gilson, "Pourquoi saint Thomas a critiqué saint Augustin," in *Archives d'histoire doctrinale et littéraire du moyen âge*, **1** (1926), *History of Christian Philosophy in the Middle Ages* (1955), and *The Christian Philosophy of St. Thomas Aquinas*, L. K. Shook, trans. (1956); Martin Grabmann, *Die Geschichte der scholastischen Methode*, II (1911, repr. 1961), *Mittelalterliches Geisteslebens*, 3 vols. (1926–1956), and *I divieti ecclesiastici di Aristotele sotto Innocenzo III e Gregorio IX* (1941); Jorge J. E. Gracia, *Introduction to the Problem of Individuation in the Early Middle Ages* (1984); Roland Hissette, *Enquête sur les 219 articles condamnés à Paris le 7 mars 1277* (1977), and "Étienne Tempier et ses condamnations," in *Recherches de théologie ancienne et médiévale*,**47** (1980); *The History of the University of Oxford*, I, *The Early Oxford Schools*, J. I. Catto, ed. (1984); David Knowles, "The Middle Ages, 604–1350," in *A History of Christian Doctrine*, Hubert Cunliffe-Jones, ed. (1978); Artur Landgraf, *Dogmengeschichte der Frühscholastik*, 8 vols. (1952–1956), and *Introduction à l'histoire de la litterature theologique de la scolastique naissante*, Albert-M. Landry, ed., Louis-B. Geiger, trans. (1973); Jean Leclercq, *The Love of Learning and the Desire for God*, Catherine Misrahi, trans. (1961); Jean Leclercq, François Vandenbrouke, and Louis Bouyer, *A History of Christian Spirituality*, II, *The Spirituality of the Middle Ages*, the Benedictines of Holme Eden Abbey, trans. (1968); Gordon Leff, *Medieval Thought* (1958); Odon Lottin, *Psychologie et morale au XIIe et XIIIe siècles*, 6 vols. in 8 (1942–1960); Henri de Lubac, *Exégèse médiévale*, 4 vols. (1959–1964).

David Edward Luscombe, *The School of Peter Abelard* (1969); Raoul Manselli, *La religion populaire au moyen âge: Problèmes de méthode et d'histoire* (1975), and *Il secolo XII: Religione popolare ed eresia*, 3rd ed. (1983); Armand A. Maurer, *Medieval Philosophy*, 2nd ed. (1982); Pierre Michaud-Quantin, *Sommes de casuistique et manuels de confession au moyen âge (XII–XVI siècles)* (1962), and *Études sur le vocabulaire philosophique du moyen âge* (1971); *The Oxford Dictionary of the Christian Church*, F. L. Cross and E. A. Livingstone, eds., 2nd ed. (1974); Jaroslav Pelikan, *The Christian Tradition*, III, *The Growth of Medieval Theology (600–1300)* (1978); Pierre Riché and Guy Lobrichon, eds., *Le moyen âge et la Bible* (1984); Reinhold Seeberg, *Lehrbuch der Dogmengeschichte*, III, *Die Dogmengeschichte des Mittelalters*, 4th ed. (1930, repr. 1953–1954), and *Text-book of the History of Doctrines*, Charles E. Hay, trans., II (1956), 57–146; Beryl Smalley, *The Study of the Bible in the Middle Ages*, 3rd ed., rev. (1983); Fernand Van Steenberghen, *La philosophie au XIIIe siècle* (1966), *Aristotle in the West*, Leonard Johnston, trans., 2nd ed. (1970), *Introduction à l'étude de la philosophie médiévale* (1974), and *Thomas Aquinas and Radical Aristotelianism* (1980); François Vandenbrouke, *La morale monastique du XIe au XVIe siècle* (1966); Gerard Verbeke, *The Presence of Stoicism in Medieval Thought* (1983); Paul Vignaux, *Philosophy in the Middle Ages*, E. C. Hall, trans. (1959); Georg Wieland, *Ethica, scientia practica: Die Anfänge der philosophischen Ethik im 13. Jahrhundert* (1981).

Studies on specific themes. Paul Anciaux, *La théologie du sacrement de pénitence au XIIe siècle* (1949); Johann Auer, *Die Entwicklung der Gnadenlehre in der Hochscholastik*, 2 vols. (1942–1951); Camille Bérubé, *La connaissance de l'individuel au moyen âge* (1964); Yves Congar, *L'église: De saint Augustin à l'époque moderne* (1970); Francis L. B. Cunningham, *The Indwelling of the Trinity: A Historico-Doctrinal Study of the Theory of St. Thomas Aquinas* (1955); Augustinus Daniels, *Quellenbeiträge und Untersuchungen zur Geschichte der Gottesbeweise im dreizehnten Jahrhundert* (1909); Bruno Decker, *Die Entwicklung der Lehre von der prophetischen Offenbarung von Wilhelm von Auxerre bis zu Thomas vōn Aquin* (1940); Georg Englhardt, *Die Entwicklung der dogmatischen Glaubenspsychologie in der mittelalterlichen Scholastik vom Abaelardstreit (um 1140) bis zu Philipp dem Kanzler (gest. 1236)* (1933); Damien van den Eynde, *Les définitions des sacrements pendant la première période de la théologie scholastique (1050–1240)* (1950); Josef Finkenzeller, *Die Lehre von den Sakramenten im allgemeinen: Von der Schrift bis zur Scholastik*, Handbuch der Dogmengeschichte, IV, fasc. 1a (1980); Edmund J. Fortman, *The Triune God: A Historical Study of the Doctrine of the Trinity* (1972, repr. 1982); Adrian Fuerst, *An Historical Study of the Doctrine of the Omnipresence of God in Selected Writings Between 1220–1270* (1951); Jean Galot, *La nature du caractère sacramentel: Étude de théologie médiévale*, 2nd ed. (1958); Louis Bertrand Gillon, *La théorie des oppositions et la théologie du péché au XIIIe siècle* (1937);

Étienne Gilson, "La notion d'existence chez Guillaume d'Auvergne," in *Archives d'histoire doctrinale et littéraire du moyen âge,* **21** (1946), and "Notes pour l'histoire de la cause efficiente," *ibid.,* **37** (1962); Elisabeth Gössmann, *Metaphysik und Heilsgeschichte: Eine theologische Untersuchung der Summa Halensis (Alexander von Hales)* (1964); Amélie Marie Goichon, *La distinction de l'essence et de l'existence d'après Ibn Sinā (Avicenne)* (1937), and *The Philosophy of Avicenna and Its Influence on Medieval Europe,* M. S. Khan, trans. (1969); Johannes Gründel, *Die Lehre von den Umständen der menschlichen Handlung im Mittelalter* (1963); Roger Guindon, *Béatitude et théologie morale chez saint Thomas d'Aquin* (1956); Nikolaus M. Häring, "The Case of Gilbert de la Porrée, Bishop of Poitiers (1142–1154)," in *Mediaeval Studies,* **13** (1951), "Character, Signum und Signaculum: Die Einführung in die Sakramententheologie des 12. Jahrhunderts," in *Scholastik,* **31** (1956), and "Sprachlogische und philosophische Voraussetzungen zum Verständnis der Christologie Gilberts von Poitiers," *ibid.,* **32** (1957); Klaus Hedwig, *Sphaera lucis: Studien zur Intelligibilität des Seienden im Kontext der mittelalterlichen Lichtspekulation* (1980); Ludwig Hödl, *Die Geschichte der scholastischen Literatur und der Theologie der Schlüsselgewalt* (1960); Robert Javelot, *Image et ressemblance au douzième siècle,* 2 vols. (1967); Wendelin Knoch, *Die Einsetzung der Sakramente durch Christus: Eine Untersuchung der Sakramententheorie der Frühscholastik von Anselm von Laon bis zu Wilhelm von Auxerre* (1960); Pius Künzle, *Das Verhältnis der Seele zu ihren Potenzen: Problemgeschichteliche Untersuchungen von Augustin bis und mit Thomas von Aquin* (1956); Gabriel Le Bras, "Mariage," in *Dictionnaire de théologie catholique,* IX, pt. 1 (1927), 2134–2220.

Kilian F. Lynch, *The Sacrament of Confirmation in the Early-middle Scholastic Period* (1957); Joseph Martos, *Doors to the Sacred: A Historical Introduction to Sacraments in the Catholic Church* (1982); James J. Megivern, *Concomitance and Communion: A Study in Eucharistic Doctrine and Practice* (1963); Michael Müller, *Die Lehre des hl. Augustinus von der Paradiesesehe und ihre Auswirkung in der Sexualethik des 12. und 13. Jahrhunderts bis Thomas von Aquin* (1954); Burkhard Neunheuser, *Eucharistie im Mittelalter und Neuzeit,* Handbuch der Dogmengeschichte, IV, fasc. 4b (1963); Joseph Marie Parent, *La doctrine de la creation dans l'école de Chartres: Étude et textes* (1938); Walter H. Principe, *The Theology of the Hypostatic Union in the Early Thirteenth Century,* 4 vols. (1963–1975); John Francis Quinn, *The Historical Constitution of St. Bonaventure's Philosophy* (1973); Heinrich J. F. Reinhardt, *Die Ehelehre der Schule des Anselm von Laon* (1974); Christopher Ryan, "Man's Free Will in the Works of Siger of Brabant," in *Mediaeval Studies,* **45** (1983); Jean Pierre Torrell, *Théorie de la prophétie et philosophie de la connaissance aux environs de 1230: La contribution d'Hugues de Saint-Cher* (1977); Roland de Vaux, *Notes et textes sur l'avicennisme latin au confins des XIIe–XIIIe siècles* (1934); Nikolaus Wicki, *Die Lehre von der himmlischen Seligkeit in der mittelalterlichen Scholastik von Petrus Lombardus bis Thomas von Aquin* (1954); Tomás Zepeda Rincón, *El matrimonio: Misterio y signo,* III, *Siglos IX–XIII* (1971), pts. 2–3.

WALTER H. PRINCIPE

[See also **Albigensians; Aristotle in the Middle Ages; Baptism; Bible; Carthusians; Christology; Church; Cistercian Order; Confession; Confirmation; Councils, Western; Dialectic; Dominicans; Dualism; Ecclesiology; Essence and Existence; Exegesis, Latin; Extreme Unction; Family and Marriage, Western European; Filioque; Florilegia; Franciscans; Indulgences; Mass; Monasticism; Mysticism; Nominalism; Oxford University; Paris, University of; Penance and Penitentials; Proverbs and Sententiae; Quaestiones; Scholasticism; Schools, Cathedral; Synagogue; Talmud; Theology, Schools of; Thomism and Its Opponents; Trinitarian Doctrine; Universities;** and individual philosophers and theologians.]

PHILOSOPHY AND THEOLOGY, WESTERN EUROPEAN: THIRTEENTH-CENTURY CRISIS. What is noteworthy about the thirteenth-century crisis between philosophy and theology is that it took over 1,000 years to develop and reached a resolution of sorts only three centuries later when Bacon and Descartes decided to pursue philosophy completely apart from theology.

From the fourth through the thirteenth centuries nearly all philosophical speculation in the Western tradition was done by theologians seeking a rational understanding of their Christian faith. Without denying the distinction between philosophy and theology, they held that the proper role of philosophy was as a handmaiden to theology.

By about 1265 at the University of Paris a growing number of masters in the faculty of arts were beginning to pursue philosophy for its own sake, quite apart from any theological considerations and seemingly regardless of whether their conclusions contradicted tenets of their own religious faith.

A number of converging factors accounted for this departure from eight centuries of philosophizing solely within the context of a faith seeking understanding. First was the sudden increase of available philosophical source material occasioned by contacts with the Islamic world. Within the span of decades, firsthand knowledge of Aristotle went from only two of his logical works to include the whole of his logic, his physics, metaphysics, ethics, politics, and psychology. In addition, works by Islamic philosophers inspired by both Aristotelian and Neoplatonic sources became available.

A second converging factor was the development of the university. Those at Oxford and Paris soon became the centers of intellectual development and formation within Christendom. By 1255, a Parisian student wishing to enter one of the professional faculties of law, medicine, or theology had first to become a master of arts. This seven-year course required a detailed study of all the works of Aristotle as well as the traditional authors of the trivium and quadrivium. Some masters of arts made a career of teaching in that faculty and provided leadership to a new movement, inspired by the works of Aristotle and the example of Ibn Rushd (Averroës) of pursuing a purely philosophical wisdom apart from theological concerns.

Some results of these pursuits quickly aroused the opposition of theologians. For example, given that Aristotle held that all coming-into-being took place through motion, then it could be demonstrated that the world had no beginning in time, which in turn entailed the eternity of species, including man. Further, given that immateriality was a necessary condition of incorruptibility and that man is a material substance, then one could not speak philosophically of personal immortality. Moreover, for Aristotle the highest Being is an Intelligence whose entire perfection consists in an eternal act of self-knowing, thus God could not be said to know, much less have a care for, men.

Theological opposition to these denials of Divine Providence, personal immortality, and creation in time was diverse. One sort came from Thomas Aquinas, who sought to challenge these positions on their own, that is, philosophical grounds. He was convinced that true philosophy and revelation could not be in contradiction for, after all, God is the author both of revealed truth and of man's rational power to acquire truth by natural means. To combat what he considered erroneous interpretations of the philosophers, Aquinas engaged in a massive program of writing commentaries on the bulk of Aristotle's works.

Another sort of opposition, led by Bonaventure, was mainly denunciatory. In a series of Lenten sermons and conferences in 1267 and 1268, he condemned the new ways of philosophizing as improper and as imperiling basic tenets of divinely revealed truth.

On 10 December 1270, Bishop Étienne Tempier of Paris formally condemned "all those who would knowingly teach or assert" any of a list of thirteen propositions regarding the eternity of the world, a single intellect for all men, and denials of both Divine Providence and human freedom of choice.

Two of the acknowledged leaders of this new breed of thinker in the faculty of arts were Siger of Brabant and Boethius of Dacia. Siger reacted to the episcopal condemnation by asserting, each time he dealt with a theologically sensitive issue, that he was merely setting forth the views of the philosophers, even though they were not the truth. In one text he added that "since a philosopher, however outstanding, could err in many matters, one ought not deny a truth of the Catholic Faith because of some philosophical argument, even though one did not know how to refute it."

The reaction of Boethius, in his *On the Eternity of the World,* was to make an impassioned plea for the right of philosophers to carry on their properly philosophical work without being subject to outside (read theological or episcopal) interference. After rigorously separating philosophy and the faith in defining their aims and procedures, he vigorously affirmed their fundamental concord provided, of course, they stuck to their respective domains. He also denounced those who were asserting that one could not be a philosopher and remain a Christian.

To many theologians, however, these and other positions were tantamount to asserting that there could be a "double truth," one for philosophy and another for theology, and on 7 March 1277 Bishop Tempier issued a new solemn condemnation of 219 propositions. All those who would profess any of these errors, or "have the audacity to defend or sustain them in any way," were subject to excommunication. Given the preeminence of the University of Paris, the effects of this local decree were felt throughout medieval Christendom. While it did not halt the study of philosophy independent of theological concerns, it did change theological perspectives. The confident use of philosophy within theology of an Aquinas gave way to more cautious, even hostile, attitudes toward philosophy. This new theological suspicion of philosophy and the philosophical indifference to theology certainly prepared the way for their ultimate divorce in the seventeenth century.

BIBLIOGRAPHY

Étienne Gilson, *History of Christian Philosophy in the Middle Ages* (1955), 387–410; Roland Hissette, *Enquête sur les 219 articles condamnés à Paris le 7 mars 1277* (1977).

WILLIAM DUNPHY

[See also **Aquinas, St. Thomas; Aristotle in the Middle Ages; Bonaventure, St.; Neoplatonism; Oxford University; Paris, University of; Quadrivium; Rushd, Ibn; Siger of Brabant; Trivium.**]

PHILOSOPHY AND THEOLOGY, WESTERN EUROPEAN: LATE MEDIEVAL. Theology, as an intellectual discipline, changed dramatically in the first three-quarters of the thirteenth century. Having encountered the newly translated works of Aristotle during their preparatory studies in the arts faculty, professors and students progressively brought to their theological studies both new methods and new content. Aristotle's newly available logical works, particularly the *Posterior Analytics,* challenged theologians on their method. The more slowly assimilated "content" or nonlogical works, especially in connection with Arabian commentaries on Aristotle's corpus, forced them to reconsider their views of God, his relation to the world, creation itself, causality, the nature and actions of man, and the other manifold connections between the more deliberately defined areas of the "natural" and the "supernatural."

THEOLOGY AS A SCIENTIFIC DISCIPLINE

During the earlier part of the thirteenth century when a university theologian asked, "Is theology science?" the answer would almost automatically be yes. For early-thirteenth-century authors "scientific" meant "having a universal dimension"; and even though theology studied the individual historical events involving God and his people, it studied the Scriptures in a universal way, searching for universal models of faith (Abraham) or patient suffering (Job), or looking at God as the creator of all things or at Christ as the universal redeemer of all men. But as Aristotle's more exacting conditions for scientific investigation became better known in university circles, the main theological question became, "Is theology a science in Aristotle's strict sense of the term?" Thomas Aquinas' distinction on this question underscores the change of perspective.

For Aquinas (1224–1274), Aristotle does offer a scientific model that can be applied to the teaching of Christian revelation. Aristotle himself did not demand that every science had to start with evident principles. He argued that optics could be a true science even though it did not itself investigate many of the principles it borrowed from geometry. Optics, as a subaltern science, received such borrowed principles from the subalternating science of geometry where they were properly and formally established as true. Aquinas admitted, of course, that theology did not provide evidence establishing the revealed principles it employed in its development. Yet, in a way parallel to Aristotle's subaltern science model, theology could be viewed as a true science borrowing its revealed principles from a subalternating science that God and the blessed possess of these same principles. God and the blessed have the evidence for these truths, and God in his revelation has passed on these principles to believers the way a geometrician passes them on to a student of optics. If Aristotle considered optics a science, though based on borrowed principles, so he could reasonably be expected to admit that theology could be a subaltern science.

Godfrey of Fontaines (*d.* 1306/1309), in his *Quodlibet IV* of 1287, accepted neither the logic of the argument nor the simile. For him Aristotle's view of science carries with it a twofold certitude: the certitude of evidence and the certitude of undoubting adherence. Formally correct arguments based on premises accepted by faith have for the believer the power to compel their acceptance; they have the certitude of adherence, and thus differ from mere opinions. However, such arguments are not based on evident principles, so they differ from science in the Aristotelian sense of the term because they lack the type of certitude guaranteed by evidence. Neither does it serve any purpose to appeal to Aristotle's subaltern model of geometry and optics. The student of optics who borrows his principles from geometry could always go back to the geometrician and demand the evidence that guarantees the borrowed principles. A theologian cannot go back to the revealed source of his premises and obtain their evidence. Although these revealed principles may be evident to God and the blessed and thus are evident in themselves, still this is of no present advantage to one studying theology without such evidence. In itself or for the blessed, theology might be a science with both the certitude of evidence and the certitude of undoubting adherence; but for a theologian in this life there is not the twofold certitude demanded by Aristotle's view of science.

In regard to the scientific character of theology Thomas Aquinas had his disciples throughout the whole of the Middle Ages. The author of the *Correctorium Corruptorii "Quare"* at the end of the thirteenth century defended him; Denys the Carthusian (*d.* 1471) repeated him; Johann Eck (*d.* 1543) summarized him; John Capreolus (*d.* 1444) and Thomas de Vio Cajetan (*d.* 1534) attempted to show that the main medieval developments regarding the nature of theology outside the Thomistic tradition were already practiced by St. Thomas in his works.

Godfrey's criticism of Aquinas' subaltern science position garnered support from John Duns Scotus (*d.* 1308), Peter Aureoli (*d.* 1322), William of Ockham (*d.* 1347), Gregory of Rimini (*d.* 1358), and their many followers. In the writings of non-Thomistic authors after Godfrey of Fontaines we find an effort to avoid what they consider two extremes: one that would claim too much for theology as a whole—namely, that its truths are as scientific as optics; the other that would hold that theology provides no evidence at all for the contents of revealed truth but merely arranges and interrelates them according to a scientific method. In avoiding these two extremes authors like Peter Aureoli, who commented on the *Sentences* of Peter Lombard at Paris in 1316–1318, developed the theory of declarative theology, while Gregory of Rimini, who began his lectures on the *Sentences* at Paris in 1343, constructed the theory of deductive theology.

Aureoli realized that many different types of intellectual activities legitimately go on in theology and that one could not reasonably limit that world to what is properly theological discourse. Sometimes, for example, theologians are no different than metaphysicians; when they argue for the unicity or infinity of God they do so demonstratively from necessary and naturally known propositions that could force the intellectual assent of a pagan philosopher. When theologians argue in this way often enough they develop a certain facility or habit; yet it is a metaphysical habit, not a properly theological one.

At other times theologians are quite different from metaphysicians. They argue from premises that have their origin in faith. In arguing correctly from premises rooted in revelation they can produce conclusions that are not evident in the way metaphysical conclusions are, but that are nonetheless certain, provided the argument consists of two revealed premises or one revealed and one necessary premise. An example of the latter type could be: In Christ there are two intellectual natures, one divine and one human; every intellectual nature has its own will; therefore, in Christ there are two wills, one divine and one human. Such a conclusion is held by faith, and Aureoli asserted that by arguments of this kind one does not acquire any habit distinct from faith. You hold unhesitatingly to the conclusion from faith, not from evidence. What takes place here is a specification or explication of faith.

Sometimes, furthermore, theologians may begin with premises that are based on faith and join them in their arguments to premises that are probable. The end result is a conclusion that is opinion. In many questions of theological treatises this procedure is the type of argument in play; it provides us with the opinions of theologians.

Granting the precision of all this detailed analysis of the knowledge value of various conclusions, and realizing that a great deal of effort in theology is given to such deductive activity, Aureoli thought that we had not yet come to what theology is properly about. Theologians, in carrying out their proper role, do not focus on conclusions drawn from articles of faith. Rather they center themselves on premises or principles, certain revealed truths that have been determined by the church—these are the articles of faith. They do not start with them as principles and unfold new conclusions of varying worth, depending on the other premises they use, but rather they focus on these very articles of faith and attempt to bring clarity to them. This, for Aureoli, is the discipline of the theologian that is most properly theological. It is not science, since they do not demonstrate such truths. Neither is it faith, since they already believe these truths before they attempt to bring clarity to them. Nor is it opinion, since they bring forth arguments from other sciences that support the articles of faith, or explain the meaning of the terms of these articles, or respond to doubts raised against them; and it is not opinion because such operations do not bring with them any hesitancy regarding the truths of faith. The theologian thus develops a habit distinct from faith, allowing him to make more clear what he already unhesitatingly believes. It was, according to Aureoli, this type of developed ability that the *quaestiones* of the theologians, the books of *sententiae,* the writings of the Fathers, and the lectures and expositions of Scripture were intended to foster. A theologian in the proper sense of the term, in contrast to the ordinary believer, is said to understand to some degree what he believes and is "to make a defense to any one who calls you to account for the hope that is in you" (1 Pet. 3:15). He knows how "to defend the faith against the impious and strengthen it in the minds of the pious" (Augustine, *De Trinitate,* XIV, c. 1). In short, a theologian differs from a simple believer in just these respects: he has developed an ability to explain terms, he can consider and respond to objections, and he is able to offer examples and supply probable arguments for the truths of faith.

So, in effect, a theologian performs a number of acts that show that he has developed many intellectual virtues. He does at times demonstrate certain truths, not as theologian but as metaphysician. And in this activity he does produce science in the strict Aristotelian sense of the term in regard to some truths. Furthermore, he makes many other deductions that render the content of the faith more explicit or provide suitable theological opinion regarding the truths of faith. But in a more special and proper way a theologian as theologian clarifies, defends, and offers probable arguments for the mysteries of faith, and he explains the terms expressing these mysteries. He provides insight. So if declarative theology is to be classified according to the catalog of intellectual virtues Aristotle provides in the *Nicomachean Ethics,* VI, it is wisdom, that is, "the science of and insight into things which are the noblest by nature." It is not wisdom under the scientific aspect of wisdom, but rather under the understanding or insight aspect of wisdom, for it brings light, understanding, clarification, or insight into the noblest things by nature, that is, the divine mysteries of Christian faith.

Gregory of Rimini, the great champion of deductive theology, simply passed over the complexity of Aureoli's own analysis of the truth and certainty value of the various conclusions arrived at by theologians. He centered his attention on Peter's insistence that theology, properly speaking, is declarative. He attacked this stance as a one-sided accent and veered strongly toward the opposite pole, arguing that the proper work of the theologian is to extend the content of belief. If a person accepts the truth of sacred Scripture, and furthermore is adept at logic, then reflection on sacred Scripture will bring him to new conclusions. This is, according to Gregory, the situation with a theologian, for a theologian sees many truths that are not formally contained as such in sacred Scripture, but that follow necessarily from what is contained there. Now whether these truths are articles of faith or not, whether they are knowable or known through other sciences or not, and whether they are determined as revealed truths by the church or not, he sees that they necessarily flow from what is formally revealed as such in sacred Scripture. These are what Rimini means by theological conclusions. The theologian in his proper role sees that these truths demanded by logic must receive the same force of assent as the truths formally found in sacred Scripture, and that they must be admitted as unhesitatingly as the principles or premises found formally in sacred Scripture itself. Theology thus extends the content of faith. A theologian develops a *habitus creditivus,* a developed ability that extends the believer's faith to its further necessary logical implications.

Generally speaking, both the declarative theology of Aureoli and the deductive theology of Rimini were viewed as extreme polarities when they were taken as exclusive positions. Peter of Candia (later Pope Alexander V, *d.* 1410), when he delivered his lectures on Lombard's *Sentences* at Paris from 1378 to 1380, argued that theologians ought to develop many habits—they should be excellent logicians, metaphysicians, and philosophers of nature. However, theologians as theologians should develop properly theological habits, and these are the declarative and deductive abilities stressed by Aureoli and Rimini. Both these properly theological habits, nonetheless, must be suitably balanced and not developed in exclusion, for both are legitimate and necessary habits of the theologian as such.

Parallel to the efforts to achieve a suitable balance for the scientific character of theology during the period after Aquinas, there were many other attempts to bring balance to what were seen as other excesses in the intellectual world during this time. The influence of Aristotle on Christian thought, for example, was judged by many as increasingly excessive. Franciscans, like John Peckham (*d.* 1292) and William de la Mare (*d. ca.* 1290), tried to restore the prestige of St. Augustine and even stimulated a vain effort to create a systematic Augustinian philosophy as a substitute for the Aristotelian metaphysical system then dominating the arts faculty. Augustine's Christian wisdom was also redeveloped and fostered by the secular priest, Henry of Ghent (*d.*

1293), and his Carmelite follower, Gerard of Bologna (*d.* 1317). The Hermits of St. Augustine (Augustinian friars) raised their own Augustinian banner under Egidius Colonna (*d.* 1316), and it was carried through the medieval centuries by Augustinus Triumphus (*d.* 1328), Gregory of Rimini (*d.* 1358), Alphonsus Vargas (*d.* 1366), Hugolinus of Orvieto (*d.* 1373), John Klenkok (*d.* 1374), Augustine Favaroni (*d. ca.* 1443), and many others.

Many also saw a problem with the decidedly academic character that theology had developed and the excessive honor given to the *doctores theologiae*. Theology had, in their judgment, lost its biblical roots and its essential spiritual and pastoral aspects. In a compensatory manner they tried to redress the imbalance. Some favored the more mystical tradition of John Scottus Eriugena (*d.* 879) and Pseudo-Dionysius the Areopagite (sixth century), as in the case of Meister Eckhart (*d. ca.* 1328) and his disciples, John Tauler (*d.* 1361), Henry Suso (*d.* 1365), and Jan van Ruusbroec (*d.* 1381). Others attempted to lead university theology in broader, more balanced theoretical, moral, and religious directions. This can be seen in the criticisms John Gerson (*d.* 1429) made about Paris, the university where he was chancellor, and his appeal for a return to the tradition of St. Anselm and St. Bonaventure. Nicholas of Cusa (*d.* 1464), likewise, protested the predominance of "the Aristotelian sect," and attempted to achieve a new synthesis, reintroducing the thinking of Thierry of Chartres (*d.* after 1151), Gilbert of Poitiers (*d.* 1154), and John of Salisbury (*d.* 1180) from the early age of Scholasticism, and the Platonism of Calcidius (*fl. ca.* 400), Macrobius (*fl. ca.* 400), "Hermes Trismegistus" (between 100 and 300), and Pseudo-Dionysius from the ancient world. Nicholas' aim was to overcome the imbalances and tendencies toward opposition he found in Aristotelian thought and bring a greater unity to the understanding of a universe created by the Christian God. Denys the Carthusian, too, aimed at a more proper synthesis between scholastic theology and mysticism. He made a staggering compilation of his vast medieval inheritance that attempted to show that a deliberate ecclecticism is much more intellectually virtuous than an unbalanced loyalty to a one-sided movement.

Not all efforts at recovering the spiritual and pastoral elements of the Christian tradition were made by trying to achieve an alternative or a broader theological base. Some attempts cut theological ties completely and constructed a more pious form of spirituality, such as that which Geert Groote (*d.* 1384) established for the Brothers of the Common Life. Of this type, likewise, is the masterpiece of Thomas à Kempis (*d.* 1471), *Imitation of Christ.*

Such tensions as these, between Aristotelian and Augustinian intellectual movements in theology, and between the demands of academic excellence and spirituality, were paralleled in many other areas of theology during the fourteenth and fifteenth centuries. The harmony between nature and grace, reason and faith, study and prayerful contemplation, sometimes approached and frequently only hoped for in different ways by different theologians in the thirteenth century, became a more fading dream. The real differences and tensions between pagan philosophy and Christian belief, and between the earthly kingdom and the Christian church, showed themselves most forcefully in the fourteenth and fifteenth centuries. The medieval intellectual synthesis, to the extent that it was achieved, was breaking down into its component elements.

THE CONTENT OF THEOLOGY

Not only did the formal structure and character of theology as a discipline alter dramatically during the later Middle Ages, but so did the treatment of its content. In the *Summa theologica* of Alexander of Hales (*d.* 1245), compiled shortly before the era of Thomas Aquinas, there are 222 citations from Aristotle's logical works, 260 quotations from the *Metaphysics,* 234 references to the *Physics,* and 188 citations from the treatise *On the Soul.* Despite over 900 citations from Aristotle's works Alexander shows no deep knowledge of the philosopher. Roger Bacon noted that Alexander himself never studied the *Physics* or the *Metaphysics* when he studied or taught in the arts faculty. His *Summa,* Bacon maintained, is weaker than all the other summae of the era and contains a lot of philosophical errors; it employs many quotations from Aristotle's works, but only for the sake of vanity.

On the other hand, Thomas Aquinas had such a masterful command of Aristotle's work that he could build his own Aristotelian philosophy within a Christian context. If the philosophy Aquinas developed differed from that of Aristotle, certainly one could not accuse him of not understanding the philosopher who most influenced him. Yet Aquinas was primarily a theologian, and as he attempted to defend, understand, and strengthen the Christian faith he did not abandon Aristotle at the arts faculty door, nor did he bring him along simply for ornamentation. Neither did he subordinate his Christian faith to Aristotle's legacy. Thomas' philosophically well-developed, Aristotle-inspired, metaphysical, cosmological, psychological, and ethical themes provide the strongest elements in the intellectual structure of his theology; it is reason at the service of faith. God's being, knowledge, power, love, and creativity were discussed both with and against Aristotle. The theological treatment of man's nature, his goals, activities, virtues, and vices show the rich influence of Aristotle's *On the Soul* and the *Nicomachean Ethics.* Thomas' study of the world and its creation is a careful effort to balance the valid points of Aristotle's *Physics,* the legitimate developments of his own metaphysical and physical insights, and the truths of the Christian faith. Later authors may have differed with Aquinas on the interpretation of Aristotle and his commentators, or on the philosophy that he developed under their inspiration, but for the most part in doing so they either provided alternate interpretations of Aristotle's texts or formed alternate philosophies, still strongly influenced by Aristotle, to serve their theological needs.

One instance of the theologians' battles over the positions of Aristotle, which also illustrates their efforts to deal with the problems raised or reset by Aristotle and his commentators, deals with the nature of God's creative act. Aquinas in his *De potentia,* I, 5, simply said that certain philosophers held that God acts out of the necessity of his nature, so that God does not create freely. Henry of Ghent specified that it is Aristotle's Arabian commentator Ibn Sīnā (*d.* 1037) who held that God creates necessarily while Aristotle himself did not admit any kind of creative act, neither free nor necessary, on the part of God. John Duns Scotus attributes necessary creation to both Aristotle and Ibn Sīnā, since Ibn Sīnā makes explicit what Aristotle's principles imply. Yet, no matter how you interpret Aristotle or his commentators, the problem still remains: How in fact can a Christian thinker explain and rationally justify the belief that God creates freely? To what extent can the Christian thinker forge a consistent philosophical instrument that would allow him to bring meaningful responses to those who had been trained in the texts of Aristotle and his commentators?

The *Sentences* of Peter Lombard, finished *ca.* 1157/1158, remained the official textbook in the theology faculty from the time of Alexander of Hales until after Luther. The commentaries on this work show more and more independence after Aquinas' era. The personal views of their authors gradually infiltrate these commentaries so that the quodlibet questions, where personal positions were more fully aired in the thirteenth and early fourteenth centuries, slowly lose their importance. The *Sentence* commentaries are our chief sources for discovering the way medieval theologians solved many thorny problems.

The logical and "content" works of Aristotle and his commentators stimulated the philosophy the medievals themselves formed as the basis for constructing their theologies. As they presented proofs for God's existence, discussed his attributes, debated his providence, examined the problem of universals, argued over the univocal or analogous character of the concept of being, fought over the nature and function of the human soul, and asked what is the ultimate purpose of man's life, they often provided us with enough elements to set the main lines of a systematic philosophy. When we approach their philosophical commentaries and treatises it is always important to distinguish—though this is sometimes quite difficult—between what they are saying in their own name and what they are presenting as an interpretation of Aristotle.

The great changes in the arts faculty at the time of Thomas Aquinas can be seen in the University of Paris statutes of 1255. On 19 March of that year the arts faculty officially became an Aristotelian philosophy faculty; one could no longer graduate without having formally heard lectures and passed examinations on the logical and "content" works of Aristotle. The arts faculty ceased officially to be a preparatory faculty of the seven liberal arts and became principally a primary source of Aristotle's philosophical world view, with its omissions as well as its declarations. The tensions that this move created are visible in the condemnations by the bishop of Paris in 1270 and 1277. A desire to remain in the arts faculty was viewed by many, and not always without some basis, as a denial of the intellectual substance of theology and even of Christian faith itself. Seemingly abstract questions such as "Is theology practical or speculative?" or "Is faith an act of the intellect?" contain this concrete tension. This tension disappeared by the end of the thirteenth century, when the choice of a predominantly arts faculty or "philosophic" career ceased to be seen as an option against faith or theology in favor of an allegiance toward Aristotle's reason and philosophy. When Walter Burley (*d.* after 1344) lectured on Aristotle's *On Interpretation* in 1301, and could be found lecturing on the same Aristotelian work in 1337, he was not challenged for allegiance; he was viewed simply as someone who explained Aristotle's texts, not as someone with rationalistic intentions.

Besides the change of atmosphere there were many other changes in the arts faculties after Aquinas. The logicians of his era provided collections of treatises: William of Sherwood (*d.* after 1267) *Introductiones in logicam*, Peter of Spain (later Pope John XXI, *d.* 1277) *Summulae logicales*, Roger Bacon (*d. ca.* 1291) *Summulae dialectices*, and Lambert of Auxerre (*fl.* 1253–1257) *Summulae logicales*. With William of Ockham in the early fourteenth century we get a completely unified treatise systematically organizing all the themes of Aristotle's *Organon* as well as the many treatises that were derived from them. In reaction to his nominalistic interpretation of Aristotle we get the strongly antagonistic *Logica contra Ockham* falsely attributed to Richard Campsall (*d. ca.* 1350) and the lightly disagreeing *Logica contra Ockham* falsely assigned, in Cod. Vat. Lat. 869, ff. lr ss., to Peter Aureoli. Such unified compendia or summaries became common after the time of Ockham and his early opponents. Their popularity can be seen, for instance, in the case of Paul of Venice's (*d.* 1429) *Logica*, the first medieval logic text ever printed (Venice, 1472). It can be found today in over eighty manuscripts and went through twenty-five editions. Humanists, like Lorenzo Valla and Marsilio Ficino, knew it; so did Thomas More, Erasmus, and Juan Luis Vives. Besides these general views of logic, which surpassed even Aristotle himself in the unity of their logical vision, the post-Thomistic medievals increased, for theory and practice, the number of separate individual logical treatises.

By far the main logical contributions in the arts faculties, however, were the commentaries and *quaestiones* on the individual logical treatises of Aristotle. These assume many dimensions. There are very elegant commentaries, with detailed exposition of the text along with special questions raised in the course of the explanation. There is a second type consisting of a collection of disputed questions corresponding to and occasioned by the text. More modestly, there are the brief summaries of Aristotle's text, such as would be given to the beginner. It is in the first two types of commentaries, especially, that we can best see the interpretative skills of the late medieval Aristotle exegetes at work.

One way to see the development of different Aristotelian interpretations is to recall the tense atmosphere occasioned by the influence of Aristotle and his commentators. This tension reached its peak between 1265 and 1285. Thomas Aquinas, early in this period, attacked some in the arts faculty who appeared to be uncritical in their loyalty to Aristotle or one of his commentators. If one wants to be a philosopher, he argued, it is not enough simply to quote other philosophers. The Franciscan Peter John Olivi (*d.* 1298) in the early 1280's bluntly accused some of his contemporaries of turning Aristotle and other philosophers into "gods of this world," and of worshiping their words. His own way of countering this effect was to point out the different interpretations that might be given to Aristotle's works. In dealing with the question of universals, with the categories, and with natural-philosophy subjects, such as motion, he offered an alternative reading to what they judged to be the common interpretation.

Alternative interpretations of Aristotle's texts had been practiced before, but in the later part of the thirteenth and early part of the fourteenth centuries alternative theories regarding philosophical interpretation grew. We can see it in Roger Bacon's *Summulae dialectices*, where, basing himself on a text of Aristotle, he distinguished between popular language employed in a philosophical work along with the vulgar understanding many take from this language and the deeper understanding that the wise give to the same works. Bacon also advised students to consider Aristotle's examples cautiously, for many examples are presented not because they are true but so that a student might get a better understanding of what he was studying. Walter Burley in his *Treatise on the Activity of Forms*, written in the 1320's, distinguished Aristotle's words when he is simply reciting a position or inquiring into an issue and when he is taking a serious stand on a question. William of Ockham's way of interpreting Aristotle's texts made such great demands on the attention of a reader that his *Summa logicae* could be considered a helpful code book for deciphering the works of Aristotle according to what he considered their intended meaning. The *Logica contra Ockham*, wrongly attributed to Campsall and written shortly after Ockham's *Summa logicae*, reveals an author who is well aware of the dangers facing the interpreter. He was not only suspicious of his contemporaries, but accused Aristotle himself of distorting the position of his teacher Plato. Yet he saved his strongest jabs for Ockham, who, in his judgment, perverted Aristotle's meanings, mainly by giving a logical meaning to every statement of Aristotle even when he speaks as a natural philosopher and not as a logician. However, even the author of this *Logica contra Ockham* realized that interpretation was unavoidable. At best he could call for such reading of the texts that would judge them in terms of "right reason" and "with good proof."

REALISM AND NOMINALISM

The main lines of philosophy and philosophical interpretation, especially after Peter John Olivi, fell into two general groups: realistic and nominalistic. They are hard to define, for two principal reasons: first, because realists and nominalists individually try to distinguish themselves from one another; and second, and less subtly, because realists portray nominalists as being in no way realistic, and nominalists tend to present all realists as "exaggerated" realists.

A concrete presentation of the conflict between realists and nominalists can be found in the writings of the "prince of the nominalists," William of Ockham, particularly as he interprets Aristotle's ten categories. Certainly, according to Ockham, individual substances are real; a tree, a dog, a man are real things. Likewise, certain qualities are real; whiteness is a real quality distinct from a wall, which inheres in or is a distinct reality from a wall, present in the wall. Yet, not all qualities are real qualities of the same sort. If we pull down a limb of a tree so that it is curved downward, is the curvedness a quality really inhering in the limb the way whiteness is a quality really inhering in the wall? Ockham would contend that the limb is really curved but that its curvedness is not a reality that inheres in the limb of a tree the way that whiteness is a real quality of a white wall. His point might come through more strongly in the category of relation. If two men are similar in color, for example white, then each of them has whiteness as a real quality existing in him. Because each is white they are similar in color. Yet though they are really similar to one another, and are similar independently of our minds that recognize their similarity, still similarity is not a characteristic inhering in each the way whiteness is in each.

Another example, belonging to the category of quantity, might better illustrate Ockham's point. If John and Mary are a happily married couple, coupledness does not exist in each of them as an inhering characteristic. If this were the case, each would be a couple. Nor can you claim that part of coupledness exists in John and part in Mary. For, if Mary were in Paris visiting friends while John stayed in London, then two parts of the same characteristic, coupledness, separated by many miles, would make up one accident—which seems unimaginable. John and Mary, according to Ockham's interpretation of reality, would really be a couple, yet coupledness is not a real characteristic inhering in them jointly or individually. For him, to think of curvedness, similarity, or coupledness after the manner of whiteness is to think realistically, that is to imagine them as inhering qualities. He wants to think of curvedness, similarity, and coupledness nominalistically, that is, a limb can be really curved, two white men can be really similar, and John and Mary can be really a couple, but the reality of each of these situations does not mean curvedness, similarity, or coupledness are real inhering qualities. In order to make this distinction, Ockham says they are names pointing to real situations but not to real inhering accidents.

In all areas of philosophy, theology, and in general discourse, according to Ockham, men have a tendency to imagine realities corresponding to the words they employ. If they say a man is white, they think that whiteness is a characteristic really existing in a man. Here they think correctly. But, when they say John and Henry are similar in color, to think that similarity is an inhering quality like whiteness would, according to Ockham, be both wrong and not speaking according to the mind of Aristotle. Because of such "reifying" tendencies it is imperative, according to Ockham, to eliminate the multiplication of such realities. This is what is meant by Ockham's razor: if you can adequately explain a real situation, for example, that John and Henry are similar in color, without postulating similarity as a distinct reality inhering in each, then you should shave off such distinct realities. Much of Ockham's philosophical and theological work was given to eliminating these unneeded extra entities. As an exegete of Aristotle's works he found it even necessary to shave the unkempt growths of the philosopher himself. For Aristotle frequently spoke loosely; he adapted his language to his audience, or used realistic phrases simply to express himself in a variant manner, or offered a realistic tone to make his text ornate or to save himself time. Imprecisions of a realistic character abound in

Aristotle's works, except when he is speaking precisely and deliberately. It is these intentional statements of his meaning, according to Ockham, that must be our key to interpret his loose statements.

This approach to Aristotle's works, and to philosophy and theology generally, points up Ockham's very precise contrast between things and names. By saying similarity is not a thing but a name, he means it is not a quality inhering in a subject after the manner of whiteness in a white wall. He does not thereby deny the real similarity between two similar white objects prior to the recognition of their similarity by the mind, but he does deny that this similarity is itself an extra thing beside the whiteness of the two objects. He might be called a nominalistic realist. Furthermore, we can see from his presentation that by implication he would hold that some of his contemporaries would say that similarity is an extra reality besides the whiteness of the two objects. They could be called, in contrast to his position, realistic realists. However, in the medieval framework of the era after Ockham, the first were called simply nominalists and the second were simply realists.

These two general approaches to the categories naturally had their applications to the other areas of Aristotle's philosophy and to the theology that employed his philosophical themes. The many commentaries and *quaestiones* on Aristotle's *Physics, Metaphysics, On the Soul, On the Heavens, Nicomachean Ethics, Politics,* and his many other works all show the influence of these opposing theories of interpretation and opposing philosophies.

During the late Middle Ages theology and philosophy predominantly show the gradual and uneasy assimilation of Aristotle's world view into the Western medieval intellectual world. Through this activity both Aristotelianism and Christian thought were profoundly changed. Before the arrival of the "new logic" and the "content" works of Aristotle, the intellectual resources of Western Christianity were largely provided from the Neoplatonic and Stoic philosophies as interpreted by the Fathers, especially St. Augustine. Through Arabian and Greek commentators new Neoplatonic elements kept appearing in the Christian intellectual world. The medieval Western European intellectual achievement in general terms was a continual work of assimilating the riches received from the Scriptures, the Fathers, and the Neoplatonic, Stoic, and Aristotelian sources and commentaries.

BIBLIOGRAPHY

E. Jennifer Ashworth, *Language and Logic in the Post-medieval Period* (1974); Stephen F. Brown, "Walter Burleigh's Treatise *De suppositionibus* and Its Influence on William of Ockham," in *Franciscan Studies,* **32** (1972), and "A Modern Prologue to Ockham's Natural Philosophy," in *Miscellanea Mediaevalia,* XIII, pt. 1, *Sprache und Erkenntnis in Mittelalter* (1981); John Buridan, *Sophisms on Meaning and Truth,* Theodore K. Scott, trans. (1966); Yves Congar, *A History of Theology,* Hunter Guthrie, trans. and ed. (1968); William J. Courtenay, *Adam Wodeham* (1978); Franz Ehrle, *Der Sentenzenkommentar Peters von Candia* (1925); Ernest L. Fortin, *Dissidence et philosophie au moyen âge* (1981); Étienne Gilson, *History of Christian Philosophy in the Middle Ages* (1955); Robert Guelluy, *Philosophie et théologie chez Guillaume d'Ockham* (1947); Aegidius Magrini, *Ioannis Duns Scoti doctrina de scientifica theologiae natura* (1952); Edward P. Mahoney, "Saint Thomas and Siger of Brabant Revisited," in *Review of Metaphysics,* **27** (1974); John E. Murdoch, "*Mathesis in philosophiam scholasticam introducta:* The Rise and Development of the Application of Mathematics in Fourteenth Century Philosophy and Theology," in Congrès international de philosophie médiévale, 4th, 1967, *Arts liberaux et philosophie au moyen âge* (1969); Calvin Normore, "Walter Burley on Continuity," in Norman Kretzmann, ed., *Infinity and Continuity in Ancient and Medieval Thought* (1982); Gabriel Nuchelmans, *Theories of the Proposition: Ancient and Medieval Conceptions of the Bearers of Truth and Falsity* (1973); Alan Perreiah, "A Biographical Introduction to Paul of Venice," in *Augustiniana,* **17** (1967); Herman Shapiro, *Motion, Time, and Place According to William Ockham* (1957); Paul V. Spade, *The Mediaeval Liar: A Catalogue of the Insolubilia-Literature* (1975); Fernand van Steenberghen, *Thomas Aquinas and Radical Aristotelianism* (1980); Severin R. Streuer, *Die theologische Einleitungslehre des Petrus Aureoli* (1968); Edward A. Synan, *The Works of Richard of Campsall,* II (1982); Damasus Trapp, "Augustinian Theology of the 14th Century," in *Augustiniana* **6** (1956); James Weisheipl, "Ockham and Some Mertonians," in *Mediaeval Studies,* **30** (1968); John F. Wippel, *The Metaphysical Thought of Godfrey of Fontaines* (1981), and *Metaphysical Themes in Thomas Aquinas* (1984).

STEPHEN F. BROWN

[See also **Aristotle in the Middle Ages; Augustinian Friars; Christology; Conciliar Theory; Dialectic; Nominalism; Paris, University of; Proverbs and Sententiae; Questiones; Quodlibet; Scholasticism, Scholastic Method; Realism; Thomism and Its Opponents; Universals; Universities;** and individual philosophers and theologians.]

PHILOSOPHY AND THEOLOGY, WESTERN EUROPEAN: TERMINOLOGY. Augustine of Hippo (354–430) provided the Latin West with a rationale for his use of the terms "philosophy" and "theology," which perdured until the innovative use of the term "theology" by Peter Abelard (*ca.* 1079–*ca.* 1142) modified the Augustinian tradition. Since God is Wisdom and "philosophy" means "love of wisdom" (*City of God* 8.1), Augustine held that the term designates accurately a reflective and penetrating study of the data proposed by Christian teaching. Given his imperfect Greek, Augustine may not have been aware of how much he was in harmony with the practice of an impressive series of Greek Christian writers, for whom "philosophy" went beyond the achievements of pagan speculation and stood for the genuine wisdom to which pagans had aspired in vain.

Before Augustine, Justin Martyr (*ca.* 100–*ca.* 165), in a purportedly autobiographical passage, recounted his successive disenchantment with a Stoic, a Peripatetic, a Pythagorean, and finally with a Platonist philosopher before discovering in Christian teaching what he felt was "alone philosophy, safe and serviceable" (*Dialogue with Trypho* 8). Adopting Christianity, Justin could say "I am a philosopher" and continue to wear the distinctive philosopher's gown, in Greek, *tribōn,* in Latin, *pallium,* by which Trypho had recognized him (*Dialogue with Trypho* 1). This usage is also found in Melito (*d.* before 190), Clement of Alexandria (*d. ca.* 215), Eusebius (*ca.* 263–*ca.* 340), Sozomen and Theodoret (*d.* before 466); Pseudo-Dionysius the Areopagite (*fl. ca.* 475–528) spoke of "monks' philosophy."

The Greek use of *oikonomia* (economy) for the divine work of salvation is not matched by Augustine. However, in 391 he asserted that "a chief point of human salvation is that philosophy, that is zeal for wisdom, is not one thing and religion another" (*On True Religion* 5.8) and in his *Confessions* (7.21.27), he contrasted the inability of Platonism to reach the goal that Platonists perceived from afar with the capacity of Jesus as Messiah to assist humans to that goal. In about 421–422 he posed the rhetorical question: "I ask you whether our Christian—which is the only genuine philosophy—is not more reputable than is the philosophy of the gentiles?" (*Against Julian the Pelagian* 5.14.72).

To this positive stance on "philosophy" Augustine added a negative judgment of the term "theology." Basing himself on Varro (116–27 B.C.), Augustine distinguished two or three sorts of "theology," all of them reprehensible: "He [Varro] says there are three sorts of theology: one called 'mythic,' a second 'natural,' a third 'civil'" (*City of God* 6.5); "Let these two theologies, then, the 'fabulous' and 'civil,' give way to Platonic philosophers" (*City of God* 8.5). If pagan "theologies" are inferior to pagan, Platonic philosophy, they are, a fortiori, inferior to the Christian Platonism that Augustine had learned from the circle of Ambrose and had so creatively developed in his own work.

Boethius (*ca.* 480–524/526) serves, however, to illustrate one disadvantage of this terminology. Counting himself an "Augustinian" (see the dedication of his *On the Trinity,* ". . . seeds sown in my mind by St. Augustine's writings . . . "), Boethius named the great work he produced under threat of execution *The Consolation of Philosophy.* Although one modern editor (Ludwig Bieler) has indexed twenty-six probable or possible echoes of the Bible in this encomium of "philosophy," critics, both medieval and modern, have put in question the Christian character of this work and its author. Those undoubtedly erroneous interpretations of this thoroughly Christian meditation on Providence, human freedom, and divine foreknowledge did not dominate the field, and the Middle Ages generally adopted the Augustinian notion of "philosophy," along with this use of it by Boethius, to designate an esteemed, and specifically Christian, "wisdom," until the intervention of Abelard.

A persistent theme of Peter Abelard is the value of ancient philosophy; what revelation had been for the ancient Hebrews, he wrote, philosophy had been for the Greeks. Indeed, their philosophy was a better preparation for receiving the Christian gospel because it included a vague notion of the Trinity and even of the cross of Jesus, which he saw in the Greek letter *X* of Plato's *Timaeus* 36 B (see Abelard's *Christian Theology* 1; see also qualification on the Trinity, *Dialectic* 5.1). Despite his admiration for the value of pagan philosophy for Christian believers, Abelard used the term "theology" in the very titles of the various recensions of three major works: *Theology for Students (Theologia scholarium), Theology of the "Highest Good" (Theologia "summi boni"),* and *Christian Theology (Theologia christiana).* Abelard did not abandon the Augustinian use of the term "philosophy." In his *Commentary on the Epistle to the*

Romans, for example, Abelard wrote that "because to discuss this is the business of a more profound philosophy, we reserve it to the perfection of our theology" (E. M. Buytaert, ed., 282, verses 275–276). His innovation in using "theology" where the tradition had consecrated "philosophy" led Bernard of Clairvaux, in a letter to Pope Innocent II (Letter 190, Benedictine Edition), to say that Abelard's "theology" (God-talk) was more properly "fools'-talk," for he counted Abelard's innovations as a scandalous paganizing of Christian teaching.

Two considerations suggest that Abelard was not indebted to Greek authors for his use of "theology" in their sense. First, he seems not to have known Greek, and second, near the beginning of his *Theology for Students,* he announced that he would deal with "faith, charity, and sacrament," a theme that a Greek writer might be expected to name "economy," whereas Abelard called his work a "theology." The future was with Abelard's terminology. Thirteenth-century universities were to grant degrees in "theology" through their faculties of "theology"; still, the triumph of the new terminology did not exclude all alternatives. Theologians were often termed "masters of the sacred page" and theology was often "sacred teaching" *(sacra doctrina),* for instance in works by Thomas Aquinas, who used "theology" in the titles of his *Summary of Theology* and *Compendium of Theology.* Fourteenth-century authors, William of Ockham for instance, distinguished between arguments that proceed "philosophically" and those that proceed "theologically," and between "philosophers" and "theologians."

BIBLIOGRAPHY

Augustine, *Confessionum libri tredecim,* Pius Knoell and Martin Skutella, eds. (1934); his works are in *Corpus scriptorum ecclesiasticorum latinorum* (1887–1922) and *Patrologia latina,* XXXII–XLVII (1841–1849); English translations are in various series: *A Library of Fathers of the Holy Catholic Church, Anterior to the Division of the East and West,* 24 vols. (1838–1885), and *A Select Library of the Nicene and Post-Nicene Fathers of the Christian Church,* Philip Schaff, ed. (1886–1890); Justin Martyr, *Dialogue with Trypho,* A. Lukyn Williams, trans. (1930); Boethius, *The Theological Tractates; The Consolation of Philosophy,* Hugh Fraser Stewart and E. K. Rand, eds. and trans. (1918); his works are in *Patrologia latina,* LXIII–LXIV (1847), and *Corpus Christianorum: Series latina,* Ludwig Bieler, ed., XCIV (1957); Peter Abelard, *Dialectica,* L. M. de Rijk, ed. (1970), and his "theologies" in *Corpus Christianorum: Continuatio mediaevalis,* E. M. Buytaert, ed., XI–XII (1969).

EDWARD A. SYNAN

[See also **Abelard, Peter; Ambrose, St.; Aquinas, St. Thomas; Aristotle in the Middle Ages; Augustine of Hippo, St.; Bernard of Clairvaux, St.; Boethius; Eusebius of Caesarea; Ockham, William of; Plato in the Middle Ages; Pseudo-Dionysius the Areopagite; Sozomen; Theodoret of Cyr.**]

PHILOSTORGIOS (*ca.* 370–after 425), a historian who wrote a continuation of Eusebius of Caesarea's (*ca.* 263–*ca.* 340) *Ecclesiastical History,* was born in Cappadocia. He came from an Arian family and seems to have lived in Constantinople for many years as well as having traveled in the Holy Land. Although probably not a cleric, he was familiar with the theological controversies of his time.

The complete text of Philostorgios' history is lost, but a number of fragments exist. The work is divided into two volumes of six books each and covers the period from the beginning of the Arian controversy to 425. The second volume is devoted exclusively to the history of the Arian church; Philostorgios has been criticized for his partiality, but he seems to have used reliable sources, although it is not known whether he read them himself.

BIBLIOGRAPHY

Joseph Bidez, "Fragments nouveaux de Philostorge sur la vie de Constantin," in *Byzantion,* 10 (1935), "L'historien Philostorge," in *Mélanges d'histoire offerts à Henri Pirenne,* I (1926), 23–30, and *idem,* ed., *Philostorgius, Kirchengeschichte* (1913, repr. 1972).

LINDA C. ROSE

[See also **Eusebius of Caesarea; Historiography, Byzantine.**]

PHILOTHEOS (*fl. ca.* 900), Byzantine court official (*protospatharios* and *atriklines*), author of a treatise known as the *Kletorologion* (899), describing the hierarchy of titles and offices. This work, which was incorporated by Constantine VII Porphyrogenitos into his *De ceromoniis aulae Byzantinae* (chaps. 52–54), is mainly concerned with the order of precedence to be followed during the imperial banquets. After having established the distinction between the honorific titles (*axiai dia brabeiōn:* bestowed for life with the investiture of certain insignia) and the high administrative positions (*axiai dia logou:* appointments for a limited time, made by the emperor's oral command), Philotheos provides detailed lists in which most of the titles and offices existing at his time appear in their hierarchical order. He also gives specific information concerning the organization of state banquets.

The *Kletorologion* is a particularly important source for our knowledge of court hierarchy during the middle Byzantine period. It can be compared with anonymous lists of officials from the same period, such as the *Taktikon Uspenski* (written *ca.* 842–843), the *Taktikon Beneševič* (written between 934 and 944), and the *Taktikon* of the Escorial (written between 971 and 975). These texts, which are now available in French translation and commented upon, allow us to reconstruct almost in its entirety the organizational diagram of the Byzantine administration in the ninth and tenth centuries.

BIBLIOGRAPHY

John B. Bury, *The Imperial Administrative System in the Ninth Century* (1911, repr. 1958); Nicolas Oikonomides, *Les listes de préséance byzantines des IXe et Xe siècles* (1972).

NICOLAS OIKONOMIDES

[See also **Byzantine Empire: Bureaucracy; Byzantine Minor Arts; Encyclopedias and Dictionaries, Byzantine.**]

PHILOTHEOS KOKKINOS (*ca.* 1300–1377), patriarch of Constantinople (1353–1354, 1364–1376) and major figure in the monastic (hesychast) revival in Byzantium. Born at Thessaloniki into a family of Jewish origin, Philotheos embraced monasticism and served as abbot of the Great Lavra (monastery) of St. Athanasius on Mt. Athos. A friend and disciple of Gregory Palamas, he was elected metropolitan of Heraclea in Thrace after the enthronement of Emperor John VI Kantakuzenos (1347). In 1353 the reigning patriarch, Kallistos, refused to crown Matthew Kantakuzenos as coemperor, since such a crowning would have been detrimental to the legitimate rights of John V Palaiologos. Philotheos was enthroned in his place and dutifully crowned Matthew. However, Philotheos was forced to leave the patriarchate after the abdication of John VI Kantakuzenos and the establishment of John V Palaiologos as sole ruler (1354). The personal prestige of Philotheos and his faithfulness to the interests of the patriarchate—which were, in his view, best served by the policies of Kantakuzenos—led to his return to the patriarchal throne in 1364. Indeed, Kantakuzenos, even after his abdication, remained influential as an elder statesman in both political and ecclesiastical affairs.

During his second patriarchate, Philotheos showed an active and independent spirit in the administration of the church, affirming "Palamite" orthodoxy and strengthening ties with the other Orthodox churches throughout Eastern Europe. In 1367 he approved the idea of an ecumenical council for the union between East and West, but the plans were thwarted following the conversion of John V to Roman Catholicism (1369). In 1368 he condemned a group of Byzantine Thomists (particularly Prochoros Kydones) and canonized Gregory Palamas as a saint. In 1375 Philotheos recognized the previously established (1346) patriarchate of Serbia, thereby ending a thirty-year schism. On various occasions he took strong measures to ensure patriarchal control over a unified metropolitanate of Russia. Philotheos was again deposed in August 1376, during the Genoese-sponsored rebellion of Andronikos IV, and died a year later.

Philotheos wrote numerous theological, hagiographical, homiletic, and hymnographical works.

BIBLIOGRAPHY

John Meyendorff, *Byzantium and the Rise of Russia* (1981); G. M. Prokhorov, "K istorii liturgicheskoi poezii: Gimny i molitvy Filofeya Kokkina," in Akademia Nauk SSR, *Trudy otdel drevne-russkoy literatury,* 27 (1973).

JOHN MEYENDORFF

[See also **Athos, Mount; Byzantine Church; Councils, Byzantine (859–1368); Gregory Palamas; Hesychasm; John V Palaiologos; John VI Kantakouzenos; Liturgy, Byzantine Church; Monasticism, Byzantine.**]

PHOKAS (547–610), Byzantine emperor (602–610). While centurion on the Danube frontier, he was brought to power by a military revolt. His reign was inept and tyrannical; the Slavs and Avars overran the Balkans, and the Persians invaded Asia

Minor (605). Phokas adopted a pro-Roman ecclesiastical policy. He was overthrown and executed by Heraklios.

BIBLIOGRAPHY

Rudolf Spintler, *De Phoca imperatore Romanorum* (1905); Andreas N. Stratos, *Byzantium in the Seventh Century*, I, Marc Ogilvie-Grant, trans. (1968), 48–89, and "An Unknown Brother of the Emperor Phocas," in *Jahrbuch der Osterreichischen Byzantinistik*, 27 (1978); Otto Veh, *Zur Geschichte des Kaisers Phokas (602–610)* (1954).

NICOLAS OIKONOMIDES

[See also **Heraklios; Maurice.**]

PHOTIOS (*ca.* 810–*ca.* 893), Byzantine scholar, twice patriarch of Constantinople. He was born into a family that was well-connected, well educated, rich, and iconophile, related to the scholar-patriarch Tarasios (*d.* 806) and allied by marriage to the empress Theodora. His father, Sergios Confessor, was an official and probably an ecclesiastical historian. Nothing is known about Photios' education, but it must have been excellent; in his youth he compiled a lexicon, which may have been an earlier version of his important *Lexicon* that survives.

During the persecution of iconophiles that began in 833, Photios' whole family was condemned as iconophile and sent into exile, in the course of which both Photios' parents died. When power passed to Theodora and the iconophiles in 842, Photios seems to have come to Constantinople and begun teaching; his students included St. Constantine Cyril (826/827–869), later missionary to the Slavs. Before leaving on an embassy to the Arabs, probably in 845, Photios composed for his brother Tarasios the work now called the *Bibliotheca*, a voluminous account of Photios' private reading. It describes some 400 works in Greek from Herodotus (*fl.* fifth century B.C.) to Photios' own time. Covering almost every subject, it remains valuable for its descriptions of material that is now lost and as a picture of Photios' scholarship and tastes.

Helped by his connections with the imperial family, Photios rose to the post of *protoasecretis* (head of the state chancery); he continued teaching informally while holding this office. In 858, though he was a layman, Photios was appointed patriarch of Constantinople to replace the deposed patriarch Ignatios. During this patriarchate Photios delivered his surviving *Homilies*. His appointment soon caused the Photian Schism with the partisans of Ignatios and with Rome, and ended in 867 with the restoration of Ignatios by the new emperor Basil I. Photios was exiled, imprisoned, and in 870 condemned by the Council of Constantinople.

During his exile he edited his collected *Letters* and composed his *Amphilochia*, a series of answers to mostly theological questions addressed to his friend Amphilochios of Kyzikos. Photios managed to gain favor with Basil, who made him tutor to his heir, the future Leo VI; when Ignatios died in 877, Basil returned Photios to the patriarchate for another nine years. In 866, however, Leo VI (*d.* 912) succeeded Basil and deposed and exiled his former teacher, making his brother, Stephen, patriarch. During this final exile, Photios wrote his *Mystagogia*, a defense of his position on the *Filioque*, which is that the Holy Spirit proceeded from the Father alone. Photios died in obscurity, no earlier than 893, but probably not much later. His canonization by the Eastern church apparently dates from the late tenth century. Photios was the outstanding figure in the revival of Byzantine learning of the ninth century and was particularly influential in promoting the study of secular literature. As patriarch he was controversial in his own time and remains controversial today, seen by some as a staunch defender of the doctrines and prerogatives of the Eastern church and by others as an ambitious and calculating politician. He was probably both.

BIBLIOGRAPHY

Sources. Photios' works in *Patrologia graeca*, CI–CIV (1860); *Bibliotheca*, R. Henry, ed. and trans. (French), 8 vols. (1959–1977). A partial English translation is *The Library of Photius*, J. H. Freese, trans. (1920). *Homilies*, Cyril Mango, trans. (1958); *Homilies*, Basil Laourdas, ed. (1959); *Lexicon*, Samuel A. Naber, ed., 2 vols. (1864–1865).

Studies. Hans Georg Beck, *Kirche und theologische Literatur im byzantinischen Reich* (1959), 520–528, includes bibliography on Photios' theological writings; Francis Dvornik, *The Photian Schism* (1948), basic and strongly pro-Photian; Joseph A. Hergenröther, *Photius, Patriarch von Constantinopel*, 3 vols. (1867–1869), old, but the most comprehensive work; Cyril Mango, "The Liquidation of Iconoclasm and the Patriarch Photios," in Anthony Bryer and Judith Herrin, eds., *Iconoclasm* (1977), a reinterpretation of Photios' experience with

The geocentric universe according to Apian (*d.* 1552). Reproduced from Petrus Apianus, *Cosmographia liber* (Antwerp, 1584). THE NEW YORK PUBLIC LIBRARY, RARE BOOKS & MANUSCRIPTS DIVISION, ASTOR, LENOX & TILDEN FOUNDATIONS

iconoclasm; Warren T. Treadgold, *The Nature of the "Bibliotheca" of Photius* (1980), includes bibliography.

WARREN T. TREADGOLD

[See also **Bardas Caesar; Basil I the Macedonian; Byzantine Church; Byzantine Empire: History (330–1025); Councils, Byzantine; Cyril and Methodius, Sts.; Filioque; Philosophy and Theology, Byzantine; Plato in the Middle Ages; Schisms, Eastern-Western Church; Schism, Photian.**]

PHYSICS. In the Middle Ages academic study of the physical world had at its core the study of books by Aristotle (384–322 B.C.), especially his *Physics,* but also his *On the Heavens, Meteorology,* and *On Generation and Corruption.* Although medieval scholars did not hold slavishly to Aristotle's views, his books were the major texts used. Consequently, medieval innovations in physics often took the form of variations on an Aristotelian theme. It will be best to begin, therefore, with the general outlines of the Aristotelian universe, indicating some of the medieval changes in his scheme.

THE ARISTOTELIAN UNIVERSE

The world as a whole, according to Aristotelian physics, was a sphere containing a nested set of spheres centered on a spherical earth. The heavens, from the moon on up, were supposed to be made of a nonearthly substance called the ether or quintessence. The idea that the heavens contain spheres rested ultimately on observation of the apparent nightly motion of the stars, which seem to rotate around the earth in concert, maintaining virtually unchanged positions relative to each other. This coordinated motion was explained by assuming that the stars are fixed to a single rotating sphere turning on its axis approximately once a day. Against this backdrop of concerted motion, seven heavenly bodies pursued deviant courses, moving relative to the stars. These seven wandering stars, or planets, including the moon and sun as well as Mercury, Venus, Mars, Jupiter, and Saturn, were given additional spheres to account for their individual motions, thus leading to a nested set of spheres filling the heavens.

For Aristotle, all of these heavenly spheres were concentric. Later Greek astronomers had, however, proposed nonconcentric spheres including spheres called epicycles centered on some point of the surface of the basic spheres, so that, for medieval Aristotelians, the exact system of heavenly spheres was open to debate. An empty rotating sphere was sometimes added outside of the sphere of the fixed stars to account for the precession of the equinoxes (that is, the very slow motion of the stars relative to the celestial poles and equator). Yet another immobile empty sphere might be added outside as the empyrean heaven or abode of God and the angels. Thus the heavens were supposed to be filled with rotating spheres of ether carrying stars and planets also made of ether. Aristotle explained that it was natural for ether to rotate with constant angular velocity around the center of the universe. Medieval Aristotelians sometimes proposed other reasons for the rotation of these spheres, for instance that they were moved by angels or that God had started them rotating when the world was created, after which they continued rotating because they encountered no resistance.

Aristotle had proposed that ultimately every motion in the universe goes back to some immaterial First or Prime Mover that causes the rotation of the heavens. The mode of action of this First Mover might be likened, to give a homely analogy, to the way that a pail of oats causes a hungry horse to move toward it, that is by creating a desire to move in the thing moved. The Christian natural philosophers of the Middle Ages identified the First Mover with God.

Aristotle had argued that there was a First Mover, but he believed that the First Mover was first logically or causally rather than first in time, because in his view the world had always existed. Aristotle's argument for the eternity of the world was a troublesome point for medieval Christians, who believed that in the beginning God created heaven and earth. Some Christian natural philosophers, often identified as followers of the Islamic commentator on Aristotle Averroës (Ibn Rushd, 1126–1198), seemed to accept the idea that as philosophers they could assert the eternity of the world while believing as Christians that it was created out of nothing. Thomas Aquinas (1224–1274) argued that physics had no way to prove whether the world was created or eternal, so that it was an open question as far as science was concerned. Later, natural philosophers agreed that if the world was created, it was a supernatural act, unexplainable by the usual physical laws.

But if Christian philosophers substituted a finite past time for Aristotle's eternal universe, they did the opposite with regard to space. Aristotle had said that outside of the finite outermost sphere of the cosmos there was nothing, not even empty space. Later medieval scholars began to develop the idea of an infinite void space outside the cosmos on the basis of considerations concerning the omnipresence of God. Whatever their thoughts about time and space, Aristotle and the medieval Aristotelians agreed that the universe was not random or accidental, but rather well designed in its structure and with discernible purpose in the relation of its parts to the whole. The heavens in particular were supposed to be a realm of constancy and perfection, where there was never a change of any kind other than the constant rotation of the ether.

The sublunar realm, that is, the part of the universe or cosmos beneath the sphere of the moon, was made of stuff quite different from the ether composing the heavens. Whereas ether was unchanging, the material below the moon was subject to changes of many sorts. Rejecting the ideas of the ancient Greek atomists, Aristotle asserted that the whole universe was full of material objects made up of continuous, ever-further divisible substance. He analyzed the substances below the sphere of the moon in terms of their material substratum or matter and their forms, including substantial forms that made a thing what it was and accidental forms such as colors and other qualities. A sublunar object might undergo any of four different types of changes. First, it could be moved from place to place. Second, its accidental forms could be altered—it could be heated, cooled, moistened, dried, and so forth. Third, it might grow or diminish, either in the proper sense, as plants and animals grow, or in a looser sense, as something elastic expands or contracts. Fourth, a thing could undergo a complete or substantial change, called corruption of the old thing and generation of a new thing, as when wood is burned and turns to smoke and ash.

Among nonliving substances, four were fundamental, namely earth, water, air, and fire. Aristotle called these four basic types of sublunar substance elements, but it should be noted that they could be transformed one into the other. Each element was characterized by two qualities: earth was cold and dry, water cold and wet, air hot and wet, and fire hot and dry. If water was heated sufficiently, it was turned into air, as happens in boiling, and similarly the other elements could be interconverted. This conception of the elements as interconvertible formed part of the background of alchemy, making transformation of other metals into gold seem possible.

Besides their temperature and relative moisture, sublunar elements were characterized by their weight or lightness. Earth and water were heavy, which meant that when released they naturally fell or moved toward the center of the universe. Earth, being heavier, tended to settle under water. On the other hand, air and fire were positively light, which meant that when released they naturally moved toward the sphere of the moon. Fire, being lighter than air, tended to end up above the air.

Thus below the moon as well as above, there was a tendency to the formation of concentric spheres, with earth at the center, surrounded in order by water, air, and fire. But the sublunar elements never all got to their natural places to form concentric shells, because of the varying action of the heavenly bodies on the sublunar realm. The sun, for instance, by heating water, tended to lift it from its natural place up into the natural place of air, from which it fell again when the sun had less effect and it was cooler. The moon and other planets were also supposed to act in ways that led to motion and circulation of the elements in the sublunar realm.

The four elements according to Isidore of Seville. Woodcut from the *editio princeps* of his *On the Nature of Things* (Augsburg, 1472). BY PERMISSION OF THE HUNTINGTON LIBRARY, SAN MARINO, CALIF.

This, then, was in outline the Aristotelian picture of the physical world. The role of physics as a discipline, according to Aristotle, was to explain what was common to all bodies within the cosmos and to explain what was naturally so as opposed to things that were the result of human artifice. Other natural sciences explained phenomena occurring only in a subclass of natural things, for instance the properties of living things or of the sublunar elements. Among the most basic principles of physics was that everything physical moves. The motions that occurred might be traced back ultimately to the First Mover, but individual natural substances also had within them natural tendencies resulting from their forms, as ether tended to circle the center of the universe and heavy bodies to seek the center.

To give a complete physical explanation of anything, according to Aristotle, one had to know the matter and form making up the thing to be explained. These were called the material and formal causes. One had also to know the efficient cause, or what made the thing in a mechanical sense. But fourth one had to know the purpose or final cause. Explanations in terms of final causes might come most easily with regard to biological subject matter, where it was natural to think there was a reason why animals have eyes (to see with) or plants roots (to absorb nutriment), but similar explanations were given concerning inanimate subject matter. Thus heavy bodies could be supposed to fall in order to get to their natural places at the center of the world. In contradistinction to natural motions, there were violent motions in which a body was moved away from its natural place or condition. Such violent motions were supposed to occur only when there was an outside power or force overcoming the body's natural inclination.

This Aristotelian view was the dominant view of physics in the Middle Ages, but it only came fully into its own in Europe after the twelfth century, when the Aristotelian physical works were translated from Greek and Arabic into Latin. Before that time, Aristotelian ideas of the cosmos were known partially, through Latin encyclopedias and the like, and Platonic conceptions, particularly those deriving from Plato's *Timaeus,* largely translated into Latin in the fourth century, had a greater influence. In the absence of any extended corpus of scientific works, the Bible and the fathers of the church were often used as authorities on scientific as well as religious matters.

Thus Isidore of Seville (*ca.* 560–636), in his treatise *On the Nature of Things,* written in the early seventh century, claims to follow the order of creation in Genesis, discussing light, the heavens, atmospheric phenomena, the sea, and finally dry land. He borrows heavily from Christian works on creation. For many terms he gives alternate allegorical or mystical senses explaining how the terms are used in the Bible: the word for universe or world (*mundus*) may also signify man, the word for heaven (*caelum*) may also signify the church, and in the plural it may signify all the saints or angels or prophets and so forth. At the same time Isidore makes use of secular sources. He describes the theory of the four elements (earth, water, air, and fire) clearly, but seems to assume that the heavens contain fire, air, and water, and has lost sight of the conception of ether as a fifth element, defining ether as "the upper, fiery air." To explain biblical references to the waters above the heavens, he assumes that God placed water in the heavens to temper the heat of fire there, possibly giving it the form of ice so that it remains in place. Although he reports that the heavens are spherical, he is uncertain whether there is only one or a separate heaven for each planet. He borrows descriptions based on the assumption of a spherical earth, but perhaps does not understand their original significance. Describing the earth as being suspended in nothing or perhaps held up by dense air or water, he is content with the idea that this, like the number of heavens, is beyond mortal understanding.

Similarly, other medieval cosmological writers in the period before the translations of Aristotle's natural works have a general but not exact familiarity with the Aristotelian world picture. Hildegard of Bingen (1098–1179) in her *Scivias,* written before 1150, conceives of the earth as spherical, but gives the outermost heavens an oval rather than spherical shape. In addition to a heaven of pure ether, she postulates heavens of watery air and of dark and bright fire. She speaks of a world spirit, emphasizing the multiform correspondences between the cosmos and human beings, both having matter animated by spirit or fire and permeated by wind or breath. Similar analogies between the cosmos or macrocosm and the human being or microcosm are common in other medieval cosmological and medical writings.

Often the analogy is taken to imply a connection: as the positions of the heavenly bodies change, so do the wind, weather, and climate change, and so is human health affected. Plagues are seen as resulting from a general corruption of the air through dryness, heat, inordinate rain, or other change of climate. On the other hand, Christian theologians sometimes sought to deny any strict connections between heavenly and earthly events, denying that astrologers could predict the future on the basis of planetary positions because this was inconsistent with human free will.

When Aristotle's physical works first became available in the Latin West, there was some initial reaction against them partly on the grounds that they too gave natural explanations too prominent a role. Nevertheless, by the mid thirteenth century Aristotelian natural works were adopted as university texts. Most extant Latin commentaries on Aristotle's *Physics* are either students' lecture notes that have happened to survive or more polished literary versions written by the lecturers themselves in connection with teaching. Although physics thus became part of the university curriculum, it was always seen only as part of a general education for people who would become clerics, lawyers, theologians, or physicians, and the like. It was not a subject for specialization.

MEDIEVAL COMMENTARIES ON ARISTOTLE'S *PHYSICS*

Modern scholars have tended to concentrate on those parts of medieval commentaries on Aristotle's *Physics* in which the commentators seem to be moving in the direction of seventeenth-century science. In some cases there was a natural development aiming to remedy weak parts of Aristotle's theories. One such weak area concerned the motions of projectiles, which fit poorly with Aristotle's analysis of the causes of motions. Aristotle said that in every violent motion the mover must be different from but in contact with the moved body. This fit well with the motion of a cart along a road, but in the case of a ball thrown through the air, it seemed to require the conclusion that the ball was moved by the air through which it moved—the air being the only other body touching the ball. This, however, was a rather implausible conclusion because common experience indicates that the air resists the motion of the ball rather than causing it.

Commentators on Aristotle therefore repeatedly suggested alternative explanations. The best-known alternative was to argue that when a projectile is put into motion some immaterial motive force, quality, or impetus is imparted to the projectile which, residing in it, causes the further motion. Jean Buridan (*ca.* 1295–*ca.* 1358) put forth a theory at the University of Paris in the mid fourteenth century, according to which the impetus imparted remained there permanently unless reduced by having to work against an outside resistance. The net result was that a projectile would tend to continue in motion if there were no action of any outside force, a view closer to seventeenth-century theories than Aristotle's had been. Buridan also used impetus to bolster other weak points in the Aristotelian theories, for instance to explain why falling bodies accelerate.

In a similar way medieval commentators on Aristotle modified other parts of his theories. They acknowledged that as bodies constantly move around on the surface of the earth, the earth as a whole may move slightly to maintain its position in the center of the universe. They considered the suggestion that the apparent daily rotation of the heavens might be more simply explained by assuming that the earth rotates daily from west to east. In the end, however, they concluded that the earth did not rotate, largely because it would be very hard to fit such rotation with the explanations of Aristotelian physics. Rotation of the earth would be classified as a violent motion, but there was no apparent force acting to cause it. If the earth were rotating through some cause, it was assumed that things thrown up from the surface would soon be left behind, which is not observed to happen. Ultimately it was mathematical astronomers starting with Copernicus (1473–1543) who instigated the development of a moving earth system. In the Middle Ages, however, mathematical astronomers were supposed to deal only with the mathematical details of the planetary motion, while it was the job of the physicists to explain the physics of the heavens as well as of the sublunar realm. Since Aristotelian physical explanations did not fit with a sun-centered moving-earth astronomy, it was unlikely that physicists would do the work to develop a moving-earth system until the barrier between physics and mathematical astronomy was broken down.

Aside from weak points within physics itself that generated innovations, the other main source of change within medieval physics was the mutual interaction between physics and other disciplines of the university curriculum. Physics and medicine had a long and close relationship. If, as is the case now, physics was more often the source of explanations for medical phenomena than the reverse, there was also a significant impact in the opposite direction based upon the influence of medical textbooks and authorities. Thus, for instance, through the widespread use of Galen's medical works as textbooks, Galen's discussions of methodology and of causation had an impact on the discussions of these topics in physics. Galen's theories of illness and of the effects of medicine on the body likewise had a major impact on general theories of alteration.

Physics was also significantly influenced by its interactions with theology. Theological doctrines might involve facts, or purported facts, that physics might need to explain. Sometimes, as in the case of the doctrine of God's creation of the world, it might be argued that the event was supernatural and so not the business of physics. In other cases, however, theological doctrines seemed to require a readjustment within physics. In this way the doctrine that God created Eve from Adam's rib might lead to reconsideration of concepts of density. If God had taken the matter from Adam's rib alone and, without any additional matter, made an adult woman of normal size and density, then density could not be determined by the amount of matter per volume. Thus consideration of God's formation of Eve led to more careful thought by authors such as Egidius Colonna about concepts of density and of quantity of matter and to new or improved concepts that might be incorporated into physics.

In the later thirteenth and fourteenth centuries theological doctrines concerning God's power had a particularly wide-ranging impact on natural philosophy through a distinction between what God might have done and what God in fact has done. Medieval Christian theology was far from seeing God as capricious. In fact it has been argued that medieval Christian theology promoted modern science through the belief that God acts in regular and lawlike ways. Nevertheless God was thought to make free choices. This potential conflict might be reconciled by saying that God does act in regular ways, since he has ordained or established laws of the universe that can be studied by physical sciences (this he does by his so-called ordained power, *potentia Dei ordinata*). On the other hand, God has established these laws freely, and, in an absolute sense, has the power to break or go beyond them (by his so-called absolute power, *potentia Dei absoluta*), as occurs in miracles.

In 1277, Étienne Tempier, the bishop of Paris, condemned as heretical 219 propositions that had been asserted by diverse unnamed people in various contexts. For physics, one upshot of this condemnation was to emphasize that God can do things according to his absolute power that are not in accordance with the accepted laws of science. A physicist might think that the world is in fact full, with no empty spaces or vacua, and this might be generally accepted as true. In line with the condemnation of 1277, however, he was ordered not to deny that God could make a vacuum if he so chose, unless it could be shown that vacua were not only physically but also logically impossible, involving some sort of self-contradiction.

Aristotle had argued that vacua are physically impossible on the grounds that a body falling in a vacuum would encounter no resistance. Since, he said, falling bodies move faster in the proportion that they encounter less resistance, a body falling with no resistance would fall infinitely fast. But an infinitely fast motion is self-contradictory: in an infinitely fast motion from *A* to *B* to *C* the body will reach *C* as soon as it reaches *B* and in fact it will be at *C* and already stopped as soon as it starts. After 1277 some philosophers concluded that the existence of a vacuum is not in itself self-contradictory. They then proceeded to try to work out how bodies might move with finite velocities within a vacuum if God made one. Some concluded that in a vacuum any body will fall with some fixed maximum rate, a conclusion that foreshadows one result of Newtonian physics. On the basis of evidence such as this, Pierre Duhem, a French scientist and one of the founders of the history of medieval science in the early twentieth century, concluded that the condemnation of 1277 promoted a questioning of Aristotelian physics that helped the development of modern science.

In addition to the influences of medicine and theology, medieval physics was also affected by interactions with other parts of the undergraduate curriculum, both with the subjects of the trivium or verbal sciences and with the subjects of the quadrivium or mathematical sciences. Aristotelian physics was qualitative rather than quantitative or mathematical. Through various routes, subsidiary mathematical sciences were added alongside physics, and mathematics was introduced into physics. Astronomy was one of the four mathematical sciences of the quadrivium along with arithmetic, geometry, and music. Between these mathematical sciences and physics there were the so-called middle sciences *(scientiae mediae)* combining mathematics and physics. Among these from Greek times were optics and statics or the science of weights. As various historians have shown, there was a strong tradition in optics in the Middle Ages, ranging from Islamic authors like al-Kindī and Ibn al-Haytham (Alhazen) through Latin authors including Albertus Magnus (*ca.* 1220–1280), Robert Grosseteste (*ca.* 1168–1253), Roger Bacon (*ca.* 1213–*ca.* 1291), Witelo (*d. ca.* after 1275), and Theodoric of Freiberg (*ca.* 1250–*ca.* 1310).

Medieval innovations with regard to such subsidiary mathematized sciences included a more general science of motion. Aristotle's remarks about the relationship of forces, resistances, and velocities in local motions were given consistent mathematical form and compared to alternate points of view. In the single most influential work in this area, *On the Ratios of Velocities in Motions,* the fourteenth-century philosopher Thomas Bradwardine (*ca.* 1300–1349) first laid out a theory of ratios and proportions and then considered the various mathematical possibilities for relating forces, resistances, and velocities, for instance that velocity varies directly as force, that velocity varies inversely as resistance, and that velocity varies as the arithmetic excess of force over resistance. The first two of these views were often ascribed to Aristotle. The third view had sometimes been suggested as a way of making motion in a vacuum possible, since it does not predict that velocity goes to infinity as the resistance diminishes to zero. Bradwardine proposed an alternative view, according to which the velocity is determined by the ratio of force to resistance—equal ratios of force to resistance always correspond to equal velocities—but when the ratio of force to resistance equals one, the velocity will be zero, and as powers of a given ratio of force to resistance are taken so the velocity will be multiplied by a like factor—for instance if the ratio of force to resistance is cubed, then the velocity will become three times faster. This view was supported by later natural philosophers partly on the grounds that it explains why there is no motion when the force is equal to or less than the resistance, whereas the Aristotelian view, as usually understood, does not.

After Bradwardine's work, which appeared in 1328, there was a long series of similar treatises relating forces and resistances to motions. The theory was taken to apply not only to local motions, but also to alterations and augmentations or diminutions. There was some background for the application to alteration both in pharmacy and in a generalization of optics called the doctrine of the multiplication of species. In pharmacy the action of a compound drug had been predicted mathematically in terms of the qualities of its components, where the dominant component might be considered analogous to the force in local motion and the weaker component analogous to the resistance—as in a body composed of earth mixed with fire, in which the earth seeks to move down and the fire up. In the doctrine of the multiplication of species any qualitative form such as hotness was supposed to propagate its effect in the surrounding region much like light, with a stronger effect near the source gradually decreasing as one moved away. Again the effect could be correlated with the causes, factored into the intensity or power of the source and the resistance of the medium.

Parallel to and combined with the study of the causes of motion, then, was the development of mathematical descriptions of the effects of motion—the spaces traversed, the qualities or quantities gained, and so forth. An extremely impressive early work devoted to the spaces traversed in local motions was the *On Motion* of Gerard of Brussels (first half of the thirteenth century). In this work, which is set up in deductive form like a work of Euclid or Archimedes, methods are developed for associating rotations at constant angular velocity with equivalent straight-line motions. In the simplest case, any part or all of a radius describing a circle is said to move as fast as its midpoint. In more complicated cases such as the rotation of a circular disk, geometrical methods are developed to take account of the fact that in a rotating body only a small part near the axis moves with slower linear velocities whereas larger parts near the outside surface move with greater velocities.

In the fourteenth century Bradwardine and his colleagues at Oxford and Nicole Oresme (*ca.* 1320–1382) at Paris also considered measures of the effects of motion. Far less sophisticated in this matter than Gerard of Brussels, Bradwardine decided to measure motions of rotation simply by the velocity of the fastest moved point of the body. For motions that vary not with respect to the parts of the body, as in rotations, but rather with respect to time, Bradwardine's colleagues developed what is now labeled the "Merton mean speed theorem" (so called because the people who developed it were mainly associated with Merton College at Oxford), according to which a uniformly accelerated motion is equivalent to a uniform or nonaccelerated motion at the speed the accelerated body had at the middle instant of its motion. This theorem had in its favor the fact that the two motions equated to each other traverse equal distances in equal times. The Mertonians also developed related concepts and theorems, such as a definition of instantaneous velocity.

For motions of augmentation and alteration, similar measures were established. The Mertonian John of Dumbleton (*d. ca.* 1349) argued that heating should be measured by the maximum degree of heat newly gained. Others argued that it should be measured by the increase in average temperature if the heat of the body varied from one part to another. For augmentations the two most common views were, first, that they should be measured by the absolute quantity added and, second, that the ratio of final to initial quantity should be used. The choice between alternative measures often depended on how the physical process being measured was conceptualized, a topic subject to intense debate. The high points of this Oxford tradition were the *Rules for Solving Sophismata* by William Heytesbury (*ca.* 1313–1372) and the *Book of Calculations* by Richard Swineshead (*fl.* 1340–1355). Echoing the last-named title, the men associated with this tradition are sometimes called the Oxford Calculators.

The Oxford Calculators developed their results verbally and calculated arithmetically. A brilliant extension of their work was carried out at Paris by Nicole Oresme. Oresme expounded, extended, and applied the theory of ratios that Bradwardine had developed, and he suggested geometrical representations of the variations of qualities or velocities that the Calculators had characterized verbally and arithmetically. The term used for measures of qualitative intervals or ranges was "latitude," a term that probably derived ultimately from Galen, who had called the range of temperature within which human life was possible a latitude, dividing it up into degrees above and below the temperate or normal temperature. Oresme treated the latitude of a quality as one dimension and extension of the quality in the body as a second dimension. The product of latitude times extension, corresponding to the area of a geometrical figure, was called the quantity of quality. For local motions, velocity took the place of latitude, and the second dimension might be either extension of the mobile or time. When the second dimension was time, the area of the figure corresponded to the distance traversed. Oresme thus developed the doctrine of the latitudes of forms into what was essentially a new middle or mathematized science.

A final area of innovation in medieval physics involved the impact of logic and of the disputations used as a method of teaching logic. Medieval logic was understood to include a study of the relations of the parts of a proposition to the things they stand for. William of Ockham (*ca.* 1285–1349), one of the most famous medieval logicians, was known for his view that one should not assume that there is some entity in nature corresponding to every noun of the language. He argued that the word "motion" does not refer to any separate entity in the outside world different from the moving body and from the spaces it successively occupies. Similarly he argued that the word "quantity" does not refer to any entities different from substances and qualities. Through his arguments Ockham helped to change medieval views of what there is in the world needing to be explained by physics. So, for instance, if motion is not any real thing or quality in the world, then one need not suppose that as a projectile continues to move there must be some force continuing to produce its motion as a new effect.

Before becoming a bachelor of arts, every medieval undergraduate had to attend, and then take part in, a certain number of disputations designed to reinforce the process of learning from lectures. In logical disputations one might be asked to analyze propositions to determine the conditions of their truth or falsity, where this might depend upon the way the proposition referred to things in the physical world. Measures of motion were sometimes involved in these analyses. One might be given the proposition, "Every part of the body *A* rotates faster and faster while the body as a whole rotates more and more slowly." Given Bradwardine's measure of rotations by the fastest moved point, one could assert that this proposition might be true of a rotating body that was constantly expanding while the outermost rim was being shaved off.

Particularly prominent in such disputations were propositions involving continuity and infinity. One might analyze the proposition, "Immediately after the present instant a body will begin to move." Given the assumption that time is continuous and contains, but is not composed of, instants, this proposition could cause difficulty because there is no first instant in which the body is moving. It is not moving in the present instant, but it will be moving before any instant that can be specified after the present instant.

A problem involving infinity might arise from the proposition, "A body *A* becomes infinitely hot at one end," if the proposition was taken to refer to a body in which the first half is two degrees hot, the next quarter four degrees hot, the next eighth eight degrees hot, and so forth. The paradox emerging from analysis of the proposition would be that the body will have temperatures beyond any given degree and yet it will not have an actually infinite degree at any point. Through debates concerning such seemingly paradoxical cases, the understanding of continuity and infinity was considerably enhanced. Often mathematics as well as logic was involved in these disputations and infinite series were used and their sums accurately taken. In this area of overlap between physical, logical, and mathematical inquiry some of the greatest achievements of medieval physics are to be found, but applied to cases that no one believed ever occurred in the natural world. So, for instance, authors like Richard Swineshead and Nicole Oresme successfully summed infinite series to calculate the average intensities of qualities with intensities approaching infinity at one end. Although these distributions were hypothetical and not believed actually to occur, historians have admired the mathematical achievement involved in summing the series derived from them.

BIBLIOGRAPHY

Sources. The most comprehensive source of translated primary sources is Edward Grant, ed., *A Source Book in Medieval Science* (1974). For physics in a narrower sense, the volumes of the University of Wisconsin Publications in Medieval Science are very important; see below.

General surveys. Alistair C. Crombie, *Augustine to Galileo: The History of Science A.D. 400–1650* (1952), revised and enlarged as *Medieval and Early Modern Science,* 2 vols. (1959); Richard Dales, *The Scientific Achievement of the Middle Ages* (1973); Edward J. Dijksterhuis, *The Mechanization of the World Picture,* C. Dikshoorn, trans. (1961); Edward Grant, *Physical Science in the Middle Ages* (1971), brief survey with a good annotated bibliography; David Lindberg, ed., *Science in the Middle Ages* (1978); Olaf Pedersen and Mogens Pihl, *Early Physics and Astronomy: A Historical Introduction* (1974); Charles J. Singer, *From Magic to Science* (1958); Nicholas H. Steneck, *Science and Creation in the Middle Ages: Henry of Langenstein (d. 1397) on Genesis* (1976), which attempts to give a general characterization of medieval science through an examination of the work of Henry of Langenstein; René Taton, ed., *History of Science: Ancient and Medieval Science from the Beginnings to 1450,* A. J. Pomerans, trans. (1963); William A. Wallace, *Causality and Scientific Explanation,* I, *Medieval and Early Classical Science* (1972); James A. Weisheipl, *The Development of Physical Theory in the Middle Ages* (1959).

Physics. The groundbreaking work on the history of medieval physics was done by Pierre Duhem, *Études sur Léonard de Vinci,* 3 vols. (1906–1913), and *Le système du monde,* 10 vols. (1913–1959); and Anneliese Maier, *Studien zur Naturphilosophie der Spätscholastic,* 5 vols. (1949–1958). More recently, fundamental work has been done by Marshall Clagett, particularly in his *The Science of Mechanics in the Middle Ages* (1957) and *Nicole Oresme and the Medieval Geometry of Qualities and Motions: A Treatise on the Uniformity and Difformity of Intensities Known as Tractatus de configurationibus qualitatum et motuum* (1968), and by the other authors in the University of Wisconsin Publications in Medieval Science series, for instance, H. Lamar Crosby, Jr., ed. and trans., *Thomas of Bradwardine: His Tractatus de proportionibus, Its Significance for the Development of Mathematical Physics* (1955); Edward Grant, ed. and trans., *Nicole Oresme: De proportionibus proportionum and Ad pauca respicientes* (1966); and Curtis Wilson, *William Heytesbury: Medieval Logic and the Rise of Mathematical Physics* (1956).

For more specialized subjects, see Edward Grant, *Much Ado About Nothing: Theories of Space and Vacuum from the Middle Ages to the Scientific Revolution* (1981); Norman Kretzmann, Anthony Kenny, and Jan Pinborg, eds., *The Cambridge History of Later Medieval Philosophy: From the Rediscovery of Aristotle to the Disintegration of Scholasticism, 1100–1600* (1982); Ernest A. Moody, *Studies in Medieval Philosophy, Science, and Logic: Collected Papers, 1933–1969* (1975); and John E. Murdoch and Edith Sylla, *The Cultural Context of Medieval Learning* (1975).

EDITH DUDLEY SYLLA

[See also **Aquinas, St. Thomas; Archimedes in the Middle Ages; Aristotle in the Middle Ages; Astronomy; Bradwardine, Thomas; Buridan, Jean; Burley, Walter; Grosseteste, Robert; Henry of Langenstein; Hildegard of Bingen, St.; Isidore of Seville, St.; Ockham, William of; Optics, Western European; Oresme, Nicole; Quadrivium; Scholasticism, Scholastic Method; Science, Islamic; Science, Jewish; Universities.**]

PIAST DYNASTY, the first ruling family of medieval Poland, took its name from a legendary mid ninth-century peasant who had established his rule over the Polanie in what became central Poland. The name "Piast" is related to the word *piastować,* "to take care of" or—in a political context—"to hold office." Linguistic scholars have thus suggested either that Piast turned his personal dominance into hereditary rule or that his name was originally a title.

The first historic member of the Piast dynasty was Mieszko I (*ca.* 922–992), who allied himself with the Přemyslid duke of Bohemia and in 965 married his daughter. The following year, Mieszko and his people accepted Christianity. Before his death Mieszko established his control over the territories to the south around Kraków and to the north along the stretches of the lower Oder. He also placed his lands under papal protection. His oldest son, Bolesław I the Brave (967–1025), was closely allied with the emperor Otto III, who confirmed the ecclesiastical organization of Poland in 1000 at the Congress of Gniezno. Bolesław subsequently, however, had to defend his territories against Emperor Henry II. He also consolidated Piast control over southern Poland and expanded to the east. On Easter Sunday 1025 Bolesław was crowned king with papal permission. This symbolic act elevated Poland into the community of nations, turned the Piast family into a royal dynasty, and established the *regnum Poloniae* as an ideal that could survive the absence of a king and the political vicissitudes of territorial fragmentation.

During the next century, however, the dynasty did not prosper, though the princely or royal capital was successfully transferred from central Poland to Kraków. Rule was sometimes disputed between brothers, and the accession of the oldest son was by no means assured. In addition, the status of the monarchy was not clear. Only some of the rulers in the eleventh century received the title of king. The early Piast monarchy had been a highly personal institution, whose support had been derived from its military retainers. By the twelfth century these followers had become an ambitious and powerful noble stratum within society. Factional strife and noble particularism were destroying the accomplishments of the early Piasts.

To regulate these centrifugal tendencies, Bolesław III the Wry-mouthed (*d.* 1138) divided the regnum among his four surviving sons, naming the eldest as grand prince (*princeps* or *senior*). Succession was to be in the line of the oldest living brother or the oldest member of the following generations. Within the century, however, this rotational system failed. Until the early fourteenth century, the kingdom was divided among a number of petty Piast princelings, many of whom pursued narrow policies of personal aggrandizement. The decades between 1138 and 1320 were the sorriest in the history of the dynasty, though all the lands ruled by the first Piasts (except for Pomerania) remained in the hands of the family. Ironically, in the midst of political disunity, there was a widespread recognition that the Piast family was an element of Polish unity. In the thirteenth century, several Silesian Piasts attempted to restore the monarchy, and the duke Przemysł II of Great Poland even accomplished it briefly. But true dynastic and political unity did not come until the reign of the Kujavian Piast, Władysław I Łokietek (Ladislas the Short) (*d.* 1333).

Władysław I gained the support of the church, the nobles, and the rising stratum of the knights. He also became identified as the defender of Polish territories against foreign threats, and he suppressed the opposition of the German merchants in such important centers as Kraków. His coronation in 1320 marked the end of territorial fragmentation. Although he strove to recover Silesia and Pomerania, at his death in 1333 the kingdom was beset by foreign attack. His inattention to internal administration and these grim military realities obscure, however, some very real accomplishments. The resurrection of the monarchy proved to be enduring. He forged ties with Hungary in 1320 by marrying his daughter to the first Angevin ruler of the Magyar kingdom, and the Polish-Hungarian alliance continued into the modern period. He married his son Casimir to a Lithuanian princess and thereby turned Polish interest to a region which became crucial by the end of the century.

His son and successor Casimir III (1310–1370) was the greatest of the royal Piasts. He purchased peace and territorial stability with Bohemia by recognizing Luxembourg's claims over Silesia (1335, 1339) and with the Teutonic Knights by recognizing their control over Pomerania (Treaty of Kalisz, 1343). In 1340 he invaded Ruthenia, captured Lwów, and eventually brought nearly the whole of that region under Polish control. In the meantime, he obtained the feudal submission of Mazovia, strengthened Poland's position in relation to Brandenburg, and extended its borders slightly in Silesia.

In internal affairs, Casimir reformed the currency, introduced new taxes, recovered royal estates, and regulated the mineral resources of the kingdom. Increased royal revenues enabled him to build more than fifty stone fortresses. Casimir reorganized the system of military recruitment, codified Polish law into two chief statutes, and founded the University of Kraków in 1364. Throughout his reign, he strove to develop an administration that was truly national and royal. All these developments greatly strengthened royal power. During Casimir's reign the concept of the *corona regni Poloniae* as something distinct from the person of an individual monarch emerged clearly.

Casimir produced no male heir, and the Piast dynasty came to an end in 1370. (By prior arrangement, he was succeeded by his nephew Louis of Hungary, whose reign saw the beginnings of the dissolution of royal power.) Other branches of the Piast family ruled in Mazovia until 1526 and in Silesia until the late seventeenth century. The Piast dynasty intermarried with many other royal or princely dynasties in central, northern, and eastern Europe. During the politically troubled times of the twelfth and thirteenth centuries, the dynasty produced a number of saints, most of them female, and also provided the chief thread of historic continuity of medieval Poland.

BIBLIOGRAPHY

Norman Davies, *God's Playground: A History of Poland,* I (1982), 61–105; Paul W. Knoll, *The Rise of the Polish Monarchy: Piast Poland in East Central Europe, 1320–1370* (1972); Tadeusz Manteuffel, *The Formation of the Polish State: The Period of Ducal Rule, 963–1194,* Andrew Gorski, trans. (1982).

PAUL W. KNOLL

[See also **Bohemia-Moravia; Hungary; Otto III; Poland.**]

PICARD LANGUAGE. Because of the distinctive characteristics and semi-independent functioning of the various dialects in the territory now known as France, it was customary in the Middle Ages to accord them the status of languages. In 1260 an Englishman, Roger Bacon, remarked that the French language comprised French, Norman, Picard, and Burgundian: "Nam et idiomata variantur eiusdem linguae apud diversos, sicut patet de lingua gallicana, quae apud Gallicos et Normannos et Picardos et Burgundos multiplici variatur idiomate" (*Opus maius,* Pt. 3). The Englishman's subdivision of French into only four dialects might well have seemed restrictive to the local inhabitants. For example, in the same century the troubadour Peire Cardinal (born at Puy-en-Velay *ca.* 1180) would have added at least one other, since he commented that he spoke neither Norman nor Poitevin. Furthermore, the fourteenth-century *Psautier de Metz* advertised itself as a psalter "in the Lorraine language." There is no doubt, however, that Picard was one of the most influential koines that developed out of Vulgar Latin.

Its distinctiveness was both phonetic and orthographic, and there were extrinsic as well as intrinsic reasons for that distinctiveness. Picardy and Flanders comprised fertile plains, drained by the Somme and the Oise. The territory was therefore coveted, and subject to invasion, beginning with the Salian Franks in the fifth century. A preponderance of Germanic topographical and agricultural terms and the persistence of Germanic speech habits were part of Picardy's enduring legacy of foreign invasion.

Its first extant literary document in the vernacular, the *Séquence de Ste. Eulalie,* records certain characteristic features of the dialect as early as 880:

PICARD LANGUAGE

the retention of velar *k* before *a* (*cose* < *causa*), diphthongization (*chielt* < *calet, maint* < *manet, buona* < *bona*), vocalization (*diaule* < *diabolum*), and the identity of masculine and feminine forms of the article (*lo* for *Eulalie*), for example. The *Eulalie* and the tenth-century *Jonas* sermon, both from St.-Amand-les-Eaux in Valenciennes, demonstrate the important role played by the church in promoting the vernacular language after the Edict of the Council of Tours in 813. Not least important in this regard was the contribution of ecclesiastical women, of whom a large proportion remained Latin-illiterate. Thus, while Latin was unchallenged as the official language of church and state, the vernacular flourished and produced in the prospering communes and urban centers of the twelfth and thirteenth centuries a vibrant literature that was unrivaled for its satire and its independence of thought.

Political and not literary dominance brought about the eventual triumph of Picard's rival, the Francien dialect. The victory was not immediate. Philip Augustus annexed Amiénois and Vermandois to the royal domain (beginning in 1185), but in 1182 Conon de Béthune, beholden to no one, reproved the French queen Alix and her son the king (Philip Augustus) for their insular rudeness. They had ridiculed his Picard accent in court, and with true Picard independence he therefore accused them of ignorance and discourtesy:

Ne chil ne sont bien apris ne cortois
Qui m'ont repris, se j'ai dit mos d'Artois
Car je ne fui pas noris à Pontoise.

Those are not well bred or courteous
Who corrected me when I used Artois words
For I was not brought up at Pontoise.

Picardy remained subject to political change. By the Treaty of Arras in 1435 Philip the Good, duke of Burgundy, won back Ponthieu and much of the Somme domain from France. Picardy was reconquered for France in 1477, but although the threats to Picardy's political autonomy never ceased, neither did its regional self-awareness and its linguistic pride. Picardisms continued to appear in the works of its major authors: for example, in the *Chronicles* of Jehan Froissart (*ca.* 1337–after 1404) and in Jean Molinet's historiography more than a century later. In the sixteenth century the Pléiade's proselytizing of the vernacular language's native resources made regionalisms fashionable again in literature.

Picard followed the same main trends as Francien (the speech of the Île-de-France) in its development from Vulgar Latin, though local patterns are visible from the earliest texts. Strong tonic stress was responsible for many of these local patterns. Listed below are the most common Picard forms for the assistance of readers who are familiar only with Francien. The treatment cannot be exhaustive, however, because of the multiplicity of possible forms within a single region and sometimes even with a single text. For example, tonic blocked vowels were, in most regions of France, immune to change because of their position behind two or more consonants, but in Picard even some tonic blocked vowels lengthened. Of the tonic blocked vowels

[a] from Latin *ā, ă* was usually preserved:
partem > *part*

However, Picard texts show much hesitation between the pronunciations [ar] and [ęr], especially in the later Middle Ages:

berbe (*cf.* Francien *barbe*), *chergeier* (*cf.* Francien *chargier*)
[ę] from Latin *ĕ* dipthongized:
servum > *sierf*
[ẹ] from Latin *ē, ĭ* remained relatively stable:
mĭssam > *messe*
[ị] from Latin *ī* also remained:
villam > *ville*
[ǫ] from Latin *ŏ* diphthongized when it occurred before *r* and *s:*
tostum > *tuest*
[ọ] from Latin *ō, ŭ* remained stable:
unquam > *onques*
[ụ] from Latin *ū* remained stable:
nullum > *nul*

The palatalization of [ụ] > [ü], which occurred first in the southern regions of France in the Gallo-Roman period, occurred relatively late in the northeast, and, in fact, did not occur at all in a few northeastern areas.

Tonic free vowels usually lengthened and diphthongized:

[a] usually diphthongized in Picard > *ei:*
patrem > *pere, peire* (*cf.* Francien *pere*)
[ę] > *ieu, iu,* which occasionally monophthongized > i:
Deus > *Dieu, Diu*
[ẹ] > *ei,* which usually developed further into *oi:*
vitrum > *voirre* (In the west of the region *ei* was more frequent than *oi.*)
[ị] > *i:*

PICARD LANGUAGE

morire > *morir*
[ǫ] diphthongized > *ue:*
cor > cuer
[ọ] diphthongized > *ou* (written also sometimes as *o*), and in most areas then moved further > *eu:*
dolorem > dolor, dolour, doleur
[ụ] was preserved, then usually palatalized
murum > mur (> mür)

Other results of heavy tonic stress upon the Picard vowel system were:

1. The disappearance of the atonic vowel *e* when in hiatus:
vestituram > vest(e)ure
2. The consonantalization of *i* before *e* in verb-endings:
Afferries is a trisyllable in the verse of *Aucassin et Nicolette.*
3. The reduction of the weak forms of the possessive pronoun and the definite article to a single form for both genders:
men, ten, sen; me, te, se; le
4. The reduction of diphthongs and triphthongs: *ie* and *ue* before [ẹ] > *i* and *u*, for example, *blechie* (*cf.* Francien *bleciée*), *puent* (*cf.* Francien *pueent*) *ieu* and *üeu* > *iu* and *ü*, for example, *liu* (*cf.* Francien *lieu*) and *fu* (from **fueu, cf.* Francien *feu*)
5. The loss of the second (less stressed) element of the diphthongs *ie* (*destrir, cf.* Francien *destrier*), *ue* (murt, *cf.* Francien *muert*), *ai* (*frales, cf.* Francien *frailes*), and *oi* (*glore, cf.* Francien *gloire*).
6. The differentiation of the triphthong *eau* to *iau* (*biaus, cf.* Francien *beaus*) and the diphthong *ou* [ǫu] to *au* or *eu:*
taut (*cf.* Francien *tout*, 3rd pers. sing. pres. indic. of *toudre < tollere*), *peu* (*cf.* Francien *pou*)

Nasalization in the Picard vowel system produced the following distinctive results:

Open and close *e* plus nasal blocked (that is, plus consonant) gave the graphy *en* [ẽ], and retained this unlowered into the Old French period (*diemenche, cf.* Francien *dimanche*). Thus, the graphies *an* and *en* do not rhyme in Picard (*cf.* Francien, where *en* and *an* could be coupled as [ã]).

Closed *i* plus nasal plus [w] gave in many areas *iun* (*chiuncquante, cf.* Francien *cinkante*).

Close *o* plus nasal gave *o* [ọ̃] and, more frequently, *ou* (*couroune, persoune*). Nasalization of close *o* was, however, later than that of [a], [ę], and [ẹ]. The graphy *ou* suggests this hesitation.

The consonantal groups *nl, nr, lr* were retained in Picard without either denasalization or the addition of an interconsonantal glide, for example, *ensanle* (*cf.* Francien *ensemble*), *estranle* (*cf.* Francien *estrangle*), *tenre* (*cf.* Francien *tendre*). Similarly, intervocalic [ẑ] and [ŝ] induced no preceding palatal glide in Picard, for example, *lazsier* (*cf.* Francien *laissier*).

Before velarized *l* [ł] and *l mouillé* [ʎ], [ẹ] was lowered to [ę] to [a]: *illos > aus* (*cf.* Francien *eus*).

Velarization and vocalization of *l mouillé* occurred after [i̯]: *fius < filius* (*cf.* Francien *fils*).

Velarization affected even the nasal vowel [ã], which became in the Old French period [ɑ̃], then [ọ̃]. Thus, in Picard *enfan* rhymed with *monde.*

In the consonant system of Picard the three most striking orthographic characteristics are:

1. Its retention of the velar articulation of *c, k,* and *g* before *a, e,* and *i*: for example, *kose* (*cf.* Francien *chose*), *gardin* (*cf.* Francien *jardin*).
2. The forward shift of *k* before *e* or *i* initial of a word or syllable merely to [tš]: *avanchier, prinche* (*cf.* Francien *avancier, prince,* in which the affricated [tš] had shifted to [ts] and later to [s].)
3. The preservation of the initial Germanic bilabial *w* in German borrowings and contaminated Latin forms: *warder* < **wardjan* (*cf.* Francien *garder*), *waaigner* < **waidanjan* (*cf.* Francien *gagner*), and *willecomme* (this Flemish word for "welcome" did not exist in Francien).

Other characteristics frequent enough to deserve mention here are the early conversion of *ts* to *s* (*enfans,* while Francien continued to use the graphy *ts* or *z* as in *enfanz*); the preservation of final *t* unsupported after a tonic vowel (*donnet* rather than the Francien *donne*); and the frequent metathesis of *r* (*affreant, cf.* Francien *afferant, kerstienté, cf.* Francien *chrestienté*). It should be noted, however, that metathesis was not unknown in Francien, and that it affected the verb endings (future and conditional) of both dialects equally.

Distinctive features of Picard's morphological system were determined to a large extent by the phonetic preferences listed above and, as in any language, by analogy.

There was an identity of masculine and feminine forms of the definitive article:

	Singular	
	Masc.	Fem.
Subject	*li*	*le* or *li*
Oblique	*le*	*le*
	Plural	
	Masc.	Fem.
Subject	*li*	*les*
Oblique	*les*	*les*

There was a preference for the stressed form of the personal pronoun *jou*, and *mihi* survived as *mi*, giving rise to analogical *ti* and *si:*

	Singular	Plural
1st person	*mi, moi*	*no(u)s*
2nd person	*ti, toi*	*vo(u)s*
3rd person (masc.)	*li, lui*	*aus*
3rd person (fem.)	*li, lui*	*eles*
Reflexive	*si, soi*	

The stressed forms of possessive adjectives *mi(e)ue, ti(e)ue* survived. A new set of unstressed plural possessive adjectives was formed analogically from the accusative plural forms:

	Singular	
	Masc.	Fem.
Subject	*nos, vos*	*no, vo*
Oblique	*no, vo*	*no, vo*
	Plural	
	Masc.	Fem.
Subject	*no, vo*	*nos, vos*
Oblique	*nos, vos*	*nos, vos*

An analogical *s* was added to the subject singular of the masculine demonstrative *cist* (< *ecce iste*) and *cil* (< *ecce ille*); then the two forms were amalgamated into (*i*)*ciz* or (*i*)*cis*.

In the verb system there was a preference for the first-person plural endings *-omes* and *-iemes* (as in *avomes*, the first-person plural present indicative of *avoir*, and *aviemes*, the first-person plural imperfect indicative), and for a first-person singular present and perfect indicative ending in *-c(h)*: fac(h) (*faire*), euc(h) (*avoir*) with, occasionally, an analogical present subjunctive form in *-che* or *-ge: meche* (*metre*).

In strong "S"-type perfects there was a preference for the third-person plural form *-is(s)ent* rather than *-rent* or *-strent: missent* (*metre*), *fisent* (*faire*).

There was a reduction of the first-conjugation endings *-ier* and *-ierent* to *-ir* and *-irent*, respectively, with a consequent coalescence of first- and second-conjugation endings in the perfect tense.

Syntactic differences between medieval Picard and neighboring dialects were not substantial enough to warrant their consideration here.

BIBLIOGRAPHY

Jules Corblet, *Glossaire étymologique et comparatif du patois picard, ancien et moderne, précédé de recherches philologiques et littéraires sur ce dialecte* (1851); Georges Doutrepont, *Étude linguistique sur Jacques de Hemricourt et son époque* (1892); Louis-Fernand Flutre, *Le moyen picard d'après les textes littéraires du temps (1560–1660)* (1970); Carl T. Gossen, *Die Pikardie als Sprachlandschaft des Mittelalters, auf Grund der Urkunden* (1942), "La scripta des chartes picardes," in *Revue de linguistique romane,* **26** (1962), and *Grammaire de l'ancien picard* (1970); Felix Lecoy, "Le vocabulaire dialectal ou régional dans les oeuvres littéraires au moyen âge," in Georges Straka, ed., *Les dialectes de France au moyen âge et aujourd'hui* (1967); Halina Lewicka, "L'élément picard dans la langue de quelques poètes arrageois des XIIe et XIIIe siècles," in Congresso internazionale di studi romanzi, 8th, *Atti,* II, 1 (1956); Auguste de Menche de Loisne, *L'ancien dialecte artésien d'après les chartes en langue vulgaire du chapitre d'Arras, 1248–1301* (1898); Mildred Katharine Pope, *From Latin to Modern French,* 2nd rev. ed. (1973); Louis Remacle, *Le problème de l'ancien wallon* (1948); M. Wilmotte, "Études de dialectologie wallonne," in *Romania,* **17–19** (1888–1890, repr. 1974).

JEANETTE M. A. BEER

[See also **French Language.**]

PICARD LITERATURE. Of all the areas of France in which literature was cultivated, the Picard-Walloon area provided the richest and most varied range of works. Moreover, its literary traditions were long—it was responsible for the first literary text of France (the ninth-century *Eulalia*) and writings in the Picard dialect continued through to "the last great Picard" of the fifteenth century, Jehan Froissart.

In the Middle Ages, "Picardy," when used in a literary or linguistic context, covered a much wider territory than the present geographical Picardy. Indeed, it extended beyond the ecclesiastical Picardy, which comprised only the dioceses of Beauvais, Senlis, Soissons, Laon, Noyon, Amiens, Arras, Cambrai, Thérouanne, and Tournai. When, in 1259, the University of Paris recognized the existence of a Picard "nation" in its organization, and when around the same time Roger Bacon in his *Opus maius* commented on the distinctiveness of French, Norman, Picard, and Burgundian, the word "Picard" broadly designated dialects spoken in Ponthieu, Vermandois, Amiénois, Flanders,

Hainaut, and beyond. The literary contribution of that Picardy was significant in all genres. In the twelfth and thirteenth centuries it may even be said to have dominated several genres, notably the fabliau, comic theater, and lyric poetry.

HAGIOGRAPHY

The first piece of French literature extant is from the Picard-Walloon region. The *Séquence de Ste. Eulalie* (*ca.* 880) is contained in a manuscript from the Benedictine monastery at St. Amand-les-Eaux near Valenciennes. In a simple, compressed style the twenty-nine-line hymn narrates the martyrdom of a young girl of noble birth, Eulalie, who was tortured, burned, and decapitated in persecutions instigated by the Roman emperors Diocletian and Maximian. The text was composed to be sung for the edification of the faithful on the saint's feast day. Although it is now the sole survivor of its kind from the ninth century, it was presumably one of many ecclesiastical texts that the church at that time converted to the vernacular.

The same monastery of St. Amand produced and preserved another early vernacular text, the tenth-century *Jonas* fragment, sometimes called the *Fragment de Valenciennes*. It contains a priest's notes for a sermon in which French is intermingled with Latin, reflecting the priest's bilingual preparation. Both the *Eulalie* sequence and the *Jonas* fragment are undoubtedly products of the Council of Tours's edict in 813 that priests should use the language of their congregations and should translate their sermons *in rusticam romanam linguam aut theotiscam*.

In the later centuries hagiography flourished and texts become more abundant. It was a frequent practice to rework lives from legendary hagiographic collections such as the *Vitae patrum* and the *Legenda aurea*. Many of the adaptations, such as *La vie saint Jehan-Baptiste, La vie saint Franchois, Les miracles de saint Eloi,* and the nine miracles in Paris, Bibliothèque Nationale, MS Fr. no. 375, are anonymous. However, prominent literary figures also chose to devote their energies to hagiographical writing, either exclusively or in combination with other literary pursuits. Wauchier de Denain made a translation (before 1212) of the *Vitae patrum* for Philippe de Namur. Apparently only eight texts of the collection were completed: *Vie de saint Paul l'ermite; Vie de saint Antoine; Vie de saint Hilarion; Vie de saint Malchus; Vie de Paul le Simple, ermite;* two books of the *Dialogue de saint Gregoire le Grand;* Rufinus of Aquileia's *Historia monachorum* and also his *Verba seniorum*. Around the same time (early thirteenth century) Pierre de Beauvais, also known as Pierre le Picard, wrote a verse *Vie de saint Eustache* and *La translation et les miracles de saint Jacques* (1212).

Jean Bodel (*ca.* 1165/1170–*ca.* 1210) wrote a semiliturgical verse drama, *Jeu de saint Nicolas,* in Arras around 1200. Despite its central subject matter, a conflict between Christians and Saracens on pagan territory and a challenge to St. Nicholas that he demonstrate his powers by protecting royal treasure, the play contains invaluable details about life in Arras. A tavern scene is clearly in Arras rather than in Africa, and local personages and idiosyncrasies are satirized. The hagiographical purpose is never lost, however. The saint intervenes to restore the pagan king's treasure, and the pagans are converted to Christianity.

The eleventh and twelfth centuries produced local collections of Mary legends all over France, and not least in the Picard region. These collections were used and reused, as, for example, by Gautier de Coinci (*ca.* 1177–1236), monk and eventually prior of St. Médard, who turned miracles from the Laon and from the Soissons collection into verse in his fifty-eight *Miracles de Nostre Dame*. He also narrated the discovery of St. Leocadia's lost relics (then at St. Ghislain in the diocese of Cambrai) in the octosyllabic *La vie de sainte Léocadie* and retold the lives of St. Bon and St. Hildefonse.

The *Conte del tumbeor Nostre Dame,* one of three pious stories attributed to a Cistercian monk in a Ponthieu abbey, was derived from Gautier's *Miracles*. It is the tale of a jongleur who offers up to the Virgin the only gift he possesses—his tumbling. Also in honor of the Virgin Huon le Roi de Cambrai wrote *Regrés Nostre Dame* (*ca.* 1250) and an *Ave Maria en roumans*. He was the author of another hagiographic piece, *La vie de saint Quentin,* around 1271.

Early in the same century Gui de Cambrai wrote an adaptation of the pious legend *Barlaam and Josaphat* for Gilles de Vermandois, interpolating a number of satirical digressions on contemporary society.

EPICS

One of the earliest epics, the late-twelfth-century *Raoul de Cambrai,* is a story of revolt in which the hero forges his own ruin by acts of cruelty and impiety, and is possibly Picard in origin. A Bertolai de Laon is named in the chanson as an eyewitness of the events described, but Joseph Bédier has argued that Bertolai was a fabrication and has suggested St. Géri near Cambrai as the place where the chanson originated. Bédier's view has been challenged by Ferdinand Lot and others, and the debate on author and origins continues even today.

The *Mort de Garin de Loherenc,* from the Lotharingian cycle of epics, is also of uncertain authorship, although Jean de Flagy probably wrote it in the latter part of the twelfth century. Its hero precipitates a war between the Lotharingians and the Bordelais by aspiring to marry Blancheflor of Arles. He is finally killed in ambush, but not before the author has narrated multiple battle scenes, truces, and renewals of battle. The Lotharingian cycle itself comprises four branches: *Hervis de Metz, Garin le Loherain, Gerbert de Metz,* and *Anseïs de Metz.* Although its extant manuscripts (numbering around sixty) are of diverse provenance, it is relevant here both for its local references and for its usefulness as an historical source to later authors.

Jean Bodel wrote an epic about Charlemagne's campaign against the Saxon Guiteclin (Witikind), the *Chanson des Saisnes* (*ca.* 1200). The events narrated are almost entirely fictional (although Jean cited St. Burgundofaro's church of Meaux as his source). The epic is unusual in that rhymes and assonanced dodecasyllables intermingle in the work.

The original version of the *Chanson d'Antioche,* narrating events in the First Crusade from Peter the Hermit's vision to the second Antioch battle, is attributed to Richard the Pilgrim from Arras. Unfortunately, the *Chanson* survives only in a version rewritten by Graindor de Douai between 1177 and 1181.

The mid-thirteenth-century *Auberi le Bourguignon* is also Picard in origin. The many love and war adventures of its hero in Bavaria and Flanders end, after 27,000 decasyllabic lines, in his marriage to the princess of Flanders.

In the same century Adenet le Roi, so called for his honorary title "king of the minstrels" in the court of Guy de Dampierre, count of Flanders, is celebrated for a skillful reworking of three old chansons de geste into *Buevon de Conmarchis, Les enfances Ogier,* and *Berthe aus grans piés.*

Jean d'Outremeuse (1338–1400) wrote *Ogier le Danois* (now lost) and the *Geste de Liège.* Another fourteenth-century chanson, the anonymous *Lion de Bourges,* incorporated romance themes in its lengthy narration of the adventures of Lion. *Lion de Bourges* probably originated in Tournai.

Walter of Châtillon (Gautier de Châtillon or de Lille) compiled a Latin epic *Alexandreis* from Quintus Curtius Rufus' *De rebus gestis Alexandri Magni* around 1180; the work is relevant here for its influence upon vernacular versions of the Alexander legend: for example, Jean le Névelon's *Venjance Alixandre* and Gui de Cambrai's poem on the same subject, the *Vengement Alixandre.*

ROMANCE

In Picardy, as in other regions, Breton material was a favorite source of exoticism and magic for romances. *Gliglois,* written anonymously in the early thirteenth century, relates the trials and triumphs of the young German Gliglois, squire to King Arthur's knight Gawain. Another squire of Gawain, Meriadeuc, is the hero of the *Chevalier as deus espees* (*ca.* 1250). His name was given to him by Kay after he succeeded in releasing a magic sword, thereby winning the Lady of Caradigan in marriage. A thirteenth-century poet, Jehan, narrated the *Merveilles de Rigomer,* a castle visited by Lancelot in quest of adventure, and from which he had to be rescued by other knights from King Arthur's court.

The fantastic adventures of a prince on a flying horse in Adenet le Roi's *Cléomadès,* written between 1274 and 1282, probably derive from Oriental tales. The author has also incorporated lyrics by his contemporaries in the narrative.

Le roman d'Abladane, a short anonymous fragment (*ca.* 1260) that provides an imaginative account of Amiens in the time of the Caesars, survives only in eighteenth-century copies. It was incorrectly attributed by Du Cange and Dom Grenier to Richard de Fournival. It claims to be a translation from Latin by one of Richard's disciples, but in fact, it was almost certainly written in the vernacular to satisfy contemporary tastes for historical romance.

Fantasy and magic are both found in the *Livre de Mélusine,* which narrates the legendary beginnings of the Lusignans. Jean d'Arras wrote it for Jean, duke of Berry, in 1393. Mélusine, the Serpent Fairy, was the wife of Raymond de Lusignan, by whom she had ten children, thus founding a dynasty.

The *Eracle,* written by Gautier d'Arras some time after 1164, was based on a Greco-Byzantine romance, set in Rome. Its hero is endowed with three invaluable gifts: the ability to assess the worth of gems, women, and horses. A prudent use of this talent causes him to be elected eventually as the emperor of Constantinople. The romance was dedicated, significantly, to Thibaut V, count of Blois, and to Baldwin V of Hainaut. Gautier's *Ille et Galeron,* written between 1167 and 1170, used the folk theme of a husband with two wives as the basis for its plot.

Another folk theme—two men wagering on the fidelity of a wife—was used by Jean Renart in *Guillaume de Dôle* (*ca.* 1210), and was reborrowed by Gerbert de Montreuil's *Roman de la violette* (*ca.* 1220). Jean Renart also wrote, *ca.* 1200, the adventure romance *Escoufle* (which he dedicated to Baldwin IX of Flanders) and the courtly *Lai de l'ombre* (*ca.* 1220). He has been suggested as the author of two satirical works—*Du plait Renart de Dammartin* and *De Renart et de Piandoue.*

Folktale elements combine with *invraisemblances* (improbabilities) in the *Manekine* (The girl without a hand), written by Philippe de Rémi, sire de Beaumanoir (*ca.* 1250–1296). A father's incestuous love for his daughter leads him to cut off her hands (which miraculously regenerate). She flees his kingdom and, after aimless wandering, marriage to a foreign king, treachery, misunderstandings, and the punishment of being set adrift at sea, is reunited with her husband.

The thirteenth-century *Fille du conte de Ponthieu* is an adventure romance from Hainaut about the vicissitudes of a count's daughter. Violated by bandits while on pilgrimage, she attempts to murder her husband, who witnessed the crime. Her father puts her adrift in a small boat; she is sold to the sultan of Aumarie, bears him a daughter and a son (his future heir), then escapes from the Holy Land with her father and husband when they come on pilgrimage.

Departing from these conventional romance peripeties, the thirteenth-century Gautier le Cordier de Tournai wrote *Gilles de Chin* about an actual personage who died in 1137. The poem was transferred into prose near the beginning of the fifteenth century. *Gilles de Chin,* which relates the imagined exploits of a historical person, is considered to be the first historico-biographical romance.

Another real person, the Picard poet Guy de Thourotte, governor of the castle of Coucy, was utilized by Jakemes (often identified with Jacques Bretiaus, the author of the *Tournoi de Chauvency, ca.* 1285) when he wrote the *Châtelain de Coucy* at the end of the thirteenth century.

Jehan Froissart's *Méliador* (completed after 1383) reverted to all the complexities of intrigue that made romance so vulnerable to parody.

Allied to romance as well as to lyric poetry and drama, the early-thirteenth-century *Aucassin et Nicolette* defies classification. Its anonymous author calls it a *cantefable,* presumably because lyrics alternate with prose throughout the narrative. A simple ten-line melody is provided for the seven syllable assonanced lyrics, each of which concludes upon a four-syllable feminine line departing from the assonance. The story has affinities with *Floire et Blancheflor* and shows Moorish influence. It parodies epic and romantic extravagance with subtle humor. Aucassin, son of Count Garin of Beaucaire, loves Nicolette, formerly a Saracen slave and now the adopted daughter of a viscount in Beaucaire. Count Garin forbids the marriage, and the lovers endure multiple adventures and mock adventures before the author reunites them in Beaucaire. (The locality described bears no resemblance to the geographic Beaucaire, and it presumably reproduces a setting in Picardy where town and castle were on one level.) *Aucassin et Nicolette* survives in only one manuscript.

Parody of epic and romance is more blatant in the rollicking animal adventures of the *Roman de Renart,* the collective name for a series of tales that arose in the twelfth and thirteenth centuries to celebrate the activities of Renard the Fox and such characters as King Noble the Lion, High Priest Bernard the Ass, and Musart the Camel, papal legate. Many of the multiple branches of the *Roman de Renart* originated in Picardy, and most of its authors were anonymous. A persistent theme was *le trompeur trompé* (the deceiver deceived). The origins of the Renard romance have aroused much debate. Popular folklore, Germanic animal tales, bourgeois irreverence, and Latin imitation have all been cited as key influences. Unquestionably, the Latin *Ysengrimus,* written by the Flemish poet Nivardus around 1150 and based upon the Latin *Ecbasis captivi,* was also a source of material for this universally popular composite of animal stories.

FABLIAUX

Picard authors also dominated the fabliau, which is why the Picard form of the word ousted other variants, such as *fabel* or *flabel.* The fabliau was typically a poem of about 350 octosyllabic lines, resembling the *Roman de Renart* in its bourgeois values and its irreverence, but without the *Roman de Renart*'s animal characters to attenuate the immoralities implicit in the plot. Moreover, humor in the fabliau was more explicit and less subtle. A favorite theme was adultery, with clerics often portrayed as lovers in a love triangle. The mood of the fabliaux was consistently anticlerical and antifemale.

One hundred and sixty fabliaux are extant. Of these the oldest is *Richeut,* written some time during the second half of the twelfth century and of unknown origin. In the thirteenth and fourteenth centuries, however, at the height of its popularity, the fabliau was favored by several well-known writers, such as Jean Bodel, Gautier de Coinci, Gautier le Leu, and Huon le Roi de Cambrai (whose *Vair Palefroi* departs by its courtliness from the customary scurrilous irreverence of the genre). As with the *Roman de Renart,* there are several schools of thought concerning the ultimate origin of fabliau material, for example, folklorist, Gallic, Indian-Persian-Oriental, and classical.

THEATER

The Walloon region was probably responsible for the first known nativity plays in the vernacular in the twelfth century; Gustave Cohen has identified the *Mystères et moralités du manuscrit 617 de Chantilly* (Musée Condé, Chantilly) as a thirteenth-century product. But it was in comic theater that the northeastern region surpassed all others.

Jean Bodel's semiliturgical *Jeu de saint Nicolas* was written around the end of the twelfth or the beginning of the thirteenth century.

The anonymous *Courtois d'Arras* from *ca.* 1220 updates the parable of the Prodigal Son, using, like the *Jeu de saint Nicolas,* an Arras tavern for part of the action. The manner of presentation for this short drama (664 rhymed octosyllables) remains in doubt. The work was probably intended as a dramatic monologue in which one jongleur would play all eight parts.

A coarse bourgeois realism reminiscent of the fabliau and portending the farce of the future characterizes the anonymous *Le garçon et l'aveugle* (*ca.* 1270–1280), which draws its humor from the tricks a derisive valet plays on a blind beggar whom he is supposed to lead around.

Arras is once more the setting for *Le jeu de la feuillée* by Adam de la Halle, also known as Adam le Bossu (Adam the Hunchback), who died *ca.* 1288. The play begins with Adam's decision to leave Arras and his wife in order to study in Paris. It combines topical allusions and satire of the locals with a fairy banquet and the Wheel of Fortune. Adam's *Jeu de Robin et de Marion* is a transposition of the lyric *pastourelle* into dramatic form. Marion's rejection of a passing knight in favor of her shepherd lover is acted out with singing and dancing in this rustic fantasy for the aristocracy. (*Le jeu de Robin et Marion* was written during the time when Adam was in Italy serving as the count of Artois's poet and musician). After Adam's death, a prologue, the *Jeu du pèlerin,* was added in which a "pilgrim" hymns Adam's praises.

In the twelfth and thirteenth centuries, when wealthy patrons and *puys* (literary societies) encouraged and supported the performance of dramatic and lyric works, more theatrical pieces were produced than at any other time in Picardy's literary history. In the fifteenth century Eustache Mercadé (*d.* 1440) wrote under different circumstances, however. He was an official at Corbie and a dean of the law faculty at Paris. His ambitious *Vengeance de Notre Seigneur* and *Mystère de la Passion* reflect the didactic religiosity of his age rather than the verve and local realism of earlier times.

LYRIC POETRY

Like drama, lyric poetry flourished in the industrial centers of the north, and at least fifty collections, or chansonniers, have been preserved. One such is Alfred Jeanroy's phototype edition of *Le chansonnier d'Arras,* which reproduces a manuscript (no. 139) now owned by the municipal library of Arras. The city of Arras was, in fact, the lyric capital of the north, and boasted that its chansons were so exquisite that God himself took time to listen to them from heaven.

The period from the end of the twelfth to the end of the thirteenth century was especially rich. Adam de Givenci, Adam de la Halle, Andrieu Contredit, Audefroi le Batard, Baude Fastoul, Colart le Bouteillier, Gillebert de Berneville, Gilles and Guillaume le Vinier, Jean Bodel, Jean Bretel, Jean de Neuville, Moniot d'Arras, Oede de la Corroierie (poetess), Perrin d'Angicourt, Pierre de Corbie, Robert de le Pierre, Robert le Clerc, and Thomas de Chastel are only some of a large number of poets who were active at that time. They utilized traditional lyric forms but allowed themselves an unusually personal approach to their subject matter—through parody (as in the *Fatrasies d'Arras*), satire and explicit invective (see Alfred Jeanroy's edition of *Chansons et dits artésiennes du XIIIe siècle*), and intimate references to their own lives (as in Jean Bodel's *Congés*, Adam de la Halle's *Congé*, and the chansons of Conon de Béthune, the *Châtelain de Coucy*, and Blondel de Nesle). On the other hand, Richard de Fournival (*b.* 1201) employed a courtly koine that betrayed neither biographical details nor dialectal idiosyncrasies. His graceful, although somewhat obscure, lyrics maintain throughout the deceptively personal set of courtly stances that had come to characterize lyrical poetry.

At the end of the thirteenth century the minstrel Baudouin de Condé and his son Jean de Condé (who wrote for the Hainaut court) composed various types of court lyrics, and Jean Baillehaut wrote *Sottes chansons*. Jehan Froissart (*ca.* 1337–after 1404) excelled in the ballade, rondeau, pastourelle, virelai, and lai as well as in longer love poems (*L'espinette amoureuse* and *Le joli buisson de Jonece*). Jean de la Motte wrote *Le regret de Guillaume, comte de Haynneau*, in 1339, the *Parfait du paon* for Simon de Lille in 1340, *Voie d'enfer et de paradis*, and several mythological ballads.

The poetic center Tournai produced the anonymous *Dame loyale en amour*, a poem written as part of the courtly debate that arose from Alain Chartier's *La belle dame sans merci* (1424). A counterresponse, *La cruelle femme en amours*, was written in Tournai by Achille Caulier, who was a member of Tournai's "Chapel vert" association. Another distinguished poet of the "Chapel vert" was Pierre de Hauteville (1376–1448), who made a contribution to the *Belle dame sans merci* cycle with his *Confession et testament de l'amant trépassé de dueil*.

Another debate in love casuistry was conducted in the late-fourteenth-century *Cent ballades*, written by Jean de Saint-Pierre, seneschal of Eu, Boucicaut, Philippe d'Artois, count of Eu, and Jean de Cresecque, while they were prisoners in the East. In the *Cent ballades* they argue the desirability of fidelity in love. Jean de Werchin (1386–1462), seneschal of Hainaut, was involved in a poetic exchange of ballades with his squire Ghillebert de Lannoy in which they debated love casuistry. Jean was the author of a longer lyric work, *Le songe de la barge*, in 1404.

In the age of the *Grands rhétoriqueurs* Georges Chastellain (1405/1415–1475) used a variety of poetic forms to express his wide political, lyrical, and official interests. (In 1455 he became official chronicler to the duke of Burgundy.) Jean Molinet (1435–1507) also wrote prolifically on a wide range of subjects. Many of his poems were addressed to his patrons' political concerns. (He became the historiographer of the Burgundy court in 1475.) It is interesting to note that, despite context and the century in which Molinet wrote, his work still contained a multitude of "Picardisms."

HISTORY

The writing of history was undertaken for a variety of reasons. Local pride was particularly strong in the towns of Picardy, and the *Chroniques de Tournai*, for example, present Tournai as a second Rome. Tournai's chronicles, which begin with Tarquin and proceed through the time of Rome's emperors, derive much material from three regional histories: *Liber Herimanni de restauratione monasterii sancti Martini Tornacensis, Liber de antiquitate urbis Tornacensis ex revelatione Heinrici*, and *Historiae Tornacenses partim ex Herimanni libris excerptae*, all written around the middle of the twelfth century. Local pride and historical fantasy were even more characteristic of the later, amplified version of the *Chroniques de Tournai* in MS L. II 15 Bibl. Nat. Turin.

The necessity for local charts and records was obvious, but a count of medieval Flanders or Hainaut was just as likely to want a *Chronique artésienne* (1296–1304), a *Chronique tournaisienne* (1296–1314), his own version of the popular pseudo-historical *Pseudo-Turpin Chronicle*, or, in a later century, richly illustrated classical compilations like Jean Mansel's *Hystores rommaines* or his *La fleur des histoires* (made for Philip the Good, duke of Burgundy). Numerous patrons in the region are known to have commissioned the writing, copying, and preservation of historical works. Among the earliest were Baldwin VIII of Flanders (Baldwin V of Hainaut, 1150–1195), his sister Yolande, countess of Saint Pol; her husband, Hugues IV, count of Saint Pol; Baldwin IX, later the emperor of Constantinople; Philippe of Namur; Laurette of Alsace; Baldwin II, count of Guines; Renaud de Dammartin, count of Boulogne; Jean II de Nesle; Philippe de Dreux and Robert II de Dreux; and Guillaume de Caieu. The so-called *Histoires de Baudouin* was supposedly written by Baldwin VI, count of Hainaut and Flanders. The manuscript cannot be found, but Louis-Fernand Flutre convincingly argues that it is to be equated with another historical compilation, the so-called *Chronique de Baudouin d'Avesnes,* written some time later (between 1295 and 1307). The latter chronicle began with the creation of the world and ended in contemporary times, giving particular attention to Hainaut and to Baldwin's family genealogy. "Baldwin's" chronicle underwent several modifications. It was reshaped and converted into Latin; then subsequently Enguerrand de Coucy (cousin of Baldwin's wife, Félicité de Coucy) extracted from the Latin version genealogical material about France's first families in a work entitled *Livre du lignage de Coucy.* A further stage in the reshaping of "Baldwin's" chronicle was its abridgment to a version now generally known as the *Chroniques abrégées de Baudouin d'Avesnes.* This was the most popular of all the versions and itself was subject to numerous rehandlings and retellings.

There was a wider public, however, whose historical tastes were diverse enough to include the *Chronique d'Ernoul et de Bernard le Trésorier,* Jean Molinet's *Chroniques,* Georges Chastellain's chronicle of the events between 1419 and 1474 (written for the duke of Burgundy), Philippe Mouskès of Tournai's monumental *Chronique rimée,* beginning with the fall of Troy and ending in the thirteenth century, and Jean d'Outremeuse's even more monumental undertaking, *Myreur des histors,* which aimed to provide a prose history of the world.

Some chronicles are anonymous, like the *Estoire des rois d'Angleterre et de Normandie* (which may have been a source for the anonymous *Récits d'un ménestrel de Reims,* written around 1260), and the *Estoire des rois de France,* a translation of the *Historia regum Francorum.* The latter two *estoires* both originated anonymously in Béthune. Little beyond his name is known of Jean de Thuim of Hainaut, who produced a romanticized translation of Lucan's *Bellum civile, Ly hystore de Julius Cesar,* around the middle of the thirteenth century.

Perhaps the best-known historical contributions from Picardy were made by three chroniclers who were of different centuries, social circumstances, and educational background: Robert de Clari (1170?–1216), Jean le Bel (*ca.* 1290–*ca.* 1370), and Jehan Froissart (*ca.* 1337–after 1404). Robert was a relatively insignificant knight and vassal of Pierre d'Amiens. His vivid eyewitness account of the Fourth Crusade in *La conquête de Constantinople* preserves the experiences and emotions of the rank and file, giving a rare and valuable record from an illiterate, undistinguished, but devout crusader.

Jean le Bel compiled for Jean de Hainaut, lord of Beaumont, the *Vraies chroniques* of the kings of England, thereby providing an excellent source of information concerning the first part of the Hundred Years War. The *Vraies chroniques* became the main source, in fact, for the first book of chronicles compiled by Jehan Froissart; later books were based upon Froissart's own experiences and upon the personal testimony of eyewitnesses he interviewed. Froissart's history is an anecdotal but valuable record of selected events and issues in England, Scotland, Ireland, France, Flanders, Italy, and elsewhere. Like Jean le Bel, Froissart had a bias toward the English, but a change in his patrons and a reversal of his political fortunes caused him to revise his attitudes and his history. Later versions of the *Chroniques* became distinctly pro-French, but the unifying theme of chivalry remained constant.

Jacques du Clercq, born in Lille in 1420, showed a similar preoccupation with chivalric and noble deeds, and a similarly anecdotal approach to history, in his *Mémoires,* concerning the years 1448–1487. Another collection of *Mémoires* was written by Pierre de Fenin, prévôt of Arras, from his knowledge of battles and diplomacy between 1407 and 1427.

DIDACTIC AND MISCELLANEOUS WORKS

The range of didactic literature in the region is so wide that complete coverage is almost impossible. Translations from Latin into the vernacular include Herman de Valencienne's *Bible de sapience* (*ca.* 1190), a résumé of the historical-narrative books of the Old and New Testaments, and Alard de Cambrai's *Moralités des philosophes,* an early thirteenth-century adaptation in verse of the *Moralium dogma.* Robert Gaguin translated Caesar's *Commentaries* (1485) and part of Livy's *History of Rome* (1493) and wrote a vernacular poem, *Le débat du laboureur, du prestre, et du gendarme* (1480).

Jean d'Outremeuse compiled a lapidary from various Latin and vernacular sources, *Trésorier de philosophie naturelle des pierres précieuses.* The thirteenth-century *Mariage des sept arts* is Jean le Teinturier d'Arras's adaptation of a fifth-century Latin work, *De nuptiis Philologiae et Mercurii,* by Martianus Capella. That allegorical poem narrates in octosyllabic couplets the marriage of the Seven

Virtues to the elements of the quadrivium and the trivium!

Pierre de Beauvais was active in translation in the early thirteenth century. He produced a vernacular version of the *Pseudo-Turpin* for Guillaume de Caieu, in which he interpolated his translation of the *Iter Hierosolymitanum,* the prose *Voyage of Charlemagne.* While in the service of Philippe de Dreux, bishop of Beauvais, he translated the Latin *Physiologus* into a French prose bestiary. His verse *Mappemonde* was adapted from Honorius Augustodunensis, and he was probably responsible for *L'Olympiade* (also entitled in one manuscript *Les prises et conquestes de Jherusalem*). Despite some debate, his source for the latter has not been determined.

Richard de Fournival (*b.* 1201 in Amiens) renewed the bestiary tradition by applying the material of the *Physiologus* to the postures of love in his *Bestiaire d'amour.* He also wrote didactic works in Latin. Several love treatises, among them *Consaus d'amours, La puissance d'amours, Commens d'amours, Amistié de vraie amour,* and *De vetula,* are all attributed to him with reasonable certitude.

The *dit* was a popular medium for didacticism, teaching a moral lesson either piously or satirically in a brief poem. *Le dis dou vrai aniel,* written between 1291 and 1294, *Drei dits de l'ame,* and the *Dits et contes de Baudouin de Condé et de son fils Jean de Condé* are just a few examples of this favorite genre.

Huon le Roi de Cambrai used verse for a didactic *ABC,* which attributes moral significance to the letters of the alphabet, and for *La descrissions des relegions,* which explains the characteristics of the religious orders. Jean de Journi was the author of *La dîme de pénitence* (1288), and Eloi d'Amerval wrote a long poem, *Livre de la deablerie,* which is encyclopedic in its biblical and literary allusions.

Reclus de Molliens's *Roman de carité* and the devotional *Miserere* were written in the early thirteenth century after he had spent years of solitude in an isolated cell. Robert le Clerc d'Arras, writing some time before 1270, used political didacticism to exhort his compatriots to join the Eighth Crusade in *Vers de la mort,* inspired by Hélinant de Froidmont's poem of the same name. Another moral treatise in verse, Sauvage's *Doctrinal sauvage,* was written at the end of the century.

To teach proper behavior, *Riote du monde* (which exists in an Anglo-Norman and a Francien version in addition to the Picard prose rendering) uses the unlikely medium of fabricated dialogue between the king of England and a jongleur. The need for appropriate conduct was treated more conventionally by Gilles li Muisis (1272–1352), abbé de Saint Martin de Tournai, in *L'estat et maintien.* Gilles also wrote *La complainte des compagnons, Lamentations, Méditations,* and prayers to the Virgin, providing spiritual if somewhat pessimistic comments upon the state of the world and the human condition.

Philippe de Rémi, sire de Beaumanoir, departed from legal convention by using the vernacular language in his treatise on *Coutumes de Beauvaisis* in 1283 (as had the earlier thirteenth-century anonymous *Coutumes d'Amiens*).

An unusual travelogue about the East, *Voyages et ambassades,* was provided by Ghillebert de Lannoy (1386–1462), based upon his experiences in the service of the dukes of Burgundy. He compiled also a practical handbook for young royalty, *Instruction d'un jeune prince.* Several decades later Georges Chastellain, in the official employ of another duke of Burgundy, wrote even more prolifically for the edification of the court. Among his didactic works were *Miroir de la mort, Dit de vérité, Les princes, Advertissement du duc Charles sous fiction de son propre entendement se parlant à lui-même, Le livre de paix,* and *Temple de Boccace.* The titles reflect the diversified interests of their author. Such diversification was not, however, atypical in the unusually heterogeneous area of Picard literature.

BIBLIOGRAPHY

Joseph Bédier, *Les fabliaux,* 4th ed. (1925), and *Les légendes épiques,* 3rd ed., 2 vols. (1926–1929); Gustave Cohen, *Le théâtre en France au moyen âge,* 2 vols. (1928), and *idem,* ed., *Nativités et moralités liégoises du moyen âge* (1953); Lucien Foulet, *Le Roman de Renard,* Bibliothèque de l'École des Hautes Études, CCXI (1914); Grace Frank, *The Medieval French Drama* (1954); Adolphe-Henri Guesnon, *La satire à Arras au XIIIe siècle* (1900, repr. 1977); Urban T. Holmes, *A History of Old French Literature* (1962); Alfred Jeanroy, ed., *Chansons et dits artésiennes du XIIIe siècle* (1898), *Les origines de la poésie lyrique en France,* 2nd ed. (1904), and *Bibliographie sommaire des chansonniers française du moyen âge* (1965); Alan E. Knight, "Drama and Society in Late Medieval Flanders and Picardy," in *Chaucer Review,* **14** (1980); Louis Kukenheim and Henri Roussel, *Guide de la littérature française du moyen âge,* 3rd ed. (1963); Pierre Le Gentil, *La littérature française du moyen âge* (1963); Anatole de Courde de Montaiglon and Gaston Raynaud, eds., *Recueil général et complet des fabliaux des XIIIe et XIVe siècles,* 6 vols. (1872–1890); Per Nykrog, *Les fabliaux* (1973); Jean Charles Payen, *Le moyen âge,* 2 vols. (1970); Léopold M. P. Sudre, *Les sources du roman de Renard* (1893); Brian Woledge and H. P. Clive, *Répertoire des plus anciens textes en prose française* (1964).

JEANETTE M. A. BEER

[See also **Adam de la Halle; Aucassin et Nicolette; Beast Epic; Beaumanoir, Philippe de; Blondel de Nesle; Bodel, Jean; Chansonnier; Chartier, Alain; Châtelain de Coucy; Chronicles, French; Drama, French; Fabliau and Comic Tale; French Literature; Froissart, Jehan; Gautier d'Arras; Gautier de Coinci; Gerbert de Montreuil; Mercadé, Eustache; Renard the Fox; Rhétoriqueurs; Troubadour, Trouvère, Trovador; Walter of Châtillon.**]

Ardross. 7th-century Pictish sandstone slab monument, Class I. INVERNESS MUSEUM AND ART GALLERY

PICTISH ART. The Picts, a people in Scotland known to recorded history from about 300 to 850, are known chiefly from their remarkable and unique artistic productions.

Their symbol stones are the most important of Pictish archaeological remains. Early in this century J. Romilly Allen first grouped these monuments into three classes for dating purposes. His first two classes fall within the Pictish Age (300–850), with the Class I stones, perhaps mainly of the seventh century, characterized by being engraved only with symbols and animals. These stones, boulders or undressed monoliths, feature many different symbols often quite abstract in character, in small groups repeated over and over again. Most frequently employed are the crescent and V-rod, the double disc and Z-rod, the serpent, and the fantastic Pictish beast or "elephant." The symbols have been variously interpreted. They have been associated with prehistoric mythology and with systems of class or tribal totems. Memorial or heraldic significance has also been suggested for them. Since they lack contemporary literary reference, however, the symbols remain wrapped in enigma.

Associated with the symbols are animals, occasionally displayed alone on the Class I stones, such as the fish, eagle, duck, bull, boar, and deer. Though somewhat stylized in their details, these creatures exude vitality and life. They seem but one step away from life sketches. Significant similarities exist between these spirited animals and certain of the animals that appear in Hiberno-Saxon illuminated manuscripts of the late seventh and early eighth centuries. These resemblances are a clue to the date of much of the Class I material. Thus the Ardross wolf displays the scrolls for musculature and articulations, the segregated muzzle, even something of the stance of the lion that is the symbol of Evangelist John in the Book of Durrow. At the same time, there is a particular elegance, precision, and delicacy of drawing unique to the Pictish animals.

Class II stones appear after 700. These shaped and dressed slabs, not always regular, depart significantly from the earlier stones in their use of relief carving and employment of a cross raised on one face. Characterized by hollows at the junction of arms and often ringed, the crosses are generally covered with a complex pattern of pure interlace, animal interlace, fretwork, scrolls, and spirals. Such ornament is also framed in surrounding panels. In form and decoration the Pictish cross is so similar to those designed by Irish and Northumbrian artists as to suggest the origin of the Class II carvings in the political and cultural contacts with Northumbria instituted by King Nechtan in 710. On the Class II stones are certain of the Pictish symbols, fanciful animals, figural scenes that may depend on pagan mythology, scenes of war and the hunt, and scenes drawn from early Christian iconography.

Of the greatest significance to an understanding of Pictish art is the hoard of twenty-eight silver objects discovered in 1958 beneath a pre-Norse church on St. Ninian's Isle, Shetland—probably a secular burial of about 800. Almost certainly of Pictish origin, this metalwork exhibits some of the same affinities with Irish and Anglo-Saxon creations noticed in the symbol stones. One of the magnificent bowls, for example, has a rhythmic frieze of interlaced animals in punched design quite like animal chains in the Lindisfarne Gospels.

Undoubtedly, Pictish art borrowed much from Hiberno-Saxon sources but should not be seen as a provincial reflection of that style. Rather, the freedom and vitality of its early animal representations and the complex assemblages of symbols and scenes and massive plasticity of its later carvings are proof of its creative spirit and separate identity.

BIBLIOGRAPHY

J. Romilly Allen and Joseph Anderson, *The Early Christian Monuments of Scotland* (1903); Isabel Henderson, *The Picts* (1967); Euan W. Mackie, *Scotland: An Archaeological Guide from Earliest Times to the 12th Century A.D.* (1975); Alan Small, Charles Thomas, and David M. Wilson, *St. Ninian's Isle and Its Treasure,* 2 vols. (1973); Robert B. K. Stevenson, "Sculpture in Scotland in the 6th–9th Centuries A.D.," in Vladimir Milojčić, ed., *Kolloquim über Spätantike und Frühmittelalterliche Skulptur,* II (1971), and "The Earlier Metalwork of Pictland," in J. W. S. Megaw, ed., *To Illustrate the Monuments: Essays on Archaeology Presented to Stuart Piggott on the Occasion of His Sixty-fifth Birthday* (1976); Frederick T. Wainwright, ed., *The Problem of the Picts* (1955, repr. 1970).

MARTIN WERNER

[See also **Durrow, Book of; Lindisfarne Gospels; Migration and Hiberno-Saxon Art; Scotland: History.**]

PICTS, the name given to a people in what is now Scotland during the period *ca.* 300–850 A.D. Although there is still much that is mysterious about the Picts (for lack of evidence), or frustrating (because the evidence is inaccessible), we are now

Silver bowl with omphalos. Pictish metalwork from the St. Ninian's Isle hoard, buried *ca.* 800. ROYAL MUSEUM OF SCOTLAND, EDINBURGH (INV. NR. FC 269)

much better informed about them than was the case even a few decades ago. Our information about them is linguistic, archaeological, and historical, with additional hints on social, political, and cultural matters.

Linguistically, we have to rely largely on the evidence provided by king lists and names of other aristocratic leaders; inscriptions on stone; and, most of all, place names. From these materials it appears that there was a sharp division between Picts speaking a *p*-Celtic language closely related to the common ancestor of Welsh and Cornish, as well as to Gaulish, and other Picts speaking a non-Celtic, to all appearances a non-Indo-European, language for which we have no analogue at present. Whereas non-Celtic Pictish was probably spoken in the northern parts of "Pictland," Celtic Pictish was the language of its more southern portion, roughly from the Forth-Clyde line to the Moray Firth, particularly in Fife and the modern central and Grampian regions of Scotland. The extent of Celtic-speaking Pictland is delineated by the distribution of place names beginning with the element *Pit-*, from Pictish *pett,* "a portion of lands." Names in this category are Pittenweem, Pitglassie, Pitlochry, Pitpointie, and Pittodrie.

Only a few of the well over 300 names formed with this generic, however, contain a specific which can also said to be Pictish (Pitpointie); many of them have second elements which are demonstrably Gaelic in origin (Pittenweem, Pittentagart, Pittencrieff, Pitcorthie, Pitcox, and so forth). Although some of these may be part-translations, most of them must be Pictish-Gaelic hybrids coined after the Gaelic occupation of Pictland. Other important Pictish place-name elements are, for example, *aber,* that is, "river-mouth" (Aberdeen, Aberdour, Aberfeldy); *lanerc,* "clear space" (Lanrick, Lanark); *pert,* "wood," "copse" (Perth, Larbert, Pappert); and *pren,* "tree" (Primrose, Primside, Prinlaws, Pirn). But none of these is as exclusively Pictish as *pett,* rather stressing a close relationship with other *p*-Celtic languages than linguistic independence. Of known Pictish personal names, Tarain, Onuist, Unuist, and Nechtan are Celtic, whereas Bliesblituth, Canutulachama, and Spusscio are non-Celtic.

The name of the Picts themselves is puzzling and has given rise to much speculation, especially through pseudo-learned association (ever since the writings of Claudian in the late fourth century) with *pictus,* past participle of the Latin verb *pingo,* "to paint, color, inscribe." We do not know what the Picts called themselves but it is highly unlikely that a Roman soldiers' nickname would, despite the folklore that went with it, give rise to the name of a whole people, particularly when phonologically appropriate forms of the same name were also known to the Norsemen and Angles. According to the fourth-century writer Ammianus Marcellinus, the Picts were then divided into two groups, the Dicalydones and the Verturiones; indeed, writers like Tacitus, Ptolemy, and Cassius Dio used the term *Caledonii* instead of *Picti,* which is first recorded by Eumenius in A.D. 297.

It is the archaeological evidence which chiefly argues for a greater extent of "Pictland" than is indicated by place names ascribable to the Pictish language. In their own way as uniquely Pictish as the *Pit-* names, the monuments known as symbol stones are found practically everywhere in Scotland north of the Forth-Clyde line, including the northern and western isles but excluding Argyll. On the mainland, this includes the seven districts of Pictland given by the twelfth-century author of *De situ Albanie* as Angus with the Mearns, Atholl and Gowrie, Strathearn with Menteith, Fife with Fothrif (Kinross), Mar with Buchan, Moray and Ross, and northern and southern Caithness. The distribution of these stones outlines the boundaries of the Pictish territory in the seventh and eighth centuries, although quite a few of them may well have been carved earlier.

The symbol stones are usually assigned to two main groups; according to Isabel Henderson, "Class I comprises erratic boulders of suitable shape with symbols incised on one side. Class II stones are properly dressed slabs with an interlaced cross carved in relief on one side and the symbols and other iconography, also in relief, on the other." It is the scatter of the later Class II stones that most closely coincides with the distribution of *Pit-* names; nevertheless, it may be a little audacious to claim that the carvers of those stones were also the coiners of these names. The congruency of material and nonmaterial evidence is never easily proved. Although the function of the symbol stones has never been satisfactorily explained, they seem to point, in the remarkable uniformity of the form and style of their designs, to a time of Pictish stability and cultural unity. Apparently their usefulness came to an end after the middle of the ninth century. Other archaeological evidence with Pictish associations is not easy to come by, partly for the lack of excavations, but we have some indication of Pictish strongholds and Pictish domestic settlement near such (ruined) fortifications and in souterrains, as well as of box shrines and monastic enclosures. The magnificent St. Ninian's Isle treasure provides poignant commentary on the richness of Pictish church life.

The exact time when the Picts first accepted Christianity is uncertain. Although Bede, in his *Ecclesiastical History* (III, 4), claims that King Brude, son of Maelchon, was converted by Columba in the ninth year of his reign (565), Adamnan in his life of the saint makes no reference to this. Whatever the beginning, Pictland was under the influence of the church at Iona until King Nechtan introduced the Roman Easter tables a little after 711.

Chronologically, the "historical Picts" have to be placed between the third century and the middle of the ninth century. There is little doubt that the Pictish kingdom was limited initially by the Roman presence in the north of Britain and later through its proximity to the encounters—sometimes victorious, sometimes not—with the Scots, the Angles, and the Britons of Strathclyde. In 367 the Picts harried the northern part of the Roman province south of Hadrian's Wall. About 558 King Brude (or Bridei) inflicted defeat on the Scots; fighting between the Picts and the Scots is reported *ca.* 650; in 658 King Oswy of Northumbria, according to Bede, "subdued the greater part of the Picts"; in 685 another Brude or Bridei, son of Bile, after subduing Orkney three years earlier, defeated Ecgfrith of Northumbria at Nechtanesmere (Dunnichen) in Angus; about 717 King Nechtan, son of Derile, removed Columban clergy from the churches in Pictland; under Óengus mac Fergus (*r.* 729–761) there was fighting against Northumbria in 740, a victorious battle against the Scots in 741 and fighting against the Britons of Strathclyde in 766; in 768 an important battle between Picts and Scots took place, and about 843 the Picts and Scots were united under the auspices of Kenneth mac Alpin, who may have had a matrilineal claim to the Pictish kingship. This union was the end of Pictland but the first stage in the formation of modern Scotland.

BIBLIOGRAPHY

Nora K. Chadwick, "The Name Pict," in *Scottish Gaelic Studies,* 8 (1958); Isabel Henderson, "The Monuments of the Picts," in *An Historical Atlas of Scotland, c. 400–c. 1600,* Peter MacNeill and Ranald Nicholson, eds. (1975), and *The Picts* (1967); W. F. H. Nicolaisen, "*P*-Celtic Place Names in Scotland: A Reappraisal," in *Studia celtica,* 7 (1972), and *Scottish Place-names: Their Study and Significance* (1976); Ian Ralston and Jim Inglis, *Foul Hordes: The Picts in the North-east and Their Background* (1984); Frederick T. Wainwright, ed., *The Problem of the Picts* (1955, repr. 1970), and *The Souterrains of Pictland* (1963); William J. Watson, *The History of the Celtic Place-names of Scotland* (1926); G. Whittington and J. A. Soulsby, "A Preliminary Report on an Investigation into *Pit* Place-names," in *Scottish Geographical Magazine,* 84 (1968).

W. F. H. NICOLAISEN

[See also **Celtic Church; Celtic Languages; Columba, St.; Dál Riata; Kenneth I Mac Alpin; Missions and Missionaries, Christian; Nechtan; Ninian, St.; Scotland: History.**]

PIERO DELLA VIGNA (*ca.* 1190–1249) was born at Capua of a judicial family and studied law at the University of Bologna. In 1221 he joined the court of Frederick II, Holy Roman emperor and king of Sicily, as a notary. After 1225 he became judge of the great court of the kingdom and one of Frederick's closest advisers. Piero participated in the signing of the Treaty of Ceprano between Frederick and Pope Gregory IX in 1230, and very likely assisted in the compilation of the Constitutions of Melfi (*Liber augustalis*) in 1231. Sent on many diplomatic missions, he became protonotary and logothete of Sicily in 1246 but was accused of treason in 1248. Paraded through the Tuscan towns in chains, he was blinded. He died, perhaps a suicide, near Pisa in April 1249.

BIBLIOGRAPHY

Jean-Louis Huillard-Bréholles, *Vie et correspondance de Pierre de la Vigne* (1865, repr. 1966); Ernest H. Kantorowicz, *Frederick the Second, 1194–1250,* E. O. Lorimer, trans. (1931, repr. 1957); Hans Martin Schaller, "Zur Entstehung der sogenannten Briefsammlung des Petrus de Vinea," in *Deutsches Archiv für Erforschung des Mittelalters,* 12 (1956).

JAMES M. POWELL

[See also **Bologna, University of; Frederick II of the Holy Roman Empire; Law Codes: 1000–1500; Melfi, Constitutions of; Tuscany.**]

St. Laurentius with adoring angels. Marble sculptures (1391–1396) by Piero di Giovanni Tedesco from the original facade of Florence Cathedral (demolished 1587). MUSEO DELL'OPERA DEL DUOMO, FLORENCE. PHOTO: BRUNO BALESTRINI, EDIZIONI ELECTA, MILAN

PIERO DI GIOVANNI TEDESCO (*fl.* late fourteenth–early fifteenth centuries), sculptor originally from northern Europe, possibly Brabant or western Germany, who worked on the sculptures of Milan Cathedral before about 1385. He arrived in Florence in 1386, bringing with him the northern Gothic style. For about fifteen years he worked steadily as part of the cathedral group, together with Giovanni d'Ambrogio and Jacopo di Piero Guidi. Between 1391 and 1396 he and his workshop executed a series of statues for the facade: four saints (Stephanus and Laurentius, Barnabas and Victor) and eight paired angels (two flanking each saint). He was also engaged in the decoration of the Loggia dei Lanzi in the Piazza della Signoria (begun 1380). Other works ascribed to Piero di Giovanni Tedesco and his workshop are a figure of a prophet on top of the Porta della Mandorla of the Florence Cathedral, a head of a king in the National Museum in Florence, and the Madonna della Rosa at Or S. Michele in Florence.

BIBLIOGRAPHY

Giulia Brunetti, "L'angelo del Metropolitan Museum di New York e qualche nuovo contributo a Piero Tedesco," in *Metropolitan Museum Journal,* **6** (1972); Claudia Freytag, "Italienische Skulptur um 1400: Untersuchungen zu den Einflussbereichen," *ibid.,* **7** (1973), 28; Gert Kreytenberg, "The Unexpected Apostle," in *Burlington Magazine,* **123** (1981); John Pope-Hennessy, *Italian Gothic Sculpture* (1972), 43, 197; Charles Seymour, Jr., "The Younger Masters of the First Campaign of the Porta della Mandorla, 1391–1397," in *Art Bulletin,* **41** (1959), and *Sculpture in Italy: 1400–1500* (1966), 26, 27, 34.

SANDRA CANDEE SUSMAN

[See also **Florence; Giovanni d'Ambrogio da Firenze; Gothic Architecture; Jacopo di Piero Guidi; Milan; Milan Cathedral.**]

PIERRE. See also **Peter; Petrus.**

PIERRE D'AILLY. See **Ailly, Pierre d'.**

PIERRE DE FONTAINES, a trusted legal adviser of St. Louis, is best known for having written the earliest legal treatise on French customary law, the *Conseil à un ami* (*ca.* 1255).

Fontaines was typical of the new class of royal servants of modest origins who contributed so much to Capetian government in the thirteenth century. He was almost certainly a native of the Vermandois; his early history is obscure, but a document from 1236 seems to indicate that he was acting as a private legal representative at that time. During the 1240's he appears in the records of a number of legal cases, and by 1253 he had been appointed bailli of the Vermandois. St. Louis returned from crusade in 1254, and by 1255 Fontaines was serving regularly in the Parlement of Paris. In 1258 he served in the Norman Exchequer. According to Joinville's *History of St. Louis,* Fontaines was among the officials who attended the royal audiences under the famous oak tree at Vincennes. Enjoying the fruits of royal service, Fontaines acquired a number of properties toward the end of his life. He appears to have died no later than 1267.

Fontaines claims he wrote the *Conseil* in order to record the customs of the Vermandois, which were in danger of being destroyed by three forces: royal baillis and *prévôts,* who ignored them; the rich, who deliberately subverted them; and a general attitude that the present was wiser than the past. The text of the *Conseil,* in fact, is a complex mixture of local custom, legal procedure of the royal courts, and Roman law, which Fontaines copied in whole or in part from contemporary vernacular versions of the Justinianic *Code* and *Digest.* Fontaines did, however, carefully distinguish the principles of Roman law from actual contemporary practices, to which he accorded priority and over which he saw the king as guardian.

It seems that the *Conseil* may have been written at the request of St. Louis for the instruction of his heir, Prince Philip, who had been assigned an appanage in the Vermandois. Although the work was widely known in its own time and directly influenced Beaumanoir, its precise significance is difficult to establish in the absence of a suitable modern edition.

BIBLIOGRAPHY

Source. A. J. Marnier, ed., *Le conseil de Pierre de Fontaines* (1846).

Studies. Quentin Griffiths, "Les origines et la carrière de Pierre de Fontaines, jurisconsulte de Saint Louis," in *Revue historique de droit français et étranger,* **48** (1970), and "New Men Among the Lay Counselors of Saint Louis' Parlement," in *Mediaeval Studies,* **32** (1970);

Pierre Petot, "Pierre de Fontaines et le droit romain," in *Études d'histoire du droit canonique dediées à Gabriel Le Bras,* II (1965); Henri Waquet, *Le bailliage de Vermandois aux XIIIe et XIVe siècles* (1919).

THEODORE EVERGATES

[See also **Bailli; Beaumanoir, Philippe de; Châtelet; Coutumes de Beauvaisis; Custumals of Normandy; Établissements de St. Louis; Joinville, Jean de; Law, Civil; Law, French; Livres de Jostice et de Plet, Li; Lo Codi; Louis IX of France; Parlement of Paris; Provost.**]

PIERRE DE MONTREUIL (de Montereau) (*d.* 1267), a leading thirteenth-century Gothic architect, active in Paris, who designed both the refectory (1239) and the Lady Chapel (1245) at St. Germain-des-Prés (both destroyed), and the south arm terminal (1258–1267) of Notre Dame de Paris. The attribution of the Ste. Chapelle to him is unsubstantiated, and his contribution to the nave of St. Denis is uncertain. He was buried in his chapel at St. Germain-des-Prés, and on his tomb (now destroyed) was called *doctor lathomorum* (doctor of masons).

BIBLIOGRAPHY

Carl F. Barnes, Jr., "Pierre and Eudes de Montreuil," in *Macmillan Encyclopedia of Architects,* Adolf K. Placzek, ed., III (1982), 228–229; Caroline A. Bruzelius, "Pierre de Montreuil [at St. Denis]," in *The 13th-century Church at St.-Denis* (1985), 173–174.

CARL F. BARNES, JR.

[See also **Gothic Architecture; Masons and Builders; Notre Dame de Paris, Cathedral of; St. Denis, Abbey Church.**]

PIERRE DE ST. CLOUD. See **Renard the Fox.**

PIERRE DES CHAMPS (Pierre Deschamps) (*fl.* late thirteenth and early fourteenth centuries) was a French Gothic master mason—possibly a son or nephew of Jean des Champs—who assumed direction of construction of the cathedral of Clermont-Ferrand when Jean died, sometime after 1287. The sole documentation for Pierre des Champs is a text of 3 August 1357 terming him *magistri edificii Claromontensis* and stating that he had been dead for some time. He may have died in or shortly before 1344, when a Pierre de Cebazat is first mentioned as master at Clermont-Ferrand.

BIBLIOGRAPHY

"Pierre Deschamps," in Ulrich Thieme and Felix Becker, eds., *Allgemeines Lexicon der bildenden Künstler von der Antike bis zur Gegenwart,* IX (1913), 116. The 1357 text is in the Archives départmentales du Puy-le-Dôme, séries 3 G, armoire 7, sac D, côte 8. See also Michael T. Davis, "The Choir of the Cathedral of Clermont-Ferrand: The Beginning of Construction and the Work of Jean Deschamps," in *Journal of the Society of Architectural Historians,* 40 (1981), 202.

CARL F. BARNES, JR.

[See also **Gothic Architecture; Jean des Champs; Masons and Builders.**]

PIERRE DUBOIS (*ca.* early 1250's–after 1313), propagandist for the interests of the French monarchy. He was almost certainly a native of Coutances in Normandy. He lived there most of his life; he gave a substantial gift to the cathedral chapter of the city and he was twice sent to meetings of the embryonic Estates General by his fellow citizens (1302 and 1308).

Pierre was probably born soon after 1250, since he was studying theology in Paris in the period when both Thomas Aquinas and Siger of Brabant were lecturing there (1269–1272). He almost certainly attended some other university to acquire his knowledge of law; Paris was weak in this subject. Pierre must have returned to Normandy soon after completing his studies, since he mentions Henri de Rie in his first treatise (the *Summaria brevis*) as viscount of Caen, a post which Henri held at least as early as 1285. He also praises Henri's knowledge of law, which suggests that Pierre was a practicing lawyer in western Normandy in the 1280's or 1290's. Certainly by 1302, and probably earlier, he was acting as permanent attorney for the king in ecclesiastical cases in the *baillage* of the Côtentin. This was not a full-time job; after the reconciliation in 1299 of Edward I of England (*r.* 1272–1307) and Philip IV the Fair of France (*r.* 1285–1314), Pierre performed similar services for Edward in Edward's duchy of Aquitaine. The arrangement did not annoy Philip; Pierre was still acting as his attorney in Coutances in 1307.

PIERRE DUBOIS

Pierre again represented Coutances at the Estates General of 1308. He was convinced of the guilt of the Templars and wrote a tract in the name of the French people (*Remontrance du peuple de France*) begging the king to press the pope to act against the Templars. He followed it up with another tract on the same subject. In speaking for the "people of France," Pierre may have strengthened the king's position slightly, but the decision to condemn the Temple had already been taken. Pierre simply helped a little on the propaganda side.

After 1308 there is almost no record of Pierre's activity. He wrote a pamphlet in 1313 or 1314 protesting a papal bull forbidding tournaments; this, he said, would make crusades impossible, since tournaments prepared knights for war. The bull was revoked in 1316.

Walther Brandt thought that a Pierre Dubois, *bailli* of the countess of Artois, who received an appointment as *rapporteur* of inquests in the Parlement of 1319, was Pierre Dubois of Coutances. This seems unlikely. Pierre Dubois was a common name and our Pierre had no connection with Artois; his entire career had been spent in the west, and most of it in Normandy. Moreover, in 1319 Pierre would have been close to seventy, rather old to begin a new career, especially in the subordinate, and at the same time strenuous, role of a *rapporteur*. He may well have survived Philip the Fair, who died in 1314, but there is no record of him in any of the acts of Philip's sons.

Pierre's real success came, not in his own life, but in the late nineteenth century, when his works were discovered by French and German scholars. They fitted in well with the interests and prejudices of that period. Attacks on the policies of the pope and the corruption of the church could be used by anticlerical writers. Pierre's vision of a world dominated by the king of France and his family could be used by German nationalists to justify their hostility to the French and their attempts to weaken French power. Probably more people read Dubois after 1891, when the first of his major works was published, than in all the centuries before.

The two major treatises of Pierre Dubois are the *Summaria brevis et compendiosa doctrina felicis expedicionis et abreviacionis guerrarum ac litium regni Francorum* (1300), and the *De recuperatione Terre Sancte* (1306). There are few new ideas in either work; what is new is the linking together of many problems that had been raised earlier and discussed separately. Thus, attacks on corruption in the church, the failure of monks to fulfill their vows, the involvement of the papacy in Italian politics through its possession of the States of the Church (Papal States), the decay of the military orders (Templars and Hospitalers), and intervention of the church in purely secular legal affairs had long been current. The collapse of the Kingdom of Jerusalem and the other crusading states was, even for the worldly and cynical, a shock. The virtual collapse of the Empire in Germany naturally made Germany's neighbors consider what faction they should support in Germany and what profit they could make out of the situation.

Dubois simply tried to find general solutions that would deal with all or most of these problems. Thus, the wealth of the church should be entrusted to laymen, who would meet legitimate expenses of the clergy from these trust funds. The Papal States, and other sources of papal income, should be treated in the same way. If churchmen were not so involved in temporal affairs they could better fulfill their spiritual duties. They would also cease trying to extend the jurisdiction of their courts to cases that concerned purely temporal affairs (Dubois, as a lawyer, was very sensitive to this matter). Meanwhile the king of France, who would help arrange these reforms, would be arbiter of Europe. Germany would become a hereditary possession of a member of the French royal family. The French king would hold all lands up to the Rhine, be overlord of Provence and Savoy, and have all imperial rights in northern Italy. A member of the royal family, as Roman senator, would rule the Papal States. A French prince would become king of Castile (here the French did have a very strong hereditary claim). In some unspecified way Charles of Valois (1270–1325, brother of the French king) would become emperor of Constantinople. Then a unified Western Europe could crush the Muslims.

It is doubtful if Philip IV the Fair knew of these proposals or, if he did, that they had any influence on him. Philip was trying to limit the jurisdiction of church courts in secular affairs by 1290, long before Dubois wrote his pamphlets. He made two feeble efforts to get a member of his family elected emperor (1308 and 1313), but he obviously did not consider this an important matter. He gave no help to his relatives who were kings of Naples and titular kings of Sicily or to his La Cerda relatives who had a legitimate claim to Castile. He talked of crusades, but did nothing to forward them.

Philip's quarrels with the church were over jurisdiction and the taxation of the clergy. His suppression of the Templars (an action which Dubois supported) was certainly not based on Dubois's arguments. He probably wanted Temple money and he probably believed that the order was corrupt.

Philip was satisfied with small but solid gains. He did acquire a little land in French-speaking areas of the empire west of the Rhine. He did curb church courts, and he did tax the clergy. Most of these gains were made before Dubois began bombarding members of the French court with pamphlets. It is quite possible that Dubois hurt rather than helped his career through his excessive zeal for rapid change and impossibly great extension of French power.

BIBLIOGRAPHY

Walther Brandt, *Pierre Dubois: The Recovery of the Holy Land* (1956). This is a translation of one of Dubois's major works, an analysis of the others, a brief biography, and a full bibliography.

JOSEPH R. STRAYER

[See also **France; Philip IV the Fair.**]

PIERRE OLIVI. See **Peter John Olivi.**

PIERS PLOWMAN. See **Langland, William.**

PIETÀ (from the Italian, meaning "pity," or "compassion"), an artistic convention depicting Mary with the dead Christ in her lap. The Pietà first appears at the turn of the fourteenth century in German convents. (The German name for the image is *Vesperbild.*) In the liturgy of Vespers, reference was made to the dead Christ and Mary's moments of calm contemplation of his death. In its artistic conception, the image is generally rendered in sculptural form.

There is often confusion over the subject matter of the Pietà and that of the Lamentation. As a station of the Passion, the Lamentation is an emotionally turbulent scene. The Pietà, in contrast, most often depicts Mary as serenely accepting her son as a divine sacrifice offered for the salvation of mankind. In later Renaissance depictions of the Pietà, other figures such as Joseph of Arimathea or Mary Magdalene were introduced into the figure group.

BIBLIOGRAPHY

Samuel G. F. Brandon, *Man and God in Art and Ritual* (1975); Émile Mâle, *L'art religieux de la fin du moyen âge en France* (1949), 122–132; Theodor Müller, *Sculpture in the Netherlands, Germany, France, and Spain, 1400 to 1500* (1966), 32, 39–41; Elisabeth Reiness-Ernst, *Das freudvolle Vesperbild und die Anfänge der Pieta-vorstellung* (1939); Gertrud Schiller, *Iconography of Christian Art,* Janet Seligman, trans., II (1972); Alessandro della Seta, *Religion and Art,* Marion H. Harrison, trans. (1914).

JENNIFER E. JONES

[See also **Crucifixion; Deposition from the Cross; Lamentation;** and frontispiece to volume V.]

PIETRO DA RIMINI (*fl.* early fourteenth century), Riminese painter active during the second half of the trecento and influenced by Giotto. He is known chiefly through a fresco depicting St. Francis, detached from a column in the church of S. Niccolò in Jesi, formerly signed and dated 1333. A signed *Crucifix* in the Chiesa dei Morti, Urbania, clearly demonstrates the influence of Giotto's S. Maria Novella *Crucifix.*

BIBLIOGRAPHY

Carlo Volpe, *La pittura riminese del trecento* (1965); John White, *Art and Architecture in Italy, 1250 to 1400* (1966), 273–274.

ADELHEID M. GEALT

[See also **Fresco Painting; Giotto di Bondone;** and illustration overleaf.]

PIETRO ODERISI. See **Oderisi, Pietro.**

PIKE. See **Lance.**

PʿILARTOS VARAŽNUNI, known to the Byzantines as Philaretos Vakhramios, imperial *mag-*

PᶜILARTOS VARAŽNUNI

St. Francis. Fresco by Pietro da Rimini (1333), formerly in S. Niccolò in Jesi. CONVENTO DI S. FRANCESCO, MONTOTTONE

istros, domesticos, curopalate, and duke of Antioch in the later part of the eleventh century. He was an Armenian Chalcedonian military leader who succeeded in creating the first major principality in southeast Anatolia after the Seljuk invasion of Bagratid Armenia. Despite the evident antagonism of most of the contemporary sources, especially of the Armenian historian Matthew of Edessa (Mattᶜēos Uřhayecᶜi), who could not forgive his adherence to Byzantine orthodoxy and even accused him of conversion to Islam, Pᶜilartos appears to have been an able and energetic, if often opportunistic and relentless, leader in a period of crisis who gathered together many of the Armenian elements set adrift by the downfall of the Bagratid dynasty.

The personal background of Pᶜilartos is obscure, and the link postulated between him and the Vakhramian family known in Byzantium since the tenth century has recently been questioned. There does not, however, seem to be any doubt that he was an Armenian, despite the rejection of that view by Matthew, who argues on purely religious grounds. Pᶜilartos first appeared in Byzantium during the reign of Emperor Romanos IV Diogenes. He was a commander of high rank as early as 1068 and participated in the Battle of Manazkert in 1071. After the fall of Romanos IV, Pᶜilartos apparently refused to recognize the authority of his successor, Michael VII Doukas, and acted independently, making the most of the vacuum of authority left by the Byzantine defeat and the disappearance of the legitimate heirs to the Armenian crowns. He acquired Melitene about 1073/1074, seized Sāsūn from its local Armenian ruler, took Edessa in 1077, and in 1078/1079 was invited to Antioch, where he avenged the murder of the preceding Armenian governor, Vasak Pahlawuni. For some fifteen years after the defeat of Manazkert Pᶜilartos controlled much of Cilicia, Mesopotamia, and northern Syria, acting as an autonomous ruler and even contriving the election of antipatriarchs when the Armenian *katᶜołikos* Grigor II Vkayasēr refused to follow his wishes and take up residence at Marash in Pᶜilartos' territory.

Pᶜilartos' negotiations with Emperor Nikephoros III Botaniates in 1078/1079 gave some legitimacy to his rule in the eyes of his Greek subjects (in exchange for his recognition of ultimate Byzantine suzerainty). In 1083 he reasserted his rule over Edessa, which had rebelled against him, and he benefited from the support of the emir of Aleppo and Mosul. In 1084, however, Pᶜilartos' power was greatly shaken by the capture of Antioch by Sulaymān ibn Qutlumish. The Seljuk sultan Malikshāh, to whom Pᶜilartos appealed for help, failed to support him, and appointed his own governor for Edessa in 1086/1087. Thereafter, Pᶜilartos disappears from the sources, though he may have survived for a time at Marash. His loyalties were ambiguous and his power transitory at best, but he provided a focus for southeast Anatolia in a period of anarchy. His transient principality may have marked a step in the formation of a more permanent Armenian principality in Cilicia.

BIBLIOGRAPHY
Nicholas Adontz (Adontc), "Notes arméno-byzantine: III. La famille de Philarète," in *Byzantion,* 9 (1934), repr. in his *Études arméno-byzantines* (1965); Viada Arutyunova-Fidanian, "Politicheskaya deyatelnost Filareta Varazhnuni v yugo-vostochnikh regionakh Vizantyskoy imperii," in *Actes du XIVe Congrès international des études byzantines,* III (1976), and *Armyane-Khalkedonity na vostochnykh granitsakh Vizantyskoy imperii* (1980), 152–169; Aleksandr P. Kazhdan, *Armyane v sostave gospodstvuyushchego klassa Vizantyskoy imperii v. XI–XII vv.* (1975), 25–28; Joseph Laurent, "Byzance et Antioche sous le curopalate Philarète," in *Revue des études arméniennes,* 9 (1929); Vitalien Laurent, *Les sceaux byzantins du médailler vatican* (1962), 115–119; C. J. Yarnley, "Philaretos: Armenian Bandit or Byzantine General?" in *Revue des études arméniennes,* n.s. 9 (1972).

NINA G. GARSOÏAN

[See also **Armenia: History; Grigor II Vkayasēr; Matthew of Edessa.**]

PILASTER, an engaged pier (rectangular column) with base and capital, projecting slightly from a wall. In classical architecture a pilaster conforms to one of the orders; in the Middle Ages the capital and base of a pilaster usually correspond to those of a freestanding column.

GREGORY WHITTINGTON

[See also **Arch; Bulgarian Art and Architecture; Capital.**]

PILASTER STRIP, an engaged pier or rectangular column that lacks the capital and base of a true pilaster; it is also called a lesene. An innovation of the Middle Ages, pilaster strips may be structural or decorative. When it is built up as a projecting piece of the wall itself, and not as a separate, addorsed construction, a pilaster strip is also called a pilaster mass.

GREGORY WHITTINGTON

Pilasters on the facade of Troia Cathedral, 1093–1130. FOTO MARBURG/ART RESOURCE

PILGRAM, ANTON (*ca.* 1455–1515), late Gothic master mason and sculptor from Brno in Moravia. First known for work on the choir and tabernacle of the church of St. Kilian in Heilbronn (1480's), Pilgram has been credited with other contemporary architectural and sculptural projects for churches in the various Swabian towns. In 1502 he returned to Brno, where he directed work on the church of St. Jacob, as well as projects on the city gates and Rathaus. From 1512 to 1515 he was Dombaumeister of St. Stephen's Cathedral, Vienna, where he produced the pulpit and organ base, on both of which he placed bust portraits of himself. In this same period he directed various projects in the Landhaus in Vienna. Several of his architectural drawings have survived, and these have been used to identify Pilgram's association with or influence on the design of several local churches in small towns near Vienna.

BIBLIOGRAPHY
Rupert Feuchtmuller, *Die spätgotische Architektur und Anton Pilgram* (1951); Hans Koepf, "Neuentdeckte Bauwerke des Meisters Anton Pilgram," in *Wiener Jahrbuch für Kunstgeschichte,* n.F. **15** (1953).

LON R. SHELBY

[See also **Masons and Builders;** and illustration overleaf.]

Anton Pilgram. Self-portrait on the base of the organ console from St. Stephen's Cathedral, Vienna, 1513. PHOTO: WIM SWAAN

PILGRIMAGE CHURCH. See **Church, Types of.**

PILGRIMAGE, ISLAMIC. The fifth of the five pillars of Islam is a pilgrimage (hajj) to Mecca. This duty, obligatory for every Muslim who has reached the age of puberty and is of sound mind, is to be performed at least once in life, provided the means are available for the trip and for the support of dependents left behind. Exempted are the insane, the destitute, and the slaves. The obligation is lifted in times of unsafe passage, wars, and epidemics. Substitutes (who could stand in for only one person) could be hired, sometimes even for those who had died. Pilgrimages of minors (with guardians) or of slaves (with their masters) were laudable but had to be repeated when the minors were of age or the slaves had been freed.

The hajj had pre-Islamic roots in annual fairs held in Arabia at the end of the date harvest, which is thought to have coincided with the autumnal equinox (hence certain features of the solar rite). The prophet Muḥammad did his best to rid that ceremony of the more obvious pagan customs, such as the prayers at sunrise. In the month of Dhu'l-Hijja (March) of 632, Muḥammad led his "farewell" pilgrimage in conformity with an earlier revelation: "Perform the hajj and the ᶜ*umra* [little pilgrimage] for Allah" (Koran 2:196). It was then that the lunar year was introduced and the intercalation was abolished, as the last vestige of paganism.

The hajj always takes place during the first two weeks of the month Dhu'l-Hijja, thus falling ten or eleven days earlier each year and rotating the whole cycle of the seasons in thirty-two to thirty-three years.

Only Muslims were allowed to enter the holy places. The pilgrims from outside Arabia formed caravans in Cairo and Damascus. From the thirteenth century on, the famous (official or ceremonial) litter (*maḥmal*) was carried to symbolize the political authority of certain Muslim lands, Egypt and Syria in particular. The Maghribi pilgrims passed through Egypt, and were sometimes joined en route by groups from western, sub-Saharan Africa. They traveled further by land, occasionally meeting the Syrian caravan in the Hejaz, or sailed up the Nile and traversed the desert to the Red Sea, which they crossed to reach Jidda. The latter was the only route during the crusaders' presence in Palestine.

Arriving at Jidda, the pilgrims were already wearing the required dress, *iḥram;* they were then in a state of purification, observing certain prohibitions (such as refraining from bloodshed, hunting, and sexual activity, as prescribed in the Koran). The individual rites on arrival at Mecca were the same for all, and might be performed any day in the holy month. Visiting the Kaaba entailed walking seven times around the Kaaba, praying two rakʿas (bowings and recitations) while facing Kaaba and two more while facing Maqām Ibrāhīm (Place of Abraham), and running seven times, at various speeds, some 400 meters between Ṣafā and Marwa, two hills near the Kaaba.

The collective ceremonies were carried out between 8 and 12 Dhu'l-Hijja. On the eighth, the pilgrims watered their animals and provided themselves with water for later, then moved east, spending the night at Minā or at ᶜArafat (twenty-five kilometers/fifteen-and-a-half miles from Mecca), the mountain where much of the Koran had been revealed to the Prophet. On the ninth a sermon was preached to the whole crowd to commemorate the one given by the Prophet; this was the apogee of the pilgrimage. The same night the mass of pilgrims left the valley of ᶜArafat, running toward Mecca. They passed the boundary marks (*ᶜalamayn*), which reminded them of their return to the area of Mecca. They prayed together at Muzdalifa, the second of the holy places outside Mecca, and on the morning of the tenth proceeded on to Minā, to stay there for three days, during which they stoned *jamra*s—three heaps of stones bounded by stone pillars or by walls. The *jamrāt* are believed to represent Satan, who is said to have appeared before Abraham and been driven out in this fashion. Afterward sheep, goats, and camels were slaughtered; the pilgrims ate some of the meat, and the rest was taken to the needy or abandoned. After the sacrifices the pilgrims had their hair shaved or cut very short. Then they returned to Mecca and circumambulated the Kaaba, by now adorned with new exterior hangings.

The presence of numerous pilgrims provided advantages for both local and visiting traders who gathered at the annual commercial fair, which peaked right after 12 Dhu'l-Hijja.

It was not unusual to combine the pilgrimage to Mecca with a visit to the Prophet's tomb in Medina, or even a stopover at Jerusalem (particularly after that town was recovered from the crusaders), where the Mosque of ᶜUmar was the main attraction.

The Shiites participated in the main Muslim pilgrimage to Mecca even though they had to pass the tombs of their archenemies, Abū Bakr and ᶜUmar. At various times the ritual was marred by tension and outbursts of violence arising from charges that Shiite pilgrims had desecrated the burial chambers of Muḥammad and his companions.

The Shiites gradually acquired their own places of pilgrimage. The first must have been Karbalāᵓ with its tomb of al-Ḥusayn, the third imam. Then followed Najaf (with ᶜAlī's tomb); Qāzimayn, near Baghdad (tombs of the seventh and ninth imams); Samarra (tombs of the tenth and eleventh imams, and the empty tomb of the twelfth); Meshed (the imam ᶜAlī al-Riḍā's tomb); and Qum (tomb of Fatima, sister of the imam ᶜAlī al-Riḍā). All the earlier visits to sepulchers must have been undertaken in secrecy, since the ruling regime was vehemently opposed to the Shiites; for instance, the caliph al-Mutawakkil (*r.* 847–861) ordered the demolition of al-Ḥusayn's tomb and banned visitors to Karbalāᵓ. The trend, however, was reversed under his son al-Muntasir (*r.* 861–862).

Other places of pilgrimage arose throughout the Muslim world because the local political and social circumstances did not always permit long-distance travel.

It is usually emphasized that the annual pilgrimage to Mecca (particularly if coupled with local ones) revealed physical mobility rare in the premodern world. These travels, by land and/or sea, were personal acts undertaken as the result of personal decisions, and were bound to have a profound impact on both the individual and the Muslim community as a whole. The pilgrimage provided a unique opportunity for coreligionists from different social strata, races, and sexes to meet, to share in the common ritual and ceremonies, and hence to establish a network of communications within the Islamic world. The pilgrimage could be also a profitable undertaking for a merchant, who would have his goods for sale either en route or at Mecca, or a worthwhile study trip for a scholar or a scribe who wanted to hear the famous lecturers of the Muslim East.

The latter two groups have left descriptions of their pilgrimages. Apparently the majority of the authors came from Spain and northwest Africa. Two major biobibliographical works for the period between 850 and 1250 list at least thirty-two scholars who traveled east, combining the quest for knowledge with their pilgrimage. The earliest known account of a pilgrimage is that of Ibn Jubayr (1145–1217), who provided a model for many later writers. Under his influence Ibn Juzayy (1321–*ca.* 1357) edited Ibn Baṭṭūṭa's (1304–1368/1377) *Riḥla* (Travels), which has become the most famous travelogue. A different type of pilgrimage-related work was written by Ibn Ruṣhayd (1259–1321), who concentrated on biographical notes of scholars like himself or of litterateurs from the places that he visited en route. A contemporary, al-ᶜAbdarī, wrote a similar work about his trip in 1289–1290, which influenced such later authors as Abu al-Baqāᵓ al-Balawī, who traveled in 1336–1340. Two later contemporaries, al-Qāsim ibn Yusuf al-Tujībī and Khalīl ibn Aybak al-Ṣafadī, seemingly wrote in the same vein, but their descriptions have been preserved only in fragments. The example was also followed by the mathematician al-Qalaṣādī (*d.* 1486).

The only topographical guide to places of pilgrimage seems to be a book by ᶜAlī al-Harawī (*d.* 1215), which covered Syria, Palestine, Egypt, North Africa, Sicily, Cyprus, Italy, Greece, Anatolia, Iraq, Arabia, Yemen, and Iran. Books on local pilgrimages often contained hagiographical stories of local saints.

The ritual portion of the main Meccan pilgrimage was also the subject of numerous theoretical elaborations and of even more numerous practical guidelines by Muslim scholars of all periods.

BIBLIOGRAPHY

Sources. Al-ᶜAbdarī, *Das nordafrikanische Itinerar des ᶜAbdari,* Wilhelm Noenerbach, trans. (1940, repr. 1966); Ibn Baṭṭūṭa, *Travels, A.D. 1325–1354,* Hamilton A. R. Gibb, trans., 3 vols., The Haklyut Society, ser. 2, **110, 117, 141** (1958–1971, vols. I and II repr. 1972); Abu al-Ḥasan al-Harawi, *Guide des lieux de pèlerinage,* Janine Sourdel-Thomine, trans. (1957); Ibn Jubair, *The Travels of Ibn Jubayr,* Ronald J. C. Broadhurst, trans. (1952).

Studies. Recent surveys on the hajj are Mohammed Arkoun, "Le hajj dans la pensée islamique," in his *Lectures du Coran* (1982); Hava Lazarus-Yafeh, "The Religious Dialectics of the Hadjdj," in her *Some Religious Aspects of Islam* (1981). Pilgrim authors are usually treated as geographers; see Régis Blachère and Henri Darmaun, *Extraits des principaux géographes arabes du moyen âge,* 2nd ed. (1957).

Other aspects of medieval pilgrimages, mainly to sites other than Mecca, are discussed in studies on Muslim saints, such as Ignác Goldziher, "Le culte des saints chez les musulmans," in *Revue de l'histoire des religions,* **2** (1880), repr. in his *Gesammelte Schriften,* Joseph Desomogyi, ed., VI (1973), and "Veneration of Saints in Islam," in his *Muslim Studies,* Samuel M. Stern, ed., C. R. Barber and Samuel M. Stern, trans. (1971); Rudolf Kriss and Hubert Kriss-Heinrich, *Volksglaube im Bereich des Islam,* I: *Wallfahrtswesen und Heiligenverehrung* (1960).

S. A. SHUISKII

[See also **ᶜAlī ibn Ṭalib; Baṭṭūṭa, Ibn; Calendars and Reckoning of Time; Fairs; Geography and Cartography, Islamic; Ḥusayn; Iḥrām; Islam, Religion; Kaaba; Mecca; Muḥammad; Travel and Transport, Islamic.**]

PILGRIMAGE, JEWISH. After the suppression of Simon Bar Kokhba's revolt in 135, Emperor Hadrian forbade Jews to live in or even enter Jerusalem. This interdiction remained in force until the Muslim conquest 500 years later. Theoretically, then, Jews were forbidden access to the city, but there is the evidence of Jerome, who in the fourth century writes in a passage of his commentary on Zephaniah 1:15 that Jews were permitted to enter the city in order to lament there on the day of the destruction of the Second Temple (A.D. 70), 9 Av. Jerome stresses the humiliating character of this Jewish pilgrimage to show how severely Jews were punished for their role in the death of Jesus. Karaite sources mention that in order to perform the pilgrimage during Roman (Byzantine) rule, Jews had to content themselves with going to other cities of Palestine that it was convenient for them to reach: Jews of the East (evidently meaning the Babylonians) to Tiberias; of the West (Egypt and nearby North Africa), to Gaza; of the South (probably Arabia), to Zoar (later called by the Arabs Zughar, east of the Dead Sea).

Things changed under Muslim rule, and in principle both Christians and Jews were then permitted to visit Jerusalem. The main season of Jewish pilgrimage was the autumn, toward the month of Tishri, at the Feast of Tabernacles (Sukkot), as was customary in antiquity. The so-called Ahimaaz Scroll mentions that one of the writer's ancestors had performed the pilgrimage (from southern Italy) three times during the ninth century; each time he took with him a hundred dinars. Many instances of pilgrimage are mentioned in the Cairo genizah letters (mainly from the eleventh century). It was common to take a vow to perform the pilgrimage in times of calamities; a Maghribite merchant says in his letter to a relative who had a death in his family: ". . . the best time for a man to set out for this house [meaning the Temple Mount, where 'the house of God' once stood] is on days of mourning, so that God will reward him with days in which people will perform this pilgrimage out of happiness and joy. . . . "

The spot where Jews gathered during the Tishri pilgrimage was the Mount of Olives. They also used to walk around the Temple Mount, saying prayers near each gate. The biblical precedent for this custom was sought in Ezekiel II:23: "And the glory of the Lord went up from the midst of the city, and stood upon the mountain which is on the east side of the city."

Important decisions and appointments of the Jerusalem yeshiva were proclaimed at a gathering called, as it was in antiquity, *ᶜaṣeret;* important donations were publicly announced there, and bans on sinners proclaimed. A Muslim writer of the eleventh century, al-Bīrunī, also has a fragment describing quite correctly this annual Jewish gathering as "the day on which the quails stood on the heads of the children of Israel."

BIBLIOGRAPHY

Moshe Gil, "The Aliya and Pilgrimage in the Early Arab Period," in *The Jerusalem Cathedra,* 3 (1983), 163–173; J. W. Hirschberg, "Concerning the Mount of Olives in the Gaonic Period" (in Hebrew), in *Bulletin of the Jewish Palestine Exploration Society,* **13** (1947).

MOSHE GIL

[See also **Jerusalem; Jews in the Middle East.**]

PILGRIMAGE, RUSSIAN. The Christian custom of making pilgrimages to sacred sites, relics of saints, wonder-working images, and popularly regarded holy men came to Russia with Byzantine Christianity in the last years of the tenth century. Anthony, the eleventh-century founder of the Caves Monastery (Pecherskaya Lavra) near Kiev, made a pilgrimage to the monasteries of Mount Athos in Greece before founding his community; his successor, St. Theodosius, had attempted when a child to join a group of pilgrims going to worship in the Holy Land, "where our Savior trod." Many other monks of the Kievan period doubtless journeyed to Palestine, Constantinople, and Athos, the major pilgrimage centers of the Christian East, often in groups. Early in the twelfth century, for example, a certain Daniel, prior of a Russian monastery, wrote a description of his pilgrimage to Palestine culminating in the Easter vigil at the Church of the Holy Sepulcher. In 1200 the future Archbishop Anthony of Novgorod penned a careful account of his pilgrimage to Constantinople. A number of later pilgrims were to follow their literary examples.

Pilgrimage was by no means a uniquely clerical preoccupation in medieval Russia. We know, for instance, of a Russian princess, Evfrosinia, who died while on pilgrimage to Jerusalem; indeed, there seem to have been sufficient numbers of pilgrims in early Russia for them to be declared a special group subject to church rather than civil law. By the twelfth century, in fact, pilgrimage had become so widespread that Bishop Nifont of Novgorod railed against pilgrimage as "a curse that is ruining the land." The pilgrims, going off to "Jerusalem and other cities" seeking salvation, lived off the generosity of others, for whom they told stories of their adventures and sang "spiritual songs." These are the "pilgrim-wanderers," the undisciplined Christian minstrel bands so often found in the byliny (sing., bylina), the early Russian folk epics, where they appear in their pilgrim cloaks and "Greek hats," going from village to village, entertaining the people in return for food and drink. From the facility with which characters commit murder and mayhem in these poems and then join pilgrim bands, one can see why church officials did not feel too kindly toward them. Certainly the actions of the group depicted in the bylina *Forty Pilgrims and a Pilgrimess* must have raised serious questions about the religious motivations of such jolly bands.

In the early thirteenth century, the Latin conquest of Constantinople, coupled with crusader losses in the Holy Land and insecure conditions in the Russian steppe area that pilgrims would normally traverse on their way to the East, slowed the pilgrim traffic abroad. Circumstances could not have interrupted the pilgrimage phenomenon completely, however, for there are passing references to pilgrims in the chronicles of this period and once again an important bishop, Theognostus of Sarai, is moved to speak out against such "pointless journeys," particularly since those returning spread untrue stories about other lands (1301). Citizens of Novgorod particularly seemed to go on pilgrimage, possibly because of their special status and comparative wealth in the years of Russia's "Tatar yoke," the period of Mongol domination that began in 1237–1240. One such traveler, Basil "the Pilgrim," was raised to the episcopal throne of that northwestern metropolis.

Pilgrimage to the Near East revived in the fourteenth and fifteenth centuries as Tatar rule weakened in the new population center of northeastern Russia, although citizens of Novgorod continued to produce a disproportionate number of pious travelers. Some of these pilgrims are known by name, and some of them left descriptions of their journeys and of the shrines they visited in the Holy Land and particularly in Constantinople, which by now had become their chief goal because of its magnificent churches and collections of relics. Indeed, some of these "pilgrims" took up temporary, or even permanent, residence in Constantinople and in the monasteries of Mount Athos, another favorite place of pilgrimage for medieval Russians. Epiphanius the Wise, the early-fifteenth-century biographer of St. Sergius of Radonezh, although he himself had traveled to the Christian East, echoed the negative feelings of the hierarchy toward pilgrimage in his praise of Sergius for becoming a saint in his rustic cell in Russia rather than "flitting hither and yon." Many of the pilgrims in the Muscovite period seem, in fact, to have added pilgrimage to other business, secular or ecclesiastical, which took them abroad.

The submission of Byzantium to the papacy and the subsequent destruction of the Byzantine Empire by the Turks in the mid fifteenth century put an end to Russian pilgrimage to the Near East almost completely. But the desire to travel to holy places remained a vital force in the Russian people. Journeys to Russian shrines and sanctuaries replaced pilgrimage abroad. By no means was this a completely new phenomenon. Even in the early medieval period the Pecherskaya Lavra, with its miraculously preserved bodies of saints the community had produced, had become a shrine of some importance. In the late fourteenth century and in subsequent centuries the famed Trinity Sergius Monastery founded by St. Sergius of Radonezh near Moscow eclipsed the Pecherskaya Lavra as a pilgrimage center. The remote monasteries of the far north, such as the St. Cyril Monastery on the White Sea and the St. Joseph Monastery at Volokolamsk, also attracted numbers of pilgrims from the fifteenth century on, as did "miraculous" icons in various places around the Muscovite state. Indeed, just as the princes of Kiev in an earlier period had journeyed to Pecherskaya Lavra to worship at its shrines and venerate its elders, in later times the grand princes and czars of Moscow made regular ceremonial pilgrimages to the Trinity Monastery as well as to various monasteries in Moscow, and sometimes even to monasteries in the far north, to fulfill special vows. Pilgrimage in fulfillment of vows had become a common custom among the people of Muscovite Russia.

BIBLIOGRAPHY

On pilgrimage in medieval Russia, see Aleksandr Nikolaevich Pypin, *Istoriia russkoi literatury,* 4th ed. (1911, repr. 1968), I, 360–409, and II, 201–245. Pilgrims in Russian folklore is the topic of I. Sreznevskii, "Russkie kaliki drevnego vremeni," in *Zapiski imperatorskoi akademii nauk,* **1,** fasc. 2 (1862). There is a translation of Prior Daniel's description of his journey to the Holy Land in *The Library of the Palestine Pilgrims' Text Society,* IV, pt. 3 (1895, repr. 1971). Several pilgrim tales dealing with Constantinople are translated in George P. Majeska, *Russian Travelers to Constantinople in the Fourteenth and Fifteenth Centuries* (1984). Klaus-Dieter Seemann, *Die altrussische Wallfahrtsliteratur* (1976), treats literary aspects of Russian pilgrim narratives and has extensive bibliographies.

GEORGE P. MAJESKA

[See also **Athos, Mount; Constantinople; Icons, Russian; Novgorod; Palestine; Pecherskaya Lavra; Sergius of Radonezh, St.**]

PILGRIMAGE, WESTERN EUROPEAN

Throughout the Middle Ages pilgrimage was one of the most popular expressions of religious devotion in the Christian world. In this article we will examine chiefly the origins and appeal of pilgrimage; the shrines available to Western European pilgrims in the central Middle Ages; and the principal developments in the last medieval centuries.

THE MAINSPRINGS OF PILGRIMAGE

The desire to visit, and worship at, places of special significance is common to most religions, but the exceptional popularity of pilgrimage in the medieval West can be attributed to three important aspects of its religious beliefs. The first of these was the dictum that the follower of Christ is ipso facto a wanderer in this world, for whom life on earth is an unavoidable but distasteful preparation for the real life in paradise. This idea, rooted in the life and teachings of Christ and St. Paul, was a part of the influential theme of "contempt for the world" and accounted for the word "pilgrim" (from the Latin *peregrinus,* stranger or foreigner). It inspired many ascetics in the early Middle Ages to commit themselves to a life of aimless and painful wandering in an attempt to come closer to Christ. This activity was especially popular with the Irish saints, missionaries, and scholars of the sixth and seventh centuries, such as St. Columbanus and Fursa. Although their wanderings were eventually curtailed by Viking raids and the greater stress that Carolingian monasticism laid on stability, the pilgrimage tradition was deeply influenced by the notion that the discomfort and suffering of travel had spiritual value in their own right.

The second contributing factor was more important, and in some ways lay at the very heart of pilgrimage: the cult relics. Western Christians believed that God and the devil fought their continual conflict not only through the minds and actions of men, but also through the events of the natural world—for example, such misfortunes as fire and flood, plague and famine, sickness and accident. The saints, men and women whose exceptional holiness enabled them when alive to act as God's agents in this conflict, continued as his supernatural soldiers after death. From at least the second century, Christians venerated the physical remains of the saints, to show reverence for what they had achieved in life, to gain their intercessory support, or because they believed that the relics themselves retained healing powers. The church hierarchy encouraged the first two practices but was very uncertain about the third, partly because of the problem of false relics. By the mid thirteenth century, influential churchmen such as Thomas Aquinas acknowledged that genuine relics had worked miracles and could function as the conductors of God's healing power. By that time most Christians had accepted that view for centuries, and the major shrines had built up impressive reputations both for the answering of prayers and for the dramatic, on-the-spot cure of pilgrims who were physically or mentally sick.

Most pilgrims, however, journeyed for the sake of their spiritual rather than their bodily health. The third factor in the popularity of pilgrimage, and the mainspring of devotional travel, was the desire to do penance for sins and the harnessing of pilgrimage to the church's penitential discipline. A compulsory pilgrimage to a distant shrine was a particularly suitable punishment for grave sins. It was expensive and laborious, gave the sinner time to repent fully, and removed him from his community long enough to let passions die down. This type of pilgrimage originated in the Irish penitential tariffs of the sixth century but was very rapidly adopted throughout the West for such sins as murder, incest, bestiality, and sacrilege. Those on judicial pilgrimages could usually be identified; they often went barefoot, and were fettered with chains. Murderers had to carry their murder weapon hanging from their fetters.

The worst crimes were punished with sentences of perpetual pilgrimage. In 585 the Council of Mâcon proclaimed such a sentence in the case of a bishop guilty of murder, and in 850 it was the punishment chosen for Frotmund, a nobleman who had killed his father. Pilgrims like these traveled from shrine to shrine, their only hope being that one saint might take pity and miraculously break their chains to signify forgiveness. The exiled Frotmund journeyed to Rome, Jerusalem, the shrine of St. Cyprian at Carthage, Rome again, then Mt. Sinai and Jerusalem, then yet again to Rome, and finally to Rédon in France, where his fetters broke in the church of St. Marcellin. The broken chains were usually left in the shrine church as a witness to a miracle, as at St. Victor in Marseilles, where there were rows of broken fetters hanging in front of the altar.

Not all those engaged in penitential pilgrimages did so because they had to. A characteristic of the late tenth and eleventh centuries was a widespread desire to increase one's chance of salvation by undertaking a voluntary pilgrimage. This sprang from changes in the sacrament of penance. The early church had imposed very severe penances, and only when these had been performed was the sinner given absolution. Toward the end of the tenth century, however, the practice began of granting absolution directly after the confession of sins. Relatively light penances were imposed, and the church taught that the difference between these and the punishment demanded by God would have to be made good by the sinner in either this life or the next (hence the doctrine of purgatory). Pilgrimages were seen as one way in which the sinner could satisfy or lessen God's punishment, for not only would the suffering (*pena*) of the journey count as penance, but the saint whose shrine was visited would intercede in the divine court. The intercession of a great saint was thought to guarantee a completely fresh start, a second baptism that pilgrims to Jerusalem celebrated by bathing in the Jordan River. The twenty-mile walk to the river became such an important part of the pilgrimage to the Holy Land that about 1172 Dietrich of Würzburg claimed to count 60,000 pilgrims on its banks. The practice was copied in a stream near Santiago de Compostela.

THE DEVELOPMENT OF PILGRIMAGE TRADITION

In a famous passage the Burgundian chronicler Raoul Glaber described the onset of a new age of religious zeal in the West in the first years of the eleventh century, when the world was covered with "a shining white robe of churches"; the roads, he wrote, became full of pilgrims. The remarkable flowering of the penitential pilgrimage at this time was undoubtedly helped by the economic recovery

 PILGRIMAGE, WESTERN EUROPEAN

of the West and its release from barbarian attacks. The bodies of the saints, which had been moved to prevent their destruction in pagan raids, were restored to their shrines and embellished by magnificent reliquaries and churches. Men and women of all social classes went on pilgrimage, but there was one group to which it had particular appeal. The knights, who formed the backbone of the new seigniorial regime, were committed to a vocation that constantly involved them in acts of violence condemned by the church. For such men, undertaking regular pilgrimages was an invaluable way of doing penance, and it was by no means a formal or ritualized act of devotion: the pilgrimages of Fulk Nerra, count of Anjou, who went at least three times to Jerusalem, gave rise to scenes of violent remorse. The Normans were among the best knights and the most frequent visitors to the shrines, but pilgrimage was very popular among the nobility of all the major feudal principalities, including Flanders, Aquitaine, Burgundy, Lorraine, and Gascony.

A characteristic of these areas was the deep influence of the monastic revival. Reformed monasteries, especially Cluny, actively encouraged the practice of pilgrimage because of their concern for the salvation of the lay order. Cluny and its dependencies had a very strong interest in the Holy Land and naturally approved of visits to the shrine of their patron, St. Peter, in Rome. But Cluny's main contribution was to the pilgrimage to Santiago. Its houses dominated the roads leading from France to Santiago and its monks almost certainly helped to write the *Liber sancti Jacobi*, the compilation that did so much to build up the shrine's popularity. The monastery also lent willingly to local noblemen who lacked the money to undertake a pilgrimage.

Together with the Peace of God and Truce of God movement, and papal sponsorship of holy war against the Muslims in Spain, Sicily and North Africa, and the Holy Land, Cluniac encouragement of pilgrimage was a feature of the church's rapprochement with the emergent feudal society of the eleventh century. Coupled with the concomitant zeal for legal clarification, this led churchmen to establish with greater exactitude than formerly the status, privileges, and obligations of the pilgrim. He or she was defined as a *miserabilis persona* and, together with widows, orphans, and other vulnerable social groups, was taken under church protection and guaranteed hospitality while fulfilling the pilgrimage vow. Similarly, the pilgrim was already under certain obligations, such as prayer and the distribution of alms, at the shrine visited.

At the end of the eleventh century, Pope Urban II gave tremendous impetus to the developing concept of the indulgence, the church's greatest contribution to pilgrimage. The indulgence was a formal remission by the church of part of the penance imposed on a repentant sinner, and Urban began to grant indulgences for visiting certain pilgrim shrines. In the twelfth century indulgences became attached to many more as bishops were persuaded to grant them to local shrines. Although the Fourth Lateran Council (1215) tried to curtail the mushroom growth of indulgences, they continued to be issued in the thirteenth century, the papacy favoring the Roman shrines. But there was more. Pressed by popular opinion, the church made a radical revision in its theology of penance. It closed the gap that had opened up between enjoined penance and God's punishment by asserting that its indulgences had a transcendental effect. Thus the pilgrim who had made a full and canonical confession of his sins and had carried out his vow properly would enjoy the remission of a specified number of days that his soul would otherwise have spent suffering in purgatory.

The fully developed pilgrimage tradition of the twelfth and thirteenth centuries was thus an imperfect but workable fusion of popular religious belief and official church doctrine. The attraction of a particular shrine lay in the efficacy of its relics and the current reputation of its saint for answering prayers. A person who had vowed to make a pilgrimage (*vovens*) but failed to make it could expect to be punished by the saint concerned by the infliction of ill fortune; thus an English knight whose broken arm was healed by St. James but who neglected to visit the saint's shrine at Reading had his other arm broken, so it was believed, by the angry apostle. But this popular belief, which was susceptible to fraud and abuse, was sanctioned and guided by the church. To symbolize the special status of the pilgrim, he or she was required to wear a distinctive uniform—consisting of a staff, a long, coarse tunic, and a pouch—that was blessed before departure. While the pilgrim was away, the church attempted to protect his or her family and property. It insisted on proof that the journey had been accomplished, a badge or token such as a palm from Jericho, or a cockleshell from Santiago. And it gave formal recognition to the intercessory powers of the saint whose shrine was visited by granting indulgences.

 PILGRIMAGE, WESTERN EUROPEAN

JERUSALEM

Of all pilgrimages, the most meritorious was that to Jerusalem. It was also the first to develop. Pilgrims traveled to Jerusalem from the early third century on, and their numbers increased in the fourth century after the construction of the city's greatest shrine, the Church of the Holy Sepulcher. By the beginning of the fifth century there were said to be 200 monasteries and hostels built to accommodate pilgrims in and around Jerusalem. This early traffic was interrupted by the Arab conquests; in the 670's it took a Frankish bishop named Arculf several years to make a complete tour of Egypt, Syria, and Palestine. There seems to have been a revival in the eighth and ninth centuries, when Charlemagne established good relations with the caliph Hārūn al-Rashīd and built hostels in Palestine for the use of pilgrims, but the practice declined again when Carolingian order collapsed.

The chief factor determining the number of Western pilgrimages to Palestine was its accessibility, which improved dramatically in the late tenth and early eleventh centuries. First, the Byzantine navy regained control of the eastern Mediterranean, so that a sea voyage became feasible, either via Constantinople or directly to a Muslim port in Syria or Egypt. Then two developments opened up the overland route: the conversion of the Hungarians to Christianity and the death of the bitterly anti-Christian caliph al-Hakim, who had destroyed the Holy Sepulcher in 1009. His successors welcomed Christian pilgrims because of the revenues they brought. Passing through Hungary, the Balkans, Anatolia, and Syria, the Western pilgrim could now reach Jerusalem by relatively safe roads maintained by friendly or well-disposed rulers, with ample provisions, accommodations, and guidance.

The greater accessibility of Palestine both by land and by sea coincided with the rise of the penitential pilgrimage in the West to make the eleventh century the period par excellence of the Jerusalem pilgrimage. It was also an age of mass pilgrimage, of large-scale regional expeditions led by high-ranking local churchmen or nobles, such as William, count of Angoulême, in 1026, and Count Guy of Limoges and his brother Bishop Hilduin a few years earlier. The biggest of such pilgrimages, those of 1033 and 1064–1065, were motivated partly by eschatological fears, the widespread belief that the end of the world was at hand. In such circumstances the best place to die was Jerusalem, where the deceased would benefit at the Last Judgment by being buried in the proximity of so many saints and martyrs.

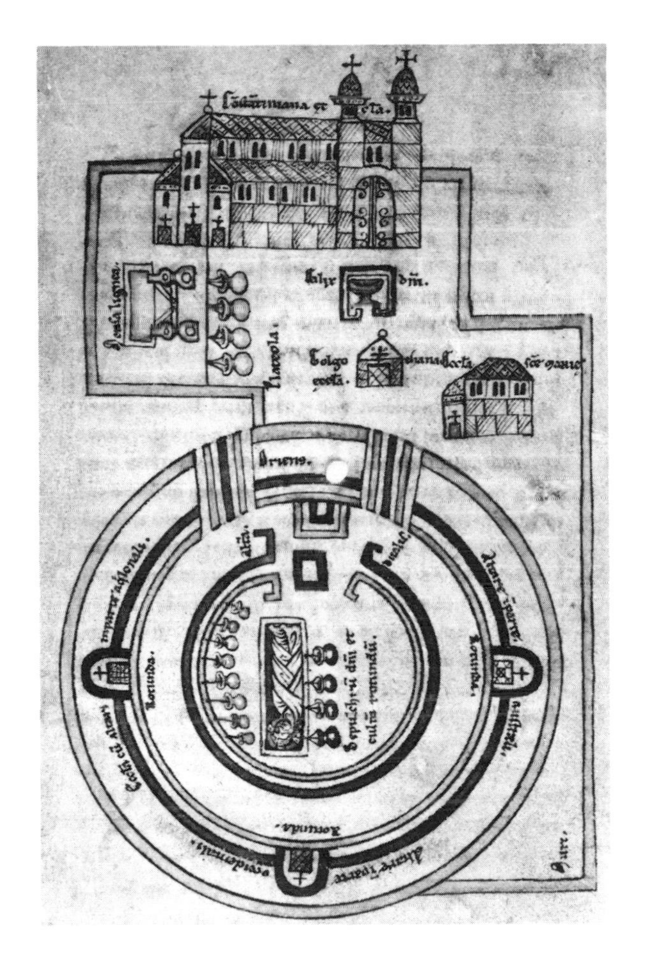

Church of the Holy Sepulcher, Jerusalem, showing Constantine's basilica (top), the gabled structure sheltering the rock of Calvary, and the circular Church of the Resurrection. From a pilgrims' guidebook from the Cistercian monastery of Reun. VIENNA, ÖSTERREICHISCHE NATIONALBIBLIOTHEK, COD. 609, fol. 4r

One good reason for traveling with a large group of compatriots was that the overland route to Jerusalem remained fairly perilous, and became more so from about 1060, when the advance of the Seljuk Turks undermined the order that Byzantium and Fatimid Egypt had jointly maintained in Anatolia and Syria. Pilgrims, who were not permitted to carry arms, came under attack, the most disastrous of which was an assault by Arab brigands on the German pilgrimage of 1064–1065. The Turks were as aware of the value of the pilgrim traffic as were their Fatimid rivals, and largely succeeded in restoring safe traveling conditions, but the situation was transformed in 1099 by the arrival of the First Crusade. From then until the fall of Jerusalem to Saladin in 1187, it was possible for pilgrims to visit the holy places under Latin occupation. Nevertheless, it remained a dangerous experience. Most pilgrims now came by sea, disembarking at Jaffa, and the road from Jaffa to Jerusalem was infested by bandits. On the other hand, the taxes paid by pilgrims at least went into Christian hands, and those who fell sick could expect to be well cared for in the great hospital maintained in Jerusalem by the Knights of St. John, where a traveler counted 2,000 beds about 1165.

The popularity of the Jerusalem pilgrimage owed much to the stress laid in the eleventh and twelfth centuries on the humanity of Christ. This meant that all the places associated with the life of Jesus, and with those of his mother and disciples, acquired sanctity in the eyes of the pilgrims. They venerated not just the shrines of Jerusalem, Bethlehem, and Nazareth but the very soil of Palestine. Returning pilgrims brought back pinches of earth or bottles of Jordan water as relics. For the most devout pilgrims, the culmination of a pilgrimage to Palestine was an intensity of spiritual feeling that no Western shrine could match. Bibles in hand, they wandered as far south as Mt. Sinai, re-creating as many events as time and money allowed. For some, the return to normal life from this spiritual level could not be endured, and they took up permanent residence in Syria as hermits.

ROME

The second great pilgrim destination was Rome. The city's chief attraction was its magnificent collection of relics. The basilicas of St. Peter, St. Paul, and St. Lawrence held the bodies of their patron saints. St. Peter's also had the tremendously popular veil (*sudarium*) of Veronica, while St. John Lateran had the heads of St. Peter and St. Paul. Dozens of other churches scattered across the city boasted the remains of more than 100 martyrs of the third-century persecutions. These were originally deposited in the catacombs outside the Aurelian walls, but barbarian attacks, together with the practice of using relics in the consecration of new churches, led to their systematic transfer to Rome between the fifth and ninth centuries. Those which remained in the catacombs were pillaged by visiting prelates from northern Europe for their own churches.

Apart from its status as a storehouse of relics, unrivaled by any other Western city, Rome had several other advantages. It was much nearer than Jerusalem and rose to fame in the seventh and eighth centuries, when Palestine was effectively closed to pilgrims by the Arab invasions. The peoples of northern Europe felt immense devotion for St. Peter, whose possession of the keys of paradise was believed to give his intercession added weight. The saint's shrine was regarded as a particularly suitable destination for criminals, and he built up a reputation as a breaker of fetters. Another advantage was Rome's classical legacy, the buildings and works of art that even in decay fascinated visitors and acted as a powerful subsidiary attraction, especially for the educated. *Mirabilia urbis Romae* (The wonders of Rome), the most widely read Roman guidebook, described and tried to account for the more famous ruins. The presence of the papal court also bolstered the city's pilgrim traffic. This was partly because of its building program, in which many of the shrine churches were enlarged and embellished, and partly because of its constant round of liturgical celebration, in which Rome's relics had a leading part. At the major Christian festivals some reliquaries were carried in procession through the streets.

The seal was set on Rome's preeminence among Western shrines by two important developments in the church's approach to the forgiveness of sins. One was the gradual process by which the absolution of certain grave offenses was reserved for the pope; by the end of the twelfth century these included sacrilege, the murder of a priest or monk, and the robbery of a church. Those guilty of such "reserved cases" had to go to Rome, and many went as pilgrims to display their contrition and mitigate the penance imposed. The other development was the introduction of indulgences for pilgrimage, from which the Roman shrines profited greatly both because the popes were generous to individual churches and because the concentration of shrines in a small area enabled energetic pilgrims to perform the devotions needed to collect the indulgences on offer in a number of churches. At the end of the twelfth century Gerald of Wales believed that he had collected ninety-two years of indulgences. In the thirteenth century a form of inflation set in, so that popes had to increase the indulgences available at the major shrines just to keep them ahead of the smaller churches that had been overly favored. By 1300 indulgences were being granted to individual altars in St. Peter's, and a pilgrim could collect several hundred years of indulgences if he or she was in the city at the right time. But the attraction of these indulgences was normally offset by the political turmoil and warfare of thirteenth-century Italy, which kept many pilgrims away from the city and may have reduced its overall share of the pilgrim traffic.

SANTIAGO DE COMPOSTELA AND OTHER SHRINES

The third great pilgrimage shrine was Santiago de Compostela in Galicia. Compared with Jerusalem and Rome, Santiago was a late starter. About 830 the news circulated that the tomb of St. James (the Greater) had been discovered there, but it was only in the mid tenth century that the shrine began to attract pilgrims, and its efflorescence was cut short by the advance of al-Mansur, who captured Compostela and looted the shrine in 997. It was several decades before the pilgrimage traffic resumed, but when it did, it was substantial; the shrine reached the peak of its popularity in the late eleventh and twelfth centuries. A large proportion of the pilgrims were French, and they reached the shrine by one of the most famous medieval trunk roads, the *camino de Santiago*.

The spectacular rise of Santiago is the best illustration of two recurring and complementary themes in medieval pilgrimage: the important role that was often played by active publicity and promotion, and the benefits that could accrue to the guardians of a popular shrine. The bishops of Santiago worked hard to spread the news of their saint's efficacy in producing miracles, all of which were noted in the *Liber sancti Jacobi*, a manuscript pilgrims could consult. They also collaborated with the kings of Navarre to ensure that the *camino de Santiago* remained in good condition, its bridges intact, its hospices, churches, and monasteries functioning properly. The profits they enjoyed, in terms of money and prestige, were impressive. In 1120 the pope was persuaded to raise the see of Santiago to metropolitan status, and its archbishops soon started to dispute the primacy of Spain with Toledo. In 1122 construction was begun on a magnificent new cathedral, which by midcentury was able to support seventy-two canons. These were the fruits of a stream of alms and legacies, but the indirect benefits of the pilgrimage traffic were of great economic importance to the town of Santiago and to all the settlements on the road to France. Such were the profits to be made that several minor shrines sprang up on the roads leading to Santiago in southern France, such as St. Gilles near Arles and St. Eutrope at Saintes.

It would be tempting to ascribe most of the newly discovered "relics" of the eleventh and twelfth centuries, and the shrines built to accommodate them, to the workings of the profit motive; but medieval psychology was too complicated for such a straightforward explanation. Certainly there was a proliferation of local shrines and relic collections that coincided with the growth of a money economy. Many of the new twelfth-century shrines were dedicated to the Virgin, relics of whom multiplied rapidly. Shrines rose to fame, and fell from it, very quickly. The tomb of St. Thomas Becket at Canterbury attracted many pilgrims in the late twelfth century but declined in the thirteenth as the news spread that the saint had lost his ability to work miracles; in the late Middle Ages pilgrimage to Canterbury was really popular only when especially generous indulgences were granted for it. Other major shrines, such as Cologne, Rocamadour, and Mont St. Michel, were just as subject to the whims of fashion.

Competition among shrines was thus intense, and was waged by the compilation of "books of miracles" and the exhibition of ex-voto offerings donated by pilgrims who had experienced miraculous cures. Some shrines became immensely rich, and were able to present their tombs and relics in a setting of overpowering splendor. When Henry VIII dissolved the cathedral priory of Canterbury, the jewels and precious metals from Becket's tomb filled twenty-six carts. But popularity had its drawbacks, notably the expense of feeding and sheltering the poorer pilgrims. Rocamadour's accounts showed a debit because of this in 1181, and in the fourteenth century the monks of Mont St. Michel claimed that providing for its poor pilgrims was proving financially crippling.

CRITICISM OF PILGRIMAGES

At its best, pilgrimage was one of the most ascetic practices of medieval Christianity, a form of *imitatio Christi* in which the ordinary hardships of travel were rigorously supplemented by a variety of self-imposed penances, such as walking barefoot, fasting, and praying day and night. But it had its critics and opponents. As early as the fourth century, St. Jerome voiced the classic criticism that seeing Jerusalem was not enough; interior, spiritual conversion was what God required. Throughout the following millennium churchmen, especially popular preachers, reiterated Jerome's point. True contrition was essential, and at the very least a pilgrim should ensure that he or she had confessed all his or her sins. Some claimed that the perils and temptations of the open road were actually detrimental to the religious purpose of the journey; and it was a constant theme of monastic writers, such as St. Bernard and Peter the Venerable, that the spiritual benefits of pilgrimage were fleeting and that the repentant sinner would do better to enter a monastery.

If the value of the voluntary pilgrimage was questioned, that of the judicial pilgrimage was open to serious criticism. Habanus Maurus, a Carolingian reformer of the ninth century, doubted whether it was an effective way of reforming the sinner. Indeed, it could lead to commission of worse crimes, and it made the roads dangerous for ordinary travelers. In the thirteenth century Jacques de Vitry complained about the Western practice of swamping Acre with hordes of exiled criminals. There were complaints too about the multiplication of saints and shrines, for which pilgrimage was partly responsible. The reputations of established saints were threatened by fashionable newcomers, and the effect was seen as a devaluation of the reverence paid to those responsible for the establishment and spread of the faith.

Several of these criticisms became more strident in the later Middle Ages (from about 1250 on), thanks to new developments that many regarded as unhealthy. One was the growing tendency for secular authorities to use the judicial pilgrimage as the punishment for relatively minor offenses. In most cases the journey could be commuted by the payment of a fine, a procedure that could only bring pilgrimage into disrepute. There were also changes in connection with the pilgrimage vow. By the mid fourteenth century the papacy had adopted the practice of selling dispensations from the vow, and of allowing minor shrines to commute vows made to travel to the major sanctuaries; a *vovens* was also allowed to send a substitute in his or her stead. Such changes, though justifiable in themselves, tended to erode the significance of the vow. The most important development, however, was a steady increase in the size and number of indulgences attached to pilgrimage shrines. A process of inflation was at work, caused by popular enthusiasm for indulgences and, especially in the late fourteenth and fifteenth centuries, by the financial needs of the papal court, which was driven to issue ever more generous indulgences in exchange for cash. There was a danger that, from being an adjunct of pilgrimage, indulgences would come to dominate it.

A major factor in the escalation of indulgences was the practice of granting a plenary indulgence, a full remission of sins, to all who visited the Roman basilicas in jubilee years. Boniface VIII was the first pope to declare a jubilee year, 1300, in response to popular pressure. Unprecedented numbers of pilgrims flocked to Rome, and in 1343 Clement VI reacted to a petition from the Romans by declaring 1350 a jubilee year on the grounds that many people born after 1300 would not live until 1400. Thereafter there were jubilee years in 1390, 1400, 1423, 1450, and 1475. By then, however, the popes had begun to issue indulgences *ad instar jubilaei* (equivalent to a jubilee indulgence) to other shrines, thus aggravating the inflationary trend and lessening the attraction even of the huge indulgences normally available in Rome. To make matters worse, there was a plethora of forged indulgences. By 1500 both official doctrine and popular belief about the indulgence were in a state of great confusion.

PILGRIMAGE IN THE LATE MIDDLE AGES

There were other, more subtle changes in the practice of pilgrimage in the late Middle Ages that confirmed critics in their belief that it had lost its spiritual value. To some extent it became an easier, more enjoyable, and more secular experience. Chaucer's pilgrims clearly had a good time on the road to Canterbury, and Venice organized its convoys to Palestine so well that a pilgrimage to the Holy Land under Muslim rule was much less risky than in the days of Latin Syria. Pilgrimage to distant shrines was beginning to resemble modern tourism, in that pilgrims took much more interest than formerly in foreign life and customs. They hired guides, bought souvenirs, and wrote up their journey in diaries. From the appearance of Sir John Mandeville's *Travels* in the mid fourteenth century, travel books became popular reading. Fewer miracles were reported at shrines and there was more trickery, like the notorious rood of Boxley, a life-size figure of Christ that rolled its eyes, shed tears, and foamed at the mouth; when it was inspected during the Reformation it was found to have "certain engines and old wires with old rotten sticks in the back of the same." The major shrines that retained their appeal became fashionable resorts for the nobility, while many minor shrines depended on a trickle of the gullible.

These changes should not be exaggerated. Raoul Glaber in the eleventh century and Jacques de Vitry in the early thirteenth complained that many pilgrims were motivated by vanity or curiosity rather than by true repentance; and it is questionable whether the sources, many of them reforming in tone, establish a radical shift in inspiration. Certainly the cult of the saints and their relics was as popular as ever, and Marian enthusiasm reached new heights. But it is true that the form taken by the most important fifteenth-century pilgrimages, especially those in France, Germany, and the Low Countries, was new and, for the church, inauspicious. They were associated with obscure cults that sprang up overnight in the wake of a miraculous event or vision, attracted crowds for months or even weeks, and were then forgotten. There were mass pilgrimages of children, most notably the Wilsnack pilgrimages of 1475 and 1487, and one Marian pilgrimage, at Nicklashausen in 1476, that had to be suppressed because its leader, a shepherd named Hans Böhm, preached social revolt. The church could control none of this.

On the eve of the Reformation, pilgrimage was in a pitiable condition typical of many popular religious practices. Literate and thoughtful churchmen such as Erasmus and Thomas More saw it as contaminated by abuses and fit only for the gullible. The religious fervor of the mass of the population still found expression in pilgrimages, but these tended to be spontaneous and nonofficial, eschewing the legal framework established by the church and leaving the big shrines high and dry. Future centuries would show that the ideal of pilgrimage had lost none of its appeal; but the creative impetus that had been given to it by the church in the eleventh and twelfth centuries had been exhausted. The movement was ripe for radical change and renewal.

BIBLIOGRAPHY

The only recent general account in English is Jonathan Sumption, *Pilgrimage: An Image of Mediaeval Religion* (1975); see also Raymond Oursel, *Pèlerins du moyen âge* (1963, repr. 1978). Of special value is Edmond-René Labande, "Éléments d'une enquête sur les conditions de déplacement du pèlerin aux xe–xie siècles," in Centro di studi sulla spiritualità medievale, *Pellegrinaggi e culto dei santi in Europa fino alla Ia Crociata* (1963), "'*Ad limina*': Le pèlerin médiéval au terme de sa démarche," in Pierre Galais and Yves-Jean Riou, eds., *Mélanges offerts à René Crozet,* I (1966), and "Recherches sur les pèlerins dans l'Europe des XIe et XIIe siècles," in *Cahiers de civilisation médiévale,* **1** (1958).

On the cult of the saints, see Peter R. L. Brown, *The Cult of the Saints: Its Rise and Function in Latin Christianity* (1981); Patrick J. Geary, *Furta Sacra: Thefts of Relics in the Central Middle Ages* (1978). For pilgrimages in the early Middle Ages, besides *Pellegrinaggi* (1963), see Kathleen Hughes, "The Changing Theory and Practice of Irish Pilgrimage," in *Journal of Ecclesiastical History,* **11** (1960). Pilgrimage in the late Middle Ages has not received detailed attention. Though dated, Johan Huizinga, *The Waning of the Middle Ages,* Frederik J. Hopman, trans. (1924, repr. 1950), chaps. 12–14, is still useful. For Nicklashausen, see Norman Cohn, *The Pursuit of the Millennium* (1957; 2nd ed., rev. and enl., 1970), 237–251.

For pilgrimages to Palestine, see Einar Joranson, "The Great German Pilgrimage of 1064–1065," in Louis J. Paetow, ed., *The Crusades and Other Historical Essays Presented to Dana C. Munro* (1928), and "The Palestine Pilgrimage of Henry the Lion," in James L. Cate and Eugene N. Anderson, eds., *Medieval and Historiographical Essays in Honor of James Westfall Thompson* (1938); Steven Runciman, "The Pilgrimages to Palestine Before 1095," in Marshall W. Baldwin, ed., *A History of the Crusades,* I, *The First Hundred Years* (1955, 2nd ed. 1969). For pilgrimages to Santiago, see Élie Lambert, "Études sur le pèlerinage de Saint-Jacques de Compostelle," in his *Études médiévales,* I (1956).

An important account of criticism is Giles Constable, "Opposition to Pilgrimage in the Middle Ages," in *Studia Gratiana,* **19** (1976), repr. in his *Religious Life and Thought (11th–12th Centuries)* (1979).

NORMAN HOUSLEY

[See also **Boniface VIII, Pope; Canterbury; Catacombs; Cluny, Abbey Church; Cologne; Crusades and Crusader States: To 1192; Indulgences; Jacques de Vitry; Jerusalem; Jubilee; Mandeville's Travels; Old Saint Peter's, Rome; Penance and Penitentials; Relics; Raoul Glaber; Rome; Santiago de Compostela; Travel and Transportation, Western European; Urban II, Pope.**]

PILGRIM'S GUIDE forms the fifth book of the *Liber sancti Jacobi* (*Codex Calixtinus*). Dated to about 1139 and often attributed to Aymeri Picaud, a priest of Parthenay-le-Vieux, Olivier d'Iscam, and Geberge la Flamande, the book plots the stages of the pilgrimage routes to Santiago de Compostela. It describes major buildings and shrines along the way (particularly the city and church at Compostela)

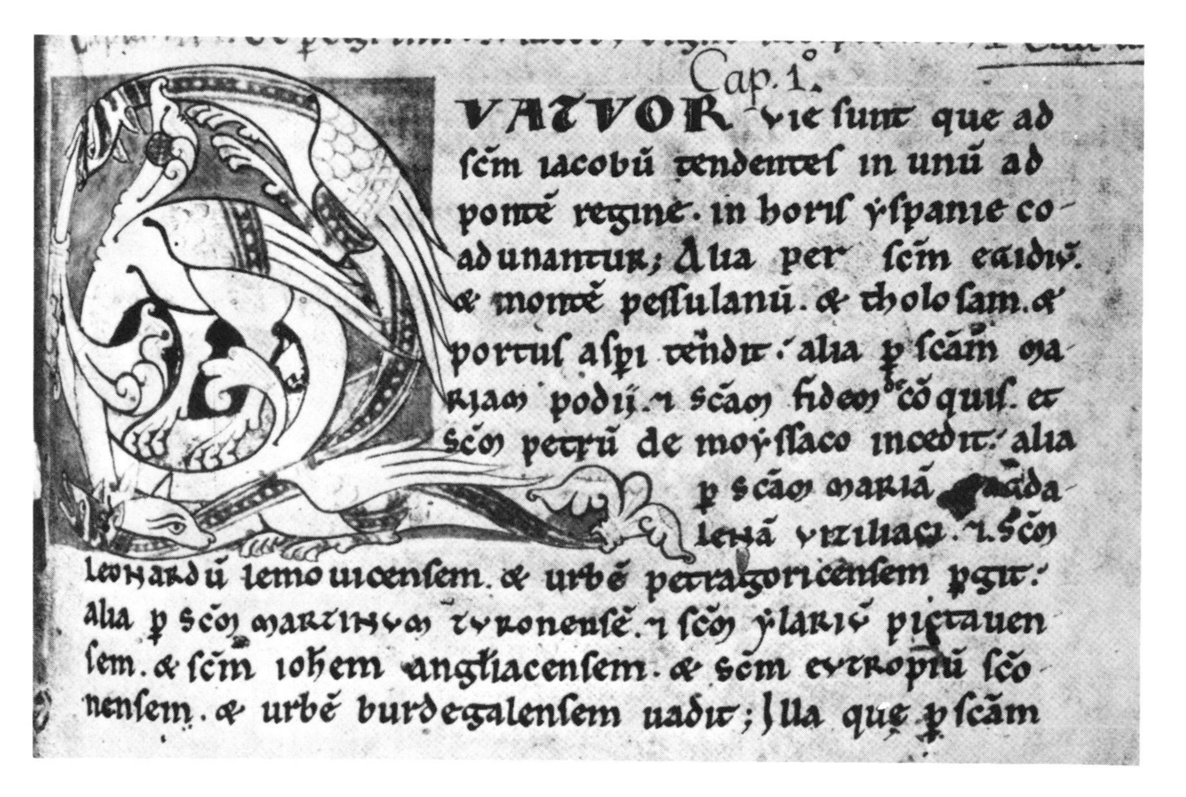
Cap. I.
VATVOR vie sunt que ad
scm iacobu tendentes in unu ad
ponte regine. in horis yspanie co
adunantur; Alia per scm egidiu.
& monte pessulanu. & tholosam. &
portus aspi tendit; alia p scam ma
riam podii. & scam fidem de conquis. &
scm petru de moyssaco incedit; alia
p scam mariam magda
lenam viziliaci. & scm
leonardu lemouicensem. & urbe petragoricensem pgit;
alia p scm martinum turonense. & scm ylariu pictauen
sem. & scm iohem angliacensem. & scm eutropiu sco
nensem. & urbe burdegalensem uadit; Illa que p scam

Initial from the first chapter of the pilgrim's guide in the *Liber sancti Jacobi*, describing the four roads leading to Santiago. Copied by Arnoldo da Monte in 1172 or 1173. SANTIAGO DE COMPOSTELA, CATHEDRAL LIBRARY, COD. CALIXTINUS, FOL. 163r

and offers practical advice to the traveler. Recently it has been suggested that the guide was designed primarily for teaching Latin and geography to schoolboys.

BIBLIOGRAPHY
Yves Bottineau, *Les chemins de Saint-Jacques* (1964), 66–124; Christopher Hohler, "A Note on *Jacobus,*" in *Journal of the Warburg and Courtauld Institutes,* 35 (1972); Émile Mâle, *Religious Art in France: The Twelfth Century,* Harry Bober, ed., Marthiel Mathews, trans. (1978), esp. 282–315; Jeanne Vielliard, trans., *Le guide du pèlerin de Saint-Jacques de Compostelle* (1938, 3rd ed. 1963).

MICHAEL T. DAVIS

[See also **Pilgrimage, Western European; Santiago de Compostela; Travel and Transport, Western European.**]

PIPE ROLLS were the financial records of the English Exchequer (treasury) listing the annual revenues and other charges owed by the sheriffs of the counties and similar accountable officers. The first extant pipe roll is for 1130, the thirty-first regnal year of Henry I, shortly after the development of the Exchequer. There are no rolls for the rest of Henry I's reign or for that of Stephen (1135–1154). In 1156, the second regnal year of Henry II, the pipe rolls are again extant, and they continue in an almost unbroken procession for almost the next 700 years. There are 676 rolls, the last dated 1832, the second regnal year of William IV. For the years the pipe rolls are missing, there are usually duplicates that were drawn up for the use of the Chancery.

Both the Exchequer and the Chancery dated their documents according to the regnal years of a king, calculated from the day of his accession or of his coronation. Unlike the Chancery year, however, the Exchequer year began and ended on Michaelmas (29 September), when the final auditing sessions were held. The earliest pipe roll, for example, covered the period from 30 September 1129 to 29 September 1130 but is referred to as from the thirty-first regnal year of Henry I, because he came to the throne on 5 August 1100 and Michaelmas 1130 therefore fell in his thirty-first year.

Called at first the roll of the treasury, the great

roll of the year, or the great roll of accounts, the pipe roll eventually became known as the great roll of the pipe. Instead of employing the later Chancery procedure of sewing parchment membranes end to end in a continuous roll, the Exchequer adopted the more convenient arrangement of fastening together a bunch of membranes at their tops and then rolling them up. Each membrane was called a "pipe" and consisted of two parchment skins sewn together to form one long sheet. A pipe was three feet to four feet, eight inches, long and an average of about fourteen inches wide. A pipe roll's resemblance to a pipe or cylinder when rolled up is the most likely explanation of the term's etymology. It has been suggested that the term derives from a comparison of the royal treasury to a reservoir into which all the royal revenues flowed through a main pipe, but this derivation lacks supporting evidence. Also unhistorical is a derivation from the roll's supposed likeness to a wine cask.

The first pipe roll is quite small, but by the fourteenth century the Exchequer's business had so expanded that the pipe rolls are about two feet in diameter. Part of this increase came from the practice of entering on the pipe rolls, in addition to the normal accounts, the so-called foreign accounts—that is, all those accounts that did not stem from the regular accounting officers at the Exchequer. This practice made the pipe rolls so bulky that Exchequer reforms between 1323 and 1326 directed the foreign accounts to be entered separately.

Concerned only with the accounts of the sheriffs and other such officials for all the counties of England, the pipe rolls give no general final statement of royal finances or what can be called a budget. They are nevertheless important for twelfth- and thirteenth-century financial and political history, for genealogy, and for the royal itineraries.

An Exchequer began functioning in Normandy almost as early as in England, but no pipe rolls or great rolls of the Norman Exchequer are extant until 1180. Except in Flanders, where comparable accounting procedures were used, there are no similar records during this period for the other states of Western Europe.

BIBLIOGRAPHY

Sources. The pipe rolls are being edited by the Pipe Roll Society, which published the first volume in its series in 1884. For translations of portions of the pipe rolls, see David C. Douglas and George W. Greenaway, eds., *English Historical Documents, 1042–1189* (1953).

Studies. The most informative discussions of the pipe rolls are in Vivian H. Galbraith, *An Introduction to the Use of the Public Records* (1934); Charles Johnson, trans., *The Course of the Exchequer by Richard, Son of Nigel* (1950); Reginald Lane Poole, *The Exchequer in the Twelfth Century* (1912, repr. 1973). Also useful is Bryce Lyon and Adriaan Verhulst, *Medieval Finance: A Comparison of Financial Institutions in Northwestern Europe* (1967).

BRYCE LYON

[See also **Accounting; Archives; Danegeld; England: Norman-Angevin; Exchequer; Flanders and the Low Countries; Normans and Normandy; Sheriff; Taxation, English.**]

PIRMIN, ST. (*d.* 753). Pirmin is first mentioned as the founder of the monastery of Reichenau about 724. Of his earlier life little is certain. His ninth-century biography indicates that he originated in Septimania or Spain, and he apparently spent some time at the abbey of Flavigny, in the diocese of Autun. Pirmin was ordained a bishop but, following the Irish custom, he had no fixed diocese. He enjoyed the support of Charles Martel, not only at Reichenau but also for his foundation of Murbach (726/728). He also established monasteries at Gegenbach (*ca.* 748) and at Hornbach, where he died. Pirmin conducted extensive missionary work in the upper Rhine area; his student Eddo became bishop of Strasbourg in 734. Pirmin was the author of a manual for missionaries, a commentary on the Apostles' Creed, and the *Dicta Pirminii* or *Scarapsus*, a brief account of salvation history.

BIBLIOGRAPHY

Arnold Angenendt, *Monachi peregrini: Studien zu Pirmin und den monastischen Vorstellung des frühen Mittelalters* (1972).

JAMES M. POWELL

[See also **Benedictines; Missions and Missionaries, Christian.**]

PISA, an Italian city located in western Tuscany on the Arno River, was an important medieval commercial center. In antiquity the city was of minor importance, but it prospered from being on the *Via Aemilia,* the coastal road to Rome. Little is known about Pisa in the early Middle Ages, but in the late tenth and eleventh centuries an aggressive group of merchant pirates took to the sea and made their presence felt in the Tyrrhenian. Pisan ships actively engaged the Saracens in southern Italy as sometime allies of the Normans, and made an early assault on the Balearic Islands in 1115. Pisa also contested with Genoa for control of nearby Corsica and Sardinia. At the time of the First Crusade, Pisan naval support appeared off the coast of Latin Syria in late 1099, and the city provided the first significant fleet in the east. The archbishop of Pisa, Daimbert, used this fleet to strengthen his hand in the new Latin Kingdom and became patriarch of Jerusalem and protector of Pisan interests in the area. In Italy, Pisa had become one of the first cities to secure, in 1080, recognition of its communal government from the German emperor Henry IV.

Situated about 10 kilometers (6.2 miles) from the mouth of the Arno, Pisa had a poor harbor because the river tended to silt up and was at best unpredictable. The city's development into the principal medieval port of Tuscany owed much to its intrepid seafarers and the establishment of more docks and warehouses at Porto Pisano downstream. Pisa had the potential to become a land power in Tuscany or to concentrate on maritime expansion, but to accomplish both goals was ultimately beyond its grasp. In the twelfth century Pisa became the entrepôt for Tuscan exports. At first local prosperity rested upon forest products, mostly timber and charcoal from the well-wooded areas north of the city, iron from the mines of the nearby island of Elba, and wheat from the marshy, disease-ridden, and fertile coastal region to the south known as the Maremma. The forests also permitted Pisa to become an important center for shipbuilding, and supported two other industries, leather and furs.

In the thirteenth century Pisa began to serve as the main port for Florence's growing trade in wool and wool cloth, and Pisa itself became a minor center for a wool industry, doomed in the next century by Florentine competition. Long-distance trade with North Africa, Sicily, and the Levant brought the city considerable prosperity and growth—reliable estimates put Pisa's population at about 11,000 in 1164 and about 38,000 in 1293, which may have been the medieval peak. Pisa's relations with the Latin Kingdom of Jerusalem brought its merchants trading concessions and colonies (quarters) in Acre, Tyre, and other cities, and after the kingdom's fall, in Cyprus. Pisa was also an important center in the development of merchant and sea law, map making, and new commercial practices and instruments of credit. The leading mathematician and proponent of Arabic numerals in the early thirteenth century, Leonardo Fibonacci, was a Pisan.

Pisa's ambitions met with two immediate rivals. Genoa too wanted naval and commercial supremacy in Corsica and Sardinia. Florence, only about 70 kilometers (43.5 miles) up the Arno, frustrated Pisa's efforts to establish an extensive area of domination, or *contado,* in Tuscany. Pisa engaged in a stiff commerical rivalry with Genoa, and often found itself at odds with its powerful neighbor Florence. In the thirteenth century Pisa experienced internal divisions among the older group of dominant aristocratic families, the merchants, and the artisans; the latter two groups assembled themselves into a *popolo* and occasionally controlled the commune. The *popolo* generally supported the Guelph (papal) party in Italy, and the aristocrats stayed loyal to the Hohenstaufen rulers and were Ghibellines. These splits in the city caused some domestic strife and occasional dramatic changes in foreign policy. With the loss of Bonifacio in Corsica to Genoa in 1195, Pisa's struggle for supremacy in the western Mediterranean became a continuous drain on the city. Catalans and Genoese became active in Sardinian trade and in North Africa, traditionally vital areas for Pisa. The central years of the thirteenth century, however, witnessed both the peak of Pisa's prosperity and the most active phase of an ambitious building program—the main legacies of which are the Baptistery (1153–1265) and the Camposanto (cemetery, 1277–1283). After a series of expensive and inconclusive wars, in 1284 the Genoese inflicted a devastating naval defeat on the Pisans at Meloria, and Pisa's naval power and role in overseas commerce never fully recovered.

In the fourteenth century Pisa suffered from protracted factional violence, and while the city retained the facade of communal government, real power was usually in the hands of a *signore.* The noble Donoratico family dominated the city from 1317 to 1347. In the next year Pisa endured an exceptionally severe visitation from the bubonic plague. The generally unhealthy and malarial climate may have contributed to the high level of mortality in the city. The most famous of early Renaissance Pisan despots, Pietro Gambacorta, presided over his faction's rule of the city from 1369 to 1392. After falling briefly under the rule of Gian Galeazzo Visconti of Milan (*r.* in Pisa 1399–1402),

Pisa Cathedral, showing baptistery, west front, and campanile. PHOTO: WIM SWAAN

Pisa was purchased from the German emperor and then conquered by Florence in 1406. The city entered a long period of decay and neglect under Florentine rule; by 1427 the city had only about 7,400 inhabitants. The invasion of Italy by Charles VIII of France in 1494 offered Pisa the opportunity to overthrow Florentine rule. The last period of Pisan independence ended when the city, after a bitter and famous siege directed in part by Niccolò Machiavelli, fell in 1509.

BIBLIOGRAPHY

Sources. Francesco Bonaini made two useful collections of source material, the Pisan law codes in *Statuti inediti della città di Pisa* (1854–1870), and the contemporary chronicles in *Archivio storico italiano,* 6 (1844–1845).

Studies. Gino Benvenuti, *Storia della repubblica di Pisa,* 3rd ed., rev. (1968), is a general survey of the medieval period. Among the monographs, see particularly Emilio Cristiani, *Nobilità e popolo nel comune di Pisa: Dalle origini del podestariata alla signoria dei Donoratico* (1962); David Herlihy, *Pisa in the Early Renaissance* (1958); G. Rossetti *et al., Pisa nei secoli XI e XII* (1979); Marco Tangheroni, *Politica, commercio, agricoltura a Pisa nel trecento* (1973); Cinzio Violante, *Economia, società, istituzioni a Pisa nel medioevo* (1980).

STEVEN EPSTEIN

[See also **Commune; Condottieri; Consulate of the Sea; Crusades and Crusader States; Florence; Genoa; Guelphs and Ghibellines; Henry IV of Germany; Italy, Rise of Towns in; Milan; Navies, Western; Podesta; Trade, European; Tuscany; Urbanism, Western European; Visconti; Warfare, Western European.**]

PISA CATHEDRAL was founded in 1063/1064, consecrated in 1118, and financed and decorated with booty from Pisa's conquests over the Saracens. It was one of the most richly adorned and largest churches of its day (96 m [315 ft] long, 48 m [157 ft] high). For the history of architecture, it is important as an early instance in which an architect, Buscheto (or Buschetus), is recorded by name and for its eclectically original design, with elements recalling ancient Roman and Islamic buildings, as well as contemporary Italian churches. Buscheto's cathedral is cruciform, with transept

Study of a horse seen from behind. Pen and ink drawing by Antonio Pisanello, before 1438. MUSÉE DU LOUVRE, PARIS, COD. VALLARDI 2444, fol. 231. Photo: Giraudon/Art Resource

arms like separate basilicas and pairs of two-storied aisles on either side of the nave. The nave was elongated in the later twelfth century and a new facade was designed by Rainaldo (Rainaldus, *fl.* 1255–1270). Bronze doors made for the facade by Bonanno of Pisa (*fl.* 1174–1186) around 1180 were destroyed in a fire of 1595; a second pair of doors by the same craftsman survives in the south transept. The elliptical brick dome on squinches over the crossing was completed in the fourteenth century; the famous campanile (the "Leaning Tower") was begun in 1173/1174.

BIBLIOGRAPHY

Piero Sanpaolesi, *Il duomo di Pisa e l'architettura romanica toscana delle origini* (1975).

DALE KINNEY

[See also **Architect, Status of; Buscheto of Pisa; Dome; Rainaldus.**]

PISA, COUNCIL OF. See **Councils, Western (1311–1449).**

PISANELLO, ANTONIO (*ca.* 1395–*ca.* 1455), painter and medalist. Antonio Pisano, known as Pisanello, was born in either Pisa or Verona. His artistic roots were in the Veronese late Gothic style and Stefano da Verona (or da Zevio, *ca.* 1374/1375–after 1438), a leading exponent of that style with whom he may have studied. Pisanello was associated with Gentile da Fabriano (*ca.* 1370/1380–1427), whose works he completed in Venice and Rome during the 1420's. Documentary evidence also confirms his presence in Mantua, Ferrara, Pavia, Milan, and Naples.

Pisanello's works include fresco and panel paintings of religious and secular subjects, many of which are lost or survive in fragmentary state; the largest number of extant drawings by any artist of the early fifteenth century; and significant activity as the first Renaissance medalist. The drawings attest to his wide-ranging interests and skill as a draftsman. While his paintings show a strong connection to the International Style, his work as a whole, particularly his drawings, provides ample evidence of his interest in the new naturalism of the early Renaissance.

BIBLIOGRAPHY

Gian Alberto dell'Acqua. *L'opera completa del Pisanello* (1972); Giovanni Paccagnini, *Pisanello,* Jane Carroll, trans. (1973); Enio Sindona, *Pisanello,* John Ross, trans. (1961).

CHRISTIANE L. JOOST-GAUGIER

[See also **Fresco Painting: Gentile da Fabriano; Gothic, International Style.**]

PISANO, ANDREA (Andrea da Pontedera) (*ca.* 1295–*ca.* 1348), sculptor and metalsmith. Born at Pontedera, a town near Pisa, Andrea was the son of a notary, Ser Ugolino Nini, and the father of the sculptor Nino Pisano. He seems to have been

Beheading of John the Baptist. Panel by Andrea Pisano from the bronze door of the baptistery of S. Maria del Fiore, Florence, 1330–1336. ALINARI/ART RESOURCE

trained as a goldsmith, possibly in Pisa, Pistoia, or Florence. Nothing is known of his sculptural activity until 1330, when he began work on the bronze door of the baptistery at Florence: in January 1330 he was first referred to as *maestro delle porte;* by 2 April 1330 a wax model of the entire door was completed; in late 1332 the first wing was completed; between July and December 1333 the second wing was finished and gilded; in August 1335 Andrea was instructed to correct flaws in the casting or alignment of the doors; on 20 June 1336 the bronze scraps and dust were weighed; and the wings were put in place in the south doorway soon after. Each wing contains fourteen rectangular fields; the upper ten reliefs are scenes from the life of John the Baptist, and the four lower reliefs contain figures of the Virtues. Andrea's work on the door shows a strong influence of French Gothic metalwork and also of the style of Giotto, particularly in the treatment of space and figures.

Following Giotto's death in 1337, Andrea continued the work of that master on the building and decoration of the cathedral campanile in Florence. (The campanile was completed 1359/1360 by Francesco Talenti.) The two rows of reliefs reflect the styles of both Giotto and Andrea, though most of the twenty-one reliefs depicting seven Virtues, seven Liberal Arts, and seven Planets are probably by the latter. Above the two cycles of reliefs on the campanile, Andrea added eight niches, four on the west face (later moved to the north) and four on the south face, to be filled with

Strength and Prudence. Marble sculptures from the Pisa pulpit of Giovanni Pisano, 1302–1311. PHAIDON PRESS LTD., OXFORD, ENGLAND

almost life-size statues representing Solomon, David, the Eritrean Sibyl, the Tiburtine Sibyl, and four prophets. The statues were carved from Andrea's designs, but he may not have executed them. Two additional marble sculptures, executed soon after 1335 and smaller in size, are generally accepted as works by Andrea: the statuettes of Christ and of S. Reparata in the Museo dell'Opera del Duomo in Florence.

In 1343 Andrea left Florence, probably for Pisa, where he may have worked at S. Maria della Spina, and from 1347 to 1348 he was in Orvieto as *capomaestro* of the cathedral. Perhaps a small Virgin and Child, originally located above a doorway of the cathedral and now in the cathedral museum, was executed by him and his son, Nino, at this time.

BIBLIOGRAPHY

Ilse Falk and Jenö Lányi, "The Genesis of Andrea Pisano's Bronze Doors," in *Art Bulletin,* **25** (1943); Gert Kreytenberg, "Andrea Pisano's Earliest Works in Marble," in *Burlington Magazine,* **122** (1980); Ilario Toesca, *Andrea e Nino Pisani* (1950); Marvin Trachtenberg, *The Campanile of Florence Cathedral* (1971); W. R. Valentiner, "Andrea Pisano as a Marble Sculptor," in *Art Quarterly,* **10** (1947).

SANDRA CANDEE SUSMAN

[See also **Baptistery; Campanile; Florence; Giotto di Bondone; Gothic Art: Sculpture; Talenti, Francesco.**]

PISANO, GIOVANNI (*fl.* 1265–*ca.* 1314), sculptor and architect, son of Nicola Pisano. His major works are the lower half of the facade of the Cathedral of Siena (*ca.* 1284–1296); the pulpit in S. Andrea, Pistoia (inscribed 1301); the pulpit in the Cathedral of Pisa (1302–1311); and the tomb of Margaret of Luxembourg (*ca.* 1312). He had a minor role in the Siena pulpit of his father, and major ones in the exterior sculpture of the baptistery at Pisa (1270's) and the Fontana Maggiore in Perugia (1278). Giovanni also sculpted a number of madonnas, including the ivory statuette in Pisa (1298), and a group of wooden crucifixes.

Giovanni was very receptive to the art of the thirteenth-century French sculptors, but this interest led him neither to slavishly imitate their forms nor to reject his father's classicism. It did, however, help him conceive his expressive and highly emotional style, arguably the sculptural counterpart of Giotto's achievement in painting. For the Siena facade Giovanni placed fourteen monumental prophets of the Virgin—including Plato, Aristotle, and a sibyl—at the level of the archivolts of the three large portals. This arrangement owes much to French inspiration, but the result is characteristically unique. The polychromy is, of course, a Tuscan practice, and the figured rinceaux of the colonnettes draw heavily on antique precedents. Of the prophets the sibyl is probably an earlier work; and Mary, the sister of Moses, with her bent neck and outthrust and turned head, a later one.

These distortions continue in the Pistoia pulpit, a hexagon set on steeply pointed, trilobe arches. Around the body of this work are reliefs of the Nativity cycle, the Crucifixion, and the Last Judgment. The iconography is close to Nicola's Siena pulpit, but the style differs. Giovanni links figures by sweeping, scythelike patterns that carry across the corner figures. Below, at the level of the archivolts, are prophets and six ecstatic sibyls.

The later Pisan pulpit is octagonal, but its geometry is complicated by the convexity of the nine reliefs. The usual Nativity segment is supplemented by the infancy of John the Baptist, and the Crucifixion is preceded by Passion scenes. Prophetic figures, including sibyls, are beneath, at the level of the classical consoles. The outstanding feature is the lowest story, which has full-size caryatid figures of the Cardinal Virtues, Ecclesia/Charity, Christ, the evangelists, St. Michael, and Hercules. The text on Christ's scroll paraphrases Psalm 85:12, which suggests that the group symbolizes divine and earthly justice. The quality of the reliefs and even of certain of the supporting figures is uneven. Some, which tend to be formularized and repetitive, are usually thought to contain much shop participation; others, especially the figures of Christ, the Virtues, and Hercules, are very strong, expressive, and reminiscent of Giovanni's earlier work.

Only dispersed fragments survive from the tomb of Margaret of Luxembourg. A central motif was the resurrection of the empress, which was based on the type of the awakening Virgin known in French sculpture.

BIBLIOGRAPHY

Enzo Carli, *Il pergamo del Duomo di Pisa* (1975), and *Giovanni Pisano* (1977); Harald Keller, *Giovanni Pisano* (1942); Antje Kosegarten, "Nicola und Giovanni Pisano 1268–1278," in *Jahrbuch der Berliner Museen,* **11** (1969); Gian Lorenzo Mellini, *Il pulpito di Giovanni Pisano a Pistoia* (1969), and *Giovanni Pisano* (*ca.* 1970); John W. Pope-Hennessy, *An Introduction to Italian Sculpture,* pt. 1: *Italian Gothic Sculpture,* 2nd ed. (1972), 7–12, 175–180; Max Seidel, "Das Fragment einer Statue Giovanni Pisanos im Museo Guarnacci in Volterra," in *Mitteilungen des Kunsthistorischen Instituts in Florenz,* **15** (1971), *La scultura lignea di Giovanni Pisano* (1971), "Die Berliner Madonna des Giovanni Pisano," in *Pantheon,* **30** (1972), "Die Elfenbeinmadonna im Domschatz zu Pisa," in *Mitteilungen des Kunsthistorischen Instituts in Florenz,* **16** (1972), and "*Ubera Matris:* Die vielschichtige Bedeutung eines Symbols in der mittelalterlichen Kunst," in *Städel-Jahrbuch,* **6** (1977).

MICHAEL D. TAYLOR

[See also **Epiphany (with illustration); Gothic Art: Sculpture; Pisa Cathedral; Trecento Art.**]

PISANO, NICOLA (*fl.* 1258–1280), sculptor and, possibly, architect. Nicola's work constituted a rupture with immediately preceding sculpture in Tuscany. His monumental figures, his spatial illusions within the reliefs, and his highly articulated architecture enrich the emotional experience of his work. The programs of the pulpits and the Perugia fountain amplify this content with their encyclopedic scope.

The most important works associated with Nicola are the pulpit in the baptistery, Pisa, inscribed with his name and the date 1259 (1260 Pisan style); the pulpit in the cathedral, Siena (1265–1268); portions of the exterior sculpture and architecture of the baptistery, Pisa (*ca.* 1270); and the Fontana Maggiore, Perugia, inscribed 1278. Other works are the Arca di S. Domenico, Bologna (*ca.* 1264–1267), worked chiefly by assistants; the font at S. Giovanni Fuorcivitas, Pistoia (probably *ca.* 1273); a relief formerly in Berlin (*ca.* 1280); and a tympanum and lintel with a Deposition and an Incarnation cycle at Lucca (date disputed).

The body of the unusual hexagonal pulpit in the Pisa baptistery is surrounded by reliefs of New Testament subjects. Beneath, in the archivolt, are virtues, prophets, and evangelists. The style of this work is strikingly classical, seen most clearly in the figure of Hercules/Fortitude. Specific sources for many other figures have been identified in antique remains at Pisa. This interest, once attributed to Nicola's probable origins in the revivalist south Italian ambience of Frederick II and to the influence of Byzantine ivories, has been attributed more recently to a tradition of classical references in earlier Pisan sculpture.

The pulpit in Siena is octagonal. Although the subjects of the reliefs are approximately those of the earlier pulpit, the supporting elements are more complex and the scale of the figures has decreased, yielding a more discursive narrative. These changes have been associated with the influence of French Gothic sculpture, seen especially in the representation of Christ in the Crucifixion and the Last Judgment. Nicola was assisted on this pulpit by Arnolfo di Cambio (*ca.* 1245–*ca.* 1310) and Lapo (*fl.* in Siena *ca.* 1265–*ca.* 1289), as well as by his son Giovanni (*ca.* 1265–*ca.* 1314).

Fixing the responsibility for the design of the last major project, the Fontana Maggiore in Perugia, has been especially troublesome. Recently Giovanni's role has been emphasized and Nicola's diminished. The lowest basin of this three-tiered fountain is twenty-five-sided, and on each face is a pair of reliefs showing the labors of the months, the liberal arts, or fables. The middle level is a twelve-sided basin which is articulated by twenty-four standing figures: per-

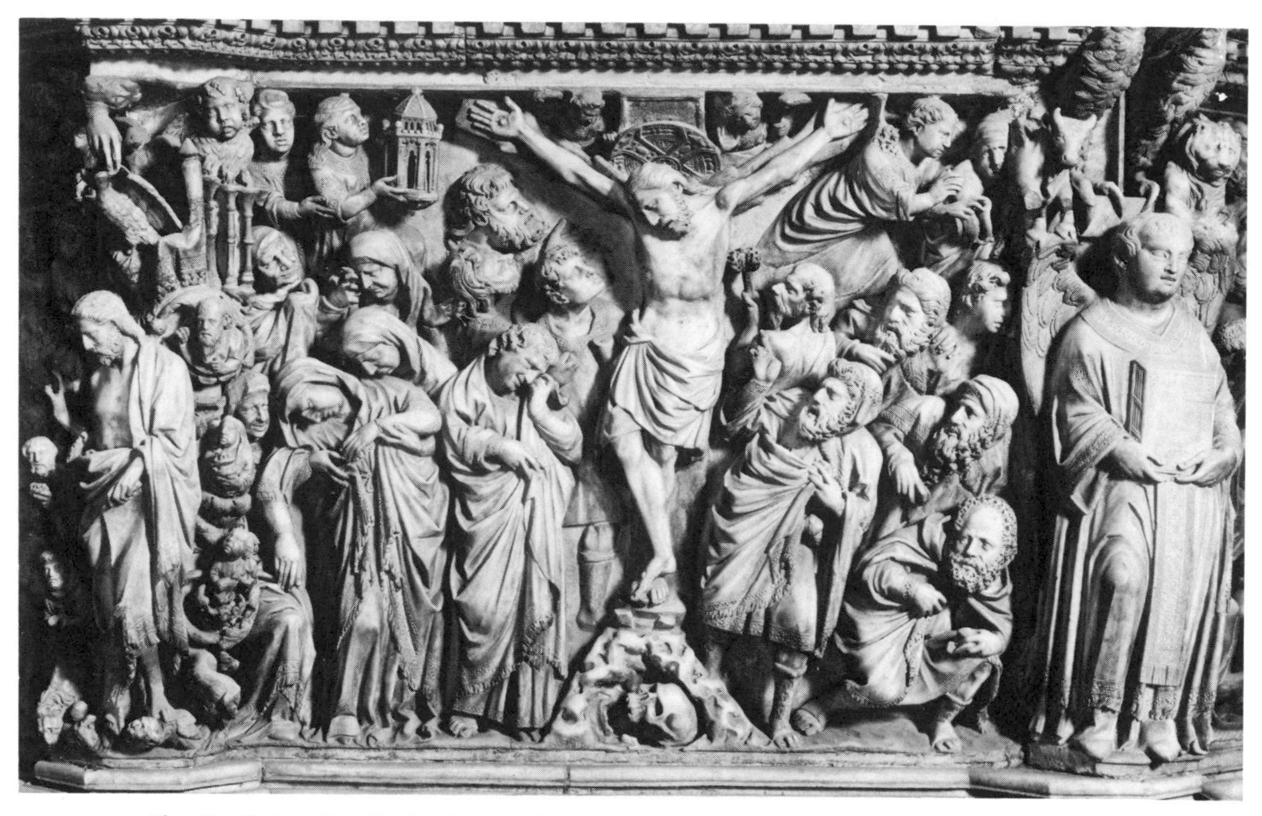

The Crucifixion (detail). Marble relief from the Siena pulpit of Nicola Pisano, 1265–1268. ALINARI/ART RESOURCE

sonifications, Old Testament personages, saints, and two portraits. The highest bronze basin is surmounted by a caryatid group derived from the ancient Hekateion group, a witness of Nicola's continued attentiveness to classical sculpture.

BIBLIOGRAPHY

Eloise M. Angiola, "Nicola Pisano, Federigo Visconti, and the Classical Style in Pisa," in *Art Bulletin,* **59** (1977); Moshe Barasch, "A Silenus Surviving in Nicola Pisano," in *Art Bulletin,* **58** (1976); Maria L. Cristiani Test, "Nicola Pisano e la committenza dell'arcivescovo Federico Visconti," in *Critica d'arte,* **21** (1975); Cesare Gnudi, *Nicola, Arnolfo, Lapo: L'arca di San Domenico in Bologna* (1948); Kathrin Hoffmann-Curtius, *Das Programm der Fontana Maggiore in Perugia* (1968); Antje Middeldorf Kosegarten, "Nicola und Giovanni Pisano 1268–1278," in *Jahrbuch der Berliner Museen,* **11** (1969), and "Identifizierung eines Grabmals von Nicola Pisano: Zur Genese des Reliefsarkophags in der Toskana," in *Mitteilungen des kunsthistorischen Instituts in Florenz,* **22** (1978); Giusta Nicco Fasola, *Nicola Pisano* (1941), and *La Fontana di Perugia* (1951); John Pope-Hennessy, *Italian Gothic Sculpture,* 2nd ed. (1972), 2–7, 169–175; F. R. Presenti, "Il XII sermone dell'archivescovo Federico Visconti e il pulpito de Battistero Pisa," in *Commentari,* **26** (1975); Max Seidel, *Il pulpito di Nicola Pisano nel Duomo di Siena* (1971), "Studien zur Antikenrezeption Nicola Pisanos," in *Mitteilungen des kunsthistorischen Institutes in Florenz,* **19** (1975), and "Una nuova opera di Nicola Pisano," in *Paragone,* **343** (1978); Georg Swarzenski, *Nicolo Pisano* (1926); John White, "The Reconstruction of Nicola Pisano's Perugia Fountain," in *Journal of the Warburg and Courtauld Institutes,* 33 (1970).

MICHAEL D. TAYLOR

[See also **Arnolfo di Cambio; Gothic Art: Sculpture.**]

PISHTAQ. Although this Persian word literally means "fore-arch," the English terms "frontispiece" and "portal" would better render respectively its symbolic and practical functions. This architectural element characterizes eastern Islamic religious buildings and comprises a narrow but monumental facade dominated by a central vaulted arch within a rectangular frame. This motif may have originated in early Islamic mausolea but quickly spread, from the tenth century onward, always connoting the major entrance, to other building types such as mosques, madrasas, and caravansaries. The selfsame element could be placed in cruciform and axial disposition around an arcaded courtyard—the celebrated "four-*eyvān*" (iwan) plan of Iranian architecture. The *pishtaq* thus articulated otherwise monotonous facades and gave them a focus.

In Iran the *pishtaq* exploited the symbolic overtones of Shiism and Sufism, and so find their appropriate apotheosis in religious shrines, whose relative importance can often be gauged by the size of the portal. This element of competition was apt to reduce the *pishtaq* to a mere screen, and incidentally explains why it so frequently displays lavish ornament and epigraphy; hence its value as an index of stylistic change in these fields over the centuries.

Early *pishtaq*s have their essential flatness masked by multiple minor recessions of their rectangular frame (Hārūniya, Tus, fourteenth century). Later a pronounced salience came into play; the central arch opened into a deep vaulted vestibule, itself often lined with benches, and was enveloped in an increasingly lofty and attenuated frame (tombs at Taybad and Balkh [Afghanistan], fifteenth century).

BIBLIOGRAPHY

Percy Brown, *Indian Architecture (The Islamic Period)* (1942); Arthur U. Pope, *Persian Architecture* (1965).

ROBERT HILLENBRAND

[See also **Eyvān; Islamic Architecture.**]

Pishtaq of the Masjid-i-Jāmiʿ, Yazd, Iran, 1324–1365. PHOTO: ARTHUR UPHAM POPE

PLACENTINUS (*ca.* 1135–1192), glossator and teacher of Roman law, and reputed founder of the law school at Montpellier. Placentinus was named after Piacenza (Latin: Placentia), where he was born. Once thought to have been of relatively humble origins, Placentinus is now known to have been a member of the Savinus family, the lords of Borgo Val di Taro. He received his legal education at Bologna under the jurists Bulgarus and Rogerius. By 1160 Placentinus was teaching law at Mantua, where he composed several minor treatises as well as his first major work of certain attribution, the *Summa cum essem Mantuae.* Before 1165, he returned to teach in Bologna, where he remained until both the predominance of the imperialist party and the hostility of a rival jurist, Henricus de Baila, drove him from the city. He found refuge in Montpellier, where, in 1170, he succeeded his former master Rogerius as teacher of law. In the introduction to his *Summa trium librorum,* Placentinus tells of his activities during the next two decades. At Montpellier he first completed the unfinished *Summa codicis* of Rogerius, then wrote his own gloss on the *Code* and a *Summa institutionum.* He returned to Italy about 1185 and, after two months in his native Piacenza, recommenced teaching at Bologna. While he does not explain why he left Montpellier, it is likely that the changed political situation and also his growing reputation as a jurist made the return to Bologna possible. There, Placentinus boasts, he had great success as a teacher but suffered the envy of those teachers whose schools were emptied of students who preferred his lectures. During these years he also composed his poetical *Sermo de legibus* at the request of the arts faculty. After two years, Placentinus left Bologna intending to retire, but, at the insistence of his colleagues and students, he taught for four additional years in Piacenza. Finally, in 1191, he returned to Montpellier, where he began the *Summa trium librorum* (on the last three books of the *Code*) and planned a major work on the *Digest*. He was still at work on the former when he died on 12 February 1192.

In the thirteenth century, the law faculty at the University of Montpellier adopted the practice, in honor of Placentinus, of observing 12 February as their annual feast day. Nevertheless, his role as the reputed founder of the law school there has often been challenged. While it is not possible to establish a direct connection between the teaching of Placentinus and the flourishing law school in Montpellier in the late thirteenth century, there can be no doubt that he did give a major stimulus to the study and teaching of Roman law in southern France. His influence in Italy was no less great among the next generation of glossators—his students include Pillius, Karolus de Tocco, and Roffredus of Benevento—than among canonists such as Sicard of Cremona and Hostiensis.

Placentinus composed glosses on nearly all of the *Code* and the *Institutes*. These works have an elegance of style and expression exceptional among the glossators. Placentinus was broadly trained in classical literature and philosophy. Skilled in dialectical reasoning, he was also a subtle and original thinker who, like Peter Abelard, suffered from excessive vanity. His notable abilities as a poet are evident in the *Sermo de legibus* (1186) as well as in the verse included in his glosses. A convincing argument has been made (by Herman Kantorowicz) that Placentinus is the author of the highly original and learned *Questiones de iuris subtilitatibus* (*ca.* 1160), but the attribution of this major work of legal scholarship remains debated. The anti-imperialist and nationalist political sympathies of Placentinus are evident in the tendency in his glosses to downgrade imperial authority and to place the emperor in a legal position subordinate to the pope; but his strongest objections are to the legality of the financial exactions attempted by Frederick I Barbarossa.

BIBLIOGRAPHY

Most of the writings of Placentinus, including the *Summa codicis* (1536, repr. 1962), remain poorly or only partially edited. For a complete bibliography of his works and their editions, see Charles Lefebvre's "Placentin" in the *Dictionnarie de droit canonique,* VII (1965).

On the life and work of Placentinus, see the Lefebvre article and H. Gilles, "L'enseignement du droit en Languedoc au XIIIe siècle," in *Les universités du Languedoc au XIIIe siècle* (1970), 206–208; André Gouron, "Les juristes de l'école de Montpellier," in *Ius romanum medii aevi,* pt. IV, 3a (1970), 3–4 and 28f; Hermann Kantorowicz, "The Poetical Sermon of a Medieval Jurist (Placentinus)," in *Journal of the Warburg and Courtald Institute,* 2 (1938), and, with William W. Buckland, *Studies in the Glossators of the Roman Law* (1938, repr. 1969), 125–126 and 181–205; Friedrich Karl von Savigny, *Geschichte de römischen Rechts im Mittelalter,* IV (1850), 244–285; Pierre Tisset, "Placentin et l'enseignement du droit à Montpellier," in *Recueil de memoires et travaux publiés par la Société d'histoire du droit et des institutions des anciens pays de droit écrit,* fasc. 2 (1951), 67–95; Pierre de Tourtoulon, *Placentin: Sa vie, ses oeuvres* (1896).

S. C. FERRUOLO

[See also **Corpus Iuris Civilis; Glossators; Law, Civil; Law, French: In South; Law, Schools of; Rogerius.**]

PLAGUES, EUROPEAN. Plagues or, more broadly speaking, infectious epidemic diseases, are considered by historians and demographers to have been a crucial element in determining preindustrial population levels and socioeconomic trends. This was especially so during the Middle Ages, part of which has been described as "the golden age of bacteria." In their etiological frameworks, plagues are caused by parasites that have relationships with other, invariably larger, host organisms, a natural part of human and animal ecology. One of the ironies of infectious diseases is that the most persistent of them are those which are not lethal to their hosts; such diseases are usually older and well established, and are only mildly deleterious to their hosts, thus ensuring a steady supply of victims. On the other hand, the spectacular diseases that periodically burst onto the historical stage by killing thousands of people are usually caused by newer parasites, which have yet to establish a balance with their hosts. An example of the older diseases is malaria, which debilitates but usually is not fatal, while an example of the newer is pneumonic plague, which is 95 to 100 percent fatal. Both diseases have been important historically, but because of the enormous mortality that they brought, plagues have been more important. The major focus of this article will be on the great killing diseases.

Infectious diseases can be classified in other ways. In historical perspective, one of the most important is by means of dissemination. One mechanism is directly from human to human, usually via the respiratory tract. Examples include influenza, diphtheria, measles, and pneumonic plague. Respiratory diseases are highly communicable, virtually impossible to prevent, and closely connected with population density. Consequently, they are common in urban societies, even highly sophisticated modern ones. The second class comprises enteric diseases, those spread through the digestive system. Examples are dysentery, diarrhea, typhoid, and cholera. Enteric diseases often reflect human social conditions, especially those conducive to poor sanitation and public health. Because of this, however, and in contrast to respiratory diseases, enteric diseases are relatively easy to eliminate. But like respiratory afflictions, certain enteric types were very common throughout the Middle Ages.

A third class of infectious diseases embraces those spread by venereal contact, the prime examples being the treponema diseases, especially syphilis and gonorrhea. The causative organisms of venereal diseases are ordinarily highly vulnerable when exposed, and were less frequent in the Middle Ages than either respiratory or enteric diseases. A fourth group, however, was very common. These are diseases transferred to humans from animal hosts, with the animals acting either as intermediaries, as with malaria and typhus, or as primary or secondary epizootic victims, as with bubonic plague. The role of animals in the transmission of disease is crucial; dogs share sixty-five different diseases with men, cattle fifty, sheep and goats forty-six, pigs forty-two, horses thirty-five, rats and mice thirty-two, and poultry twenty-six. While not always as common as respiratory or enteric diseases, those transmitted by animals are often more lethal, since most viruses and bacteria tend to gain in virulence as they pass through chains of hosts.

Diseases facilitated by animal intermediaries are important for another reason. In themselves, they represent an additional disease classification and interpretation. Their dissemination and frequency are based primarily on the animal host rather than man. Some scholars have suggested that communicable diseases are a basic part of human environment and a function of population density, and that civilization and disease travel hand in hand. Hence the incidence of a given epidemic hinges on patterns of settlement. Certainly, this is the case with respiratory, enteric, and venereal diseases, but it is not the case with those diseases spread by animal intermediaries. They are primarily dependent on factors exogenous to civilization, such as insect and rodent population density and ecology, and on climate. There is great danger in being too anthropocentric when stressing solely the human element. In terms of epidemic diseases, men are perhaps most effective as carriers when entering new ecospheres, such as the Americas in the sixteenth century, rather than in older areas, such as Europe throughout the Middle Ages.

A key factor in the incidence of infectious diseases is immunity. Humans have complex mechanisms for defending themselves against pathogens, with individual resistance varying with many factors such as protective antibodies. Immunity is either innate or acquired, with the latter being either passive or active. Active immunity comes when the host generates his own defenses, passive when generated defenses are introduced, the latter often being only temporary. In the Middle Ages, active immunity was particularly important in determining the extent and intensity of an epidemic. Some infectious diseases, especially respiratory types such as smallpox and measles, do not change a great deal in their etiology. Hence, survival of an initial attack confers immunity, limiting recurrence to younger members of society, born after the last epidemic. These diseases had less of an impact on medieval Europe than more complex, multiple infections such as dysentery, influenza, and plague, for which immunity is quite limited, if it exists at all.

The background to medieval patterns of infectious disease consists of the general confluence of Eurasian and North African disease gene pools during the period 500 B.C. to about A.D. 250, when the Mediterranean basin received most of the infectious diseases it was ever to get. Despite the arrival of the diseases, however, and with the exception of a few general instances such as the Athenian plague of the fifth century B.C., the classical world was remarkably free from major killing epidemics. This was basic to its consistent population increases, which continued almost unabated until about the year 250. Also crucial to the plague patterns that would develop in the Middle Ages was the system of commerce and communication established in the ancient world, particularly by the Romans. Although their road system was excellent, most commerce in the Roman Empire was sea-based, with major trading routes converging on the Levantine coast, then branching east across the northern part of the Arabian Peninsula, to the Arabian Sea, the Indian Ocean, and south Asia; and west to Italy, southern Gaul, and Iberia, where goods then proceeded inland through major river valleys like the Rhône. Sea travel was relatively quick, and thus allowed a disease organism to spread before it could dispose of all its shipboard hosts. Cargoes were also bulky enough to conceal potential insect and rodent intermediaries. This, coupled with the linking of south and central Asia, the Middle East, the Nile Delta, and the European coast of the Mediterranean, brought about the fruition of disease pools.

SMALLPOX, MEASLES, AND PLAGUE

From the second through the sixth centuries A.D., this confluence carried at least three new infections to Europe, bringing an end to the ecological peace of the ancient world, and marking the disease watershed between classical and medieval. From 165 to 180, an epidemic called the Antonine Plague raged throughout Italy and most of the Western part of the empire. It seems to have been brought from the East by Roman legions, and probably marks the introduction into Mediterranean Europe of smallpox. Some authorities believe smallpox was concurrently present among the Germans north and east of the Rhine-Danube frontier, but the barbarian tribes seem never to have transmitted it into the empire, at least not before the third century. Smallpox is one of man's most communicable diseases and, among a virgin population with no immunity, can be very deadly. This was the case in Rome. During the fifteen years in which smallpox raged, the physician Galen estimated that between a quarter and a third of the population of Italy died.

So introduced into Europe, smallpox would persist as a major killer throughout the Middle Ages. Caused by a virus and transferred by droplets through the respiratory system, it comes in three strains: *variola major,* the true, most virulent form; *variola minor,* a much milder form of the same; and *variola vaccinae,* principally a cattle disease also known as cowpox. Because the virus seems to change very rarely, survival of an attack confers immunity, and smallpox becomes a once in a lifetime experience. This limited its role as a medieval plague to areas that had yet to experience it, and eventually to people who had never had it, primarily children. It would be as a killer of children that smallpox would make its biggest mark. Aside from the second century, smallpox seems to have been most virulent in the fourteenth and fifteenth centuries. In the 1440's and 1460's successive waves swept through Central and Western Europe and seem to have been particularly severe in the British Isles. It was the subject of an early English treatise on medicine, the *Rosa angelica* (or *Rosa medicinae*) by John Gaddesden (*ca.* 1280–1349), written early in the fourteenth century (probably 1314); and it ultimately proved to be the deadliest disease that Europeans would introduce into other parts of the world.

Smallpox was joined in 251 by the second of the great plagues that marked the classical/medieval disease watershed. This was measles, which at its peak between 251 and 266 was said to have killed 5,000 people a day in Rome. Measles is like smallpox in many ways. It is caused by a virus and transmitted through the respiratory system, and is highly lethal to a population without immunity. Like smallpox, it was described in great detail by Gaddesden, but was not distinguished as a peculiar disease until the sixteenth century. And also like smallpox, survival of an attack confers immunity from future visitations, so that measles too was to become primarily a childhood disease throughout the Middle Ages. Nevertheless, it is important not to underrate the effects of either smallpox or measles, especially on their initial appearance. Measles depleted population, facilitated the desertion of many rural areas, particularly in North Africa and Sicily, and hence cut the rolls of the Roman army and taxpayers. It caused at least a temporary reduction in East-West trade, and has formed the cornerstone of a major theory of the decline of the Roman Empire.

Important as smallpox and measles were in the natural history of infectious disease, their combined role is dwarfed by the arrival of a third disease. This was plague, a complex series of disease strains caused by the bacillus *Yersinia pestis.* There are four variations: bubonic, pneumonic, septicemic, and enteric. The latter two are quite rare, and their presence in most epidemics is very hard to document; one of the reasons is that septicemic as well as enteric plague are literally 100 percent fatal, killing their victims within hours of infection. Pneumonic plague, almost as deadly, is the one variety of plague that is respiratory in its spread, and hence communicable directly from person to person, rather than through insect and rodent intermediaries. Bubonic plague is by far the most common strain, and thus the most important historically. It too is lethal, killing about half of those infected. It was generally seasonal in occurrence, coming in spring and autumn, and depended on local climatic conditions and the activity of the host flea. Bubonic plague tended to come in pandemic cycles lasting hundreds of years, with individual epidemics recurring every three to twenty years. Herein lay its importance to medieval Europe. Plague combined virulence and frequency to a degree matched by no other infectious disease. Its multiple varieties and frequent permutations, perhaps the result of its complicated mechanism of infection, make innate immunity rare, and perhaps even nonexistent. Because of all of these biological and ecological factors, plague served as one of the major checks on population expansion for much of the Middle Ages.

THE FIRST PLAGUE PANDEMIC

Plague is indigenous to several areas in east Africa and south and perhaps central Asia. It is likely that the first medieval plague pandemic came to Europe from east Africa, down the Nile and through Egypt, into the relatively populous eastern Mediterranean. The first outbreak of this pandemic, called Justinian's Plague, arrived in 541, when the Byzantine emperor was in the midst of his attempt to regain the Western half of the old Roman Empire from its new Germanic overlords. The Byzantine court historian, Procopius, wrote:

> During these times there was a pestilence, by which the whole human race came near to being annihilated. Now in the case of all other scourges sent from Heaven some explanation of a cause might be given by daring men, such as the many theories propounded by those who are clever in these matters; for they love to conjure up causes which are absolutely incomprehensible to man, and to fabricate outlandish theories of natural philosophy, knowing well that they are saying nothing sound, but considering it sufficient for them, if they completely deceive by their argument some of those whom they meet and persuade them to their view. But for this calamity it is quite impossible now to express in words or conceive in thought any explanation, except indeed to refer it to God. . . .
>
> It started from the Egyptians who dwell in Pelusium. Then it divided and moved in one direction towards Alexandria and the rest of Egypt and in other directions; it came to Palestine on the borders of Egypt and from here it spread over the whole world, always moving forward and traveling at times favorable to it. For it seemed to move by fixed arrangement, and to tarry for a specified time in each country, casting its blight slightingly upon none, but spreading in either direction right out to the ends of the world, as if fearing lest some corner of the earth might escape it. For it left neither island nor cave nor mountain ridge which had human inhabitants; and if it passed by any land, either not affecting the men there or touching them in indifferent fashion, still at a later time it came back. . . .
>
> With the majority it came about that they were seized by the disease without becoming aware of what was coming either through a waking vision or a dream. And they were taken in the following manner. They had a sudden fever, some when just roused from sleep, others while walking about, and others while otherwise engaged, without any regard to what they were doing. And the body showed no change from its previous color, nor was it as hot as it might be expected when attacked by fever, nor indeed did any inflamation set in, but the fever was of such a languid sort from its commencement and until evening that neither to the sick themselves nor to a physician who touched them would it afford any suspicion of danger. It was natural, therefore, that not one of those who contracted the disease expected to die from it. But on the same day in some cases, in others on the following day, and in the rest not many days later, a bubonic swelling developed and this took place not only in the particular part of the body which is called the groin, that is, below the abdomen, but also inside the armpit, and in some cases besides the ears, and at different points on the thighs.

In a sixth-century context, Justinian's Plague was nearly worldwide in scope, striking central and south Asia, North Africa and Arabia, and Europe as far north as Denmark and west to Ireland, where mortality proved especially severe. In Constantinople, the center of the Byzantine Empire, the plague was at its most virulent from autumn 541 until spring 542. During a four-month peak, it allegedly killed 200,000 of the city's people, perhaps 40 percent of the total population. It had a devastating effect in Italy, southern France, the Rhine Valley and Iberia, where it lingered until autumn of 544. When Justinian's Plague had finally spent itself, between a fifth and a quarter of Europe's population south of the Alps had perished. In political terms, it dealt a crippling blow to Byzantine plans to conquer the western Mediterranean, and perhaps so weakened Byzantium as to set up its defeat by the Arabs a few generations later. From the perspective of the history of infectious disease, it marked the arrival of the third major disease into Europe in a four-hundred-year period, and the last major disease to come to the West from the lands abutting the Indian Ocean for close to a thousand years.

Justinian's Plague established a reservoir of the bacillus *y. pestis* among European fleas and rodents, ensuring that subsequent epidemics of the pandemic would recur in ten-to-twelve-year cycles for the next two hundred years. Plague returned from 558 to 561, again beginning in Constantinople, spreading throughout the eastern Mediterranean, then west through the Italian ports of Ravenna and Genoa, and through southern France. It came again from 580 to 582, and 588 to 591, the latter spreading from Spain to southern France and then Italy, the reverse of most of the patterns of dissemination. There is some evidence that these third, fourth, and fifth plague epidemics were exacerbated by accompanying sieges of smallpox. The sixth plague epidemic occurred from 599 through 600; in Italy and southern France, it is considered the most lethal epidemic after Justinian's Plague, killing up to 15 percent of the population.

After 599–600, successive epidemics of the first plague pandemic were less virulent but about as frequent. Large areas of Mediterranean Europe were afflicted in 608, 618, 628, 640, 654, 684–686, 694–700, 718, and 740 to 750. More localized plague epidemics struck Sicily and Calabria in 746, and Naples and southern Italy in 767. In both instances, the epidemics remained restricted, suggesting that they were introduced by foreign ships, and that *y. pestis* was no longer enzootic among the indigenous rodent populations, the result perhaps of a mutation in the bacillus or a change in rodent and insect ecology. By the late eighth century, the first plague pandemic had come to its end in Europe.

The first pandemic, although restricted primarily to the Mediterranean basin and primarily bubonic plague, left an indelible mark on early medieval Europe. Because of its cyclic, recurrent nature, it helped restrict population levels below those of 541; the demographic historian J. C. Russell has estimated total population loss from 541 to 700 at 50 to 60 percent. Contemporaries were baffled by the new disease, as would be their counterparts in the fourteenth and fifteenth centuries. Explanations of its causation were usually taken from biblical exegesis, and high mortality attributed to divine judgment. Pilgrimages and at least visible remonstrances of piety increased, and the church seems to have gained in influence during the pandemic. There is little statistical evidence that can be used to measure the plague's impact on economy and society, but it must have disrupted trade routes and patterns, at least during flare-ups, and changed patterns of food production and distribution. It was a major retardant during Europe's early Middle Ages.

THE PERIOD FROM ABOUT 700 TO 1347

From the eighth through the mid fourteenth century, Europe was remarkably free from most epidemic diseases. There were isolated, often severe infections, such as the unidentifiable epidemic of 870, which swept through Western Europe killing perhaps a tenth of the populations of England and France. Most infectious diseases in this period were endemic, or closely linked to famine, malnutrition, or plant diseases, such as recurring epidemics of ergotism, or St. Anthony's disease, which struck from the mid tenth through mid eleventh centuries. With the exception of a few isolated coastal epidemics, plague would not strike again en masse until 1347, and smallpox and measles were restricted to younger members of society. Since in demographic terms childhood diseases are the least important, their effect on population levels was limited. At the same time, influenza and typhus, scourges of the late fifteenth and early sixteenth centuries, did not yet make a significant impact. Not coincidentally, much of the period from the ninth through the mid fourteenth centuries corresponded to medieval Europe's most extended period of demographic and economic expansion, as a major constraint on population was curbed.

Leprosy. The most important infectious disease of high medieval Europe was leprosy, or Hansen's disease. It is a chronic infection that develops slowly over a number of years and by itself rarely kills its victims. But it does produce decades of pain and suffering, and renders the afflicted vulnerable to respiratory and enteric ailments. Leprosy is not very contagious, but because it so horribly mutilates and scars its victims, it was feared and dreaded. One extremity after another rots away, including those of the face, until the latter appears as an almost formless mass. Compounding this horrible visage is a foul odor coming from the gangrenous parts, all combining to make the disease and its victims repulsive.

Medieval society was unable to provide preventive or curative treatment for the leper, and its best alternative was isolation. Upon diagnosis, the leper was counted among the dead, and a quasi-requiem mass was sung for his or her soul. Earth was shoveled on the victim's feet to symbolize the departure from the mainstream of society, and the patient was removed to a leper hospital, where, isolated from the rest of society including family and friends, he lived out his days. Most medical authorities considered that the disease was caused by divine judgment, and felt that mortal men could never develop a proper cure for it. One of the few exceptions was the English physician Gilbertus Anglicus (*fl.* 1245). Having observed a number of lepers over several years, he concluded that it was not highly communicable, and was primarily a nervous affliction, which might be treated in the same fashion as other nerve-related diseases. But even Gilbert was generally bereft of concrete ideas, suggesting only a few ways to balance the body humors, a favorite cure carried over from the Greeks by medieval doctors. Isolation was the most practical and in many ways the most humane treatment.

Incidence of leprosy seems to have increased from the eighth through the thirteenth century, reaching a peak in the fourteenth century, and then disappearing almost entirely by 1400. Several theories have been offered to explain its rise and fall. The rise is usually connected with parallel movements among the general population; as there were more people, so there were more potential and actual leprosy victims. The decline, however, is much harder to explain, and has elicited several theories. One explains the disappearance by the Black Death; as the great plague swept away 25 percent to 45 percent of Europe's people, it took a much higher percentage of lepers, already weakened by the debilitating effects of their disease. The subsequent plague epidemics of the second pandemic had similar impact, until by 1400 most of Europe's lepers had been killed. A second theory credits advancing medical analysis. Leprosy with its characteristic skin eruptions manifests itself in a fashion similar to that of many common skin diseases. Some modern authorities believe that high medieval chroniclers and physicians simply called all or most people with any skin disease lepers without regard to whether they had the real thing, smallpox, measles, or just a severe case of acne. By the late fourteenth century physicians, and even surgeons and apothecaries, had become much more discriminating in their diagnoses. Leechbooks and pharmaceuticals identified and typed a wide variety of skin conditions, and were more accurate when identifying Hansen's disease per se. A third theory credits the advancing state of hygiene, especially in urban areas, which followed the Black Death; while proponents of a fourth theory argue that leprosy retreated because of the rising incidence of pulmonary tuberculosis. Whatever the precise cause, with the exception of a few isolated regions in Norway and Poland, the incidence of leprosy declined markedly, and many of Europe's leper houses closed down, changed their focus toward new ailments, or became almshouses and retirement homes.

Leprosy was probably more important in a cultural rather than demographic or economic sense. It killed relatively few people, and engendered little real social change in its own right, but it did enter the psyche, religion, and art of Europe. The church regarded lepers as unclean; it became the "disease of the soul." Because of their forced isolation from society, lepers' legal identities became muddled. In many north Italian cities, canon lawyers were called to discuss the alienation of property, and in several Rhineland cities, including Trier and Mainz, an elaborate set of rules was drawn up to guide lepers through their everyday routines. They were barred from all churches, markets, shops, and other public places. They could not wash or drink from any civic water sources, and had to wear distinctive clothing. The leper had to touch everything with a rod, and could not enter inns or taverns. Sexual intercourse, even with spouses, was strictly forbidden. No public building could be touched without gloves, and shoes had to be worn at all times. Lepers were even required to stand downwind of those ordinary folks who chose to address them.

Sympathy for lepers was often restricted to abstract representations in art and literature. In the thirteenth-century epic *Der Arme Heinrich,* by Hartmann von Aue, the self-sacrificing heroine, a young peasant girl, offers to give her life to cure her lord of leprosy. And in the fourteenth-century painting *The Triumph of Death* in the Campo Santa, Pisa, a group of lepers beseech Death to take them away and relieve their misery. But Death bypasses them to claim young and healthy victims, dooming the lepers to further suffering.

THE SECOND PLAGUE PANDEMIC

Europe's relatively disease-free era ended rather abruptly in the middle of the fourteenth century. Population had increased about 300 percent from the tenth to the thirteenth century, to 75–80 million, and militant expansionism had extended the boundaries of Christendom east into Russia and southwest and southeast into Iberia and Palestine.

Internal European trade and travel had improved dramatically, with new Alpine passes opened, a direct sea link established between Italy and the Netherlands, and the integration of the Baltic and North Sea hinterlands with the rest of the continent. As the result of this upswing in commerce and improvement in communications, urban and rural population density was higher than it had been for a thousand years.

Perhaps even more important, closer connections were established between Europe, Asia, and Africa. To ease a bullion shortage, Italian merchants forged links with Arab middlemen in order to gain access to sub-Saharan gold supplies. As demand for luxury goods and spices rose, more ships and caravans journeyed to south and central Asia. Much of this trade was made through Middle Eastern intermediaries, but from the twelfth century on, Europeans played a large role. In all, contacts between East and West flourished as never before. But these contacts also changed the balance and pattern of infectious epidemic disease throughout Eurasia.

By 1250, Europe's disease pool had become relatively stable. Smallpox, measles, leprosy, and a few other diseases had established a tentative equilibrium within the European population. Plague, the greatest killer, had disappeared. By the mid thirteenth century, however, the Mongol conquest of much of central Asia began to tilt this balance. It caused considerable dislocation and migration, east, west, and south. By the 1270's, Mongol horsemen had penetrated the Hindu Kush into the Indian subcontinent, and a few years later had made their way into Yunan in southwest China, one of the traditional homes of *y. pestis.* As contacts between south and central Asia increased, the likelihood of a transfer of diseases also increased. Scholars debate whether central Asian rodents were indigenous plague carriers before the thirteenth century, whether plague was introduced through contacts with south Asian rodents, or whether south Asian rodents simply rekindled dormant central Asian reservoirs. At all events, by 1300, plague was enzootic among rodents in the Gobi Desert. By 1320, it was epizootic among the rodents, and by 1330 plague had become epidemic among the central Asian human population. By 1340 it had reached east to China, and by 1346 it reached the Crimea. By 1347, plague was back in Europe. This outbreak was the Black Death, the herald of the second plague pandemic, which lasted in Europe until the early eighteenth century.

The Black Death is discussed in detail in a separate article. Briefly, it ravaged various parts of Europe from 1347 to 1351, and was a rare combination of all the plague varients. In some towns and regions, mortality ranged as high as 45 percent to 75 percent. It is likely that no major area escaped with less than 15 percent mortality, and the best estimates of European-wide mortality range between 25 percent and 45 percent of the total population. It changed Europe's social, economic, and demographic structure, and ranks as the greatest natural disaster and one of the most significant events in European history.

Devastating as the Black Death was, it proved to be only the initial epidemic of the second plague pandemic. Plague became ingrained among Europe's rodent population and would remain so throughout the remainder of the Middle Ages. In 1361–1362, it struck the entire continent once again. The recurrence is extremely important. Human population levels are highly resilient and will respond to almost any single check, no matter how severe, within a generation or two through subsequent declines in mortality, earlier and higher marriage ratios, and higher fertility. In most preindustrial societies, given the general absence of constraints on fertility other than later age of first marriage for females, low levels of mortality meant rising populations. The most successful, indeed the only agent that could assure relatively high levels of mortality was a continual positive check. This role was assumed by the plague from 1347 until at least 1479–1480.

The plague of 1361–1362 was called the *pestis secunda* or *pestis puerorum,* the latter reference to the large numbers of young people it killed. While not as severe as the Black Death and predominantly an epidemic of bubonic plague, this second pestilence still took a tremendous toll. In upper Normandy, rural mortality in some villages exceeded 20 percent; in urban Florence, it was about the same. In England, for which local research has been the most intensive, the death figures seem to have been even higher. *Inquisitiones post mortem* indicate that mortality among the gentry approached 25 percent. In the East Anglian town of Bury St. Edmunds, testamentary mortality in the spring of 1361 was nine times higher than that of the next seasonal quarter for the ensuing forty years. Close to 20 percent of the beneficed clergy of York perished, and a national mortality estimate of 18 to 20 percent seems reasonable.

PLAGUES, EUROPEAN

Except for the high levels of child mortality, the narrative sources do little more than mention the *pestis secunda*. But the shock at the return of so great an affliction, which most people thought had departed, must have been very deep. Europe's aristocracy seems to have been afflicted severely; Guy de Chauliac, the papal surgeon and physician, contrasted the mortality patterns of 1347–1351 with those of 1361–1362, claiming that the former were most lethal to the poor, and the latter to the rich. Coming little more than a decade after the Black Death, the second plague epidemic thwarted the recovery of the late 1350's.

The *pestis secunda* established a plague cycle, and in 1369 the dreaded disease returned. By then, plague was becoming a part of daily life. Chroniclers rather blandly noted its presence, and moved on to discussion of other, often trivial topics. The 1369 death count was less severe than either of its predecessors, perhaps killing 10 to 15 percent. In England, mortality among both the gentry and the clergy of Yorkshire ran close to 13 percent, and it became clear that future generations would experience similar visitations. Langland's Piers Plowman believed that "the rain that raineth where we rest should, be sickness and the sorrow we suffer oft." And indeed, after 1369, the most important aspect of the plague pandemic was its frequency. No subsequent outbreak would kill more than 15 percent of the population in any given region or country, and some took barely 5 percent. But plague entered a cycle in which it recurred from five or six to ten or twelve years, depending on local insect and rodent ecological conditions. There was a national plague outbreak in England in 1375, followed by one in the north country in 1379, the midlands in 1381–1382, East Anglia, Essex, and Kent in 1383 and 1387, and severe national epidemics that killed in excess of 10 percent of the population in 1390 and 1399–1400. There was another national epidemic in 1405–1406, making for three major blows in a fifteen-year period, a plague in Wales and the west country in 1410–1411, followed by yet another national epidemic in 1411–1412. Two years later in 1413–1414, all Britain was afflicted, followed by plague in East Anglia in 1420, a national epidemic in 1423, a London visitation in 1426, and a national epidemic once more in 1428–1429. England may have been a bit atypical, but data from other areas in Western Europe, including the Low Countries and Normandy, show broadly similar trends of frequency and virulence. The effect of two, three, or even more epidemics in each generation ensured high mortality, and prevented population from reaching its pre-plague levels.

Recurrent plague and its disruptive effects became part of everyday life. In England, it interrupted parliament at least six times between 1376 and 1479; and throughout Europe it helped keep royal courts on the move, lest some of their members become infected. It had other institutional ramifications, including responsibility for a number of improvements in urban sanitation systems. In Italy, towns like Ragusa, Milan, and Venice enacted strict laws of quarantine by the mid fifteenth century. In England, the council of Edward III promulgated between 1369 and 1371 a series of public health ordinances for London. Slaughterhouse offal could no longer be dumped in the streets, nor in the streams and brooks that fed the Thames. Rather, the offal and all rubbish and garbage had to be carried to a special dump between the river and Baynard's Castle. Eventually, the slaughter of animals in the streets rather than the shops and most aspects of noxious industries like textile dying and fulling and leatherworking and tanning were banned. The catalyst in all of these improvements was plague.

Plague had important psychological effects on late medieval society. Its role in shaping the themes of the plastic arts was enormous. In literature, the great figures of the era, Petrarch, Boccaccio, Langland, Chaucer, Villon, and Erasmus, would incorporate it into the themes of many of their major works. A 1499 woodcut in Lyons, *La grand danse macabre,* shows Death in the form of plague, visiting first a printer and then a bookseller, showing them their craft, so that they might glorify his image. Later editions of Petrarch's *Trionfi* are illustrated with a series of engravings that interpret life and death through representations of plague, themes subsequently taken up in a number of books of hours. It persisted in spiritual life; in a famous sermon delivered in 1496, Savonarola evoked to a Florentine audience the images of Petrarch from 150 years earlier:

> There will not be enough men left to bury the dead, nor means to dig enough graves. So many will lie dead in the houses that men will go through the streets crying, "Set forth your dead." And the dead will be heaped in carts and on horses; they will be piled up and buried. Men will pass through the streets crying aloud, "Are there any dead? Are there any dead?"

PLAGUES, EUROPEAN

Death visits the printers. Woodcut (detail) from *La grande danse macabre,* printed by Mathias Huss at Lyons, 1499. BY PERMISSION OF THE BRITISH LIBRARY, LONDON, MS IB.41735, fol. b1r

Bad as things were from 1369 to 1430, they proved even worse in the half century that followed. Again England provides a good example. In the 1430's, plague entered a shorter frequency cycle, in which it recurred about once every four years. In 1431, all of eastern England from Kent north to Lincolnshire and west to Hampshire was stricken. This was surpassed in scope and virulence by a national epidemic that began in 1433 and lasted until 1435; it was facilitated by a dramatic drop in temperature late in November 1434, which apparently allowed bubonic plague to become pneumonic. There were local plague epidemics in 1437 in London, Canterbury, St. Albans, Bristol, and Bury St. Edmunds, followed in 1438–1439 by yet another national epidemic. Another cold autumn probably brought on the deadlier pneumonic strain, and mortality from plague was exacerbated by one of the few crop failures in the fifteenth century. In East Anglia, mortality during 1438–1439 reached 12 percent, and while no national mortality data are available, crude figures indicate that the death rate in two provincial towns (Norwich and Bury St. Edmunds) rose from 3 to over 10 percent.

Parts of England experienced plague epidemics in eleven of the eighteen years between 1442 and 1459. London was particularly hard hit, suffering on at least six separate occasions. From 1463 to 1464, another severe epidemic hit the entire kingdom, followed by still one more in 1467. But all this simply set the stage for the terrible 1470's. Perhaps England's increased trade with the Continent brought in new bacterial strains, or perhaps there was a change in the primary and secondary animal vectors. Whatever the cause, in 1471 all of England was overwhelmed. In East Anglia, adult mortality reached 20 percent. John Paston, a Norfolk gentleman then in London, wrote home to his family:

> I pray you send me word if any of our friends or well wishers be dead, for I fear that there is great death in Norwich and in other boroughs and towns in Norfolk, for I assure you that this is the most universal death that I ever witnessed in England. For by my trowth, I can hear from the pilgrims who travel through the country that no man who rides or goes in any country or borough town in England is free from the sickness.

The epidemic of 1471 was brief in duration but extreme in virulence, a classic example of bubonic plague at its most destructive. It began in late August, peaking through September and the first week in October, until it disappeared with the frosts in November. In its wake, 10 to 15 percent of England's population perished.

There were additional, localized plague epidemics in the mid 1470's, but all served as preludes for the epidemic of 1479–1480. From autumn to autumn, a combination of bubonic and pneumonic plague devastated the entire British Isles. Total mortality, where it can be measured accurately, ranged up to 20 percent, close to the levels of the *pestis secunda* of 1361–1362. The narrative sources raised their voices as one to lament its tithing; indeed, records such as the stately Great Chronicle of London, which never before mentioned a plague epidemic, drew attention to this one. Parliament was cancelled and the king's court dismissed from Easter 1480 to midsummer. All activity in the London Guildhall ceased, and at least three members of the Paston clan perished.

In most cases, the local evidence for the Continent is not as good as that for England, but what has been studied corroborates the English image. Normandy had plague cycles approximately as frequent as those of East Anglia, ranging from five to twelve years, with especially virulent cycles in the 1390's, 1440's, 1450's, and 1470's. In Cambrai there was also a similar frequency pattern, with particularly bad decades in the 1430's and 1450's. Paris was struck eight times between 1414 and 1439, and Barcelona eleven times between 1396 and 1437. The Iberian Peninsula was visited fourteen times between 1391 and 1459. In the Umbrian town of Perugia, plague was present for nineteen years in the fifteenth century, while Hamburg, Nuremberg, and Cologne suffered through at least ten epidemics each. As in England, the continental patterns suggest that plague came at least two or three times each generation, and was sufficently virulent to keep population levels low. Scholarly consensus, as it exists, estimates that from 1349 to 1450 European population declined between 60 and 75 percent, with the bulk of the depopulation coming in rural areas. This in turn had profound social and economic effects, and was a major reason for European stagnation and malaise in the later Middle Ages.

The epidemics of the 1470's were significant for reasons other than their ferocity. They marked an etiological turning point for plague. Again using England as an example, the insect/rodent vectors appear to have undergone considerable change after the 1479/1480 epidemic, shifting to a longer-cycle frequency. There were to be no more major epidemics for close to twenty years. Plague had by no means disappeared; there were national outbreaks in 1499, 1509–1510, 1516–1517, and a very severe one from 1528 to 1530. All of these epidemics rank in virulence with those of the fifteenth century, and that of 1528–1530 with the epidemics of 1361–1362, 1438–1439, and 1479–1480. But the major difference was in frequency; with the post-1470's broadening of cycles, there was greater opportunity for recovery between major epidemics. Accordingly, population began to expand once again. In those parts of the Continent where good local evidence survives and has been studied, trends of plague cycles and population expansion are similar to those of the British Isles, suggesting broad continental patterns.

OTHER DISEASES OF THE LATE MIDDLE AGES

The fourteenth and fifteenth centuries were unique not just because of the presence of plague, but for the presence and in some cases arrival of several other infectious diseases. Smallpox, *la petite vérole*, remained a major problem. It continued to be chronic among children, and in the 1440's and 1460's was epidemic in parts of Western Europe. The "red plague," as it became known, killed over 20 percent of the population of one English town in 1463, and may have killed more people in France during the 1440's than even plague. Malaria, or the ague, was chronic in several areas, including parts of Italy, southern France, southern Spain, the Low Countries, Denmark, southern Sweden, and eastern and southern England. More important were the enteric fevers, water-borne diseases associated with poor sanitation still present in many urban areas despite post–Black Death public health reforms. Of these, the deadliest were infantile diarrhea, dehydration from which was a major cause of infant mortality rates that could range as high as 50 percent; and intestinal dysentery, the "bloody flux." Dysentery proved especially lethal to armies and could flare up in a given area after a campaign. In 1411, a severe epidemic of dysentery swept through Savoy, France, and England; in 1473, another visited East Anglia and killed 15 to 20 percent of the adult male population in a three-month period. When these diseases are combined with the omnipresent plague epidemics, the general frequency of major infectious "killing" diseases was as little as three to five years apart from 1370 to 1470.

Late in the fifteenth century, Europe began the transition to the "modern" disease era; while the natural history of these diseases falls largely outside the Middle Ages, their origins do not. The first continuous records of typhus, or gaol fever, appear from about 1400. A disease facilitated by filth, typhus is caused by the microorganism *Rickettsia*, which is carried by the human body louse. It is highly contagious and relatively lethal, and by the sixteenth century some typhus epidemics proved almost as deadly as those of plague. Typhus originated in India, and its precise European beginnings are uncertain; since famine and malnutrition exacerbate it, the conditions of depopulation brought on by the Black Death may have delayed its spread. But by the 1430's, there are increasing indications of its possible presence—heavy spring mortality without mention of "pockys" diseases and smaller than usual harvests. In Germany and France, typhus may have struck in the 1430's, 1450's, and 1470's. England may have experienced it in the 1430's, and in 1414 Newgate prison in London was almost certainly visited; in the course of one week, five gaolers and sixty-four prisoners died from a disease that sounds like a textbook description of gaol fever. The major depredations of typhus would come in the sixteenth and seventeenth centuries, but its European roots are clearly medieval.

Influenza was present throughout the Middle Ages, but seems to have become more virulent in the fifteenth century. It is one of the most common of infectious diseases, and because over 300,000 different strains of influenza virus have been identified, specific immunity to more than a tiny fraction of its variations is impossible. Further, since it is airborne and respiratory in communication, it is a disease that virtually everyone experiences a few times in a lifetime. Generally, it produces a mild reaction, dangerous only to the very young, very old, or sick. But occasionally a highly lethal strain appears, and influenza can become a major killer. Such was the case in 1918–1919 when the Spanish flu killed more people than World War I, and such was the case several times in the fifteenth century. In 1426–1427, a flu epidemic swept through France, the Low Countries, Spain, and the British Isles, and in eastern England, where data are available, killed about 7 percent of the population. More infamous was the Sweating Sickness, or Picardy Sweat, which first appeared in 1485 in the lands touching the English Channel, and came back at least six times until 1551. It first swept through England in autumn 1485 and killed two lord mayors of London in as many months. The Sweat would ultimately prove less deadly than plague epidemics, but did in some places kill up to 10 percent of selected local populations.

Of all the new diseases of the later Middle Ages, the most intriguing was syphilis. Venereal diseases, especially gonorrhea, had been present since the classical era, and proved a particular curse to soldiers. After his 1475 campaign in France, Edward IV of England commented on the frequency among his troops of the "French Pox," to which he "lost many a man that fell to the lust of women and were burned by them, and their penises rotted away and fell off and they died." But the medieval origins of syphilis, the most deadly of the venereal diseases in the modern era, are more mysterious. Two principal theories have been offered to explain its appearance in Europe at the very end of the Middle Ages. One, the Columbian theory, attributes the arrival to the discovery of the New World. Archaeological and paleological evidence suggests that syphilis was well established among the Amerindian population, and was brought to Europe by Columbus, his sailors, and a few Indian captives. There are weaknesses in this theory, especially concerning the rapidity of the spread from so few sources, but new diseases often spread quickly in unexposed populations, and even more important, contemporaries seem to stress its American origins and timing.

The second theory, the unitarian, stresses the African origins of syphilis through the guise of yaws, a skin disease that is caused by treponema, the same spirochete responsible for syphilis. In the mid fifteenth century, in search of gold, slaves, and a sea route to India, Portuguese sailors began to establish trading posts along the west coast of Africa; within a few years, they brought African slaves, some of whom may have had yaws, back to the Mediterranean. For treponema to survive as a skin disease, the climate must be very hot and damp; in the cooler north, it was forced to mutate. The unitarians claim that it retreated deep into the body to the nervous system, and over a period of several decades became transmitted venereally, always protected in the warm, damp recesses of the human body. This argument has the strength of numbers—there were many more Africans in Europe by 1490 than there were Amerindians or Europeans who had had sexual contact with them—and is also supported by the long incubation period of syphilis. The weakness of the argument lies in the Columbian theory's strength, the conviction of contemporaries, and the 1490's timing.

Whatever syphilis's actual cause, its impact was staggering. The army of the French king, Charles VIII, brought it north with them after a campaign in 1493–1494 in Spanish-held southern Italy. Made up of Frenchmen, Germans, Walloons, Swiss, Scots, and Irishmen, the army disbanded after the campaign, and the soldiers took the disease to their respective homes. By summer 1495, it had spread across all of German-speaking Central Europe; by winter 1496, it was in the Low Countries and the British Isles; and by 1499 in Russia. Italians called it the French Pox, which proved its most popular name, but the French called it the Italian Pox. The English called it the Spanish Pox, the Poles the German Pox, and the Russians the Polish Pox. The German humanist Ulrich von Hutton wrote a treatise describing his personal experiences with it, and among those alleged to have been infected were Christopher Columbus, Ferdinand I of Spain, Henry VIII of England, his minister Cardinal Wolsey, Charles VIII and Francis I of France, Pope Alexander Borgia, Ivan IV of Russia, and even

PLAGUES, EUROPEAN

Erasmus. As with plague, syphilis entered the art and literature of everyday experience, with one of the best examples being Albrecht Dürer's 1496 woodcut *The Syphilitic.*

Syphilis is not an immediate killer. It more commonly takes the form of a wasting disease, and therefore has less immediate consequences than plague, smallpox, and several other infections. But it has a terrible debilitating effect on its victims, and leaves a mark on future generations, often rendering victims or their offspring sterile. Further, the 1490's–1500's epidemic was so severe that it may well have been communicable by nonvenereal means.

The arrival of syphilis ends the medieval era of infectious diseases. In medical terms, the Middle Ages was the key era in the formation of Europe's disease pools. Successive migrations and contacts with Africa and Asia brought to Europe smallpox, measles, plague, leprosy, dysentery, influenza, typhus, and other infectious diseases, and when Europeans began their global expansion in the sixteenth century, they passed these diseases to new areas. In demographic terms, infectious diseases were the most crucial element controlling mortality, itself the most important part of the demographic equation. In crude terms, when plague and other diseases were rife, as in the fifth through the eighth and in the fourteenth and fifteenth centuries, population contracted; when they were less frequent, population expanded.

BIBLIOGRAPHY

The best books dealing with the broad effects of disease and its relationship with society include Macfarlane Burnet and David O. White, *Natural History of Infectious Disease,* 4th ed. (1972); Robert Forster and Orest Ranum, eds., *Biology of Man in History* (1975); A. H. Gale, *Epidemic Diseases* (1951); William H. McNeill, *Plagues and People* (1976); Henry E. Sigerist, *Civilization and Disease* (1943). The Burnet and Gale books have bibliographies that list medical studies on particular diseases.

Sources for disease in the early Middle Ages include Julius Beloch, *Bevölkerungsgeschichte Italiens* (1961); Arthur E. R. Boak, *Manpower Shortage and the Fall of the Roman Empire in the West* (1955); Georges Duby, *The Early Growth of the European Economy,* Howard B. Clarke, trans. (1974); Josiah C. Russell, *Late Ancient and Medieval Population* (1958).

For the tenth through the fifteenth centuries, the literature broadens considerably, and the best approach is probably national. For England see Jonathan D. Chambers, *Population, Economy, and Society in Pre-industrial England* (1972); Charles Creighton, *A History of Epidemics in Britain,* 2 vols. (1891–1894, 2nd ed. 1965); Robert S. Gottfried, *Epidemic Disease in Fifteenth Century England* (1978); John Hatcher, *Plague, Population and the English Economy, 1348–1530* (1977); Josiah C. Russell, *British Medieval Population* (1948); John F. D. Shrewsbury, *A History of Bubonic Plague in the British Isles* (1970).

For France see Édouard Baratier, *La démographie provençale du XIIIe au XIVe siècle* (1961); Robert-Henri Bautier, "Feux, population, et structure sociale au milieu du XVe siècle," in *Annales: E.S.C.,* **14** (1959); Charles R. de Beaurepaire, *Recherches sur la population de la généralité et du diocèse de Rouen* (1971); Guy Bois, *Crise de féodalisme* (1976); Elisabeth Carpentier, "La peste noire: Famines et épidémies au XIVe siècle," in *Annales: E.S.C.,* **17** (1962). For the Netherlands, see W. P. Blockmans, "Effects of Plague in the Low Countries," in *Revue belge de philologie et d'histoire,* **58** (1980).

For Italy see David Herlihy, *Medieval and Renaissance Pistoia* (1967), and, with Christiane Klapisch-Zuber, *Tuscans and Their Families* (1985); Katharine Park, *Doctors and Medicine in Early Renaissance Florence* (1985). For Germany and Eastern Europe a fine text with a full bibliography is Wilhelm Abel, *Agrarkrisen und Agrarkonjunktur,* 3rd ed. (1978). A good source for urban areas is Roger Mols, *Introduction à la démographie historique des villes d'Europe du XIVe au XVIIIe siècles,* 3 vols. (1954–1956).

For the first plague pandemic see Jean-Noël Biraben and Jacques Le Goff, "The Plague in the Early Middle Ages," in Forster and Ranum, eds., *Biology of Man;* Josiah C. Russell, "The Earlier Plague," in *Demography,* **5** (1968). Jean-Noël Biraben, *Les hommes et la peste en France et dans les pays européens et mediterranéens* (1975–), is definitive for plague. Vern L. Bullough, *The Development of Medicine as a Profession* (1966), describes the role of the physician in treating epidemics. Additional books on medical treatment are Luke E. Demaitre, *Doctor Bernard de Gordon* (1980); Robert S. Gottfried, *Doctors and Medicine in Medieval England* (1986); Nancy G. Siraisi, *Taddeo Alderotti and His Pupils* (1981).

Historical studies on particular diseases include, for leprosy, Saul N. Brody, *The Disease of the Soul: Leprosy in Medieval Literature* (1974); for syphilis, Alfred Crosby, *The Columbian Exchange* (1972); for influenza, Robert S. Gottfried, "Population, Plague, and the Sweating Sickness," in *Journal of British Studies,* 17 (1977–1978); and for smallpox, Donald R. Hopkins, *Princes and Peasants: Smallpox in History* (1983).

ROBERT S. GOTTFRIED

[See also **Black Death; Death and Burial; Demography; Feudalism; Leprosy; Medicine.**]

PLAGUES IN THE ISLAMIC WORLD. Epidemic disease was a scourge as common and persistent in the medieval Near East as it was in Europe. Smallpox and measles were already well known in various parts of the Near East by the time of Muḥammad's birth in the sixth century. Leprosy and various other skin afflictions, though not actually epidemic diseases, were also common and much feared. The evidence for typhus, tuberculosis, and dysentery is less compelling, but it is very likely that they too were prevalent. Medieval Arabic authors also mention outbreaks of "fever," which in both the Near East and Europe was regarded as a disease in itself. Given the conditions of stagnation around the great river systems in Egypt and Iraq, as well as in parts of Syria and Arabia, indications of malaria could be expected, although there are no descriptions of outbreaks unequivocally identifiable as such. Cholera, which has repeatedly devastated the area in modern times, appears to have been unknown in the medieval period.

These afflictions are generally difficult to distinguish in the sources. It is often unclear what is meant by references, for example, to pustules, ulcerations, and swellings, and medieval writers frequently subsumed these terms under the general rubric of "pestilence." As a result, the history of these diseases (with the exception, perhaps, of leprosy) and their impact on medieval Near Eastern society cannot be reconstructed in any detail.

The sole exception to this is the plague, the most terrible epidemic disease ever to strike medieval man. The plague was already known in the first century A.D., but its first historically significant outbreak was the Plague of Justinian in 541–543. This great epidemic, which spread from Egypt to lands as distant as Spain, Britain, the Balkans, and Iraq, began the first plague pandemic, or cycle of outbreaks recurring in the same areas over an extended span of time. There were at least five more plague epidemics in the Near East in the sixth and early seventh centuries (558, 573–574, 592, 599–600, 628), so the disease was already firmly established by the time the Arab conquests began in 634. In 638–639, just as the Arab occupation of Syria was nearing completion, both this area and Iraq were devastated by a plague that killed many thousands among both the conquerors and the native populations. During the Umayyad caliphate (661–749) the Near East was frequently seized by plague: 673, 698–699, 705–706, 713, 718, 725, 729, 733–734, 734–735, 744, 745, and 749 in Syria; 669–670, 673, 687, 699, 705–706, 718–719, 725, 732–733, 734–735, 743, 744, 745, and 749 in Iraq; 689–690, 714–715, 724, 733–734, 744, and 745–752 in Egypt (some of these are doubtful); and 745–752 in North Africa, particularly Ifrīqiya, the old Roman province of Africa. This list is by no means complete, and for Syria, which suffered worst in this pandemic, it is all but certain that other plagues did occur. This pandemic did not, however, spread to Arabia, or any further east than Iraq.

For the last four years of Umayyad rule the plague was practically incessant. But in 749, and for reasons unknown, the pandemic faded out and the plague rapidly disappeared, not to return again until 913, when it struck Baghdad. There were occasional outbreaks in the tenth to thirteenth centuries, but it becomes increasingly difficult to identify them since the formerly precise terminology for plague was by this time taking on the more general signification of "epidemic" or "pestilence." Also, these outbreaks were of more sporadic occurrence and did not subject any particular areas to repeated devastation, as had happened in the pandemic of the sixth to eighth centuries. By the mid thirteenth century even those sporadic epidemics had ceased.

In 1347–1349, the Black Death, which marks the beginning of the second plague pandemic, spread westward from central Asia and engulfed the Near East. Once the plague reached the Crimean ports along the northern shore of the Black Sea in 1346, it passed to Constantinople, which it ravaged in mid 1347, and from there spread throughout the Mediterranean basin. Egypt was infected by the fall of that year, and Syria by the following spring. From the ports in these areas the epidemic penetrated more slowly, but with no less devastating effect, into the inland regions of Asia Minor, Azerbaijan, and Armenia. The ports of North Africa also fell victim in rapid succession, and there too the pestilence spread from the major centers to the smaller towns and the villages of the agrarian hinterlands. In 1348–1349, the plague struck Arabia for the first time and infected the holy city of Mecca.

It is now clear that the Black Death was fully as devastating in the Near East as it was in Europe. And in the long term its implications were far worse, since in the Near East this epidemic initiated a series of recurrences of the disease which struck more frequently and with greater severity than in

PLAGUES IN THE ISLAMIC WORLD

Europe. In particular, pneumonic plague, the disease's most lethal form, continued to reappear in the Near East after the Black Death; and whereas plague had disappeared from most parts of Europe by the seventeenth century, it was still a recurrent and common scourge in the Near East until the late nineteenth, when the advent of modern plague epidemiology made it possible to suppress the disease. The frequency and geographical distribution of these later outbreaks are still under investigation, but from what we know thus far it appears that Egypt and Syria were the areas primarily affected by these recurrences. North Africa also suffered serious epidemics in later medieval times, although not to the extent that Egypt and Syria did. Iraq and Iran seem to have been affected very little, but this impression may be more indicative of the biases of our sources than of the historical facts.

The question of the impact of epidemic disease on the course of medieval Near Eastern history is a very vexed one. Once the historical importance of epidemic disease is established, it is tempting to view incidences of it as significant causal factors in any events or developments, particularly those involving great changes, which occurred concurrently or shortly thereafter. But at the same time it is worth noting that epidemic disease was a threat that almost constantly confronted medieval people, even in periods of great prosperity and achievement, and that individual epidemics only rarely had an immediately significant impact. It is, therefore, dangerous to argue for the important effects of epidemics unless convincing positive evidence can be advanced. As we so far know little about most of the epidemic diseases in the medieval Near East, it is not yet possible to determine their impact on the course of historical events.

The exception is again plague, the importance of which derives from its extremely high mortality rate (50–100 percent), its recurrence at frequent intervals in the same regions, and the fact that, unlike populations exposed to such diseases as smallpox and malaria, peoples exposed to pandemic plague over a long period do not build up a clinical immunity to the disease. The proportion of the population at risk thus remains high regardless of how often previous plagues have already decimated the area. Over an extended period of time this epidemiological pattern results in a significant decline in population. There is considerable evidence for this fact in both the first and the second pandemics in the Near East. In the cities and towns, some households perished completely, and many quarters and neighborhoods were left desolate; in rural areas it was not uncommon for entire villages to disappear under the impact of one or two severe outbreaks. On numerous occasions large extended families in a region lost all but one or two of their members.

The problem of mortality was compounded by that of large-scale flight from infected areas. The Islamic dictums denying contagion and prohibiting flight from the plague had not yet gained currency during the first pandemic, and even in the second did not prevent peasants and townsmen from fleeing from infected areas. Fleeing served only to aggravate the effects of the epidemic, since it often led to the introduction of the disease into previously unaffected areas, as well as to the deaths of many of the refugees, either from the plague itself, or from other diseases, starvation, or exposure.

Repeated plague epidemics on a massive scale, and the demographic decline that they precipitated, had profound effects on the social and economic structure of those areas of the medieval Near East where the pandemics were focused: Syria and Iraq in the sixth to eighth centuries, and Syria and Egypt from the fourteenth century onward. The most disruptive impact was felt in the critically important relationship between the cities and their agricultural hinterlands. Agricultural land frequently fell out of cultivation due to the deaths or flight among the peasantry; this reduced both the amount of food available for the cities, which depended on surplus rural production, and the tax revenues of the governments involved. These demands did not diminish but rather were imposed with greater rigor on the peasants who survived. Such impositions only made the lot of the cultivators more insufferable and further encouraged the abandonment of arable land. The plague itself, however, was a scourge which was worst in large urban areas, and famine, caused by hoarding, profiteering, and the declining amount of food supplies available from the countryside, often added to the disorder. During epidemics social and economic order often collapsed entirely: markets were closed, trade was disrupted, and government functions of all kinds were suspended. Sources often speak of times in which people abandoned all activities except for tending to the dead and searching for food, and these accounts are probably quite accurate.

The repeated devastation of the sedentary populations of the Near East was all the more serious for them since it was not accompanied by a comparable level of destruction among the nomadic peoples of the region. Bedouins had from pre-Islamic times been extremely sensitive to the threat posed by epidemic disease and avoided towns and areas where it was known to be present. In the case of plague, the bedouins were even more secure, since the disease is carried by the rats and other vermin hosts that thrive in unsanitary urban conditions but find it difficult to sustain themselves in other less densely settled surroundings. Thus the periods from 541 to 749 and from 1347 to the end of medieval times were stages in Near Eastern history which we must view as eras characterized by the erosion of sedentary life and culture, to the distinct advantage of nomadic elements of society.

The most uncertain aspect of epidemic disease and its impact on the medieval Near East is the extent to which it influenced great historical events. Medieval authors seldom speak of this, and any attempt to address the question must invariably be somewhat speculative. We do know that epidemics, particularly of smallpox and plague, at times decimated armies and made military operations impossible. Here again, plague draws our primary attention because of its recurrent and highly lethal character. The Arab conquest of Syria and Iraq in the early seventh century was probably facilitated by the repeated decimation of sedentary populations in these areas by plague outbreaks over the previous eighty years. And it is perhaps no coincidence that the Abbasid revolution of 747–750 succeeded, where other rebellions had failed, at a time when the Umayyad bases of power in Syria and Iraq were being ravaged by terrible plague outbreaks, which appear to have reduced the state of affairs in both regions to one of unmitigated chaos. In the period following the Black Death, the steady decline discernible in population, urban life, and trade, industry, and other economic affairs is without doubt related to the plagues which repeatedly struck Egypt and Syria.

BIBLIOGRAPHY

Literature on epidemic disease in the medieval Near East is as yet sparse. For good introductions to the problem in general, see Henry E. Sigerist, *Civilization and Disease* (1943, repr. 1962) and William H. McNeill, *Plagues and Peoples* (1976); and on the Islamic world in particular, Edward G. Browne, *Arabian Medicine* (1921); and Manfred Ullmann, *Die Medizin im Islam* (1970), and his *Islamic Medicine,* Jean Watt, trans. (1978). Smallpox in the medieval era is discussed, though with little historical emphasis, by Paul Richter, "Beiträge zur Geschichte der Pocken bei den Arabern," in *(Sudhoffs) Archiv für Geschichte der Medizin,* **5** (1912).

The literature on the plague is much more informative. On the first pandemic, see Lawrence I. Conrad, "The Plague in the Early Medieval Near East" (diss., Princeton, 1981); and on the Black Death, Michael W. Dols, *The Black Death in the Middle East* (1977). Both of these works provide extensive bibliographies and assessments of earlier literature. The plagues following the Black Death are discussed in Dols's "The Second Plague Pandemic and Its Recurrences in the Middle East," in *Journal of the Economic and Social History of the Orient,* **23** (1979).

Beginning with the Black Death, medieval Muslim authors wrote plague treatises addressing problems identical to those facing their European contemporaries. Very few of these works have thus far been made available to nonspecialists; for some of them, see Taha Dinānah, "Die Schrift von Abī Ǧaʿfar Aḥmed ibn ʿAlī ibn Moḥammed ibn ʿAlī ibn Hātimah aus Almeriah über die Pest," in *(Sudhoffs) Archiv für Geschichte der Medizin,* **19** (1927); Michael W. Dols, "Ibn al-Wardī's *Risālah al-nabaʾ ʿan al-wabaʾ*: A Translation of a Major Source for the History of the Black Death in the Middle East," in Dickran K. Kouymjian, ed., *Near Eastern Numismatics, Iconography, Epigraphy, and History: Studies in Honor of George C. Miles* (1974); M. J. Muller, "Ibnulkhatîb's Bericht über die Pest," in *Sitzungsberichte der Königlich Bayerischen Akademie der Wissenschaften zu München,* II (1863), 1–34;

On this literature see also Michael W. Dols, *The Black Death in the Middle East* (1977), 110–121, 320–335; Lawrence I. Conrad, "Arabic Plague Chronologies and Treatises: Social and Historical Factors in the Formation of a Literary Genre," in *Studia islamica,* **54** (1981); Jacqueline Sublet, "La peste prise aux rêts de la jurisprudence: Le traité d'Ibn Ḥagar al-ʿAsqualānī sur la peste," *ibid.,* **33** (1971).

LAWRENCE I. CONRAD

[See also **Black Death; Medicine, History of.**]

PLAINCHANT/PLAINSONG. See **Gregorian Chant.**

PLAINSONG, EASTERN EUROPE. Plainsong as a technical term refers to the regulated chanting in unison in Christian religious services. The roots of this monophonic singing are found in the synagogal

PLAINSONG, EASTERN EUROPE

practice of the Palestinian Jews and in the musical traditions of early converts to Christianity, most of whom were Greek-speaking and lived in the eastern Mediterranean. It is customary to refer to the Greek Christians as "Eastern Orthodox," and in some respects the repertory of chants of the Greek Orthodox church is a part of the Eastern European musical heritage.

With the spread of missionary activity from Constantinople, particularly to the eastern Slavs (Russians), Christianity and its religious services, including its musical practices, became accepted. The first missionary activity took place in the 860's with the mission of Constantine (who later became the monk Cyril) and Methodios to Moravia; they brought translations of scriptural and liturgical books and created a new alphabet for use by the Slavs. The strong opposition of Roman (Frankish) missionaries in the area caused the pupils of the "Apostles to the Slavs" to abandon the territory and move south to the Bulgarian region, where they continued their work. The official conversion of Russia to Christianity took place in 988, though the earlier presence of Christians in Russia is presumed.

Records of religious practices suggest that from the late tenth century on, services included chanting. Musical sources for this earliest period are extremely sparse. The earliest manuscript with musical notation above texts used in services dates from the eleventh/twelfth century and contains, in addition to Slavic texts, transliterations of Greek texts in the Slavic alphabet, suggesting the existence of bilingual liturgical practice at first. Additional musical manuscripts from the twelfth and thirteenth centuries contain substantial parts of services for the whole yearly cycle that document the existence of a specific variant of Byzantine chant.

The relationship of the early Slavic chant to its Byzantine roots is complex. The musical notation in Slavic manuscripts is unquestionably Byzantine in its origin; but even in the early stages there are specific notational signs for which there is no known Byzantine counterpart. It would seem that while accepting the framework of Byzantine melodies and musical practices, the Slavs from the outset may have created original ways to adapt the transmitted body of music. At present there is no reliable way of reconstructing the Russian chant that existed before about 1600. Any attempt is experimental and relies heavily on the degree of relationship of the notational signs to the then-current Byzantine performance of the same hymns. The overwhelming majority of texts in Slavic musical manuscripts are literal translations of Greek originals, though from the eleventh century on a few original texts begin to appear. Texts in two languages (Greek and Old Church Slavonic) often contain almost identical musical notations, with slight adjustments due to the difference in the number of syllables in corresponding verses. From this evidence it is certain that the earliest Slavic musical notation is an adaptation of the Byzantine Coislin notation, which was faithfully copied even later in Byzantium, when the so-called middle Byzantine notation prevailed.

After the Tatar invasion (1237–1240) the direct contacts with Byzantium ceased to influence the musical traditions of Russia. It is likely that new and original developments of Russian church music began to take place in the fourteenth century, and even more in the fifteenth. In the sixteenth century, names of Russian musicians and composers began to appear, and the formation of a specifically Russian musical style occurred through the interaction of orally transmitted traditional melodies and indigenous melodies based on folk songs and composed works of then-active musicians.

Viewed as a whole, Russian chants in medieval manuscripts contain the main body of the Greek repertory of plainsong: syllabic and more ornate types of chants. Among the latter there is a special small group of manuscripts containing kontakia and having a notation at one time believed to be an original Russian creation, the "kondakarian" notation (it has been located in Byzantine sources as well). It is presumed that at least during the Middle Ages and before 1500, Russian plainsong must have remained monophonic and represented a variant of its Byzantine roots with the use of Slavic language, then experienced gradually greater differentiation, leading to the later Russian church music that accepted polyphonic practices in the sixteenth and seventeenth centuries.

BIBLIOGRAPHY

Dimitri E. Conomos, *The Late Byzantine and Slavonic Communion Cycle: Liturgy and Music* (1985); Johann von Gardner, *Bogosluzhebnoe pienie russkoi pravoslavnoi tserkvi* [Liturgical chant of the Russian Orthodox Church], 2 vols. (1978–1982); Nicolas Schidlovsky, "The Notated Lenten Prosomois in the Byzantine and Slavic Traditions" (diss., Princeton, 1983); Miloš Velimirović, *Byzantine Elements in Early Slavic Chant,* 2 vols. (1960). See also "Plainchant," in *New*

Grove Dictionary of Music and Musicians, XIV (1980), and "Russian and Slavonic Church Music," *ibid.,* XVI (1980).

MILOŠ VELIMIROVIĆ

[See also **Cyril and Methodios, Sts.; Music, Byzantine; Music, Slavic; Musical Notation, Byzantine; Russian Orthodox Church.**]

PLAINSONG, SOURCES OF. Plainsong, commonly known as Gregorian chant, is a liturgical music of the Catholic church that began to be written down in the ninth and early tenth centuries and of which editions are still being published today. It consists of settings of sacred Latin texts, most of them from the Vulgate and earlier Latin versions of the Bible (in particular, from the book of Psalms). The chants fall into categories according to the services for which they are intended—for the Mass, for the Divine Office, and for other liturgical observances—and according to the roles they play in those services. Some chants belong to the Proper—that is, they are intended for use only for one particular day or event; others are Ordinary chants, which can be used on many different days and occasions.

Relatively little is known about the early development of Gregorian chant. Since even in the New Testament there are references to singing, there is no question that from the very beginning Christians sang together when they met for worship. But the precise texts that were employed in those times, and the melodies to which they were set, remain unknown. In following the course of development of Gregorian chant, one must begin with the early documents that testify to the use of certain texts in certain liturgical roles. The history of the melodies is more difficult to trace, for the idea of writing out a collection of chant texts and including the melodies (in musical notation of an early kind) did not find realization until the ninth and early tenth centuries. And—if the surviving sources can be relied on to give a true picture of the historical development—this idea did not originate in Rome but in the Frankish Empire. Once the repertory had been fixed in writing, there was relatively little change in it.

The chants of the Proper of the Mass (introit, gradual, alleluia or tract, offertory, and communion) are often found written down in the order in which they appear in one service after another through the course of the liturgical year; such a collection is called a gradual. Usually graduals include musical notation (as, for example, in Paris, Bibliothèque Mazarine, MS 384, eleventh century [Fig. 2]), but a few early examples lack it (Laon, Bibliothèque Municipale, MS 118, tenth century [Fig. 1]). A cantatorium includes only the chants between the lessons of the Mass, the gradual, and the alleluia (or tract). A missal presents the prayers and lessons of the Mass along with its chants (as does the missal of Paris, Bibliothèque Nationale, MS lat. 1107, thirteenth century [Fig. 4]), while the missal of BN, MS lat. 9436, eleventh century (Fig. 3) contains prayers and chants, but not lessons. For the Divine Office, if the chants alone are written, the collection is called an antiphonary; if there are full services (prayers, lessons, and chants), it is a breviary. The names for the collections in which certain types of chants appear are often self-explanatory: troper, hymnal, sequentiary, processional, and so on.

Though it is sometimes possible to speak of a certain book as "a gradual" or "a cantatorium," very often a volume will contain more than one of the kinds of collections mentioned above. Thus the thirteenth-century manuscript in Figure 4 includes a missal, a sequentiary, and a kyriale (a collection of Ordinary chants of the Mass). The St. Denis gradual in Figure 2 begins with a gradual, follows with some offices for specific days, and then continues with a list of text incipits for chants of the Divine Office through the whole year.

Among the developments in the chant repertory that can be observed in medieval liturgical books are the addition of new chants to the repertory, the adapting of old chants to new uses (such as when a feast is added to the calendar), and modifications in the performance of existing chants (such as shortening through the suppression of verses). Both kinds of change are evident in the first four manuscripts illustrated here, as is the difference in appearance between a missal and a gradual, between manuscripts with and without musical notation, and those with notation of different kinds.

These chant manuscripts all come from the abbey church of St. Denis, just north of Paris, and all are manuscripts of the Mass, ranging in date from the beginning of the tenth century to the second half of the thirteenth. Each of the first three manuscripts includes the introit for the feast of St. Gregory the Great (12 March), *Sacerdotes Dei*

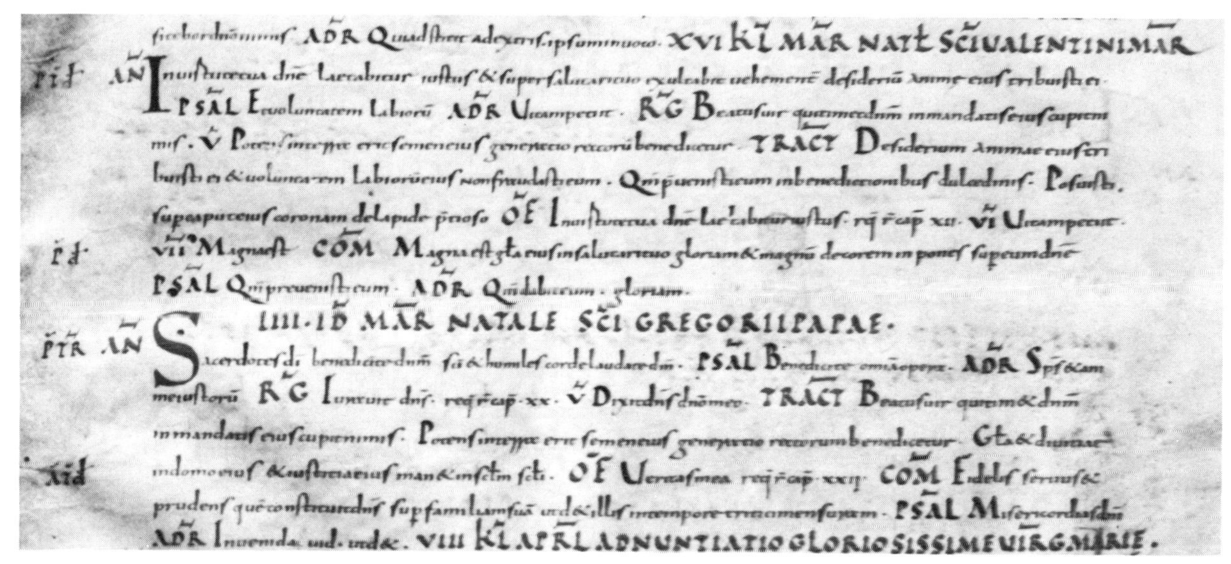

Figure 1. LAON, BIBLIOTHÈQUE MUNICIPALE, MS 118, fol. 5r (10th century)

benedicite Dominum; Figures 2, 3, and 4 contain the communion, *Tu es Petrus,* for the feast of St. Peter's Chair (22 February). Thus the same part of the liturgical year is shown for all four sources.

The tenth-century Laon manuscript lacks musical notation, as do all the graduals written in the ninth century which have been studied by Hesbert in *Antiphonale missarum sextuplex.* But certain guides in it allowed choristers to read and sing the service. A rubric halfway down the page shown in Figure 1 reads "IIII ID MAR NATALE SCI GREGORII PAPAE," thus identifying the date and the feast. The texts of the Proper chants follow. These include the introit (here given the rubric AN, for "antiphon") *Sacerdotes Dei,* with its verse (PSAL, for "psalm" or "psalm verse" despite the fact that here an Old Testament canticle is called for) *Benedicite omnia opera,* and *versus ad repetendum* (ADR) *Spiritus et animae iustorum.* (The verse "ad repetendum" is given in conformity with a practice—to which reference is made, for example, in the *Ordo romanus* I—according to which the verses of the introit psalm were followed by a special verse designated to introduce the return of the introit antiphon.) There follow the gradual (RG) *Iuravit Dominus* (the full text has been given earlier in the book, on the feast of another saint, and so only the incipit is given here), with the verse *Dixit Dominus Domino meo;* the tract *Beatus vir,* given in full; the offertory *Veritas mea* (incipit only); and the communion *Fidelis servus,* with a verse *Misericordias Domini* and *versus ad repetendum Inveni David.* Though there is no musical notation, the melodic formulas to which the verses of both the introit and the communion are chanted are identified through letters in the margin that designate the mode of each of these chants.

The preceding service in this manuscript is for St. Valentine (14 February), and here a parallel series of chants is given—introit, gradual, tract, offertory (in this case, *In virtute tua,* with the first verse [VI] *Vitam petiit* and the second [VII] *Magna est*), and communion (*Magna est gloria*) with verse and *versus ad repetendum.* In the Mazarine manuscript (Fig. 2), a notated gradual of the eleventh century, the feast of St. Gregory the Great is preceded by that of St. Peter's Chair, and apparently a cycle of Proper chants for that day had not yet been organized at the time at which the Laon manuscript was written; there is none in any of the ninth-century graduals studied by Hesbert. The chants for this feast are in some cases borrowed—the communion *Tu es Petrus* comes from the feast of Sts. Peter and Paul (29 June). In other cases they appear to be of relatively recent composition: the offertory *Tu es Petrus* (of which one sees in the upper half of Figure 2 the end of the verse) does not appear in any of the earliest sources. It contains several long melismas (chains of notes sung to a single syllable) on "tibi," "est," and "alleluia." In some of these melismas musical phrases are repeated exactly, a procedure that characterizes the later chant style.

In Mazarine MS 384, neither the communion

PLAINSONG, SOURCES OF

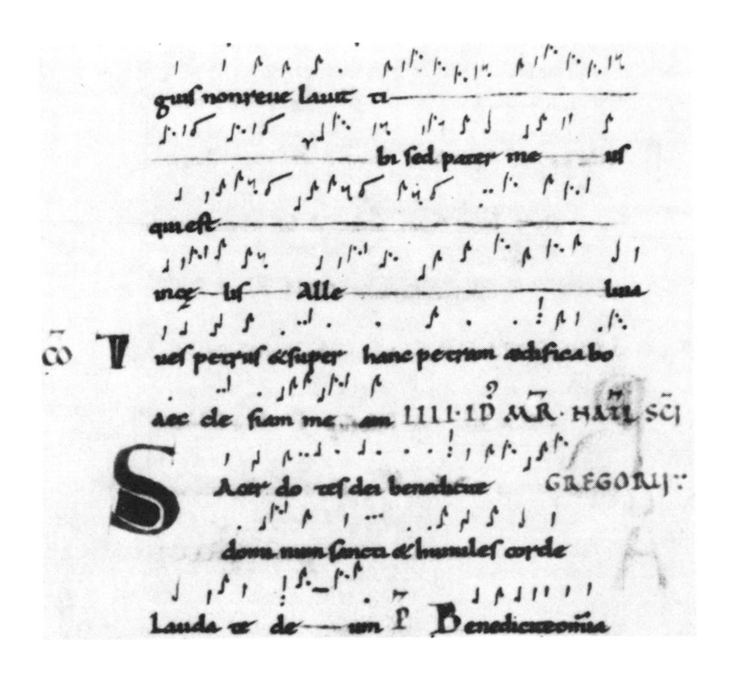

Figure 2. PARIS, BIBLIOTHÈQUE MAZARINE, MS 384, fol. 45r (11th century)

Tu es Petrus nor the introit *Sacerdotes Dei* has a *versus ad repetendum;* the communion has not even a psalm verse. The text is written without abbreviations, except where incipits are given. This is necessary because of the musical notation; in most chant manuscripts musical notation and text are carefully aligned, with the symbol representing the notes for a particular syllable being placed directly over its vowel. The distinctive forms of St. Denis neumes of the eleventh century can also be seen in the Paris MS lat. 9436 (Fig. 3), which, though a missal, lacks lessons. The page begins with the Preface for the feast of St. Peter's Chair. Then comes the communion antiphon, *Tu es Petrus,* and then a choice of prayers for the post-communion. There follow a series of prayers (including a Proper Preface) foı the feast of St. Matthew (24 February), and then—at the very end of the page—come the first two words of the introit for the feast of St. Gregory. For the celebration of Mass, the only book needed to supplement this one would be a Bible (or lectionary).

The fourth example is a manuscript that contains all the chants, lessons, and prayers of the Mass. Its thirteenth-century date was at a time when private Masses were coming into use, and when there was a practical need for books that contained all that would be necessary for such ceremonies. But it is far from utilitarian in its appearance. (And, in a private Mass, would the chants actually have been sung?) The page shown in Figure 4 begins with the end of the antiphon of the offertory *Tu es Petrus;* its verse is omitted. The secret (a prayer) follows, then the communion *Tu es Petrus,* and a post-communion prayer, *Letificet nos quaesumus,* which is the first of the two offered as alternates in lat. 9436. Then comes the rubric "In dedicatione ecclesie," and the introit, *Terribilis est locus iste,* for the dedication of a church.

Given at this point in the year, the service marks the anniversary of the consecration not of the Gothic building still standing at St. Denis (of which the nave, under construction at about the time this manuscript was written, is evoked—even if not actually depicted—in the illumination of the initial letter *T*), but an earlier church, that of the abbot Fulrad; the ceremony took place on 24 February 775, with Charlemagne in attendance.

Earlier manuscripts of St. Denis also include this Mass Proper, but they set it on 13 May, where it commemorates the dedication of the Roman church of St. Maria ad Martyres—the conversion of the Pantheon to Christian use, which took place in 608. There is no specific reference in the service to St. Denis or to Paris, but to anyone knowing the liturgical calendar of that abbey, finding this service at this point in the year would have a clear meaning: it would identify the place for which the manuscript was intended, an identification which—for this particular source—could be corroborated in a number of ways. (There is a good deal of variety among manuscripts in their placement of this service; it corresponds, one assumes, to variety in medieval practices in respect to the observation of this feast. But when it is set on the actual day of dedication of a church, it helps to identify the manuscript as belonging to that particular place.)

Comparison of the four manuscripts has thus far revealed differences in the handling of the verses of the offertory, introit, and communion (and of the *versus ad repetendum* of the latter two); what remains to be pointed out is the dramatic change in the character of musical notation that took place at St. Denis (and in many other places) between the eleventh and the thirteenth centuries.

The notation of the thirteenth-century Paris missal (Fig. 4) offers few problems today: a person with ordinary musical training could after just a few minutes' special instruction play or sing melodies from that source. However, certain informa-

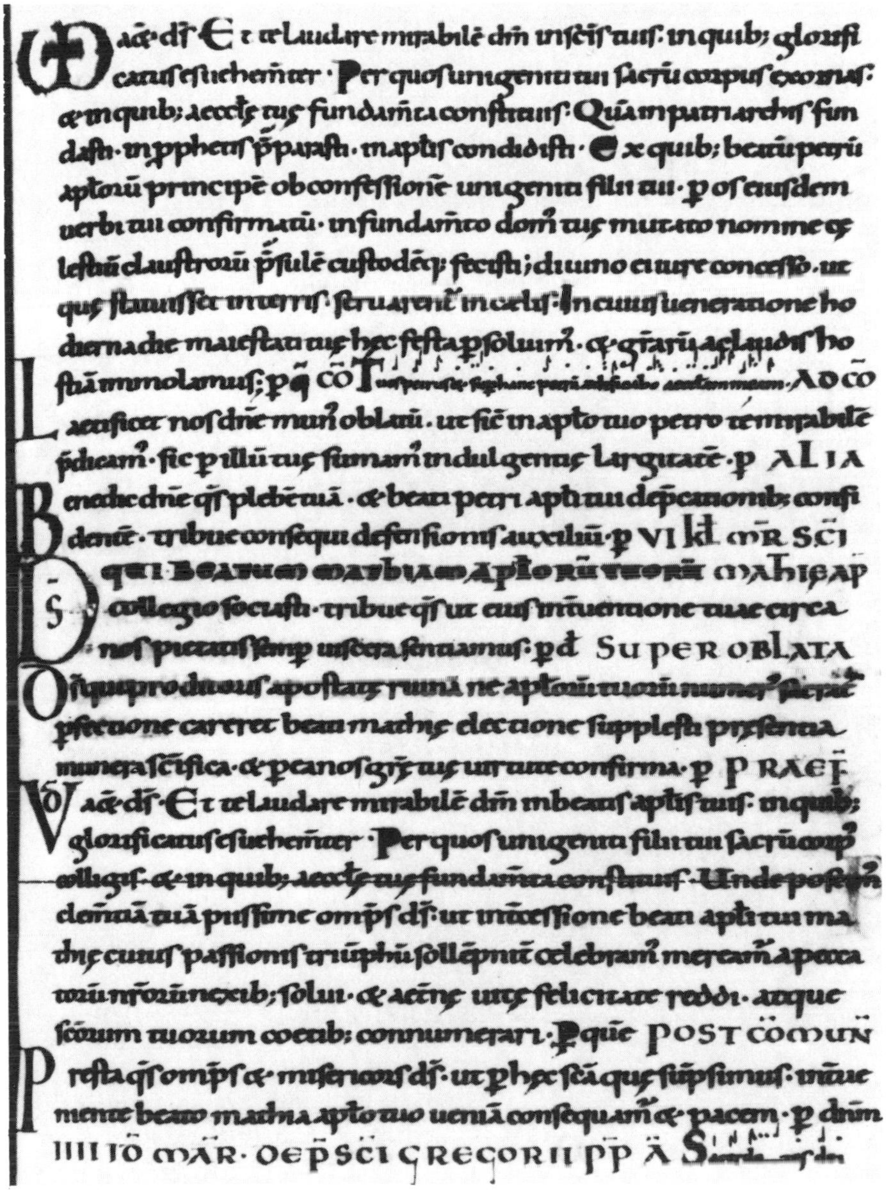

Figure 3. PARIS, BIBLIOTHÈQUE NATIONALE, MS LAT. 9436, fol. 81r (11th century)

tion about the music is not conveyed by that notation: it says nothing about rhythm, phrasing or articulation, dynamics, or tempo. It is a good deal less complete than modern musical notation, as commonly employed. But it is more precise with respect to musical intervals than are the neumes employed in earlier sources of St. Denis—the Mazarine manuscript, for example; these show the number of notes on a syllable, and the direction of the movement, but not the size of the intervals. A melody preserved only in neumes cannot be transcribed and sung today.

Some types of neumes convey information about rhythm and articulation. Of these the most fully studied appear in manuscripts from the monastery of St. Gall. Figure 5 shows a leaf from the most famous of these, an Office antiphonal copied around the year 1000 by the recluse monk Hartker (and edited by Hesbert in *Corpus antiphonalium officii*). The illustration shows part of the office for the patron saint of the abbey—St. Gall, who was one of the Irish monks who came with St. Columbanus to the Continent, and who died near Bregenz around 650. His vita, by Walafrid Strabo,

PLAINSONG, SOURCES OF

Figure 4. PARIS, BIBLIOTHÈQUE NATIONALE, MS LAT. 1107, fol. 228r (after 1254)

is drawn in the texts of the antiphons and responsories of the Divine Office on his feast day, 16 October; and excerpts from it formed the lessons on that day. Figure 5 shows the rubric for the third nocturn of matins (the words "SUPER III CANT." refer to the canticles that took the place of psalms at the beginning of the third nocturn of matins in the monastic cursus), the antiphon for those canticles, and the first and second responsories of the third nocturn. The responsory *Pater sanctus* is a condensed account of the death of the saint, based on chapter twenty-nine of the vita; it is given two verses, rather than the usual one; and a melisma is provided for the word "perennibus" as it occurs in

Figure 5. SANKT GALLEN, STIFTSBIBLIOTHEK, MS 390-391, p. 324-130 (*ca.* 1000)

the refrain of the chant after the second verse. These features are out of the ordinary, and identify the day on which they are found as one of special importance.

The neumes include a number of special forms and modifications that bear on performance: for example, the letter *c* with its tail extended into a horizontal stroke identifies neumes that are to be sung more swiftly than usual.

This Office for St. Gall appears in only a few sources, but the main contents of both the antiphonal and the gradual are found in hundreds of manuscripts. Comparison of the readings given in these sources reveals for many chants a remarkable degree of uniformity in the tradition, with relatively few minor variants. But for some chants (these are more numerous in the Office than in the Mass) the differences in the readings are more pronounced, and for a few chants the editing problems are quite serious. A consensus concerning goals and methodology for a modern critical edition of Gregorian chant is still being sought.

BIBLIOGRAPHY

John Emerson, "Sources, MS, II,1: Western Plainchant," in *New Grove Dictionary of Music and Musicians,* XVII (1980), with an excellent list of sources; *Le graduel romain: Édition critique par les moines de Solesmes* (1957–; sources are listed in vol. II); René Jean Hesbert, ed., *Antiphonale missarum sextuplex* (1935, repr. 1967), and *Corpus antiphonalium officii,* 6 vols. (1963–1979); Andrew Hughes, *Medieval Manuscripts for the Mass and Office* (1982); Victor Leroquais, *Les sacramentaires et les missels manuscripts des bibliothèques publiques en France,* 3 vols. (1924).

RUTH STEINER

[See also **Gregorian Chant; Hymns, Latin; Mass, Liturgy of the; Neume;** and individual liturgical books and Mass sections.]

PLANCTUS (Latin: *planctus;* Middle English: *playnte, pleynte, plaint,* and other forms; Old French: *plainte;* Provençal: *planh;* Italian: *pianto*), a lament, usually for deceased royalty or high church officials, though the *planctus Mariae* and the cycle of Old Testament *planctus* suggest that they are not always occasional pieces. A large number of medieval *planctus* with music are preserved in Latin, Old French, Provençal, and Italian. Because they are sometimes cast in forms that resemble both the sequence and the *lai,* some scholars have tried to show genetic relationships among the three. This is not true of all *planctus,* however, and thus the word does not seem to imply a special kind of poetic and musical form, as "sequence" and *lai* almost always do.

The best-known examples of the genre are Peter Abelard's cycle of six *planctus* "in which Old Testament personages, men and women, are brought to life and lament their tragic fates," as Peter Dronke puts it. Their music has been transcribed and, if Abelard is the composer, establishes his reputation as a musician of significant stature. The late-twelfth-century *planctus Mariae* ("Planctus ante nescia") is also cast in sequence form, presumably under the influence of Abelard. The *planctus,* particularly the Marian variety, also formed the core of the Passion plays that appeared beginning in the thirteenth century. Some notable examples of more conventional *planctus* that survive with musical notation are "Planctus Karoli," for Charlemagne; "Fortz causa," by Gaucelm Faidit (*fl.* 1172–1203) for Richard the Lionhearted; and "Pange melos lacrimosum," for Frederick I Barbarossa.

BIBLIOGRAPHY

Peter Dronke, *The Medieval Lyric* (1968, 2nd ed. 1977), 27, 53–55, and *Poetic Individuality in the Middle Ages* (1970), 26–31, 114–149, 203–209; Hans Spanke, "Über das Fortleben der Sequenzenform in den romanischen Sprachen," in *Zeitschrift für romanische Philologie,* 51 (1931); Bruno Stablein, "Die Schwanenklage: Zum Problem Lai-Planctus-Sequenz," in *Festschrift Karl Gustav Fellerer* (1962); Lorenz Weinrich, "Peter Abelard as Musician," in *Musical Quarterly,* 55 (1969).

ROBERT FALCK

[See also **Abelard, Peter; ¡Ay, Iherusalem!; Carolingian Latin Poetry; Lai, Lay; Latin Literature; Music, Western European; Passion Plays, French.**]

PLANO CARPINI, JOHN OF. See **John of Plano Carpini.**

PLANTAGENETS. Geoffrey V, count of Anjou, married Matilda, daughter of Henry I of England. Their son, Henry, after a long struggle with King Stephen of England (1135–1154), was recognized as heir to the throne and became king after Stephen's death. Geoffrey V had acquired the nickname Plantegenet, probably because he liked to hunt in gorse-covered country (*plante genêt* = gorse). It became a family name with his son Henry II of England and all the kings of England descended in the male line from Henry. The last Plantagenet king was Richard III (1483–1485). The Tudors, who succeeded him, were descended from a daughter of a Plantagenet duke. While the word is usually spelled "Plant*a*genet," its origin suggests that "Plant*e*genet" would be more accurate.

BIBLIOGRAPHY

Charles E. Petit-Dutaillis, *Feudal Monarchy in France and England* (1936), 100; Austin L. Poole, *From Domesday Book to Magna Carta* (1951), 129 and chap. 5.

JOSEPH R. STRAYER

[See also **Angevins; Henry II of England.**]

PLASHCHANITSA (plural, *plashchanitsy;* Greek: *epitaphios, epitaphion*), a richly embroidered full-length cloth depiction of the dead Christ often surrounded with mourning figures of the Virgin, angels, and saints. In Orthodox churches, the

Detail from the Salonika Epitaphios (*plashchanitsa*). Embroidery in gold and silver thread with blue silk, 14th century. BY COURTESY OF THE BYZANTINE MUSEUM, ATHENS

plashchanitsa, sometimes called the "winding sheet" or "shroud" of Christ, is carried in solemn procession on Good Friday to a "tomb" arranged in the front of the church, where it is an object of veneration until Easter services.

BIBLIOGRAPHY

Aleksei N. Svirin, *Drevnerusskoe shit'e* (1963); Arthur Voyce, *The Art and Architecture of Medieval Russia* (1967), 271.

GEORGE P. MAJESKA

[See also **Holy Week.**]

PLATERESQUE STYLE. "Plateresque" refers to a uniquely Spanish architectural style of the late fifteenth and sixteenth centuries. Though the term literally means "like silverwork," plateresque monuments have little relationship to contemporary minor arts; rather, they recall jewelry through the intricacy of complex reliefs on otherwise austere exteriors. Important in this respect are the designs of the master of plateresque, Alonso de Covarrubias (*ca.* 1488–1564/1570), and such works as the building of the University of Salamanca and the new cathedral in that city. Many plateresque motifs derive from Spain's long-lived Gothic style, and others reflect a new Renaissance vocabulary. However, their application ignores the values of both styles, conforming neither to architectonic laws nor to concern with decorative harmony. Though Islamic or Mudéjar motifs are rarely used, there is reason to believe that the taste for overall surface decoration on a building's exterior might ultimately be derived from Spain's recently severed contact with Islam.

BIBLIOGRAPHY

José Camón Aznar, *La arquitectura plateresca* (1945); George Kubler, "The Plateresque and Purist Styles," in George Kubler and Martin Soria, *Art and Architecture in Spain and Portugal and Their American Dominions, 1500–1800* (1959, repr. 1969).

JERRILYNN DODDS

[See also **Mudéjar Art.**]

PLATO IN THE MIDDLE AGES. The philosophy of Plato (429–347 B.C.), the Athenian philosopher, transmitted both directly and indirectly, had a powerful effect upon the intellectual and cultural life of the Middle Ages, as upon all other periods of

Plateresque ornament over the main portal of the New Cathedral, Salamanca. Attributed to Juan Gil de Hontañón, early 16th century. FOTO MAS, BARCELONA

Western civilization. Much of this effect may be traced to the impact of Plato's own works, or works attributed to him, upon medieval thinkers. The medieval Byzantines possessed all thirty-six of the dialogues ascribed to him by his ancient editors (the great majority of which are now accepted as genuine) as well as the standard collection of ancient spuria, and a number of other anepigraphic writings of later date and various origin that were attached to the name of Plato during the medieval period. The Latin West and Arabic South were less well supplied, but even there the handful of dialogues known in Latin and Arabic, when combined with the reports of Plato's thought in various compendia and in the works of other ancient authors, were sufficient to guarantee Plato's position as a leading authority in philosophy.

Yet even this direct transmission of Plato's thought was of less significance in the Middle Ages than the indirect tradition. Already, prior to the

PLATO IN THE MIDDLE AGES

medieval period, Plato's thought had formed the basis of the most important philosophical traditions of late ancient times, now known as Middle Platonism and Neoplatonism, and it was primarily within these traditions that the Christian, Jewish, and Islamic theologies had attained their intellectual majority. Thus, at an early period of their development, the sacred literatures of the three great medieval religions were seeded with Platonic themes and language and informed by Platonic habits of thought, and this (as it were) latent Platonism in religion was responsible for much of the vitality Platonic philosophy enjoyed even after the Aristotelian revolution of the twelfth century.

In this article, however, we shall not consider that broader and more diffuse stream of Platonic philosophy transmitted by the pagan and Christian writers of the later Roman Empire, but shall concern ourselves solely with the relatively smaller subject of the study and impact of Plato's own works between A.D. 500 and 1500.

PLATO IN THE BYZANTINE WORLD

By rights the Byzantine East ought to have been the most fruitful field for the study of Plato during the Middle Ages. Unlike Latin, Arabic, and Jewish students of Plato, the Byzantines had available the entire corpus of Plato's writings, and in their own language. That Byzantium was not in fact, relatively speaking, greatly productive of Platonic scholarship was no doubt largely a result of the separation and polarization of inner (sacred) and outer (pagan) knowledge fostered by Orthodox Christianity, and the relatively greater importance within it of the mystical tradition and the doctrine of the unknowability of God. This led, despite the example of the three Cappadocian fathers and St. Maximus the Confessor (*ca.* 580–662), to an ambivalence about—often even to a positive hostility toward—the use of philosophical methods in theological speculation, a hostility much greater than existed in the West, and a consequent devaluation of philosophy as an autonomous science.

Moreover, Platonic scholarship was in many cases actually hindered by the very availability of Plato's works. In the West, Plato's thought was gradually assimilated by Christian thinkers over a period of several centuries, and his unorthodoxy and "immorality" were in many cases concealed by bowdlerized and even Christianized translations. The Greek East had no opportunity for such gradual and painless assimilation; there, the heretical and "immoral" features of Platonic thought were instantly evident to the (in the early period) more sophisticated theologians of Orthodoxy, and were only disguised with difficulty.

The suspicion that attached to philosophy as an autonomous discipline thus prevented the Byzantines from accepting the Aristotelian view that philosophy was the architectonic science, and encouraged the tendency, going back to Isocrates in the fourth century B.C., to subordinate philosophy to rhetoric and literary purposes generally. The approach of the Byzantine scholar to the texts of Plato was thus that of the philologist, the educator, and the man of letters, rather than that of the pure philosopher. This meant that Byzantine disputes about Plato's value rarely followed the lines they did in Latin scholasticism, where Plato's scientific authority was defended or challenged according as his doctrines exhibited a logical consistency with one or another system of Christian philosophy. Instead, these Byzantine disputes were cast in the form of a debate (similar to that of the early Italian Renaissance) between a Christian humanism and a philistine fundamentalism. The defense of Plato made part of a general defense of the value of pagan literature, a defense drawing heavily on such sources as St. Basil of Caesarea's epistolatory tract *Ad adolescentes* (To the young), in which Plato was highly praised. Byzantine humanists lauded Plato's works both as models of pure style and as sources of pious doctrine, the contemplation of which even in a pagan would strengthen a Christian in his faith. Much was made of the seeming consonance between Christian beliefs and the Platonic doctrines of creation, immortality, providence and free will, evil, rewards and punishments, and *homoiōsis theō* (becoming like God). Alternatively, doctrines considered immoral or heretical would be isolated and cauterized, and the rest declared fit for Christian association. Such an orientation did not entirely preclude free philosophical speculation on Platonic themes, but it was by nature a fragmentary and literary approach to Plato's thought, an approach that stood in the way of a genuine grasp of Plato's philosophical system, such as was achieved at a surprisingly early date in the Latin West. It was the Byzantine humanists who initiated the tendency, later followed by the Italian humanists of the fifteenth century, to reduce Plato to a set of pious and melodious *loci communes,* stripped of their connecting tissue of dialectical reasoning, and hence of their systematic force.

PLATO IN THE MIDDLE AGES

Platonic studies in Constantinople. It has sometimes been asserted that there was an unbroken continuity of the Platonic tradition in Byzantium from antiquity to the fall of Constantinople in 1453. And if the mere existence of manuscripts of Plato's works were the sufficent condition of such continuity, the point would have to be granted. It is nevertheless difficult to find evidence for the study of the Platonic dialogues between what may be considered the end of the ancient Platonic school in the early seventh century, when Stephen of Alexandria lectured on Plato in Constantinople at the court of Emperor Heraklios (610–641), and the second and third decades of the ninth century, which find Leo the Mathematician teaching philosophy privately in Constantinople. Leo is thought to have made a recension (*diorthōsis*) of Platonic texts, a fact which fits well with what is otherwise known of the philological orientation of his teaching. Leo was likewise the key figure in the attempt by Caesar Bardas (*d.* 866) to found a school in the Magnaura Palace (*ca.* 855/856), where the second important student of Plato of the ninth century, Photios (*ca.* 810–*ca.* 897), also taught. Photios was later the patriarch of Constantinople (858) and one of the most powerful political figures of the age. Notwithstanding his declared preference for Aristotle, Photios was well informed about Plato's works, though his knowledge seems to have come chiefly, if not entirely, from intermediary sources. At least in the famous *Bibliotheca* (*ca.* 837/838), Photios relied for his information and opinions entirely on Hierokles, a Christian Platonist of the fifth century, the second-century rhetorician Aristides, and an anonymous life of Pythagoras. With Hierokles, Photios approves the view that Plato and Aristotle are fundamentally in accord on providence, the immortality of the soul, and cosmology, while reproving Plato for his belief in the preexistence of the soul and in the eternity of prime matter, and for his immoral and utopian political views. With Aristides, he admits that Plato is a great stylist, but faults him for his attacks on Homer, Pericles, and rhetoric and poetry in general; rhetoric is in fact more useful and complete (*teleōteros*) than philosophy, Photios declares, because while the latter merely avoids injustice, the former actively causes justice.

Whatever Photios' dependence on intermediaries, there can be no doubt that the text of Plato was thoroughly familiar to the next great figure of Byzantine Platonic scholarship, Photios' student Arethas of Patras, later the archbishop of Caesarea (*fl.* 895–*ca.* 944). Four surviving manuscripts and three sets of scholia have been plausibly associated with his studium, and to him also may probably be attributed the most important collection of philosophical prolegomena to Plato. As this last bit of evidence indicates, Arethas' interest in Plato was more than merely philological. While many of his scholia are textual and grammatical, a sizable number (especially in Vienna, Nat. Libr., MS Phil. gr. 314) show a keen interest in philosophical issues. Though something of a Platonist himself, Arethas does not hesitate to reprove Plato (in the second person) for doctrines he considers contrary to Christian truth, and to warn future readers of potential dangers to their faith.

The Platonic renaissance. The revival of humanistic studies in the mid tenth century under Emperor Constantine VII Porphyrogenitos (905–959) apparently did not lead immediately to a revival of philosophy, for Michael Psellos (1018–1078) in an autobiographical passage of his *Chronographia* claims sole credit for resuscitating the moribund discipline of philosophy, presumably in the middle years of the eleventh century. This cannot have been literally true, however, since Psellos himself shortly afterward speaks of having had teachers in philosophy; and the manuscript evidence for Plato's text, at least, shows that a considerable number were copied and annotated in the later tenth and eleventh centuries (like the well-known Vienna, Nat. Libr., MS Suppl. gr. 7). Psellos may have meant that he was the first in his day to take more than a literary interest in the philosophical authors of antiquity, an impression borne out by the list he gives of his reading—Plato, Aristotle, Plotinus, Porphyry, Iamblichus—and by his own numerous writings on philosophical subjects. Psellos' claim to have personally revived philosophy is further strengthened by the necessity he was under of defending philosophical study against the attacks of religious anti-intellectualism, as in his famous letter to his friend John Xiphilinos (patriarch, 1063–1073) in 1054. Yet despite his plea there to follow the example of the church fathers in using philosophy to refute heretics and strengthen faith, Psellos' own philosophical works, as far as they are presently known, do not attempt to execute such a program. His works on Platonic philosophy in particular are highly derivative, being based more or less closely on works of Proclus (as in his commentary *On Plato's Psychogony*),

 PLATO IN THE MIDDLE AGES

Hermeias (in his *Explanation of the Platonic Chariot-driving of Souls in the Phaedrus and of the Campaigns of the Gods*), Plotinus (in his treatise *On the Ideas Which Plato Mentions*), and other Neoplatonic intermediaries.

The Platonic renaissance of the eleventh century culminated in the career of Psellos' student, the philosopher John Italos (*ca.* 1025–after 1082), who of all Byzantine philosophers came nearest to the methods and outlook of Western Scholasticism. For Italos was a genuine dialectician who wanted to use philosophical doctrines to elucidate truths of faith and who was even willing to entertain, hypothetically, philosophical theses contrary to Orthodoxy. But Italos might be viewed as well as having revived the tradition of Christian Platonism handed down by the Cappadocian fathers, John Philoponus, and St. Maximus the Confessor. His doctrines are in many respects similar to theirs, and his doctrines which appear novel are developments very much in their spirit. Italos used Platonic methods to prove the anti-Platonic doctrines that the world was created *ex nihilo* and that the soul was immortal but not eternal. He held that both the Forms and particulars were causally dependent on God and contingent on his Will, an idea ultimately destructive of the notion of ontological hierarchy, since contingency is the differentia of what "has nonbeing." His psychology was a complicated mixture of Aristotelian and Platonic doctrines. What is interesting for our purposes is that Italos apparently based his teaching in great part upon a reading of Plato's dialogues themselves (particularly the *Timaeus*) as explained by the Neoplatonic commentators and illuminated by the Christian Platonism of the Fathers.

Yet despite Italos' adherence to the example of the Fathers, and despite, indeed, his complete orthodoxy, Italos ran into trouble with the regime of Alexios I Komnenos (*r.* 1081–1118), which in a frenzy of politically motivated anti-intellectualism condemned him and his doctrines in a famous trial on the Feast of Orthodoxy, 13 March 1082. A number of years later appeared one of Italos' pupils, Eustratios, bishop of Nicaea (*fl.* end of eleventh–early twelfth centuries), who wrote, among other works, a Platonizing commentary on the *Nicomachean Ethics* (which when translated into Latin in the thirteenth century by Grosseteste had a powerful yet hitherto unrealized impact on the understanding of Aristotle's text in the Latin West); he, too, was condemned (on more substantial grounds) for theological error in 1117. These two condemnations reveal at once the difficulties serious students of philosophy faced in the Eastern empire, and help explain the general transfer of philosophical interests in the twelfth century to the safer waters of Aristotelian-school philosophy.

Later Byzantine students of Plato. The greatest setback for medieval Greek Platonism, as for Byzantine culture in general, was the disaster of 1204. Aside from some copies of Plato's works dating from the early Palaiologan period there are few signs of interest in Platonic philosophy until the time of the great fourteenth-century polyhistor and humanist Theodore Metochites, who praises Plato as the "Olympus of Wisdom," and cites him many times in his *Hupomnematismoi* or *Commentaries.* He too defends the orthodoxy of Plato's cosmology. Although his knowledge of it would seem to be largely derived from Iamblichus' (*d. ca.* 330) *De communi mathematica scientia,* the knowledge of it possessed by his opponent in the controversy that developed, Nikephoros Choumnos (*ca.* 1250–1327), was certainly based on a firsthand knowledge of the *Timaeus* and was probably informed by the speculation of the Cappadocian fathers as well. Metochites' interest in Plato was continued by his student, the little-studied Nikephoros Gregoras (1290–1359/1360), who is regarded by some scholars as a forerunner of Georgios Gemistos Plethon (*d.* 1452).

In the later fourteenth century, intellectual energies were absorbed in the hesychast controversy, in which Platonism took a part, but more as a rallying cry for the humanists than as an object of serious study. The last act of Byzantine Platonism came in the fifteenth century and was played out mostly on Italian soil by Byzantine emigrés. One of the earliest, Manuel Chrysoloras (*d.* 1415), translated the *Republic* into Latin (*ca.* 1402) and inspired the first generation of Italian humanists, especially Guarino da Verona (1374–1460) and Leonardo Bruni (1370–1444), with a keen interest in Plato. Gemistos Plethon, who had founded a school of Platonic philosophy in Mistra, near ancient Sparta, is credited with having inspired Cosimo de' Medici with the idea of founding a Platonic Academy, if this story is not (as it is likely to be) an invention of Marsilio Ficino. Plethon's political views (based obscurely on the *Republic*) and his even more bizarre proposals for the revival of a Neoplatonized paganism to replace Christianity and Islam as a unified world religion gave rise to the important

PLATO IN THE MIDDLE AGES

Plato-Aristotle controversy of the mid fifteenth century, and to Cardinal Bessarion's famous reply to George of Trebizond, the *In calumniatorem Platonis* (Against the calumniator of Plato, 1469), a book which shaped the Western reading of Plato for more than a century.

PLATO IN THE ARAB WORLD

The study of Plato in the Arabic world began at about the same time that it was being revived in the Byzantine East, in the early ninth century. This age saw a number of Plato's works translated into Arabic by Nestorian Christians working in the court of the caliphs in Baghdad. In the early ninth century the *Timaeus* was translated by Yaḥyā ibn al-Biṭrīq; later in the century the famous Syrian Nestorian Christian Ḥunain ibn Isḥāq (Johannitius, 808–873) and his school translated at least the *Republic*, the *Laws*, the *Sophist* (with Olympiodorus' sixth-century commentary) and, again, the *Timaeus*, as well as Proclus' commentary on the *Timaeus* and Galen's medical commentary on the same work. The Jacobite Yaḥyā ibn ᶜAdī in the tenth century retranslated the *Laws* and revised the earlier translation of the *Timaeus;* to him may also be attributed the translations of the *Apology, Crito,* and *Phaedo* quoted by later philosophers. Of these translations, nothing today survives but fragments of Proclus' and Galen's commentaries on the *Timaeus* and some collections of *sententiae.*

The translators not only provided the Arabic world with translations of Plato himself, they also made versions of a number of later ancient commentaries and compilations based on his work. In addition to the works of Olympiodorus, Galen, and Proclus already mentioned, they turned Galen's *Synopsis of the Platonic Dialogues* (of which a part survives), Plutarch's commentary on the *Timaeus* (now lost, or perhaps identical with his *De animae procreatione in Timaeo* [On the creation of the soul in the Timaeus] handed down with many Greek manuscripts of Plato), and a work on the order of Plato's books by Theon of Smyrna (*fl.* second century), of which a fragment survives. A compilation based on Proclus and known later in the West as the *Liber de causis* was probably translated into Arabic from a late Greek source and became an important authority in Islamic philosophy, just as did the *Theologia Aristotelis,* a work based loosely on *Enneads* IV–VI of Plotinus. A collection known as the *Platonica* (İstanbul, Aya Sophia MS 2821) contains a variety of political and moral maxims from Plato, with a commentary on the last book of the *Laws* at the end. There were in addition a number of apocryphal works attributed to Plato of apparently Arabic origin, including two letters (İstanbul, University Library, MS 1458, fols. 105–106 and fols. 206–211), a collection of medical recipes (Paris, Bibliothèque Nationale, MS arab. 2577, fol. 104), the *Liber de tredecim clavibus sapientiae majoris* (surviving in Latin in Venice, Biblioteca Marciana, MS Zan. lat. 324), and the so-called *Liber quartus,* which was translated into Latin around 1200 with commentary and had some influence in the West.

As the range and character of these texts suggest, the interest of the Arabs in Plato's works was chiefly scientific, moral, and metaphysical, and their interpretation of his philosophy regularly Neoplatonic. Philosophical ethics as a whole in the Islamic crescent was based on Plato rather than Aristotle, although it remains a matter of some doubt whether this situation reflected a genuine preference or arose merely from the accident that Plato's *Republic* and *Laws* were available in Arabic, whereas Aristotle's *Politics* was not. With Plato's metaphysics, or his metaphysics as interpreted by Neoplatonic commentators, Islam had an obvious affinity, for the doctrine of emanation was the cornerstone of Arabic philosophy until the time of al-Ghazālī (1058–1111). All Arabic philosophers, it may be said, were Platonists insofar as they were metaphysicians, but the degree to which this Platonism was the result of reading Plato himself was in most cases probably rather small.

The Islamic philosopher most influenced by Plato was al-Fārābī (Alfarabius), who flourished in the first half of the tenth century (*d.* 950). Al-Fārābī seems to have known nearly all of Plato's works—at least he quotes their titles—as well as the important *conciliatio* of Plato and Aristotle preserved in Simplicius' (sixth century) commentaries on the *De caelo* and the *Categoriae*, which the Islamic philosopher repeated with approval. He wrote a treatise on the order of Plato's books and made an abridgment of the *Laws* with commentary; both works survive. In his theological works he shows himself a Neoplatonist, and his political philosophy makes interesting use of the *Republic* by introducing the notion of the philosopher-king as a way of reforming the Islamic caliphate.

Other Islamic philosophers had less close relations with the text of Plato. Ibn Sīnā (Avicenna, 980–1037) was a Neoplatonist who espoused a

PLATO IN THE MIDDLE AGES

hierarchical emanationism and shows considerable acquaintance with Plato's cosmological and political doctrines. Ibn Rushd (Averroës, 1126–1198), though he wrote a commentary on the *Republic,* was chiefly concerned with cleansing the interpretation of Aristotle of Neoplatonic elements. So, too, al-Ghazālī attacked Avicenna's Neoplatonizing theology and cosmology in the name of Islamic fundamentalism, but by a curious irony became himself an important source of Neoplatonic doctrine for the West when the first book of his *Incoherence of the Philosophers* (*Tahafut al-Falasifah*), which summarized the doctrine of the philosophers (that is, Neoplatonists) as a prelude to refuting them, was translated into Latin and taken by the Scholastics as representative of al-Ghazālī's own views.

Jewish philosophy. Within the orbit of Islamic philosophy, at least until the early thirteenth century, moved also the Jewish philosophers of the Middle Ages, who indeed wrote most of their philosophical works in Arabic until the early twelfth century. There are, as far as is known, no Hebrew translations of Plato and no direct study of the dialogues by any medieval Jewish philosopher, yet most of the Jewish philosophy before the later twelfth century was marked more or less deeply by the Neoplatonism widely diffused in Arabic lands, and especially by the doctrine of the *Theologia Aristotelis.* Such philosophers as Isaac ben Solomon Israeli (*ca.* 855–*ca.* 955), who was translated into Latin in the mid twelfth century, Joseph ibn Saddiq (early twelfth century), and Solomon ben Judah ibn Gabirol (Avicebron, *ca.* 1021–*ca.* 1058) can be plausibly classified as Neoplatonists; the latter's *Fountain of Life,* translated into Latin (as *Fons vitae*) in the thirteenth century, evidently influenced Bonaventure with its odd doctrine that spiritual substances were composed of matter and form. But in the later twelfth century, along with its Byzantine, Islamic, and Latin cousins, Jewish philosophy, led by Moses Maimonides, (1135–1204), became rigorously focused on the works of Aristotle. In the thirteenth century, Jewish philosophy shifted to Latin Christian lands, a circumstance which only reinforced the Aristotelian bias. It is indeed difficult to find any examples of Jewish study of Plato in Arabic or Christian lands in the later Middle Ages, aside from Samuel ben Judah ha-Marsili's fourteenth-century Hebrew translation of Averroës' commentary on the *Republic,* which in the fifteenth century was translated into Latin by the Jewish teacher of Giovanni Pico della Mirandola, Elijah ben Moses Delmedigo (*ca.* 1460–1497), and is preserved in Siena (Biblioteca Comunale, MS G.VII. 32, fols. 158–188).

PLATO IN THE LATIN WEST

It was within Latin Christianity, the last of the three medieval traditions to reach philosophical maturity, that the future of Platonic studies and the Platonic tradition lay. The Latin West had initially the smallest firsthand knowledge of Plato. The only dialogue it possessed until the twelfth century was the first third of the *Timaeus,* translated in late ancient times by Calcidius (Chalcidius) and provided by him with a commentary whose philosophical character was highly eclectic. In the mid twelfth century (between 1154 and 1160), Henricus Aristippus, archdeacon of Catania under William I of Sicily (*d.* 1166), translated the *Meno* and the *Phaedo,* and in the later thirteenth century (between 1274 and 1286) the Flemish Dominican William of Moerbeke (*ca.* 1215–1286) translated, at the request of Thomas Aquinas, Proclus' commentary on the *Parmenides,* which included a substantial part of the dialogue itself. But the ad verbum technique employed by both translators rendered much of these versions obscure and thus limited their impact on medieval thinkers. It was chiefly the *Timaeus,* with Calcidius' commentary, that represented Plato's thought to the medieval Latin West; it has survived in over 165 manuscripts and was glossed and commented upon dozens of times between the late eleventh and the fifteenth centuries, though only a handful of these glosses have seen print.

For the rest, Plato's writings and opinions were preserved in testimonia and summaries contained in the writings of ancient Latin authors, particularly Cicero, Seneca, Apuleius, Macrobius, St. Augustine, and Martianus Capella. In late antiquity there was also translated into Latin a Middle Platonic summary of Plato's dialogues, called by Raymond Klibansky the *Summarium librorum Platonis,* but whose correct medieval title was *De Platonis pluribus libris compendiosa expositio.* This unpublished work had some circulation and was apparently known to Albertus Magnus (*ca.* 1200–1280) and Thomas Aquinas (1224–1274). Boethius among other quotations reports the teaching of the *Timaeus* in metrum 9 of book III in his *De consolatione Philosophiae* (Consolation of Philosophy), a poem that was commented upon frequently in the early Middle Ages. Porphyry in his

PLATO IN THE MIDDLE AGES

Isagoge and Pseudo-Dionysius, translated respectively in the sixth and ninth centuries, gave accounts of a number of Plato's doctrines. The great wave of Aristotelian translations in the thirteenth century further increased the West's knowledge of the dialogues, for Nemesius, Themistius (both fourth century), Proclus (*d.* 485), Simplicius (*fl.* early sixth century), Avicenna, and Averroës between them provided a copious store of Platonic testimonia. Most important of all, ironically enough, was Aristotle himself, who in many of his works, especially the *Metaphysics, Ethics, Politics,* and *De anima,* gives Plato's views on a given question (however tendentiously), thus supplying the matter for a revival within Latin Scholasticism of the ancient tradition of the *comparatio,* or comparison, of Plato and Aristotle.

The net effect of this profusion of texts was, as might be expected, considerable confusion. Unlike the situation in Byzantium and Islam, where the Neoplatonic interpretation of Plato reigned relatively undisturbed, in the West Plato's thought was presented by Academic skeptics, Stoics, Aristotelians, and eclectics as well as Neoplatonists. In the books of *auctoritates* there thus appeared many doctrines ascribed to Plato which a modern scholar would have great difficulty in recognizing as Platonic. In some few cases this was a *fructuosa confusio* which allowed men of learning and philosophical penetration, such as Albertus Magnus, Thomas Aquinas, and John Duns Scotus (*ca.* 1266–1308), to develop a fairly sophisticated grasp of Plato's doctrines concerning the forms, participation, the soul, and the process of cognition. But for most medieval thinkers, if the philosophy of Plato meant anything coherent at all, it meant the natural philosophy and cosmology of the *Timaeus.*

Importance of the Timaeus. It was the *Timaeus,* certainly, that occupied the efforts of the early medieval students of Plato. John Scottus Eriugena in the ninth century was familiar with the dialogue, and through it scholars of the tenth and eleventh centuries were able to recognize the philosophical paternity of Boethius' *Consolatio* (III, 9), thus giving rise to a lively debate whether the latter was in his *Consolatio* writing as a Christian Platonist or as a Platonist simpliciter. This controversy was, however, largely a mask for a more fundamental debate on the value of secular learning. In it, Plato became the symbol of secular learning (or "philosophy"), just as Aristotle was to become in the thirteenth century. Bovo II of Corvei (*d.* 916) regarded the *Consolatio* as a work of pagan philosophy, and hence as a book to be studied with caution, if at all; yet, like Augustine, he would take the trouble for apologetic purposes at least to attempt to understand its doctrines and identify its errors. A more positive attitude is represented by Adalbold of Utrecht (*d.* 1026), who regarded Boethius as a Christian philosopher and Platonism as a kind of secondary source of divine wisdom. Of yet greater interest is a controversy with political overtones in the late eleventh century (*ca.* 1085), this time between the Gregorian Manegold of Lautenbach and Wolfhelm of Cologne, a Benedictine who was at once an opponent of Gregory VII and (through Boethius) a *sectator Platonis.* Wolfhelms' uncritical acceptance of heretical Platonic doctrines, says Manegold, has led to his refusal to obey the will of God in political matters, and to his belief that "we have no pontiff but Caesar." Manegold admits that the Fathers did well to take over certain Platonic ethical doctrines, but he rejects the cosmological speculations of the early medieval schools as representing a dangerous challenge to the truths revealed in Genesis.

It was within this context that the Platonist masters of the cathedral schools of northern France set about their mission in the early twelfth century of reconciling the cosmology of Plato with the doctrines of Genesis. To counter the hostility exhibited in some quarters to pagan philosophy, they recurred to the position of Christian Platonism of the Greek Fathers, derived, perhaps, from Eriugena. Nature, and all objects presented to man's senses and reason, they argued, are sources of divine light provided by God to pagan and Christian alike—inferior, no doubt, to Scripture, yet useful to bring the pagan to the truth and to enlarge the Christian's knowledge of the divine wisdom. For since all nature was modeled on Ideas contained within the mind of God, which were engendered in matter (*hyle, materia, silva*) by his Word (Christ), a knowledge of creation will lead ultimately to a knowledge of the mind of the Creator.

With this conviction, and with a new and broader literary culture, the Platonists associated with Chartres and other cathedral schools of northern France developed in the course of the twelfth century an important body of commentaries and glosses on the *Timaeus* (mostly unpublished), which drew upon an ever-wider range of sources in the design to comprehend Plato's thought, and especially upon Boethius, Macrobius, Apuleius, and

PLATO IN THE MIDDLE AGES

Seneca. Although the central orientation of these works remained toward reconciling the Platonic and biblical accounts of creation, and hence toward physics and cosmology, the commentary form allowed digression into such diverse areas as medicine, politics, number theory, optics, and music. This is a progressive movement: While in Bernard of Chartres's (*d. ca.* 1130) recently identified commentary on the *Timaeus* the concerns remained primarily moral and theological, by the time of William of Conches (*d. ca.* 1154) the text of the *Timaeus* had become the focus of the entire range of twelfth-century learning. The study of the *Timaeus* and other Platonic texts moreover gave rise for the first time in the Latin West to a large and independent body of Platonic literature, such as Thierry of Chartres's (*fl.* 1121–1148) and Clarembald of Arras's (*d. ca.* 1187) treatises on Genesis. Bernard Silvester's (*fl.* 1141–*ca.* 1160) visionary dialogue, the *Cosmographia,* modeled on Boethius and Martianus Capella, gave literary expression to the Chartrean vision of God's glory reflected in the order of nature. The most interesting of the group from the philosophical point of view was Gilbert of Poitiers (Gilbert de la Porrée, *ca.* 1076–1154), whom Étienne Gilson credits with having encouraged "the diffusion of that particular form of Platonism we might call the realism of essences," a form of Platonism that was to culminate in the metaphysics of Duns Scotus.

Platonic studies and the universities. The later twelfth and thirteenth centuries saw the universities mature into the leading centers of learning; they saw a movement away from the literary concerns of the twelfth-century masters, and the various branches of learning transformed into well-defined and ordered bodies of scientific knowledge, fully synthesized with Christian theology. Contact with Islam and heretical sects imparted a new apologetical direction to university studies, especially in the new preaching orders. All these changes were inimical to the study of Plato's works, with their literary dress, dialogic uncertainties, and suspect doctrine. The works of Aristotle, now translated in great numbers, satisfied much better the new orientation of medieval learning; they had encyclopedic range, apparent scientific certainty, and a textbook approach ideal for university teaching. Moreover, their doctrine, if no less heretical in places than Plato's, had had many of its blemishes disguised or excused by the Islamic commentaries that were translated at about the same time: hence, the Aristotelian revolution of the later twelfth and early thirteenth centuries and the consequent eclipse of Plato.

Yet, though no longer the leading auctor in philosophy, Plato continued to be studied. The *Timaeus* was still copied and glossed, and remained an important authority in cosmology, physics, mathematics, and optics. The new translations of Aristotle and his commentators cast more light on Plato's metaphysical, psychological, and political doctrines. Plato's theory of forms and his notion of being exercised some influence (mostly indirectly) on realist metaphysicians; his psychology and cosmology were still adhered to by Albertus Magnus and his disciples when the rest of the intellectual globe had turned to Aristotle; his doctrine of participation figured in Thomas Aquinas' teachings on natural law. Plato's political views, on the other hand, known chiefly through the inaccurate report of Aristotle in book II of the *Politics,* were routinely condemned as impracticable and perverse. In the later thirteenth and fourteenth centuries, though the so-called light-metaphysics of the Neoplatonists enjoyed a renewed vogue, the study of Plato remained restricted to a few scholars, such as Henry of Ghent (*d.* 1397), Henry Bate of Malines, Petrarch, and Antonius de Romagno. In the theological faculties of the universities the doctors had taken warning from the condemnation of 1277 and had begun to dissociate themselves from the thirteenth-century program of reconciling theology and philosophy. In the arts faculties, philosophical studies were concentrated upon logic, physics, and moral philosophy, and in all of these disciplines Aristotle was taken as the authority par excellence, although there are some signs that the *Timaeus* was occasionally used as a text in physics. Petrarch summed up the situation in his well-known dictum, "A pluribus Aristoteles, a majoribus Plato laudatus est" (More men praise Aristotle; better ones, Plato).

The Italian humanists and Christian Platonism. The revival of Platonic study in the West had to await the fifteenth century and the first generation of Italian humanists instructed in Greek. A new wave of Latin versions then appeared, this time translated into readable literary prose, often with bowdlerizations and Christianizations of passages the humanists thought inappropriate. The emigré Greek Manuel Chrysoloras translated the *Republic* with his student Uberto Decembrio around 1402; this translation was thoroughly revised in the late 1430's by Uberto's son Pier Candido, who also

PLATO IN THE MIDDLE AGES

translated the *Lysis* (1456). Another student of Chrysoloras, Leonardo Bruni (1370–1444), translated the *Phaedo* (1405), *Gorgias* (1409), *Letters* (1411), part of the *Phaedrus* (1424), the *Crito* and the *Apology* (in two redactions, both before 1427), and a speech from the *Symposium* (1435). Francesco Filelfo translated (1430's) three of the *Letters* and the *Euthyphro*. At mid century George of Trebizond (Georgius Trapezuntius), for all his anti-Platonic convictions, translated the *Parmenides* for Nicolas of Cusa (1459) and the *Laws* (1450/1451). Perhaps the most popular dialogue was the pseudo-Platonic *Axiochus*, which was put into Latin by four different translators and had a wide circulation. The translation activity of the fifteenth century culminated in the work of Marsilio Ficino, who published the first complete translation of the nine tetralogies in 1484; this version became the most important channel of Plato's thought to early modern Europe.

Despite this extraordinary burst of translations, Plato did not succeed in reentering the universities during the fifteenth century. Platonism and the study of Plato flourished indeed, but outside the universities, among the educated gentlemen who formed the audience of the humanists, and in the courts of popes and princes. The early humanists had themselves no very profound understanding of Platonic philosophy and were chiefly interested in Plato as an example of one of their favorite themes (borrowed from their Byzantine teachers), the necessity of joining wisdom with eloquence. Then too they sought to use Plato in the defense of the *studia humanitatis* against the philistines by showing how his philosophical arguments strengthened Christian beliefs in such doctrines as the immortality of the soul and rewards and punishments after death. But the dialogic form of Plato's works presented them with severe difficulties when it came to the task of interpreting Plato's philosophy, and Bruni, Guarino, and Uberto Decembrio at least, like John of Salisbury and Petrarch earlier, tended consequently to the easier Academic interpretation of Plato found in Cicero and in Augustine's *Contra academicos*.

The revival of Christian Platonism as a real philosophical alternative came in the mid and late fifteenth century with Nicholas of Cusa (1401–1464), Cardinal Bessarion (*ca.* 1403–1472), Marsilio Ficino (1433–1499), and Giovanni Pico della Mirandola (1463–1494). Nicholas of Cusa possessed and annotated copies of most of the medieval and humanistic translations of Plato; and though he wrote no study of Plato himself, he did much to spread Platonic thought in Italy and Germany by means of the original blend of mystical and Neoplatonic elements in his own philosophical works. The Plato-Aristotle controversy of mid century, incited by Georgios Gemistos Plethon and continued by both Greek and Latin scholars, was a channel for the introduction to the West of the Byzantine study and interpretation of Plato; the two major works it produced, George of Trebizond's *Comparatio Platonis et Aristotelis* (1458) and Bessarion's *In calumniatorem Platonis* (1469), began the Renaissance tradition of comparing or synthesizing Plato and Aristotle which was to reach its peak in the sixteenth century. Bessarion was moreover responsible for the preservation of much of ancient Platonic philosophy through the donation of his large collection of Greek books to the city of Venice, a gift which became the nucleus of the present-day Biblioteca Marciana.

There is, however, little doubt that the greatest contribution to Platonic study in the fifteenth century was made by Marsilio Ficino, who in addition to his own original synthesis of Christianity and Platonism translated the entire corpus of Plato's dialogues into Latin and provided with them lengthy commentaries and arguments explaining the text. In these commentaries a Christian Neoplatonic interpretation of Plato predominated, but he exploited other sources as well, as in his *Compendium in Timaeum*, which draws much of its material from the medieval glossary tradition of the dialogue. Ficino also translated Plotinus (1492) and several Neoplatonic commentaries on Plato. These translations were extremely influential; they were reprinted many times and successfully ousted all rival versions for several centuries. Ficino also exercised a personal influence as head of the Platonic Academy founded by Cosimo de' Medici, which, with its lectures and discussions, provided for several decades a center for the dissemination of Platonic thought. Thus it was Ficino's work, built upon centuries of medieval thought and learning, that presented Plato and Platonism to the modern world.

BIBLIOGRAPHY

General works. Arthur Hilary Armstrong, ed., *The Cambridge History of Later Greek and Early Medieval Philosophy* (1967, repr. with corrections 1970); Raymond Klibansky, *The Continuity of the Platonic*

Tradition During the Middle Ages (1939; repr. with supplement 1981); Paul Oskar Kristeller, "Renaissance Platonism," in his *Renaissance Thought: The Classic, Scholastic, and Humanist Strains* (1961), 48–69.

Plato in the Byzantine world. Lowell Clucas, *The Trial of John Italos and the Crisis of Intellectual Values in Byzantium in the Eleventh Century* (1981); Paul Oskar Kristeller, "Byzantine and Western Platonism in the Fifteenth Century," in his *Renaissance Thought and Its Sources* (1979); Leendert Gerrit Westerink, *Texts and Studies in Neoplatonism and Byzantine Literature* (1980); Christopher Montague Woodhouse, *George Gemistos Plethon, the Last of the Hellenes* (1986).

Plato in the Arab world. Alexander Altmann, ed., *Jewish Medieval and Renaissance Studies* (1967); *Alfarabi's Philosophy of Plato and Aristotle*, Muhsin Mahdi, trans., rev. ed. (1969); Franz Rosenthal, "On the Knowledge of Plato's Philosophy in the Islamic World," in *Islamic Culture*, **14** (1940); Richard Walzer, "Platonism in Islamic Philosophy," in his *Greek into Arabic: Essays on Islamic Philosophy* (1962, 1970), 236–252.

Plato in the Latin West. Michael J. B. Allen, *The Platonism of Marsilio Ficino: A Study of His Phaedrus Commentary, Its Sources and Genesis* (1984); F. Edward Cranz, "The Transmutation of Platonism in the Development of Nicolaus Cusanus and of Martin Luther," in *Nicolò Cusano agli inizi del mondo moderno* (1964); Peter Dronke, *Fabula: Explorations into the Uses of Myth in Medieval Platonism* (1974); Paul Edward Dutton, "The Uncovering of the *Glosae super Platonem* of Bernard of Chartres," in *Mediaeval Studies*, **46** (1984); Margeret Gibson, "The Study of the *Timaeus* in the Eleventh and Twelfth Centuries," in *Pensamiento*, **25** (1969); Nikolaus M. Häring, "Chartres and Paris Revisited," in *Essays in Honour of Anton Charles Pegis*, J. Reginald O'Donnell, ed. (1974); Robert John Henle, *Saint Thomas and Platonism* (1956); Édouard Jeauneau, "*Lectio philosophorum*": *Recherches sur l'école de Chartres* (1973); Raymond Klibansky, "The School of Chartres," in *Twelfth-century Europe and the Foundations of Modern Society* (1961, repr. 1966), "Plato's *Parmenides* in the Middle Ages and the Renaissance," in *Mediaeval and Renaissance Studies*, **1**, no. 2 (1943); Paul Oskar Kristeller, *The Philosophy of Marsilio Ficino*, Virginia Conant, trans. (1943, repr. 1964), *Studies in Renaissance Thought and Letters* (1956), and *Renaissance Thought II: Papers on Humanism and the Arts* (1965); Stephan Kuttner, "Gratian and Plato," in *Church and Government in the Middle Ages*, C. N. L. Brooke *et al.*, eds. (1976), 93–118, reprinted in Kuttner, *The History of Ideas and Doctrines of Canon Law in the Middle Ages* (1980); Arthur Little, *The Platonic Heritage of Thomism* (1950); Edward Patrick Mahoney, "Metaphysical Foundations of the Hierarchy of Being According to Some Late Medieval and Renaissance Philosophers," in *Philosophies of Existence, Ancient and Modern*, Parviz Morewedge, ed. (1982), 165–257; John Monfasani, *George of Trebizond: A Biography and a Study of His Rhetoric and Logic* (1976); Richard W. Southern, "Humanism and the School of Chartres," in his *Medieval Humanism and Other Studies* (1970), 61–85, and "The Schools of Paris and the School of Chartres," in *Renaissance and Renewal in the Twelfth Century*, Robert L. Benson and Giles Constable, eds. (1982), 173–200; Eugène N. Tigerstedt, *The Decline and Fall of the Neoplatonic Interpretation of Plato* (1974); Winthrop Wetherbee, *Platonism and Poetry in the Twelfth Century: The Literary Influence of the School of Chartres* (1972).

JAMES HANKINS

[See also **Abelard, Peter; Adalbold of Utrecht; Albertus Magnus; Aquinas, St. Thomas; Aristotle in the Middle Ages; Augustine of Hippo, St.; Bardas Caesar; Basil the Great of Caesarea, St.; Bernard of Chartres; Bernard Silvester; Bessarion; Boethius; Bonaventure, St.; Bovo II of Corvei; Bruni, Leonardo; Classical Literary Studies; Constantine VII Porphyrogenitos; Dun Scotus, John; Fārābī, al-; George of Trebizond; Ghazālī, al-; Henry of Ghent; Hesychasm; John Italos; John Scottus Eriugena; Joseph ibn Saddiq; Leo the Mathematician; Macrobius; Maimonides, Moses; Manegold of Lautenbach; Manuel Chrysoloras; Martianus Capella; Maximus the Confessor, St.; Neoplatonism; Nicholas of Cusa; Philosophy and Theology; Photios; Psellos, Michael; Pseudo-Dionysius the Areopagite; Rushd, Ibn; Sīnā, Ibn; Solomon ben Judah ibn Gabirol; Theodore Metochites; William of Conches; William of Moerbeke.**]

PLATO OF TIVOLI (*fl.* 1135–1145), one of several translators of scientific works from Arabic and Hebrew into Latin who worked in Spain in the first half of the twelfth century. Nothing is known about his life beyond what can be gleaned from his translations. These are often characterized by a horoscope indicating the position of the planets, the date (in several different eras) at the time of the completion of the work, and the place of composition. From these horoscopes we know that Plato was active in Barcelona between 1135 and 1145. His translations include: a work on trigonometry by Abraham bar Ḥiyya (Savasorda) called the *Liber embadorum;* a textbook on astronomy and astronomical tables by al-Battānī (Albategnius); Ptolemy's introduction to astrology (the *Quadripartitum*) and a set of astrological aphorisms falsely attributed to Ptolemy; works on horoscopes and anniversary horoscopes by Abū ᶜAlī al-Khayyāṭ

(Abuali sutor) and Abū Bakr al-Ḥasan (Albubather); a treatise on the use of the astrolabe by Abūʾl-Qāsim (Albucasis); and an introduction to the divinatory science of geomancy. While he probably did not translate Theodosius' *Spherics,* he is quite possibly the translator of Archimedes' important text on the squaring of the circle. He may have been helped by a well-known scholar belonging to the large Jewish population in Barcelona, Abraham bar Ḥiyya, for the latter, as well as being the author of the original Hebrew version of the *Liber embadorum,* is described as being the "interpreter" (*interpres*) of a text on astrological elections by ʿAlī ibn Aḥmad al-ʿImrānī (Haly), which is in the same style and has the same form of horoscope as works translated (*translata*) by Plato.

Later astronomers such as Edmund Halley (1656–1742) and Jean-Sylvain Bailly (1736–1793) did not have a high opinion of Plato's competence in astronomy or in languages. However, the *Liber embadorum,* which provided the first complete solution of the quadratic equation $x^2 - ax + b = 0$ in Europe, was a major source for Leonardo Fibonacci's (*ca.* 1170–after 1240) *Practica geometriae,* and the works on astrology and al-Battānī's treatise were frequently copied in the Middle Ages and printed in Renaissance editions.

BIBLIOGRAPHY

Baldassarre Boncompagni-Ludovisi, *Delle versioni fatte da Platone Tiburtino, traduttore del secolo duodecimo* (1851); Lorenzo Minio-Paluello, "Plato of Tivoli," in *Dictionary of Scientific Biography,* XI (1975); Moritz Steinschneider, "Abraham Judaeus-Savasorda und Ibn Ezra," in his *Gesammelte Schriften,* Heinrich Malter and Alexander Marx, eds. (1925). For the version of Archimedes probably by Plato see Marshall Clagett, *Archimedes in the Middle Ages,* I (1964), 16–17. The Theodosius attribution is based entirely on an unsubstantiated statement in Jean Pena's preface to his edition of the Greek text of the *Spherics* (1558).

CHARLES S. F. BURNETT

[See also **Abraham bar Ḥiyya; Archimedes in the Middle Ages; Astrology/Astronomy; Translation and Translators.**]

PLATYTERA, a figural type of the Madonna and Child in which a portrait of the Christ Child is suspended in front of the Virgin standing in *orans* position. Some scholars suggest this is a variation of the Annunciation motif, representing Christ at his inception. The motif is found in Christian iconography of the Eastern and Western churches, but reached its greatest popularity in the post-Iconoclastic period in the Greek East.

BIBLIOGRAPHY

Ormond Maddock Dalton, *Byzantine Art and Archaeology* (1911), 674; André Grabar, *Christian Iconography* (1968), 128.

JENNIFER E. JONES

[See also **Blachernitissa; Orant** (both with illustrations).]

PLAY OF DANIEL, an ecclesiastical music drama from the twelfth and thirteenth centuries, based on Old Testament material. The play, presenting the story of Daniel, begins with the ceremonial entrance of King Belshazzar and his use of sacred vessels pillaged from the Temple of Jerusalem at a riotous feast. When a warning appears written on the wall, Daniel is summoned to interpret it for the king. Belshazzar's predicted defeat in battle ensues, and Daniel is appointed counselor to the new king, Darius. When Daniel's power arouses jealousy among the courtiers, he is accused of treason and sent to a den of lions, from which he emerges unharmed, whereupon Darius accepts Daniel's God as his own. The play ends with a prophecy of the coming of Christ.

Two versions of the Daniel play survive in manuscript sources, both written in Latin verse of various metric types. The earlier one is from the late twelfth century and was written by Hilarius, a student of Abelard. It appears in the manuscript Paris, Bibliothèque Nationale, MS lat. 11331. The manuscript contains no music, although the play includes rubrics directing the actors to sing. This version contains an apocryphal episode in which a sword-wielding angel closes the mouths of the lions, while another summons the prophet Habakkuk to bring food to Daniel.

The second play, better known to modern scholars because of its impressive music, is from the cathedral school of Beauvais. It was probably written slightly later than the Hilarius version, in the early thirteenth century, and appears in British Library MS Egerton 2615. The Beauvais play follows the presentation of the earlier one, including the apocryphal incident. It differs, however, in the inclusion of a prologue sung by the courtiers of Belshazzar, in extensive use of dialogue between Daniel and the two kings, and in the character of Darius, who is far nobler and less irascible. The text of the Beauvais play includes a few phrases in French, which seem to provide more emphasis than explanation.

Much of the music for the Beauvais play is in the form of the liturgical prosa, that is, syllabic declamation of text with some ornamented passages, and melodies that are largely diatonic and triadic in motion. The melodic lines are extremely well crafted, and some—most notably the processionals *Astra tenenti* and *Jubilemus regi nostro*—have strongly marked declamatory rhythms that suggest metrical interpretation. There are over fifty distinct melodies in the play, of which only one—the concluding hymn *Nuntium vobis fero*—can be placed in the liturgical repertory. It points to the Christmas season, as does the inclusion of a prophecy concerning Christ. The play cannot be identified with any specific day in the liturgical calendar, but it would seem to have been performed during Advent or the week of Christmas.

BIBLIOGRAPHY

Solange Corbin, "Le *Jeu de Daniel* à l'abbaye de Royaumont," in *Cahiers de civilisation médiévale,* 3 (1960); Noah Greenberg, ed., *The Play of Daniel* (1959); William L. Smoldon, ed., *The Play of Daniel* (1960).

MARCIA J. EPSTEIN

[See also **Drama, Liturgical.**]

PLAY OF HEROD, one of the themes in liturgical music drama in the twelfth and thirteenth centuries. It is also known in various sources as the *Officium stellae* or *Officium regum trium.* The play represents the journey of the Magi to Herod's court and their visit to the newborn Christ. Some versions of the play, of which there are twelve in various states of preservation, include the Annunciation to the Shepherds. A number of apocryphal details are also found: the presence of midwives at the birth, the identification of the Magi as kings, and the assignment to them of dominions (Tarsus, Arabia, and Saba) and of proper names (usually Melchior, Caspar, and Balthasar). The Herod play is intended for performance on Epiphany (6 January) and is usually followed in the manuscript sources by plays of the Holy Innocents ("Slaughter of the Innocents" or *Ordo Rachelis*). Both plays typically depict the character of Herod as a madman prone to fits of rage, represented on stage with stylized histrionics.

The best-known Herod play is the one appearing in the so-called Fleury Playbook (Orléans, Bibliothèque Municipale, MS 201). Its text is drawn in part from the Gospels of Matthew and Luke, but much of the text and most of the music are newly composed. A number of rubrics indicating dramatic gestures and staging are included in the manuscript.

BIBLIOGRAPHY

Madeleine Bernard, "L'Officium Stellae nivernais," in *Revue de musicologie,* 51 (1965); Walther Lipphardt, "Das Herodesspiel von Le Mans nach den Handschriften Madrid, Bibl. Nac. 288 und 289," in *Organicae voces: Festschrift Joseph Smits van Waseberghe* (1963); William L. Smoldon and Noah Greenberg, eds., *The Play of Herod* (1965).

MARCIA J. EPSTEIN

[See also **Drama, Liturgical; Fleury Playbook.**]

PLAYING CARDS, MASTER OF THE (*fl.* 1430–1445), an anonymous engraver active along the upper Rhine, probably in Strasbourg and Alsace. The most accomplished early engraver before Master E. S. (*d. ca.* 1467), he employed outline and delicate parallel hatching to suggest texture and light. His playing cards include elegant and varied single figures for the court cards. Animals, birds, flowers, and wild-appearing men are arranged in decorative combinations to form the numbered cards.

Designs from his series of playing cards, which are preserved largely in the Kupferstich-kabinett, Dresden, and the Bibliothèque Nationale, Paris, were widely copied, especially in manuscripts after about 1440. As the playing cards incorporate designs used in earlier manuscript illuminations, the engravings evidently served to transmit established designs.

The few surviving engravings of religious subjects that can be attributed to the engraver show links to Upper Rhenish painting and were also influential, though in a more limited geographical area.

BIBLIOGRAPHY
Anne H. van Buren and Sheila Edmunds, "Playing Cards and Manuscripts: Some Widely Disseminated Fifteenth-century Model Sheets," in *Art Bulletin,* 56 (1974); Max Geisberg, *Das älteste gestochene deutsche Kartenspiel vom Meister der Spielkarten (vor 1446)* (1905), and *Die Anfänge des Kupferstiches,* 2nd ed. (1924); Hellmut Lehmann-Haupt, *Gutenberg and the Master of the Playing Cards* (1966); Max Lehrs, *Geschichte und kritischer Katalog des deutschen, niederländischen und französischen Kupferstichs im XV. Jahrhundert,* I (1908); Martha Wolff, "The Master of the Playing Cards: An Early Engraver and His Relationship to Traditional Media" (diss., Yale, 1979).

MARTHA WOLFF

[See also **E. S., Master; Engraving.**]

"Three of Birds." Engraved playing card by the Master of the Playing Cards, before *ca.* 1440. (Designs copied in the later *Hours of Catherine of Cleves.*) PARIS, BIBLIOTHÈQUE NATIONALE, KH 25 rés. 4°

PLEIER, DER (*fl.* mid thirteenth century), an epigonic author of three lengthy Arthurian epics (romances): *Garel von dem blüenden Tal* (Garel of the flowering valley), 21,310 short lines in rhymed couplets, with about 100 lines missing from the beginning; *Tandareis und Flordibel,* 18,339 short lines mostly in rhymed couplets; and *Meleranz,* 12,834 short lines in rhymed couplets. Very little is known about the author. He wrote between 1260 and 1280, and his rhymes point to Austria, perhaps to the Salzburg area. His pen name may very well mean "(glass) blower," perhaps referring metaphorically to his writing technique of using old materials, melting them down, and fusing them into new works.

Garel. Ekunaver of Kanadic provokes Arthur and his court by sending his messenger, the giant Karabin, who announces, after a year's term, a revenge campaign. Arthur accepts this declaration of war. Garel, one of his young knights, follows Karabin in order to explore Ekunaver's lands. On his trip Garel gets involved in several adventures, defeats many knights and princes and helps others, obliging all of them to provide him with manpower, and finally frees Queen Laudamie of Anferre from her oppressor, the monster Vulganus, and marries her. With his old and new troops he is able to defeat Ekunaver before Arthur arrives at the battlefield. The enemies arrange a reconciliation and join for a splendid celebration. Garel arranges several marriages, and Ekunaver and Garel found a monastery on the battlefield.

The *Garel* was written as a reaction to *Daniel von dem blüenden Tal* by Der Stricker (*ca.* 1230). Daniel is an overly cunning hero, an antihero in Pleier's view. Garel, in contrast, is again on the level of high knightly ideals.

Tandareis. At Arthur's court the youthful crown prince Tandareis of Tandernas and Flordibel, an oriental princess, fall in love, but they cannot admit this publicly because Arthur had promised to guard Flordibel's honor and to kill anybody who might want to gain her love. The couple flee to Tandernas. Arthur besieges the castle, and several fights occur. But Gawan, one of Arthur's knights, is able to reconcile Arthur and the couple under the condition that Flordibel entrust herself to his wife, Jenover, whereas Tandareis shall travel to foreign countries in order to establish himself as a real knight. In two series of adventures he defeats many robbers and giants and frees numerous imprisoned knights and captive ladies, including the oppressed Queen Albiun. Arthur keeps learning about his many victories and tries to get him back to his court, but his attempts fail. He then decides to organize a tournament once a month for one year. Tandareis appears three times incognito and wins, every time in a different guise. He is recognized, however, but refuses to return to court. Arthur tries other ways to get him back and finally succeeds. Arthur and Tandareis come to a definitive reconciliation, Tandareis is reunited with Flordibel, and, after some more complications (other ladies claim Tandareis!), the marriage takes place at Arthur's court, at a splendid celebration during which several other couples are also married. Tandareis and Flordibel return to the kingdom of Karmil, where the coronation is celebrated at Pentecost.

Meleranz. Meleranz, the crown prince of France, decides to go to Arthur's court at the age of twelve. On his way he encounters the young Queen Tydomie of Kameric under a lime tree. They fall in love, but Meleranz rides on to court. Two years later he is dubbed a knight; at this occasion he receives from Tydomie a belt, a wreath, and a clasp, clear signs of her lasting love, and he resolves to return to the place under the lime tree. On his way back he gets involved in three interconnected adventures; he is victorious in each, but learns that Tydomie is about to be married to King Libers by her uncle Malloas. Meleranz conquers both. During a splendid celebration, which Arthur as well as the king of France attend, the wedding takes place; the marriage will be happy and blessed with two sons and one daughter.

Although the Pleier claims French narratives as sources for his works, none has been found. Instead, his achievement appears to consist of using narrative plots and motifs as they occur in "classical" Arthurian works by Hartmann von Aue, Wolfram von Eschenbach, Wirnt von Grafenberg, and others, as well as in Gottfried's *Tristan* and in *Daniel* by the Stricker, and recombining them into new stories, which are generally well constructed and pleasantly narrated. Most characters are taken from such earlier German epics; the author draws heavily and without making mistakes upon the genealogies of the Arthurian and other dynasties that are to be found in Wolfram's *Parzival* and *Titurel,* adding on to the characters, filling narrative lacunae, and raising minor figures to major protagonists. There are strong restorative trends in these works, and there is a decidedly nostalgic flavor (see the twenty *Garel* frescoes from about 1400 in Runkelstein Palace near Bozen). From the way the Pleier writes, it may be inferred that he appeals to a reading public well versed in Arthurian fiction; thus he consciously and adroitly establishes an encompassing but specific narrative world. The reading pleasure of his public consisted mainly in recognizing and enjoying the old in the new as well as the new in the old.

BIBLIOGRAPHY

Sources. Garel von dem blüenden Tal: Ein höfischer Roman aus dem Artussangenkreise von dem Pleier, Michael Walz, ed. (1892); *Meleranz,* Karl Bartsch, ed. (1861, repr. 1974); *Tandareis und Flordibel: Ein höfischer Roman,* Ferdinand Khull, ed. (1885).

Studies. Karin R. Gürttler, *"Künec Artûs der guote": Das Artusbild der höfischen Epik des 12. und 13. Jahrhunderts* (1976), esp. 239–262; Walter Haug, "Paradigmatische Poesie: Der spätere deutsche Artusroman auf dem Weg zu einer 'nachklassischen' Ästhetik," in *Deutsche Vierteljahrsschrift für Literaturwissenschaft und Geistesgeschichte,* **54** (1980); Michel Huby, *L'adaptation des romans courtois en Allemagne au XIIe et au XIIIe siècle* (1968); Peter Kern, *Die Artusromane des Pleier: Untersuchungen über den Zusammenhang von Dichtung und literarischer Situation* (1981); Paul Piper, *Höfische Epik,* II (1892/1895), 302–369; John Lancaster Riordan, "A Vindication of the Pleier," in *Journal of English and Germanic Philology,* **47** (1948).

PETRUS W. TAX

[See also **Arthurian Literature; German Literature; Romance; Gottfried von Strassburg; Hartmann von Aue; Stricker, Der; Wirnt von Grafenberg; Wolfram von Eschenbach.**]

PLENITUDO POTESTATIS, the fullness of power ascribed to the pope in canonist writings. Leo I (440–461) first used the term to describe the relation of pope and bishops (Letter 14.1). The power of binding and loosing given by Jesus to Peter (Matthew 16:19) was the spiritual basis of *plenitudo;* the recognition of this grant in the so-called Donation of Constantine (*ca.* 754–796) provided a secular basis.

In the thirteenth and fourteenth centuries, *plenitudo* was debated between expansionists, usually decretalists connected with the centralizing tendencies of the Roman curia, and limitationists, usually decretists and those who emphasized an episcopal framework for papal authority.

Whereas early decretists proposed a jurisdictional *plenitudo* exercised for the good of the church, comparing it to the *plena potestas* invested in any administrator, expansionists dominated the period after Innocent III (1198–1216). Decretalists such as James of Viterbo (*ca.* 1255–1308), Matthew of Aquasparta (1240–1302), and Egidius Colonna (*ca.* 1247–1316) greatly expanded the concept, making *plenitudo* the personal possession of the pope. As vicar of Christ and vicar of God, the pope stood above church law and could even change the natural (divine) law; this line of argument was most fully realized by Boniface VIII (1294–1303). Scholastic theologians especially opposed this interpretation.

The abdication of Celestine V (1294) and the perceived excesses of Boniface VIII and John XXII (1316–1334) encouraged a renewed emphasis on limitation, often from episcopal or regal perspective, as exemplified by Marsilius of Padua (*ca.* 1275–1342) and John of Paris (*ca.* 1240–1306): the pope exercised *plenitudo* for the good of the church and only in emergencies. The Western schism ended the debate, with conciliarists such as Francesco Zabarella (1360–1417) and John Gerson (1363–1429) arguing for limitation of the pope's power.

Official use of the term—in letters of Innocent III and Innocent IV (1243–1254) and in a decree of Lyons II (1274)—usually appeared in documents addressed to Eastern Christians. Clement VI employed the phrase in a letter to the Armenians in 1351. The Council of Ferrara-Florence reverted to *plena potestas* in *Laetentur coeli* (1439), and, following its reasoning, Vatican I (1870) defined *plenitudo* as the pope's jurisdictional authority over other bishops.

BIBLIOGRAPHY

Walter Ullmann, *Medieval Papalism* (1949); Brian Tierney, *Foundations of the Conciliar Theory* (1968); John A. Watt, *The Theory of Papal Monarchy in the Thirteenth Century* (1966).

STEPHEN WAGLEY

Pleurants from the tomb of Philip the Bold by Claus Sluter, Dijon, 1404–1405. PHOTO: WIM SWAAN

Descent from the Cross. Panel from the Breslau altarpiece by Hans Pleydenwurff, 1462. GERMANISCHES NATIONALMUSEUM, NUREMBERG, INV. NR. GM 1127

[See also **Boniface VIII, Pope; Church, Latin; Conciliar Theory; Councils, Western (1311–1449); Egidius Colonna; Gerson, John; Innocent III, Pope; John XXII, Pope; John of Paris; Leo I, Pope; Marsilius of Padua; Matthew of Aquasparta; Papacy, Origins and Development of; Pope; Schism, Great; Zabarella, Francesco.**]

PLEURANT, a mourning figure (weeper), usually a statue, placed on or near a tomb. First used in the thirteenth century to indicate a funeral, *pleurants* were carved with great emotional effectiveness for the tomb of Philip the Bold by Claus Sluter and Claus de Werve (1404/1405, Dijon, Musée des Beaux Arts), and frequently imitated by their followers during the fifteenth century.

BIBLIOGRAPHY

Henri David, *Claus Sluter* (1951), 107–128, 143–160; Musée des Beaux Arts, *Les pleurants dans l'art du moyen âge en Europe,* 2nd ed., rev. (1971).

ROBERT G. CALKINS

[See also **Burgundy, Duchy of; Sluter, Claus.**]

PLEYDENWURFF, HANS (*ca.* 1420–1472), painter in Nuremberg. Like Caspar Isenmann and Hans Schüchlein, he was strongly influenced by contemporary Flemish art, particularly in details of surfaces, lights, and textures. Pleydenwurff trained Michael Wolgemut. His major works are *Calvary* (*ca.* 1460), *Descent from the Cross* of the Breslau altarpiece (1462), and a portrait diptych of Count George of Löwenstein (*ca.* 1456) with *Man of Sorrows.*

BIBLIOGRAPHY

Alte Pinakothek München, *Altdeutsche Malerei* (1963), 166–170; Alfred Stange, *Deutsche Malerei der Gotik,* IX (1958), 41–44.

LARRY SILVER

[See also **Flemish Painting; Gothic Art: Painting; Isenmann, Caspar; Schüchlein, Hans; Wolgemut, Michael.**]

PLICA (Latin, "fold"), the square-notation equivalent of the liquescent neumes of early plainsong notation. The plica appears as a line added to the ordinary form of a single-note symbol or ligature, and indicates a second pitch either lower (, , etc.) or higher (, , etc.) than the last notated pitch. The melodic interval between the two notes is left unspecified, but usually is a second. In polyphonic notation, however, the plica lost its connection with liquescence, and instead indicated the rhythmic division into two shorter notes of the note to which it is attached. In Notre Dame notation the plica was common, since it was the simplest way to break the regular pattern of the rhythmic mode *(fractio modi)*, whereas in later polyphony not based on the rhythmic modes, it was less useful, and is rarely found after the *Roman de Fauvel.*

BIBLIOGRAPHY
David Hiley, "Plica," in *The New Grove Dictionary of Music and Musicians,* XV (1980).

DIANE L. DROSTE

[See also **Fauvel, Roman de; Musical Notation; Neumes; Plainsong.**]

POCKETBOOKS. Miniature, pocket-sized codices were a not uncommon feature of ancient and medieval book production in both the Latin West and Byzantine East. Such books often have a "private" character and seem to have served essentially personal needs. Among the most popular works transcribed in this format were Psalters and texts useful to people who traveled extensively.

BIBLIOGRAPHY
Annemarie Weyl Carr, "Diminutive Byzantine Manuscripts," in *Codices Manuscripti: Zeitschrift für Handschriftenkunde,* **6** (1980); Monique-Cécile Garand, "Livres de poche médiévaux à Dijon et à Rome," in *Scriptorium,* **25** (1971).

MICHAEL MCCORMICK

[See also **Manuscript Books, Binding of; Manuscript Books, Production of.**]

PODESTA (from the Latin *potestas,* power), the highest official in a medieval Italian commune. The term apparently first applied to officials appointed to or recognized for north Italian towns about 1160 by the emperor Frederick I Barbarossa. Most central and north Italian towns were experimenting with the appointment of their own podestas by the closing decades of the twelfth century.

The institution of the podesta resulted from efforts to limit family and factional strife within towns. Some towns briefly appointed natives to that office, but in an effort to ensure impartiality, the selection of men from another town or rural area, thought of as foreigners, quickly became the rule. The appearance of the podesta also reflected the attempt of wealthy burghers of non-noble origin, especially merchants, bankers, and manufacturers, to share governmental power with members of the hitherto dominant urban nobility that controlled the communal consular regimes. While in some towns for a few decades the offices of consul and podesta might alternate or even coexist, by about the 1220's podestarile regimes were the rule. Communal councils offered the podestaship to nobles from friendly towns or to rural lords. Some nobles seemed to make partial careers of holding podestaships and other high offices; a minority actually studied law themselves.

The podesta exercised a wide variety of important executive, legislative, judicial, military, and police functions during his six- or twelve-month term of office. Accompanied by an entourage of his own judges, armed cavalrymen, and lesser followers whom he ordinarily paid from his own stipend, the podesta presided over major communal councils, headed the communal court system, commanded a town police force, and often led the town's military forces in time of war.

Communal governments hedged these powerful officials with numerous and minute restrictions to prevent favoritism to local persons or factions, abuses of power, and, worst of all, attempted subversion or overthrow of the communal regime itself. A podesta generally could not succeed himself or even return to office until the passage of a constitutionally designated period of time, usually a year or more. A podesta was paid in installments (typically every two months), and a portion of his stipend was withheld until the completion of the "syndication" or official review and audit of his regime at the end of his term of office.

As early as the mid thirteenth century, in many towns the authority of the podesta was limited by the appearance of a rival official, the captain of the people (*capitano del popolo*), who headed an organization composed largely of middle- or upper-ranking burghers that tended to become incorporated within the communal constitution. In many late-thirteenth-century towns dominant urban oligarchies gradually restricted the powers of the podesta, exercising increasing authority themselves. In other towns native or foreign *signori* or lords assumed rule for themselves, their families, or factions. The *signori* either took the title of podesta themselves or turned that official into a functionary who served their own interests under the guise of continuing the previous podestarile regime.

BIBLIOGRAPHY
William M. Bowsky, *A Medieval Italian Commune: Siena Under the Nine, 1287–1355* (1981); Vittorio Franchini, *Saggio di ricerche su l'instituto del podestà nei comuni medievali* (1912); John Kenneth Hyde, *Society and Politics in Medieval Italy* (1973), 101–123; Daniel P. Waley, *The Italian City-Republics* (1969).

WILLIAM M. BOWSKY

[See also **Commune; Consuls, Consulate; Italy, Rise of Towns in.**]

POETA SAXO (*fl.* late ninth century), the name ascribed to the author of the four books of the *Annales de gestis Caroli Magni imperatoris* (Annals of the deeds of the emperor Charlemagne), to which a fifth book, *De vita et obitu eiusdem* (About the life and death of Charlemagne), is added. The whole work, comprising 2,693 lines, is sometimes referred to as the *Gesta Caroli metrica* (The metrical deeds of Charlemagne) and was composed approximately one hundred years after the events it describes. Each of the first four books covers a decade in the typical year-by-year manner of historical annals—they are in fact closely modeled on the so-called *Annals of Einhard*—while the fifth book gives a summary of the life and personality of Charlemagne using Einhard's *Vita Caroli Magni* as its basis. From a historical point of view, Saxo's work is virtually unoriginal and therefore of little interest, though it should be noted that Saxo stops using the *Annals of Einhard* at the year 801 and thereafter apparently follows another brief, faulty, and no longer extant source. This unknown work—perhaps written in Halberstadt—would appear to have been related to the *Annals of Hersfeld,* and there may also have been other sources. The first four books are written in simple hexameters, the fifth in elegiac distichs.

Historians have been especially disturbed by Saxo's report that Charlemagne made a peace treaty with the Saxons in Salz in 803, a treaty which has been variously declared spurious and defended as genuine. Georg Hüffer strongly endorses the latter view in his *Korveier Studien,* where he also argues that Saxo's epic is of considerable poetic value. Hüffer's methods of historical investigation are, however, highly questionable. Thus his opinion, for instance, that the Poeta Saxo was a well-read man who knew among others the works of Jerome, Vergil, Ovid, Statius, Boethius, Isidore, Sedulius, Arator, Venantius Fortunatus, and even the *Annals,* as well as the *Germania,* of Tacitus, cannot be conclusively proven.

The identity of the Poeta Saxo has not been settled. In the fifth book he refers to himself as a Saxon, and most investigators believe that he came from the monastery in Corvey. Some credence has been given to Pertz's identification of Saxo with Agius, the author of the *Dialogus Hathumothae* (Hathumod's dialogue, referring to the famous ninth-century abbess of Gandersheim) and the *Agii versus computistici* (The verse about numbers). But this attempt, despite Hüffer's revival of it, has not been successful. Interestingly enough, Paul von Winterfeld, the chief editor of the Poeta Saxo's work, accepts Hüffer's arguments.

Two manuscripts of Saxo's work are extant. *G,* now in Wolfenbüttel (no. 601), originally from the Saxon nunnery Lamespringe in the diocese of Hildesheim, thereafter in Helmstedt (no. 553), dates from the eleventh or twelfth century. Most of the early editions follow this manuscript, which was first inadequately edited by R. Reineccius in 1594 and copied by all later editors until Paul von Winterfeld reedited the text. The second manuscript, *B,* in Brussels (no. 1638–1649), dates from the fifteenth century. Winterfeld recognized that both *G* and *B* go back to the same archetype.

BIBLIOGRAPHY
Texts and translation. Monumenta Germaniae historica: Scriptores, I (1826), 227–279; *Monumenta Germaniae historica: Poetae latini aevi carolini,* IV (1909), 1–71; Mary E. McKinney, trans., *The Saxon Poet's Life of Charles the Great* (1956).

Studies. Bernhard E. Simson, "Der Poeta Saxo und der Friede zu Salz," in *Forschungen zur deutschen Geschichte,* **1** (1862); Georg Hüffer, *Korveier Studien: Quellenkritische Untersuchungen zur Karoliner-Geschichte* (1898), and reviews of Hüffer, by K. Brandi in *Westdeutsche Zeitschrift* (1900), W. Erben in *Historische Vierteljahrschriften,* **3** (1900), and O. Holder-Egger in *Deutsche Literaturzeitung,* **14** (1900); Max Manitius, *Geschichte der lateinischen Literatur des Mittelalters,* I (1911), 583–584.

EVELYN SCHERABON FIRCHOW

[See also **Agius of Corvey; Carolingian Latin Poetry; Carolingians; Charlemagne; Einhard; Epic, Latin.**]

POETRY, LITURGICAL. The religious poetry that is used in the established liturgy of the church is

POETRY, LITURGICAL

called liturgical poetry. Other religious poetry, which remained only marginal to the liturgy, is called paraliturgical. Liturgical poetry consists predominantly of lyric hymns of praise, occasionally intermingled with legendary, epic, or biblical elements.

Beyond its function in the liturgy, liturgical poetry served European cultural development in many ways. It created standards for the poetic expression of Christian religious sentiments and established a poetic style and imagery that are often reflected even in the secular poetry of the Middle Ages and afterward. In addition, poets often experimented with new poetic forms while writing hymns. Perhaps the outstanding instance of this is Peter Abelard (*ca.* 1079–*ca.* 1142), whose 133 surviving hymns display an astonishing variety of innovative forms while also drawing on many literary sources that other hymn writers were not accustomed to use. Further, liturgical poetry contributed significantly to the growth of medieval music by providing new texts that could be set to new music.

The Latin hymns of the liturgy also formed the basis of religious poetry in the vernacular languages. Recent research indicates that the bulk of early vernacular religious poetry consists of translations of Latin liturgical poetry. These vernacular works served the needs of both lay people and the members of religious communities.

EARLY DEVELOPMENT

The earliest liturgical chants follow no metrical or rhythmic pattern and display no stanzaic character. Among these early chants are "Gloria in excelsis," "Te Deum laudamus," and the Easter chant "Exsultet iam angelica turba." The first is entirely anonymous. The second may have been written by Nicetas of Remesiana. The third has been attributed to Ambrose of Milan (*ca.* 340–397), but some scholars have disputed this attribution. In these early, free compositions, the exclusive theme is the praise of God.

We also have from Ambrose fourteen hymns with a recognizable metric structure and stanzaic form. All these hymns have the same form: eight stanzas, each with four iambic lines without regular rhymes. These hymns often reflect classical rhetoric and have poetic value.

Ambrose did not originally write these hymns for a definite place in the liturgy. Rather, they were "protest songs" that he used in his struggle against the Arians in Milan and in his resistance to imperial interference in church affairs. Still, the contents of some of them clearly indicate that they were to be associated with some of the feasts of the ecclesiastical year or with the cult of saints.

The Ambrosian hymns found their way into the usage of Benedictine monasteries. Other early hymns were not so fortunate. Only three fragments of the first known Latin hymns survive from the work of Hilary of Poitiers (*ca.* 320/325—*ca.* 367), who was unable to establish his hymns in permanent liturgical use.

In general, during this early period, local traditions prevailed over any unifying tendencies. Thus, Milan adopted the Ambrosian hymnal, but other areas of Italy created their own hymns, and Rome remained largely hostile to the use of hymns until the thirteenth century. Hymns of the Iberian Peninsula were often very long and involved, and they display few links with the religious poetry being produced elsewhere. On the other hand, hymns produced in England and Ireland often found their way into continental hymnbooks. Bede the Venerable, best known as a historian, was also the first important English hymnodist of the eighth century.

CAROLINGIAN INNOVATIONS

The early Carolingian poets produced several remarkable hymns—"Veni creator spiritus," "Ave maris stella," "Ut queant laxis resonare fibris," and "Gloria, laus, et honor tibi sit," the last, by Theodulf of Orléans, being intended for the Palm Sunday procession. In general, however, the production of the first Carolingian generation was thin. In later generations, hymn production picked up considerably.

The mid Carolingian era brought several important novelties into liturgical hymnody. It is at this time that tropes and sequences emerge as new hymn types in the liturgy. The tropes were additions to extant liturgical texts. These additions, many of them written in hexameters, show a great variation in form, style, and function. Numerous tropes were written in an esoteric style. They frequently contained classical allusions, and a dialogue format was not unusual. The sequence was a new form that relied heavily on repetition. Apart from the initial versicle, all the others are structured according to the scheme *aa, bb, cc,* etc. The sequence played an important role in the development of music throughout the Middle Ages.

Other formal developments of this period are the *versus* and the *Historia.* The *versus,* a processional hymn, came from St. Gall. In the *versus*, distichs are the normal form, and dramatizing tendencies are common. The *Historia* is a versified Divine Office. Its origins can be placed around the year 900. At first the *historia* had a mixed structure, largely prose, with the inclusion of a limited number of preexisting verses (such as antiphons and responsories). Only later did this form evolve into a predominantly versified entity. This development reached its peak in the twelfth and thirteenth centuries, when it was the norm for a single artist to create the entire Office, writing both the poetry and the music.

THE ELEVENTH CENTURY

From the middle of the eleventh century, Western hymnody was strongly influenced by the Byzantine akathistos hymn. This influence showed itself in the use of rich symbolism and imagery, of epitheta, and of salutation formulas, most of which derive directly from the akathistos hymn. The influence of this hymn lasted throughout the Middle Ages and even reached vernacular religious poetry by way of Latin intermediaries.

Also in the eleventh century, the sequence underwent a rapid development. Early sequences had displayed no regular rhythm and no rhyme, apart from occasional assonance at the end of versicles. Eleventh-century sequences show a gradual turn toward regularity. This is particularly visible in the famous Easter sequence "Victimae paschali laudes," by Wipo of Burgundy (*ca.* 1040), which is an outstanding representative of the transitional stage of sequence development. The dramatic elements in this sequence are very conspicuous, especially in the dialogue on the Resurrection between Mary Magdalene and the community of Christians.

Half a century after the composition of "Victimae paschali," the existence of a large number of rhythmically highly developed sequences with rhymes can be established in liturgical sources. They are called "regular" or "rhyming" sequences, and they represent a revolutionary stage in the history of Western versification.

THE TWELFTH CENTURY

The twelfth century saw the production of sequences that must be considered among the finest work in medieval Latin poetry. The name of the poet Adam of St. Victor has been attached to a number of outstanding "regular" sequences, although all may not have been composed by him.

A most remarkable monument of the twelfth century is the *Hymnarius Paraclitensis*, which Peter Abelard wrote for the convent of Heloise. Both formally and in terms of their content, Abelard's 133 surviving hymns are the most important liturgical poems of their time. In the hymns, Abelard employs twenty-one different stanza forms; most of these forms are his own creations. Abelard's sources go far beyond those employed by most hymnodists. Although he receives regular inspiration from the Bible and patristic writings, he also uses his own writings, anecdotes borrowed from Orosius and Macrobius, legends, Platonic ideas and terminology, and theological speculation.

Other twelfth-century hymn writers include Abelard's old adversary Bernard of Clairvaux, whose work is of decidedly inferior quality. Bernard's secretary Nicholas of Clairvaux did better. Other liturgical poets of the twelfth century are Peter the Venerable, Hugh of Orléans, Adalbert of Mende (or Adalbert III, bishop of Tournel), and Alan of Lille. Many hymns of this period are anonymous.

LATER DEVELOPMENTS

In the thirteenth century the most conspicuous liturgical hymns were composed by members of the Franciscan and Dominican orders. The versified Divine Office reached a high point in the work of the Franciscan Julian of Speyer. The Dominican Thomas Aquinas, best known as a theologian, may have written hymns for the feast of Corpus Christi that are among the most outstanding memorials of this new feast. The Franciscan John Peckham, archbishop of Canterbury, produced important liturgical texts for the feast of the Holy Trinity. Quantitatively the Milanese Origo Scaccabarozzi (*d.* 1293) stands in the foregound with his extensive production in a variety of forms.

Meanwhile, in the north and east of Europe, the work of missionaries was bearing fruit. Local saints gave local poets many opportunities to enrich the liturgy, and many of the new texts became popular beyond the lands of their origin. In Sweden, in particular, the fourteenth and fifteenth centuries brought a flourishing of compositions for the Divine Office.

Political events also occasionally contributed to the growth of hymnody. On the Iberian Peninsula, hymns celebrated Christian victories over the Muslims—in particular the battle of Río Salado in 1340.

The new Marian feasts required new hymns.

These were supplied by Philippe de Mézières, Johannes of Jetzenstein (Jan of Jenštejn), Adam Easton, and Raymond de Vineis, among others. The cult of the four doctors of the church also inspired new hymns.

In the fifteenth century the field of hymnody was invaded by humanism. The invasion was not successful. The production of new hymns according to pre-humanist models went on into the early seventeenth century, and only a close scrutiny of the individual texts reveals their late origins.

BIBLIOGRAPHY

Higinio Anglés, *Scripta musicologica,* José López-Calo, ed., 3 vols. (1975–1976); John F. Benton, "Nicolas of Clairvaux and the Twelfth-century Sequence," in *Traditio,* **18** (1962); S. Corbin, "Fêtes portugaises: Commémoraison de la victoire chrétienne de 1340 (Río Salado)," in *Bulletin hispanique,* **49** (1947); Richard L. Crocker, *The Early Medieval Sequence* (1977); Jacques Fontaine, *Études sur la poésie latine tardive d'Ausone à Prudence* (1980); Helmut Gneuss, *Hymnar und Hymnen im englischen Mittelalter* (1968); Heinrich Lausberg, *Der Hymnus "Ave maris stella"* (1976), and *Der Hymnus "Veni Creator Spiritus"* (1979); G. G. Meersseman, *Der Hymnos Akathistos im Abendland,* 2 vols. (1958–1960); Dag Norberg, *Notes critiques sur l'Hymnarius Severinianus* (1977), and *L'oeuvre poétique de Paulin d'Aquilée* (1979); Alf Önnerfors, *Mediaevalia: Abhandlungen und Aufsätze* (1977); Alejandro E. Planchart, *The Repertory of Tropes at Winchester,* 2 vols. (1977); Bruno Stäblein, *Monumenta monodica medii aevi,* I, *Hymnen* (1956); Wolfram von den Steinen, *Notker der Dichter und seine geistige Welt,* 2 vols. (1948); Joseph Szövérffy, *Peter Abelard's Hymnarius Paraclitensis,* 2 vols. (1975), *Psallat chorus caelestium: Religious Lyrics of the Middle Ages* (1983), and *A Concise History of Medieval Latin Hymnody* (1985); Kees Veelekoop, *Dies ire, dies illa: Studien zur Frühgeschichte einer Sequenz* (1978).

JOSEPH SZÖVÉRFFY

[See also **Abelard, Peter; Adam of St. Victor; Akathistos; Alan of Lille; Ambrose, St.; Carolingian Latin Poetry; Divine Office; Hilary of Poitiers, St.; Hugh (Primas) of Orléans; Hymns, Latin; Latin Meter; Mass Cycles; Music; Notre Dame School; Peckham, John; Peter the Venerable; Sequence; Theodulf of Orléans; Tropes.**]

POGOST, in medieval Russia, a permanently staffed tax-collecting point. Examples were those established by Princess Olga of Kiev in the mid tenth century to make annual tribute-gathering journeys unnecessary for the princes. The term *pogost* was also used to refer to a settlement in northern Russia large enough to have a church.

GEORGE P. MAJESKA

POILLEVILLAIN, NICHOLAS. See **Nicholas of Clamanges.**

POINTED ARCH. See **Arch.**

POITIERS, BATTLE OF. On 25 October 732 Charles Martel, the Frankish mayor of the palace, led a Frankish army to victory—somewhere between Poitiers and Tours—over a Muslim raiding party commanded by ᶜAbd al-Raḥman Ghāfiqī (emir of Spain, 731–732). From 721 to 732 Duke Eudo of Aquitaine had been campaigning unsuccessfully against several Muslim raiding bands operating in the south of Gaul. Not until the summer of 732 did these forces penetrate as far north as Bordeaux and Poitiers, and shortly before Charles gained his victory Eudo had been soundly defeated near the Garonne not far from Bordeaux.

Charles did not save Europe from Muslim conquest, as romantic traditions maintain. Indeed, conquest had never been in prospect for the Muslim raiders from Spain. Charles did, however, put an end to successful Muslim raiding while at the same time solidifying his own position of leadership in Frankish society.

The Battle of Poitiers has become famous for both historical and historiographical reasons. In the latter regard the battle is seen by many as a confirmation of views represented by Paul Roth, Heinrich Brunner, and Lynn T. White, Jr., that under Charles Martel the Franks changed from infantry to heavy cavalry, began using stirrups and specially fitted saddles for mounted shock combat, and plundered the church to create benefices, or fiefs, for vassals in an incipient feudal system. Almost every component of this famous old argument has been shown to be untenable, but the argument continues to circulate.

This Battle of Poitiers should not be confused with the English victory over a much larger French force during the Hundred Years War (19 September 1356). In that encounter, at nearby Maupertuis, the forces of Edward the Black Prince devastated the French army and took captive King John II, thus inaugurating one of the most difficult periods for the French monarchy.

BIBLIOGRAPHY

The battle and attendant circumstances, especially developments in the Arab world, are well treated in Jean-Henri Roy and Jean Deviosse, *La bataille de Poitiers* (1966). Military matters are well covered in Bernard S. Bachrach, *Merovingian Military Organization, 481–751* (1972), 92–112, esp. 101–105; Philippe Contamine, *La guerre au moyen âge* (1980), 315–320, and, in English, *War in the Middle Ages,* Michael Jones, trans. (1984). The bibliographical quarrels surrounding the battle and its significance are expertly discussed in Bernard S. Bachrach, "Charles Martel, Mounted Shock Combat, the Stirrup, and Feudalism," in *Studies in Medieval and Renaissance History,* 7 (1970).

THOMAS F. X. NOBLE

[See also **Carolingians and the Carolingian Empire; Charles Martel; Islam, Conquests of.**]

POKROV, meaning veil or protection, refers to a festival of the Orthodox church that was particularly venerated in Russia. The festival of Pokrov commemorated the miraculous appearance of the Mother of God in a church in Constantinople in the tenth century. She was seen by St. Andrew the Fool to remove her shining veil and extend it above the people praying—a symbol of the Virgin as the protectress of mankind and their intercessor before God. The icon which marks this festival pictures the miraculous event, with the Virgin in a pose of prayerful intercession.

ANN E. FARKAS

[See also **Icons, Russian; Russian Orthodox Church.**]

POLAND. Medieval Poland had no "ancient" history, for its lands and peoples had lain largely outside the sphere of classical civilization. Its history begins properly only in the tenth century with the formation of the state under the rule of the Piast dynasty and its entry into the historical consciousness of Christian Europe. Before this time, however, important developments had taken place that were the prerequisites for the achievements of the tenth century. This article begins therefore with a discussion of Poland's prehistory. The subsequent narrative utilizes chiefly a political framework, but includes at appropriate points a discussion of social and economic developments and of cultural achievements.

PREHISTORY

In the last centuries before the Christian era, the Slavic peoples were gradually differentiated into separate groups. Among the western tribes were those that eventually came to form the population of the Polish state. During the crucial period of the fifth, sixth, and seventh centuries of the Christian era, their previous material prosperity and relatively sophisticated political and social organization declined, in part because they themselves participated in the great disruptive völkerwanderungen of these years and in part because they were often subject, in greater or lesser degree, to other powerful groups such as the Huns and the Avars. By about 700 the proto-Polish population in the valleys of the Oder, Warta, and Vistula rivers could begin the recovery from this time of troubles. Their simple economy was based upon stockbreeding and farming, with iron plowshares in use in some areas as early as the fifth century. Indirect testimony from Byzantine sources provides a picture of a primitive social organization in which tribal assemblies of freemen (the *wiec*), presided over by elders, discussed all problems common to the group. This body decided issues democratically and chose military leaders who were given limited authority to rule. Such a society was not markedly different from that of contemporary Scandinavian and Baltic peoples. The following three centuries brought great changes.

One of these was economic. The proto-Polish tribes developed commercial contacts with the outside world. Trade with the Carolingians, Kievan Rus, Great Moravia, and the peoples of the Baltic and North seas is reflected in both archaeological artifacts and fragmentary written records. Another change was political. The military leaders (sing., *dux;* Polish *knędz,* later *książę*) sought to transform their tenuous political control into something more substantial, attempting to secure wealth and office for themselves and their heirs. They and their families established fortified settlements (*castrum;* Polish *gród*), which enabled them to extend their authority over the surrounding territory. They were supported in this by military retainers similar to the Germanic war band (*comitatus;* Polish *drużyna*). Gradually, through generations of protracted conflict, the earlier, more democratic tribal structure was replaced by one dominated by a new political aristocracy, which was able to reduce some of the peasantry to servitude and to obtain tribute from the remainder of the free population. These new leaders were thus able to exercise administrative control over their region, and throughout the eventual Polish lands there emerged a number of small-scale territorial organizations. At least five were located in Silesia in the upper Oder Valley; in central Poland, the most important center among several was that of the duke of the Polanie tribe (Polanes) in the vicinity of Gniezno; and in the south, the Wiślanie (Vislanes) controlled the region around Kraków.

These tribal states under the leadership of the dukes also waged war upon one another in an effort to consolidate even larger areas of control. Eventually, the whole region was dominated by only two, the Wiślanie and the Polanie. The duke of the former was sufficiently powerful (according to the ninth-century *Life of Methodius*) to be able for a while to resist expansion by Great Moravia to the south. Subsequently, however, this area fell under Moravian control. Along the reaches of the middle Warta, the state of the Polanes (from Polish *pole,* field) grew to include such previously independent fortified settlements as Poznań, Kruszwica, Ląd, and Kalisz (the last site having been mentioned as early as the second century by Ptolemy). Later medieval legend recorded the rise to power of the wheelwright Piast, from whom the future ruling dynasty took its name. More reliable tradition provides the names of several of his supposed descendants. They succeeded in making the Polanes so dominant that when their state came into contact with the medieval West, the whole region it eventually controlled became known as *Polonia,* that is, the land of the field-dwellers, the Poles.

From a cultural standpoint, the Slavic peoples of Poland shared a common heritage. Their language was sophisticated enough to include vocabulary for not only concrete objects but also abstract ideas. The religion included many fertility elements, reflecting the agricultural origins of the people. It also provided for the worship of personified deities derived from various natural phenomena and the physical environment. These were represented in stone and wooden images. The most important religious cult was fire or sun worship, and the chief god was called Swarog (Swarożyc). There is some evidence to suggest that by the tenth century a few political leaders were attempting to invest this religious heritage with political associations by identifying it with their authority.

THE FORMATION OF THE STATE (TO 1025)

In 963, according to the contemporary chronicler Widukind of Corvei and the somewhat later writer Thietmar of Merseburg, the Saxon count Gero came into contact with "King Misaca (Mieszko), under whose rule the Slavs were living." This took place in conjunction with efforts by both rulers to pacify the Veleti tribe, which lived between them. Eventually, Mieszko agreed to pay tribute to the Holy Roman emperor for the lands of the Veleti he might conquer along the western bank of the lower course of the Oder. This first historic mention of the Polish ruler suggests that the state over which he ruled was not merely a primitive organization. Additional testimony from 966 confirms this. The wandering Jewish merchant Ibrāhīm ibn-Ya^{c}qūb of Tortosa, who was in Prague early in that year, described Mieszko as the "king of the north" and the ruler of the most powerful of all the Slavic states. According to Ibrāhīm, Mieszko's territory stretched from the coasts of Prussia east to the Russian lands. He attributed to Mieszko an army of retainers numbering 3,000 knights, supported by tribute raised from the countryside. The lifetime of Mieszko (*d.* 992) was devoted to the twin goals of consolidating the Polish state and expanding its territory so as to enable it to compete with the other emerging states of Central and Eastern Europe.

One of the events closely connected with the first of these goals was the introduction into Poland of Christianity, which to this point had been without influence among the ruling groups in society. Mieszko recognized the cultural and political importance of conversion. In 964 (or 965), as part of an alliance with Bohemia, he arranged to marry Dobrava, the daughter of the Přemyslid duke there. She came to Poland with priests and Christian literature, and in 966 Mieszko and his court retinue were baptized. The importance of this for Poland's development cannot be overemphasized.

In the first place, Poland gained international respectability as a civilized nation. It ceased to be an outsider to the emerging civilization of the Latin and Germanic West. In the second place, by choos-

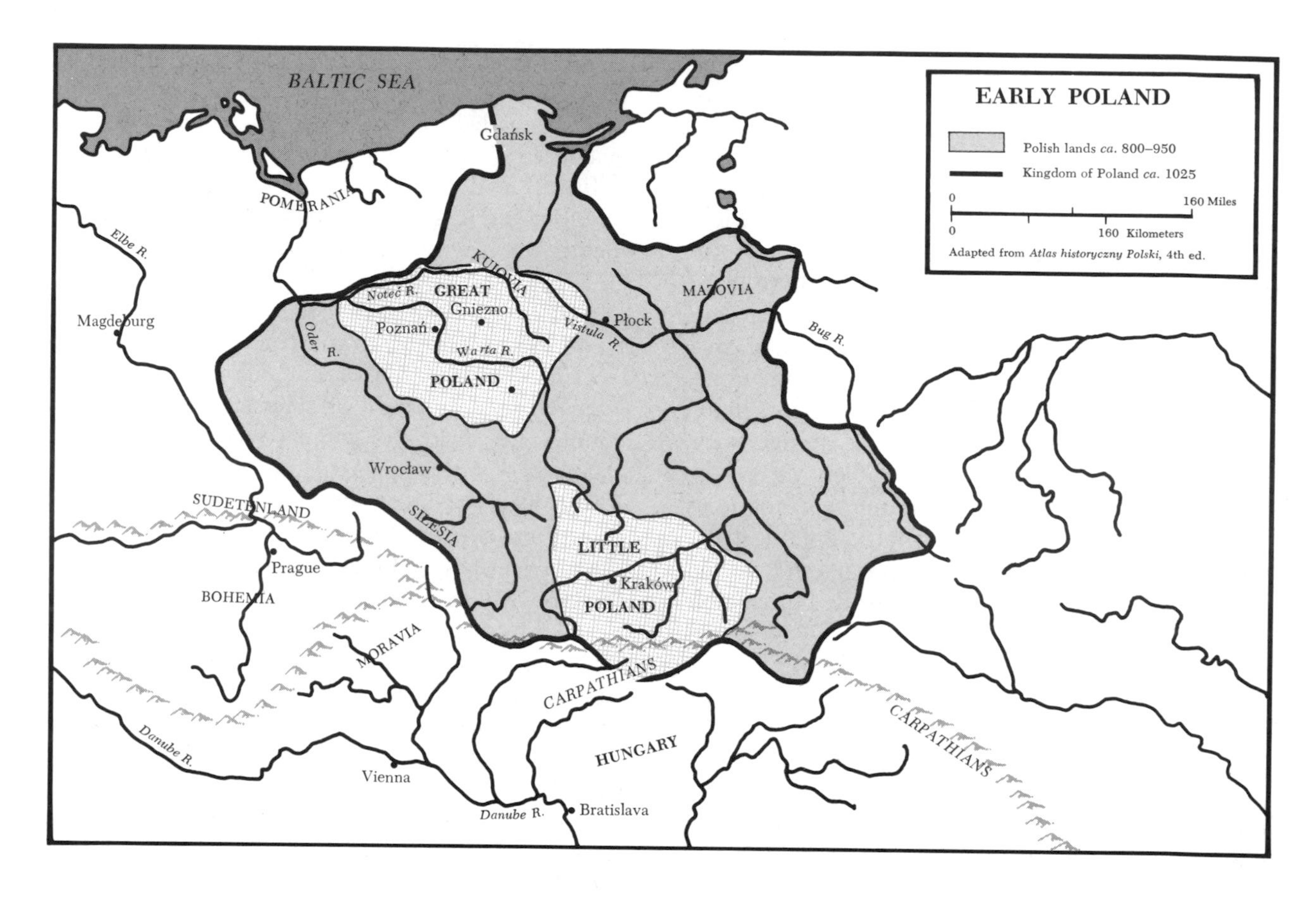

ing Latin and not Eastern Christianity (though there was probably no real alternative for Mieszko), Poland became by culture and religion an integral part of the Western, rather than the Byzantine, tradition. By contact with more highly developed Western centers of culture, education, and art, it was able to assimilate their achievements and produce its own distinctive culture. In the third place, the Christianization of Poland provided religious sanction for the new political framework that had been previously introduced into Polish society. The church supported Mieszko's authority as duke. In addition, by providing organizational models and trained officials, it helped him extend that authority and consolidate his internal administration. Finally, Mieszko's acceptance of Christianity and the eventual (though gradual) conversion of his people was implemented in such a way as to ensure religious and even political independence from any of Poland's neighbors. The Polish church was organized as a missionary diocese that included all of Mieszko's territories; under its bishop it was directly subject to the papacy. This direct dependency of Poland upon the Apostolic See was based in a grant by Mieszko to the pope, which dedicated Gniezno and its environs to St. Peter, thereby placing Poland under the special protection of the pope. (This grant is known only from an eleventh-century transcription entitled, from its incipit, the donation of *Dagome iudex*.) This ecclesiastical independence enabled Mieszko and his successors to resist much of the political dependence that accompanied the extension of the imperial German church with its proprietary character.

In the realm of international politics, Mieszko was also successful. By virtue of his alliance with Bohemia, he was for the time protected on the south so that he could pursue the conquest of the lower Oder territories. As imperial *amicus* and tributary, he reached the mouth of the Oder in 967. In 972 he defeated the German margrave Hodo, consolidating his control of the lands at the confluence of the Warta and Oder. Seven years later he successfully defended his Pomeranian holdings against Emperor Otto II. This ensured his control of the Baltic ports, such as Szczecin and Wolin, and allowed Poland to participate in the extensive commerce of the northern seas. The other focus of Mieszko's territorial policy was the south. In the 980's relations with Bohemia grew strained over control of Silesia and the region of Little Poland around Kraków (*Polonia minor*, in contrast to Great Poland, *Polonia maior*, the original state of the Polanes in central Poland). In the last four years of his life, Mieszko waged war successfully to incorporate these lands into Poland. At his death, Mieszko had united Slavic lands that were henceforth collectively to be known as Poland, rebuilt many castle towns and founded others, consolidated the political control of the duke, and successfully brought Poland into the economic, political, and cultural mainstream of Western civilization.

The oldest son of Mieszko was Bolesław, surnamed in Polish historiography "the Brave" (*r.* 992–1025). He quickly established himself as sole ruler. A personal friendship with the youthful Emperor Otto III ensured early cooperation between Germany and Poland. Otto came to Poland in 1000 to worship at the shrine of the martyred St. Adalbert (Vojtěch) from the Bohemian Slavnik family, who had been killed in 997 while trying to convert the Prussians. (This mission had political overtones, for Adalbert was acting on behalf of Bolesław in the duke's efforts to extend his own political control.) At Gniezno, the idealistic emperor confirmed the independence of the duke of Poland, and treated Bolesław as an equal partner with himself and the pope in the imperial program that Otto had formulated. The emperor also authorized the reorganization of the Polish church, with an archbishop in Gniezno as Polish metropolitan and bishoprics in Wrocław, Kołobrzeg, and Kraków.

This promising beginning was reversed following Otto's death in 1002. The new emperor, Henry II, allied with the pagan Veleti to attack Poland. Bolesław successfully defended himself in three separate, but related, wars. He was also able to pursue this conflict by diplomatic means, marrying his son Mieszko to the daughter of the count palatine of Lorraine, thus undermining Henry's support in the west. The peace between the empire and Poland, which was signed at Budziszyn (now Bautzen) in 1018, confirmed the territorial integrity of the Polish state and Bolesław's independence.

Another diplomatic marriage brought Bolesław and Poland into the affairs of the east. In 1018 he intervened in Russia on behalf of his son-in-law, Prince Svjatopolk. Bolesław led a successful expedition to Kiev, which he entered in triumph and from where he wrote the Holy Roman and Byzantine emperors to announce his victory. Bolesław gained important territories in the east as a result of this expedition, although Polish intervention was occasioned more by family loyalties than by any conscious expansionism to the east.

A third area of Bolesław's territorial ambitions was the south and southwest. He tried to unite Poland and Bohemia under his control, in part to present a stronger front against Emperor Henry II. He had only qualified success, however, retaining only Moravia for part of his reign. In 1025, Bolesław was crowned king, thus raising Poland to the same level as its neighbor Hungary. This coronation took place, probably with papal permission, shortly after the death in 1024 of Bolesław's enemy Henry II and only a few months before his own death (June 1025).

THE EARLY PIAST STATE (1025–1138)

In the four generations following the death of Bolesław the Brave, the fortunes of the Polish state and monarchy underwent several important changes. Mieszko II Lambert (*r.* 1025–1034) succeeded his father and for several years continued his expansionistic policies. His rule was not, however, without challenge. Internally, Mieszko's older brother Bezprym disputed his position as king. He was supported by segments of the Polish nobility, which resisted royal centralization. Externally, the Holy Roman Empire and Kievan Russia allied with one another both to regain and to obtain territories held by Mieszko. In 1031, the king fled the country, and Bezprym seized control. He renounced the royal title, recognized the suzerainty of the emperor, and deeded away several territories gained by previous rulers. Bezprym's rule was very precarious, however, and he died in 1032, probably at the hands of disappointed former supporters. In the aftermath, Mieszko was able to return to Poland, although his rule was now shared with relatives and he was unable to recover the royal dignity. At his death in 1034, the Polish state of the early Piasts lay in ruins.

Several factors helped account for this. The nobility, who had prospered under the rulers of the tenth and early eleventh centuries, now sought greater political and economic power for themselves. In addition, the earlier opportunities for expansion were no longer available, and the dissatisfied nobility were consequently less inclined to follow ducal or royal leadership. When Casimir I, eventually surnamed "the Restorer," succeeded his father, Mieszko II, in 1034, he was confronted by a Poland that had broken up into regional factions led by petty princelings. In this anarchy there occurred a widespread peasant insurrection directed in part against political and social authority, especially in the countryside. But it was also directed against the church and its leadership, and resulted in a nearly full-scale reversion to paganism. At the same time, the duke of Bohemia took advantage of the chaos in Poland to seize Silesia and ravage Great Poland. Only gradually was Casimir I able to rally support within the country from the threatened great nobles. Abroad, his support came especially from the empire, which feared Bohemia's rise at Poland's expense. By the late 1040's and early 1050's, order was beginning to be restored; but in comparison with the Poland of his grandfather, the state of Casimir I was a much reduced and weakened one at his death in 1058.

The Restorer's son, Bolesław II the Bold, was still a teenager in that year. Nevertheless, he pursued from the beginning an activist policy, both internally and in foreign affairs. He intervened in Russia and in Hungary, regained Silesia, and took the side of Pope Gregory VII on the eve of the investiture conflict. This support won him papal authorization for a royal coronation on Christmas Day 1076. In addition, he was able to complete the resurrection of the Polish church under the archbishop of Gniezno, now with bishops in Poznań, Wrocław, Płock, and Kraków, which henceforth became the royal capital. Bolesław's very aggressiveness, however, roused the opposition of the nobility. They successfully challenged the king and eventually drove him into Hungarian exile in 1079; he died there two or three years later. One figure in the opposition was apparently Bishop Stanisław of Kraków, whom Bolesław executed and who ironically became, through his putative martyrdom, the patron saint of Poland. Another figure was the king's younger brother, Władysław Hermann (*d.* 1102), a puppet of the centrifugal forces within the country. His nominal rule as his brother's successor was characterized by the decline of Poland's international position and the acceptance of imperial influence. Internally, central power was destroyed by the great nobles, who successfully partitioned rule of Poland between Władysław and his two sons after 1097.

The younger son, Bolesław III the Wry-mouthed, restored some of the dignity and authority of the duke. He relied chiefly upon the lesser knights, who were anxious to aggrandize themselves at the expense of the greater nobility. After his father's death, he drove his brother into exile, made alliances with Hungary and Kievan Russia, and repelled an invasion by Emperor Henry V. By successfully pursuing the recovery of lost territories and by bringing new ones, such as the district of Lubusz, under Polish political and ecclesiastical control, Bolesław III was able to provide the knights with opportunities for the power and wealth they sought. Not surprisingly, however, the nobles resisted, and the end of Bolesław's reign was clouded by factional strife.

TERRITORIAL DISINTEGRATION (1138–CA. 1300)

At his death in 1138, Bolesław attempted to reach a compromise with the decentralizing tendencies that beset the monarchy. In his will he sought to regularize them by dividing the country into duchies, based roughly upon the older provinces. These were to be given to his sons, with the eldest entitled grand duke and holding Little Poland and Pomerania. Succession to the grand duchy was to be in the line of the oldest living brother or the oldest member of following generations. In order that some semblance of unity be preserved in disunity, the grand duke was to be accepted as *principatus,* or *senior,* as far as foreign and military affairs were concerned, and he was to have considerable say in ecclesiastical matters. This effort to stabilize the political organization of Poland was a daring experiment. Within two generations, however, it had failed. For the next century and a half, Poland was riven by petty particularism and political fragmentation.

Throughout the thirteenth century the political history of Poland was the history of these individual duchies. Eventually there were several branches of the dynasty ruling in Great Poland, Little Poland, Mazovia, Kujavia, and Silesia. Szczecin Pomerania (Western) and Gdańsk Pomerania (Eastern) came to be ruled by local dynasties. In Silesia and Mazovia further subdivisions into petty principalities took place. Beneath the surface of individual events, two major trends dominated the century. One was the interplay between centrifugal and centripetal forces in which narrow efforts by rulers of various Piast lines to aggrandize themselves were balanced by successive attempts of a more statesmanlike character that aimed at reunification. The other was the growing threat from abroad to the territorial integrity of the *regnum Poloniae,* a kingdom that continued to exist in the abstract despite the political disunity.

The first major effort at reunification came from Silesia. Duke Henry the Bearded of Wrocław (*r.* 1202–1238) and his son, Henry the Pious, united Silesia and Little Poland. This effort was cut short by the death of the latter in 1241 during the Mongol invasion of East Central Europe. Only in the 1280's was Duke Henry IV Probus of Wrocław able to revive these goals. He had obtained hegemony over Silesia and Little Poland and was making plans for a royal coronation when he died prematurely in 1290. A second effort to reestablish the Polish monarchy came from Great Poland. There was broad support for such a development there. The nobility feared foreign intervention. The Polish church, reformed under Archbishop Henry Kietlicz early in the thirteenth century, had never been territorially fragmented and favored the reestablishment of the monarchy. The knights saw in such a development their best hope for order and protection. Thus when Duke Przemysł II of Great Poland inherited Gdańsk Pomerania in 1294, giving him a claim to have united some Polish territories, Archbishop Jakub Świnka moved to crown him king the following year. Unfortunately, Przemysł was assassinated in 1296, probably at the hands of agents of the dukes of Brandenburg.

A third effort at reunification came, ironically, from abroad. King Václav (Wenceslas) II of Bohemia, who may have envisioned some kind of great Slav state, extended his control over most of Silesia in the wake of the death of Duke Henry IV Probus. In 1291 Václav seized control of Kraków and Little Poland from Duke Władysław Łokietek of Kujavia. Less than a decade later the Bohemian king moved to conquer Great Poland, which was by this time held by the same Władysław Łokietek. In 1300 Václav was crowned Polish king and, in an effort to legitimize his rule, married the daughter of Przemysł II. Thus at the beginning of the fourteenth century Poland had been reunited, though at the hands of a foreigner.

This foreign impact upon, and threat to, Poland was felt in other ways. In Silesia, for example, the gradual immigration of German settlers, the growth of a foreign bourgeoisie in the prosperous cities, and the successful extension of Czech political control caused the region to become increasingly detached from the *regnum*. To the west, the aggressive Ascanian duchy of Brandenburg sought to expand at Polish expense. Its dukes were successful in establishing the New March, a territorial wedge driven up the Warta, separating Great Poland and Western Pomerania. To the east, the Mongol invasions in 1241 and after initiated a menace to Polish security that lasted for more than a century. To the northeast, pagan tribes such as the Prussians, Yotvingians, and Lithuanians constantly harassed the borders. But it was in the north that the greatest threat lay. In 1226 the Knights of the Teutonic Order, a military-crusading group originally founded in the Holy Land in the late twelfth century, had accepted a vague invitation from Duke Conrad of Mazovia to assist him in the pacification and conversion of the aforementioned pagan tribes. The order did more than this, however. In the half century after 1230 they completed the conquest of Prussia and permanently established a powerful centralized state. They were territorially ambitious and increasingly hostile to Poland. That they were a major threat to the kingdom's territorial integrity was shown by their conquest of Gdańsk Pomerania in 1308 and 1309. By this time, however, a new era of political unification and development had begun.

SOCIETY AND ECONOMY

The economy of early medieval Poland was at first closely tied to the fortified castle towns, originally established by local rulers and later incorporated into the state of Mieszko I and his successors. The duke (or king) and his representatives (who were eventually called castellans) organized the economy of the surrounding countryside in order to support their own social, military, and nutritional requirements. The crafts and services that may be observed in the tenth and eleventh centuries were closely regulated by those who controlled the castle towns. Eventually around these castra there grew up suburbs whose function was in part tied to the needs of the ruler of the castle town. But in addition these suburbia had lives of their own, and their inhabitants engaged in trade, services, and specialized production. With this development in the twelfth and thirteenth centuries, a new form of town life may be observed. (One indication of this transition is the change in the word commonly used for town/city in Polish from *gród*, a fortified place, to *miasto*, from *miejsce*, place, that is, market or settlement place.) Poland's fortunate location on the trade routes, both north-south and east-west, facilitated and stimulated this development.

These changes in the urban life of Poland were complemented by developments in the countryside.

The nobility, which had previously been dependent upon the duke or his representatives, became wealthy and powerful, with estates of varying size, as the result of the evolution of the state in the tenth and early eleventh centuries. They gained numerous immunities and strove to limit the authority of the ruler over them on these estates. By the twelfth century, several families had been so successful in consolidating their holdings and rights that they formed an oligarchical challenge to central authority. The church also, which in the tenth century had derived most of its support from payments out of the duke's treasury, sought to obtain landed estates, the revenues and services from which would be directly controlled by individual bishops and abbots. For example, in the mid twelfth century it is estimated that the archbishop of Gniezno held more than a thousand peasant farms. In the face of these changes, it is not surprising that the position of the peasantry was also altered. The majority of them had held their land freely, though their economic service had been organized by the duke. Now they became increasingly dependent upon the local nobles. Particularly after the suppression of the peasant insurrection of the mid eleventh century, the peasantry was fundamentally a subject, servile population. Documents from this period and after refer less and less frequently to *rustici ducis* (the duke's peasants) and more and more to *servi* (serfs).

Not all the rural population sank into servitude. Relatively sparse settlement patterns, a steadily growing population, and technological improvements such as the wheeled plow, the three-field system, and new crops allowed many peasants to colonize areas not previously developed. Just as in Western Europe, the rural settlements that developed in Poland as a result were inhabited by free peasants who paid rent in either kind or money instead of owing services for their land. This internal colonization came earliest in Silesia and the foothills of Little Poland, but it eventually can be observed in Great Poland, Kujavia, and, to a lesser extent, Mazovia.

Such opportunities also attracted immigrants from abroad. The nature of their impact upon Polish society and culture has long been a controversial topic. In the course of the twelfth and thirteenth centuries, several waves of both rural and urban colonists from the west settled in Poland. Much of the colonization was carried out under the terms of German law (*de iure Teutonico*), most frequently in the Magdeburg version developed at Środa in Silesia (*ius Novi Fori Stredense*). Many of the settlers came from territories in the empire, though the Low Countries were also represented. Those who came into Lower Silesia, Western Pomerania, and Prussia ultimately changed the linguistic, cultural, and political character of the region, for these districts tended to become Germanized. In other areas, such as Upper Silesia, Little Poland, most of Great Poland, and (before 1308) Gdańsk Pomerania, the influx was less numerous, and the foreigners were eventually absorbed into Polish society. But the process was often a difficult one. Frequently, severe tensions existed between German artisans and merchants, who emerged as the urban patriciate in many places, and the lower social strata, who remained ethnically and linguistically Polish. In 1311 in Kraków, for example, there was open conflict when the German *advocatus* Albert, a civil administrator responsible to Duke Władysław Łokietek, led a revolt of burghers against Polish political authority.

Eventually, by the beginning of the fourteenth century, this colonization stimulated a Polish society and economy whose main characteristics had been defined in the early Middle Ages. Once their initial rents had been satisfied, the peasantry became an important part of a reciprocal economy with the relatively prosperous cities. This contributed greatly to the flourishing of Polish civilization in the late Middle Ages.

EARLY MEDIEVAL CULTURE

Polish cultural achievements in the period prior to 1300 were rooted in native traditions and local needs, but stimulated and shaped by developments and influences from the West. Out of the spiritual needs of the people came a number of religious compositions in both Latin and the vernacular. Saints' lives, for example, were particularly popular. One of the most important was the *Vita maior* (*ca.* 1253) of St. Stanisław. In addition to its religious content, it also had a political dimension. In describing how the dismembered body of the saint had miraculously grown together and become whole again, the author expressed the hope that this reunion might also be the destiny of divided Poland. The hymn was also a popular form of religious literature. Many hymns that were used in Poland were simply compositions in Latin from the West. In the case of the vernacular *Hymn to the Virgin* (*Bogurodzica,* literally Mother of God, from the Byzantine "Theotokos"), however, a native version was developed, perhaps as early as the end of the eleventh century. Beyond these contributions, mention should be made of a few fragments of court and folk literature and of now-lost writings. For example, Duke Henry IV Probus of Wrocław wrote excellent poetry in both Latin and the vernacular, though none of it is now extant.

Formal historical writing was also an important achievement in this period. There were a number of court annals, one of which rose above a narrow preoccupation with the local scene. Between 1116 and 1119 a Benedictine monk known as Gallus Anonymous composed his *Cronicae et gesta ducum sive principum Polonorum.* This rhythmical narrative of great power and beauty retold some of the early legends of Poland and celebrated the ideal of Polish unity. It concentrated, in much the same way as the Western chansons de geste, upon the great deeds of the ruling dukes of Poland (the *domini naturales*), in particular those of Bolesław the Wrymouthed. Though a foreigner, Gallus was sympathetic to, and proud of, Poland. According to him, it was "rich in gold and silver, bread and meat . . . and has never been conquered by anyone. The air is healthy, the land fertile, and there are valiant soldiers and hardworking peasants. . . ." The *Chronicon comitis Petri* stands in this same literary tradition. Written also in the twelfth century (though transmitted only in several versions at a later date), this Latin chanson concentrated upon the legendary activities of one of the great nobles, Peter Włostowicz of Silesia, whose historical deeds had been a challenge to ducal authority.

Two great historiographical monuments were written in the thirteenth century. The first was the *Cronica de gestis principum ac regum Poloniae* of Vincent Kadłubek, the bishop of Kraków (*d.* 1223). Educated in the West, perhaps at Paris and Bologna, Kadłubek was a great admirer of Duke Casimir the Just of Little Poland (*d.* 1194), who figures as one of the heroes of the narrative. The literary quality of this work is high, though the style is typical of the grandiloquent rhetorical tradition of the age. The author conceived his work as a linkage of Poland to the glories of antiquity, and as a result the early sections are full of legend. As Kadłubek approached the events of his own age, the historical quality of the narrative improved markedly. He told the story of all the divided Polish duchies, but he emphasized Little Poland as the focus and bearer of the true tradition of the united regnum. The second history of importance was the *Chronica Poloniae Maioris,* prepared by Godisław Baszko, an ecclesiastic in Ponznań who died prior to 1297/1298. Baszko told the history of the Poles from legendary times until 1272. He was a fierce partisan of Duke, eventually King, Przemysł II, and he emphasized the leadership of the Great Poland tradition within the regnum. Although he presented forcibly the ideal of a unified kingdom, he was systematic and critical in his utilization of sources. As a result, his narrative has a high value.

In the area of the fine arts and architecture there were several important achievements. The sculptural styles of the Rhineland, Burgundy, and northern Italy were adapted to the aesthetic needs of the native aristocracy. For example, in the Premonstratensian nunnery in Strzelno, the sculpture from the last third of the twelfth century, particularly on the church columns, depicted the moral and religious implications of the conflict between the material and the spiritual. In these representations, an artistic naturalism and a feeling for nature are quite evident. One of the best examples of Romanesque art from the period is the set of great bronze doors on the cathedral in Gniezno. Eighteen separate panels, dating from the late twelfth century, retell the legend of the life and martyrdom of St. Adalbert. The contemporary bronze doors of the cathedral in Płock, while also impressive, are inferior to Gniezno in their fluidity and depiction of nature. In architecture, the Romanesque dominated through much of this period. The major cathedral, collegiate, and monastic churches all adapted this style to Polish needs. Early in the thirteenth century the Gothic style began to be introduced, particularly by the Cistercians in Wachock and elsewhere. By the end of the century the shortage of native stone for church construction was being compensated for by the introduction of brick. First used in the late Romanesque church of St. James in Sandomierz, it produced distinctive forms of the Polish Gothic in later buildings.

REUNION AND THE LAST PIASTS (1306–1386)

Václav II died unexpectedly in 1305. His young son was murdered the following year and never ruled in Poland. By the end of 1306 Władysław I Łokietek (this sobriquet, by which he is usually known, implies "short" in Polish) had gained control of Little Poland and Gdańsk Pomerania. Despite the eventual loss of this latter territory to the Teutonic Order and his failure to recover any of the Silesian principalities, Łokietek consolidated his

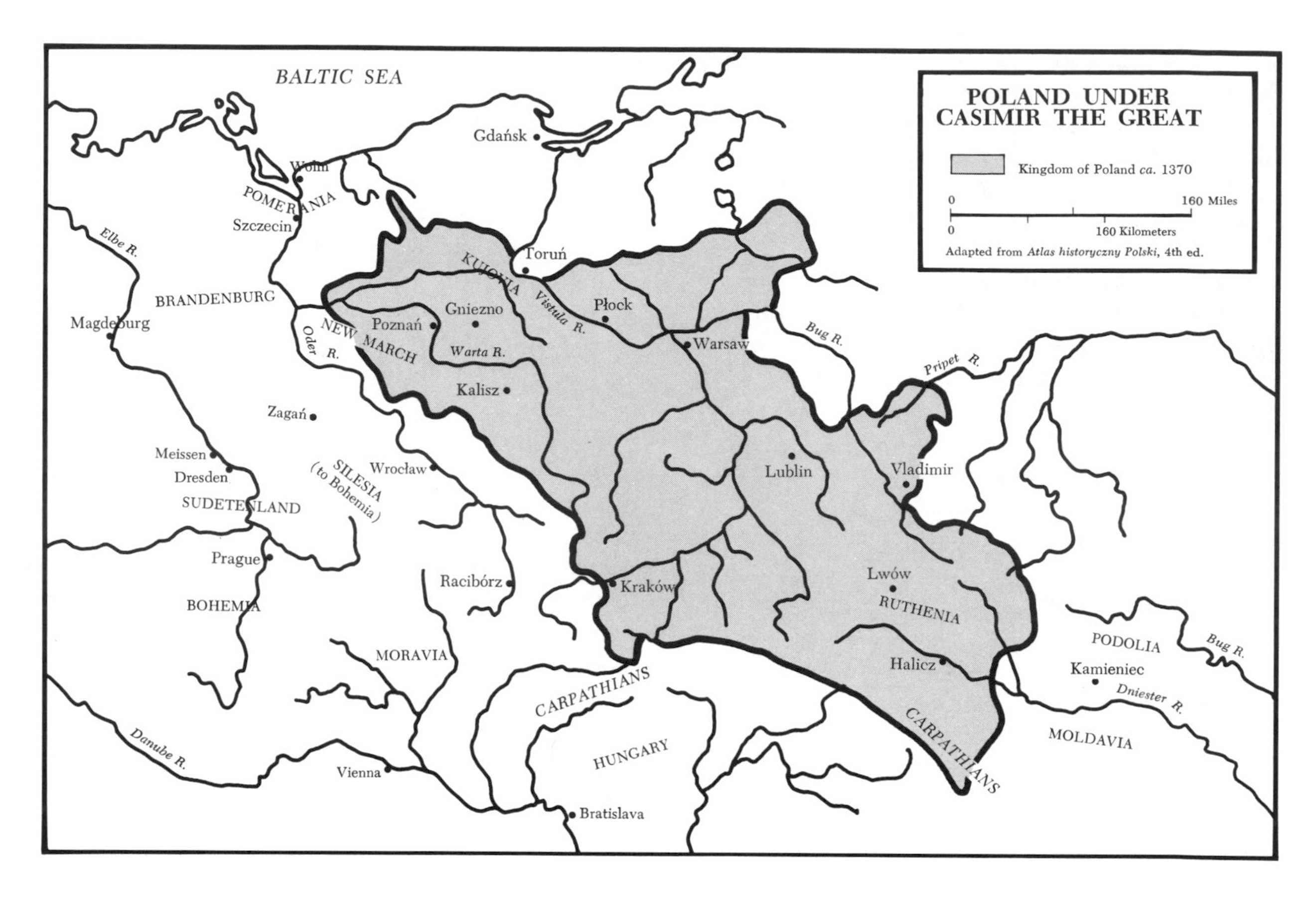

hold on Kraków (putting down the revolt fomented by Albert in 1311) and gained dominion over Great Poland in 1314. With the approval of the Polish church and the support of both the great and small nobility and town dwellers, Łokietek eventually received papal permission to assume the royal title. When he was crowned king in 1320, Poland's long generations of division came to an end.

In the next thirteen years Łokietek concentrated upon the pressing problems of foreign policy. He allied Poland with the Angevin rulers of Hungary by marrying his daughter Elizabeth to King Charles Robert in 1320. He tried legal and diplomatic means to recover Gdańsk Pomerania, but in vain; and when relations with the Teutonic Knights worsened, he went to war to protect Polish interests. After 1326 he waged almost annual campaigns. Although the Poles did win a major military victory at Płowce in 1331, the Knights conquered important border districts in Kujavia. To the west, the Wittelsbach dynasty in Brandenburg continued the Ascanian policy of aggression against Poland. In Bohemia, King John of Luxembourg, who had succeeded the Přemyslid dynasty upon its extinction, consolidated his control over Silesia and declared himself to be Václav's rightful heir to the Kingdom of Poland. He allied himself with the Teutonic Knights and mounted several expeditions against Poland. Internally, Władysław Łokietek had little opportunity to pursue systematic administration, and a contemporary chronicler described Poland as a "great chaos of error and license." When Łokietek died in 1333, the newly resurrected kingdom was sorely beset within and without.

His son and successor, Casimir III, was the only Polish king to be accorded the title "the Great." In the first decade of his reign, he resolved the foreign policy problems left by his father. He realistically recognized that Poland's resources were too limited to pursue the military recovery of its lost territories for the time being. He allied himself with the Wittelsbachs in order to bring pressure upon their archfoes, the Luxembourgs. Then in the late 1330's he negotiated peace with Bohemia. In return for King John's renunciation of claims to Poland, Casimir recognized Bohemian control over Silesia. With the Teutonic Order he arranged for, and then extended, truces immediately upon his accession. Then, when legal suits failed to recover Polish lands, Casimir negotiated the Peace of Kalisz in

1343. By its terms Poland agreed to renounce its claim to Gdańsk Pomerania, and the Knights returned the other territories they had conquered from Łokietek.

In the meantime, beginning in 1340, Casimir had intervened in Ruthenia. He acted in part to protect Poland from the resurgent Mongols. But he also sought to incorporate territories in the east to strengthen Poland sufficiently so that it could return to the question of Silesia and Pomerania more successfully. By 1366, Casimir had conquered almost the whole of the Ruthenian territories of Halicz and Vladimir, thus doubling the size of the Polish state. In this protracted conflict Casimir also successfully fought the pagan Lithuanians, who were interested in expanding into this region. Casimir's several efforts to christianize the Lithuanians failed, but they were the basis for later successful attempts. While he was pursuing these goals in the east, Casimir improved slightly, by both limited military campaigns and diplomacy, the Polish western boundaries in Silesia and elsewhere. These successes in foreign policy heightened Poland's international prestige. Casimir was able to arbitrate conflicts between the Luxembourg, Habsburg, and Angevin dynasties in the 1360's, and in 1364, in order to help the king of Cyprus to launch a crusade, he hosted in Kraków the most glittering international congress of the century.

Casimir's greatness was not only based upon foreign policy. In internal affairs he reformed the currency, introduced new taxes, obtained the return of royal lands that had earlier been alienated or let out on unprofitable leases, and developed the mineral resources of the kingdom, especially the salt mines. The result of this activity was an increase in the crown's annual income, which in turn enabled him to effect other important reforms. One of these was military. He commissioned the building of more than fifty fortresses in the kingdom, encouraged the construction of stone defensive walls around at least twenty-seven cities, and organized a defensive force for the kingdom, the *pospolite ruszenie* (a nonfeudal *levée en masse* of both the greater and lesser nobles organized under native administrators). Casimir also encouraged the building of new churches and public buildings. A later medieval historian paraphrased the Roman writer Livy by saying that Casimir "found a Poland of wood and left one of stone."

In the area of administrative centralization, Casimir was particularly successful. He strove to develop an administration that was not merely local and regional, but national and royal. This strengthened the king's authority, but at the same time required that Polish law be revised. In two codes, published at Piotrków and Wiślica in the 1340's and 1350's, the king moved far toward the creation of one royal law applied in common through Poland. Casimir also protected the rights of Jews in Poland and encouraged further immigration. He took care that the peasantry in Poland should not suffer at the hands of rapacious landlords; and in recognition of this, he was popularly known as "king of the peasants." It is not surprising, therefore, that when he died at the age of sixty in 1370 his last royal chancellor, the historian Janko of Czarnków, reported that the princes, prelates, and populace of Poland mourned his passing with grief that was beyond human ability to describe.

THE EARLY JAGIELLONIAN STATE (1386–1492)

Since Casimir left no direct heir at his death, rule in Poland for the next twelve years was exercised by his older sister, Queen Elizabeth of Hungary, on behalf of her son, Louis. His right of succession had been negotiated earlier with the nobility, particularly those from Little Poland. This period was marked by factional strife and political drift, for Louis ruled in absentia and his mother was resented. Janko of Czarnków commented bitterly that "at the time of that king there was neither stability nor justice in the Kingdom of Poland." Louis also had no male heir, and in 1384 (after a two-year interregnum) the Polish nobility accepted his daughter Jadwiga as their ruler. (These failures of the dynastic line allowed the nobility each time to extend their rights and limit royal authority.) In 1385, the magnates arranged for Jadwiga to marry the grand prince of pagan Lithuania. This mature and experienced ruler became a convert, Polonized his given name to Jagiełło, took the additional Christian name Władysław (and became Władysław II), and with the urging and support of his pious wife effected the conversion of his people. Jadwiga died childless at the age of twenty-six in 1399, but by virtue of a later marriage Jagiełło became the founder of a new dynasty, which ruled Poland and Lithuania until 1572.

The personal, dynastic union negotiated by nobles of both countries in the Treaty of Krewo in 1385, followed by the accession of Jagiełło, was one of the most important events in the history of

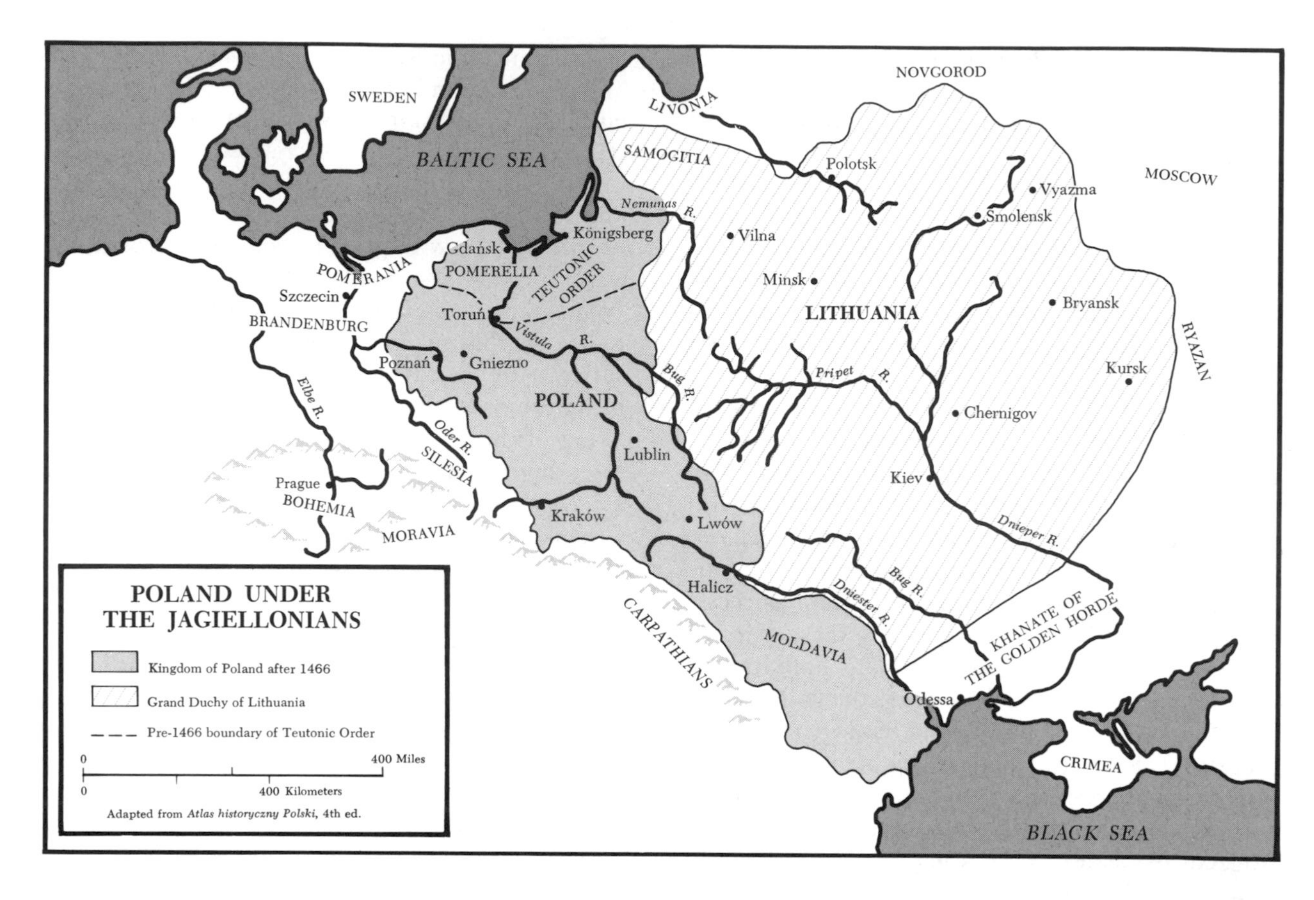

Poland. It drew the state into the affairs of the East, opened the possibility for expanded colonization and control of vast reaches of land in the area for the nobility, and raised fundamental constitutional questions about the relationship between the two countries. Many, though not all, of these were eventually resolved. In 1401 Jagiełło's cousin Witold (Vytautas) was named grand prince of Lithuania, recognizing Jagiełło's vague suzerainty as supreme prince. Then, in 1413, in part as the result of the Mongols having temporarily thwarted Lithuanian plans for expansion and in part as the result of the common threat from the Teutonic Order, a new treaty of union was signed at Horodło. By its terms the respective rights of the Polish and Lithuanian nobility were defined. Through the following century the federation of the two states was the basis for making the union a great power in Central and Eastern Europe.

Beyond the dynastic and constitutional issue, the overriding problem of Jagiełło's reign was the Teutonic Order. The order believed that the conversion of Jagiełło and the Lithuanians was merely a political sham. The Knights were consequently unwilling to give up their crusading activity and territorial expansion. Although Witold had at first, in pursuit of his own ambitions, allied with the order, after 1401 he and his cousin acted in concert. War broke out in 1409, and a joint Polish-Lithuanian army met the order at Grunwald (Tannenberg) in 1410 in a decisive battle. The Teutonic Knights were routed, the grand master and hundreds of other important officers were killed, and numerous divisional flags fell into Polish and Lithuanian hands. Henceforth the order was considerably weakened, both militarily and financially. Jagiełło did not, or could not, follow up his victory, however, and the outcome of the war at the first Peace of Toruń in 1411 was curiously unsatisfactory for Poland. The order's territory remained largely intact, and the conflict continued for another generation. Jagiełło sent ambassadors to the Council of Constance to argue before the assembled representatives of Christendom that on the basis of canon and natural law the order should be forced to give back Poland's territories and be dissolved. But eloquent argument and scholastic logic brought no satisfaction for Poland. Jagiełło again waged war against the order in a series of campaigns from 1414 to 1422, and by the Treaty of Mielno in the latter year the order lost the territory of Samogitia, thus separating their Prussian and Livonian holdings.

In internal affairs, Jagiełło followed closely the guidance of the church, which, in teaching the former pagan prince how to rule as a Western Christian monarch, ensured that he would be not only pupil, but also protector of its privileges. Especially after 1424 was Jagiełło dependent upon the advice provided by Bishop Zbigniew Oleśnicki of Kraków, the de facto leader of the hierarchy. Thus, for example, the king refused to accept the throne of Bohemia when it was offered by the Hussite leaders, even though this could have meant the return of some of the Piast territories in the west. Jagiełło was also unable to retain and recover the royal prerogatives of the last Piast ruler. In order to consolidate his support among the nobility, in 1386 he confirmed all of the traditional rights that Louis of Hungary had granted in the Charter of Koszyce (1374). Then, in order to ensure the succession in Poland of his son, Władysław (*b.* 1424), he was forced to extend and make uniform these privileges. At Brześć (Brest Oblast) in 1425, the charter *Neminem captivabimus nisi jure victum* granted wide personal immunities; five years later at Jedlnia and in 1432 at Kraków many of these privileges were extended to the *szlachta* (the gentry, or lesser landed nobility). Thus when Jagiełło died in 1434, the monarchy was increasingly circumscribed and limited.

The reign of Władysław III (1434–1444) reinforced these tendencies. A regency was established, headed by Bishop Oleśnicki, who was the leader of the great nobles from Little Poland. This group had risen to economic and political strength in the previous three-quarters of a century because of the great estates and wealth they held in Ruthenia and the east. Their power was shown in 1439 when they successfully defeated a military confederation of the *szlachta* and some members of the court. The gentry, many of whom held Hussite sympathies, had aimed at putting Władysław's younger brother, Casimir, on the throne of Bohemia. The next year, however, the magnates suffered a political reverse when the Lithuanians chose Casimir as their new grand prince instead of King Władysław. This theoretically disrupted the union. To compensate, Oleśnicki and his party obtained for Władysław the throne of Hungary. The young king spent the next years there, while the great nobles exacted further liberties in Poland. Władysław's tragic death in 1444 at Varna in the ill-fated crusade against the Turks brought an end to a short and unhappy reign.

For many months after Varna, the Poles refused to believe their king would not return. Eventually the crown council elected Władysław's brother to succeed him. Casimir IV, the Jagiellonian, retained his hereditary position in Lithuania in addition to assuming his elected kingship, thus reestablishing a "fraternal union," as he called it, in which he guaranteed the integrity of Lithuania's frontiers and regarded it as a sovereign nation, coequal with Poland. Casimir's policy from the beginning was to reestablish strong central authority in Poland, restore lost territories, and extend his dynasty's influence over the whole of the region.

To accomplish the first, he refused at his accession to recognize any of the privileges that restricted royal authority. To break the opposition of the magnates, he relied upon their natural enemies, the gentry; upon the so-called "new" nobility, that is, those who in the previous generation had risen out of the gentry, particularly in Great Poland; and, to a limited extent, upon the towns. During the first years of his reign he was strikingly successful. He was also able to revise to royal advantage the system of ecclesiastical taxation and to obtain, over the opposition of the clergy, control over the appointments of bishops. In attempting to restrict the oligarchy of the magnates, however, Casimir widened the prerogatives of the gentry. In the Charter of Nieszawa (1454), he bound the crown not to raise troops or impose new taxes without the approval of the *szlachta* expressed in local diets (*conventiones particulares, sejmiki*).

In the territories of the Teutonic Order, Casimir was able to take advantage of political unrest. The ruling oligarchy of such towns as Toruń and Gdańsk felt themselves exploited by the Knights. Dissident members of the order's military ranks formed a secret society called the Order of the Salamander. Finally, after 1440, the several estates of Prussia formed the Prussian Union to rectify what they felt to be unjust tax policy. When this was repressed, representatives of the union appealed to Casimir. He incorporated the union into the Polish crown and declared war on the Teutonic Order. The resultant conflict dragged on for thirteen years. It was not popular in Lithuania and was not well received by contemporary rulers and observers. But Casimir's dogged pursuit of his goal and the willingness of the populace to bear both physical and fiscal hardships ultimately brought victory. By the second Peace of Toruń in 1466, the lands of the defeated order were partitioned. Gdańsk Pomerania and parts of western Prussia were incorporated into the Polish crown as Royal Prussia. The rest remained in the hands of the grand master, who moved his residence to Königsberg (now Kaliningrad in the Soviet Union) from where he did homage to Casimir, recognizing him as suzerain.

Casimir was also successful in his third goal. By his death, his eldest son, Władysław, had been accepted as king by the estates of both Bohemia and Hungary. This Jagiellonian hegemony over the region had little real substance, however, for the lands were not homogeneous, Władysław was not an energetic ruler, and royal power in Bohemia and Hungary was extremely limited. Ironically, despite Casimir's early policy, the same thing was becoming true in Poland. The privileges that he had granted to the *szlachta* provided the basis for them to extend their power in later years. The assemblies eventually developed in the modern period into the means by which the "golden freedom" of the Polish nobility was exercised at all levels. As an elective ruler, the monarch was becoming increasingly the plaything of other groups in society. Thus the Middle Ages in Poland end, politically, with the future triumph of the nobility assured. To a certain degree the character of this triumph lay at the heart of the disasters Poland suffered in the early centuries of the modern period.

SOCIETY AND ECONOMY IN THE LATE MIDDLE AGES

Many of the trends discussed above continued in the fourteenth and fifteenth centuries. New rural and urban settlements were common, and with the acquisition of Ruthenia and the eastern regions there was a vigorous colonization movement there. In general, the countryside was prosperous. The agricultural overextension evident in Western Europe had not developed so far in Poland. Thus the climatic changes that precipitated retrenchment elsewhere, with resultant social dislocation, were less evident in Poland. In addition, the Black Death, while by no means unknown in the kingdom, wreaked less havoc than in the West.

An important agricultural development, with closely associated social implications, began in the late fourteenth century. In Western Europe there was a shift in the use of land from field to pasture, and the population began to look to Central and Eastern Europe for crop production. This made the utilization of great estates for grain growing increasingly profitable. First monastic landlords, and then the new landholders who had risen to prominence with the expansion of the state, reaped the benefits of this economic shift. They expanded their estates to increase grain production, much of which, incidentally, was shipped down the Vistula, making Gdańsk one of the great ports of Europe. In the process, the tenant farmer was unable to keep pace, and he was gradually brought under the economic and social control of the great landowners. At the very time when serfdom was disappearing in Western Europe, it was growing in Poland. Some peasants resisted exploitation by flight. But at the Diet of Piotrków in 1496 King John Albert allowed landlords to bind their serfs to the soil. Although scholars in Poland today refer to this as a feudal economy and society, it is more closely approximate to the manorial, or seigniorial, tradition Western scholars talk about in connection with medieval Europe.

In another sector of the economy, mining showed considerable progress, especially in the mineral-rich territories of Silesia and Little Poland. New deposits of iron, copper, lead, zinc, sulphur, and salt were all brought into production during the fourteenth century. Kraków was one of the important smelting centers, and a contemporary remarked that the area "looked like Mt. Etna, with furnaces burning full of . . . [metals] . . . being joined in the fire." In addition, there were iron foundries nearby, and the processing of lead was a lucrative business.

The Polish towns in these centuries experienced a general prosperity. Many were small by Western standards. At the beginning of the fifteenth century, Wrocław and Gdańsk were the largest, with about 20,000 inhabitants, Kraków had perhaps 14,000, Poznań only about 4,000–5,000, and few others exceeded 2,000. But there was considerable economic vitality in these cities. Both local trade and long-distance commerce with Western Europe and the Black Sea area is reflected in the records of the merchants. Cloth, especially fine woolens from the Low Countries, was one of the most important commodities traded. In Kraków, the more wealthy merchants, supported by Casimir the Great, constructed a large Drapers' Hall in the central market square. Similar developments may be observed elsewhere.

Eventually both merchants and the numerous craftsmen organized into guilds, as they had earlier done in the West, to protect their interests. Sometimes these guilds created unrest within cities. For example, in 1333 the weavers in Wrocław rose against the town council for a greater share in the government. On other occasions, tensions within the guilds themselves created problems. In 1375 apprentice bakers in Kraków rebelled against their masters. And sometimes ethnic conflicts resulted in riots. In the 1360's the largely Polish-speaking craft guilds of Gdańsk organized against the predominantly German great merchants with the politically potent cry of "Kraków, Kraków" on their lips.

This phenomenon of social and ethnic tension points up one of the most important characteristics of the cities at the end of the Middle Ages. By 1500 in most of the larger towns, the great merchant patricians had effectively assumed control over the political and economic fortunes of the cities. They were chiefly of German extraction, though there were important groups of Italians in Kraków and Armenians in such eastern cities as Lwów. Below them were the smaller merchants and the artisans and craftsmen, the majority of whom were ethnically and linguistically Polish. Finally, there were the poor and the unskilled, who in this period also, as in all times and all urban places, lived on the margins of society. The character of this stratification helps in part to explain the weakness of the Polish monarchy. The patricians had little national consciousness, and the king could consequently draw little support from the cities.

One final ethnic group that does not fit neatly into the foregoing framework should be mentioned here, the Jews. The liberties extended to Jews by Casimir the Great were confirmed by Casimir IV in 1453. (Some were, however, later revoked by the Statutes of Nieszawa.) Jews were directly subject to the jurisdiction of the king's regional administrator, the *wojewoda,* and the state recognized the validity of their courts. In the fifteenth century, immigration to Poland in the wake of persecutions in the West increased the number of Jews. Their growing involvement in craft production was often a source of conflict with town guilds. Eventually towns began to limit Jewish residence to separate districts, as in Kazimierz, a city just south of Kraków. The decision in 1483 of the city council in Warsaw to require Jews to live outside the city walls was unusual.

CULTURE IN THE LATE MIDDLE AGES

The following comments touch only selectively upon the cultural achievements of this period. In the field of education, Poland's schools, libraries, and educators, many of them having attended universities in the West, convinced Casimir the Great that he could found a university that would, among other functions, train lawyers to help in the administration of the kingdom. He obtained papal permission, and in 1364 chartered in Kraków a school on the model of Bologna. It was given one chair in arts, two in medicine, three in canon law, and five in civil law. Salaries were derived from the income of the royal salt mines at nearby Wieliczka. This foundation never prospered, and after Casimir's death it gradually declined. Efforts to revive it in the 1390's, including the establishment of a theological faculty, were fruitless. Only in 1400 did Władysław Jagiełło, fulfilling the educational dream of his wife Jadwiga, effect a successful new foundation, modeled upon Paris.

The new university prospered. The king endowed it with living and teaching quarters, the eventual Collegium Maius, and with professorships. The Polish church and private benefactors also contributed endowments, including specific chairs in rhetoric and astronomy. Students came to the school in considerable numbers. By the 1490's more than 290 new matriculations were recorded annually, and in the first century of the school's functioning about 18,700 students attended one or more years. More than forty percent of these came from abroad. The faculty was active in the national life of Poland as well as contributing to the intellectual achievement of late medieval Europe. Rector Paul Vladimiri argued the Polish case at Constance; professors such as John of Regulus were elected to the city council of Kraków; several faculty members, including former rector Thomas Strzempiński, became bishops and archbishops; Jakub Parkosz helped standardize the Polish language by preparing a manual on orthography; and Jan Dąbrówka, many-time rector and former vice-chancellor, prepared a commentary upon Polish history emphasizing patriotism and moral virtue. The theologians of the university refined and defended conciliar theory within the church; the natural scientists undermined Aristotelian approaches to the external world; the mathematicians and astronomers made the school an international center of learning in this field by the end of the fifteenth century; and faculty members introduced and supported humanistic interests in Poland after mid century, thus drawing to Kraków such noted figures as the German poet and humanist Conrad Celtis.

This period was also important in historiography. The Silesian *Chronica principum Poloniae,* probably by Peter of Byczyna (*d.* 1388), presented a vivid picture of a region whose political and cultural character was in transition. Janko of Czarnków (*d.* 1387) wrote a lively political memoir, *Chronica Polonorum.* This work is sophisticated in its use of documents, does not adhere rigidly to an annalistic framework, and, by celebrating the strength of the Polish monarchy and its fate in the 1370's, provides a striking picture of its time. Jan Długosz (1415–1480) was the greatest medieval Polish historian. A protégé of Bishop Oleśnicki and canon of the Kraków cathedral, Długosz had access to royal archives and to collections of historical material that gave his *Annales seu cronicae incliti regni Poloniae* in twelve books both authority and reliability. In addition, he prepared long historical studies on the insignia of the Polish kingdom, lives of the bishops of Kraków, a detailed catalog of the benefices belonging to the diocese of Kraków, and a study of the banners won from the Teutonic Order at Grunwald. Długosz consciously modeled his *Annales* upon Livy, and his work has justly been called "a monument to patriotism and historical knowledge." Phillip Buonaccorsi, called Callimachus (*d.* 1496), was an Italian humanist who spent the last twenty-five years of his life in Poland in the service of the Jagiellonian monarchy. His *Historia de rege Vladislao* (1485) and his biographies of Archbishop Gregory of Sanok, Zbigniew Oleśnicki, and others brought to Poland the traditions of Renaissance historiography. He was also part of the Sodalitas Litteraria Vistulana, a literary circle in Kraków inspired by Celtis.

In the arts, this was a productive period. Gothic churches were built throughout the kingdom, but with the greatest success in Kraków (Wawel cathedral). In Silesia, Wrocław could boast a fine cathedral and several other churches; and in Gdańsk, the church of St. Mary was one of the largest ecclesiastical structures in Europe. Though built in different regions and reflecting regional styles, these structures have in common brick construction, a medium that alters the architectural message. Their ratio of height-to-width makes them appear narrower than their Western counterparts and gives them a greater sense of verticality. This impression is reinforced by the fact that buttresses are not freestanding ("flying"), but abut directly and completely the segment they support. Among the secular buildings of this period, the town halls in Wrocław, Poznań, Kraków, and Toruń, the Drapers' Hall in Kraków, and the castle of the Teutonic Knights in Malbork are some of the finest examples of late medieval civilian architecture available. Late in the fifteenth century, early Renaissance architectural influences may be observed, particularly in the Collegium Maius in Kraków.

In sculpture, the delicate figure of the Krużlowa Madonna (now in the National Museum in Kraków) bears similarities to the Rhineland tradition, though it clearly reflects a native school. But the most outstanding sculptor active in Poland was Wit Stwosz (Veit Stoss) of Nuremberg. His ten-meter-high polychromed triptych altar in St. Mary's church in Kraków is a masterpiece. In the central grouping the Virgin dominates the larger-than-life-size figures. Her lyrical grace, the expressive and plastic qualities of the carving, the dramatic elements reflected in the group scenes, and the realistic representations mark this altar as one of the highest achievements of the late Gothic style. Stwosz also executed a sarcophagus for Casimir the Jagiellonian, a memorial epitaph for Callimachus, and several other examples of funeral art.

BIBLIOGRAPHY

Sources. The literary and diplomatic sources for medieval Poland have, for the most part, been published, though some need reedition. The most important collections, some of which contain multivolume subsets, are the following: *Monumenta Poloniae historica: Pomniki dziejowe Polski,* 6 vols. (1864–1893), and *Nova series* (1946–); *Monumenta medii aevi historica res gestas Poloniae illustrantia,* 19 vols. (1874–1927); Augustin Theiner, ed., *Vetera monumenta Poloniae et Lithuaniae . . . ,* 4 vols. (1860–1864); *Codex diplomaticus Majoris Poloniae documenta,* 5 vols. (1877–1908); *Codex diplomaticus Poloniae,* 4 vols. in 6 (1847–1887). A more detailed listing of source materials pertaining to Poland may be found in *Repertorium fontium historiae medii aevi,* I: *Series collectionum* (1962), and *Additamenta,* I: *Series collectionum continuata et aucta* (1977). The corpus of Jan Długosz's writings is in Alexander Przeździecki, ed., *Opera omnia,* 14 vols. (1863–1887), and Jan Dąbrowski, ed., *Annales seu cronicae incliti regni Poloniae* (1964–). A useful survey article describing the edition of Polish sources is Brygida Kürbis and Jerzy Luciński, "Les éditions polonaises de sources médiévales entre 1945 et 1965," in International Congress of Historical Sciences, Vienna, 1965, *La Pologne au XIIe Congrès international des sciences historiques à Vienne* (1965). The two most convenient guides to the sources are Jan Dąbrowski, *Dawne dziejopisarstwo polskie (do roku 1480)* (1964); and Pierre David, *Les sources de l'histoire de Pologne à l'époque des Piasts (963–1386)* (1934).

Bibliographies. From the nineteenth century, see

Ludwik Finkel, *Bibliografia historii polskiej,* 3 vols. (1891–1914, repr. 1956). More modern, though more selective, is Helena Madurowicz-Urbańska, *Bibliografia historii Polski,* I, in 3 pts., *Do roku 1795* (1965). A comprehensive annual bibliography is Polska akademia nauk, Instytut historii, *Bibliografia historii polskiej* (1962–). In English, the most helpful bibliography is that by Norman Davies, ed., *Poland, Past and Present* (1977).

Histories of Poland. The semiofficial Polska akademia nauk, Instytut historii, *Historia Polski,* I, in 3 pts. (1958 and later editions), reflects orthodox Polish scholarship under the postwar regime. Jerzy Wyrozumski, *Historia Polski do roku 1505* (1978), has an excellent description of medieval Polish sources and a good bibliography. See also *The Cambridge History of Poland,* I, William F. Reddaway *et al.,* eds. (1950), useful, but in many ways already antiquated when it appeared; Alexander Gieysztor, "Medieval Poland," Krystyna Cękalska, trans., in *History of Poland,* Stefan Kieniewicz, ed., 2nd ed. (1979); Oskar Halecki, *A History of Poland,* rev. ed. (1976, 1978, 1983); Gotthold Rhode, *Geschichte Polens: Ein Überblick,* 3rd rev. ed. (1980).

General works. František Dvorník's many books are all useful; see particularly *The Making of Central Europe,* 2nd ed. (1974), *The Slavs: Their Early History and Civilization* (1956), and *The Slavs in European History and Civilization* (1962). See also Geoffrey Barraclough, ed., *Eastern and Western Europe in the Middle Ages* (1970); Colloque international sur les origines des États européens aux IXe–XIe siècles, *L'Europe aux IXe–XIe siècles aux origines des états nationaux* (1968); A. P. Vlasto, *The Entry of the Slavs into Christendom* (1970).

Special studies. Jan Białostocki, *The Art of the Renaissance in Eastern Europe* (1976); Paul W. Knoll, *The Rise of the Polish Monarchy* (1972), dealing with foreign affairs in the fourteenth century, and "The Arts Faculty at the University of Cracow at the End of the Fifteenth Century," in Robert S. Westman, ed., *The Copernican Achievement* (1975); Brian Knox, *The Architecture of Poland* (1971); Kazimierz Lepszy, ed., *Dzieje Uniwersytetu Jagiellońskiego,* I, *W latach 1364–1764* (1964); Michał Walicki, ed., *Sztuka polska przedromańska i romańska do schyłku XIII wieku,* 2 vols. (1971), with useful plates illustrating all areas of arts and architecture in the thirteenth century.

Biography. Polski słownik biograficzny (1935–) is authoritative and by 1986 had reached Sz; Polska akademia nauk, Instytut badań literackich, *Nowy Korbut,* 3 vols. (1963–1965), concentrates on literary figures, but for the early period almost all literate individuals are included.

Paul W. Knoll

[See also **Agriculture and Nutrition; Baltic Countries, Balts; Bohemia-Moravia; Hungary; Jagiełło Dynasty; Lithuania; Piast Dynasty.**]